Conversion Tables

Conversion Tables

LC-Dewey
Dewey-LC

Mona L. Scott

With the assistance of
Christine E. Alvey

1993
Libraries Unlimited, Inc.
Englewood, Colorado

LIBRARIES UNLIMITED, INC.
P.O. Box 6633
Englewood, CO 80155-6633
1-800-237-6124

Library of Congress Cataloging-in-Publication Data

Scott, Mona L.
   Conversion tables : LC-Dewey, Dewey-LC / Mona L. Scott.
   viii, 365 p. 22x28 cm.
   ISBN 1-56308-017-6 (Print version)
   ISBN 1-56308-152-0 (Disk version)
   1. Classification, Library of Congress.   2. Classification, Dewey decimal.   I. Title.
Z696.U4S36   1993
025.4'31--dc20   93-26938
                                                 CIP

Contents

Introduction

While Head of Cataloging at the United States Bureau of the Census Library outside Washington, D.C., I was frequently frustrated by the lack of Library of Congress call numbers on non-LC MARC records available from our cataloging utility. My staff had to stop the routine copy cataloging process in order to identify a call number. I began a search for a conversion manual to assist the Cataloging Department, and the only one I found was twenty years out of date, incomplete, lacking any subject reference to the list of class numbers, and was limited to class numbers downloaded from LC MARC records. I decided I would create a cataloging tool that could be a standard reference in any cataloging department for daily copy cataloging activities, as well as massive projects of converting from one class system to the other. The project began with an analysis of the scope of each system.

The Library of Congress and Dewey Decimal classification schemes approach the organization of knowledge from different perspectives, with one system emphasizing an area that the other may just briefly explore. In addition, the manner in which they organize the topics differ. For example, the Library of Congress classes all aspects of the Methodist Christian denomination together, while Dewey classes some aspects (as missions and church discipline) with those from all Christian denominations.

Conversion Tables: LC-Dewey; Dewey-LC is a resource to be used for conversion of entire libraries, but it will be most frequently used to convert individual MARC records from bibliographic utilities that include only one classification number. For example, a record concerning a census of India may contain only a Dewey class number when a LC number is needed. These tables will provide that number without the necessity for extensive examination of the LC tables. Depending upon the specificity of the subject, these tables may provide the entire class number, or may direct you to the area to search for a more refined notation.

To help clarify the meaning of the lists of numbers, descriptors, or brief explanations, will be found beside each set of class numbers.

In the LC-Dewey table you will find:

LC	Dewey	Descriptor
BD646-648	117	Structure of matter and form

In the Dewey-LC table you will find:

Dewey	LC	Descriptor
117	BD646-648	Structure of matter and form

The following conventions will be used to accommodate the differences.

- Ranges of numbers will be used in one system, especially LC in which many class numbers convert to a single Dewey number. At times portions of these number ranges will be broken down further where it is reasonable to do so.

- In the world and local history sections, and in some areas of literature, dates and date ranges for the two systems can only approximate each other.

- The following symbols are used in the class numbers:

    / indicates a choice (122/124 is 122 *or* 124)
    - indicates a range (PQ8230-8239 is PQ8230 *through* PQ8239)

- ( ) indicates a further choice (380.1(42) means that 42 can be added to further refine the subject)

- Within the descriptors, the following conventions are observed:

  Education refers to any type of teaching or study
  Oceania is used to include all South Pacific islands

  Serials is used to refer to periodicals and serials of all types
  / between words will indicate either word

To use the tables, select the part for the classification system to convert *from*, either from LC to Dewey or from Dewey to LC. Begin by locating the number converting *from* in the left column, which lists those numbers or alphanumeric notations in order. Because of the broad differences in the two class systems, in many areas the notations will be displayed as ranges of numbers. Frequently this broad range of numbers will be broken down concisely in lines following them. For example:

LC	Dewey	Descriptor
ML1610-1751	782.409	History secular music, By place
ML1611	782.40973	United States
ML1613	782.40971	Canada

If you find a range of numbers, look below to see if there is a further breakdown. When the closest number is found, across from it in the middle column will be the equivalent in the other scheme. The right column will be the descriptor to help identify the class number sought.

LC-Dewey Conversion Table

LC	Dewey	Descriptor	LC	Dewey	Descriptor
AC	080	General collections	AM41-43	069.0941	Great Britain
AC1-8	081/082	American/English collections	AM46-48	069.0944	France
			AM49-51	069.0943	Germany
AC9	080	General collections	AM52-53	069.09495	Greece
AC16-19	083.931	Dutch collections	AM54-55	069.0945	Italy
AC20	084.1	French collections	AM60	069.0974	European Russia
AC30-35	083.1	German collections	AM61.5-64	069.0948	Scandinavia
AC40-45	085.1	Italian collections	AM65-66	069.0946(9)	Spain/Portugal
AC50-55	088	Scandinavian	AM69	069.09496	Balkan states
AC60-65	087	Slavic	AM71-79	069.095	Asia
AC70-75	086.(1/69)	Spanish/Portuguese	AM72	069.0951	China
AC80-85	089.945	Finno-Ugrian	AM77-78	069.0952	Japan
AC95	089.(7-9)	Other European	AM80-91	069.096	Africa
AC101-102	089.92	Semitic	AM93-100	069.099(3-6)	Australia/New Zealand/Oceania
AC103-104	083.7	Yiddish			
AC105-106	089.927	Arabic	AM111-157	069.(01)	Museology/Methods
AC111-125	089.911	Indo-Aryan	AM200-401	790.132/069.5	Collectors/Collecting
AC126-127	089.915	Persian	AM200-207	790.1320/069.50(5/6)	Serials/Societies
AC132-133	089.91992	Armenian	AM221	790.13209/069.509	History of collecting
AC140-141	089.9435	Turkish	AM223	790.132092/069.5092	Biography
AC145-146	089.956	Japanese	AM301-396	790.13209/069.509	Collecting, By place
AC147-148	089.957	Korean	AM303-311	790.132/069.5 (0973)	United States
AC149-150	089.951	Chinese	AM313	790.132/069.5 (0971)	Canada
AC156-160	089.59	Indo-Chinese	AM314-322	790.132/069.5 + 0972(8)	Mexico/Central America
AC166-167	089.992	Malay	AM323-329	790.132/069.5 (09729)	West Indies
AC168-169	089.9922	Indonesian	AM330-341	790.132/069.5 (098)	South America
AC177-189	089.96	African	AM342-371	790.132/069.5 (094)	Europe
AC195	089.97	American Indian	AM343-347	790.132/069.5 (0941)	Great Britain
AC801-895	Varies	Dissertations	AM349	790.132/069.5 (0944)	France
AC901-995	Varies	Pamphlets	AM350	790.132/069.5 (0943)	Germany
AC999	Varies	Scrapbooks	AM356	790.132/069.5 (0947)	European Russia
AE	030	Encyclopedias	AM362-363	790.132/069.5 + 0946(9)	Spain/Portugal
AE2-4	030-039	Early	AM372-385	790.132/069.5 (095)	Asia
AE5-88	030-039	Modern, By language	AM387-389	790.132/069.5 (096)	Africa
AE5-10	031/032	American/English	AM390-396	790.132/069.5 + 099(3-6)	Australia/New Zealand/Oceania
AE7-10	036	American, Other than English			
AE61-65	036.1	Spanish	AP	050	General periodicals
AG	413/423-490.3/028.7	Dictionaries/General reference	AP1	050	Periodicals, Polyglot
			AP2-95	051-059	By language
AG1-90	413/423-490.3	Dictionaries	AP2-9	052/051	English
AG103-196	028.7	Reference, General	AP14-17	053.931	Dutch/Flemish
AG240-243	030	Wonders/Curiosities	AP18	053.936	Afrikaans
AG250	Varies	Pictorial works	AP20-28	054.1	French
AG305-313	031/032.02	Notes/Queries	AP30-36.7	053.1	German
AG500-551	027	Information centers/Bureaus	AP37-39	055.1	Italian
AG521-527	027.073	United States	AP40-49	058	Scandinavian
AG531	027.0(71-8)	Other American countries	AP50-58	057	Slavic
AG540	027.04	Europe	AP60-64	056.1	Spanish
AG551	027.0(5-9)	Other countries	AP65-68	056.9	Portuguese
AI	016	Indexes	AP73-77	059.916	Celtic
AI1	050	Periodical indexes	AP80	058.94541	Finnish
AI3-19	016	Indexes, By language	AP82-83	059.94511	Hungarian
AI21	016.07	Newspaper indexes	AP85	059.89	Modern Greek
AM	069	Museums/Collecting	AP86	055.91	Romanian
AM1	069.05	Serials/Societies	AP91-93	059.924	Jewish
AM8	069.083	Children's museums	AP101-115	Varies	Humorous
AM10-101	069.09	History, By place	AP200-230	050	Juvenile periodicals
AM11-13	069.0973	United States	AP(250)-(265)	050.24042	Women's
AM21-22	069.0971	Canada	AP(270)-(271)	050.240396073	Afro-American
AM23-35	069.09(72-8)	Latin/Spanish America	AS	060	Learned societies
AM40-70	069.094	Europe	AS1-2	060.5	Serials
			AS2.5-4	060	Congresses

1

LC	Dewey	Descriptor
AS5	060.9	History
AS6	060.6	Organization
AS8	060.25	Directories
AS9-911	061-068	By place
AS21-36	061.(3-9)	United States
AS40-42	061.1	Canada
AS60-70	068.728	Central America
AS71-75	068.729	West Indies
AS77-90	068.8	South America
AS91-348	062-068	Europe
AS111-122	062	Great Britain
AS151-162	064	France
AS171-182	063	Germany
AS191-202	068.495	Greece
AS211-222	065	Italy
AS251-262	067	European Russia
AS271-284	068.48	Scandinavia
AS300-304	066.(9)	Spain/Portugal
AS401-599	068.5	Asia
AS441-452	068.51	China
AS461-472	068.54	India
AS541-552	068.52	Japan
AS600-699	068.6	Africa
AS701-785	068.9(3-6)	Australia/New Zealand/Oceania
AY	050/030	Yearbooks/Almanacs/Directories
AY30-1730	030	Almanacs
AY30-39	030.9	History
AY51-1730	030.9(4-9)	By place
AY51-425	030.97	North America
AY51-381	030.973/031	United States
AY410-425	030.971/031	Canada
AY430-499	030.9728/036	Central America
AY510-581	036	West Indies
AY600-729	036	South America
AY750-789	032	Great Britain
AY830-839	034.1	France
AY850-860	033.1	Germany
AY890-899	035.1	Italy
AY950-989	038	Scandinavia
AY1000-1009	036.1	Spain
AY1010-1019	036.9	Portugal
AY1050-1188	039.5	Asia
AY1600-1636	032/030.994	Australia
AY1651-1652	032/030.993	New Zealand
AY1671-1730	039.99	Oceania
AY2001	011.7	Compilation of directories
AZ	001	Scholarship/Learning/Errors
AZ(20)-(48)	001.090(1-4)	By date
AZ101-(181)	001.01	Philosophy/Theory
AZ200-361	001.090(1-4)	History, By date
AZ301-311	001.0901	Ancient
AZ321	001.0902	Medieval
AZ331	001.090(23-31)	Renaissance
AZ341-361	001.090(3-4)	Modern
AZ501-908	001.09	By place
AZ501-516	001.097	North America
AZ503-513	001.0973	United States
AZ517-588	001.09(72-8)	Spanish America
AZ600-765	001.094	Europe
AZ770-795	001.095	Asia
AZ800-821	001.096	Africa
AZ850-908	001.099(3-6)	Australia/New Zealand/Oceania
AZ999	001.9	Popular errors
B	100	Philosophy
B1-8	105	Serials
B11-18	106	Societies
B20	106	Congresses
B31	105	Yearbooks
B35	102.5	Directories
B40-48	103	Dictionaries
B49-50	101.4	Terminology
B51	103	Encyclopedias
B52-59.5	107	Education
B53-67	101	Methodology
B104	109.22	Collective biography
B108-118	180	Ancient philosophy
B121-162.7	181	Ancient Oriental philosophy
B125-128	181.11(2-5)	Chinese, Ancient
B130-133	181.4	India, Ancient
B135-138	181.(12/09561)	Japanese, Ancient
B139.1-.4	181.119	Korean, Ancient
B140-143	181.2	Egyptian, Ancient
B145-148	181.6	Assyrian-Babylonian, Ancient
B149.2-.23	181.9	Armenian, Ancient
B150-153	181.5	Iranian, Ancient
B154-159	181.06	Jewish, Ancient
B162	181.043	Buddhist, Ancient
B162.5	181.044	Jainist, Ancient
B162.6	181.09561	Shinto, Ancient
B162.7	181.114	Taoist, Ancient
B165-708	182-188	Ancient Occident philosophy
B165-491	182-185	Ancient Greek
B188-258	182	Greek, Ancient (First period)
B265-320	182.7-183	Greek, Ancient (Second period)
B310-318	183	Greek, Ancient (Socratic)
B335-491	184-186	Greek, Ancient (Third period)
B350-398	184	Greek, Ancient (Plato)
B400-491	185	Greek, Ancient (Aristotle)
B505-626	183.4/186-187	Greco-Roman
B630-708	186.4/190	Alexandrian/Early Christian
B720-753	189	Medieval philosophy
B728	189.5	Mystic philosophy
B734	189.4	Scholasticism
B755-759	181.3/296.3	Jewish philosophers
B770-785	190	Renaissance
B790-5739	190	Modern philosophy
B850-945	191	Philosophy, United States
B981-995	191	Philosophy, Canada
B1001-1084	199.(72/8)	Philosophy, Latin America
B1111-1682	192	Philosophy, England
B1801-2430	194	Philosophy, France
B2521-3396	193	Philosophy, Germany/Austria
B3501-3515	199.495	Philosophy, Greece
B3551-3656	195	Philosophy, Italy
B3801-4030	199.492	Philosophy, Low Countries
B4041-4095	199.492	Philosophy, Netherlands
B4151-4175	199.493	Philosophy, Belgium
B4201-4279	197	Philosophy, Russia
B4301-4315	198	Philosophy, Scandinavia
B4325-4395	198.9	Philosophy, Denmark
B4402-4406	199.4912	Philosophy, Iceland
B4411-4445	198.1	Philosophy, Norway
B4455-4495	198.5	Philosophy, Sweden
B4561-4568	196.1	Philosophy, Spain
B4591-4598	198.9	Philosophy, Portugal

LC	Dewey	Descriptor
B4625-4651	199.494	Philosophy, Switzerland
B4687-4691	199.438	Philosophy, Poland
B4711-4715	198.8	Philosophy, Finland
B4801-4805	199.437	Philosophy, Czechoslovakia
B4811-4815	199.439	Philosophy, Hungary
B4821-4825	199.498	Philosophy, Romania
B4831-4835	199.4977	Philosophy, Bulgaria
B4841-4845	199.497	Philosophy, Yugoslavia
B4851-4855	199.4965	Philosophy, Albania
B4871-4875	199.561	Philosophy, Turkey
B5017-5289	181	Philosophy, Asia
B5040-5044	181.6	Philosophy, Iraq
B5045-5054	181.8	Philosophy, Lebanon/Syria
B5055-5059	181.3	Philosophy, Israel/Palestine
B5060-5069	181.9	Philosophy, Jordan/Arabia
B5070-5074	181.5	Philosophy, Iran
B5130-5134	181.4	Philosophy, India
B5135-5289	181.1	Philosophy, South/Eastern Asia
B5300-5679	199.6	Philosophy, Africa
B5685-5739	199.9(3-6)	Philosophy, Aust./N.Z./Oceania
BC	160	Logic
BC1	160.5	Serials
BC4-5	160.(5/6)	Societies/Congresses
BC9	160.3	Dictionaries/Encyclopedias
BC11-39	160-169.9	History
BC25-32	160-169.9(01/3)	Ancient
BC34-35	160-169.902	Medieval
BC38-39	160-169	Modern
BC39.5	160-169.9(4-9)	Logic, By place
BC50-57	160.1	Methodology
BC59	160.7	Education
BC60-78	162	Deductive
BC80-99	161	Inductive
BC101-117	160.202	Outlines/Etc.
BC131-135	511.3	Symbolic/Mathematical logic
BC175	165	Fallacies
BC177	168	Reasoning/Argument
BC183	167	Hypotheses
BC185	166	Syllogisms/Dilemma
BD	110-121	Speculative philosophy
BD10-28	100	Philosophy, Introductions
BD30-38	110-121.0202	Outlines/Etc.
BD95-131	110	Metaphysics
BD131	110.202	Outlines/Etc.
BD143-237	121	Epistemology
BD181	121.3	Origin/Sources of knowledge
BD182	121.65	Criterion
BD183	121.6	Inquiry
BD201	121.2	Limits of knowledge
BD215	121.(6/7)	Belief/Faith
BD220	121.4	Objectivity
BD222	121.4	Subjectivity
BD232	121.8	Value/Worth
BD300-450	111	Ontology
BD331	111.1	Being/Substance
BD352	111.8	Attributes of being
BD396	111.82	Whole/Parts
BD398	111.5	Nothingness
BD411	111.6	Finite/Infinite
BD450	128	Philosophical anthropology
BD493-708	113	Cosmology
BD494-496	113.09	History
BD530-595	122/124	Causation/Teleology
BD620-655	114-117	Space/Time/Matter/Motion
BD621-626	114	Space/Space and matter
BD632-638	115	Time/Space and time
BD646-648	117	Structure of matter and form
BD652	116/117	Matter and motion/Force
BF	150	Psychology
BF1-8	150.5	Serials
BF11-20	150.6	Societies/Congresses
BF30	150.25	Directories
BF31	150.3	Dictionaries/Encyclopedias
BF32	150.14	Terminology
BF38-.8	150.1	Philosophy
BF76.5	150.724	Research
BF77-80.7	150.7	Education
BF81-105	150.9	History
BF109	150.9(4-9)/155.89 (4-9)	By place
BF109	150.92	Biography
BF173-175.5	150.195	Psychoanalysis
BF176-.5	150.287	Testing/Tests
BF180-198.7	150.724	Experimental psychology
BF199	150.1943	Behaviorism
BF203	150.1982	Gestalt
BF207-210	154.4	Drugs/Electronic effects
BF231-299	152.1	Sensation
BF319.5-499	153.4	Cognition/Consciousness
BF315	154.2	Subconsciousness
BF318-319.5	153.15	Learning
BF321-323	153.73	Apperception/Attention
BF335-337	152.33	Habits
BF353-.5	155.9	Environmental psychology
BF365-395	153.2	Association/Ideas
BF408-426	153.3	Imagination/Creativity
BF431-433	153.9	Intelligence
BF441-449	153.42	Thought/Thinking
BF501-504.3	153.8	Motivation
BF511-593	152.4	Emotion/Feeling
BF608-635	153.8	Will/Choice
BF636-637	158	Applied psychology
BF660-687	156	Comparative psychology
BF692-.5	155.3	Sexual behavior (Psychology)
BF697-.5	155	Differential psychology
BF698	155.2	Personality
BF698.4-.9	155.28	Personality assessment/Tests
BF699-711	155.7	Genetic psychology
BF712-724.85	155	Developmental psychology
BF719-723	155.4	Infant/Child psychology
BF724-.85	155.5	Adolesence/Young adult
BF795-811	155.26	Temperament
BF818-839	155.2	Character
BF839.8-861	138	Physiognomy
BF866-885	139	Phrenology
BF889-905	137	Graphology
BF908-990	133.6	Palmistry
BF1001-1389	133	Parapsychology
BF1001-1008	133.05	Serials
BF1009-1021	133.06	Societies/Congresses
BF1024.4	133.025	Directories
BF1025	133.03	Dictionaries/Encyclopedias
BF1026-1027	133.092	Biography
BF1028-.5	133.09	History
BF1040.5	133.07	Education
BF1068-1073	154.64	Somnambulism/Sleep
BF1074-1099	135.3	Dreaming
BF1111-1156	133.8	Hypnotism
BF1161-1175	133.82	Telepathy

LC	Dewey	Descriptor
BF1228-1389	133.9	Spiritualism
BF1404-1999	133	Occult sciences
BF1404	133.06	Congresses
BF1407	133.03	Dictionaries/Encyclopedias
BF1408-.2	133.092	Biography
BF1409	133.025	Directories
BF1421-1429	133.09	History
BF1434	133.09(4-9)	By place
BF1444-1486	133.1	Ghosts/Apparitions
BF1501-1562	133.42	Demonology
BF1546-1550	133.422	Satanism
BF1562.5-1623	133.43	Witchcraft/Magic
BF1651-1729	133.5	Astrology
BF1745-1779	133.3248	Oracles/Divinations
BF1783-1815	133.3	Seers/Prophets
BF1845-1999	133.3	Fortune-telling
BH	111.85	Aesthetics
BH1-8	111.8505	Serials
BH11-19	111.8506	Societies/Congresses
BH39-41	111.8501	Philosophy
BH56	111.8503	Dictionaries/Encyclopedias
BH61-62	111.8507	Education
BH81-208	111.8509	History
BH221	111.8509(4-9)	By place
BJ	170	Ethics
BJ1-8	170.5	Serials
BJ10-11	170.6	Societies
BJ19	170.6	Congresses
BJ37-60	170.1	Philosophy/Methodology
BJ63	170.3	Dictionaries/Encyclopedias
BJ66-68	170.7	Education
BJ71-982	170.9	History of ethics
BJ101-214	170.9	Ancient
BJ116-118	170.9	China/Japan
BJ121-123	170.954/294.5	India
BJ131-133	170.932/299.3	Egypt
BJ136-143	170.9(35/55)	Assyria-Babylonia/Persia
BJ160-214	170.93(7-8)	Greece/Rome
BJ231-255	170.902	Medieval
BJ271-285	170.90(23-31)	Renaissance
BJ301-944	170.90(3-4)	Modern
BJ351-354	170.973	United States
BJ401-404	170.971	Canada
BJ421-424	170.972	Mexico
BJ431-434	170.9728	Central America
BJ441-444	170.9729	West Indies
BJ441-564	170.98	South America
BJ591-594	170.9436	Austria
BJ595-598	170.94977	Bulgaria
BJ601-654	170.941	Great Britain
BJ701-704	170.944	France
BJ751-759	170.943	Germany
BJ801-804	170.9495	Greece
BJ805-808	170.9439	Hungary
BJ811-814	170.945	Italy
BJ831-834	170.9492	Netherlands
BJ841-844	170.9493	Belgium
BJ847-850	170.9438	Poland
BJ851-854	170.947	European Russia
BJ861-894	170.948	Scandinavia
BJ871-874	170.9489	Denmark
BJ881-884	170.9481	Norway
BJ891-894	170.9485	Sweden
BJ911-914	170.946	Spain
BJ921-924	170.9469	Portugal
BJ941-944	170.9494	Switzerland
BJ961-964	170.95	Asia
BJ965-968	170.951	China
BJ971	170.952	Japan
BJ973-976	170.9519	Korea
BJ980-982	170.96	Africa
BJ901-1185	170	Textbooks, By language
BJ1075-1077	170.202	Outlines/Etc.
BJ1188-1295	291.5	Religious ethics
BJ1238-1278.5	241	Christian ethics
BJ1279-1287	296.385	Jewish ethics
BJ1289	294.35	Buddhist ethics
BJ1292	297.5	Islamic ethics
BJ1518-1535	179.(8/9)	Virtue/Vices/Character
BJ1725	174	Professional ethics
BJ1801-2195	395	Etiquette
BJ1801	395.0(5/6)	Serials/Societies
BJ1815	395.03	Dictionaries/Encyclopedias
BJ1821	395.09	History
BJ1843	395.0207	Satire/Etc.
BJ2018-2019.5	395.53	Church etiquette
BJ2021-2078	395.3	Entertaining/Hospitality
BJ2081-2115	395.4	Correspondence/Stationery
BJ2120-2128	395.59	Conversation etiquette
BJ2139-2156	395.5	Specific situations
BJ2195	395.59	Telephone etiquette
BL	200	Religion
BL1-10	200.5	Serials
BL11-21	200.6	Societies/Congresses
BL31	200.3	Dictionaries/Encyclopedias
BL35	200.25	Directories
BL41-42	200.7	Education
BL51-54	200.1	Philosophy of religion
BL70-71	291.82	Sacred books
BL71.5-72	200.92	Biography
BL74-98	290-299	Religions of the world
BL175-290	210	Natural theology
BL239-265	291.175	Religion and science
BL300-325	291.13	Myth
BL350-385	291.14	Classification of religions
BL390	292-299	World religions
BL410	291.172	Inter-relations of religions
BL425-490	291.2	Religious doctrines
BL500-547	291.23	Eschatology
BL550-619	291.(3/43)	Worship
BL624-627	291.4	Religious life
BL630-632	291.65	Religious organizations
BL633	291.63	Prophets
BL635	291.61	Priests
BL637	291.7	Missionaries
BL639	291.42	Religious conversion
BL640	291.1772	Religious liberty
BL660-2670	291.09	History
BL660-687	291.0956	Middle East
BL690-980	291.094	Europe
BL700-820	292	Classical religions/Myths
BL740-760	299.92	Etruscan
BL780-795	292.08	Greek
BL800-820	292.07	Roman
BL830-875	293	Germanic/Norse
BL900-980	291.094/299.16	Other European religions
BL1000-2370	294/299.5	Asian/Oriental
BL1100-1295	294.5	Hinduism
BL1112.2-1137.5	294.5921	Vedic texts
BL1141.2-1142.6	294.59(2/5)	Tantric texts
BL1213.32-1215.7	294.52	Doctrines/Theology
BL1216-1225	294.5211	Pantheon/Deities
BL1225.2-1243.58	294.54	Practice/Worship
BL1238	294.5657	Monasticism

LC	Dewey	Descriptor	LC	Dewey	Descriptor
BL1239.32	294.5446	Pilgrims	BM328-330	296.09469	Portugal
BL1239.72-.82	294.536	Festivals	BM331-333	296.0947	European Russia
BL1243.32-.36	294.57	Missionaries	BM334-336	296.094897	Finland
BL1243.72-.78	294.5657	Monasteries	BM337-339	296.09438	Poland
BL1271.2-1295	294.55	Sects/Cults	BM340-353	296.0948	Scandinavia
BL1300-1380	294.4	Jainism	BM342-344	296.09489	Denmark
BL1310-1314.2	294.482	Sacred books	BM348-350	296.09481	Norway
BL1356-1375	294.42	Doctrine	BM351-353	296.09485	Sweden
BL1376-1380	294.44	Practice/Worship	BM354-356	296.0946	Spain
BL1324-1327	294.409	By place	BM357-359	296.09494	Switzerland
BL1500-1590	295	Zoroastrianism	BM364-366	296.094977	Bulgaria
BL1510-1525	295.82	Sacred books	BM370-372	296.09498	Romania
BL1600-1710	299.2	Semitic religions	BM373-375	296.09497	Yugoslavia
BL1750-2375	299.5	Asian religions, By place	BM377-431	296.095	Asia
BL1800-1975	299.51	China	BM386.4-.6	296.09567	Iraq/Mesopotamia
BL2000-2032	299.141(1-44)	India	BM387-389	296.09569(1/4)	Syria/Palestine
BL2035	299.1412	Pakistan	BM390-392	296.095694	Israel
BL2050-2150	299.95(8-95)	Southeast Asia	BM393-395	296.0953	Arabia
BL2200-2228	299.956	Japan	BM396-398	296.0955	Iran
BL2230-2240	299.957	Korea	BM400	296.09581	Afghanistan
BL2270-2280	299.915	Iran	BM406-410	296.0954	India
BL2290	299.919	Phrygia	BM423-425	296.0951	China
BL2300	299.95	Siberia	BM426-428	296.0952	Japan
BL2320-2370	291.093	Mediterranean region	BM432-440	296.096	Africa
BL2400-2490	299.6	Africa	BM434-436	296.0962	Egypt
BL2420-2460	299.62	Egyptian	BM437	296.0968	South Africa
BL2462	299.61	North Africa	BM443-445	296.099(3-4)	Australia/New Zealand
BL2463	299.68	Southern Africa	BM447-449	296.099(5-6)	Oceania
BL2464	299.676	East Africa	BM480-488	296.1	Pre-Talmudic literature
BL2465	299.696	West Africa	BM495-532	296.(12-8)	Rabbinical literature
BL2520-2560	299.7	North America	BM497-509	296.12	Talmudic literature
BL2580-2592	299.8	South America	BM510-518	296.14	Midrash
BL2600-2630	299.92	Oceania	BM520-523	296.18	Halacha
BL2670	299.92	Arctic	BM525-526	296.16	Cubala
BL2700-2790	211.4	Rationalism	BM600-652	296.3	Dogmatic Judaism
BM	296	Judaism	BM615-625	296.33	Messiah
BM1	296.0(5/6)	Serials/Societies	BM650-747	296.7	Practice of Judaism
BM11	296.05	Yearbooks	BM653-655	296.65	Congregations/Temples
BM21-30	296.06	Societies/Congresses	BM656-685	296.72	Worship
BM50	296.03	Dictionaries/Encyclopedias	BM690-720	296.43	Festivals
BM51	296.076	Questions/Answers	BM730-747	296.42	Preaching
BM55-65	296.025	Directories	BM750-755	296.092	Biography
BM70-135	296.68	Education	BM900-990	296.81	Samaritans
BM150-449	296.09	History	BP	297	Islam
BM165-178	296.81	Ancient	BP1-9	297.05	Serials
BM180-185	296.82	Medieval	BP10-15	297.06	Societies/Congresses
BM190-199	296.83	Modern	BP40	297.03	Dictionaries/Encyclopedias
BM193	296.0903(1-3)	16th-18th centuries	BP42-48	297.07	Education
BM195	296.090(34-4)	19th-20th centuries	BP50-68	297.09	History
BM197.5	296.8342	Conservative	BP70-80	297.092	Biography
BM198	296.8332	Hasidism	BP100-137	297.12	Sacred books
BM201-449	296.09(4-9)	By place	BP100-134	297.122	Koran
BM205-225	296.0973	United States	BP135-136	297.124	Hadith literature
BM227-229	296.0971	Canada	BP140-165	340.59	Islamic law
BM230-232	296.0972	Mexico	BP166	297.2	Theology
BM233-247	296.09728	Central America	BP174-190	297.(3-4)	Practice/Worship
BM248-260	296.09729	West Indies	BP184	297.38	Ceremonies/Rites
BM261-289	296.098	South America	BP186	297.3(6/8)	Feasts/Festivals
BM290-376	296.094	Europe	BP187	297.35	Shrines
BM292-305	296.0941	Great Britain	BP188-190	297.4	Religious life
BM307-309	296.09436	Austria	BP192-194	297.82	Shiites
BM310-312	296.09493	Belgium	BP195-253	297.8	Other sects
BM313-315	296.0944	France	BP300-395	297.93	Bahaism
BM316-318	296.0943	Germany	BP500-585	299.934	Theosophy
BM319-321	296.09495	Greece	BP595-597	299.935	Anthroposophy
BM322-324	296.0945	Italy	BP600-610	297.(8/9)	Other beliefs/Movements
BM325-327	296.09492	Netherlands	BQ	294.3	Buddhism

LC	Dewey	Descriptor	LC	Dewey	Descriptor
BQ1-10	294.305	Serials	BR	200	Christianity
BQ12-93	294.306	Societies/Clubs	BR1-9	205	Serials
BQ96-99	294.306	Financial institutions	BR21-29	206	Societies
BQ141-209	294.307	Religious education	BR41-43	206	Congresses
BQ210-219	294.307	Research	BR95-99	203	Encyclopedias/Dictionaries
BQ251-799	294.309	History	BR100-114	201	Philosophy
BQ286-317	294.3090(1-4)	By period	BR115	261	And other subjects
BQ320-799	294.309(4-9)	By place	BR117-126	808.0662/270	Christian literature
BQ330-349	294.30954	India	BR127-128	261.2	And other religions
BQ350-379	294.3095493	Sri Lanka	BR138-1500	209/270	History
BQ380-396	294.3095496	Nepal	BR160-481	209.0(1-4)/270.(1-82)	By period
BQ416-439	294.309591	Burma	BR160.3-275	209.0 (1-2)/270.(1-4)	Early/Medieval
BQ440-509	294.30959(4-7)	Indochina	BR280	209.0(23-31)/270.(5-7)	Renaissance/Reformation
BQ510-539	294.309598	Indonesia	BR290-481	209.0(3-4)/270.8	Modern
BQ540-549	294.309595	Malaysia	BR500-1500	209.(4-9)/274-279	Christianity, By place
BQ550-568	294.309593	Thailand	BR513-563	209.73/277.3	United States
BQ570-609	294.30958	Central Asia	BR610-615	209.72/277.2	Mexico
BQ610-699	294.3095	Far East	BR620-625	209.728/277.28	Central America
BQ620-649	294.30951	China	BR640-655	209.729/277.29	Caribbean
BQ650-669	294.309519	Korea	BR660-730	209.8/278	South America
BQ670-699	294.30952	Japan	BR740-799	209.41/274.1	Great Britain
BQ700-709	294.3094	Europe	BR840-849	209.44/274.4	France
BQ710-719	294.3096	Africa	BR850-859	209.43/274.3	Germany
BQ720-760	294.309(7-8)	America	BR930-939	209.47/274.7	European Russia
BQ730-739	294.30973	United States	BR970-1019	209.48/274.8	Scandinavia
BQ740-749	294.30971	Canada	BR1020-1029	209.46/274.6	Spain
BQ770-799	294.3099(3-6)	Pacific area	BR1060-1357	209.5/275	Asia
BQ800-829	294.3	Persecutions	BR1150-1156	209.54/275.4	India
BQ840-999	294.3092	Biography	BR1178-1261	209.59/275.9	Southeast Asia
BQ860-939	294.363	Buddha	BR1280-1297	209.51/275.1	China
BQ1100-3340	294.382	Tripitaka (Canon literature)	BR1300-1317	209.52/275.2	Japan
BQ1170-3340	294.382(2-4)	By version	BR1320-1337	209.519/275.19	Korea
BQ4061-4570	294.34	Doctrinal/Systematic	BR1359-1470	209.6/276	Africa
BQ4080-4125	294.3409	History	BR1369-1415	209.61/276.1	North Africa
BQ4180-4565	294.34	Special doctrines	BR1430	209.67/276.7	Central Africa
BQ4195-4250	294.34	Dharma	BR1440-1445	209.676/276.76	East Africa
BQ4260-4263	294.34	Seal of 3 laws	BR1446-1458	209.68/276.8	Southern Africa
BQ4401-4430	294.345	Virtues/Vices	BR1460-1470	209.66/276.6	West Africa
BQ4475-4525	294.3423	Eschatology	BR1480-1495	209.9(3-6)/279.(3-6)	Australia/New
BQ4600-4610	294.33172	Buddhism and other			Zealand/Oceania
		religions	BR1500	209.98/279.8	Polar regions
BQ4620-4890	294.34211	Pantheism	BR1600-1609	272	Persecutions/Martyrs
BQ4911-5720	294.34(3-4)	Practice/Worship	BR1610-1617	261.72	Tolerance/Liberalism
BQ4965-5030	294.3438	Ceremonies	BR1690-1725	209.2	Biography
BQ5035-5065	294.3438	Hymns/Chants	BS	220	Bible
BQ5070-5075	294.3437	Altar/etc.	BS1-355	220.(4-5)	Versions
BQ5100-5125	294.3437	Symbols	BS11-115	220.4	Early
BQ5130-5137	294.3435	Temple	BS125-355	220.5	Modern
BQ5140-5355	294.361	Ministry/Priesthood	BS390-399	220.520 (1-9)6	Selections/Quotes
BQ5360-5680	294.344	Religious life	BS405-408	220.52	Abridged
BQ5485-5530	294.3(4-5)	Precepts	BS410-680	220.(6-7)	Works about the Bible
BQ5535-5594	294.3443	Meditation/Prayer	BS420-429	220.3	Concordances
BQ5700-5720	294.3436	Festivals	BS482-498	220.7	Commentaries
BQ5720-5845	294.34	Folklore	BS500-534	220.6	Criticism/Interpretation
BQ5851-5899	294.337832	Welfare work	BS535-537	809.93522	As literature
BQ5901-5975	294.37	Missionary work	BS546-559	220/226.9505	Bible stories
BQ6001-6160	294.3657	Monasticism	BS569-580	221/225.92	People of the Bible
BQ6200-6240	294.34447	Asceticism	BS580	221.092	People in the Old Testament
BQ6300-6388	294.3(657/435)	Monasteries/Shrines	BS585-613	220.07	Education
BQ6400-6495	294.34446	Pilgrims	BS635-636	220.095	And history
BQ7001-9800	294.39	Modifications/Schools	BS647-649	220.15	Prophecy
BQ7100-7285	294.391	Theravada Buddhism	BS701-1830	221	Old Testament
BQ7300-7522	294.392	Mahayana Buddhism	BS701-1013	221.(4-5)	Texts and versions
BQ7530-7950	294.3923	Lamaism	BS705-815	221.4	Early
BQ8000-9800	294.392	Special sects	BS737-765	221.48	Ancient Greek
BQ8500-8769	294.3926	Pure Land	BS767-815	221.47	Latin
BQ9250-9519	294.3927	Zen	BS825-1013	221.5	Modern

LC	Dewey	Descriptor	LC	Dewey	Descriptor
BS1091-1099	221.520(1-9)6	Selections/Quotes	BT650-654	232.917	Miracles/Shrines
BS1104	221.65	Harmonies	BT683-694	235.2	Misc. Saints
BS1121-1128	221.520(1-9)3	Concordances	BT695-748	231.765	Creation
BS1130-1136	221.09	History	BT700-745	233	Man
BS1143-1158	221.7	Commentaries	BT750-810	234	Salvation
BS1160-1191	221.6	Criticism/Interpretation	BT809-810	234.9	Freedom/Predestination
BS1192	230	Theology of	BT819-891	236	Eschatology
BS1193-1195	221.07	Education	BT834-842	236.25	Hades
BS1200-1830	222-224	Special parts	BT844-849	236.24	Heaven
BS1221-1285	222.1	Pentateuch	BT875-891	236.9	End of world
BS1401-1490	223	Political books	BT899-940	236.2	Future life/State
BS1419-1450	223.2	Psalms	BT919-925	236.22	Immortality
BS1455-1490	223	Wisdom literature	BT960-985	235	Invisible world
BS1501-1675	224	Prophetic books	BT968	235.3	Angels
BS1691-1830	229	Apocrypha	BT975-981	235.4	Demons
BS1901-2970	225-228	New Testament	BT990-1010	238	Creeds/Etc.
BS1901-2213	225.(4-5)	Texts and versions	BT1029-1040	238	Catechisms
BS1937-2020	225.4	Early	BT1095-1253	239	Apologetics
BS2025-2213	225.5	Modern	BT1109-1115	239.009	History
BS2260-2269	225.520(1-9)6	Selections/Quotes	BT1313-1480	230.(1-9)/270-273	History of doctrines/ Movements
BS2280-2545	225.(6-7)	Works about New Testament	BT1319-1480	230.(1-9)/270-273	By periods
BS2301-2312	225.520(1-9)3	Concordances	BV	248	Christian practical theology
BS2315-2318	225.09	History	BV1	248.05	Serials
BS2333-2348	225.7	Commentaries	BV2.5	248.03	Dictionaries
BS2350-2393	225.6	Criticism/Interpretation	BV5-530	248.3/264	Worship
BS2397-2405	230	Theology of	BV5-8	248.309	History
BS2415-2417	232.954	Teachings of Jesus	BV15-29	264	Public worship
BS2430-2520	225.092	People of the Bible	BV30-135	263.9	Church year
BS2525-2544	225.07	Education	BV43-64	263.9(1-7)	Feast days
BS2547-2970	226-228	Special parts	BV65-70	263.98	Saints' days
BS2549-2619	226.(2-5)	Gospels	BV80-105	263.9	Fast days
BS2620-2629	226.6	Acts	BV107-133	263.4	Lord's day
BS2630-2638	227	Epistles	BV150-168	246.55	Symbols
BS2640-2815	227	Pauline Epistles	BV169-199	264	Liturgy/Rituals
BS2820-2827	228	Apocalypse	BV195-196	247.1	Altars
BS2831-2970	229	Apocrypha	BV198-199	264	Books/Liturgies
BT	230	Christian doctrinal theology	BV200	249	Family worship
BT19-33	230-236	Doctrine and dogma	BV205-287	248.32	Prayer
BT20-30	230.09	History	BV290-530	264.2	Music/Hymns
BT40-55	230.01	Philosophical theology	BV343-520	264.2	Hymn books
BT65-84	230-239	Doctrinal/Dogmatic/ Systematic	BV590-1652	260	Ecclesiastical theology
BT94	231.72	Kingdom of God	BV598-603	260	The church
BT95-97	241.2	Divine law	BV629-633	261.7	Church and state
BT98-180	231	God	BV646-651	262	Church polity
BT109-115	231.(1-3)	Trinity	BV652-.9	262.0068	Church management
BT117-123	231.3	Holy Spirit	BV652.95-657	254.3	Mass media
BT130-157	231.4	Divine attributes	BV659-690	262.14	Clergy/Ministry
BT160-180	231.8	Theodicy	BV700-741	262	Parish/Congregation/ Authority
BT198-590	232	Christology	BV770-774	254.8	Church finance
BT230-245	232.1	Messiahship	BV775-777	247/254.7/262.933	Property
BT250-270	232.8	Offices of Jesus Christ	BV800-838	265	Sacraments/Ordinances
BT296-500	232.9	Life of Christ	BV800-813	265.1	Baptism
BT304	232.903	Character/Personality (Jesus)	BV823-828	264.36	Holy Communion
BT306	232.9(01/5)	Words of Jesus	BV835-838	265.5	Marriage
BT340-500	232.95	Public life of Jesus	BV900-1450	267	Societies/Associations
BT373-378	226.8/232.954	Parables	BV1000-1220	267.3	YMCA
BT380-382	226.9/232.954	Sermon on the Mount	BV1300-1393	267.5	YWCA
BT400-420	232.9 (56-97)	Transfiguration to Ascension	BV1420-1430	267.613	YPSCE
BT430-470	232.96	Passion	BV1460-1615	268	Religious education/ Schools
BT580	232.955	Miracles/Shrines	BV1500-1579	268	Sunday schools
BT587	232.966	Relics	BV1534-1536	268.6	Teaching methods
BT595-680	232.91	Mary	BV1607-1612	207	In public/Private schools
BT610-640	232.91	Theology	BV1620-1652	259.8	Social life/Recreation
			BV2000-3705	266	Missions

LC	Dewey	Descriptor	LC	Dewey	Descriptor
BV2000-2121	266.02	General/Foreign	BX515-558	262.01947	Organization
BV2130-2300	266.2	Roman Catholic	BX560-573	264.01947	Worship
BV2350-2595	266.(4-9)	Protestant	BX575-577	281.947092	Saints
BV2400-2595	266.(4-9)09	History	BX580-583	255.(8/98)	Monasticism
BV2495-2525.2	266.(4-9)	By denomination	BX595-597	281.947092	Biography
BV2750-3695	266.023	In specific countries	BX610-619	281.9495	Greek
BV2762-2808	266.0230973	United States	BX630-639	281.943(6/9)	Austria/Hungary
BV2810-2820	266.0230971	Canada	BX650-754	281.9(4-9)	Other areas
BV2829-2853	266.02309(72-8)	Latin America	BX800-4795	282	Roman Catholic
BV2855-3145	266.023094	Europe	BX800-816	282.0(5/6)	Serials/Societies
BV2860-2875	266.0230941	Great Britain	BX820-837	262.52	Councils
BV2940-2945	266.0230944	France	BX841-847	282.03	Dictionaries
BV2950-2957	266.0230943	Germany	BX895-939	268.82/207	Education
BV2970-2975	266.0230945	Italy	BX940-1745	282.09	History
BV3120-3127	266.0230946	Spain	BX950-961	262.13	Papacy
BV3147	266.023091822	Mediterranean region	BX965-1397	262.13090(1-4)/270.(1-5)	By date
BV3149-3487	266.023095	Asia	BX1070-1176	262.1309021/270.(1-3)	590-1049
BV3160-3217	266.0230956	Near East	BX1178-1200	262.1309021/270.4	1049-1122
BV3220-3240	266.0230958	Central Asia	BX1210-1263	262.1309022/270.(4-5)	1122-1305
BV3250-3290	266.0230954	South Asia	BX1270-1302	262.130902(3-4)/270.5	1305-1447
BV3260-3290	266.0230954	India	BX1304-1329	262.13090(24-3)/270.5	1447-1572
BV3298-3390	266.0230959	Southeast Asia	BX1330-1361	262.130903(1-3)/270.(6-7)	1572-1789
BV3400-3457	266.023095	East Asia	BX1365-1390	262.13090(34-4)/270.8	1789-
BV3410-3427	266.0230951	China	BX1401-1695	282.(4-9)	By place
BV3440-3457	266.0230952	Japan	BX1404-1418	282.73	United States
BV3470-3487	266.0230957	North Asia	BX1419-1424	282.71	Canada
BV3500-3630	266.023096	Africa	BX1427-1431	282.72	Mexico
BV3560-3625	266.023096(1-9)	Africa, By country	BX1432-1447	282.728	Central America
BV3640-3680	266.023099(3-6)	Oceania	BX1448-1459	282.729	West Indies
BV3650-3667	266.023099(3-4)	Australia/New Zealand	BX1460-1489	282.8	South America
BV3670-3680	266.023099(5-6)	Oceania	BX1490-1612	282.4	Europe
BV3690-3695	266.0230998	Polar regions	BX1491-1514	282.41	Great Britain
BV3750-3799	269.2	Evangelism/Revivals	BX1528-1533	282.44	France
BV4000-4470	253	Pastoral theology	BX1534-1539	282.43	Germany
BV4012	253.52	Psychology	BX1543-1548	282.45	Italy
BV4019-4180	253.07	Education	BX1558-1560	282.47	European Russia
BV4200-4317	251	Preaching/Homiletics	BX1583-1588	282.46	Spain
BV4239-4317	252	Sermons	BX1615-1673	282.5	Asia
BV4390-4399	253.2	Personal life	BX1617-1636	282.56	Middle East
BV4485-5099	248	Christian life	BX1637-1642	282.58	Central Asia
BV4520-4526	248.(4-5)/249	Religious duties	BX1643-1661	282.54	South Asia
BV4527-4599	248.8(2-9)	For special persons	BX1662-1670	282.5	East Asia
BV4625-4780	241	Moral theology	BX1675-1682	282.6	Africa
BV4625-4627	241.3	Sins/Vices	BX1685-1695	282.9(3-6)	Australia/New Zealand/Oceania
BV4630-4647	241.4	Virtues			
BV4650-4715	241.5(2-4)	Biblical precepts	BX1700-1745	272.2	Inquisition
BV4720-4780	241.57	Church precepts	BX1746-1755	230.2	Theology/Doctrine
BV4800-4897	242	Meditation/Devotion	BX1756	252.02	Sermons/Etc.
BV4912-4950	248.24	Religious conversion	BX1781-1789	282	And other churches
BV5015-5068	248.47	Asceticism	BX1790-1795	261.7	And the state
BV5070-5095	248.22	Mysticism	BX1800-1920	262.02	Organization
BV5099	248.47	Quietism	BX1805-1815	262.13	Pope
BX	280-289	Christian church denominations	BX1818-1899	262.136	Curia romana
			BX1905-1920	262.1	Priests/Bishops/Etc.
BX1-9	261.001	Church unity	BX1958-1968	238.2	Creeds/Catechisms
BX100-754	281	Eastern/Oriental	BX1970-2175	264.02	Liturgy and ritual
BX200-754	281.9	Orthodox Eastern	BX1973-1975	264.020090(1-4)	By period
BX290-310	281.909	Eastern/Orthodox history	BX1977	264.02009(4-9)	By place
BX350-376	264.019	Liturgy and ritual	BX1980-1990	264.02(1-9)	Books/Texts
BX377-378	264.019	Sacraments	BX1999-2045	264.02 (1-9)	Special liturgical books
BX380	235.2/270.092	Saints	BX2000	264.024	Breviaries
BX385-388	255.(8/98)	Monasticism	BX2010	264.0272	Holy week
BX390-359	281.9092	Biography	BX2015	264.023	Missals
BX400-754	281.9(4-9)	Divisions	BX2030-2031	264.025	Pontificals
BX460-605	281.947	Russian Orthodox	BX2035	264.025	Rituals
BX485-492	281.94709	History	BX2037	264.023	Sacramentaries
BX494-500	281.94709(4-9)	By place	BX2050-2155	242.802	Prayer books

LC	Dewey	Descriptor
BX2159	231.73/232.96	Devotions to Jesus
BX2160-2161	231.73/232.91	Devotions to Virgin Mary
BX2164-2167	231.73/232.932	Devotions to St. Joseph
BX2169	264.02	Eucharistic devotions
BX2178-2198	242	Meditations
BX2200-2292	264.0208	Sacraments
BX2215-2239	264.02036	Eucharist
BX2240	264.02084	Ordination (Holy Order)
BX2250-2254	264.02085	Marriage
BX2260-2267	264.02086	Penance
BX2270	264.020864	Absolution
BX2279-2283	264.020866	Indulgences
BX2295-2310	264.02091	Sacramentals
BX2320-2321	263.042(3-9)	Shrines
BX2323	248.463	Pilgrimages
BX2325-2333	282.0922	Saints
BX2347-2348	248.482	Practical religion
BX2349-2377	248.482	Christian life
BX2380-2386	248.482	Religious life
BX2400-4556	255.(1-7/9)	Monasticism/Orders
BX2433-2434	255.(1-7)	Superiors/Administration
BX2435-2438	255.(1-7)06	Life/Rules
BX2460-2749	255.(1-7)009	History
BX2465-2475	255.(1-7)0090(1-4)	By period
BX2501-2749	255.(1-7)009	By place
BX2505-2525	255.(1-7)00973	United States
BX2527-2529	255.(1-7)00971	Canada
BX2530-2532	255.(1-7)00972	Mexico
BX2533-2547	255.(1-7)009728	Central America
BX2548-2560	255.(1-7)009729	Caribbean
BX2561-2589	255.(1-7)0098	South America
BX2631-2676	255.(1-7)0094	Europe
BX2677-2731	255.(1-7)0095	Asia
BX2732-2740	255.(1-7)0096	Africa
BX2747-2749	255.(1-7)0099(3-6)	Australia/New Zealand/Oceania
BX2890-4192	255.(1-7)	Individual orders/Men
BX4200-4250	255.9	General orders for women
BX4262-4556	255.9(1-7)	Individual orders for women
BX4600-4644	282.(4-9)	Churches, By place
BX4600-4603	282.73	United States
BX4605	282.71	Canada
BX4610	282.72	Mexico
BX4615	282.728	Central America
BX4618	282.729	West Indies
BX4620-4625	282.8	South America
BX4627-4638	282.4	Europe
BX4629	282.44	France
BX4630	282.43	Germany
BX4631	282.41	Great Britain
BX4634	282.45	Italy
BX4635	282.469	Portugal
BX4636	282.46	Spain
BX4640	282.5	Asia
BX4642	282.6	Africa
BX4644	282.9(3-6)	Australia/New Zealand/Oceania
BX4650-4705	282.092	Biography
BX4654-4660	282.0922	Saints/Martyrs, Collected bios.
BX4700-4705	282.092	Saints/Martyrs, Biographies
BX4800-9999	283-289/280.4	Protestantism
BX4800-4801	280.40(5/6)	Serials/Societies
BX4804-4807	280.407/283-289.09	Protestantism, History
BX4818	280.4	And other Christians
BX4819-4821	280.4	Anti-Protestant
BX4825-4827	280.4092	Biography
BX4833-4861	280.409(4-9)	Protestantism, By place
BX4833	280.40972	Mexico
BX4833.5-4834	280.409728	Central America
BX4835	280.409729	West Indies
BX4836	280.4098	South America
BX4837-4854	280.4094	Europe
BX4838-4840	280.40941	Great Britain
BX4843	280.40944	France
BX4844	280.40943	Germany
BX4847	280.40945	Italy
BX4849	280.40947	European Russia
BX4851	280.40945	Spain
BX4857	280.4095	Asia
BX4861	280.4099(3-6)	Australia/New Zealand/Oceania
BX4872-4924	280.4	Pre-Reformation
BX4872-4893	284.4	Waldenses/Albiegenses
BX4900-4906	284.3	Lollards/Wycliffites
BX4913-4924	284.3	Hussites
BX4929-4946	284.3	Anabaptists
BX5001-6093	283	Anglican Communion
BX5001-5002	283.0(5/6)	Serials/Societies
BX5005	283.090 (1-5)	Anglican history
BX5008.11	252.03	Sermons
BX5011-5740	283.42	Church of England
BX5011-5023	283.420(5/6)	Serials/Societies
BX5031	283.42025	Directories
BX5041-5050	207/268.8342	Education
BX5051-5101	283.4209	Church of England, History
BX5067-5101	283.4209(1-5)	By period
BX5103-5110	283.(4-9)	By place
BX5115-5126	283.42	Movements
BX5127-5129	283.42	And other churches
BX5137-5140	230.342	Dogma
BX5140.5-5147	264.0342	Liturgy and ritual
BX5145	264.03	Prayer books
BX5146	264.038	Psalter
BX5148-5149	264.035	Sacraments
BX5150-5182	262.0342	Organization
BX5194-5195	283.42	Churches
BX5197-5199	283.42092	Biography
BX5210-5395	283.411	Episcopal Church in Scotland
BX5300-5310	293.41109	Church in Scotland, History
BX5335-5337	264.03411	Liturgy and ritual
BX5340-5355	262.03411	Organization
BX5369-5370	283.411	Churches
BX5390-5395	283.411092	Biography
BX5410-5595	283.417	Church in Ireland
BX5500-5510	283.41709	Church in Ireland, History
BX5535-5537	264.03415	Liturgy and ritual
BX5540-5555	262.03415	Organization
BX5569-5570	283.415	Churches
BX5590-5595	283.415092	Biography
BX5596-5598	283.3	Anglican Church in Wales
BX5600-5740	283	Church of England abroad
BX5601-5620	283	Anglican Church of Canada
BX5601-5604	283.0(5/6)	Serials/Societies/Congresses
BX5610-5613	283.09	In Canada, History
BX5617	283	Churches
BX5619-5620	283.092	Biography
BX5661-5680	283	Asia
BX5681-5700	283	Africa
BX5701-5720	283	Australia/New Zealand
BX5721-5740	283	Oceania
BX5800-6093	283.73	Episcopal Church

LC	Dewey	Descriptor	LC	Dewey	Descriptor
BX5869-5876	207/268.873(5-9)	Education	BX6901-6997	289.5	Christian Science
BX5879-5919	283.709	Episcopal Church, History	BX6901-6903	289.50(5/6)	Serials/Societies
BX5881-5882	283.709(34-4)	By period	BX6905-6907	289.506	Congresses
BX5885-5919	283.7(4-9)	Episcopal Church, By place	BX6917	268.895/207	Education
BX5926-5928	283.73	And other Churches	BX6931-6935	289.509	Christian Science, History
BX5929-5930	230.373	Doctrines	BX6950	234.13/289.5	Healing
BX5939	238.373	Creeds	BX6958	262.095	Organization
BX5940	264.0373	Liturgy and ritual	BX6960	264.095	Service/Liturgy
BX5943-5945	264.0373	Book of common prayer	BX6980-6985	289.5	Individual churches
BX5946	264.03873	Psalter	BX6990-6996	289.5092	Biography
BX5947-5948	264.0373	Other rituals	BX7020-7097	286.73	Church of God
BX5949	264.03573	Sacraments	BX7101-7260	285.8	Congregationalism
BX5950-5968	262.0373	Organization	BX7101-7105	285.80(5/6)	Serials/Societies
BX5969	266.373	Missions	BX7106-7109	285.806	Congresses
BX5970-5974	255.(8/98)	Religious orders	BX7119-7127	268.858/207	Education
BX5971-5972	255.8	Men	BX7131-7228	285.809	Congregationalism, History
BX5973-5974	255.98	Women	BX7133-7228	285.8(4-9)	Congregationalism, By place
BX5980-5983	283.7(4-9)	Churches	BX7135-7149	285.87(3-9)	United States
BX5990	283.73092	Biography	BX7151-7173	285.871	Canada
BX5996-6030	283.7309(4-9)	By place (Abroad)	BX7175-7210	285.84	Europe
BX6051-6093	283.3	Reformed Episcopal	BX7215-7216	285.85	Asia
BX6051-6055	283.30(5/6)	Serials/Societies	BX7220-7222	285.86	Africa
BX6061-6064	268.83/207	Education	BX7225-7228	285.89(3-6)	Australia/New Zealand/Oceania
BX6065-6069	283.309 (34-4)	Episcopal Reformed, History	BX7233	252.058	Sermons
BX6074	238.33	Creeds	BX7235-7236	238.58	Creeds
BX6075	264.033	Liturgy and ritual	BX7237	264.058	Service/Liturgy
BX6076	262.033	Organization	BX7238-7239	264.058	Sacraments
BX6081-6083	283.7(4-9)	Churches	BX7240-7246	262.058	Organization
BX6091-6093	283.3092	Biography	BX7250-7252	230.58	Special doctrines
BX6101-6194	286.7	Adventists	BX7255-7257	285.8	Individual churches
BX6101-6193	286.73	Millerites	BX7259-7260	285.8092	Biography
BX6101-6105	286.70(5/6)	Serials/Societies	BX7301-7343	286.6	Disciples of Christ
BX6113	268.8673/207	Education	BX7433-7435	289.9	Dukhobors
BX6115-6117	286.709	Adventists, History	BX7451-7571	285.734	Evangelical and Reformed
BX6123	252.067	Sermons	BX7601-7795	289.6	Society of Friends (Quakers)
BX6124.3-.6	264.067	Ordinances/Sacraments	BX7601-7606	289.605	Serials/Societies
BX6131-6184	286.73	Branches	BX7606.5-7608	289.606	Congresses
BX6151-6154	286.732	Seventh-Day Adventists	BX7619-7627	268.896/207	Education
BX6185	286.7	Individual churches	BX7630-7732	289.609	Friends, History
BX6191-6193	286.7092	Biography	BX7633-7728	289.6(4-9)	By place
BX6195-6198	284.9	Arminians	BX7635-7649	289.67(3-9)	United States
BX6201-6495	286.(1-5)	Baptist	BX7650-7653	289.671	Canada
BX6201-6206	286.(1-5)0(5/6)	Serials/Societies/Congresses	BX7655-7673	289.6(72-8)	Latin America
BX6211-6213	286.(1-5)0(3/25)	Dictionaries/Directories	BX7675-7710	289.64	Europe
BX6219-6227	268.86(1-5)/207	Education	BX7676-7693	289.641	Great Britain
BX6231-6328	286.(1-5)09	History	BX7715-7716	289.65	Asia
BX6233-6328	286.(1-5)	History, By place	BX7720-7723	289.66	Africa
BX6235-6249	286.(1-5)7(3-9)	United States	BX7725-7728	289.69(3-6)	Australia/New Zealand/Oceania
BX6251-6253	286.(1-5)71	Canada	BX7733	252.096	Sermons
BX6254-6273	286.(1-5)(72/8)	Latin America	BX7737	264.096	Liturgy/Ritual
BX6275-6310	286.(1-5)4	Europe	BX7740-7746	262.096	Organization
BX6315-6316	286.(1-5)5	Asia	BX7751-7783	289.63	Individual branches/Meetings
BX6320-6322	286.(1-5)6	Africa	BX7790-7795	289.6092	Biography
BX6325-6326	286.(1-5)9(3-4)	Australia/New Zealand	BX7800-7843	286.5	German Baptist
BX6327-6328	286.(1-5)9(5-6)	Oceania	BX8001-8080	284.1	Lutheran
BX6330-6331	230.6(1-5)	Doctrine	BX8001-8011	284.10(5/6)	Serials/Etc.
BX6332-6333	252.06(1-5	Sermons	BX8012-8016	268.841/207	Education
BX6335-6336	238.6(1-5)	Creeds/Catechisms	BX8018-8063	284.109	Lutheran Church, History
BX6337-6339	264.06(1-5)	Liturgy/Ritual	BX8020-8063	284.1(4-9)	By place
BX6340-6346	262.06(1-5)	Organization	BX8020-8023	284.143	Germany
BX6349-6462	286.(1-5)	Branches	BX8025-8040	284.14	Other European areas
BX6475-6476	269.24	Meetings/Camps	BX8041-8061	284.173	United States
BX6480-6490	286.(1-5)	Individual churches			
BX6493-6495	286.1092	Biography			
BX6751-6799	286.63	Christian Church			
BX6801-6843	285.731	Christian Reformed			

LC	Dewey	Descriptor	LC	Dewey	Descriptor
BX8063.7	284.1	Relations with others	BX8622-8631	289.32	Sacred books
BX8066	252.041	Sermons	BX8639	252.093	Sermons
BX8067	264.041	Liturgy/Ritual	BX8649	238.93	Catechisms/Creeds
BX8071	262.041	Organization	BX8651	264.093	Liturgy/Ritual
BX8072-8073	264.041	Sacraments	BX8655	264.093	Sacraments
BX8075-8077	284.1	Individual churches	BX8657-8659	262.093	Organization
BX8079-8080	284.1092	Biography	BX8661	266.93	Missions
BX8101-8143	289.7	Mennonites	BX8670-8687	289.3	Individual branches/Temples
BX8101-8105	289.70(5/6)	Serials/Societies/Congresses			
BX8106	289.703	Dictionaries/Encyclopedias	BX8701-8749	289.4	New Jerusalem Church
BX8111-8114	268.897/207	Education	BX8701	289.405	Serials
BX8115-8119	289.709	History	BX8703-8705	289.406	Societies/Congresses
BX8116-8119	289.7(4-9)	Mennonites, By place	BX8714	268.894/207	Education
BX8116-8118	289.773	United States	BX8715-8719	289.409	History
BX8118.5-.7	289.771	Canada	BX8724	252.094	Sermons
BX8124	238.97	Catechism and creeds	BX8733	238.94	Creeds/Catechism
BX8125	264.097	Liturgy and ritual	BX8735	264.094	Liturgy/Ritual
BX8126	262.097	Organization	BX8736	264.094	Sacraments
BX8127	252.097	Sermons	BX8737	262.094	Organization
BX8129	289.73	Branches	BX8741-8743	289.4	Individual churches
BX8131-8132	289.7	Individual churches	BX8747-8749	289.4092	Biography
BX8141-8143	289.7092	Biography	BX8762-8780	289.94	Pentecostal churches
BX8201-8495	287	Methodism	BX8901-9225	285	Presbyterian
BX8201-8207	287.0(5/6)	Serials/Societies/Congresses	BX8901-8907	285.0(5/6)	Serials/Societies/Congresses
BX8219-8227	268.87/207	Education	BX8917-8925	268.85/207	Education
BX8231-8328	287.09	History	BX8930-9169	285.(1/2)09	Presbyterian, History
BX8233-8328	287.(1-8)(4-9)	Methodism, By place	BX8933-9169	285.(1/2)(4-9)	By place
BX8235-8249	287.(1-8)73	United States	BX8935-8999	285.1	United States
BX8251-8253	287.(1-8)71	Canada	BX8990-8998	285.136	Reformed Presbyterian
BX8254-8273	287.(1-8)(72-8)	Latin America	BX9001-9003	285.(1/2)71	Canada
BX8275-8310	287.(1-8)4	Europe	BX9011-9043	285.(1/2)(72-8)	Latin America
BX8276-8293	287.(1-8)41	Great Britain	BX9050-9140	285.(1/2)4	Europe
BX8315-8316	287.(1-8)5	Asia	BX9052-9105	285.2	Great Britain
BX8320-8322	287.(1-8)6	Africa	BX9150-9151	285.(1/2)5	Asia
BX8325-8328	287.(1-8)9(3-6)	Australia/New Zealand/Oceania	BX9160-9162	285.(1/2)6	Africa
			BX9168-9169	285.(1/2)9(3-6)	Australia/New Zealand/Oceania
BX8330-8331	287	And other churches			
BX8333	252.7	Sermons	BX9178	252.05	Sermons
BX8335	238.7	Catechisms/Creeds	BX9183-9184	238.5	Creeds/Catechisms
BX8336-8337	264.07	Worship/Liturgy/Ritual	BX9185-9187	264.05	Liturgy/Ritual
BX8338	264.07	Sacraments	BX9188-9189	264.05	Sacraments
BX8339-8346	262.07	Organization	BX9190-9195	262.05	Organization
BX8350-8473	287.(1-8)	Branches	BX9211-9215	285	Individual churches
BX8350-8359	287.1	Wesleyan	BX9220-9225	285.092	Biography
BX8370-8379	287.4	Primitive Methodist	BX9301-9359	285.9	Puritanism
BX8380-8389	287.6	United Methodist	BX9301-9303	285.90(5/6)	Serials/Societies
BX8390-8399	287.63(2-3)	Methodist Episcopal	BX9331-9359	285.909(4-9)	Puritanism, By place
BX8435-8473	287.8	Black Methodist	BX9401-9640	284.2	Reformed/Calvinist
BX8481-8483	287	Individual churches	BX9401	284.205	Serials
BX8491-8495	287.092	Biography	BX9403	284.206	Societies/Congresses
BX8525-8528	289.92	Jehovah's Witnesses	BX9412-9413	268.842/207	Education
BX8530	284.6	Moravian	BX9415	284.209	Reformed/Calvinist history
BX8551-8593	284.6	Moravian/United Brethren	BX9417-9419	284.2092	Biography
BX8551-8555	284.60(5/6)	Serials/Societies/Congresses	BX9420-9422	230.42	Doctrine
BX8561-8564	268.846/207	Education	BX9425	262.042	Organization
BX8565-8569	284.609	Moravian Church, History	BX9426	252.042	Sermons
BX8566-8569	284.6(4-9)	By place	BX9427	264.042	Liturgy/Ritual
BX8574-8575	264.046	Liturgy/Ritual/Devotions	BX9428-9429	238.42	Creeds/Catechisms
BX8576	262.046	Organization	BX9430-9640	284.2(4-9)	Reformed/Calvinist, By place
BX8577	252.046	Sermons			
BX8578	238.46	Catechisms/Creeds	BX9430-9480	284.24	Europe
BX8581-8583	284.6	Branches/Churches	BX9430-9439	284.2494	Switzerland
BX8591-8593	284.6092	Biography	BX9450-9459	284.244	France
BX8601-8695	289.3	Mormons	BX9470-9479	284.2492	Netherlands
BX8601-8605	289.30(5/6)	Serials/Societies/Congresses	BX9495-9593	284.273	United States
BX8610	268.893/207	Education	BX9596	284.271	Canada
BX8611-8617	289.309	History	BX9615	284.25	Asia

LC	Dewey	Descriptor	LC	Dewey	Descriptor
BX9618-9640	284.26	Africa	CC72-80.6	930.101	Philosophy/Theory
BX9701-9743	287.96	Salvation Army	CC83-97	930.107	Education
BX9751-9793	289.8	Shakers	CC107	930.1023	As a profession
BX9751-9755	289.80(5/6)	Serials/Societies/Congresses	CC110-115	930.1092	Biography
BX9761-9764	268.898/207	Education	CC120-125	930.1025	Directories
BX9765-9769	289.809	Shakers, History	CC135-137	930.1028	Preservation
BX9766-9769	289.809(4-9)	History, By place	CC140	930.1	Forgeries
BX9766-9768	289.80973	United States	CC300-350	910(4-9)	Crosses
BX9776	262.098	Organization	CC310-350	910(4-9)	Crosses, By place
BX9777	252.098	Sermons	CC600-605	910(4-9)	Boundary stones
BX9791-9793	289.8092	Biography	CC700-705	910(4-9)	Stone heaps
BX9801-9869	289.1	Unitarianism	CC900-950	910(4-9)	Hill figures/Tombs
BX9801	289.105	Serials	CC908-950	910(4-9)	By place
BX9803-9807	289.106	Societies/Congresses	CC960	910(4-9)	Lanterns of the dead
BX9817-9823	268.891/207	Education	CD	027/327.2/737.6	Diplomatics/Archives/Seals
BX9831-9835	289.109	History	CD1-511	027/327.2	Diplomatics
BX9833-9835	289.1(4-9)	Unitarianism, By place	CD1-15	027.005/327.205	Serials
BX9833	289.173	United States	CD20-29	027.006/327.206	Societies/Congresses
BX9842-9843	252.091	Sermons	CD40	027.003/327.203	Dictionaries/Encyclopedias
BX9850	262.091	Organization	CD46	027.001/327.201	Philosophy/Theory
BX9854	264.091	Sacraments	CD47	027.009/327.209	History
BX9861-9863	289.1	Individual churches	CD50-69	027.0090/327.2090(1-5)	General diplomatics, By date
BX9867-9869	289.1092	Biography			
BX9875-9877	289.9	United Brethren in Christ	CD70-79	354.(3-9)061	Chancelleries, By place
BX9875	289.905	Serials/Societies/Congresses	CD101-392	027.0(3-9)	Documents, By place
BX9876	252.099	Sermons	CD101-215	027.04	Europe
BX9877	289.9092	Biography	CD221-254	027.05	Asia
BX9881-9883	287.92	United Church of Canada	CD255-269	027.06	Africa
BX9884-9886	285.834	United Church of Christ	CD271-290	027.09(3-4)	Australia/New Zealand
BX9887	289.95	United Evangelical Church	CD291	027.09(5-6)	Oceania
BX9901-9969	289.134	Universalism	CD309-311	027.073	United States
BX9901	289.13405	Serials	CD331-332	027.071	Canada
BX9903-9907	289.13406	Societies/Congresses	CD333-334	027.072	Mexico
BX9917-9923	268.89134/207	Education	CD335-350	027.0728	Central America
BX9931-9935	289.13409	Universalism, History	CD351-362	027.0729	Caribbean area
BX9942-9943	252.09134	Sermons	CD365-392	027.08	South America
BX9953	264.09134	Services	CD501-511	354.(3-9)061007/027.007	Education
BX9954	264.09134	Sacraments	CD921-4280	027	Archives
BX9961-9962	289.134	Individual churches	CD921	027.00(5/6)	Serials/Societies
BX9967-9969	289.134092	Biography	CD941	027.0025	Directories
C	900	Auxiliary sciences of history	CD945	027.003	Dictionaries/Encyclopedias
			CD947-972	027.001	Philosophy/Theory
C2	906	Societies	CD973-976	027.0028	Methods/Techniques
C3	906	Congresses	CD981-985	022	Buildings/Furnishings
C4	905	Yearbooks	CD987-988	027.007	Education
C8	903	Dictionaries/Encyclopedias	CD995-4280	027.009	History
C20	907	Education	CD996-.4	027.0090(1-4)	By period
CB	909	History of civilization	CD1000-4280	027.0(1-9)	National archives, By place
CB3-4	905/906	Serials/Societies/Congresses	CD1000-2000	027.04	Europe
CB9	903	Dictionaries/Encyclopedias	CD1040-1199.5	027.041	Great Britain
CB13	902.22	Pictorial works	CD1120-1149.5	027.0436	Austria
CB15-18	907.2	Historiography	CD1150-1169.5	027.0437	Czechoslovakia
CB19	901	Philosophy	CD1170-1189.5	027.0439	Hungary
CB20	907	Education	CD1190-1219.5	027.044	France
CB23-151	909	World history, General	CD1220-1378.195	027.043	Germany
CB156	001.94	Alien evidences	CD1400-1658	027.045	Italy
CB158-161	003.2	Future forecasts	CD1670-1689.5	027.0493	Belgium
CB195-481	909.04	Civilization and race	CD1690-1709.5	027.0492	Netherlands
CB203-281	930-998.004	By place	CD1710-1739.5	027.047	Russia
CB305-430	930-998.004	By date	CD1740-1759.5	027.0438	Poland
CB311	909/93(4-9).004	Ancient history	CD1770-1789.5	027.0489	Denmark
CB351-355	940.1/909.07	Medieval history	CD1790-1809.5	027.04912	Iceland
CB357-430	909.82	Modern history	CD1810-1829.5	027.0481	Norway
CC	930.1	Archaeology	CD1830-1849.5	027.0485	Sweden
CC1-15	930.105	Serials	CD1850-1879.5	027.046	Spain
CC20-51	930.106	Societies/Congresses	CD1880-1899.5	027.0469	Portugal
CC70	930.103	Dictionaries/Encyclopedias	CD1900-1929.5	027.0494	Switzerland

LC	Dewey	Descriptor	LC	Dewey	Descriptor
CD1930-1989.5	027.0496	The Balkans	CJ59-62	737.409	History
CD2001-2291	027.05	Asia	CJ109-119	737.4028	Materials
CD2010-2919.5	027.05694	Israel	CJ201-1397	737.493	Ancient
CD2030-2059.5	027.051	China	CJ301-763	737.493	Greek
CD2080-2099.5	027.054	India	CJ425-763	737.493(2-9)	By place
CD2160-2189.5	027.052	Japan	CJ427-499	737.4938	Greece
CD2300-2491	027.06	Africa	CJ517-542	737.4937	Italy
CD2500-2789.5	027.09(3-4)	Australia/New Zealand	CJ573-647	737.493(1-5)	Asia
CD2795	027.09(5-6)	Oceania	CJ725-763	737.49397	Africa
CD3020-3615	027.073	United States	CJ801-1139	737.493	Roman
CD3070-3609	027.07(4-9)	By state	CJ1021-1139	737.493(1-9)	By place
CD3620-3649.6	027.071	Canada	CJ1021-1070	737.4937	Italy
CD3650-3679.5	027.072	Mexico	CJ1071-1085	737.49397	Africa
CD3690-3859.5	027.0728	Central America	CJ1087-1099	737.493(1-5)	Asia
CD3860-3985	027.0729	Caribbean area	CJ1101-1139	737.493(6/98)	Europe
CD4000-4279.5	027.08	South America	CJ1201-1291	737.49495	Byzantine
CD5001-6471	737.6	Seals (Numismatics)	CJ1301-1397	737.4	African/Oriental
CD5001	737.605	Serials	CJ1509-4625	737.49(4-9)	Medieval and modern
CD5005-5009	737.606	Societies/Congresses	CJ1601-1715	737.49(4-9)	Medieval/Modern, By place
CD5011	737.605	Yearbooks	CJ1735-1743	737.49(4-9)	Renaissance
CD5017-5022	737.6074	Museums/Exhibitions	CJ1747-1758	737.49(4-9)	Modern coins
CD5029-5041	737.601	Philosophy/Theory	CJ1800-4625	737.49(4-9)	Coins, By place
CD5045	737.607	Education	CJ1820-1845	737.4973	United States
CD5049	737.609	History of seals	CJ1860-1879	737.4971	Canada
CD5051-5052	737.6092	Biography	CJ1889-2449	737.49(72-8)	Latin America
CD5053	737.6025	Directories	CJ2450-3369	737.494	Europe
CD5055	737.603	Dictionaries/Encyclopedias	CJ3370-3889	737.495	Asia
CD5085-5175	737.6028	Technique	CJ3900-4389	737.496	Africa
CD5201-5391	737.60901	Ancient	CJ4400-4625	737.499(3-6)	Australia/New Zealand/Oceania
CD5501-5557	737.60902	Medieval			
CD5561	737.6090(23-31)	Renaissance	CJ4801-5450	737.3	Tokens
CD5575-6471	737.6090(3-4)	Modern	CJ4801	737.30(5/6)	Serials/Societies
CD5601-5619	737.60973	United States	CJ4805-4808	737.3074	Exhibitions/Museums
CD5621-5700	737.609728	Central America	CJ4813	737.303	Dictionaries/Encyclopedias
CD5701-5741	737.609729	West Indies	CJ4861-4889	737.3	Tokens, By period
CD5751-5870	737.6098	South America	CJ4901-5336	737.309(4-9)	By place
CD5871-6151	737.6094	Europe	CJ4901-4910	737.30973	United States
CD5881-5899.1	737.60941	Great Britain	CJ4921-4985	737.309(72-8)	Latin America
CD5921-5939	737.60944	France	CJ4986-5045	737.3098	South America
CD5941-5960.2	737.60943	Germany	CJ5046-5185	737.3094	Europe
CD5971-5989	737.60945	Italy	CJ5186-5243	737.3095	Asia
CD6161-6295	737.6095	Asia	CJ5246-5275	737.3096	Africa
CD6171-6180	737.60951	China	CJ5281-5336	737.3099(3-6)	Australia/New Zealand/Oceania
CD6191-6200	737.60954	India			
CD6241-6250	737.60952	Japan	CJ5501-6661	737.22	Medals/Medallions
CD6301-6365	737.6096	Africa	CJ5501-5502	737.220(5/6)	Serials/Societies/Congresses
CD6371-6471	737.6099(3-6)	Australia/New Zealand/Oceania	CJ5517-5521	737.2201	Philosophy/Theory
			CJ5525	737.2207	Education
CE	529	Chronology/Calendars	CJ5581-5690	737.22093	Ancient
CE1	529.0(5/6)	Serials/Societies	CJ5625	737.220938	Greek
CE1.5	529.06	Congresses	CJ5641-5685	737.220937	Roman
CE4	529.03	Dictionaries/Encyclopedias	CJ5723-5780	737.22	Medieval/Modern
CE6-8	529.09	History	CJ5795-6661	737.2209(4-9)	Medals, By place
CE21-46	529.3	Ancient	CJ5801-5812	737.220973	United States
CE31-39	529.32(2-9)	Asian	CJ5830-6090	737.2209(72-8)	Latin America
CE42	529.32208	Greek	CJ6091-6380	737.22094	Europe
CE46	529.32207	Roman	CJ6381-6485	737.22095	Asia
CE51-77	529.(3/4)	Medieval/Modern	CJ6491-6559	737.22096	Africa
CE81-85	529.(32/44)	Church/Religious	CJ6561-6661	737.22099(3-6)	Australia/New Zealand/Oceania
CJ	737	Numismatics			
CJ1-4625	737.4	Coins	CN	411.7	Epigraphy/Inscriptions
CJ1-9	737.405	Serials	CN1	411.70(5/6)	Serials/Societies
CJ14-27	737.406	Societies/Congresses	CN15	411.706	Congresses
CJ31	737.403	Yearbooks	CN25-30	411.7074	Museums/Collections
CJ39-45	737.4074	Exhibitions/Museums	CN40-42	411.701	Philosophy/Theory
CJ53	737.401	Philosophy/Theory	CN50	411.707	Education
CJ55	737.407	Education	CN55	411.709	History

LC	Dewey	Descriptor	LC	Dewey	Descriptor
CN70	411.703	Dictionaries/Encyclopedias	CR760-769	929.920951	China
CN120-760	411.7	By period	CR800-809	929.920952	Japan
CN120-740	411.7	Ancient	CR869-920	929.92096	Africa
CN340-740	471.1/481.1	Classical languages	CR930-1020	929.92099(3-6)	Australia/New Zealand/Oceania
CN350-455	481.1/487.4	Classical Greek			
CN380-455	481.1	Classical Greek, By place	CR1101-1131	929.82	Ecclesiastical/Sacred
CN400	481.1	Asia	CR1179-3395	929.6	Family
CN405	487.4	Near East	CR3599-4420	929.7	Titles/Nobility
CN410-415	481.1	Asia Minor	CR4480-4485	929.7	Royalty
CN420	481.1	Crete	CR4501-6305	929.7	Knighthood
CN430	481.1	Cyprus	CR4801-6305	929.7(2-3/09)	By place
CN440-441	481.1	Egypt	CR4801-4941	929.72	Great Britain
CN470-499	451.1	Ancient dialects of Italy	CR4951-5005	929.736	Austria
CN510-740	471.1	Latin	CR5025-5085	929.74	France
CN530-730	471.1	By place	CR5100-5475	929.73	Germany
CN745	492.411	Early Jewish inscriptions	CR5485-5489	929.795	Greece
CN750-753	487.4	Early Christian inscriptions	CR5500-5580	929.75	Italy
CN755-760	421.1-499.11	Medieval/Modern inscriptions	CR5657-5703	929.77	Russia
			CR5713-5737	929.738	Poland
CN805-865	421.1-499.11	By language	CR5745-5809	929.48	Scandinavia
CN900-1355	411-499.1	By place	CR5819-5889	929.76	Spain
CN900-1130	421-461.1	Europe	CR5900-5925	929.769	Portugal
CN910-915	431.1	Austria	CR6000-6150	929.7095	Asia
CN945-948	441.1	France	CR6160-6190	929.7096	Africa
CN950-957	431.1	Germany	CR6250-6261	929.7097	North America
CN960-997	421.1	Great Britain	CR6270-6305	929.7098	South America
CN1000-1005	489.311	Greece	CS	929.1	Genealogy
CN1010-1015	451.1	Italy	CS1	929.10(5/6)	Serials/Societies
CN1060-1065	491.7011	European Russia	CS2	929.106	Congresses
CN1090-1095	461.1	Spain	CS5	929.1025	Directories
CN1150-1230	495.1-9	Asia	CS6	929.103	Dictionaries/Encyclopedias
CN1160-1161	495.11	China	CS7	929.109	History
CN1170-1175	491.4	India	CS25-35	929.(2-5)	Lists
CN1180-1181	495.611	Japan	CS38-39	929.2	Family history
CN1193-1194	492.411	Israel	CS42-2209	929.10720(4-9)	Genealogy, By place
CN1300-1320	496	Africa	CS42-71	929.1072073	United States
CN1340-1355	421.1/499	Australia/New Zealand/ Oceania	CS80-90	929.1072071	Canada
			CS100-110	929.10720(72-8)	Latin America
CR	929.6	Heraldry	CS400-1059	929.107204	Europe
CR1	929.60(5/6)	Serials/Societies	CS410-499	929.1072041	Great Britain
CR2	929.606	Congresses	CS610-699	929.1072043	Germany
CR9	929.6076	Museums/Exhibitions	CS780-839	929.10720492	Low Countries
CR11	929.6025	Directories	CS890-939	929.1072048	Scandinavia
CR13	929.603	Dictionaries/Encyclopedias	CS1080-1549	929.107205	Asia
CR14-16	926.601	Philosophy/Theory	CS1550-1779	929.107206	Africa
CR51-79	929.82	Crests	CS2000-2209	929.107209(3-6)	Australia/New Zealand/Oceania
CR91-93	929.82	Shields			
CR101-115	929.92	Flags	CS2300-3090	929.4	Personal/Family names
CR151-159	929.609	History	CS2347-2357	929.409(4-9)	By place
CR165-185	929.6	Law/Regulations	CS2367-2377	929.44	Forenames
CR191-1020	929.92	Public/Official heraldry	CS2385-2391	929.42	Surnames
CR199-1020	929.9209(3-9)	By place	CS3010-3090	929.4209(4-9)	By place
CR199-229	929.92097	North America	CT	920	Biography
CR200-209	929.920973	United States	CT25-83	920	History of the literature
CR210-219	929.920971	Canada	CT93-206	920	Collective, General
CR220-229	929.920972	Mexico	CT100-120	921.0(73/41)	American/English
CR230-294	929.9209728	Central America	CT130-139	920.0492	Dutch
CR304-350	929.9209729	West Indies	CT140-149	920.044	French
CR369-479	929.92098	South America	CT150-159	920.043	German
CR489-739	929.92094	Europe	CT160-169	920.045	Italian
CR490-524	929.920941	Great Britain	CT170-179	920.048	Scandinavian
CR540-549	929.920944	France	CT180-189	920.046(9)	Spanish/Portuguese
CR550-559.2	929.920943	Germany	CT190-199	920.0437	Slavic
CR570-579	929.920954	Italy	CT210-3150	920.0(4-9)	National
CR610-614	929.920947	European Russia	CT210-275	920.073	United States
CR670-679	929.920946	Spain	CT280-310	920.071	Canada
CR749-850	929.92095	Asia	CT339-410	920.0729	West Indies

LC	Dewey	Descriptor	LC	Dewey	Descriptor
CT550-558	920.072	Mexico	D200-203	909.07	11th-15th centuries
CT570-638	920.0728	Central America	D205-472	909.08	Modern (1453-)
CT640-758	920.08	South America	D205	909.0803	Dictionaries
CT759-1458	920.04	Europe	D206	909.08072	Historiography
CT770-868	920.041	Great Britain	D214	355.0090 (3-4)	Modern military history
CT100-1018	920.044	France	D215	359.0090 (3-4)	Modern naval history, General
CT1050-1099	920.043	Germany			
CT1240-1328	920.048	Scandinavia	D217	909.08	Political/Diplomatic history
CT1399-1458	920.0496	Balkan	D219-234	909.(4-6)	1453-1648
CT1500-1919	920.05	Asia	D242-283	909.6	1601-1715
CT1820-1848	920.05	Far East	D251-270	940.24	Thirty Years' War
CT1870-1919	920.056	Near East	D274.5-.6	940.252	Anglo/French war
CT1920-2750	920.06	Africa	D275-276	940.252	War of Revolution (1667-1668)
CT2800-3090	920.09(3-6)	Australia/New Zealand/ Oceania	D277-278	940.252	Dutch war
CT3200-9999	001-999.092	By subject	D279-280	940.2525	War of Grand Alliance
CT3200-3830	920.72	Women	D281-283	942.2526	War of Spanish Succession
CT3230-3830	920.7209(3-9)	Women, By place	D284-297	909.7	1715-1789
D	900	History (General)	D291-294	940.2532	War of Austrian Succession
D1	905/906	Serials/Societies	D295	909.7	Political/Military history
D2	905	Yearbooks	D297	940.2534	Seven Years' War
D3	906	Congresses	D299-309	909.(7-8)	1789-1800
D9	903	Dictionaries	D304-309	940.27	French Revolution
D13-15	907.2	Historiography	D351-400	909.8(1-21)	1801-1920
D16-.8	901	Methodology	D410-472	909.82	20th century
D16.2-.5	907	Education	D431-436	909.82	Military/Naval history
D16.7-.9	901	Philosophy of history	D501-680	940.3	World War I
D17-24	909	World histories	D501	940.305	Serials
D25	355.009	Military history	D502	940.306	Societies
D27	359.009	Naval history	D503	940.3074	Museums/Exhibitions
D31-34	909	Political/Diplomatic history	D504	940.306	Congresses
D51-95	930	Ancient history, General	D507	940.3092	Biography
D51-53	930.0(5/6)	Serials/Societies	D511-520	940.311	Causes
D54	930.03	Dictionaries/Encyclopedias	D522-528	940.30222	Pictures/Etc.
D55	930.0099	Biography	D529-578	940.4	Military operations
D56	930.072	Historiography	D530-549	940.4144	Western
D65-90	930.1(1-6)	Earliest	D531-538	940.4143	German
D70	936.4	Celts	D539	940.4144	Austrian
D95	359.00901	Naval history	D540	940.4144	Hungarian
D101-110	909.0(7-8)	Medieval-Modern (General)	D541	940.4144	Belgian
D101	909.0(7/8)03	Dictionaries	D544-545	940.4144	Anglo/French combined
D105	909.0(7/8)	Political/Diplomatic	D546-547	940.4144	English
D107-110	909.0(7/8)092	Biography	D548-549	940.4144	French
D111-203	909.07	Medieval	D550-569	940.4147	Eastern
D111	909.070(5/6)	Serials/Societies	D551-559	940.4147	Russian
D113-114	909.0703	Dictionaries	D566-568	940.416	Turkey/Near East
D115	909.07092	Biography	D569	940.4145	Italian
D116	909.07072	Historiography	D570-578	940.41273	United States
D121-123	909.1	By date	D580-589	940.45	Naval operations
D128	355/359.00902	Military/Naval	D581-582	940.45	Anglo-German
D131-134	909.07	Political	D583-584	940.45	Franco-Austrian
D135-149	304.80902	Migrations	D590-595	940.451	Submarine
D151-173	909.07	Crusades	D600-607	940.44	Aerial operations
D151-155	909.0703	Dictionaries	D609	940.467	Registers of the dead
D156	909.07092	Biography	D610-621	940.32	Diplomacy
D156.58	909.07072	Historiography	D640	940.48(1-2)	Personal narratives
D161	909.07	First crusade	D641-651	940.439	Peace
D162	909.07	Second crusade	D652-658	940.3144	Reconstruction
D163	909.07	Third crusade	D663-680	940.46	Celebration/Monuments
D164	909.07	Fourth crusade	D720-728	940.5(1-2)	Between World Wars
D165	909.07	Fifth crusade	D731-838	940.53	World War II
D166	909.07	Sixth crusade	D731	940.5305	Serials
D167	909.07	Seventh crusade	D732	940.5306	Societies
D168	909.07	Eighth crusade	D733	940.53074	Museums/Exhibitions
D169	909.07	Juvenile works	D734	940.5306	Congresses
D171-172	909.07	13th/15th century crusades	D736	940.53092	Biography
D175-195	909.(1-2)	Latin Kingdom of Jerusalem	D741-742	940.5311	Causes

15

LC	Dewey	Descriptor
D745	940.54002	Satire/Caricature
D748-754	940.532	Diplomatic
D755-769	940.54	Military operations
D756-769	940.542	By place
D756-763	940.5421	Western
D757	940.542143	Germany
D759-760	940.542141	Great Britain
D761-762	940.542144	France
D764-767	940.5425	Eastern
D765	940.5421	Poland/Czechoslovakia/Etc.
D766	940.542(1-3)	Balkan/Middle East/Africa
D766.3-.32	940.5421495	Greece
D766.4-.42	940.5421498	Romania
D766.6-.62	940.5421497	Yugoslavia
D766.8-.97	940.5423	Africa
D767	940.542(5-6)	Far East/Pacific Battles
D767.2-.82	940.5425	China/Japan/ Philippines/Etc.
D767.9-.99	940.5426	Pacific islands
D768	940.54127(1/2)	Canada/Mexico
D769	940.541273	United States
D770-779	940.545	Naval operations
D771-772	940.545	Anglo-German
D772.3	940.545	Russo-German
D773-774	940.545973	American
D775	940.545	Anglo-Italian
D777	940.545952	Japanese
D778-784	940.5451	Submarine operations
D785-792	940.544	Aerial operations
D793	940.541	Tank
D794	940.541	Cavalry
D797	940.5467	Registers of the dead
D801	940.5316	Alien enemies
D802	940.5336	Occupied areas
D803-804	940.5(405/31)/341.690268	Atrocities
D805	940.547	Prisoners
D806-807	940.547(5-6)	Medical/Sanitation
D809	940.5477	Relief
D811	940.548(1-2)	Personal narrative
D812-821	940.5312	Peace
D824-829	940.53144	Reconstruction
D830-838	940.546	Celebrations
D839-845.2	940.55	Post war
D839	940.550(5/6)	Serials/Societies
D839.2	940.5506	Congresses
D839.5-.7	940.550099	Biography
D842.5-847	940.55(4-6)	1945-1965
D848-850	940.55(6-9)	1965-
D880-888	909.091724	Developing countries
D890-893	909.091811	Eastern Hemisphere
D900-1075	940	Europe, General
D901-980	914	Description/Travel
D911-923	940.(1-559)	By date
D965-975	940-949	By place
D1050-1065	940.55	1945-
D1050	940.5505	Serials
D1050.8-.82	940.5507	Education
D1056	940.55004	Ethnography
D1058-1065	940.55	Political/Diplomatic history
D1070-1075	940.550099	Biography
DA	941/936.(1-2)	History, Great Britain
DA10-18	941.0(6-85)	Empire/Commonwealth
DA20-690	942/936.2	England
DA20-22	942.00(5-6)	Serials/Societies
DA28-592	936.2/942	History
DA28	942.0099	Biography
DA40-47	942	Political/Diplomatic
DA49-69	355.00942	Military
DA70-89.1	359.00942	Naval
DA89.5	358.400942	Air Force
DA110-115	942	Social life
DA120-125	942.004	Ethnography
DA129-592	936.2/942.0(1-8)	By date
DA129-162	936.2/942.01	Early-1065
DA170-260	942.0(2-46)	1066-1485
DA300-592	942.0(5-8)	1485-
DA310-360	942.05	Tudors (1485-1603)
DA331-339	942.052	Henry VIII
DA350-360	942.055	Elizabeth I (1558-1603)
DA370-462	942.06	1603-1702
DA385-398	942.06(1-2)	Stuarts (early)
DA400-429	942.06(1-2)	Civil war/Commonwealth
DA430-462	942.06(4-9)	Stuarts (late)
DA499	942.071	George I (1714-1727)
DA500	942.072	George II (1727-1760)
DA505-522	942.073	George III (1760-1820)
DA537-538	942.074	George IV (1820-1830)
DA539-542	942.075	William IV (1830-1837)
DA550-565	942.081	Victoria (1837-1901)
DA566-592	942.08(2-5)	20th century
DA600-632	914.204	Travel
DA670	942.(1-8)	Local history
DA675-689	942.1	London
DA677-684	942.1	History
DA685	942.1(3-7)	Parishes
DA690	942.(2-8)	Other cities/Towns
DA700-745	942.9	Wales
DA700	942.900(5/6)	Serials/Societies
DA710	942.90099	Biography
DA711.5	942.9	Social life
DA712	942.9004	Ethnography
DA713.5-722.1	942.9	History
DA725-731.2	914.29(04)	Geography/Travel
DA750-890	941.1	Scotland
DA750	941.100(5/6)	Serials/Societies
DA751-.5	941.10074	Museums/Exhibitions
DA753	941.1005	Yearbooks
DA757-.7	914.11	Geography
DA758-826	936.1/941.1	History
DA775-826	936.1/941.10(1-8)	By date
DA778	941.101	844-1057
DA779-782	941.102	1057-1278
DA783	941.10(2-4)	1278-1488
DA784-790	941.10(4-5)	1488-1603
DA800-807	941.10(61-69)	1603-1707
DA809-814	941.10(69-73)	1707-1800
DA815-818	941.10(73-81)	19th century
DA821-826	941.108(2-5)	20th century
DA850-878	914.1104	Travel
DA880-890	941.1(1-4)	Local history
DA900-995	941.5	Ireland
DA900	941.500(5/6)	Serials/Societies
DA909-965	941.5	History
DA930-965	941.5(1-84)	By date
DA930-932	936.1/941.501	To 1172
DA933-937	941.50(3-5)	1172-1603
DA938-946	941.506	17th century
DA947-949	941.507	18th century
DA950-958	941.5081	19th century
DA959-965	941.5082	20th century
DA969-988	914.1504	Travel
DA990-995	941.(6-9)	Local history
DAW	940/943	Central Europe
DAW1001	940/943.000(5/6)	Serials/Societies

16

LC	Dewey	Descriptor	LC	Dewey	Descriptor
DAW1004	940/943.0006	Congresses	DB955	943.9051	1918-1945
DAW1006	940/943.0003	Gazetteers/Dictionaries	DB956-957	943.9052	1945-1956 (Revolution of 1956)
DAW1010-1015	941/914.3	Travel	DB956	943.9053	1953-
DAW1024	940/943	Social life	DB974.9-999	943.9(1-9)	Local history/Description
DAW1026-1028	940/943.004	Ethnography	DB981-999	943.912	Budapest
DAW1031-1051	940/943	History	DB2000-3150	943.7	Czechoslovakia
DAW1046-1051	940.(1-5)	By period	DB2000	943.700(5/6)	Serials/Societies
DAW1046	940.(1-21)	Early to 1500	DB2001-2002	943.70074	Museums/Exhibitions
DAW1047	940.2(1-7)	1500-1815	DB2003	943.7006	Congresses
DAW1048	940.(28-48)	1815-1918	DB2007	943.7003	Gazetteers/Dictionaries
DAW1049	940.5	1918-1945	DB2009	943.70025	Directories
DAW1050	940.55(4-8)	1945-1989	DB2018-2022	914.37(04)	Geography/Travel
DAW1051	940.558-	1989-	DB2017-2022	943.7	Social life
DB	943.6/943.(7-9)	Austria/Hungary/ Czechoslovakia	DB2040-2043	943.7004	Ethnography
DB1-879	943.6	Austria	DB2044-2232	943.7	History
DB1-5	943.600(5/6)	Serials/Societies	DB2080-2133	943.702(1-24)	Early to 1526
DB14	943.6003	Gazetteers	DB2085-2088	943.7021	To 904 (Great Moravian Empire)
DB20-27.5	914.36(04)	Geography/Travel	DB2088.7-2133	943.7022	907-1526
DB33-34	943.6004	Ethnography	DB2088.7-2091	943.70223	907-1306 (Premyslid Dynasty)
DB30	943.6	Social life			
DB35-99.2	936.3/943.6	History	DB2095-2111	943.70224	1306-1526 (Luxembourg Dynasty)
DB35	943.6003	Dictionaries			
DB36-.7	943.60099	Biography	DB2135-2181	943.7022(3-4)	Hapsburg rule (1526-1918)
DB36.8-.9	943.60072	Historiography	DB2145-2171	943.7023	1526-1815
DB42-44	355.009436	Military history	DB2145-2151	943.70232	1526-1620
DB45	359.009436	Naval history	DB2155-2171	943.70233	1620-1800
DB51-99.2	936.3/943.60(2-4)	History, By date	DB2175-2182	943.7024	1815-1915
DB51	936.3	Ancient	DB2185-2211	943.703	1918-1945
DB51-59	936.3/943.602	To Medieval	DB2195-2202	943.7032	1918-1939 (Republic)
DB51	943.6022	481-976	DB2205-2211	943.7033	1939-1945 (World War II)
DB56-57	943.6024	1246-1273	DB2215-2232	943.704	1945-
DB58-59	943.6025	1273-1500	DB2215-2222	943.7042	1945-1968 (Reform/ Repression)
DB65.2-77	943.603	1521-1815			
DB80-99.2	943.60(3-53)	19th-20th centuries	DB2225-2232	943.7043	1968-
DB83	943.6043	Revolution (1848)	DB2300-2650	943.7(1-3)	Local history/Description
DB96-99.2	943.605	Republic (1918-)	DB2300-2421	943.72	Moravia
DB99-.1	943.6052	WW II/occupation (1938-1955)	DB2600-2649	943.712	Prague
DB99.2	943.6053	1955-	DB2700-3150	943.73	Slovakia
DB101-879	943.6(1-3)	Local history/Description	DC	936.4/944	France
DB841-860	943.613	Vienna	DC1	944.005	Serials
DB881-898	936.3/943.648	Liechtenstein	DC2	944.006	Societies
DB881	943.64800(5/6)	Serials/Societies	DC14	944.003	Dictionaries/Gazetteers
DB888	914.364804	Travel	DC15	944.0025	Directories
DB891-894	936.3/943.648	History	DC20.5-29.3	914.4(04)	Geography/Travel
DB901-999	939.8/943.9	Hungary	DC33	936.4/944	Social life
DB901	943.900(5/6)	Serials/Societies	DC34-.5	944.004	Ethnography
DB904	943.9003	Dictionaries/Gazetteers	DC35-423	936.4/944	History
DB906.9-917	914.3904	Travel	DC35	944.003	Dictionaries
DB919	943.9004	Ethnography	DC36-.8	944.0099	Biography
DB920.5	943.9	Social life	DC36.9-.985	944.007	Education
DB921-957	939.8/943.9	History	DC60-423	936.4/944.0(1-83)	By date
DB921	943.9003	Dictionaries	DC60-64	936.4	Ancient
DB922	943.90099	Biography	DC64.7-69.85	944.013	Merovingian Dynasty (486-751)
DB927-957	939.8/943.9	By date			
DB927.3	939.8	Ancient	DC70-73.9	944.014	Carolingian Dynasty (751-987)
DB929-.9	943.902	Arpad Dynasty (894-1301)			
DB930-931.9	943.903	Elective kings (1301-1526)	DC82-120	944.02	987-1589 (Royal power)
DB932-933	943.904	1526-1918 (Turkish/ Hapsburgs)	DC82-94	944.021	House of Capet (987-1328)
DB932-.3	943.9041	1526-1686 (Turkish)	DC87-.7	944.022	Philip I-Louis VII (1060-1180)
DB932.5-934	943.9042	1686-1918 (Hapsburgs)			
DB933-945	943.9043	1867-1918 (Austria-Hungary)	DC90-91.6	944.023	Philip II-Louis IX (1180-1270)
DB940-945	943.9043	1849-1900	DC91.7-93.7	944.024	Philip III-Charles IV
DB947-957	943.90(43-53)	20th century	DC95-109	944.025	House of Valois (1328-1589)

LC	Dewey	Descriptor	LC	Dewey	Descriptor
DC101-105.9	944.026	Charles VI, VII (1380-1461)	DD145-155	943.024	Hohenstaufen (1125-1273)
DC106-109	944.027	Louis XI-Louis XII (1461-1515)	DD156-174.6	943.02(6-9)	1273-1519
DC110-120	944.028	House of Angouleme (1515-1589)	DD156-174	943.02(6-7)	House of Habsburg/Luxemburg
DC120.8-138	944.03	Bourbons (1589-1789)	DD175-289	943.0(3-7)	1519-
DC122-.9	944.031	Henry IV (1589-1610)	DD175-189	943.03	1519-1648 (Reformation/Counter)
DC123-.9	944.032	Louis XIII (1610-1643)			
DC133-138	944.03(4-5)	Louis XV, XVI (1715-1789)	DD181-183	943.031	Peasants' War (1524-1525)
DC139-249	944.04	Revolution/Napoleon (1789-1815)	DD184	943.031	Schmalkaldic League (1530-1547)
DC161-185.9	944.041	Assemblies			
DC175-190.8	944.042	First republic (1792-1799)	DD189	943.041	Thirty Years' War (1618-1648)
DC175-185.9	944.043	Nat'l. convention (1792-1795)			
			DD190-199	943.0(43-6)	1648-1815
DC183-185	944.044	Reign of Terror (1793-1794)	DD201-289	943.0(6-84)	19th century -
			DD206-216	943.0(7-82)	1815-1871
DC186-190.8	944.045	Directory (1795-1799)	DD217-231	943.08(3-4)	New Empire (1871-1918)
DC191-193.8	944.046	Consulate (1799-1804)	DD228.8	943.084	World War I (1914-1918)
DC197-219	944.05	First Empire (1804-1815)	DD233-289	943.08(5-7)	Revolution/Republic
DC256-260	944.06	Restoration (1815-1830)	DD253-256.5	943.086	Hitler
DC256-257	944.061	Louis XVIII (1815-1830)	DD256	943.086	World War II
DC258-259.5	944.062	Charles X (1824-1830)	DD257-.4	943.087	Allied occupation (1945-)
DC266	944.063	Louis Philippe (1830-1848)	DD258-262	943.087	West Germany
DC270-274.5	944.07	Second Republic/Empire (1848-1870)	DD280-289	943.1087	East Germany
			DD301-454	943	Prussia
DC281-423	944.08	1870 to present	DD301	943.005	Serials
DC281-354	944.0812	1870-1899 (Paris Commune)	DD302	943.006	Societies
			DD308	943.003	Gazetteers/Dictionaries
DC334-354.9	944.081	Third Republic (1870-1945)	DD314-320	914.3804	Travel
DC385	944.0814	World War I (1914-1918)	DD335-339	943.(004)	Social life/Ethnography
DC389-396	944.0815	Between wars (1918-1939)	DD341-454	936.3/943	History
DC397	944.0816	World War II (1940-1946)	DD341	943.003	Dictionaries
DC398-409	944.082	Fourth Republic (1947-1958)	DD343-.8	943.0099	Biography
			DD345	943.0072	Historiography
DC411-423	944.083	Fifth Republic (1958-)	DD354-370	355/359/943	Military/Naval/Political
DC600-801	944.(1-9)	Local history/Description	DD375-454	936.3/943.0(1-76)	By date
DC701-790	944.36	Paris	DD375-387	943.0(1-43)	To 1640
DC921-930	946.79	Andorra	DD389-454	943.0(34-57)	1640-
DC941-947	944.949	Monaco	DD390-414.9	943.05	17th-18th centuries
DD	936.3/943	Germany	DD406-407.5	943.05(3-4)	Silesian Wars (1740-1745)
DD1	943.005	Serials	DD409-412.8	943.055	Seven Years' War (1756-1763)
DD1.5-.6	943.0074	Museums/Exhibitions			
DD2	943.006	Societies	DD415-446	943.0(6-84)	19th century
DD14	943.003	Gazetteers/Dictionaries	DD423	943.07(3-6)	Confederation (1816-1866)
DD15.5	943.0025	Directories	DD436-440	943.076	Austro-Prussian war (1866)
DD21.5-43	914.3(04)	Travel	DD442	943.081	North German Confederation
DD51-78	943.(004)	Social life/Ethnography			
DD84-262	936.3/943	History	DD446	943.082	Franco-German War (1870-1871)
DD84	943.003	Dictionaries			
DD85-.8	943.0099	Biography	DD448-451	943.08(3-4)	1871-1918 (New Empire)
DD86	943.0072	Historiography	DD452-454	943.085	Between World Wars
DD99-120	355/359/943	Military/Naval/Political	DD701-901	943.(1-5)	Local history
DD121-289	936.3/943.0(1-87)	By date	DD801	943.(1)1-5	By state/Province
DD121-124	936.3/943.012	Earliest to 481	DD851-900	943.155	Berlin
DD125-174.6	943.0(13-29)	To 1519	DD900.2	943.5518	Bonn
DD126-155	943.0(13-25)	Medieval Empire (481-1273)	DE	909.09638/937/938	Mediterranean/Greco-Roman
DD127-135	943.021	481-918	DE1-4	90(5/6)/(937/938).00(5/6)	Serials/Societies
DD128	943.013	Merovingians (481-752)	DE5	903/(937/938).003	Dictionaries
DD129-135	943.014	Carolingians (752-911)	DE7	909/(937/938).0099	Biography
DD136-144	943.022	919-1125	DE8-9	907.2/(937/938).0072	Historiography
DD136-140.7	943.022	House of Saxony (919-1024)	DE15	907/(937/938).007	Education
			DE23-31	911/913.(7-8)	Geography
DD141-144	943.023	House of Franconia (1024-1125)	DE46-71	909.638/(937/938)	Civilization
			DE72	937/938/939	During life of Christ
			DE73	909.04/(937/938).004	Ethnography
			DE80-100	909.09638/937/938	History
			DE86-92	937/938	Ancient to 476

LC	Dewey	Descriptor
DE94	909.0963801	Medieval to 1453
DE96	909.096380(4-7)	1453-1800
DE98	909.0963808(1-24)	1801-1945
DE100	909.0963808(24-3)	1945-
DF	938/949.5	Greece
DF10-289	938	Ancient Greece
DF10	938.005	Serials
DF11	938.006	Societies
DF11.2-.3	938.0074	Museums/Exhibitions
DF16	938.0025	Dictionaries
DF27-41	913.8(04)	Geography/Travel
DF135	938.004	Ethnography
DF207-241	938	History
DF220-241	938.0(1-9)	By date
DF220-221	938.01	Mythical/Minoan/ Mycenaean
DF222-224	938.02	Early/Tyrants (775-500 BC)
DF225-226	938.03	Persian wars (499-479 BC)
DF227-228	938.04	Athenian/Pericles (479-431 BC)
DF229-230	938.05	Peloponnesian War (431-404 BC)
DF231-232	938.07	Spartan/Theban (404-362 BC)
DF233-.8	938.07	Macedonia/Philip (359-336 BC)
DF234-.9	938.07	Alexander the Great
DF235-238.9	938.08	Hellenistic (323-146 BC)
DF239-241	938.09	Roman (146 BC-476 AD)
DF251-289	938.(1-9)	Local history/Description
DF501-649	949.50(1-4)	Byzantine Empire (323-1453)
DF501	949.50(1-4)00(5/6)	Serials/Societies
DF501.5	949.50(1-4)006	Congresses
DF505-.7	949.50(1-4)0072	Historiography
DF505.8-.82	949.50(1-4)007	Education
DF506-.5	949.50(1-4)0099	Biography
DF518	914.95	Geography
DF542-.4	949.50(1-4)004	Ethnography
DF543	355.009495	Military history
DF544	359.009495	Naval history
DF548	949.5	Empire/Papacy (Political)
DF550-649	949.50(1-4)	History
DF553-599.5	949.50(1-2)	Eastern Empire (323/476-1057)
DF557	949.501	Constantine the Great (323-337)
DF599.8-649	949.50(3-4)	1057-1453
DF610-629	949.504	Latin Empire (1204-1261)
DF630-649	949.504	Palaeologi (1261-1453)
DF645-649	949.504	Fall of Constantinople (1453)
DF701-854.32	949.50(5-7)	Modern Greece
DF701	949.50(5-7)00(5/6)	Serials/Societies/etc.
DF721-728	914.9504	Travel
DF741-748	949.50(5-7)004	Ethnography
DF750-854.32	949.5	History
DF765-775	355/359.009495	Military/Naval
DF801-854.32	949.50(5-7)	By date
DF801-.9	949.505	Turkish rule (1453-1821)
DF803-832	949.506	1821-1913
DF804-815	949.506	War of Independence (1821-1829)
DF816-818	949.506	Kapodistrias (1827-1831)
DF833-854.32	949.50(6-7)	20th century
DF848	949.5073	Republic (1924-1935)
DF895-951	949.5(1-7)	Local history

LC	Dewey	Descriptor
DF901	949.5(1-7)	Provinces/Islands
DF901.C78-.C89	949.98	Crete
DF915-936	949.512	Athens
DG	937/945	Italy
DG11-365	937	Roman Empire to 476
DG11	937.005	Serials
DG12	937.006	Societies
DG12.2-.3	937.0074	Museums/Exhibitions
DG12.5	937.006	Congresses
DG16	937.003	Dictionaries
DG27-41	913.7	Geography
DG51-59	937.(1-9)	Local history
DG51-55	937.(1-7)	Areas inside Italy
DG59	936/937.(8-9)	Areas outside Italy
DG61-69	937.6	Rome (city) to 476
DG70	937.(1-7)	Other towns
DG75-190	937.004	Ethnography
DG201-365	937	History, Ancient Italy
DG203-204	937.0099	Biography
DG205-206	937.0072	Historiography
DG206.5	937.007	Education
DG221-365	937.0(1-9)	By date
DG221-225	937.5	Pre-Roman/Etruria/ Etruscans
DG231-269	937.01	Kings/Republic (753-727 BC)
DG233-.9	937.01	Foundations/Kings (753-510 BC)
DG235-269	937.02	Republic (509-27 BC)
DG237-238	937.03	Conquest of Italy (343-290 BC)
DG241-253	937.04	Conquest of Med. (264-133 BC)
DG242-249.4	937.04	Punic/Illyrain wars (264-201)
DG250-253	937.04	East/West wars (200-133 BC)
DG253.5-269	937.05	Fall of Republic/ New Empire
DG256-260	937.05	Marius/Sulla (111-78 BC)
DG261-267	937.05	Julius Caesar/Triumvirate
DG268-269	937.05	2nd Triumvirate (43-31 BC)
DG269.5-365	937.06	Empire (27 BC-476 AD)
DG272	937.06	Civilization/Social life
DG274-.3	937.060099	Biography
DG275-309.3	937.07	Constitutional Empire
DG311-365	937.0(8-9)	Decline/Fall (284-476 AD)
DG401-583	945	Medieval/Modern (476-)
DG401	945.005	Serials
DG402	945.006	Societies
DG413	945.0025	Directories
DG415	945.003	Gazetteers/Dictionaries
DG421	914.5	Geography
DG421.5-430.2	914.504	Travel
DG455-457	945.004	Ethnography
DG461-583	945	History
DG461	945.003	Dictionaries
DG463-.8	945.0099	Biography
DG465-.7	945.0072	Historiography
DG465.8	945.007	Education
DG480-499	355/359.00945	Military/Naval
DG500-583	945.0(1-9)	By date
DG500-537	945.0(1-5)	Medieval (476-1492)
DG503-529	945.0(1-4)	476-1268
DG506-509	945.01	Goth kingdom (489-553)
DG510	945.01	Byzantine Exarchate (553-568)

LC	Dewey	Descriptor
DG511-514.7	945.01	Lombard kingdom
DG515-529	945.02	Frankish emperors (774-962)
DG520-529	945.0(3-4)	German emperors (962-1268)
DG530-537.8	945.0(4-5)	1268-1492
DG532-537.8	945.05	Renaissance
DG538-583	945.0(6-9)	1492-
DG539-545.8	945.07	16th-18th centuries
DG546-549	945.082	Napoleonic (1792-1815)
DG548-549	945.082	Kingdom of Italy
DG551-564	945.08(2-4)	19th century
DG552-554.5	945.083	Risorgimento (1848-1871)
DG553-.5	945.084	Austro-Sardinian war
DG555-575	945.0(84-91)	Monarchy (1871-1947)
DG571-572	945.091	Fascism (1919-1945)
DG576-579	945.092	Republic (1948-)
DG600-684.72	945.(1-3)	Northern Italy
DG610-618.75	945.1	Piedmont
DG631-645	945.182	Genoa
DG651-664.5	945.2	Milan/Lombardy
DG670-684.72	945.31	Venice
DG691-817.3	945.(5-6)	Central Italy
DG731-759.3	945.5	Tuscany/Florence
DG791-800	945.634	Papal states/Vatican
DG803-818	945.632	Modern Rome
DG819-875	945.(7-8)	Southern Italy
DG831	945.8(5)	Sicily/Malta
DG840-857.5	945.73	Naples
DG861-875	945.8(1-2)	Sicily
DG987-999	945.85	Malta/Maltese islands
DH	936.3/949.2	Low Countries (General)/Belgium
DH1	949.200(5/6)	Serials/Societies
DH14	949.2003	Gazetteers/Dictionaries
DH31-40	914.9204	Travel
DH71	949.2	Social life
DH91	949.2004	Ethnography
DH95-207	936.3/949.2	History
DH101	949.2003	Dictionaries
DH103	949.20099	Biography
DH113	355.009492	Military history
DH121	359.009492	Naval history
DH141-207	936.3/949.20(2-7)	By date
DH141-162	936.3/949.201	Early/Medieval to 1384
DH171-184	949.20(1-2)	House of Burgundy (1384-1555)
DH185-207	949.203	Wars/Independence (1555-1648)
DH401-811	936.4/949.3	Belgium
DH401	949.300(5/6)	Serials/Societies
DH414	949.3003	Dictionaries/Gazetteers
DH430-435	914.93(04)	Geography/Travel
DH471	949.3	Social life
DH491-492	949.3004	Ethnography
DH503-692	936.4/949.3	History
DH511	949.3003	Dictionaries
DH513-516	949.30099	Biography
DH540-545	355.009493	Military history
DH551	359.009493	Naval history
DH571-692	936.4/949.30(1-4)	By date
DH571-584	936.4/949.30(1-2)	Early and Medieval to 1555
DH585-619	949.302	1555-1794 (Austrian era)
DH620-676	949.30(2-3)	1794-1909 (French era)
DH677-692	949.304	20th century
DH801-811	949.3(1-48)	Local history/Description
DH802-809.95	949.332	Brussels
DH901-925	949.35	Luxembourg
DJ	949.2	Netherlands (Holland)
DJ1	949.200(5/6)	Serials/Societies
DJ14	949.2003	Gazetteers/Dictionaries
DJ30-40	914.92(04)	Geography/Travel
DJ51	936.3/949.2	Social life
DJ91-92	949.2004	Ethnography
DJ95-292	936.3/949.2	History
DJ101	949.2003	Dictionaries
DJ103-106	949.20099	Biography
DJ124	355.009492	Military history
DJ130-138	359.009492	Naval history
DJ151-292	936.3/949.20(1-7)	By date
DJ151-152	936.3/949.20(1-2)	Early and Medieval to 1555
DJ154-210	949.20(3-4)	1555-1795 (United Provinces)
DJ180-182	949.204	Anglo-Dutch (1652-1667)
DJ190-191	949.204	War with France (1672-1678)
DJ193	949.204	Anglo-Dutch War (1672-1674)
DJ196-199.2	949.204	Stadtholders (1702-1747)
DJ205-206	949.204	Anglo-Dutch War (1780-1784)
DJ208-209	949.204	War with France (1793-1795)
DJ211	949.205	Batavian Republic (1795-1806)
DJ215-292	949.20(5-7)	19th-20th centuries
DJ219	949.20(5-7)0099	Biographies
DJ226	949.205	Kingdom of Holland (1806-1810)
DJ228	949.205	Union with France (1810-1813)
DJ236	949.205	Netherlands kingdom (1813-1830)
DJ241-263	949.20(5-6)	1815-1890
DJ281-283	949.20(6-71)	Willhelmina (1890-1948)
DJ285	949.2071	World War I (1914-1918)
DJ286	949.2071	Between wars (1918-1939)
DJ287	949.2071	World War II (1939-1948)
DJ288-289	949.2072	Juliana (1948-1980)
DJ290-292	949.2073	Beatrix (1980-)
DJ401-411	949.2(1-4)	Local history/Description
DJ411.A5-59	949.2352	Amsterdam
DJK	947	Eastern Europe (General)
DJK1	947.000(5/6)	Serials/Societies
DJK1.5	947.0006	Congresses
DJK6	947.0003	Gazetteers/Dictionaries
DJK11-18	914.7(04)	Geography/Travel
DJK24	947	Social life
DJK26-28	947.0004	Ethnography
DJK31	947.00099	Biography
DJK32-34	947.00072	Historiography
DJK35-36	947.0007	Education
DJK61-66	947.7	Black Sea region
DJK71-76	947.718	Carpathian Mountain region
DJK76.2-.8	949.6	Danube River valley
DJK77	939.8	Pannonia
DK	947/943.8	Russia/Poland
DK1-949.5	947	Russia (Soviet Union)
DK1	947.00(5/6)	Serials/Societies
DK2.5	947.006	Congresses
DK14	947.003	Gazetteers/Dictionaries
DK18.7-29	914.7(04)	Geography/Travel
DK32-.7	947	Social life
DK33-35	947.004	Ethnography

LC	Dewey	Descriptor	LC	Dewey	Descriptor
DK36-290.3	947	History	DL1-87	948/936.3	Scandinavia, General
DK70-112	947.0(1-45)	To 1613	DL1	936.300(5/6)/948.00(5/6)	Series/Societies
DK112.8-264.8	947.0(46-83)	House of Romanov (1613-1917)	DL1.5	936.3006/948.006	Congresses
			DL4	936.3003/948.003	Gazetteers/Dictionaries
DK265-.95	947.0841	Revolution (1917-1921)	DL6.7-11.5	913.63(04)/914.8(04)	Geography/Travel
DK266-290.3	947.08(4-54)	Soviet Regime (1917-)	DL30-33	936.3/948	Social life
DK266.A2	947.08400(5-)	Serials/Etc.	DL41-42	936.3004/948.004	Ethnography
DK266.A33	947.0840072	Historiography	DL43-87	936.3/948	History
DK267-273	947.0842	Stalin (1925-1953)	DL61-87	936.3/948.0(1-8)	By date
DK273	947.0842	World War II (1939-1945)	DL61-65	936.3/948.0(1-2)	To 1387 (Northmen/ Vikings)
DK274-282	947.085(2-3)	1953-1982			
DK285-290	947.0854	1982-	DL75-81	948.0(3-7)	1387-1900
DK501-949.5	947.(2-9)/957	Local history/Description	DL83-87	948.08	1901-
DK502.3-.7	947.4	Baltic states	DL101-291	936.3/948.9	Denmark
DK503-.95	947.41	Estonia	DL101	936.300(5/6)/948.900(5/6)	Serials/Societies
DK504-.95	947.43	Latvia	DL105	936.3003/948.9003	Gazetteers/Dictionaries
DK505-.95	947.5	Lithuania	DL115-120	913.6304/914.8904	Travel
DK507-.95	947.65	Belorussia	DL131-133	936.3/948.9	Social life
DK507.92-.939	947.652	Minsk	DL141-142	936.3004/948.9004	Ethnography
DK508-.95	947.71	Ukraine	DL160-263.3	936.30(1-2)/948.90(1-5)	By date
DK508.92-.939	947.714	Kiev	DL160-183.9	936.3/948.90(1-2)	Early/Medieval to 1523
DK509.1-.95	947.75	Moldavia/Bessarabia	DL162-173.8	948.901	750-1241 (Norwegian rule)
DK510-651	947	Russia	DL174-183.9	948.90(1-2)	1241-1523 (Union of Kalmar)
DK541-579	947.45	Leningrad			
DK588-609	947.312	Moscow	DL184-263.3	948.90(3-5)	Modern 1523-
DK670-679.5	947.95	Georgia	DL185-192.8	948.903	1523-1670 (War with Sweden)
DK680-689.5	947.92	Armenia			
DK690-699.5	947.91	Azerbaijan	DL193-199.8	948.903	1670-1808
DK751-781	957	Siberia	DL196.6	948.903	Northern War (1700-1721)
DK845-860	958.4	Asian Russia/ West Turkestan	DL201-249	948.904	1808-1906
			DL217-239.6	948.904	Schleswig-Holstein wars
DK901-909.5	958.45	Kazakh/Kazakhstan	DL250-263.3	948.905	20th century
DK911-919.5	958.43	Kirghiz/Kirghizia	DL269-291	948.9(1-5)	Local history/Description
DK921-929.5	958.6	Tajik/Tadzhikistan	DL276	948.913	Copenhagen
DK931-939.5	958.5	Turkmen/Turkmenia	DL301-398	949.12	Iceland
DK941-949.5	958.7	Uzbek/Uzbekistan	DL301	949.1200(5/6)	Serials/Societies
DK4010-4800	943.8	Poland	DL304	949.12003	Gazetteers
DK4010	943.800(5/6)	Serials/Societies	DL309-315	914.91204	Travel
DK4018	943.8006	Congresses	DL331-334	949.12004	Ethnography
DK4030	943.8003	Gazetteers/Dictionaries	DL351-380	949.12	History
DK4045-4081	914.38(04)	Geography/Travel	DL351-356	949.120(1-2)	Early to 1540
DK4120-4122	943.8004	Ethnography	DL357-360	949.1203	1540-1800
DK4123-4442	943.8	History	DL365-373	949.120(3-4)	1801-1918
DK4130-4138	943.80099	Biography	DL375	949.120(4-5)	1918-
DK4139	943.80072	Historiography	DL401-596	936.3/948.1	Norway
DK4186-4348	943.802	Early to 1795	DL401-403	936.300(5/6)/948.100(5/6)	Serials/Societies
DK4189-4289	943.802(2-3)	To 1572	DL405	936.3003/948.1003	Gazetteers/Dictionaries
DK4210	943.8022	To 960	DL415-419.2	913.6304/914.8104	Travel
DK4211-4249	943.8022	960-1386	DL431-433	936.3/948.1	Social life
DK4249.7-4289	943.8023	1386-1575	DL441-442	936.3004/948.1004	Ethnography
DK4290-4328	943.802(4-5)	1572-1763	DL443-535	936.3/948.1	History
DK4328.9-4348	943.8025	Partition (1763-1795)	DL443	936.3003/948.1003	Dictionaries
DK4348.5-4395	943.803	1795-1918	DL444	936.30099/948.10099	Biography
DK4366-4378	943.8033	Revolution (1863-1864)	DL445	936.30072/948.10072	Historiography
DK4379.5-4395	943.8033	1864-1918	DL460-535	936.30(1-2)/948.10(1-4)	By date
DK4397-4420	943.804(4-53)	1918-1945	DL460-478	936.3/948.101	Early and Medieval to 1387
DK4404-4409	943.804	Wars (1918-1921)	DL480-502	948.102	1387-1814 (Union of Kalmar)
DK4409.4	943.804	Coup d'etat (1926)			
DK4410-4415	943.8053	1939-1945	DL500-502	948.103	Union with Sweden (1814)
DK4419-4420	943.80(4-5)0099	Biography	DL503-526	948.103	19th century
DK4429-4442	943.805(4-)	1945- (People's Republic)	DL525	948.1041	Dissolution of Union (1905)
DK4434-4435	943.805092	Biography	DL527-535	948.104	20th century (World War II)
DK4600-4800	943.8(1-6)	Local history/Description	DL576-596	948.(2-8)	Local history/Description
DK4610-4645	943.84	Warsaw (Warszawa)	DL581	948.23	Oslo (Christiania)
DK4650-4685	943.82	Gdansk (Danzig)	DL601-991	936.3/948.5	Sweden
DK4700-4735	943.86	Krakow (Cracow)	DL601	936.300(5/6)/948.500(5/6)	Serials/Societies
DL	948/936.3	Scandinavia	DL605	936.3003/948.5003	Gazetteers/Dictionaries

21

LC	Dewey	Descriptor
DL614.55-619.5	913.6304/914.8504	Travel
DL631-635	936.3/948.5	Social life
DL639-641	936.3004/948.5004	Ethnography
DL643-879	936.3/948.5	History
DL643	936.3003/948.5003	Dictionaries
DL644	936.30099/948.90099	Biography
DL645	936.3007(2)/948.5007(2)	Education/Historiography
DL660-879	936.30(1-2)/948.50(1-5)	By date
DL660-700.9	936.3/948.501	Early to 1523 (Union of Kalmar)
DL701-879	948.50(2-5)	Modern (1523-)
DL701-719.9	948.502	1523-1654 (Vasa Dynasty)
DL721-743	948.503	Zweibrucken Dynasty (1654-1718)
DL733-743	947.05	Northern War (1700-1721)
DL747-805	948.503	1718-1818
DL805	948.503	Union with Norway (1814)
DL807-859	948.504	1814-1907
DL860-879	948.505	20th century
DL971-991	948.(6-8)	Local history/Description
DL976	948.73	Stockholm
DL1002-1180	948.97	Finland
DL1002	948.9700(5/6)	Serials/Societies
DL1004	948.97006	Congresses
DL1007	948.97003	Gazetteers/Dictionaries
DL1015-.4	914.89704	Travel
DL1017	948.97	Social life
DL1018-1020	948.97004	Ethnography
DL1024-1141.6	948.97	History
DL1024	948.970099	Biography
DL1025-1027	948.97007(2)	Education/Historiography
DL1050-1141.6	948.970(1-34)	By date
DL1050-1052.9	948.9701	Early to 1523
DL1055-1141.6	948.970(1-34)	Modern (1523-)
DL1058-1063	948.9701	1523-1809
DL1065-.805	948.9702	1809-1917 (Russian period)
DL1066-1141.6	948.9703	20th century
DL1170-1180	948.97(1-7)	Local history/Description
DL1175-.95	948.971	Helsinki (Helsingfors)
DP	936.6/946.(9)	Spain/Portugal
DP1-402	936.6/946	Spain
DP1	936.600(5/6)/946.00(5/6)	Serials/Societies
DP2	936.6006/946.006	Congresses
DP11	936.60025/946.0025	Directories
DP12	936.6003/946.003	Gazetteers/Dictionaries
DP27-43.2	913.6604(04)/914.6(04)	Geography/Travel
DP48-.9	936.6/946	Social life
DP52-53	936.6004/946.004	Ethnography
DP58	936.60099/946.0099	Biography
DP63-.83	936.60072/946.0072	Historiography
DP76-78	355.00946	Military history
DP80-81	359.00946	Naval history
DP91-272.4	936.60(1-2)/946.0(1-8)	History, By date
DP91-96	936.6/946.01	Earliest to 711
DP97.3-160.8	946.0(2-3)	(711-1516)
DP161-272.4	946.0(4-8)	Modern Spain (1516-)
DP161.5-166	946.03	Fernando V/Isabel I (1479-1516)
DP170-189	946.04	Habsburgs (1516-1700)
DP192-200.8	946.054	Bourbons (1700-1808)
DP201-232.6	946.0(6-74)	19th century
DP204-208	946.06	Napoleonic period (1808-1814)
DP212-220	946.072	Bourbon restoration (1814-1868)
DP222-232.6	946.07(3-4)	1868-1886
DP233-272.4	946.0(74-8)	1886-

LC	Dewey	Descriptor
DP250-269.9	946.081	Second republic (1931-1939)
DP269.97-271	946.082	1939-1975 (Franco)
DP272-.4	946.083	1975-
DP285-402	946.(1-88)	Local history/Description
DP350-374	946.41	Madrid
DP501-802	936.6/946.9	Portugal
DP501	936.600(5/6)/946.900(5/6)	Serials/Societies/Congresses
DP513	936.60025/946.90025	Directories
DP514	936.6003/946.9003	Gazetteers/Dictionaries
DP520-526.5	913.66(04)/914.69(04)	Geography/Travel
DP532-.7	936.6/946.9	Social life
DP533-534.5	936.6004/946.9004	Ethnography
DP535-682.2	936.6/946.9	History
DP535	936.6003/946.9003	Dictionaries
DP536	936.60099/946.90099	Biography
DP536.8-.96	936.60072/946.90072	Historiography
DP547	355.009469	Military history
DP550-551	359.009469	Naval history
DP558-682.2	936.60(1-3)/946.90(1-4)	By date
DP558-618	936.6/946.901	Early to 1143
DP568-629	946.90(1-2)	House of Burgundy (1095-1640)
DP620-682.2	946.90(2-4)	1580-
DP622-629	946.902	1580-1640 (Spanish Dynasty)
DP632-644.9	946.903(2-4)	House of Braganza (1640-1816)
DP645-669	946.903(4-6)	1816-1908
DP650-657	946.9035	Revolution/Wars of 1820-1840
DP670-682.2	946.904	20th century
DP674-682.2	946.904	Revolution/Republic (1910-)
DP702-802	946.9(1-9)	Local history/Description
DP752-776	946.9425	Lisbon
DQ	936.4/949.4	Switzerland
DQ1	936.400(5/6)/949.400(5/6)	Serials/Societies
DQ2	936.4006/949.4006	Congresses
DQ14	936.4003/949.4003	Gazetteers/Dictionaries
DQ20-26	913.64(04)/914.94(04)	Geography/Travel
DQ36-39	936.4/949.4	Social life
DQ48-49	936.4004/949.4004	Ethnography
DQ51-210	936.4/949.4	History
DQ51	936.4003/949.4003	Dictionaries
DQ52-.7	936.40099/949.40099	Biography
DQ52.8-.95	936.4007(2)/949.4007(2)	Historiography
DQ59	355.009494	Military history
DQ78-210	936.40(1-2)/949.40(1-7)	By date
DQ78-110	936.4/949.40(1-3)	Early and Medieval to 1516
DQ79-84	936.4	Celts and Romans (To 687)
DQ85-87	949.401	Carlovingian/German (687-1291)
DQ88-110	949.40(2-3)	1291-1516 (Independence)
DQ111-123	949.40(3-4)	1516-1798
DQ124-191	949.40(5-6)	19th century
DQ131-151	949.405	Helvetic Republic (1798-1803)
DQ154-191	949.406	Sonderbund (1815-1900)
DQ201-210	949.407	20th century
DQ301-851	949.4(3-79)	Local history/Description
DQ820-829	949.47	Alps
DR	939.8/949.6	Balkan Peninsula
DR1	939.8/949.6 + 00(5/6)	Serials/Societies
DR1.5	939.8/949.6(006)	Congresses
DR5	939/949.6(003)	Gazetteers/Dictionaries
DR11-16	913.98/914.96 + (04)	Geography/Travel

LC	Dewey	Descriptor
DR22-23	939.8/949.6	Social life
DR24-27	939.8/949.6 + (004)	Ethnography
DR32-48.5	949.6	History
DR32	949.6003	Dictionaries
DR33	949.60092	Biography
DR39	949.6101(1-4)	Ancient to Medieval to 1500
DR41-43	949.61015	1500-1900 (Ottoman Empire)
DR45-48	949.610(2-3)	1900-present
DR50-.84	949.61	Thrace
DR51-98	939.8/949.77	Bulgaria
DR51	939.8/949.77 + 00(5/6)	Serials/Societies
DR51.3-.4	939.8/949.77 + (0074)	Museums/Exhibitions
DR53	939.8/949.77 + (003)	Gazetteers/Dictionaries
DR53.7	939.8/949.77 + (0025)	Directories
DR57-61	913.98/914.977 + (04)	Geography/Travel
DR63	939.8/949.6	Social life
DR64	939.8/949.7 + (004)	Ethnography
DR65-93.34	939.8/949.77	History
DR65	939.8/949.77 + (003)	Dictionaries
DR66	939.8/949.77 + (0099)	Biography
DR66.7-.97	939.8/949.77 + (0072)	Historiography
DR70	355.0094977	Military history
DR73.7-93.34	939.8/949.770(1-3)	By date
DR74-81.6	939.8/949.7701	Early and Medieval
DR75-77.8	939.8/949.77013	1st Bulgarian Empire (681-1018)
DR79-80.8	949.77014	1018-1396 (2nd Empire)
DR82-.5	949.77015	Turk rule/Uprising (1396-1878)
DR84.9-.8	949.7702	1878-1946
DR89.9-93.34	949.7703	1946-
DR95-98	949.77(2-8)	Local history/Description
DR97	949.773	Sofia
DR201-296	939.8/949.8	Romania
DR201	939.8/949.8 + 00(5/6)	Serials/Societies
DR201.2	939.8/949.8(006)	Congresses
DR204	939.8/949.8(003)	Gazetteers/Dictionaries
DR207-210	913/914.98(04)	Travel
DR212	939.8/949.8	Social life
DR213-214	939.8/949.8 + (004)	Ethnography
DR215-267.5	939.8/949.80(1-3)	History
DR215	939.8/949.8 + (003)	Dictionaries
DR216	939.8/949.8 + (0099)	Biography
DR216.7-.92	939.8/949.8 + 007(2)	Education/Historiography
DR219	355.009498	Military history
DR225	359.009498	Naval history
DR238-267.5	939.8/949.80(1-3)	By date
DR238-239.22	939.8	Early Roman period
DR241-.5	949.8015	Phanariote Regime (1601-1822)
DR242-250	949.8016	1822-1866
DR250-266	949.802	1881-1944
DR267-.5	949.803	1944-
DR279-296	949.80(2-4)	Local history/Description
DR279-280.74	949.84	Transylvania
DR286	949.82	Bucharest
DR401-741	939.2/956.1	Turkey
DR401	939.2/956.1 + 00(5/6)	Serials/Societies
DR401.2	939.2/956.1 + (006)	Congresses
DR413	939.2/956.1 + (0025)	Directories
DR414	939.2/956.1 + (003)	Gazetteers/Dictionaries
DR421-429.4	913.92/915.61 + (04)	Travel
DR432	939.2/956.1	Social life
DR434-435	939.2/956.1 + (004)	Ethnography
DR436-603	939.2/956.1	History

LC	Dewey	Descriptor
DR436	939.2/956.1 + (003)	Dictionaries
DR438-.7	939.2/956.1 + (0099)	Biography
DR438.8-.95	939.2/956.1 + 007(2)	Education/Historiography
DR448	355.009561	Military history
DR451	359.009561	Naval history
DR481-603	939.2/956.10(1-3)	By date
DR481	939.2/956.101(3-4)	Early to 1281/1453
DR511-529	956.1015	1566-1640
DR515-516	956.1015	1570-1571 (Cyprian War)
DR531-555.7	956.1015	1640-1789
DR576-603	956.102	20th century republic
DR701-741	956.(2-6)	Local history/Description
DR716-739	949.618	Istanbul (Constantinople)
DR901-998	938.1/949.65	Albania
DR901	938.1/949.65 + 00(5/6)	Serials/Societies
DR903.5	938.1/949.65 + (006)	Congresses
DR907	938.1/949.65 + (003)	Gazetteers/Dictionaries
DR914-918	913.81/914.965 + (04)	Geography/Travel
DR922	938.1/949.65	Social life
DR923-925	938.1/949.65 + (004)	Ethnography
DR927-977.25	938.1/949.65	History
DR927	938.1/949.65 + (003)	Dictionaries
DR928-934	938.1/949.65 + (0099)	Biography
DR954-977.25	938.1/949.650(1-3)	By date
DR954-960.5	938.1	Early
DR961-969	949.6501	1912 (Turkish rule)
DR970-977.25	949.650(2-3)	1912-
DR1202-2285	939.8/949.7	Yugoslavia
DR1202	939.8/949.7 + 00(5/6)	Serials/Societies
DR1205	939.8/949.7 + (006)	Congresses
DR1209	939.8/949.7 + (003)	Gazetteers/Dictionaries
DR1212	939.8/949.7 + (0025)	Directories
DR1218-1224	913.98/914.97 + (04)	Geography/Travel
DR1228	939.8/949.7	Social life
DR1229-1230	939.8/949.7 + (004)	Ethnography
DR1232-1321	939.8/949.7	History
DR1233-1235	939.8/949.7 + (0099)	Biography
DR1239-1243	939.8/949.7 + 007(2)	Education/Historiography
DR1250-1251	355.009497	Military history
DR1252-1253	359.009497	Naval history
DR1259-1312	939.8/949.70(1-2)	By date
DR1259-1265	939.8/949.701	Early and Medieval
DR1266-1280	949.701	1500 to 1918
DR1281-1312	949.702	1918-
DR1350-2285	949.7(1-6)	Local history/Description
DR1352-1485	949.73	Slovenia
DR1502-1645	949.72	Croatia
DR1652-1785	949.742	Bosnia and Hercegovina
DR1802-1928	949.745	Montenegro
DR1932-2125	949.71	Serbia
DR2152-2285	949.76	Macedonia
DS	950	Asia
DS1-3	950.0(5/6)	Serials/Societies
DS4	950.03	Gazetteers/Dictionaries
DS5.9-10	915	Geography
DS13-28	950.04	Ethnography
DS31-35.2	950	Asia (General)
DS33.5	950.1	Ancient to 1162
DS33.5	950.2	Mongol/Tatar eras (1162-1480)
DS33.7	950.3	European entry (1480-1905)
DS34	950.4	1905-
DS34	950.41	1905-1945
DS34	950.424	1945-1949
DS34	950.425	1950-1959
DS34	950.426	1960-1969
DS34	950.427	1970-1979

LC	Dewey	Descriptor	LC	Dewey	Descriptor
DS34	950.428-	1980-	DS86	956.92035	Mandate period (1920-1941)
DS36-39.2	909.09174927	Arab countries	DS86	956.9204	1926-
DS36-.28	909.091749270(5/6)	Serials/Societies/Congresses	DS86	956.92042	1926-1941
DS36.55	909.0917492703	Gazetteers/Directories	DS87-.53	956.92043	1941-
DS36.59-.65	910.91	Travel	DS87.53	956.92044	1975- (Civil war)
DS36.77-.88	909.09174927	Social life	DS92-99	939.43/956.91	Syria
DS36.9	909.0917492704	Ethnography	DS92	939.43/956.91 + 00(5/6)	Serials/Societies
DS37-39.2	909.09174927	History	DS92.6	939.43003/956.91003	Gazetteers
DS38	939.49	Arab countries, Ancient to 622	DS92.8	939.430025/956.910025	Directories
DS38.1-.7	953.02	622-1517	DS94	913.94304/915.69104	Travel
DS38.8	953.03	Ottoman Empire (1517-1740)	DS94.7-.8	939.43004/956.91004	Ethnography
DS38.9	953.04	1740-1926	DS94.9-98.3	939.43/956.91	History
DS39	953.05	1926-	DS96-.2	939.43	Ancient to 640
DS39	953.052	1926-1964	DS97-.4	956.9102	640-1516
DS39	953.053	1964-	DS97.5-.6	956.9103	Ottoman Empire (1516-1920)
DS41-66	939.4/956	Near East	DS98-.3	956.9104	1920-
DS41-.5	939.400(5/6)/956.00(5/6)	Serials/Societies/Congresses	DS98	956.91041	Mandate period (1920-1945)
DS43	939.4003/956.003	Gazetteers/Dictionaries	DS98	956.91042	Republic (1945-)
DS44.9-49.7	913.94/915.6	Geography	DS99	956.91(2-44)	Local history/Description
DS54-.95	939.37/956.45	Cyprus	DS101-151	933/956.94	Israel/Palestine
DS54.6	939.37	Cyprus, Ancient to 640	DS101	933/956.94 + 00(5/6)	Serials/Societies
DS54.6	939.37/956.4501	To 1571	DS102.9	933.0025/956.940025	Directories
DS54.7	956.4502	1571-1878	DS103-107.4	913.304/915.69404	Travel
DS54.8-.83	956.4503	British era (1878-1960)	DS109-.94	956.9442	Jerusalem
DS54.9	956.4504	1960-	DS113-.8	933.004/956.94004	Ethnography
DS61-66	939.4/956	Near East, History (General)	DS114-128.19	933/956.94	History
DS62.2-.25	939.4	Near East, Ancient to 640	DS122-.8	933	Israel/Palestine, to 70
DS62.4	956.01	To 1900	DS122.9-123.5	956.9402	Mishnaic/Talmudic eras (70-640)
DS62.4	956.015	1300-1900 (Ottoman Empire)	DS124-125.5	956.9403	640-1917 (Ottoman Empire)
DS62.4	956.02	1900-1918	DS126-.4	956.9404	British era (1917-1948)
DS62.4	956.03	1918-1945	DS126.5-128	956.9405	1948-
DS62.4	956.04	1945-1980	DS126.5-127	956.94052	1948-1967
DS62.4	956.042	Arab/Israel War (1948-1949)	DS127-128	956.94053	1967-1974
DS62.4	956.044	Arab/Israel War (1956)	DS127-128	956.94054	1974-
DS62.4	956.046	Arab/Israel War (1967)	DS133-151	909.04924	Jews outside Palestine/Israel
DS62.4	956.048	Arab/Israel War (1973)	DS153-154.9	933/956.95	Jordan
DS62.4	956.05	1980-	DS153.A2-.A5	933/956.95 + 00(5/6)	Serials/Societies
DS67-79.9	935/956.7	Iraq (Babylonia/Mesopotamia)	DS153.2	913.304/915.69504	Travel
DS67	935.00(5/6)/956.700(5/6)	Serials/Societies	DS153.5-.55	933.004/956.95004	Ethnography
DS67.8	935.003/956.7003	Dictionaries/Gazetteers	DS153.7-154.55	933/956.95	History
DS70.8	935.004/956.7004	Ethnography	DS154.2	933	Jordan, Ancient to 70
DS70.82-79.66	935/956.7	History	DS154.3	956.9502	70-640
DS71-75	935	Iraq, Ancient to 637	DS154.4	956.9503	640-1923 (Ottoman Empire)
DS76-.4	956.702	637-1553	DS154.5-.55	956.9504	1923-
DS77	956.703	Ottoman Empire (1553-1920)	DS154.5	956.95042	Mandate period (1923-1946)
DS79	956.704	1920-	DS154.5	956.95043	Hashemite kingdom (1946-)
DS79.5	956.7041	Mandate period (1920-1932)	DS154.55	956.95044	1967-
DS79.52-.53	956.7042	Monarchy (1932-1958)	DS154.9	956.95(1-8)	Local history
DS79.65	956.7043	Republic (1958-)	DS155-156	939.2/956.(1-8)	Asia Minor
DS80-90	939.44/956.92	Lebanon	DS161-195.5	939.55/956.62	Armenia
DS80.A2	929.44/956.92 + 00(5/6)	Serials/Societies	DS174-.9	956.620072	Historiography
DS80.A5	939.44003/956.92003	Gazetteers/Dictionaries	DS181-184	939.55	Ancient to 640
DS80.2	913.94404/915.69204	Travel	DS186-188	956.601(3-5)	428-1522
DS80.5	939.44004/956.92004	Ethnography	DS191-193	956.6015	1522-1800 (Ottoman Empire)
DS80.7-87.53	939.44/956.92	History	DS194-.5	956.6015	1801-1900
DS81-82	939.44	Lebanon, Ancient to 640	DS195-.5	956.60(2-39)	1901-
DS83-85	956.9203	640-1926	DS201-248	939.49/953	Arabian Peninsula/Saudi Arabia
DS83	956.92032	640-1517	DS201	939.49/953. + 00(5/6)	Serials/Societies
DS84-85	956.92034	Ottoman Empire (1517-1920)	DS204.5-208	913.94904/915.304	Travel

LC	Dewey	Descriptor	LC	Dewey	Descriptor
DS218-219	939.49004/953.004	Ethnography	DS461.1	954.0252	Babur reign (1526-1530)
DS221-244.63	939.49/953	History	DS461.2	954.0253	Humayun (1530-1556)
DS231	939.49	Ancient to 622	DS461.3-.4	956.0254	Akbar reign (1556-1605)
DS232-238.7	953.02	622-1517	DS461.5	954.0256	Jahangir reign (1605-1627)
DS239-241	953.03	Ottoman Empire (1517-1740)	DS461.6	954.0257	Shahjahan reign (1628-1658)
DS242-244.5	956.04	1740-1926 (Freedom from Turks)	DS461.7	954.0258	Aurangzib reign (1658-1707)
DS244.512-.63	956.05	1926-	DS461.8	954.029	European entry (1707-1785)
DS244.512-.56	956.052	1926-1964	DS461.8	954.0292	1707-1744
DS244.6-.63	956.053	1964-	DS461.8	954.0294	Anglo-French War (1744-1757)
DS251-326	935/955	Iran (Persia)			
DS251-.5	935./955. + 00(5/6)	Serials/Societies/Congresses	DS463-472.9	954.0296	1757-1772
DS253	935.003/955.003	Gazetteers	DS473-.5	954.0298	Governor Hastings (1772-1785)
DS254.8-259.2	913.5/915.5 + (04)	Geography/Travel			
DS268-269	935.004/955.004	Ethnography	DS474-480.83	954.03	British period (1785-1947)
DS270-318.85	935/955	History	DS474-478.3	954.031	East India Co. (1785-1858)
DS275-287.8	935	Iran, Ancient to 637	DS479-480.83	954.035	Crown rule (1858-1947)
DS288-290	955.02	637-1499 (Foreign rule)	DS480.84-.85	954.042	Jawaharlal Nehru (1947-1964)
DS292-297	955.03	Persian dynasties (1499-1794)			
DS298-311	955.04	1794-1906	DS480.852	954.043	Lal Bahadur Shastri (1964-1966)
DS313-318.85	955.05	1906-			
DS313-316	955.051	1906-1925	DS480.852	954.045	Indira Gandhi (1966-1977)
DS316.2-317	956.052	Reza Shah Pahlavi (1925-1941)	DS480.853	954.05	1971-
			DS483-486.8	954.(1-8)	Local history/Description
DS318.72-.85	955.054	1979-	DS488-490	954.93	Sri Lanka
DS327-329.4	939.68/958	Central Asia	DS489.6-.73	954.9301	Ancient to 1795
DS331-349.9	909.09824	Indian Ocean region	DS489.7-.73	954.9302	British era (1795-1948)
DS350-375	939.6/958.1	Afghanistan	DS489.8-.86	954.9303	1948-
DS358	939.6	Afghanistan, Ancient to 640	DS493-495.8	954.96	Nepal
DS358	958.101	640-1221	DS498-.8	954.799	Goa
DS358	958.102	1221-1709	DS520-589	959	Southeast Asia
DS358-368	958.103	1709-1919	DS527-530.9	959.1	Burma
DS369-371.2	958.104	1919-	DS529.2-.3	959.102	Ancient to 1826
DS369.4-371	958.1043	Muhammad Zahir Shah (1933-1973)	DS529.7	959.103	British conquest (1826-1885)
DS371.2	958.1044	Republic (1973-1978)	DS530-.32	959.104	British era (1886-1948)
DS376-392.2	954.91	Pakistan	DS530.4-.53	959.105	1948-
DS384-387	954.9104	West/East union (1947-1971)	DS554-.98	959.6	Cambodia
			DS554.6-.73	959.603	Ancient to 1949
DS388	954.9105	1971-	DS554.7-.842	959.604	1949-
DS393-396.9	954.92	Bangladesh	DS555-.98	959.4	Laos
DS395	954.9204	East/West union (1947-1971)	DS556.6-.73	959.403	Ancient to 1949
			DS559.7-.86	959.404	1949-
			DS556-559.93	959.7	Vietnam
DS395.5-.7	954.9205	1971-	DS556.6-.83	959.703	Ancient to 1949
DS421-486.8	934/954	India	DS556.8-559.916	959.704	1949-
DS430-432	934.004/954.004	Ethnography	DS556-.83	959.7041	Indochinese War (1946-1954)
DS433-481	934/954	History			
DS451-.9	934	India, Ancient to 647	DS556-.93	959.7042	1954-1961
DS451-473.5	954.02	647-1785	DS557-559.8	959.7043	Vietnamese War (1961-1975)
DS451	954.021	647-997			
DS452-458.7	954.022	Moslem conquests (997-1206)	DS559.912-.916	959.7044	1975-
			DS561-589	959.3	Thailand
DS458-.3	954.0223	Ghazni Dynasty (997-1196)	DS576-577	959.302	Ancient to 1782
DS458.5-.7	954.0225	Ghor Dynasty (1196-1206)	DS576-577	959.3021	Ancient to 1219
DS459-.52	954.023	1206-1414	DS577-582	959.303	1782-1910 (Rama IV)
DS459-.15	954.0232	Delhi Slave Kings (1206-1290)	DS583-586	959.304	1910- (Rama VI-)
			DS591-599	959.5	Malaysia
DS459.2-.3	954.0234	Khilji Dynasty (1290-1320)	DS596.5-.63	959.503	Ancient to 1946
DS459.4-.52	954.0236	Tughlak Dynasty (1320-1414)	DS597-.215	959.504	1946-1963
			DS597.2-.215	959.505	1963- (Federation period)
DS459.6-.95	954.024	1414-1526	DS597.22-599	959.5(1-7)	Local history/Description
DS459.6	954.0242	Sayyid Dynasty (1414-1451)	DS600-649	959.8	Indonesia
			DS646.1-.15	959.81	Sumatra
DS459.7-.95	954.0245	Lodi Dynasty (1451-1526)	DS646.17-.29	959.82	Java
DS461-.9	954.025	Mogul Empire (1526-1707)	DS646.3-.34	959.83	Borneo

LC	Dewey	Descriptor	LC	Dewey	Descriptor
DS646.4-.49	959.84	Celebes/Sulawesi	DT15-16	960.04	Ethnography
DS646.5-.59	959.86	Timor	DT17-39	960	General history
DS646.6-.69	959.85	Moluccas/Maluku	DT24	960.1	Ancient to 640
DS650-.99	959.55	Brunei	DT25	960.2	640-1885
DS651-689	959.9	Philippines	DT25	960.21	640-1450
DS665-666	959.9004	Ethnography	DT25-57	960.22	1450-1799
DS667-686.6	959.9	History	DT28	960.23	1800-1885
DS673.8	959.901	Ancient to 1564	DT29-30.5	960.3	1885-
DS674-678	959.902	Spanish era (1564-1898)	DT29	960.31	1885-1945
DS679-686.4	959.903	United States era (1898-1946)	DT30-.5	960.32	1945-
DS686.5-.6	959.904	Republic (1946-)	DT43-154	932/962	Egypt
DS701-799.9	951	China	DT63-.5	932	Pyramids
DS741-748.76	931	China, Ancient to 420	DT71	932.004/962.004	Ethnography
DS748.45-.76	951.015	420-581	DT74-107.87	932/962.0(2-55)	History
DS749.2-.29	951.016	Sui Dynasty (581-618)	DT83-93	932	Egypt, Ancient to 640
DS749.3-.47	951.017	T'ang Dynasty (618-907)	DT95-96.7	962.02	Arab era (640-1517)
DS749.5-.76	951.018	907-960	DT97-106	962.03	Ottoman Empire (1517-1882)
DS750.52-753.7	951.02	960-1644	DT107-.8	962.04	British era (1882-1922)
DS751-.6	951.024	Sung Dynasty (960-1279)	DT107.8-.87	962.05	1922-
DS752-.6	951.025	Yuan Dynasty (1271-1368)	DT107.8	962.051	Faud I (1922-1936)
DS753-.7	951.026	Ming Dynasty (1368-1644)	DT107.82	962.052	Faruk/Regency (1936-1952)
DS753.82-773.6	951.03	Ch'ing Dynasty (1644-1912)	DT107.83	962.053	Naguib/Nasser (1953-1970)
DS753.82-754.84	951.032	1644-1795	DT107.85	962.054	Anwar Sadat (1970-1981)
DS755-757.7	951.033	1796-1850 (Opium War)	DT107.87	962.055	1981-
DS758.7-759.4	951.034	Taiping Rebellion (1850-1864)	DT154.1-159.9	962.4	Sudan
DS763.5-773.23	951.035	1864-1911 (Boxer Rebellion)	DT155-.2	962.4004	Ethnography
DS773.32-.6	951.036	Revolution (1911-1912)	DT155.3-157.67	962.4	History
DS773.83-777.544	951.04	Republic (1912-1949)	DT156	962.401	Ancient to 500
DS773.83-777.46	951.041	1912-1927	DT156-.3	962.402	500-1820
DS777.47-.544	951.042	Nationalist era (1927-1949)	DT156-.3	962.4022	Christian Kingdoms (500-1504)
DS777.545-779.29	951.05	People's Republic (1949-)	DT156.3	962.4023	Funj Sultanate (1504-1820)
DS781-796	951.(1-6)	Local history/Description	DT156.4-.7	962.403	Anglo/Egyptian era (1820-1956)
DS781-784.2	951.8	Manchuria	DT157-.67	962.404	1956-
DS785-786	951.5	Tibet	DT159.6-.9	962.(5-9)	Local history/Description
DS798	951.73	Outer Mongolia	DT160-177	939.7/961	North Africa
DS798.92-799.9	951.249	Taiwan/Formosa	DT167-176	939.7/961	History
DS799.64-.66	951.24902	Ancient to 1683	DT168-169.5	939.7	Carthaginian era
DS799.64-.66	951.24903	Chinese era (1683-1895)	DT168-171	939.7	Ancient to 640
DS799.69-.72	951.24904	Japanese era (1895-1945)	DT172-176	961.02	Arab/Ottoman rule (640-1830)
DS799.77-.833	951.24905	Nationalist China (1945-)	DT173	961.022	Arab era (640-1520)
DS801-897	952	Japan	DT174	961.023	Ottoman Empire (1520-1830)
DS851-856.72	952.01	Ancient to 1185	DT176	961.03	European entry (1830-1950)
DS856.75-881.84	952.02	Feudal era (1185-1868)	DT176	961.04	1950-
DS856.75-861	952.021	Kamakura era (1185-1334)	DT176	961.045	1950-1959
DS863-865.5	952.022	Namboku era (1334-1392)	DT176	961.046	1960-1969
DS868-869.6	952.023	Muromachi era (1392-1573)	DT176	961.047	1970-1979
DS869.5-.6	952.024	Momoyama era (1573-1603)	DT176	961.048	1980-1989
DS870-881.84	952.025	Takugawa era (1603-1868)	DT176	961.049	1990-
DS881.85-888.5	952.03	1868-1945	DT179.2-.9	939.71/964	Northwest Africa
DS881.98-884	952.031	Meiji era (1868-1912)	DT211-346	939.7/961/964	Libya/Tunisia/Morocco
DS885.8-888	952.032	Taisho era (1912-1926)	DT211-239	939.74/961.2	Libya
DS888.15-890	952.033	Showa era (1926-1945)	DT223-.2	939.74/961.2 + (004)	Ethnography
DS888.84-890.3	952.04	1945-	DT223.2-236	939.74/961.2	History
DS901-937	951.9	Korea	DT228	939.74	Libya, Ancient to 644
DS911-912.43	951.901	Ancient to 1392	DT229-231	961.202	Arab/Ottoman eras (644-1911)
DS913-915.5	951.902	Yi Dynasty (1392-1910)	DT235	961.203	Italian era (1911-1952)
DS916.525-.58	951.903	Japanese era (1910-1945)	DT235.5-236	961.204	1952-
DS916.6-922.42	951.904	1945-	DT235.5	961.2041	Idris I (1952-1969)
DS916.6-.92	951.9041	1945-1950	DT236	961.2042	Muammar Qaddafi (1969-)
DS918-921.8	951.9042	Korean War (1950-1953)			
DS922-.42	951.9043	1953-			
DT	960	Africa	DT241-269	939.73/961.1	Tunisia

LC	Dewey	Descriptor
DT253-.2	939.73/961.1 + (004)	Ethnography
DT253.4-264.49	939.73/961.1	History
DT258	939.73	Tunisia, Ancient to 647
DT259	961.102	Arab era (647-1516)
DT261-263.76	961.103	Ottoman Empire (1516-1881)
DT263.9-264.3	961.104	1881-1956
DT264.35-.49	961.105	1956-
DT264.35-.364	961.1051	Habib Bourguiba (1956-1987)
DT264.35-.49	961.1052	1987-
DT271-299	939.71/965	Algeria
DT283-.6	939.71/965. + (004)	Ethnography
DT283.7-295.55	939.71/965	History
DT288	939.71	Algeria, Ancient to 647
DT289-292	965.02	Arab/Berber/Ottoman (647-1830)
DT294-295.3	965.03	French era (1830-1962)
DT294.5-295.3	965.04	1900-1962
DT295.5-.55	965.05	1962-
DT298-299	965.(1-7)	Local history/Description
DT301-330	939.71/964	Morocco
DT313-.6	939.71/964. + (004)	Ethnography
DT313.7-325.92	939.71/964.0(2-5)	History
DT318	939.71	Morocco, Ancient to 647
DT319-323.5	964.02	Arab/Berber eras (647-1830)
DT324-.92	964.03	1830-1899
DT324-.92	964.04	1900-1956
DT325-.92	964.05	1956-
DT331-346	966	Sahara
DT348-363.3	967	Central Sub-Sahara
DT365-469	967.6	East Africa
DT365.5-.8	967.60(1-4)	History
DT365.65	967.601	Ancient to 1894
DT365.7-.75	967.603	1894-1961
DT365.8	967.604	1961-
DT371-398	963	Ethiopia
DT380-.4	963.004	Ethnography
DT380.5-387.954	963	History
DT383	963.01	Ancient to 640
DT383	963.02	640-1543
DT384-386	963.03	1543-1855 (John IV)
DT386.3-387.3	963.04	1855-1913 (Theodore II)
DT387.5-.92	963.05	1913-1941 (WW I - WW II)
DT387.7-.92	963.05(4-5)	Haile Selassie (1917-1974)
DT387.9-.92	963.06	1941-1974 (WW II and after)
DT387.95-.954	963.07	1974-
DT391-398	963.5	Eritrea
DT401-409	967.73	Somalia
DT402.3-.45	967.73004	Ethnography
DT402.5-407.3	967.73	History
DT403.5-.7	967.7301	Ancient to 1884
DT404-406.3	967.7303	British/Italian era (1884-1960)
DT407-.3	967.7305	1960-
DT411-.9	967.71	Djibouti
DT411.42-.45	967.71004	Ethnography
DT411.5-.83	967.71	History
DT411.65	967.7101	Ancient to 1881
DT411.75-.77	967.7103	French era (1881-1977)
DT411.8-.83	967.7104	1977-
DT421-432.5	967.6	British East Africa
DT433.2-.29	967.61	Uganda
DT433.242-.245	967.61004	Ethnography
DT433.252-.287	967.61	History

LC	Dewey	Descriptor
DT433.265-.267	967.6101	Ancient to 1894
DT433.27-.273	967.6103	British era (1894-1962)
DT433.275-.287	967.6104	1962-
DT436-449	967.8	Tanzania
DT443-.2	967.8004	Ethnography
DT443.5-448.25	967.8	History
DT450-.49	967.571	Rwanda
DT450.24-.25	967.571004	Ethnography
DT450.26-.437	967.571	History
DT450.435-.437	967.57104	1962-
DT450.5-.95	967.572	Burundi
DT450.64-.65	967.572004	Ethnography
DT450.66-.855	967.572	History
DT450.85-.855	967.57204	1962-
DT468-469	969	Islands (East African coast)
DT469.M21-.M38	969.1	Madagascar
DT469.M31-.M335	969.101	Ancient to 1895
DT469.M34-.M342	969.103	French era (1895-1960)
DT469.M343-.M345	969.105	1960-
DT469.M39	969.8	Mascarene Islands
DT469.M4-.M495	969.82	Mauritius
DT469.M465-.M467	969.8201	Ancient to 1810
DT469.M47-.M473	969.8202	British rule (1810-1968)
DT469.M48-.M483	969.8203	1968-
DT469.M497	969.4	Mayotte
DT469.R3-.R5	969.81	Reunion
DT469.R44-.R453	969.8102	Ancient to 1946
DT469.R455-.R458	969.8104	As a French dept. (1946-)
DT469.S4-.S49	969.6	Seychelles
DT470-671	966	West Africa
DT477	966.52	Guinea
DT479	966.57	Guinea-Bissau
DT491-516.9	966	British West Africa
DT509-.9	966.51	Gambia
DT509.42-.45	966.51004	Ethnography
DT509.5-.83	966.51	History
DT509.65	966.5101	Ancient to 1806
DT509.65-.7	966.5012	British era (1807-1965)
DT509.8-.83	966.5103	1965-
DT509.97-512.9	966.7	Ghana
DT510.42-.43	966.7004	Ethnography
DT510.5-512.34	966.7	History
DT511-.3	966.701	Ancient to 1874
DT511-.3	966.703	Gold Coast era (1874-1957)
DT512-.34	966.705	1957-
DT515-.9	966.9	Nigeria
DT515.42-.45	966.9004	Ethnography
DT515.53-.84	966.9	History
DT515.65-.73	966.901	Ancient to 1886
DT515.7-.77	966.903	British era (1886-1960)
DT515.8-.84	966.905	1960-
DT516-.9	966.4	Sierra Leone
DT516.42-.45	966.4004	Ethnography
DT516.5-.82	966.4	History
DT516.65	966.401	Ancient to 1787
DT516.7-.72	966.402	British era (1787-1896)
DT516.7-.72	966.403	1896-1961 (Protectorate)
DT516.8-.82	966.404	1961-
DT521-555.9	966/967	French West Africa (Sahara)
DT541-.9	966.83	Benin
DT541.42-.45	966.83004	Ethnography
DT541.5-.845	966.83	History
DT541.65-.67	966.8301	Ancient to 1904
DT541.65-.67	966.83018	Dahomey Kingdom (1600-1904)
DT541.75	966.8303	French era (1904-1960)

LC	Dewey	Descriptor
DT541.8-.845	966.8305	1960-
DT543-.9	966.52	Guinea
DT543.42-.45	966.52004	Ethnography
DT543.5-.827	966.52	History
DT543.65	966.5201	Ancient to 1882
DT543.75-.77	966.5203	French era (1882-1958)
DT543.8-.827	966.5205	1958-
DT545-.9	966.68	Ivory Coast
DT545.42-.45	966.68004	Ethnography
DT545.52-.82	966.68	History
DT545.7-.73	966.6801	Ancient to 1904
DT545.75-.77	966.6903	French era (1904-1960)
DT545.8-.83	966.6805	1960-
DT546.1-.19	967.21	Gabon
DT546.142-.145	967.21004	Ethnography
DT546.15-.183	967.21	History
DT546.165	967.2101	Ancient to 1839
DT546.165-.175	967.2102	French era (1839-1960)
DT546.18-.183	967.2104	1960-
DT546.2-.29	967.24	Republic of the Congo
DT546.242-.245	967.24004	Ethnography
DT546.25-.283	967.24	History
DT546.265-.267	967.2401	Ancient to 1885
DT546.265-.275	967.2403	Middle Congo era (1885-1960)
DT546.28-.283	967.2405	1960-
DT546.3-.39	967.41	Central African Republic
DT546.342-.345	967.41004	Ethnography
DT546.348-.384	967.41	History
DT546.365	967.4101	Ancient to 1890
DT546.365-.37	967.4103	Ubangi-Shari era (1890-1960)
DT546.375-.384	967.4105	1960-
DT546.4-.49	967.43	Chad
DT546.422-.445	967.43004	Ethnography
DT546.457-.483	967.43	History
DT546.47-.473	967.4301	Ancient to 1850
DT546.47-.477	967.4302	French era (1850-1960)
DT546.48-.483	967.4304	1960-
DT547-.9	966.26	Niger
DT547.42-.45	966.26004	Ethnography
DT547.5-.83	966.26	History
DT547.65	966.2601	Ancient to 1900
DT547.75	966.2603	French era (1900-1960)
DT547.8-.83	966.2605	1960-
DT548	966	West Sahara
DT549-.9	966.3	Senegal
DT549.42-.45	966.3004	Ethnography
DT549.47-.83	966.3	History
DT549.7-.73	966.301	Ancient to 1895
DT549.75-.77	966.303	French era (1895-1960)
DT549.8-.83	966.305	1960-
DT551-.9	966.23	Mali (French Sudan)
DT551.42-.45	966.23004	Ethnography
DT551.5-.82	966.23	History
DT551.65	966.2301	Ancient to 1902
DT551.7-.72	966.2303	French Sudan (1902-1960)
DT551.8-.82	966.2305	1960-
DT554-.9	966.1	Mauritania
DT554.42-.45	966.1004	Ethnography
DT554.52-.83	966.1	History
DT554.65-.67	9066.101	Ancient to 1903
DT554.65-.67	966.1016	300-1200 (Ghana Empire)
DT554.65-.67	966.1017	1200-1500 (Mali Empire)
DT554.75-.77	966.103	French era (1903-1960)
DT554.8-.83	966.105	1960-
DT555-.9	966.25	Burkina Faso (Upper Volta)

LC	Dewey	Descriptor
DT555.42-.45	966.25004	Ethnography
DT555.52-.83	966.25	History
DT555.65-.67	966.2501	Ancient to 1897
DT555.75-.77	966.2503	French era (1897-1960)
DT555.8-.83	966.2505	1960-
DT561-581	967.11	Cameroon
DT570-571	967.11004	Ethnography
DT572-578.4	967.11	History
DT574-575	967.1101	Ancient to 1884
DT574-575	967.1102	1884-1916 (German era)
DT574-575	967.1103	Anglo/French era (1916-1959)
DT575.5-578.4	967.1104	1960-
DT582-.9	966.81	Togo
DT582.42-.45	966.81004	Ethnography
DT582.5-.82	966.81	History
DT582.65	966.8101	Ancient to 1894
DT582.7	966.8102	German era (1894-1914)
DT582.75	966.8103	Ango-French era (1914-1960)
DT582.8-.82	966.8104	1960-
DT591-615.9	966.5/967.15	Portuguese West Africa
DT613-.9	966.57	Guinea-Bissau
DT613.42-.45	966.57004	Ethnography
DT613.5-.83	966.57	History
DT613.65	966.5701	Ancient to 1879
DT613.75-.78	966.5702	Portuguese era (1879-1974)
DT613.8-.83	966.5703	1974-
DT615-.9	967.15	Sao Tome/Principe
DT615.42-.45	967.15004	Ethnography
DT615.5-.8	967.15	History
DT615.65-.7	967.1501	Ancient to 1975
DT615.8	967.1502	Republic 1975-
DT620-.9	967.18	Equatorial (Spanish) Guinea
DT620.42-.45	967.18004	Ethnography
DT620.46-.83	967.18	History
DT620.65-.67	967.1801	Ancient to 1469
DT620.65-.73	967.1802	European eras (1469-1968)
DT621-637	966.62	Liberia
DT630-.5	966.62004	Ethnography
DT630.8-636.53	966.62	History
DT633-.3	966.6201	Ancient to 1847
DT634-.3	966.6202	1847-1945
DT635-636.53	966.6203	1945-
DT639	967.2	Congo River area
DT641-665	967.51	Zaire
DT649.5-650	967.51004	Ethnography
DT650.2-683	967.51	History
DT654-.3	967.5101	Ancient to 1885
DT655-657.2	967.5102	Belgian era (1885-1960)
DT658-.25	967.5103	1960-
DT665	967.51(1-8)	Local history/Description
DT669-671	964.9/966.58	West Coast islands
DT671.C2-.C29	966.58	Cape Verde
DT671.C242-.C245	966.58004	Ethnography
DT671.C25-.C28	966.58	History
DT671.C265	966.580(1-2)	Early to 1975
DT671.C28	966.5803	1975-
DT671.S2	997.3	St. Helena
DT671.T8	997.3	Tristan da Cunha
DT1001-1190	968	Southern Africa
DT1054-1058	968.004	Ethnography
DT1062-1177	968	History
DT1107-1123	968.02	Ancient to 1488
DT1107-1123	968.03	European entry (1488-1814)
DT1107-1144	968.04	1814-1910

LC	Dewey	Descriptor	LC	Dewey	Descriptor
DT1107-1123	968.041	1814-1835 (Mfecane/ Difaqane)	DT2225-2278	968.4	History
DT1107-1123	968.042	Great Trek (1835-1838)	DT2232-2238	968.403	Ancient to 1824
DT1107-1123	968.044	1838-1854	DT2232-2267	968.404	1824-1910 (Zululand)
DT1107-1123	968.045	1854-1899	DT2240	968.4041	British entry (1824-1835)
DT1125-1144	968.048	2nd Anglo-Boer War (1899-1902)	DT2242	968.4042	Great Trek (1835-1843)
DT1125-1144	968.049	1902-1910	DT2250-2263	968.4045	British colony (1843-1899)
DT1144-1147	968.05	Union (1910-1961)	DT2265	968.4048	2nd Anglo-Boer War (1899-1902)
DT1147-1177	968.06	Republic (1961-)	DT2267	968.4049	1902-1910
DT1190	968.(2-9)	Local history	DT2270-2278	968.40(5-6)	Union/Republic (1910-)
DT1251-1465	967.3	Angola	DT2291-2378	968.2	Transvaal
DT1304-1308	967.3004	Ethnography	DT2322	968.2004	Ethnography
DT1341-1436	967.3	History	DT2325-2378	968.2	History
DT1357-1369	967.301	Ancient to 1648	DT2332-2344	968.203	Ancient to 1835
DT1373-1382	967.302	1648-1899	DT2332-2371	968.204	1835-1910
DT1385-1417	967.303	1900-1975	DT2342	968.2042	Great Trek (1835-1852)
DT1420-1436	967.304	1975-	DT2344-2359	968.2045	South Africa (1852-1877)
DT1501-1685	968.81	Namibia	DT2354-2359	968.2046	British era (1877-1881)
DT1554-1558	968.81004	Ethnography	DT2361-2368	968.2048	2nd Anglo-Boer War (1899-1902)
DT1564-1648	968.81	History	DT2371	968.2049	Transvaal Colony (1902-1910)
DT1587-1601	968.8101	Ancient to 1884			
DT1603-1622	968.8102	German era (1884-1915)	DT2375-2378	968.20(5-6)	Union/Republic (1910-)
DT1625-1648	968.8103	South African era (1915-)	DT2421-2525	968.83	Botswana
DT1701-2405	968	South Africa	DT2454-2458	968.83004	Ethnography
DT1754-1770	968.004	Ethnography	DT2464-2502	968.83	History
DT1772-1969	968	History	DT2483-2488	968.8301	Ancient to 1885
DT1807-1810	968.02	Ancient to 1488	DT2490-2493	968.83C	Bechuanaland (1885-1966)
DT1807-1845	968.03	European entry (1488-1814)	DT2496-2502	968.8303	1966-
DT1837-1922	968.04	1814-1922	DT2541-2686	968.85	Lesotho (Basutoland)
DT1837-1845	968.041	1814-1835 (Mfecane/ Difaqane)	DT2592-2596	968.85004	Ethnography
DT1853	968.042	Great Trek (1834-1838)	DT2604-2660	968.85	History
DT1853-1861	968.044	1838-1854	DT2630-2636	968.8501	Ancient to 1868
DT1861-1889	968.045	1854-1899	DT2638-2648	968.8502	Basutoland (1868-1966)
DT1890-1920	968.048	2nd Anglo-Boer war (1899-1902)	DT2652-2660	968.8503	1966-
			DT2701-2825	968.87	Swaziland
DT1921-1922	968.049	1902-1910	DT2744-2746	968.87004	Ethnography
DT1924-1941	968.05	Union (1910-1961)	DT2754-2806	968.87	History
DT1945-1969	968.06	Republic (1961-)	DT2777-2786	968.8701	Ancient to 1840
DT1991-2054	968.7	Cape of Good Hope (Province)	DT2777-2795	968.8702	British era (1840-1968)
DT2032	968.7004	Ethnography	DT2797-2806	968.8703	1968-
DT2035-2054	968	History	DT2831-2864	967	British Central Africa
DT2042-2044	968.703	European entry (1488-1814)	DT2871-3025	968.91	Zimbabwe
DT2042-2049	968.704	1806-1920	DT2910-2913	968.91004	Ethnography
DT2042-2044	968.7042	British control (1806-1854)	DT2914-3000	968.91	History
DT2042-2044	968.7045	Self-government (1854-1899)	DT2937-2957	968.9101	Ancient to 1889
			DT2959-2975	968.9102	British era (1889-1953)
DT2046-2049	968.7048	2nd Anglo-Boer War (1899-1902)	DT2976-2979	968.9103	Confederation (1953-1963)
DT2051-2054	968.70(5-6)	Union/Republic (1910-)	DT2981-2994	968.9104	Zimbabwe (1964-1980)
DT2075-2145	968.5	Orange Free State	DT2996-3000	968.9105	Republic (1980-)
DT2102	968.5004	Ethnography	DT3031-3145	968.94	Zambia
DT2105-2145	968.5	History	DT3054-3058	968.94004	Ethnography
DT2112-2118	968.503	Ancient to 1828	DT3064-3119	968.94	History
DT2118-2139	968.504	1828-1910	DT3079-3089	968.9401	Ancient to 1890
DT2120	968.5042	1835-1854 (Great Trek)	DT3091-3106	968.9402	British era (1890-1953)
DT2124-2137	968.5045	Orange Free State (1854-1899)	DT3108-3111	968.9403	Federation (1953-1963)
			DT3113-3119	968.9404	Republic (1946-)
DT2137-2139	968.5048	2nd Anglo-Boer War (1899-1902)	DT3161-3257	968.97	Malawi
DT2139	968.5049	Orange River Colony(1902-1910)	DT3189-3192	968.97004	Ethnography
			DT3194-3237	968.97	History
DT2142-2145	968.50(5-6)	Union/Republic (1910-)	DT3211-3214	968.9701	Ancient to 1891
DT2181-2278	968.4	Natal	DT3216-3225	968.9702	Nyasaland (1891-1953)
DT2222	968.4004	Ethnography	DT3227-3230	968.9703	Federation (1953-1963)
			DT3232-3237	968.9704	1964-
			DT3291-3415	967.9	Mozambique
			DT3324-3328	967.9004	Ethnography
			DT3330-3398	967.9	History

LC	Dewey	Descriptor
DT3345-3359	967.901	Ancient to 1648
DT3361-3383	967.902	1648-1900 (Portuguese era)
DT3383-3387	967.903	1900-1975
DT3389-3398	967.905	1975-
DU	993-996	Australia/New Zealand/Oceania
DU1	993-996.00(5/6)	Serials/Societies
DU10	993-996.003	Gazetteers/Dictionaries
DU19-23.5	919.(3-6)04	Travel
DU28.11-66	993-996	History
DU80-398	994	Australia
DU96.5-105.2	919.4(04)	Geography/Travel
DU98-117.2	994	History
DU98.1	994.01	Ancient to 1788
DU114-115.2	994.02	British settlement (1788-1851)
DU114-115.2	994.03	Self-government (1851-1901)
DU116-117.2	994.04	Commonwealth (1901-)
DU116-.2	994.04(1-2)	1900-1945
DU116.9-117.2	994.05	1945-1966
DU116.9-117.2	994.06	1966-
DU120-125	994.004	Ethnography
DU145	994.7	Canberra
DU150-180	994.4	New South Wales
DU182-198	994.6	Tasmania
DU200-230	994.5	Victoria
DU250-280	994.3	Queensland
DU300-330	994.23	South Australia
DU350-380	994.1	Western Australia
DU390	994.2	Central Australia
DU392-398	994.29	Northern Territory
DU400-430	993	New Zealand
DU419-422	993	History
DU420.12-.14	993.01	Ancient to 1840
DU420.16-.24	993.02	Colonial era (1840-1908)
DU420.16-.18	993.021	Crown colony (1840-1853)
DU420.16-.24	993.02(2-3)	Self-government (1853-1908)
DU420.22-.34	933.03	Dominion era (1908-)
DU420.22-.24	993.031	1908-1918
DU420.26-.28	993.032	1918-1945
DU420.32-.34	933.035	1945-1969
DU420.32-.34	933.037	1970-
DU422.5-424.5	993.004	Ethnography
DU490	995	Melanesia (General)
DU500	996.5	Micronesia (General)
DU510	996	Polynesia (General)
DU520-950	995-996	Island groups
DU550-553	995.8	Bismarck Archipelago
DU560-568	996.6	Caroline Islands
DU600	996.11	Fiji Islands
DU615	996.81	Kiribati (Gilbert Islands)
DU620-629	996.9	Hawaiian Islands
DU622	996.9003	Gazetteers
DU624.5	996.9	Social life
DU624.6-.7	996.9004	Ethnography
DU624.9-.96	996.90099	Biography
DU625-627.83	996.9	History
DU627-.2	996.902	Early to 1898
DU627.5-.7	996.903	1900-1959 (Territory)
DU627.8-.83	996.904	State (1959-)
DU640-648	996.7	Mariana Islands
DU650	996.4	Line Islands
DU700-701	996.31	Marquesas Islands
DU710	996.83	Marshall Islands
DU720	995.97	New Caledonia

LC	Dewey	Descriptor
DU739-747	995	New Guinea
DU740	995.3	Papua New Guinea
DU760	995.95	Vanuatu (New Hebrides)
DU780	996.6	Pelew (Palau) Islands
DU790	996.81	Phoenix Islands
DU800	996.18	Pitcairn Island
DU810-819	996.1(3-4)	Western/American Samoa
DU850	995.93	Solomon Islands
DU870	996.21	Society Islands (Tahiti)
DU880	996.12	Tonga (Friendly Islands)
DU910	996.15	Tokelau (Union Islands)
DU920	996.16	Wallis and Futuna Islands
DX	909.0491497	Gypsies
E	970/980	America
E11	970/980. + 00(5/6)	Serials/Societies
E14	970.003/980.003	Dictionaries/Gazetteers
E16-18.85	970/980	History
E16	970.0072/980.0072	Historiography
E16.5	970.007/980.007	Education
E17	970.0099/980.0099	Biography
E18.7	970/980	Juvenile works
E29	970.004/980.004	Populations
E31-45	970	North America
E31	970.00(5/6)	Serials/Societies
E35	970.003	Dictionaries/Gazetteers
E36	970.00992	Biography (Collective)
E38.5	970	Juvenile works
E40	970	Civilization/Social life
E41	917.04	Travel
E45	970	History
E51-74	970.011	Pre-Columbian America/Indians
E51	970.01100(5/6)	Serials/Societies
E56	970.0110074	Museums/Exhibitions
E65	972.(8/9)/980. + (01)	Latin America (General)
E77-99	970.00497	Indians (North America)
E101-135	970.01(5-9)/980.013	Discovery/Early explorations
E103-110	970.011	Pre-Columbian period
E105	970.013	Norse/Vinland
E111-120	970.015	Columbus
E121-135	970.01(6-9)	Post-Columbian
E123-125	970.016	Spanish/Portuguese
E127-129	970.017	English
E131-133	970.018	French
E141-143	970	Description
E141	972.01	Earliest to 1606
E143	972.02	Latin America (1607-1810)
E151-839	973	United States
E151	973.0(5/6)	Serials/Societies
E154	973.03	Gazetteers
E154.5-.7	973.025	Directories
E159	974-979	Monuments
E161.5-169	917.304	Travel
E171-183.9	973	History
E171	973.05	Serials
E172	973.06	Societies
E174	973.03	Dictionaries/Encyclopedias
E175-.4	973.0072	Historiography
E176-.8	973.099	Biography
E179.5	917.3	Historical geography
E184-185.97	973.04	Population elements
E185-.93	973.0496	Afro-Americans
E185.18-.3	973.(1-9)0496	History, By date
E185.18	973.(1-732)0496	Free Negroes/South before 1863
E185.2	973.(7-82)0496	1863-1877

LC	Dewey	Descriptor
E185.3	973.(83-927)0496	1877-
E185.5-.89	973.714	Emancipation
E185.5	973.7140(5/6)	Serials/Societies
E185.61-.625	305.896073	Black-White relations
E185.63	355/359. + (008996073)	Afro-American soldiers/Seamen
E185.65	364.3496073	Crime
E185.7	200.8996073	Religion
E185.8	331.6396073	Occupations
E185.82	331.71208996073	Afro-American professionals
E185.86	305.896073	Social/Moral conditions
E185.88	613.08996073	Health
E185.9-.93	974-979. + (0496)	By region/State
E185.96-.97	920.009296073	Biography
E186-199	973.2	Colonial history
E186-.99	973.20(5/6)	Serials/Societies
E186.3-.99	369.12	Patriotic societies
E187.5	973.2099	Biographies
E191-199	973.2(1-7)	By date
E191	973.2(1-4)	1607-1689
E195-199	973.2(5-7)	1689-1775
E196	973.25	King William's War (1689-1697)
E197	973.25	Queen Anne's War (1702-1713)
E198	973.26	King George's War (1744-1748)
E199	973.26	French & Indian War (1755-1763)
E201-298	973.3	The Revolution (1775-1783)
E201	973.305	Serials
E202-.99	973.306	Societies
E206-207	973.3099	Biography
E210-216	973.31	Political history
E221	973.313	Declaration of Independence
E230-241	979.33	Military operations
E230.5	974-979.03	By region
E231-239	973.33(1-9)	Campaigns, By year
E241	973.33(1-9)	Individual battles
E249	973.317	Treaty of Paris (1783)
E251-268	973.34	Armies/Troops
E255-265	973.34(4-5)	American army
E263	973.34(4-5)	By state
E265	973.346	Auxiliaries
E267-268	973.341	British army
E271	973.35	Naval history
E275	973.38	Personal accounts
E276	973.30082	Women & the war
E278	973.38(1-6)	Loyalists/Traitors
E279-280	973.38(5-6)	Secret service/Spies
E281	973.37(1-2)	Prisoners/Prisons
E283	973.375	Medical services
E285-286	973.36	Celebrations/Exhibits
E295-298	973.3022	Illustrative material
E301-453	973.(318-68)	Revolution-Civil War (1775-1861)
E302.1	973.(521/621)	Political history
E302.5-.6	973.(4-6)099	Biographies
E303-440.5	973.(318-68)	By date
E303-309	973.318	1775-1789 (The Confederation)
E310-337	973.4	1789-1809 (Constitutional era)
E311-320	973.4(1-3)	Washington (1789-1797)

LC	Dewey	Descriptor
E321-330	973.4(4-8)	John Adams (1797-1801)
E323	973.44	French dispute (1796-1800)
E331-337	973.46	Jefferson (1801-1809)
E333	973.46	Louisiana purchase (1803)
E335	973.47	War with Tripoli (1801-1805)
E337.5-400	973.(46-89)	19th century
E337.8-400	973.(46-58)	Early 19th century (1801-1845)
E339-340	973.(46-89)099	Biography
E341-370	973.51	Madison (1809-1817)
E351-364.9	973.52	War of 1812
E365	973.53	War with Algeria (1815)
E371-375	973.54	Monroe (1817-1825)
E373	973.54	Missouri Compromise (1820)
E374	973.54	Annexation of Florida (1819)
E376-380	973.55	John Quincy Adams (1825-1829)
E381-385	973.56	Jackson (1829-1837)
E384.3	973.561	Nullification
E386-390	973.57	Van Buren (1837-1841)
E391-392	973.58	William H. Harrison (1841)
E396-400	973.58	Tyler (1841-1845)
E401-415.2	973.62	War with Mexico (1845-1848)
E408	973.62	Mexican Cession of 1848
E415.6-440.5	973.6	1845-1861
E415.8-.9	973.6099	Biography
E416-420	973.61	Polk (1845-1849)
E421-423	973.63	Taylor (1849-1850)
E423	973.6(3-4)	Slavery question (1849-1853)
E426-430	973.64	Fillmore (1850-1853)
E431-435	973.66	Pierce (1853-1857)
E433	973.66	Slavery question (1853-1857)
E436-440.5	973.68	Buchanan (1857-1861)
E438	973.68	Slavery question (1857-1861)
E456-655	973.7	Civil War (1861-1865)
E456-459	973.7	Lincoln (1861-1865)
E461-655	973.7	Civil War (1861-1865)
E482-489	973.713	Confederate States
E660-738	973.8	1865-1900
E661.7	973.892	Diplomacy
E663-664	973.8099	Biography
E666-670	973.81	Johnson (1865-1869)
E668	973.8(1-2)	Reconstruction (1865-1877)
E669	973.81	Alaska purchase (1867)
E671-680	973.82	Grant (1869-1877)
E681-685	973.83	Hayes (1877-1881)
E686-687.9	973.84	Garfield (1881)
E691-695	973.84	Arthur (1881-1885)
E696-700	973.85	Cleveland (1885-1889)
E701-705	973.86	Benjamin Harrison (1889-1893)
E706-710	973.87	Cleveland (1893-1897)
E711-751	973.88	McKinley (1897-1901)
E714-735	973.89	Spanish-American War (1898)
E740-839	973.9	20th century
E740	973.90(5/6)	Serials/Societies
E743-.5	973.9	Political history
E745	940.(4/54)/959.70434	Military history
E746	940.(45/545)/959.704345	Naval history

LC	Dewey	Descriptor
E747-748	973.9099	Biography
E749	973.88	McKinley (1901)
E756-760	973.911	T. Roosevelt (1901-1909)
E761-765	973.912	Taft (1909-1913)
E766-783	973.913	Wilson (1913-1921)
E768	973.913	Virgin Islands purchase (1917)
E780	973.913	World War I (Internal)
E784	973.91(3-6)	1919-1933
E785-786	973.914	Harding (1921-1923)
E791-796	973.915	Coolidge (1923-1929)
E801-805	973.916	Hoover (1929-1933)
E806-812	973.917	F.D. Roosevelt (1933-1945)
E813-816	973.918	Truman (1945-1953)
E835-839	973.921	Eisenhower (1953-1961)
F	971-989	The Americas
F1-15	974	New England
F16-30	974.1	Maine
F31-45	974.2	New Hampshire
F46-60	974.3	Vermont
F61-75	974.4	Massachusetts
F76-90	974.5	Rhode Island
F91-105	974.6	Connecticut
F106	974	Middle Atlantic States
F116-130	974.7	New York
F131-145	974.9	New Jersey
F146-160	974.8	Pennsylvania
F161-175	975.1	Delaware
F176-190	975.2	Maryland
F191-205	975.3	District of Columbia
F206-220	975	South Atlantic States
F221-235	975.5	Virginia
F236-250	975.4	West Virginia
F251-265	975.6	North Carolina
F266-280	975.7	South Carolina
F281-295	975.8	Georgia
F296-301	975.9-976.4	Gulf states
F306-320	975.9	Florida
F321-335	976.1	Alabama
F336-350	976.2	Mississippi
F351-355	977	Mississippi River and valley
F366-380	976.3	Louisiana
F381-395	976.4	Texas
F396	977	Lower Mississippi valley
F406-420	976.7	Arkansas
F431-445	976.8	Tennessee
F446-460	976.9	Kentucky
F461-475	977.8	Missouri
F476-485	977	Old Northwest/N.W. Territory
F486-500	977.1	Ohio
F516-520	977	Ohio River and valley
F521-535	977.2	Indiana
F536-550	977.3	Illinois
F561-575	977	Michigan
F576-590	977.5	Wisconsin
F591-596	977/978	West/Trans-Mississippi region
F597	977	Upper Mississippi valley
F598	978	Missouri River valley
F601-615	977.6	Minnesota
F616-630	977.7	Iowa
F631-645	978.4	North Dakota
F646-660	978.3	South Dakota
F661-675	978.2	Nebraska
F676-690	978.1	Kansas

LC	Dewey	Descriptor
F691-705	976.6	Oklahoma
F721-722	978.(752)	Rocky Mountains/ Yellowstone Pk.
F726-740	978.6	Montana
F741-755	979.6	Idaho
F756-770	978.7	Wyoming
F771-785	978.8	Colorado
F786-788	979.(13)	New Southwest/Colorado River
F791-805	978.9	New Mexico
F806-820	979.1	Arizona
F821-835	979.2	Utah
F836-850	979.3	Nevada
F851	979	Pacific states
F852-853	979.7	Columbia River and valley
F856-870	979.4	California
F871-885	979.5	Oregon
F886-900	979.7	Washington
F904-915	979.8	Alaska
F975	972.8	Central America
F1001-1035	971	Canada
F1035.8	971.5	Maritime provinces
F1036-1040	971.6	Nova Scotia
F1041-1045	971.51	New Brunswick
F1046-1049.7	971.7	Prince Edward Island
F1050	971.4	St. Lawrence Gulf and valley
F1051-1055	971.4	Quebec
F1056-1059.7	971.3	Ontario
F1060-.92	971.92	Canadian northwest
F1061-1065	971.27	Manitoba
F1067	971.273	Assiniboine Region
F1070-1074.7	971.24	Saskatchewan
F1075-1080	971.23	Alberta
F1086-1089.7	971.1	British Columbia
F1090	971.1	Rocky Mountains of Canada
F1091-1095.5	971.91	Yukon
F1096-1100.5	971.93	Mackenzie
F1101-1105.5	971.95	Franklin
F1106-1110.5	971.94	Keewatin
F1121-1139	971.8	Newfoundland
F1136-1139	971.82	Labrador
F1140	971.82	Labrador peninsula
F1170	971.88	Saint Pierre/Miquelon
F1201-1392	972.0(1-8)	Mexico
F1401-1419	980	Latin/Spanish America (General)
F1421-1577	972.8	Central America
F1441-1457	972.83	British Honduras
F1461-1477	972.81	Guatemala
F1481-1497	972.84	El Salvador
F1501-1517	972.83	Honduras
F1521-1537	972.85	Nicaragua
F1541-1557	972.86	Costa Rica
F1561-1577	972.87	Panama
F1601-2175	972.9	West Indies
F1630-1640	972.99	Bermuda
F1650-1660	972.96	Bahamas
F1741-1991	972.9	Greater Antilles
F1751-1849	972.91	Cuba
F1861-1896	972.92	Jamaica
F1900-1940	972.94	Haiti
F1912-1930	972.94	Haiti (Republic)
F1931-1940	972.93	Dominican Republic
F1951-1983	972.95	Puerto Rico
F2001-2151	972.9	Lesser Antilles

LC	Dewey	Descriptor
F2006	972.97	Leeward Islands
F2011	972.984	Windward Islands
F2016	987	Venezuela coast islands
F2136	972.972	Virgin Islands
F2141	972.986	Netherlands West Indies
F2151	972.976	French West Indies
F2161-2175	972.9	Caribbean Sea/Spanish Main
F2201-2239	980	South America
F2251-2299	986.1	Colombia
F2301-2349	987	Venezuela
F2351	988	Guiana
F2361-2391	988.1	British Guiana
F2401-2431	988.3	Suriname
F2441-2471	988.2	French Guiana
F2501-2659	981	Brazil
F2661-2699	989.2	Paraguay
F2701-2799	989.5	Uruguay
F2801-3021	982	Argentina
F3031	997.1	Falkland Islands
F3051-3285	983	Chile
F3301-3559	984	Bolivia
F3401-3619	985	Peru
F3701-3799	986.6	Ecuador
G	910/912	Geography/Maps
G1	910.5/912.05	Serials
G2-55	910.6/912.06	Societies
G56	910.6/912.06	Congresses
G63	910.3/912.03	Dictionaries/Encyclopedias
G64	910.25/912.025	Directories
G65	910.23/912.023	As a profession
G67-69	910.92/912.092	Biography
G70-.4	910.01/912.01	Philosophy
G72-76.5	910.7/912.07 + (02)	Education/Research
G77	910.71/912.071	Schools
G77.8-78	910.74/912.074	Museums/Exhibitions
G80-99	910.9/912.09	History
G100.5-108.5	910.014	Toponymy
G141	911	Historical geography
G149-180	910.4	Travel and voyages (General)
G149-.5	910.40(5/6)	Serials/Societies/Congresses
G149.9-153	910.202	Instructions/Guidebooks
G155-180	338.4791	Tourist trade
G200-336	910.9	Discoveries/Explorations
G220-336	910.9(3-9)	By nationality
G220-226	910.973	American
G230-236	910.9492	Dutch
G240-246	910.942	English
G250-256	910.944	French
G260-266	910.943	German
G270-276	910.945	Italian
G280-286	910.9469	Portuguese
G287-289	910.946	Spanish
G290-296	910.947	Russian
G300-306	910.948	Scandinavian
G320-326	910.951	Chinese
G330-336	910.952	Japanese
G369-503	910.4	Special voyages/Travels
G369-370	940-990	Medieval voyages/Travels
G400-401	940-990	Travels, 1400-1520
G419-503	940-990	1521-
G419-420	910.45	Circumnavigations
G445	910.41	Flights around the world
G460-503	910.4	To several parts
G521-539	910.45	Shipwreck/Buried treasure
G540-550	910.45	Seafaring life/Ocean travel
G570	910.4083	Juvenile voyages and travels
G575-890	919.8/998	Arctic/Antarctic regions
G575-599	910.998/919.8/998	Polar regions
G600-839	910.998	Arctic explorations
G725-765	910.9982/919.82/998.2	Greenland
G778-810	910.9481/914.81/948.1	Norwegian regions
G820-839	910.957/915.7/957	Siberia
G845-890	910.9989/919.89/998.9	Antarctica
G905-910	911.3	Tropics (General)
G912-922	911.81(3-4)	Northern/Southern Hemispheres
G1000.3-.5	912.99	Planets (Atlases)
G1001-1046	912	World atlases
G1050-1052	912.198(3-4)	Northern/Southern Hemispheres
G1053	912.193	Tropics (Atlases)
G1054-1055	912.191	Polar regions (Atlases)
G1059-1061	912.1962	Maritime atlases (General)
G1100-3102	912.(3-9)	Atlases, By specific place
G1100-1779	912.19812	America/Western Hemisphere
G1105-1694	912.7	North America
G1110-1114	912.982	Greenland
G1115-1193	912.71	Canada
G1200-1534.24	912.73	United States
G1535-1537	912.729	Caribbean area
G1540-1542	912.(72-8)	Latin America (General)
G1545-1549	912.72	Mexico
G1550-1594	912.728	Central America
G1600-1694	912.729	West Indies
G1700-1779	912.8	South America
G1780-2799	912.19811	Eastern Hemisphere/Eurasia
G1791-2082	912.4	Europe
G1791-1799	912.4090(1-4)	Europe, By date
G1807-1834	912.41	Great Britain/Ireland
G1837-1844	912.44	France
G1850-1874	912.49(2-3)	Low Countries
G1895-1899	912.494	Switzerland
G1907-1924	912.43	Germany
G1935-1939	912.436	Austria
G1940-1944	912.439	Hungary
G1945-1949	912.437	Czechoslovakia
G1950-1954	912.438	Poland
G1965-1969	912.46	Spain
G1975-1979	912.469	Portugal
G1980-1981	911.37	Roman Empire
G1983-1989	912.45	Italy
G2000-2004	912.495	Greece
G2005-2009	912.4965	Albania
G2010-2032	912.497	Yugoslavia
G2035-2039	912.498	Romania
G2040-2044	912.4977	Bulgaria
G2055-2059	912.489	Denmark
G2060-2064	912.4912	Iceland
G2065-2069	912.481	Norway
G2070-2074	912.485	Sweden
G2075-2079	912.4897	Finland
G2110-2193	912.47	European Russia
G2200-2444	912.5	Asia
G2210-2214	912.561	Turkey
G2215-2219	912.5645	Cyprus
G2220-2224	912.5691	Syria
G2225-2229	912.5692	Lebanon
G2235-2239	912.5694	Israel/Palestine
G2240-2244	912.5695	Jordan
G2245-2249	912.53	Arabian peninsula

LC	Dewey	Descriptor
G2250-2254	912.567	Iraq
G2255-2259	912.55	Iran
G2265-2269	912.581	Afghanistan
G2270-2274	912.5491	Pakistan
G2275-2279	912.5492	Bangladesh
G2280-2284	912.54	India
G2285-2289	912.591	Burma
G2290-2294	912.5493	Sri Lanka
G2295-2299	912.5496	Nepal
G2305-2326	912.51	China
G2330-2334	912.519	Korea
G2340-2344	912.51249	Taiwan
G2353-2357	912.52	Japan
G2370-2374	912.597	Vietnam
G2374	915.596	Cambodia
G2374.5-.54	912.594	Laos
G2375-2379	912.593	Thailand
G2445-2739	912.6	Africa
G2455-2499	912.61	North Africa
G2560-2584	912.68	Southern Africa
G2590-2639	912.67	Central Africa
G2640-2739	912.66	West Africa
G2740-2799	912.9	Australasia
G2750-2793	912.94	Australia
G2795-2799	912.93	New Zealand
G2800-3064	912.19162	Oceans (General)
G2805-2839	912.1963	Atlantic Ocean/Islands
G2850-2857	912.1965	Indian Ocean islands
G2860-3012	912.1964	Pacific Ocean
G2870-2894	912.95	Melanesia
G2900-2934	912.965	Micronesia
G2970-2984	912.96	Polynesia
G3012	912.19642	East Pacific islands
G3050-3064	912.19632	Arctic Ocean
G3100-3102	912.1967	Antarctica
G3190-9980	912	Maps
G3190-3192	912.(99/19)	Celestial maps
G3195-3199	912.991	Moon
G3210-3222	912.1981(3-4)	Northern/Southern Hemispheres
G3240-3241	912.193	Tropics
G3250-3251	912.192	Temperate zones
G3260-3272	912.998	Polar regions
G3290-5668	912.19812	Western Hemisphere
G3300-5184	912.7	North America
G3380-3384	912.982	Greenland
G3400-3612	912.71	Canada
G3410-3412	912.715	Maritime provinces
G3450-3454	912.714	Quebec
G3460-3464	912.713	Ontario
G3470-3504	912.712	Prairie provinces
G3510-3514	912.711	British Columbia
G3520-3524	912.7191	Yukon
G3530-3532	912.7192	N.W. Territories
G3600-3612	912.718	New Foundland/Labrador
G3690-4383	912.73	United States
G3701	911.73	History
G3709.3-.32	912.7(4-5)	Atlantic states
G3715-3717	912.74	Northeast Atlantic states
G3720-3784	912.74	New England
G3790-3854	912.74	Mid-Atlantic states
G3870-3933	912.75	Southeast Atlantic states
G3935-3937	912.76	South Central states
G3990-4033	912.76	West South Central states
G4040-4042	912.77	Central states
G4050-4052	912.78	The West
G4070-4123	912.77	Old Northwest

LC	Dewey	Descriptor
G4125-4203	912.79	Northwestern states
G4220-4222	912.78	Rocky Mountain states
G4240-4293	912.795	Pacific Northwest
G4295-4364	912.79	Southwestern
G4370-4373	912.798	Alaska
G4380-4383	912.969	Hawaii/Sandwich Islands
G4390-4392	912.729	Caribbean area
G4410-4763	912.72	Mexico
G4800-4884	912.728	Central America
G4900-5184	912.729	West Indies
G5200-5668	912.8	South America
G5240-5274	912.88	Guianas
G5280-5284	912.87	Venezuela
G5290-5294	912.861	Colombia
G5300-5302	912.866	Ecuador
G5310-5314	912.85	Peru
G5330-5334	912.83	Chili
G5350-5352	912.82	Argentina
G5670-9084	912.19811	Eastern Hemisphere/ Eurasia/Etc.
G5700-6966	912.4	Europe
G5740-5814	912.41	Great Britain
G5830-5973	912.44	France
G5990-6023	912.49(2-3)	Low Countries
G6035-6043	912.494	Alps/Switzerland
G6070-6428	912.43	Germany
G6490-6494	912.436	Austria
G6500-6503	912.439	Hungary
G6510-6513	912.437	Czechoslovakia
G6520-6523	912.438	Poland
G6560-6563	912.46	Spain
G6670-6672	912.4689	Gibraltar
G6680-6694	912.469	Portugal
G6700-6701	911.37	Roman Empire
G6705-6773	912.45	Italy
G6810-6813	912.495	Greece
G6830-6834	912.4965	Albania
G6840-6877	912.497	Yugoslavia
G6880-6883	912.498	Romania
G6890-6894	912.4977	Bulgaria
G6920-6923	912.489	Denmark
G6930-6934	912.4912	Iceland
G6940-6944	912.481	Norway
G6950-6954	912.485	Sweden
G6960-6963	912.4897	Finland
G7000-7342	912.47	European Russia
G7400-8198.54	912.5	Asia
G7420-7623	912.56	Near East
G7500-7504	912.5694	Israel/Palestine
G7520-7604	912.53	Arabian peninsula
G7610-7614	912.567	Iraq
G7620-7624	912.55	Iran
G7630-7634	912.581	Afghanistan
G7640-7644	912.5491	Pakistan
G7645-7649	912.5492	Bangladesh
G7650-7654	912.54	India
G7720-7724	912.591	Burma
G7750-7754	912.5493	Sri Lanka
G7760-7764	912.5496	Nepal
G7810-7892	912.51	China
G7895-7899	912.5173	Mongolia
G7900-7907	912.519	Korea
G7910-7914	912.51249	Taiwan
G7940-7944	912.5125	Hong Kong
G7950-7963	912.52	Japan
G8010-8014	912.596	Cambodia
G8015-8017	912.594	Laos

LC	Dewey	Descriptor
G8020-8022	912.597	Vietnam
G8025-8029	912.593	Thailand
G8030-8034	912.595	Malaysia
G8040-8044	912.5957	Singapore
G8060-8064	912.599	Philippines
G8070-8132	912.598	Indonesia
G8140-8192	912.95	New Guinea
G8200-8904	912.6	Africa
G8230-8234	912.64	Morocco
G8240-8244	912.65	Algeria
G8250-8254	912.611	Tunisia
G8260-8264	912.612	Libya
G8300-8304	912.62	Egypt
G8330-8334	912.63	Ethiopia
G8350-8364	912.6773	Somalia
G8410-8414	912.6762	Kenya
G8420-8424	912.6761	Uganda
G8425-8439	912.6757(1/2)	Rwanda/Burundi
G8440-8444	912.678	Tanzania
G8450-8454	912.679	Mozambique
G8460-8464	912.691	Madagascar
G8500-8542	912.68	South Africa
G8550-8562	912.689	Zimbabwe
G8640-8644	912.673	Angola
G8650-8654	912.6751	Zaire
G8660-8664	912.6718	Equatorial Guinea
G8720-8724	912.6743	Chad
G8730-8734	912.6711	Cameroon
G8760-8764	912.6681	Togo
G8770-8774	912.6626	Niger
G8780-8784	912.6668	Ivory Coast
G8810-8814	912.663	Senegal
G8840-8844	912.669	Nigeria
G8850-8854	912.667	Ghana
G8880-8884	912.6662	Liberia
G8950-9084	912.9	Australasia
G8960-9063	912.94	Australia
G9080-9084	912.93	New Zealand
G9095-9794	912.1962	Oceans (General)
G9100-9177	912.1963	Atlantic Ocean
G9180-9217	912.1965	Indian Ocean area
G9230-9762	912.1964	Pacific Ocean
G9800-9804	912.989	Antarctica
G9900-9980	912	Unlocalized
GA	526	Cartography
GA1	526.0(5/6)	Serials/Societies
GA2.7-.9	526.07	Education
GA3	526.09	History
GA101	526.0(5/6)	Serials/Societies
GA101.2	526.06	Congresses
GA102	526.03	Dictionaries/Encyclopedias
GA102.2	526.014	Terminology
GA102.25	526.025	Directories
GA102.3	526.01	Philosophy
GA102.5-.7	526.07	Education
GA109	526.982	Aerial cartography
GA110-115	526.8	Projection
GA125-155	526.0221	Map drawing/Modeling/Etc.
GA190	526.074	Exhibitions/Museums
GA192-197.3	026.526	Map libraries/Collections
GA197.5	526.023	As a profession
GA201-246	912.09	History
GA300-325	912	World maps/Atlases
GA341-1776	912.(3-9)	Maps, by region or country
GA368-381	912.1963	Atlantic Ocean area
GA383-390	912.1964	Pacific Ocean area
GA392-397	912.1965	Indian Ocean
GA405-460	912.73	United States
GA409-460	912.7(4-9)	By state and city
GA471-475	912.71	Canada
GA481-485	912.72	Mexico
GA491-555	912.728	Central America
GA511-515	912.7286	Costa Rica
GA521-525	912.7281	Guatemala
GA531-535	912.7283	Honduras
GA541-545	912.7285	Nicaragua
GA546-550	912.7287	Panama
GA551-555	912.7284	El Salvador
GA561-621	912.729	West Indies
GA571-575	912.7296	Bahamas
GA581-585	912.7291	Cuba
GA591-595	912.7294	Haiti
GA601-605	912.7292	Jamaica
GA611-615	912.7295	Puerto Rico
GA641-775	912.8	South America
GA651-655	912.82	Argentina
GA661-665	912.84	Bolivia
GA671-675	912.81	Brazil
GA681-685	912.83	Chile
GA691-695	912.861	Colombia
GA701-705	912.866	Ecuador
GA711-730	912.88	Guianas
GA741-745	912.892	Paraguay
GA751-755	912.85	Peru
GA761-765	912.895	Uruguay
GA771-775	912.87	Venezuela
GA781-1077	912.4	Europe
GA791-825	912.41	Great Britain
GA831-834	912.436	Austria
GA861-865	912.44	France
GA871-880	912.43	Germany
GA881-885	912.495	Greece
GA891-895	912.45	Italy
GA911-915	912.493	Belgium
GA921-925	912.492	Netherlands
GA931-935	912.47	European Russia
GA951-995	912.48	Scandinavia
GA961-965	912.489	Denmark
GA971-975	912.4912	Iceland
GA981-985	912.481	Norway
GA991-995	912.485	Sweden
GA1005	912.46	Spain
GA1011-1015	912.469	Portugal
GA1021-1025	912.494	Switzerland
GA1031-1075	912.496	Balkan states
GA1081-1340	912.5	Asia
GA1101-1105	912.53	Arabia
GA1121-1125	912.51	China
GA1131-1135	912.54	India
GA1136-1140	912.5491	Pakistan
GA1141-1195	912.59(4-7)	Indochina
GA1201-1205	912.595	Malaysia
GA1221-1225	912.598	Indonesia
GA1231-1235	912.599	Philippines
GA1241-1245	912.52	Japan
GA1251-1255	912.519	Korea
GA1261-1265	912.55	Iran
GA1271-1295	912.57	Asian Russia
GA1301-1305	912.561	Turkey
GA1321-1325	912.5694	Israel/Palestine
GA1331-1335	912.5691	Syria
GA1341-1673	912.6	Africa
GA1348-1414	912.61	North Africa
GA1428-1499	912.676	East Africa

LC	Dewey	Descriptor	LC	Dewey	Descriptor
GA1500-1543	912.67	Central Africa	GF3	304.206	Congresses
GA1550-1603	912.66	West Africa	GF4	304.203	Dictionaries/Encyclopedias
GA1604-1673	912.68	Southern Africa	GF4.5	304.2014	Terminology
GA1681-1685	912.94	Australia	GF5	304.2025	Directories
GA1765-1769	912.93	New Zealand	GF13	304.209	History
GA1771-1776	912.9(5-6)	Oceania	GF15-16	304.2092	Biography
GB	551	Physical geography	GF51-71	304.2(3-5)	Environmental influence
GB400-649	551.41	Geomorphology/Land formations	GF75	304.28	Man in environment
GB447	551.41	Climatic geomorphology	GF101-127	307	Settlements
GB448	551.436	Slopes	GF125	307.76/912.19732	Cities/Urban geography
GB450-460	551.45(7/8)	Coasts	GF127	307.72/912.191734	Rural settlements/ Geography
GB461-468	551.424	Reefs	GF500-895	304.209(4-9)	Human ecology, By place
GB471-478	551.42	Islands	GF500-532	304.209(7/8)	America
GB500-555	551.432	Mountains	GF503-504	304.20973	United States
GB561-649	554.4(15-58)	Other natural landforms	GF511-512	304.20971	Canada
GB651-2998	551.48	Hydrology/Water	GF516-517	304.20972	Mexico
GB980-992	551.488	Watersheds/Runoff/ Drainage	GF521-522	304.209728	Central America
GB1001-1199.8	551.49	Groundwater/Hydrogeology	GF526-527	304.209729	West Indies
GB1201-1598	551.483	River/Stream measurements	GF531-532	304.2098	South America
GB1601-1798.9	551.48(2)	Limnology/Lakes	GF540-645	304.2094	Europe
GB2401-2598	551.31	Ice/Glaciers/Ice sheets	GF541	304.2091822	Mediterranean region
GB2601-2798	551.5784	Snow/Snow surveys	GF545	304.2094947	Alps
GB2801-2998	551.57	Hydrometeorology	GF547	304.209474	Baltic region
GB5000-5030	904.5	Natural disasters	GF551-562	304.20941	Great Britain
GC	551.46	Oceanography	GF552	304.20942	England
GC1	551.4600(5/6)	Serials/Societies	GF555-556	304.209411	Scotland
GC2	551.46006	Congresses	GF561.562	304.209416	Northern Ireland
GC9	551.46003	Dictionaries/Encyclopedias	GF563	304.209415	Ireland
GC9.2	551.460014	Terminology	GF565-567	304.209436	Austria
GC10.2-.4	551.46001	Philosophy	GF568	304.209437	Czechoslovakia
GC20	551.4600202	Outlines/Etc.	GF569	304.209439	Hungary
GC29-.2	551.46009	History	GF571-572	304.20944	France
GC30	551.460092	Biography	GF576-579	304.20943	Germany
GC30.5	551.460023	As a profession	GF581-582	304.209495	Greece
GC31-.7	551.46007	Education	GF586-587	304.20945	Italy
GC35-.2	551.460074	Museums/Exhibitions	GF593-594	304.209492	Netherlands
GC41	551.460028	Instruments/Apparatus	GF596-597	304.209493	Belgium
GC57-59	551.460072	Research	GF601-602	304.20947	European Russia
GC63	551.4607	Oceanographic expeditions	GF604	304.2094897	Finland
GC65-78	551.4607	Underwater exploration	GF611	304.20948	Scandinavia
GC83-87.6	551.46084	Submarine topography	GF612-613	304.209481	Norway
GC96-97.8	551.4609	Estuarine oceanography	GF614-615	304.209485	Sweden
GC100-103	551.4601	Seawater	GF616-617	304.209489	Denmark
GC109-149	551.4601	Chemical oceanography	GF621-622	304.20946	Spain
GC150-181	551.4601	Physical oceanography	GF623-624	304.209469	Portugal
GC190-.5	551.47	Ocean-atmosphere interaction	GF631-632	304.209494	Switzerland
GC200-376	551.47	Dynamics of the ocean	GF641-642	304.209496	Balkan states
GC205-226	551.4702	Waves	GF651-696	304.2095	Asia
GC228.5-.6	551.47	Ocean circulation	GF656-657	304.20951	China
GC229-296.8	551.4701	Currents	GF659	304.209519	Korea
GC297-299	551.47	Water masses and ocean mixing	GF661-662	304.20954	India
GC300-376	551.4708	Tides	GF664	304.2095491	Pakistan
GC377-399	551.46083	Marine sediments	GF666-667	304.20952	Japan
GC401-881	551.46(1-9)	By place	GF669	304.209595	Malaysia
GC401-455	551.468	Arctic Ocean	GF670	304.20956	Near East (General)
GC461-462	551.469	Antarctic Ocean	GF671-672	304.20955	Iran
GC481-711	551.461	Atlantic Ocean	GF674	304.209581	Afghanistan
GC721-761	551.467	Indian Ocean	GF675	304.209567	Iraq
GC771-871	551.46(5-6)	Pacific Ocean	GF676-677	304.20957	Asian Russia
GC1000-1023	551.46	Marine resources	GF678-679	304.209561	Turkey
GC1080-1581	363.7394	Marine pollution	GF681-682	304.209538	Saudi Arabia
GF	304.2	Human ecology	GF685-686	304.2095694	Israel/Palestine
GF1	304.20(5/6)	Serials/Societies	GF687-688	304.2095691	Syria
			GF698	304.209174927	Arab countries
			GF701-758	304.2096	Africa
			GF702-706	304.20961	North Africa

LC	Dewey	Descriptor	LC	Dewey	Descriptor
GF711-712	304.20962	Egypt	GR265-345	398.095	Asia
GF720-729	304.209676	East Africa	GR350-360	398.096	Africa
GF730	304.20967	Central Africa	GR365-385	398.099(3-6)	Australia/New Zealand/ Oceania
GF740-758	304.20966	West/South Africa			
GF801-802	304.20994	Australia	GR430-487	398.35(3-4)	Relating to private life
GF805-806	304.20993	New Zealand	GR500-615	398.4	Supernatural Beings/Demonology
GF851-852	304.2099(5-6)	Oceania			
GF891	304.20998	Arctic regions	GR620-635	398.362	Cosmic phenomena
GF895	304.20913	Tropics	GR650-690	398.3	Geographical subjects
GN	301/573	Anthropology	GR700-860	398.46	Animals/Plants/Minerals
GN1	301.05/573.05	Serials	GR865-874	398.355	Transportation/Travel/ Commerce
GN2-3	301.06/573.06	Societies/Congresses			
GN11	301.03/573.03	Dictionaries/Encyclopedias	GR880	398.353/615.882	Folk medicine
GN12	301.014/573.014	Terminology	GR890-910	398.355	Occupations
GN17	301.09/573.09	History	GR931-940	001.51/398.042	Signs and symbols
GN20-21	301.092/573.092	Biography	GT	390-395	Manners and customs
GN33-34.3	301.01/573.01	Philosophy	GT1	390.00(5/6)	Serials/Societies
GN35-41	301.074/573.074	Museums/Exhibitions	GT3	390.006	Congresses
GN42-46	301.07/573.07	Education	GT31	390.003	Dictionaries/Encyclopedias
GN49-296	573	Physical anthropology/ Somatology	GT41	390.009	History of manners and customs
GN62.8-263	573.22	Human variation	GT51-53	390.0092	Biography
GN66-69	573.6	Body dimensions	GT61	390.001	Philosophy
GN70-161	573.671	Skeleton	GT170-474	392.36	Houses/Dwellings
GN171	573.673	Muscular system	GT175-195	392.360090(1-4)	By date
GN181-190	573.68	Nervous system/Brain	GT175	392.3600901	Ancient
GN191-199	573.677	Skin	GT180	392.3600902	Medieval
GN209	573.314	Teeth	GT185	392.360090(23-31)	Renaissance
GN211	573.6(3-7)	Sex organs	GT190	392.360090(1-3)	16th-18th centuries
GN221-263	573	Physiological anthropology	GT195	392.360090(34-4)	1801-
GN269-279	572	Race (General)	GT201-384	392.36009(4-9)	Dwellings, By place
GN280.7	304.5/573.2	Man as an animal	GT205-227	392.3600973	United States
GN281-289	573.2	Human evolution	GT228-229	392.3600971	Canada
GN282-286.7	573.3	Fossil man	GT231-232	392.3600972	Mexico
GN296	306.461	Medical anthropology	GT235-236	392.360097282	Belize
GN301-673	305.8/306	Ethnology/Social anthropology	GT237-238	392.360097286	Costa Rica
GN357-367	306	Culture/Cultural processes	GT239-240	392.360097281	Guatemala
GN378-395	305.8	Collected ethnographies	GT241-242	392.360097283	Honduras
GN406-442	306.46	Technology/Material culture	GT243-244	392.360097285	Nicaragua
			GT245-.5	392.360097287	Panama
GN448-450.7	306.3	Economic anthropology	GT246-.5	392.360097284	El Salvador
GN451-477.7	306.42	Intellectual life	GT249-250	392.360097296	Bahamas
GN478-491.7	305	Social organization	GT251-252	392.360097291	Cuba
GN492-495	306.2	Political anthropology	GT253-254	392.360097294	Haiti
GN495.4-498	305	Societal groups	GT255-256	392.360097292	Jamaica
GN502-517	155.8/305.8	Psychological anthropology	GT257-.5	392.360097295	Puerto Rico
GN537-673	305.8/572	Ethnic groups/Races	GT261-262	392.3600982	Argentina
GN550-673	305.8009/572.09	Ethnic groups/Races, By place	GT263-264	392.3600984	Bolivia
			GT265-266	392.3600981	Brazil
GN550-560	305.80097/572.097	North America	GT267-268	392.3600983	Chile
GN562-564	305.80/572. + 09(728/8)	Central/South America	GT269-270	392.36009861	Colombia
GN575-585	305.80094/572.094	Europe	GT271-272	392.36009866	Ecuador
GN625-635	305.80095/572.095	Asia	GT273-274	392.3600988	Guianas
GN643-661	305.80096/572.096	Africa	GT275-276	392.36009892	Paraguay
GN662-671	305.80/572. + 099(3-6)	Australia/New Zealand/ Oceania	GT277-278	392.3600985	Peru
			GT279-280	392.36009895	Uruguay
GN673	305.800998/572.998	Arctic	GT281-282	392.3600987	Venezuela
GN700-875	573.3	Prehistoric archaeology	GT285-294	392.3600941	Great Britain
GR	398	Folklore	GT294.5-.6	392.3600941(6-7)	Ireland
GR72-79	398.2	Folk literature (General)	GT295-296	392.36009436	Austria
GR81	398.41	Folk beliefs/ Superstitions/Etc.	GT296.5-.6	392.36009439	Hungary
			GT297-298	392.3600944	France
GR100-390	398.09(3-9)	By place	GT298.9-299	392.3600943	Germany
GR101-113	398.097	North America	GT301-302	392.36009495	Greece
GR114-133	398.09(72/8)	Spanish America	GT303-304	392.3600945	Italy
GR135-263	398.094	Europe	GT307-308	392.36009492	Netherlands
			GT311-312	392.3600947	Russia

LC	Dewey	Descriptor	LC	Dewey	Descriptor
GT315-316	392.36009489	Denmark	GV201-555	796.07/372.86	Physical education/Training
GT317-318	392.360094912	Iceland	GV346-350	796.(07/32363/33263)	School/College athletics
GT319-320	392.36009481	Norway	GV401-433	796.068	Sports facilities
GT321-322	392.36009485	Sweden	GV435-436.5	613.7	Physical tests
GT323-324	392.3600946	Spain	GV450	613.19(3-4)	Sunbathing/Nudism
GT325-326	392.36009469	Portugal	GV460-555	796.44	Gymnastics
GT327-328	392.36009494	Switzerland	GV561-1198.995	796	Sports
GT331-341	392.36009496	Balkan states	GV711	796.077	Coaching
GT343-372	392.360095	Asia	GV735	790.1	Umpires
GT344-.2	392.360095691	Syria	GV743-749	796.028	Sporting goods/Supplies
GT345-346	392.36009561	Turkey	GV750-770	797.5	Air sports
GT346.5-.6	392.36009567	Iraq	GV770.3-840	797.(1-3)	Water sports
GT347-348	392.3600955	Iran	GV840.7-857	796.9	Winter sports
GT349-350	392.3600958	Central Asia	GV861-1017	796.3	Ball games
GT351-352	392.3600954	India	GV1020-1034	796.7	Automobile travel
GT352.5-.6	392.360095493	Sri Lanka	GV1040-1060.2	796.6	Bicycling/Motorcycling
GT355-356	392.36009593	Thailand	GV1060.5-1098	796.42	Track and field
GT357-358	392.36009595	Malaysia	GV1101-1150.6	796.8	Fighting sports
GT359-360	392.36009598	Indonesia	GV1151-1190	799.3	Shooting/Archery
GT361-362	392.36009599	Philippine Islands	GV1195-1198.995	796.812	Wrestling
GT365-366	392.3600951	China	GV1199-1570	793	Games and amusements
GT367-368	392.3600952	Japan	GV1201.5	790.13	Hobbies (General)
GT369-370	392.36009519	Korea	GV1203-1218	793.02405(4-5)	Children's games
GT373-377	392.360096	Africa	GV1218.5-1220.7	790.133	Toys
GT375-376	392.3600962	Egypt	GV1221-1469	793	Indoor games
GT379-380	392.3600994	Australia	GV1232-1299	795.4	Card games
GT381-382	392.3600993	New Zealand	GV1301-1311	795	Gambling
GT383-384	392.360099(5-6)	Oceania	GV1312-1469	794	Board games
GT485	395.53	Churches	GV1470-1511	793.2	Parties
GT500-2370	391	Dress/Fashion	GV1541-1561	793.8	Parlor magic/Tricks
GT530-596	391.0090(1-4)	By date	GV1580-1799	793.3	Dancing
GT530-560	391.00901	Ancient	GV1800-1860	791	Circuses/Spectacles
GT575	391.00902	Medieval	H	300	Social Sciences
GT580-596	391.0090(3-4)	Modern	H1-9	300.5	Serials
GT601-1605	391.009(3-9)	By place	H10-29	300.6	Societies/Congresses
GT603-620	391.0097	North America	H50	300.25	Directories
GT623-716	391.009(72-8)	Latin America	H51-53	300.9	History
GT720-1330	391.0094	Europe	H57-59	300.92	Biography
GT1370-1570	391.0095	Asia	H61	300.1	Theory/Method
GT1580-1589	391.0096	Africa	H62	300.7	Education
GT1590-1599	391.0099(3-6)	Australia/New Zealand/ Oceania	H63-64	300.74	Museums/Exhibits
			H65-87	300.711	Schools
GT1710-1950	391.0(1-4)	By class	HA	310	Statistics
GT2050-2370	391.4	Materials/Accessories	HA1-15	310.(5/6)	Serials/Societies
GT2400-3390	392	Customs of private life	HA17	310.3	Dictionaries/Encyclopedias
GT2450-2487	392.14	Children/Adolescence	HA19	310.9	History
GT2600-2810	392.(4-6)	Love/Sex/Marriage	HA22-23	310.92	Biography
GT2660-2810	392.5	Marriage	HA29-31.9	310.1	Theory/Method
GT2701-2796	392.509(3-9)	By place	HA35	310.7	Education
GT2805-2955	394.1	Eating/Drinking	HA36-37	310.6	Organizations/Bureaus
GT3150-3390	393.1	Burial	HA38-39	350.714/304.6	Registration of vital events
GT3400-5090	394	Customs of public social life	HA154-4737	310	Statistical data
			HA154-155	310	Statistics (General)
GT3925-4995	394.26	Festivals/Holidays	HA175-4737	314-319	By place
GT5010-5090	390.22	Royalty/Nobility	HA201-730	317.3	United States
GT5320-6720	390.(1-4)	Customs of special classes	HA251-730	31(7.4-7.9)	By state
GT5320-5680	390.2	By birth/Rank/Etc.	HA740	319.82	Greenland
GT5750-6390	390.4	By occupation	HA741-750	317.1	Canada
GV	790-799	Recreation/Leisure	HA761-770	317.2	Mexico
GV181.35-.55	790.069	Recreation leadership	HA791-800	317.282	Belize
GV182-.5	790.068	Recreational facilities	HA801-810	317.286	Costa Rica
GV191.2-200.6	796.5	Outdoor recreation	HA811-820	317.281	Guatemala
GV191.68-198.9	796.54	Camping	HA821-830	317.283	Honduras
GV199-.6	796.51	Hiking	HA831-840	317.285	Nicaragua
GV199.8-200.3	796.522	Mountaineering	HA841-850	317.284	El Salvador
GV200.5	796.5	Wilderness survival	HA851-854	317.287	Panama
GV200.6	797.(1-3)	Water recreation	HA855	317.2875	Panama Canal Zone

LC	Dewey	Descriptor	LC	Dewey	Descriptor
HA861	317.296	Bahamas	HA2303	316.94	Comoro Islands
HA865	317.2981	Barbados	HA2305	316.982	Mauritius
HA866	317.297	Leeward Islands	HA2307	316.981	Reunion
HA867	317.2983	Trinidad/Tobago	HA2309	316.99	Kerguelen Islands
HA868	317.2984	Windward Islands	HA3001-3010	319.4	Australia
HA871-880	317.291	Cuba	HA3171-3190	319.3	New Zealand
HA881-885	317.294	Haiti	HA4012	319.67	Guam
HA886-890	317.293	Dominican Republic	HA4013	319.53	Papua New Guinea
HA891-900	317.292	Jamaica	HA4014	319.593	Solomon Islands
HA901-910	317.295	Puerto Rico	HA4015	319.597	New Caledonia
HA911-915	317.29722	Virgin Islands of the U.S.	HA4015.5	319.595	Vanuatu
HA917	317.2886	Netherlands Antilles	HA4016	319.611	Fiji Islands
HA918.7	317.2976	Guadeloupe	HA4016.7	319.681	Kiribati and Tuvalu (Gilbert
HA918.9	317.2982	Martinique			and Ellice Islands)
HA921-930	317.299	Bermuda	HA4017	319.612	Tonga
HA941-960	318.2	Argentina	HA4017.5	319.623	Cook Islands
HA961-970	318.4	Bolivia	HA4018.5	319.613	American Samoa
HA971-990	318.1	Brazil	HA4018.7	319.614	Western Samoa
HA991-1010	318.3	Chile	HA4020-.5	319.89	Polar regions
HA1011-1020	318.61	Colombia	HA4551-4555	315	Asia
HA1021-1030	318.66	Ecuador	HA4556.5	315.61	Turkey
HA1033	318.81	Guyana	HA4557	315.645	Cyprus
HA1035	318.83	Suriname	HA4558	315.691	Syria
HA1037	318.82	French Guiana	HA4559	315.692	Lebanon
HA1041-1050	318.92	Paraguay	HA4560	315.694	Israel
HA1051-1070	318.5	Peru	HA4561	315.695	Jordan
HA1071-1090	318.95	Uruguay	HA4563	315.38	Saudi Arabia
HA1091-1100	318.7	Venezuela	HA4564	315.332	Yemen
HA1107	314	Europe	HA4565	315.353	Oman
HA1121-1140	314.1	Great Britain/England	HA4566	315.357	United Arab Emirates
HA1141-1150	314.16	Northern Ireland	HA4567	315.363	Qatar
HA1151-1160	314.11	Scotland	HA4568	315.365	Bahrein
HA1161-1170	314.29	Wales	HA4569	315.367	Kuwait
HA1170.1-.5	314.15	Ireland	HA4570	315.67	Iraq
HA1171-1190	314.36	Austria	HA4570.2	315.5	Iran
HA1191-1200	314.37	Czechoslovakia	HA4570.6	315.81	Afghanistan
HA1201-1210	314.39	Hungary	HA4570.7	315.91	Burma
HA1210.5	314.3648	Liechtenstein	HA4570.8	315.493	Sri Lanka
HA1211-1230	314.4	France	HA4570.9	315.496	Nepal
HA1231-1349	314.3	Germany	HA4581-4590	315.4	India
HA1351-1359	314.95	Greece	HA4590.3	315.498	Bautan
HA1361-1379	314.5	Italy	HA4590.5	315.491	Pakistan
HA1381-1390	314.92	Netherlands	HA4590.6	315.492	Bangladesh
HA1391-1410	314.93	Belgium	HA4600.3	315.96	Cambodia
HA1411-1420	314.935	Luxembourg	HA4600.4	315.94	Laos
HA1431-1450	314.7	Russia	HA4600.5	315.97	Vietnam
HA1450.5	314.897	Finland	HA4600.55	315.93	Thailand
HA1451-1460	314.38	Poland	HA4600.6	315.95	Malaysia
HA1471-1490	314.89	Denmark	HA4601-4610	315.98	Indonesia
HA1491-1500	314.912	Iceland	HA4611-4620	315.99	Philippine Islands
HA1501-1520	314.81	Norway	HA4621-4630	315.2	Japan
HA1521-1540	314.85	Sweden	HA4630.5-.6	315.19	Korea/North Korea
HA1541-1560	314.6	Spain	HA4630.8	315.17	Mongolia
HA1571-1580	314.69	Portugal	HA4631-4640	315.1	China
HA1591-1610	314.94	Switzerland	HA4641-4645	315.26	Macao
HA1620.5	314.965	Albania	HA4646-4650	315.1249	Taiwan
HA1621-1630	314.977	Bulgaria	HA4651-4655	315.125	Hong Kong
HA1631-1635	314.971	Yugoslavia	HA4682	316.4	Morocco
HA1641-1650	314.98	Romania	HA4683	316.5	Algeria
HA2280	314.699	Azores	HA4684	316.11	Tunisia
HA2285	314.698	Madeira Islands	HA4685	316.12	Libya
HA2287	316.49	Canary Islands	HA4686	316.2	Egypt
HA2289	316.658	Cape Verde Islands	HA4687	316.24	Sudan
HA2291	319.73	St. Helena	HA4689	316.3	Ethiopia
HA2295	319.711	Falkland Islands	HA4690	316.773	Somalia
HA2300	315.495	Maldive Islands	HA4691	316.771	Djibouti
HA2301	316.96	Seychelles	HA4693	316.762	Kenya

LC	Dewey	Descriptor	LC	Dewey	Descriptor
HA4694	316.761	Uganda	HB848-849	304.60(5/6)	Serials/Societies/Congresses
HA4695	316.7571	Rwanda	HB850	304.607	Education
HA4696	316.7572	Burundi	HB851-853	304.609	History
HA4697	316.78	Tanzania	HB855-865	304.6092	Biography
HA4698	316.79	Mozambique	HB884	304.6071724	Developing countries
HA4699	316.91	Madagascar	HB901-1108	304.63	Births/Fertility
HA4701	316.8	South Africa	HB911-1107	304.6309	By place
HA4702	316.89	Zimbabwe/Zambia/Malawi	HB915-916	304.630973	United States
HA4703	316.894	Zambia	HB935	304.63097(4-9)	By state
HA4704	316.885	Lesotho	HB937	304.63097(4-9)	By city
HA4705	316.887	Swaziland	HB939-940	304.630971	Canada
HA4706	316.883	Botswana	HB941-942	304.630972	Mexico
HA4707	316.897	Malawi	HB945-946	304.63097282	Belize
HA4708	316.881	Namibia	HB947-948	304.63097286	Costa Rica
HA4710	316.73	Angola	HB949	304.63097281	Guatemala
HA4711	316.751	Zaire	HB950	304.63097283	Honduras
HA4712	316.718	Equatorial Guinea	HB951	304.63097285	Nicaragua
HA4713	316.715	Sao Tome/Principe	HB952-953	304.63097287	Panama
HA4714	316.72	French Equatorial Africa	HB953.5	304.630972875	Panama Canal Zone
HA4715	316.721	Gabon	HB954	304.63097284	El Salvador
HA4716	316.724	Congo	HB957-958	304.63097296	Bahamas
HA4717	316.741	Central African Republic	HB959-960	304.63097291	Cuba
HA4718	316.743	Chad	HB961	304.63097294	Haiti
HA4719	316.711	Cameroon	HB962	304.63097293	Dominican Republic
HA4722	316.683	Benin (Dahomey)	HB963-964	304.63097292	Jamaica
HA4723	316.681	Togo	HB965-966	304.63097295	Puerto Rico
HA4724	316.626	Niger	HB966.3	304.6309729722	Virgin Islands of the U.S.
HA4725	316.668	Ivory Coast	HB966.57	304.630972981	Barbados
HA4726	316.652	Guinea	HB966.72	304.630972973	Anguilla
HA4727	316.623	Mali	HB966.74	304.630972974	Antigua/Barbuda
HA4728	316.625	Burkina Faso	HB966.76	304.630972975	Montserrat
HA4729	316.63	Senegal	HB966.78	304.630972973	Saint Kitts-Nevis
HA4730	316.61	Mauritania	HB966.93	304.6309729841	Dominica
HA4731	316.69	Nigeria	HB966.95	304.6309729845	Grenada
HA4732	316.67	Ghana	HB966.97	304.6309729843	Saint Lucia
HA4733	316.64	Sierra Leone	HB966.99	304.6309729844	Saint Vincent/Grenadines
HA4734	316.651	Gambia	HB967	304.630972983	Trinidad/Tobago
HA4735	316.662	Liberia	HB967.35	304.630972986	Aruba
HA4736	316.657	Guinea-Bissau	HB967.36	304.630972986	Bonaire
HA4737	316.48	Spanish Sahara	HB967.37	304.630972986	Curacao
HB	330	Economics/Economic theory	HB967.38	304.630972977	Saba
HB1-9	330.0(5/6)	Serials/Societies	HB967.385	304.630972977	Saint Eustatius
HB21	330.06	Congresses	HB967.39	304.630972977	Saint Martin
HB61	330.03	Dictionaries/Encyclopedias	HB967.7	304.630972976	Guadeloupe
HB63	330.025	Directories	HB967.9	304.630972982	Martinique
HB71-74	330	Economics (General)	HB969-970	304.630982	Argentina
HB75-130	330.09	History	HB971-972	304.630984	Bolivia
HB131-145	330.01	Methodology	HB973-974	304.630981	Brazil
HB135-145	330.1543	Mathematical economics	HB975-976	304.630983	Chile
HB201-205	338.521	Value/Utility	HB977-978	304.6309861	Colombia
HB221-236	338.52	Price	HB979-980	304.6309866	Ecuador
HB238	338.6048	Competition	HB982.3	304.6309881	Guyana
HB241	338	Production	HB982.5	304.6309883	Suriname
HB251	330.16/339.2	Wealth	HB982.7	304.6309882	French Guiana
HB401	339.21	Rent	HB983-984	304.6309892	Paraguay
HB501	330.122	Capital/Capitalism	HB985-986	304.630985	Peru
HB522-715	339.3/338	Income/Factor shares	HB987-988	304.6309895	Uruguay
HB531-551	332.82	Interest	HB989-990	304.630987	Venezuela
HB551	332.83	Usury	HB995-996	304.630942(9)	England/Wales
HB601	338.516	Profit	HB997-998	304.6309411	Scotland
HB615-715	338.(04/5)	Entrepreneurship/Risk	HB998.5	304.6309416	Northern Ireland
HB701-715	330.17	Property	HB999-1000	304.6309417	Irish Republic
HB801-843	339.47	Consumption	HB1001-1002	304.6309436	Austria
HB842-843	338.5212	Demand	HB1002.3	304.6309437	Czechoslovakia
HB846-.8	330.156	Welfare theory	HB1002.5	304.6309439	Hungary
HB848-3697	304.6	Demography/Vital events	HB1002.9	304.630943648	Liechtenstein
			HB1003-1004	304.630944	France

LC	Dewey	Descriptor	LC	Dewey	Descriptor
HB1004.5	304.630944949	Monaco	HB1072.5	304.63096762	Kenya
HB1004-1006.5	304.630943	Germany	HB1072.6	304.63096761	Uganda
HB1009-1010	304.630945	Italy	HB1072.7	304.630967571	Rwanda
HB1013-1014	304.6309493	Belgium	HB1072.8	304.630967572	Burundi
HB1015-1016	304.6309492	Netherlands	HB1072.9	304.6309678	Tanzania
HB1016.5	304.63094935	Luxembourg	HB1073	304.6309679	Mozambique
HB1017-1018	304.630947	European Russia	HB1073.2	304.6309691	Madagascar
HB1018.3	304.63094897	Finland	HB1073.4	304.630968	South Africa
HB1018.7	304.6309438	Poland	HB1073.5	304.6309689	Zimbabwe/Zambia/Malawi
HB1021-1022	304.6309489	Denmark	HB1073.6	304.63096894	Zambia
HB1023-1024	304.63094912	Iceland	HB1073.7	304.63096885	Lesotho
HB1025-1026	304.6309481	Norway	HB1073.8	304.63096887	Swaziland
HB1027-1028	304.6309485	Sweden	HB1073.9	304.63096883	Botswana
HB1029-1030	304.630946	Spain	HB1074	304.63096897	Malawi
HB1031-1032	304.6309469	Portugal	HB1074.2	304.63096881	Namibia
HB1033-1034	304.6309494	Switzerland	HB1074.4	304.63096673	Angola
HB1036.5	304.63094965	Albania	HB1074.5	304.63096751	Zaire
HB1037-1038	304.63094977	Bulgaria	HB1074.6	304.63096718	Equatorial Guinea
HB1038.5	304.6309497	Yugoslavia	HB1074.7	304.63096715	Sao Tome/Principe
HB1041-1042	304.6309498	Romania	HB1074.8	304.6309672	French Equatorial Africa
HB1042.5	304.6609495	Greece	HB1074.9	304.63096721	Gabon
HB1043.4	304.6309561	Turkey	HB1075	304.63096724	Congo
HB1043.5	304.63095645	Cyprus	HB1075.2	304.63096741	Central African Republic
HB1043.7	304.63095691	Syria	HB1075.3	304.63096743	Chad
HB1043.9	304.63095692	Lebanon	HB1075.4	304.63096711	Cameroon
HB1044	304.63095694	Israel/Palestine	HB1075.7	304.63096683	Benin (Dahomey)
HB1044.3	304.63095695	Jordan	HB1075.8	304.63096681	Togo
HB1044.7	304.6309538	Saudi Arabia	HB1075.9	304.63096626	Niger
HB1044.9-1045	304.63095332	Yemen	HB1076	304.63096668	Ivory Coast
HB1045.3	304.63095353	Oman	HB1076.2	304.63096652	Guinea-Bissau
HB1045.5	304.63095357	United Arab Emirates	HB1076.3	304.63096623	Mali
HB1045.7	304.63095363	Qatar	HB1076.4	304.63096625	Burkina Faso
HB1045.9	304.63095365	Bahrein	HB1076.5	304.6309663	Senegal
HB1046	304.63095367	Kuwait	HB1076.6	304.6309661	Mauritania
HB1046.3	304.6309567	Iraq	HB1076.7	304.6309669	Nigeria
HB1046.4	304.630955	Iran	HB1076.8	304.6309667	Ghana
HB1046.6	304.6309581	Afghanistan	HB1076.9	304.6309664	Sierra Leone
HB1046.7	304.6309591	Burma	HB1077	304.63096651	Gambia
HB1046.8	304.63095493	Sri Lanka	HB1077.2	304.63096662	Liberia
HB1046.9	304.63095496	Nepal	HB1077.3	304.63096657	Guinea-Bissau
HB1049-1050	304.630954	India	HB1077.4	304.6309648	Spanish Sahara
HB1050.3	304.63095498	Bhutan	HB1077.5	304.63094699	Azores
HB1050.5	304.63095491	Pakistan	HB1078	304.63097299	Bermuda
HB1050.6	304.63095492	Bangladesh	HB1078.5	304.63094698	Madeira Islands
HB1054.3	304.6309596	Cambodia	HB1079	304.6309649	Canary Islands
HB1054.4	304.6309594	Laos	HB1079.5	304.63096658	Cape Verde Islands
HB1054.5	304.6309597	Vietnam	HB1080	304.6309973	St. Helena
HB1054.55	304.6309593	Thailand	HB1080.5	304.6309973	Tristan da Cunha
HB1054.6	304.6309595	Malaysia	HB1081	304.6309971	Falkland Islands
HB1057-1058	304.6309598	Indonesia	HB1081.5	304.63095495	Maldive Islands
HB1059-1060	304.6309599	Philippine Islands	HB1082	304.6309696	Seychelles
HB1061-1062	304.630952	Japan	HB1082.5	304.6309694	Comoro Islands
HB1062.5-.6	304.6309519	Korea/North Korea	HB1803	304.63096982	Mauritius
HB1062.8	304.6309517	Mongolia	HB1083.5	304.63096981	Reunion
HB1064	304.630951	China	HB1084	304.6309699	Kerguelen Islands
HB1065	304.63095126	Macao	HB1085-1086	304.630994	Australia
HB1066	304.630951249	Taiwan	HB1102.5	304.630993	New Zealand
HB1067	304.63095125	Hong Kong	HB1102.7	304.6309967	Guam
HB1071.3	304.630964	Morocco	HB1102.8	304.6309953	Papua New Guinea
HB1071.4	304.630965	Algeria	HB1102.9	304.63099681	Kiribati (Gilbert Islands)
HB1071.5	304.6309611	Tunisia	HB1103	304.63099593	Solomon Islands
HB1071.6	304.6309612	Libya	HB1103.3	304.63099597	New Caledonia
HB1071.7	304.630962	Egypt	HB1103.4	304.63099595	Vanuatu
HB1071.8	304.6309624	Sudan	HB1103.5	304.63099611	Fiji Islands
HB1072	304.630963	Ethiopia	HB1103.6	304.63099612	Tonga
HB1072.2	304.63096773	Somalia	HB1103.65	304.63099623	Cook Islands
HB1072.3	304.63096771	Djibouti	HB1103.7	304.63099613	American Samoa

LC	Dewey	Descriptor	LC	Dewey	Descriptor
HB1103.8	304.63099614	Western Samoa	HB1214.5	306.810944949	Monaco
HB1103.9	304.6309962	French Polynesia	HB1215-1216.5	306.810943	Germany
HB1105	304.630998(1-8)	Polar regions	HB1219-1220	306.810945	Italy
HB1106	304.6309982	Greenland	HB1223-1224	306.8109493	Belgium
HB1108	304.63091724	Developing countries	HB1225-1226	306.8109492	Netherlands
HB1111-1317	306.81	Marriage	HB1226.5	306.810994935	Luxembourg
HB1121-1317	306.8109	Marriage, By place	HB1227-1228	306.810947	European Russia
HB1125-1126	306.810973	United States	HB1228.3	306.81094897	Finland
HB1145	306.81097(4-9)	By state	HB1228.7	306.8109438	Poland
HB1147	306.81097(4-9)	By city	HB1231-1232	306.8109489	Denmark
HB1149-1150	306.810971	Canada	HB1233-1234	306.810994912	Iceland
HB1151-1152	306.810972	Mexico	HB1235-1236	306.8109481	Norway
HB1155-1156	306.81097282	Belize	HB1237-1238	306.8109485	Sweden
HB1157-1158	306.81097286	Costa Rica	HB1239-1240	306.810946	Spain
HB1159	306.81097281	Guatemala	HB1241-1242	306.8109469	Portugal
HB1160	306.81097283	Honduras	HB1243-1244	306.8109494	Switzerland
HB1161	306.81097285	Nicaragua	HB1246.5	306.81094965	Albania
HB1162-1163	306.81097287	Panama	HB1247-1248	306.81094977	Bulgaria
HB1163.5	306.810972875	Panama Canal Zone	HB1248.5	306.8109497	Yugoslavia
HB1164	306.81097284	El Salvador	HB1251-1252	306.8109498	Romania
HB1167-1168	306.81097296	Bahamas	HB1252.5	306.8109495	Greece
HB1169-1170	306.81097291	Cuba	HB1253.4	306.8109561	Turkey
HB1171	306.81097294	Haiti	HB1253.5	306.81095645	Cyprus
HB1172	306.81097293	Dominican Republic	HB1253.7	306.81095691	Syria
HB1173-1174	306.81097292	Jamaica	HB1253.9	306.81095692	Lebanon
HB1175-1176	306.81097295	Puerto Rico	HB1254	306.81095694	Israel/Palestine
HB1176.3	306.8109729722	Virgin Islands of the U.S.	HB1254.3	306.81095695	Jordan
HB1176.57	306.810972981	Barbados	HB1254.7	306.8109538	Saudi Arabia
HB1176.72	306.810972973	Anguilla	HB1254.9-1255	306.81095332	Yemen
HB1176.74	306.810972974	Antigua/Barbuda	HB1255.3	306.81095353	Oman
HB1176.76	306.810972975	Montserrat	HB1255.5	306.81095357	United Arab Emirates
HB1176.78	306.810972973	Saint Kitts-Nevia	HB1255.7	306.81095363	Qatar
HB1176.93	306.8109729841	Dominica	HB1255.9	306.81095365	Bahrein
HB1176.95	306.8109729845	Grenada	HB1256	306.81095367	Kuwait
HB1176.97	306.8109729843	Saint Lucia	HB1256.3	306.8109567	Iraq
HB1176.99	306.8109729844	Saint Vincent/Grenadines	HB1256.4	306.810955	Iran
HB1177	306.810972983	Trinidad/Tobago	HB1256.6	306.8109581	Afghanistan
HB1177.35	306.810972986	Aruba	HB1256.7	306.8109591	Burma
HB1177.36	306.810972986	Bonaire	HB1256.8	306.81095493	Sri Lanka
HB1177.37	306.810972986	Curacao	HB1256.9	306.81095496	Nepal
HB1177.38	306.810972977	Saba	HB1259-1260	306.810954	India
HB1177.385	306.810972977	Saint Eustatius	HB1260.3	306.81095498	Bhutan
HB1177.39	306.810972977	Saint Martin	HB1260.5	306.81095491	Pakistan
HB1177.7	306.810972976	Guadeloupe	HB1260.6	306.81095492	Bangladesh
HB1177.9	306.810972982	Martinique	HB1264.3	306.8109596	Cambodia
HB1179-1180	306.810982	Argentina	HB1264.4	306.810954	Laos
HB1181-1182	306.810984	Bolivia	HB1264.5	306.8109597	Vietnam
HB1183-1184	306.810981	Brazil	HB1264.55	306.8109593	Thailand
HB1185-1186	306.810983	Chile	HB1264.6	306.8109595	Malaysia
HB1187-1188	306.8109861	Colombia	HB1267-1268	306.8109598	Indonesia
HB1189-1190	306.8109866	Ecuador	HB1269-1270	306.8109599	Philippine Islands
HB1192.3	306.8109881	Guyana	HB1271-1272	306.810952	Japan
HB1192.5	306.8109883	Suriname	HB1272.5-.6	306.8109519	Korea/North Korea
HB1192.7	306.8109882	French Guiana	HB1272.8	306.8109517	Mongolia
HB1193-1194	306.8109892	Paraguay	HB1274	306.810951	China
HB1195-1196	306.810985	Peru	HB1275	306.81095126	Macao
HB1197-1198	306.8109895	Uruguay	HB1276	306.810951249	Taiwan
HB1199-1200	306.810987	Venezuela	HB1277	306.81095125	Hong Kong
HB1205-1206	306.810942(9)	England/Wales	HB1281.3	306.810964	Morocco
HB1207-1208	306.8109411	Scotland	HB1281.4	306.810965	Algeria
HB1208.5	306.8109416	Northern Ireland	HB1281.5	306.8109611	Tunisia
HB1209-1210	306.8109417	Irish Republic	HB1281.6	306.8109612	Libya
HB1211-1212	306.8109436	Austria	HB1281.7	306.810962	Egypt
HB1212.3	306.8109437	Czechoslovakia	HB1281.8	306.8109624	Sudan
HB1212.5	306.8109439	Hungary	HB1282	306.810963	Ethiopia
HB1212.9	306.810943648	Liechtenstein	HB1282.2	306.81096773	Somalia
HB1213-1214	306.810944	France	HB1282.3	306.81096771	Djibouti

LC	Dewey	Descriptor	LC	Dewey	Descriptor
HB1282.5	306.81096762	Kenya	HB1313.8	306.81099614	Western Samoa
HB1282.6	306.81096761	Uganda	HB1313.9	306.8109962	French Polynesia
HB1282.7	306.810967571	Rwanda	HB1315	306.810998(1-8)	Polar regions
HB1282.8	306.810967572	Burundi	HB1316	306.8109982	Greenland
HB1282.9	306.8109678	Tanzania	HB1321-1528	304.64	Deaths
HB1283	306.8109679	Mozambique	HB1322	304.64	Life tables
HB1283.2	306.8109691	Madagascar	HB1331-1528	304.6409(3-9)	By place
HB1283.4	306.810968	South Africa	HB1335	304.640973	United States
HB1283.5	306.8109689	Zimbabwe/Zambia/Malawi	HB1355	304.64097(4-9)	By state
HB1283.6	306.81096894	Zambia	HB1357	304.64097(4-9)	By city
HB1283.7	306.81096885	Lesotho	HB1359-1360	304.640971	Canada
HB1283.8	306.81096887	Swaziland	HB1361-1362	304.640972	Mexico
HB1283.9	306.81096883	Botswana	HB1365-1366	304.64097282	Belize
HB1284	306.81096897	Malawi	HB1367-1368	304.64097286	Costa Rica
HB1284.2	306.81096881	Namibia	HB1369	304.64097281	Guatemala
HB1284.4	306.8109673	Angola	HB1370	304.64097283	Honduras
HB1284.5	306.81096751	Zaire	HB1371	304.64097285	Nicaragua
HB1284.6	306.81096718	Equatorial Guinea	HB1372-1373	304.64097287	Panama
HB1284.7	306.81096715	Sao Tome/Principe	HB1373.5	304.640972875	Panama Canal Zone
HB1284.8	306.8109672	French Equatorial Africa	HB1374	304.64097284	El Salvador
HB1284.9	306.81096721	Gabon	HB1377-1378	304.64097296	Bahamas
HB1285	306.81096724	Congo	HB1379-1380	304.64097291	Cuba
HB1285.2	306.81096741	Central African Republic	HB1381	304.64097294	Haiti
HB1285.3	306.81096743	Chad	HB1382	304.64097293	Dominican Republic
HB1285.4	306.81096711	Cameroon	HB1383-1384	304.64097292	Jamaica
HB1285.7	306.81096683	Benin (Dahomey)	HB1385-1386	304.64097295	Puerto Rico
HB1285.8	306.81096681	Togo	HB1386.3	304.6409729722	Virgin Islands of the U.S.
HB1285.9	306.81096626	Niger	HB1386.57	304.640972981	Barbados
HB1286	306.81096668	Ivory Coast	HB1386.72	304.640972973	Anguilla
HB1286.2	306.81096652	Guinea-Bissau	HB1386.74	304.640972974	Antigua/Barbuda
HB1286.3	306.81096623	Mali	HB1386.76	304.640972975	Montserrat
HB1286.4	306.81096625	Burkina Faso	HB1386.78	304.640972973	Saint Kitts-Nevia
HB1286.5	306.8109663	Senegal	HB1386.93	304.6409729841	Dominica
HB1286.6	306.8109661	Mauritania	HB1386.95	304.6409729845	Grenada
HB1286.7	306.8109669	Nigeria	HB1386.97	304.6409729843	Saint Lucia
HB1286.8	306.8109667	Ghana	HB1386.99	304.6409729844	Saint Vincent/Grenadines
HB1286.9	306.8109664	Sierra Leone	HB1387	304.640972983	Trinidad/Tobago
HB1287	306.81096651	Gambia	HB1387.35	304.640972986	Aruba
HB1287.2	306.81096662	Liberia	HB1387.36	304.640972986	Bonaire
HB1287.3	306.81096657	Guinea-Bissau	HB1387.37	304.640972986	Curacao
HB1287.4	306.8109648	Spanish Sahara	HB1387.38	304.640972977	Saba
HB1287.5	306.81094699	Azores	HB1387.385	304.640972977	Saint Eustatius
HB1288	306.81097299	Bermuda	HB1387.39	304.640972977	Saint Martin
HB1288.5	306.81094698	Madeira Islands	HB1387.7	304.640972976	Guadeloupe
HB1289	306.8109649	Canary Islands	HB1387.9	304.640972982	Martinique
HB1289.5	306.81096658	Cape Verde Islands	HB1389-1390	304.640982	Argentina
HB1290	306.8109973	St. Helena	HB1391-1392	304.640984	Bolivia
HB1290.5	306.8109973	Tristan da Cunha	HB1393-1394	304.640981	Brazil
HB1291	306.8109971	Falkland Islands	HB1395-1396	304.640983	Chile
HB1291.5	306.81095495	Maldive Islands	HB1397-1398	304.6409861	Colombia
HB1292	306.8109696	Seychelles	HB1399-1400	304.6409866	Ecuador
HB1292.5	306.8109694	Comoro Islands	HB1402.3	304.6409881	Guyana
HB1293	306.81096982	Mauritius	HB1402.5	304.6409883	Suriname
HB1293.5	306.81096981	Reunion	HB1402.7	304.6409882	French Guiana
HB1294	306.8109699	Kerguelen Islands	HB1403-1404	304.6409892	Paraguay
HB1295-1296	306.810994	Australia	HB1405-1406	304.640985	Peru
HB1312.5	306.810993	New Zealand	HB1407-1408	304.6409895	Uruguay
HB1312.7	306.8109967	Guam	HB1409-1410	304.640987	Venezuela
HB1312.8	306.8109953	Papua New Guinea	HB1415-1416	304.640942(9)	England/Wales
HB1312.9	306.81099681	Kiribati (Gilbert Islands)	HB1417-1418	304.6409411	Scotland
HB1313	306.81099593	Solomon Islands	HB1418.5	304.6409416	Northern Ireland
HB1313.3	306.81099597	New Caledonia	HB1419-1420	304.6409417	Irish Republic
HB1313.4	306.81099595	Vanuatu	HB1421-1422	304.6409436	Austria
HB1313.5	306.81099611	Fiji Islands	HB1422.3	304.6409437	Czechoslovakia
HB1313.6	306.81099612	Tonga	HB1422.5	304.6409439	Hungary
HB1313.65	306.81099623	Cook Islands	HB1422.9	304.640943648	Liechtenstein
HB1313.7	306.81099613	American Samoa	HB1423-1424	304.640944	France

LC	Dewey	Descriptor
HB1424.5	304.640944949	Monaco
HB1425-1426.5	304.640943	Germany
HB1429-1430	304.640945	Italy
HB1433-1434	304.64409493	Belgium
HB1435-1436	304.64409492	Netherlands
HB1436.5	304.64094935	Luxembourg
HB1437-1438	304.640947	European Russia
HB1438.3	304.64094897	Finland
HB1438.7	304.6409438	Poland
HB1441-1442	304.6409489	Denmark
HB1443-1444	304.64094912	Iceland
HB1445-1446	304.6409481	Norway
HB1447-1448	304.6409485	Sweden
HB1449-1450	304.640946	Spain
HB1451-1452	304.6409469	Portugal
HB1453-1454	304.6409494	Switzerland
HB1456.5	304.64094965	Albania
HB1457-1458	304.64094977	Bulgaria
HB1458.5	304.6409497	Yugoslavia
HB1461-1462	304.6409498	Romania
HB1462.5	304.6409495	Greece
HB1463.4	304.6409561	Turkey
HB1463.5	304.64095645	Cyprus
HB1463.7	304.64095691	Syria
HB1463.9	304.64095692	Lebanon
HB1464	304.64095694	Israel/Palestine
HB1464.3	304.64095695	Jordan
HB1464.7	304.6409538	Saudi Arabia
HB1464.9-1465	304.64095332	Yemen
HB1465.3	304.64095353	Oman
HB1465.5	304.64095357	United Arab Emirates
HB1465.7	304.64095363	Qatar
HB1465.9	304.64095365	Bahrein
HB1466	304.64095367	Kuwait
HB1466.3	304.6409567	Iraq
HB1466.4	304.640955	Iran
HB1466.6	304.6409581	Afghanistan
HB1466.7	304.6409591	Burma
HB1466.8	304.64095493	Sri Lanka
HB1466.9	304.64095496	Nepal
HB1469-1470	304.640954	India
HB1470.3	304.64095498	Bhutan
HB1470.5	304.64095491	Pakistan
HB1470.6	304.64095492	Bangladesh
HB1474.3	304.6409596	Cambodia
HB1474.4	304.6409594	Laos
HB1474.5	304.6409597	Vietnam
HB1474.55	304.6409593	Thailand
HB1474.6	304.6409595	Malaysia
HB1477-1478	304.6409598	Indonesia
HB1479-1480	304.6409599	Philippine Islands
HB1481-1482	304.640952	Japan
HB1482.5-.6	304.6409519	Korea/North Korea
HB1482.8	304.6409517	Mongolia
HB1484	304.640951	China
HB1485	304.64095126	Macao
HB1486	304.640951249	Taiwan
HB1487	304.64095125	Hong Kong
HB1491.3	304.640964	Morocco
HB1491.4	304.640965	Algeria
HB1491.5	304.64409611	Tunisia
HB1491.6	304.64409612	Libya
HB1491.7	304.640962	Egypt
HB1491.8	304.64409624	Sudan
HB1492	304.640963	Ethiopia
HB1492.2	304.64096773	Somalia
HB1492.3	304.64096771	Djibouti
HB1492.5	304.64096762	Kenya
HB1492.6	304.64096761	Uganda
HB1492.7	304.640967571	Rwanda
HB1492.8	304.640967572	Burundi
HB1492.9	304.6409678	Tanzania
HB1493	304.6409679	Mozambique
HB1493.2	304.6409691	Madagascar
HB1493.4	304.640968	South Africa
HB1493.5	304.6409689	Zimbabwe/Zambia/Malawi
HB1493.6	304.64096894	Zambia
HB1493.7	304.64096885	Lesotho
HB1493.8	304.64096887	Swaziland
HB1493.9	304.64096883	Botswana
HB1494	304.64096897	Malawi
HB1494.2	304.64096881	Namibia
HB1494.4	304.6409673	Angola
HB1494.5	304.64096751	Zaire
HB1494.6	304.64096718	Equatorial Guinea
HB1494.7	304.64096715	Sao Tome/Principe
HB1494.8	304.6409672	French Equatorial Africa
HB1494.9	304.64096721	Gabon
HB1495	304.64096724	Congo
HB1495.2	304.64096741	Central African Republic
HB1495.3	304.64096743	Chad
HB1495.4	304.64096711	Cameroon
HB1495.7	304.64096683	Benin (Dahomey)
HB1495.8	304.64096681	Togo
HB1495.9	304.64096626	Niger
HB1496	304.64096668	Ivory Coast
HB1496.2	304.64096652	Guinea-Bissau
HB1496.3	304.64096623	Mali
HB1496.4	304.64096625	Burkina Faso
HB1496.5	304.6409663	Senegal
HB1496.6	304.6409661	Mauritania
HB1496.7	304.6409669	Nigeria
HB1496.8	304.6409667	Ghana
HB1496.9	304.6409664	Sierra Leone
HB1497	304.64096651	Gambia
HB1497.2	304.64096662	Liberia
HB1497.3	304.64096657	Guinea-Bissau
HB1497.4	304.6409648	Spanish Sahara
HB1497.5	304.64094699	Azores
HB1498	304.64097299	Bermuda
HB1498.5	304.64094698	Madeira Islands
HB1499	304.6409649	Canary Islands
HB1499.5	304.64096658	Cape Verde Islands
HB1500	304.6409973	St. Helena
HB1500.5	304.6409973	Tristan da Cunha
HB1501	304.6409971	Falkland Islands
HB1501.5	304.64095495	Maldive Islands
HB1502	304.6409696	Seychelles
HB1502.5	304.6409694	Comoro Islands
HB1503	304.64096982	Mauritius
HB1503.5	304.64096981	Reunion
HB1504	304.6409699	Kerguelen Islands
HB1505-1506	304.640994	Australia
HB1522.5	304.640993	New Zealand
HB1522.7	304.6409967	Guam
HB1522.8	304.6409953	Papua New Guinea
HB1522.9	304.64099681	Kiribati (Gilbert Islands)
HB1523	304.64099593	Solomon Islands
HB1523.3	304.64099597	New Caledonia
HB1523.4	304.64099595	Vanuatu
HB1523.5	304.64099611	Fiji Islands
HB1523.6	304.64099612	Tonga
HB1523.65	304.64099623	Cook Islands
HB1523.7	304.64099613	American Samoa

LC	Dewey	Descriptor	LC	Dewey	Descriptor
HB1523.8	304.64099614	Western Samoa	HB1634.5	304.620944949	Monaco
HB1523.9	304.6409962	French Polynesia	HB1635-1636.5	304.620943	Germany
HB1525	304.640998(1-8)	Polar regions	HB1639-1640	304.620945	Italy
HB1526	304.6409982	Greenland	HB1643-1644	304.6209493	Belgium
HB1528	304.64091724	Developing countries	HB1645-1646	304.6209492	Netherlands
HB1531-1737	304.62	Age distribution	HB1646.5	304.62094935	Luxembourg
HB1541-1737	304.6209	By place	HB1647-1648	304.620947	European Russia
HB1545-1546	304.620973	United States	HB1648.3	304.62094897	Finland
HB1565	304.62097(4-9)	By state	HB1648.7	304.6209438	Poland
HB1567	304.62097(4-9)	By city	HB1651-1652	304.6209489	Denmark
HB1569-1570	304.620971	Canada	HB1653-1654	304.62094912	Iceland
HB1571-1572	304.620972	Mexico	HB1655-1656	304.6209481	Norway
HB1575-1576	304.62097282	Belize	HB1657-1658	304.6209485	Sweden
HB1577-1578	304.62097286	Costa Rica	HB1659-1660	304.620946	Spain
HB1579	304.62097281	Guatemala	HB1661-1662	304.6209469	Portugal
HB1580	304.62097283	Honduras	HB1663-1664	304.6209494	Switzerland
HB1581	304.62097285	Nicaragua	HB1666.5	304.62094965	Albania
HB1582-1583	304.62097287	Panama	HB1667-1668	304.62094977	Bulgaria
HB1583.5	304.620972875	Panama Canal Zone	HB1668.5	304.6209497	Yugoslavia
HB1584	304.62097284	El Salvador	HB1671-1672	304.6209498	Romania
HB1587-1588	304.62097296	Bahamas	HB1672.5	304.6209495	Greece
HB1589-1590	304.62097291	Cuba	HB1673.4	304.6209561	Turkey
HB1591	304.62097294	Haiti	HB1673.5	304.62095645	Cyprus
HB1592	304.62097293	Dominican Republic	HB1673.7	304.62095691	Syria
HB1593-1594	304.62097292	Jamaica	HB1673.9	304.62095692	Lebanon
HB1595-1596	304.62097295	Puerto Rico	HB1674	304.62095694	Israel/Palestine
HB1596.3	304.6209729722	Virgin Islands of the U.S.	HB1674.3	304.62095695	Jordan
HB1596.57	304.620972981	Barbados	HB1674.7	304.6209538	Saudi Arabia
HB1596.72	304.620972973	Anguilla	HB1674.9-1675	304.62095332	Yemen
HB1596.74	304.62097294	Antigua/Barbuda	HB1675.3	304.62095353	Oman
HB1596.76	304.620975	Montserrat	HB1675.5	304.62095357	United Arab Emirates
HB1596.78	304.620972973	Saint Kitts-Nevia	HB1675.7	304.62095363	Qatar
HB1596.93	304.6209729841	Dominica	HB1675.9	304.62095365	Bahrein
HB1596.95	304.6209729845	Grenada	HB1676	304.62095367	Kuwait
HB1596.97	304.6209729843	Saint Lucia	HB1676.3	304.6209567	Iraq
HB1596.99	304.6209729844	Saint Vincent/Grenadines	HB1676.4	304.620955	Iran
HB1597	304.620972983	Trinidad/Tobago	HB1676.6	304.6209581	Afghanistan
HB1597.35	304.620972986	Aruba	HB1676.7	304.6209591	Burma
HB1597.36	304.620972986	Bonaire	HB1676.8	304.62095493	Sri Lanka
HB1597.37	304.620972986	Curacao	HB1676.9	304.62095496	Nepal
HB1597.38	304.620972977	Saba	HB1679-1680	304.620954	India
HB1597.385	304.620972977	Saint Eustatius	HB1680.3	304.62095498	Bhutan
HB1597.39	304.620972977	Saint Martin	HB1680.5	304.62095491	Pakistan
HB1597.7	304.620972976	Guadeloupe	HB1680.6	304.62095492	Bangladesh
HB1597.9	304.620972982	Martinique	HB1684.3	304.6209596	Cambodia
HB1599-1600	304.620982	Argentina	HB1684.4	304.6209594	Laos
HB1601-1602	304.620984	Bolivia	HB1684.5	304.6209597	Vietnam
HB1603-1604	304.620981	Brazil	HB1684.55	304.6209593	Thailand
HB1605-1606	304.620983	Chile	HB1684.6	304.6209595	Malaysia
HB1607-1608	304.6209861	Colombia	HB1687-1688	304.6209598	Indonesia
HB1609-1610	304.6209866	Ecuador	HB1689-1690	304.6209599	Philippine Islands
HB1612.3	304.6209881	Guyana	HB1691-1692	304.620952	Japan
HB1612.5	304.6209883	Suriname	HB1692.5-.6	304.6209519	Korea/North Korea
HB1612.7	304.6209882	French Guiana	HB1692.8	304.6209517	Mongolia
HB1613-1614	304.6209892	Paraguay	HB1694	304.620951	China
HB1615-1616	304.620985	Peru	HB1695	304.62095126	Macao
HB1617-1618	304.6209895	Uruguay	HB1696	304.620951249	Taiwan
HB1619-1620	304.620987	Venezuela	HB1697	304.62095125	Hong Kong
HB1625-1626	304.620942(9)	England/Wales	HB1701.3	304.620964	Morocco
HB1627-1628	304.6209411	Scotland	HB1701.4	304.620965	Algeria
HB1628.5	304.6209416	Northern Ireland	HB1701.5	304.6209611	Tunisia
HB1629-1630	304.6209417	Irish Republic	HB1701.6	304.6209612	Libya
HB1631-1632	304.6209436	Austria	HB1701.7	304.620962	Egypt
HB1632.3	304.6209437	Czechoslovakia	HB1701.8	304.6209624	Sudan
HB1632.5	304.6209439	Hungary	HB1702	304.620963	Ethiopia
HB1632.9	304.620943648	Liechtenstein	HB1702.2	304.62096773	Somalia
HB1633-1634	304.620944	France	HB1702.3	304.62096771	Djibouti

LC	Dewey	Descriptor	LC	Dewey	Descriptor
HB1702.5	304.62096762	Kenya	HB1733.8	304.62099614	Western Samoa
HB1702.6	304.62096761	Uganda	HB1733.9	304.6209962	French Polynesia
HB1702.7	304.620967571	Rwanda	HB1735	304.620998(1-8)	Polar regions
HB1702.8	304.620967572	Burundi	HB1736	304.6209982	Greenland
HB1702.9	304.6209678	Tanzania	HB1741-1947	304.6	Sex
HB1703	304.6209679	Mozambique	HB1751-1947	304.609(4-9)	By place
HB1703.2	304.6209691	Madagascar	HB1755-1756	304.60973	United States
HB1703.4	304.620968	South Africa	HB1775	304.6097(4-9)	By state
HB1703.5	304.6209689	Zimbabwe/Zambia/Malawi	HB1777	304.6097(4-9)	By city
HB1703.6	304.62096894	Zambia	HB1779-1780	304.60971	Canada
HB1703.7	304.62096885	Lesotho	HB1781-1782	304.60972	Mexico
HB1703.8	304.62096887	Swaziland	HB1785-1786	304.6097282	Belize
HB1703.9	304.62096883	Botswana	HB1787-1888	304.6097286	Costa Rica
HB1704	304.62096897	Malawi	HB1789	304.6097281	Guatemala
HB1704.2	304.62096881	Namibia	HB1790	304.6097283	Honduras
HB1704.4	304.6209673	Angola	HB1791	304.6097285	Nicaragua
HB1704.5	304.62096751	Zaire	HB1792-1793	304.6097287	Panama
HB1704.6	304.62096718	Equatorial Guinea	HB1793.5	304.60972875	Panama Canal Zone
HB1704.7	304.62096715	Sao Tome/Principe	HB1794	304.6097284	El Salvador
HB1704.8	304.6209672	French Equatorial Africa	HB1797-1798	304.6097296	Bahamas
HB1704.9	304.62096721	Gabon	HB1799-1800	304.6097291	Cuba
HB1705	304.62096724	Congo	HB1801	304.6097294	Haiti
HB1705.2	304.62096741	Central African Republic	HB1802	304.6097293	Dominican Republic
HB1705.3	304.62096743	Chad	HB1803-1804	304.6097292	Jamaica
HB1705.4	304.62096711	Cameroon	HB1805-1806	304.6097295	Puerto Rico
HB1705.7	304.62096683	Benin (Dahomey)	HB1806.3	304.609729722	Virgin Islands of the U.S.
HB1705.8	304.62096681	Togo	HB1806.57	304.60972981	Barbados
HB1705.9	304.62096626	Niger	HB1806.72	304.60972973	Anguilla
HB1706	304.62096668	Ivory Coast	HB1806.74	304.60972974	Antigua/Barbuda
HB1706.2	304.62096652	Guinea-Bissau	HB1806.76	304.60972975	Montserrat
HB1706.3	304.62096623	Mali	HB1806.78	304.60972973	Saint Kitts-Nevia
HB1706.4	304.62096625	Burkina Faso	HB1806.93	304.609729841	Dominica
HB1706.5	304.6209663	Senegal	HB1806.95	304.609729845	Grenada
HB1706.6	304.6209661	Mauritania	HB1806.97	304.609729843	Saint Lucia
HB1706.7	304.6209669	Nigeria	HB1806.99	304.609729844	Saint Vincent/Grenadines
HB1706.8	304.6209667	Ghana	HB1807	304.60972983	Trinidad/Tobago
HB1706.9	304.6209664	Sierra Leone	HB1807.35	304.60972986	Aruba
HB1707	304.62096651	Gambia	HB1807.36	304.60972986	Bonaire
HB1707.2	304.62096662	Liberia	HB1807.37	304.60972986	Curacao
HB1707.3	304.62096657	Guinea-Bissau	HB1807.38	304.60972977	Saba
HB1707.4	304.6209648	Spanish Sahara	HB1807.385	304.60972977	Saint Eustatius
HB1707.5	304.62094699	Azores	HB1807.39	304.60972977	Saint Martin
HB1708	304.62097299	Bermuda	HB1807.7	304.60972976	Guadeloupe
HB1708.5	304.62094698	Madeira Islands	HB1807.9	304.60972982	Martinique
HB1709	304.6209649	Canary Islands	HB1809-1810	304.60982	Argentina
HB1709.5	304.62096658	Cape Verde Islands	HB1811-1812	304.60984	Bolivia
HB1710	304.6209973	St. Helena	HB1813-1814	304.60981	Brazil
HB1710.5	304.6209973	Tristan da Cunha	HB1815-1816	304.60983	Chile
HB1711	304.6209971	Falkland Islands	HB1817-1818	304.609861	Colombia
HB1711.5	304.62095495	Maldive Islands	HB1819-1820	304.609866	Ecuador
HB1712	304.6209696	Seychelles	HB1822.3	304.609881	Guyana
HB1712.5	304.6209694	Comoro Islands	HB1822.5	304.609883	Suriname
HB1713	304.62096982	Mauritius	HB1822.7	304.609882	French Guiana
HB1713.5	304.62096981	Reunion	HB1823-1824	304.609892	Paraguay
HB1714	304.6209699	Kerguelen Islands	HB1825-1826	304.60985	Peru
HB1715-1716	304.620994	Australia	HB1827-1828	304.609895	Uruguay
HB1732.5	304.620993	New Zealand	HB1829-1830	304.60987	Venezuela
HB1732.7	304.6209967	Guam	HB1835-1836	304.60942(9)	England/Wales
HB1732.8	304.6209953	Papua New Guinea	HB1837-1838	304.609411	Scotland
HB1732.9	304.62099681	Kiribati (Gilbert Islands)	HB1838.5	304.609416	Northern Ireland
HB1733	304.62099593	Solomon Islands	HB1839-1840	304.609417	Irish Republic
HB1733.3	304.62099597	New Caledonia	HB1841-1842	304.609436	Austria
HB1733.4	304.62099595	Vanuatu	HB1842.3	304.609437	Czechoslovakia
HB1733.5	304.62099611	Fiji Islands	HB1842.5	304.609439	Hungary
HB1733.6	304.62099612	Tonga	HB1842.9	304.60943648	Liechtenstein
HB1733.65	304.62099623	Cook Islands	HB1843-1844	304.60944	France
HB1733.7	304.62099613	American Samoa	HB1844.5	304.60944949	Monaco

LC	Dewey	Descriptor	LC	Dewey	Descriptor
HB1845-1846.5	304.60943	Germany	HB1912.6	304.6096761	Uganda
HB1849-1850	304.60945	Italy	HB1912.7	304.60967571	Rwanda
HB1853-1854	304.609493	Belgium	HB1912.8	304.60967572	Burundi
HB1855-1856	304.609492	Netherlands	HB1912.9	304.609678	Tanzania
HB1856.5	304.6094935	Luxembourg	HB1913	304.609679	Mozambique
HB1857-1858	304.60947	European Russia	HB1913.2	304.609691	Madagascar
HB1858.3	304.6094897	Finland	HB1913.4	304.60968	South Africa
HB1858.7	304.609438	Poland	HB1913.5	304.609689	Zimbabwe/Zambia/Malawi
HB1861-1862	304.609489	Denmark	HB1913.6	304.6096894	Zambia
HB1863-1864	304.6094912	Iceland	HB1913.7	304.6096885	Lesotho
HB1865-1866	304.609481	Norway	HB1913.8	304.6096887	Swaziland
HB1867-1868	304.609485	Sweden	HB1913.9	304.6096883	Botswana
HB1869-1870	304.60946	Spain	HB1914	304.6096897	Malawi
HB1871-1872	304.609469	Portugal	HB1914.2	304.6096881	Namibia
HB1873-1874	304.609494	Switzerland	HB1914.4	304.609673	Angola
HB1876.5	304.6094965	Albania	HB1914.5	304.6096751	Zaire
HB1877-1878	304.6094977	Bulgaria	HB1914.6	304.6096718	Equatorial Guinea
HB1878.5	304.609497	Yugoslavia	HB1914.7	304.6096715	Sao Tome/Principe
HB1881-1882	304.609498	Romania	HB1914.8	304.609672	French Equatorial Africa
HB1882.5	304.609495	Greece	HB1914.9	304.6096721	Gabon
HB1883.4	304.69561	Turkey	HB1915	304.6096724	Congo
HB1883.5	304.6095645	Cyprus	HB1915.2	304.6096741	Central African Republic
HB1883.7	304.6095691	Syria	HB1915.3	304.6096743	Chad
HB1883.9	304.6095692	Lebanon	HB1915.4	304.6096711	Cameroon
HB1884	304.6095694	Israel/Palestine	HB1915.7	304.6096683	Benin (Dahomey)
HB1884.3	304.6095695	Jordan	HB1915.8	304.6096681	Togo
HB1884.7	304.609538	Saudi Arabia	HB1915.9	304.6096626	Niger
HB1884.9-1885	304.6095332	Yemen	HB1916	304.6096668	Ivory Coast
HB1885.3	304.6095353	Oman	HB1916.2	304.6096652	Guinea-Bissau
HB1885.5	304.6095357	United Arab Emirates	HB1916.3	304.6096623	Mali
HB1885.7	304.6095363	Qatar	HB1916.4	304.6096625	Burkina Faso
HB1885.9	304.6095365	Bahrein	HB1916.5	304.609663	Senegal
HB1886	304.6095367	Kuwait	HB1916.6	304.609661	Mauritania
HB1886.3	304.609567	Iraq	HB1916.7	304.609669	Nigeria
HB1886.4	304.60955	Iran	HB1916.8	304.609667	Ghana
HB1886.6	304.609581	Afghanistan	HB1916.9	304.609664	Sierra Leone
HB1886.7	304.609591	Burma	HB1917	304.6096651	Gambia
HB1886.8	304.6095493	Sri Lanka	HB1917.2	304.6096662	Liberia
HB1886.9	304.6095496	Nepal	HB1917.3	304.6096657	Guinea-Bissau
HB1889-1890	304.60954	India	HB1917.4	304.609648	Spanish Sahara
HB1890.3	304.6095498	Bhutan	HB1917.5	304.6094699	Azores
HB1890.5	304.6095491	Pakistan	HB1918	304.6097299	Bermuda
HB1890.6	304.6095492	Bangladesh	HB1918.5	304.6094698	Madeira Islands
HB1894.3	304.609596	Cambodia	HB1919	304.609649	Canary Islands
HB1894.4	304.609594	Laos	HB1919.5	304.6096658	Cape Verde Islands
HB1894.5	304.609597	Vietnam	HB1920	304.609973	St. Helena
HB1894.55	304.609593	Thailand	HB1920.5	304.609973	Tristan da Cunha
HB1894.6	304.609595	Malaysia	HB1921	304.609971	Falkland Islands
HB1897-1898	304.609598	Indonesia	HB1921.5	304.6095495	Maldive Islands
HB1899-1900	304.609599	Philippine Islands	HB1922	304.609696	Seychelles
HB1901-1902	304.60952	Japan	HB1922.5	304.609694	Comoro Islands
HB1902.5-.6	304.609519	Korea/North Korea	HB1923	304.6096982	Mauritius
HB1902.8	304.609517	Mongolia	HB1923.5	304.6096981	Reunion
HB1904	304.60951	China	HB1924	304.609699	Kerguelen Islands
HB1905	304.6095126	Macao	HB1925-1926	304.60994	Australia
HB1906	304.60951249	Taiwan	HB1942.5	304.60993	New Zealand
HB1907	304.6095125	Hong Kong	HB1942.7	304.609967	Guam
HB1911.3	304.60964	Morocco	HB1942.8	304.609953	Papua New Guinea
HB1911.4	304.60965	Algeria	HB1942.9	304.6099681	Kiribati (Gilbert Islands)
HB1911.5	304.609611	Tunisia	HB1943	304.6099593	Solomon Islands
HB1911.6	304.609612	Libya	HB1943.3	304.6099597	New Caledonia
HB1911.7	304.60962	Egypt	HB1943.4	304.6099595	Vanuatu
HB1911.8	304.609624	Sudan	HB1943.5	304.6099611	Fiji Islands
HB1912	304.60963	Ethiopia	HB1943.6	304.6099612	Tonga
HB1912.2	304.6096773	Somalia	HB1943.65	304.6099623	Cook Islands
HB1912.3	304.6096771	Djibouti	HB1943.7	304.6099613	American Samoa
HB1912.5	304.6096762	Kenya	HB1943.8	304.6099614	Western Samoa

LC	Dewey	Descriptor	LC	Dewey	Descriptor
HB1943.9	304.609962	French Polynesia	HB2052.5	304.609439	Hungary
HB1945	304.60998(1-8)	Polar regions	HB2052.9	304.60943648	Liechtenstein
HB1946	304.609982	Greenland	HB2053-2054	304.60944	France
HB1951-2577	304.(6/8)	Population geography/ Migration	HB2054.5	304.60944949	Monaco
HB1952	304.809	Internal migration	HB2045-2056.5	304.60943	Germany
HB1953	304.61	Population density	HB2059-2060	304.60945	Italy
HB1955-1956	307.2	Urban/Rural migration	HB2063-2064	304.609493	Belgium
HB1961-2151	304.609	Population geography, By place	HB2065-2066	304.609492	Netherlands
			HB2066.5	304.6094935	Luxembourg
HB1965-1966	304.60973	United States	HB2067-2068	304.60947	European Russia
HB1985	304.6097(4-9)	By state	HB2068.3	304.6094897	Finland
HB1987	304.6097(4-9)	By city	HB2068.7	304.609438	Poland
HB1989-1990	304.60971	Canada	HB2071-2072	304.609489	Denmark
HB1991-1992	304.60972	Mexico	HB2073-2074	304.6094912	Iceland
HB1995-1996	304.6097282	Belize	HB2075-2076	304.609481	Norway
HB1997-1998	304.6097286	Costa Rica	HB2077-2078	304.609485	Sweden
HB1999	304.6097281	Guatemala	HB2079-2080	304.60946	Spain
HB2000	304.6097283	Honduras	HB2081-2082	304.609469	Portugal
HB2001	304.6097285	Nicaragua	HB2083-2084	304.609494	Switzerland
HB2002-2003	304.6097287	Panama	HB2086.5	304.6094965	Albania
HB2003.5	304.60972875	Panama Canal Zone	HB2087-2088	304.6094977	Bulgaria
HB2004	304.6097284	El Salvador	HB2088.5	304.609497	Yugoslavia
HB2007-2008	304.6097296	Bahamas	HB2091-2092	304.609498	Romania
HB2009-2010	304.6097291	Cuba	HB2092.5	304.609495	Greece
HB2011	304.6097294	Haiti	HB2093.4	304.609561	Turkey
HB2012	304.6097293	Dominican Republic	HB2093.5	304.6095645	Cyprus
HB2013-2014	304.6097292	Jamaica	HB2093.7	304.6095691	Syria
HB2015-2016	304.6097295	Puerto Rico	HB2093.9	304.6095692	Lebanon
HB2016.3	304.609729722	Virgin Islands of the U.S.	HB2094	304.6095694	Israel/Palestine
HB2016.57	304.60972981	Barbados	HB2094.3	304.6095695	Jordan
HB2016.72	304.60972973	Anguilla	HB2094.7	304.609538	Saudi Arabia
HB2016.74	304.60972974	Antigua/Barbuda	HB2094.9-2095	304.6095332	Yemen
HB2016.76	304.60972975	Montserrat	HB2095.3	304.6095353	Oman
HB2016.78	304.60972973	Saint Kitts-Nevia	HB2095.5	304.6095357	United Arab Emirates
HB2016.93	304.609729841	Dominica	HB2095.7	304.6095363	Qatar
HB2016.95	304.609729845	Grenada	HB2095.9	304.6095365	Bahrein
HB2016.97	304.609729843	Saint Lucia	HB2096	304.6095367	Kuwait
HB2016.99	304.609729844	Saint Vincent/Grenadines	HB2096.3	304.609567	Iraq
HB2017	304.60972983	Trinidad/Tobago	HB2096.4	304.60955	Iran
HB2017.35	304.60972986	Aruba	HB2096.6	304.609581	Afghanistan
HB2017.36	304.60972986	Bonaire	HB2096.7	304.609591	Burma
HB2017.37	304.60972986	Curacao	HB2096.8	304.6095493	Sri Lanka
HB2017.385	304.60972977	Saba	HB2096.9	304.6095496	Nepal
HB2017.385	304.60972977	Saint Eustatius	HB2099-2100	304.60954	India
HB2017.39	304.60972977	Saint Martin	HB2100.3	304.6095498	Bhutan
HB2017.7	304.60972976	Guadeloupe	HB2100.5	304.6095491	Pakistan
HB2017.9	304.60972982	Martinique	HB2100.6	304.6095492	Bangladesh
HB2019-2020	304.60982	Argentina	HB2104.3	304.609596	Cambodia
HB2021-2022	304.60984	Bolivia	HB2104.4	304.609594	Laos
HB2023-2024	304.60981	Brazil	HB2104.5	304.609597	Vietnam
HB2025-2026	304.60983	Chile	HB2104.55	304.609593	Thailand
HB2027-2028	304.609861	Colombia	HB2104.6	304.609595	Malaysia
HB2029-2030	304.609866	Ecuador	HB2107-2108	304.609598	Indonesia
HB2032.3	304.609881	Guyana	HB2109-2110	304.609599	Philippine Islands
HB2032.5	304.609883	Suriname	HB2111-2112	304.60952	Japan
HB2032.7	304.609882	French Guiana	HB2112.5-.6	304.609519	Korea/North Korea
HB2033-2034	304.609892	Paraguay	HB2112.8	304.609517	Mongolia
HB2035-2036	304.60985	Peru	HB2114	304.60951	China
HB2037-2038	304.609895	Uruguay	HB2115	304.6095126	Macao
HB2039-2040	304.60987	Venezuela	HB2116	304.60951249	Taiwan
HB2045-2046	304.60942(9)	England/Wales	HB2117	304.6095125	Hong Kong
HB2047-2048	304.609411	Scotland	HB2121.3	304.60964	Morocco
HB2048.5	304.609416	Northern Ireland	HB2121.4	304.60965	Algeria
HB2049-2050	304.609417	Irish Republic	HB2121.5	304.609611	Tunisia
HB2051-2052	304.609436	Austria	HB2121.6	304.609612	Libya
HB2052.3	304.609437	Czechoslovakia	HB2121.7	304.60962	Egypt
			HB2121.8	304.609624	Sudan

LC	Dewey	Descriptor	LC	Dewey	Descriptor
HB2122	304.60963	Ethiopia	HB2153.6	304.6099612	Tonga
HB2122.2	304.6096773	Somalia	HB2153.65	304.6099623	Cook Islands
HB2122.3	304.6096771	Djibouti	HB2153.7	304.6099613	American Samoa
HB2122.5	304.6096762	Kenya	HB2153.8	304.6099614	Western Samoa
HB2122.6	304.6096761	Uganda	HB2153.9	304.609962	French Polynesia
HB2122.7	304.60967571	Rwanda	HB2155	304.60998(1-8)	Polar regions
HB2122.8	304.60967572	Burundi	HB2156	304.609982	Greenland
HB2122.9	304.609678	Tanzania	HB2160	304.6091724	Developing countries
HB2123	304.609679	Mozambique	HB2161-2367	307.216	Urban population
HB2123.2	304.609691	Madagascar	HB2171-2367	307.21609	By place
HB2123.4	304.60968	South Africa	HB2175-2176	307.2160973	United States
HB2123.5	304.609689	Zimbabwe/Zambia/Malawi	HB2195	307.216097(4-9)	By state
HB2123.6	304.6096894	Zambia	HB2197	307.216097(4-9)	By city
HB2123.7	304.6096885	Lesotho	HB2199-2200	307.2160971	Canada
HB2123.8	304.6096887	Swaziland	HB2201-2202	307.2160972	Mexico
HB2123.9	304.6096883	Botswana	HB2205-2206	307.216097282	Belize
HB2124	304.6096897	Malawi	HB2207-2208	307.216097286	Costa Rica
HB2124.2	304.6096881	Namibia	HB2209	307.216097281	Guatemala
HB2124.4	304.609673	Angola	HB2210	307.216097283	Honduras
HB2124.5	304.6096751	Zaire	HB2211	307.216097285	Nicaragua
HB2124.6	304.6096718	Equatorial Guinea	HB2212-2213	307.216097287	Panama
HB2124.7	304.6096715	Sao Tome/Principe	HB2213.5	307.2160972875	Panama Canal Zone
HB2124.8	304.609672	French Equatorial Africa	HB2214	307.216097284	El Salvador
HB2124.9	304.6096721	Gabon	HB2217-2218	307.216097296	Bahamas
HB2125	304.6096724	Congo	HB2219-2220	307.216097291	Cuba
HB2125.2	304.6096741	Central African Republic	HB2221	307.216097294	Haiti
HB2125.3	304.6096743	Chad	HB2222	307.216097293	Dominican Republic
HB2125.4	304.6096711	Cameroon	HB2223-2224	307.216097292	Jamaica
HB2125.7	304.6096683	Benin (Dahomey)	HB2225-2226	307.216097295	Puerto Rico
HB2125.8	304.6096681	Togo	HB2226.3	307.21609729722	Virgin Islands of the U.S.
HB2125.9	304.6096626	Niger	HB2226.57	307.2160972981	Barbados
HB2126	304.6096668	Ivory Coast	HB2226.72	307.2160972973	Anguilla
HB2126.2	304.6096652	Guinea-Bissau	HB2226.74	307.2160972974	Antigua/Barbuda
HB2126.3	304.6096623	Mali	HB2226.76	307.2160972975	Montserrat
HB2126.4	304.6096625	Burkina Faso	HB2226.78	307.2160972973	Saint Kitts-Nevis
HB2126.5	304.609663	Senegal	HB2226.93	307.21609729841	Dominica
HB2126.6	304.609661	Mauritania	HB2226.95	307.21609729845	Grenada
HB2126.7	304.609669	Nigeria	HB2226.97	307.21609729843	Saint Lucia
HB2126.8	304.609667	Ghana	HB2226.99	307.21609729844	Saint Vincent/Grenadines
HB2126.9	304.6096664	Sierra Leone	HB2227	307.2160972983	Trinidad/Tobago
HB2127	304.6096651	Gambia	HB2227.35	307.2160972986	Aruba
HB2127.2	304.6096662	Liberia	HB2227.36	307.2160972986	Bonaire
HB2127.3	304.6096657	Guinea-Bissau	HB2227.37	307.2160972986	Curacao
HB2127.4	304.609648	Spanish Sahara	HB2227.38	307.2160972977	Saba
HB2127.5	304.6094699	Azores	HB2227.385	307.2160972977	Saint Eustatius
HB2128	304.6097299	Bermuda	HB2227.39	307.2160972977	Saint Martin
HB2128.5	304.6094698	Madeira Islands	HB2227.7	307.2160972976	Guadeloupe
HB2129	304.609649	Canary Islands	HB2227.9	307.2160972982	Martinique
HB2129.5	304.6096658	Cape Verde Islands	HB2229-2230	307.2160982	Argentina
HB2130	304.609973	St. Helena	HB2231-2232	307.2160984	Bolivia
HB2130.5	304.609973	Tristan da Cunha	HB2233-2234	307.2160981	Brazil
HB2131	304.609971	Falkland Islands	HB2235-2236	307.2160983	Chile
HB2131.5	304.6095495	Maldive Islands	HB2237-2238	307.21609861	Colombia
HB2132	304.609696	Seychelles	HB2239-2240	307.21609866	Ecuador
HB2132.5	304.609694	Comoro Islands	HB2242.3	307.21609881	Guyana
HB2133	304.6096982	Mauritius	HB2242.5	307.21609883	Suriname
HB2133.5	304.6096981	Reunion	HB2242.7	307.21609882	French Guiana
HB2134	304.609699	Kerguelen Islands	HB2243-2244	307.21609892	Paraguay
HB2135-2136	304.60994	Australia	HB2245-2246	307.2160985	Peru
HB2152.5	304.60993	New Zealand	HB2247-2248	307.21609895	Uruguay
HB2152.7	304.609967	Guam	HB2249-2250	307.2160987	Venezuela
HB2152.8	304.609953	Papua New Guinea	HB2255-2256	307.2160942(9)	England/Wales
HB2152.9	304.6099681	Kiribati (Gilbert Islands)	HB2257-2258	307.21609411	Scotland
HB2153	304.6099593	Solomon Islands	HB2258.5	307.21609416	Northern Ireland
HB2153.3	304.6099597	New Caledonia	HB2259-2260	307.21609417	Irish Republic
HB2153.4	304.6099595	Vanuatu	HB2261-2262	307.21609436	Austria
HB2153.5	304.6099611	Fiji Islands	HB2262.3	307.21609437	Czechoslovakia

LC	Dewey	Descriptor
HB2262.5	307.21609439	Hungary
HB2262.9	307.2160943648	Liechtenstein
HB2263-2264	307.2160944	France
HB2264.5	307.2160944949	Monaco
HB2265-2266.5	307.2160943	Germany
HB2269-2270	307.2160945	Italy
HB2273-2274	307.21609493	Belgium
HB2275-2276	307.21609492	Netherlands
HB2276.5	307.216094935	Luxembourg
HB2277-2278	307.2160947	European Russia
HB2278.3	307.216094897	Finland
HB2278.7	307.21609438	Poland
HB2281-2282	307.21609489	Denmark
HB2283-2284	307.216094912	Iceland
HB2285-2286	307.21609481	Norway
HB2287-2288	307.21609485	Sweden
HB2289-2290	307.21609469	Spain
HB2291-2292	307.21609469	Portugal
HB2293-2294	307.21609494	Switzerland
HB2296.5	307.216094965	Albania
HB2297-2298	307.216094977	Bulgaria
HB2298.5	307.21609497	Yugoslavia
HB2301-2302	307.21609498	Romania
HB2302.5	307.21609495	Greece
HB2303.4	307.21609561	Turkey
HB2303.5	307.216095645	Cyprus
HB2303.7	307.216095691	Syria
HB2303.9	307.216095692	Lebanon
HB2304	307.216095694	Israel/Palestine
HB2304.3	307.216095695	Jordan
HB2304.7	307.21609538	Saudi Arabia
HB2304.9-2305	307.216095332	Yemen
HB2305.3	307.216095353	Oman
HB2305.5	307.216095357	United Arab Emirates
HB2305.7	307.216095363	Qatar
HB2305.9	307.216095365	Bahrein
HB2306	307.216095367	Kuwait
HB2306.3	307.21609567	Iraq
HB2306.4	307.2160955	Iran
HB2306.6	307.21609581	Afghanistan
HB2306.7	307.21609591	Burma
HB2306.8	307.216095493	Sri Lanka
HB2306.9	307.216095496	Nepal
HB2309-2310	307.2160954	India
HB2310.3	307.216095498	Bhutan
HB2310.5	307.216095491	Pakistan
HB2310.6	307.216095492	Bangladesh
HB2314.3	307.21609596	Cambodia
HB2314.4	307.21609594	Laos
HB2314.5	307.21609597	Vietnam
HB2314.55	307.21609593	Thailand
HB2314.6	307.21609595	Malaysia
HB2317-2318	307.21609598	Indonesia
HB2319-2320	307.21609599	Philippine Islands
HB2321-2322	307.2160952	Japan
HB2322.5-.6	307.21609519	Korea/North Korea
HB2322.8	307.21609517	Mongolia
HB2324	307.2160951	China
HB2325	307.216095126	Macao
HB2326	307.2160951249	Taiwan
HB2327	307.216095125	Hong Kong
HB2331.3	307.2160964	Morocco
HB2331.4	307.2160965	Algeria
HB2331.5	307.21609611	Tunisia
HB2331.6	307.21609612	Libya
HB2331.7	307.2160962	Egypt
HB2331.8	307.21609624	Sudan
HB2332	307.2160963	Ethiopia
HB2332.2	307.216096773	Somalia
HB2332.3	307.216096771	Djibouti
HB2332.5	307.216096762	Kenya
HB2332.6	307.216096761	Uganda
HB2332.7	307.2160967571	Rwanda
HB2332.8	307.2160967572	Burundi
HB2332.9	307.21609678	Tanzania
HB2333	307.21609679	Mozambique
HB2333.2	307.21609691	Madagascar
HB2333.4	307.2160968	South Africa
HB2333.5	307.21609689	Zimbabwe/Zambia/Malawi
HB2333.6	307.216096894	Zambia
HB2333.7	307.216096885	Lesotho
HB2333.8	307.216096887	Swaziland
HB2333.9	307.216096883	Botswana
HB2334	307.216096897	Malawi
HB2334.2	307.216096881	Namibia
HB2334.4	307.21609673	Angola
HB2334.5	307.216096751	Zaire
HB2334.6	307.216096718	Equatorial Guinea
HB2334.7	307.216096715	Sao Tome/Principe
HB2334.8	307.21609672	French Equatorial Africa
HB2334.9	307.216096721	Gabon
HB2335	307.216096724	Congo
HB2335.2	307.216096741	Central African Republic
HB2335.3	307.216096743	Chad
HB2335.4	307.216096711	Cameroon
HB2335.7	307.216096683	Benin (Dahomey)
HB2335.8	307.216096681	Togo
HB2335.9	307.216096626	Niger
HB2336	307.216096668	Ivory Coast
HB2336.2	307.216096652	Guinea-Bissau
HB2336.3	307.216096623	Mali
HB2336.4	307.216096625	Burkina Faso
HB2336.5	307.21609663	Senegal
HB2336.6	307.21609661	Mauritania
HB2336.7	307.21609669	Nigeria
HB2336.8	307.21609667	Ghana
HB2336.9	307.21609664	Sierra Leone
HB2337	307.216096651	Gambia
HB2337.2	307.216096662	Liberia
HB2337.3	307.216096657	Guinea-Bissau
HB2337.4	307.21609648	Spanish Sahara
HB2337.5	307.216094699	Azores
HB2338	307.216097299	Bermuda
HB2338.5	307.216094698	Madeira Islands
HB2339	307.21609649	Canary Islands
HB2339.5	307.216096658	Cape Verde Islands
HB2340	307.21609973	St. Helena
HB2340.5	307.21609973	Tristan da Cunha
HB2341	307.21609971	Falkland Islands
HB2341.5	307.216095495	Maldive Islands
HB2342	307.21609696	Seychelles
HB2342.5	307.21609694	Comoro Islands
HB2343	307.216096982	Mauritius
HB2343.5	307.216096981	Reunion
HB2344	307.21609699	Kerguelen Islands
HB2345-2346	307.2160994	Australia
HB2362.5	307.2160993	New Zealand
HB2362.7	307.21609967	Guam
HB2362.8	307.21609953	Papua New Guinea
HB2362.9	307.216099681	Kiribati (Gilbert Islands)
HB2363	307.216099593	Solomon Islands
HB2363.3	307.216099597	New Caledonia
HB2363.4	307.216099595	Vanuatu
HB2363.5	307.216099611	Fiji Islands

LC	Dewey	Descriptor	LC	Dewey	Descriptor
HB2363.6	307.216099612	Tonga	HB2472.9	307.2120943648	Liechtenstein
HB2363.65	307.216099623	Cook Islands	HB2473-2474	307.2120944	France
HB2363.7	307.216099613	American Samoa	HB2474.5	307.2120944949	Monaco
HB2363.8	307.216099614	Western Samoa	HB2475-2476.5	307.2120943	Germany
HB2363.9	307.21609962	French Polynesia	HB2479-2480	307.2120945	Italy
HB2365	307.2160998(1-8)	Polar regions	HB2483-2484	307.21209493	Belgium
HB2366	307.21609982	Greenland	HB2485-2486	307.21209492	Netherlands
HB2371-2577	307.212	Rural population	HB2486.5	307.212094935	Luxembourg
HB2381-2577	307.21209(4-9)	By place	HB2487-2488	307.2120947	European Russia
HB2385-2386	307.2120973	United States	HB2488.3	307.212094897	Finland
HB2405	307.212097(4-9)	By state	HB2488.7	307.21209438	Poland
HB2407	307.212097(4-9)	By city	HB2491-2492	307.21209489	Denmark
HB2409-2410	307.2120971	Canada	HB2493-2494	307.212094912	Iceland
HB2411-2412	307.2120972	Mexico	HB2495-2496	307.21209481	Norway
HB2415-2416	307.212097282	Belize	HB2497-2498	307.21209485	Sweden
HB2417-2418	307.212097286	Costa Rica	HB2499-2500	307.2120946	Spain
HB2419	307.212097281	Guatemala	HB2501-2502	307.21209469	Portugal
HB2420	307.212097283	Honduras	HB2503-2504	307.21209494	Switzerland
HB2421	307.212097285	Nicaragua	HB2506.5	307.212094965	Albania
HB2422-2423	307.212097287	Panama	HB2507-2508	307.212094977	Bulgaria
HB2423.5	307.2120972875	Panama Canal Zone	HB2508.5	307.21209497	Yugoslavia
HB2424	307.212097284	El Salvador	HB2511-2512	307.21209498	Romania
HB2427-2428	307.212097296	Bahamas	HB2512.5	307.21209495	Greece
HB2429-2430	307.212097291	Cuba	HB2513.4	307.21209561	Turkey
HB2431	307.212097294	Haiti	HB2513.5	307.212095645	Cyprus
HB2432	307.212097293	Dominican Republic	HB2513.7	307.212095691	Syria
HB2433-2434	307.212097292	Jamaica	HB2513.9	307.212095692	Lebanon
HB2435-2436	307.212097295	Puerto Rico	HB2514	307.212095694	Israel/Palestine
HB2436.3	307.21209729722	Virgin Islands of the U.S.	HB2514.3	307.212095695	Jordan
HB2436.57	307.2120972981	Barbados	HB2514.7	307.21209538	Saudi Arabia
HB2436.72	307.2120972973	Anguilla	HB2514.9-2515	307.212095332	Yemen
HB2436.74	307.2120972974	Antigua/Barbuda	HB2515.3	307.212095353	Oman
HB2436.76	307.2120972975	Montserrat	HB2515.5	307.212095357	United Arab Emirates
HB2436.78	307.2120972973	Saint Kitts-Nevis	HB2515.7	307.212095363	Qatar
HB2436.93	307.21209729841	Dominica	HB2515.9	307.212095365	Bahrein
HB2436.95	307.21209729845	Grenada	HB2516	307.212095367	Kuwait
HB2436.97	307.21209729843	Saint Lucia	HB2516.3	307.21209567	Iraq
HB2436.99	307.21209729844	Saint Vincent/Grenadines	HB2516.4	307.2120955	Iran
HB2437	307.2120972983	Trinidad/Tobago	HB2516.6	307.21209581	Afghanistan
HB2437.35	307.2120972986	Aruba	HB2516.7	307.21209591	Burma
HB2437.36	307.2120972986	Bonaire	HB2516.8	307.212095493	Sri Lanka
HB2437.37	307.2120972986	Curacao	HB2516.9	307.212095496	Nepal
HB2437.38	307.2120972977	Saba	HB2519-2520	307.2120954	India
HB2437.385	307.2120972977	Saint Eustatius	HB2520.3	307.212095498	Bhutan
HB2437.39	307.2120972977	Saint Martin	HB2520.5	307.212095491	Pakistan
HB2437.7	307.2120972976	Guadeloupe	HB2520.6	307.212095492	Bangladesh
HB2437.9	307.2120972982	Martinique	HB2524.3	307.212095596	Cambodia
HB2439-2440	307.2120982	Argentina	HB2524.4	307.21209594	Laos
HB2441-2442	307.2120984	Bolivia	HB2524.5	307.21209597	Vietnam
HB2443-2444	307.2120981	Brazil	HB2524.55	307.21209593	Thailand
HB2445-2446	307.2120983	Chile	HB2524.6	307.21209595	Malaysia
HB2447-2448	307.21209861	Colombia	HB2527-2528	307.21209598	Indonesia
HB2449-2450	307.21209866	Ecuador	HB2529-2530	307.21209599	Philippine Islands
HB2452.3	307.21209881	Guyana	HB2531-2532	307.2120952	Japan
HB2452.5	307.21209883	Suriname	HB2532.5-.6	307.21209519	Korea/North Korea
HB2452.7	307.21209882	French Guiana	HB2532.8	307.21209517	Mongolia
HB2453-2454	307.21209892	Paraguay	HB2534	307.2120951	China
HB2455-2456	307.2120985	Peru	HB2535	307.212095126	Macao
HB2457-2458	307.21209895	Uruguay	HB2536	307.2120951249	Taiwan
HB2459-2460	307.2120987	Venezuela	HB2537	307.212095125	Hong Kong
HB2465-2466	307.2120942(9)	England/Wales	HB2541.4	307.2120965	Algeria
HB2467-2468	307.21209411	Scotland	HB2541.5	307.21209611	Tunisia
HB2468.5	307.21209416	Northern Ireland	HB2541.6	307.21209612	Libya
HB2469-2470	307.21209417	Irish Republic	HB2541.7	307.2120962	Egypt
HB2471-2472	307.21209436	Austria	HB2541.8	307.21209624	Sudan
HB2472.3	307.21209437	Czechoslovakia	HB2542	307.2120963	Ethiopia
HB2472.5	307.21209439	Hungary	HB2542.2	307.212096773	Somalia

LC	Dewey	Descriptor	LC	Dewey	Descriptor
HB2542.3	307.212096771	Djibouti	HB2573.7	307.212099613	American Samoa
HB2542.5	307.212096762	Kenya	HB2573.8	307.212099614	Western Samoa
HB2542.6	307.212096761	Uganda	HB2573.9	307.21209962	French Polynesia
HB2542.7	307.2120967571	Rwanda	HB2575	307.2120998(1-8)	Polar regions
HB2542.8	307.2120967572	Burundi	HB2576	307.21209982	Greenland
HB2542.9	307.21209678	Tanzania	HB2581-2787	331.7	Professions/Occupations
HB2543	307.21209679	Mozambique	HB2591-2787	331.7009(4-9)	Professions, By place
HB2543.2	307.21209691	Madagascar	HB2595-2596	331.700973	United States
HB2543.4	307.2120968	South Africa	HB2615	331.70097(4-9)	By state
HB2543.5	307.21209689	Zimbabwe/Zambia/Malawi	HB2617	331.70097(4-9)	By city
HB2543.6	307.212096894	Zambia	HB2619-2620	331.700971	Canada
HB2543.7	307.212096885	Lesotho	HB2621-2622	331.700972	Mexico
HB2543.8	307.212096887	Swaziland	HB2625-2626	331.70097282	Belize
HB2543.9	307.212096883	Botswana	HB2627-2628	331.70097286	Costa Rica
HB2544	307.212096897	Malawi	HB2629	331.70097281	Guatemala
HB2544.2	307.212096881	Namibia	HB2630	331.70097283	Honduras
HB2544.4	307.21209673	Angola	HB2631	331.70097285	Nicaragua
HB2544.5	307.2120967 51	Zaire	HB2632-2633	331.70097287	Panama
HB2544.6	307.212096718	Equatorial Guinea	HB2633.5	331.700972875	Panama Canal Zone
HB2544.7	307.212096715	Sao Tome/Principe	HB2634	331.70097284	El Salvador
HB2544.8	307.21209672	French Equatorial Africa	HB2637-2638	331.70097296	Bahamas
HB2544.9	307.212096721	Gabon	HB2639-2640	331.70097291	Cuba
HB2545	307.212096724	Congo	HB2641	331.70097294	Haiti
HB2545.2	307.212096741	Central African Republic	HB2642	331.70097293	Dominican Republic
HB2545.3	307.212096743	Chad	HB2643-2644	331.70097292	Jamaica
HB2545.4	307.212096711	Cameroon	HB2645-2646	331.70097295	Puerto Rico
HB2545.7	307.212096683	Benin (Dahomey)	HB2646.3	331.7009729722	Virgin Islands of the U.S.
HB2545.8	307.212096681	Togo	HB2646.57	331.700972981	Barbados
HB2545.9	307.212096626	Niger	HB2646.72	331.700972973	Anguilla
HB2546	307.212096668	Ivory Coast	HB2646.74	331.700972974	Antigua/Barbuda
HB2546.2	307.212096652	Guinea-Bissau	HB2646.76	331.700972975	Montserrat
HB2546.3	307.212096623	Mali	HB2646.78	331.700972973	Saint Kitts-Nevis
HB2546.4	307.212096625	Burkina Faso	HB2646.93	331.7009729841	Dominica
HB2546.5	307.21209663	Senegal	HB2646.95	331.7009729845	Grenada
HB2546.6	307.21209661	Mauritania	HB2646.97	331.7009729843	Saint Lucia
HB2546.7	307.21209669	Nigeria	HB2646.99	331.7009729844	Saint Vincent/Grenadines
HB2546.8	307.21209667	Ghana	HB2647	331.700972983	Trinidad/Tobago
HB2546.9	307.21209664	Sierra Leone	HB2647.35	331.700972986	Aruba
HB2547	307.212096651	Gambia	HB2647.36	331.700972986	Bonaire
HB2547.2	307.212096662	Liberia	HB2647.37	331.700972986	Curacao
HB2547.3	307.212096657	Guinea-Bissau	HB2647.38	331.700972977	Saba
HB2547.4	307.21209648	Spanish Sahara	HB2647.385	331.700972977	Saint Eustatius
HB2547.5	307.212094699	Azores	HB2647.39	331.700972977	Saint Martin
HB2548	307.212097299	Bermuda	HB2647.7	331.700972976	Guadeloupe
HB2548.5	307.212094698	Madeira Islands	HB2647.9	331.700972982	Martinique
HB2549	307.21209649	Canary Islands	HB2649-2650	331.700982	Argentina
HB2549.5	307.212096658	Cape Verde Islands	HB2651-2652	331.700984	Bolivia
HB2550	307.21209973	St. Helena	HB2653-2654	331.700981	Brazil
HB2550.5	307.21209973	Tristan da Cunha	HB2655-2656	331.700983	Chile
HB2551	307.21209971	Falkland Islands	HB2657-2658	331.7009861	Colombia
HB2551.5	307.212095495	Maldive Islands	HB2659-2660	331.7009866	Ecuador
HB2552	307.21209696	Seychelles	HB2662.3	331.7009881	Guyana
HB2552.5	307.21209694	Comoro Islands	HB2662.5	331.7009883	Suriname
HB2553	307.212096982	Mauritius	HB2662.7	331.7009882	French Guiana
HB2553.5	307.212096981	Reunion	HB2663-2664	331.7009892	Paraguay
HB2554	307.21209699	Kerguelen Islands	HB2665-2666	331.700985	Peru
HB2555-2556	307.2120994	Australia	HB2667-2668	331.7009895	Uruguay
HB2572.5	307.2120993	New Zealand	HB2669-2670	331.700987	Venezuela
HB2572.7	307.21209967	Guam	HB2675-2676	331.700942(9)	England/Wales
HB2572.8	307.21209953	Papua New Guinea	HB2677-2678	331.7009411	Scotland
HB2572.9	307.212099681	Kiribati (Gilbert Islands)	HB2678.5	331.7009416	Northern Ireland
HB2573	307.212099593	Solomon Islands	HB2679-2680	331.7009417	Irish Republic
HB2573.3	307.212099597	New Caledonia	HB2681-2682	331.7009436	Austria
HB2573.4	307.212099595	Vanuatu	HB2682.3	331.7009437	Czechoslovakia
HB2573.5	307.212099611	Fiji Islands	HB2682.5	331.7009439	Hungary
HB2573.6	307.212099612	Tonga	HB2682.9	331.700943648	Liechtenstein
HB2573.65	307.212099623	Cook Islands	HB2683-2684	331.700944	France

LC	Dewey	Descriptor
HB2684.5	331.700944949	Monaco
HB2685-2686.5	331.700943	Germany
HB2689-2690	331.700945	Italy
HB2693-2694	331.7009493	Belgium
HB2695-2696	331.7009492	Netherlands
HB2696.5	331.70094935	Luxembourg
HB2697-2698	331.700947	European Russia
HB2698.3	331.70094897	Finland
HB2698.7	331.7009438	Poland
HB2701-2702	331.7009489	Denmark
HB2703-2704	331.70094912	Iceland
HB2705-2706	331.7009481	Norway
HB2707-2708	331.7009485	Sweden
HB2709-2710	331.700946	Spain
HB2711-2712	331.7009469	Portugal
HB2713-2714	331.7009494	Switzerland
HB2716.5	331.70094965	Albania
HB2717-2718	331.70094977	Bulgaria
HB2718.5	331.7009497	Yugoslavia
HB2721-2722	331.7009498	Romania
HB2722.5	331.7009495	Greece
HB2723.4	331.7009561	Turkey
HB2723.5	331.70095645	Cyprus
HB2723.7	331.70095691	Syria
HB2723.9	331.70095692	Lebanon
HB2724	331.70095694	Israel/Palestine
HB2724.3	331.70095695	Jordan
HB2724.7	331.7009538	Saudi Arabia
HB2724.9-2725	331.70095332	Yemen
HB2725.3	331.70095353	Oman
HB2725.5	331.70095357	United Arab Emirates
HB2725.7	331.70095363	Qatar
HB2725.9	331.70095365	Bahrein
HB2726	331.70095367	Kuwait
HB2726.3	331.7009567	Iraq
HB2726.4	331.700955	Iran
HB2726.6	331.7009581	Afghanistan
HB2726.7	331.7009591	Burma
HB2726.8	331.70095493	Sri Lanka
HB2726.9	331.70095496	Nepal
HB2729-2730	331.700954	India
HB2730.3	331.70095498	Bhutan
HB2730.5	331.70095491	Pakistan
HB2730.6	331.70095492	Bangladesh
HB2734.3	331.7009596	Cambodia
HB2734.4	331.7009594	Laos
HB2734.5	331.7009597	Vietnam
HB2734.55	331.7009593	Thailand
HB2734.6	331.7009595	Malaysia
HB2737-2738	331.7009598	Indonesia
HB2739-2740	331.7009599	Philippine Islands
HB2741-2742	331.700952	Japan
HB2742.5-.6	331.7009519	Korea/North Korea
HB2742.8	331.7009517	Mongolia
HB2744	331.700951	China
HB2745	331.70095126	Macao
HB2746	331.700951249	Taiwan
HB2747	331.70095125	Hong Kong
HB2751.3	331.700964	Morocco
HB2751.4	331.700965	Algeria
HB2751.5	331.7009611	Tunisia
HB2751.6	331.7009612	Libya
HB2751.7	331.700962	Egypt
HB2751.8	331.7009624	Sudan
HB2752	331.700963	Ethiopia
HB2752.2	331.70096773	Somalia
HB2752.3	331.70096771	Djibouti
HB2752.5	331.70096762	Kenya
HB2752.6	331.70096761	Uganda
HB2752.7	331.700967571	Rwanda
HB2752.8	331.700967572	Burundi
HB2752.9	331.7009678	Tanzania
HB2753	331.7009679	Mozambique
HB2753.2	331.7009691	Madagascar
HB2753.4	331.700968	South Africa
HB2753.5	331.7009689	Zimbabwe/Zambia/Malawi
HB2753.6	331.70096894	Zambia
HB2753.7	331.70096885	Lesotho
HB2753.8	331.70096887	Swaziland
HB2753.9	331.70096883	Botswana
HB2754	331.70096897	Malawi
HB2754.2	331.70096881	Namibia
HB2754.4	331.7009673	Angola
HB2754.5	331.70096751	Zaire
HB2754.6	331.70096718	Equatorial Guinea
HB2754.7	331.70096715	Sao Tome/Principe
HB2754.8	331.7009672	French Equatorial Africa
HB2754.9	331.70096721	Gabon
HB2755	331.70096724	Congo
HB2755.2	331.70096741	Central African Republic
HB2755.3	331.70096743	Chad
HB2755.4	331.70096711	Cameroon
HB2755.7	331.70096683	Benin (Dahomey)
HB2755.8	331.70096681	Togo
HB2755.9	331.70096626	Niger
HB2756	331.70096668	Ivory Coast
HB2756.2	331.70096652	Guinea-Bissau
HB2756.3	331.70096623	Mali
HB2756.4	331.70096625	Burkina Faso
HB2756.5	331.7009663	Senegal
HB2756.6	331.7009661	Mauritania
HB2756.7	331.7009669	Nigeria
HB2756.8	331.7009667	Ghana
HB2756.9	331.7009664	Sierra Leone
HB2757	331.70096651	Gambia
HB2757.2	331.70096662	Liberia
HB2757.3	331.70096657	Guinea-Bissau
HB2757.4	331.7009648	Spanish Sahara
HB2757.5	331.70094699	Azores
HB2758	331.70097299	Bermuda
HB2758.5	331.70094698	Madeira Islands
HB2759	331.7009649	Canary Islands
HB2759.5	331.70096658	Cape Verde Islands
HB2760	331.7009973	St. Helena
HB2760.5	331.7009973	Tristan da Cunha
HB2761	331.7009971	Falkland Islands
HB2761.5	331.70095495	Maldive Islands
HB2762	331.7009696	Seychelles
HB2762.5	331.7009694	Comoro Islands
HB2763	331.70096982	Mauritius
HB2763.5	331.70096981	Reunion
HB2764	331.7009699	Kerguelen Islands
HB2765-2766	331.700994	Australia
HB2782.5	331.700993	New Zealand
HB2782.7	331.7009967	Guam
HB2782.8	331.7009953	Papua New Guinea
HB2782.9	331.70099681	Kiribati (Gilbert Islands)
HB2783	331.70099593	Solomon Islands
HB2783.3	331.70099597	New Caledonia
HB2783.4	331.70099595	Vanuatu
HB2783.5	331.70099611	Fiji Islands
HB2783.6	331.70099612	Tonga
HB2783.65	331.70099623	Cook Islands
HB2783.7	331.70099613	American Samoa

LC	Dewey	Descriptor	LC	Dewey	Descriptor
HB2783.8	331.70099614	Western Samoa	HB3599-3600	304.60945	Italy
HB2783.9	331.7009962	French Polynesia	HB3603-3604	304.609493	Belgium
HB2785	331.700998(1-8)	Polar regions	HB3605-3606	304.609492	Netherlands
HB2786	331.7009982	Greenland	HB3606.5	304.6094935	Luxembourg
HB3501-3697	304.609	Demography, By place	HB3607-3608	304.60947	European Russia
HB3505-3506	304.60973	United States	HB3608.3	304.6094897	Finland
HB3525	304.6097(4-9)	By state	HB3608.7	304.609438	Poland
HB3527	304.6097(4-9)	By city	HB3611-3612	304.609489	Denmark
HB3529-3530	304.60971	Canada	HB3613-3614	304.6094912	Iceland
HB3531-3532	304.60972	Mexico	HB3615-3616	304.609481	Norway
HB3535-3536	304.6097282	Belize	HB3617-3618	304.609485	Sweden
HB3537-3538	304.6097286	Costa Rica	HB3619-3620	304.60946	Spain
HB3539	304.6097281	Guatemala	HB3621-3622	304.609469	Portugal
HB3540	304.6097283	Honduras	HB3623-3624	304.609494	Switzerland
HB3541	304.6097285	Nicaragua	HB3626.5	304.6094965	Albania
HB3542-3543	304.6097287	Panama	HB3627-3628	304.6094977	Bulgaria
HB3543.5	304.60972875	Panama Canal Zone	HB3628.5	304.609497	Yugoslavia
HB3544	304.6097284	El Salvador	HB3631-3632	304.609498	Romania
HB3547-3548	304.6097296	Bahamas	HB3632.5	304.609495	Greece
HB3549-3550	304.6097291	Cuba	HB3633.4	304.609561	Turkey
HB3551	304.6097294	Haiti	HB3633.5	304.6095645	Cyprus
HB3552	304.6097293	Dominican Republic	HB3633.7	304.6095691	Syria
HB3553-3554	304.6097292	Jamaica	HB3633.9	304.6095692	Lebanon
HB3555-3556	304.6097295	Puerto Rico	HB3634	304.6095694	Israel/Palestine
HB3556.3	304.609729722	Virgin Islands of the U.S.	HB3634.3	304.6095695	Jordan
HB3556.57	304.60972981	Barbados	HB3634.7	304.609538	Saudi Arabia
HB3556.72	304.60972973	Anguilla	HB3634.9-3635	304.6095332	Yemen
HB3556.74	304.60972974	Antigua/Barbuda	HB3635.3	304.6095353	Oman
HB3556.76	304.60972975	Montserrat	HB3635.5	304.6095357	United Arab Emirates
HB3556.78	304.60972973	Saint Kitts-Nevis	HB3635.7	304.6095363	Qatar
HB3556.93	304.609729841	Dominica	HB3635.9	304.6095365	Bahrein
HB3556.95	304.609729845	Grenada	HB3636	304.6095367	Kuwait
HB3556.97	304.609729843	Saint Lucia	HB3636.3	304.60.95367	Iraq
HB3556.99	304.609729844	Saint Vincent/Grenadines	HB3636.4	304.60955	Iran
HB3557	304.60972983	Trinidad/Tobago	HB3636.6	304.609581	Afghanistan
HB3557.35	304.60972986	Aruba	HB3636.7	304.609591	Burma
HB3557.36	304.60972986	Bonaire	HB3636.8	304.6095493	Sri Lanka
HB3557.37	304.60972986	Curacao	HB3636.9	304.6095496	Nepal
HB3557.38	304.60972977	Saba	HB3639-3640	304.60954	India
HB3557.385	304.60972977	Saint Eustatius	HB3640.3	304.6095498	Bhutan
HB3557.39	304.60972977	Saint Martin	HB3640.5	304.6095491	Pakistan
HB3557.7	304.60972976	Guadeloupe	HB3640.6	304.6095492	Bangladesh
HB3557.9	304.60972982	Martinique	HB3644.3	304.609596	Cambodia
HB3559-3560	304.60982	Argentina	HB3644.4	304.609594	Laos
HB3561-3562	304.60984	Bolivia	HB3644.5	304.609597	Vietnam
HB3563-3564	304.60981	Brazil	HB3644.55	304.609593	Thailand
HB3565-3566	304.60983	Chile	HB3644.6	304.609595	Malaysia
HB3567-3568	304.609861	Colombia	HB3647-3648	304.609598	Indonesia
HB3569-3570	304.609866	Ecuador	HB3649-3650	304.609599	Philippine Islands
HB3572.3	304.609881	Guyana	HB3651-3652	304.60952	Japan
HB3572.5	304.609883	Suriname	HB3652.5-.6	304.609519	Korea/North Korea
HB3572.7	304.609882	French Guiana	HB3652.8	304.609517	Mongolia
HB3573-3574	304.609892	Paraguay	HB3654	304.60951	China
HB3575-3576	304.60985	Peru	HB3655	304.6095126	Macao
HB3577-3578	304.609895	Uruguay	HB3656	304.60951249	Taiwan
HB3579-3580	304.60987	Venezuela	HB3657	304.6095125	Hong Kong
HB3585-3586	304.60942(9)	England/Wales	HB3661.3	304.60964	Morocco
HB3587-3588	304.609411	Scotland	HB3661.4	304.60965	Algeria
HB3588.5	304.609416	Northern Ireland	HB3661.5	304.609611	Tunisia
HB3589-3590	304.609417	Irish Republic	HB3661.6	304.609612	Libya
HB3591-3592	304.609436	Austria	HB3661.7	304.60962	Egypt
HB3592.3	304.609437	Czechoslovakia	HB3661.8	304.609624	Sudan
HB3592.5	304.609439	Hungary	HB3662	304.60963	Ethiopia
HB3592.9	304.60943648	Liechtenstein	HB3662.2	304.6096773	Somalia
HB3593-3594	304.60944	France	HB3662.3	304.6096771	Djibouti
HB3594.5	304.60944949	Monaco	HB3662.5	304.6096762	Kenya
HB3595-3596.5	304.60943	Germany	HB3662.6	304.6096761	Uganda

LC	Dewey	Descriptor	LC	Dewey	Descriptor
HB3662.7	304.60967571	Rwanda	HB3695	304.60998(1-8)	Polar regions
HB3662.8	304.60967572	Burundi	HB3696	304.609982	Greenland
HB3662.9	304.609678	Tanzania	HB3711-3840	338.54	Business/Economic cycles
HB3663	304.609679	Mozambique	HB3730	330.900112	Economic forecasting
HB3663.2	304.609691	Madagascar	HB3732	339.5	Economic stabilization
HB3663.4	304.60968	South Africa	HB3741-4840	338.54209(4-9)	Business cycles, By place
HB3663.5	304.609689	Zimbabwe/Zambia/Malawi	HC	330.9	Economic history/
HB3663.6	304.6096894	Zambia			Conditions
HB3663.7	304.6096885	Lesotho	HC10-14	330.0(5/6)	Serials/Societies
HB3663.8	304.6096887	Swaziland	HC15	330.03	Encyclopedias/Dictionaries
HB3663.9	304.6096883	Botswana	HC26	330.1	Theory/Method
HB3664	304.6096897	Malawi	HC28	330.07	Education
HB3664.2	304.6096881	Namibia	HC29	330.9092	Biography
HB3664.4	304.609673	Angola	HC31-60	330.909	History
HB3664.5	304.6096751	Zaire	HC31-39	330.93	Ancient
HB3664.6	304.6096718	Equatorial Guinea	HC41-42	330.902	Middle Ages
HB3664.7	304.6096715	Sao Tome/Principe	HC51-53	330.903	16th-19th centuries
HB3664.8	304.609672	French Equatorial Africa	HC54-60	330.9	20th century
HB3664.9	304.6096721	Gabon	HC92	333.916 4	Economics of the ocean
HB3665	304.6096724	Congo	HC94-1085	330/338.9(1-9)	By place
HB3665.2	304.6096741	Central African Republic	HC106.2-.8	330/338.973	United States
HB3665.3	304.6096743	Chad	HC107-110	330/338.97(4-9)	By state
HB3665.4	304.6096711	Cameroon	HC110.5	330/338.9982	Greenland
HB3665.7	304.6096683	Benin (Dahomey)	HC111-120	330/338.9971	Canada
HB3665.8	304.6096681	Togo	HC131-140	330/338.972	Mexico
HB3665.9	304.6096626	Niger	HC141-148	330/338.9728	Central America
HB3666	304.6096668	Ivory Coast	HC151-158	330/338.9729	West Indies
HB3666.2	304.6096652	Guinea-Bissau	HC161-239	330/338.98	South America
HB3666.3	304.6096623	Mali	HC171-180	330/338.982	Argentina
HB3666.4	304.6096625	Burkina Faso	HC181-185	330/338.984	Bolivia
HB3666.5	304.609663	Senegal	HC186-189	330/338.981	Brazil
HB3666.6	304.609661	Mauritania	HC191-195	330/338.983	Chile
HB3666.7	304.609669	Nigeria	HC196-200	330/338.9861	Colombia
HB3666.8	304.609667	Ghana	HC201-204	330/338.9866	Ecuador
HB3666.9	304.609664	Sierra Leone	HC205-220	330/338.988	Guyanas
HB3667	304.6096651	Gambia	HC221-225	330/338.9892	Paraguay
HB3667.2	304.6096662	Liberia	HC226-230	330/338.985	Peru
HB3667.3	304.6096657	Guinea-Bissau	HC231-235	330/338.9895	Uruguay
HB3667.4	304.609648	Spanish Sahara	HC236-239	330/338.987	Venezuela
HB3667.5	304.6094699	Azores	HC240-407	330/338.94	Europe
HB3668	304.6097299	Bermuda	HC245-246	330/338.917241	Commonwealth
HB3668.5	304.6094698	Madeira Islands	HC251-257	330/338.941	Great Britain
HB3669	304.609649	Canary Islands	HC258	330/338.9417	Ireland
HB3669.5	304.6096658	Cape Verde Islands	HC261-270	330/338.9436	Austria
HB3670	304.609973	St. Helena	HC270.2-.295	330/338.9437	Czechoslovakia
HB3670.5	304.609973	Tristan da Cunha	HC271-280	330/338.944	France
HB3671	304.609971	Falkland Islands	HC280-290	330/338.943	Germany
HB3671.5	304.6095495	Maldive Islands	HC291-300	330/338.9495	Greece
HB3672	304.609696	Seychelles	HC301-310	330/338.945	Italy
HB3672.5	304.609694	Comoro Islands	HC311-320	330/338.9493	Belgium
HB3673	304.6096982	Mauritius	HC321-329	330/338.9492	Netherlands
HB3673.5	304.6096981	Reunion	HC330	330/338.94935	Luxembourg
HB3674	304.609699	Kerguelen Islands	HC331-340	330/338.947	European Russia
HB3675-3676	304.60994	Australia	HC340.3	330/338.9438	Poland
HB3692.5	304.60993	New Zealand	HC341-380	330/338.948	Scandinavia
HB3692.7	304.609967	Guam	HC351-360	330/338.9489	Denmark
HB3692.8	304.609953	Papua New Guinea	HC361-370	330/338.9481	Norway
HB3692.9	304.6099681	Kiribati (Gilbert Islands)	HC371-380	330/338.9485	Sweden
HB3693	304.6099593	Solomon Islands	HC381-390	330/338.946	Spain
HB3693.3	304.6099597	New Caledonia	HC391-394	330/338.9469	Portugal
HB3693.4	304.6099595	Vanuatu	HC395-400	330/338.9494	Switzerland
HB3693.5	304.6099611	Fiji Islands	HC401-407	330/338.9496	Balkans
HB3693.6	304.6099612	Tonga	HC402	330/338.94965	Albania
HB3693.65	304.6099623	Cook Islands	HC403	330/338.94977	Bulgaria
HB3693.7	304.6099613	American Samoa	HC405	330/338.9498	Romania
HB3693.8	304.6099614	Western Samoa	HC407	330/338.9497	Yugoslavia
HB3693.9	304.609962	French Polynesia	HC411-495	330/338.95	Asia

LC	Dewey	Descriptor
HC415.23	330/338.95691	Syria
HC415.24	330/338.95692	Lebanon
HC415.25	330/338.95694	Israel/Palestine
HC415.26	330/338.95695	Jordan
HC415.33	330/338.9538	Saudi Arabia
HC415.34	330/338.95332	Yemen
HC415.35	330/338.95353	Oman
HC415.36	330/338.95357	United Arab Emirates
HC415.37	330/338.95363	Qatar
HC415.38	330/338.95365	Bahrein
HC415.39	330/338.95367	Kuwait
HC415.4	330/338.9567	Iraq
HC416-420	330/338.9581	Afghanistan
HC422	330/338.9591	Burma
HC424	330/338.95493	Sri Lanka
HC425	330/338.95496	Nepal
HC426-430	330/338.951	China
HC430.5	330/338.951249	Taiwan
HC431-440	330/338.954	India
HC440.5	330/338.95491	Pakistan
HC440.8	330/338.95492	Bangladesh
HC442	330/338.9596	Cambodia
HC443	330/338.9594	Laos
HC444	330/338.9597	Vietnam
HC445	330/338.9593	Thailand
HC446-450	330/338.9598	Indonesia
HC451-460	330/338.9599	Philippine Islands
HC461-465	330/338.952	Japan
HC466-470	330/338.9519	Korea
HC471-480	330/338.955	Iran
HC491-495	330/338.9561	Turkey
HC592-595	330/338.997	Atlantic Ocean Islands
HC601-610	330/338.994	Australia
HC661-670	330/338.993	New Zealand
HC681-688	330/338.99(5-6)	Pacific Ocean Islands
HC721-740	330/338.998(1-8)	Arctic regions
HC800-1085	330/338.96	Africa
HC810	330/338.964	Morocco
HC815	330/338.965	Algeria
HC820	330/338.9611	Tunisia
HC825	330/338.9612	Libya
HC830	330/338.962	Egypt
HC835	330/338.9624	Sudan
HC845	330/338.963	Ethiopia
HC850	330/338.96773	Somalia
HC865	330/338.96762	Kenya
HC870	330/338.96761	Uganda
HC875	330/338.967571	Rwanda
HC880	330/338.967572	Burundi
HC885	330/338.9678	Tanzania
HC890	330/338.9679	Mozambique
HC895	330/338.9691	Madagascar
HC905	330/338.968	South Africa
HC910	330/338.9689	Zimbabwe
HC915	330/338.96894	Zambia
HC925	330/338.96887	Swaziland
HC950	330/338.9673	Angola
HC955	330/338.96751	Zaire
HC975	330/338.96721	Gabon
HC980	330/338.96724	Congo
HC990	330/338.96743	Chad
HC995	330/338.96711	Cameroon
HC1020	330/338.96626	Niger
HC1025	330/338.96668	Ivory Coast
HC1030	330/338.96652	Guinea
HC1055	330/338.9669	Nigeria
HD	330.9	Economic history/Conditions
HD28-88	338	Production
HD28-70	658	Industrial management
HD39-40.7	332.041	Capital/Capital investments
HD41	338.6048	Competition
HD45-.2	658.(3/5)	Control of industry/Technology
HD47-.4	338.51	Costs/Cost control
HD49-.5	332.41	Overproduction/Inflation
HD50	658.402	Delegation of authority
HD56-57.5	338.06	Industrial productivity
HD58	338.09(4-9)	Location of industry
HD58.7-.95	302.35	Organizational behavior
HD59-.2	659	Public relations/Publicity
HD60-.5	658.408	Social responsibilities
HD61	658.155	Risk/Risk management
HD62	658.562	Simplification/Standardization
HD62.2-.8	338.76	Special enterprises
HD66	658.3128	Work groups/Team work
HD72-88	338.9	Economic growth/Development
HD101-1395	333.73	Land use
HD101-107	333.730(5/6)	Serials/Societies
HD107.7-.8	333.7303	Encyclopedias/Dictionaries
HD108	333.7301	Theory
HD110	333.7307	Education
HD113-156	333.7309	History
HD113-139	333.730901	Ancient
HD141-150	333.730902	Medieval
HD151-156	333.73090(3-4)	Modern
HD166-1130.5	333.7309(4-9)	Land use, By place
HD170-279	333.730973	United States
HD311-320	333.730971	Canada
HD321-330	333.730972	Mexico
HD336-340	333.73097282	Belize
HD341-350	333.73097286	Costa Rica
HD351-360	333.73097281	Guatemala
HD361-370	333.73097283	Honduras
HD371-380	333.73097285	Nicaragua
HD381-385	333.73097287	Panama
HD386-390	333.730972875	Panama Canal Zone
HD391-400	333.73097284	El Salvador
HD406-410	333.73097296	Bahamas
HD411-420	333.73097291	Cuba
HD421-425	333.73097294	Haiti
HD426-430	333.73097293	Dominican Republic
HD431-440	333.73097292	Jamaica
HD441-450	333.73097295	Puerto Rico
HD450.3	333.7309729722	Virgin Islands of the U.S.
HD451.5	333.730972981	Barbados
HD453.2	333.730972973	Anguilla
HD453.4	333.730972974	Antigua/Barbuda
HD453.6	333.730972975	Montserrat
HD453.8	333.730972973	Saint Kitts-Nevis
HD454.3	333.7309729841	Dominica
HD454.5	333.7309729845	Grenada
HD454.7	333.7309729843	Saint Lucia
HD454.9	333.7309729844	Saint Vincent/Grenadines
HD455	333.730972983	Trinidad/Tobago
HD456.5	333.730972986	Aruba
HD456.6	333.730972986	Bonaire
HD456.7	333.730972986	Curacao
HD456.8	333.730972977	Saba
HD456.85	333.730972977	Saint Eustatius
HD456.9	333.730972977	Saint Martin

LC	Dewey	Descriptor	LC	Dewey	Descriptor
HD458	333.730972976	Guadeloupe	HD880.6	333.73095492	Bangladesh
HD459	333.730972982	Martinique	HD890.3	333.7309596	Cambodia
HD471-480	333.730982	Argentina	HD890.4	333.7309594	Laos
HD481-490	333.730984	Bolivia	HD890.5	333.7309597	Vietnam
HD491-500	333.730981	Brazil	HD890.55	333.7309593	Thailand
HD501-510	333.730983	Chile	HD890.6	333.7309595	Malaysia
HD511-520	333.7309861	Colombia	HD891-900	333.7309598	Indonesia
HD521-530	333.7309866	Ecuador	HD901-910	333.7309599	Philippine Islands
HD540.3	333.7309881	Guyana	HD911-920	333.730952	Japan
HD540.5	333.7309883	Suriname	HD920.5-.6	333.7309519	Korea/North Korea
HD540.7	333.7309882	French Guiana	HD920.8	333.7309517	Mongolia
HD541-550	333.7309892	Paraguay	HD921-930	333.730951	China
HD551-560	333.730985	Peru	HD931-935	333.73095126	Macao
HD561-570	333.7309895	Uruguay	HD936-940	333.730951249	Taiwan
HD571-580	333.730987	Venezuela	HD941-945	333.73095125	Hong Kong
HD601-610	333.730942(9)	England/Wales	HD972	333.730964	Morocco
HD611-620	333.7309411	Scotland	HD973	333.730965	Algeria
HD620.5	333.7309416	Northern Ireland	HD974	333.7309611	Tunisia
HD621-630	333.7309417	Irish Republic	HD975	333.7309612	Libya
HD631-640	333.7309436	Austria	HD976	333.730962	Egypt
HD640.3	333.7309437	Czechoslovakia	HD977	333.7309624	Sudan
HD640.5	333.7309439	Hungary	HD979	333.730963	Ethiopia
HD640.9	333.730943648	Liechtenstein	HD980	333.73096773	Somalia
HD641-650	333.730944	France	HD981	333.73096771	Djibouti
HD650.5	333.730944949	Monaco	HD983	333.73096762	Kenya
HD651-660.5	333.730943	Germany	HD984	333.73096761	Uganda
HD671-680	333.730945	Italy	HD985	333.730967571	Rwanda
HD691-700	333.7309493	Belgium	HD986	333.730967572	Burundi
HD701-710	333.7309492	Netherlands	HD987	333.7309678	Tanzania
HD710.5	333.73094935	Luxembourg	HD988	333.7309679	Mozambique
HD711-720	333.730947	European Russia	HD989	333.7309691	Madagascar
HD721-725	333.73094897	Finland	HD991	333.730968	South Africa
HD726-729.5	333.7309438	Poland	HD992	333.7309689	Zimbabwe/Zambia/Malawi
HD731-740	333.7309489	Denmark	HD993	333.73096894	Zambia
HD741-750	333.73094912	Iceland	HD994	333.73096885	Lesotho
HD751-760	333.7309481	Norway	HD995	333.73096887	Swaziland
HD761-770	333.7309485	Sweden	HD996	333.73096883	Botswana
HD771-780	333.730946	Spain	HD997	333.73096897	Malawi
HD781-790	333.7309469	Portugal	HD998	333.73096881	Namibia
HD791-800	333.7309494	Switzerland	HD1000	333.7309673	Angola
HD810.5	333.73094965	Albania	HD1001	333.73096751	Zaire
HD811-820	333.73094977	Bulgaria	HD1002	333.73096718	Equatorial Guinea
HD821-825	333.7309497	Yugoslavia	HD1003	333.73096715	Sao Tome/Principe
HD831-840	333.7309498	Romania	HD1004	333.7309672	French Equatorial Africa
HD840.5	333.7309495	Greece	HD1005	333.73096721	Gabon
HD846.5	333.7309561	Turkey	HD1006	333.73096724	Congo
HD847	333.73095645	Cyprus	HD1007	333.73096741	Central African Republic
HD848	333.73095691	Syria	HD1008	333.73096743	Chad
HD849	333.73095692	Lebanon	HD1009	333.73096711	Cameroon
HD850	333.73095694	Israel/Palestine	HD1012	333.73096683	Benin (Dahomey)
HD851	333.73095695	Jordan	HD1013	333.73096681	Togo
HD853	333.7309538	Saudi Arabia	HD1014	333.73096626	Niger
HD854-.5	333.73095332	Yemen	HD1015	333.73096668	Ivory Coast
HD855	333.73095353	Oman	HD1016	333.73096652	Guinea
HD856	333.73095357	United Arab Emirates	HD1017	333.73096623	Mali
HD857	333.73095363	Qatar	HD1018	333.73096625	Burkina Faso
HD858	333.73095365	Bahrein	HD1019	333.7309663	Senegal
HD859	333.73095367	Kuwait	HD1020	333.7309661	Mauritania
HD860	333.7309567	Iraq	HD1021	333.7309669	Nigeria
HD860.2	333.730955	Iran	HD1022	333.7309667	Ghana
HD860.6	333.7309581	Afghanistan	HD1023	333.7309664	Sierra Leone
HD860.7	333.7309591	Burma	HD1024	333.73096651	Gambia
HD860.8	333.73095493	Sri Lanka	HD1025	333.73096662	Liberia
HD860.9	333.73095496	Nepal	HD1026	333.73096657	Guinea-Bissau
HD871-880	333.730954	India	HD1027	333.7309648	Spanish Sahara
HD880.3	333.73095498	Bhutan	HD1028	333.73094699	Azores
HD880.5	333.73095491	Pakistan	HD1028.3	333.73097299	Bermuda

LC	Dewey	Descriptor
HD1028.5	333.73094698	Madeira Islands
HD1028.7	333.7309649	Canary Islands
HD1028.9	333.73096658	Cape Verde Islands
HD1029	333.7309973	St. Helena
HD1029.3	333.7309973	Tristan da Cunha
HD1029.5	333.7309971	Falkland Islands
HD1029.7	333.73095495	Maldive Islands
HD1029.9	333.7309696	Seychelles
HD1030	333.7309694	Comoro Islands
HD1030.3	333.73096982	Mauritius
HD1030.5	333.73096981	Reunion
HD1030.7	333.7309699	Kerguelen Islands
HD1031-1040	333.730994	Australia
HD1120.5	333.730993	New Zealand
HD1121.5	333.7309967	Guam
HD1122	333.7309953	Papua New Guinea
HD1122.3	333.73099681	Kiribati (Gilbert Islands)
HD1123	333.73099593	Solomon Islands
HD1124	333.73099597	New Caledonia
HD1125	333.73099595	Vanuatu
HD1126	333.73099611	Fiji Islands
HD1127	333.73099612	Tonga
HD1127.5	333.73099623	Cook Islands
HD1128	333.73099613	American Samoa
HD1129	333.73099614	Western Samoa
HD1129.5	333.7309962	French Polynesia
HD1130	333.730998(1-8)	Polar regions
HD1130.5	333.7309982	Greenland
HD1241-1339	333.3	Land tenure
HD1259-1265	333.13	Eminent domain
HD1262-1265	333.1309(4-9)	By place
HD1262-1263	333.130973	United States
HD1265	333.1309(4-9)	Other places
HD1286-1289	333.2	Communal ownership
HD1290-1291	333.1	Municipal ownership
HD1294-1295	336.22	Taxation
HD1301-1313	333.14	Agrarian socialism
HD1326-1329	333.3	Large holdings
HD1330-1331	333.54	Landlord/Peasant
HD1332-1333.5	333.31	Land/Agrarian reform
HD1334-1335	333.33	Consolidation of land holdings
HD1336-1339	333.322	Peasant/Small holdings
HD1361-1395	333.33	Real estate business
HD1401-2210	338.1	Agriculture
HD1428-1431	338.181	International cooperation
HD1470.5-1476	338.16	Size of farms
HD1478	333.335563	Sharecropping
HD1483-1486	338.106	Agricultural associations
HD1491-.5	334.683/338.1	Cooperative agriculture
HD1492-.5	335	Collective farms
HD1493	338.763	Government owned/ Operated farms
HD1501-1540	305.555	Social classes (Agricultural)
HD1549	631.55	Gleaning
HD1580	333.7153	Melioration/Reclamation
HD1635-1702	333.7(36-83)	Special classes of lands
HD1711-1741	333.(7153/913)	Irrigation/Reclamation
HD2321-4730.9	338	Industry
HD2329	338.9	Industrialization
HD2330	338.091734	Rural industry
HD2331-2336	338.634	House industry
HD2337-2339	338.634	Sweating system
HD2340.8-2346	338.642	Small-medium industry/ Artisans
HD2350.8-2356	338.644	Large industry/Factory system
HD2365-2385	658.723	Contracting
HD2421-2429	060	Trade/Industrial associations
HD2709-2932	338.7	Corporation/Cartels/Trusts
HD2709-2711	338.70(5/6)	Serials/Societies
HD2713	338.703	Encyclopedias/Dictionaries
HD2741-2748	338.7068	Organization/ Administration
HD2753	336.243	Taxation of
HD2757-2768	338.8	Monopolies/Trusts/Etc.
HD2763-2768	363.6	Public utilities
HD2770-2930.7	338.709	Corporations/Etc., By place
HD2771-2798	338.70973	United States
HD2807-2810	338.70971	Canada
HD2811	338.70972	Mexico
HD2813.5-2819	338.709728	Central America
HD2820.5-2825.9	338.709729	West Indies
HD2827-2843	338.7098	South America
HD2846-2891.83	338.7094	Europe
HD2846-2847.5	338.70941	Great Britain
HD2853-2856	338.70944	France
HD2857-2860.5	338.70943	Germany
HD2862-2865	338.70945	Italy
HD2865.5-2873.5	338.709492	Low Countries
HD2874-2877	338.70947	European Russia
HD2885-2888	338.70946	Spain
HD2889	338.709469	Portugal
HD2891.83	338.709495	Greece
HD2891.93-2892.53	338.70956	Middle East
HD2892.2	338.7095694	Israel/Palestine
HD2892.55	338.709567	Iraq
HD2892.56	338.70955	Iran
HD2892.7-2913	338.7095	Far East
HD2897-2900	338.70954	India
HD2905	338.709599	Philippine Islands
HD2907	338.70952	Japan
HD2910	338.70951	China
HD2918.3-2929.3	338.7096	Africa
HD2930-.68	338.7099(3-6)	Australia/New Zealand/ Oceania
HD2951-3575	334.6	Industrial cooperation
HD2951-2953	334.60(5/6)	Serials/Societies
HD2954	334.603	Encyclopedias/Dictionaries
HD2955	334.607	Education
HD2956	334.609	History
HD2961	334.601	Theory/Method
HD2970-3110	331.2164	Profit sharing
HD2981-3110.9	331.216409(4-9)	Profit sharing, By place
HD3120-3260.9	334.6	Cooperative production
HD3131-3260.9	334.609(4-9)	Production, By place
HD3271-3410.9	334.5	Cooperative distribution
HD3281-3410.9	334.681380109(4-9)	Distribution, By place
HD3441-3570.9	334.09	Cooperation, By place
HD3611-4730.9	346.0(65-78)	Industry and the state
HD3612	346.0(65-78)	Regulation
HD3641-3646	338.922	Subsidies
HD3656-3790.9	658.568	Inspections
HD3661-3790	658.56809(4-9)	Inspections, By place
HD3860-4420.7	338.9	Government ownership
HD4001-4420.7	338.909(4-9)	Government ownership, By place
HD4801-8943	331	Labor
HD4861-4895	331.117	Labor systems
HD4906-5100.7	331.21	Wages
HD4909-4912	331.2101	Theory
HD4915-4916	331.21021	Statistics
HD4917-4924	331.23	Minimum wage

58

LC	Dewey	Descriptor
HD4918-4924	331.2309(4-9)	Minimum wage, By place
HD4925	331.21	Family allowance
HD4926-4928	331.216	Remuneration
HD4938-4946	331.2813	State labor wages
HD4964-4965	331.216 6	Professional salary/Fee
HD4965.2	331.281331714/658.407	Businessmen's executive salary
HD4967	331.291724	Wages, developing countries
HD4971-5100.7	331.29(4-9)	Wages, By place
HD4973-4976	331.2973	United States
HD4977-4980	331.2971	Canada
HD4981	331.2972	Mexico
HD4983.5-4989	331.29728	Central America
HD4990-4995.9	331.29729	West Indies
HD4996-5013	331.298	South America
HD5014-5061.83	331.294	Europe
HD5015-5017.5	331.2941	Great Britain
HD5023-5026	331.2944	France
HD5027-5030.5	331.2943	Germany
HD5032-5035	331.2945	Italy
HD5035.5-5043.5	331.29492	Low Countries
HD5044-5047	331.2947	European Russia
HD5055-5058	331.2946	Spain
HD5059	331.29469	Portugal
HD5061.83	331.29495	Greece
HD5061.93-5062.53	331.2956	Middle East
HD5062.2	331.295694	Israel/Palestine
HD5062.55	331.29567.	Iraq
HD5062.56	331.2955	Iran
HD5062.7-5083	331.295	Far East
HD5067-5070	331.2954	India
HD5075	331.29599	Philippine Islands
HD5077	331.2952	Japan
HD5080	331.2951	China
HD5088.3-5099.3	331.296	Africa
HD5100-.68	331.299(3-6)	Australia/New Zealand/ Oceania
HD5106-5267	331.257	Hours
HD5109	331.2572	Flexible
HD5110	331.2572	Part time/Job sharing
HD5115.5-.6	331.25762	Sick leave
HD5255-5257	331.25763	Leave of absence
HD5260-5267	331.2576	Vacations
HD5306-5474	331.89	Labor disputes/Strikes/Etc.
HD5321-5450.7	331.8909(4-9)	By place
HD5481-5630.7	331.8914	Arbitration/Conciliation
HD5501-5630.7	331.891409(4-9)	Arbitration, By place
HD5650-5660	331.0112/658.1147	Employees in management
HD5701-6000.7	331.12	Labor market
HD5702	331.107	Education
HD5707.5-5710.2	331.137	Unemployment
HD5711-5712	331.1021	Statistics
HD5713-.6	331.12042	Manpower policy
HD5715-.5	331.2592	Occupational training
HD5716-5717	331.127	Labor mobility
HD5721-5851	331.1209(4-9)	Labor market, By place
HD5723-5726	331.120973	United States
HD5727-5730	331.120971	Canada
HD5731	331.120972	Mexico
HD5733.5-5739	331.1209728	Central America
HD5740.5-5745.9	331.1209729	West Indies
HD5747-5763	331.12098	South America
HD5764-5811.83	331.12094	Europe
HD5765-5767.5	331.120941	Great Britain
HD5773-5776	331.120944	France
HD5777-5780.5	331.120943	Germany

LC	Dewey	Descriptor
HD5782-5785	331.120945	Italy
HD5785.5-5793.5	331.1209492	Low Countries
HD5794-5797	331.120947	European Russia
HD5805-5808	331.120946	Spain
HD5810	331.1209494	Switzerland
HD5811.83	331.1209495	Greece
HD5811.93-5812.53	331.120956	Middle East
HD5812.2	331.12095694	Israel/Palestine
HD5812.55	331.1209567	Iraq
HD5812.56	331.120955	Iran
HD5812.7-5833	331.12095	Far East
HD5817-5820	331.120954	India
HD5825	331.1209599	Philippine Islands
HD5827	331.120952	Japan
HD5830	331.120951	China
HD5837-5849.3	331.12096	Africa
HD5850-.68	331.12099(3-6)	Australia/New Zealand/ Oceania
HD5860-6000.7	331.128	Labor/Employment agencies
HD5871-6000.7	331.12809(4-9)	Employment agencies, By place
HD6050-6305	331.(3-6)	Classes of labor
HD6050-6220.7	331.4	Women
HD6091-6220.7	331.409(4-9)	Women's labor, By place
HD6229-6276	331.3(1-47)	Child/Youth labor
HD6276.5-6278	331.34	College students
HD6279-6283	331.39(4-8)	Middle East
HD6304-6305	331.6	Minorities
HD6350-6940.7	331.8	Trade/Labor union
HD6350	331.80(5/6)	Serials/Societies
HD6451-6481	331.809	History
HD6500-6940.5	331.809(4-9)	Labor unions, By place
HD6500-6519	331.80973	United States
HD6521-6530	331.80971	Canada
HD6531-6535	331.80972	Mexico
HD6540.5-6570	331.809728	Central America
HD6571-6595.95	331.809729	West Indies
HD6596-6655	331.8098	South America
HD6656-6795.5	331.8094	Europe
HD6661-6670	331.80941	Great Britain
HD6681-6690	331.80944	France
HD6691-6700.5	331.80943	Germany
HD6706-6715	331.80945	Italy
HD6716-6730.5	331.809492	Low Countries
HD6731-6735	331.80947	European Russia
HD6761-6765	331.80946	Spain
HD6771-6775	331.809494	Switzerland
HD6795.5	331.809495	Greece
HD6796.5-6804	331.80956	Middle East
HD6798.5	331.8095694	Israel/Palestine
HD6805	331.809567	Iraq
HD6805.2	331.80955	Iran
HD6805.7-6851	331.8095	Far East
HD6811-6815	331.80954	India
HD6826-6830	331.809599	Philippine Islands
HD6831-6835	331.80952	Japan
HD6836-6840	331.80951	China
HD6861-6888.5	331.8096	Africa
HD6891-6938.9	331.8099(3-6)	Australia/New Zealand/ Oceania
HD6951-6957	306.36	Industrial sociology
HD6958.5-6976	331	Industrial relations
HD6977-7080	331.21/339.42	Wages/Cost of living
HD7088-7250.7	368.43	Social security/Insurance
HD7088-7090	368.430(5/6)	Serials/Societies
HD7090.5	368.4303	Encyclopedias/Dictionaries

LC	Dewey	Descriptor	LC	Dewey	Descriptor
HE199.9	388.042	Passenger traffic	HE2846-2850	385.097285	Nicaragua
HE305-311	388.4	Urban transportation	HE2851-2855	385.097284	El Salvador
HE323-328	387.52	Ocean/Trade routes	HE2860-2865	385.097296	Bahamas
HE331-380	388.1	Roads/Highways/Traffic	HE2891-3000	385.098	South America
HE369-373	388.314	Traffic surveys	HE2901-2910	385.0982	Argentina
HE374-377	388.132	Bridges	HE2911-2920	385.0984	Bolivia
HE379-380	388.13	Vehicular tunnels	HE2921-2930	385.0981	Brazil
HE380.8-971	386/387	Water transportation	HE2931-2940	385.0983	Chile
HE380.8-560	386.(3-5)	Waterways	HE2941-2950	385.09861	Colombia
HE380.8	386.0(5/6)	Serials/Societies	HE2951-2960	385.09866	Ecuador
HE384-389	343.0(96/66-68)	Control/Taxation	HE2962	385.09881	Guyana
HE392.8-520.9	386.09(4-9)	By place	HE2963	385.09883	Suriname
HE392.8-398	386.0973	United States	HE2964	385.09882	French Guiana
HE397-400	386.0971	Canada	HE2966-2970	385.09892	Paraguay
HE401	386.0972	Mexico	HE2971-2980	385.0985	Peru
HE403.5-520.9	386.09(4-9)	Other countries	HE2981-2990	385.09895	Uruguay
HE528-545	386.42	Interoceanic canals	HE2991-3000	385.0987	Venezuela
HE550-560	386.8	Ports	HE3011-3020	385.0941	Great Britain
HE561-971	387.5	Shipping/Merchant Marine	HE3041-3050	385.09416	Northern Ireland
HE561	387.50(5/6)	Serials/Societies	HE3051-3059.2	385.09436	Austria
HE562	387.5(06)	Congresses	HE3059.3	385.09437	Czechoslovakia
HE564	387.506	Associations of owners	HE3059.5	385.09439	Hungary
HE565	386.2	Tests of vessels	HE3060.5	385.09438	Poland
HE567-568	387.503	Encyclopedias/Dictionaries	HE3061-3070	385.0944	France
HE568.9	387.5092	Biography	HE3071-3080.5	385.0943	Germany
HE570	387.507	Education	HE3091-3100	385.0945	Italy
HE587-589	343.0(66-68)/096	Taxation/Registration	HE3111-3120	385.09493	Belgium
HE593-601	387.544	Traffic/Freight	HE3121-3130	385.09492	Netherlands
HE617-720	623.89229	Interior navigation	HE3131-3140	385.0947	European Russia
HE623-720	623.89229(4-9)	Interior navigation, By place	HE3151-3160	385.09489	Denmark
HE623-633	623.8922973	United States	HE3161-3170	385.094912	Iceland
HE635-720	623.89229(4-9)	Other countries	HE3171-3180	385.09481	Norway
HE730-943	387.5	Merchant Marine	HE3181-3190	385.09485	Sweden
HE730-736	387.50(5/6)	Serials/Societies	HE3191-3200	385.0946	Spain
HE737-738	387.5	Manuals	HE3201-3210	385.09469	Portugal
HE740-743	387.51	Subsidies	HE3211-3220	385.09494	Switzerland
HE745-943	387.509(4-9)	Merchant Marine, By place	HE3231-3240	385.094977	Bulgaria
HE745-767	387.50973	United States	HE3241-3245	385.09497	Yugoslavia
HE769-937	387.509(4-9)	Other countries	HE3251-3260	385.09498	Romania
HE943	387.5091724	Developing countries	HE3281-3290	385.0951	China
HE951-953	387.16	Port guides/Charges	HE3291-3300	385.0954	India
HE961-971	368.2(2-3)	Marine insurance/Damage	HE3300.3	385.095493	Sri Lanka
HE1001-5600	385	Railways	HE3300.5	385.095491	Pakistan
HE1001-1007	385.0(5/6)	Serials/Societies	HE3300.6	385.095492	Bangladesh
HE1009	385.03	Encyclopedias/Dictionaries	HE3320.3	385.09597	Vietnam
HE1021	385.09	History	HE3320.4	385.09594	Laos
HE1051-1081	343.095	Government control	HE3321-3330	385.09595	Malaysia
HE1601-2591	385.068	Administration	HE3331-3340	385.09598	Indonesia
HE1821-2591	385.2	Traffic	HE3341-3350	385.09599	Philippine Islands
HE1831-2220	385.1	Rates	HE3351-3360	385.0952	Japan
HE1951-2100	385.22	Passenger	HE3360.5	385.09519	Korea/North Korea
HE2231-2261	385.1	Finance	HE3380.3	385.09538	Saudi Arabia
HE2271-2273	385.021	Statistics	HE3401-3410	385.0962	Egypt
HE2301-2547	385.24	Freight	HE3411	385.0964	Morocco
HE2330-2345	385.22	Car service/Delay transit	HE3412	385.0965	Algeria
HE2351-2547	385.2209(4-9)	Passengers, By place	HE3413	385.09611	Tunisia
HE2556	385.22	Baggage	HE3414	385.09612	Libya
HE2561-2591	385.22	Passengers	HE3415	385.09624	Sudan
HE2701-3560	385.09(4-9)	Railroads, By place	HE3416	385.0963	Ethiopia
HE2704-2791	385.0973	United States	HE3417	385.096773	Somalia
HE2801-2810	385.0971	Canada	HE3419	385.096762	Kenya
HE2811-2820	385.0972	Mexico	HE3420	385.096761	Uganda
HE2825.5	385.097282	Belize	HE3421	385.0967571	Rwanda
HE2831-2835	385.097286	Costa Rica	HE3422	385.0967572	Burundi
HE2836-2840	385.097281	Guatemala	HE3423	385.09678	Tanzania
HE2841-2845	385.097283	Honduras	HE3424	385.09679	Mozambique
			HE3425	385.09691	Madagascar

LC	Dewey	Descriptor	LC	Dewey	Descriptor
HE3426	385.0968	South Africa	HE7601	384.05	Serials
HE3428	385.096894	Zambia	HE7603-7604	384.06	Societies/Congresses
HE3429	385.096885	Lesotho	HE7621-7625	384.03	Encyclopedias/Dictionaries
HE3430	385.096887	Swaziland	HE7661	384.068	Administration
HE3431	385.096883	Botswana	HE7669-7679	384.14	Codes
HE3432	385.096897	Malawi	HE7681-7695	384.13	Rates/Finances
HE3432.3	385.096881	Namibia	HE7709-7741	384.1	Ocean cables
HE3433	385.09673	Angola	HE7761-8630.7	384.09(4-9)	Telecommunications, By place
HE3434	385.096751	Zaire			
HE3435	385.096718	Equatorial Guinea	HE7761-7798	384.0973	United States
HE3436	385.096715	Sao Tome/Principe	HE7811-7820	384.0971	Canada
HE3437	385.09672	French Equatorial Africa	HE7821-7830	384.0972	Mexico
HE3438	385.096721	Gabon	HE7831-7900	384.09728	Central America
HE3439	385.096724	Congo	HE7901-7959	384.09729	West Indies
HE3441	385.096743	Chad	HE7961-8080	384.098	South America
HE3442	385.096711	Cameroon	HE8081-8340.5	384.094	Europe
HE3444	385.096683	Benin (Dahomey)	HE8091-8120.5	384.0941	Great Britain
HE3445	385.096681	Togo	HE8141-8150	384.0944	France
HE3446	385.096626	Niger	HE8151-8160.5	384.0943	Germany
HE3447	385.096668	Ivory Coast	HE8171-8180	384.0945	Italy
HE3448	385.096652	Guinea	HE8181-8210.5	384.09492	Low Countries
HE3449	385.096623	Mali	HE8211-8220	384.0947	European Russia
HE3450	385.096625	Burkina Faso	HE8271-8280	384.0946	Spain
HE3451	385.09663	Senegal	HE8291-8300	384.09494	Switzerland
HE3452	385.09661	Mauritania	HE8340.5	384.09495	Greece
HE3453	385.09669	Nigeria	HE8346-8359	384.0956	Middle East
HE3454	385.09667	Ghana	HE8350	384.095694	Israel/Palestine
HE3455	385.09664	Sierra Leone	HE8360	384.09567	Iraq
HE3456	385.096651	Gambia	HE8360.2	384.0955	Iran
HE3457	385.096662	Liberia	HE8360.7-8445	384.095	Far East
HE3458	385.096657	Guinea-Bissau	HE8371-8380	384.0954	India
HE3458.2	385.09648	Spanish Sahara	HE8401-8410	384.09599	Philippine Islands
HE3461-3550	385.0994	Australia	HE8411-8420	384.0952	Japan
HE3550.5	385.0993	New Zealand	HE8421-8430	384.0951	China
HE3601-4043	385.5/388.4	Light rails	HE8461-8527	384.096	Africa
HE3601	385.5/388.4 + 0(5/6)	Serials/Societies	HE8531-8629.5	384.099(3-6)	Australia/New Zealand/ Oceania
HE3651-4043	385.5/388.4 + 09(4-9)	Light rails, By place			
HE4201-5600	388.4	Rapid transit	HE8635	384.091724	Developing countries
HE4201-4202	388.40(5/6)	Serials/Societies	HE8660-8688	384.5	Wireless
HE4301-4391	388.4068	Administration	HE8690-8699	384.54	Radio
HE4401-5600	388.409(4-9)	Rapid transit, By place	HE8700-.9	384.55	Television
HE4401-4491	388.40973	United States	HE8701-9680.7	384.6	Telephone industry
HE4501-5600	388.409(4-9)	Other countries	HE8701	384.60(5/6)	Serials/Societies
HE5601-5720	388.3	Automotive transportation	HE8721	384.6025	Directories
HE5623-5720	388.309(4-9)	Auto transportation, By place	HE8728	384.6021	Statistics
			HE8761-8783	384.6068	Administration
HE5746-5749	388.3228	Stage lines	HE8777-8779	384.63	Rates
HE5751-5870	386.6	Ferries	HE8801-9680.7	384.609(4-9)	Telephone industry, By place
HE5880-5990	388.044	Express service			
HE5880	388.0440(5/6)	Serials/Societies	HE8801-8846	384.60973	United States
HE5889	388.049	Rates	HE8861-9680.7	384.609(4-9)	Other countries
HE5893-5990	388.04409(4-9)	Express service, By place	HE9713-9715	384.53	Wireless telephone industry
HE5893-5904	388.0440973	United States	HE9719-9721	384.51	Satellite telecommunications
HE5905-5990	388.04409(4-9)	Other countries			
HE6000-7496	383	Postal services/Stamps	HE9723-9737	384.1	Signaling
HE6000-6025	383.0(5/6)	Serials/Societies	HE9751-9755	651.79	Messenger service
HE6031-6035	383.03	Encyclopedias/Dictionaries	HE9761-9900	387.7	Air transportation
HE6036	383.07	Education	HE9761-9765	387.70(5/6)	Serials/Societies
HE6041-6055	383.49	History	HE9768-9769	387.703	Encyclopedias/Dictionaries
HE6061	383.492	Biography	HE9774-9775	387.709	History
HE6182-6228	383.23	Stamps/Postmarks	HE9780-9789	387.7068	Administration
HE6246-6278	383.41	International	HE9801-9900	387.709(4-9)	Air transportation, By place
HE6300-7496	383.49(4-9)	Postal service, By place	HE9803-9814	387.70973	United States
HE6300-6500	383.4973	United States	HE9815	387.70971	Canada
HE6651-7496	383.49(4-9)	Other countries	HE9816	387.70972	Mexico
HE7511-7549	651.79	Pneumatic services	HE9817.5-9823	387.709728	Central America
HE7601-8700.9	384. (1-7)	Telecommunications	HE9824.5-9829.9	387.709729	West Indies

LC	Dewey	Descriptor
HE9830-9841	387.7098	South America
HE9842-9867.5	387.7094	Europe
HE9843-9845.5	387.70941	Great Britain
HE9848	387.70944	France
HE9849-.5	387.70943	Germany
HE9851	387.70945	Italy
HE9852-9854.5	387.709492	Low Countries
HE9855	387.70947	European Russia
HE9861	387.70946	Spain
HE9863	387.709494	Switzerland
HE9867.5	387.709495	Greece
HE9868.2-.95	387.70956	Middle East
HE9868.45	387.7095694	Israel/Palestine
HE9869	387.709567	Iraq
HE9869.2	387.70955	Iran
HE9869.7-9881	387.7095	Far East
HE9871	387.70954	India
HE9876	387.709599	Philippine Islands
HE9877	387.70952	Japan
HE9878	387.70951	China
HE9882.3-9888.4	387.7096	Africa
HE9889-9898.9	387.7099(3-6)	Australia/New Zealand/ Oceania
HF	380.1	Commerce
HF1-53	380.10(5/6)	Serials/Societies
HF54	380.1025	Directories
HF55	380.106	Associations/Congresses
HF61	380.1074	Museums
HF71-81	353.82	Ministries/Bureaus
HF351	380.109	History
HF357-389	380.10901	Ancient
HF391-475	380.10902	Medieval
HF479-499	380.1090(3-4)	Modern
HF1001-1002	380.03	Dictionaries/Encyclopedias
HF1014	382.17	Balance of trade
HF1016-1017	380.1021	Statistics
HF1040-1054	338.02	Commodities
HF1101-1186	380.107	Commercial education
HF1101	380.1070(5/6)	Serials/Societies
HF1102	380.10706	Congresses
HF1108	380.10709	History
HF1131-1186	380.1070(4-9)	Commercial education, By place
HF1131-1134	380.107073	United States
HF1135	380.1070(72-8)	Spanish America
HF1140-1165	380.10704	Europe
HF1171	380.10705	Asia
HF1176	380.10706	Africa
HF1181-1186	380.10709(3-4)	Australia/New Zealand
HF1371-1379	382	International trade
HF1401-1647	381/382.3	Commercial policies
HF1413.5-1414	338.6048	Boycotts/Competition
HF1414	338.6048	Competition
HF1414.5-1417	382.6	Exports/Controls/Etc.
HF1419-1420	382.5	Imports
HF1451-1647	382.309(4-9)	Commercial policies, By place
HF1701-2701	382.7	Tariff policy
HF1750-2580.7	382.709(4-9)	Tariff policy, By place
HF1750-1757	382.70973	United States
HF1761-2580.9	382.709(4-9)	Other countries
HF3000-4050	380.109(4-9)	Commerce, By place
HF3000-3163	380.10973	United States
HF3001-3006	380.10973021	Statistics
HF3010-3012	380.10973025	Directories
HF3021-3031	380.10973	History
HF3041-3050	382.0973	Foreign commerce
HF3151-3163	381.0973	Local commerce
HF3221-3230	380.10971	Canada
HF3231-3240	380.10972	Mexico
HF3246-3310	380.109728	Central America
HF3311-3369	380.109729	West Indies
HF3371-3490	380.1098	South America
HF3491-3750.5	380.1094	Europe
HF3501-3530.5	380.10941	Great Britain
HF3551-3560	380.10944	France
HF3561-3570.5	380.10943	Germany
HF3581-3590	380.10945	Italy
HF3590-3620.5	380.109492	Low Countries
HF3621-3630	380.10947	European Russia
HF3681-3690	380.10946	Spain
HF3701-3710	380.109494	Switzerland
HF3750.5	380.109495	Greece
HF3756-3769	380.10956	Middle East
HF3760	380.1095694	Israel/Palestine
HF3770	380.109567	Iraq
HF3770.2	380.10955	Iran
HF3770.3-3855	380.1095	Far East
HF3781-3790	380.10954	India
HF3811-3820	380.109599	Philippine Islands
HF3821-3830	380.10952	Japan
HF3831-3840	380.10951	China
HF3872-3937	380.1096	Africa
HF3941-4039.5	380.1099(3-6)	Australia/New Zealand/ Oceania
HF5001-6182	650	Business
HF5381-5386	331.702	Vocational guidance
HF5387	174.4	Business ethics
HF5410-5417.5	380.1/658.8	Marketing/Distribution
HF5419-5422	381.2	Wholesale trade
HF5428-5429.6	381.1	Retail trade
HF5429.7-5430.6	381.1	Shopping centers
HF5460-5469.5	381.1(42)	Stores/Mail order
HF5469.7-5481	381.18	Markets/Fairs
HF5482-.3	381.19	Secondhand trade
HF5484-5495	388.044	Warehousing/Storage
HF5500.2-5506	651.3	Personnel
HF5520-5541	651.2	Equipment
HF5546-5548.6	651	Office management
HF5548.7-.85	158.7	Industrial psychology
HF5549-.5	658.3	Personnel management
HF5601-5689	657	Accounting/Bookkeeping
HF5717-5746	651.7	Business communications
HF5761-5780	658.788	Shipping/Delivery of goods
HF5801-6182	659.1	Advertising
HF5801-5802	659.10(5/6)	Serials/Societies
HF5802.5	659.106	Congresses
HF5803	659.103	Dictionaries/Encyclopedias
HF5804-5808	659.1025	Directories
HF5810	659.1092	Biography
HF5811-5813	659.109	History
HF5814-5815	659.107	Education
HF5833	343.082	Regulation
HF5837-6146	659.101	Methods
HF5861-5863	659.133	Direct mail
HF5871-6141	659.132	Newspaper/Magazine
HF5901-6097	659.13209(4-9)	Newspaper/Magazine, By place
HF6103	659.13209	History
HF6178-6182	659.1125	Agencies
HG	332	Finance
HG1-52	332.0(5/6)	Serials/Societies
HG63	332.06	Congresses
HG64-96	332.025	Directories

LC	Dewey	Descriptor
HG151	332.03	Encyclopedias/Dictionaries
HG152	332.07	Education
HG171	332.09	History
HG172	332.092	Biography
HG176-.5	332.021	Statistics
HG177	657.48	Liquidity
HG179	332.024	Personal finance
HG201-1496	332.4	Money
HG261-312	332.42(2-4)	Precious metals/Bullion
HG315	332.404(2-3)	Small coins
HG321-329	351.822/332.46/669.92	Mints/Assaying
HG335-341	332.9	Counterfeiting
HG348-353.5	332.4044	Paper money
HG361-363	332.42042	Legal tender
HG381-395	332.45	International currency
HG401-421	332.423	International bimetallism
HG451-1496	332.49(4-9)	Money, By place .
HG451-645	332.4973	United States
HG501-540	332.4973	History, U.S. money
HG656-1496	332.49(4-9)	Other countries
HG1501-3550	332.1	Banking
HG1621-1638	332.82	Rate of interest
HG1641-1643	332.1753	Loans/Bank credits
HG1651-1654	332.84	Discounts
HG1655	332.77	Acceptances
HG1656	332.1	Reserves/Liquidity
HG1660	332.1752	Accounts and deposits
HG1662	368.854	Insurance of deposits
HG1685-1703	332.76	Drafts/Checks
HG1706-1708	657.(2)	Accounting/Bookkeeping
HG1709	332.10285	Electronic data processing
HG1722	332.16	Mergers
HG1723	332.6722	Bank stocks
HG1725-1778	346.082	Banks and the state
HG1811-2351	332.(1-3)	Special classes of banks
HG1811-1855	332.11	Central banks
HG1881-1966	332.21	Savings banks
HG1968-1969	334.2	Trade/Union banks
HG1975-1976	332.28	Development banks
HG1978-2031	332.123	Private banks
HG2032-2039	334.2	Cooperative banks
HG2040	332.722	Mortgage credit agencies
HG2041-2051	332.31	Agriculture credit
HG2070-2106	332.34	Pawn brokering
HG2121-23156	332.32	S & L Associations
HG2251-2256	332.178	Safe deposit companies
HG2301-2351	332.12	Clearing houses
HG2401-3550	332.109(4-9)	Banking, By place
HG2401-2626	332.10973	United States
HG2461-2491	332.10973	History
HG2493	332.10973021	Statistics
HG2535-2543	353.2	Treasury/Currency comptroller
HG3691-3769	332.7	Credit
HG3810-4000	332.45	Foreign exchange
HG3810	332.450(5/6)	Serials/Societies
HG3810.5	332.4503	Encyclopedias/Dictionaries
HG3811-3815	332.4509	History
HG3821-3823	332.4501	Theory/Method
HG3853-3877	332.(450212/042)	Tables/Cambistry
HG3861-3877	332.45609(4-9)	Tables, By place
HG3879-3898	332.(042/15)	Intern'l. finance/ Banking/Etc.
HG3901-4000	332.45609(4-9)	Foreign exchange, By place
HG4001-4280.7	658.15	Financial management
HG4001-4007	658.150(5/6)	Serials/Societies
HG4008	658.1503	Dictionaries/Encyclopedias
HG4009	658.15025	Directories
HG4011-4012	658.1501	Theory/Method
HG4014-4016	658.1507	Education
HG4017	658.1509	History
HG4027-.15	658.15021	Statistics
HG4050-4280.7	658.1509(4-9)	Financial management, By place
HG4050-4070	658.15097(3-9)	United States
HG4090-4280.7	658.1509(4-9)	Other countries
HG4301-4480.9	332.(26-178)	Trust services
HG4301-4305	332.260(5/6)	Serials/Societies
HG4307	332.26025	Directories
HG4311	332.2609	History
HG4341-4480.9	332.2609(4-9)	Trust services, By place
HG4341-4356	332.260973	United States
HG4357-4480.9	332.2609(4-9)	Other countries
HG4501-6051	332.6	Investments
HG4530	332.6327	Mutual funds
HG4538	332.673	Foreign investments
HG4551-4598	332.64	Stock exchanges
HG4621	332.62	Stock brokerage
HG4651-4751	332.632	Securities
HG4905-5993	332.609(4-9)	Investment, By place
HG4905-5131	332.60973	United States
HG4928.5-4930.5	332.620973	Investment companies/ Dealers
HG4931-4955	332.632320973	Government securities
HG4961-4965	332.63220973	Industrial securities
HG5125-5131	332.6097(4-9)	Local, By place
HG5151-5992.7	332.609(4-9)	Other countries
HG6001-6051	332.645	Speculation
HG6105-6270.9	336.17	Lotteries
HG6105	336.1709	History
HG6126-6270.9	336.1709(4-9)	Lotteries, By place
HG7920-7933	332.024/339.43	Thrift/Saving
HG8011-9999	368	Insurance
HG8053.5-8054.4	368.564	Malpractice insurance
HG8059	368.81	Business insurance
HG8075-8107	368.0065	Insurance business
HG8111-8123	346.086	Insurance (State supervision)
HG8205-8220	368.4	Government insurance
HG8501-8740.5	368.9(4-9)	Insurance, By place
HG8501-8540	368.973	United States
HG8550-8740.5	368.9(4-9)	Other countries
HG8751-9271	368.32	Life insurance
HG8779-8793	368.01	Actuarial science
HG8799-8830	368.32	By class insured/By risk
HG8835-8899	368.32065	Life insurance business
HG8901-8914	346.08632/368.32019	State supervision (Life ins.)
HG8941-9200.5	368.32009(4-9)	Life insurance, By place
HG9201-9245	368.363	Mutual life insurance
HG9251-9262	368.362	Industrial life insurance
HG9271	368.32	Child life insurance
HG9291-9295	368.424	Maternity insurance
HG9301-9343	368.384	Accident insurance
HG9371-9399	368.382	Health insurance
HG9651-9899	368.11	Fire insurance
HG9651-9655	368.1100(5/6)	Serials/Societies
HG9657	368.110025	Directories
HG9657.5	368.11003	Encyclopedias/Dictionaries
HG9660	368.11009	History
HG9663	368.110021	Statistics
HG9671-9731	368.110068	Business/Management
HG9689	368.1100212	Tables
HG9711-9725	368.11014	Inspectors/Claims
HG9733-9735	368.11019	State regulations

LC	Dewey	Descriptor	LC	Dewey	Descriptor
HG9751-9866	368.11009(4-9)	Fire insurance, By place	HJ2445-3192.7	336.2009(4-9)	Other countries
HG9751-9780	368.1100973	United States	HJ3231-5957	351.724	Taxation, Administration of
HG9781-9866	368.11009(4-9)	Other places	HJ3241-3245	351.724001	Theory
HG9956-9969	368.8	Casualty insurance	HJ3251-3696	351.724009(4-9)	Tax administration, By place
HG9969.5-9999	368.(1-8)	Other insurance	HJ3251-3361.9	353.00724	United States
HG9970	368.(09-8)	Auto insurance	HJ3260-3361.9	353.9(7-9)00724	By state
HG9972	368.093	Aviation insurance	HJ3370-3696	351.724009(4-9)	Other countries
HG9979	368.122	Disaster insurance	HJ3801-3844	336.1	Income other than taxation
HG9990	368.5	Liability	HJ3851-4939	336.2	Direct taxes
HG9997	368.8(3-4)	Fidelity/Surety insurance	HJ3871-4056.7	336.2009(4-9)	Direct taxes, By place
HG9999	368.88	Title insurance	HJ4101-4939	336.2(2-78)	Specific direct taxes
HJ	336	Public finance	HJ4120-4449	336.2209(4-9)	Land/Real estate tax, By place
HJ9-99.6	351.(02/72)	Documents, By place			
HJ101-119	336.00(5/6)	Serials/Societies	HJ5001-5225	336.2	Indirect taxes
HJ120-129	336.003	Encyclopedias/Dictionaries	HJ5018-5225	336.2009(4-9)	Indirect taxes, By place
HJ131-132	336.001	Theory	HJ5018-5074	336.200973	United States
HJ203-209	330.007	Education	HJ5075-5508	336.2009(4-9)	Other countries
HJ210-1620	336.09(4-9)	History/Conditions	HJ5301-5508	336.(16/272)	Fees/Licenses/Stamp tax
HJ213-227	336.093	Ancient	HJ5321-5508	336.1609(4-9)	Fees/Licenses/Etc., By place
HJ230-240	336.090(3-4)	Medieval/Modern			
HJ241-789	336.73	United States	HJ5321-5374	336.160973	United States
HJ276-789	336.7(4-9)	Local United States, By place	HJ5323-5519	336.1609(4-9)	Other countries
			HJ5521-5957	336.2	Other forms of tax
HJ790-799	336.71	Canada	HJ5703-5797	336.207	Raw materials/ Manufacturing
HJ800-809	336.72	Mexico			
HJ810-844	336.728	Central America	HJ5801-5923	336.276	Inheritance/Transfer
HJ844.3-889.5	336.729	West Indies	HJ5951-5957	336.278388	Transportation/Traffic
HJ890-999	336.8	South America	HJ6603-7390	351.7246	Customs administration
HJ1000-1616	336.4	Europe	HJ6603-6605	351.72460(5/6)	Serials/Societies
HJ1001-1039.7	336.41	Great Britain	HJ6606-6607	351.724603	Dictionaries/Encyclopedias
HJ1071-1099	336.44	France	HJ6619	364.133	Smuggling
HJ1101-1150.5	336.43	Germany	HJ6620-7390	351.724609(4-9)	Administration, By place
HJ1151-1155	336.495	Greece	HJ6620-6740	351.72460973	United States
HJ1156-1188	336.45	Italy	HJ6750-7174.7	351.724609(4-9)	Other countries
HJ1190-1204.5	336.492	Low Countries	HJ7451-7977	336.(39/206)	Expenditure
HJ1205-1211.5	336.47	European Russia	HJ7531-7977	336.3909(4-9)	Expenditure, By place
HJ1241-1249	336.46	Spain	HJ7531-7654	336.390973	United States
HJ1255-1264	336.494	Switzerland	HJ7660-7977	336.3909(4-9)	Other countries
HJ1302-1316	336.56	Middle East	HJ8003-8899	336.3	Public credit/Debts/Loans
HJ1306	336.5694	Israel/Palestine	HJ8003-8011	336.309	History
HJ1317	336.567	Iraq	HJ8034	336.34	Public credits/Creditors
HJ1318	336.55	Iran	HJ8046-8049	336.344	Borrowing/Forms of loans
HJ1320.7-1425	336.5	Far East	HJ8052	336.363	Amortization/Sinking funds
HJ1331-1340	336.54	India	HJ8055	336.363	Reduction/Liquidation
HJ1381-1390	336.599	Philippine Islands	HJ8061-8079	336.368	Insolvency
HJ1391-1400	338.52	Japan	HJ8101-8899	336.3409(4-9)	Public credit, By place
HJ1401-1410	336.51	China	HJ9000-9694.7	336.01 (3-4)	Local finance
HJ1441-1507	336.6	Africa	HJ9011-9109	336.01(3-4)0(5/6)	Serials/Societies
HJ1511-1609.5	336.9(3-6)	Australia/New Zealand/ Oceania	HJ9115-9123	336.201(3-4)	Revenue/Tax
			HJ9125-9127	336.3909(4-9)	Expenditure
HJ2005-2347	336.(1-3)	Income/Expenditure	HJ9141-9694.7	336.01(3-4)(4-9)	Local finance, By place
HJ2005-2216	336/351.722	The budget	HJ9141-9343	336.01(3-4)7(4-9)	United States
HJ2005-2043	336.001/351.72201	Theory	HJ9170-9343	336.01(3-4)097(4-9)	U.S. local, By place
HJ2050-2053	353.00722	United States	HJ9350-9694.7	336.01(3-4)(4-9)	Other countries
HJ2054-2215	354.(4-9)00722	Other countries	HJ9701-9995	657.61	Public accounting
HJ2240-3192.7	336.(02/2)	Revenue/Taxation	HJ9701-9741	657.610(5/6)	Serials/Societies
HJ2240	336.200(5/6)	Serials/Etc.	HJ9745-9769	657.6101	Methods
HJ2250-2279	336.2009	History	HJ9801-9940	657.6109(4-9)	Public accounting, By place
HJ2300-2323	336.2001	Theory	HJ9801-9920	657.610973	United States
HJ2326-2327	336.293	Progressive/Taxation	HJ9817-9920	657.61097(4-9)	Local, By place
HJ2336-2337	336.206	Exemption	HJ9921-9940	657.6109(4-9)	Other countries
HJ2341-2343	336.294	Double taxation	HM	301	Sociology
HJ2348.5	364.133	Tax evasion	HM1-7	301.05	Serials
HJ2351.4	336.20015195	Tax revenue estimating	HM9-13	301.06	Societies/Congresses
HJ2360-3192.7	336.2009(4-9)	Revenue/Taxation, By place	HM17	301.03	Dictionaries/Encyclopedias
HJ2360-2442	336.200973	United States	HM19-22	301.09	History
HJ2385-2442	336.20097(4-9)	Local, By place			

LC	Dewey	Descriptor	LC	Dewey	Descriptor
HM22	301.09(4-9)	By place	HN261-270	361.982	Argentina
HM24-37	301.01	Theory/Etc.	HN271-280	361.984	Bolivia
HM41-43	301.074	Museums	HN281-290	361.981	Brazil
HM45-48	301.07(2)	Education/Research	HN291-300	361.983	Chile
HM101-121	306	Civilization/Culture	HN301-310	361.9861	Colombia
HM131-134	305	Social groups	HN311-320	361.9866	Ecuador
HM132	302	Interpersonal relations	HN330.3	361.9881	Guyana
HM136-146	302.54	Individualism	HN330.5	361.9883	Suriname
HM201-221	303-306	Social forces/Laws	HN330.7	361.9882	French Guiana
HM206-208	304.2	Environment	HN331-340	361.9892	Paraguay
HM211	306.3	Economic	HN341-350	361.985	Peru
HM213	306.42	Intellectual	HN351-360	361.9895	Uruguay
HM216	303.372	Moral	HN361-370	361.987	Venezuela
HM219	306.6	Religious	HN381-400	361.941	Great Britain
HM221	306.46	Technological	HN400.3	361.9417	Ireland/Irish Republic
HM251-291	302	Social psychology	HN401-420	361.9436	Austria
HM258	302.2	Communication	HN420.3	361.9437	Czechoslovakia
HM261	303.38	Public opinion	HN420.5	361.9439	Hungary
HM263	303.375	Public relations/Propaganda	HN420.9	361.943648	Liechtenstein
HM281-283	302.33/303.6	Crowds/Violence	HN421-440	361.944	France
HN	361	Social history/Problems	HN440.5	361.944949	Monaco
HN1	361.00(5/6)	Serials/Societies	HN441-460.5	361.943	Germany
HN3	361.006	Congresses	HN471-490	361.945	Italy
HN8-19	361.9	History	HN501-510	361.9493	Belgium
HN9-10	361.901	Ancient	HN511-520	361.9492	Netherlands
HN11	361.902	Medieval	HN520.5	361.94935	Luxembourg
HN13-18	361.9(3-4)	Modern	HN521-530	361.947	European Russia
HN14	361.90(31-33)	Medieval to 1800	HN531-535	361.94897	Finland
HN15-.5	361.9034	19th century	HN536-539.5	361.9438	Poland
HN16-18	361.904	20th century	HN541-550	361.9489	Denmark
HN25	361.0021	Statistics	HN551-560	361.94912	Iceland
HN28	361.001	Theory	HN561-570	361.9481	Norway
HN29	361.007	Education	HN571-580	361.9485	Sweden
HN30-39	261.83	Church and social problems	HN581-590	361.946	Spain
HN39	261.8309(4-9)	Religion/Etc., By place	HN591-600	361.9469	Portugal
HN40	291.1783	Non-Christian & social problems	HN601-610	361.9494	Switzerland
HN41-46	790.068	Community/Social centers	HN620.5	361.94965	Albania
HN41	790.0680(5/6)	Serials/Societies	HN621-630	361.94977	Bulgaria
HN43-46	790.06809(4-9)	Community centers, By place	HN631-635	361.9497	Yugoslavia
HN43-45	790.0680973	United States	HN641-650	361.9498	Romania
HN50-981	361.9(4-9)	Social problems, By place	HN650.5	361.9495	Greece
HN51-90	361.973	United States	HN656.5	361.9561	Turkey
HN101-110	361.971	Canada	HN657	361.95645	Cyprus
HN111-120	361.972	Mexico	HN658	361.95691	Syria
HN126-130	361.97282	Belize	HN659	361.95692	Lebanon
HN131-140	361.9728	Costa Rica	HN660	361.95694	Israel/Palestine
HN141-150	361.97281	Guatemala	HN661	361.95695	Jordan
HN151-160	361.97283	Honduras	HN663	361.9538	Saudi Arabia
HN161-170	361.97285	Nicaragua	HN664-.5	361.95332	Yemen
HN171-175	361.97287	Panama	HN665	361.95353	Oman
HN176-180	361.972875	Panama Canal Zone	HN666	361.95357	United Arab Emirates
HN181-190	361.97284	El Salvador	HN667	361.95363	Qatar
HN196-200	361.97296	Bahamas	HN668	361.95365	Bahrein
HN201-210	361.97291	Cuba	HN669	361.95367	Kuwait
HN211-215	361.97294	Haiti	HN670	361.9567	Iraq
HN216-220	361.97293	Dominican Republic	HN670.2	361.955	Iran
HN221-230	361.97292	Jamaica	HN670.6	361.9581	Afghanistan
HN231-240	361.97295	Puerto Rico	HN670.7	361.9591	Burma
HN241	361.9729722	Virgin Islands of the U.S.	HN670.8	361.95493	Sri Lanka
HN244	361.97297	Leeward Islands	HN670.9	361.95496	Nepal
HN245	361.972984	Windward Islands	HN681-690	361.954	India
HN246	361.972983	Trinidad and Tobago	HN690.3	361.95498	Bhutan
HN247	361.972986	Netherlands Antilles	HN690.5	361.95491	Pakistan
HN249	361.972976	Guadeloupe	HN690.6	361.95492	Bangladesh
HN250	361.972982	Martinique	HN700.3	361.9596	Cambodia
			HN700.4	361.9594	Laos
			HN700.5	361.9597	Vietnam

LC	Dewey	Descriptor
HN700.55	361.9593	Thailand
HN700.6	361.9595	Malaysia
HN700.67	361.95957	Singapore
HN700.68	361.95955	Brunei
HN701-710	361.9598	Indonesia
HN711-720	361.9599	Philippine Islands
HN721-730	361.952	Japan
HN730.5-.6	361.9519	Korea/North Korea
HN730.8	361.9517	Mongolia
HN731-740	361.951	China
HN746-750	361.951249	Taiwan
HN751-755	361.95125	Hong Kong
HN782	361.964	Morocco
HN783	361.965	Algeria
HN784	361.9611	Tunisia
HN785	361.9612	Libya
HN786	361.962	Egypt
HN787	361.9624	Sudan
HN789	361.963	Ethiopia
HN790	361.96773	Somalia
HN791	361.96771	Djibouti
HN793	361.96762	Kenya
HN794	361.96761	Uganda
HN795	361.967571	Rwanda
HN796	361.967572	Burundi
HN797	361.9678	Tanzania
HN798	361.9679	Mozambique
HN801	361.968	South Africa
HN802	361.9689	Zimbabwe (Southern Rhodesia)
HN803	361.96894	Zambia (Northern Rhodesia)
HN804	361.96885	Lesotho
HN805	361.96887	Swaziland
HN806	361.96883	Botswana
HN807	361.96897	Malawi (Nyasaland)
HN808	361.96881	Namibia
HN810	361.9673	Angola
HN811	361.96751	Zaire
HN812	361.96718	Equatorial Guinea
HN813	361.96715	Sao Tome/Principe
HN814	361.9672	French Equatorial Africa
HN815	361.96721	Gabon
HN816	361.96724	Congo
HN817	361.96741	Central African Republic
HN818	361.96743	Chad
HN819	361.96711	Cameroon
HN822	361.96683	Benin (Dahomey)
HN823	361.96681	Togo
HN824	361.96626	Niger
HN825	361.96668	Ivory Coast
HN826	361.96652	Guinea
HN827	361.96623	Mali
HN828	361.96625	Burkina Faso
HN829	361.9663	Senegal
HN830	361.9661	Mauritania
HN831	361.9669	Nigeria
HN832	361.9667	Ghana
HN833	361.9664	Sierra Leone
HN834	361.96651	Gambia
HN835	361.96662	Liberia
HN836	361.96657	Guinea-Bissau
HN837	361.9648	Spanish Sahara
HN838	361.94699	Azores
HN838.3	361.97299	Bermuda
HN838.5	361.94698	Madeira Islands
HN838.7	361.9649	Canary Islands
HN838.9	361.96658	Cape Verde Islands
HN839	361.9973	St. Helena
HN839.3	361.9973	Tristan da Cunha
HN839.5	361.9971	Falkland Islands
HN839.7	361.95495	Maldive Islands
HN839.9	361.9696	Seychelles
HN840	361.9694	Comoro Islands
HN840.3	361.96982	Mauritius
HN840.5	361.96981	Reunion
HN840.7	361.9699	Kerguelen Islands
HN841-850	361.994	Australia
HN930.5	361.993	New Zealand
HN931.5	361.9967	Guam
HN932	361.9953	Papua New Guinea
HN932.3	361.99681	Kiribati (Gilbert Islands)
HN933	361.99593	Solomon Islands
HN934	361.99597	New Caledonia
HN935	361.99595	Vanuatu
HN936	361.99611	Fiji Islands
HN937	361.99612	Tonga
HN938	361.99613	American Samoa
HN939	361.99614	Western Samoa
HN939.5	361.9962	French Polynesia
HN940	361.98	Arctic regions
HN942.5	361.982	Greenland
HN942.7	361.989	Antarctic regions
HN958-962	361.91717	Communist countries
HN978-981	361.91724	Developing countries
HQ	306.8	Marriage/The family/Woman
HQ1	306.805	Serials
HQ3/7	306.806	Societies/Congresses
HQ9	306.803	Dictionaries/Encyclopedias
HQ10-.5	306.807	Education
HQ12-449	306.7	Sexual life
HQ12-18	306.709	Sexual life, history
HQ13-16	306.7090(1-4)	By date
HQ18	306.709(3-9)	By place
HQ18.3-.32	306.7092	Biography
HQ19-30.7	306.7	Sexuality/Sexual behavior
HQ27-.5	306.70835	Adolescents/Young adults
HQ27.3	306.708351	Boys
HQ27.5	306.708352	Girls
HQ28	306.7081	Men
HQ29	306.7082	Women
HQ30	306.70846	Aged
HQ30.5	306.7087	Handicapped
HQ30.7	306.70877	The sick
HQ31-64	613.9/176	Sex instruction/Ethics
HQ35	613.90835	Adolescents
HQ36	613.9081	Men
HQ46	613.9082	Women
HQ53	613.9083	Children
HQ54-.3	613.9087	Handicapped adults
HQ55	613.90846	Aged
HQ56-57.6	613.9	Teaching
HQ57.5-.6	613.909(4-9)	Teaching sex, By place
HQ60	613.9072	Sex research
HQ71-72	364.1536/616.8583	Sexual deviations/Crimes
HQ74	306.765	Bisexuality
HQ75-76.8	306.766/616.85834	Homosexuality/Lesbianism
HQ77	306.77	Transvestitism
HQ77.7-.9	305.3	Transsexualism
HQ79	306.77(5-6)/616.85835	Sadism/Masochism/Fetishism
HQ101-440.7	306.74/363.44	Prostitution
HQ111-117	306.7409	History

LC	Dewey	Descriptor
HQ121-125	364.1534	Regulation/And the law
HQ141-270.7	306.7409(4-9)	Prostitution, By place
HQ143-146	306.740973	United States
HQ147-150	306.740971	Canada
HQ151	306.740972	Mexico
HQ153-159	306.7409728	Central America
HQ160-165.9	306.7409729	West Indies
HQ166-183	306.74098	South America
HQ184-231.84	306.74094	Europe
HQ185-187.5	306.740941	Great Britain
HQ193-196	306.740944	France
HQ197-200.5	306.740943	Germany
HQ202-205	306.740945	Italy
HQ206-213.5	306.7409492	Low Countries
HQ214-217	306.740947	European Russia
HQ225-228	306.740946	Spain
HQ230	306.7409494	Switzerland
HQ231.83	306.7409495	Greece
HQ231.93-232.56	306.740956	Middle East
HQ232.2	306.74095694	Israel
HQ232.55	306.7409567	Iraq
HQ232.56	306.740955	Iran
HQ232.7-253	306.74095	Far East
HQ237-240	306.740954	India
HQ245	306.7409599	Philippine Islands
HQ247	306.740952	Japan
HQ250	306.740951	China
HQ257-269.3	306.74096	Africa
HQ270-.43	306.74099(3-6)	Australia/New Zealand/ Oceania
HQ280-285	363.44/364.1534/380.144	Traffic in women
HQ301-440.7	362.8	Rescue work
HQ311-440.7	362.809(4-9)	Rescue work, By place
HQ447	306.772	Masturbation
HQ450-471	808.803538	Erotica
HQ461-470	306.7/420-490.0803538	Erotic literature, By language
HQ471	808.803538	Pornography
HQ503-2039	306.8	The family/Marriage/Home
HQ503-727	306.809	The family/Etc., History
HQ505-518	306.809	By date
HQ505-512	306.80901	Ancient
HQ513	306.80902	Medieval
HQ515-518	306.809	Modern
HQ525	306.8089(03-99)	By race/Nationality/Etc.
HQ531-727	306.809(4-9)	The family/Marriage, By place
HQ535-557	306.80973	United States
HQ559-560	306.80971	Canada
HQ561-562	306.80972	Mexico
HQ563-574	306.809728	Central America
HQ575-587.9	306.809729	West Indies
HQ588-610	306.8098	South America
HQ611-662.7	306.8094	Europe
HQ613-618.5	306.80941	Great Britain
HQ623-624	306.80944	France
HQ625-626.5	306.80943	Germany
HQ629-630	306.80945	Italy
HQ631-636.5	306.809492	Low Countries
HQ637-638	306.80947	European Russia
HQ649-650	306.80946	Spain
HQ653-654	306.809494	Switzerland
HQ662.5	306.809495	Greece
HQ663.3-666.4	306.80956	Middle East
HQ664	306.8095694	Israel/Palestine
HQ666.3	306.809567	Iraq
HQ666.4	306.80955	Iran

LC	Dewey	Descriptor
HQ666.7-687	306.8095	Far East
HQ669-670	306.80954	India
HQ679-680	306.809599	Philippine Islands
HQ681-682	306.80952	Japan
HQ684	306.80951	China
HQ691-697.4	306.8096	Africa
HQ705-723.9	306.8099(3-6)	Australia/New Zealand/Oceania
HQ745-746	392.5/395.22	Weddings
HQ750-755.5	363.92	Eugenics
HQ755.7-759.92	306.874	Parents
HQ756.-.5	306.8742	Husbands/Fathers
HQ759-.6	306.8743	Wives
HQ760-767.7	304.63/363.96	Family size
HQ762	304.6309/363.9609	Family size, By place
HQ763-767.7	304.6/363.96	Family planning/Birth control
HQ767.8-792.2	305.23	Children/Child development
HQ767.8	305.230(5/6)	Serials/Societies
HQ767.82	305.2306	Congresses
HQ767.84	305.2303	Dictionaries/Encyclopedias
HQ767.85	305.2307	Education
HQ767.87	305.2309	History
HQ768-778.7	392.13/649.1	Child rearing
HQ781-784	305.23	Child life/Activities
HQ792-.2	305.2309(4-9)	Conditions, By place
HQ793-799.2	305.235	Youth/Adolescence
HQ796-798	305.2350973	United States
HQ799	305.23509(4-9)	Other countries
HQ799.5-.9	305.235	Young adults
HQ799.95-.97	305.24	Adulthood
HQ800-.4	305.90652	Single people
HQ801-802.5	306.734	Courtship/Dating/Etc.
HQ805-806	306.88	Desertion/Adultery
HQ811-960.7	306.89	Divorce
HQ831-960.7	306.8909(4-9)	Divorce, By place
HQ833-836	306.890973	United States
HQ837-960.9	306.8909(4-9)	Other countries
HQ961-967	306.735	Free love
HQ970-972	307.774	Communal living
HQ981-997	306.8423	Polygamy/Polyandry
HQ998-999	306.856	Unmarried mothers
HQ1001-1006	346.016	Marriage and the state
HQ1018-1043	306.84	Misc. marriage situations
HQ1059.4-.5	305.244	Middle age
HQ1060-1064	305.26	Aged
HQ1073-.5	306.9	Death/Dying
HQ1075-.5	305.3	Sex roles
HQ1088-1090.7	305.31	Men
HQ1101-2039	305.4	Women/Feminism
HQ1121-1154	305.409	History
HQ1180-1181	305.407	Education/Women's studies
HQ1236-.5	323.34	Women and the state/Rights
HQ1240-1399	305.4	Misc. aspects of women/ Society
HQ1402-1870.5	305.409(4-9)	Women, By place
HQ1402-1439	305.40973	United States
HQ1451-1870.9	305.409(4-9)	Other countries
HQ1871-2030.7	305.4(06/8)/367	Women's clubs/Societies
HS	366-367/369	Societies (Secret/ Benevolent)
HS1	366.0(5/6)	Serials/Societies
HS5	366.06	Congresses
HS8	366.05	Yearbooks
HS12	366.05	Dictionaries/Encyclopedias
HS17	366.025	Directories

LC	Dewey	Descriptor
HS25	366.09	History
HS61-89	366.09(4-9)	Organization, By place
HS61	366.0973	United States
HS63	366.0971	Canada
HS65	366.09(728-8)	Central/South America
HS67	366.0941	Great Britain
HS71	366.094	Other European countries
HS81	366.095	Asia
HS84	366.096	Africa
HS87	366.099(3-4)	Australia/New Zealand
HS89	366.099(5-6)	Oceania
HS101-330.7	366.(1-5)	Secret societies
HS101-106	366.(1-5)05	Serials
HS110	366.(1-5)06	Congresses
HS113	366.(1-5)05	Yearbooks/Almanacs
HS119	366.(1-5)03	Dictionaries/Encyclopedias
HS125-148	366.(1-5)09	History
HS131	366.(1-5)093	Ancient
HS137	366.(1-5)090(2-31)	Medieval to 1600
HS146	366.(1-5)09033	18th century
HS147	366.(1-5)09034	19th century
HS148	366.(1-5)	20th century
HS162	728.4	Halls/Buildings
HS181-191	366.(1-5)	Anti-secret society
HS201-330.7	366.(1-5)09(4-9)	Secret societies, By place
HS203-206	366.(1-5)0973	United States
HS207-330.7	366.(1-5)09(4-9)	Other places
HS351-929	366.1	Freemasons
HS351-359	366.105	Serials
HS365	366.105	Yearbooks
HS375	366.103	Dictionaries/Encyclopedias
HS381-390	366.1025	Directories
HS383-387	366.10973	United States
HS390	366.109(4-9)	Other countries
HS392-394	366.107	Education/Research
HS399-400	366.1092	Biography
HS403-420	366.109	History
HS455-459	366.12	Rituals
HS469	728.4	Halls/Buildings
HS503-680.7	366.109(4-9)	Freemasons, By place
HS503-539	366.10973	United States
HS557-680.7	366.109(4-9)	Other countries
HS701-833	366.1(6-7)	Other Masonic bodies
HS851-859	366.18	Women in Masonry
HS875-895	366.1089036	Freemasonry and blacks
HS951-1179	366.3	Odd Fellows
HS951-953	366.305	Serials
HS963-975	366.3025	Directories
HS987-991	366.309	History
HS1029	728.4	Buildings/Halls
HS1041-1051	366.309(4-9)	Odd Fellows, By place
HS1041-1045	366.30973	United States
HS1051	366.309(4-9)	Other countries
HS1161	366.38	Women in Odd Fellows
HS1171-1179	366.3089036	Odd Fellows and blacks
HS1201-1350	366.2	Knights of Pythias
HS1201	366.205	Serials
HS1205	366.203	Dictionaries/Encyclopedias
HS1207-1213	366.2025	Directories
HS1219	366.209	History
HS1238	728.4	Buildings/Halls
HS1251-1261	366.209	By place
HS1251-1254	366.20973	United States
HS1261	366.209(4-9)	Other countries
HS1355-3369	369	Other societies
HS1501-1510	334.7	Benevolent/Friendly societies
HS1525-1560	291.65	Religious societies
HS1601-2265	369.3(03-9)	Race societies
HS2301-2460.7	369.2	Political/Patriotic societies
HS2321-2330	369.1	United States
HS2501-3365	367	Clubs
HS2501-2503	367.05	Serials
HS2507-2515	367.025	Directories
HS2521	367.01	Theory
HS2721-3200	367.9(4-9)	Clubs, By place
HS2721-2725	367.973	United States
HS2731-3200	367.9(4-9)	Other countries
HS3250-3270	367.4	Children's clubs
HS3250-.2	369.406	Congresses
HS3252	369.403	Dictionaries/Encyclopedias
HS3254	369.409	History
HS3256-.2	369.4092	Biography
HS3260	369.409(4-9)	Children's clubs, By place
HS3265-3270	369.4(3/6)	Scouts/Scouting (General)
HS3270	369.4(3/6)09(4-9)	Scouting, By place
HS3301-3325	369.42	Boys' societies
HS3312-3315	369.43	Boy Scouts
HS3341-3365	369.4(6-7)	Girls' societies
HT	305-307	Communities/Classes/Races
HT51	305.05	Serials
HT53-55	305.06	Societies/Congresses
HT101-395	307.76	Urban sociology/Groups/ City
HT101-103	307.7605	Serials
HT105-107	307.7606	Societies/Congresses
HT108.5	307.7603	Dictionaries/Encyclopedias
HT109	307.7607	Education/Museums
HT110	307.76072	Research
HT111-149.5	307.7609	History
HT114	307.76093	Ancient cities
HT115	307.760902	Medieval cities
HT119	307.76	Modern cities
HT121-149.5	307.7609(4-9)	Cities, By place
HT123-.5	307.760973	United States
HT127	307.760971	Canada
HT127.7	307.760972	Mexico
HT128-.5	307.760972 (8/9)	Central America/West Indies
HT129	307.76098	South America
HT131-145	307.760094	Europe
HT133	307.760941	Great Britain
HT135	307.760944	France
HT137	307.760943	Germany
HT147	307.76095	Asia
HT147.5	307.7609174927	Arab countries
HT148	307.76096	Africa
HT149	307.76099(3-6)	Australia/New Zealand/ Oceania
HT149.5	307.76091724	Developing countries
HT165.5-169.9	307.1216/711.4	City planning
HT165.5-.53	307.1207/711.407	Education
HT167-169.5	307.1216/711.4 + 09(4-9)	By place
HT167-168	307.1216/711.4 + 0973	United States
HT169-.5	307.1216/711.4 + 09(4-9)	Other countries
HT169.55-.57	307.768	New towns
HT169.6-.9	333.7717	Zoning
HT170-178	307.3416	Urban renewal
HT175-177	307.34160973	United States
HT178	307.341609(4-9)	Other countries
HT201-221	307.76	City population (Life, etc.)
HT330-334	307.764	Metropolitan areas
HT351	307.74	Suburban cities/Towns
HT381	307.26	Movement to country

LC	Dewey	Descriptor
HT390-395	307.12	Regional planning
HT392-394	307.120973	United States
HT395	307.1209(4-9)	Other countries
HT401-485	307.72	Rural groups/Sociology
HT401-403	307.7205	Serials
HT405-407	307.7206	Societies/Congresses
HT411	307.7207	Education
HT415	307.7209	History
HT601-1445	305.5	Classes
HT601	305.505	Serials
HT603	305.506	Societies
HT607	305.509	History
HT641-657	305.522	Classes, By birth
HT647-653	305.522(2-3)	Royalty/Nobility
HT655-657	305.5	Commons
HT675-690	305.5	Classes, By occupations
HT680-690	305.55	Middle class
HT690	305.5(5-6)09(4-9)	By place
HT713-725	305.5122	Caste system
HT751-815	306.365	Serfdom
HT775	306.365090(1-4)	By date
HT781-815	306.36509(4-9)	Serfdom, By place
HT781	306.3650941	Great Britain
HT785	306.3650944	France
HT791-801	306.3650943	Germany
HT803	306.3650943(6/9)	Austria/Hungary
HT807-809	306.3650947	Russia
HT815	306.36509(4-9)	Other countries
HT851-1445	305.567	Slavery
HT851	305.56705	Serials
HT853-855	305.56706	Societies/Congresses
HT861-867	305.56709	History
HT910-921	261.8/291.17834567	Religion and slavery
HT941-950	326/342.085	Law and slavery
HT975-999	380.144	Slave trade
HT1025-1037	326	Abolition of slavery
HT1048-1445	305.56709(4-9)	Slavery, By place
HT1051-1052	305.5670971	Canada
HT1053-1054	305.5670972	Mexico
HT1055-1056	305.56709728	Central America
HT1071-1119	305.56709729	West Indies
HT1121-1152	305.567098	South America
HT1155-1240	305.567094	Europe
HT1161-1165	305.5670941	Great Britain
HT1176-1180	305.5670944	France
HT1181-1185	305.5670943	Germany
HT1191-1195	305.5670945	Italy
HT1196-1205	305.56709492	Low Countries
HT1206-1210	305.5670947	European Russia
HT1216-1220	305.5670946	Spain
HT1227-1228	305.56709494	Switzerland
HT1234	305.56709495	Greece
HT1240.5-1315	305.567095	Far East
HT1241-1245	305.5670951	China
HT1271-1275	305.56709599	Philippine Islands
HT1276-1280	305.5670952	Japan
HT1321-1427	305.567096	Africa
HT1431-1445	305.567099(3-6)	Australia/New Zealand/ Oceania
HT1501-1595	305.8	Races
HT1501	305.8005	Serials
HT1503-1505	305.8006	Societies/Congresses
HT1506	305.8007	Education
HT1507	305.8009	History
HT1561	177.5	Ethics of race questions
HT1575-1595	305.8(03-99)	By race
HT1575	305.8034	Caucasian
HT1577	305.8034	Aryan/Indo-European
HT1581-1589	305.8(036/93)	Black/Hamitic
HV	361.1/364	Social pathology/ Criminology
HV1-4	361.105	Serials
HV6	361.106	Societies
HV7	361.1025	Directories
HV8	361.106	Congresses
HV10	361.1074	Exhibitions/Museums
HV10.5	361.3023	Social work as a profession
HV11	361.107	Education
HV11.5	361.1076	Examinations/ Questions/ Etc.
HV12	361.103	Dictionaries/Encyclopedias
HV16-25	361.709	History of philanthropy
HV27-28	361.1092	Biography
HV29	361.1021	Statistics
HV29.2-.5	361.10285	Computer applications
HV40-525	361.(3/7)	Social work/Charities
HV40.3-.32	361.3092	Biography
HV40.4-.42	361.37	Non-professional workers
HV41.2-.9	361.706 81	Fund raising
HV42	659.293613	Mass media/Public relations
HV46-.2	331.88113613	Social workers' trade unions
HV48	361.7	Private relief/Aid
HV51-57	361.6	Public relief/Aid
HV59-61	361.05	Institutional/Indoor relief
HV65	361.05	Noninstitutional/Outdoor aid
HV67	361.3091734	Rural social work
HV70-72	344.032	Public welfare laws
HV85-520.5	361.309(4-9)	Social work, By place
HV85-99	361.30973	United States
HV98-99	361.3097(4-9)	By state/City
HV101-520.5	361.309(4-9)	Other countries
HV530	261.832/361.75	The church and charity
HV547	374.22	Self-help groups
HV553-639	363.348	Disaster relief
HV555	363.34809(4-9)	Disaster relief, By place
HV560-583	361.77	Red Cross/Crescent
HV568	361.7709	History
HV569	361.77092	Biography
HV575-580	361.7709(4-9)	By place
HV589-593	361.7(4-6)	Other relief associations
HV599-639	363.349	Types of disasters
HV599-600	363.34958	Earthquakes
HV609-610	363.34938	Floods
HV620	363.37	Fires
HV625-626	363.34928	Droughts
HV630-635	363.8	Famines
HV636	363.34928	Storms/Hurricanes/ Typhoons
HV638	363.119622	Mine disasters
HV638.5	363.34958	Volcanoes
HV639	363.34988	War
HV640-645	362.87	Refugee problems
HV675-677	363.107	Accident prevention
HV680-685	362.58	Legal aid
HV687-694	362.1(1-6)	Medical charities/Advice/ Aid
HV689-690	362.20425	Psychiatric social work
HV694	363.883	Soup kitchens
HV697-4959	362	Protection/Assistance/Relief
HV697-700.7	362.82	Families
HV699-700	362.8209(4-9)	By place
HV700.5	362.8294	Unmarried mothers
HV700.7	362.8294	Unmarried fathers

LC	Dewey	Descriptor	LC	Dewey	Descriptor
HV701-1420.5	362.7	Children	HV4102-4105	362.50945	Italy
HV701-707	362.70(5/6)	Serials/Societies/Congresses	HV4105.5-4113.5	362.509492	Low Countries
HV741-803	362.709(4-9)	By place	HV4114-4117	362.50947	European Russia
HV741-743	362.70973	United States	HV4125-4128	362.50946	Spain
HV745-804	362.709(4-9)	Other countries	HV4131.9-4132.56	362.50956	Near East
HV835-847	362.73	Foundlings	HV4132.6-4153	362.5095	Asia
HV851-861	362.712	Day care centers	HV4137-4140	362.50954	India
HV862-866	362.732	Residential care/Group homes	HV4147	362.50952	Japan
HV873-887	362.7(3/6)	Destitute/Neglected/ Abandoned	HV4150	362.50951	China
			HV4157-4169.3	362.5096	Africa
HV874.8-875.7	362.734	Adoption	HV4170-.68	362.5099(4-6)	Australia/New Zealand/ Oceania
HV877-878	369.42	Boys (Clubs/Etc.)	HV4173	362.5091724	Developing countries
HV879	369.46	Girls (Societies/Etc.)	HV4480-4630	362.5	Mendicancy/Vagabondism/ Tramps
HV880-887	362.7309(4-9)	Destitute, By place			
HV880-885	362.730973	United States	HV4997-5000	362.29	Substance abuse
HV888-907	362.(3-4)	Handicapped children	HV4999.2-5000	362.2909(4-9)	By place
HV891-901	362.3	Mentally handicapped	HV5001-5720.5	362.292	Alcoholism/Intemperance
HV903-907	362.4	Physically handicapped	HV5001-5002	362.29205	Serials
HV959-1420.5	362.732	Orphans/Orphanages	HV5006-5009	362.29206	Societies/Congresses
HV971-1420.5	362.73209(4-9)	Orphanages, By place	HV5020-5025	362.29209	History
HV971-995	362.7320973	United States	HV5030-5032	362.292092	Biography
HV1421-1441	362.7083	Young men/Women	HV5045	616.86107	Psychology of alcoholism
HV1442-1448	362.83	Women	HV5081-5095	344.044 61	Alcoholism and the state
HV1449	363.49	Homosexuals	HV5203-5247	362.2927	Women and temperance reform
HV1450-1493	362.6	Aged			
HV1454-.2	362.61	Life care communities	HV5275-5283	362.2928	Care/Rehabilitation
HV1457-1493	362.609(4-9)	Aged, By place	HV5285-5720.5	362.29209(4-9)	Alcoholism, By place
HV1551-3024	362.(3-4)	Handicapped adults	HV5285-5298	362.2920973	United States
HV1570-.5	362.1968	Developmentally disabled	HV5301-5720.5	362.29209(4-9)	Other countries
HV1571-2349	362.41	Blind	HV5725-5770	362.296	Tobacco habit
HV1584	362.41092	Biography	HV5755-5770	362.29609(4-9)	By place
HV1597-.2	362.41	Deaf-blind	HV5755-5768	362.2960973	United States
HV1618-1708	371.911	Education of the blind	HV5770	362.296(4-9)	Other countries
HV1783-2220.5	362.4109(4-9)	Blind persons, By place	HV5800-5840	362.29(3-9)	Drug habits/Abuse
HV1783-1796	362.410973	United States	HV5810	362.298	Cocaine/Crack
HV1801-2220.5	362.4109(4-9)	Other countries	HV5813	362.293	Morphine
HV2350-2990.5	362.42	Deaf	HV5816	362.293	Opium
HV2373	362.42092	Biography	HV5823-.5	616.86	Drug testing
HV2402	362.4283	Interpreters	HV5825-5840	362.29(3-8)09(4-9)	Drug habits, By place
HV2417-2500	371.912	Education of the deaf	HV5825-5833	362.29(3-8)0973	United States
HV2502-2503	362.4283	Communication devices for	HV5840	362.29(3-8)09(4-9)	Other countries
HV2510-2990.5	362.4209(4-9)	Deaf persons, By place	HV6001-7220.5	364	Criminology
HV2510-2561	362.420973	United States	HV6001-6006	364.05	Serials
HV3004-3009.5	362.38	Mentally handicapped	HV6008-6010	364.06	Societies/Congresses
HV3006	362.380973	United States	HV6011	364.074	Exhibitions/Museums
HV3008	362.3809(4-9)	Other countries	HV6017	364.03	Encyclopedias/Dictionaries
HV3011-3024	362.48	Physically handicapped	HV6018-6023	364.09	History of criminology
HV3023-3024	362.4809(4-9)	By place	HV6024	364.07	Education
HV3023	362.480973	United States	HV6024.5	364.072	Research
HV3024	362.4809(4-9)	Other countries	HV6035-6197	364.2	Criminal anthropology
HV3025-3174	362.858	Classed by occupation	HV6045-6054	364.2	Criminal type
HV3176-3199	362.84(03-99)	Classed by race/Ethnic group	HV6065-6079	364.24	Criminal anthropometry
			HV6080-6113	364.3	Criminal psychology
HV3181-3185	362.8496073	Afro-Americans	HV6115-6190	364.2	Causes of crime/Etiology
HV4023-4470.7	362.5	City poor/Slums	HV6121-6125	364.24	Hereditary causes
HV4041-4170.7	362.509(4-9)	By place	HV6150-6190	364.22	Environmental causes
HV4043-4046	362.50973	United States	HV6191-6197	364.256	Caused by race/Nationality
HV4047-4050	362.50971	Canada	HV6250-.4	362.88	Victims of crime
HV4051	362.50972	Mexico	HV6251-6773.3	364.1	Crimes and offenses
HV4053-4059	362.509728	Central America	HV6254-6321	364.13	Political crimes
HV4060-4065.9	362.509729	West Indies	HV6303-6316	364.130973	United States
HV4066-4083	362.5098	South America	HV6321	364.1309(4-9)	Other countries
HV4084-4131.84	362.5094	Europe	HV6323-6335	364.134	Offenses against justice
HV4085-4087.5	362.50941	Great Britain	HV6337-6351	364.133	Offenses against the revenue
HV4093-4096.5	362.50944	France			
HV4097-4100	362.50943	Germany	HV6419-6433	364.142	Against public safety

71

LC	Dewey	Descriptor
HV6435-6492	364.143	Against the public order
HV6437-6453	364.106	Outlaws/Gangs/Etc.
HV6455-6471	364.134	Lynching
HV6474-6485	364.143	Riots/Mobs/Unlawful assemblies
HV6486-6491	364.143	Disorderly conduct
HV6493-6626.5	364.15	Against persons
HV6499-6535	364.152	Murder/Homicide
HV6518-6535	364.15209(4-9)	Murder, By place
HV6518-6534	364.1520973	United States
HV6535	364.15209(4-9)	Other countries
HV6537-6541	364.1523	Infanticide
HV6543-6548	364.1522	Suicide
HV6549-6555	364.1791	Poisoning
HV6558-6569	364.1532	Rape
HV6571-6574	364.154	Abduction
HV6584-6589	364.153	Seduction
HV6595-6604	364.154	Kidnapping
HV6618	364.1555	Bodily assault
HV6625-6626.5	364.1555(3-4)	Abuse of persons
HV6629-6633	364.156	Against reputation/Honor
HV6635-6700	364.16	Against property
HV6638-.5	364.164	Arson
HV6640	364.164	Bombings
HV6646-6665	364.162	Theft
HV6666-6669	364.164	Vandalism
HV6675-6685	364.162	Embezzlement/Forgery/Etc.
HV6688	364.165	Extortion
HV6691-6700	364.163	Frauds/Quacks/Etc.
HV6705-6722	364.17	Against public morals
HV6708-6722	364.172	Gambling
HV6763-6771	364.168	Financial crimes
HV6773-.3	364.168	Computer crimes
HV6774-7220.5	364.(1/3)09(4-9)	Crimes/Criminals, By place
HV6774-6795	364.(1/3)0973	United States
HV6801-7220.5	364.(1/3)09(4-9)	Other countries
HV7231-9481	364	Criminal justice admin.
HV7231-7239	364.05	Serials
HV7240-7243	364.06	Societies/Congresses
HV7245-7400	364.02109(4-9)	By place (Statistics/Etc.)
HV7245-7300	364.0210973	United States
HV7250-7300	364.021097(4-9)	By state
HV7315	364.0210971	Canada
HV7316	364.0210972	Mexico
HV7317-7323	364.02109728	Central America
HV7324-7329.9	364.02109729	West Indies
HV7330-7341	364.021098	South America
HV7342-7367.7	364.021094	Europe
HV7343-7345.5	364.0210941	Great Britain
HV7348	364.0210944	France
HV7349-.5	364.0210943	Germany
HV7351	364.0210945	Italy
HV7355	364.0210947	European Russia
HV7361	364.0210946	Spain
HV7368.2-7369.2	364.0210956	Middle East
HV7368-7381	364.0210995	Asia
HV7371	364.0210954	India
HV7377	364.0210952	Japan
HV7378	364.0210951	China
HV7382-7388.4	364.021096	Africa
HV7389-7398.9	364.021099(3-6)	Australia/New Zealand/ Oceania
HV7411	364.03	Dictionaries/Encyclopedias
HV7419.5	364.072	Research
HV7435-7439	363.33	Gun control
HV7551-8280.7	363.2(89)	Police/Detectives
HV7900	363.2025	Directories
HV7901	363.203	Dictionaries/Encyclopedias
HV7903-7909	363.209	History
HV7911	363.2092	Biography
HV7923	363.207	Education
HV7935-8025	351.74	Administration/ Organization
HV8031-8080	363.23	Police duty/Investigation/ Etc.
HV8081-8099	363.289	Private detectives
HV8130-8280.7	363.209(4-9)	Police, By place
HV8130-8148	363.20973	United States
HV8157-8160	363.20971	Canada
HV8161	363.20972	Mexico
HV8163-8169	363.209728	Central America
HV8170-8175.9	363.209729	West Indies
HV8176-8193	363.2098	South America
HV8194-8217.7	363.2094	Europe
HV8195-8197.5	363.20941	Great Britain
HV8203-8206	363.20944	France
HV8207-8210	363.20943	Germany
HV8212-8215	363.20945	Italy
HV8215.5-8223.5	363.209492	Low Countries
HV8224-8227	363.20947	European Russia
HV8235-8238	363.20946	Spain
HV8239	363.209469	Portugal
HV8241.83	363.209495	Greece
HV8241.85-8263	363.2095	Asia
HV8241.9-8242.56	363.20956	Middle East
HV8247-8250	363.20954	India
HV8255	363.209599	Philippines
HV8257	363.20952	Japan
HV8260	363.20951	China
HV8267-8279.3	363.2096	Africa
HV8280-.68	363.2099(3-6)	Australia/New Zealand/ Oceania
HV8290	363.289	Guards/Watchmen/Etc.
HV8301-9920.5	364.6	Penology
HV8482-8488	364.6021	Statistics
HV8482	364.60973	United States
HV8483	364.60971	Canada
HV8484	364.609(72-8)	Other American countries
HV8485	364.6094	Europe
HV8486	364.6095	Asia
HV8487	364.6096	Africa
HV8488	364.60994	Australia
HV8497-8654	364.609	History
HV8508-8526	364.60903	Ancient
HV8529-8532	364.60902	Medieval
HV8545-8654	364.6(3-8)	Forms of punishment
HV8551-8586	364.66	Capital punishment
HV8593-8599	364.67	Torture
HV8613-8621	364.67	Flogging/Flagellation
HV8657-8658	365.4092	Biography of prisoners
HV8675-8686	365.601	Theory of punishment
HV8705-8749	365	Imprisonment
HV8751-8931	365.01	Prison methods/Practice
HV8935-8962	365	Penal colonies/ Transportation
HV8971-9018	365.7	Prison reform
HV9025	365.641	Prison violence
HV9051-9230.7	364.36	Juvenile offenders
HV9051-9058	364.360(5/6)	Serials/Societies/Congresses
HV9068	364.3607	Education
HV9101-9230.7	364.3609(4-9)	Juvenile offenders, By place
HV9103-9106	364.360973	United States
HV9107-9230.7	364.3609(4-9)	Other countries

LC	Dewey	Descriptor
HV9261-9430.7	364.601	Reforming of adult prisoners
HV9441-9920.5	364.609(4-9)	Penology, By place
HV9456-9481	364.60973	United States
HV9501-9920.5	364.609(4-9)	Other countries
HV9501-9510	364.60971	Canada
HV9511-9515	364.60972	Mexico
HV9516-9550	364.609728	Central America
HV9551-9575.95	364.609729	West Indies
HV9576-9635	364.6098	South America
HV9636-9775.7	364.6094	Europe
HV9641-9650	364.60941	Great Britain
HV9661-9670	364.60944	France
HV9671-9680.5	364.60943	Germany
HV9686-9695	364.60945	Italy
HV9696-9710.5	364.609492	Low Countries
HV9711-9715	364.60947	European Russia
HV9741-9745	364.60946	Spain
HV9775.5	364.609495	Greece
HV9776.5-9785.2	364.60956	Middle East
HV9785.7-9831	364.6095	Asia
HV9791-9795	364.60954	India
HV9806-9810	364.609599	Philippines
HV9811-9815	364.60952	Japan
HV9816-9820	364.60951	China
HV9836-9868.5	364.6096	Africa
HV9871-9918.9	364.609(3-6)	Australia/New Zealand/ Oceania
HV9950-9956	364.973	U.S. criminal justice admin.
HV9960	364.9(4-9)	In other countries
HX	335.(4/83)	Socialism/Communism/ Anarchism
HX1-9	335.005	Serials
HX11-13	335.006	Societies/Congresses
HX17	335.003	Dictionaries/Encyclopedias
HX18	335.0014	Terminology
HX19-.2	335.007	Education
HX21-54	335.009	History
HX26	335.0093	Ancient
HX31	335.00902	Medieval
HX36-44	335.009	Modern
HX51-54	335.7	Christian Socialism
HX77	335.43	Democratic Centralism
HX80-517.5	335.009(4-9)	Socialism/Etc., By place
HX81-92	335.00973	United States
HX101-517.5	335.009(4-9)	Other countries
HX101-110	335.00971	Canada
HX111-115	335.00972	Mexico
HX116-150	335.009728	Central America
HX151-175.95	335.009729	West Indies
HX176-235	335.0098	South America
HX236-375.5	335.0094	Europe
HX241-250	335.00941	Great Britain
HX261-270	335.00944	France
HX271-280.5	335.00943	Germany
HX286-295	335.00945	Italy
HX296-310.5	335.009492	Low Countries
HX311-315	335.00947	European Russia
HX341-345	335.00946	Spain
HX375.5	335.009495	Greece
HX376.5-385.2	335.00956	Middle East
HX385.7-431	335.0095	Asia
HX385.8	335.0095493	Sri Lanka
HX391-395	335.00954	India
HX395.5	335.0095491	Pakistan
HX406-410	335.009599	Philippines
HX411-415	335.00952	Japan
HX416-420	335.00951	China
HX436-468.5	335.0096	Africa
HX471-518.5	335.0099(3-6)	Australia/New Zealand/ Oceania
HX626-780.7	335.(43/12)	Communism/Utopian Socialism
HX626-632	335.4309	History
HX635	335.9	Management of collectives
HX651-780.7	335.4309(4-9)	Communism, By place
HX653-656	335.430973	United States
HX657-660	335.430971	Canada
HX661	335.430972	Mexico
HX663-669	335.4309728	Central America
HX670-675.9	335.4309729	West Indies
HX676-693	335.43098	South America
HX694-741.84	335.43094	Europe
HX695-697.5	335.430941	Great Britain
HX703-706	335.430944	France
HX707-710.5	335.430943	Germany
HX712-715	335.430945	Italy
HX715.5-723.5	335.4309492	Low Countries
HX724-727	335.430947	European Russia
HX735-738	335.430946	Spain
HX741.83	335.4309495	Greece
HX741.9-742.56	335.430956	Middle East
HX742.7-763	335.43095	Asia
HX742.8	335.43095493	Sri Lanka
HX747-750	335.430954	India
HX750.5	335.43095491	Pakistan
HX755	335.4309599	Philippines
HX757	335.430952	Japan
HX760	335.430951	China
HX767-779.3	335.43096	Africa
HX780-.68	335.43099(3-6)	Australia/New Zealand/ Oceania
HX806-810.5	321.07	Utopias/Ideal states
HX821-970.7	335.83	Anarchism
HX841-970.7	335.8309(4-9)	Anarchism, By place
J	328/353/354.(3-9)0005	Official documents/Gazettes
J1-9	353.0005/354.(3-9)0005	Official gazettes
J1	353.0005	United States
J2	354.710005	Canada
J3	354.7290005	West Indies
J4	354.72(8) + 0005	Mexico/Central America
J6	354.80005	South America
J7	354.40005	Europe
J10-981	328.(4-9)/353/354.(4-9)	Official documents
J10-87	328.7304/353.0006	United States, Official docs.
J10	328.73	Continental Congress
J11-15	328.7301	Congress (Annuals/ Record/Etc.)
J21-34	328.7309	Congress 1-14th
J35-75	328.7309	15th and later
J80-82	353.035	Presidential messages/ Documents
J82	353.03509	By President
J83-85	353.(1-87)	Department reports/ Documents
J86-87	353.9(4-9)0006/328.7(4-9)	State documents
J100-981	328/354.(3-9)	Documents of other countries
J100-125	328/354.71	Canada
J162-163	328/354.7291	Cuba
J164-165	328/354.7295	Puerto Rico
J166-168	328/354.729	Other Caribbean islands
J170-172	328/354.72	Mexico
J175-185	328/354.728	Central America

LC	Dewey	Descriptor
J200-259	328/354.8	South America
J301-462	328/354.4	Europe
J301-309	328/354.41	Great Britain
J310-340	328/354.436	Austria/Hungary
J341-345	328/354.44	France
J351-383	328/354.43	Germany
J385	328/354.495	Greece
J388-389	328/354.45	Italy
J391-395	328/354.492	Low Countries/Netherlands
J397-400	328/354.47	European Russia
J402-406	328/354.48	Scandinavia
J409-411	328/354.46(9)	Spain/Portugal
J415-442	328/354.494	Switzerland
J450-459	328/354.496	Balkans
J450	328/354.4965	Albania
J451-452	328/354.4977	Bulgaria
J459	328/354.497	Yugoslavia
J500-693	328/354.5	Asia
J500-593	328/354.54	India
J577	328/354.5491	Pakistan
J579	328/354.5492	Bangladesh
J611	328/354.5493	Sri Lanka
J612	328/354.5645	Cyprus
J613	328/354.5125	Hong Kong
J615-618	328/354.5951	Malaysia
J625	328/354.5496	Nepal
J631	328/354.598	Indonesia
J642	328/354.596	Cambodia
J643	328/354.594	Laos
J644	328/354.597	Vietnam
J655	328/354.57	Asian Russia
J661-663	328/354.599	Philippines
J671-681	328/354.5	Far East
J671	328/354.51	China
J672	328/354.51249	Taiwan
J674	328/354.52	Japan
J677-.5	328/354.519	Korea
J681	328/354.593	Thailand
J685	328/354.581	Afghanistan
J688-689	328/354.55	Iran
J691	328/354.561	Turkey
J693.I6	328/354.567	Iraq
J693.J6	328/354.5965	Jordan
J693.L5	328/354.5692	Lebanon
J693.P2	328/354.5694	Palestine/Israel
J693.Q37	328/354.5363	Qatar
J693.S3	328/354.538	Saudi Arabia
J693.S8	328/354.5691	Syria
J693.U54	328/354.5357	United Arab Emirates
J693.Y4	328/354.5332	Yemen
J700-881	328/354.6	Africa
J705-719	328/354.68	South Africa
J720	328/354.6887	Swaziland
J722	328/354.6885	Lesotho
J723	328/354.6883	Botswana
J725	328/354.6891	Zimbabwe/Zambia/Malawi
J731	328/354.6762	Kenya
J732	328/354.6761	Uganda
J733	328/354.6781	Zanzibar
J741.G3	328/354.667	Ghana/Gold Coast
J745-.7	328/354.669	Nigeria
J747	328/354.664	Sierra Leone
J753-755	328/354.97	Atlantic Ocean Islands
J758-759	328/354.69	Indian Ocean Islands
J763	328/354.65	Algeria
J765	328/354.611	Tunisia
J768	328/354.6683	Benin (Dahomey)

LC	Dewey	Descriptor
J771	328/354.6652	Guinea
J773	328/354.6668	Ivory Coast
J774	328/354.6623	Mali
J775	328/354.661	Mauritania
J777	328/354.6626	Niger
J779	328/354.663	Senegal
J780	328/354.6625	Burkina Faso
J784	328/354.6741	Central African Republic
J785	328/354.6743	Chad
J786	328/354.6724	Congo
J787	328/354.6721	Gabon
J801	328/354.678	Tanzania
J805	328/354.6711	Cameroon
J809	328/354.6681	Togo
J812	328/354.6881	Namibia
J814-816	328/354.6757	Ruanda-Urundi
J825	328/354.6773	Somalia
J826	328/354.612	Libya
J831	328/354.6751	Zaire
J841	328/354.673	Angola
J844	328/354.6658	Cape Verde Islands
J849	328/354.679	Mozambique
J850	328/354.6652	Equitorial Guinea
J851	328/354.6715	Sao Tome/Principe
J857	328/354.642	Tangier
J861	328/354.63	Ethiopia
J866	328/354.62	Egypt
J868	328/354.624	Sudan
J875	328/354.6662	Liberia
J881	328/354.64	Morocco
J903-936	328/354.94	Australia
J941	328/354.93	New Zealand
J951-981	328/354.9(5-6)	Oceania
JA	320	Political science
JA1-26	320.05	Serials
JA27-34	320.06	Societies
JA35-.5	320.06	Congresses
JA50-59	320.05	Yearbooks
JA61-64	320.03	Dictionaries/Encyclopedias
JA71-80	320.011	Theory
JA81-84	320.09	History
JA82	320.090(1-2)	Ancient/Medieval
JA83	320	Modern
JA84	320.09(3-9)	By place
JA86-89	320.07	Education
JA92-98	320.092	Biography of writers
JC	320.011	Political theory
JC11-323	320.1	The state
JC20-46	321.1	The primitive state
JC26-29	321.1	Tribal
JC31-46	321.1	Village
JC47-50	294.3377/297.1977	Oriental state
JC51-95	321.1(2/4)	Ancient state
JC61	320.935	Assyro-Babylonian
JC66	320.932	Egypt
JC67	320.933	Hebrews
JC71-79	320.938	Greece
JC81-90	320.9376	Rome
JC91-95	320.9495	Byzantine
JC101-126	321.14	Medieval state
JC109-113	321.3	Feudal
JC131-273	321	Treatises on the modern state
JC134-273	321	Treatises, By date
JC311-323	320.54	Nationalism
JC325-341	320.1	Nature/Concept of the state
JC345-347	929.(82/92)	Flags/Seals/Etc.

LC	Dewey	Descriptor
JC348-497	321	Forms of the state
JC352	321.06	City/State
JC359	321.03	Empire
JC361-363	321.04	The world state
JC374-393	321.6	Monarchy
JC401-408	342	Constitutional
JC411-417	321.5	Aristocracy
JC419	321.5	Oligarchy
JC421-458	321.(4/8)	Democracy
JC474	321.92	Communistic state
JC478	321.94	Corporate state
JC481	321.94	Totalitarianism/Fascism
JC490-497	321.09	Change of form
JC501-628	320.1-323	Purpose/Relations of the state
JC510-514	322.1	Church and state
JC571-609	323.(01)	Individual/Natural rights
JF	350-352	Political administration
JF31-36	353-354	History, By place
JF107-109	350-352.000202	Compends./Outlines/Etc.
JF201-723	328/351	Organs/Functions of government
JF251-314	350-352	Executive
JF255	351.00313	President
JF256	351.00322	Military/War powers
JF260-261	351.00322	Legislative power (Veto/Etc.)
JF265	351.00322	Judicial/Pardoning power
JF269	351.00322	Treaty making
JF274	351.00322	Appointments
JF285	321.8042	Election/Succession
JF289	351.00354/394.4	Oath/Inauguration
JF290-297	351.003(4/6)	Term/Leaving office
JF305-309	351.00328	Privileges
JF401-637	328	Legislation/Lawmaking
JF411-416	328.09	History
JF424-427	328.37	Lawmaking
JF441-483	328.34	Legislative powers
JF488-497	328.2	Direct legislation
JF488-495	328.2	Initiative/Referendum
JF493-495	328.2(4-9)	Direct legislation, By place
JF501-540.5	328.3	Legislative bodies
JF541-567	328.31	Upper house
JF601-637	328.32	Lower house
JF700-723	347	Judiciary
JF711	347.012	Perogatives/Jurisdiction
JF723	347.052	Jury system
JF751-786	320.8/321.023	Federal-State relations
JF800-1191	323-324	Political rights/Guaranties
JF800-823	323.6	Citizenship
JF825-943	324.62	Suffrage
JF1001-1043	324.63	Electoral systems/Voting
JF1051-1077	324.63	Representation
JF1081-1085	324.66	Corruption/Electoral fraud
JF1091-1177	324.65	The ballot
JF1321-2111	351	Government/Administration
JF1601-1671	351.1	Officials/Bodies/Etc.
JF1800	343.015	Military government
JF1800	355.49	Military government
JF1900	350	Federal districts
JF2011-2112	324.2	Political parties
JK	342.73029/353	U.S. (Admin./Constitutional hist.)
JK1	353.0005	Serials
JK3	353.0006	Societies
JK4	353.00074	Exhibitions
JK9	353.0003	Dictionaries

LC	Dewey	Descriptor
JK11-371	342.73029	Constitutional history
JK14-19	342.7302	Charters/Constitutions
JK54-103	342.73029033	Colonial period
JK111-181	342.73029033	1776-1820
JK201-227	342.73029034	1821-1865
JK231-254	342.73029034	1866-1908
JK261-289	342.7302904	1908-
JK305-306	342.73044	Separation of powers
JK310-331	342.73042	Federal-State relations
JK404-1686	353	Government/Administration
JK501-901	353.03	Executive
JK511-609	353.0313	The president
JK609.5	353.0318	The vice president
JK610-616	353.04	The cabinet
JK631-901	353.(1-87)/353.006	Departments/Civil service
JK730-761	353.0013	Appointments/Etc.
JK765-770	353.001	Personnel administration
JK771-849	353.00123	Salaries/Pensions
JK851-901	353.(1-87)	The departments
JK1001-1447	328.73	Congress/Legislative branch
JK1021-1059	328.7309	History
JK1061-1081	342.7305	Constitutional powers
JK1151-1276	328.73071	Senate
JK1166-1197	328.73074	Constitutional powers
JK1304-1447	328.73072	House of Representatives
JK1326-1391	328.73074	Constitutional powers
JK1507-1598	347.73	The Judiciary
JK1551-1598	347.732	Federal courts
JK1606-1686	353.00713	Government property
JK1711-2246	323.0973	Politics/Civil rights
JK1751-1788	323.60973	Citizenship
JK1800-1836	323.6230973	Naturalization
JK1846-1936	324.60973	Suffrage
JK1951-2225	324.60973	Electoral/Ballot systems
JK2251-2391	324.273	Political parties
JK2301-2391	324.273(2-8)	Particular parties
JK2403-9501	353.9	State governments
JK2410-2411	353.9(7-9)	Admission to statehood
JK2430-2441	328.7(4-9)	Legislation
JK2443-2525	353.9(7-9)	Administration
JK2447-2474	353.97(4-9)0313	The executive
JK2484-2508	328.7(4-7)07	The legislature
JK2521-2525	347.733	The judiciary
JK2701-9501	353.9(7-9)	By state
JK9661-9993	353.75	Confederate States
JK9695-9704	328.7507	Legislative
JK9705-9710	328.75071	Senate
JK9711-9716	328.75072	House of Representatives
JK9718-9719	353.7503	Executive
JK9778-9799	973.713	Secession of states
JK9803-9993	342.75029	Constitutional history
JL	354.(7-8)/342.(7-8)029	Americas (Admin./Constitution)
JL1-500	354.71/342.71029	Canada
JL1-3	354.71000(5/6)	Serials/Societies/Etc.
JL11-65	342.71029	Constitutional history
JL41-65	342.71029	By date
JL71-198	354.71	Government administration
JL88-111	354.7103	The executive
JL131-179	328.71	The legislative
JL181-185	347.71	The judiciary
JL198-500	354.71(1-9)	Provincial government
JL590-599	354.7299/342.7299029	Bermuda
JL610-619	354.7296/342.7296029	Bahamas
JL620-629	354.72981/342.72981029	Barbados
JL629.5	354.72921/342.72921029	Cayman Islands
JL629.6	354.729845/342.729845029	Grenada

LC	Dewey	Descriptor
JL630-639	354.7292/342.7292029	Jamaica
JL640-649	354.7297/342.7297029	Leeward Islands
JL650-659	354.72983/342.72983029	Trinidad
JL659.5	354.72961/342.72961029	Turks/Caicos Islands
JL660-669	354.72984/342.72984029	Windward Islands
JL670-679	354.7282/342.7282029	Belize
JL680-689	354.881/342.881029	Guyana
JL690-699	354.9711/342.9711029	Falkland Islands
JL770-779	354.72986/342.72986029	Curacao
JL780-789	354.883/342.883029	Suriname
JL810-819	354.882/342.882029	French Guiana
JL820-829	354.72976/342.72976029	Guadeloupe
JL830-839	354.72982/342.72982029	Martinique
JL1000-1019	354.7291/342.7291029	Cuba
JL1040-1059	354.7295/342.7295029	Puerto Rico
JL1080-1099	354.7294/342.7294029	Haiti
JL1120-1139	354.729375/342.729375029	Santo Domingo
JL1200-1299	354.72/342.72029	Mexico
JL1440-1459	354.7286/342.7286029	Costa Rica
JL1480-1499	354.7281/342.7281029	Guatemala
JL1520-1539	354.7283/342.7283029	Honduras
JL1560-1579	354.7284/342.7284029	El Salvador
JL1600-1619	354.7285/342.7285029	Nicaragua
JL1630-1679	354.7287/342.7287029	Panama
JL2000-2099	354.82/342.82029	Argentina
JL2200-2299	354.84/342.84029	Bolivia
JL2400-2499	354.81/342.81029	Brazil
JL2600-2699	354.83/342.83029	Chile
JL2800-2899	354.861/342.861029	Colombia
JL3000-3099	354.866/342.866029	Ecuador
JL3200-3299	354.892/342.892029	Paraguay
JL3400-3499	354.85/342.85029	Peru
JL3600-3699	354.895/342.895029	Uruguay
JL3800-3899	354.87/342.87029	Venezuela
JN	342.4029/354.4	Europe (Admin./ Constitution)
JN1-97	342.4029/354.4	Europe, General
JN101-1179	342.41029/354.41	Great Britain
JN101-102	354.41000(5/6)	Serials/Societies/Etc.
JN111-248	342.41029	Constitutional history
JN128-237	342.410290(1-4)	By date
JN175-237	342.410290(23-4)	Modern (1485-)
JN301-329	354.41	Government/Administration
JN331-453	354.4103	The executive
JN500-695	328.41	Parliament
JN751-829	347.41	Judiciary
JN901-1097	323.0941	Civil/Political rights
JN1111-1129	324.241	Political parties
JN1150-1159	342.429029/354.429	Wales
JN1187-1371	342.411029/354.411	Scotland
JN1400-1571.5	342.417029/354.417	Ireland
JN1572	342.416029/354.416	Northern Ireland
JN1601-2199	342.436029/354.436	Austria/Hungary
JN2210-2229	342.437029/354.437	Czechoslovakia
JN2301-3007	342.44029/354.44	France
JN3201-4980	342.43029/354.43	Germany
JN5001-5191	342.495029/354.495	Greece
JN5201-5697	342.45029/354.45	Italy
JN5701-5999	342.492029/354.492	The Netherlands
JN6101-6371	342.493029/354.493	Belgium
JN6500-6747	342.47029/354.47	European Russia
JN6750-6769	342.438029/354.438	Poland
JN7001-7066	342.48029/354.48	Scandinavia (General)
JN7101-7367	342.489029/354.489	Denmark
JN7370-7379	342.982029/354.982	Greenland
JN7300-7389	342.4912029/354.4912	Iceland
JN7390-7399	342.4897029/354.4897	Finland

LC	Dewey	Descriptor
JN7401-7695	342.481029/354.481	Norway
JN7721-7997	342.485029/354.485	Sweden
JN8101-8399	342.46029/354.46	Spain
JN8423-8661	342.469029/354.469	Portugal
JN8701-9599	342.494029/354.494	Switzerland
JN9600-9689	342.496029/354.496	Balkan states
JQ	342.(5-9)029/354.(5-9)	Asia/Africa/Oceania (Admin./Etc.)
JQ20-1825	342.5029/354.5	Asia
JQ200-620	342.54029/354.54	India
JQ540-559	342.5491029/354.5491	Pakistan
JQ630-639	342.5492029/354.5492	Bangladesh
JQ650-659	342.5493029/354.5493	Sri Lanka
JQ670-679	342.5125029/354.5125	Hong Kong
JQ710-719	342.595029/354.595	Malaysia
JQ760-779	342.598029/354.598	Indonesia
JQ800-899	342.59(7)029/354.59(7)	Vietnam/Indochina
JQ930-939	342.596029/354.596	Cambodia
JQ950-959	342.594029/354.594	Laos
JQ1089-1199	342.57029/354.57	Asian Russia
JQ1269-1419	342.599029/354.599	Philippines
JQ1519	342.51029/354.51	China
JQ1539	342.51249029/354.51249	Taiwan
JQ1699	342.52029/354.52	Japan
JQ1729-.5	342.519029/354.519	Korea
JQ1749	342.593029/354.593	Thailand
JQ1769	342.581029/354.581	Afghanistan
JQ1789	342.55029/354.55	Iran
JQ1809	342.561029/354.561	Turkey
JQ1825.A75	342.53029/354.53	Arabia
JQ1825.B34	342.5365029/354.5365	Bahrein
JQ1825.C93	342.5645029/354.5645	Cyprus
JQ1825.I7	342.567029/354.567	Iraq
JQ1825.J6	342.5695029/354.5695	Jordan
JQ1825.K8	342.5367029/354.5367	Kuwait
JQ1825.L4	342.5692029/354.5692	Lebanon
JQ1825.N4	342.5496029/354.5496	Nepal
JQ1825.O42	342.5353029/354.5353	Oman
JQ1825.P3	342.5694029/354.5694	Israel/Palestine
JQ1825.Q37	342.5363029/354.5363	Qatar
JQ1825.S3	342.538029/354.538	Saudi Arabia
JQ1825.S8	342.5691029/354.5691	Syria
JQ1825.U5	342.5357029/354.5357	United Arab Emirates
JQ1825.Y4-.Y5	342.5332029/354.5332	Yemen
JQ1850	342.53029/354.53	Arab countries
JQ1870-3981	342.6029/354.6	Africa
JQ3995-6651	342.9(3-6)029/354.9(3-6)	Australia/New Zealand/Oceania
JS	352	Local government
JS13-37	352.000(5/6)	Municipal serial documents
JS13	352.07(4-9)000(5/6)	United States
JS14	352.071000(5/6)	Canada
JS15	352.0(72-8)000(5/6)	Other American areas
JS16-31	352.04000(5/6)	Europe
JS33	352.05000(5/6)	Asia
JS35	352.06000(5/6)	Africa
JS37	352.09(3-6)000(5/6)	Australia/New Zealand/Oceania
JS39-41	352.0005	Serials
JS42	352.0006	Societies/Congresses
JS48	352.0003	Dictionaries
JS49	352.0007	Education
JS50	352.0001	Theory
JS55-67	352.0009	History
JS141-231	352	Municipal government
JS141-163	352.008	Executive (Mayor/Etc.)
JS185-188	347.02	Judiciary (City courts)

LC	Dewey	Descriptor
JS301-1583	352.07(4-9)	United States (Local gov't.)
JS301	352.07(4-9)0005	Serials
JS302-303	352.07(4-9)0006	Societies
JS304	352.07(4-9)	Congresses
JS309-323	352.07(4-9)0009	History
JS356-365	352.008097(4-9)	Executive (Mayor)
JS381-385	347.7(4-9)02	Judiciary (City courts)
JS393-399	324.973	Suffrage/Elections
JS408-425	352.07(4-9)	Other than municipal
JS431-1583	352.07(4-9)	Municipalities (United States)
JS1701-1800	352.071	Canada
JS1811-1819	352.0718	Newfoundland
JS1840-2059	352.0729	West Indies
JS2101-2143	352.072	Mexico
JS2145-2219	352.0728	Central America
JS2300-2778	352.08	South America
JS3000-69549	352.04	Europe
JS3001-4280	352.041	Great Britain
JS4501-4650	352.0436	Austria
JS4661-4696	352.0439	Hungary
JS4721-4756	352.0437	Czechoslovakia
JS4801-5249	352.044	France
JS5301-5598	352.043	Germany
JS5701-5925	352.045	Italy
JS5931-5998	352.0492	Netherlands
JS6001-6048	352.0493	Belgium
JS6051-6120	352.047	European Russia
JS6151-6189	352.0489	Denmark
JS6201-6235	352.0481	Norway
JS6251-6285	352.0485	Sweden
JS6301-6335	352.046	Spain
JS6341-6375	352.0469	Portugal
JS6401-6889	352.0494	Switzerland
JS6900-6949	352.0496	Balkan states
JS6950-7499	352.05	Asia
JS7001-7090	352.054	India
JS7300-7335	352.0599	Philippines
JS7351-7365	352.051	China
JS7371-7385	352.052	Japan
JS7510	352.053	Arab countries
JS7525-7829	352.06	Africa
JS8001-8310	352.094	Australia
JS8331-8399	352.093	New Zealand
JS8450-8455	352.09(5-6)	Oceania
JV	325	Colonization/Migration
JV1-5399	325.3	Colonies and colonization
JV1-9	325.305	Serials
JV10-21	325.306	Societies/Congresses
JV51	325.301	Philosophy/Theory
JV55-59	325.307	Education
JV201-246	325.(4-9)	By area
JV261-291	325.3(3-9)	Colonists by nationality/Race
JV305-317	306.089	Natives
JV351-381	325.3	Types of colonies
JV412-485	325.31	Administration/ Organization
JV500-5399	325.3(3-9)	Colonizing nations
JV500-599	325.373	United States
JV1000-1099	325.341	Great Britain
JV1800-1899	325.344	France
JV2000-2099	325.343	Germany
JV2200-2299	325.345	Italy
JV2500-2899	325.349(2-3)	Netherlands/Belgium
JV3000-3099	325.347	Russia
JV3300-3399	325.348(9)	Scandinavia/Denmark

LC	Dewey	Descriptor
JV4000-4299	325.346(9)	Spain/Portugal
JV5200-5299	325.352	Japan
JV5300-5399	325.394	Australia
JV6001-9500	325.(1-2)	Immigration/Emigration
JV6001-6006	325.(1-2)05	Serials
JV6021-6033	325.(1-2)09	History
JV6061-6149	325.2	Emigration
JV6061-6081	325.2090(1-4)	History, By date
JV6065-6066	325.20901	Ancient
JV6068-6069	325.20902	Medieval
JV6071-6072	325.209032	17th century
JV6074-6075	325.309033	18th century
JV6077-6078	325.309034	19th century
JV6080-6081	325.20904	20th century
JV6135-6149	325.(4-9)	To specific areas
JV6137	325.7	To North America
JV6139	325.(8/728)	South/Central America
JV6141-6149	325.(4-9)	Europe/Asia/Africa/Oceania
JV6201-6348	325.1	Immigration
JV6403-7127	325.(73/273)	U.S. (Immigration/ Emigration)
JV6403-6405	325.7306	Societies/Congresses
JV6421-6429	342.73082	Laws/Regulations
JV6431-6445	325.273	Emigration
JV6450-6479	325.73	Immigration
JV6610-6895	325.73089	By race/Nationality
JV6905-7127	325.7(4-9)	By state
JV7200-7299	325.(72/271)	Canada
JV7320-7339	325.(729/2729)	British West Indies
JV7346	325.(881/2881)	British Guiana
JV7347	325.(7282/27282)	British Honduras
JV7353-7359	325.(729/2729)	Danish/Dutch/French Caribbean
JV7370-7379	325.(7291/27291)	Cuba
JV7380-7389	325.(7295/27295)	Puerto Rico
JV7393	325.(7294/27294)	Haiti
JV7395	325.(7293/27293)	Dominican Republic
JV7397	325.(729722/2729722)	U.S. Virgin Islands
JV7400-7409	325.(72/272)	Mexico
JV7413	325.(7286/27286)	Costa Rica
JV7416	325.(7281/27281)	Guatemala
JV7419	325.(7283/27283)	Honduras
JV7423	325.(7284/27284)	El Salvador
JV7426	325.(7285/27285)	Nicaragua
JV7429	325.(7287/27287)	Panama
JV7432	325.(72875/272875)	Panama Canal Zone
JV7440-7449	325.(82/282)	Argentina
JV7450-7459	325.(84/284)	Bolivia
JV7460-7469	325.(81/281)	Brazil
JV7470-7479	325.(83/283)	Chile
JV7480-7489	325.(861/2861)	Colombia
JV7490-7499	325.(866/2866)	Ecuador
JV7500-7509	325.(892/2892)	Paraguay
JV7510-7519	325.(85/285)	Peru
JV7520-7529	325.(895/2895)	Uruguay
JV7530-7539	325.(87/287)	Venezuela
JV7600-7729	325.(41/241)	Great Britain
JV7700-7709	325.(411/2411)	Scotland
JV7710-77i9	325.(415/2415)	Ireland
JV7800-7899	325.(436/2436)	Austria/Hungary
JV7900-7999	325.(44/244)	France
JV8000-8099	325.(43/243)	Germany
JV8110-8119	325.(495/2495)	Greece
JV8130-8139	325.(45/245)	Italy
JV8150-8159	325.(492/2492)	Netherlands
JV8160-8169	325.(493/2493)	Belgium
JV8175	325.(4935/24935)	Luxembourg

LC	Dewey	Descriptor
JV8180-8189	325.(47/247)	European Russia
JV8193	325.(4897/24897)	Finland
JV8195	325.(438/2438)	Poland
JV8200-8209	325.(489/2489)	Denmark
JV8210-8219	325.(481/2481)	Norway
JV8220-8229	325.(485/2485)	Sweden
JV8250-8259	325.(46/246)	Spain
JV8260-8269	325.(469/2469)	Portugal
JV8280-8289	325.(494/2494)	Switzerland
JV8300-8339	325.(496/2496)	Balkan states
JV8490-8749	325.(5/25)	Asia
JV8500-8509	325.(54/254)	India
JV8683-8685	352.(599/2599)	Philippines
JV8700-8709	325.(51/251)	China
JV8710-8719	325.(51249/251249)	Taiwan
JV8720-8729	325.(52/252)	Japan
JV8739-8749	325.(56/256)	Near East
JV8760	325.(53/253)	Arab countries
JV8790-9025	325.(6/26)	Africa
JV9100-9259	325.(94/294)	Australia
JV9260-9269	325.(93/293)	New Zealand
JV9290-9500	325.9(5-6)/325.29(5-6)	Oceania
JX	341	International law
JX1-18	341.05	Serials
JX24-54	341.06	Societies/Congresses
JX63-191	341.026	Documents/Cases
JX221-1195	341.0268(1-9)	Cases, By place
JX231-245	341.026873	United States
JX351-360	341.026871	Canada
JX361-370	341.026872	Mexico
JX371-450	341.0268728	Central America
JX451-496	341.0268729	West Indies
JX501-620	341.02688	South America
JX621-899	341.02684	Europe
JX900-1015	341.02685	Asia
JX1031-1145	341.02686	Africa
JX1161-1195	341.02689(3-6)	Australia/New Zealand/Oceania
JX1261-1283	341.026 7	Codification
JX1305-1598	327	Foreign relations
JX1305-1395	327.09	History
JX1305-1395	327.090(1-4)	By date
JX1315-1395	327	Modern
JX1391-1395	327	20th century
JX1404-1598	327.(3-9)	By place
JX1405-1428	327.73	United States
JX1515	327.71	Canada
JX1516	327.72	Mexico
JX1517.5	327.7282	Belize
JX1518	327.7286	Costa Rica
JX1519	327.7281	Guatemala
JX1520	327.7283	Honduras
JX1521	327.7285	Nicaragua
JX1522	327.7287	Panama
JX1522.5	327.72875	Panama Canal Zone
JX1523	327.7284	El Salvador
JX1524.5	327.7296	Bahamas
JX1525	327.7291	Cuba
JX1526	327.7294	Haiti
JX1526.5	327.7293	Dominican Republic
JX1527	327.7292	Jamaica
JX1528	327.7295	Puerto Rico
JX1528.5	327.729722	U.S. Virgin Islands
JX1531	327.82	Argentina
JX1532	327.84	Bolivia
JX1533	327.81	Brazil
JX1534	327.83	Chile
JX1535	327.861	Colombia
JX1536	327.866	Ecuador
JX1537.1	327.881	Guyana
JX1537.3	327.883	Suriname
JX1537.5	327.882	French Guiana
JX1538	327.892	Paraguay
JX1539	327.85	Peru
JX1540	327.895	Uruguay
JX1541	327.87	Venezuela
JX1543	327.42	England
JX1545	327.411	Scotland
JX1546	327.415	Ireland
JX1547	327.436	Austria
JX1547.3	327.437	Czechoslovakia
JX1548	327.44	France
JX1549	327.43	Germany
JX1550	327.495	Greece
JX1550.5	327.439	Hungary
JX1551	327.45	Italy
JX1553	327.493	Belgium
JX1554	327.492	Netherlands/Holland
JX1554.5	327.4935	Luxembourg
JX1555	327.47	European Russia
JX1555.3	327.4897	Finland
JX1555.7	327.438	Poland
JX1557	327.489	Denmark
JX1558	327.4912	Iceland
JX1559	327.481	Norway
JX1560	327.485	Sweden
JX1562	327.469	Portugal
JX1563	327.494	Switzerland
JX1564	327.4977	Bulgaria
JX1564.5	327.4497	Yugoslavia
JX1566	327.498	Romania
JX1568	327.561	Turkey
JX1570	327.51	China
JX1571	327.54	India
JX1572-1573	327.59(3-6)	Indochina
JX1574	327.598	Indonesia
JX1576	327.599	Philippines
JX1577	327.52	Japan
JX1577.5	327.519	Korea
JX1578	327.55	Iran
JX1579.5	327.593	Thailand
JX1579.7	327.51249	Taiwan
JX1583	327.62	Egypt
JX1589-1597	327.9(3-4)	Australia/New Zealand
JX1598	327.9(5-6)	Oceania
JX1625-1896	327.2/351.89	Diplomacy/Diplomatic service
JX1635-1662	327.209/351.8909	History, By date
JX1705-1894	327.(4-9)/354.(4-9)0089	Diplomacy, By place
JX1705-1725	327.73/353.0089	United States
JX1729-1730	327.71/354.710089	Canada
JX1731-1732	327.72/354.720089	Mexico
JX1735-1736	327.7282/354.72820089	Belize/British Honduras
JX1737-1738	327.7286/354.72860089	Costa Rica
JX1739	327.7281/354.72810089	Guatemala
JX1741	327.7285/354.72850089	Nicaragua
JX1742-1743	327.7287/354.72870089	Panama
JX1743.5	327.72875/354.728750089	Panama Canal Zone
JX1744	327.7284/354.72840089	El Salvador
JX1749-1750	327.7291/354.72910089	Cuba
JX1751	327.7294/354.72940089	Haiti
JX1752	327.7293/354.72930089	Dominican Republic
JX1753	327.7292/354.72920089	Jamaica
JX1755-1756	327.7295/354.72950089	Puerto Rico

LC	Dewey	Descriptor
JX1756.5	327.729722/354.7297220089	U.S. Virgin Islands
JX1759-1760	327.82/354.820089	Argentina
JX1761-1762	327.84/354.840089	Bolivia
JX1763-1764	327.81/354.810089	Brazil
JX1767-1768	327.861/354.8610089	Colombia
JX1769-1770	327.866/354.8660089	Ecuador
JX1772	327.881/354.8810089	Guyana
JX1772.5	327.883/354.8830089	Suriname
JX1772.7	327.882/354.8820089	French Guiana
JX1773-1774	327.892/354.8920089	Paraguay
JX1775-1776	327.85/354.850089	Peru
JX1777-1778	327.895/354.8950089	Uruguay
JX1779-1780	327.87/354.870089	Venezuela
JX1783-1784	327.42/354.420089	England
JX1787-1788	327.411/354.4110089	Scotland
JX1789-1790	327.415/354.4150089	Ireland
JX1791-1792	327.436/354.4360089	Austria
JX1792.5	327.437/354.4370089	Czechoslovakia
JX1793-1794	327.44/354.440089	France
JX1795-1796	327.43/354.430089	Germany
JX1797-1798	327.495/354.4950089	Greece
JX1798.5	327.439/354.4390089	Hungary
JX1799-1800	327.45/354.450089	Italy
JX1803-1804	327.493/354.4930089	Belgium
JX1805-1806	327.492/354.4920089	Netherlands
JX1806.5	327.4935/354.49350089	Luxembourg
JX1807-1808	327.47/354.470089	European Russia
JX1808.3	327.4897/354.48970089	Finland
JX1808.7	327.438/354.4380089	Poland
JX1811-1812	327.489/354.4890089	Denmark
JX1813-1814	327.4912/354.49120089	Iceland
JX1815-1816	327.481/354.4810089	Norway
JX1817-1818	327.485/354.4850089	Sweden
JX1819-1820	327.46/354.460089	Spain
JX1821-1822	327.469/354.4690089	Portugal
JX1823-1824	327.494/354.4940089	Switzerland
JX1825-1826	327.561/354.5610089	Turkey
JX1826.5	327.4965/354.49650089	Albania
JX1827-1828	327.4977/354.49770089	Bulgaria
JX1828.5	327.497/354.4970089	Yugoslavia
JX1831-1832	327.498/354.4980089	Romania
JX1837-1838	327.51/354.510089	China
JX1838.5	327.51249/354.512490089	Taiwan
JX1839-1840	327.54/354.540089	India
JX1841-1844	327.59(3-7)/354.59(3-7)0089	Indochina
JX1845-1848	327.598/354.5980089	Indonesia
JX1849-1850	327.599/354.5990089	Philippines
JX1851-1852	327.52/354.520089	Japan
JX1853-1854	327.55/354.550089	Iran
JX1863-1864	327.62/354.620089	Egypt
JX1875-1876	327.9(3-4)/354.9(3-4)0089	New Zealand/Australia
JX1891-1894	327.9(5-6)/354.9(5-6)0089	Oceania
JX1901-1995	341.522	International arbitration
JX1905.5-1908	341.52206	Societies
JX1910-1935	341.52206	Congresses
JX1937-1962	341.55209	History
JX1941-1954	341.522090(1-4)	By date
JX1961	341.52209(1-9)	By place
JX1975	341.22	League of Nations
JX1976-1977	341.23	United Nations
JX2001-3695	341.0(9/1)	History/Theory
JX2001-2035	341.093(8/7)	Ancient (Greece/Rome)
JX2041-2060	341.0902	Medieval
JX2061-2182	341.0903(1-3)	1500-1713
JX2206-2435	341.09033	18th century
JX2441-3085	341.09034	19th century
JX3091-3695	341.0904	20th century

LC	Dewey	Descriptor
JX4161-4171	341.37	Treaties
JX4203-4270	341.482	Nationality/Citizenship
JX4275-4399	341.488	Asylum/Extradition
JX4408-4449	341.7566	Maritime law
JX4471-5397	341.5	International disputes
JX5401-5486	341.26	International responsibility
JX6001-6953	340.9	Private (Conflict of laws)
JX6001-6008	340.905	Serials
JX6009-6025	340.906	Societies/Congresses
JX6041-6048	340.903	Dictionaries
JX6051-6053	340.901	Theory
JX6071	340.909	History
JX6085	340.907	Education
JX6111-6242	340.909	By place
JX6271-6339	340.97	Commercial law (International)
JX6351	340.92	Contracts/Obligations
JX6411-6433	340.915	Family
JX6501-6510	340.95	Inheritance/Succession
JX6561-6570	340.94	Property
JX6708-6953	341.77	Criminal law
K	340-349	Law (General)
K1-36	340.05	Serials
K48	340.03	Encyclopedias
K50-54	340.03	Dictionaries
K64	340.05	Yearbooks
K68-70	340.025	Directories
K85-88	340.072	Legal research
K100-103	340.07	Legal education
K110	340.06	Bar associations
K115-129	340.023	The legal profession
K133	347.017	Legal aid
K140-165	340.(09/5)	History of law
K170	340.092	Biography
K175	340.06	Congresses
K181-184.7	340.02	Miscellany
K190-195	340.52	Primitive law
K237-487	340.1	Philosophy/Theory of law
K237-264	340	The concept of law
K270-274	340.11	Acts and events
K280-286	340.11	Sources of law
K321-474	340.109	Legal theory
K325-328	340.1	Historical jurisprudence
K330-344	340.112	Positivism
K368-380	340.115	Sociology of law/Jurisprudence
K400-474	340.112	Natural law
K540-5582	340.2/341	Comparative/International law
K540-546	347.07	Trials
K583-591	340.5(2-9)	Legal systems compared
K600-619	346	Private law
K623-968	346	Civil law
K625-709	346.012	Persons
K670-709	346.015	Domestic relations
K720-792	346.04	Property
K795-798	346.059	Trusts and trustees
K805-821	346.052	Succession upon death
K830-968	346.02	Obligations
K840-917	346.02(2-5)	Contracts
K920	346.029	Restitution/Quasi contracts
K923-968	346.03	Torts
K970	342.03288	Victims compensation
K1000-1388	346.07	Commercial law
K1010-1016	346.065	Merchants/Business enterprises
K1024-1132	346.02	Commercial contracts

LC	Dewey	Descriptor	LC	Dewey	Descriptor
K1026-1045	346.072	Sale of goods	K4028-4045	343.0942	Roads
K1054-1065	346.096	Negotiable instruments	K4061-4070	343.095	Railroads
K1066-1088	346.08	Banking	K4080	343.098	Local transportation
K1100-1104	346.074	Secured transactions	K4091-4124	343.097	Aviation
K1112-1116	346.092	Investments	K4135	341.47/343.0979	Space law
K1150-1231	343.096	Maritime law	K4150-4235	346.04691	Water
K1226-1231	346.0862	Marine insurance	K4157-4180	343.0965	Ships
K1241-1287	346.086	Insurance	K4182-4194	343.0967	Navigation/Pilotage
K1301-1366	346.06	Business associations	K4198-4200	343.0967	Harbors/Ports
K1370-1388	346.078	Bankruptcy	K4240-4343	343.099	Communication
K1401-1578	346.048	Intellectual property	K4245-4279	343.0992	Postal service
K1411-1485	346.0482	Copyright	K4285-4290	343.0998	The press
K1500-1578	346.048	Industrial property	K4301-4343	343.0994	Telecommunication
K1700-1970	344	Social legislation	K4360-4375	344.01712	Professions
K1701-1841	344.01	Labor law	K4430-4675	343.03	Public finance
K1861-1929	344.02	Social insurance	K4453-4640	343.036	National revenue
K1960-1970	344.03	Public welfare	K4456-4590	343.04	Taxation
K2100-2385	347	Court procedures	K4501-4558	343.052	Income/Profit tax
K2110-2155	347.01(2-7)	Court organization/	K4560-4566	343.054	Property tax
		Procedure	K4568	343.053	Inheritance/Estate
K2201-2385	347.05	Civil procedure	K4572-4580	343.0553	Excise tax
K2390	347.09	Negotiated settlement	K4600-4640	343.056	Tariffs
K2400-2405	347.09	Arbitration	K4650-4675	343.043	State/Local finance
K3150	342	Public law	K4700-4705	342.02	Government emergencies
K3154-3367	342	Constitutional law	K4720-4760	343.01	National defense
K3161	342.029	Constitutional history	K4725-4734	343.015	Armed forces
K3169	320.1	The state	K4740-4760	343.014	Military criminal law
K3171-3179	342.02	Constitutional principles	K5000-5570	345	Criminal law
K3185-3188	342.04	Structure of government	K5018-5022	345.001	Philosophy/Theory
K3201-3205	342.0412	Foreign relations	K5032-5033	345.009	History
K3224-3278	342.08	Individual and state	K5036-5048	345.01	Criminal jurisdiction
K3280-3282	322.1	Church and state	K5055-5056	345.02	Criminal offense
K3285	321	Forms of government	K5064-5083	345.04	Criminal liability
K3290-3367	342.0(5-68)	Organs of government	K5090-5098	345.02	Forms of offense
K3290-3304	342.08	The people	K5101-5136	345.077	Punishment
K3310-3329	342.05	The legislature	K5165-5316	345.02	Offenses
K3332-3363	342.062	Heads of state	K5401-5570	345.05	Criminal procedure
K3367	347	The judiciary	K5404	345.0501	Philosophy/Theory
K3375	341.28	Colonial law	K5409-5410	345.0509	History
K3400-3431	342.066	Administrative law	K5412-5418	345.05	Principles of procedure
K3403-3416	342.066	The administrative process	K5423	345.01	Jurisdiction
K3420-3431	342.06	Administrative organization	K5425	345.072	Indictment
K3440-3460	342.068	Civil service	K5430-5447	345.072	Preliminary proceedings
K3476-3558	343.02	Public property	K5452-5453	345.056	Rights of suspects
K3478-3486	346.044	Natural resources	K5460-5492	345.075	Trial
K3492	343.0942	Roads	K5465-5490	345.06	Evidence
K3496-3501	346.04691	Water resources	K5492	345.075	Jury
K3511-3512	343.0252	Eminent domain	K5495-5497	345.01	Appellate/Etc.
K3514-3525	343.025	Public land	K5510-5570	345.077	Execution of sentence
K3531-3544	346.045	Regional/City planning	K5575-5582	345.08	Juvenile criminal law
K3550-3553	344.063635	Housing	K7000-7720	342.042	Conflict of laws
K3558-3560	343.02	Government property	K7000	016.3409	Bibliographies
K3566-3609	344.04	Public health/Medical law	K7010-7011	348.022	Statutes
K3615-3617	344.049	Veterinary laws	K7015	340.903	Encyclopedias/Dictionaries
K3625-3649	344.0423	Food/Drugs/Cosmetics	K7019	340.906	Societies
K3651-3654	344.042	Alcohol	K7021	340.1	Philosophy/Theory
K3661-3674	344.047	Public safety	K7030	340.9	History
K3740-3762	344.07	Education	K7033	340.6	Congresses
K3770-3793	344.09	Science/Arts/Research	K7051-7054	341.7	International unification
K3820-3823	343.07	Economics	K7120-7197	340.912	Persons
K3840-4375	343.07	Business regulations	K7120-7148	340.913	Status/Capacity
K3842-3862	343.08	Trade regulations	K7125-7140	340.983	Natural persons
K3870-3918	343.075	Primary production	K7145-7148	340.913	Juristic persons
K3941-3974	343.08	Trade and commerce	K7155-7197	340.915	Family law
K3978-3990	343.09	Public utilities	K7157-7178	340.916	Marriage
K4011-4339	343.093	Transportation/	K7181-7192	340.917	Parent and child
		Communication	K7197	340.918	Guardian and ward

LC	Dewey	Descriptor	LC	Dewey	Descriptor
K7200-7222	340.94	Property	KD1034-1195	343.4202	Public property
K7230-7245	340.952	Succession upon death	KD1035	346.42044	Natural resources
K7260-7335	340.92	Obligations	KD1040-1048	343.420942	Roads
K7265-7305	340.92(2-5)	Contracts	KD1070	346.4204691	Water resources
K7310	340.929	Restitution/Quasi contracts	KD1090-1107	343.42025	Public land
K7315-7335	340.93	Torts	KD1125-1162	346.42045	Planning/Zoning
K7340-7512	340.97	Commercial law	KD1185-1189	343.420252	Eminent domain
K7350-7444	340.97	Commercial contracts	KD1195	343.420256	Public works
K7350	340.972	Sale	KD1205-1465	346.42047	Personal property
K7360-7370	340.996	Negotiable instruments	KD1238-1450	346.42048	Intangible
K7380-7390	340.982	Banking/Loans	KD1261-1450	346.42048	Intellectual/Industrial
K7410-7418	340.992	Investments	KD1281-1325	346.420482	Copyright
K7430-7444	343.093	Carriers	KD1345	346.420484	Design protection
K7449-7460	343.096	Maritime law	KD1361-1413.3	346.420486	Patent law
K7470	340.986	Insurance	KD1431-1445	346.420488	Trademarks
K7485-7495	340.96	Associations/Corporations	KD1450	346.42048	Business names
K7550-7582	340.948	Intellectual property	KD1465	343.42023	Government personal property
K7555-7557	340.9482	Copyright	KD1480-1495	346.42059	Trust/Trustees
K7570-7582	340.948	Industrial property	KD1497	343.42053/346.42052	Estate planning
K7585-7595	344	Social legislation	KD1500-1534	346.42052	Succession upon death
K7616-7686	347.05	Civil procedure	KD1554-1920	346.4202	Contracts
K7625-7627	340.9/347.012	Jurisdiction	KD1610-1613	346.42023	Government contracts
K7640-7646	347.0(72/52)	Pleading/Motions	KD1621-1920	346.4202	Types of contracts
K7650-7655	347.052	Parties	KD1621-1630	346.4202	Commercial
K7660-7673	347.07	Trial	KD1634	346.42024	Service contracts
K7680	340.9	Foreign judgments	KD1638-1642	344.420189	Labor contracts
K7681-7686	347.077	Remedies	KD1650-1675	346.42072	Sale of goods
K7690	347.09	Arbitration	KD1679-1685	346.42025	Bailments
KD	349.42	Law (England)	KD1695-1699	346.42096	Negotiable instruments
KD51-59	016.34942	Bibliography	KD1715-1737	346.42082	Banking
KD125-180	328.42	Legislation	KD1740-1742	346.42073	Financial loans
KD125-150	348.42022	Statutes	KD1752	346.42074	Guaranty/Secured transactions
KD190-300	348.4204	Law reports, Etc.			
KD310	340.03	Encyclopedias	KD1755-1763	346.42092	Securities/Investments
KD313	340.03	Dictionaries	KD1800-1847	343.42093	Carriers
KD318	347.42055	Form books	KD1802	343.4209(4-5)	Carriage by land
KD325	340.05	Yearbooks	KD1804	343.42097	Carriage by air
KD327-332	347.42013	Judicial statistics	KD1811-1834	343.42096	Carriage by sea
KD336-340	340.025	Directories	KD1845-1847	346.420862	Marine insurance
KD347	340.06	Congresses	KD1851-1913	346.42086	Insurance
KD370-379.5	347.4207	Trials	KD1924	346.42029	Quasi contracts
KD370-376	345.4207	Criminal trials	KD1941-2004	346.4203	Torts
KD378-379.5	347.4207	Civil trials	KD2007	344.4203288	Victim compensation
KD392-400	349.42072	Legal research	KD2020-2024	346.42029	Agency/Power of attorney
KD411	348.4204	Reporting	KD2040-2127	346.4206	Associations
KD417-452	340.07	Education	KD2046-2054	346.42064	Unincorporated associations
KD456	340.06042	Societies	KD2049-2054	346.420682	Partnership
KD460-510	340.023	Legal profession	KD2057-2127	346.42066	Corporations
KD512	347.42017	Legal aid	KD2061-2062	346.42064	Nonprofit
KD530-632	340.0942	History	KD2071-2127	346.42065	Businesses/Companies
KD640	340.1	Philosophy	KD2139-2172	346.42078	Bankruptcy
KD674	346.42004	Equity	KD2200-2990	343.4207	Business regulation
KD680-685	342.42042	Conflict of laws	KD2204-2231	343.4208	Trade regulations
KD691-703	349.42	General principles/Concepts	KD2204	343.42072	Unfair trade practices
KD720-721	347.42	Civil law	KD2206	343.42082	Advertising
KD723-746	346.42013	Persons (Status/Capacity)	KD2208-2209	343.42082	Labeling
KD750-785	346.42015	Family law	KD2212	343.420723	Restraint of trade
KD810-1465	346.4204	Property	KD2215	343.42083	Price regulation
KD810-815	346.420432	Possession	KD2218-2220	343.42072	Monopolies
KD821-1195	346.42043	Real property/Land law	KD2225-2226	343.420725	Unfair competition
KD833-1020.6	346.420432	Real estate management/Etc.	KD2228	346.4206	Trade associations
KD833-960	346.420432	Land tenure	KD2230-2231	343.42075	Weights/Measures/Containers
KD834-839	346.420434	Feudal systems			
KD841-960	346.420432	Estates	KD2241-2370	343.4207(6-7)	Primary production industries
KD966-992	346.420(4363/052)	Sale/Inheritance			
KD1010-1016	346.4204364	Mortgages/Liens	KD2241-2295	343.42076	Agriculture/Forestry

LC	Dewey	Descriptor	LC	Dewey	Descriptor
KD2310-2315	343.4207692	Fishery	KD5295	343.42034	Public auditing
KD2331-2370	343.420775	Mining/Quarrying	KD5300	343.42037	National debt
KD2375-2398	343.42078	Manufacturing industries	KD5320-5694	343.42036	National income
KD2405-2430	343.4207833847664	Food processing industry	KD5320-5341	343.4203609	History
KD2435	343.42078624	Construction industry	KD5351-5694	343.420(4-68)	Sources of national income
KD2455-2530	343.4208	Commerce/Trade	KD5351-5605	343.4204	Taxation
KD2535-2560	343.4209	Public utilities	KD5641-5694	343.42056	Tariffs
KD2571-2915	343.4209(3-9)	Transportation/ Communication	KD5710-5752	343.42(1-9)	Local finance
KD2940-2990	344.42201712	The professions	KD6000-6355	343.4201	National defense
KD3000-3315	344.42	Social legislation	KD6030-6335	343.42013	Armed forces
KD3001-3177	344.4201	Labor law	KD6086-6228	343.4201(6-9)	Branches of service
KD3191-3273	344.4202	Social insurance	KD6240-6248	343.4201	Auxiliary services (War time)
KD3291-3315	344.4203	Public welfare			
KD3351-3375	344.4204(6)	Public health/Pollution	KD6250	343.42014	Military discipline
KD3395-3413	344.42041	Medicine	KD6270-6332	343.42015	Military criminal law
KD3420-3422	344.42049	Veterinary medicine	KD6335	343.42015/347.42	Civil law/Armed forces
KD3450-3462	344.420423	Food/Drugs/Cosmetics	KD6338	343.4201	Other defense agencies
KD3466-3480	344.42042	Alcohol	KD6340	344.420535	Civil defense
KD3490-3516	344.4205	Public safety	KD6355	343.42011	Veterans
KD3492	344.420533	Weapons/Firearms	KD6850-7640	347.42	Courts (Procedure)
KD3494-3507	344.420472	Hazards	KD6850-6855	347.4209	History
KD3510	344.42047	Accidents	KD6870-6992	347.42	Justice before 1873
KD3515-3516	344.420537	Fire	KD7100-7312	347.42	Justice after 1873
KD3523	344.42099	Amusements	KD7111-7312	347.420(1-5)	Court organization/ Procedures
KD3525	344.42099	Sports			
KD3527	344.420542	Gambling	KD7645-7647	347.4209	Arbitration
KD3600-3689	344.4207	Education	KD7850-8090	345.42	Criminal law
KD3710-3758	344.4209(5/7)	Science/Arts	KD8220-8464	345.4205	Criminal procedure
KD3720-3731	344.42097	The arts	KD8850-9355	349.42(1-9)	Local laws
KD3736	344.42093	Museums/Galleries	KD8850-9312	349.42	England
KD3746	344.42092	Libraries	KD8850-9150	349.42(1-8)	Counties/Shires/Cities/Etc.
KD3753-3755	344.42092	Archives	KD8860-9142	342.4212	London
KD3758	344.4208	Scientific/Cultural exchanges	KD9320-9355	349.429	Wales (Local law)
			KD9320-9325	349.429 (1-9)	Counties/Shires/Cities/Etc.
KD3930-4645	342.42	Constitutional law	KD9400-9500	349.429	Law of Wales
KD3931-3966	342.42029	History	KD9407	348.429022	Statutes
KD3931-3932	342.42024	Sources	KD9410-9417	348.42904	Law reports
KD3938-3966	342.420290(1-4)	By date	KD9420	349.42903	Law dictionaries
KD3981-3990	342.42	Constitutional law, General	KD9423	345.42907	Criminal trials
KD3995-4018	342.42	Constitutional principles	KD9430	340.09429	History
KD4000-4010	342.42044	Separation of powers	KD9460	344.42907	Education (Law)
KD4015-4018	342.42024	Sources of law	KD9480	347.429	Courts and procedure
KD4030	342.420412	Foreign relations	KD9490	345.429	Criminal law
KD4050-4139	342.4208	Individual and state	KDC	349.411	Law (Scotland)
KD4050-4058	342.42083	Citizenship	KDC70-90	328.411	Legislation
KD4080-4119	342.42085	Civil rights	KDC110-113	347.41103	Courts of Appeal
KD4130-4139	342.42083	Aliens	KDC150-152	340.41103	Dictionaries/Encyclopedias
KD4185-4645	342.4204	Organs of government	KDC184-188	347.41107/345.41107	Trials (Civil/Criminal)
KD4190-4381	342.4205	Parliament	KDC220	340.06411	Societies
KD4430-4531	342.4206	The crown/Central government	KDC225-247	340.023411	The legal profession
			KDC270-320	340.09411	History
KD4435-4456	342.4206	The crown	KDC350-378	346.411012	Persons
KD4462	342.4206(2-4)	Prime minister/Cabinet	KDC390-452	346.41104	Property
KD4467-4531	342.4206(4/8)	Departments/Civil service	KDC462-470	346.411052	Succession upon death
KD4645	347.42	Judiciary	KDC482-545	346.4110(2/96)	Obligations/Negotiable instruments
KD4650	344.4209	National emblem/Seals			
KD4656-4657	344.4209	Honors/Dignities	KDC635-674	344.411	Social legislation
KD4746-4840	342.4209/349.4(2-9)	Local government	KDC680-695	344.41104	Health/Medical legislation
KD5020-5025	349.42	Commonwealth/Empire	KDC750-785	342.411	Constitutional law
KD5110-5133	343.4201	Government emergencies/ War	KDC807-825	343.41103	Public finance
			KDC840-948	347.41105	Courts (Procedure)
KD5280-5752	343.4203	Public finance	KDC875-902.6	347.41105	Civil procedure
KD5280	343.420309	History	KDC910-948	345.4110(7/5)	Criminal law/Procedure
KD5284-5286	343.42032	Currency/Coinage	KDC958-974	349.411	Ecclesiastical law
KD5288	343.42032	Foreign exchange	KDC980-990	349.411(2-9)	Local laws
KD5292	343.42034	Budget	KDE	349.416	Law (Northern Ireland)
			KDE42-50	328.416	Legislation

LC	Dewey	Descriptor
KDE55-60	348.41604	Law reports
KDE90-98	346.416012	Persons
KDE110-137	346.41604	Property
KDE140-142	346.416059	Trust/Trustees
KDE145-151	346.416052	Succession upon death
KDE235-282	343.41607	Business regulation
KDE320-348	344.416	Social legislation
KDE410-462	342.416	Constitutional law
KDE510-530	347.41605	Courts (Procedure)
KDE525-530	347.41605	Civil procedure
KDE540-562	345.416(075)	Criminal law/Procedure
KDE570-580	349.416(1-98)	Local laws
KDG	349.4234	Law (Channel Islands, Britain)
KDG26-170	349.4279	Isle of Man
KDG220-380	349.42341	Channel Islands, Jersey
KDG421-440	349.42342	Channel Islands, Guernsey
KDG532-540	349.42345	Channel Islands, Sark
KDK	349.417	Law (Ireland)
KDK38-51	328.417	Legislation
KDK61-80	348.41704	Law reports
KDK84	340.03	Dictionaries
KDK93	340.06	Societies
KDK102-106	347.41707	Trials
KDK120-134	340.023417	The legal profession
KDK141-161	340.09417	History
KDK185-205	346.417012	Persons
KDK215-345	346.41704	Property
KDK350-354	346.417059	Trust/Trustees
KDK360-365	346.417052	Succession upon death
KDK370-437	346.41702	Contracts
KDK450-469	346.41703	Torts
KDK550-769	343.41707	Business regulation
KDK800-895	344.417	Social legislation
KDK910-932	344.41704	Medical/Health legislation
KDK1200-1350	342.417	Constitutional law
KDK1430-1526	343.41703	Public finance
KDK1580-1713	347.41705	Courts (Procedure)
KDK1660-1713	347.41705	Civil procedure
KDK1750-1831	345.4170(7/5)	Criminal trial/Procedure
KDK1910-1950	349.4(6-9)	Local laws
KDZ	349.7	North America
KDZ0-999	349.7	General
KDZ1100-1199	341.245	Organization of American States
KDZ2000-2499	349.7299	Bermuda
KDZ3000-3499	349.982	Greenland
KDZ4000-4499	349.7188	St. Pierre and Miquelon
KE	349.71	Law (Canada)
KE1-8	016.34971	Bibliography
KE78-125	328.71	Legislation
KE132-176	348.7104	Law reports
KE198-206	347.71013	Judicial statistics
KE225-237	347.7107	Trials
KE225-229	345.7107	Criminal trials
KE234-237	347.7107	Civil trials
KE250-259	349.71072	Legal research
KE273-322	340.07	Education
KE325	340.06071	Legal institutes/Societies
KE330-372	340.02371	Legal profession
KE335-355	347.710504	Practice of law
KE359-372	340.06071	The bar/Associations
KE376-378	347.71017	Legal aid
KE427	340.1	Philosophy
KE457	346.71004	Equity
KE470-474	342.71042	Conflict of laws
KE495	347.71	Civil law
KE498-606	346.71012	Persons
KE531-606	346.71015	Family law
KE618-781	346.7104	Property
KE625-754	346.71043	Real property
KE765-781	346.71047	Personal property
KE787-799	346.71059	Trusts
KE806-833	346.71052	Succession upon death
KE850-1225	346.7102	Contracts
KE899-906	346.71023	Government contracts
KE924	346.71024	Service contracts
KE928-936	344.710189	Labor contracts
KE943-966	346.71072	Sale of goods
KE970-972	346.71025	Bailments
KE980-986	346.71096	Negotiable instruments
KE991-1026	346.71082	Banking
KE1030-1034	346.71073	Loans
KE1042-1056	346.71074	Secured transactions
KE1060-1089	346.71092	Investments
KE1099-1135	343.71093	Carriers
KE1141-1220	346.71086	Insurance
KE1229	344.71032	Restitution
KE1232-1309	346.7103	Torts
KE1312	344.7103288	Victims' compensation
KE1328-1332	346.7102	Agency
KE1345-1465	346.7106	Associations
KE1351-1361	346.71064	Unicorporated associations
KE1369-1465	346.71066	Corporations
KE1485-1520	346.71078	Bankruptcy
KE1589-2742	343.7107	Business regulation
KE1591-1660	343.7108	Trade regulation
KE1610-1614	343.71082	Advertising
KE1616-1618	343.71082	Labeling
KE1620-1622	343.71075	Weights/Measures/ Containers
KE1631-1655	343.710721	Competition
KE1671-1830	343.7107(6-7)	Primary production
KE1671-1745	343.71076	Agriculture/Forestry
KE1760-1765	343.71076392	Fishing industry
KE1790-1830	343.71077	Mining/Quarrying/ Petroleum
KE1840-1858	343.71078	Manufacturing industries
KE1867-1906	343.710783847664	Food processing industries
KE1915	343.71078624	Construction industry
KE1935-1999	343.7108	Trade/Commerce
KE2020-2061	343.7109	Public utilities
KE2071-2649	343.7109(3-9)	Transportation/ Communication
KE2700-2742	344.7101712	The professions
KE2771-2998	346.71048	Intellectual property
KE3098-3542	344.71	Social law
KE3375-3635	344.7104(632)	Public health/Pollution
KE3646-3660	344.71041	Medical legislation
KE3696-3725	344.710423	Food/Drugs/Cosmetics
KE3756-3778	344.7105	Public safety
KE3805-3917	344.7107	Education
KE3950-4000	344.7109(5/7)	Science/Arts
KE4120	342	Public law
KE4125-4775	342.71	Constitutional law
KE4228	342.71032	Amending process
KE4270-4285	342.7104	Structure of government
KE4310	342.710412	Foreign relations
KE4335	342.710418	Public policy/Police
KE4345-4486	342.71085	Civil rights
KE4526-4775	342.71044	Organs of government
KE4529-4665	342.7105	The legislature
KE4705-4765	342.7106	The Crown/Executive branch

LC	Dewey	Descriptor
KE4775	347.71	The judiciary
KE4900-4934	342.71	Local government
KE4940-4995	342.71068	Civil service
KE5006-5010	342.710418	Power of police
KE5015-5036	342.71066	Administrative procedure
KE5105-5420	343.7102	Public property
KE5145-5165	346.7104691	Water resources
KE5184-5217	343.71025	Public land law
KE5258-5284	346.71045	Regional/City planning
KE5460-5484	343.7101	Government emergency
KE5600-6328	343.7103	Public finance
KE6800-7240	343.7101	National defense
KE8200-8605	347.7101	Courts
KE8212-8332	347.7101	Court organization
KE8341-8605	347.7105	Civil procedure
KE8615	347.7109	Negotiated settlement
KE8618	347.7109	Arbitration
KE8801-9440	345.71	Criminal law
KEA	349.7123	Law, Alberta
KEB	349.711	Law, British Columbia
KEM	349.7127	Law, Manitoba
KEN0-599	349.7151	Law, New Brunswick
KEN1200-1799	349.718	Law, Newfoundland
KEN5400-5999	349.7192	Law, Northwest Territories
KEN7400-7999	349.716	Law, Nova Scotia
KEO	349.713	Law, Ontario
KEQ	349.714	Law, Quebec
KES	349.7124	Law, Saskatchewan
KEY	349.7191	Law, Yukon Territory
KEZ	349.71(1-9)	Law, Canadian Cities
KF	349.73	Law (United States)
KF1-8	016.34973	Bibliography
KF16-49	348.73	Legislative documents
KF50-90	348.73022	Statutes
KF101-153	348.7304	Law reports
KF154	340.03	Encyclopedias
KF156	340.03	Law dictionaries
KF165	348.7(4-9)	Uniform state laws
KF170	347.73055	Form books
KF178	340.05	Yearbooks
KF180-185	347.73013	Judicial statistics
KF190-195	340.02573	Directories
KF202	340.06	Congresses
KF220-224	345.7307	Criminal trials
KF228	347.7353	Civil suits
KF240-246	349.73072	Legal research
KF255	348.7304	Law reporting
KF260	348.7304	Cases
KF262-292	340.07	Legal education
KF294	340.06	Law societies
KF297-334	340.02373	Legal profession
KF336-337	347.7317	Legal aid
KF350-374	340.0973	History
KF350	342.73024	Sources
KF379-382	340.01	Jurisprudence/Philosophy
KF398-400	346.73004	Equity
KF410-418	342.73042	Conflict of law
KF425-450	342.73	Principles/Concepts
KF465-553	346.73012	Persons
KF465-485	346.73013	Status/Capacity
KF501-553	346.73015	Family law
KF560-720	346.7304	Property
KF560-562	346.730432	Ownership
KF566-698	346.73043	Real property
KF701-720	346.73047	Personal property
KF726-745	346.73059	Trusts
KF746-750	346.73052/343.73053	Estate planning
KF753-780	346.73052	Succession upon death
KF801-1241	346.7302	Contracts
KF807-839	346.7302	Contracts (Principles)
KF841-869	346.73023	Government contracts
KF871-890	346.7302	Commercial/Mercantile contracts
KF894	346.73024	Service contracts
KF898-905	344.7301891	Labor contracts
KF911-935	346.73072	Sale of goods
KF939-951	346.73025	Bailments
KF956-962	346.73096	Negotiable instruments
KF966-1032	346.73082	Banking
KF1033	343.73032	Foreign-exchange
KF1035-1040	346.73073	Loans
KF1045	346.73074	Guaranty
KF1046-1062	346.73074	Chattel mortgages/Liens
KF1066-1083	346.73092	Securities/Investments
KF1085-1086	343.7308	Commodity exchanges
KF1091-1137	343.73093	Carriers
KF1092	343.7309(4-5)	By land
KF1093	343.73097	By air
KF1096-1114	343.73096	By sea
KF1121-1132	344.73017613875	Maritime labor law
KF1135-1137	346.730862	Marine insurance
KF1146-1238	346.73086	Insurance
KF1241	344.730542	Gambling/Wagering contracts
KF1244	346.73029	Restitution
KF1246-1327	346.7303	Torts
KF1328	344.7303288	Victims' compensation
KF1341-1348	346.73029	Power of attorney/Brokers
KF1355-1480	346.7306	Associations
KF1361-1380	346.73064	Unincorporated
KF1365-1380	346.730682	Partnership
KF1384-1480	346.73066	Corporations
KF1388-1389	346.73064	Nonprofit corporations
KF1396-1477	346.73066	Business corporations
KF1480	346.73067	Government-owned
KF1501-1548	346.73078	Bankruptcy
KF1600-2940	343.7307	Business regulations
KF1601-1666	343.7308	Trade regulations
KF1601-1611	343.73072	Unfair trade practices
KF1614-1617	343.73082	Advertising
KF1619-1620	343.73082	Labeling
KF1624-1625	343.730723	Restraint of trade
KF1626-1629	343.730725	Price fixing
KF1631-1657	343.73072	Monopolies
KF1659-1659.1	343.7307	Small business
KF1661	346.73064	Trade associations
KF1663	343.73088	State/Trade barriers
KF1665-1666	343.73075	Weights/Measures/Containers
KF1681-1873	343.7307(6-7)	Primary production
KF1681-1750	343.7307(6-7)	Agriculture/Forestry
KF1770-1773	343.7307692	Fishery
KF1801-1873	343.73077	Mining/Quarrying/Petroleum
KF1875-1893	343.73078	Manufacturing industry
KF1900-1944	344.7307833847664	Food processing industry
KF1950	343.73078624	Construction industry
KF1970-2057	343.7308	Trade/Commerce
KF2076-2140	343.7309	Public utilities
KF2161-2849	343.7309(3/9)	Transportation/Communication
KF2901-2940	344.7301712	The professions
KF2971-3192	346.73048	Intellectual property
KF2986-3080	346.730482	Copyright

LC	Dewey	Descriptor		LC	Dewey	Descriptor
KF3084	070.509730687	Publishing contracts		KF5130	347.73	Judiciary
KF3086	346.730484	Design protection		KF5150	344.7309	National emblems/Seals
KF3091-3192	346.73048(6/8)	Patent law/Trademarks		KF5152	344.73091	Patriotic customs
KF3195-3198	343.730721	Unfair competition		KF5153-5154	344.7309	Honors/Awards
KF3300-3750	344.73	Social legislation		KF5155-5156	344.7309	Commemorative medals
KF3301-3580	344.7301	Labor law		KF5300-5332	342.7309	Local government
KF3600-3686	344.7302	Social insurance		KF5336-5398	342.73068	Civil service
KF3720-3745	344.7303	Public welfare/Assistance		KF5399	342.730418	Power of police
KF3750	344.730534	Disaster relief		KF5401-5425	342.73066	Administration and procedures
KF3775-3813	344.7304	Public health/Sanitation		KF5500-5865	343.7302	Public property
KF3821-3829	344.73041	Medical legislation		KF5505-5508	346.73044	Natural resources
KF3832	344.73048	Eugenics/Sterilization		KF5521-5536	343.730942	Roads
KF3835-3838	344.73049	Veterinary medicine		KF5551-5590	346.7304691	Water resources
KF3861-3894	344.730423	Food/Drugs/Cosmetics		KF5594	344.73065515	Meteorology
KF3901-3925	344.73042	Alcohol		KF5599	343.730252	Eminent domain
KF3941-3977	344.7305	Public safety		KF5601-5646	343.73025	Public land law
KF3941-3942	344.730533	Weapons/Firearms		KF5670-5673	343.730253	Homesteads
KF3945-3965	344.730472	Hazardous items/Processes		KF5675-5677	343.730253	Land grants
KF3970	344.73047	Accident control		KF5691-5710	346.73045	Planning/Zoning
KF3975-3977	344.73053(7/33)	Fire/Explosives		KF5721-5740	344.73063635	Public housing/ Redevelopment
KF3987	344.73099	Amusements		KF5750-5857	343.7302	Government property
KF3989	344.73099	Sports		KF5750-5755	343.7302	Administration
KF3992	344.730542	Lotteries		KF5760-5810	343.73025	Land/Real property
KF4101-4258	344.7307	Education		KF5820-5857	343.73023	Personal property
KF4124	344.730796	Church and education		KF5865	344.7306	Public works
KF4125-4143	344.73076	School finance/Etc.		KF5900-6075.5	343.7301	Government emergencies
KF4150-4166	344.73079	Students		KF6200-6795	343.7303	Public finance
KF4175-4190	344.73078	Teachers		KF6201-6219	343.73032	Currency/Coinage
KF4192	344.7307	Other personnel		KF6221-6225	343.73034	Budget
KF4195-4223	344.73074	Through high school		KF6231-6236	343.73034	Public auditing
KF4225-4258	344.73074	Higher education		KF6241-6245	343.73037	Public debts
KF4270-4330	344.7309(5/7)	Science/Arts		KF6251-6708	343.73036	National revenue
KF4288-4302	344.73097	The arts		KF6251-6256	343.7303609	History
KF4305	344.73093	Museums/Galleries		KF6256-6708	343.730(4-68)	Sources of revenue
KF4310-4312	344.73094	Monuments/Historical sites		KF6271-6645	343.7304	Taxation
KF4315-4319	344.73092	Libraries		KF6296-6297	343.7304	Tax planning
KF4325	344.73092	Archives		KF6298	343.7304	Tax expenditures
KF4330	344.7308	Scientific/Cultural exchanges		KF6300-6328	343.7304	Tax administration
KF4501-5130	342.73	Constitutional law		KF6310-6316	343.73042	Tax collection
KF4501-4515	342.73024	Sources		KF6320-6328	343.73042	Procedures
KF4520	348.731	Legislative history		KF6329-6330	343.7304	Exemption
KF4525-4528	342.73023	The Constitution (Texts)		KF6334	345.730233	Tax evasion
KF4530	342.7302	State constitutions		KF6335-6636	343.7305	Kinds of taxes
KF4541-4545	342.73029	Constitutional history		KF6351-6499	343.73052	Income tax
KF4546-4554	342.73001	Theory/Interpretation		KF6525-6558	343.73054	Property tax
KF4555	342.73032	Amending process		KF6566-6594	343.730524	Taxes on capital and income
KF4558	342.73032	Amendments		KF6598-6636	343.730526	Indirect taxes
KF4565-4578	342.73044	Separation of powers		KF6651-6708	343.73056	Tariffs
KF4581-4583	342.73024	Sources of law		KF6720-6795	343.73043	State/Local finance
KF4600-4629	342.73042	Federal-State relations		KF7201-7755	343.7301	National defense/Military
KF4635	342.730413	Territories		KF7250-7680	343.73013	Armed forces
KF4650-4694	342.730412	Foreign relations		KF7305-7479	343.7301(6-9)	Branches of service
KF4695	342.73041(8)	Public policy/Police		KF7305-7335	343.7301(6-82)	Army
KF4700-4856	342.7308	Individual and state		KF7345-7375	343.73019	Navy
KF4700-4720	342.73083	Citizenship		KF7385-7395	343.7301996	Marine Corps
KF4741-4783	342.73085	Civil rights		KF7405-7430	343.730184	Air Force
KF4788	342.73087	Political parties		KF7445-7479	343.7301997	Coast Guard
KF4791-4856	342.7308	Control of individuals		KF7485-7488.7	343.7301997	Services during war/ Emergency
KF4794-.5	342.73082	Passports		KF7590	343.73014	Military discipline
KF4800-4848	342.73083	Aliens		KF7595-7596	343.73014	Law enforcement
KF4850-4856	344.7305	Internal security		KF7601-7679	343.730143	Military criminal law
KF4865-4869	342.730852	Church and state		KF7625-7659	343.730143	Courts martial
KF4881-5130	342.73044	Organs of government		KF7631-7642	343.7301(6-82)	Army
KF4881-4921	342.7307	Election law				
KF4930-5005	342.7305	The legislature				
KF5050-5125	342.7306	Executive branch				

LC	Dewey	Descriptor
KF7646-7652	343.73019	Navy
KF7654	343.7301996	Marine Corps
KF7657	343.730184	Air Force
KF7659	343.7301997	Coast Guard
KF7665	343.730143	Appellate
KF7675-7677	343.730146	Punishment
KF7679	343.730146	Probation
KF7680	347.73	Civil status
KF7685	344.730535	Civil defense
KF7701-7755	343.73011	War veterans
KF8201-8228	342.730872	Indians
KF8700-9075	347.730(1-5)	Courts/Procedure
KF8711-8807	347.730(1-5)	Court organization/ Procedures
KF8732-8733	347.7313	Administration (Courts)
KF8736	347.733	State courts
KF8737	347.734	Local courts
KF8741-8745	347.7326	Supreme court
KF8750-8752	347.7324	Appeals courts
KF8754-8755	347.7322	District/Circuit courts
KF8760	347.7328	Claims courts
KF8770-8807	347.731(4-6)	Judicial officers/Employees
KF8810-9075	347.735	Civil procedures
KF8815	348.7322	Statutes
KF8816-8902	347.7351	Court rules
KF8820-8821	347.7351	District courts
KF8858-8861	347.7351	Jurisdiction
KF8863-8865	347.7353	Action/Process
KF8866-8885	347.734(82/52)	Pleading/Motions
KF8890-8896	347.7352	Parties
KF8900-8902	347.7372	Pretrial
KF8910-9075	347.737	Trial
KF8911-8925	347.7375	Trial practice
KF8931-8969	347.736	Evidence
KF8971-8986	347.73752	Jury
KF8990-9002	347.7377	Judgment
KF9010-9039	347.7377	Remedies
KF9050-9058	347.738	Appellate
KF9084	347.739	Negotiated settlement
KF9085	347.739	Arbitration
KF9201-9461	345.73	Criminal law
KF9225-9227	345.73077	Punishment
KF9300	345.7302	Kinds of offenses
KF9304-9345	345.73025	Against persons
KF9350-9379	345.73026	Against property
KF9390-9456	345.730232	Against government/Public
KF9460-9461	345.730236	Through the mail
KF9625	345.730527	Arrest
KF9630	345.730522	Searches
KF9632	345.73056	Bail
KF9635	345.73052	Extradition
KF9640-9642	345.73072	Indictment
KF9641-9760	345.7305	Criminal procedure
KF9645-9650	345.73072	Arraignment
KF9655-9688	345.7307	Trial
KF9660-9677	345.7306	Evidence
KF9680	345.73075	Jury
KF9685-9688	345.73077(2)	Judgment/Sentence
KF9690	347.738	Appeals
KF9695	345.73077	Pardon
KF9725-9756	345.73077	Execution of sentence
KF9763	344.7303288	Victims of crimes
KF9771-9827	345.7308	Juvenile criminal law
KFA0-599	349.761	Law of Alabama
KFA1200-1799	349.798	Law of Alaska
KFA2400-2999	349.791	Law of Arizona
KFA3600-4199	349.767	Law of Arkansas
KFC0-1199	349.794	Law of California
KFC1800-2399	349.788	Law of Colorado
KFC3600-4199	349.746	Law of Connecticut
KFD0-599	349.751	Law of Delaware
KFD1200-1799	349.753	Law of District of Columbia
KFF0-599	349.759	Law of Florida
KFG0-599	349.758	Law of Georgia
KFH0-599	349.969	Law of Hawaii
KFI0-599	349.796	Law of Idaho
KFI1200-1799	349.773	Law of Illinois
KFI3000-3599	349.772	Law of Indiana
KFI4200-4799	349.777	Law of Iowa
KFK0-599	349.781	Law of Kansas
KFK1200-1799	349.769	Law of Kentucky
KFL0-599	349.763	Law of Louisiana
KFM0-599	349.741	Law of Maine
KFM1200-1799	349.752	Law of Maryland
KFM2400-2999	349.744	Law of Massachusetts
KFM4200-4799	349.774	Law of Michigan
KFM5400-5999	349.776	Law of Minnesota
KFM6600-7199	349.762	Law of Mississippi
KFM7800-8399	349.778	Law of Missouri
KFM9000-9599	349.786	Law of Montana
KFN0-599	349.782	Law of Nebraska
KFN600-1199	349.793	Law of Nevada
KFN1200-1799	349.742	Law of New Hampshire
KFN1800-2399	349.749	Law of New Jersey
KFN3600-4199	349.789	Law of New Mexico
KFN5000-6199	349.747	Law of New York
KFN7400-7999	349.756	Law of North Carolina
KFN8600-9199	349.784	Law of North Dakota
KFO0-599	349.771	Law of Ohio
KFO1200-1799	349.766	Law of Oklahoma
KFO2400-2919	349.795	Law of Oregon
KFP0-599	349.748	Law of Pennsylvania
KFR0-599	349.745	Law of Rhode Island
KFS1800-2399	349.757	Law of South Carolina
KFS3000-3599	349.783	Law of South Dakota
KFT0-599	349.768	Law of Tennessee
KFT1200-1799	349.764	Law of Texas
KFU0-599	349.792	Law of Utah
KFV0-599	349.743	Law of Vermont
KFV2400-2999	349.755	Law of Virginia
KFW0-599	349.797	Law of Washington
KFW1200-1799	349.754	Law of West Virginia
KFW2400-2999	349.775	Law of Wisconsin
KFW4200-4799	349.787	Law of Wyoming
KFX	349.7(41-98 7)	Law of United States cities
KFZ1800-2399	349.7192	Law of Northwest Territory
KFZ8600-9199	349.75	Confederate States of America
KG	349.(72/8)	Latin America
KG0-999	349.(72/8)	Latin America, General
KG3000-3999	349.72(9)	Mexico/Central America
KGA	349.7282	Belize
KGA0-5999	349.7282	General
KGB	349.7286	Costa Rica
KGB0-5999	349.7286	General
KGB6200-7499	349.7286(1-7)	Provinces
KGB6200-6299	349.72865	Alajuela
KGB6400-6499	349.72862	Cartago
KGB6600-6699	349.72866	Guanacaste
KGB6800-6899	349.72864	Heredia
KGB7000-7099	349.72861	Limon
KGB7200-7299	349.72867	Puntarenas
KGB7400-7499	349.72863	San Jose
KGB8000-8019	349.72863	San Jose (City)

LC	Dewey	Descriptor	LC	Dewey	Descriptor
KGC	349.7284	El Salvador	KGF	349.72	Mexico
KGC0-5999	349.7284	General	KGF0-5999	349.72	General
KGC6200-8899	349.7284(11-34)	Departments	KGF6200-9399	349.72(1-7)	States
KGC6200-6299	349.728411	Ahuachapan	KGF6200-6299	349.7242	Aguascalientes
KGC6400-6499	349.728426	Cabanas	KGF6300-6399	349.7223	Baja California/Baja California Norte
KGC6600-6699	349.728421	Chalatenango			
KGC6800-6899	349.728424	Cuscatlan	KGF6400-6499	349.7224	Baja California Sur
KGC7000-7099	349.728422	La libertad	KGF6500-6599	349.7264	Campeche
KGC7200-7299	349.728425	La Paz	KGF6600-6699	349.7275	Chiapas
KGC7400-7499	349.728434	La Union	KGF6700-6799	349.7216	Chihuahua
KGC7600-7699	349.728433	Morazan	KGF6800-6899	349.7214	Coahuila
KGC7800-7899	349.728432	San Miguel	KGF6900-6999	349.7236	Colima
KGC8000-8099	349.728423	San Salvador	KGF7000-7099	349.7215	Durango
KGC8200-8299	349.728427	San Vicente	KGF7100-7199	349.7241	Guanajuato
KGC8400-8499	849.728412	Santa Ana	KGF7200-7299	349.7273	Guerrero
KGC8600-8699	349.728413	Sonsonate	KGF7300-7399	349.7246	Hidalgo
KGC8800-8899	349.728431	Usulutan	KGF7400-7499	349.7235	Jalisco
KGC9600-9619	349.728423	San Salvador (City)	KGF7500-7599	349.7252	Mexico (State)
KGC9640-9659	349.728412	Santa Ana (City)	KGF7600-7699	349.7253	Mexico City (Federal District)
KGD	349.7281	Guatemala			
KGD0-5999	349.7281	General	KGF7700-7799	349.7237	Michoacan
KGD6100-9899	349.7281(1-84)	Departments	KGF7800-7899	349.7249	Morelos
KGD6100-6199	349.728151	Alta Verapaz	KGF7900-7999	349.7234	Nayarit
KGD6200-6299	349.728152	Baja Verapaz	KGF8000-8099	349.7213	Nuevo Leon
KGD6300-6399	349.728161	Chimaltenango	KGF8100-8199	349.7274	Oaxaca
KGD6500-6599	349.728141	Chiquimula	KGF8200-8299	349.7248	Puebla
KGD6700-6799	349.728153	El Progreso	KGF8300-8399	349.7245	Queretaro
KGD6900-6999	349.728163	Escuintla	KGF8400-8499	349.7267	Quintana Roo
KGD7000-7099	349.72811	Guatemala (Dept.)	KGF8500-8599	349.7244	San Luis Potosi
KGD7100-7199	349.728171	Huehuetenango	KGF8600-8699	349.7232	Sinaloa
KGD7300-7399	349.728131	Izabal	KGF8700-8799	349.7217	Sonora
KGD7500-7599	349.728142	Jalapa	KGF8800-8899	349.7263	Tabasco
KGD7700-7799	349.728143	Jutiapa	KGF8900-8999	349.7212	Tamaulipas
KGD7900-7999	349.72812	Peten	KGF9000-9099	349.7247	Tlaxcala
KGD8100-8199	349.728182	Quezaltenango	KGF9100-9199	349.7262	Veracruz
KGD8300-8399	349.728172	Quiche	KGF9200-9299	349.7265	Yucatan
KGD8500-8599	349.728183	Retalhuleu	KGF9300-9399	349.7243	Zacatecas
KGD8700-8799	349.728162	Sacatepequez	KGG	349.7285	Nicaragua
KGD8900-8999	349.728184	San Marcos	KGG0-5999	349.7285	General
KGD9100-9199	349.728144	Santa Rosa	KGG6200-9499	349.7285(11-32)	Departments/Territory
KGD9300-9399	349.728164	Solola	KGG6200-6299	349.728526	Boaco
KGD9500-9599	349.728165	Suchitepequez	KGG6400-6499	349.728532	Cabo Gracias a Dios
KGD9700-9799	349.728181	Totonicapan	KGG6600-6699	349.728516	Carazo
KGD9800-9899	349.728132	Zacapa	KGG6800-6899	349.728511	Chinandega
KGD9920-9939	349.72811	Guatemala City	KGG7000-7099	349.728527	Chontales
KGE	349.7283	Honduras	KGG7200-7299	349.728524	Estelf
KGE0-5999	349.7283	General	KGG7400-7499	349.728515	Granada
KGE6100-9599	349.7283(11-85)	Departments	KGG7600-7699	349.728522	Jinotega
KGE6100-6199	349.728315	Atlantida	KGG7800-7899	349.728512	Leon
KGE6300-6399	349.728351	Choluteca	KGG8000-8099	349.728523	Madriz
KGE6500-6599	349.728313	Colon	KGG8200-8299	349.728513	Managua
KGE6700-6799	349.728372	Comayagua	KGG8400-8499	349.728514	Masaya
KGE6900-6999	349.728384	Copan	KGG8600-8699	349.728525	Matagalpa
KGE7100-7199	349.728311	Cortes	KGG8800-8899	349.728521	Nueva Segovia
KGE7300-7399	349.72834	El Paraiso	KGG9000-9099	349.728531	Rio San Juan
KGE7500-7599	349.728371	Francisco Morazan	KGG9200-9299	349.728517	Rivas
KGE7700-7799	349.72832	Gracias a Dios	KGG9400-9499	349.728532	Zelaya
KGE7900-7999	349.728381	Intibuca	KGG9600-9619	349.728513	Managua (City)
KGE8100-8199	349.728315	Islas de la Bahia	KGH	349.7287	Panama
KGE8300-8399	349.72836	La Paz	KGH0-5999	349.7287	General
KGE8500-8599	349.728382	Lempira	KGH6100-7799	349.7287(1-5)	Provinces
KGE8700-8799	349.728383	Octepeque	KGH6100-6199	349.728712	Bocas del Toro
KGE8900-8999	349.72833	Olancho	KGH6300-6399	349.728711	Chiriqui
KGE9100-9199	349.728385	Santa Barbara	KGH6500-6599	349.728721	Cocle
KGE9300-9399	349.728352	Valle	KGH6700-6799	349.728732	Colon
KGE9500-9599	349.728314	Yoro	KGH6900-6999	349.72874	Darien
KGE9960-9979	349.728371	Tegucigalpa	KGH7100-7199	349.728724	Herrera

LC	Dewey	Descriptor	LC	Dewey	Descriptor
KGH7300-7399	349.728723	Los Santos	KGR3000-3499	349.72976	French West Indies
KGH7500-7599	349.728731	Panama	KGR4000-4499	349.729845	Grenada
KGH7700-7799	349.728722	Veraguas	KGR5000-5499	349.72976	Guadeloupe
KGH7820-7839	349.728732	Colon (City)	KGS	349.7294	Haiti
KGH7840-7859	349.728731	Panama City	KGS0-5999	349.7294	General
KGH9000-9499	349.72875	Panama Canal Zone	KGS6200-7899	349.7294(2-6)	Departments
KGJ-KGZ	349.729	West Indies/Caribbean area	KGS6200-6299	349.72944	Artibonite
KGJ7000-7499	349.72973	Anguilla	KGS6800-6899	349.72943	Nord
KGK0-499	349.72974	Antigua and Barbuda	KGS7200-7299	349.72942	Nord-Ouest
KGK1000-1499	349.72986	Aruba	KGS7400-7499	349.72945	Ouest
KGL0-499	349.7296	Bahamas	KGS7600-7699	349.72946	Sud
KGL1000-1499	349.72981	Barbados	KGS8000-8019	349.72945	Port-au-Prince
KGL2000-2499	349.72986	Bonaire	KGT0-499	349.7292	Jamaica
KGL4000-4499	349.729725	British Virgin Islands	KGT1000-1499	349.72982	Martinique
KGM0-499	349.72921	Cayman Islands	KGT2000-2499	349.72975	Montserrat
KGN	349.7291	Cuba	KGV	349.7295	Puerto Rico
KGN0-5999	349.7291	General	KGV0-5999	349.7295	General
KGN6200-8899	349.7291(1-67)	Provinces	KGV8000-8019	349.72952	Bayamon
KGN6200-6299	349.729156	Camaguey	KGV8060-8079	349.72956	Mayaguez
KGN6400-6499	349.729153	Ciego de Avila	KGV8080-8099	349.72957	Ponce
KGN6600-6699	349.729143	Cienfuegos	KGV8100-8119	349.72951	San Juan
KGN6800-6899	349.729163	Granma	KGW0-499	349.72977	Saba
KGN7000-7099	349.729167	Guantanamo	KGW2000-2499	349.72973	St. Kitts/Nevis/Anguilla
KGN7200-7299	349.729123	Havana (City)	KGW3000-3499	349.729843	St. Lucia
KGN7400-7499	349.729124	Havana (Province)	KGW5000-5499	349.729844	St. Vincent and the Grenadines
KGN7600-7699	349.729164	Holguin			
KGN7800-7899	349.729162	Las Tunas	KGW7000-7499	349.72977	St. Eustatius
KGN7900-7999	349.72914	Las Villas	KGW8000-8499	349.72977	St. Martin
KGN8000-8099	349.72913	Matanzas	KGX0-499	349.72983	Trinidad/Tobago
KGN8100-8199	349.72916	Oriente	KGY0-499	349.72961	Turks/Caicos Islands
KGN8200-8299	349.72911	Pina del Rio	KGZ0-499	349.729722	Virgin Islands of U.S.
KGN8400-8499	349.729145	Sancti Spiritus	KH	349.8	South America
KGN8600-8699	349.729165	Santiago de Cuba	KH0-999	349.8	General
KGN8800-8899	349.729142	Villa Clara	KHA	349.82	Argentina
KGP0-499	349.72986	Curacao	KHA0-5999	349.82	General
KGP2000-2499	349.729841	Dominica	KHA6200-8799	349.8211	Buenos Aires (Federal Dist.)
KGQ	349.7293	Dominican Republic			
KGQ0-5999	349.7293	General	KHA6300-6399	349.8212	Buenos Aires (Province)
KGQ6200-8899	349.7293(2-85)	Provinces/National district	KHA6400-6499	349.8245	Catamarca
KGQ6200-6299	349.729372	Azua	KHA6500-6599	349.8234	Chaco (President Peron)
KGQ6300-6399	349.729326	Bahoruco	KHA6600-6699	349.8274	Chubut
KGQ6400-6499	349.729324	Barahona	KHA6700-6799	349.8254	Cordoba
KGQ6500-6599	349.729345	Dajabon	KHA6800-6899	349.8222	Corrientes
KGQ6600-6699	349.729367	Duarte	KHA6900-6999	349.8221	Entre Rios (Federal District)
KGQ6700-6799	349.729384	El Seibo	KHA7000-7099	349.8235	Formosa
KGQ6800-6899	349.729362	Espaillat	KHA7200-7299	349.8241	Jujuy
KGQ6900-6999	349.729325	Independencia	KHA7300-7399	349.8213	La Pampa (Eva Peron)
KGQ7000-7099	349.729385	La Altagracia	KHA7400-7499	349.8246	La Rioja
KGQ7100-7199	349.729343	La Estrelleta (San Rafael)	KHA7600-7699	349.8264	Mendoza
KGQ7200-7299	349.729383	La Romana	KHA7700-7799	349.8223	Misiones
KGQ7300-7399	349.729369	La Vega	KHA7800-7899	349.8272	Neuquen
KGQ7400-7499	349.729364	Maria Trinadad Sanchez	KHA7900-7999	349.8273	Rio Negro
KGQ7500-7599	349.729352	Montecristi	KHA8000-8099	349.8242	Salta
KGQ7600-7699	349.729323	Pedernales	KHA8100-8199	349.8263	San Juan
KGQ7700-7799	349.729373	Peravia	KHA8200-8299	349.8262	San Luis
KGQ7800-7899	349.729358	Puerto Plata	KHA8300-8399	349.8275	Santa Cruz
KGQ7900-7999	349.729363	Salcedo	KHA8400-8499	349.8224	Santa Fe
KGQ8000-8099	349.729365	Samana	KHA8500-8599	349.8252	Santiago del Estero
KGQ8100-8199	349.729374	San Cristobal	KHA8600-8699	349.8276	Tierra del Fuego
KGQ8200-8299	349.729342	San Juan	KHA8700-8799	349.8243	Tucuman
KGQ8300-8399	349.729382	San Pedro de Macoris	KHC	349.84	Bolivia
KGQ8500-8599	349.729356	Santiago	KHC0-5999	349.84	General
KGQ8600-8699	349.729353	Santiago Rodriguez	KHC6200-7899	349.84(1-43)	Departments
KGQ8700-8799	349.729375	Santo Domingo (National dist)	KHC6200-6299	349.8424	Chuquisaca
			KHC6400-6499	349.8423	Cochabamba
KGQ8800-8899	349.729357	Valverde	KHC6600-6699	349.8442	El Beni
KGR1000-1499	349.72986	Netherlands Antilles	KHC6800-6899	349.8412	La Paz

LC	Dewey	Descriptor	LC	Dewey	Descriptor
KHC7000-7099	349.8413	Oruro	KHF8600-8699	349.83255	Valparaiso/Easter Island
KHC7200-7299	349.8443	Pando	KHF9600-9619	349.8313	Antofagasta (City)
KHC7400-7499	349.8414	Potosi	KHF9640-9659	349.83315	Santiago (City)
KHC7600-7699	349.843	Santa Cruz	KHF9700-9719	349.83255	Valparaiso (City)
KHC7800-7899	349.8425	Tarija	KHH	349.861	Colombia
KHC8000-8019	349.8423	Cochabamba (City)	KHH0-5999	349.861	General
KHC8020-8039	349.8412	La Paz (City)	KHH6200-9399	349.861(12-8)	Departments
KHD	349.81	Brazil	KHH6200-6299	349.8617	Amazonas
KHD0-5999	349.81	General	KHH6300-6399	349.86126	Antioquia
KHD6200-8999	349.81(1-7)	States/Federal district	KHH6400-6499	349.86138	Arauca
KHD6200-6299	349.8112	Acre	KHH6500-6599	349.86115	Atlantico
KHD6300-6399	349.8135	Alagoas	KHH6600-6699	349.86148	Bogota (Special district)
KHD6400-6499	349.8116	Amapa	KHH6700-6799	349.86114	Bolivar
KHD6500-6599	349.8113	Amazonas	KHH6800-6899	349.86137	Boyaca
KHD6600-6699	349.8142	Bahia	KHH6900-6999	349.86135	Caldas
KHD6700-6799	349.8174	Brasilia (Federal District)	KHH7000-7099	349.86164	Caqueta
KHD6800-6899	349.8131	Ceara	KHH7100-7199	349.86143	Casanore
KHD6900-6999	349.8152	Espirito Santo	KHH7200-7299	349.86153	Cauca
KHD7000-7099	349.8136	Fernando de Noronha	KHH7300-7399	349.86127	Choco
KHD7100-7199	349.8173	Goias	KHH7400-7499	349.86112	Cordoba
KHD7200-7299	349.8153	Guanabara	KHH7500-7599	349.86146	Cundinamarca
KHD7300-7399	349.8121	Maranhao	KHH7600-7699	349.86123	El Cesar
KHD7400-7499	349.8172	Mato Grosso	KHH7700-7799	349.86167	Guainia
KHD7500-7599	349.8151	Minas Gerais	KHH7800-7899	349.86154	Huila
KHD7600-7699	349.8115	Para	KHH7900-7999	349.86117	La Guajira
KHD7700-7799	349.8133	Paraiba	KHH8000-8099	349.86116	Magdelena
KHD7800-7899	349.8162	Parana	KHH8100-8199	349.86156	Meta
KHD7900-7999	349.8134	Pernambuco	KHH8200-8299	349.86162	Narino
KHD8000-8099	349.8122	Piaui	KHH8300-8399	349.86124	Norte de Santander
KHD8100-8199	349.8153	Rio de Janeiro	KHH8400-8499	349.86163	Putamayo
KHD8200-8299	349.8132	Rio Grande do Norte	KHH8500-8599	349.86134	Quindio
KGD8300-8399	349.8165	Rio Grande do Sul	KHH8600-8699	349.86132	Risaralda
KHD8400-8499	349.8175	Rondonia (Guapore)	KHH8700-8799	349.8618	San Andres y Providencia
KHD8500-8599	349.8114	Roraima	KHH8800-8899	349.86125	Santander
KHD8600-8699	349.8164	Santa Catarina	KHH8900-8999	349.86113	Sucre
KHD8700-8799	349.8161	Sao Paulo	KHH9000-9099	349.86136	Tolima
KHD8800-8899	349.8141	Sergipe	KHH9100-9199	349.86152	Valle de Cauca
KHD8900-8999	349.8171	Mato Grosso do Sul	KHH9200-9299	349.86165	Vaupes
KHD9800-9819	349.8153	Rio de Janeiro (City)	KHH9300-9399	349.86139	Vichada
KHD9840-9859	349.8161	Sao Paulo (City)	KHK	349.866	Ecuador
KHF	349.83	Chile	KHK0-5999	349.866	General
KHF0-5999	349.83	General	KHK6100-9899	349.866(11-5)	Provinces
KHF6200-8699	349.83(1-6)	Provinces	KHK6100-6199	349.86624	Azuay
KHF6200-6299	349.8324	Aconcagua	KHK6300-6399	349.86616	Bolivar
KHF6300-6399	349.8313	Antofagasta	KHK6500-6599	349.86623	Canar
KHF6400-6499	349.8342	Arauco	KHK6700-6799	349.86611	Carchi
KHF6500-6599	349.8314	Atacama	KHK6900-6999	349.86617	Chimborazo
KHF6600-6699	349.83622	Aysen	KHK7100-7199	349.86614	Cotopaxi
KHF6700-6799	349.8341	Bio-Bio	KHK7300-7399	349.86631	El Oro
KHF6800-6899	349.8346	Cautin	KHK7500-7599	349.86635	Esmeraldas
KHF6900-6999	349.8356	Chiloe	KHK7700-7799	349.8665	Galapagos Islands (Colon)
KHF7000-7099	349.8333	Colchagua	KHK7900-7999	349.86632	Guayas
KHF7100-7199	349.8339	Concepcion	KHK8100-8199	349.86612	Imbabura
KHF7200-7299	349.8323	Coquimbo	KHK8300-8399	349.86625	Loja
KHF7300-7399	349.8334	Curico	KHK8500-8599	349.86633	Los Rios
KHF7400-7499	349.8337	Linares	KHK8700-8799	349.86634	Manabi
KHF7500-7599	349.8354	Llanquihue	KHK8900-8999	349.86643	Morona-Santiago
KHF7600-7699	349.8364	Magallanes	KHK9100-9199	349.86641	Napo
KHF7700-7799	349.8345	Malleco	KHK9300-9399	349.86642	Pastaza
KHF7800-7899	349.8335	Maule	KHK9500-9599	349.86613	Pichincha
KHF7900-7999	349.8338	Nuble	KHK9700-9799	349.86615	Tungurahua
KHF8000-8099	349.8332	O'Higgins	KHK9800-9899	349.86644	Zamora-Chinchipe
KHF8100-8199	349.8353	Osorno	KHK9960-9979	349.86613	Quito (City)
KHF8200-8299	349.8331	Santiago	KHL	349.9711	Falkland Islands
KHF8300-8399	349.8335	Talca	KHL0-5999	349.9711	General
KHF8400-8499	349.8312	Tarapaca	KHM	349.882	Guyane/French Guiana
KHF8500-8599	349.8352	Valdivia	KHM0-5999	349.882	General

LC	Dewey	Descriptor	LC	Dewey	Descriptor
KHN	349.88	Guyana	KHU6600-6699	349.89524	Durazno
KHN0-5999	349.88	General	KHU6700-6799	349.89526	Flores
KHP	349.892	Paraguay	KHU6800-6899	349.89525	Florida
KHP0-5999	349.892	General	KHU6900-6999	349.89521	Lavelleja
KHP6100-9399	349.892(1-27)	Departments	KHU7000-7099	349.89515	Maldonado
KHP6100-6199	349.892132	Alto Parana	KHU7100-7199	349.89513	Montevideo
KHP6300-6399	349.892137	Amambay	KHU7200-7299	349.89531	Paysandu
KHP6500-6599	349.892121	Asuncion (Federal District)	KHU7300-7399	349.89528	Rio Negro
KHP6700-6799	349.89224	Boqueron	KHU7400-7499	349.89534	Rivera
KHP6900-6999	349.892134	Caaguazu	KHU7500-7599	349.89516	Rocha
KHP7100-7199	349.892127	Caazapa	KHU7600-7699	349.89535	Salto
KHP7300-7399	349.892122	Central	KHU7700-7799	349.89512	San Jose
KHP7500-7599	349.892138	Concepcion	KHU7800-7899	349.89527	Soriano
KHP7700-7799	349.892135	Cordillera	KHU7900-7999	349.89532	Tacuarembo
KHP7900-7999	349.892128	Guaira	KHU8000-8099	349.89522	Treinta y Tres
KHP8100-8199	349.892126	Itapua	KHU9620-9639	349.89513	Montevideo
KHP8300-8399	349.892125	Misiones	KHU9640-9659	349.89531	Paysandu
KHP8500-8599	349.892124	Neembucu	KHU9660-9679	349.89535	Salto
KHP8900-8999	349.892123	Paraguari	KHW	349.87	Venezuela
KHP9300-9399	349.892136	San Pedro	KHW0-5999	349.87	General
KHQ	349.85	Peru	KHW6200-6299	349.8764	Amazonas
KHQ6200-6299	349.8546	Amazonas	KHW6300-6399	349.8752	Anzoategui
KHQ6300-6399	349.8521	Ancash	KHW6400-6499	349.8742	Apure
KHQ6400-6499	349.85294	Apurimac	KHW6500-6599	349.8734	Aragua
KHQ6500-6599	349.8522	Arequipa	KHW6600-6699	349.8743	Barinas
KHQ6600-6699	349.85292	Ayacucho	KHW6700-6799	349.8763	Bolivar
KHQ6700-6799	349.8525	Cajamarca	KHW6800-6899	349.8732	Carabobo
KHQ6800-6899	349.8526	Callao	KHW6900-6999	349.877	Carascas (Federal district)
KHQ6900-6999	349.8537	Cuzco	KHW7000-7099	349.8746	Cojedes
KHQ7000-7099	349.8528	Huancavelica	KHW7100-7199	349.8762	Delta Amacuro
KHQ7100-7199	349.8522	Huanuco	KHW7200-7299	349.8724	Falcon
KHQ7200-7299	349.8527	Ica	KHW7300-7399	349.8747	Guarico
KHQ7300-7399	349.8524	Junin	KHW7400-7499	349.8725	Lara
KHQ7400-7499	349.8516	La Libertad	KHW7500-7599	349.8713	Merida
KHQ7500-7599	349.8514	Lambayeque	KHW7600-7699	349.8735	Miranda
KHQ7600-7699	349.8525	Lima	KHW7700-7799	349.8756	Monagas
KHQ7700-7799	349.8543	Loreto	KHW7800-7899	349.8754	Nueva Esparta
KHQ7800-7899	349.8542	Madre de Dios	KHW7900-7999	349.8745	Portuguesa
KHQ7900-7999	349.8534	Moquegua	KHW8000-8099	349.8753	Sucre
KHQ8000-8099	349.8523	Pasco	KHW8100-8199	349.8712	Tachira
KHQ8100-8199	349.8513	Piura	KHW8200-8299	349.8714	Trujillo
KHQ8200-8299	349.8536	Puno	KHW8300-8399	349.8726	Yaracuy
KHQ8300-8399	349.8545	San Martin	KHW8400-8499	349.8723	Zulia
KHQ8400-8499	349.8535	Tacna	KHW9660-9679	349.8763	Ciudad Bolivar
KHQ8500-8599	349.8512	Tumbes	KJG	349.4965	Law of Albania
KHQ9600-9619	349.8532	Arequipa (City)	KJH	349.4679	Law of Andorra
KHQ9620-9639	349.8526	Callao (City)	KJJ	349.436	Law of Austria
KHQ9660-9679	349.8537	Cuzco (City)	KJK	349.493	Law of Belgium
KHQ9680-9699	349.8525	Lima (City)	KJM	349.4977	Law of Bulgaria
KHS	349.883	Suriname	KJN	349.5645	Law of Cyprus
KHS0-5999	349.883	General	KJP	349.437	Law of Czechoslovakia
KHS6200-6299	349.8839	Brokopondo	KJR	349.489	Law of Denmark
KHS6400-6499	349.8837	Commewijne	KJT	349.4897	Law of Finland
KHS6600-6699	349.8832	Coronie	KJV	349.44	Law of France
KHS6800-6899	349.8838	Marowijne	KK	349.43	Law of Germany
KHS7000-7099	349.8831	Nickerie	KKE	349.495	Law of Greece
KHS7200-7299	349.8834	Para	KKF	349.439	Law of Hungary
KHS7400-7499	349.8835	Paramaribo	KKG	349.4912	Law of Iceland
KHS7600-7699	349.8833	Saramacca	KKH	349.45	Law of Italy
KHS7800-7899	349.8836	Suriname	KKJ	349.43648	Law of Liechtenstein
KHU	349.895	Uruguay	KKK0-499	349.4935	Law of Luxembourg
KHU0-5999	349.895	General	KKK1000-1499	349.4585	Law of Malta
KHU6200-8099	349.895(1-36)	Departments	KKL	349.44949	Law of Monaco
KHU6200-6299	349.89536	Artigas	KKM	349.492	Law of Netherlands
KHU6300-6399	349.89514	Canalones	KKN	349.481	Law of Norway
KHU6400-6499	349.89523	Cerro Largo	KKP	349.438	Law of Poland
KHU6500-6599	349.89511	Colonia	KKQ	349.469	Law of Portugal

LC	Dewey	Descriptor
KKR	349.498	Law of Romania
KKS	349.4549	Law of San Marino
KKT	349.46	Law of Spain
KKV	349.485	Law of Sweden
KKW	349.494	Law of Switzerland
KKX	349.561	Law of Turkey
KKY	349.45634	Law of Vatican City
KKZ	349.497	Law of Yugoslavia
L	370	Education (General)
L7-97	370.5	Serials
L10-94	370.5	By language/Place
L101	370.5	Yearbooks
L106-107	370.6	Congresses
L111-791	370.9(4-9)	By place
L111-219	370.973	United States
L116-219	370.97(4-9)	Local, By place
L221-223	370.971	Canada
L227-229	370.972	Mexico
L231-249	370.9728	Central America
L251-267	370.9729	West Indies
L291-335	370.98	South America
L341-551	370.94	Europe
L341-359	370.941	Great Britain
L346-348	370.9415	Ireland
L361-366	370.9436	Austria
L381-383	370.9439	Hungary
L385-387	370.9437	Czechoslovakia
L391-396	370.944	France
L401-410	370.943	Germany
L411-416	370.9495	Greece
L421-426	370.945	Italy
L431-436	370.9493	Belgium
L441-446	370.9492	Netherlands
L451-466	370.947	European Russia
L471-476	370.9489	Denmark
L481	370.94912	Iceland
L491-496	370.9481	Norway
L501-506	370.9485	Sweden
L511-516	370.946	Spain
L521-526	370.9469	Portual
L531-536	370.9494	Switzerland
L539-540	370.9561	Turkey
L541-542	370.94977	Bulgaria
L545-546	370.9498	Romania
L549-550	370.9497	Yugoslavia
L561-642	370.95	Asia
L571-573	370.951	China
L577-578	370.954	India
L578.5-.6	370.95491	Pakistan
L583-584	370.9595	Maylay Peninsula
L585-586	370.959(4-7)	Indochina
L597-598	370.9598	Indonesia
L601-602	370.9599	Philippines
L611-612	370.952	Japan
L613-614	370.9519	Korea
L615-616	370.955	Iran
L617-620	370.957	Asian Russia
L627-628	370.9567	Iraq
L631-632	370.95694	Israel/Palestine
L651-742	370.96	Africa
L750-791	370.99(3-6)	Australia/New Zealand/ Oceania
L797-899	370.74	Exhibitions/Museums
L801-899	370.74(4-9)	By place
L801-803	370.7473	United States
L805-806	370.7471	Canada
L808-809	370.7472	Mexico

LC	Dewey	Descriptor
L811-812	370.74728	Central America
L814-815	370.74729	West Indies
L816-817	370.748	South America
L818-885	370.744	Europe
L887-889	370.745	Asia
L890-891	370.746	Africa
L893-898	370.749(3-6)	Australia/New Zealand/ Oceania
L900-991	373/378.0 + (025)	Directories
L901-991	373/378.0 + (025 4-9)	By place
L901-903	373/378.0 + (02573)	United States
L905-906	373/378.0 + (02571)	Canada
L907-908	373/378.0 + (02572)	Mexico
L909-910	373/378.0 + (025728)	Central America
L911-912	373/378.0 + (025729)	West Indies
L913-914	373/378.0 + (0258)	South America
L914.5-957	373/378.0 + (0254)	Europe
L915-918	373/378.0 + (02541)	Great Britain
L919-920	373/378.0 + (025415)	Ireland
L921-922	373/378.0 + (025436)	Austria
L927-928	373/378.0 + (02544)	France
L929-930	373/378.0 + (02543)	Germany
L931-932	373/378.0 + (025495)	Greece
L935-936	373/378.0 + (02545)	Italy
L937-938	373/378.0 + (025493)	Belgium
L939-940	373/378.0 + (025492)	Netherlands
L941-942	373/378.0 + (02547)	European Russia
L943-944	373/378.0 + (025489)	Denmark
L945-946	373/378.0 + (025481)	Norway
L947-948	373/378.0 + (025485)	Sweden
L949-950	373/378.0 + (02546)	Spain
L951-952	373/378.0 + (025469)	Portugal
L953-954	373/378.0 + (025494)	Switzerland
L960-961	373/378.0 + (0255)	Asia
L967	373/378.0 + (025174927)	Arab countries
L970-971	373/378.0 + (0256)	Africa
L981-982	373/378.0 + (02594)	Australia
L985-986	373/378.0 + (02593)	New Zealand
L991	373/378.0 + (0259 5-6)	Oceania
LA	371-379. + (09)	History of education
LA31-133	371-379.090(1-4)	By date
LA31-81	371-379.093	Ancient
LA34-66	371-379.0934	Oriental
LA71-81	371-379.093(8/7)	Classic (Greek/Roman)
LA95-98	268	Christian education
LA106-108	371-379.090(23-24)	Renaissance
LA116-118	371-379.090(31-32)	16th-17th centuries
LA121-124	371-379.090 33	18th century
LA126-133	371-379.090 (34-4)	19th-20th centuries
LA173-186	378.009	Higher education
LA177-186	378.0090(1-4)	By date
LA190-2284	371-379.09	By place
LA201-398	371-379.0973	United States
LA410-419	371-379.0971	Canada
LA420-430	371-379.0972	Mexico
LA435-474	371-379.09728	Central America
LA475-505	371-379.09729	West Indies
LA540-609	371-379.098	South America
LA545-549	371-379.0982	Argentina
LA550-554	371-379.0984	Bolivia
LA555-559	371-379.0981	Brazil
LA560-564	371-379.0983	Chile
LA565-569	371-379.09861	Colombia
LA570-574	371-379.09866	Ecuador
LA575-579	371-379.09881	Guyana
LA580-584	371-379.09882	French Guiana
LA585-589	371-379.09883	Suriname

LC	Dewey	Descriptor	LC	Dewey	Descriptor
LA590-594	371-379.09892	Paraguay	LA1815-1819	371-379.09611	Tunisia
LA595-599	371-379.0985	Peru	LA1840-1844	371-379.09678	Tanzania
LA600-604	371-379.09895	Uruguay	LA1850-1854	371-379.096711	Cameroon
LA605-609	371-379.0987	Venezuela	LA1910-1914	371-379.096751	Zaire
LA620-1040	371-379.094	Europe	LA1920-1924	371-379.096662	Liberia
LA630-669.5	371-379.0941	Great Britain	LA1940-1944	371-379.0964	Morocco
LA670-679	371-379.09436	Austria	LA2010-2014	371-379.0968	South Africa
LA680-687	371-379.09439	Hungary	LA2070-2074	371-379.09612	Libya
LA690-716	371-379.0944	France	LA2100-2189	371-379.09(3-4)	Australia/New Zealand
LA720-779	371-379.0943	Germany	LA2200-2270	371-379.099(5-6)	Oceania
LA780-789	371-379.09495	Greece	LA2277-2279	371-379.0998(1-8)	Polar regions
LA790-799	371-379.0945	Italy	LA2280-2284	371-379.09982	Greenland
LA810-819	371-379.09493	Belgium	LA2301-2396	371-379.092	Biography
LA820-820	371-379.09492	Netherlands	LB	370.1	Education/Theory/Practice
LA830-838	371-379.0947	European Russia	LB5-45	370.1	General
LA840-844	371-379.09438	Poland	LB51-885	370.1	Theories by date/Person
LA870-879	371-379.09489	Denmark	LB51-95	370.1093	Ancient
LA880-889	371-379.094912	Iceland	LB125	268/370.1 + 090(1-2)	Early Christian/Medieval
LA890-899	371-379.09481	Norway	LB175-375	370.109(23-31)	Renaissance/Humanists
LA900-909	371-379.09485	Sweden	LB472-475	370.109(31-32)	16th-17th centuries
LA910-919	371-379.0946	Spain	LB501-575	370.10933	18th century
LA920-929	371-379.09469	Portugal	LB621-695	370.10934	19th century
LA930-939	371-379.09494	Switzerland	LB775-885	370.1094	20th century
LA950-959	371-379.094977	Bulgaria	LB1025-1050.7	371.(102/3)	Teaching (Principles/ Practice)
LA970-979	371-379.09498	Romania			
LA1000-1009	371-379.09497	Yugoslavia	LB1027.5-.9	371.4	Guidance/Counseling
LA1045	371-379.0956	Near East	LB1042.5-1044.8	371.335	Audio visual education
LA1050-1484	371-379.095	Asia	LB1049.9-1050.7	372.4	Reading (General)
LA1130-1134	371-379.0951	China	LB1050.9-1091	370.15	Educational psychology
LA1145-1149	371-379.095493	Sri Lanka	LB1101-1139	155.4	Child study
LA1150-1154	371-379.0954	India	LB1140-.5	372.216	Nursery schools
LA1155-1159	371-379.095491	Pakistan	LB1141-1499	372.218	Kindergarten
LA1165-1169	371-379.095492	Bangladesh	LB1501-1547	372.241	Primary education
LA1180-1189	371-379.09597	Vietnam	LB1555-1601	372	Elementary education
LA1190-1194	371-379.09596	Cambodia	LB1603-1695	373	Secondary education
LA1205-1209	371-379.09594	Laos	LB1705-2286	370.71/371.122	Training of teachers
LA1220-1224	371-379.09593	Thailand	LB1771-1773	379.157	Certification (Teachers)
LA1235-1239	371-379.09595	Malaysia	LB1775-1785	371.10023	Teaching as a profession
LA1270-1274	371-379.09598	Indonesia	LB1805-2151	370.73	State teachers' colleges
LA1290-1299	371-379.09599	Philippines	LB1805-1987	370.730973	United States
LA1310-1319	371-379.0952	Japan	LB1991-1998	370.730971	Canada
LA1330-1339	371-379.09519	Korea	LB2001-2003	370.730972	Mexico
LA1350-1354	371-379.0955	Iran	LB2005-2019	370.7309728	Central America
LA1370-1394	371-379.0957	Asian Russia	LB2020-2032	370.7309729	West Indies
LA1440-1444	371-379.095694	Israel/Palestine	LB2035-2058	370.73098	South America
LA1455-1459	371-379.095691	Syria	LB2059-2124	370.73094	Europe
LA1460-1464	371-379.095692	Lebanon	LB2061-2068	370.730941	Great Britain
LA1465-1469	371-379.09567	Iraq	LB2125-2128	370.73095	Asia
LA1470-1474	371-379.095695	Jordan	LB2129	370.7309174927	Arab countries
LA1480-1484	371-379.095645	Cyprus	LB2130-2133	370.73096	Africa
LA1490-1493	371-379.09174927	Arab countries	LB2135-2149	370.73099(3-4)	Australia/New Zealand
LA1500-2090	371-379.096	Africa	LB2150-2151	370.73099(5-6)	Oceania
LA1545-1549	371-379.096885	Lesotho	LB2300-2430	378	Higher education
LA1550-1554	371-379.096897	Malawi	LB2326.4-2330	378.0(4/5)	Institutions
LA1560-1564	371-379.096762	Kenya	LB2331.7-2335.7	378.12	Teaching personnel
LA1565-1569	371-379.096761	Uganda	LB2335.86-.88	331.88113711	Trade unions
LA1595-1599	371-379.096894	Zambia	LB2337.3-2340.8	378.3	Student finance
LA1600-1604	371-379.096883	Botswana	LB2341-.8	378.107	Supervision/Administration
LA1620-1624	371-379.096651	Gambia	LB2351-2359	378.105	Admission requirements
LA1625-1629	371-379.09667	Ghana	LB2361-2365	378.199	Curriculum
LA1630-1634	371-379.09669	Nigeria	LB2366-2367.6	378.168	College examinations
LA1640-1644	371-379.09664	Sierra Leone	LB2371-2372	378.1553	Academic degrees
LA1645-1649	371-379.0962	Egypt	LB2801-3095	371.2	School administration
LA1670-1674	371-379.0965	Algeria	LB2831.6-.99	371.201	Administrative personnel
LA1780-1784	371-379.09672	French Equatorial Africa	LB2832-2844.1	371.1	Teaching personnel
LA1790-1794	371-379.09691	Madagascar	LB2844.52-.63	331.88113711	Trade unions
LA1810-1814	371-379.09624	Sudan	LB3011-3095	371.5	Management/Discipline

LC	Dewey	Descriptor
LB3045-3048	371.32	Textbooks
LB3050-3060.87	371.27	Tests/Measurements
LB3201-3325	371.6	Architecture/Equipment
LB3401-3495	371.7	School hygiene
LB3497-3499	378.197	Universities/Colleges/ Hygiene
LB3525-3575	371.24	Special days
LB3602-3640	371.8	School life
LC	370-379	Education (Special aspects)
LC25-33	371.3944	Self-education
LC37-44.3	649.68	Home education
LC45-.8	371.04	Nonformal education
LC47-58.7	371.02	Private school education
LC58-.7	373.222	Preparatory schools
LC59	371.01	Public school education
LC65-245	370.19	Social aspects
LC65-67.68	370.19341	Economic aspects
LC68-70	370.1934(6-8)	Demographic aspects
LC71-120.4	370.19349	And the state
LC72-.4	371.104	Academic freedom
LC73-97	371.01	Popular education
LC107-120.4	377	Secularization
LC129-139	379.23	Compulsory education
LC142-148.5	370.19341	Attendance
LC149-160	302.2244	Literacy/Illiteracy
LC165-182	379.344	Higher education and state
LC184-188	336.27837	Schools/College taxation
LC189-214.53	370.1934	Educational sociology
LC212-.863	370.19344	Discrimination
LC215-238.4	370.1931	And the community
LC225-.5	370.19	School and home
LC230-235	370.19312	Parent-teacher associations
LC237-238.4	378.103	And colleges/Universities
LC251-951	370.114	Moral/Religious education
LC251-318	370.114	Moral education
LC311-318	370.11409(4-9)	Moral education, By place
LC321-951	377.(8/9)	Religion and education
LC361-629	268	Christian education
LC461-510	268.8282	Roman Catholic
LC531-629	268.828(3-9)	Protestant
LC701-775	296.68	Jewish education
LC901-915	297.7	Islamic education
LC921-929.7	294.37	Buddhist education
LC1001-1021	370.112	Humanistic/Liberal education
LC1025-1027	370.0907	Collective education
LC1030	370.91717	Communist education
LC1031-1034.5	370.1	Competency based education
LC1035-.8	370.11	Basic education
LC1037-.8	370.113	Career education
LC1041-1048	373.113	Vocational education (General)
LC1051-1072	378.013	Professional education
LC1081-1085	370.113	Industrial education
LC1090-1091	370.115	Political education
LC1099	370.196	Intercultural education
LC1390	372-378	Education of boys
LC1401-2571	376	Education of women
LC1401	376.0(5/6)	Serials/Societies
LC1402	376.06	Congresses
LC1421-1486	376.90(1-4)	By date
LC1500-1506	370.113	Vocational education
LC1551-1651	376.65	Higher education
LC1660-1666	374	Adult education
LC1701-2571	376.90(1-4)	History
LC1751-2571	376.9(4-9)	By place

LC	Dewey	Descriptor
LC2601-2611	370-379.091724	In developing countries
LC2667-2674	371.9768	Latin Americans
LC2680-2688	371.976872	Mexican Americans
LC2690-2698	371.97687295	Puerto Ricans
LC2701-2913	371.9796	Blacks
LC3001-3501	371.9795	Asians
LC3503-3520	371.9791497	Gypsies
LC3530-3540	371.979455	Lapps
LC3701-3740	371.97	Immigrants/Minorities
LC3950-4803	371.9	Exceptional children
LC3991-4000	371.95	Gifted children
LC4001-4803	371.9(1-4)	Handicapped children
LC4051-4100	371.967	Socially handicapped
LC4165-4184	371.94	Mentally ill
LC4501-4543	371.91	Physically handicapped
LC4580-4700	371.92	Mentally handicapped
LC4704-4803	371.9	Learning disabilities
LC5161-5163	370.194	Fundamental education
LC5201-6660.4	374	Education extension/Adult
LC5501-5560	378.1544	Evening schools
LC5701-5771	371.232	Vacation
LC5900-6101	374.4	Correspondence schools
LC6201-6401	378.1554	University extension
LC6501-6560.4	373.241	Lyceums/Lecture courses
LC6571-6581	374.26	Radio/Television courses
LC6601-6660.4	374.22	Reading circles
LC6681	371.38	Education and travel
LC6691	370.74	Traveling exhibits
LD	378/373.73	Individual institutions/U.S.
LD13-7251	378.7(4-9)	Universities/Colleges
LD6501	378.1543097(4-9)	Junior colleges
LD7020-7251	378.(4-9)	Women's colleges
LD7501	373/372.97(4-9)	Secondary/Elementary schools
LE	373-378.(7-8)	Institutions, The Americas
LE3-5	373-378.71	Canada
LE7-9	373-378.72	Mexico
LE11-13	373-378.728	Central America
LE15-17	373-378.729	West Indies
LE21-78	373-378.8	South America
LE21-23	373-378.82	Argentina
LE27-29	373-378.84	Bolivia
LE31-33	373-378.81	Brazil
LE36-38	373-378.83	Chile
LE41-43	373-378.861	Colombia
LE46-48	373-378.866	Ecuador
LE51-59	373-378.88	Guianas
LE61-63	373-378.892	Paraguay
LE66-68	373-378.85	Peru
LE71-73	373-378.895	Uruguay
LE76-78	373-378.87	Venezuela
LF	373-378.4	Institutions, Europe
LF20-1257	373-378.41	Great Britain
LF20-797	373-378.42	England
LF800-957	373-378.415	Ireland
LF960-1137	373-378.411	Scotland
LF1140-1257	373-378.429	Wales
LF1311-1537	373-378.436	Austria
LF1541-1549	373-378.437	Czechoslovakia
LF1551-1697	373-378.439	Hungary
LF1705-1709	373-378.4897	Finland
LF1711-2397	373-378.44	France
LF2402-3197	373-378.43	Germany
LF3211-3247	373-378.495	Greece
LF3251-3897	373-378.45	Italy
LF3911-4067	373-378.493	Belgium
LF4069	373-378.4935	Luxemburg

LC	Dewey	Descriptor	LC	Dewey	Descriptor
LF4071-4197	373-378.492	Netherlands	M	780	Music
LF4203-4209	373-378.438	Poland	M1.A1-.A15	780.262090(1-34)	Manuscript before 1860
LF4211-4437	373-378.47	European Russia	M2-2.3	780.264	Musical sources
LF4451-4487	373-378.489	Denmark	M3-3.1	780.92	Individual composers
LF4489-4491	373-378.4912	Iceland	M6-1490	784.19	Instrumental music
LF4493-4537	373-378.481	Norway	M6-175	786-788	Solo instruments
LF4539-4607	373-378.485	Sweden	M6-39	786.5	Organs/Pianos
LF4610-4827	373-378.46	Spain	M40-59	787	String instruments
LF4831-4887	373-378.469	Portugal	M60-110	788	Wind instruments
LF4901-5047	373-378.494	Switzerland	M115-142	787.7	Plectral instuments
LF5051-5477	373-378. (561/474)	Turkey/Baltic	M145-175	786.8	Percussion instruments
LG	373-378.(5-9)	Institutions, By place	M176	781.542	Motion pictures (Music)
LG21-395	373-378.5	Asia	M176.5	781.54(4-6)	Radio/Televison
LG21	373-378.581	Afghanistan	M177-990	786-788	Solo instruments
LG31	373-378.53	Arabia	M180-298.5	785.12	Duets
LG51-53	373-378.51	China	M300-386	785.13	Trios
LG55-57	373-378.51249	Taiwan	M400-486	785.14	Quartets
LG60-170.2	373-378.54	India	M500-586	785.15	Quintets
LG60-170.2	373-378.5491	Pakistan	M600-686	785.16	Sextets
LG60-170.2	373-378.5492	Bangladesh	M700-786	785.17	Septets
LG60-170.2	373-378.591	Burma	M800-886	785.18	Octets
LG60-170.2	373-378.5493	Sri Lanka	M900-986	785.19	Nonets chamber music
LG60-170.2	373-378.5496	Nepal	M990	784.1909033	18th century instruments
LG171-172	373-378.59(3-7)	Indochina	M1000-1075	784.2	Orchestra
LG173	373-378.595	Malaysia	M1100-1160	784.7	String orchestra
LG181-184	373-378.598	Indonesia	M1200-1269	784.(8-9)	Band
LG185-187	373-378.953	Papua New Guinea (Territory)	M1270	784.8(3-4)	File/Drum/Field music
LG200-227	373-378.599	Philippines	M1350-1353	784.4	Reduced orchestra
LG240-277	373-378.52	Japan	M1356-.2	784.48	Dance orchestra
LG281-285	373-378.519	Korea	M1360	787.84	Mandolin/Plectral instruments
LG291	373-378.55	Iran	M1362	788.86	Accordion band
LG301-320	373-378.57	Asian Russia	M1365	791.12	Minstrel music
LG321	373-378.561	Asia Minor	M1366	781.65	Jazz ensembles
LG338	373-378.567	Iraq	M1375-1420	784.02405(4-5)	Instrumental music (Children's)
LG341-345	373-378.5694	Israel	M1450	781.554	Dance music
LG351-357	373-378.5692	Lebanon	M1470	781.3	Chance compositions
LG361	373-378.5691	Syria	M1473	786.7	Electronic music
LG401-681	373-378.6	Africa	M1490	780.262090(1-32)	In manuscript before 1700
LG401	373-378.63	Ethiopia	M1497-5000	782-783	Vocal music
LG405-411	373-378.68	South Africa	M1497-1998	782.(1/4)	Secular vocal music
LG418	373-378.6762	Kenya	M1500-1527.8	782.1	Dramatic music
LG421-423	373-378.6761	Uganda	M1528-1529.5	783.12	Duets/Trios
LG441	373-378.689(7)	Nyasaland/Malawi	M1530-1546.5	782.5	Choruses (Orchestra/Ensemble)
LG461	373-378.6891	Zimbabwe	M1547-1600	782.5	Choruses (Solo unaccompanied)
LG468	373-378.678	Tanzania	M1608	782.5	Choruses (Sol-fa notation)
LG469	373-378.6894	Zambia	M1609	782.5	Unison choruses
LG481-491	373-378.66	West Africa	M1610	782.48	Cantatas (Unaccompanied)
LG511	373-378.62	Egypt	M1611-1624.8	783	Songs for one voice
LG513-514	373-378.624	Sudan	M1625-1626	780.268	Recitations (Accompaniment)
LG521	373-378.6(5/11)	Algeria/Tunisia	M1627-1853	781.599	National music
LG531	373-378.672(4)	French Equatorial Africa/ Congo	M1900-1980	781.5	Special songs
LG541	373-378.691	Madagascar	M1985	793.4	Musical games
LG545	373-378.67571	Rwanda	M1990-1998	782.402405(4-5)	Secular music (Children's)
LG551	373-378.663	Senegal	M1999-2199	781.7	Sacred vocal music
LG561	373-378.6623	Mali	M2000-2007	782.23	Oratorios
LG615	373-378.6751	Zaire	M2010-2017.7	782.3	Services
LG621	373-378.6662	Liberia	M2018-2019.5	783.1(2/3)	Duets/Trios (Solo voices)
LG631	373-378.64	Morocco	M2020-2036	782.24	Choruses/Cantatas/Etc.
LG681	373-378.612	Libya	M2060-2101.5	782.5	Choruses (Accompaniment)
LG715-720	373-378.94	Australia	M2101-2114.8	783.2	For one voice
LG741-745	373-378.93	New Zealand	M2115-2146	782.27	Hymnals
LG961	373-378.9(5-6)	Pacific Islands	M2147-2188	782.3	Liturgy and ritual
LH	371.897	College/School publications			
LJ	371.85(5/6)	Student fraternities (U.S.)			
LT	371.32/100-999	Textbooks			

LC	Dewey	Descriptor
M2147-2155.6	782.3222	Roman Catholic
M2156-2160.87	782.33	Orthodox churches
M2161-2183	782.322(4-89)	Protestant churches
M2184	782.322(1-8)	Other Christian churches
M2186-2187	782.36	Jewish
M2188	782.3(4-9)	Other non-Christian
M2190-2196	782.25	Sacred vocal music (Children's)
M2198-2199	782.25	Gospel/Revival
M5000	781.3	Unidentified compositions
ML	780-788	Literature on music
ML1-5	780.5	Serials
ML12-21	780.25	Directories
ML25-28	780.6	Societies
ML29-31	781	Music foundations
ML35-38	780.79	Festivals/Congresses
ML40-44	780.78	Programs
ML48-54.8	780	Librettos
ML90	780.92(2)	Writings of musicians
ML93-97	780.262	Manuscripts/Autographs
ML100-102	780.3	Dictionaries/Encyclopedias
ML105-109	780.92(2)	Biobibliography
ML111-158	016.78	Bibliography
ML132	780.216	Graded lists
ML135	780.262	Manuscripts
ML136-158	780.216	Catalogs
ML159-3797	780.9	History/Criticism
ML162-169	780.901	Ancient
ML170-190	780.902	Medieval
ML193-197	780.90(32-4)	1600-
ML198-350.5	780.9(4-9)	History/Criticism, By place
ML200-.9	780.973	United States
ML205.9	780.971	Canada
ML207	780.9729	West Indies
ML210-.9	780.972	Mexico
ML220	780.9728	Central America
ML230-239	780.98	South America
ML240-325	780.94	Europe
ML330-345	780.95	Asia
ML350-.5	780.96	Africa
ML385-429	780.92	Biography
ML430-455	781.3	Composition
ML460-1354	784.1909(4-9)	Instruments, By place
ML475-486	784.19097	America
ML476	784.190973	United States
ML478	784.190971	Canada
ML480	784.1909729	West Indies
ML482	784.190972	Mexico
ML484	784.1909728	Central America
ML486	784.19098	South America
ML489-522	784.19094	Europe
ML491	784.1909436	Austria
ML493	784.1909437	Czechoslovakia
ML494	784.1909439	Hungary
ML496	784.1909493	Belgium
ML497	784.190944	France
ML499-500	784.190943	Germany
ML501	784.190941	Great Britain
ML503	784.190945	Italy
ML505	784.1909492	Netherlands
ML507-511	784.190947	European Russia
ML513-516	784.190948	Scandinavia
ML514	784.1909489	Denmark
ML515	784.1909481	Norway
ML516	784.1909485	Sweden
ML518	784.190946	Spain
ML519	784.1909469	Portugal
ML520	784.1909494	Switzerland
ML525	784.19095	Asia
ML527	784.1909538	Saudia Arabia
ML531	784.19095	China
ML533	784.190954	India
ML535	784.190952	Japan
ML537	784.1909519	Korea
ML539	784.190955	Iran
ML544	784.19096	Africa
ML547	784.19099(3-6)	Australia/New Zealand/ Oceania
ML549-1092	786-788.09	Instruments
ML550-649	786.509	Organs
ML650-747	786.(2/3)09	Piano/Clavichord
ML750-927	787.09	String instruments
ML930-990	788.09	Wind instruments
ML1000-1018	787.709	Plectral instruments
ML1030-1040	786.809	Percussion instruments
ML1050-1055	786.609	Mechanical/Other instruments
ML1100-1165	785.009	Chamber music
ML1200-1270	784.209	Orchestral music
ML1300-1354	784.09	Band music
ML1400-3275	782.009	Vocal music
ML1402-1406	782.0090(1-4)	History vocal music, By date
ML1410-1451	782.009(4-9)	History vocal music, By place
ML1500-1554	782.509	Choral music
ML1600-2881	782.409	Secular vocal music
ML1602-1606	782.4090(1-4)	History secular music, By date
ML1610-1751	782.409	History secular music, By place
ML1611	782.40973	United States
ML1613	782.40971	Canada
ML1614	782.409729	West Indies
ML1615	782.40972	Mexico
ML1616	782.409728	Central America
ML1617	782.4098	South America
ML1620-1649	782.4094	Europe
ML1700-2881	782.1	Dramatic music
ML1702-1706	782.1090(1-4)	Dramatic music, By date
ML1710-1751	782.109(4-9)	Dramatic music, By place
ML1711	782.10973	United States
ML1713	782.10971	Canada
ML1714	782.109729	West Indies
ML1715	782.10972	Mexico
ML1716	782.109728	Central America
ML1717	782.1098	South America
ML1720-1749	782.1094	Europe
ML2500-2551	782.4209	Songs
ML2600-2770	783.109	Part songs
ML2800-2862	783.209	Solo songs
ML2900-3275	782.2209	Sacred vocal music
ML2902-2906	782.22090(1-4)	By date
ML2910-2951	782.2209(4-9)	By place
ML3000-3197	782.3(22)009	Religious/Denominational
ML3002-3051	782.3222009	Roman Catholic
ML3100-3188	782.322(4-8)009	Protestant
ML3300-3354	781.5609	Program music
ML3400-3465	781.55409	Dance music
ML3545-3775	781.59909	National music
ML3800-3923	780.1	Philosophy/Physics (Music)
ML3845-3877	781.17	Aesthetics
ML3880-3923	780.9	Criticism
ML3930	780	Literature (Children's)

LC	Dewey	Descriptor
MT	780.7/782-788	Musical instruction and study
MT2-5	780.9/782-788.009	History/Criticism
MT6-7	781	Music theory
MT20-32	780.77	Special methods
MT40-67	781.3	Composition
MT68	781.36	Improvisation/Accompaniment
MT70-71	784/785	Orchestras
MT73	784/785	Bands
MT90-145	780.15	Analytical guides
MT95-100	781.556/782.1	Opera/Ballet
MT110-115	782.2 (3/4)	Oratorios/Cantatas
MT125-130	784.207	Orchestral music
MT140-145	785	Chamber music
MT170-810	784.193	Instrumental techniques
MT180-198	786.5193	Organ
MT192-.8	786.59193	Electronic keyboard instruments
MT200-208	786.55193	Harmonium (Reed organ)
MT220-255	786.2193	Piano
MT259-338	787.193	String instruments
MT260-279	787.2193	Violin
MT280-298	787.3193	Viola
MT300-318	787.4193	Violoncello
MT320-334	787.5193	Double bass
MT339-538	788.193	Wind instruments
MT340-359	788.3193	Flute
MT360-376	788.52193	Oboe
MT380-388	788.62193	Clarinet (A/Bb/C/Eb, Etc.)
MT400-408	788.58193	Bassoon
MT418	788.9193	Brass insturments
MT539-654	787.(7-9)193	Plectral instruments
MT540-557	787.9193	Harp
MT560-570	787.88193	Banjo
MT580-599	787.87193	Guitar
MT600-612	787.84193	Mandolin
MT620-634	787.75193	Zither
MT655-722	786.8193	Percussion/Other instruments
MT728	785	Chamber music
MT730	784.207	Orchestral instruction
MT733-733.6	784.(6-9)	Band instruction
MT820-949	782/783	Singing/Voice culture
MT825-850	783/784. + (0077)	Systems/Methods
MT855-883	782/783. + (0077)	Special techniques
MT898-949	782/783. + (0077)	Children's techniques
N	702-709	Visual arts
N1-9	705	Serials
N10-17	706	Societies
N21-23	706	Congresses
N31-33	703	Encyclopedias/Dictionaries
N40-43	709.2	Biographies
N50-55	702.5	Directories
N61-72	701	Theory/Philosophy
N81-390	707	Education
N90-284	707	Art education, History
N325-333	707.1	Art schools
N328-330	707.1073	United States
N331	707.10(7-8)	Other American countries
N332-333	707.104	Europe
N340	707.6	Examinations
N345-365	707.11	Art study (Other schools)
N380-390	707.2	Study of art history
N400-4040	708	Art museums/Galleries
N570-880	708.1(3-9)	United States
N908-910	708.(11/972-8)	Cities of other American areas
N1010-3690	708.(2-9)	Europe
N1020-1560	708.2	Great Britain
N1610-1710	708.3(6/7)	Austria-Hungary/Czechoslovakia
N1750-1850	708.93	Belgium
N1880-1935	708.89	Denmark
N2010-2180	708.4	France
N2210-2406	708.3	Germany
N2410-2425	708.95	Greece
N2450-2505	708.92	Netherlands
N2510-3065	708.5	Italy
N3110-3135	708.81	Norway
N3150-3165	708.38	Poland
N3210-3236	708.69	Portugal
N3310-3375	708.7	Russia
N3410-3497	708.6	Spain
N3510-3570	708.85	Sweden
N3610-3655	708.94	Switzerland
N3690	708.(3-8)	Other European countries
N3700-3750	708.95	Asia
N3720-3730	708.954	India
N3735	708.952	Japan
N3800-3885	708.96	Africa
N3910-3975	708.994	Australia
N3976-3980	708.993	New Zealand
N3990	708.99(5-6)	Oceania
N4010-4015	708	Public collections
N4020-4025	708	Private collections
N4390-5098	707.4	Exhibitions
N4397-4877	707.4	International exhibitions
N5015-5098	707.4(1-9)	Other exhibitions, By place
N5015-5020	707.473	United States
N5050-5080	707.44	Europe
N5051-5056	707.441	Great Britain
N5063-5069	707.444	France
N5085	707.45	Asia
N5090	707.46	Africa
N5095	707.494	Australia
N5097	707.493	New Zealand
N5098	707.49(5-6)	Oceania
N5200-5299	708	Private collections
N5213-5230	708.(1/972-98)	The Americas
N5215-5220	708.1(3-9)	United States
N5240-5280	708.(2-8)	Europe
N5284-5285	708.95	Asia
N5289-5290	708.96	Africa
N5295-5298	708.99(3-4)	Australia/New Zealand
N5299	708.99(5-6)	Oceania
N5300-7418	709	Visual art history
N5310-5313	709.01	Primitive/Prehistoric
N5315-5899	709.01	Ancient
N5350-5351	709.32	Egypt
N5460	709.33	Judea/Syria
N5470	709.3949	Arabia
N5480-5560	709.392	Asia Minor
N5603-5899	709.3(7-8)	Classical art
N5630-5720	709.38	Greece
N5740-5790	709.37	Italy
N5940-6311	709.02	Medieval art
N6350-6494	709.0(3-4)	Modern art
N6370-6375	709.0(24-31)	Renaissance/16th century
N6410-6415	709.032	17th century
N6420-6425	709.033	18th century
N6450-6465	709.034	19th century
N6485-6494	709.04	20th century

LC	Dewey	Descriptor	LC	Dewey	Descriptor
N6501-7413	709	By place	NA803-805	720.97291	Cuba
N6510-6512.5	709.73	United States	NA806-808	720.97294	Haiti
N6767-6988.5	709.4	Europe	NA809-810	720.97292	Jamaica
N6767-6868.5	709.41	Great Britain	NA812-814	720.97295	Puerto Rico
N6847-6848.5	709.44	France	NA820-939	720.98	South America
N6866-6868.5	709.43	Germany	NA830-839	720.982	Argentina
N6917-6918.5	709.45	Italy	NA840-849	720.984	Bolivia
N6948-.5	709.492	Netherlands	NA850-859	720.981	Brazil
N6988-.5	709.47	European Russia	NA860-869	720.983	Chile
N7430-7433	701.8/702.8	Technique/Composition	NA870-879	720.9861	Colombia
N7475-7483	701.18/709	Art criticism	NA880-889	720.9866	Ecuador
N7560-8266	704.94(2-9)	By subject	NA895	720.9881	Guyana
N8350-8356	702.3	Art as a profession	NA896	720.9883	Suriname
N8510-8553	702.8	Studios/Materials	NA897	720.9882	French Guiana
N8555-8580	702.88	Art conservation	NA900-909	720.9892	Paraguay
N8600-8675	380.1457/706.88	Dealers/Etc.	NA910-919	720.985	Peru
N8700-9165	344.097	Art and the state	NA920-929	720.9895	Uruguay
N8750-9084	069.54/702.8(8-9)	Protection/Cultivation of art	NA930-939	720.987	Venezuela
N9100-9165	069.53/363.3498	Art and war (Loss/ Damage/Etc.)	NA950-1455	720.94	Europe
			NA961-997	720.941	Great Britain
NA	720	Architecture	NA1001-1011.5	720.9436	Austria
NA1-9	720.5	Serials	NA1012-1022.5	720.9439	Hungary
NA10-21	720.6	Societies/Congresses	NA1023-1034	720.9437	Czechoslovakia
NA31	720.3	Encyclopedias/ Dictionaries/Etc.	NA1041-1053	720.944	France
			NA1068-1088	720.943	Germany
NA40	720.92	Biography	NA1091-1103	720.9495	Greece
NA50-60.5	720.25	Directories	NA1111-1123	720.945	Italy
NA105-109	363.69/725.0288	Monuments (Preserve/ Restore)	NA1131-1153	720.9492	Netherlands
			NA1161-1173	720.9493	Belgium
NA106-108	725.940973	Monuments, United States	NA1181-1188	720.947	European Russia
NA109	725.9409(4-9)	Other countries	NA1191	720.9438	Poland
NA120-130	720.76	Examination/Licensing	NA1193	720.94897	Finland
NA200-1613	722-724	History	NA1201-1293	720.948	Scandinavia
NA205	722	Primitive	NA1211-1223	720.9489	Denmark
NA210-340	722	Ancient	NA1241-1253	720.94912	Iceland
NA280-283	722.80938	Athens (Parthenon/Etc.)	NA1261-1273	720.9481	Norway
NA295-340	722.7	Italy	NA1281-1293	720.9485	Sweden
NA300-301	722.62	Etruscan	NA1301-1313	720.946	Spain
NA310-340	722.7	Roman	NA1321-1333	720.9469	Portugal
NA350-489	723	Medieval	NA1341-1353	720.9494	Switzerland
NA390-391	723.4	Romanesque	NA1361-1373	720.9561	Turkey
NA423	723.4	Norman	NA1381-1393	720.94977	Bulgaria
NA440-489	723.5	Gothic	NA1421-1433	720.9498	Romania
NA490-497	725.18	Military (Walls/Gates/Etc.)	NA1441-1453	720.9497	Yugoslavia
NA500-680	724	Modern	NA1460-1569.6	720.95	Asia
NA510	724.1(2-4)	Renaissance (16th century)	NA1467-1469	720.9567	Iraq
NA590	724.1(6-9)	Baroque/Rococo	NA1470-1472	720.9538	Saudi Arabia
NA600	724.2	Neoclassicism	NA1476.6-.8	720.95692	Lebanon
NA610	724.3	Gothic revival	NA1477-1479	720.95694	Israel/Palestine
NA627-640	724.19	18th century	NA1479.6-.8	720.95695	Jordan
NA630	720.94209033	Queen Anne	NA1480-1489	720.955	Iran
NA640	724.19	Georgian	NA1489.6-.8	720.95691	Syria
NA645-670	724.5	19th century	NA1492-.3	720.9581	Afghanistan
NA680	724.6	20th century	NA1492.6-1499	720.958	Asian Russia (Siberia)
NA701-1613	720.9(4-9)	By place	NA1501-1510	720.954	India
NA705-738	720.973	United States	NA1510.6-.63	720.95493	Sri Lanka
NA740-749	720.971	Canada	NA1510.7-.8	720.95491	Pakistan
NA750-759	720.972	Mexico	NA1512-.3	720.9591	Burma
NA760-790	720.9728	Central America	NA1514-.3	720.9597	Vietnam
NA773-775	720.97286	Costa Rica	NA1515-.3	720.9596	Cambodia
NA776-778	720.97281	Guatemala	NA1516-.3	720.9594	Laos
NA779-781	720.97283	Honduras	NA1521-1523	720.9593	Thailand
NA782-784	720.97285	Nicaragua	NA1525-.6	720.9595	Malaysia
NA785-787	720.97287	Panama	NA1526-.6	720.9598	Indonesia
NA788-790	720.97284	El Salvador	NA1527-1532	720.9599	Philippines
NA791-815	720.9729	West Indies	NA1540-1549.6	720.951	China
NA800-802	720.97296	Bahamas	NA1550-1559.6	720.952	Japan

LC	Dewey	Descriptor	LC	Dewey	Descriptor
NA1560-1569.6	720.9519	Korea	NA4259-4281	725.1098	South America
NA1580-1599	720.96	Africa	NA4261	725.10982	Argentina
NA1581-1585	720.962	Egypt	NA4263	725.10984	Bolivia
NA1586	720.963	Ethiopia	NA4265	725.10981	Brazil
NA1588	720.965	Algeria	NA4267	725.10983	Chile
NA1589	720.9612	Libya	NA4269	725.109861	Colombia
NA1590	720.964	Morocco	NA4271	725.109866	Ecuador
NA1591	720.9611	Tunisia	NA4273-.4	725.10988	Guianas
NA1591.7-1596.6	720.968	Southern Africa	NA4275	725.109892	Paraguay
NA1597-.6	720.9676	East Africa	NA4277	725.10985	Peru
NA1598-1599	720.966	West Africa	NA4279	725.109895	Uruguay
NA1600-1605	720.994	Australia	NA4281	725.10987	Venezuela
NA1606-1608	720.993	New Zealand	NA4283-4341	725.1094	Europe
NA1610-1613	720.99(5-6)	Oceania	NA4285-4293	725.10941	Great Britain
NA1995-1997	720.23	As a profession	NA4295	725.109436	Austria
NA2000-2320	720.7	Education	NA4297	725.10944	France
NA2101-2284	720.710(4-9)	Education, By place	NA4299-4300.6	725.10943	Germany
NA2300-2320	720.71	Special schools	NA4301	725.109495	Greece
NA2300-2304	720.71073	United States	NA4303	725.10945	Italy
NA2305	720.710(7-8)	Other American	NA4307	725.109492	Netherlands
NA2310	720.7104	Europe	NA4309	725.109493	Belgium
NA2320	720.710(4-9)	Other countries	NA4311	725.10947	European Russia
NA2335-2360	720.79	Competitions	NA4313-4321	725.10948	Scandinavia
NA2400-2460	720.74	Museums/Exhibitions	NA4315	725.109489	Denmark
NA2500	720.1	Theory/Aesthetics	NA4317	725.1094912	Iceland
NA2530	720.202	Outlines/Syllabi/Etc.	NA4319	725.109481	Norway
NA2590	720.212	Tables/Etc.	NA4321	725.109485	Sweden
NA2700-2725	720.222	Architectural drawing	NA4323	725.10946	Spain
NA2750-2790	721	Design	NA4325	725.109469	Portugal
NA2835-3070	721	Architectual details/Motives	NA4327	725.109494	Switzerland
NA3310-4050	729	Architectural decoration	NA4329	725.109561	Turkey
NA3330-3485	729.090(1-4)	Decoration, By date	NA4331-4338	725.109496	Balkan states
NA3330-3370	729.0901	Ancient	NA4343-4372	725.1095	Asia
NA3390-3420	729.0902	Medieval	NA4345-4346.6	725.1095(6-61)	Near East/Asia Minor
NA3450-3485	729.090(3-4)	Modern	NA4346.6	725.1095694	Israel/Palestine
NA3501-3596	729.09(4-9)	Decoration, By place	NA4347	725.10955	Iran
NA3750-3860	729.7	Mosaic/Terrazzo work	NA4349.6	725.109581	Afghanistan
NA3755	729.7074	Museums/Exhibitions	NA4350	725.10957	Asian Russia
NA3760-3780	729.70901	Ancient	NA4351	725.10954	India
NA3788-3792	729.70902	Medieval	NA4352.6	725.1095493	Sri Lanka
NA3810-3850	729.7090(3-4)	Modern	NA4353	725.1095491	Pakistan
NA4100-8480	721-728	Classes of buildings	NA4356.C3	725.109596	Cambodia
NA4100-4145	721.044	By material (Wood/Stone/ Etc.)	NA4356.L3	725.109594	Laos
NA4150-4160	721.042	Classed by form(Basilicas/ Etc.)	NA4356.V5	725.109597	Vietnam
			NA4356.6	725.109593	Thailand
NA4170-8480	725-728	Classed by use	NA4357	725.109595	Malaysia
NA4170-7010	725	Public buildings	NA4359	725.109598	Indonesia
NA4180-4193	725.1	International (Hague/Etc.)	NA4361	725.109599	Philippines
NA4195-4510	725.1	National/State/Municipal	NA4365	725.10951	China
NA4201-4384	725.109(4-9)	By place	NA4367	725.10952	Japan
NA4205-4228	725.10973	United States	NA4368.6	725.109519	Korea
NA4229	725.10971	Canada	NA4373-4378.6	725.1096	Africa
NA4231	725.10972	Mexico	NA4374-.8	725.10961	North Africa
NA4233-4246	725.109728	Central America	NA4375	725.10962	Egypt
NA4237	725.1097286	Costa Rica	NA4376.7	725.10963	Ethiopia
NA4239	725.1097281	Guatemala	NA4376.8-.9	725.109676	East Africa
NA4241	725.1097283	Honduras	NA4377-.6	725.10966	West Africa
NA4243	725.1097285	Nicaragua	NA4378-.6	725.10968	Southern Africa
NA4245	725.1097287	Panama	NA4379-4380	725.10994	Australia
NA4246	725.1097284	El Salvador	NA4381	725.10993	New Zealand
NA4247-4258	725.109729	West Indies	NA4383-4384	725.1099(5-6)	Oceania
NA4249	725.1097296	Bahamas	NA4410-4417	725.11	Capitols
NA4251	725.1097291	Cuba	NA4411-4413	725.110973	United States
NA4253	725.1097294	Haiti	NA4415	725.1109(4-9)	Other countries
NA4255	725.1097292	Jamaica	NA4420-4427	725.1(1-9)	Government offices/Bureaus
NA4257	725.1097295	Puerto Rico	NA4430-4437	725.13	City/Town halls

LC	Dewey	Descriptor	LC	Dewey	Descriptor
NA4440-4447	725.17	Official residences	NA5801-5813	726.0946	Spain
NA4450-4457	725.16	Post offices	NA5821-5833	726.09469	Portugal
NA4490-4497	725.18	Police stations	NA5841-5853	726.09494	Switzerland
NA4590-6199	726	Religious buildings	NA5861-5873	726.09561	Turkey
NA4590	726.0(5/6)	Serials/Societies	NA5881-5893	726.09497	Bulgaria
NA4595	726.06	Congresses	NA5921-5933	726.09498	Romania
NA4610-4710	726.(1-3)	Non-Christian	NA5941-5953	726.09497	Yugoslavia
NA4790-5095	726.509	Christian architecture, History	NA5960-6069.6	726.095	Asia
			NA5967-5969	726.09567	Iraq
NA4817-4825	726.5090(1-4)	Christian architecture, By date	NA5970-5972	726.09538	Saudi Arabia
			NA5976.6-.8	726.095692	Lebanon
NA4828-4829	726.58(1-9)	By denomination	NA5977-5979	726.095694	Israel/Palestine
NA4830-4910	726.(1/4)	Special (Chapels/Shrines/ Etc.)	NA5979.6-.8	726.095695	Jordan
			NA5980-5989	726.0955	Iran
NA5000	726.5(1-28)	Interior decoration	NA5989.6-.8	726.095691	Syria
NA5050-5095	247/726.529	Ecclesiastical furnishings	NA5992-.3	726.09581	Afghanistan
NA5201-6113	726.09	Religious buildings, By place	NA5992.6-5999	726.0957	Asian Russia (Siberia)
			NA6001-6010	726.0954	India
NA5205-5238	726.0973	United States	NA6010.6-.63	726.095493	Sri Lanka
NA5240-5249	726.0971	Canada	NA6010.7-.8	726.095491	Pakistan
NA5250-5259	726.0972	Mexico	NA6012-.3	726.09591	Burma
NA5260-5290	726.09728	Central America	NA6014-.3	726.09597	Vietnam
NA5273-5275	726.097286	Costa Rica	NA6015-.3	726.09596	Cambodia
NA5276-5278	726.097281	Guatemala	NA6016-.3	726.09594	Laos
NA5279-5281	726.097283	Honduras	NA6021-1523	726.09593	Thailand
NA5282-5284	726.097285	Nicaragua	NA6025-.6	726.09595	Malaysia
NA5285-5287	726.097287	Panama	NA6026-.6	726.09598	Indonesia
NA5288-5290	726.097284	El Salvador	NA6027-6029	726.09599	Philippines
NA5291-5315	726.09729	West Indies	NA6040-6049.6	726.0951	China
NA5300-5302	726.097296	Bahamas	NA6050-6059.6	726.0952	Japan
NA5303-5305	726.097291	Cuba	NA6060-6069.6	726.09519	Korea
NA5306-5308	726.097294	Haiti	NA6080-6099	726.096	Africa
NA5309-5311	726.097292	Jamaica	NA6081-6085	726.0962	Egypt
NA5312-5314	726.097295	Puerto Rico	NA6086	726.0963	Ethiopia
NA5320-5439	726.098	South America	NA6088	726.0965	Algeria
NA5330-5339	726.0982	Argentina	NA6089	726.09612	Libya
NA5340-5349	726.0984	Bolivia	NA6090	726.0964	Morocco
NA5350-5359	726.0981	Brazil	NA6091-.6	726.09611	Tunisia
NA5360-5369	726.0983	Chile	NA6092-6096.6	726.0968	Southern Africa
NA5370-5379	726.09861	Colombia	NA6097-.6	726.09676	East Africa
NA5380-5389	726.09866	Ecuador	NA6098-6099	726.0966	West Africa
NA5395	726.09881	Guyana	NA6100-6105	726.0994	Australia
NA5396	726.09883	Suriname	NA6106-6108	726.0993	New Zealand
NA5397	726.09882	French Guiana	NA6110-6113	726.099(5-6)	Oceania
NA5400-5409	726.09892	Paraguay	NA6120-6199	726.8	Sepulchral monuments
NA5410-5419	726.0985	Peru	NA6132-6142	726.80901	Ancient
NA5420-5429	726.09895	Uruguay	NA6143-6147	726.80902	Medieval
NA5430-5439	726.0987	Venezuela	NA6148	726.8090(3-4)	Modern
NA5450-5955	726.094	Europe	NA6149-6199	726.809	Sepulchrals, By place
NA5461-5497	726.0941	Great Britain	NA6150-6152	726.80973	United States
NA5501-5511.5	726.09436	Austria	NA6153-6154	726.80971	Canada
NA5512-5522.5	726.0939	Hungary	NA6155	726.80972	Mexico
NA5523-5534.5	726.0937	Czechoslovakia	NA6154-6157	726.809728	Central America
NA5541-5553	726.0944	France	NA6158-6159	726.809729	West Indies
NA5568-5588	726.0943	Germany	NA6160-6161	726.8098	South America
NA5591-5603	726.09495	Greece	NA6162-6178	726.8094	Europe
NA5611-5623	726.0945	Italy	NA6163	726.80941	Great Britain
NA5641-5638	726.09492	Netherlands	NA6165	726.80944	France
NA5661-5673	726.09493	Belgium	NA6166	726.80943	Germany
NA5681-5688	726.0947	European Russia	NA6167	726.80945	Italy
NA5691	726.09438	Poland	NA6170	726.80947	European Russia
NA5693	726.094897	Finland	NA6174	726.80946	Spain
NA5701-5793	726.0948	Scandinavia	NA6179-6190	726.8095	Asia
NA5711-5723	726.09489	Denmark	NA6183	726.80954	India
NA5741-5753	726.094912	Iceland	NA6183.2	726.8095491	Pakistan
NA5761-5773	726.09481	Norway	NA6183.5	726.8095493	Sri Lanka
NA5781-5793	726.09485	Sweden	NA6188	726.80951	China

LC	Dewey	Descriptor
NA6189	726.80952	Japan
NA6189.5	726.809519	Korea
NA6191-6194	726.8096	Africa
NA6192	726.80962	Egypt
NA6195-6196	726.80994	Australia
NA6197	726.80993	New Zealand
NA6198-6199	726.8099(5-6)	Oceania
NA6210-6280	725.2	Commercial buildings
NA6290-6327	725.3	Transportation (Airports/Etc.)
NA6330-6360	725.3(5/6)	Grain elevators/Warehouses/Etc.
NA6400-6589	725.4	Industrial buildings
NA6590-6605	727	Educational buildings
NA6700	727.6	Museums
NA6800-6810	725.8	Recreational buildings
NA6815-6840	725.822	Theaters/Opera houses
NA7100-7880	728	Domestic architecture
NA7100	728.0(5/6)	Serials/Societies
NA7102	728.06	Congresses
NA7105	728.09	History
NA7150-7180	721.044	Types of materials
NA7201-7476	728.09(4-9)	Houses/Etc., By place
NA7205-7239	728.0973	United States
NA7241	728.0971	Canada
NA7244	728.0972	Mexico
NA7247-7267	728.09728	Central America
NA7253	728.097286	Costa Rica
NA7256	728.097281	Guatemala
NA7259	728.097283	Honduras
NA7262	728.097285	Nicaragua
NA7265	728.097287	Panama
NA7267	728.097284	El Salvador
NA7268-7286	728.09729	West Indies
NA7271	728.097296	Bahamas
NA7274	728.097291	Cuba
NA7277	728.097294	Haiti
NA7280	728.097292	Jamaica
NA7283	728.097295	Puerto Rico
NA7289-7322	728.098	South America
NA7292	728.0982	Argentina
NA7295	728.0984	Bolivia
NA7298	728.0981	Brazil
NA7301	728.0983	Chile
NA7304	728.09861	Colombia
NA7307	728.09866	Ecuador
NA7310-.4	728.0988	Guianas
NA7313	728.09892	Paraguay
NA7316	728.0985	Peru
NA7319	728.09895	Uruguay
NA7322	728.0987	Venezuela
NA7325-7412	728.094	Europe
NA7328-7342	728.0941	Great Britain
NA7343	728.09436	Austria
NA7346	728.0944	France
NA7349-7351.6	728.0943	Germany
NA7352	728.09495	Greece
NA7355	728.0945	Italy
NA7361	728.09492	Netherlands
NA7364	728.09493	Belgium
NA7367	728.0947	European Russia
NA7370-7382	728.0948	Scandinavia
NA7373	728.09489	Denmark
NA7376	728.094912	Iceland
NA7379	728.09481	Norway
NA7382	728.09485	Sweden
NA7385	728.0946	Spain

LC	Dewey	Descriptor
NA7388	728.09469	Portugal
NA7391	728.09494	Switzerland
NA7394	728.09561	Turkey
NA7397-7412	728.09496	Balkan states
NA7415-7459	728.095	Asia
NA7418-7422	728.095(6-61)	Near East/Asia Minor
NA7420	728.095694	Israel/Palestine
NA7421	728.0955	Iran
NA7424.6	728.09581	Afghanistan
NA7425	728.0957	Asian Russia
NA7427	728.0954	India
NA7430	728.095493	Sri Lanka
NA7431	728.095491	Pakistan
NA7434.C3	728.09596	Cambodia
NA7434.L3	728.09594	Laos
NA7434.V5	728.09597	Vietnam
NA7435	728.09593	Thailand
NA7436	728.09595	Malaysia
NA7439	728.09598	Indonesia
NA7442	728.09599	Philippines
NA7448	728.0951	China
NA7451	728.0952	Japan
NA7453.6	728.09519	Korea
NA7460-7468.6	728.096	Africa
NA7461-7465.6	728.0961	North Africa
NA7463	728.0962	Egypt
NA7465.7	728.0963	Ethiopia
NA7466-.6	728.09676	East Africa
NA7467-.6	728.0966	West Africa
NA7478-.6	728.0968	Southern Africa
NA7479-7480	728.0994	Australia
NA7481	728.0993	New Zealand
NA7483-7484	728.099(5-6)	Oceania
NA7511-7515	728.(1-31/8)	City houses
NA7560-7566	728.(37/6/8)	Country homes
NA7570-7572.5	728.373	Suburban homes/Bungalows
NA7574-7579	728.7	Summerhouses/Vacation houses
NA7580-7596	728.8	Villas
NA7600-7625	728.8	Manor houses
NA7710-7786	728.8(1-2)	Castles/Palaces
NA7800-7850	728.5	Hotels/Inns
NA7860	728.314	Apartment houses/Flats
NA7910-8125	728.4	Clubhouses
NA8050-8125	728.4	Guild houses
NA8200-8260	728.6	Farm architecture
NA8300-8392	728.9	Minor buildings/Gates/Fences
NA8480	721.04497	Prefabricated buildings
NA9000-9425	711	City planning/Aesthetics
NA9000	711.0(5/6)	Serials/Societies
NA9010	711.06	Congresses
NA9012	711.07	Education
NA9013	711.023	As a profession
NA9015-9016	711.074	Exhibitions
NA9080-9085	711.092	Biography
NA9090-9095	711.09	History
NA9101-9284	711.09(4-9)	City planning, By place
NA9320-9425	725	Ornamental structures
NA9325-9330	725.94	War memorials
NA9335-9355	725.94	Monuments
NA9360-9380	725.94	Memorial/Triumphal arches
NA9400-9425	714	Fountains
NB	730	Sculpture
NB1	730.(5/6)	Serials
NB16-30	730.74	Museums/Exhibitions

LC	Dewey	Descriptor	LC	Dewey	Descriptor
NB33-35	730.294	Catalogs/Trade catalogs	NB841-853	730.9494	Switzerland
NB38	730.6	Congresses	NB861-873	730.9561	Turkey
NB50	730.3	Dictionaries/Encyclopedias	NB818-893	730.94977	Bulgaria
NB60-1113	730.9	History	NB921-933	730.9498	Romania
NB61.5-64	732	Primitive/Prehistoric	NB941-953	730.9497	Yugoslavia
NB69-169	732	Ancient	NB960-1069.6	730.95	Asia
NB90-105	733.3	Greek	NB967-969	730.9567	Iraq
NB115-120	733.5	Roman	NB970-972	730.9538	Saudi Arabia
NB135-159	731.2	Special materials used	NB976.6-.8	730.95692	Lebanon
NB135-143	731.456	Bronze	NB977-979	730.95694	Israel/Palestine
NB145-159	731.47	Terra cottas	NB979.6-.8	730.95695	Jordan
NB170-180	734	Medieval	NB980-989	730.955	Iran
NB172	734.224	Byzantine	NB989.6-.8	730.95691	Syria
NB180	734.25	Gothic	NB992-.3	730.9581	Afghanistan
NB185-198	735	Modern	NB992.6-999	730.957	Asian Russia (Siberia)
NB201-1113	730.9	By country	NB1001-1010	730.954	India
NB205-238	730.973	United States	NB1010.6-.63	730.95493	Sri Lanka
NB240-249	730.971	Canada	NB1010.7-.73	730.95491	Pakistan
NB250-259	730.972	Mexico	NB1012-.3	730.9591	Burma
NB260-290	730.9728	Central America	NB1014-.3	730.9597	Vietnam
NB273-275	730.97286	Costa Rica	NB1015-.3	730.9596	Cambodia
NB276-278	730.97281	Guatemala	NB1016-.3	730.9594	Laos
NB279-281	730.97283	Honduras	NB1021-1023	730.9593	Thailand
NB282-284	730.97285	Nicaragua	NB1025-.6	730.9595	Malaysia
NB285-287	730.97287	Panama	NB1026-.6	730.9598	Indonesia
NB288-290	730.97284	El Salvador	NB1027-1032	730.9599	Philippines
NB291-215	730.9729	West Indies	NB1040-1049.6	730.951	China
NB300-302	730.97296	Bahamas	NB1050-1059.6	730.952	Japan
NB303-305	730.97291	Cuba	NB1060-1069.6	730.9519	Korea
NB306-308	730.97294	Haiti	NB1080-1099	730.96	Africa
NB309-311	730.97292	Jamaica	NB1081-1085	730.962	Egypt
NB312-314	730.97295	Puerto Rico	NB1086	730.963	Ethiopia
NB320-439	730.98	South America	NB1088	730.965	Algeria
NB330-339	730.982	Argentina	NB1089	730.9612	Libya
NB340-349	730.984	Bolivia	NB1090	730.964	Morocco
NB350-359	730.981	Brazil	NB1091	730.9611	Tunisia
NB360-369	730.983	Chile	NB1092-1096.6	730.968	Southern Africa
NB370-379	730.9861	Colombia	NB1097-.6	730.9676	East Africa
NB380-389	730.9866	Ecuador	NB1098-1099	730.966	West Africa
NB395	730.9881	Guyana	NB1100-1105	730.994	Australia
NB396	730.9883	Suriname	NB1106-1108	730.993	New Zealand
NB397	730.9882	French Guiana	NB1110-1113	730.99(5-6)	Oceania
NB400-409	730.9892	Paraguay	NB1120-1133	730.7	Education
NB410-419	730.985	Peru	NB1160-1195	731.028	Designs/Techniques
NB420-429	730.9895	Uruguay	NB1199	731.48	Restoration
NB430-439	730.987	Venezuela	NB1208-1270	731.2	Materials
NB450-955	730.94	Europe	NB1208-1210	731.463	Stone
NB461-497	730.941	Great Britain	NB1215	731.452	Concrete
NB501-511.5	730.9436	Austria	NB1220-1240	731.4(1/56-57)	Metals
NB512-522.5	730.9439	Hungary	NB1250-1255	731.462	Wood
NB523-534.5	730.9437	Czechoslovakia	NB1265-1793	731.47	Terra cotta
NB541-553	730.944	France	NB1272	731.55	Mobiles
NB568-588	730.943	Germany	NB1280-1291	731.54	Sculpture in relief
NB591-603	730.9495	Greece	NB1293-1310	731.82	Portrait sculpture
NB611-623	730.945	Italy	NB1312	731.81	Equestrian statues
NB641-653	730.9492	Netherlands	NB1330-1684	731.76	Sculptured monuments
NB661-673	730.9493	Belgium	NB1501-1684	731.7609(4-9)	Monuments, By place
NB681-699	730.947	European Russia	NB1750-1793	726	Religious monuments/
NB691	730.9438	Poland			Shrines
NB693	730.94897	Finland	NB1800-1880	736.5	Sepulchral monuments
NB701-793	730.948	Scandinavia	NB1910-1950	731.8(2-9)	Special subjects
NB711-723	730.9489	Denmark	NB1910	731.88	Religious subjects
NB741-753	730.94912	Iceland	NB1920	731.87	Mythology
NB761-773	730.9481	Norway	NB1940	731.832	Animals
NB781-793	730.9485	Sweden	NB1950	731.834	Plants
NB801-813	730.946	Spain	NC	741.(6)/745.4	Drawing/Design/Illustration
NB821-833	730.9469	Portugal	NC1	741.(6)05/745.405	Serials

LC	Dewey	Descriptor
NC5	741.(6)06/745.406	Congresses
NC15-17	741.(6)074/745.4074	Exhibitions
NC20-33	741.(6)074/745.4074	Museums/Collections of drawings
NC37-38	741.(6)0294/745.40294	Catalogs of drawings
NC45	741.(6)092/745.4092	Biography
NC50-376	741.09	History of drawings
NC54	741.0901	Primitive
NC55-65	741.0901	Ancient
NC70-75	741.0902	Medieval
NC80-95	741.090(3-4)	Modern
NC85	741.090(23-31)	Renaissance/16th century
NC86	741.09132	17th century
NC87	741.09033	18th century
NC90	741.09034	19th century
NC95	741	20th century
NC101-376	741.(09/9) (3-9)	History of drawings, By place
NC105-139	741.(09/9)73	United States
NC141	741.(09/9)71	Canada
NC144	741.(09/9)72	Mexico
NC147-167	741.(09/9)728	Central America
NC153	741.(09/9)7286	Costa Rica
NC156	741.(09/9)7281	Guatemala
NC159	741.(09/9)7283	Honduras
NC162	741.(09/9)7285	Nicaragua
NC165	741.(09/9)7287	Panama
NC167	741.(09/9)7284	El Salvador
NC168-186	741.(09/9)729	West Indies
NC171	741.(09/9)7296	Bahamas
NC174	741.(09/9)7291	Cuba
NC177	741.(09/9)7294	Haiti
NC180	741.(09/9)7292	Jamaica
NC183	741.(09/9)7295	Puerto Rico
NC189-222	741.(09/9)8	South America
NC192	741.(09/9)82	Argentina
NC195	741.(09/9)84	Bolivia
NC198	741.(09/9)81	Brazil
NC201	741.(09/9)83	Chile
NC204	741.(09/9)861	Colombia
NC207	741.(09/9)866	Ecuador
NC210-.4	741.(09/9)88	Guianas
NC213	741.(09/9)892	Paraguay
NC216	741.(09/9)85	Peru
NC219	741.(09/9)895	Uruguay
NC222	741.(09/9)87	Venezuela
NC225-415	741.(09/9)4	Europe
NC228-242	741.(09/9)41	Great Britain
NC246	741.(09/9)44	France
NC249-251.6	741.(09/9)43	Germany
NC252	741.(09/9)495	Greece
NC255	741.(09/9)45	Italy
NC267	741.(09/9)47	European Russia
NC270-282	741.(09/9)48	Scandinavia
NC273	741.(09/9)489	Denmark
NC276	741.(09/9)4912	Iceland
NC279	741.(09/9)481	Norway
NC282	741.(09/9)485	Sweden
NC285	741.(09/9)46	Spain
NC288	741.(09/9)469	Portugal
NC291	741.(09/9)494	Switzerland
NC294	741.(09/9)561	Turkey
NC297-308	741.(09/9)496	Balkan states
NC315-359	741.(09/9)5	Asia
NC318-320	741.(09/9) + 5(6-61)	Near East/Asia Minor
NC320	741.(09/9)5694	Israel/Palestine
NC321	741.(09/9)55	Iran
NC324.6	741.(09/9)581	Afghanistan
NC325	741.(09/9)57	Asian Russia
NC327	741.(09/9)54	India
NC330	741.(09/9)5493	Sri Lanka
NC331	741.(09/9)5491	Pakistan
NC334.C3	741.(09/9)596	Cambodia
NC334.L3	741.(09/9)594	Laos
NC334.V5	741.(09/9)597	Vietnam
NC335	741.(09/9)593	Thailand
NC336	741.(09/9)595	Malaysia
NC339	741.(09/9)598	Indonesia
NC342	741.(09/9)599	Philippines
NC348	741.(09/9)51	China
NC351	741.(09/9)52	Japan
NC353.6	741.(09/9)519	Korea
NC360-368.6	741.(09/9)6	Africa
NC361-.8	741.(09/9)61	North Africa
NC363	741.(09/9)62	Egypt
NC365.7	741.(09/9)63	Ethiopia
NC366.6	741.(09/9)676	East Africa
NC367.6	741.(09/9)66	West Africa
NC368-.6	741.(09/9)68	Southern Africa
NC369-370	741.(09/9)94	Australia
NC372	741.(09/9)93	New Zealand
NC375-376	741.(09/9) + 9(5-6)	Oceania
NC390-670	741.07	Education
NC390-584	741.07	History of drawing study
NC401-584	741.070 (4-9)	Study, By country
NC597	741.0202	Outlines/Syllabi/Etc.
NC599	741.076	Examinations/Questions
NC610-635	372.52	In elementary schools
NC703	745.401	Design theory
NC730-757	741.2	Technique
NC760-825	743	Special subjects
NC765-776	743.4	Human figure
NC780-783	743.6	Animal drawing
NC790-800	743.836	Landscapes
NC805-815	743.7	Trees/Plants/Flowers
NC850-915	741.2	Graphic art materials
NC850	741.22	Charcoal
NC855-875	741.23	Crayon
NC880-885	741.235	Pastels
NC890-895	741.24	Pencil drawings
NC900	741.25	Silverpoint
NC905	741.26	Pen and ink
NC910	741.7	Silhouettes (Cutting/Etc.)
NC930	741.218	Conservation/Restoration
NC950-995.8	741.6	Illustration
NC975-995.8	741.609 (4-9)	Illustration, By place
NC997-1003	741.6	Commercial/Advertising art
NC997.A1	741.60(5/6)	Serials/Societies
NC997.A2	741.606	Congresses
NC997.A4	741.6074	Exhibitions
NC998-.4	741.609	History
NC999	741.6025	Directories
NC999.2	741.6092	Biography
NC1000	741.607	Education
NC1001	741.6023	As a profession
NC1300-1766	741.5	Pictorial humor/Caricature/Etc.
NC1300	741.50(5/6)	Serials/Societies
NC1310-1312	741.5074	Exhibitions
NC1313-1318	741.5074	Museums/Collections
NC1325-1762	741.509	History
NC1400-1762	741.5(09/9) + (4-9)	Caricatures, By place
NC1420-1429	741.5(09/9)73	United States
NC1440-1449	741.5(09/9)71	Canada

LC	Dewey	Descriptor	LC	Dewey	Descriptor
NC1450-1460	741.5(09/9) + (728/8)	Central/South America	ND410-419	759.985	Peru
NC1465-1670	741.5(09/9)4	Europe	ND420-429	759.9895	Uruguay
NC1470-1479	741.5(09/9)41	Great Britain	ND430-439	759.987	Venezuela
NC1490-1499	741.5(09/9)44	France	ND450-955	759.(3-8)	Europe
NC1500-1509	741.5(09/9)43	Germany	ND461-497	759.2	Great Britain
NC1510-1519	741.5(09/9)495	Greece	ND501-511.5	759.36	Austria
NC1520-1529	741.5(09/9)45	Italy	ND512-522.5	759.39	Hungary
NC1570-1579	741.5(09/9)47	European Russia	ND523-534.5	759.37	Czechoslovakia
NC1580-1629	741.5(09/9)78	Scandinavia	ND541-553	759.4	France
NC1630-1649	741.5(09/9)4609)	Spain/Portugal	ND568-588	759.3	Germany
NC1680-1729	741.5(09/9)5	Asia	ND591-603	759.9495	Greece
NC1690-1699	741.5(09/9)51	China	ND611-623	759.5	Italy
NC1700-1709	741.5(09/9)52	Japan	ND641-653	759.9492	Netherlands
NC1710-1719	741.5(09/9)54	India	ND661-673	759.9493	Belgium
NC1730-1749	741.5(09/9)6	Africa	ND681-699	759.7	European Russia
NC1750-1761	741.5(09/9) + 9(3-4)	Australia/New Zealand	ND691	759.38	Poland
NC1765-1766	741.58	Motion picture cartoons	ND693	759.897	Finland
NC1800-1855	741.674	Posters	ND701-793	759.8	Scandinavia
NC1860-1890	741.684	Greeting cards/Invitations/ Etc.	ND711-723	759.89	Denmark
NC1920-1940	741.217	Copying/Enlarging of drawings	ND741-753	759.94912	Iceland
			ND761-773	759.81	Norway
ND	750	Painting	ND781-793	759.85	Sweden
ND30	750.3	Encyclopedias	ND801-813	759.6	Spain
ND31	750.3	Dictionaries	ND821-833	759.69	Portugal
ND34-38	759	Biography	ND841-853	759.9494	Switzerland
ND40-45	750.294	Catalogs of paintings/Etc.	ND861-873	759.9561	Turkey
ND49-1113	759	History	ND881-893	759.94977	Bulgaria
ND70-130	759.01	Ancient	ND921-933	759.9498	Romania
ND135	759.0212	Early Christian (Catacombs/ Etc.)	ND941-953	759.9497	Yugoslavia
ND140-146	759.02	Medieval	ND960-1069.6	759.95	Asia
ND160-196	759.06(3-6)	Modern	ND967-969	759.9567	Iraq
ND170-172	759.03	Renaissance (15-16th centuries)	ND970-972	759.9538	Saudi Arabia
ND180-182	759.046	17th century	ND976.6-.8	759.95692	Lebanon
ND186-188	759.047	18th century	ND977-979	759.95694	Israel/Palestine
ND190-192	759.05	19th century	ND979-.8	759.95695	Jordan
ND195-196	759.06	20th century	ND980-989	759.955	Iran
ND204-1113	759.(1-9)	Painting, By place	ND989.6-.8	759.95691	Syria
ND205-238	759.13	United States	ND992-.3	759.9581	Afghanistan
ND240-249	759.11	Canada	ND992.6-999	759.957	Asian Russia (Siberia)
ND250-259	759.972	Mexico	ND1001-1010	759.954	India
ND260-290	759.9728	Central America	ND1010.6-.63	759.95493	Sri Lanka
ND273-275	759.97286	Costa Rica	ND1010.7-.73	759.95491	Pakistan
ND276-278	759.97281	Guatemala	ND1012-.3	759.9591	Burma
ND279-281	759.97283	Honduras	ND1014-.3	759.9597	Vietnam
ND282-284	759.97285	Nicaragua	ND1015-.3	759.9596	Cambodia
ND285-287	759.97287	Panama	ND1016-.3	759.9594	Laos
ND288-290	759.97284	El Salvador	ND1021-1023	759.9593	Thailand
ND291-315	759.9729	West Indies	ND1025-.6	759.9595	Malaysia
ND300-302	759.97296	Bahamas	ND1026-.6	759.9598	Indonesia
ND303-305	759.97291	Cuba	ND1027-1029	759.9599	Philippines
ND306-308	759.97294	Haiti	ND1040-1049.6	759.951	China
ND309-311	759.97292	Jamaica	ND1050-1059.6	759.952	Japan
ND312-314	759.97295	Puerto Rico	ND1060-1069.6	759.9519	Korea
ND320-439	759.98	South America	ND1080-1099	759.96	Africa
ND330-339	759.982	Argentina	ND1081-1085	759.962	Egypt
ND340-349	759.984	Bolivia	ND1086	759.963	Ethiopia
ND350-359	759.981	Brazil	ND1088	759.965	Algeria
ND360-369	759.983	Chile	ND1089	759.9612	Libya
ND370-379	759.9861	Colombia	ND1090	759.964	Morocco
ND380-389	759.9866	Ecuador	ND1091	759.9611	Tunisia
ND395	759.9881	Guyana	ND1092-1096.6	759.968	Southern Africa
ND396	759.9883	Suriname	ND1097-.6	759.9676	East Africa
ND397	759.9882	French Guiana	ND1098-1099	759.966	West Africa
ND400-409	759.9892	Paraguay	ND1100-1105	759.994	Australia
			ND1106-1108	759.993	New Zealand
			ND1110-1113	759.99(5-6)	Oceania
			ND1115-1120	750.7	Education

LC	Dewey	Descriptor
ND1290-1293	757	Human figure
ND1300-1337	757	Portraits
ND1303-1327	757.09	History
ND1305	757.0901	Ancient
ND1307	757.0902	Medieval
ND1308	757.090(24-31)	15th-16th centuries
ND1309-.6	757.090(3-4)	Modern
ND1309.2	757.09031	16th century
ND1309.3	757.09032	17th century
ND1309.4	757.09033	18th century
ND1309.5	757.09034	19th century
ND1309.6	757	20th century
ND1311-.9	757.0973	Portraits, United States
ND1313-1324	757.094	Europe
ND1314-.6	757.0941	Great Britain
ND1316-.6	757.0944	France
ND1317-.6	757.0943	Germany
ND1318-.6	757.0945	Italy
ND1319-.6	757.09492	Netherlands
ND1320-.6	757.0947	European Russia
ND1322-.6	757.0946(9)	Spain/Portugal
ND1325-1327	757.095	Asia
ND1326-.6	757.095(1/2)	China/Japan
ND1328-1329	757.092	Biography
ND1330-1337	757.7	Portrait miniatures
ND1340-1367	758.1	Landscape painting
ND1343-1367	758.109	History
ND1351-1367	758.109(3-9)	Landscape painting, By place
ND1351-.6	758.10973	United States
ND1352	758.109(71-8)	Other American
ND1353-1364	758.1094	Europe
ND1354-.6	758.10941	Great Britain
ND1356-.6	758.10944	France
ND1357-.6	758.10943	Germany
ND1358-.6	758.10945	Italy
ND1362-.6	758.10946(9)	Spain/Portugal
ND1366-.96	758.1095	Asia
ND1370-1373	758.2	Marine painting
ND1380-1383	758.3	Animals/Birds
ND1385-1388	758.3	Sport/Hunting/Fishing
ND1390-1393	758.4	Still life
ND1400-1403	758.42	Flowers/Fruit
ND1420-1422	753	Mythological/Symbolical
ND1430-1432	755	Religious
ND1455-1457	745.61	Calligraphy as painting
ND1470-1495	751.4	Techniques
ND1480-1482	751.4/759.0(2-6)	Styles (Abstract/Impressionism)
ND1486-1495	752	Color
ND1500-1660	751	Materials/Methods
ND1510-1535	751.2	Pigments/Varnishes
ND1538-1539	751.3	Brushes/Knives
ND1560-1625	750/751.7	Surfaces (Canvas/Glass/Metal)
ND1630-1660	751.6	Conservation of paintings
ND1700-2495	751.422	Watercolor painting
ND1700	751.42205	Serials
ND1711-1721	751.42206	Societies
ND1725-1735	751.422074	Museums/Collections/Exhibition
ND1760-2094	751.42209	History
ND1801-2094	751.42209(4-9)	Watercolors, By place
ND1805-1839	751.4220973	United States
ND1889-1922	751.422098	South America
ND1925-2012	751.422094	Europe
ND1928-1942	751.4220941	Great Britain
ND1947	751.4220944	France
ND1949-1951.6	751.4220943	Germany
ND1955	751.4220945	Italy
ND1961	751.42209492	Netherlands
ND1964	751.4220947	European Russia
ND1985-1988	751.4220946(9)	Spain/Portugal
ND2015-2059	751.422095	Asia
ND2048-2051	751.422095(1-2)	China/Japan
ND2110-2115	751.42207	Education
ND2190-2192	751.42242	Human figure
ND2200-2202	751.42242	Portraits
ND2240-2243	751.422436	Landscapes
ND2270-2272	751.422437	Marine
ND2280-2282	751.422432	Animals/Birds
ND2290-2292	751.422435	Still life
ND2300-2302	751.422435	Flowers/Fruit
ND2360-2362	751.42248	Religious
ND2550-2888	751.73	Mural painting
ND2555-2590	751.73090(1-4)	By date
ND2601-2876	751.7309(4-9)	Mural painting, By place
ND2880	751.74	Panoramas
ND2882	751.74	Dioramas
ND2885-2888	751.75	Scene painting (As the stage)
ND2890-3416	745.67	Illuminating (Manuscripts/Etc.)
ND2890	745.67092	Biographical dictionaries
ND2893	745.67074	Exhibitions
ND2900-3294	745.6709	History
ND2910-2990	745.67090(1-4)	By date
ND2910	745.670901	Ancient
ND2920-2980	745.670902	Medieval
ND2990	745.67090(23-31)	Renaissance
ND3001-3294	745.6709(4-9)	By place
ND3410-3416	745.67	Modern illuminated books
NE	760/769	Print media
NE1-978	760-767	Printmaking/Engraving
NE1	760.(5/6)	Serials/Societies
NE3	760.6	Congresses
NE10	760.5	Yearbooks
NE20	760.3	Encyclopedias
NE30	760.25	Directories
NE42-59	760.74	Museums/Exhibitions
NE60	760.75	Organization (Gallery/Museum)
NE61	760.23	As a profession
NE63-75	760.294	Catalogs (Sales/Dealers)
NE218-310	769.420216	Catalogs of engraved portraits
NE380	769.18	Conservation/Restoration
NE400-794	769.9	History of printmaking
NE405-420	769.901	Ancient
NE430-492	769	Modern
NE440-468	769.90(23-31)	14th-16th centuries
NE475-476	769.9032	17th century
NE480-481	769.9033	18th century
NE485-486	769.9034	19th century
NE490-492	769.904	20th century
NE501-794	769.9(4-9)	By place
NE800	769.92	Biography
NE820	760.278	Engravers' marks
NE953-962	769.4	Special subjects
NE953	769.435	Flowers/Fruit
NE955-.3	769.4949355	Military
NE957-.3	769.437	Naval/Marine prints
NE958-.3	769.48	Religious
NE960-.3	769.949796	Sports

LC	Dewey	Descriptor
NE965-.3	741.685	Tradesmen's cards/Billheads
NE970-973	760.7	Education
NE977-978	760.28	Equipment/Apparatus
NE1000-1352	761.2	Wood engraving/Woodcuts
NE1000	761.20(5/6)	Serials/Societies
NE1010-1012	761.2074	Exhibitions
NE1030-1196	761.209	History
NE1035	761.20901	Ancient
NE1040-1047	761.20902	Medieval
NE1048-1097	761.2090(3-4)	Modern
NE1050-1055	761.2090(24-32)	15th-17th centuries
NE1085-1088	761.209033	18th century
NE1090-1093	761.209034	19th century
NE1095-1097	761.2	20th century
NE1101-1196	761.209(4-9)	Wood engraving, By place
NE1310-1325	769	Japanese/Ukiyoe prints
NE1314-1318	769.074	Museums/Exhibitions
NE1321-1323	769.09	History
NE1330-1336	769	Linoleum block prints
NE1332	769.973	United States
NE1334	769.9(4-9)	Other countries
NE1350-1352	769	Other materials used
NE1400-1879	765/761.8	Metal engraving
NE1400	765.0(5/6)	Serials/Societies
NE1410-1412	765.074	Exhibitions
NE1430-1749	765.09	History
NE1637	765.093	Ancient
NE1637.5	765.0902	Medieval
NE1638	765.09023	14th century
NE1639-1749	765.090(3-4)	Modern
NE1655-1656	765.09024	15th century
NE1665-1666	765.09031	16th century
NE1670-1690	765.09032	17th century
NE1710-1719	765.09033	18th century
NE1720.5-1739	765.09034	19th century
NE1740-1749	765.0904	20th century
NE1850-1879	769	Color prints
NE1855	769.9033	18th century color prints
NE1857	769.9034	19th century color prints
NE1858	769.904	20th century color prints
NE1940-2230	766.3/767.2	Etching/Aquatint
NE1940	766.3/767.2 + 0(5/6)	Serials/Societies
NE1945-1955	766.3/767.2 + 074	Museums/Exhibitions
NE1960	766.3/767.2 + 0294	Dealers' catalogs
NE1980-1998	766.3/767.2 + 09	History
NE1984-1985	766.3/767.2 + 090(24-32)	15th-17th century folios/Etc.
NE1990-1992	766.3/767.2 + 09033	18th century folios/Etc.
NE1994-1995	766.3/767.2 + 09034	19th century folios/Etc.
NE1997-1998	766.3/767.2 + 0904	20th century folios/Etc.
NE2001-2096	767.209(4-9)	Etching/Etc., By place
NE2110	767.2092	Biography
NE2141-2149	769.4	Special subject
NE2141	769.48	Religious
NE2142	769.42	Human figures
NE2143	769.436	Landscapes
NE2144	769.437	Marine/Naval
NE2145	769.432	Animals/Birds
NE2146-2147	769.435	Flowers/Fruit/Still life
NE2148	769.44	Architectural subjects
NE2220-2225	767.3	Dry point
NE2230	766.3	Aquatint
NE2236-2240	764.8	Serigraphy (Silk screen print)
NE2237-.5	764.80973	United States
NE2238-.5	764.809(4-9)	Other countries
NE2239-.7	769.4	Special subjects

LC	Dewey	Descriptor
NE2239	769.42	Human figures
NE2239.1	769.437	Marine/Landscapes
NE2239.2	769.432	Animals/Birds
NE2239.(3-4)	769.435	Still life
NE2239.6	769.48	Religious subjects
NE2250-2529	763	Lithography
NE2250	763.0(5/6)	Serials/Societies
NE2260-2275	763.074	Museums/Exhibitions
NE2280	763.0294	Dealers' catalogs
NE2283	763.025	Directories
NE2295-2396	763.09	History
NE2297	763.09034	19th century
NE2298	763.0904	20th century
NE2301-2396	763.09(4-9)	Lithography, By place
NE2410	763.092	Biography
NE2452	769.48	Religious subjects
NE2453	769.42	Human figures
NE2454	769.436	Landscapes/Etc.
NE2480	763.07	Education
NE2490-2495	763.028	Equipment/Apparatus
NE2500-2529	764.2	Chromolithography
NE2690	748.6	Engraving on glass
NE2715	769.5	Stationery engraving
NE2800-2890	769	Printing of engravings
NE2800	769.0(5/6)	Serials/Societies
NE2802	769.09	History
NE2803	769.092	Biography
NK	745	Decorative arts
NK1-9	745.05	Serials
NK11-21	745.06	Societies/Congresses
NK28	745.03	Encyclopedias
NK30	745.03	Dictionaries
NK50-440	745.07	Education
NK101-376	745.070(1-9)	Education, By place
NK410	745.0710(71-8)	Special schools, America
NK420	745.07104	Special schools, Europe
NK430	745.0710(5-9)	Special schools, Other places
NK450-490	745.074	Museums/Galleries
NK460	745.07473	Galleries, United States
NK470	745.074(71-8)	Other American countries
NK475-480	745.0744	Europe
NK530-570	745.074	Private collections
NK530-535	745.07473	Collections, United States
NK540	745.074(71-8)	Other American countries
NK550	745.0744	Europe
NK560	745.074(5-9)	Other countries
NK600-1133	745.09	History
NK605	745.093	Primitive
NK610-685	745.0901	Ancient
NK700-740	745.0902	Medieval
NK750-789	745.090(3-4)	Modern
NK801-1094	745.09(4-9)	By place
NK1133	745.0294	Catalogs
NK1135-1149	745	Arts and crafts
NK1135	745.05	Serials
NK1136	745.06	Societies
NK1137	745.074	Exhibitions
NK1140-1142	745.09	History
NK1160-1590	745.4	Decoration/Ornament/Design
NK1160	745.40(5/6)	Serials/Societies
NK1165	745.403	Dictionaries
NK1170	745.407	Education
NK1175-1496	745.44	History
NK1177-1250	745.441	Ancient/Primitive
NK1260-1295	745.442	Medieval

LC	Dewey	Descriptor	LC	Dewey	Descriptor
NK1330	745.443	15th-16th centuries	NK3800-3855	738.093	Ancient
NK1340-1365	745.443	17th-18th centuries	NK3870-3880	738.0902	Medieval
NK1370-1382	745.4441	19th century	NK3900-3930	738	Modern
NK1390-1394	745.4442	20th century	NK4001-4184	738.09(4-9)	Ceramic arts, By place
NK1505	745.01	Theory	NK4200	738.092	Biography
NK1648-1678	704.948	Religious art	NK4260-4340	738.3	Earthenware/Terra cotta
NK1650-1657	704.9482	Christian	NK4360-4367	738.3	Stoneware
NK1670-1678	704.9489	Non-Christian	NK4370-4584	738.2	Porcelain
NK1672	704.94896	Jewish	NK4700-4890	746.92	Costume/Accessories
NK1674	704.94897	Islamic	NK4700-.5	746.920(5/6)	Serials/Societies
NK1676	704.948943	Buddhist	NK4701-4703	746.92074	Exhibitions/Museums
NK1700-3505	747	Interior/House decoration	NK4706-4710	746.9209	Costume history
NK1700	747.0(5/6)	Serials/Societies	NK4712	746.920973	United States
NK1750	747.025	Directories	NK4712.5	746.9209(72-8)	Spanish/Latin America
NK1710-2096	747.2	History/Styles, By place	NK4713-4796	746.9209(4-9)	Other countries
NK1720-1780	747.201	Ancient	NK4799	746.920294	Catalogs
NK1800-1840	747.202	Medieval	NK5100-5440	748	Glass (Stained/Leaded/Etc.)
NK1860-1986	747.20(3-4)	Modern	NK6200-6210	745.531	Leatherwork
NK1870	747.203(4-5)	15th-16th centuries	NK6400-8459	739	Metalwork
NK1880-1940	747.203(6-7)	17th-18th centuries	NK8800-9505	746	Textile arts
NK1960-1972	747.2048	19th century	NK9509-.8	745.592	Toys (Handicrafted)
NK1980-1986	747.2049	20th century	NK9600-9699	745.51	Woodworking
NK2000-2096	747.2(1-9)	Interior decoration, By place	NX	700	Arts (General)
NK2001	747.27	North America	NX1-9	705	Serials
NK2003-2012	747.273	United States	NX20-50	706	Societies/Congresses
NK2013	747.271	Canada	NX70	703	Encyclopedias
NK2014	747.272	Mexico	NX80	703	Dictionaries
NK2015-2022	747.2728	Central America	NX90	709.2	Biography
NK2023-2029	747.2729	West Indies	NX100-120	702.5	Directories
NK2030-2041	747.28	South America	NX163	702.3	As a profession
NK2042-2071	747.24	Europe	NX280-410	707	Education
NK2072-2086	747.25	Asia	NX420-430	707.4	Exhibitions
NK2087-2089.8	747.26	Africa	NX440-600	709	History of the arts
NK2090-2096	747.29(3-6)	Australia/New Zealand/ Oceania	NX448-458	709.0(1-49)	By date
			NX501-596	709.(3-9)	By place
NK2116-.2	747.023	As a profession	NX503-512	709.73	United States
NK2116.4-.6	747.07	Education	NX513	709.71	Canada
NK2117-2121	747.(3-7)	Special areas/Parts of house	NX514	709.72	Mexico
NK2140-2180	747.3	Decorative painting	NX515-522	709.728	Central America
NK2190	747.86	Church decoration	NX517	709.7286	Costa Rica
NK2195	747.8(5-7)	Other buildings	NX518	709.7281	Guatemala
NK2200-2750	749	Furniture	NX519	709.7283	Honduras
NK2200	749.05	Serials	NX520	709.7285	Nicaragua
NK2205	749.03	Dictionaries	NX521	709.7287	Panama
NK2210-2220	747.074	Exhibitions/Museums	NX522	709.7284	El Salvador
NK2265	747.0294	Catalogs	NX523-529	709.729	West Indies
NK2267-2268	749.07	Education	NX524	709.7296	Bahamas
NK2270-2694	749.20(1-5)	Furniture, History	NX525	709.7291	Cuba
NK2401-2694	749.2(1-9)	Furniture, By place	NX526	709.7294	Haiti
NK2775-2896	747.5	Rugs/Carpets	NX527	709.7292	Jamaica
NK2775	747.505	Serials	NX528	709.7295	Puerto Rico
NK2780-2786	747.5074	Exhibitions/Museums	NX530-541	709.8	South America
NK2808-2896	747.509(4-9)	Rugs/Carpets, By place	NX531	709.82	Argentina
NK2910	749.3	Screens	NX532	709.84	Bolivia
NK2975-3096	746.3	Tapestries	NX533	709.81	Brazil
NK3175-3296	747.(5/3)	Upholstery/Wall hangings	NX534	709.83	Chile
NK3375-3496	747.3	Wallpapers	NX535	709.861	Colombia
NK3600-9955	738-749	Misc. arts	NX536	709.866	Ecuador
NK3600-3640	745.61	Alphabets/Calligraphy/ Initials	NX537-.4	709.88	Guianas
			NX538	709.892	Paraguay
NK3603-3631	745.61978	Roman	NX539	709.85	Peru
NK3632-3639	745.619(8-9)	Non-Roman	NX540	709.895	Uruguay
NK3700-4695	738	Ceramic arts	NX541	709.87	Venezuela
NK3712-3745	738.074	Exhibitions/Museums	NX542-571	709.4	Europe
NK3770	738.03	Dictionaries/Encyclopedias	NX543-547	709.41	Great Britain
NK3780-4184	738.09	History	NX548	709.436	Austria
			NX549	709.44	France

LC	Dewey	Descriptor
NX550-.6	709.43	Germany
NX551	709.495	Greece
NX552	709.45	Italy
NX554	709.492	Netherlands
NX555	709.493	Belgium
NX556	709.47	European Russia
NX557-561	709.48	Scandinavia
NX558	709.489	Denmark
NX559	709.4912	Iceland
NX560	709.481	Norway
NX561	709.485	Sweden
NX562	709.46	Spain
NX563	709.469	Portugal
NX564	709.494	Switzerland
NX565	709.561	Turkey
NX566-569	709.496	Balkan states
NX572-586	709.5	Asia
NX573-.7	709.5(6-61)	Near East/Asia Minor
NX573.7	709.5694	Israel/Palestine
NX574	709.55	Iran
NX575.6	709.581	Afghanistan
NX575.7	709.57	Asian Russia
NX576	709.54	India
NX576.6	709.5493	Sri Lanka
NX576.7	709.5491	Pakistan
NX578.6.C3	709.596	Cambodia
NX578.6.L3	709.594	Laos
NX578.6.V5	709.597	Vietnam
NX578.7	709.593	Thailand
NX579	709.595	Malaysia
NX580	709.598	Indonesia
NX581	709.599	Philippines
NX583	709.51	China
NX584	709.52	Japan
NX584.6	709.519	Korea
NX587-589.8	709.6	Africa
NX587.6-588.6	709.61	North Africa
NX588	709.62	Egypt
NX588.7	709.63	Ethiopia
NX588.8-.9	709.676	East Africa
NX589-.6	709.66	West Africa
NX589.7-.8	709.68	Southern Africa
NX590-591	709.94	Australia
NX593	709.93	New Zealand
NX595-596	709.9(5-6)	Oceania
NX654-694	704.948	Religious arts
NX655-663	704.9482	Christian art
NX670-692	704.9489	Non-Christian art
NX700-750	700.79	Patronage of the arts
NX800-820	700.74	Special art centers
P	400/410	Philology/Linguistic
P1-10	405/410.5	Serials
P11-23	406/410.6	Societies/Congresses
P29	403/410.3	Encyclopedias/Dictionaries
P33-41	401/410.1	Theory
P51-59	407/410.7	Education
P61-81	409/410.9	History of philology
P63-77	409/410.9 + 0(1-4)	By date
P81	409.(4-9)	By place
P101-410	400	Language/Comparative philology
P101-106	401	Philosophy, By date
P121-149	410	Science of language
P151-259	415	Grammar
P151-152	415	Theory
P201-299	415	Comparative grammar
P215-240	414	Phonetics/Phonology
P241-259	415	Morphology
P270-298	415	Parts of speech
P291-298	415	Syntax
P321	412	Etymology
P331-365.5	413	Comparative lexicography
P501-769	420-480	Indo-European philology
P501	420-480. + (5)	Serials
P503-505	420-480. + (6)	Societies/Congresses
P518	420-480. + (3)	Encyclopedias/Dictionaries
P541-551	420-480. + (9)	History
P575-769	410.5	Comparative grammar
P583-610	410.15	Phonology
P611-627	410.5	Morphology
P631-663	410.5	Parts of speech
P671	410.5	Syntax
P721-725	410.2	Etymology
P761-769	410.3028	Lexicography
P901-1099	417	Extinct Asiatic/European
PA	480/880	Classical (Greek/Latin)
PA1-895	480	Classical philology
PA1-9	480.05	Serials
PA11-23	480.06	Societies/Congresses
PA31	480.03	Encyclopedias/Dictionaries
PA35-37	480.01	Philosophy/Theory
PA39-49	480.802	Criticism (Hermeneutics)
PA51-72	480.09	History
PA53-67	480.090(1-4)	By date
PA55	480.0902	Medieval
PA57	480.090(23-31)	Renaissance
PA59-67	480.090(3-4)	Modern
PA61	480.0903(1-2)	16th-17th centuries
PA63	480.0903(2-3)	17th-18th centuries
PA65	480.09034	19th century
PA67	480	20th century
PA70	480.09(4-9)	History, By place
PA74-79	480.07	Education
PA83-85	480.092	Biography
PA111-199	470/480	Greek/Latin languages
PA111	475/485	Comparative grammar
PA119	470/480.(76)	Examination questions
PA121	471/481.(5)	Phonology
PA141-155	475/485	Morphology
PA161	475/485	Syntax
PA181-184	871-878/881-888.(9)	Style
PA185-190	871/881	Prosody/Metrics
PA191	472/482	Etymology
PA195	470/480.(143)	Semantics
PA227-1179	480	Greek philology/Language
PA227-379	480	Language
PA231-241	480.7	Education
PA251-379	485	Grammar
PA265-281	481.5	Phonology
PA283-287	485	Morphology
PA303-361	485	Parts of speech
PA367-379	485	Syntax
PA401-407	488/881-888.09	Style/Rhetoric/Composition
PA411-419	481	Prosody/Metrics
PA421-430	482	Etymology
PA431-459	483.028	Lexicography
PA441-459	483	Dictionaries
PA500-591	487	Dialects
PA600-695	487.4	Hellenistic Greek
PA700-895	487.4	Biblical Greek
PA700-791	487.4	Septuagint (Rabbinic Greek)
PA800-895	487.4	New Testament/Early Christian

LC	Dewey	Descriptor	LC	Dewey	Descriptor
PA813-857	487.45	Grammar	PA3403	888.01008	Prose
PA881	487.43	Dictionaries	PA3423-3427	881-888.(0108)	By date
PA1001-1179	487.3/489.3	Medieval/Modern Greek	PA3423-3424	881-888.(0108)	Hellenistic (300-31 B.C.)
PA1001-1009	487.305/489.305	Serials	PA3427	881-888.(0108)	Roman (31 B.C.-100 A.D.)
PA1011-1023	487.306/489.306	Societies/Congresses	PA3431-3459	881.0108	Poetry
PA1031	487.303/489.303	Encyclopedias/Dictionaries	PA3437-3439	883.0108	Epic
PA1041-1049	487/489. + 30(7/9)	Education/History	PA3443-3447	884.0108	Lyric poetry
PA1051-1099	487.35/489.35	Grammar	PA3461-3466	882.0108	Drama
PA1061-1071	487.315/489.315	Phonology	PA3473-3515	888.010080008	Prose
PA1076	487.35/489.35	Morphology	PA3479-3482	885.0108	Oratory
PA1081-1089	487.35/489.35	Parts of speech	PA3520-3564	881-888.(09)	Criticism/Interpretation
PA1091-1097	487.35/489.35	Syntax	PA3527	881-888.(0109)	Hellenistic (300-31 B.C.)
PA1101-1105	487.38/489.38/881-888.09	Style/Rhetoric	PA3531	881-888.(0109)	Roman (31 B.C.-600 A.D.)
PA1106	889.1/881-888.0(3-4)	Prosody/Metrics	PA3537-3543	881.0109	Poetry
PA1111	487.32/489.32	Etymology	PA3545-3551	882.0109	Drama
PA1123-1145	487.33/489.33	Dictionaries	PA3553	887.0109	Comedy
PA1151-1155	487.37/489.37	Dialects	PA3556-3558	888.010080009	Prose
PA2001-2915	470	Latin philology/Language	PA3561-3564	885.0109	Oratories
PA2001-2009	470.5	Serials	PA3818-4500	881-888.(01)	By author (to 700 A.D.)
PA2011-2019	470.6	Societies	PA5000-5665	881-888.(2-3)/889	Byzantine/Modern Greek
PA2041-2055	470.9	History	PA5000-5040	881-888.(2-3)09/889.09	History/Criticism
PA2043-2052	470.90(1-4)	By date	PA5070-5075	881-888.(2-3)08/889.08	Collections
PA2045	470.902	Medieval	PA5101-5395	881-888.(2)/889.1	Medieval/Byzantine
PA2047	470.90(23-31)	Renaissance	PA5101-5167	881-888.(0209)/889.109	History/Criticism
PA2049-2052	470.90(3-4)	Modern	PA5150-5155	881.0209/889.1109	Poetry
PA2051	470.903(2-3)	17th-18th centuries	PA5160-5163	882.0209/889.2109	Drama
PA2052	470.90(34-4)	19th-20th centuries	PA5165	888.020080009/889.810809	Prose/Fiction
PA2055	470.9(4-9)	History, By place	PA5167	887.0209/889.7109	Humor/Satire
PA2061-2067	470.7	Education	PA5170-5198	881-888.(0208)/889.108	Collections
PA2071-2309	475	Grammar	PA5170-5172	881-888.(0208)/889.108	By date
PA2111-2131	471.5	Phonology	PA5178-5179	881-888.(0208)/889.108	By place
PA2133-2158	475	Morphology	PA5180-5189	881.0208/889.1108	Poetry
PA2161-2281	475	Parts of speech	PA5190-5194	882.0208/889.2108	Drama
PA2285-2297	475	Syntax	PA5195-5196	889.810808/888.010080008	Prose/Fiction
PA2311-2320	478/871-878.09	Style/Rhetoric	PA5197-5198	887.0208/889.7108	Humor/Satire
PA2329-2340	871	Prosody/Metrics	PA5201-5298	881-888.(03)/889.(1-3)	Renaissance and modern
PA2341-2350	472	Etymology	PA5201-5267	881-888.(309)/889.(1-3)09	History/Criticism
PA2351-2359	473.028	Lexicography	PA5259-5255	889.1(1-3)09/881.0309	Poetry
PA2361-2389	473	Dictionaries	PA5260-5263	889.2(1-3)09/882.0309	Drama
PA2391-2550	477	Ancient dialects of Italy	PA5265	889.7(1-3)09/887.0309	Humor/Satire
PA2420-2550	479	Italic dialects	PA5270-5298	881-888.(0308)/889.(1-3)	Collections
PA2600-2748	477	Vulgar Latin	PA5270-5272	881-888.(0308)/889.(1-3)	By date
PA2801-2899	478	Medieval Latin	PA5280-5289	889.1(1-3)08/881.0308	Poetry
PA2901-2915	478	Modern Latin (1350-)	PA5290-5294	889.2(1-3)08/882.0308	Drama
PA3001-3044	881-888.(09)	Classical literature (History)	PA5295-5296	889/888. + (1-3)08008	Prose/Fiction
PA3005-3006	881-888.(09)	Biography (Collected)	PA5297-5298	889.7(1-3)08/887.0308	Humor/Satire
PA3019-3022	871/881.(09)	Poetry	PA5301-5610	889.(1-3)08/881-888.0308	By author/Date
PA3024-3034	872/882.(09)	Drama	PA5301-5395	881-888.(208)/889.108	Byzantine to 1600
PA3035-3044	878/888.(0080009)	Prose	PA5609-5610	889.(1-3)08/881-888.308	Modern (1600-)
PA3051-4500	881-888.(01)	Ancient Greek (to 600 A.D.)	PA5650-5665	881-888.0308/889.(1-3)08	In other countries
PA3051-3191	881-888.(0109)	Literary history	PA6001-6971	871-878	Latin/Ancient Roman literature
PA3081-3086	881-888. + 0(1-3)09	By date	PA6001-6095	871-878.(09)	Literary history
PA3081-3084	881-888.(0109)	Hellenistic (300-31 B.C.)	PA6035-6043	871-878.0(1-4)09	By date
PA3086	881-888.(0109)	Roman	PA6035	871-878.(0109)	Early (To 240 B.C.)
PA3092-3125	881.0109	Poetry	PA6041-6043	871-878.(0109)	Empire period
PA3105-3107.5	883.0109	Epic poetry	PA6047-6063	871.0109	Poetry
PA3110-3111	884.0109	Lyric poetry	PA6067-6075	872.0109	Drama
PA3131-3136	882.0109	Drama	PA6081-6095	878.010080009	Prose
PA3160	887.0109	Satire	PA6101-6140	871-878.(0108)	Collections
PA3161-3191	887.0109	Comedy	PA6119	871-878.(0108)	By date
PA3201-3251	792.0938	Theater/Stage	PA6121-6135	871.0108	Poetry
PA3255-3273	888.01008	Prose	PA6123	871.0108	By date
PA3285	398.20	Folk literature	PA6125	873.0108	Epic
PA3301-3516	881-888.(0108)	Collections	PA6127	874.0108	Lyric
PA3301-3371	881-888.(0108)	Papyri/Ostraka	PA6137	872.0108	Drama
PA3401-3516	881-888.(0108)	Printed editions	PA6138-6139	878.010080008	Prose

LC	Dewey	Descriptor
PA6141-6144	871-878.(0109)	Criticism/Interpretation
PA6142	871.0109	Poetry
PA6143	872.0109	Drama
PA6144	878.010080009	Prose
PA6202-6971	871-878.(0108)	By author
PA8001-8595	871-878.(3-4)	Medieval/Modern Latin
PA8001-8045	871-878.0(3-4)09	History/Criticism
PA8001-8002	870.(5/6)	Serials/Societies/Congresses
PA8035-8043	871-878.0(3-4)09	By date
PA8050-8096	871-878.0(3-4)	By form
PA8050-8065	871.0(3-4)	Poetry
PA8073-8079	872.0(3-4)	Drama
PA8081-8096	878.0(3-4)008	Prose
PA8101-8199	871-878.0(3-4)08	Collections
PA8112-8117	871-878.0(3-4)08	By date
PA8120-8149	871-878.0(3-4)08	By form
PA8120-8133	871.0(3-4)08	Poetry
PA8135-8142	872.0(3-4)08	Drama
PA8145	878.0(3-4)0080008	Prose/Fiction
PA8200-8595	871-878.0(3-4)	By author/Date
PA8200-8445	871-878.0308	Medieval to 1350
PA8450-8595	871-878.0408	Modern (1350-)
PB	491.6	Celtic languages
PB1-5	491.605	Serials
PB6-11	491.606	Societies/Congresses
PB67.9	491.609	History/Criticism
PB328	491.603	Dictionaries
PB1001-1013	491.6	Philology
PB1001	491.60(5/6)	Serials/Societies
PB1005	491.601	Philosophy
PB1007	491.609	History
PB1009	491.6092	Biography
PB1011	491.607	Education
PB1014-1095	491.6	Celtic language
PB1015	491.609	History
PB1019-1071	491.65	Grammar
PB1083-1085	491.62	Etymology
PB1087-1089	491.63028	Lexicography
PB1096-1100	891.6	Literature
PB1101-1195	491.6(2/3)	Gaelic
PB1101-1113	491.6(2/3)	Philology
PB1101	491.6(2-3)0(5/6)	Serials/Societies
PB1105	491.6(2-3)01	Philosophy
PB1107	491.6(2-3)09	History
PB1109	491.6(2-3)092	Biography
PB1111	491.6(2-3)07	Education
PB1114-1195	491.6(2-3)	Gaelic language
PB1115	491.6(2-3)09	History
PB1119-1171	491.6(2-3)5	Grammar
PB1183-1185	491.6(2-3)2	Etymology
PB1187-1189	491.6(2-3)3028	Lexicography
PB1196-1200	891.6(2-3)	Literature
PB1201-1449	491.62	Irish
PB1201-1213	491.62	Philology
PB1201	491.620(5/6)	Serials/Societies
PB1205	491.6201	Philosophy
PB1207	491.6209	History
PB1211	491.6207	Education
PB1214-1299	491.62	Language
PB1215	491.6209	History
PB1221-1273	491.625	Grammar
PB1283-1284	491.622	Etymology
PB1287-1295	491.623028	Lexicography
PB1299	491.627	Slang
PB1306-1449	891.62	Literature
PB1306-1337	891.6209	History
PB1501-1709	491.63	Scottish Gaelic
PB1501-1599	491.63	Language
PB1501-1213	491.63	Philology
PB1501	491.630(5/6)	Serials/Societies
PB1505	491.6301	Philosophy
PB1507	491.6309	History
PB1511	491.6307	Education
PB1514-1599	491.63	Language
PB1515	491.6309	History
PB1521-1573	491.635	Grammar
PB1583-1584	491.632	Etymology
PB1587-1595	491.633028	Lexicography
PB1605-1709	891.63	Literature
PB1605-1613	891.6309	History
PB1801-1888	491.64	Manx
PB1801-1847	491.64	Language
PB1801	491.640(5/6)	Serials/Societies
PB1806	491.64092	Biography
PB1807	491.6407	Education
PB1809	491.6409	History
PB1811-1847	491.645	Grammar
PB1851-1888	891.64	Literature
PB1950	491.6	Pict (Pre-Celtic)
PB2001-3029	491.6	Brittanic
PB2001	491.680(5/6)	Serials/Societies
PB2005	491.6807	Education
PB2007	491.6809	History
PB2009-2015	491.685	Grammar
PB2021	491.682	Etymology
PB2023	491.683028	Lexicography
PB2101-2499	491.66	Welsh/Cymric
PB2101-2113	491.66	Philology
PB2101	491.660(5/6)	Serials/Societies
PB2105	491.6601	Philosophy
PB2107	491.6609	History
PB2109	491.66092	Biography
PB2111	491.6607	Education
PB2114-2199	491.66	Language
PB2115	491.6609	History
PB2121-2173	491.665	Grammar
PB2183-2184	491.662	Etymology
PB2187-2195	491.663028	Lexicography
PB2206-2450	891.66	Literature
PB2206-2237	891.6609	History
PB2501-2621	491.67	Cornish
PB2501-2549	491.67	Language
PB2501	491.670(5/6)	Serials/Societies
PB2506	491.67092	Biography
PB2507	491.6707	Education
PB2509	491.6709	History
PB2511-2547	491.675	Grammar
PB2551-2621	891.67	Literature
PB2551-2552	891.6709	History
PB2801-2931	491.68	Breton
PB2801-2849	491.68	Language
PB2801	491.680(5/6)	Serials/Societies
PB2806	491.68092	Biography
PB2807	491.6807	Education
PB2809	491.6809	History
PB2811-2847	491.685	Grammar
PB2856-2931	891.68	Literature
PB2856-2858	891.6809	History
PB3001-3029	491.6	Gaulish
PC	440	Romance languages
PC1-5	440.05	Serials
PC6-11	440.06	Societies/Congresses
PC19	440.03	Encyclopedias
PC21-23	440.01	Philosophy/Theory

LC	Dewey	Descriptor	LC	Dewey	Descriptor
PC35-39	440.07	Education	PC2620-2693	443.(028)	Dictionaries/Lexicography
PC43-400	440	Languages	PC2700-3761	447-449	Dialects/Provincialisms/Etc.
PC60-201	445	Grammar	PC2700	447	Geographic variations
PC301-319	442	Etymology	PC2701	447.00(5/6)	Serials/Societies/Congresses
PC320-335	443.028	Lexicography	PC2721-2746	447.5	Grammar
PC601-872	459	Romanian	PC2761	447.2	Etymology
PC601-623	459	Philology	PC2766	447.3028	Lexicography
PC601-603	459.0(5/6)	Serials/Societies	PC2801-2898	447.01	Old French
PC615	459.09	History	PC2813-2896	447.01	Language
PC619	459.07	Education	PC2821-2873	447.015	Grammar
PC624-799	459	Language	PC2883-2886	447.012	Etymology
PC625	459.09	History	PC2887-2895	447.013028	Lexicography
PC631-725	459.5	Grammar	PC3201-3366	449	Provencal (Old)
PC761-767	459.2	Etymology	PC3201-3213	449	Philology
PC775-784	459.3028	Lexicography	PC3201	449.0(5/6)	Serials/Societies
PC787-799	459.7	Geographic linguistics	PC3207	449.09	History
PC799	459.7	Slang	PC3209	449.092	Biography
PC800-872	859	Literature	PC3214-3273	449	Language
PC800-812	859.09	History	PC3215	449.09	History
PC901-986	459.9	Romansh	PC3219-3273	449.5	Grammar
PC901-949	459.9	Language	PC3283-3286	449.2	Etymology
PC901	459.90(5/6)	Serials/Societies	PC3287-3295	449.3028	Lexicography
PC905-906	459.909	History	PC3296	449.7	Geographic variations
PC906	459.9092	Biography	PC3299	449.7	Slang
PC907	459.907	Education	PC3301-3359	849	Literature
PC911-923	459.95	Grammar	PC3301-3321	849.09	History
PC931	459.92	Etymology	PC3371-3420	449	Neo-Provencal
PC937	459.93	Dictionaries	PC3371-3378	449	Language
PC941-949	459.97	Geographic variation/ Dialects	PC3381-3415	849	Literature
PC949	459.97	Slang	PC3721-3761	447	Slang
PC951-986	859.9	Literature	PC3801-3975	449.9	Catalan
PC951	859.909	History	PC3801-3813	449.9	Philology
PC953	859.9092	Biography	PC3801	449.90(5/6)	Serials/Societies
PC1001-1977	450	Italian	PC3807	449.909	History
PC1001-1071	450	Philology	PC3809	449.9092	Biography
PC1001-1011	450.(5/6)	Serials/Societies	PC3814-3873	449.9	Language
PC1035	450.1	Philosophy/Theory	PC3815	449.909	History
PC1051-1060	450.9	History	PC3819-3873	449.95	Grammar
PC1063-1064	450.92	Biography	PC3883-3886	449.92	Etymology
PC1065	450.7	Education	PC3887-3895	449.93028	Lexicography
PC1073-1693	450	Language	PC3901-3947	849.9	Literature
PC1075	450.9	History	PC3901-3917	849.909	History of literature
PC1099-1400	455	Grammar	PC4001-4977	460	Spanish
PC1571-1580	452	Etymology	PC4001-4071	460	Philology
PC1620-1693	453.028	Lexicography	PC4001-4009	460.5	Serials
PC1620-1645	453	Dictionaries	PC4011-4019	460.6	Societies
PC1700-1977	457	Geographic variation/ Dialects	PC4035	460.1	Philosophy/Theory
PC1704	457.003	Encyclopedias	PC4051-4060	460.9	History
PC1713-1718	457.009	History	PC4063-4064	460.92	Biography
PC1951-1977	457	Slang	PC4065	460.7	Education
PC2001-3761	440	French	PC4073-4693	460	Language
PC2001-2071	440	Philology	PC4075	460.9	History
PC2001-2009	440.5	Serials	PC4099-4400	465	Grammar
PC2011-2019	440.6	Societies	PC4571-4580	462	Etymology
PC2035	440.1	Philosophy/Theory	PC4620-4693	463.028	Lexicography
PC2051-2060	440.9	History	PC4620-4645	463	Dictionaries
PC2063-2064	440.92	Biography	PC4700-4941	467	Geographic variation/ Dialects
PC2065	440.7	Education	PC4951-4977	467	Slang
PC2073-2400	440	Language	PC5001-5491	469	Portuguese
PC2101-2400	445	Grammar	PC5001-5041	469	Philology
PC2113-2117	448.6	Readers	PC5001	469.005	Serials
PC2131-2151	441.5	Phonology	PC5003	469.006	Societies
PC2171-2175	445	Morphology	PC5025-5034	469.009	History
PC2201-2321	445	Parts of speech	PC5035-5039	469.007	Education
PC2571-2591	442	Etymology	PC5043-5231	469	Language
			PC5061-5231	469.5	Grammar

LC	Dewey	Descriptor
PC5301-5315	469.2	Etymology
PC5320-5348	469.3028	Lexicography
PC5325-5348	469.3	Dictionaries
PC5350-5498	469.7	Geographic variation/Dialects
PC5498	469.709	Slang
PD	430	Germanic languages/Literature
PD1-9	430.05	Serials
PD11-21	430.06	Societies/Congresses
PD31	430.03	Encyclopedias
PD35	430.01	Philosophy/Theory
PD51-60	430.09	History
PD63-64	430.092	Biography
PD65-69	430.07	Education
PD73-361	430	Language
PD99-321	435	Grammar
PD571-599	432	Etymology
PD601-660	433.028	Lexicography
PD625-660	433	Dictionaries
PD700-777	437	Geographic variation/Dialects
PD1001-1350	439.(1-4)	Old Germanic
PD1115-1211	439.9	Gothic
PD1115	439.909	History
PD1119-1167	439.95	Grammar
PD1193	439.93	Dictionaries
PD1501-5929	439.(5-6)	North Germanic/Scandinavian
PD1501-1541	439.(5-6)	Philology
PD1501-1504	439.(5-6)05	Serials
PD1505-1507	439.(5-6)06	Societies
PD1519	439.(5-6)03	Encyclopedias
PD1525-1531	439.(5-6)09	History
PD1533-1534	439.(5-6)092	Biography
PD1535-1539	439.(5-6)07	Education
PD1543-1855	439.(5-6)	Language
PD1559-1701	439.(5-6)5	Grammar
PD1801-1819	439.(5-6)2	Etymology
PD1823	439.(5-6)3028	Lexicography
PD1850-1893	439.(5-6)7	Geographic variations/Dialects
PD2201-2392	439.6	Old Norse/Icelandic
PD2201-2223	439.6	Philology
PD2224-2392	439.6	Language
PD2229-2331	439.605	Grammar
PD2361-2369	439.602	Etymology
PD2376-2385	439.603028	Lexicography
PD2387-2392	439.607	Geographic variation/Dialects
PD2401-2447	439.69	Modern Icelandic
PD2401	439.690(5/6)	Serials/Societies
PD2407	439.6907	Education
PD2409	439.6909	History
PD2411-2423	439.695	Grammar
PD2431	439.692	Etymology
PD2437	439.693	Dictionaries
PD2447	439.697	Slang
PD2483-2489	439.67	Old Norse dialects
PD2501-2999	439.82	Norwegian
PD2571-2578	439.82	Middle Norwegian
PD2601-2999	439.83	Modern
PD2601	439.830(5/6)	Serials/Societies
PD2611-2612	439.8307	Education
PD2619-2673	439.835	Grammar
PD2683-2684	439.832	Etymology
PD2687-2695	439.833028	Lexicography
PD2688-2695	439.833	Dictionaries
PD2696-2699	439.837	Geographic variation/Dialects
PD2699	439.837	Slang
PD3001-3929	439.81	Danish
PD3001-3071	439.81	Philology
PD3001-3019	439.810(5/6)	Serials/Societies
PD3035	439.8101	Philosophy/Theory
PD3051	439.8109	History
PD3063-3064	439.81092	Biography
PD3065	439.8107	Education
PD3073-3400	439.81	Language
PD3075	439.8109	History
PD3101-3400	439.815	Grammar
PD3571-3599	439.812	Etymology
PD3601-3693	439.813028	Lexicography
PD3625-3693	439.813	Dictionaries
PD3700-3929	439.817	Geographic variation/Dialects
PD3901-3929	439.817	Slang
PD5001-5929	439.7	Swedish
PD5001-5071	439.7	Philology
PD5035	439.701	Philosophy/Theory
PD5051	439.709	History
PD5063-5064	439.7092	Biography
PD5065	439.707	Education
PD5073-5400	439.7	Language
PD5075	439.709	History
PD5101-5400	439.75	Grammar
PD5571-5599	439.72	Etymology
PD5611-5693	439.73028	Lexicography
PD5625-5693	439.73	Dictionaries
PD5700-5929	439.77	Geographic variation/Dialects
PE	420	English
PE1-71	420	Philology
PE1-9	420.5	Serials
PE11-13	420.6	Societies/Congresses
PE31	420.3	Encyclopedias
PE35-37	420.1	Philosophy/Theory
PE51-60	420.9	History
PE63-64	420.92	Biography
PE65-69	420.7	Education
PE101-408	429	Anglo-Saxon
PE101-123	429	Philology
PE124-231	429	Language
PE129-231	429.5	Grammar
PE261-269	429.2	Etymology
PE274-285	429.3028	Lexicography
PE275-285	429.3	Dictionaries
PE287-299	429.7	Geographic variation/Dialects
PE451-693	427.02	Middle English
PE501-523	427.02	Philology
PE524-531	427.02	Language
PE529-531	427.025	Grammar
PE561-569	427.022	Etymology
PE574-585	427.023028	Lexicography
PE575-585	427.023	Dictionaries
PE688	427.027	Geographic variation/Dialects
PE801-896	420	Early modern
PE821-873	425	Grammar
PE887-895	423.028	Lexicography
PE1001-1693	420	Modern
PE1001-1400	420	Language
PE1001-1010	420.5	Serials

LC	Dewey	Descriptor
PE1011	420.6	Societies
PE1065-1069	420.7	Education
PE1075-1087	420.9	History
PE1097-1105	425	Grammar
PE1117-1130	428.6	Readers
PE1133-1168	421.5	Phonology
PE1171-1197	425	Morphology
PE1199-1359	425	Parts of speech
PE1402-1497	808.042	Rhetoric
PE1404-1405	808.04207	Education
PE1571-1599	422	Etymology
PE1601-1693	423.028	Lexicography
PE1620-1693	423	Dictionaries
PE1700-3601	427	Geographic variation/Dialects
PE3701-3729	427.09	Slang
PF	430	Teutonic languages
PF1-979	439.31	Dutch
PF1-9	439.3105	Serials
PF11-19	439.3106	Societies
PF21	439.3106	Congresses
PF31	439.3103	Encyclopedias
PF35-37	439.3101	Philosophy/Theory
PF51-60	439.3109	History
PF63-64	439.31092	Biography
PF65-69	439.3107	Education
PF73-693	439.31	Language
PF97	439.315	Grammar
PF131-168	439.3115	Phonology
PF171-197	439.315	Morphology
PF199-335	439.315	Parts of speech
PF410-497	808.043931	Rhetoric
PF571-599	439.312	Etymology
PF601-693	439.313028	Lexicography
PF620-693	439.313	Dictionaries
PF700-979	439.317	Geographic variation/Dialects
PF951-979	439.31709	Slang
PF1001-1184	439.31	Flemish
PF1001-1023	439.31	Philology
PF1001-1003	439.310(5/6)	Serials/Societies
PF1015	439.3109	History
PF1019	439.3107	Education
PF1024-1125	439.31	Language
PF1033-1125	439.315	Grammar
PF1161-1167	439.312	Etymology
PF1175-1184	439.313	Dictionaries
PF1401-1558	439.2	Frisian
PF1401-1411	439.2	Philology
PF1415-1497	439.2	Language
PF1501-1558	839.2	Literature
PF3001-5999	430	German
PF3001-3009	430.5	Serials
PF3011-3019	430.6	Societies
PF3021	430.6	Congresses
PF3031	430.3	Encyclopedias
PF3035-3037	430.1	Philosophy/Theory
PF3051-3060	430.9	History
PF3063-3064	430.92	Biography
PF3065-3069	430.7	Education
PF3073-3095	430	Language
PF3097-3400	435	Grammar
PF3131-3168	431.5	Phonology
PF3171-3197	435	Morphology
PF3199-3335	435	Parts of speech
PF3410-3497	808.0431	Rhetoric
PF3571-3599	432	Etymology
PF3601-3693	433.028	Lexicography
PF3620-3693	433	Dictionaries
PF3801-3991	437.01	Old High German
PF3801-3823	437.01	Philology
PF3824-3977	437.01	Language
PF3831-3931	437.015	Grammar
PF3985-3991	839	Literature
PF3992-4000	439.1	Old Saxon
PF3992-3996	439.1	Language
PF3997-4000	839.1	Literature
PF4043-4350	437.02	Middle High German
PF4043-4111	437.02	Language
PF4061-4171	437.025	Grammar
PF4327-4345	437.023028	Lexicography
PF4333-4345	437.023	Dictionaries
PF4501-4596	430	Early Modern German
PF4514-4595	430	Language
PF5000-5951	437.(1-6)	Dialects/Provincialisms
PF5971-5999	437.09	Slang
PG	491.(7-9)	Slavic/Balto-Slavic/Albanian
PG1-7948	491.8	Slavic
PG1-41	491.8	Philology
PG1-11	491.80(5/6)	Serials/Societies
PG19	491.83	Encyclopedias
PG21-23	491.801	Philosophy/Theory
PG25-31	491.809	History
PG33-34	491.8092	Biography
PG35-39	491.807	Education
PG43-400	491.8	Language
PG59-97	491.85	Grammar
PG301-319	491.82	Etymology
PG320-335	491.83028	Lexicography
PG331-335	491.83	Dictionaries
PG350-400	491.87	Geographic variation/Dialects
PG400	491.8709	Slang
PG500-583	891.8	Literature
PG501-512	891.809	History
PG601-789	491.81701	Church Slavic
PG601-698	491.81701	Language
PG661-698	491.817015	Grammar
PG701-705	891.81	Literature
PG801-1158	491.81	Bulgarian
PG801-823	491.81	Philology
PG824-993	491.81	Language
PG831-925	491.815	Grammar
PG975-984	491.813	Dictionaries
PG1000-1158	891.81	Literature
PG1000-1012	891.8109	History
PG1201-1798	491.82	Serbo-Croatian
PG1201-1223	491.82	Philology
PG1224-1399	491.82	Language
PG1229-1313	491.825	Grammar
PG1374-1384	491.823(028)	Dictionaries/Lexicography
PG1399	491.827	Slang
PG1400-1696	891.82	Literature
PG1400-1412	891.8209	History
PG1801-1998	491.84	Slovenian
PG1801-1813	491.84	Philology
PG1814-1899	491.84	Language
PG1819-1881	491.845	Grammar
PG1887-1894.5	491.843028	Lexicography
PG1888-1894.5	491.843	Dictionaries
PG1900-1962	891.84	Literature
PG1900-1962	891.8409	History
PG2001-3698	491.7	Russian

LC	Dewey	Descriptor
PG2001-2072	491.7	Philology
PG2001-2009	491.705	Serials
PG2011-2019	491.706	Societies
PG2021	491.706	Congresses
PG2031	491.703	Encyclopedias
PG2035-2037	491.701	Philosophy/Theory
PG2063-2064	491.7092	Biography
PG2065-2069	491.707	Education
PG2073-2850	491.7	Language
PG2097-2127	491.75	Grammar
PG2131-2161	491.715	Phonology
PG2171-2197	491.75	Morphology
PG2199-2321	491.75	Parts of speech
PG2571-2591	491.72	Etymology
PG2601-2693	491.73028	Lexicography
PG2625-2693	491.73	Dictionaries
PG2700-2850	491.77	Geographic variation/ Dialects
PG2850	491.7709	Slang
PG2900-3698	891.7	Literature
PG3801-3998	491.79	Ukranian
PG3801-3813	491.79	Philology
PG3814-3899	491.79	Language
PG3819-3881	491.795	Grammar
PG3887-3894.5	491.793028	Lexicography
PG3888-3894.5	491.793	Dictionaries
PG3900-3987	891.79	Literature
PG4001-4599	491.86	Bohemian (Czech)
PG4004-4771	491.86	Language
PG4601-4693	491.863028	Lexicography
PG4625-4693	491.863	Dictionaries
PG4700-4771	491.867	Geographic variation/ Dialects
PG5000-5146	891.86	Literature
PG5201-5598	491.87	Slovak
PG5201-5223	491.87	Philology
PG5224-5293	491.87	Language
PG5231-5325	491.875	Grammar
PG5375-5384	491.873	Dictionaries
PG5400-5546	891.87	Literature
PG5631-5698	491.88	Sorbish/Wendish
PG5631-5659	491.88	Language
PG5661-5698	891.88	Literature
PG6001-7498	491.85	Polish
PG6001-6790	491.85	Philology/Language
PG6625-6638	491.853028	Lexicography
PG6700-6790	491.857	Geographic variation/ Dialects
PG7001-7446	891.85	Literature
PG7012-7129	891.8509	History
PG7900-7925	491.(85-89)	Minor Slavic dialects
PG8001-9198	491.8	Balto-Slavic languages
PG8201-8208	491.91	Old Prussian
PG8206	491.913	Dictionaries
PG8501-8798	491.92	Lithuanian
PG8501-8693	491.92	Philology/Language
PG8701-8798	891.92	Literature
PG8801-9198	491.93	Lettish
PG8801-8993	491.93	Philology/Language
PG9000-9198	891.93	Literature
PG9501-9678	491.991	Albanian
PG9501-9513	491.991	Philology
PG9514-9599	491.991	Language
PG9601-9678	891.991	Literature
PH	494.5	Finno-Ugrian/Basque
PH1-11	494.5	Philology
PH1	494.505	Serials
PH4	494.53	Encyclopedias
PH5	494.501	Philosophy/Theory
PH9	494.5092	Biography
PH11	494.507	Education
PH14	494.5	Language
PH21-41	494.55	Grammar
PH101-498	494.541	Finnish
PH101-123	494.541	Philology
PH101-103	494.5410(5/6)	Serials/Societies
PH124-293	494.541	Language
PH131-225	494.541	Grammar
PH300-405	894.541	Literature
PH300-337	894.54109	History
PH501-509	494.54	Karelian
PH541-549	494.54	Vepsish (Chudish, N.)
PH561-569	494.5	Votish (Chudish, S.)
PH581-589	494.54	Livonian
PH601-688	494.545	Estonian
PH601-629	494.545	Language
PH630-671	894.545	Literature
PH701-735	494.55	Lappish
PH701-729	494.55	Language
PH731-735	894.55	Literature
PH751-785	494.56	Mordvinian
PH751-779	494.56	Language
PH781-785	894.56	Literature
PH801-809	494.56	Cheremissian
PH1001-1109	494.53	Permian
PH1201-3718	494.51	Ugrian languages
PH1251-1409	494.51	Ob-Ugrian
PH2001-3718	494.511	Hungarian
PH2001-2071	494.511	Philology
PH2073-2800	494.511	Language
PH2097-2410	494.5115	Grammar
PH2601-2693	494.5113028	Lexicography
PH2625-2693	494.5113	Dictionaries
PH2800	494.511709	Slang
PH3001-3445	894.511	Literature
PH3012-3132	894.51109	History
PH5001-5490	499.92	Basque
PH5001-5022	499.92	Philology
PH5023-5259	499.92	Language
PH5280-5490	899.92	Literature
PJ	490/890	Oriental philology/ Literature
PJ1-187	492-493	Languages
PJ1-10	492-493.(05)	Serials
PJ20-21	492-493.(06)	Congresses
PJ31	492-493.(03/3)	Encyclopedias/Dictionaries
PJ37	492-493.(01)	Philosophy/Theory
PJ51-60	492-493.(09)	History
PJ63-64	492-493.(092)	Biography
PJ65-69	492-493.(07)	Education
PJ120-171	492-493.(5)	Grammar
PJ183	492-493.(02)	Etymology
PJ187	492-493.(3028)	Lexicography
PJ306-489	892-893	Oriental literature (General)
PJ306-345	892-893.(09)	History
PJ347-489	892-893.(08)	Collections
PJ601-621	493/230-280	Christian Oriental
PJ701-908	492/493	Mohammedan
PJ701-761	492/493	Languages
PJ735-745	492/493.(5)	Grammar
PJ806-908	892/893	Literature
PJ1001-1989	493.1	Egyptology
PJ1001-1009	493.105	Serials
PJ1011-1021	493.106	Societies/Congresses

LC	Dewey	Descriptor	LC	Dewey	Descriptor
PJ1031	493.103	Encyclopedias/Dictionaries	PJ4501-5192	492.4	Hebrew
PJ1035	493.101	Philosophy/Theory	PJ4501-4541	492.4	Philology
PJ1051-1069	493.109	History	PJ4501-4504	492.405	Serials
PJ1091-1097	493.1	Hieroglyphic	PJ4505-4509	492.406	Societies/Congresses
PJ1111-1439	493.1	Language	PJ4519	492.403	Encyclopedias
PJ1121-1201	493.15	Grammar	PJ4521	492.401	Philosophy/Theory
PJ1350-1371	493.12	Etymology	PJ4525-4531	492.409	History
PJ1401-1439	493.13028	Lexicography	PJ4543-4937	492.4	Language
PJ1423-1439	493.13	Dictionaries	PJ4553-4731	492.45	Grammar
PJ1481-1921	893.1	Literature	PJ4576-4583	492.415	Phonology/Phonetics
PJ1481-1488	893.109	History	PJ4601-4677	492.45	Morphology
PJ1501-1571	493.111	Texts (Inscriptions/Papyri)	PJ4801-4819	492.42	Etymology
PJ1801-1921	493.1	Demotic literature	PJ4820-4847	492.43028	Lexicography
PJ2001-2199	493.2	Coptic	PJ4825-4847	492.43	Dictionaries
PJ2001	493.20(5/6)	Serials/Societies	PJ4855-4937	492.47	Dialects/Provincialisms
PJ2019	493.207	Education	PJ4860	492.29	Samaritan
PJ2029-2113	493.25	Grammar	PJ4901-4937	492.47	Talmudic (Mishnaic)
PJ2161	493.22	Etymology			Hebrew
PJ2181	493.23(028)	Dictionaries/Lexicography	PJ4911-4925	492.475	Grammar
PJ2190-2199	893.2	Literature	PJ4931-4933	492.472	Etymology
PJ2340-2399	493.3	Libyco/Berber languages	PJ4934-4937	492.473028	Lexicography
PJ2345	493.35	Grammar	PJ4935-4937	492.473	Dictionaries
PJ2347	493.32	Etymology	PJ5001-5060	892.4	Literature
PJ2349	493.303	Dictionaries	PJ5001-5004	892.40(5/6)	Serials/Societies/Congresses
PJ2353-2367	493.3	Libyan languages	PJ5007	892.407	Education
PJ2369-2399	493.3	Berber languages	PJ5008-5034.2	892.409	History
PJ2401-2594	493.5	Cushitic languages	PJ5016-5021	892.4(1-6)	By period
PJ2405	493.55	Grammar	PJ5022-5033.9	892.4(1-8)	By form
PJ2409	493.52	Etymology	PJ5034.4-.9	492.411	Inscriptions
PJ2413	493.53	Dictionaries	PJ5035-5047.9	892.408	Collections
PJ2425-2594	493.509	By dialect	PJ5048	398.204924	Folk literature
PJ3001-3097	492	Semitic philology	PJ5049	892.4	By place
PJ3001-.5	492.0(5/6)	Serials/Societies/Congresses	PJ5050-5060	892.4(1-6)	By date/Author
PJ3004	492.03	Dictionaries/Encyclopedias	PJ5061-5192	492.47	Mixed Jewish dialects
PJ3005	492.01	Philosophy/Theory	PJ5111-5192	437.947	Yiddish
PJ3011-3013	492.07	Education	PJ5115-5116.5	437.9475	Grammar
PJ3021-3041	492.5	Grammar	PJ5117	437.9473	Dictionaries
PJ3065	492.2	Etymology	PJ5120-5129	839.09	Literature
PJ3071-3075	492.3	Lexicography	PJ5140-5168	839.09	By place
PJ3081-3095	492.11	Texts/Inscriptions	PJ5201-5329	492.2	Aramaic
PJ3097	892.(09)	Literature (History/ Criticism)	PJ5208-5209	492.211	Texts/Inscriptions
PJ3101-4083	492.1	East Semitic languages	PJ5211-5289	492.29	West Aramaic
PJ3101-3953	492.1	Assyriology	PJ5211-5219	492.29	Biblical (Chaldaic)
PJ3101-3121	492.10(5/6)	Serials/Societies	PJ5271-5279	492.29	Samaritan
PJ3191-3225	492.111	Cuneiform writing	PJ5301-5329	492.3	East Aramaic
PJ3231-3595	492.1	Language	PJ5321-5329	496.391	Mandaean
PJ3231-3311	492.15	Grammar	PJ5401-5909	492.3	Syriac
PJ3450-3471	492.12	Etymology	PJ5401-5411	492.3	Philology
PJ3511-3547	492.13028	Lexicography	PJ5414-5493	492.3	Language
PJ3523-3547	492.13	Dictionaries	PJ5419-5471	492.35	Grammar
PJ3550-3595	492.17	Linguistic geography/ Dialects	PJ5483	492.32	Etymology
PJ3601-3941	892.1	Literature	PJ5490-5493	492.33	Dictionaries
PJ3601-3671	892.109	History	PJ5601-5695	892.3	Literature
PJ3701-3941	492.111	Texts/Inscriptions	PJ5601-5607	892.309	History
PJ4001-4083	499.95	Sumerian	PJ5611-5647	892.308	Collections
PJ4001-4007	499.950(5/6)	Serials/Societies	PJ5701-5709	492.37	East Syriac (Nestorian)
PJ4010-4041	499.95	Language	PJ5711-5719	492.37	West Syriac (Jacobite)
PJ4011-4025	499.955	Grammar	PJ5801-5809	492.37	Neo-Syriac
PJ4037	499.953	Dictionaries	PJ5901-5909	492.9	South Semitic languages
PJ4045-4075	899.95	Literature	PJ6001-8517	492.7	Arabic
PJ4101-4197	492	West/North Semitic languages	PJ6001-6071	492.7	Philology
PJ4149	492.6	Moabite	PJ6001-6021	492.70(5/6)	Serials/Societies/Congresses
PJ4150	492.6	Ugaritic	PJ6031	492.7(3/03)	Dictionaries/Encyclopedias
PJ4171-4197	492.6	Phoenician-Punic	PJ6035	492.701	Philosophy/Theory
			PJ6065-6069	492.707	Education
			PJ6073-6697	492.7	Language
			PJ6101-6599	492.75	Grammar

LC	Dewey	Descriptor
PJ6101-6199.5	492.7	Arabic
PJ6172-6199	492.72	Etymology
PJ6201-6209	491.5	Persian
PJ6209	491.53	Dictionaries
PJ6231-6239	494.35	Turkish
PJ6601-6680	492.73028	Lexicography
PJ6620-6680	492.73	Dictionaries
PJ6690-6695	492.77	Ancient Arabic
PJ6701-6901	492.7	Modern Arabic dialects (North)
PJ6707	492.707	Education
PJ6737	492.73	Dictionaries
PJ6751-6760	492.77	Spain
PJ6771-6799	492.77	Egypt
PJ6777-6785	492.775	Grammar
PJ6795	492.773	Dictionaries
PJ6805-6808	492.77	Palestine
PJ6810	492.77	Lebanon
PJ6811-6820	492.77	Syria
PJ6821-6830	492.77	Mesopotamia/Iraq
PJ6841-6880	492.77	Arabic peninsula
PJ6950-7144	492.9	South Arabic
PJ7501-8517	892.7	Arabic literature
PJ7501-7600	892.709	History/Criticism
PJ7526-7538	892.7(1-6)09	By date
PJ7541-7561	892.7109	Poetry
PJ7565	892.7209	Drama
PJ7571-7577	892.7808009	Prose
PJ7580	398.204927	Folk literature
PJ7593-7600	492.711	Inscriptions/Papyri
PJ7601-7680	892.708	Collections
PJ7611-7625	892.7(1-6)08	By date
PJ7631-7661	892.7108	Poetry
PJ7665	892.7208	Drama
PJ7671-7677	892.7808008	Prose
PJ7680	398.204927	Folk literature
PJ7695.8-7876	892.7(1-6)	By date/Author
PJ8000-8517	892.77	Provincial/Colonial/Local
PJ8025-8517	892.(7-9)	By place
PJ8025-8190	892.(7-9)	In Asia
PJ8030-8129	892.(7-9)	In the Near East
PJ8130-8167	892.(7-9)	In India/Pakistan
PJ8195-8390	892.(7-9)	In Africa
PJ8395-8490	892.(7-9)	In Europe
PJ8500-8517	892.(7-9)	In America
PJ8991-9293	492.8	Ethiopian languages
PK	491.1	Indo-Iranian languages
PK1-14	491.1	Philology
PK1	491.10(5/6)	Serials/Societies
PK11-13	461.107	Education
PK14	491.1(3/03)	Dictionaries/Encyclopedias
PK15-79	491.1	Languages
PK21-41	491.15	Grammar
PK75-77	491.13	Dictionaries
PK80-85	891.1	Literature
PK101-185	491.(2-4)	Indo-Aryan languages
PK207-379	491.2	Vedic
PK223-379	491.2	Language
PK231-313	491.25	Grammar
PK361-369	491.22	Etymology
PK375-379	491.23	Dictionaries
PK401-976	491.2	Sanskrit
PK401-420	491.2	Philology
PK423-976	491.2	Language
PK501-811	491.25	Grammar
PK901-919	491.22	Etymology
PK920-969	491.23028	Lexicography
PK925-969	491.23	Dictionaries
PK1001-1095	491.37	Pali
PK1001-1081	491.37	Philology
PK1017-1073	491.375	Grammar
PK1083-1086	491.372	Etymology
PK1087-1093	491.373028	Lexicography
PK1089-1095	491.373	Dictionaries
PK1201-1409	491.3	Prakrit languages
PK1206-1215	491.35	Grammar
PK1223-1225	491.33	Dictionaries
PK1471-1490	491.1	Middle Indo-Aryan
PK1501-2899	491.4	Modern Indo-Aryan
PK1511-1523	491.45	Grammar
PK1537	491.43	Dictionaries
PK1550-2899	491.4(1-9)	Dialects/Languages
PK1550-1569	491.451	Assamese
PK1651-1730.46	491.44	Bengali
PK1801-1831	491.454	Bihari
PK1841-1859	491.47	Gujarati
PK1931-1970	491.43	Hindi language
PK1971-1979	491.439	Urdu language
PK2030-2142	891.43	Hindustani literature
PK2151-2212	891.439	Urdu literature
PK2261-2270	491.419	Lahnda
PK2351-2418	491.46	Marathi
PK2461-2479	491.4797	Marawari
PK2561-2579.5	491.45	Oriya
PK2591-2610	491.49	Pahari
PK2631-2659	491.42	Panjabi
PK2701-2709	491.479	Rajasthani
PK2781-2790	491.41	Sindhi
PK2801-2891	491.48	Sinhalese
PK2902-2979	891.1	Indo-Aryan literature
PK2902-2947	891.109	History/Criticism
PK2911-2915	891.109	By date
PK2916-2929	891.1109	Poetry
PK2931-2933	891.1209	Drama
PK2941-2943	891.10802309	Narratives
PK2945-2947	891.17009	Wit/Humor
PK3591-4485	891.2	Sanskrit
PK3791-3799	891.2	By author
PK4501-4681	891.37	Pali literature
PK4990-5046	891.3	Prakrit/Jaina literature
PK5401-5471	891.4	Modern Indo-Aryan literature
PK6001-6996	491.5/891.5	Iranian philology/Literature
PK6001-6091	491.5	Philology
PK6097-6099	891.509	History of literature
PK6101-6118	491.52	Avestan
PK6121-6129	491.51	Old Persian
PK6135-6199.5	491.53	Middle Iranian (Pahlavi)
PK6201-6599	491.55	New Persian
PK6201-6399	491.55	Language
PK6400-6599	891.55	Literature
PK6400-6427.6	891.5509	History/Criticism
PK6416-6420	891.55109	Poetry
PK6421-6422	891.55209	Drama
PK6423	891.55(808/3)09	Prose/Fiction
PK6426	398.2049155	Folk literature
PK6428-6450	891.5508	Collections
PK6433-6439	891.55108	Poetry
PK6440	891.55208	Drama
PK6443	891.55(808/3)08	Prose/Fiction
PK6450.9-6561	891.55	By author
PK6701-6820	491.593	Afghan
PK7001-7075	491.499	Dardic (Pisacha)
PK7021-7037	491.499	Kashmiri

LC	Dewey	Descriptor
PK7040-7045	491.499	Kohistani
PK7050-7065	491.499	Kafir group
PK7070	491.499	Khowar
PK8001-8835	491.992	Armenian
PK8001-8499	491.992	Language
PK8501-8835	891.992	Literature
PK8501-8546	891.9920(9/8)	History and collections
PK8547-8548	891.992	By author
PK8561-8699	891.992	By place
PK8601-8661	891.992	Europe
PK8681-8689	891.992	United States/Canada
PK9001-9201	499.96	Caucasian languages
PK9001	499.960(5/6)	Serials/Societies
PK9005	499.9607	Education
PK9007-9015	499.965	Grammar
PK9025	499.963	Dictionaries
PK9030-9040	899.96	Literature, By language
PK9101-9169	499.96	Georgian
PK9106-9115	499.965	Grammar
PK9125	499.963	Dictionaries
PK9160-9169	899.96	Literature
PK9201	499.96	Other languages
PL	494-499	East Asian/African/ Oceanian
PL1-481	494	Ulra-Altaic
PL21-396	494.3	Turkic languages
PL31	494.3	Old Turkic
PL41-45	494.3	Siberian (Northeastern) group
PL51-56	494.36	Chagatai (Southeastern) group
PL61-65	494.3	Kipchak (Northwestern) group
PL63	494.3	Kipchak
PL65.B2	494.3	Balkar
PL65.C74	494.3	Crimean Tatar
PL65.T3	494.3	Tatar
PL91-396	494.36	Oghuz (Southwestern) group
PL101-275	494.35	Turkish (Osmanic/Ottoman)
PL201-248	894.3(5-6)	Literature
PL248	894.3(5-6)	By author
PL311-314	494.361	Azerbaijani
PL331-334	494.36	Turkmen
PL400-431	494.2	Mongolian languages
PL401-409	494.2	Mongol language
PL410-419	894.2	Mongol literature
PL450-481	494.1	Tungus-Manchu
PL471-479	494.1	Manchu
PL491-495	495	Far eastern languages
PL495	494.6	Ainu
PL501-889	495.6	Japanese
PL501-699	495.6	Language
PL525-.6	495.609	History
PL531.3-532.5	495.65	Grammar
PL674.5-677.6	495.63	Dictionaries
PL700-889	895.6	Literature
PL700-751.5	895.609	History/Criticism
PL700-701	895.605	Serials
PL702-703	895.606	Societies/Congresses
PL703.5	895.6074	Museums/Exhibitions
PL709-711	895.607	Education
PL714-715	895.609	Criticism
PL716-751.5	895.609	History
PL727-733	895.6109	Poetry
PL734-739	895.6209	Drama
PL740-747	895.6(808/3)09	Prose/Fiction
PL748-749	398.204956	Folk literature
PL750-751	495.611	Inscriptions
PL751.5	895.6(1-9) + (0809282)	Juvenile literature
PL752-783	895.6(1-8)08	Collections
PL757-763	895.6108	Poetry
PL764-769	895.6208	Drama
PL770-777	895.6(808/3)08	Prose/Fiction
PL784-866	895.6(1-5)	By author/Date
PL787-789	895.614	Heian period (794-1185)
PL790-792	895.62(2-4)	Kamakura-Monoyama (1185-1600)
PL793-795	895.632	Early Edo (1600-1788)
PL796-799	895.634	Late Edo (1789-1867)
PL800-820	895.642	Meiji-Taisho (1868-1926)
PL821-866	895.6(44-5)	Showa (1926-)
PL885-889	895.6(1-8)	Local/In other countries
PL901-998	495.7/895.7	Korean language/Literature
PL901-949	495.7	Language
PL935-.6	495.73	Dictionaries
PL950-998	895.7	Literature
PL950.2-969.5	895.709	History/Criticism
PL950.2-.4	895.705	Serials
PL950.6-.8	895.706	Societies/Congesses
PL951.6	895.73	Dictionaries/Encyclopedias
PL952-.4	895.707	Education
PL955-969.5	895.709	History
PL959-961.23	895.7109	Poetry
PL962-964	895.7209	Drama
PL965-967	895.7(808/3)09	Prose/Fiction
PL968.2-.4	398.204957	Folk literature
PL969.2-.4	495.711	Inscriptions
PL969.5	895.7(1-8)	Juvenile literature
PL969.8-985	895.7(1-8)08	Collections
PL974-976.23	895.7108	Poetry
PL977-979	895.7208	Drama
PL980-981	895.7(808/3)08	Prose/Fiction
PL986-993	895.7(1-4)	By author/Date
PL987	895.71	Koryo period (935-1392)
PL988	895.72	1392-1598
PL989-96	895.72	1598-1894
PL990-.96	895.728	1894-1919
PL991-.96	895.73	1919-1945
PL992-993	895.74	1945-
PL997-998	895.7(1-8)	Local/In other countries
PL1001-(3208)	495.1/895.1	Chinese language/Literature
PL1001-1940	495.1	Language
PL1001-1010	495.105	Serials
PL1011-1021	495.106	Societies/Congresses
PL1031	495.103	Encyclopedias
PL1065-1069	495.107	Education
PL1075-1083	495.109	History of the language
PL1099-1241	495.15	Grammar
PL1201-1219	495.115	Phonology
PL1281-1315	495.12	Etymology
PL1401-1498	495.13028	Lexicography
PL1420-1498	495.13	Dictionaries
PL1501-1940	495.17	Dialects
PL1731-1740	495.17	Cantonese
PL1861-1870	495.17	Hsiang (Hunanese)
PL1891-1900	495.1	Mandarin
PL1931-1940	495.17	Wu
PL2250-(3208)	895.1	Literature
PL2250-2443	895.109	History/Criticism
PL2250-2251	895.105	Serials
PL2252-2253	895.106	Societies/Congresses
PL2253.5	895.1074	Exhibitions/Museums
PL2257	895.103	Encyclopedias

LC	Dewey	Descriptor
PL2258-2260	895.107	Education
PL2260-.52	895.1092	Biography
PL2261-2262.2	895.109	Criticism
PL2263-2443	895.109	History
PL2277	895.10922	Biography (Collective)
PL2306-2355.8	895.1109	Poetry
PL2356-2393	895.1209	Drama
PL2395-2413	895.1409	Essays
PL2415-2443	895.1309	Fiction
PL2445-2446	398.204951	Folk literature
PL2450-2653	895.1(1-8)08	Collections
PL2517-2565.8	895.1108	Poetry
PL2566-2603	895.1208	Drama
PL2606-2623	895.14008	Essays
PL2625-2653	895.1308	Fiction
PL2661-2929.5	895.1(1-52)	By author/Date
PL2661-2662	895.11	Early to 221 B.C.
PL2663-2669	895.12	221 B.C.-618 A.D.
PL2670-2677	895.13	618-907 (T'ang Dynasty)
PL2679-2687	895.142	Sung Dynasty (960-1279)
PL2688-2694	895.144	Yuan Dynasty (1260-1368)
PL2694.5-2698	895.146	Ming Dynasty (1368-1644)
PL2699-2735	895.148	Ch'ing Dynasty (1644-1912)
PL2735.5-2832.3	895.151	1912-1949
PL2832.5-2929.5	895.152	1949-
PL3030-(3208)	895.1(1-8)	Provincial/Local
PL3033-(3208)	895.1(1-8)	In other countries
PL3521-4001	495	Sino-Tibetan
PL3551-4001	495.4	Tibeto-Burman
PL3561-3801	495.4	Tibeto-Himalayan
PL3601-3775	495.4	Tibetan
PL3601-3651	495.4	Language
PL3701-3775	895.4	Literature
PL3781-3801	495.49	Himalayan languages
PL3851-4001	491.451/495.8	Assamese and Burmese
PL3921-3988	495.8	Burmese
PL3921-3969	495.8	Languages
PL3970-3988	895.8	Literature
PL4051-4054	495	Karen languages
PL4111-4251	495.91	Thai languages
PL4151-4209	495.91	Thai/Siamese
PL4151-4199	495.91	Language
PL4200-4209	895.91	Literature
PL4281-4587	495.93	Austroasiatic languages
PL4301-4351	495.932	Mon-Khmer languages
PL4371-4379	495.922	Vietnamese/Annamese
PL4401-4471	499.2	Malay languages
PL4501-4587	495.95	Munda (Kolarian) languages
PL4601-4794	494.8	Dravidian languages
PL4641-4659	494.814	Kannada/Kanarese
PL4711-4718.9	494.812	Malayalam (Malabar)
PL4751-4758.9	494.811	Tamil
PL4771-4780.9	494.827	Telugu
PL5001-7511	499	Languages of Oceania
PL5001-7101	499.(2/12/15)	Austronesian/Papuan/Australian
PL5051-5490	499.2(8/21)	Malayan (Indonesian)
PL5071-5089	499.221	Indonesian
PL5101-5139	499.28	Malay
PL5161-5179	499.222	Javanese
PL5501-6135	499.21	Philippine languages
PL6191-6341	499.5	Micronesian/Melanesian
PL6401-6551	499.4	Polynesian languages
PL6601-6621	499.12	Papuan languages
PL7001-7101	499.15	Australian languages

LC	Dewey	Descriptor
PL8000-8839	496/896	African languages/Literature
PL8000-8009	496	Languages
PL8000-8002	496.0(5/6)	Serials/Societies/Congresses
PL8004	496.07	Education
PL8008	496.5	Grammar
PL8009.5-8014	896	Literature
PL8015-8021	496	Languages by country
PL8024-8027	496.(1-5)	Families of languages
PL8025	496.39	Bantu
PL8027	496.5	Sudanian
PL8035-8839	496.(1-5)	Languages, Alphabetically
PM	494.6/497/499.99	Hyperborean/Indian/Artifical
PM1-95	494.6	Hyperborean languages
PM31-34	497.1	Aleut
PM61-64	497.1	Eskimo
PM101-2711	497	American aboriginal
PM231-355	497	Of Canada/Newfoundland/Etc.
PM421-501	497	Of United States and Mexico
PM549-2711	497.(1-9)	Languages, Alphabetical
PM3001-4566	497	Of Mexico and Central America
PM3100-3281	497	Of Mexico, By state
PM3301-3393	497	Of Central America, By country
PM3501-4566	497	Languages, Alphabetical
PM5001-7356	497/498	Of South America & West Indies
PM5071-5099	497	Of West Indies
PM5100-5295	498	Of South America
PM5301-7356	498.(2-4)	Languages, Alphabetical
PM7831-7875	447.9	Creole
PM8001-8995	499.99	Artificial languages
PM8201-8298	499.992	Esperanto
PM8999	499	Picture languages (Isotype)
PM9001-9021	417.2	Secret languages (Slang/Argot)
PN	800	Literature (General)
PN1-19	805	Serials, By language
PN20-30	806	Societies/Congresses
PN35-37	808	Collections
PN41-43	803	Dictionaries/Encyclopedias
PN45-57	801	Theory/Philosophy
PN59-72	807	Education
PN70-71	807.0(1-9)	By place
PN80-99	809	Criticism
PN80-.5	809.00(5/6)	Serials/Societies
PN86-94	809	History
PN101-245	808.02	Authorship
PN167-171	808	Plagiarism
PN149.8-163	808.02	As a profession
PN172-239	808.808(06)	Technique/Composition/Rhetoric
PN441-1009.5	809	Literary history
PN451-497	809.2	Biography
PN500-519	808	Collections
PN599-605	809.9(1-2)	Movements of literature
PN599	809.913	Idealism
PN601	809.912	Realism/Naturalism
PN603	809.9145	Romanticism
PN610-779	809.0(1-5)	By date
PN610-649	809.01	Ancient
PN661-694	809.02	Medieval to 1500
PN683-687	398.2	Legends

LC	Dewey	Descriptor
PN688-691	809.102	Poetry
PN692-694	809.(888/83)	Prose/Fiction
PN695-779	809.0(3-4)	Modern
PN715-749	809.0(3-32)	Renaissance (1500-1700)
PN801-820	809.9145	Romance literatures
PN821-840	839	Germanic literatures
PN841	809.836	Black literature (General)
PN851-883	809	Comparative literature
PN905-1008	398.209	Folk literature
PN953-963	398.2090(1-4)	By date
PN1008.2-1009.5	809	Juvenile literature (General)
PN1010-1525	808.1	Poetry
PN1031-1049	808.1001	Theory/Philosophy
PN1010	808.1005	Serials
PN1012-1014	808.1006	Societies/Congresses
PN1021	808.1003	Dictionaries
PN1065-1085	808.819	Special subjects
PN1105-1279	809.1	History/Criticism
PN1301-1333	808.132	Epic poetry
PN1341-1347	398.2	Folk poetry
PN1351-1389	808.14	Lyric poetry
PN1530	808.8245	The monologue
PN1551	808.8026	The dialogue
PN1560-1590	790.2	Performing arts/Show business
PN1560-1569	790.205	Serials
PN1570-1575	790.206	Societies/Congresses
PN1576-1578	790.207	Education
PN1579	790.203	Dictionaries
PN1581	790.209	History
PN1583	790.2092	Biography
PN1585-1589	790.2	Performing arts centers
PN1600-3307	808.2	Drama
PN1600-1610	808.2005	Serials
PN1611-1620	808.200(6/74)	Societies/Congresses/Museums
PN1621-1623	808.82	Collections
PN1631-1633	808.2001	Philosophy
PN1660-1693	808.2	Technique/Dramatic composition
PN1720-1861	809	History
PN1741-1861	809.0(1-5)	By date
PN1741	809.01	Ancient
PN1751-1771	809.02	Medieval
PN1785-1801	809.0(23-31)	Renaissance
PN1811-1861	809.0(3-4)	Modern
PN1865-1988	808.(8-9)	Special types
PN1990-1992.92	808.822	Broadcasting
PN1991-.9	808.8222	Radio broadcasts
PN1992-.92	808.8225	Television broadcasts
PN1993-1999	808.823	Motion pictures
PN1997-.85	808.82	Plays/Scenarios/Etc.
PN2000-3307	792	The theater
PN2061-2071	792.028	Art of acting
PN2085-2091	792.025	The stage/Accessories
PN2100-2193	792.09	History
PN2131-2193	792.090(1-4)	By date
PN2131-2145	792.0901	Ancient
PN2152-2160	792.0902	Medieval
PN2171-2179	792.090(23-31)	Renaissance
PN2181-2193	792.090(3-4)	Modern
PN2220-2298	792.0973	United States
PN2300-2308.5	792.0971	Canada
PN2310-2318	792.0972	Mexico
PN2320-2384	792.09728	Central America
PN2390-2440	792.09729	West Indies
PN2445-2554	792.098	South America

LC	Dewey	Descriptor
PN2570-2859	792.094	Europe
PN2575-2609	792.0941	Great Britain
PN2610-2618	792.0943(6/9)	Austria (Hungary)
PN2620-2639	792.0944	France
PN2640-2659.5	792.0943	Germany
PN2660-2668	792.09495	Modern Greece
PN2670-2688	792.0945	Italy
PN2690-2719	792.09492	Low Countries
PN2720-2728	792.0947	European Russia
PN2730-2778	792.0948	Scandinavia
PN2780-2788	792.0946	Spain
PN2790-2798	792.09469	Portugal
PN2800-2808	792.09494	Switzerland
PN2818.5-2858	792.09496	Balkans
PN2860-2960	792.095	Asia
PN2870-2878	792.0951	China
PN2919-.8	792.095694	Israel/Palestine
PN2920-2928	792.0952	Japan
PN2930-2939.8	792.09519	Korea
PN2969-3000	792.096	Africa
PN2970-2978	792.0962	Egypt
PN3010-3018	792.099(3-4)	Australia/New Zealand
PN3030	792.099(5-6)	Oceania
PN3151-3171	792.0222	Amateur theatricals
PN3175-3191	792.022	Colleges/School theatricals
PN3203-3299	791.62/793.24	Tableaux/Pageants/Happenings
PN3311-3503	808.3	Prose (Fiction)
PN3311-3319	808.300(5/6)	Serials/Societies
PN3321-3324	808.83	Collections
PN3329-3352	808.3001	Philosophy/Theory
PN3355-3383	808.3	Technique/Authorship
PN3428-3448	808.3(1-8)	Special kinds of fiction
PN3451-3503	809.83	History of fiction
PN3466-3503	809.830(1-4)	By date
PN3466	809.8301	Ancient
PN3481	809.830(23-31)	Renaissance
PN3491-3503	809.830(3-4)	Modern (18th-20th centuries)
PN4001-4355	808.5	Oratory/Elocution
PN4071-4095	808.5007	Education
PN4001-4005	808.5005	Serials
PN4007	808.50025	Directories
PN4009	808.5006	Societies
PN4016	808.5003	Dictionaries
PN4021-4055	809.5	History
PN4031-4051	809.50(1-4)	By date
PN4057-4059	809.50092	Biographies
PN4061	808.5001	Philosophy/Theory
PN4177-4191	808.53	Debating
PN4199-4355	808.54	Recitations
PN4699-5650	070.4	Journalism/Period press
PN4699-4705	050-059	Serials
PN4712-4715	070.406	Societies
PN4717	070.406	Congresses
PN4722-4726	070.4	Collections
PN4728	070.403	Dictionaries
PN4735-4748	323.445	Relation to the state
PN4775-4784	070.4028	Practical journalism/Techniques
PN4785-4823	070.407	Education
PN4832-4836	050	Magazines/Other periodicals
PN4840-5648	071-079	Journalism, By place
PN4841-4900	071.(3-9)	United States
PN4901-4920	071.1	Canada
PN4930.5-4959	079	Caribbean/West Indies

LC	Dewey	Descriptor	LC	Dewey	Descriptor
PN5000-5106	079	South America	PQ601-771	848.0809	Prose/Fiction
PN5110-5355	073-078	Europe	PQ611-629	848.089009	Modern French prose/ Fiction
PN5111-5160	072	Great Britain			
PN5171-5790	074	France	PQ631-671	843.009	Fiction
PN5201-5220	073	Germany	PQ781-841	398.20441	Folk literature
PN5271-5280	077	European Russia	PQ1101-1413	841-848.(008)	Collections
PN5280.5-5310	078	Scandinavia	PQ1121-1125	841-848.(2-3)08	15th-16th centuries
PN5359	079(56/174927)	Near East/Arab countries	PQ1126-1130	841-848.(408)	17th century
PN5360-5449	079.5	Asia	PQ1131-1135	841-848.(508)	18th century
PN5450-5499	079.6	Africa	PQ1141	841-848.(908)	20th century
PN5511-5590	079.9(4/3)	Australia/New Zealand	PQ1161-1193	841.08	Poetry
PN5620-5639	079.9(5-6)	Oceania	PQ1211-1241	842.008	Drama
PN6010-6790	808	Collections-General literature	PQ1243-1297	848.0808	Prose
			PQ1261-1275	843.008	Fiction
PN6080-6095	808.882	Quotations	PQ1281-1283	845.01008	Oratory
PN6081-6084	820.802	English	PQ1300-1595	841-848.8	Old French, Collections
PN6086-6089	840.802	French	PQ1308-1339	841.08	Poetry
PN6090-6093	830.802	German	PQ1341-1365	842.008	Drama
PN6099-6110	808.81	Poetry	PQ1371-1385	842.05161008	Moralities/Farces
PN6110.5-6120	808.82	Drama	PQ1391	848.0808	Prose
PN6120.15-.95	808.83	Fiction	PQ1411-2651	841-848.(1-914)	By author/Date
PN6121-6129	808.851	Orations	PQ1411-1545	841-848.(1)	1350-1400
PN6130-6140	808.86	Letters	PQ1551-1595	841-848.(2)	14th-15th centuries
PN6141-6145	808.84	Essays	PQ1600-2651	841-848.(3-9)	Modern
PN6147-6231	808.87	Wit and humor	PQ1600-1709	841-848.(3)	16th century
PN6157-6222	808.87	By place	PQ1710-1935	841-848.(4)	17th century
PN6157-6163	808.87	United States	PQ1947-2147	841-848.(5)	18th century
PN6173-6178	808.87	Great Britain	PQ2149-2551	841-848.(7-8)	19th century
PN6183-6222	808.87	Other European countries	PQ2600-2651	841-848.(9-914)	20th century
PN6231	808.879(1-3)	By topic	PQ3801-3999	849	Provincial/Colonial
PN6233-6238	808.803538	Anacreontic (Erotic/ Pleasures)	PQ3809-3999	849	By place
			PQ3810-3858	849	Belgium
PN6259-6268	808.882	Anecdotes/Table talk	PQ3860	849	Netherlands
PN6269-6278	398.9	Aphorisms/Apothegms	PQ3861	849	Germany
PN6279-6288	808.882	Epigrams	PQ3862	841-848	Great Britain
PN6299-6308	398.9	Maxims	PQ3863	841-848	Italy
PN6340-6348	808.851	Toasts	PQ3865	841-848	European Russia
PN6366-6377	398.6/793.24	Riddles/Charades	PQ3867	841-848	Scandinavia
PN6400-6525	398.9	Proverbs	PQ3870-3888	841-848	Switzerland
PN6700-6790	070.444/741.5	Comic books/Comic strips	PQ3890	841-848	Other Europe
PQ	840	Romance language literature	PQ3900-3919	841-848	Canada
			PQ3940-3949	841-848	West Indies
PQ1-3999	840	French literature	PQ3950-3959	841-848	South America/Central America
PQ1-841	840.9	History/Criticism			
PQ1-19	840.5	Serials	PQ3960-3979	841-848	Asia
PQ21-31	840.6	Societies/Congresses	PQ3980-3989	841-848	Africa
PQ41	840.3	Encyclopedias	PQ3990-3999	841-848	Oceania
PQ51-65	840.7	Education	PQ4001-5991	850	Italian literature
PQ75	840.9	History	PQ4001-4199	850.9	History and criticism
PQ82-96	840.900(1-914)	By date	PQ4001	850.(5/6)	Serials/Societies
PQ100-771	840.9	History of French literature	PQ4003-4005	850.8	Collections
PQ115-128	840.202	Compendiums	PQ4006	850.3	Encyclopedias
PQ146-150	840.9	Authors, Biographies	PQ4013-4023	850.7	Education
PQ151-221	841-848.(109)	Medieval	PQ4025-4034	850.9	Criticism
PQ201-205	841.032109	Epics	PQ4035-4047	850.9	History
PQ207-211	841.109	Poetry	PQ4057-4059	850.9	Biography
PQ226-307	841-848. + (3-914)09	Modern	PQ4064-4073	851-858.(109)	Medieval
PQ230-239	841-848.(309)	Renaissance/16th century	PQ4075	851-858.(209)	Renaissance
PQ241-251	841-848.(409)	17th century	PQ4077-4087	851-858. + (3-9)09	Modern
PQ261-276	841-848.(509)	18th century	PQ4091-4130	851.09	Poetry
PQ281-299	841-848. + (7-8)09	19th century	PQ4133-4160	852.009	Drama
PQ305-307	841-848.(909)	20th century	PQ4161-4185	858.0809	Prose
PQ400-491	841.9	History of Poetry	PQ4186-4199	398.20451	Folk literature
PQ411-443	841.(3-8)09	Modern (16-19th centuries)	PQ4201-4263	851-858.(008)	Collections
PQ500-558	842.009	Drama, History	PQ4207-4225	851.08	Poetry
PQ511-515	842.109	Medieval	PQ4227-4245	852.008	Drama
PQ516-558	842.(3-9)09	Modern	PQ4247-4263	858.0808	Prose

LC	Dewey	Descriptor
PQ4265-4556	851-858.(1)	Authors and works to 1400
PQ4561-4664	851-858.(2-5)	Individual authors (1400-1700)
PQ4675-4734	851-858.(5-8)	Individual authors (1701-1900)
PQ4800-4851	851-858.(9-914)	By author (20th century)
PQ5901-5991	851-858	Provincial/Local/Colonial
PQ6001-8921	860	Spanish literature
PQ6001-6167	861-868.(009)	History/Criticism
PQ6001	860.5	Serials
PQ6002	860.6	Societies/Congresses
PQ6003-6005	861-868.(008)	Collections
PQ6006	860.3	Encyclopedias
PQ6013-6020	860.7	Education
PQ6022-6030	861-868.(009)	Criticism
PQ6031-6167	860.9	History of literature
PQ6051-6055	860.9	Biography
PQ6057-6060	861-868. + (1-2)09	Early to 1500
PQ6063-6072	861-868. + (3-6)09	Modern
PQ6076-6098	861.09	Poetry
PQ6099-6029	862.009	Drama
PQ6131-6153	868.0809	Prose
PQ6155-6167	398.20461	Folk literature
PQ6171-6264	861-868.(008)	Collections
PQ6175-6215	861.08	Poetry
PQ6217-6239	862.008	Drama
PQ6247-6264	868.0808	Prose
PQ6271-6498	861-868.(1-3)	By author, To 1700
PQ6500-6576	861-868.(4-5)	By author, 1700-1868
PQ6600-6647	861-868.(5-6)	By author, 1868-
PQ7000-8921	861-868	Provincial/Local/Colonial
PQ7000-7011	861-868	Spain
PQ7020-8921	861-868	Outside of Spain
PQ7031-7061	861-868	Europe
PQ7071-8560	861-868	America
PQ7071-7079	861-838	United States and Canada
PQ7079	861-868	Individual authors
PQ7081-8560	861-868	Spanish America
PQ7100-7300	861-868	Mexico
PQ7296-7297	861-868	By author
PQ7310-7349	861-868	In the United States
PQ7361-7451	861-868	West Indies
PQ7370-7389	861-868	Cuba
PQ7389	861-868	Individual authors
PQ7400-7409	861-868	Dominican Republic
PQ7409	861-868	By author
PQ7420-7439	861-868	Puerto Rico
PQ7439	861-868	By author
PQ7451	861-868	Other islands
PQ7471-7539	861-868	Central America
PQ7480-7489	861-868	Costa Rica
PQ7489	861-868	By author
PQ7490-7499	861-868	Guatemala
PQ7499	861-868	By author
PQ7500-7509	861-868	Honduras
PQ7509	861-868	By author
PQ7510-7519	861-868	Nicaragua
PQ7519	861-868	By author
PQ7520-7529	861-868	Panama
PQ7529	861-868	By author
PQ7530-7539	861-868	El Salvador
PQ7539	861-868	By author
PQ7551-8549	861-868	South America
PQ7600-7799	861-868	Argentine Republic
PQ7797	861-868	By author
PQ7801-7819	861-868	Bolivia
PQ7819	861-868	By author
PQ7900-8099	861-868	Chile
PQ8097	861-868	By author
PQ8160-8179	861-868	Colombia
PQ8179	861-868	By author
PQ8200-8219	861-868	Ecuador
PQ8219	861-868	By author
PQ8230-8239	861-868	Guiana
PQ8239	861-868	By author
PQ8250-8259	861-868	Paraguay
PQ8259	861-868	By author
PQ8300-8499	861-868	Peru
PQ8496-8497	861-868	By author
PQ8510-8519	861-868	Uruguay
PQ8519	861-868	By author
PQ8530-8549	861-868	Venezuela
PQ8549	861-868	By author
PQ8600-8619	861-868	Africa
PQ8650-8911	861-868	Asia
PQ8700-8899	861-868	Philippine Islands
PQ8921	861-868	Australia/Pacific islands
PQ9001-9991	869	Portuguese literature
PQ9001-9128	869.09	History and criticism
PQ9000-9001	869.05	Serials
PQ9002-9003	869.06	Societies/Congresses
PQ9004-9006	869.08	Collections
PQ9008-9009.5	869.07	Education
PQ9010-9023	869.09	History
PQ9027-9033	869.09	Biography
PQ9035-9055	869.(1-4)09	By date
PQ9061-9081	869.109	Poetry
PQ9083-9095	869.2009	Drama
PQ9097-9119	869.80809	Prose
PQ9121-9128	398.20469	Folk literature
PQ9131-9187	869.08	Collections
PQ9149-9163	869.108	Poetry
PQ9164-9170	869.2008	Drama
PQ9172-9187	869.80808	Prose
PQ9191-9260	869.(1-2)	By author, To 1700
PQ9261	869.(3-4)	By author, 1701-
PQ9400-9991	869	Provincial/Local/Colonial
PQ9400-9411	869	Portugal
PQ9421-9991	869	Other countries
PQ9431-9470	869	Europe
PQ9471-9699	869	America
PQ9471-9479	869	United States/Canada
PQ9500-9699	869	Brazil
PQ9696-9697	869.(1-3)	By author, To 1800
PQ9901	869	Africa
PQ9951	869	Asia
PQ9991	869	Australia/Oceania
PR	820	English literature
PR1-56	820.9	Literary history/Criticism
PR1-3	820.5	Serials
PR5-7	820.6	Societies/Congresses
PR13-14	820.8	Collections
PR19	820.3	Dictionaries/Encyclopedias
PR31-55	820.7	Education
PR57-78	820.9	Criticism
PR81-990	820.9	History
PR111-116	820.928709	Women authors
PR161-479	820.(1-914)	By date
PR171-236	829	Anglo-Saxon to 1066
PR201-217	829.1	Poetry
PR221-236	829.8	Prose
PR251-369	821-828. + (1-2)009	Medieval/Middle (1066-1500)
PR311-369	821. (1-2)09	Poetry

LC	Dewey	Descriptor	LC	Dewey	Descriptor
PR321-347	821.032(1-2)09	Epics/Metrical	PR1215-1219	821.(5-6)08	18th century
PR351-369	821.04(1-2)09	Lyric	PR1221-1223	821.(7-8)08	19th century
PR401-479	821-828. + (3-914)009	Modern	PR1224-1227	821.(9-914)08	20th century
PR421-429	821-828.(3009)	Elizabethan era (1066-1500)	PR1241-1273	822.008	Drama
PR431-439	821-828.(4009)	17th century	PR1248-1259	822.0(2-57)008	Special types
PR441-449	821-828. + (5-6)009	18th century	PR1260-1273	822.(1-914)08	By date
PR451-469	821-828. + (7-8)009	19th century	PR1260-1261	822.108	Medieval
PR471-479	821-828. + (9914)009	20th century	PR1262	822.208	Pre-Shakespeare
PR500-681	821.09	Poetry	PR1263	822.308	Elizabethan era
PR500	821.005	Serials	PR1265.3-1266	822.408	17th century
PR505-508	821.09(1-9)	Special topics	PR1269	822.(5-6)08	18th century
PR521-611	821.(1-914)09	By date	PR1271	822.(7-8)08	19th century
PR521-529	821.(1-3)09	15th-16th centuries	PR1272	822.(9-914)08	20th century
PR531-539	821.309	Elizabethan era	PR1281-1309	828.08008	Prose (General)
PR541-549	821.409	17th century	PR1293-1307	828.(1-914)0808	By date
PR551-575	821.(5-6)09	18th century	PR1293	828.30808	16th century
PR581-595	821.(7-8)09	19th century	PR1295	828.40808	17th century
PR601-611	821.(9-914)09	20th century	PR1297	828.(5-6)0808	18th century
PR621-739	822.009	Drama	PR1301-1304	828.(7-8)0808	19th century
PR621	822.00(5/6)	Serials/Societies	PR1307	828.(9-914)0808	20th century
PR623	822.003	Dictionaries	PR1321-1329	825.01008	Oratory
PR631-635	822.0(2-57)009	Special forms/Topics	PR1330	828.03008	Diaries
PR641-739	822.(1-914)09	Drama (History/Critcism), By date	PR1341-1349	826.008	Letters
			PR1361-1369	824.008	Essays
PR641-644	822.109	Medieval	PR1490-6076	821-828.(1-914)	Literature by author/Date
PR646-649	822.2 (2-3)009	16th century	PR1490-1799	829	Anglo-Saxon literature
PR651-658	822.3009	Elizabethan era	PR1803-2165	821-828.(1)	Early/Middle English
PR671-698	822.4009	17th century	PR2199-3195	821-828.(3)	English Renaissance (1500-1640)
PR701-719	822.(5-6)009	18th century			
PR721-734	822.(7-8)009	19th century	PR3291-3785	821-828.(4-6)	17th-18th centuries
PR735-739	822. (9-914)009	20th century	PR3991-5990	821-828.(7-8)	19th century
PR750-888	828.08009	Prose	PR6000-6049	821-828.912	1900-1960
PR750	828.0800(5/6)	Serials/Societies	PR6050-6076	821-828.914	1961-
PR756	828.08009(1-9)	Special topics	PR8309-9680	821-828.	Provincial/Local
PR767-808	828.(1-914)08	By date	PR8309-8489	821-828	England
PR821-888	823.009	Fiction/The novel	PR8490-8499	891.6	Celtic
PR830	823.009(1-9)	By topic	PR8500-8697	821-828	Scotland
PR833-888	823.(1-914)09	By date	PR8700-8807	821-828	Ireland
PR833	823.209	16th century	PR8900-8997	821-828.	Wales
PR836-839	823.309	Elizabethan era	PR9080-9680	821-828	English literature abroad
PR841-844	823.409	17th century	PR9090-9170	821-828	Europe
PR851-858	823.(5-6)09	18th century	PR9175-9199	811-818	America
PR861-878	823.(7-8)09	19th century	PR9180-9199.3	811-818	Canada
PR881-888	823. (9-914)09	20th century	PR9200	811-818.	Mexico
PR901-907	825.01009	Oratory	PR9210-9275	811-818	West Indies
PR908	828.03009	Diaries	PR9280-9298	811-818	Central America
PR911-917	826.009	Letters	PR9300-9333	811-818	South America
PR921-927	824.009	Essays	PR9340-9408	811-818	Africa
PR931-937	827.009	Wit and humor	PR9420-9570	811-818.	Asia
PR951-981	398.2042	Folk literature	PR9600-9619.3	811-818	Australia
PR1098-1369	821-828.008	Collections	PR9620-9639.2	811-818	New Zealand
PR1110	821-828.89(1-9)	Authors (Special classes)	PR9645-9670	811-818	Oceania
PR1111	821-828.0803	Special topics	PS	810	American literature
PR1119-1150	821-828. + (1-914)08	By date	PS1-3	810.5	Serials
PR1120	821-828.(108)	Medieval	PS5-7	810.6	Societies/Congresses
PR1121-1125	821-828.(308)	Renaissance	PS21	810.3	Encyclopedias/Dictionaries
PR1127-1131	821-828.(408)	17th century	PS31	810.1	Philosophy
PR1134-1139	821-828. + (5-6)08	18th century	PS41-49	810.7	Education
PR1143-1145	821-828. + (7-8)08	19th century	PS55-79	810.9	Criticism
PR1148-1150	821-828. + (9-914)08	20th century	PS85-111	810.9	History
PR1170-1227	821	Poetry	PS85-96	811-828.(009)	English
PR1170	821.0(5/6)	Serials/Societies	PS102	841-848.(009)	French
PR1171-1174	821.08	Collections	PS106	831-838.(009)	German
PR1181-1195	821.0(2-8)09(1-9)	Special forms/Subjects	PS126-138	816/818.(009)	Biography/Memoirs/Letters
PR1203-1227	821.(1-914)08	By date	PS147-152	811-818.(99287)	Women authors
PR1207	821.308	Elizabethan era	PS153-490	811-818.(009)	History
PR1209-1213	821.408	17th century	PS163-169	811-818.(0803)	Special subjects

LC	Dewey	Descriptor
PT1141	831-838 + (9-914)08	20th century
PT1151-1241	831.08	Poetry
PT1163-1175	831.(1-914)08	By date
PT1163-1165	831.(3-5)08	15th-17th centuries
PT1167	831.608	18th century
PT1171-1173	831.(7-8)08	19th century
PT1174-1175	831.(9-914)08	20th century
PT1179-1181	831.03208	Epic poetry
PT1185	831.04408	Ballads
PT1187	831.0408	Lyric poetry
PT1229	831.08382	Religious poetry
PT1251-1299	832.08	Drama
PT1263-1268	832.(1-914)08	By date
PT1263	832.408	16th century
PT1264	832.508	17th century
PT1265	832.608	18th century
PT1266	832.(7-8)08	19th century
PT1268	832.(9-914)08	20th century
PT1271-1299	832.0(2-57)08	By type of drama
PT1271-1273	832.051208	Tragedies
PT1275-1277	832.052308	Comedies
PT1301-1318	838.08008	Prose
PT1313	838.40808	16th century
PT1314	838.80808	17th century
PT1315	838.60808	18th century
PT1316	838.70808	19th century
PT1318	838.(9-914)0808	20th century
PT1321-1340	833.008	Fiction
PT1332-1334	833.(1-914)08	By date
PT1332	833.(7-8)08	19th century
PT1334	833.(9-914)08	20th century
PT1337-1340	833.0108	Short stories
PT1344-1345	835.0108	Oratory
PT1348-1352	836.008	Letters
PT1354	834.008	Essays
PT1371-1372	830.(1-3)08	By date, to 1500
PT1375-1479	831-838.(208)	Middle High German-Collections
PT1391-1429	831.208	Poetry
PT1411-1418	831.03208	Epic poetry
PT1419	831.0408	Lyric poetry
PT1434-1477	832.(2-4)08	Drama (1300-1600)
PT1438-1477	832.0803	Special subjects
PT1479	838.08008	Prose
PT1501-2688	831-838.(9-914)	By author/Date
PT1501-1695	831-838.(2)	Middle High German (1050-1500)
PT1505	220.531092	The Bible
PT1701-1797	831-838.(4-5)	1500-1700
PT1799-2592	831-838.(6-7)	1700-1870
PT1891-2239	832.62	Goethe
PT2600-2653	831-838.(8-914)	1870-1960
PT2660-2688	831-838.(914)	1961-
PT3701-3971	831-838	Provincial/Colonial
PT3701-3807	831-838	Germany
PT3808-3971	831-838	Outside Germany
PT3810-3895	831-838	Europe
PT3810-3828	831-838	Austria
PT3830-3837.5	831-838	Czechoslovakia
PT3840-3848	831-838	Hungary
PT3850-3858	831-838	European Russia
PT3860	831-838	Switzerland
PT3900-3919	831-838	North America/United States
PT3951	831-838	Africa
PT3961	831-838	Asia
PT3971	831-838	Oceania

LC	Dewey	Descriptor
PT4801-4897	839.4	Low German literature
PT4801-4828	839.4(1-8)09	History/Criticism
PT4801	839.40(5/6)	Serials/Societies
PT4802	839.403	Encyclopedias/Dictionaries
PT4803	839.407	Education
PT4805-4814	839.409	History
PT4815	839.409	Collective biography
PT4817-4820	839.4109	Poetry
PT4821	839.4209	Drama
PT4823	839.4309	Fiction
PT4829-4830	398.204394	Folk literature
PT4831-4845	839.4(1-8)08	Collections
PT4834-4836	839.4108	Poetry
PT4837-4838	839.4208	Drama
PT4839-4845	839.4808008	Prose
PT4846-4897	839.4(1-3)	By author/Date
PT4846	839.41	To 1600
PT4847	839.42	17th-18th centuries
PT4848	839.42	19th century
PT4849	839.43	20th century
PT4851-4855	839.4(1-8)	Germany
PT4859	839.4(1-8)	Europe
PT4860-4869	839.4(1-8)	United States
PT4870	839.4(1-8)	Canada
PT4875-4877	839.4(1-8)	Spanish America
PT4880	839.4(1-8)	Africa
PT4885	839.4(1-8)	Asia
PT4887-4890	839.4(1-8)	Australia/New Zealand/ Oceania
PT5001-5980	839.31	Dutch literature
PT5001-5003	839.3105	Serials
PT5005-5007	839.3106	Societies/Congresses
PT5019	839.3103	Encyclopedias/Dictionaries
PT5021	839.3101	Theory
PT5029	839.3101	Philosophy/Esthetics
PT5040-5044	839.3107	Education
PT5050-5054	839.3109	Criticism
PT5060-5185	839.3109	History
PT5085-5095	839.31093	Special subjects
PT5100-5110	839.3109	Biography
PT5121-5185	839.31(1-64)	By date
PT5121-5137	839.311	Medieval to 1500
PT5141-5155	839.31(2-3)	16th-17th centuries
PT5160-5165	839.314	18th century
PT5170-5175	839.315	19th century
PT5180-5185	839.316	20th century
PT5201-5245	839.311	Poetry
PT5250-5295	839.312	Drama
PT5300-5336	839.31808	Prose
PT5351-5395	398.2043931	Folk literature
PT5400-5547	839.31(1-8)08	Collections
PT5420-5460	839.31(1-64)08	Collections, By date
PT5470-5488	839.31108	Collections, Poetry
PT5490-5515	839.31208	Collections, Drama
PT5517-5547	839.31808008	Collections, Prose
PT5535-5547	839.31(5/4/7)008	Oratory/Essays/Wit and humor
PT5555-5880	839.31(1-64)	By date/Author
PT5901-5903	839.31(1-8)	Provincial/Local, By place
PT5905-5907	839.31(1-8)	In Belgium (Pre-1830)
PT5910-5928	839.31(1-8)	Dutch East Indies
PT5931-5949	839.31(1-8)	Dutch West Indies
PT5950-5975	839.31(1-8)	North America
PT6000-6471	839.31(1-8)	Flemish, Post-1830
PT6000-6003	839.3105	Serials
PT6005-6007	839.3106	Societies/Congresses
PT6019	839.3103	Encyclopedias/Dictionaries

LC	Dewey	Descriptor
PT6021	839.3101	Theory
PT6029	839.3101	Philosophy
PT6040	839.3107	Education
PT6050	839.3109	Criticism
PT6060-6199	839.3109	History
PT6120-6130	839.31(1-64)09	By date
PT6140-6199	839.31(1-8)09	By form
PT6200-6230	398.209493	Folk literature
PT6300-6397	839.3108	Collections
PT6330-6340	839.31108	Poetry
PT6350-6360	839.31208	Drama
PT6365-6397	839.31808008	Prose
PT6400-6465	839.31(1-8)	By author
PT6500-6590	839.36	Afrikaans literature
PT6500	839.360(5/6)	Serials/Societies
PT6510-6530	839.3609	History
PT6540-6545	398.2043936	Folk literature
PT6550-6575	839.3608	Collections
PT6590	839.36	By author
PT7001-7099	839.(5-8)	Scandinavian literature
PT7001-7029	839.(5-8)09	History/Criticism
PT7035-7039	839.(5-8)07	Education
PT7045-7054	839.(5-8)09	Criticism
PT7051-7054	839.(5-8)(1-74)	By date
PT7060-7087	839.(6-8)09	History, By language
PT7075-7078	839.(5-8)(1-74)	By date
PT7080-7087	839.(5-8)(1-8)	By form
PT7088-7089	398.204395	Folk literature
PT7090-7099	839.(5-8)08	Collections
PT7093-7099	839.(5-8)(1-8)08	By form
PT7101-7338	839.6	Old Norse (Icelandic/ Norwegian)
PT7101-7129	839.609	History/Criticism
PT7135-7139	839.607	Education
PT7145-7149	839.609	Criticism
PT7150-7211	839.609	History
PT7150-7157	839.6	By language
PT7170-7174	839.6109	Poetry
PT7177-7211	839.6808009	Prose
PT7181-7188	839.609	Sagas
PT7195-7211	808.066(001-999)03961	Scientific/Learned
PT7220-7262	839.608	Collections
PT7230-7252	839.6108	Poetry
PT7255-7262	839.6808008	Prose
PT7261-7296	839.608	Sagas
PT7263-7296	839.6	Individual sagas/Histories
PT7269	839.6	Sagas of Icelandic families
PT7271-7272	839.6	Icelandic church sagas
PT7276-7279	839.6	Sagas of kings
PT7281	839.6	Sagas of Norwegian colonies
PT7282	839.6	Sagas of Denmark/Sweden
PT7285-7287	839.6	Mythical sagas
PT7288	398.2043961/839.63	Novels/Fairy tales
PT7298-7309	839.6080382	Religious works
PT7312-7318	808.066(001-999)03961	Scientific/Learned
PT7326-7338	839.6	By author (Pre-1540)
PT7351-7550	839.69	Modern Icelandic literature
PT7351-7418	839.6909	History/Criticism
PT7370-7373	839.6907	Education
PT7395-7402	839.69(1-4)09	History, By date
PT7410-7418	839.69(1-8)09	By form
PT7420-7438	398.20439691	Folk literature
PT7420-7426	398.2043969109	History of folk literature
PT7430-7438	398.20439691	Collections (Folk literature)
PT7451-7495	839.6908	Collections
PT7465-7467	839.69108	Poetry
PT7470-7477	839.69208	Drama
PT7480-7495	839.69808008	Prose
PT7485-7487	839.69308	Fiction
PT7500-7511	839.69(1-4)	By author/Date
PT7520-7521	839.69	Provincial
PT7525-7550	839.69	In other countries
PT7526-7545	839.69	North America
PT7581-7599	839.699	Faroese literature
PT7584	839.69909	Biography (Collected)
PT7586-7588	839.699	By date
PT7590-7592	839.699(1-8)	By form
PT7593-7596	839.69908	Collections
PT7601-8260	839.81	Danish literature
PT7601-7869	839.8109	History/Criticism
PT7640-7644	839.8107	Education
PT7650-7654	839.8109	Criticism
PT7660-7869	839.8109	History
PT7700-7710	839.8109	Biography/Etc.
PT7721-7760	839.81(1-74)09	By date
PT7721-7738	839.81109	Medieval to 1500
PT7741-7747	839.81(2-5)09	16th-18th centuries
PT7751-7756	839.81609	19th century
PT7760	839.81(1-74)09	20th century
PT7770-7795	839.81109	Poetry
PT7800-7832	839.81209	Drama
PT7835-7862	839.81808009	Prose
PT7847-7862	839.81309	Fiction
PT7900-7930	398.2043981	Folk literature
PT7950-8046	839.8108	Collections
PT7975-7994	839.81108	Poetry
PT7999-8020	839.81208	Drama
PT8021-8046	839.81808008	Prose
PT8022-8024	839.81308	Fiction
PT8050-8175	839.81(1-74)	By author/Date
PT8050	839.811	Medieval
PT8060-8098	839.81(2-5)	16th-18th centuries
PT8100-8167	839.816	19th century
PT8174-8175	839.81	20th century
PT8205-8207	839.81	Provincial
PT8210-8260	839.81	In other countries
PT8211-8229	839.81	West Indies/Virgin Islands
PT8231-8250	839.81	North America
PT8301-9155	839.82	Norwegian literature
PT8301-8574	839.8209	History/Criticism
PT8340-8344	839.8207	Education
PT8350-8354	839.8209	Criticism
PT8405-8415	839.8209	Biography/Etc.
PT8425-8450	839.82(1-74)09	By date
PT8460-8490	839.82109	Poetry
PT8500-8534	839.82209	Drama
PT8540-8567	839.82808009	Prose
PT8555-8567	839.82309	Fiction
PT8600-8635	398.2043982	Folk literature
PT8650-8733	839.8208	Collections
PT8675-8695	839.82108	Poetry
PT8699-8718	839.82208	Drama
PT8719-8722	839.82808008	Prose
PT8750-8961	839.82(1-74)	By author/Date
PT8750-8775	839.82(2-5)	16th-18th centuries
PT8800-8942	839.826	19th century
PT8949-8950	839.82(7-74)	20th century
PT9000-9094	839.83	Landsmaal/New Norwegian
PT9000-9019	839.8309	History/Criticism
PT9025-9055	839.8308	Collections
PT9064-9094	839.83	By author
PT9100-9155	839.82	Norwegian (Provincial/ Foreign)

LC	Dewey	Descriptor
PT9131-9150	839.82	North America
PT9201-9999	839.7	Swedish literature
PT9201-9499	839.709	History/Criticism
PT9240-9245	839.707	Education
PT9250-9254	839.709	Criticism
PT9260-9499	839.709	History
PT9305-9315	839.709	Biography/Etc.
PT9320-9370	839.7(1-74)09	By date
PT9320-9339	839.7109	Medieval to 1540
PT9345-9361	839.7(2-5)09	16th-18th centuries
PT9365-9367	839.7609	19th century
PT9368-9370	839.7(7-74)09	20th century
PT9375-9405	839.7109	Poetry
PT9415-9449	839.7209	Drama
PT9460-9492	839.7808009	Prose
PT9480-9492	839.7309	Fiction
PT9509-9542	398.209485	Folk literature
PT9509-9520	398.20439709	History
PT9525-9542	398.204397	Collections (Folk literature)
PT9550-9639	839.708	Collections
PT9580-9599	839.7108	Poetry
PT9605-9625	839.7208	Drama
PT9626-9630	839.7808008	Prose
PT9627-9630	839.7308	Fiction
PT9650-9881	839.7(1-74)	By author/Date
PT9650-9651	839.71	Medieval
PT9674-9715	839.7(2-5)	16th-18th centuries
PT9725-9850	839.76	19th century
PT9870-9875	839.7((7-74)	20th century
PT9950-9952	839.7	Provincial
PT9955-9999	839.7	In other countries
PT9960-9975	893.7	Finland
PT9980-9995	839.7	North America
PZ	808.83/811-899.(0809282)	Fiction/Juvenile Belles-letter
PZ1-4	813/823	Fiction in English
PZ5-90	811-899.(0809282)	Juvenile Belles-letters
PZ5-8.3	811-818/821-828+(0809282)	American/English
PZ8.72-.78	892.7(1-8) + 0809282	Arabic
PZ8.82-.88	895.1(1-8) + (0809282)	Chinese
PZ11-14.9	839.3(1/6)(1-8)+(0809282)	Dutch/Flemish/Afrikaans
PZ21-28	841-848.(0809282)	French
PZ31-38	831-838.(0809282)	German
PZ41-48	851-858.(0809282)	Italian
PZ49.2-.8	895.6(1-8) + (0809282)	Japanese
PZ50.52-.58	895.7(1-8) + (0809282)	Korean
PZ51-60.3	839.5(1-8) + (0809282)	Scandinavian
PZ61-68	891.7(1-8) + (0809282)	Russian
PZ69-70	891.85(1-8) + (0809282)	Polish
PZ71-78	861-868.(0809282)	Spanish
PZ81-88	869.(1-8) + (0809282)	Portuguese
Q	500	Science, General
Q1-9	505	Serials
Q10-101	506	Societies/Congresses
Q105	507.4	Museums/Exhibitions
Q115-116	508	Scientific voyages/Expeditions
Q121-123	503	Encyclopedias/Dictionaries
Q124.6-127.2	509	History
Q124.95	509.01	Ancient
Q124.97	509.02	Medieval
Q125-.2	509.(3-4)	Modern
Q127-.2	509.(4-9)	By place
Q141-143	509.2	Biography
Q145	502.5	Directories
Q147-149	502.3	As a profession
Q161.7	502.22	Pictorial works

LC	Dewey	Descriptor
Q174-175.3	501	Philosophy/Methodology
Q175.4-.55	303.483	Impact on society
Q177	501.2	Classification of the sciences
Q179	501.4	Terminology
Q179.9-180.7	507.2	Research
Q181-183.4	507	Education
Q183.9	502.85	Computers/Data processing
Q184-185.7	502.8	Instruments/Apparatus
Q300-385	003.5	Cybernetics
Q300	003.50(5/6)	Serials/Societies/Congresses
Q304	003.503	Dictionaries/Encyclopedias
Q305	003.509	History
Q316	003.507	Education
Q317-321	003.5	Bionics
Q334-336	006.3/003.52	Artificial intell./Perception
Q350-385	003.54	Information theory
QA	510	Mathematics
QA1	510.(5/6)	Serials/Societies/Congresses
QA5	510.3	Dictionaries/Encyclopedias
QA8-10.4	510.1	Philosophy
QA9-10.3	511.3	Mathematical logic
QA11-20	510.7	Education
QA21-27	510.9	History
QA22	510.93	Ancient
QA23	510.902	Medieval
QA24-26	510.90(3-4)	Modern
QA27	510.9(4-9)	By place
QA28-29	510.92	Biography
QA30	510.25	Directories
QA47-59	510.212	Tables
QA75-76.95	004/510.28	Calculating machines/Computers
QA75.5	004.0(5/6)/510.(5/6)	Serials/Societies/Congresses
QA76.15	004.03/510.3	Dictionaries/Encyclopedias
QA76.17	004.09/510.9	History
QA76.2	004.092/510.92	Biography
QA101-141.8	513	Elementary math/Arithmetic
QA150-272	512	Algebra
QA150	512.00(5/6)	Serials/Societies/Congresses
QA157	512.0076	Exercises/Examinations
QA159	512.007	Education
QA164-167.2	511.6	Combinatorial analysis
QA171	512.2	Theory of groups
QA184-205	512.5	Linear/Multilinear algebra
QA211-218	512.94	Equation theory
QA241-.7	512.7	Number theory
QA267-268.5	511.3	Machine theory
QA269-272	519.3	Game theory
QA273-274.76	519.2	Probabilities
QA276-280	519.5	Mathematical statistics
QA299.6-433	515	Analysis
QA303-316	515	Calculus
QA319-329.9	515.7	Functional analysis
QA370-379	515.35	Differential equations
QA401-425	515	Analytical methods
QA440-699	516	Geometry
QA451-469	516.2	Elementary geometry
QA474	516.05	Plane geometry
QA475	516.06	Solid geometry
QA501-521	516.6	Descriptive geometry
QA531-538	516.24	Trigonometry
QA551-563	516.3	Analytic geometry
QA564-608	516.35	Algebraic geometry
QA611-614.97	514	Topology
QA615-639	516.36	Infinitesimal geometry

LC	Dewey	Descriptor	LC	Dewey	Descriptor
QA641-660	516.36	Differential geometry	QB500.5-785	523.2	Solar system
QA801-939	531.01515	Analytical mechanics	QB520-544	523.7	Sun
QA801	531.015150(5/6)	Serials/Societies/Congresses	QB580-595	523.3	Moon
QA821-835	531.12	Statics	QB600-701	523.4	Planets
QA841-842	531.112	Kinematics	QB717-732	523.6	Comets
QA843-871	531.11	Dynamics	QB740-759	523.5	Meteors/Meteorites
QA901-930	531.38	Mechanics of deformable bodies	QB790-792	523.1125	Interstellar matter
			QB799-903	523.8	Stars
QA931-939	531.38	Elasticity/Plasticity	QB980-991	523.1(2)	Cosmology/Cosmogony
QB	520	Astronomy	QC	530	Physics
QB1	520.(5/6)	Serials/Societies/Congresses	QC1	530.0(5/6)	Serials/Societies/Congresses
QB2	520.74	Museums/Exhibitions	QC5	530.03	Dictionaries/Encyclopedias
QB4-.9	522.1	Observations	QC5.56-6.4	530.01	Philosophy/Methodology
QB7-9	528	Ephermerides	QC6.8	530.014	Terminology/Nomenclature
QB14	520.3	Dictionaries/Encyclopedias	QC6.9-9	530.09	History
QB14.5	520.1	Philosophy	QC9	530.09(4-9)	By place
QB15-34	520.9	History	QC15-16	530.092	Biography
QB16-22	520.901	Ancient	QC16.2	530.025	Directories
QB23	520.902	Medieval	QC19.2-20.85	530.15	Mathematical physics
QB28-33	520.90(3-4)	Modern	QC19.2	530.150(5/6)	Serials/Societies/Congresses
QB35-36	520.92	Biography	QC20.52-.54	530.1207	Education
QB51.5	520.23	As a profession	QC29	530.023	Physics as a profession
QB54	999	Extraterrestrial life	QC30-47	530.07	Education
QB61-62.7	520.7	Education	QC51	530.072	Laboratories
QB65	912	Atlases/Charts	QC52	530.0285	Computers/Data processing
QB81-84	522.1	Observatories	QC53	530.028	Instruments/Apparatus
QB82	522.19(1-9)	Observatories, By place	QC60	530.074	Museums/Exhibitions
QB84.5-115	522.2	Astronomical instruments	QC72-73.8	531.6	Force/Energy
QB121	522.6	Photography/Etc.	QC81-114	530.81	Weights/Measures
QB136	523.111	Space/Astronautics in	QC81	530.810(5/6)	Serials/Societies/Congresses
QB140-237	522.7	Practical/Spherical astronomy	QC81.5	530.81074	Museums/Exhibitions
			QC82	530.8103	Dictionaries/Encyclopedias
QB151-168	522.9	Correction/Reduction	QC83-86	530.8109	History
QB201-205	526.6	Geodetic astronomy	QC90.8-94	530.812	Metric system
QB209-224	529	Time (Sundials/Sunsets/Etc.)	QC100.5-.8	530.7	Measuring instruments
QB224.5-237	526.6	Longitude/Latitude	QC101-114	530.81	Measurement (Length/Area/Etc.)
QB275-343	526.1	Geodesy			
QB275	526.10(5/6)	Serials/Societies/Congresses	QC120-168.85	531-533	Experimental mechanics
QB279	526.103	Dictionaries/Encyclopedias	QC120	531.0(5/6)	Serials/Societies/Congresses
QB280.5	526.109	History	QC133-136	531.1	Dynamics
QB283	526	Mathematical theory of earth	QC138-168.85	532	Fluids/Fluid mechanics
			QC145.5-148.4	532.2	Hydrostatics/Floating bodies
QB297	526.10285	Computers/Data processing	QC150-159	532.5	Fluid/Hydrodynamics
QB297.9-298	526.1092	Biography	QC161-167	533.6	Gases/Pneumatics
QB301-328	526.3	Geodetic surveying	QC167.5-168.85	533.2	Gas dynamics/Motion of gases
QB330-339	526.7	Gravity determinations			
QB349-421	521	Theory/Celestial mechanics	QC170-197	539.7	Atomic physics
			QC170	539.70(5/6)	Serials/Societies/Congresses
QB361-407	521.4	Perturbations	QC172-173.4	530	Matter/Antimatter
QB361-389	523.4	Planetary theory	QC173.5-.65	530.11	Relativity
QB391-399	523.3	Lunar theory	QC173.68-.75	530.14	Field theory
QB401-407	523.9	Satellites	QC173.96-174.52	530.12	Quantum theory/Mechanics
QB421	521	Double star theory	QC174.2-.26	530.124	Wave mechanics
QB450	523.02	Cosmochemistry	QC174.3-.35	530.122	Matrix mechanics
QB460-466	523.01	Astrophysics (General)	QC174.4-.43	530.133	Quantum statistics
QB468-480	522.68	Non-optical methods	QC174.45-.52	530.143	Quantum field theory
QB470	522.68	Infrared astronomy	QC174.7-175.36	530.13	Statistical physics
QB471-.7	522.6862	Gamma ray	QC175-.16	533.7	Kinetic gas theory
QB472-473	522.6863	X-ray astronomy	QC175.2-.25	530.138	Transport theory
QB475-479.3	522.682	Radio astronomy	QC175.3-.36	532.5	Kinetic liquid theory
QB480	522.684	Radar astronomy	QC175.4-.45	530.42	Superfluid physics
QB495-991	520	Descriptive astronomy	QC176-.9	531	Solids/Solid-state physics
QB495	520.(5/6)	Serials/Societies/Congresses	QC176.82-.9	530.4175	Thin films
QB497	520.3	Dictionaries/Encyclopedias	QC221-246	534	Acoustics/Sound
QB498-.2	520.9	History	QC221	534.0(5/6)	Serials/Societies/Congresses
QB500.25-.268	500.5	Universe/Space sciences	QC226-227	534.07	Education

LC	Dewey	Descriptor
QC228	534.072	Laboratories
QC231	534.5	Vibrations/Wave motion
QC233	534.2	Propagation of sound
QC235-241	534.5	Vibrations
QC242-.4	534.23	Underwater acoustics
QC244	534.55	Ultrasonics
QC251-338.5	536	Heat
QC251	536.0(5/6)	Serials/Societies/Congresses
QC270-275	536.50287	Thermometers
QC290-297	536.6	Calorimeters
QC301-310	536.4	Change of state
QC310.15-319	536.7	Thermodynamics
QC319.8-338.5	536.2	Heat transfer
QC320.8-323	536.23	Conduction
QC326-330	536.25	Convection
QC331-338.5	536.3	Radiation/Absorption/Cooling
QC350-467	535	Optics/Light
QC350	535.0(5/6)	Serials/Societies/Congresses
QC363-366	535.07(2)	Education/Research
QC370.5-379	535.028	Optical instruments/Apparatus
QC391	535.220287	Photometery/Microphotometry
QC392-449	535.2	Physical optics
QC410.9-411	535.4	Interference
QC414.8-417	535.4	Diffraction
QC425-.4	535.323	Reflection
QC425.9-426.8	535.324	Refraction
QC440-446	535.52	Polarization
QC446.15-.3	535.(15/2)	Quantum/Nonlinear optics
QC447.9-448.2	621.3692	Fiber optics
QC449	535.4	Holography
QC450-464	535.84	Spectroscopy
QC474-496.9	539.2	Radiation physics
QC474	539.20(5/6)	Serials/Societies/Congresses
QC476.4-480.2	535.35	Luminescence
QC480.8-482.3	539.7222	X-rays
QC484.2-.6	539.7222	Bremsstrahlung
QC484.8-485.9	539.7223	Cosmic ray physics
QC494-496.9	535.6	Color
QC501-766	537-538	Electricity/Magnetism
QC501-718.8	537	Electricity
QC543-544	537.028	Instruments/Apparatus
QC570-596.9	537.2	Electrostatics/Friction
QC584-585.8	537.24	Dielectrics
QC601-625	537.6	Electric current
QC610.3-612	537.62	Electric conductivity
QC610.9-611.8	537.622	Semiconductor physics
QC630-648	537.6	Electrodynamics
QC660.5-678.6	537.534	Electric oscillations/Waves
QC669-675.8	537	Electromagnetism
QC676-678.6	537.534	Radio waves
QC679-680.5	537.67	Quantum electrodynamics
QC685-689.5	537.5	Quantum electronics
QC717.6-718.8	530.44	Plasma physics/Ionized gases
QC750-755.65	538	Magnetism
QC756.7-757.9	538.4	Magnets
QC770-798	539.7(2)	Nuclear/Particle physics
QC770	539.70(5/6)	Serials/Societies/Congresses
QC785.5-787	539.7028	Instruments/Apparatus
QC786.4-.8	621.483	Nuclear reactors for research
QC788-789.2	539.7072	Research
QC789.7-790.8	539.762	Nuclear fission
QC790.95-791.8	539.764	Nuclear fusion
QC791.9-792.8	539.7	Atomic energy
QC793-.5	539.72	Elementary particle physics
QC793.9-794.8	539.75	Nuclear interactions
QC794.95-798	539.752	Radioactivity/Substances
QC801-809	550	Geophysics/Cosmic physics
QC801	550.(5/6)	Serials/Societies/Congresses
QC811-849	538.7	Geomagnetism
QC811	538.70(5/6)	Serials/Societies/Congresses
QC825-826	538.78	Magnetic surveys
QC830-845	538.79	Magnetic observations
QC851-999	551.(5/6)	Meteorology/Climatology
QC851	551.50(5/6)	Serials/Societies/Congresses
QC854.2	551.5014	Terminology
QC855-857	551.509	History
QC858	550.50092	Biography
QC875.5-876.7	551.5028	Instruments
QC877-.5	551.632	Broadcasts/Warnings
QC878.5-879.59	551.5	Aeronomy
QC879.6-.8	551.511	Atmospheric chemistry
QC880-.4	551.52	Dynamic meteorology
QC881-.2	551.514	Atmospheric shells
QC882	551.5113	Pollutants (Dust/Smoke/Etc.)
QC883.7-.86	551.66	Micrometerology
QC884-.2	551.69	Paleoclimatology
QC885-896	551.54	Atmospheric pressure
QC901-913	551.52(5/7)	Temperature/Radiation
QC915-929	551.57	Aqueous vapor
QC915-917	551.571	Humidity/Hygrometry
QC920.7-921.6	551.576	Clouds
QC924.5-926.2	551.577	Rainfall
QC926.6-928.74	551.68	Weather/Cloud modification
QC930.5-959	551.518	Wind
QC940.6-959	551.55	Storms/Cyclones
QC960.5-969	551.56	Electrical phenomena
QC966-.7	551.5632	Lightning
QC968-.2	551.554	Thunderstorms
QC972.6-973.8	551.635	Radio meteorology
QC973.45-.8	551.6353	Radar meteorology
QC974.5-976	551.56	Meteorological optics
QC980-999	551.6	Climatology/Weather
QC980	551.60(5/6)	Serials/Societies/Congresses
QC982-994.9	551.65(1-9)	Geographic divisions
QC983-984	551.6573	United States
QC985-.5	551.6571	Canada
QC986	551.6572(8)	Mexico/Central America
QC987	551.65729	West Indies
QC988	551.658	South America
QC989	551.654	Europe
QC990	551.655	Asia
QC991	551.656	Africa
QC992-993	551.659(3-6)	Australia/New Zealand/ Oceania
QC993.5	551.6513	Tropics
QC993.6	551.65143	Mountains
QC993.7	551.65154	Arid/Desert areas
QC993.83-.9	551.65162	Ocean/Maritime meteorology
QC994.95-999	551.63	Weather forecasting
QD	540	Chemistry
QD1	540.(5/6)	Serials/Societies/Congresses
QD2	540.74	Museums/Exhibitions
QD4-5	540.3	Encyclopedias/Dictionaries
QD6	540.1	Philosophy
QD7	540.14	Terminology
QD11-18	540.9	History

LC	Dewey	Descriptor
QD18	540.9(4-9)	By place
QD21-22	540.92	Biography
QD23	540.25	Directories
QD23.3-26.5	540.112	Alchemy
QD39.5	540.23	As a profession
QD40-49	540.7	Education
QD51-63	542.1	Laboratories
QD71-142	543	Analytical chemistry
QD71	543.00(5/6)	Serials/Societies/Congresses
QD81-96	544	Qualitative analysis
QD101-117	545	Quantitative analysis
QD130-139	546.3	Technical analysis (Metals)
QD142	543.08	Water analysis
QD146-197	546	Inorganic chemistry
QD146	546.0(5/6)	Serials/Societies/Congresses
QD161-169	546.7	Nonmetals
QD171-172	546.3	Metals
QD181-197	546.(2-6)	Other elements
QD241-441	547	Organic chemistry
QD241	547.00(5/6)	Serials/Societies/Congresses
QD271-272	547.3	Organic analysis
QD273	541.37	Electrochemistry
QD300-315	547.4	Alphatic compounds
QD320-327	547.78	Carbohydrates
QD330-341	547.6	Aromatic compounds
QD375-377	547.76	Antibiotics
QD380-388	547.7	Polymers
QD390-395	547.611	Condensed benzene rings
QD399-406	547.59	Heterocyclic compounds
QD410-412	547.05	Organometallic compounds
QD415-441	574.192	Biological chemistry
QD450-731	541	Physical/Theoretical chemistry
QD450	541.0(5/6)	Serials/Societies/Congresses
QD462-.9	541.28	Quantum chemistry
QD463-464	541.242	Atomic/Nuclear weights
QD466-469	546	Chemical elements
QD501-505.5	541.39	Conditions/Law of reactions
QD506-508	541.33	Surface chemistry
QD510-536	541.36	Thermochemistry
QD540-549	541.34	Theory of solution
QD551-562	541.37	Electrochemistry/Electrolysis
QD601-608	541.38	Nuclear/Radiochemistry
QD625-655	541.382	Radiation chemistry
QD701-731	541.35	Photochemistry
QD901-999	548	Crystallography
QD901	548.0(5/6)	Serials/Societies/Congresses
QD911-915	548.(81/7)	Geometrical/Mathematical
QD921-932	548.(5/81)	Crystal growth/Structure
QD931-947	548.8	Crystals, Physical properties
QE	551	Geology
QE1	551.0(5/6)	Serials/Societies/Congresses
QE5	551.03	Dictionaries/Encyclopedias
QE6	551.01	Philosophy
QE7	551.014	Terminology
QE11-13	551.09	History
QE21-22	551.092	Biography
QE23	551.025	Directories
QE34	551.023	As a profession
QE36	526/912	Geological maps
QE40-48	551.07	Education
QE48.8	551.0285	Computers/Data processing
QE49	551.072	Laboratories
QE49.5	551.028	Instruments/Apparatus
QE51	551.074	Museums/Exhibitions
QE65-350.52	554-559	Geographical divisions
QE70	559.8(1/2)	Arctic regions/Greenland
QE71-217	557	North America
QE72-182	557.3	United States
QE81-182	557.(4-9)	By state
QE81-82	557.61	Alabama
QE83-84	557.98	Alaska
QE85-86	557.91	Arizona
QE87-88	557.67	Arkansas
QE89-90	557.94	California
QE91-92	557.88	Colorado
QE93-94	557.46	Connecticut
QE95-96	557.51	Delaware
QE97-98	557.53	District of Columbia
QE99-100	557.59	Florida
QE101-102	557.58	Georgia
QE103-104	557.96	Idaho
QE105-106	557.73	Illinois
QE109-110	557.72	Indiana
QE111-112	557.77	Iowa
QE113-114	557.81	Kansas
QE115-116	557.69	Kentucky
QE117-118	557.63	Louisiana
QE119-120	557.41	Maine
QE121-122	557.52	Maryland
QE123-124	557.44	Massachusetts
QE125-126	557.74	Michigan
QE127-128	557.76	Minnesota
QE129-130	557.62	Mississippi
QE131-132	557.78	Missouri
QE133-134	557.86	Montana
QE135-136	557.82	Nebraska
QE137-138	557.93	Nevada
QE139-140	557.42	New Hampshire
QE141-142	557.49	New Jersey
QE143-144	557.89	New Mexico
QE145-146	557.47	New York
QE147-148	557.56	North Carolina
QE149-150	557.84	North Dakota
QE151-152	557.71	Ohio
QE153-154	557.66	Oklahoma
QE155-156	557.95	Oregon
QE157-158	557.48	Pennsylvania
QE159-160	557.45	Rhode Island
QE161-162	557.57	South Carolina
QE163-164	557.83	South Dakota
QE165-166	557.68	Tennessee
QE167-168	557.64	Texas
QE169-170	557.92	Utah
QE171-172	557.43	Vermont
QE173-174	557.55	Virginia
QE175-176	557.97	Washington
QE177-178	557.54	West Virginia
QE179-180	557.75	Wisconsin
QE181-182	557.87	Wyoming
QE185-199	557.1	Canada
QE201-203	557.2	Mexico
QE210-217	557.28	Central America
QE220-226	557.29	West Indies
QE230-251	558	South America
QE260-287.8	554	Europe
QE289-319	555	Asia
QE320-339	556	Africa
QE340-349	559.(3-6)	Australia/New Zealand/ Oceania
QE350	559.89	Antarctic
QE351-399.2	549	Mineralogy
QE351	549.0(5/6)	Serials/Societies/Congresses

LC	Dewey	Descriptor	LC	Dewey	Descriptor
QE367-369	549.1	Determinative mineralogy	QE901	561.0(5/6)	Serials/Societies/Congresses
QE371	549.13	Mineralogical chemistry	QE914-932	551.7	Stratigraphic divisions
QE388	549.012	Classification	QE914	551.73	Precabrian
QE390-.2	553	Ore minerals	QE915-920	551.72	Paleozoic
QE392-394	553.8	Precious stones	QE921-924	551.76	Mesozoic
QE420-499	552	Petrology	QE925-931.3	551.78	Cenozoic
QE420	552.00(5/6)	Serials/Societies/Congresses	QE934-950	561.19(1-9)	Geographical divisions
QE443-456.5	552.09(1-9)	Geographical divisions	QE934	561.19981	Arctic regions
QE444-445	552.0973	United States	QE936-937	561.1973	United States
QE445.5-446	552.0971	Canada	QE938	561.1971	Canada
QE446.5-.6	552.0972	Mexico	QE939	561.1972	Mexico
QE447	552.09728	Central America	QE940	561.19729	West Indies
QE448	552.09729	West Indies	QE941	561.19728	Central America
QE449	552.098	South America	QE942	561.198	South America
QE451	552.094	Europe	QE943-945	561.194	Europe
QE452	552.095	Asia	QE946	561.195	Asia
QE453	552.096	Africa	QE947	561.196	Africa
QE453.5-454	552.0994	Australia	QE948	561.1994	Australia
QE454.5-.6	552.0993	New Zealand	QE948.2	561.1993	New Zealand
QE455	552.099(5-6)	Oceania	QE949	561.199(5-6)	Oceania
QE456	552.09981	Arctic regions	QE950	561.19989	Antarctic regions
QE456.5	552.09989	Antarctic regions	QE955-983	561.(2-93)	Systematic divisions
QE461-462	552.1	Igneous rocks/Volcanic ash	QE975-978	561.5/585	Gymnosperms/Pinophyta
QE471-.15	552.5	Sedimentary rocks	QE980-983	561.(3-4)/585.114	Angiospermophyta/
QE475	552.4	Metamorphic rocks			Magnoliophyta
QE500-625	551.(1-4/8)	Dynamic/Structural geology	QH	508/574	Natural history/Biology
QE500	551.10(5/6)	Serials/Societies/Congresses	QH1-278.5	508	Natural history
QE514-516.5	551.9	Geochemistry	QH1-7	508.0(5/6)	Serials/Societies/Congresses
QE517-.5	551.3	Dynamic geology	QH13	508.03	Dictionaries/Encyclopedias
QE521.5-527	551.21	Volcanoes	QH15-21	508.09	History
QE528	551.23	Geysers/Hot springs/Etc.	QH26-31	508.092	Biography
QE531-545	551.22	Earthquakes/Seismology	QH35	508.025	Directories
QE570	551.302	Weathering	QH46	508.0222	Pictorial works
QE571-597	551.303	Sedimentation	QH51-58	508.07	Education
QE598-600.3	551.307	Earth/Mass movements	QH61-63	579	Collecting/Preservation
QE601-613.5	551.8	Structural geology	QH68	635.9824	Terrariums/Vivariums
QE640-699	551.7	Stratigraphy	QH70	508.074	Museums/Exhibitions
QE640	551.700(5/6)	Serials/Societies/Congresses	QH75-77	333.72	Nature conservation
QE654-674	551.72	Paleozoic	QH83	508.014	Terminology
QE675-688	551.76	Mesozoic	QH84-198	508.3(1-3)	Geographical distribution
QE691-699	551.78	Cenozoic	QH84.8-89	508.314	Land
QE701-760	560	Paleontology	QH90-100	508.316(2-9)/574.92	Water/Aquatic biology
QE701	560.(5/6)	Serials/Societies/Congresses	QH91-95.59	574.92	Marine biology
QE724-742	560.17	Stratigraphic divisions	QH92-95.59	574.9(2-9)	Marine biology, By place
QE725-730	560.172	Paleozoic	QH92-93.9	574.921	Atlantic Ocean
QE731-734	560.176	Mesozoic	QH94-.7	574.927	Indian Ocean
QE736-741.3	560.178	Cenozoic	QH95-.55	574.925	Pacific Ocean
QE743-760	560.9(1-9)	Geographical divisions	QH95.56-.57	574.928	Arctic seas
QE744	560.9981	Arctic regions	QH95.58	574.924	Antarctic Ocean
QE746-747	560.973	United States	QH95.8	574.92142	Coral reefs
QE748	560.971	Canada	QH95.9	574.92169	Brackish/Saline water
QE749	560.972	Mexico	QH96-100	574.929	Freshwater biology/
QE750	560.9729(9)	West Indies/Bermuda			Limnology
QE751	560.9728	Central America	QH101-198	508.(4-9)	Topographical divisions
QE752	560.98	South America	QH104-105	508.73	United States
QE753-755	560.94	Europe	QH106-.2	508.71	Canada
QE756	560.95	Asia	QH107	508.72	Mexico
QE757	560.96	Africa	QH108	508.728	Central America
QE758-759	560.99(3-6)	Australia/New	QH109	508.729	West Indies
		Zealand/ Oceania	QH111-130	508.8	South America
QE760	560.9989	Antarctic regions	QH135-178	508.4	Europe
QE760.8-899	560	Paleozoology	QH179-193	508.5	Asia
QE760.8	560.(5/6)	Serials/Societies/Congresses	QH194-195	508.6	Africa
QE767	562	Plankton	QH197-198	508.9(3-6)	Australia/New
QE770-832	562-565	Invertebrates			Zealand/ Oceania
QE840.5-882	566-569	Chordata/Vertebrates	QH201-278.5	502.82/578	Microscopy
QE901-996.5	561	Paleobotany	QH201	502.820(5/6)	Serials/Societies/Congresses

LC	Dewey	Descriptor	LC	Dewey	Descriptor
QH211-212	502.82(2-5)	Microscopes	QK201-203	581.971	Canada
QH231-278.5	578.(6-9)	Preparation of objects	QK211	581.972	Mexico
QH301-705	574	Biology	QK215-222	581.9728	Central America
QH301	574.0(5/6)	Serials/Societies/Congresses	QK225-231	581.9729	West Indies
QH302.5	574.03	Dictionaries/Encyclopedias	QK241-273	581.98	South America
QH305-.2	574.09	History	QK281-339	581.97	Europe
QH314	574.023	As a profession	QK341-379	581.95	Asia
QH315-320	574.07	Education	QK353	581.953	Arabia
QH321-323.2	574.072	Laboratories/Stations	QK360-368	581.959	Southeast Asia
QH325	577	Origin/Beginning of life	QK381-424	581.96	Africa
QH327	574.999	Space biology	QK431-473	581.99(3-6)	Australia/New Zealand/Oceania
QH331	574.01	Philosophy			
QH359-425	575	Evolution	QK474-.3	581.9981	Arctic regions
QH401-411	575.2	Variation	QK474.4	581.9989	Antarctic regions
QH421-425	575.132	Hybridization	QK474.5	581.90913	Tropics
QH426-470	575.1	Genetics	QK474.8-495	582	Spermatophyta/Phanerogams
QH426	575.10(5/6)	Serials/Societies/Congresses			
QH443-450.5	575.13	Recombination mechanisms	QK474.8-480	582.1(6-7)	Trees/Shrubs
QH460-468	575.292	Mutations	QK494-.5	585	Gymnosperms
QH471-489	574.16	Reproduction	QK495	582.13	Angiosperms
QH491	574.3(32)	Development/Morphogenesis	QK504-635	586	Cryptogams
			QK520-532	587	Pteridophyta (Ferns)
QH499	574.31	Regeneration	QK532.4-563.7	588	Bryophyta/Bryology
QH501-531	574.1	Life (Growth/Respiration/Etc.)	QK564-580.5	589.(3-4)	Algae/Algology
			QK580.7-597.5	589.1	Lichens
QH540-549	574.5	Ecology	QK600-635	589.2	Fungi
QH540	574.50(5/6)	Serials/Societies/Congresses	QK640-673	581.4	Plant anatomy
QH543-.2	551.66/574.5222	Bio/Microclimatology	QK710-899	581.1	Plant physiology
QH545-549	574.5(3-7)	Influence of factors	QK825-830	581.16	Reproduction
QH573-705	574.87	Cytology	QK861-899	581.1334	Phytochemistry
QH573	574.870(5/6)	Serials/Societies/Congresses	QK900-989	581.5	Plant ecology
QH585-.5	574.87072	Research/Culture	QK900-.2	581.50(5/6)	Serials/Societies/Congresses
QH591-601.2	574.872	Cell structure	QK930-938	581.9(09-99)	Physiographic regions
QH604-.3	574.876	Cell regulation/Control	QK930-935	581.90916(2-9)	Water
QH605-.3	574.8762	Cell division	QK936-938	581.90914	Land
QH611-623	574.821(2)	Physical/Chemical properties	QK980-989	581.15	Evolution of plants
			QL	591	Zoology
QH631-647	574.876	Physiological properties	QL1	591.0(5/6)	Serials/Societies/Congresses
QH650-659	574.191	Physical/Chemical agent effects	QL7-9	591.03	Encyclopedias/Dictionaries
			QL10	591.014	Terminology
QH651	574.19153	Light	QL15-21	591.09	History
QH652-.7	574.1915	Radiation	QL26-31	591.092	Biography
QH653	574.1916	Temperature	QL35	591.025	Directories
QH671	574.8765	Pathology and death	QL46-.5	591.0222	Pictorial/Illustrations
QK	581	Botany	QL51-58	591.07	Education
QK1	581.0(5/6)	Serials/Societies/Congresses	QL61-67	579	Collecting/Preservation
QK7	581.03	Encyclopedias	QL69	591.072	Laboratories
QK9	581.03	Dictionaries	QL71	591.074	Museums/Exhibitions
QK10	581.014	Terminology	QL73-77.5	590.744	Menageries/Zoological gardens
QK15-21	581.09	History			
QK26-31	581.092	Biography	QL78-79	597.0074	Public aquariums
QK35	581.025	Directories	QL81.5-84.28	333.9516	Wildlife conservation
QK51-57	581.07	Education	QL88-.5	560	Extinct animals/Fossils
QK71-73	580.744	Botanical gardens	QL100	591.69	Poisonous animals
QK75-77	580.742	Herbariums	QL101-345	591.9(09-99)	Geographical distribution
QK78-.5	581.72	Laboratories	QL111-118	591.90914	Land
QK79-.5	581.074	Museums	QL120-149	591.90916(2-9)	Water
QK86	333.953	Conservation	QL126	591.9091632	Arctic Ocean
QK91-97	581.012	Classification	QL126.5	591.909167	Antarctic Ocean
QK98-.3	581.0222	Pictorial/Illustrations	QL127-135	591.909163	Atlantic
QK98.5	581.632	Edible plants	QL137	591.909165	Indian Ocean
QK98.7	581.64	Dye plants	QL138	591.909164	Pacific Ocean
QK100	581.69	Poisonous plants	QL139	591.909169	Brackish water
QK101-474.5	581.9(09-99)	Geographical distribution	QL141-149	591.909169(2-8)	Fresh water
QK102-105	581.92	Aquatic	QL150-345	591.9(3-9)	Topographical divisions
QK115-195	581.973	United States	QL155-215	591.973	United States
QK145-195	581.97(4-9)	By state	QL159-215	591.97(4-9)	By state

LC	Dewey	Descriptor
QL219-221	591.971	Canada
QL225	591.972	Mexico
QL227	591.9728	Central America
QL229	591.9729	West Indies
QL235-251	591.98	South America
QL253-298	591.94	Europe
QL300-334	591.95	Asia
QL336-337	591.96	Africa
QL338-345	591.99(3-6)	Australia/New Zealand/ Oceania
QL362-599.82	592	Invertebrates
QL366-369.2	593.1	Protozoa
QL371-374.2	593.4	Porifera (Sponges)
QL375-379	593.5	Coelenterata
QL380-.8	593.8	Ctenophora
QL381-385.2	593.9	Echinodermata
QL386-394	595.1	Worms
QL401-432	594.6	Mollusca
QL434-599.82	595.2	Arthropoda
QL449.5-.65	595.6(1/2)	Millipedes/Centipedes
QL451-459.2	595.4	Arachnida (Spiders/ Scorpions)
QL461-599.82	595.7	Insects
QL605-739.3	597-599	Vertebrates/Chordates
QL605	597-599.00(5/6)	Serials/Societies/Congresses
QL614-639.6	597	Fishes
QL640-666	597.9	Reptiles
QL667-668	597.6	Amphibians
QL671-699	598	Birds
QL700-739.3	599	Mammals
QL750-795	591.51	Animal behavior
QL750	591.510(5/6)	Serials/Societies/Congresses
QL753-755.5	591.52	Seasonal habits
QL758-.5	591.5(3/6)	Predation/Agression
QL799	591.4	Morphology
QL801-950.9	591.4	Anatomy
QL801	591.40(5/6)	Serials/Societies/Congresses
QL821-831	591.47	Muscular/Skeletal
QL835-841	591.41	Vascular system
QL845-855	591.42	Respiratory organs
QL856-867	591.43	Digestive organs
QL871-881	591.4(4-6)	Urogenital system
QL921-938	591.48	Nervous system
QL945-949	591.48	Sense organs
QL950-.9	591.49	Regional anatomy
QL951-991	574.33	Embryology
QL951	574.330(5/6)	Serials/Societies/Congresses
QM	611	Human anatomy
QM1	611.00(5/6)	Serials/Societies/Congresses
QM 7	611.003	Dictionaries/Encyclopedias
QM11	611.009	History
QM16	611.0092	Biography
QM17	611.0025	Directories
QM25	611.00222	Pictorial works
QM30-33.3	611.007	Education
QM41-43	611.0072	Laboratories
QM51	611.0074	Museums/Exhibitions
QM81	611.0014	Terminology
QM100-170	611.7(1-5)	Musculoskeletal system
QM105-117	611.71	Skeleton/Osteology
QM151-170	611.73	Muscles
QM178-197	611.1	Vascular system
QM251-265	611.2	Respiration/Voice organs
QM301-367	611.3	Digestive organs
QM368-371	611.4	Glands
QM401-421	611.6	Urinary/Reproductive organs

LC	Dewey	Descriptor
QM451-471	611.8(1-3)	Nervous system
QM481-495	611.77	Integument
QM501-511	611.8(4-8)	Sense organs
QM535-549	611.9	Regions of the body
QM550-577.8	611.018	Histology
QM550	611.0180(5/6)	Serials/Societies/Congresses
QM601-695	611.013	Embryology
QP	612	Physiology
QP1	612.00(5/6)	Serials/Societies/Congresses
QP11	612.003	Dictionaries/Encyclopedias
QP13	612.0014	Terminology
QP21	612.009	History
QP25-26	612.0092	Biography
QP39-47	612.007	Education
QP51-53	612.0072	Laboratories
QP54-55	612.0028	Instruments/Technique
QP82-.2	612.0144	Physiological adaptation
QP84-87	612.6(5-8)	Growth to death
QP91-99.5	612.11	Blood
QP101-110	612.13	Circulation system
QP111-114	612.17	Heart
QP115	612.42	Lymphatic system
QP121-124	612.2	Respiratory organs
QP135	612.01426	Body temperature/ Regulation
QP136-139	612.391	Hunger/Thirst/Etc.
QP141-185.3	612.3	Nutrition
QP145-159	612.3(1-6)	Physiology of digestive tract
QP186-188.5	612.4	Glands/Endocrinology
QP190-246	612.(4/7921)	Secretions (Milk/Sweat)
QP247-285	612.(46/6)	Urinary/Reproductive organs
QP248-250.8	612.46	Urinary organs
QP251-285	612.6	Reproduction/Physiology of sex
QP301-321	612.7(4-6)	Musculoskeletal system
QP351-495	612.8	Neurophysiology/ Psychology
QP351	612.80(5/6)	Serials/Societies/Congresses
QP361-430	612.81	Nervous system
QP376-430	612.82	Brain
QP431-495	612.8(4-8)	Senses
QP460-471	612.85	Hearing/Equilibrium
QP474-495	612.84	Vision
QP501-801	612.015	Animal biochemistry
QP531-535	612.01524	Inorganic substances
QP550-801	612.0157	Organic substances
QP551-619	612.01575	Proteins/Amino acids
QP561-563	612.01575	Amino acids
QP571-572	612.405	Hormones
QP601-619	612.0151	Enzymes
QP620-625	612.01579	Nucleic acids
QP670-671	612.01528	Pigments
QP701-702	612.01578	Carbohydrates
QP751-752	612.01577	Lipids
QP771-772	612.399	Vitamins
QP901-981	612.0158	Experimental pharmacology
QP901	612.01580(5/6)	Serials/Societies/Congresses
QR	576/616.01	Microbiology
QR1	576/616.010 + 0(5/6)	Serials/Societies/Congresses
QR9	576/616.010(03)	Dictionaries/Encyclopedias
QR11	576/616.010(014)	Terminology
QR12	576/616.010(012)	Classification
QR21-22	576616.010(09)	History
QR30-31	576/616.010(092)	Biography
QR46-47	616.01	Medical/Etc. microbiology

LC	Dewey	Descriptor	LC	Dewey	Descriptor
RA421-790.85	613/614.(4-5)	Prevention/Public health	RA794	613.122	Health resorts/Spas/Etc.
RA421	613/614.(4-5) + 0(5/6)	Serials/Societies	RA801-954	613.109(3-9)	By place
RA422	613/614.(4-5) + (06)	Congresses	RA801-844	613.109(7/8)	America
RA423	613/614.(4-5) + (03)	Dictionaries/Encyclopedias	RA802-816	613.1097	North America
RA424	613/614.(4-5) + (09)	History	RA804-807	613.10973	United States
RA424.4-.5	613/614.(4-5) + (092)	Biography	RA809-810	613.10971	Canada
RA428-.5	613/614.(4-5) + (072)	Public health laboratories	RA811-812	613.10972	Mexico
RA430	613/614.(4-5) + (076)	Examinations	RA813-814	613.109728	Central America
RA437-438	613/614.(4-5) + (074)	Museums/Exhibitions	RA815-816	613.109729	West Indies
RA440-.8	613/614.(4-5) + (07)	Education	RA817-844	613.1098	South America
RA440.85	613/614.(4-5) + (072)	Research	RA845-887	613.1094	Europe
RA440.9	613/614.(4-5) + (023)	The profession	RA891-934	613.1095	Asia
RA441-.5	613/614.(4-5) + (09)	World health	RA943-949	613.1096	Africa
RA443-558	613/614.(4-5) + 09(3-9)	By place	RA951-952	613.10994	Australia
RA443-482	613/614.(4-5) + 09(7-8)	America	RA952.5	613.10993	New Zealand
RA443-456	613/614.(4-5) + (097)	North America	RA953-954	613.1099(5-6)	Pacific Islands
RA445-448.5	613/614.(4-5) + (0973)	United States	RA960-998	362.1(1-2)	Medical centers/Hospitals
RA449-450	613/614.(4-5) + (0971)	Canada	RA960	362.110 (5/6)	Serials/Societies
RA450.5-482	613/614.(4-5) + (098)	Latin America	RA961	362.1106	Congresses
RA451-452	613/614.(4-5) + (0972)	Mexico	RA962.2	362.11014	Terminology
RA453-454	613/614.(4-5) + (09728)	Central America	RA964	362.1109	History
RA455-456	613/614.(4-5) + (09729)	West Indies	RA964.5	362.11072	Research
RA457-482	613/614.(4-5) + (098)	South America	RA966	362.12	Medical centers/Clinics
RA483-523	613/614.(4-5) + (094)	Europe	RA967-971.8	362.11	Hospitals
RA525-541	613/614.(4-5) + (095)	Asia	RA968	362.11028	Equipment
RA545-552	613/614.(4-5) + (096)	Africa	RA971.3	362.110681	Finance/Business management
RA561-563	613/614.(4-5) + (089)	By ethnic group/Etc.			
RA564.5-.9	613/614.(4-5) + (04)	By age group/Class/Etc.	RA971.35	362.110683	Personnel management
RA565-600	628	Environmental health	RA977-979	362.11025	Directories
RA601-602	363.192	Food and public health	RA980-993	362.1109	Medical facilities, By place
RA604-618	363.729(2/4)	Parks/Public baths/Etc.	RA981-982	362.110973	United States
RA619-636.7	614.6	Undertaking/ Cemeteries/ Etc.	RA983	362.110971	Canada
			RA984	362.1109(7-8)	Other American areas
RA638	614.47	Immunization & public health	RA985-989	362.11094	Europe
			RA986-988	362.110941	Great Britain
RA639-642	614.4(3-8)	Transmission of disease	RA990	362.11095	Asia
RA643-645	614.(44-59)	Disease and public health	RA990.5	362.1109174927	Arab countries
RA645.3-.37	362.14	Home health care services	RA991	362.11096	Africa
RA645.5-.8	362.18	Emergency medical services	RA992-.3	362.110994	Australia
RA646-648.3	363.3(49 8/5)	War and public health	RA992.5-.7	362.110993	New Zealand
RA648.5-653	614.4	Epidemics	RA993	362.11099(5-6)	Oceania
RA650-653.5	614.409(4-9)	By place	RA995	362.188	Ambulance service
RA650.5-.55	614.409(7-8)	America	RA997-998	362.16	Nursing homes/Extended care
RA650.6	614.4094	Europe			
RA650.7	614.4095	Asia	RA1001-1171	614.1	Forensic medicine
RA650.8	614.4096	Africa	RA1001	614.10(5/6)	Serials/Societies
RA650.9	614.4099 (3-6)	Australia/New Zealand/ Oceania	RA1016	614.106	Congresses
			RA1017	614.103	Dictionaries/Encyclopedias
RA655-758	614.46	Quarantine	RA1018.5	614.1021	Statistics
RA664-758	614.4609 (4-9)	By place	RA1021-1022	614.109	History
RA664-677	614.46097	North America	RA1025	614.1092	Biography
RA665-667	614.460973	United States	RA1027	614.107	Education
RA671	614.460971	Canada	RA1028	614.10202	Outlines
RA673	614.460972	Mexico	RA1032-1038	614.1072	Laboratories
RA675	614.4609728	Central America	RA1042-.2	614.1074	Museums/Exhibitions
RA677	614.4609729	West Indies	RA1055-1056	347.067/614.1	Medicolegal exam/ Testimony
RA678-699	614.46098	South America			
RA700-737	614.46094	Europe	RA1056.5	346.0332	Malpractice
RA738-751	614.46095	Asia	RA1063-.4	616.078	Death determination/Etc.
RA753-755	614.46096	Africa	RA1071-1081	617.18	Asphyxia
RA756-.5	614.46099(3-4)	Australia/New Zealand	RA1085	617.11	Burns
RA758	614.46099(5-6)	Pacific islands	RA1091	617.122	Electricity
RA761-766	614.48	Disinfection/Sterilization	RA1101	612.014465	Cold
RA771-.7	614.091734	Rural health and hygiene	RA1116	616.399	Starvation
RA773-788	613	Personal health and hygiene	RA1121	617.14	Wounds/Injuries/Accidents
RA791-954	613.11	Climatology/Meteorology	RA1122-.5	364.1555	Assault/Battery
RA791-.2	613.10(5/6)	Serials/Societies/Congresses	RA1123	364.152	Homicide

LC	Dewey	Descriptor	LC	Dewey	Descriptor
RA1136	364.1522	Suicide	RC168.M8	616.313	Mumps
RA1141	364.153	Sexual offenses/Diseases/ Etc.	RC171-179	616.9232	Plague (Bubonic)
RA1148	614.1	Forensic psychology	RC180-181	616.835	Poliomyelitis
RA1151	614.1	Forensic psychiatry	RC182.R4	616.991	Rheumatic fever
RA1190-1270	615.9	Toxicology/Poisons	RC182.R8	616.916	Rubella/German measles
RA1195-1197	615.9009	History	RC182.S12	616.927	Salmonella infections
RA1198-.3	615.9007	Education	RC182.S2	616.917	Scarlet fever
RA1199	615.90072	Research	RC183-.9	616.912	Smallpox
RA1215.5-.52	615.90021	Statistics	RC185	616.9318	Tetanus
RA1221-1223	615.907	Examination for poisons	RC187-197	616.9272	Typhoid fever
RA1229	615.902	Industrial toxicology	RC199-.9	616.9222	Typhus
RA1230-1270	615.9(1-54)	Poisons, By type	RC200-203	616.951	Venereal diseases
RA1230-1231	615.92	Inorganic poisons	RC204	616.204	Whooping cough
RA1235-1242	615.95	Organic poisons	RC206-216	616.928	Yellow fever
RA1245-1247	615.91	Gaseous poisons	RC254-282	616.992	Neoplasms/Tumors/ Oncology
RA1250	615.952	Vegetable poisons	RC306-320.5	616.995	Tuberculosis
RA1255	615.94	Animal poisons	RC321-571	616.8	Neurology/Psychiatry
RA1258-1260	615.954	Food poisons	RC346-429	616.8	Neurology
RB	616.07	Pathology	RC435-571	616.89	Psychiatry
RB1	616.0700(5/6)	Serials/Societies	RC475-489	616.8914	Psychotherapy
RB3	616.07006	Congresses	RC490-499	616.89162	Hypnotism/Suggestion therapy
RB10	616.070025	Directories	RC500-510	616.8917	Psychoanalysis
RB15-.2	616.07009	History	RC512-571	616.89	Psychopathology
RB16-17	616.070092	Biography	RC512-528	616.89(2-8)	Psychoses
RB24-33	611. (018)	Pathological anatomy/ Histology	RC530-552	616.852	Neuroses
RB37-55.2	616.075	Clinical/Laboratory pathology	RC554-569.5	616.858	Personality disorders
RB57	616.0759	Autopsies	RC569.7-571	616.8588	Mental retardation
RB113	612	Physiological pathology	RC581-951	616	Internal medicine specialities
RB115	616.070014	Terminology	RC581-606	616.97	Immunological diseases
RB119	616.070076	Examinations	RC627.5-632	616.39	Metabolic diseases
RB120	616.0700202	Outlines	RC620-627	616.39	Nutritional diseases
RB123-124	616.07007	Education	RC627.5-632	616.39	Metabolic diseases
RB127-150	616.047	Manifestations of diseases	RC633-647.5	616.15	Blood diseases
RB127	616.0472	Pain	RC648-665	616.4	Endocrine gland diseases
RB131	616.0473	Inflammation	RC666-701	616.1	Cardiovascular diseases
RB140-.5	616.47	Growth disorders	RC666	616.100(5/6)	Serials/Societies
RB151-214	616.071	Theories of disease/ Etiology	RC666.2	616.1006	Congresses
RB153-154	616.047	Infection (And resistance)	RC666.3	616.1003	Dictionaries/Encyclopedias
RB155	616.042	Heredity/Medical genetics	RC666.5	616.1009	History
RB157	616.(1-9)	Acquired disease	RC666.7-.72	616.10092	Biography
RB210-212	613.04	Age/Sex influence on disease	RC669.9	616.107	Pathology
			RC670-.5	616.1075	Examination/Diagnosis
RC	616	Internal medicine	RC674	610.73691	Cardiovascular disease nursing
RC41	616.003	Dictionaries/Encyclopedias	RC681-688	616.12	Diseases of the heart
RC49-52	616.08	Psychosomatic medicine	RC682.9	616.1207	Pathology
RC71-78.7	616.075	Examination/Diagnosis	RC683-.5	616.12075	Examination/Diagnosis
RC81-82	616.024	Popular medicine	RC683.8-684	616.1206	Therapeutics
RC86-88.9	616.025	Medical emergencies	RC685	616.12 (2-9)	Individual diseases (Heart)
RC91-103	616.989	Diseases by physical agents	RC687	616.12043	Congenital anomalies
RC110-216	616.9	Infectious/Parasitic diseases	RC688	616.96	Parasites
RC114-.7	616.92(2/5)	Rickettsial diseases/Viruses	RC691-701	616.13	Diseases of the blood vessels
RC115-116	616.92	Bacterial diseases	RC691.4	616.1307	Pathology
RC118-.7	616.93	Spirochetal/Protozoan diseases	RC691.5-.6	616.13075	Examination/Diagnosis
RC119-.7	616.96	Parasitic diseases	RC692-700	616.1(1-8)	Diseases
RC125	616.914	Chicken pox	RC701	616.13043	Congenital anomalies
RC126-134	616.932	Cholera	RC705-779	616.2	Respiratory system diseases
RC138-.9	616.9313	Diphtheria	RC711	616.207	Pathology
RC140	616.935	Dysentery	RC733-734	616.2075	Examination/Diagnosis
RC148	616.953	Hydrophobia/Rabies	RC735	616.206	Special therapies
RC150-.9	616.203	Influenza	RC735.5	610.73692	Nursing
RC154-.9	616.998	Leprosy	RC737-.5	616.2	Apnea
RC156-166	616.9362	Malaria	RC742	616.2	Empyema
			RC746	616.201	Croup

LC	Dewey	Descriptor
RC751	616.25	Pleurisy
RC754	616.27	Diseases of the mediastinum
RC756-776	616.24	Diseases of the lungs
RC778	616.23	Diseases of the bronchi
RC779	616.2(01-49)	Other respiratory diseases
RC799-869	616.33	Gastroenterology
RC799	616.3300 (5/6)	Serials/Societies
RC802.9	616.3307	Pathology
RC803-805	616.33075	Examination/Diagnosis
RC805	616.330028	Instruments/Etc.
RC810	616.31	Visceroptosis/ Splanchnoptosis
RC815-.6	616.31	Diseases of the mouth
RC815.7	616.32	Diesases of the esophagus
RC816-840	616.3 (3-4)	Stomach/Duodenum diseases
RC845-858	616.362	Diseases of the liver/Etc.
RC846.9	616.3607	Pathology
RC847	616.36075	Examination/Diagnosis
RC848-858	616.36(2-5)	Individual diseases (Liver)
RC860-862	616.34	Diseases of the intestines
RC861	616.3428	Constipation
RC862	616.34(2-4)	Other diseases
RC864-866	616.35	Proctology
RC870-923	616.6	Urology
RC870	616.600(5/6)	Serials/Societies
RC870.9-.92	616.60092	Biography
RC873	616.60076	Examinations/Problems
RC873.9	616.607	Pathology
RC874	616.6075	Examination/Diagnosis
RC875-899.5	616.6(5/8)	Diseases/Disorders of genitals
RC881.5-883.5	616.65043	Congenital anomalies
RC884	618.175	Climacteric
RC888	613.94	Male contraception
RC889	616.692	Impotence/Infertility
RC892	616.62	Diseases of the urethra
RC894	616.66	Diseases of the prepuce
RC896	616.66	Diseases of the penis
RC897	616.67	Diseases of the scrotum
RC898-.3	616.68	Diseases of the testes/Etc.
RC899	616.65	Diseases of the prostate
RC900-923	616.63	Diseases of the urinary organs
RC900.9	616.6307	Pathology
RC901	616.63075	Examination/Diagnosis
RC901.5-.7	616.630028	Instruments/Etc.
RC901.8	616.624	Urinary tract infections
RC902-918	616.61	Diseases of the kidneys
RC902.A1	616.6100(5/6)	Serials/Societies
RC902.A2	616.61006	Congresses
RC903.9	616.6107	Pathology
RC904	616.61075	Examination/Diagnosis
RC905	616.63	Albuminuria/Etc.
RC907	616.612	Nephritis/Etc.
RC912	616.633	Pyuria
RC915	616.635	Uremia
RC916	616.622	Urinary calculi
RC919-921	616.62	Diseases of the bladder
RC921	616.62(2-4)	Individual bladder diseases
RC922	616.61	Diseases of the ureters
RC923	616.63043	Congenital anomalies
RC924-.5	616.77	Connective tissue diseases
RC925-935	616.7	Musculoskeletal system disease
RC952-954.6	618.97	Geriatrics
RC955-958	616.9881	Arctic medicine
RC960-962	616.9883	Tropical medicine
RC963-969	616.9803	Industrial medicine
RC970-971	616.98023	Military medicine
RC981-986	616.98024	Naval medicine
RC1000-1015	616.98022	Submarine medicine
RC1030-1160	616.9802	Travel/Transportation medicine
RC1200-1245	617.1027	Sports medicine
RD	617	Surgery
RD1	617.00(5/6)	Societies/Serials
RD9	617.005	Yearbooks
RD9.2	617.006	Congresses
RD10	617.0025	Directories of surgeons
RD16	617.0014	Nomenclature/Etc.
RD17	617.003	Dictionaries/Encyclopedias
RD19-27.3	617.09	History
RD22	617.0901	Primitive
RD23	617.0901	Ancient
RD25	617.0902	Medieval
RD27	617.090(3-4)	Modern
RD27.3	617.09(4-9)	By place
RD27.34-.35	617.092	Biography
RD27.4-.44	617.023	Practice of surgery/ Economics
RD27.42-.44	617.023(4-9)	By place
RD27.42-.43	617.02373	United States
RD27.43	617.0237(4-9)	By state
RD27.44	617.023(4-9)	Other areas
RD27.5	617.023	Profession of surgery
RD27.7	174.2	Surgical ethics
RD28	617.007	Education
RD29-.5	617.0072	Research/Experimentation
RD32-33.9	617.91	Operative surgery
RD49-52	617.919	Pre/Post operative care
RD57	617.07	Surgical pathology
RD58	617.919	Processes after operations
RD59	617.21	Surgical/Traumatic shock
RD63-73	617.917	Operating rooms/ Instruments
RD78.3-87.3	617.96	Anesthesiology
RD91-.5	617.9101	Sterilization (Operative)
RD92-97.8	617.026	Emergency surgery
RD98-.4	617.01	Surgical complications
RD99-.35	610.73677	Surgical nursing
RD101-103	617.15	Fractures (General)
RD118-120.5	617.95	Plastic surgery
RD120.7-129.5	617.95	Transplantation
RD130	617.95	Prosthesis/Artificial organs
RD151-498	617.99	Military/Naval surgery
RD156	617.044	War wounds
RD200-498	617.9909(3-9)	By place
RD200-214	617.990973	United States
RD216	617.990971	Canada
RD221	617.990972	Mexico
RD224-225	617.9909728	Central America
RD231-232	617.9909729	West Indies
RD235-267	617.99098	South America
RD268-441	617.99094	Europe
RD445-476	617.99095	Asia
RD481-489	617.99096	Africa
RD493	617.990994	Australia
RD493.5	617.990993	New Zealand
RD498	617.99099(5-6)	Oceania
RD520-599.5	617.4	Surgery by system/Organ
RD651-678	616.992	Neoplasms/Tumors/ Oncology

LC	Dewey	Descriptor	LC	Dewey	Descriptor
RD680-688	617.47	Locomotor system (Surgery)	RE401-461	617.742	Diseases of the lens
			RE501	617.746	Diseases of the vitreous body
RD701-811	617.3	Orthopedic surgery			
RD701	617.300(5/6)	Societies/Serials	RE551-661	617.73	Diseases of the retina
RD705-706	362.11	Hospitals	RE711	617.78	Diseases of the orbit
RD705.5-706	362.1109(4-9)	By place	RE714-715	617.74	Diseases of the eyeball
RD705.5	362.110973	United States	RE725-780	617.73	Neuro-ophthalmology
RD706	362.1109(4-9)	Other areas	RE831-840	617.713	Wounds/Injuries
RD711	617.3005	Yearbooks	RE871	617.741	Glaucoma
RD715	617.3006	Congresses	RE906	617.7043	Congenital abnormalities
RD723	617.3003	Dictionaries/Encyclopedias	RE918-921	617.759075	Color vision tests/Charts
RD725-726	617.309	History	RE925-939	617.755	Errors of refraction
RD726	617.309(4-9)	By place	RE940-981	617.75(2)	Optometry/Opticians
RD727-728	617.3092	Biography	RE986-988	617.79	Artificial eyes
RD732.3	617.3008	By age group/Class/Etc.	RF	617.51	Otorhinolaryngology
RD732.6	617.30076	Problems/Exercises/ Examination	RF1	617.5100(5/6)	Serials/Societies
			RF5-6	362.1(1-2)	Hospitals
RD732.7	617.300202	Outlines/Syllabi/Etc.	RF6	362.1109(4-9)	Hospitals, By place
RD733.2	617.300222	Pictorial works	RF11	617.51005	Yearbooks
RD734	617.30754	Examination/Diagnoses	RF16	617.51006	Congresses
RD736	617.06	Special therapies	RF23	617.51003	Dictionaries/Encyclopedias
RD755-757	617.30028	Orthopedic instruments/Etc.	RF24	617.510014	Nomenclature/Etc.
RD755.5	617.470592	Implants	RF25-26	617.5109	History
RD756	617.470592	Artificial limbs	RF26	617.5109(4-9)	Otorhinolaryngology, By place
RD757	617.30028	Other apparatus			
RD761-789	617.3(7-9)	Deformities/Disorders	RF28	617.510025	Directories
RD762	617.37	Posture disorders	RF29-30	617.510072	Laboratories
RD763	617.371	Head/Neck	RF32-33	617.510074	Museums/Etc.
RD766	617.374	Trunk	RF37-38	617.510092	Biography
RD768-771	617.375	Spine/Back	RF47	617.51008	By age group/Class/Etc.
RD772	617.376	Hip	RF47.5	617.5107	Pathology
RD775-789	617.39	Extremities	RF48-.5	617.510754	Examination/Diagnosis
RD776-778.5	617.397	Upper extremities/Arm	RF49	617.51(1-86)	Diseases
RD779-789	617.398	Lower extremities/Leg	RF50	617.51044	Wounds/Injuries
RD792-811	617.303	Physical rehabilitation	RF51-52	617.51059	Surgery
RD792	617.30300(5/6)	Serials/Societies	RF52.5	610.73	Nursing
RD792.5	617.303006	Congresses	RF53-54	617.5106	Therapeutics
RD794	617.3030025	Directories	RF55	617.51061	Materia medica/ Pharmacology
RD795-.5	617.30309	History			
RD796	617.303092	Biography	RF57	617.80076	Problems/Exercises/Etc.
RD807-809	617.303007	Education	RF58	617.800202	Outlines/Syllabi/Etc.
RE	617.7	Opthalmology	RF62	617.8007	Education
RE1	617.700(5/6)	Serials/Societies	RF63	617.8027	Research/Experimentation
RE6	617.7005	Yearbooks	RF81	617.800222	Pictorial works
RE11	617.7006	Congresses	RF85-.7	617.8023	Practice/Economics
RE20	617.70014	Nomenclature/ Terminology/Etc.	RF87	617.80028	Instruments/Etc.
			RF110-320	617.8	Otology/Diseases of ear
RE21	617.7003	Dictionaries/Encyclopedias	RF110-111	617.809	Otology, History
RE22	617.70025	Directories	RF111	617.809(4-9)	Otology, By place
RE26-30	617.709	Ophthalmology, History	RF122.5	617.8008(1-8)	By age group/Class/Etc.
RE30	617.709(4-9)	By place	RF122.7	617.80089	By race/Ethnic group/Etc.
RE31-36	617.7092	Biography	RF123	617.80754	Examination/Diagnosis
RE46-52	617.7(2-8)	Diseases of the eye	RF124	617.806	Therapeutics
RE56-58	617.70072	Research/Experimentation	RF126-127	617.8059	Surgery
RE71	617.700222	Pictorial works	RF131-132	617.80076	Examinations/Problems
RE72-.5	617.7023	Practice of	RF145	617.800222	Pictorial works
RE73	617.70028	Instruments/Apparatus/Etc.	RF155	617.801	Complications/Sequelae
RE75-79	617.70754	Examination/Diagnosis	RF175-200	617.8(1-2)	External ear/Auricle diseases
RE80-87	617.7059	Surgery			
RE91-94	617.7(5/12)	Vision disorders/Blindness	RF210	617.85	Tympanic membrane diseases
RE121-155	617.771	Diseases of the eyelids			
RE201-216	617.764	Lacrimal gland/Duct diseases	RF220-228	617.84	Middle ear diseases
			RF230	617.86	Eustachian tubes
RE310-326	617.773	Diseases of the conjunctiva	RF235	617.87	Mastoid process diseases
RE328	617.719	Diseases of the sclera	RF260-275	617.882	Internal ear diseases
RE336-340	617.719	Diseases of the cornea	RF286-320	617.89	Audiology
RE350-355	617.72	Diseases of the uvea	RF286	617.8900(5-6)	Serials/Societies

LC	Dewey	Descriptor	LC	Dewey	Descriptor
RF286.5	617.89006	Congresses	RG316	618.1	Diseases of the endrometrium
RF291.3	617.890076	Problems/Exercises/Etc.	RG421-481	618.1(1/2)	Diseases of the ovary/ Oviducts
RF291.5	617.89008	By age group/Class/Etc.	RG482-483	617.55	Diseases of the pelvis
RF292	617.804(2-3)	Hereditary deafness/ Congenital	RG484-485	616.6	Female urology
RF295	617.8059	Surgery	RG491-499	618.19	Diseases of the breast
RF298-310	617.80028	Instruments/Etc.	RG500-991	618.(2-8)	Obstetrics
RF320	617.8	Deaf-mutism	RG502	618.20072	Laboratories/Institutes/Inc.
RF341-437	616.212	Rhinology	RG504-505	618.20025	Directories
RF345	616.212075	Examination/Diagnosis	RG509-510	618.20092	Biography
RF348-349	616.21206	Therapeutics	RG511-51⁸	618.2009	History
RF350	617.523	Surgery	RG512-513	618.200901	Primitive/Ancient
RF361	616.212	Rhinitis	RG514	618.200902	Medieval
RF460-547	616.22	Laryngology	RG515	618.200903(1-3)	Modern through 1800
RF476	616.22075	Examination/Diagnosis	RG516	618.20090(34-4)	19th-20th centuries
RF481-499	616.32	Pharynx/Tonsil diseases	RG520	618.200222	Pictorial works
RF482	616.32075	Examination/Diagnosis	RG527-.5	618.207	Examination/Diagnosis
RF483	616.3206	Therapeutics	RG528	618.2061	Pharmacology
RF484-.5	617.531	Surgery	RG530-.3	618.2021	Statistics
RF491-496	616.314	Tonsillitis/Etc.	RG532	618.20076	Exercises/Exams/Problems
RF510-540	616.2(2-3)	Larynx/Trachea/Etc.	RG533	618.200202	Outlines/Etc.
RF511	616.2(2-3)008	By age group/Class/Etc.	RG545	618.20028	Instruments/Apparatus/Etc.
RF511.5	616.2(2-3)07	Pathology	RG547	618.200285	Computer applications
RF512-514	616.2(2-3)075	Examination/Diagnosis	RG551-591	618.(2-3)	Pregnancy
RF516-517	617.533	Surgery	RG559	618.24	Nutritional aspects
RF522	616.22	Larynx neurological disorders	RG560	618.2019	Psychology aspects
RF526	616.22	Diseases of the vocal cords	RG563-564	618.22	Examination/Diagnosis
RF529	616.23	Diseases of the trachea	RG567	618.25	Multiple pregnancy
RF540	616.2(2-3)03	Rehabilitation	RG571-580	618.3	Diseases/Conditions
RG	618	Gynecology and obstetrics	RG586	618.31	Extrauterine pregnancy
RG1	618.100(5/6)	Serials/Societies	RG600-631	618.32	Embryo/Fetus
RG12-16	362.11	Hospitals/Clinics/Etc.	RG628-.3	618.320754	Examination/Diagnosis
RG17-18	618.10072	Laboratories/Institutes/Etc.	RG629	618.32(6-8)	Specific diseases of fetus
RG21-.2	618.10074	Museums/Exhibitions	RG648	618.392	Spontaneous abortion
RG26	618.1005	Yearbooks	RG649	618.397	Premature labor
RG31	618.1006	Congresses	RG651-721	618.4	Labor
RG32-33	618.10025	Directories of gynecologists	RG661	618.45	Natural childbirth
RG45	618.1003	Dictionaries/Encyclopedias	RG671-693	618.42	Presentations/Positions
RG47	618.10014	Nomenclature/Etc.	RG696	618.25	Multiple birth
RG51-67	618.1009	History of gynecology	RG701-721	618.5	Complicated labor
RG53	618.100901	Primitive	RG705-707	618.51	Anomalies/Mechanical obstacles
RG55	618.100939	Oriental	RG709	618.53	Fetal size/Etc.
RG57-59	618.100901	Ancient	RG711	618.54	Hemorrhage
RG61	618.100902	Medieval	RG715	618.56	Placenta complications
RG67	618.09(4-9)	Gynecology, By place	RG719	618.58	Umbilical cord complications
RG71-76	618.10092	Biography	RG725-791	618.8	Obstetric operations
RG77	618.07	Pathology	RG730	618.89	Asepsis/Antisepsis
RG79	618.100222	Pictorial works	RG741	618.82	Extraction/Version
RG103.5	618.10019	Psychological aspects	RG761	618.86	Cesarean section
RG104-.6	618.145	Operative gynecology	RG781	618.83	Embryotomy/Craniotomy
RG136-.6	613.94	Contraception	RG801-871	618.7	Puerperal state
RG138	613.942	Sterilization of women	RG831	618.75	Convulsions/Eclampsia
RG159-208	618.17	Functional/Systemic disorders	RG851	618.76	Psychoses/Mental disorders
RG211-485	618.1(1-7)	Female genital organs/ Diseases	RG861-866	618.71	Lactation diseases
RG218	618.142	Infectious diseases	RG950	618.2	Midwives
RG261-266	618.16	Diseases of the vulva	RG951	610.73678	Obstetric nursing
RG268-272	618.15	Diseases of the vagina	RJ	618.92	Pediatrics
RG301-391	618.14	Diseases of the uterus	RJ1	618.92000(5/6)	Serials/Societies
RG304	618.10754	Examination/Diagnosis	RJ16	618.920005	Yearbooks
RG306	618.106	Therapeutics	RJ21	618.920006	Congresses
RG310-314	618.14	Diseases of the cervix uteri	RJ26	618.920003	Dictionaries/Encyclopedias
RG312	618.142	Cervicitis	RJ27-28	362.11	Hospitals/Clinics/Etc.
RG314	618.143	Erosion	RJ27.2-.5	362.1109(4-9)	Hospitals, By place
			RJ27.2-.3	362.110973	United States

LC	Dewey	Descriptor	LC	Dewey	Descriptor
RJ27.5.....................362.11097(4-9).........................By areas			RJ466-478.5............618.926...............................Urology		
RJ29	618.9200025	Directories	RJ486-496	618.928	Nervous system diseases
RJ31-32	618.9200072	Laboratories/Institutes/Etc.	RJ499-507	618.9289	Mental disorders
RJ33.5-.8	338.473621/618.92023	Practice of/Economics of	RJ499.A1	618.9289000(5/6)	Serials/Societies
RJ33.6-.8	618.92023(4-9)	Practice, By place	RJ500	618.92890007	Education
RJ33.6-.7 ....618.9202373...............United States			RJ500.2................618.928900072................Research		
RJ33.7	618.920237(4-9)	By region or state	RJ501-502	618.92890009(4-9)	Mental disorders, By place
RJ33.8	618.92023(4-9)	Other areas	RJ501	618.9289000973	United States
RJ34	618.9200028	Instruments/Etc.	RJ502	618.92890009(4-9)	Other regions or countries
RJ36-42	618.920009	History of pediatrics	RJ502.3	610.7368	Psychiatric nursing
RJ38......................618.92000901........................Ancient			RJ502.5-503............616.89022..........................Child/Adolescent psychiatry		
RJ39	618.92000902	Medieval	RJ504-505	618.928914	Child psychotherapy
RJ40	618.9200090(3-4)	Modern	RJ504.2	618.928917	Analysis
RJ42	618.920009(4-9)	By place	RJ504.4	618.9289025	Crisis intervention
RJ43	618.9200092	Biography	RJ504.7	618.928918	Chemotherapy
RJ47.3-.4 ....618.92002...................Genetic aspects			RJ505....................618.92891(2-8)...............Specific therapies		
RJ50-51	618.92007	Examination	RJ506	618.9289(5-8)	Specific disorders
RJ52-53	615.542	Therapeutics	RJ511-516	618.925	Diseases of the skin
RJ91	618.24	Prenatal influence/Culture	RJ560-570	618.92(1-9)061	Materia medica
RJ101-111	613.0432	Hygiene/Care of children	RK	617.6	Dentistry
RJ125-145 ....612................Child/Adolescent physiology			RK1.......................617.600(5/6)..................Serials/Societies		
RJ206-235	612.3	Child/Adolescent feeding	RK3-.5	362.11	Hospitals/Clinics/Etc.
RJ240	613.0432	Child immunization (General)	RK3.5	362.1109(4-9)	Hospitals, By place
			RK4-15	344.0413	Examination/Registration
RJ245	610.7362	Pediatric nursing	RK5-15	344.(4-9)0413	Registration, By place
RJ250	618.92011	Premature infants	RK16.....................617.6005.................Yearbooks		
RJ251-325 ....618.9201..................Newborn infants			RK21	617.6006	Congresses
RJ252	612	Physiology	RK27	617.6003	Dictionaries/Encyclopedias
RJ254-320	618.92(1-9)	Diseases	RK28	617.60014	Nomenclature
RJ255.5-.6	618.920075	Examination/Diagnosis	RK29-34	617.6009	History of dentistry
RJ256	618.922	Asphyxia	RK31.....................617.600901...........................Ancient		
RJ267......................618.923...........................Colic			RK32	617.600902	Medieval
RJ269	618.9212	Heart diseases/ Abnormalities	RK33	617.60090(3-4)	Modern
			RK34	617.6009(4-9)	Dentistry, By place
RJ269.5-271	618.9215	Hematologic diseases	RK37	617.60025	Directories
RJ272	618.923623	Hepatitis	RK38-39 ....617.60072.............................Laboratories		
RJ274	618.922	Hyaline membrane disease/Etc.	RK41-43	617.60092	Biography
			RK52-.4	617.60021	Statistics
RJ275......................618.929...................Infectious diseases			RK53	617.60019	Psychological aspects
RJ276	618.923625	Jaundice/Icterus	RK55	617.6008(3-6)	By age group/Class/Etc.
RJ278	618.9261	Kidney diseases	RK55.3..................617.60089.............................By race/Ethnic group/Etc.		
RJ281	618.92011	Low birth weight	RK57	617.60076	Problems/Examinations/Etc.
RJ286	618.9239	Metabolic disorder	RK57.5	617.600202	Outlines/Syllabi/Etc.
RJ290......................618.928...................Nervous system diseases			RK68-69	617.60074	Museums/Exhibitions
RJ296	618.920977	Ophthalmia/Conjunctivitis	RK71-231	617.6007	Education
RJ301	618.92842	Paralysis	RK80.....................617.60072...................Research/Experimentation		
RJ312	618.922	Respiratory diseases	RK86-231	617.6070(1-9)	Education, By place
RJ316	618.58	Umbilical diseases	RK86-106	617.60707	North America
RJ370-520 ....618.92(1-9)...................Diseases of children			RK91-97	617.607073	United States
RJ370	618.920025	Critical diseases/ Emergencies	RK98	617.607071	Canada
			RK100...................617.607072...................Mexico		
RJ385-387	618.92979	Immunologic diseases	RK102-103	617.6070728	Central America
RJ386-.5	618.9297	Allergy	RK105-106	617.6070729	West Indies
RJ401-406	618.92(6)	Infectious/Parasitic diseases	RK111-113	617.60708	South America
RJ411-416 ....618.92(15/42).......................Hematology/Lymph diseases			RK114-184	617.60704	Europe
			RK186-207 ....617.60705.............................Asia		
RJ418-420	618.9242	Endocrine system diseases	RK214-221	617.60706	Africa
RJ421-426	618.921	Cardiovascular system/ Diseases	RK227	617.607094	Australia
			RK227.5	617.607093	New Zealand
RJ423-.5	618.921075	Examination/Diagnosis	RK231	617.60709(5-6)	Oceania
RJ424	615.542	Therapeutics	RK240...................617.600285...................Computer applications		
RJ431-436 ....618.922........................Respiratory system diseases			RK301-493	617.6(07/3)	Oral/Dental pathology/Diseases
RJ433-.5	618.922075	Examination/Diagnosis			
RJ434	615.542	Therapeutics	RK306	617.6008(3-6)	By age group/Class/Etc.
RJ446-456	618.9233	Gastroenterology	RK307	617.6307	Pathology
RJ460-463	618.9231	Diseases of the mouth	RK308-310	617.630754	Examination/Diagnosis
			RK318-320 ....617.606...................Therapeutics		

LC	Dewey	Descriptor
RK331	617.67	Caries
RK340-341	617.634	Diseases of enamel/Dentine
RK351-356	617.6342	Endodontics
RK361-450	617.632	Periodontics
RK490-493	617.6044	Wounds/Injuries
RK501-519	617.605	Operative dentistry
RK520-528	617.64	Orthodontics
RK529-535	617.605	Oral surgery
RK529.5	617.605008(3-6)	By age group/Class/Etc.
RK531	617.66	Exodontics
RK533	617.60592	Transplants
RK641-667	617.69	Prosthetic dentistry
RL	616.5	Dermatology
RL1	616.500(5/6)	Serials/Societies
RL20-21	362.11	Hospitals/Clinics/Etc.
RL26	616.5005	Yearbooks
RL31	616.5006	Congresses
RL39	616.50014	Nomenclature/Terminology
RL41	616.5003	Dictionaries/Encyclopedias
RL43	616.50025	Directories
RL46	616.5009	History
RL46.2-.3	616.50092	Biography
RL46.9-47	616.50074	Museums/Exhibitions
RL48-49	616.50072	Laboratories
RL55	616.50028	Instruments
RL73	616.5008(3-6)	By age group/Class/Etc.
RL74.2	616.50076	Problems/Examinations/Etc.
RL74.3	616.500202	Outlines/Syllabi/Etc.
RL77	616.5007	Education
RL79	616.5027	Research/Experimentation
RL81	616.500222	Pictorial works
RL87-94	613	Care/Hygiene
RL110-120	616.506	Therapeutics
RL130-169	616.5	Glands/Hair/Nail diseases
RL201-331	616.52	Skin inflammations/Infections
RL221	616.523	Boils/Etc.
RL231-241	616.51	Dermatitis
RL251	616.521	Eczema
RL283	616.524	Impetigo
RL321	616.526	Psoriasis
RL401-489	616.544	Hypertrophies
RL411	616.544	Corns/Callosities
RL431	616.546	Hypertrichosis
RL435	616.544	Keratosis/Ichthyosis
RL451	616.544	Scleroderma
RL471	616.544	Verrucae/Warts
RL675	616.545	Chronic ulcers/Bedsores
RL701-751	616.08	Psychosomatic/Nerve disorders
RL760-785	616.57	Diseases due to parasites
RL790	616.55	Pigmentations/Albinism
RL793	616.(042/55)	Congential disorders/Moles/Etc.
RM	615.(5)	Pharmacology/Therapeutics
RM1	615.(5)0(5/6)	Serials/Societies
RM16	615.(5)05	Yearbooks
RM21	615.(5)06	Congresses
RM36	615.(5)03	Dictionaries/Encycliopedias
RM38	615.(5)014	Terminology/Nomenclature
RM39	615.(5)025	Directories
RM41-47	615.(5)09	History
RM43	615.(5)0901	Ancient
RM44	615.(5)0902	Medieval
RM45	615.(5)090(3-4)	Modern
RM47	615.(5)09(4-9)	By place
RM61-62	615.(5)092	Biography
RM105	615.(5)076	Problems/Exercises/Exams
RM106	615.(5)0202	Outlines/Syllabi/Etc.
RM108	615.(5)07	Education
RM111	615.(5)072	Experimental therapeutics
RM121-127	615.5	Therapeutics
RM122	615.50202	Outlines/Syllabi/Etc.
RM123	615.5078	Laboratory manuals
RM125	610.73	Nurses' manuals
RM126	615.5076	Problems/Exercises/Exams
RM138	615.14	Drug prescribing
RM139	615.14	Prescription writing
RM147-180	615.6	Administration of drugs
RM182-190	615.(5/8)	Other therapeutic procedures
RM214-258	615.854	Diet therapy
RM259	615.328	Vitamin therapy
RM260-263	615.58	Chemotherapy
RM265-267	615.329	Antibiotic therapy
RM270-282	615.37	Serum therapy/Immunotherapy
RM283-298	615.36	Endocrinotherapy/Organotherapy
RM300-666	615.7	Drugs and their actions
RM301.25	615.7072	Research
RM301.3	615.704	Drug response/Special factors
RM301.5	615.7	Pharmacokinetics
RM301.55	615.7	Drug metabolism
RM302-.3	615.7045	Drug interactions
RM303-309	615.778	Drugs acting on the skin
RM312	615.773	On the skeletal muscles
RM315-333	615.78	Neuropsychopharmacology
RM335	615.718	On blood cells/Etc.
RM340	615.718	On blood coagulation
RM345-349	615.71	On the cardiovascular system
RM355-365	615.73	On the digestive system
RM370-371	615.37	On the immune system
RM375-377	615.761	On the urinary organs
RM380-386	615.766	On reproductive organs
RM388-.5	615.72	On respiratory system
RM409	615.329	Antibacterial agents
RM671-.5	615.886	Patent medicines
RM695-890	615.82	Physical medicine/Therapy
RM695	615.820(6/5)	Serials/Societies
RM696	615.8206	Congresses
RM696.5	615.8203	Dictionaries/Encyclopedias
RM697	615.82025	Directories
RM698-.5	615.82028	Instruments/Apparatus/Etc.
RM699-.3	615.8209	Physical medicine, History
RM699.3	615.8209(4-9)	Physical medicine, By place
RM699.5-.7	615.82092	Biography
RM701.6	615.82076	Problems/Exercises/Exams
RM705	615.82023	The profession
RM706-707	615.8207	Education
RM708	615.82072	Research
RM713	615.82023/338.473621	Practice/Economics of
RM719-727	615.822	Mechanotherapy
RM733	615.836	Respiration as a remedy
RM735-.7	615.8515	Occupational therapy
RM736.7	615.85153	Recreational therapy
RM801-822	615.853	Hydrotherapy
RM824-827	615.836	Aerotherapy
RM831-862.5	615.8(31/4)	Phototherapy/Radiotherapy/Etc.
RM831	615.830(5/6)	Serials/Societies
RM831.5	615.83106	Congresses

LC	Dewey	Descriptor	LC	Dewey	Descriptor
RV401-411	615.(1/5)	Materia medica/ Therapeutics	RZ243.2	615.5340202	Outlines/Syllabi/Etc.
RV415-431	615.11	Pharmacy	RZ260-265	616-618.(062)	Diseases/Injuries/Treatment
RX	615.532	Homeopathy	RZ270-275	617.1062	Wounds/Injuries
RX1	615.5320(5/6)	Serials/Societies	RZ301-399	615.533	Osteopathy
RX6-.5	362.11	Hospitals/Clinics/Etc.	RZ301	615.5330(5/6)	Serials/Societies
RX11	615.53205	Yearbooks	RZ302-304	362.11	Hospitals/Clinics/Etc.
RX21	615.53206	Congresses	RZ311	615.53305	Yearbooks
RX41	615.53203	Dictionaries/Encyclopedias	RZ313	615.53306	Congresses
RX46	615.532025	Directories	RZ321-325	615.53309	Osteopathy, History
RX51	615.53209	History	RZ325	615.53309(4-9)	By place
RX61-66	615.532092	Biography	RZ331-332	615.533092	Biography
RX73.3	615.532076	Problems/Exercises/Exams	RZ333	615.533025	Directories
RX81-85	615.53201	Theory/Principles	RZ336	615.533023	The profession
RX91-101	615.53207	Education	RZ337-338	615.53307	Education
RX211-581	616-618	Diseases/Treatment/Etc.	RZ343	615.533076	Problems/Exercises/Exams
RX211	615.8325	Fevers	RZ343.2	615.5330202	Outlines/Syllabi/Etc.
RX221-226	616.9	Diseases/Specific infections	RZ347-397.5	616-618.(062)	Diseases/Treatment/Etc.
RX281-301	616.8	Diseases of the nervous system	RZ400-408	615.851	Mental healing
RX305-309	616.(15/42)	Blood/Lymphatics/Etc. diseases	RZ409.7-999	615.53	Miscellaneous treatments
RX309	616.(151-7/42)	Individual diseases	RZ430	615.851	Mesmerism/Animal magnetism/Etc.
RX311-316	616.13	Diseases of circulatory system	RZ433-445	615.535	Naturopathy
RX321-326	616.2	Diseases of respiratory system	RZ510	615.88/139	Phrenology
RX331-336	616.3	Diseases of digestive system	RZ600	615.88/133.323	Radiesthesia
RX332	616.33	Diseases of the stomach	S	630-638	Agriculture
RX333	616.362	Diseases of the liver	S1-19	630.5	Serials
RX341-346	616.35	Diseases of the rectum	S20	630.6	Societies
RX351-356	616.6	Genitourinary system diseases	S21-400	630-638.09(4-9)	Documents/Etc., By place
RX360	617.54	Diseases of the chest	S21-131	630-638.(0973)	United States
RX366-376	617	Surgery adapted to homeopathy	S21	353.81	Federal documents
RX410-431	617.7	Diseases of the eye	S22	630-638.06073	National societies/ Congresses
RX441-456	617.(8/523/531)	Diseases of ear/Nose/Throat	S22.7-131	630-638. + 097(4-9)	By state
RX446	617.8	Diseases of the ear	S133-164	630-638.(09071)	Canada
RX451	617.523	Diseases of the nose	S165-166	630-638.(0972)	Mexico
RX456	617.531	Diseases of the throat	S167-174	630-638.(09728)	Central America
RX460-476	618	Gynecology/Obstetrics	S175-183	630-638.(09729)	West Indies
RX460	618.00(5/6)	Gyn. serials/Societies	S184	630-638.(097299)	Bermuda
RX467	618.172	Menstruation	S185-212	630-638.(098)	South America
RX469	618.175	Menopause	S187-188	630-638.(0982)	Argentina
RX471	618.173	Leucorrhea	S189-190	630-638.(0984)	Bolivia
RX476	618.2	Obstetrics	S191-192	630-638.(0981)	Brazil
RX501-531	618.92	Diseases of children	S193-194	630-638.(0983)	Chile
RX540	617.63	Diseases of the teeth	S195-196	630-638.(09861)	Colombia
RX561-581	616.5	Diseases of the skin	S197-198	630-638.(09866)	Ecuador
RX601-675	615.(1/5)	Materia medica/ Therapeutics	S199-204	630-638.(0988)	The Guianas
RZ	615.53	Other systems of medicine	S205-206	630-638.(09892)	Paraguay
RZ210-275	615.534	Chiropractic	S207-208	630-638.(0985)	Peru
RZ201	615.5340(5/6)	Serials/Societies	S209-210	630-638.(09895)	Uruguay
RZ211	615.53405	Yearbooks	S211-212	630-638.(0987)	Venezuela
RZ213	615.53406	Congresses	S215-269	630-638.(094)	Europe
RZ221-225	615.53409	Chiropractic, History	S217-224	630-638.(0941)	Great Britain
RZ225	615.53409(4-9)	By place	S220.5-.6	630-638.(09416)	Northern Ireland
RZ231-232	615.534092	Biography	S225-226	630-638.(09436)	Austria
RZ232.2-.4	615.534023/338.473621	Practice/Economics of	S227-228	630-638.(09439)	Hungary
RZ233	615.534025	Directories	S229-230	630-638.(0944)	France
RZ235	615.5340222	Pictorial works	S231-232.6	630-638.(0943)	Germany
RZ236	615.534023	The profession	S233-234	630-638.(09495)	Greece
RZ237-238	615.53407	Education	S235-236	630-638.(0945)	Italy
RZ243	615.534076	Problems/Exercises/Exams	S237-238	630-638.(09493)	Belgium
			S239-240	630-638.(09492)	Netherlands
			S241-242	630-638.(0947)	European Russia
			S245-246	630-638.(09489)	Denmark
			S247-248	630-638.(094912)	Iceland
			S249-250	630-638.(09481)	Norway
			S251-252	630-638.(09485)	Sweden
			S253-254	630-638.(0946)	Spain

LC	Dewey	Descriptor
S255-256	630-638.(09469)	Portugal
S257-258	630-638.(09494)	Switzerland
S261-262	630-638.(094977)	Bulgaria
S265-266	630-638.(09498)	Romania
S267-268	630-638.(09497)	Yugoslavia
S270-322	630-638.(095)	Asia
S277-278	630-638.(0951)	China
S279-280	630-638.(0954)	India
S281-282	630-638.(095493)	Sri Lanka
S285-286	630-638.(09597)	Vietnam
S287-288	630-638.(09596)	Cambodia
S293-294	630-638.(09593)	Thailand
S295-296	630-638.(09595)	Malay peninsula
S297-298	630-638.(09598)	Indonesia
S301-302	630-638.(09599)	Philippine Islands
S303-304	630-638.(0952)	Japan
S305-306	630-638.(09519)	Korea
S307-308	630-638.(0955)	Iran
S313-314	630-638.(095)	Asian Russia
S315-316	630-638.(09561)	Turkey
S323-338	630-638.(096)	Africa
S325-326	630-638.(0963)	Ethiopia
S328-336	630-638.(0968)	South/southern Africa
S339-340	630-638.(096751)	Zaire
S341-342	630-638.(0962)	Egypt
S345-346	630-638.(0965)	Algeria
S346.5-.6	630-638.(09611)	Tunisia
S347-348	630-638.(0966)	West Africa
S349-350	630-638.(09691)	Madagascar
S357-358	630-638.(09678)	Tanzania
S359-360	630-638.(096711)	Cameroon
S365-366	630-638.(096662)	Liberia
S367-368	630-638.(0964)	Morocco
S371-372	630-638.(09679)	Mozambique
S373-374	630-638.(09673)	Angola
S381-397.5	630-638.(0994)	Australia
S397.7-.8	630-638.(0993)	New Zealand
S398-400	630-638. + 099(5-6)	Oceania
S419-481	630.9	History
S421-431	630.901	Ancient
S435	630.903(1-2)	16th-17th centuries
S437	630.903(3-4)	18th-19th centuries
S441-481	630.9(4-9)	By place
S441-451	630.973	United States
S443-451	630.97(4-9)	By state
S451.5	630.971	Canada
S451.7	630.972	Mexico
S453-460.6	630.941	Great Britain
S463-464	630.944	France
S465-466	630.943	Germany
S469	630.94(1-9)	Other European countries
S470-471	630.95	Asia
S472-473	630.96	Africa
S474-475	630.98	South America
S476	630.9728	Central America
S477	630.9729	West Indies
S478	630.994	Australia
S478.5	630.993	New Zealand
S479-.3	630.99(5-6)	Oceania
S480	630.998(1-8)	Arctic regions
S519	630-638	Juvenile literature
S530-559	630.7	Education
S539.5-542	630.72	Research/Experimentation
S560-572	338.13/630.68	Farm economics/ Management
S583-587.5	631	Agricultural chemistry
S590-599.9	631.4	Soils/Soil science

LC	Dewey	Descriptor
S600-.7	630.2515	Agricultural meteorology
S602.5-604.37	631.5	Methods of culture
S604.5-605.64	631.45	Agricultural conservation
S604.8-621.5	631.6	Melioration/Reclamation
S622-627	631.45	Soil conservation
S631-667	631.8	Fertilizers/Soil improvement
S671-760	630.208/631.3	Farm machinery/ Engineering
S770-790.3	631.2	Structures/Buildings
S900-954	333.72/631.45	Conservation (Natural resources)
SB	630	Plant culture
SB1-13	630.(5/6)	Serials/Societies
SB16	630.6	Congresses
SB19-29	630.9	Documents, By place
SB19-21	630.973	United States
SB23	630.941	Great Britain
SB25	630.944	France
SB27	630.943	Germany
SB44	630.25	Directories
SB45	630.3	Encyclopedias/Dictionaries
SB46	631.208	Calendars/Rules
SB51-56	630.7(2)	Education/Research
SB57-60	630.74	Exhibitions/Museums
SB61-63	630.92	Biography
SB71-87	630.9	History
SB73-77	630.901	Ancient
SB79	630.902	Medieval
SB83-85	630.973	United States
SB87	630.9(4-9)	Other countries
SB110	631.586	Dry farming
SB111	631.58	Tropical farming
SB113-118.45	631.521	Seeds
SB118.5-.75	631.52	Nurseries
SB119-124	631.5(2-36)	Propagation
SB125	631.54	Training/Pruning
SB126.5	631.585	Hydroponics
SB129	631.55	Harvesting/Curing
SB170-171	634.99	Tree crops
SB175-177	635	Food crops (Legumes/Etc.)
SB183-317	633	Field crops
SB183	633.00(5/6)	Serials/Societies
SB183.2	633.006	Congresses
SB185.8	631.5	Planting/Harvesting
SB188-192	633.1	Grain/Cereal
SB193-207	633.2	Forage/Feed crops
SB197-202	633.2(1-5)	Grasses
SB203-205	633.3	Legumes
SB209-211	635.(1-2)	Root/Tuber crops
SB215-239	633.6	Sugar plants (Beets/Cane)
SB241-261	633.5	Textile/Fiber plants (Hemp/Etc.)
SB267-279	633.7	Alkaloidal (Cocao/ Tea/Tobacco)
SB281-283	633.58	Basketwork/Matwork plants
SB285-287	633.86	Dye plants
SB290-291	633.895	Gum/Resin plants
SB292	633.898	Insecticidal plants
SB293-295	633.88	Medicinia plant culture
SB298-299	633.85	Oil-bearing/Wax (Poppy/Palm)
SB301-303	633.81	Aromatic (Jasmine/ Lavender)
SB305-307	633.8(3-4)	Condiments/Spices
SB317.5-319.77	635	Horticulture
SB320-353	635	Vegetables

LC	Dewey	Descriptor
SB354-402	634	Fruits/Orchards
SB403-450.87	635.9	Flowers/Ornamentals
SB414.6-417	631.583/635.0483	Greenhouses
SB418-419.5	635.986	Container/Indoor gardening
SB421-439.8	633-635	Classes of plants
SB433-.34	635.964(2/7)	Lawns/Turf
SB434	635.932	Perennials
SB435-437	635.976	Shrubs/Ornamental trees
SB439	635.9676	Wild plants
SB441-.75	635.9074	Flower shows/Exhibitions
SB442.8-443.4	380.14159	Marketing (Florists/Etc.)
SB449-450.87	745.92	Flower arrangements
SB450.9-467	635	Gardens/Gardening
SB469-476	635.967	Landscape gardening
SB481-485	363.68	Parks/Public reservations
SB481	363.680(5/6)	Serials/Societies/Congresses
SB482-483	363.680973	United States
SB484-485	363.6809(4-9)	Other countries
SB599-989	632	Pests/Diseases
SB599	632.0(5/6)	Serials/Societies
SB599.2	632.06	Congresses
SB600	632.03	Dictionaries
SB600.5	632.025	Directories
SB603.5	635.92	Garden pests/Diseases
SB605	632.09(4-9)	By place
SB608	635.(1-8)	By plant type
SB610-615	632.5	Weeds/Parasitic plants/Etc.
SB617-618	581.69	Poisonous plants
SB621-795	581.2	Plant pathology
SB744.5-746	632.19	Pollution
SB761-795	635.97(6/7)9(3-6)	Trees/Shrubs (Pest/Diseases)
SB781-793	635.(6/7)91	Effect of elements on
SB818-945	632.7	Economic entomology
SB945	632.7(1-9)	Specific insects
SB950-989	632.9	Pest control/Disease remedy
SB950.9-970.41	632.95	Pesticides
SB951.145-952	632.95(1-4)	By type/Name
SB952.5	632.95042	Safety measures
SB935-955	632.94	Methods of application
SB957-969.8	632	Resistance to pesticides
SB970-.4	344.04633	Policy
SB974-989	632.96	Organic control/Protection
SB992-998	632.6	Economic zoology
SB992	632.60(5/6)	Serials/Societies/Congresses
SB993.3-.34	632.609	By place
SB993.3-32	632.60973	United States
SB993.34	632.609(4-9)	Other countries
SB993.5-994	632.69	Mammals (Deer/Rabbits/Rats)
SB995-996	632.68	Birds
SD	634.9	Forestry
SD1	634.90(5/6)	Serials/Societies
SD11-115	634.909	Documents, By place
SD11-12	634.90973	United States
SD12	634.9097(4-9)	By state
SD13-14	634.90971	Canada
SD15-16	634.90972	Mexico
SD17-18	634.909728	Central America
SD19	634.909729	West Indies
SD21-44	634.9098	South America
SD23-24	634.90982	Argentina
SD25-26	634.90984	Bolivia
SD27-28	634.90981	Brazil
SD29-30	634.90983	Chile
SD31-32	634.909861	Colombia
SD33-34	634.909866	Ecuador

LC	Dewey	Descriptor
SD35-36	634.90988	Guianas
SD37-38	634.909892	Paraguay
SD39-40	634.90985	Peru
SD41-42	634.90985	Uruguay
SD43-44	634.90987	Venezuela
SD45-83	634.9094	Europe
SD45-50	634.90941	Great Britain
SD51-52	634.909415	Ireland
SD53-54	634.909436	Austria
SD59-60	634.90944	France
SD61-62	634.90943	Germany
SD63-64	634.909495	Greece
SD67-68	634.90945	Italy
SD73-74	634.90947	European Russia
SD75-76	634.90946	Spain
SD77-78	634.909485	Sweden
SD79-80	634.909494	Switzerland
SD85-97	634.9095	Asia
SD85-86	634.90951	China
SD87-88	634.90954	India
SD89-90	634.90952	Japan
SD93-94	634.909599	Philippine islands
SD99-105	634.9096	Africa
SD110-111	634.90994	Australia
SD112-113	634.90993	New Zealand
SD115	634.9099(5-6)	Oceania
SD131-247.5	634.9090(1-4)	History of forest conditions
SD250-381	634.907	Education
SD356	634.9072	Research/Experimentation
SD383-385	634.97	Description (Trees/Forests)
SD388	634.9028	Equipment/Etc.
SD391-409.5	634.95	Silviculture
SD395-397	634.97	By type
SD411-428	333.75/634.9	Conservation/Protection
SD430-557	634.98	Exploitation/Utilization
SD561-668	634.92	Administration policy
SF	636	Animal culture
SF1	636.00(5/6)	Serials/Societies
SF5	636.006	Congresses
SF11-13	636.00973	Documents, United States
SF15	636.009(4-9)	Documents, Other countries
SF19	636.005	Yearbooks
SF21	636.003	Dictionaries/Encyclopedias
SF23-27	636.0025	Directories
SF31-33	636.0092	Biography
SF41-55	636.09	History
SF51	636.0973	United States
SF53	636.0941	Great Britain
SF55	636.09(4-9)	Other countries
SF61	636	Textbooks
SF63-75.3	636	Handbooks
SF75.5	636	Juvenile works
SF81-83	636.007(2)	Education/Research
SF84-.45	338.176	Economic zoology
SF84.82-85.6	636.01	Stock ranges
SF95-99	636.08(4-5)	Feeds/Feeding/Nutrition
SF101-103.5	636.0812	Branding/Etc.
SF105-109	636.082	Breeding
SF114-121	636.0074	Exhibitions
SF170-180	636.0886	Working animals
SF191-275	636.2	Cattle
SF198-199	636.2(2-8)	Breeds
SF221-250	636.2142	Dairying
SF250.5-275	637	Dairy Processing/Products
SF277-359.7	636.1	Horses
SF290-293	636.1(1-7)	Breeds
SF294.2-.35	798	Sports

143

LC	Dewey	Descriptor
SF294.5-297	798.24	Shows
SF308.5-310.5	798.2	Horsemanship
SF321-359.7	798.4	Racing
SF361	636.18	Donkeys
SF362	636.18	Mules
SF371-379	636.3	Sheep
SF380-388	636.39	Goats
SF391-397.4	636.4	Swine
SF399-401	636.(5-8)	Other domesticated animals
SF402-405	636.(7-9)	Fur-bearing animals
SF405.5-407	636.0885	Laboratory animals
SF409	636.(3-8)	Small animal culture
SF411-459	636.0887	Pets
SF421-440.2	636.7	Dogs
SF441-450	636.8	Cats
SF451-455	636.9322	Rabbits/Hares
SF456-458.83	597.0074/639.3(4)	Fishes/Aquariums
SF459	636.0887	Other animals
SF461-473	636.5	Birds
SF481-507	636.5	Poultry
SF508-510	636.63	Game birds
SF511-513	636.6	Other birds
SF518	638	Insect rearing
SF521-539	638.1	Bee culture
SF541-560	638.2	Sericulture
SF561-562	638.5	Other insects
SF600-1100	636.089	Veterinary medicine
SF600-604	636.0890(5/6)	Serials/Societies
SF605	636.08906	Congresses
SF606	636.089074	Exhibitions
SF609	636.08903	Dictionaries/Encyclopedias
SF610	636.089014	Terminology
SF611	636.089025	Directories
SF612-613	636.089092	Biography
SF615-724	636.08909	History
SF740	636.0894	Veterinary public health
SF775-779	636.08907	Education
SF781-809	636.08969	Communicable diseases
SF810	636.089696	Parasitology, By pest
SF910	636.0896	Other diseases/Conditions
SF910.5	636.08973	Orthopedics
SF911-914	636.0897	Surgery
SF914.3-.4	636.0896025	Emergencies
SF914.5	636.0895892	Acupuncture
SF915-919.5	636.08951	Pharmacology
SF951-997.5	636.0896(1-9)	Diseases of classes of animals
SH	639.(2/8)/799.1	Aquaculture/Fisheries/Angling
SH1	639.(2/8)00(5/6)	Serials/Societies/Congresses
SH3	639.(2/8)006	Congresses
SH11	639.(2/8)00973	Documents, United States
SH20	639.(2/8)0092	Biography
SH20.5-191	639.8	Aquaculture
SH20.5	639.8025	Directories
SH21	639.809	History (General)
SH34-133	639.809(4-9)	By place
SH34-36	639.80973	United States
SH37	639.80971	Canada
SH39	639.80972	Mexico
SH41-.5	639.809728	Central America
SH42-.5	639.809729	West Indies
SH43-65	639.8098	South America
SH67-101	639.8094	Europe
SH103-117	639.8095	Asia
SH121-125	639.8096	Africa
SH131	639.8099(3-4)	Australia/New Zealand

LC	Dewey	Descriptor
SH133	639.8099(5-6)	Oceania
SH138	639.8	Mariculture
SH151-179	639.3(1-4)	Fish culture
SH167	639.(1-4)	By species or class
SH171-179	636.0896	Diseases/Adverse factors
SH185	639.3789	Frog culture
SH187	639.7545	Leech culture
SH191	639.(37-7)	Other (Not fish or shellfish)
SH201-400.8	639.2/338.3727	Fisheries
SH201	639.2/338.3727(03)	Dictionaries/Encyclopedias
SH203	639.2/338.3727(025)	Directories
SH211	639.2/338.3727(09)	History
SH213-.77	639.2/338.3727(09163)	Atlantic Ocean
SH214-215	639.2/338.3727(09164)	Pacific Ocean
SH216-.55	639.2/338.3727(09165)	Indian Ocean
SH219-321	639.2/338.3727 + 09(4-9)	By place
SH221-222	639.2/338.3727(0973)	United States
SH223-229	639.2/338.3727(0971)	Canada
SH231	639.2/338.3727(0972)	Mexico
SH232	639.2/338.3727(09728)	Central America
SH233	639.2/338.3727(09729)	West Indies
SH234-251	639.2/338.3727(098)	South America
SH235	639.2/338.3727(0982)	Argentina
SH236	639.2/338.3727(0981)	Brazil
SH237	639.2/338.3727(0983)	Chile
SH239	639.2/338.3727(09861)	Colombia
SH241	639.2/338.3727(09866)	Ecuador
SH242	639.2/338.3727(09881)	Guyana
SH243	639.2/338.3727(09883)	Suriname
SH244	639.2/338.3727(09882)	French Guiana
SH245	639.2/338.3727(09892)	Paraguay
SH247	639.2/338.3727(0985)	Peru
SH249	639.2/338.3727(09895)	Uruguay
SH251	639.2/338.3727(0987)	Venezuela
SH253-293	639.2/338.3727(094)	Europe
SH255-260	639.2/338.3727(0941)	Great Britain
SH261-262	639.2/338.3727(09415)	Ireland
SH263-264	639.2/338.3727(09436)	Austria
SH265-266	639.2/338.3727(09493)	Belgium
SH267-268	639.2/338.3727(09489)	Denmark
SH268.G83	639.2/338.3727(09982)	Greenland
SH269-270	639.2/338.3727(0944)	France
SH271-272	639.2/338.3727(0943)	Germany
SH273-274	639.2/338.3727(09495)	Greece
SH275-276	639.2/338.3727(09492)	Netherlands
SH277-278	639.2/338.3727(0945)	Italy
SH279-280	639.2/338.3727(09481)	Norway
SH281-282	639.2/338.3727(09469)	Portugal
SH283-284	639.2/338.3727(0947)	European Russia
SH285-286	639.2/338.3727(0946)	Spain
SH287-288	639.2/338.3727(09485)	Sweden
SH289-290	639.2/338.3727(09494)	Switzerland
SH291-292	639.2/338.3727(09561)	Turkey
SH295-307	639.2/338.3727(095)	Asia
SH297-298	639.2/338.3727(0951)	China
SH299-300	639.2/338.3727(0954)	India
SH301-302	639.2/338.3727(0952)	Japan
SH302.5-.7	639.2/338.3727(09519)	Korea
SH303-304	639.2/338.3727(0955)	Iran
SH305-306	639.2/338.3727(0957)	Siberia
SH311-315	639.2/338.3727(096)	Africa
SH313-314	639.2/338.3727(0962)	Egypt
SH317-318	639.2/338.3727(0994)	Australia
SH318.5	639.2/338.3727(0993)	New Zealand
SH319	639.2/338.3727 + 099(5-6)	Oceania
SH320	639.2/338.3727(09989)	Arctic regions
SH327.7	639.977	Conservation

LC	Dewey	Descriptor	LC	Dewey	Descriptor
SH328-329	639.2068	Management	SK43	799.2975	The South
SH332-.2	639.207(2)	Education/Research	SK45	799.2978	The West
SH334.9-336.5	639.94	Processing	SK47-145	799.297(4-9)	By state
SH337	639.20688	Packing, Transporting	SK151-152	799.2971	Canada
SH338-343	639.2074	Exhibitions	SK153	799.2972	Mexico
SH343.8	623.89	Navigation	SK155	799.29728	Central America
SH343.9	623.888	Safety	SK157	799.29729	West Indies
SH344-.8	623.86	Methods/Gear	SK159-181	799.298	South America
SH346-351	639.27(2-5)	Fishery for individual species	SK183-223	799.294	Europe
SH360-363	639.29	Seal fisheries	SK185-191	799.2941	Great Britain
SH364	639.2	Sea otters	SK231-247	799.295	Asia
SH365-380.92	639.4	Shellfish fisheries/Culture	SK251-255	799.296	Africa
SH365-367	639.409(4-9)	By place	SK261	799.2994	Australia
SH371-374.52	639.4	Mollusks	SK262	799.2993	New Zealand
SH375-377	639.412	Pearl fisheries	SK265	799.29989	Arctic/Antarctic
SH378-379	639.48	Freshwater mollusks	SK267	799.299(5-6)	Oceania
SH380-.92	639.5	Crustaceans	SK271	799.2022	Illustrations (Hunting scenes)
SH381-385	639.28	Whaling	SK273-275	799.2028	Equipment
SH387	639.2	Porpoises/Dolphins	SK274-.8	799.2028(2-5)	Guns/Ballistics
SH389-391.5	639.7	Algae culture/Seaweed	SK275	799.20216	Catalogs
SH393	639.89	Seagrasses	SK276	799.2074	Museums/Collections
SH396	639.734	Sponge fisheries	SK281-293	799.20282	Special types of hunting
SH400-.8	639.(2-7)	Seafood gathering	SK284-287	799.25974442	Fox hunting
SH401-691	799.12	Angling	SK293	799.23	Ferreting
SH401	799.120(5/6)	Serials/Societies	SK295-305	799.26	Big game, By animal type
SH403	799.1206	Fishing clubs	SK311-335	799.24	Bird hunting
SH411	799.1203	Dictionaries/Encyclopedias	SK323-325	799.242	Land birds
SH414-415	799.12092	Biography	SK324	799.24209(4-9)	By country
SH421	799.1209	History	SK325	799.248(5-9)	By kind of bird
SH447-453	799.12028	Equipment/Tackle	SK327-329	799.243	Bay birds
SH454	799.12	Casting	SK331-335	799.244	Waterfowl
SH455.4-458	799.12	Angling methods	SK335	799.2028	Decoys
SH461-601	799.1209(7-8)	America	SK336	799.2	Varmint hunting (General)
SH462	799.12097	North America	SK341	799.25(4-9)/799.27(1-9)	Other game
SH463-565	799.120973	United States	SK351-579	639.9	Wildlife management
SH571-572	799.120971	Canada	SK351	639.90(5/6)	Serials/Societies
SH573	799.120972	Mexico	SK352	639.906	Congresses
SH575-576	799.1209728	Central America	SK354	639.9092	Biography
SH577-578	799.1209729	West Indies	SK357	639.95	Game preserves/Refuges/Etc.
SH579-601	799.12098	South America	SK361-579	639.909(4-9)	By place
SH603-643	799.12094	Europe	SK361-465	639.90973	United States
SH651-667	799.12095	Asia	SK470-471	639.90971	Canada
SH669	799.120998	Arctic/Antarctic	SK473	639.90972	Mexico
SH671-675	799.12096	Africa	SK475	639.909728	Central America
SH677-679	799.12099(3-6)	Australia/New Zealand/ Oceania	SK477	639.909729	West Indies
SH681-691	799.17	Angling for special fish	SK479-501	639.9098	South America
SH681	799.1758	Bass	SK503-543	639.9094	Europe
SH684-686.7	799.1755	Salmon	SK505-511	639.90941	Great Britain
SH687-688	799.1755	Trout	SK553-567	639.9095	Asia
SK	799.2	Hunting sports	SK571-575	639.9096	Africa
SK1	799.20(5/6)	Serials/Societies/Congresses	SK577-578	639.9099(3-6)	Australia/New Zealand/ Oceania
SK3	799.206	Hunting clubs	SK579	639.90998	Arctic/Antarctic
SK7	799.205	Yearbooks	T	600	Technology
SK11	799.203	Dictionaries/Encyclopedias	T1-5	605/606	Serials/Societies
SK12	799.2025	Directories	T6	606	Congresses
SK15-17	799.2092	Biography	T8	601.48	Symbols/Abbreviations
SK21	799.209	History	T9-10	603	Dictionaries/Encyclopedias
SK36	799.215	Bow hunting	T14	601	Philosophy/Theory
SK36.2	799.2028	Dressing/Skinning	T15-33	609	History
SK36.3	799.2028	Flying	T21-31	609.(1-9)	By place
SK36.7	799.2028	Poaching	T54-55	363.11	Industrial accidents/Safety
SK37-39.5	799.213	Shooting	T55.4-60.8	670	Industrial engineering
SK40-267	799.29	By country	T55.4-.45	670.(5/6)	Serials/Societies/Congresses
SK40-157	799.297	North America	T55.5	670.3	Dictionaries/Encyclopedias
SK41-145	799.2973	United States			

LC	Dewey	Descriptor	LC	Dewey	Descriptor
T55.52	670.148	Symbols/Abbreviations	TA41-42	624/620.(0981)	Brazil
T55.54	670.25	Directories	TA43-44	624/620.(0983)	Chile
T55.6	670.9	History	TA45-46	624/620.(09861)	Colombia
T56.3	670.23	As a profession	TA47	624/620.(09866)	Ecuador
T57-59	519/670.42	Applied mathematics	TA48	624/620.(09881)	Guyana
T58.7	338/670.42	Production/Productivity	TA49	624/620.(09883)	Suriname
T59.5	670.427	Automation	TA50	624/620.(09882)	French Guiana
T59.7-.77	620.82	Human engineering	TA51	624/620.(09892)	Paraguay
T61-173	607	Technical education	TA52	624/620.(0985)	Peru
T66-69	607	History	TA53	624/620.(09895)	Uruguay
T71-170	607.(4-9)	By place	TA54	624/620.(0987)	Venezuela
T73-75	607.73	United States	TA57-64.5	624/620.(0941)	Great Britain
T76-77	607.71	Canada/Newfoundland	TA65-.2	624/620.(09436)	Austria
T78-79	607.72	Mexico	TA65.3-.4	624/620.(09437)	Czechoslovakia
T80-81	607.728	Central America	TA65.5-66	624/620.(09439)	Hungary
T82-83	607.729	West Indies	TA67-68	624/620.(09493)	Belgium
T84-104	607.8	South America	TA69-70	624/620.(09489)	Denmark
T105-147	607.4	Europe	TA71-72.5	624/620.(0944)	France
T107-114	607.41	Great Britain	TA73-74.5	624/620.(0943)	Germany
T121-122	607.44	France	TA75-76	624/620.(09495)	Greece
T123-124	607.43	Germany	TA77-78	624/620.(09492)	Netherlands
T149-163	607.5	Asia	TA79-80	624/620.(0945)	Italy
T151-152	607.51	China	TA81-82	624/620.(09481)	Norway
T155-156	607.52	Japan	TA83-84.5	624/620.(09469)	Portugal
T165-166	607.6	Africa	TA85-86	624/620.(0947)	European Russia
T167-170	607.9(3-6)	Australia/New Zealand/ Oceania	TA87-88	624/620.(0946)	Spain
T173.2-174.5	338.(064/926)	Technology transfer/ Innovation	TA88.5	624/620.(0948)	Scandinavia
			TA89-90	624/620.(09485)	Sweden
T175-178	607.2	Industrial research	TA91-92	624/620.(09494)	Switzerland
T201-342	608	Patents	TA95.A2	624/620.(09496)	Balkans
T201-203	608.0(5/6)	Serials/Societies/Congresses	TA95.F5	624/620.(094897)	Finland
T215-323.3	608.7	History	TA95.Y8	624/620.(09497)	Yugoslavia
T212-323.3	608.7	By place	TA101-102	624/620.(0951)	China
T223-225	608.773	United States	TA103-104	624/620.(0954)	India
T226-227	608.771	Canada	TA104.5-.6	624/620.(095491)	Pakistan
T228-229	608.772	Mexico	TA104.7-.8	624/620.(095493)	Sri Lanka
T230-231	608.7728	Central America	TA105-106	624/620.(0952)	Japan
T232-233	608.7729	West Indies	TA107-108	624/620.(0955)	Iran
T234-254	608.78	South America	TA109-110	624/620.(0957)	Asian Russia
T255-295	608.74	Europe	TA111-112	624/620.(09561)	Turkey
T257-264.5	608.741	Great Britain	TA113.I55	624/620.(09598)	Indonesia
T271-272.5	608.744	France	TA113.I7	624/620.(09567)	Iraq
T273-274.5	608.743	Germany	TA113.I75	624/620.(095694)	Israel/Palestine
T299-313	608.75	Asia	TA113.P6	624/620.(09599)	Philippines
T305-306	608.752	Japan	TA115-119	624/620.(096)	Africa
T315-319	608.76	Africa	TA117-118	624/620.(0962)	Egypt
T321-322.6	608.79(3-4)	Australia/New Zealand	TA119	624/620. + 096(1-9)	Africa, By country
T323-324	608.79(5-6)	Oceania	TA121-122	624/620.(0994)	Australia
T325-326	608.798	Polar areas	TA122.5-.6	624/620.(0993)	New Zealand
T351-385	604.2	Mechanical drawing	TA123-124	624/620. + 099(5-6)	Oceania
T391-999	607.34	Technical exhibitions	TA125-126	624/620.(0998)	Polar areas
T400-999	607.3409	By city/Date	TA139-140	624/620.(092)	Biography
TA	620/624	Engineering, General/Civil	TA152	624/620.(078)	Laboratory manuals
TA1-5	624/620. + 0(5/6)	Serials/Societies/Congresses	TA157-158	624/620.(023)	The profession
TA9	624/620.(03)	Dictionaries/Encyclopedias	TA160	624/620.(072)	Research
TA11	624/620.(0148)	Symbols/Abbreviations	TA165	624/620.(028)	Instruments
TA12	624/620.(025)	Directories	TA174-175	624/620.(0222)	Engineering drawing/ Designs
TA15-19	624/620.(09)	History	TA177	624/620.(0228)	Models
TA21-126	624/620. + 09(4-9)	By place	TA177.4-185	624/620.(0681)	Economics
TA23-25	624/620.(0973)	United States	TA190-194	624/620.(068)	Management
TA26-27	624/620.(0971)	Canada	TA201-210	624/620. + 0(687/28)	Contracting/Equipment
TA28-29	624/620.(0972)	Mexico	TA329-348	624/620.(0151)	Mathematics
TA30-31	624/620.(09728)	Central America	TA349-360	620.10(3-7)	Applied mechanics
TA32-33	624/620.(09729)	West Indies	TA365-367	620.2(1-5)	Acoustical engineering
TA36-37	624/620.(0982)	Argentina	TA401-492	624.18/620.11	Materials
TA38-39	624/620.(0984)	Bolivia	TA401-.3	624.18/620.11 + 0(5/6)	Serials/Societies/Congresses

LC	Dewey	Descriptor	LC	Dewey	Descriptor
TA402	624.18/620.11(03)	Dictionaries/Encyclopedias	TA1107-1108	629.040955	Iran
TA402.5	624.18/620.11(09)	By place	TA1109-1110	629.040957	Asian Russia
TA404-.3	624.18/620.11(07)	Education/Research	TA1111-1112	629.0409561	Turkey
TA410-418.34	624.18/620.11(0287)	Testing	TA1113.I55	629.0409598	Indonesia
TA418.95-492	624.11/620.1(2-9)	By type of material	TA1113.I7	629.0409567	Iraq
TA501-625	624.1517	Surveying	TA1113.I75	629.04095694	Israel/Palestine
TA535-538	624.151707	Education	TA1113.P6	629.0409599	Philippines
TA562-595	624.1517028	Instruments/Methods	TA1115-1119	629.04096	Africa
TA630-695	624.1	Structural engineering	TA1117-1118	629.040962	Egypt
TA630	624.10(5/6)	Serials/Societies/Congresses	TA1119	629.04096(1-9)	Africa, By country
TA638-.5	624.107(2)	Education/Research	TA1121-1122	629.040994	Australia
TA645-656.5	624.1(01/7)	Structural theory/Analysis	TA1122.5-.6	629.040993	New Zealand
TA658-.6	624.1771	Structural design	TA1123-1124	629.04099(5-6)	Oceania
TA663-695	624.1771	Design/Construction	TA1125-1126	629.040998	Polar areas
TA705-770	624.15	Geology/Earthworks	TA1160	629.04023	As a profession
TA715-770	624.152	Earthworks/Excavations	TA1163	629.0407	Education
TA775-787	624.15(3-8)	Foundations	TA1205	388.4	Urban transportation systems
TA800-820	624.19	Tunneling/Tunnels			
TA1001-1280	629.04	Transportation engineering	TA1225	388.47	Terminals
TA1001-1005	629.040(5/6)	Serials/Societies/Congresses	TA1245-1250	388.41312	Signaling/Equipment
TA1009	629.0403	Dictionaries/Encyclopedias	TC	627	Hydraulic engineering
TA1015	629.0409	History	TC1-5	627.0(5/6)	Serials/Societies/Congresses
TA1021-1126	629.0409(3-9)	By place	TC6	627.074	Exhibitions/Museums
TA1023-1025	629.040973	United States	TC9	627.03	Encyclopedias
TA1026-1027	629.040971	Canada	TC15-20	627.09	History
TA1028-1029	629.040972	Mexico	TC21-126	627.09(3-9)	By place
TA1030-1031	629.0409728	Central America	TC23-25	627.0973	United States
TA1032-1033	629.0409729	West Indies	TC26-27	627.0971	Canada
TA1036-1037	629.040982	Argentina	TC28-29	627.0972	Mexico
TA1038-1039	629.040984	Bolivia	TC30-31	627.09728	Central America
TA1041-1042	629.040981	Brazil	TC32-33	627.09729	West Indies
TA1043-1044	629.040983	Chile	TC36-37	627.0982	Argentina
TA1045-1046	629.0409861	Colombia	TC38-39	627.0984	Bolivia
TA1047	629.0409866	Ecuador	TC41-42	627.0981	Brazil
TA1048	629.0409881	Guyana	TC43-44	627.0983	Chile
TA1049	629.0409883	Suriname	TC45-46	627.09861	Colombia
TA1050	629.0409882	French Guiana	TC47	627.09866	Ecuador
TA1051	629.0409892	Paraguay	TC48	627.09881	Guyana
TA1052	629.040985	Peru	TC49	627.09883	Suriname
TA1053	629.0409895	Uruguay	TC50	627.09882	French Guiana
TA1054	629.040987	Venezuela	TC51	627.09892	Paraguay
TA1057-1064.5	629.040941	Great Britain	TC52	627.0985	Peru
TA1065-.2	629.0409436	Austria	TC53	627.09895	Uruguay
TA1065.3-.4	629.0409437	Czechoslovakia	TC54	627.0987	Venezuela
TA1065.5-1066	629.0409439	Hungary	TC57-64.5	627.0941	Great Britain
TA1067-1068	629.0409493	Belgium	TC59-.3	627.09417	Ireland
TA1069-1070	629.0409489	Denmark	TC61-62	627.09411	Scotland
TA1071-1072.5	629.040944	France	TC65-.2	627.09436	Austria
TA1073-1074.5	629.040943	Germany	TC65.3-.4	627.09437	Czechoslovakia
TA1075-1076	629.0409495	Greece	TC65.5-66	627.09439	Hungary
TA1077-1078	629.0409492	Netherlands	TC67-68	627.09493	Belgium
TA1079-1080	629.040945	Italy	TC69-70	627.09489	Denmark
TA1081-1082	629.0409481	Norway	TC71-72.5	627.0944	France
TA1083-1084.5	629.0409469	Portugal	TC73-74.5	627.0943	Germany
TA1085-1086	629.040947	European Russia	TC75-76	627.09495	Greece
TA1087-1088	629.040946	Spain	TC77-78	627.09492	Netherlands
TA1088.5	629.040948	Scandinavia	TC79-80	627.0945	Italy
TA1089-1090	629.0409485	Sweden	TC81-82	627.09481	Norway
TA1091-1092	629.0409494	Switzerland	TC83-84.5	627.09469	Portugal
TA1095.A2	629.0409496	Balkans	TC85-86	627.0946	Spain
TA1095.F5	629.04094897	Finland	TC88.5	627.0948	Scandinavia
TA1095.Y8	629.0409497	Yugoslavia	TC89-90	627.09485	Sweden
TA1101-1102	629.040951	China	TC91-92	627.09494	Switzerland
TA1103-1104	629.040954	India	TC95.A2	627.09496	Balkans
TA1104.5-.6	629.04095491	Pakistan	TC95.F5	627.094897	Finland
TA1104.7-.8	629.04095493	Sri Lanka	TC95.P7	627.09438	Poland
TA1105-1106	629.040952	Japan	TC95.Y8	627.09497	Yugoslavia

LC	Dewey	Descriptor	LC	Dewey	Descriptor
TC101-102	627.0951	China	TC495.F5	628.1094897	Finland
TC103-104	627.0954	India	TC495.P7	628.109438	Poland
TC104.5-.6	627.094591	Pakistan	TC495.Y8	628.109497	Yugoslavia
TC104.7-.8	627.094593	Sri Lanka	TC501-502	628.10951	China
TC105-106	627.0952	Japan	TC503-504	628.10954	India
TC107-108	627.0955	Iran	TC504.5-.6	628.1095491	Pakistan
TC109-110	627.0947	Asian Russia	TC504.7-.8	628.1095493	Sri Lanka
TC111-112	627.09561	Turkey	TC505-506	628.10952	Japan
TC113.I55	627.09598	Indonesia	TC507-508	628.10955	Iran
TC113.I7	627.09567	Iraq	TC509-510	628.10957	Asian Russia
TC113.I75	627.095694	Israel/Palestine	TC511-512	628.109561	Turkey
TC113.P6	627.09599	Philippines	TC513.I55	628.109598	Indonesia
TC115	627.096	Africa, General	TC513.I7	628.109567	Iraq
TC117-118	627.0962	Egypt	TC513.I75	628.1095694	Israel/Palestine
TC119	627.096(1-9)	Africa, By country	TC513.P6	628.109599	Philippines
TC121-122	627.0994	Australia	TC515	628.1096	Africa, General
TC122.5	627.0993	New Zealand	TC517-518	628.10962	Egypt
TC123-124	627.099(5-6)	Oceania	TC519	628.1096(1-9)	Africa, By country
TC125-126	627.0998	Polar regions	TC521-522	628.10994	Australia
TC139-140	627.092	Biography	TC522.5	628.10993	New Zealand
TC157-.5	627.07	Education	TC523-524	628.1099(5-6)	Oceania
TC158	627.072	Laboratories	TC525-526	628.10998	Polar areas
TC160-181	532.5	Hydrodynamics/Etc.	TC530-537	627.4	Protective works/Flood control
TC183-201	627.702	Dredging/Preliminaries			
TC195-201	627.7	Submarine building	TC540-558	627.8	Dams
TC203-365	627.2	Harbors/Coast protective works	TC601-791	627.13/629.048	Canals/Waterways
			TC615-726	627.13/629.048 + 09(4-9)	History, By place
TC375-381	627.922	Lighthouses	TC623-625	627.13/629.048(0973)	United States
TC401-526	628.1	River/Water supply engineering	TC626-627	627.13/629.048(0971)	Canada
			TC628-629	627.13/629.048(0972)	Mexico
TC401	628.10(5/6)	Serials/Societies/Congresses	TC630-631	627.13/629.048(09728)	Central America
TC415-526	628.109	History, By place	TC632-633	627.13/629.048(09729)	West Indies
TC423-425	628.10973	United States	TC636-637	627.13/629.048(0982)	Argentina
TC426-427	628.10971	Canada	TC638-639	627.13/629.048(0984)	Bolivia
TC428-429	628.10972	Mexico	TC641-642	627.13/629.048(0981)	Brazil
TC430-431	628.109728	Central America	TC643-644	627.13/629.048(0983)	Chile
TC432-433	628.109729	West Indies	TC645-646	627.13/629.048(09861)	Colombia
TC436-437	628.10982	Argentina	TC647	627.13/629.048(09866)	Ecuador
TC438-439	628.10984	Bolivia	TC648	627.13/629.048(09881)	Guyana
TC441-442	628.10981	Brazil	TC649	627.13/629.048(09883)	Suriname
TC443-444	628.10983	Chile	TC650	627.13/629.048(09882)	French Guiana
TC445-446	628.109861	Colombia	TC651	627.13/629.048(09892)	Paraguay
TC447	628.109866	Ecuador	TC652	627.13/629.048(0985)	Peru
TC448	628.109881	Guyana	TC653	627.13/629.048(09895)	Uruguay
TC449	628.109883	Suriname	TC654	627.13/629.048(0987)	Venezuela
TC450	628.109882	French Guiana	TC657-664.5	627.13/629.048(0941)	Great Britain
TC451	628.109892	Paraguay	TC665-.2	627.13/629.048(09436)	Austria
TC452	628.10985	Peru	TC665.3-.4	627.13/629.048(09437)	Czechoslovakia
TC453	628.109895	Uruguay	TC665.5-666	627.13/629.048(09439)	Hungary
TC454	628.10987	Venezuela	TC667-668	627.13/629.048(09493)	Belgium
TC457-464.5	628.10941	Great Britain	TC669-670	627.13/629.048(09489)	Denmark
TC465-.2	628.109436	Austria	TC671-672.5	627.13/629.048(0944)	France
TC465.3-.4	628.109437	Czechoslovakia	TC673-674.5	627.13/629.048(0943)	Germany
TC465.5-466	628.109439	Hungary	TC675-676	627.13/629.048(09495)	Greece
TC467-468	628.109493	Belgium	TC677-678	627.13/629.048(09492)	Netherlands
TC469-470	628.109489	Denmark	TC679-680	627.13/629.048(0945)	Italy
TC471-472.5	628.10944	France	TC681-682	627.13/629.048(09481)	Norway
TC473-474.5	628.10943	Germany	TC683-684.5	627.13/629.048(09469)	Portugal
TC475-476	628.109495	Greece	TC685-686	627.13/629.048(0947)	European Russia
TC477-478	628.109492	Netherlands	TC687-688	627.13/629.048(0946)	Spain
TC483-484.5	628.109469	Portugal	TC688.5	627.13/629.048(0948)	Scandinavia
TC485-486	628.10947	European Russia	TC689-690	627.13/629.048(09485)	Sweden
TC487-488	628.10946	Spain	TC691-692	627.13/629.048(09494)	Switzerland
TC488.5	628.10948	Scandinavia	TC695.A2	627.13/629.048(09496)	Balkans
TC489-490	628.109485	Sweden	TC695.F5	627.13/629.048(094897)	Finland
TC491-492	628.109494	Switzerland	TC695.Y8	627.13/629.048(09497)	Yugoslavia
TC495.A2	628.109496	Balkans	TC701-702	627.13/629.048(0951)	China

LC	Dewey	Descriptor	LC	Dewey	Descriptor
TC703-704	627.13/629.048(0954)	India	TC907-908	627.50955	Iran
TC704.5-.6	627.13/629.048(095491)	Pakistan	TC909-910	627.50957	Asian Russia
TC704.7-.8	627.13/629.048(095493)	Sri Lanka	TC911-912	627.509561	Turkey
TC705-706	627.13/629.048(0952)	Japan	TC913.I55	627.509598	Indonesia
TC707-708	627.13/629.048(0955)	Iran	TC913.I7	627.509567	Iraq
TC709-710	627.13/629.048(0957)	Asian Russia	TC913.I75	627.5095694	Israel/Palestine
TC711-712	627.13/629.048(09561)	Turkey	TC913.P6	627.509599	Philippines
TC713.I55	627.13/629.048(09598)	Indonesia	TC915	627.5096	Africa
TC713.I7	627.13/629.048(09567)	Iraq	TC917-918	627.50962	Egypt
TC713.I75	627.13/629.048(095694)	Israel/Palestine	TC919	627.5096(1-9)	Africa, By country
TC713.P6	627.13/629.048(09599)	Philippines	TC921-922	627.50994	Australia
TC715	627.13/629.048(096)	Africa	TC922.5	627.50993	New Zealand
TC717-718	627.13/629.048(0962)	Egypt	TC923-924	627.5099(5-6)	Oceania
TC719	627.13/629.048 + 096(1-9)	Africa, By country	TC925-926	627.50998	Polar areas
TC721-722	627.13/629.048(0994)	Australia	TC970-978	627.54	Drainage
TC722.5	627.13/629.048(0993)	New Zealand	TC1501-1645	620.4162	Ocean engineering
TC723-724	627.13/629.048 + 099(5-6)	Oceania	TC1501	620.41620(5/6)	Serials/Societies
TC725-726	627.13/629.048(0998)	Polar areas	TC1505	620.416206	Congresses
TC773-788	627.137	Isthmain canal projects	TD	628	Environmental engineering
TC774-781	627.137	Panama Canal	TD1-5	628.0 5/6)	Serials/Societies/Congresses
TC791	627.13	Suez Canal	TD6	628.074	Exhibitions/Museums
TC801-967	627.5	Irrigation/Land reclamation	TD9	628.03	Dictionaries/Encyclopedias
TC815-926	627.509(4-9)	By place	TD12	628.025	Directories
TC823-825	627.50973	United States	TD15-20	628.09	History
TC826-827	627.50971	Canada	TD16-20	628.090(1-4)	By date
TC828-829	627.50972	Mexico	TD21-126	628.09(4-9)	By place
TC830-831	627.509728	Central America	TD23-25	628.0973	United States
TC832-833	627.509729	West Indies	TD26-27	628.0971	Canada
TC836-837	627.50982	Argentina	TD28-29	628.0972	Mexico
TC838-839	627.50984	Bolivia	TD30-31	628.09728	Central America
TC841-842	627.50981	Brazil	TD32-33	628.09729	West Indies
TC843-844	627.50983	Chile	TD36-37	628.0982	Argentina
TC845-846	627.509861	Colombia	TD38-39	628.0984	Bolivia
TC847	627.509866	Ecuador	TD41-42	628.0981	Brazil
TC848	627.509881	Guyana	TD43-44	628.0983	Chile
TC849	627.509883	Suriname	TD45-46	628.09861	Colombia
TC850	627.509882	French Guiana	TD47	628.09866	Ecuador
TC851	627.509892	Paraguay	TD48	628.09881	Guyana
TC852	627.50985	Peru	TD49	628.09883	Suriname
TC853	627.509895	Uruguay	TD50	628.09882	French Guiana
TC854	627.50987	Venezuela	TD51	628.09892	Paraguay
TC857-864.5	627.50941	Great Britain	TD52	628.0985	Peru
TC865-.2	627.509436	Austria	TD53	628.09895	Uruguay
TC865.3-.4	627.509437	Czechoslovakia	TD54	628.0987	Venezuela
TC865.5-866	627.509439	Hungary	TD57-64.5	628.0941	Great Britain
TC867-868	627.509493	Belgium	TD65-.2	628.09436	Austria
TC869-870	627.509489	Denmark	TD65.3-.4	628.09437	Czechoslovakia
TC871-872.5	627.50944	France	TD65.5-66	628.09439	Hungary
TC873-874.5	627.50943	Germany	TD67-68	628.09493	Belgium
TC875-876	627.509495	Greece	TD69-70	628.09489	Denmark
TC877-878	627.509492	Netherlands	TD71-72.5	628.0944	France
TC879-880	627.50945	Italy	TD73-74.5	628.0943	Germany
TC881-882	627.509481	Norway	TD75-76	628.09495	Greece
TC883-884.5	627.509469	Portugal	TD77-78	628.09492	Netherlands
TC885-886	627.50947	European Russia	TD79-80	628.0945	Italy
TC887-888	627.50946	Spain	TD81-82	628.09481	Norway
TC888.5	627.50948	Scandinavia	TD83-84.5	628.09469	Portugal
TC889-890	627.509485	Sweden	TD85-86	628.0947	European Russia
TC891-892	627.509494	Switzerland	TD87-88	628.0946	Spain
TC895.A2	627.509496	Balkans	TD88.5	628.0948	Scandinavia
TC895.F5	627.5094897	Finland	TD89-90	628.09485	Sweden
TC895.Y8	627.509497	Yugoslavia	TD91-92	628.09494	Switzerland
TC901-902	627.50951	China	TD95.A2	628.09496	Balkans
TC903-904	627.50954	India	TD95.F5	628.094897	Finland
TC904.5-.6	627.5095491	Pakistan	TD95.Y8	628.09497	Yugoslavia
TC904.7-.8	627.5095493	Sri Lanka	TD101-102	628.0951	China
TC905-906	627.50952	Japan	TD103-104	628.0954	India

LC	Dewey	Descriptor	LC	Dewey	Descriptor
TD104.5-.6	628.095491	Pakistan	TD273-274.5	628.10943	Germany
TD104.7-.8	628.095493	Sri Lanka	TD275-276	628.109495	Greece
TD105-106	628.0952	Japan	TD277-278	628.109492	Netherlands
TD107-108	628.0955	Iran	TD279-280	628.10945	Italy
TD109-110	628.0957	Asian Russia	TD281-282	628.109481	Norway
TD111-112	628.09561	Turkey	TD283-284.5	628.109469	Portugal
TD113.I55	628.09598	Indonesia	TD285-286	628.10947	European Russia
TD113.I7	628.09567	Iraq	TD287-288	628.10946	Spain
TD113.I75	628.095694	Israel/Palestine	TD288.5	628.10948	Scandinavia
TD113.P6	628.09599	Philippines	TD289-290	628.109485	Sweden
TD115-119	628.096	Africa	TD291-292	628.109494	Switzerland
TD117-118	628.0962	Egypt	TD295.A2	628.109496	Balkans
TD119	628.096(1-9)	Africa, By country	TD295.F5	628.1094897	Finland
TD121-122	628.0994	Australia	TD295.Y8	628.109497	Yugoslavia
TD122.5-.6	628.0993	New Zealand	TD301-302	628.10951	China
TD123-124	628.099(5-6)	Oceania	TD303-304	628.10954	India
TD125-126	628.0998	Polar areas	TD304.5-.6	628.1095491	Pakistan
TD139-140	628.092	Biography	TD304.7-.8	628.1095493	Sri Lanka
TD156	628.023	As a profession	TD305-306	628.10952	Japan
TD158-167	628	Municipal engineering	TD307-308	628.10955	Iran
TD160-167	307.1216	Planning/Laying out cities	TD309-310	628.10957	Asian Russia
TD172-192	363.73/628.5	Environmental pollution	TD311-312	628.109561	Turkey
TD178-.8	628.507(2)	Education/Research	TD313.I55	628.109598	Indonesia
TD179	628.509	History	TD313.I7	628.109567	Iraq
TD179.5-190.7	628.509(4-9)	By place	TD313.I75	628.1095694	Israel/Palestine
TD180-181	628.50973	United States	TD313.P6	628.109599	Philippines
TD182-.4	628.50971	Canada	TD315-319	628.1096	Africa
TD182.6-.7	628.50972	Mexico	TD317-318	628.10962	Egypt
TD183-.5	628.509728	Central America	TD319	628.1096(1-9)	Africa, By country
TD184-.5	628.509729	West Indies	TD321-322	628.10994	Australia
TD185-.5	628.5098	South America	TD322.5-.6	628.10993	New Zealand
TD186-.5	628.5094	Europe	TD323-324	628.1099(5-6)	Oceania
TD187-.5	628.5095	Asia	TD325-326	628.10998	Polar areas
TD188-.5	628.5096	Africa	TD360	351.871044	Water rates
TD189-.5	628.5099(3-6)	Australia/New Zealand/ Oceania	TD365-387	628.16	Water quality
TD190-.7	628.50998	Polar regions	TD388-.5	628.13	Water conservation
TD192	628.5028	Pollution control equipment	TD390-418	628.11	Sources of water supply
TD201-500	363.61/628.1	Water supply	TD420-427	628.168	Water pollution
TD215-220	628.109	History	TD429	628.162	Water reuse
TD216-220	628.1090(1-4)	By date	TD430-477	628.162	Water purification/Etc.
TD221-326	628.109(4-9)	Water supply, By place	TD478-480.7	628.167	Saline water conversion
TD223-225	628.10973	United States	TD481-491	628.14	Water distribution
TD226-227	628.10971	Canada	TD511-780	628.3	Sewage collection/ Sewerage
TD228-229	628.10972	Mexico	TD511	628.30(5/6)	Serials/Societies/Congresses
TD230-231	628.109728	Central America	TD515-520	628.309	History
TD232-233	628.109729	West Indies	TD516-520	628.3090(1-4)	By date
TD236-237	628.10982	Argentina	TD521-626	628.309(4-9)	Sewerage, By place
TD238-239	628.10984	Bolivia	TD523-525	628.30973	United States
TD241-242	628.10981	Brazil	TD526-527	628.30971	Canada
TD243-244	628.10983	Chile	TD528-529	628.30972	Mexico
TD245-246	628.109861	Colombia	TD530-531	628.309728	Central America
TD247	628.109866	Ecuador	TD532-533	628.309729	West Indies
TD248	628.109881	Guyana	TD536-537	628.30982	Argentina
TD249	628.109883	Suriname	TD538-539	628.30984	Bolivia
TD250	628.109882	French Guiana	TD541-542	628.30981	Brazil
TD251	628.109892	Paraguay	TD543-544	628.30983	Chile
TD252	628.10985	Peru	TD545-546	628.309861	Colombia
TD253	628.109895	Uruguay	TD547	628.309866	Ecuador
TD254	628.10987	Venezuela	TD548	628.309881	Guyana
TD257-264.5	628.10941	Great Britain	TD549	628.309883	Suriname
TD265-.2	628.109436	Austria	TD550	628.309882	French Guiana
TD265.3-.4	628.109437	Czechoslovakia	TD551	628.309892	Paraguay
TD265.5-266	628.109439	Hungary	TD552	628.30985	Peru
TD267-268	628.109493	Belgium	TD553	628.309895	Uruguay
TD269-270	628.109489	Denmark	TD554	628.30987	Venezuela
TD271-272.5	628.10944	France	TD557-564.5	628.30941	Great Britain

LC	Dewey	Descriptor	LC	Dewey	Descriptor
TD565-.2	628.309436	Austria	TD878-893.5	628.5	Special types of pollution
TD565.3-.4	628.309437	Czechoslovakia	TD878-879	628.55	Soil
TD565.5-566	628.309439	Hungary	TD881-890	628.53	Air
TD567-568	628.309493	Belgium	TD891-893.5	363.74	Noise
TD569-570	628.309489	Denmark	TD895-899	628.51	Industrial/Factory sanitation
TD571-572.5	628.30944	France	TD920-929	628.7	Rural sanitary engineering
TD573-574.5	628.30943	Germany	TE	625.(7-8)	Highway engineering
TD575-576	628.309495	Greece	TE1-4	625.70(5/6)	Serials/Societies
TD577-578	628.309492	Netherlands	TE5	625.706	Congresses
TD579-580	628.30945	Italy	TE6	625.7074	Museums/Exhibitions
TD581-582	628.309481	Norway	TE9	625.703	Dictionaries/Encyclopedias
TD583-584.5	628.309469	Portugal	TE12	625.7025	Directories
TD585-586	628.30947	European Russia	TE15-19	625.709	History
TD587-588	628.30946	Spain	TE21-126	625.709(4-9)	By place
TD588.5	628.30948	Scandinavia	TE23-25	625.70973	United States
TD589-590	628.309485	Sweden	TE26-27	625.70971	Canada
TD591-592	628.309494	Switzerland	TE28-29	625.70972	Mexico
TD595.A2	628.309496	Balkans	TE30-31	625.709728	Central America
TD595.F5	628.3094897	Finland	TE32-33	625.709729	West Indies
TD595.Y8	628.309497	Yugoslavia	TE36-37	625.70982	Argentina
TD601-602	628.30951	China	TE38-39	625.70984	Bolivia
TD603-604	628.30954	India	TE41-42	625.70981	Brazil
TD604.5-.6	628.3095491	Pakistan	TE43-44	625.70983	Chile
TD604.7-.8	628.3095493	Sri Lanka	TE45-46	625.709861	Colombia
TD605-606	628.30952	Japan	TE47	625.709866	Ecuador
TD607-608	628.30955	Iran	TE48	625.709881	Guyana
TD609-610	628.30957	Asian Russia	TE49	625.709883	Suriname
TD611-612	628.309561	Turkey	TE50	625.709882	French Guiana
TD613.I55	628.309598	Indonesia	TE51	625.709892	Paraguay
TD613.I7	628.309567	Iraq	TE52	625.70985	Peru
TD613.I75	628.3095694	Israel/Palestine	TE53	625.709895	Uruguay
TD613.P6	628.309599	Philippines	TE54	625.70987	Venezuela
TD615-619	628.3096	Africa	TE57-64.5	625.70941	Great Britain
TD617-618	628.30962	Egypt	TE65-.2	625.709436	Austria
TD619	628.3096(1-9)	Africa, By country	TE65.3-.4	625.709437	Czechoslovakia
TD621-622	628.30994	Australia	TE65.5-66	625.709439	Hungary
TD622.5-.6	628.30993	New Zealand	TE67-68	625.709493	Belgium
TD623-624	628.3099(5-6)	Oceania	TE69-70	625.709489	Denmark
TD625-626	628.30998	Polar areas	TE71-72.5	625.70944	France
TD662-670	628.2	Sewerage systems	TE73-74.5	625.70943	Germany
TD675-725	628.2	Sewers	TE75-76	625.709495	Greece
TD730-737	628.3	Sewage	TE77-78	625.709492	Netherlands
TD741-780	628.36	Sewage disposal	TE79-80	625.70945	Italy
TD785-812	628.44	Municipal refuse/Solid wastes	TE81-82	625.709481	Norway
			TE83-84.5	625.709469	Portugal
TD785	628.440(5/6)	Serials/Societies/Congresses	TE85-86	625.70947	European Russia
TD788-.4	628.440973	United States	TE87-88	625.70946	Spain
TD789	628.4409(3-9)	Other countries	TE88.5	625.70948	Scandinavia
TD793.3	628.44072	Research	TE89-90	625.709485	Sweden
TD793.7	628.440299	Estimates/Costs	TE91-92	625.709494	Switzerland
TD794	628.442	Collection	TE95.A2	625.709496	Balkans
TD795-812	628.445	Special disposal methods	TE95.F5	625.7094897	Finland
TD813-870	628.46	Street cleaning/Litter	TE95.Y8	625.709497	Yugoslavia
TD815-849	628.4609(3-9)	By place	TE101-102	625.70951	China
TD817-819	628.460973	United States	TE103-104	625.70954	India
TD820-822	628.460971	Canada	TE104.5-.6	625.7095491	Pakistan
TD824-825	628.460972	Mexico	TE104.7-.8	625.7095493	Sri Lanka
TD826-827	628.4609728	Central America	TE105-106	625.70952	Japan
TD829-830	628.4609729	West Indies	TE107-108	625.70955	Iran
TD832-833	628.46098	South America	TE109-110	625.70957	Asian Russia
TD835-836	628.46094	Europe	TE111-112	625.709561	Turkey
TD838-839	628.46095	Asia	TE113.I55	625.709598	Indonesia
TD841-843	628.46096	Africa	TE113.I7	625.709567	Iraq
TD845-849	628.46099(3-6)	Australia/New Zealand/ Oceania	TE113.I75	625.7095694	Israel/Palestine
			TE113.P6	625.709599	Philippines
TD860	628.46028	Tools/Appliances	TE115-119	625.7096	Africa
TD868-870	625.763	Snow/Ice on streets	TE117-118	625.70962	Egypt

151

LC	Dewey	Descriptor	LC	Dewey	Descriptor
TF668	385.22/625.23	Dining car service	TF1121-1122	625.100994	Australia
TF670-851	385.5/625.(4-6)	Local and light railways	TF1122.5-.6	625.100993	New Zealand
TF677-851	385.5(2-4)/625.(4-6)	By type	TF1124-1124	625.10099(5-6)	Oceania
TF701-851	385.5/625.(4-6)	Municipal railways	TF1125-1126	625.100998	Polar areas
TF855-1126	621.33/625.263	Electric railways	TG	624.(2-3)	Bridge engineering
TF858-859	621.33	Electrification	TG1-4	624.20(5/6)	Serials/Societies
TF863-912	621.33/625.1	Construction	TG5	624.206	Congresses
TF960-970	385.068	Operation and management	TG6	624.2074	Exhibitions/Museums
TF975	385.363/625.26	Electric locomotives	TG9	624.203	Dictionaries/Encyclopedias
TF1021-1126	625.1009(4-9)	By country and system	TG12	624.2025	Directories
TF1023-1025	625.100973	United States	TG15-20	624.209	History
TF1026-1027	625.100971	Canada	TG21-126	624.209(3-9)	By place
TF1028-1029	625.100972	Mexico	TG23-25	624.20973	United States
TF1030-1031	625.1009728	Central America	TG26-27	624.20971	Canada
TF1032-1033	625.1009729	West Indies	TG28-29	624.20972	Mexico
TF1036-1037	625.100982	Argentina	TG30-31	624.209728	Central America
TF1038-1039	625.100984	Bolivia	TG32-33	624.209729	West Indies
TF1041-1042	625.100981	Brazil	TG36-37	624.20982	Argentina
TF1043-1044	625.100983	Chile	TG38-39	624.20984	Bolivia
TF1045-1046	625.1009861	Colombia	TG41-42	624.20981	Brazil
TF1047	625.1009866	Ecuador	TG43-44	624.20983	Chile
TF1048	625.1009881	Guyana	TG45-46	624.209861	Colombia
TF1049	625.1009883	Suriname	TG47	624.209866	Ecuador
TF1050	625.1009882	French Guiana	TG48	624.209881	Guyana
TF1051	625.1009892	Paraguay	TG49	624.209883	Suriname
TF1052	625.100985	Peru	TG50	624.209882	French Guiana
TF1053	625.1009895	Uruguay	TG51	624.209892	Paraguay
TF1054	625.1009987	Venezuela	TG52	624.20985	Peru
TF1057-1064.5	625.100941	Great Britain	TG53	624.209895	Uruguay
TF1059-.3	625.1009417	Ireland	TG54	624.20987	Venezuela
TF1061-1062	625.1009411	Scotland	TG57-64.5	624.20941	Great Britain
TF1065-.2	625.1009436	Austria	TG65-.2	624.209436	Austria
TF1065.3-.4	625.1009437	Czechoslovakia	TG65.3-.4	624.209437	Czechoslovakia
TF1065.5-1066	625.1009439	Hungary	TG65.5-66	624.209439	Hungary
TF1067-1068	625.1009493	Belgium	TG67-68	624.209493	Belgium
TF1069-1070	625.1009489	Denmark	TG69-70	624.209489	Denmark
TF1071-1072.5	625.100944	France	TG71-72.5	624.20944	France
TF1073-1074.5	625.100943	Germany	TG73-74.5	624.20943	Germany
TF1075-1076	625.1009495	Greece	TG75-76	624.209495	Greece
TF1077-1078	625.1009492	Netherlands	TG77-78	624.209492	Netherlands
TF1079-1080	625.100945	Italy	TG79-80	624.20945	Italy
TF1081-1082	625.1009481	Norway	TG81-82	624.209481	Norway
TF1083-1084.5	625.1009469	Portugal	TG83-84.5	624.209469	Portugal
TF1085-1086	625.100947	European Russia	TG85-86	624.20947	European Russia
TF1087-1088	625.100946	Spain	TG87-88	624.20946	Spain
TF1088.5	625.100948	Scandinavia	TG88.5	624.20948	Scandinavia
TF1089-1090	625.1009485	Sweden	TG89-90	624.209485	Sweden
TF1091-1092	625.1009494	Switzerland	TG91-92	624.209494	Switzerland
TF1095.A2	625.1009496	Balkans	TG95.A2	624.209496	Balkans
TF1095.F5	625.10094897	Finland	TG95.F5	624.2094897	Finland
TF1095.P7	625.1009438	Poland	TG95.Y8	624.209497	Yugoslavia
TF1095.Y8	625.1009497	Yugoslavia	TG101-102	624.20951	China
TF1101-1102	625.100951	China	TG103-104	624.20954	India
TF1103-1104	625.100954	India	TG104.5-.6	624.2095491	Pakistan
TF1104.5-.6	625.10095491	Pakistan	TG104.7-.8	624.2095493	Sri Lanka
TF1104.7-.8	625.10095493	Sri Lanka	TG105-106	624.20952	Japan
TF1105-1106	625.100952	Japan	TG107-108	624.20955	Iran
TF1107-1108	625.100955	Iran	TG109-110	624.20957	Asian Russia
TF1109-1110	625.100957	Asian Russia	TG111-112	624.209561	Turkey
TF1111-1112	625.1009561	Turkey	TG113.I55	624.209598	Indonesia
TF1113.I55	625.1009598	Indonesia	TG113.I7	624.209567	Iraq
TF1113.I7	625.1009567	Iraq	TG113.I75	624.2095694	Israel/Palestine
TF1113.I75	625.10095694	Israel/Palestine	TG113.P6	624.209599	Philippines
TF1113.P6	625.1009599	Philippines	TG115-119	624.2096	Africa
TF1115-1119	625.10096	Africa	TG117-118	624.20962	Egypt
TF1117-1118	625.100962	Egypt	TG119	624.2096(1-9)	Africa, By country
TF1119	625.10096(1-9)	Africa, By country	TG121-122	624.20994	Australia

LC	Dewey	Descriptor	LC	Dewey	Descriptor
TG122.5-.6	624.20993	New Zealand	TH95.F5	690.094897	Finland
TG123-124	624.2099(5-6)	Oceania	TH95.Y8	690.09497	Yugoslavia
TG125-126	624.20998	Polar areas	TH101-102	690.0951	China
TG139-140	624.2092	Biography	TH103-104	690.0954	India
TG215-255	343.09(4-5)	Bridge legislation and laws	TH104.5-.6	690.095491	Pakistan
TG265-270	624.201	Theory of structures, Bridges	TH104.7-.8	690.095493	Sri Lanka
			TH105-106	690.0952	Japan
TG301-304	624.25	Bridge design and drafting	TH107-108	690.0955	Iran
TG305	624.20287	Testing	TH109-110	690.0957	Asian Russia
TG307	624.20228	Models	TH111-112	690.09561	Turkey
TG310	624.20(212/687)	Specifications/Contracts	TH113.I55	690.09598	Indonesia
TG313	624.20299	Estimates/Quantities/Costs	TH113.I7	690.09567	Iraq
TG315	624.28	Maintenance/Repair	TH113.I75	690.095694	Israel/Palestine
TG320	624.284	Bridge foundations	TH113.P6	690.09599	Philippines
TG325	624.28	Abutments/Retaining walls	TH115-119	690.096	Africa
TG325.6	624.283	Floors	TH117-118	690.0962	Egypt
TG326	624.28	Details (Bearings/Etc.)	TH119	690.096(1-9)	Africa, By country
TG327-340	624.6	Arched bridges	TH121-122	690.0994	Australia
TG350-360	624.37	Beam and girder bridges	TH122.5-.6	690.0993	New Zealand
TG365-370	624.32	Trustle bridges	TH123-124	690.099(5-6)	Oceania
TG375-380	624.38	Trussed bridges	TH125-126	690.0998	Polar areas
TG470	624.20289	Accidents	TH139-140	690.092	Biography
TH	690	Building construction	TH165-213	690.07	Education
TH1-4	690.0(5/6)	Serials/Societies	TH219-255	343.078690	Laws/Legislation
TH5	690.06	Congresses	TH375-383	690.2	Building/Site
TH6	690.074	Exhibitions/Museums	TH434-437	690.0299	Estimates/Costs
TH9	690.03	Dictionaries/Encyclopedias	TH845-895	690	Engineering
TH15-126	690.09	History	TH900-915	690.028	Equipment
TH15-19	690.090(1-4)	By date	TH1061-1725	693	Systems of construction
TH21-126	690.09(3-9)	By place	TH1061-1093	693.82	Fire-resistive/Fireproof
TH23-25	690.0973	United States	TH1199-1501	693.(1/5)	Masonry/Concrete
TH26-27	690.0971	Canada	TH1610-1675	693.7	Metals
TH28-29	690.0972	Mexico	TH1715	691.95	Insulation
TH30-31	690.09728	Central America	TH2031-3000	690.1	Details in design/ Construction
TH32-33	690.09729	West Indies			
TH36-37	690.0982	Argentina	TH2101	690.11	Foundations/Supports/Etc.
TH38-39	690.0984	Bolivia	TH2201-2251	690.12	Walls
TH41-42	690.0981	Brazil	TH2261-2279	690.182	Windows/Doors/Etc.
TH43-44	690.0983	Chile	TH2281-2288	690.15	Chimneys
TH45-46	690.09861	Colombia	TH2301-2311	694.2	Framing
TH47	690.09866	Ecuador	TH2391-2495	690.15	Roofs
TH48	690.09881	Guyana	TH2521-2529	690.16	Flooring
TH49	690.09883	Suriname	TH2531	690.17	Ceilings
TH50	690.09882	French Guiana	TH3301-3411	690.24	Maintenance/Repair
TH51	690.09892	Paraguay	TH4021-4970	690.(5-8)	Buildings by type/Use
TH52	690.0985	Peru	TH4021-4221	690.(5-6)	Public
TH53	690.09895	Uruguay	TH4221	690.6	Churches
TH54	690.0987	Venezuela	TH4311	690.52	Commercial/Office
TH57-64.5	690.0941	Great Britain	TH4451-4499	690.53	Storage/Warehouses
TH65-.2	690.09436	Austria	TH4511-4591	690.54	Factories
TH65.3-.4	690.09437	Czechoslovakia	TH4711	690.58	Recreation
TH65.5-66	690.09439	Hungary	TH4805-4850	690.8	Houses
TH67-68	690.09493	Belgium	TH4911-4935	690.8(6/92)	Farm buildings
TH69-70	690.09489	Denmark	TH5011-5701	690-697	By phase of work
TH71-72.5	690.0944	France	TH5201	690.11	Foundations
TH73-74.5	690.0943	Germany	TH5311-5511	624.183/693.(1-2)	Masonry/Bricklaying
TH75-76	690.09495	Greece	TH5601-5691	694	Carpentry/Joinery
TH77-78	690.09492	Netherlands	TH6010-6013	696-697	Fittings/Etc./Mechanical equip.
TH79-80	690.0945	Italy			
TH81-82	690.09481	Norway	TH6014-6085	697	Environmental engineering
TH83-84.5	690.09469	Portugal	TH6101-6887	696.1	Plumbing and pipefitting
TH85-86	690.0947	European Russia	TH6485-6500	696.182	Bathrooms
TH87-88	690.0946	Spain	TH6507-6512	696.184	Kitchens
TH88.5	690.0948	Scandinavia	TH6521-6569	696.12	Water supply
TH89-90	690.09485	Sweden	TH6571-6675	696.1(3/8)	House drainage
TH91-92	690.09494	Switzerland	TH6681-6685	696.10288	Maintenance of plumbing
TH95.A2	690.09496	Balkans	TH6800-6887	696.2	Gas supply

LC	Dewey	Descriptor	LC	Dewey	Descriptor
TH7005-7699	697	Heating and ventilation	TJ109-110	621.0957	Asian Russia
TH7201-7643	697.(1-8)	Heating of buildings	TJ111-112	621.09561	Turkey
TH7400-7413	697.04	Heating by special fuels	TJ113.I55	621.09598	Indonesia
TH7418-7458	697.(02/1-2)	Local heating	TJ113.I7	621.09567	Iraq
TH7461-7638	697.03	Central heating	TJ113.I75	621.095694	Israel/Palestine
TH7601-7635	697.3	Warm air heating	TJ113.P6	621.09599	Philippines
TH7647-7699	697.92	Ventilation of buildings	TJ115-119	621.096	Africa
TH7687-7688	697.93	Air conditioning and cooling	TJ117-118	621.0962	Egypt
TH7700-7975	621.32/644.3	Illumination, lighting	TJ119	621.096(1-9)	Africa, By country
TH8001-8581	698	Decoration	TJ121-122	621.0994	Australia
TH9025-9745	690.22	Protection of buildings	TJ122.5-.6	621.0993	New Zealand
TH9111-9599	693.82	From fire, Fire prevention	TJ123-124	621.099(5-6)	Oceania
TJ	621	Mechanical engineering	TJ125-126	621.0998	Polar areas
TJ1-4	621.0(5/6)	Serials/Societies	TJ139-140	621.092	Biography
TJ5	621.06	Congresses	TJ158-159	621.07	Education
TJ6	621.074	Exhibitions/Museums	TJ164	621.3121	Power plants
TJ9	621.03	Dictionaries/Encyclopedias	TJ166	621.0289	Safety
TJ11-13	621.025	Directories	TJ168	621.0294	General catalogs
TJ14	621.01	Philosophy	TJ170-173	620.1	Mechanics
TJ15-20	621.09	History	TJ177	621.811	Machinery vibration
TJ21-126	621.09(4-9)	By place	TJ181-210	621.811	Mechanical movements
TJ23-25	621.0973	United States	TJ189-204	621.83	Special gears
TJ26-27	621.0971	Canada	TJ212-225	621.317	Control engineering
TJ28-29	621.0972	Mexico	TJ227-240	621.815	Machine design
TJ30-31	621.09728	Central America	TJ255-265	621.4	Heat engines
TJ32-33	621.09729	West Indies	TJ268-280.5	621.1	Steam engineering
TJ36-37	621.0982	Argentina	TJ281-393	621.183	Boilers
TJ38-39	621.0984	Bolivia	TJ290-295	621.18	Construction
TJ41-42	621.0981	Brazil	TJ310-318	621.1(5-9)	Types of boilers
TJ43-44	621.0983	Chile	TJ320-393	621.197	Details/Accessories
TJ45-46	621.09861	Colombia	TJ320-358	621.183	Furnaces
TJ47	621.09866	Ecuador	TJ395-444	621.3121	Powerplants
TJ48	621.09881	Guyana	TJ415-444	621.185	Pipe and fittings
TJ49	621.09883	Suriname	TJ461-567	621.1	Steam engines
TJ50	621.09882	French Guiana	TJ485-507	621.1(5-6)	Special types
TJ51	621.09892	Paraguay	TJ515-551	621.1(5-6)	Design/Construction
TJ52	621.0985	Peru	TJ603-695	625.261	Locomotives
TJ53	621.09895	Uruguay	TJ700-740	621.1(5-6)	Other steam engines
TJ54	621.0987	Venezuela	TJ731-830	621.4(2-3)	Misc. motors/Engines
TJ57-64.5	621.0941	Great Britain	TJ770-780	621.433	Gas engines
TJ65-.2	621.09436	Austria	TJ795-799	621.436	Diesel engines
TJ65.3-.4	621.09437	Czechoslovakia	TJ823-827	621.453	Windmills
TJ65.5-66	621.09439	Hungary	TJ840-935	621.2	Hydraulic machinery
TJ67-68	621.09493	Belgium	TJ900-925	621.69	Pumps
TJ69-70	621.09489	Denmark	TJ930-933	621.8672	Pipelines
TJ71-72.5	621.0944	France	TJ940	621.55	Vacuum technology
TJ73-74.5	621.0943	Germany	TJ950-1030	621.6	Fans/Blowers/Air pumps
TJ75-76	621.09495	Greece	TJ1061-1073	621.822	Bearings
TJ77-78	621.09492	Netherlands	TJ1100-1119	621.852	Belts
TJ79-80	621.0945	Italy	TJ1125-1345	621.9	Machine shops
TJ81-82	621.09481	Norway	TJ1135-1150	621.9068	Management
TJ83-84.5	621.09469	Portugal	TJ1180-1313	621.90(2/8)	Machine/Handtools/Etc.
TJ85-86	621.0947	European Russia	TJ1185-1191	621.902	Machine tools
TJ87-88	621.0946	Spain	TJ1195-1201	621.908	Handtools
TJ88.5	621.0948	Scandinavia	TJ1233-1240	621.93	Cutting/Sawing tools
TJ89-90	621.09485	Sweden	TJ1320-1340	621.88	Fastenings
TJ91-92	621.09494	Switzerland	TJ1345	621.91(4)	Milling/Crushing
TJ95.A2	621.09496	Balkans	TJ1357-1383	621.862	Hoisting
TJ95.F5	621.094897	Finland	TJ1385-1418	621.867	Conveying
TJ95.Y8	621.09497	Yugoslavia	TJ1425-1475	621.(86/98)	Lifting/Pressing machinery
TJ101-102	621.0951	China	TJ1480-1496	631.3	Agricultural machinery
TJ103-104	621.0954	India	TJ1501-1519	646.2044	Sewing machines
TJ104.5-.6	621.095491	Pakistan	TK	621.3	Electrical/Nuclear engineering
TJ104.7-.8	621.095493	Sri Lanka	TK1-4	621.30(5/6)	Serials/Societies
TJ105-106	621.0952	Japan	TK5	621.306	Congresses
TJ107-108	621.0955	Iran	TK6	621.3074	Exhibitions/Museums

155

LC	Dewey	Descriptor
TK9	621.303	Dictionaries/Encyclopedias
TK12	621.3025	Directories
TK15-18	621.309	History
TK21-126	621.309(4-9)	By place
TK23-25	621.30973	United States
TK26-27	621.30971	Canada
TK28-29	621.30972	Mexico
TK30-31	621.309728	Central America
TK32-33	621.309729	West Indies
TK36-37	621.30982	Argentina
TK38-39	621.30984	Bolivia
TK41-42	621.30981	Brazil
TK43-44	621.30983	Chile
TK45-46	621.309861	Colombia
TK47	621.309866	Ecuador
TK48	621.309881	Guyana
TK49	621.309883	Suriname
TK50	621.309882	French Guiana
TK51	621.309892	Paraguay
TK52	621.30985	Peru
TK53	621.309895	Uruguay
TK54	621.30987	Venezuela
TK57-64.5	621.30941	Great Britain
TK65-.2	621.309436	Austria
TK65.3-.4	621.309437	Czechoslovakia
TK65.5-66	621.309439	Hungary
TK67-68	621.309493	Belgium
TK69-70	621.309489	Denmark
TK71-72.5	621.30944	France
TK73-74.5	621.30943	Germany
TK75-76	621.309495	Greece
TK77-78	621.309492	Netherlands
TK79-80	621.30945	Italy
TK81-82	621.309481	Norway
TK83-84.5	621.309469	Portugal
TK85-86	621.30947	European Russia
TK87-88	621.30946	Spain
TK88.5	621.30948	Scandinavia
TK89-90	621.309485	Sweden
TK91-92	621.309494	Switzerland
TK95.A2	621.309496	Balkans
TK95.F5	621.3094897	Finland
TK95.Y8	621.309497	Yugoslavia
TK101-102	621.30951	China
TK103-104	621.30954	India
TK104.5-.6	621.3095491	Pakistan
TK104.7-.8	621.3095493	Sri Lanka
TK105-106	621.30952	Japan
TK107-108	621.30955	Iran
TK109-110	621.30957	Asian Russia
TK111-112	621.309561	Turkey
TK113.I55	621.309598	Indonesia
TK113.I7	621.309567	Iraq
TK113.I75	621.3095694	Israel/Palestine
TK113.P6	621.309599	Philippines
TK115-119	621.3096	Africa
TK117-118	621.30962	Egypt
TK119	621.3096(1-9)	Africa, By country
TK121-122	621.30994	Australia
TK122.5-.6	621.30993	New Zealand
TK123-124	621.3099(5-6)	Oceania
TK125-126	621.30998	Polar areas
TK165-213	621.307	Education
TK215-255	343.0786213	Laws/Legislation
TK275-277	621.37	Standards/Measurements
TK301-396	621.373	Meters
TK401-415	621.37	Testing
TK431-451	621.30221	Drawings
TK452-454.4	621.3028	Apparatus/Materials
TK1001-1841	621.3121	Production of electric energy
TK1041-1081	621.3121	Production methods
TK1191-1841	621.3121	Powerplants
TK2000-2891	621.3132	Dynamoelectric machinery/Etc.
TK2411-2491	621.313	Generators
TK2511-2541	621.313	Motors
TK2611-2699	621.3132	Direct current
TK2711-2799	621.3133	Alternating current
TK2805	621.315	Condensers
TK2811-2891	621.317	Meters/Switches
TK2896-2970	621.3121	Production of electricity
TK3001-3511	621.319	Distribution of electric power
TK3101-3171	621.3191	Systems
TK3201-3351	621.3193	Wiring/Cables
TK4001-4101	621.3(2-9)	Applications of electric power
TK4125-4399	621.32	Electric lighting
TK4134-4156	621.3209(4-9)	By place
TK4135-4137	621.320973	United States
TK4138-4139	621.320971	Canada
TK4140	621.320972	Mexico
TK4141-4142	621.3209728	Central America
TK4143-4144	621.3209729	West Indies
TK4145-4146	621.32098	South America
TK4147-4148	621.32094	Europe
TK4149-4150	621.32095	Asia
TK4151-4152	621.32096	Africa
TK4153-4154.5	621.32099(3-4)	Australia/New Zealand
TK4155-4156	621.32099(5-6)	Oceania
TK4303-4391	621.32(5-7)	Lighting systems
TK4311-4335	621.325	Arc
TK4341-4367	621.326	Incandescent
TK4500	621.362	Infrared technology
TK4601-4661	621.4028	Electric heating
TK5101-6525	621.382	Telecommunication
TK5107-5865	621.383	Telegraph
TK5107	621.3830(5/6)	Serials/Societies/Etc.
TK5301-5385	384.15/621.383	Plants/Stations/The line
TK5401-5491	621.383	Distribution/Construction
TK5451-5468	384.15/621.383	The line
TK5501-5585	384.15/621.383	Systems/Instruments
TK5601-5681	384.1	Submarine telegraph
TK5700-5865	621.3842	Radiotelegraph
TK5981-5986	621.3828	Electroacoustics
TK6001-6525	621.38(5-7)	Telephone
TK6001-6005	621.3850(5/6)	Serials/Societies/Congresses
TK6201-6285	621.38(5-7)	Plants/Stations/The line
TK6301-6397	621.387	Distribution/Construction
TK6401-6500	621.387	Systems/Instruments
TK6540-6571.5	621.384	Radio
TK6540-6542	621.3840(5/6)	Serials/Societies/Congresses
TK6560-6595	621.3841(1/8)	Receivers/Senders
TK6573-6600	621.3848	Radar
TK6573	621.38480(5/6)	Serials/Societies/Congresses
TK6585-6592	621.384135	Antennas
TK6630-6720	621.388	Television
TK6630	621.38800(5/6)	Serials/Societies/Congresses
TK6650-6655	621.3883	Tubes/Antennas
TK7018-7725	621.38928	Bells/Alarms/Etc.
TK7800-8360	621.381	Electronics
TK7800-7801	621.3810(5/6)	Serials/Societies/Congresses
TK7867-7868	621.3815	Circuits

LC	Dewey	Descriptor	LC	Dewey	Descriptor
TK7870-7872	621.3815	Amplifiers/Tubes/Diodes	TL107-108	629.20955	Iran
TK7876	621.3813	Microwaves	TL109-110	629.20957	Asian Russia
TK7878-7879	621.3810287	Electronic measurements	TL111-112	629.209561	Turkey
TK7885-7895	621.39	Computer engineering	TL113.I55	629.209598	Indonesia
TK7887	621.390288	Maintenance/Repair	TL113.I7	629.209567	Iraq
TK7888	621.3919	Analog	TL113.I75	629.2095694	Israel/Palestine
TK7888.3	621.39	Digital	TL113.P6	629.209599	Philippines
TK7889	621.391	Special computers	TL115-119	629.2096	Africa
TK7895	621.397	Tapes/Memory	TL117-118	629.20962	Egypt
TK8300-8360	621.381542	Photoelectronic devices	TL119	629.2096(1-9)	Africa, By country
TK9001-9401	621.48	Nuclear engineering	TL121-122	629.20994	Australia
TK9001-9006	621.480(5/6)	Serials/Societies/Congresses	TL122.5-.6	629.20993	New Zealand
TK9151.4-9152.2	621.4835	Radiation procedures	TL123-124	629.2099(5-6)	Oceania
TK9202-9230	621.483	Nuclear reactors	TL125-126	629.20998	Polar areas
TL	629.(2/1)	Motor vehicles/Aeronautics	TL139-140	629.2092	Biography
TL1-480	629.2	Motor vehicles	TL151.5-.7	629.283	Operation (Driving)
TL1-5	629.20(5/6)	Serials/Societies	TL200-229	629.250(1-9)	Automobiles (By power type)
TL6	629.206	Congresses			
TL7	629.2074	Exhibitions/Museums	TL240-275	629.23	Design/Construction/Equipment
TL9	629.203	Dictionaries			
TL12	629.2025	Directories	TL400-460	629.227	Cycles
TL15	629.209	History	TL439-448	629.2275	Motorcycles
TL21-126	629.209(4-9)	By place	TL500-777	629.13	Aeronautics
TL23-25	629.20973	United States	TL500-505	629.1300(5/6)	Serials/Societies/Congresses
TL26-27	629.20971	Canada	TL515-516	629.13009	History
TL28-29	629.20972	Mexico	TL521-532	629.13009(4-9)	By place
TL30-31	629.209728	Central America	TL521-522	629.13009973	United States
TL32-33	629.209729	West Indies	TL523	629.1300971	Canada
TL36-37	629.20982	Argentina	TL524-525	629.13009(72-8)	Mexico/West Indies/Latin Amer.
TL38-39	629.20984	Bolivia			
TL41-42	629.20981	Brazil	TL526	629.130094	Europe
TL43-44	629.20983	Chile	TL527	629.130095	Asia
TL45-46	629.209861	Colombia	TL528	629.130096	Africa
TL47	629.209866	Ecuador	TL529-530	629.130099(3-6)	Australia/New Zealand/ Oceania
TL48	629.209881	Guyana			
TL49	629.209883	Suriname	TL539-540	629.130092	Biography
TL50	629.209882	French Guiana	TL553.5	629.130684	Accidents
TL51	629.209892	Paraguay	TL556-558	629.1324	Meteorology
TL52	629.20985	Peru	TL570-574	629.1323	Aerodynamics
TL53	629.209895	Uruguay	TL586-589.7	629.13(251/5)	Navigation and instruments
TL54	629.20987	Venezuela	TL600-688	629.133	Aircraft type
TL57-64.5	629.20941	Great Britain	TL605-668	629.1332	Lighter than air
TL65-.2	629.209436	Austria	TL670-688	629.1333	Heavier than air
TL65.3-.4	629.209437	Czechoslovakia	TL692-694	629.135	Communication
TL65.5-66	629.209439	Hungary	TL695-696	629.1351	Electronic aids to navigation
TL67-68	629.209493	Belgium			
TL69-70	629.209489	Denmark	TL710-713	629.1325	Flying
TL71-72.5	629.20944	France	TL725-733	629.136	Airways/Airports/Fields
TL73-74.5	629.20943	Germany	TL780-785.8	621.4356	Rockets
TL75-76	629.209495	Greece	TL787-4050	629.4	Astronautics/Space travel
TL77-78	629.209492	Netherlands	TL789	001.942	UFOs
TL79-80	629.20945	Italy	TL789.8	629.409(4-9)	By place
TL81-82	629.209481	Norway	TL795	629.47	Spaceships
TL83-84.5	629.209469	Portugal	TL796-798	629.46	Artificial satellites
TL85-86	629.20947	European Russia	TL799	629.455	Flights (By planet)
TL87-88	629.20946	Spain	TL844	621.43560228	Model rockets
TL88.5	629.20948	Scandinavia	TL845-849	629.407	Education
TL89-90	629.209485	Sweden	TL867	629.40289	Safety
TL91-92	629.209494	Switzerland	TL869	629.4068	Contracts
TL95.A2	629.209496	Balkans	TL870-873	629.47	Systems engineering
TL95.F5	629.2094897	Finland	TL875-940	629.47(1/3)	Vehicle design/Construction
TL95.Y8	629.209497	Yugoslavia			
TL101-102	629.20951	China	TL945	629.4774	Sterilization (Vehicle)
TL103-104	629.20954	India	TL950-953	629.472	Materials (Vehicle)
TL104.5-.6	629.2095491	Pakistan	TL1050-1060	629.4(5/11)	Astrodynamics/Flight mechanics
TL104.7-.8	629.2095493	Sri Lanka			
TL105-106	629.20952	Japan	TL1065-1080	629.453	Space navigation

LC	Dewey	Descriptor
TL1082	629.4742	Instruments
TL1085	629.4507	Space flight training
TL1090-1095	629.458	Piloting
TL1100-1102	629.474	Electric equipment on vehicles
TL1500-1575	629.477	Human engineering/Life support
TL3000-3280	629.453	Astrionics/Electronics
TL4000-4050	629.478	Ground support
TN	622/669	Mining engineering/ Metallurgy
TN1-4	622.0(5/6)	Serials/Societies
TN5	622.06	Congresses
TN6	622.074	Exhibitions/Museums
TN9-10	622.03	Dictionaries/Encyclopedias
TN12	622.025	Directories
TN15-19	622.09	History
TN21-126	622.09(4-9)	Mine engineering, By place
TN23-25	622.0973	United States
TN26-27	622.0971	Canada
TN28-29	622.0972	Mexico
TN30-31	622.09728	Central America
TN32-33	622.09729	West Indies
TN36-37	622.0982	Argentina
TN38-39	622.0984	Bolivia
TN41-42	622.0981	Brazil
TN43-44	622.0983	Chile
TN45-46	622.09861	Colombia
TN47	622.09866	Ecuador
TN48	622.09881	Guyana
TN49	622.09883	Suriname
TN50	622.09882	French Guiana
TN51	622.09892	Paraguay
TN52	622.0985	Peru
TN53	622.09895	Uruguay
TN54	622.0987	Venezuela
TN57-64.5	622.0941	Great Britain
TN65-.2	622.09436	Austria
TN65.3-.4	622.09437	Czechoslovakia
TN65.5-66	622.09439	Hungary
TN67-68	622.09493	Belgium
TN69-70	622.09489	Denmark
TN71-72.5	622.0944	France
TN73-74.5	622.0943	Germany
TN75-76	622.09495	Greece
TN77-78	622.09492	Netherlands
TN79-80	622.0945	Italy
TN81-82	622.09481	Norway
TN83-84.5	622.09469	Portugal
TN85-86	622.0947	European Russia
TN87-88	622.0946	Spain
TN88.5	622.0948	Scandinavia
TN89-90	622.09485	Sweden
TN91-92	622.09494	Switzerland
TN95.A2	622.09496	Balkans
TN95.F5	622.094897	Finland
TN95.Y8	622.09497	Yugoslavia
TN101-102	622.0951	China
TN103-104	622.0954	India
TN104.5-.6	622.095491	Pakistan
TN104.7-.8	622.095493	Sri Lanka
TN105-106	622.0952	Japan
TN107-108	622.0955	Iran
TN109-110	622.0957	Asian Russia
TN111-112	622.09561	Turkey
TN113.I55	622.09598	Indonesia
TN113.I7	622.09567	Iraq
TN113.I75	622.095694	Israel/Palestine
TN113.P6	622.09599	Philippines
TN115-119	622.096	Africa
TN117-118	622.0962	Egypt
TN119	622.096(1-9)	Africa, By country
TN121-122	622.0994	Australia
TN122.5-.6	622.0993	New Zealand
TN123-124	622.099(5-6)	Oceania
TN125-126	622.0998	Polar areas
TN139-140	622.092	Biography
TN165-213	622.07	Education
TN215-257	343.0775	Mining laws/Legislation
TN270-271	622.18	Prospecting
TN272-274	622.2	Mines
TN275-292	622.2(2-9)	Practical mining operations
TN295-319	622.8	Safety and ventilation
TN331-342	622.6	Transportation
TN343	622.48	Electrical engineering
TN345	622.2	Machinery/Tools/Etc.
TN400-580	622.34	Ores and mining
TN400-409	622.341	Iron ore
TN600-799	669	Metallurgy
TN600-605	669.0(5/6)	Serials/Societies/Congresses
TN612	669.025	Directories
TN615-620	669.09	History
TN621-655	669.09(4-9)	By place
TN672	669.8	Heat treatment of metals
TN675.3	669.07	Education
TN681-687	669.0284	Electrometallurgy
TN688	669.0283	Hydrometallurgy
TN690-693	669	Metallurgy
TN695-799	669.(1-7)	Types of metallurgy
TN799.5-948	622.33	Nonmetallic minerals
TN800-842	622.334	Coal
TN845-859	622.33(8-9)	Other natural carbons
TN860-879	622.338	Petroleum
TN880-883	622.3385	Natural gas
TN885	622.339	Amber/Fossil gums
TN890	622.3668	Sulphur
TN895-897	669.725	Alkalies
TN899-909	622.363	Sodium salts, Soda deposits
TN911	622.364	Nitrates
TN913	622.364	Phosphates
TN917	622.3633	Borax/Borates
TN919	622.3636	Potassium salts/Potash
TN923-929	622.373	Mineral waters
TN930	622.3672	Asbestos
TN933	622.3674	Mica
TN936	622.365	Abrasives
TN939	622.3626	Sand/Gravel
TN941-943	622.361	Clay
TN945	622.368	Cement materials
TN946	622.3635	Gypsum
TN948	622.3(5-9)	Other nonmetalic minerals
TN950-997	622.35	Building/Ornamental stones
TP	660	Chemical technology
TP1	660.0(5/6)	Serials/Societies
TP5	660.06	Congresses
TP6	660.074	Exhibitions/Museums
TP9	660.03	Dictionaries/Encyclopedias
TP12	660.025	Directories
TP15-20	660.09	History
TP21-126	660.09(4-9)	Chemical technology, By place
TP23-25	660.0973	United States
TP26-27	660.0971	Canada
TP28-29	660.0972	Mexico

LC	Dewey	Descriptor	LC	Dewey	Descriptor
TP30-31	660.09728	Central America	TP249-261	661	Industrial chemistry
TP32-33	660.09729	West Indies	TP265-267	662	Chemistry of fire
TP36-37	660.0982	Argentina	TP267.5-301	662.(1-2)	Explosives and pyrotechnics
TP38-39	660.0984	Bolivia			
TP41-42	660.0981	Brazil	TP310	662.5	Matches
TP43-44	660.0983	Chile	TP315-360	662.6	Fuel
TP45-46	660.09861	Colombia	TP361	665.(5-8)/662.66	Inflammable liquids and gases
TP47	660.09866	Ecuador			
TP48	660.09881	Guyana	TP363	660.2842(6-7)	Heating, drying, cooling
TP49	660.09883	Suriname	TP365	660.2961	By products of combustion
TP50	660.09882	French Guiana	TP368-465	664	Food processing/ Manufacture
TP51	660.09892	Paraguay			
TP52	660.0985	Peru	TP480-482	660.29686	Low-temperature engineering
TP53	660.09895	Uruguay			
TP54	660.0987	Venezuela	TP490-498	664.0285(2/3)	Refrigeration/Icemaking
TP57-64.5	660.0941	Great Britain	TP500-659	663.13	Fermentation industries
TP65-.2	660.09436	Austria	TP670-699	665.(2-4)	Oils/Fats/Waxes
TP65.3-.4	660.09437	Czechoslovakia	TP680-684	665.(3-4)	Vegetable oils/Fats/Waxes
TP65.5-66	660.09439	Hungary	TP685-699	665.4	Mineral oils/Fats/Waxes
TP67-68	660.09493	Belgium	TP690-692.5	665.5	Petroleum
TP69-70	660.09489	Denmark	TP700-746	621.32	Illuminating industries
TP71-72.5	660.0944	France	TP751-762	665.706	Gas industry
TP73-74.5	660.0943	Germany	TP785-871	666.(1-7)	Glass/Clay industries/Etc.
TP75-76	660.09495	Greece	TP870-873	666.8(6-9)	Artificial stones/Gems
TP77-78	660.09492	Netherlands	TP875-889	666.9	Cement industries/ Lime/Etc.
TP79-80	660.0945	Italy			
TP81-82	660.09481	Norway	TP890-933	677	Textile processing
TP83-84.5	660.09469	Portugal	TP934-944	667.(6-7)	Paints/Pigments/Varnishes
TP85-86	660.0947	European Russia	TP946-949.95	667.(4-5)	Inks
TP87-88	660.0946	Spain	TP950-994	661.8	Organic chemical industries
TP88.5	660.0948	Scandinavia	TP995-996	658.567	Utilization of wastes
TP89-90	660.09485	Sweden	TP997	662.65	Wood distillation
TP91-92	660.09494	Switzerland	TP1101-1185	668.4	Plastics (Manufacture)
TP95.A2	660.09496	Balkans	TP1101-1105	668.40(5/6)	Serials/Societies/Congresses
TP95.F5	660.094897	Finland	TP1107	668.4074	Exhibitions/Museums
TP95.Y8	660.09497	Yugoslavia	TP1110	668.403	Dictionaries/Encyclopedias
TP101-102	660.0951	China	TP1112	668.4025	Directories
TP103-104	660.0954	India	TP1116-1118	668.409	History
TP104.5-.6	660.095491	Pakistan	TP1150-1175	668.4(2-5)	Processes
TP104.7-.8	660.095493	Sri Lanka	TP1177-1185	668.4(2-9)	By type
TP105-106	660.0952	Japan	TR	770	Photography
TP107-108	660.0955	Iran	TR1	770.(5/6)	Serials/Societies
TP109-110	660.0957	Asian Russia	TR5	770.6	Congresses
TP111-112	660.09561	Turkey	TR6	770.74	Exhibitions/Museums
TP113.I55	660.09598	Indonesia	TR9	770.3	Dictionaries/Encyclopedias
TP113.I7	660.09567	Iraq	TR12	770.25	Directories
TP113.I75	660.095694	Israel/Palestine	TR15	770.9	History
TP113.P6	660.09599	Philippines	TR21-126	770.9(4-9)	By place
TP115-119	660.096	Africa	TR22-25	770.973	United States
TP117-118	660.0962	Egypt	TR26-27	770.971	Canada
TP119	660.096(1-9)	Africa, By country	TR28-29	770.972	Mexico
TP121-122	660.0994	Australia	TR30-31	770.9728	Central America
TP122.5-.6	660.0993	New Zealand	TR32-33	770.9729	West Indies
TP123-124	660.099(5-6)	Oceania	TR34-54	770.98	South America
TP125-126	660.0998	Polar areas	TR36-37	770.982	Argentina
TP139-140	660.092	Biography	TR38-39	770.984	Bolivia
TP155-156	660	Chemical engineering	TR41-42	770.981	Brazil
TP157-159	660.28(2-3)	Apparatus and supplies	TR43-44	770.983	Chile
TP165-183	660.07	Education	TR45-46	770.9861	Colombia
TP187-197	660.076	Laboratories	TR47	770.9866	Ecuador
TP200-245	661	Chemicals	TR48-50	770.988	Guianas
TP217	661.2	Acids	TR51	770.9892	Paraguay
TP222-223	661.03	Alkalies	TR52	770.985	Peru
TP230-240	661.(4-6)	Salts	TR53	770.9895	Uruguay
TP245	661.(1-7)	Inorganic chemicals	TR54	770.987	Venezuela
TP247-248	661.8	Organic chemicals/ Preparations	TR55-95	770.94	Europe
			TR57-64.5	770.941	Great Britain

LC	Dewey	Descriptor
TR59.3	770.9415	Ireland
TR65-.2	770.9436	Austria
TR71-72.5	770.944	France
TR73-74.5	770.943	Germany
TR75-76	770.9495	Greece
TR79-80	770.945	Italy
TR77-78	770.9492	Netherlands
TR81-82	770.9481	Norway
TR85-86	770.947	European Russia
TR87-88	770.946	Spain
TR89-90	770.9485	Sweden
TR91-92	770.9494	Switzerland
TR99-113	770.95	Asia
TR101-102	770.951	China
TR103-104	770.954	India
TR105-106	770.952	Japan
TR107-108	770.955	Iran
TR109-110	770.957	Asian Russia
TR111-112	770.9561	Turkey/Asia Minor
TR115-119	770.96	Africa
TR117-118	770.962	Egypt
TR121-122	770.994	Australia
TR122.5-.6	770.993	New Zealand
TR123-124	770.99(5-6)	Oceania
TR139-140	770.92	Biography
TR149	770	Juvenile
TR151	770.212	Tables/Formulas
TR154	770.232	As a profession
TR161	770.7	Education
TR162	770.76	Examinations/Questions
TR196-199	771	Materials/Supplies/Etc.
TR200-220	770.1	Theory of general processes
TR225	771.47	Recovery of wastes
TR250-265	771.3	Cameras
TR268	771	Pinhole photography
TR270	771.352	Lenses
TR280-285	771.532(2-4)	Plates/Films/Paper
TR287-500	772-774	Processing techniques
TR504-508	778.2	Transparencies/Diapositives
TR515-545	778.6	Color photography
TR550-581	771.1	Studio/Laboratory
TR590-605	778.72	Lighting
TR624-835	778	Applied photography
TR640-685	778	Artistic
TR692-780	778.99(5-6)	Scientific/Technological
TR721-729	778.93	Nature
TR786-810	778.93(6-7)	Mountains/Travel/ Submarine
TR818	371.897	School photography
TR820	070.49	Journalism
TR821	070.449796	Sports journalism
TR845-899	778.5	Cinematography
TR900-923	771.4	Industrial production
TR905	771.44	Enlargements
TR910	771.44	Reductions
TR920-923	686.42	Blue print reproductions
TR925-1045	686.232	Photomechanical processes
TR930-937	686.2325	Collotype process
TR940-950	686.2325	Photolithography
TR970	686.2327	Photoengraving/Relief
TR975	686.2327	Halftone
TR977	778.6	Color process
TR980	686.2327	Photogravure/Intaglio process
TR1010	686.22544	Phototypeset
TR1025-1045	686.44	Electrophotography
TS	670	Manufacturing

LC	Dewey	Descriptor
TS1-5	670.(5/6)	Serials/Societies/Congresses
TS9	670.3	Dictionaries/Encyclopedias
TS15	670.9	History
TS21-126	670.9(4-9)	Manufacturing, By place
TS23-25	670.973	United States
TS26-27	670.971	Canada
TS28-29	670.972	Mexico
TS30-31	670.9728	Central America
TS32-33	670.9729	West Indies
TS36-37	670.982	Argentina
TS38-39	670.984	Bolivia
TS41-42	670.981	Brazil
TS43-44	670.983	Chile
TS45-46	670.9861	Colombia
TS47	670.9866	Ecuador
TS48	670.9881	Guyana
TS49	670.9883	Suriname
TS50	670.9882	French Guiana
TS51	670.9892	Paraguay
TS52	670.985	Peru
TS53	670.9895	Uruguay
TS54	670.987	Venezuela
TS57-64.5	670.941	Great Britain
TS65-.2	670.9436	Austria
TS65.3-.4	670.9437	Czechoslovakia
TS65.5-66	670.9439	Hungary
TS67-68	670.9493	Belgium
TS69-70	670.9489	Denmark
TS71-72.5	670.944	France
TS73-74.5	670.943	Germany
TS75-76	670.9495	Greece
TS77-78	670.9492	Netherlands
TS79-80	670.945	Italy
TS81-82	670.9481	Norway
TS83-84.5	670.9469	Portugal
TS85-86	670.947	European Russia
TS87-88	670.946	Spain
TS88.5	670.948	Scandinavia
TS89-90	670.9485	Sweden
TS91-92	670.9494	Switzerland
TS95.A2	670.9496	Balkans
TS95.F5	670.94897	Finland
TS95.Y8	670.9497	Yugoslavia
TS101-102	670.951	China
TS103-104	670.954	India
TS104.5-.6	670.95491	Pakistan
TS104.7-.8	670.95493	Sri Lanka
TS105-106	670.952	Japan
TS107-108	670.955	Iran
TS109-110	670.957	Asian Russia
TS111-112	670.9561	Turkey
TS113.I55	670.9598	Indonesia
TS113.I7	670.9567	Iraq
TS113.I75	670.95694	Israel/Palestine
TS113.P6	670.9599	Philippines
TS115-119	670.96	Africa
TS117-118	670.962	Egypt
TS119	670.96(1-9)	Africa, By country
TS121-122	670.994	Australia
TS122.5-.6	670.993	New Zealand
TS123-124	670.99(5-6)	Oceania
TS125-126	670.998	Polar areas
TS139-140	670.92	Biography
TS155-174	658.5	Production management
TS195-198.8	688.8	Packaging
TS200-770	671	Metal manufacturing
S200	671.0(5/6)	Serials/Societies/Congresses

LC	Dewey	Descriptor	LC	Dewey	Descriptor
TS214	363.7288	Scrap metals	TT12	745.5025	Directories
TS215	671.35	Metalworking machinery	TT15-126	745.509(4-9)	Handicrafts, By place
TS225-.2	671.332	Forging	TT23-25	745.50973	United States
TS226-228.9	671.5	Joining of metals	TT26-27	745.50971	Canada
TS228.99-239	671.2	Casting	TT28-29	745.50972	Mexico
TS300-360	672	Iron/Steel	TT30-31	745.509728	Central America
TS370-377	673	Nonferrous metals (General)	TT32-33	745.509729	West Indies
TS400-405	683	Hardware	TT36-37	745.50982	Argentina
TS500-518	681	Instrument manufacture	TT38-39	745.50984	Bolivia
TS519-530	683.3	Locksmithing	TT41-42	745.50981	Brazil
TS532-538.5	683.4	Firearms	TT43-44	745.50983	Chile
TS540-549	681.11(3-4)	Watches/Clocks	TT45-46	745.509861	Colombia
TS551-650	669	Metals	TT47	745.509866	Ecuador
TS653-718	671	Metal finishing (General)	TT48	745.509881	Guyana
TS720-770	669.2	Precious metals	TT49	745.509883	Suriname
TS740-761	739.27	Jewelry	TT50	745.509882	French Guiana
TS800-915	674	Wood technology/Lumber	TT51	745.509892	Paraguay
TS800-801	674.0(5/6)	Serials/Societies	TT52	745.50985	Peru
TS840-915	674.8/684.104	Wood products/Furniture	TT53	745.509895	Uruguay
TS840	674.80(5/6)	Serials/Societies	TT54	745.50987	Venezuela
TS850-851	674.8	Machinery/Mills	TT57-64.5	745.50941	Great Britain
TS880-889	684.104	Furniture	TT65-.2	745.509436	Austria
TS890	674.82	Barrels	TT65.3-.4	745.509437	Czechoslovakia
TS920-937	674.386	Chemical processing of wood	TT65.5-66	745.509439	Hungary
TS940-1067	675/685	Leather industries/Tanning	TT67-68	745.509493	Belgium
TS940	675.0(5/6)	Serials/Societies	TT69-70	745.509489	Denmark
TS970-980	675	Kinds of leather	TT71-72.5	745.50944	France
TS989-1025	685.31	Boots/Shoemaking	TT73-74.5	745.50943	Germany
TS1030-1035	685.1	Harnesess/Saddles	TT75-76	745.509495	Greece
TS1060-1067	675.3/685.24	Furs	TT77-78	745.509492	Netherlands
TS1080-1268	676	Paper manufacture/Trade	TT79-80	745.50945	Italy
TS1080	676.0(5/6)	Serials/Societies/Congresses	TT81-82	745.509481	Norway
TS1090-1096	676	Manufacturing	TT83-84.5	745.509469	Portugal
TS1124-1165	676.28(2-9)	Paper types	TT85-86	745.50947	European Russia
TS1171-1177	676.12	Woodpulp industry	TT87-88	745.50946	Spain
TS1228-1268	676.2823	Stationery	TT88.5	745.50948	Scandinavia
TS1262-1268	674.88/681.6	Pens/pencils	TT89-90	745.509485	Sweden
TS1300-1865	677	Textile industries	TT91-92	745.509494	Switzerland
TS1300-1301	677.00(5/6)	Serials/Societies/Congresses	TT95.A2	745.509496	Balkans
TS1480-1487	677.02822	Spinning	TT95.F5	745.5094897	Finland
TS1488-1520	677.028	Other processes	TT95.Y8	745.509497	Yugoslavia
TS1540-1549	677.(1-5)	Textile fibers	TT101-102	745.50951	China
TS1550-1590	677.21	Cotton manufacture	TT103-104	745.50954	India
TS1600-1635	677.31	Woolen manufacture	TT104.5-.6	745.5095491	Pakistan
TS1640-1688	677.39	Silk manufacture	TT104.7-.8	745.5095493	Sri Lanka
TS1700-1750	677.1	Flax/Hemp/Jute	TT105-106	745.50952	Japan
TS1760-1768	677.02864	Dry goods/Fabrics	TT107-108	745.50955	Iran
TS1870-1935	678.2	Rubber industry	TT109-110	745.50957	Asian Russia
TS1950-1981	664.(34/9)	Meats/Lard/Etc.	TT111-112	745.509561	Turkey
TS1960-1967	664.902	Butchering/Meat curing	TT113.I55	745.509598	Indonesia
TS2001-2035	688.6	Carriage/Wagon making	TT113.I7	745.509567	Iraq
TS2120-2159	664.7	Cereals/Grain milling	TT113.I75	745.5095694	Israel/Palestine
TS2156-2159	664.72	Cereal products	TT113.P6	745.509599	Philippines
TS2157	664.755	Macaroni/Spaghetti	TT115-119	745.5096	Africa
TS2158	664.76	Feeds	TT117-118	745.50962	Egypt
TS2159	664.725	Individual cereals (Corn/Rice)	TT119	745.5096(1-9)	Africa, By country
TS2160-2193	685.(4/2)/687.4	Gloves/Hats	TT121-122	745.50994	Australia
TS2220-2283	679.7	Tobacco	TT122.5-.6	745.50993	New Zealand
TS2255	679.7	Nicotine (Preparation/Use)	TT123-124	745.5099(5-6)	Oceania
TS2260	679.7(2/3)	Cigars/Cigarettes	TT125-126	745.50998	Polar areas
TS2270	688.42	Pipes	TT151	620.0046/646.(2/6)	Mending/Repairing
TT	745.5	Handicrafts/Arts and crafts	TT152-153	684.08	Workshops
TT1	745.50(5/6)	Serials/Societies	TT154-.5	688.1/745.5928	Models/Modelmaking
TT6	745.5074	Exhibitions/Museums	TT161-169	373.246	Industrial arts training
TT9	745.503	Dictionaries/Encyclopedias	TT174-176	745.592	Toys/Etc. for children
			TT180-203	745.51	Woodworking
			TT205-214	739/745.56	Metalworking

LC	Dewey	Descriptor	LC	Dewey	Descriptor
TT215-240	739.14	Ironworking/Forging	TX73-74.5	640.943	Germany
TT267	739.14	Soldering/Brazing	TX75-76	640.9495	Greece
TT270	745.73	Stencil cutting	TX79-80	640.945	Italy
TT288	745.584	Bone/Horn crafts	TX77-78	640.9492	Netherlands
TT290	745.531	Leatherwork	TX81-82	640.9481	Norway
TT297	745.572	Plastic crafts	TX85-86	640.947	European Russia
TT300-382.8	745.723	Painting/Varnishing/Etc.	TX87-88	640.946	Spain
TT310-315	745.723	Paint mixing/Spraying	TX89-90	640.9485	Sweden
TT320-324	698.1	House painting	TX91-92	640.9494	Switzerland
TT325-345	745.51	Wood finishing	TX99-113	640.95	Asia
TT360	745.61	Lettering/Etc.	TX101-102	640.951	China
TT370	745.7	Coloring of stone/Etc.	TX103-104	640.954	India
TT380	745.75	Gilding/Bronzing	TX105-106	640.952	Japan
TT382-.8	739.15/745.56	Metal finishing	TX107-108	640.955	Iran
TT387-410	646.21	Soft home furnishings	TX109-110	640.957	Asian Russia
TT490-695	646.4	Clothing manufacture	TX111-112	640.9561	Turkey/Asia Minor
TT490	646.40(5/6)	Serials/Societies	TX115-119	640.96	Africa
TT498	687	Factories	TX117-118	640.962	Egypt
TT499	646.40212/687.0212	Tables/Calculations/Etc.	TX121-122	640.994	Australia
TT500-565	646.404/687.082	Women's fashions	TX122.5-.6	640.993	New Zealand
TT570-630	646.4/687.081	Men's fashions	TX123-124	640.99(5-6)	Oceania
TT635-645	646.406/687.083	Children's clothing	TX165-286	640.7	Education
TT647	646.40088092	Ecclesiastical vestments	TX298-399	643	The house
TT650-665	646.5/687.4	Millinery	TX340	646.3	Clothing
TT670-678	646.42/687.2	Underwear	TX341-641	641	Nutrition/Foods/Food supply
TT679-695	677.028245/746.432	Knit goods/Machine knitting	TX356	641.31	Marketing for food economy
TT697-910	640	Home arts/Homecrafts	TX360	641.59(3-9)	Diet of special countries
TT697	640.(5/6)	Serials/Societies	TX361	641.592(03-9)	Diet of special groups
TT699-715	646.2/746.4	Textile arts/Crafts	TX364-365	641.07	Education
TT700-715	646.2/746.4	Sewing/Needlework	TX371-389	641.306	Animal foods
TT720-730	646.(2/6)	Mending	TX391-401	641.303	Vegetable foods
TT740-829	746.4(3-4)	Decorative needlework	TX406-407	641.6382	Condiments/Spices
TT845	646.1	Tools/Supplies	TX409	641.6	Baking powders/Etc.
TT848-849	746.42	Hand weaving	TX412-415	641.2	Beverages
TT855-910	745	Decorative crafts	TX501-597	641.300287	Examination/Analysis
TT950-979	646.724(2)	Barbering/Hairdressing	TX515	641.3009	History
TT980-999	648.1	Laundry work	TX551-560	641.1	Dietary studies/Etc.
TX	640	Home economics	TX599-612	641.4	Preservation/Storage
TX1-5	640.(5/6)	Serials/Societies/Congresses	TX607-612	641.4(6-7)	Chemical treatment
TX6	640.74	Exhibitions/Museums	TX631-641	641.013	Gastronomy
TX11	640.3	Dictionaries/Encyclopedias	TX645-840	641.5	Cookery
TX13	640.1	Theory/Philosophy	TX653-655	643.3	Kitchen
TX15-19	640.9	History	TX656-658	643.3	Equipment/Appliances/Etc.
TX21-126	640.9(4-9)	By place	TX661-669	641.507	Education
TX22-25	640.973	United States	TX681-693	641.7	Cooking Processes
TX26-27	640.971	Canada	TX703-725	641.5	Cookbooks
TX28-29	640.972	Mexico	TX726	641.62(2-5)	Cookery with alcohol
TX30-31	640.9728	Central America	TX727-739	642	Menus/Etc.
TX32-33	640.9729	West Indies	TX743-759	641.66	Animal foods
TX34-54	640.98	South America	TX761-799	641.8(53-65)	Baking/Confectionery
TX36-37	640.982	Argentina	TX801-814	641.6(3-7)	Preparation by food type
TX38-39	640.984	Bolivia	TX815-817	641.87	Beverages
TX41-42	640.981	Brazil	TX818	641.84	Sandwiches
TX43-44	640.983	Chile	TX819	641.814	Condiments/Sauces/Etc.
TX45-46	640.9861	Colombia	TX820	641.57	Cooking for large numbers
TX47	640.9866	Ecuador	TX821-840	641.55/642.3	Fast food/Picnics/Etc.
TX48-50	640.988	Guianas	TX851-885	642.(6-8)	Dining-room service/ Tables/Etc.
TX51	640.9892	Paraguay	TX901-953	642.5	Hotels/Restaurants/Etc.
TX52	640.985	Peru	TX955-985	648	Bldg. operation/ Housekeeping
TX53	640.9895	Uruguay	TX1100-1105	643.2	Mobile home living
TX54	640.987	Venezuela	U	355	Military science (General)
TX55-95	640.94	Europe	U1-4	355.00(5/6)	Serials/Societies
TX57-64.5	640.941	Great Britain	U7	355.006	Congresses
TX59.3	640.9417	Ireland			
TX65-.2	640.9436	Austria			
TX71-72.5	640.944	France			

LC	Dewey	Descriptor	LC	Dewey	Descriptor
U9-10	355.005	Yearbooks/Almanacs	U825-897	623.44(1-7)	By type
U11	355.3	Army lists	U850-870	623.441	Swords/Daggers
U13	355.0074	Museums/Exhibitions	U872	623.441	Lances/Spears
U21-22.3	355.02	War (Philosophy/ Psychology)	U877-878	623.441	Bows
			U880-897	623.44	Guns
U24-25	355.003	Dictionaries/Encyclopedias	U900	355.54	Drill manuals for nonmilitary
U26	355.00148	Symbols/Abbreviations			
U27-43	355.009	History of military science	UA	355.3	Armies (Organization/Etc.)
U29-42	355.0090(1-4)	By date	UA11	355.0335	Military policy
U51-55	355.0092	Biography	UA11.5	355.0215	Limited war
U56-59	369.2	Clubs	UA12	355.031	Mutual security
U110-145	355.5	Handbooks	UA12.5	355.03	Disarmament inspection
U161-163	355.4	Strategy	UA13	355.37	General organization (Militia)
U164-167.5	355.42	Tactics			
U168	355.411	Logistics	UA14	355.352	Colonial/Native troops
U169	355.547	Drill manuals (Arms)	UA15	355.31	Armies of the world
U170-185	355.35	Field service/Encampments	UA16	355.032	Military missions
U190-195	355.35	Guard duty/Outposts/Etc.	UA17	355.622	Costs/Budgets/Etc.
U200	355.422	Debarkation/Landing maneuvers	UA17.5	355.22	Manpower
			UA18	355.26	Industrial mobilization
U205	355.423	Stream crossing	UA19	355.0021	Statistics
U210	355.422	Skirmishing	UA21-876	355.309	Organization, By place
U220	355.413	Reconnaissance	UA22-605	355.3097	North America
U230	363.32	Riot duty	UA23-585	355.30973	United States
U240	355.0215	Small wars	UA23.2-.6	353.6	Dept. of Defense
U250-255	355.4	Maneuvers	UA42-560	355.370973	Reserves/National Guard/Etc.
U260	355.46	Combined operations			
U261	355.46/359.9646	Amphibious warfare	UA45	355.3480973	Women's reserves
U262	355.422	Commando tactics	UA50-549	355.3097(4-9)	By state
U265	355.352	Military expeditions	UA50-59	355.309761	Alabama
U280-313	355.4(8)	Maneuvers/War games/Etc.	UA60-69	355.309798	Alaska
U320-328	355.5	Training/Military sports	UA70-79	355.309791	Arizona
U350-365	355.17	Salutes/Ceremonials	UA80-89	355.309767	Arkansas
U370-375	355.35	Garrison service	UA90-99	355.309794	California
U380-385	355.00289/623.75	Safety	UA100-109	355.309788	Colorado
U390-395	355.0(7/072)	Military research	UA110-119	355.309746	Connecticut
U400-717	355.(007/5)	Military education/Training	UA120-129	355.309751	Delaware
U400-403	355.(007/509)	History	UA130-139	355.309753	District of Columbia
U401-403	355.(007/5090) + (1-4)	By date	UA140-149	355.309759	Florida
U407-714	355.(0070/509) + (4-9)	By place	UA150-159	355.309758	Georgia
U408-439	355.(007073/50973)	United States	UA159.1-.9	355.309969	Hawaii
U409	355.(00707/5097) + (4-9)	By state	UA160-169	355.309796	Idaho
U410-430	355.00710747	West Point/Etc.	UA170-179	355.309773	Illinois
U440-444	355.(007071/50971)	Canada	UA180-189	355.309772	Indiana
U445-449	355.(007072/50972)	Mexico	UA190-199	355.309777	Iowa
U450-454	355.(0070728/509728)	Central America	UA200-209	355.309781	Kansas
U455-459	355.(0070729/509729)	West Indies	UA210-219	355.309769	Kentucky
U465-499	355.(00708/5098)	South America	UA220-229	355.309763	Louisiana
U505-630	355.(00704/5094)	Europe	UA230-239	355.309741	Maine
U510-549.3	355.(007041/50941)	Great Britain	UA240-249	355.309752	Maryland
U550-554	355.(0070436/509436)	Austria	UA250-259	355.309744	Massachusetts
U570-574.54	355.(007043/50943)	Germany	UA260-269	355.309774	Michigan
U635-660	355.(00705/5095)	Asia	UA270-279	355.309776	Minnesota
U640-644	355.(007051/50951)	China	UA280-289	355.309762	Mississippi
U645-649	355.(007054/50954)	India	UA290-299	355.309778	Missouri
U650-654	355.(007052/50952)	Japan	UA300-309	355.309786	Montana
U655-659	355.(007055/50955)	Iran	UA310-319	355.309782	Nebraska
U670-695	355.(00706/5096)	Africa	UA320-329	355.309793	Nevada
U700-714	355.(00709/5099) + (3-6)	Australia/New Zealand/ Oceania	UA330-339	355.309742	New Hampshire
			UA340-349	355.309749	New Jersey
U719-740	355.48	Observations on special wars	UA350-359	355.309789	New Mexico
			UA360-369	355.309747	New York
U750-773	355.1	Life/Manners/Customs/Etc.	UA370-379	355.309756	North Carolina
U800-897	623.4409	History of arms/Armor	UA380-389	355.309784	North Dakota
U804	623.44074	Museums/Exhibitions	UA390-399	355.309771	Ohio
U805-815	623.44090(1-4)	By date	UA400-409	355.309766	Oklahoma
U818-823.5	623.4409(4-9)	By place	UA410-419	355.309795	Oregon

LC	Dewey	Descriptor	LC	Dewey	Descriptor
UA420-429	355.309748	Pennsylvania	UB105-106	355.60952	Japan
UA430-439	355.309745	Rhode Island	UB115-119	355.6096	Africa
UA440-449	355.309757	South Carolina	UB121-122.5	355.6099(3-4)	Australia/New Zealand
UA450-459	355.309783	South Dakota	UB123-124	355.6099(5-6)	Oceania
UA460-469	355.309768	Tennessee	UB147	355.(0023/1)	Military service as a profession
UA470-479	355.309764	Texas			
UA480-489	355.309792	Utah	UB160-165	355.6	Records/Accounts/Etc.
UA490-499	355.309743	Vermont	UB180-197	355.61	Civilian personnel depts.
UA500-509	355.309755	Virginia	UB200-235	355.33	Commanders/Staffs/ Headquarters
UA510-519	355.309797	Washington			
UA520-529	355.309754	West Virginia	UB240-245	355.63	Inspection
UA530-539	355.309775	Wisconsin	UB246-249	355.3433	Security
UA540-549	355.309787	Wyoming	UB250-271	355.3432	Intelligence
UA580-585	973.742	Confederacy	UB273-277	355.34(37)	Propaganda/Sabotage
UA600-602	355.30971	Canada	UB280-285	358.24	Cryptography
UA603-605	355.30972	Mexico	UB320-338	355.223	Enlistment/Recruiting/Etc.
UA606-608	355.309728	Central America	UB320-336	355.2236	Medical exams
UA609-611	355.309729	West Indies	UB337-338	355.6	Personnel classification
UA612-645	355.3098	South America	UB340-345	355.22363	Compulsory service
UA646-829	355.3094	Europe	UB350-355	355.225	Universal service
UA647-668	355.30941	Great Britain	UB356-385	362.1608697	Veterans/Soldiers' homes
UA670-679	355.309436	Austria	UB407-409	355.332	Warrant officers
UA700-709	355.30944	France	UB410-415	355.332	Officers
UA710-719	355.30943	Germany	UB420-425	355.113	Furloughs
UA830-853	355.3095	Asia	UB430-435	355.134	Rewards
UA835-839.3	355.30951	China	UB461-736	343.01	Law
UA840-844	355.30954	India	UB505-509	343.7101	Canada
UA845-849	355.30952	Japan	UB510-514	343.7201	Mexico
UA855-868	355.3096	Africa	UB515-519	343.72801	Central America
UA870-876	355.3099(3-6)	Australia/New Zealand/ Oceania	UB520-524	343.72901	West Indies
			UB530-589	343.801	South America
UA910-915	355.28	Mobilization	UB530-534	343.8201	Argentina
UA920-925	355.4	Attack/Defense plans	UB545-549	343.8301	Chile
UA926-929	363.35	Civil defense	UB550-554	343.86101	Colombia
UA929.5-.95	355.26	Industrial war damage/Defense	UB585-589	343.8701	Venezuela
			UB590-684	343.401	Europe
UA930	355.7	Strategic lines/Bases	UB615-619	343.4401	France
UA940-945	355.85/623.73	Military communications	UB620-624	343.4301	Germany
UA980	623.73(2/42)	Telegraphic connections	UB630-634	343.49501	Greece
UA985-997	355.47	Military geography/Charts	UB640-644	343.4501	Italy
UB	355.6	Military administration	UB650-654	343.46901	Portugal
UB1	355.60(5/6)	Serials/Societies	UB655-659	343.4701	European Russia
UB15	355.609	History (General)	UB660-664	343.4601	Spain
UB21-124	355.609(4-9)	By place	UB685-710	343.501	Asia
UB23-25	353.6/355.60973	United States	UB690-694	343.5101	China
UB26-27	355.60971	Canada	UB695-699	343.5401	India
UB28-29	355.60972	Mexico	UB700-704	343.5201	Japan
UB30-31	355.609728	Central America	UB715-729	343.601	Africa
UB32-33	355.609729	West Indies	UB730-734.5	343.9(3-4)01	Australia/New Zealand
UB34-54	355.6098	South America	UB735-736	343.9(5-6)01	Oceania
UB36-37	355.60982	Argentina	UB780-789	355.1334	Crimes/Offenses
UB43-44	355.60983	Chile	UB790-815	343.014/355.13	Military discipline/ Punishment
UB45-46	355.609861	Colombia			
UB54	355.60987	Venezuela	UB820-825	355.13323	Military police
UB55-95	355.6094	Europe	UB840-867	343.0143	Judiciary/Courts
UB57-64	355.60941	Great Britain	UB880	394.(7-8)	Court of honor/Dueling
UB71-72	355.60944	France	UB890	343.0143	Procedure/Appeals
UB73-74	355.60943	Germany	UC	355.8/358.25	Maintenance/Transportation
UB75-76	355.609495	Greece	UC15	355.(28/8)	Requisitions
UB79-80	355.60945	Italy	UC20-258	355.809	Organization, By place
UB83-84	355.609469	Portugal	UC20-88	355.80973	United States
UB85-86	355.60947	European Russia	UC90-93	355.80971	Canada
UB86.5	355.60948	Scandinavia	UC94-97	355.80972	Mexico
UB87-88	355.60946	Spain	UC98-99	355.809728	Central America
UB99-113	355.6095	Asia	UC104-105	355.809729	West Indies
UB101-102	355.60951	China	UC106-154	355.8098	South America
UB103-104	355.60954	India	UC158-233	355.8094	Europe

LC	Dewey	Descriptor
UC180-183	355.80943	Germany
UC184-187	355.80941	Great Britain
UC234-245	355.8095	Asia
UC241	355.80952	Japan
UC247-253	355.8096	Africa
UC255-258	355.8099(3-6)	Australia/New Zealand/ Oceania
UC260-267	355.8	Supplies
UC270-360	358.25	Transportation
UC400-440	355.71	Quarters/Barracks
UC460-585	355.81	Clothing/Equipment
UC590-595	355.15	Flags/Colors
UC600-695	357.1	Horses/Mules
UC700-780	355.81	Subsistence
UD	356.1	Infantry
UD1	356.10(5/6)	Serials/Societies
UD10	356.189	Organization (General)
UD15	356.109	History
UD21-124	356.109(4-9)	By place
UD23-25	356.10973	United States
UD26-27	356.10971	Canada
UD28-29	356.10972	Mexico
UD30-31	356.109728	Central America
UD32-33	356.109729	West Indies
UD34-54	356.1098	South America
UD36-37	356.10982	Argentina
UD43-44	356.10983	Chile
UD45-46	356.109861	Colombia
UD54	356.10987	Venezuela
UD55-95	356.1094	Europe
UD57-64	356.10941	Great Britain
UD71-72	356.10944	France
UD73-74.5	356.10943	Germany
UD75-76	356.109495	Greece
UD79-80	356.10945	Italy
UD83-84	356.109469	Portugal
UD85-86	356.10947	European Russia
UD86.5	356.10948	Scandinavia
UD87-88	356.10946	Spain
UD99-113	356.1095	Asia
UD101-102	356.10951	China
UD103-104	356.10954	India
UD105-106	356.10952	Japan
UD115-119	356.1096	Africa
UD121-122.5	356.1099(3-4)	Australia/New Zealand
UD123-124	356.1099(5-6)	Oceania
UD150-155	356.1	Manuals
UD157-302	356.109	Tactics/Maneuvers, By place
UD317	355.183	Stream crossing
UD320-325	356.184	Manual of arms
UD330-335	356.184/623.44(2-3)	Firing
UD340-345	356.184	Bayonet drill
UD370-375	356.186	Equipment
UD380-425	355.824/623.44	Small arms
UD430	356.1	Militia/Reserves
UD440-445	356.183	Field service
UD450-485	356.1(1-67)	Troops (By type)
UD450-455	356.1	Mounted infantry
UD460-465	356.164	Mountain troops
UD470-475	356.164	Ski troops
UD480-485	356.166	Airborne/Parachute troops
UE	357/358.18	Cavalry/Armor
UE1	357/358.18 + 0(5/6)	Serials/Societies
UE10	357/358.18(043)	Cavalry organization (General)
UE15	357/358.18(09)	History
UE21-124	357/358.18 + 09(4-9)	By place
UE23-25	357/358.18(0973)	United States
UE26-27	357/358.18(0971)	Canada
UE28-29	357/358.18(0972)	Mexico
UE30-31	357/358.18(09728)	Central America
UE32-33	357/358.18(09729)	West Indies
UE34-54	357/358.18(098)	South America
UE36-37	357/358.18(0982)	Argentina
UE43-44	357/358.18(0983)	Chile
UE45-46	357/358.18(09861)	Colombia
UE54	357/358.18(0987)	Venezuela
UE55-95	357/358.18(094)	Europe
UE57-64	357/358.18(0941)	Great Britain
UE71-72	357/358.18(0944)	France
UE73-74	357/358.18(0943)	Germany
UE75-76	357/358.18(09495)	Greece
UE79-80	357/358.18(0945)	Italy
UE83-84	357/358.18(09469)	Portugal
UE85-86	357/358.18(0947)	European Russia
UE86.5	357/358.18(0948)	Scandinavia
UE87-88	357/358.18(0946)	Spain
UE99-113	357/358.18(095)	Asia
UE101-102	357/358.18(0951)	China
UE103-104	357/358.18(0954)	India
UE105-106	357/358.18(0952)	Japan
UE115-119	357/358.18(096)	Africa
UE121-122.5	357/358.18 + 099(3-4)	Australia/New Zealand
UE123-124	357/358.18 + 099(5-6)	Oceania
UE144-145	357.1	Horse cavalry
UE147	358.18	Armor
UE150-155	357/358.18	Manuals
UE157-158	357.184	Tactics, Horse cavalry
UE159	357.584/358.184	Armored/Mechanized cavalry
UE160-302	357.5/358.184 + 09(4-9)	Tactics/Maneuvers, By place
UE160-162	357.5/358.184(0973)	United States
UE163-165	357.5/358.184(0971)	Canada
UE166-168	357.5/358.184(0972)	Mexico
UE169-170	357.5/358.184(09728)	Central America
UE172-173	357.5/358.184(09729)	West Indies
UE175-211	357.5/358.184(098)	South America
UE176-178	357.5/358.184(0982)	Argentina
UE185-187	357.5/358.184(0983)	Chile
UE188-190	357.5/358.184(09861)	Colombia
UE215-269	357.5/358.184(094)	Europe
UE228-230	357.5/358.184(0944)	France
UE231-233.53	357.5/358.184(0943)	Germany
UE234-236	357.5/358.184(0941)	Great Britain
UE237-239	357.5/358.184(09495)	Greece
UE243-245	357.5/358.184(0945)	Italy
UE249-251	357.5/358.184(09469)	Portugal
UE252-254	357.5/358.184(0947)	European Russia
UE255-257	357.5/358.184(0946)	Spain
UE270-280	357.5/358.184(095)	Asia
UE271-273	357.5/358.184(0951)	China
UE274-276	357.5/358.184(0954)	India
UE277-279	357.5/358.184(0952)	Japan
UE285-292	357.5/358.184(096)	Africa
UE295-298	357.5/358.184 + 099(3-4)	Australia/New Zealand
UE300-302	357.5/358.184 + 099(5-6)	Oceania
UE360	357.584/358.184	Cavalry reconnaissance
UE400-435	357.(1/5)85/358.185	Training/Instructions/Etc.
UE440-445	357.(1/5)88/358.188	Equipment
UE460-475	357.188	Horses/Equitation
UE500	357	Camel troops
UF	358.12	Artillery

LC	Dewey	Descriptor
UF1	358.120(5/6)	Serials/Societies
UF6	358.12074	Museums/Exhibitions
UF9	358.1203	Dictionaries/Encyclopedias
UF10	358.123	Artillery organization (General)
UF15	358.1209	History (General)
UF21-124	358.1209(4-9)	By place
UF23-25	358.120973	United States
UF26-27	358.120971	Canada
UF28-29	358.12O972	Mexico
UF30-31	358.1209728	Central America
UF32-33	358.1209729	West Indies
UF34-54	358.12098	South America
UF36-37	358.120982	Argentina
UF43-44	358.120983	Chile
UF45-46	358.1209861	Colombia
UF54	358.120987	Venezuela
UF55-95	358.12094	Europe
UF57-64	358.120941	Great Britain
UF71-72	358.120944	France
UF73-74	358.120943	Germany
UF75-76	358.1209495	Greece
UF79-80	358.120945	Italy
UF83-84	358.12209469	Portugal
UF85-86	358.120947	European Russia
UF86.5	358.120948	Scandinavia
UF87-88	358.120946	Spain
UF99-113	358.12095	Asia
UF101-102	358.120951	China
UF103-104	358.120954	India
UF105-106	358.120952	Japan
UF115-119	358.12096	Africa
UF121-122.5	358.12099(3-4)	Australia/New Zealand
UF123-124	358.12099(5-6)	Oceania
UF150-155	358.12	Manuals
UF157-302	358.12409(4-9)	Tactics/Maneuvers, By place
UF160-162	358.1240973	United States
UF163-165	358.1240971	Canada
UF166-168	358.1240972	Mexico
UF169-170	358.12409728	Central America
UF172-173	358.12409729	West Indies
UF175-211	358.124098	South America
UF176-178	358.1240982	Argentina
UF185-187	358.1240983	Chile
UF188-190	358.12409861	Colombia
UF209-211	358.1240987	Venezuela
UF215-269	358.124094	Europe
UF228-230	358.1240944	France
UF231-233.53	358.1240943	Germany
UF234-236	358.1240941	Great Britain
UF237-239	358.12409495	Greece
UF243-245	358.1240945	Italy
UF249-251	358.12409469	Portugal
UF252-254	358.1240947	European Russia
UF255-257	358.1240946	Spain
UF270-280	358.124095	Asia
UF271-273	358.1240951	China
UF274-276	358.1240954	India
UF277-279	358.1240952	Japan
UF285-292	358.124096	Africa
UF295-298	358.124099(3-4)	Australia/New Zealand
UF300-302	358.124099(5-6)	Oceania
UF320	358.124	Stream crossing
UF340-345	358.125	Target practice
UF356	358.12	Reserves/Militia
UF360-365	358.128	Equipment/Harness/Etc.
UF390	358.25	Motor transportation
UF400-495	358.1(2-6)	Artillery/Batteries (By type)
UF520-780	355.82/623.4	Ordnance
UF520-537	355.824/623.44	Small arms
UF560-780	355.824/623.4	Ordnance material
UF563	355.82/623.4(0973)	United States
UF565	355.82/623.4 + 09(4-9)	Other countries
UF620	355.8224/623.4424	Machine guns
UF625	358.13	Antiaircraft guns
UF750-770	355.82513/623.4513	Projectiles
UF800-805	623.55	Gunnery
UF820-830	623.51	Ballistics
UF845	355.8	Telescopes/Binoculars
UF848-856	623.46	Artillery instruments
UF857	623.46	Range tables
UF860-880	623.452	Explosives/Pyrotechnics
UF890	623.40287	Ordnance tests
UF910	355.81	Bulletproof clothing
UG	358.22/623.(1-7)	Military engineering
UG1	358.22/623. + 0(5/6)	Serials/Societies
UG5	358.22/623.(06)	Congresses
UG6	358.22/623.(074)	Museums/Exhibitions
UG15	358.22/623.(09)	History
UG21-124	358.22/623. + 09(4-9)	By place
UG127-128	358.22/623.(092)	Biography
UG130-135	343.01822	Laws
UG150-155	358.22	Manuals
UG157	358.2207/623.07	Education
UG160-302	358.224	Tactics/Regulations
UG320-325	358.224	Maneuvers
UG330	623.62	Roads
UG335	623.67	Bridges
UG340	623.68	Tunnels
UG345	623.63	Railroads
UG350	623.047	Hydraulic engineering
UG360-390	358.2/623.(1-3)	Field engineering
UG400-442	623.1	Fortification
UG443-449	355.4(2/4)	Siege warfare (Attack/Defense)
UG447-.6	358.34	Chemical warfare
UG450	623.045	Mechanical engineering
UG470-474	623.71	Military surveying/Mapping
UG476	623.72	Photography
UG480	623.76	Electricity
UG485	623.043	Electronics
UG487	623.942	Infrared rays
UG490	623.45115	Mines
UG500-565	358-359	Technical/Special troops
UG570-613.5	358.24/623.73	Communication
UG570-582	623.731	Signaling
UG590-613.5	623.73 (2-4)	Telegraph/Telephone
UG612-.5	623.7348	Radar
UG615-620	358.5/623.74	Motor vehicles
UG622-1425	358.4	Air forces/Air warfare
UG622-623	358.400(5/6)	Serials/Societies/Congresses
UG623-624	358.40074	Museums/Exhibitions
UG625	358.4009	History
UG626-.2	358.40092	Biography
UG628	358.4003	Dictionaries/Encyclopedias
UG633-635	358.4009	By place
UG633-634.5	358.400973	United States
UG635	358.4009(4-9)	Other countries
UG637-639	358.4(007/15)	Education/Training
UG638.5	358.40071173	U.S. Air Force Academy
UG670-675	358.4	Manuals
UG700-705	358.414	Tactics
UG730-735	358.4145	Air defenses

LC	Dewey	Descriptor	LC	Dewey	Descriptor
UG760-765	358.45	Aerial reconnaissance	V43-46	359.00902	Medieval
UG770-1045	358.413	Organization	V47	359.00903(2/3)	17th-18th centuries
UG1100-1425	358.418	Equipment/Supplies	V51	359.009034	19th century
UH	355.(3-6)	Other services	V53	359	20th century
UH20-25	355.347	Chaplains	V55	359.009(4-9)	By place
UH40-45	784.84	Bands	V61-64	359.0092	Biography
UH70	355.345	Orderlies	V66-69	369.2(3-9)	Clubs, By place
UH80-85	355.693	Postal service	V110-145	359	Handbooks
UH87-100	355.424	Animals in military science	V160-178	359.42	Strategy/Tactics
UH201-630	355.345	Medical/Sanitary service	V210-214	359.93	Submarine warfare
UH201	355.3450(5/6)	Serials/Societies	V215	359.9641	Marine camouflage
UH205	355.34506	Congresses	V220-240	359.7/623.64	Stations/Ports/Bases/Yards
UH206	355.345074	Museums/Exhibitions	V260-265	359.5	Physical Training
UH215-324	355.34509	History	V280-285	623.8561	Naval signaling
UH223-225	355.3450973	United States	V300-305	359.15	Flags (Not signaling)
UH226-227	355.3450971	Canada	V303-304	359.15	Flags, United States
UH228-229	355.3450972	Mexico	V305	359.15	Flags, Other countries
UH230-231	355.34509728	Central America	V310	359.1(6-7)	Ceremonies/Honors
UH232-233	355.34509729	West Indies	V380-386	623.(75/888)	Safety
UH234-254	355.345098	South America	V390-395	359.0072	Research
UH236-237	355.3450982	Argentina	V398	359.8	Electronic data processing
UH243-244	355.3450983	Chile	V400-699	359.(007/5)	Naval education/Training
UH245-246	355.34509861	Colombia	V401-409	359.(007/509)	History
UH254	355.3450987	Venezuela	V402-409	359.(007/50901-4)	By date
UH255-295	355.345094	Europe	V411-695	359.(0070/509) + (4-9)	By place
UH257-264	355.3450941	Great Britain	V411-438	359.(0070/509)73	United States
UH271-272	355.3450944	France	V437	359.9707073	Coast Guard
UH273-274	355.3450943	Germany	V438	973.757	Confederate States
UH275-276	355.34509495	Greece	V440-444	359.(0070/509)71	Canada
UH279-280	355.3450945	Italy	V445-449	359.(0070/509)72	Mexico
UH283-284	355.34509469	Portugal	V450-453	359.(0070/509)728	Central America
UH285-286	355.3450947	European Russia	V455-458	359.(0070/509)729	West Indies
UH286.5	355.3450948	Scandinavia	V465-496	359.(0070/509)8	South America
UH287-288	355.3450946	Spain	V500-623	359.(0070/509)4	Europe
UH299-313	355.345095	Asia	V510-530	359.(0070/509)41	Great Britain
UH301-302	355.3450951	China	V570-574	359.(0070/509)43	Germany
UH303-304	355.3450954	India	V630-650	359.(0070/509)5	Asia
UH305-306	355.3450952	Japan	V630-634	359.(0070/509)51	China
UH315-319	355.345096	Africa	V635-639	359.(0070/509)54	India
UH321-322.5	355.345099(3-4)	Australia/New Zealand	V640-644	359.(0070/509)52	Japan
UH323-324	355.345099(5-6)	Oceania	V645-649	359.(0070/509)55	Iran
UH341-347	355.3450992	Biography	V660-680	359.(0070/509)6	Africa
UH398-399	355.34450711	Army medical schools	V690-695	359.(0070/509) + 09(3-6)	Australia/New
UH399.5-.7	355.345072	Research/Labs			Zealand/ Oceania
UH400-485	355.345068	Organization and service	V720-743	359.1	Life/Manners/Customs/Etc.
UH487	355.345	Diet/Cooking for sick/	V750-995	359.(32/8)/623.825	War vessels/Material
		Wounded	V755-767	359.(32/8)/623.825+0901-4	By period
UH490-495	355.345	Nursing	V795-805.5	623.818	Construction/Materials
UH500-505	355.345	Ambulances	V810	623.888	Damage control
UH510-515	355.345028	Equipment	V820-.5	359.3253/623.8253	Cruisers
UH520-551	361.77	Relief societies	V825-.5	359.3254/623.8254	Destroyers
UH535-537	361.77	Red Cross	V830-840	359.3258/623.8258	Torpedo boats
UH570	355.699	Treatment of dead	V857-859	359.3257/623.8257	Submarines
UH600-629.5	355.345	Hygiene/Sanitation	V874-875	359.3255/623.8255	Aircraft carriers
UH630	355.34(5/7)	Health/Morals	V990-995	359.9817/623.45195	Fleet Ballistic Missile
UH650-655	355.345	Veterinary service			Systems
UH700-705	355.342	Public relations	VA	359	Navies/Naval situations
UH750-769	306.27	Social work/Welfare	VA20-25	359.622	Costs/Expenditures
UH800-910	355.34(2/6)	Recreation/Information	VA45	359.373	Militia/Reserves
		service			(Organization)
V	359	Naval science	VA48	359.28	Mobilization
V1-5	359.00(5/6)	Serials/Societies	VA49-750	359.309(4-9)	By place
V7	359.006	Congresses	VA49-395	359.30973	United States
V13	359.0074	Exhibitions/Museums	VA393-395	973.757	Confederate States Navy
V25-55	359.009	History	VA400-402	359.30971	Canada
V29-53	359.0090(1-4)	History, By date	VA403-405	359.30972	Mexico
V29-41	359.00901	Ancient	VA406-407	359.309728	Central America

LC	Dewey	Descriptor
VA409-410	359.309729	West Indies
VA415-445	359.3098	South America
VA416-418	359.30982	Argentina
VA425-427	359.30983	Chile
VA428-430	359.309861	Colombia
VA450-619	359.3094	Europe
VA452-467	359.30941	Great Britain
VA510-519.39	359.30943	Germany
VA520-529	359.309495	Greece
VA530-539	359.309492	Netherlands
VA540-549	359.30945	Italy
VA560-569	359.309469	Portugal
VA570-579	359.30947	European Russia
VA580-589	359.30946	Spain
VA620-667	359.3095	Asia
VA630-639	359.30951	China
VA650-659	359.30952	Japan
VA710-719	359.30994	Australia
VA720-729	359.30993	New Zealand
VA730-750	359.3099(5-6)	Oceania
VB	359.6	Naval administration
VB15	359.609	History
VB21-124	359.609(4-9)	By place
VB23-25	353.7/359.60973	United States
VB26-27	359.60971	Canada
VB28-29	359.60972	Mexico
VB30-31	359.609728	Central America
VB32-33	359.609729	West Indies
VB34-54	359.6098	South America
VB36-37	359.60982	Argentina
VB43-44	359.60983	Chile
VB45-46	359.609861	Colombia
VB55-96	359.6094	Europe
VB57-64	359.60941	Great Britain
VB71-72	359.60944	France
VB73-74.5	359.60943	Germany
VB75-76	359.609495	Greece
VB79-80	359.60945	Italy
VB83-84	359.609469	Portugal
VB85-86	359.60947	European Russia
VB87-88	359.60946	Spain
VB99-113	359.6095	Asia
VB101-102	359.60951	China
VB105-106	359.60952	Japan
VB115-119	359.6096	Africa
VB121-122.5	359.6099(3-4)	Australia/New Zealand
VB123-124	359.6099(5-6)	Oceania
VB160	359.31	Administration (Fleets/Etc.)
VB170-187	359.61	Civil department
VB220-225	359.63	Inspection
VB230-250	359.3432	Intelligence
VB257-258.5	359.61	Personnel management
VB260-275	359.338	Enlisted men
VB280-285	362.86	Pensions/Disability benefits
VB307-309	359.332	Warrant officers
VB310-315	359.332	Officers
VB330-335	359.134	Rewards
VB350-785	343.019	Naval law
VB790-815	343.019	Judiciary/Courts/Etc.
VB840-910	343.019/359.13	Discipline/Crimes/ Punishment
VB920-955	359.13323	Military police
VC	359.8	Naval maintenance
VC20-258	359.809(4-9)	Organization, By place
VC20-65	359.80973	United States
VC90-93	359.80971	Canada
VC94-97	359.80972	Mexico
VC98-99	359.809728	Central America
VC104-105	359.809729	West Indies
VC110-150	359.8098	South America
VC160-229	359.8094	Europe
VC180-183.53	359.80943	Germany
VC184-187	359.80941	Great Britain
VC230-245	359.8095	Asia
VC241	359.80952	Japan
VC247-253	359.8096	Africa
VC255-258	359.8099(3-6)	Australia/New Zealand/ Oceania
VC260-268	359.8	Supplies/Stores
VC270-279	359.8	Equipment of vessels
VC280-410	359.81	Clothing/Subsistence
VC412-425	359.7/623.83	Navy yards/Stations
VC500-505	359.62(2)	Ship records/Accounting
VC530-580	359.985	Transportation/Shipping
VD	359.3	Naval seamen
VD15	359.309	History
VD21-124	359.309(4-9)	By place
VD23-25	359.30973	United States
VD26-27	359.30971	Canada
VD28-29	359.30972	Mexico
VD30-31	359.309728	Central America
VD32-33	359.309729	West Indies
VD34-54	359.3098	South America
VD55-96	359.3094	Europe
VD57-64	359.30941	Great Britain
VD71-72	359.30944	France
VD73-74.5	359.30943	Germany
VD75-76	359.309495	Greece
VD79-80	359.30943	Italy
VD83-84	359.309469	Portugal
VD85-86	359.30947	European Russia
VD86.5	359.30948	Scandinavia
VD87-88	359.30946	Spain
VD99-113	359.3095	Asia
VD101-102	359.30951	China
VD105-106	359.30952	Japan
VD115-119	359.3096	Africa
VD121-122.5	359.3099(3-4)	Australia/New Zealand
VD123-124	359.3099(5-6)	Oceania
VD150-155	359	Manuals
VD160-302	359.509 (4-9)	Drill regulations, By place
VD160-162	359.50973	United States
VD163-165	359.50971	Canada
VD166-168	359.50972	Mexico
VD169-170	359.509728	Central America
VD172-173	359.509729	West Indies
VD175-211	359.5098	South America
VD215-269	359.5094	Europe
VD228-230	359.5094	France
VD231-233	359.50943	Germany
VD234-236	359.50941	Great Britain
VD249-251	359.509469	Portugal
VD255-257	359.50946	Spain
VD270-280	359.5095	Asia
VD277-279	359.50952	Japan
VD285-292	359.5096	Africa
VD295-298	359.5099(3-4)	Australia/New Zealand
VD300-302	359.5099(5-6)	Oceania
VD320-345	359.547	Manual of arms/Bayonet/ Etc.
VD350-355	359.824	Equipment/Small arms
VD400-405	359.323	Small boat service
VE	359.96	Marines
VE15	359.96309	History

LC	Dewey	Descriptor
VE21-124	359.96309(4-9)	By place
VE23-25	359.9630973	United States
VE26-27	359.9630971	Canada
VE28-29	359.9630972	Mexico
VE30-31	359.96309728	Central America
VE32-33	359.96309729	West Indies
VE34-54	359.963098	South America
VE55-96	359.963094	Europe
VE57-64	359.9630941	Great Britain
VE71-72	359.9630944	France
VE73-74.5	359.9630943	Germany
VE79-80	359.9630945	Italy
VE85-86	359.9630947	European Russia
VE86.5	359.9630948	Scandinavia
VE87-88	359.9630946	Spain
VE99-113	359.963095	Asia
VE105-106	359.9630952	Japan
VE115-119	359.963096	Africa
VE121-122.5	359.963099(3-4)	Australia/New Zealand
VE123-124	359.963099(5-6)	Oceania
VE150-155	359.965	Handbooks/Manuals
VE160-302	359.96509(4-9)	Drill regulations, By place
VE160-162	359.9650973	United States
VE163-165	359.9650971	Canada
VE166-168	359.9650972	Mexico
VE169-170	359.96509728	Central America
VE172-173	359.96509729	West Indies
VE175-211	359.965098	South America
VE215-269	359.965094	Europe
VE228-230	359.9650944	France
VE231-233	359.9650943	Germany
VE234-236	359.9650941	Great Britain
VE243-245	359.9650945	Italy
VE252-254	359.9650947	European Russia
VE270-280	359.965096	Asia
VE277-279	359.9650952	Japan
VE285-292	359.965096	Africa
VE295-298	359.965099(3-4)	Australia/New Zealand
VE300-302	359.965099(5-6)	Oceania
VE330-340	359.9654	Manual of arms/Shooting/ Etc.
VE350-390	359.96824	Equipment/Small arms
VE400-405	359.9614	Uniforms
VE420-425	359.9671	Quarters/Barracks
VE430-435	359.965	Training camps
VE480-490	359.96622	Accounting/Pay/Allowances
VF	359.82/623.8251	Naval ordnance
VF1	359.82/623.8251 + 0(5/6)	Serials/Societies
VF6	359.82/623.8251(074)	Exhibitions/Museums
VF15	359.82/623.8251(09)	History
VF21-124	359.82/623.8251 + 09(4-9)	By place
VF23-25	359.82/623.8251(0973)	United States
VF26-27	359.82/623.8251(0971)	Canada
VF28-29	359.82/623.8251(0972)	Mexico
VF30-31	359.82/623.8251(09728)	Central America
VF32-33	359.82/623.8251(09729)	West Indies
VF34-54	359.82/623.8251(098)	South America
VF36-37	359.82/623.8251(0982)	Argentina
VF43-44	359.82/623.8251(0983)	Chile
VF45-46	359.82/623.8251(09861)	Colombia
VF55-96	359.82/623.8251(094)	Europe
VF57-64	359.82/623.8251(0941)	Great Britain
VF71-72	359.82/623.8251(0944)	France
VF73-74.5	359.82/623.8251(0943)	Germany
VF79-80	359.82/623.8251(0945)	Italy
VF83-84	359.82/623.8251(09469)	Portugal
VF85-86	359.82/623.8251(0947)	European Russia

LC	Dewey	Descriptor
VF86.5	359.82/623.8251(0948)	Scandinavia
VF87-88	359.82/623.8251(0946)	Spain
VF101-113	359.82/623.8251(095)	Asia
VF105-106	359.82/623.8251(0952)	Japan
VF111-112	359.82/623.8251(09561)	Turkey
VF115-119	359.82/623.8251(096)	Africa
VF121-122.5	359.82/623.8251+ 099(3-4)	Australia/New Zealand
VF123-124	359.82/623.8251+ 099(5-6)	Oceania
VF150-155	359.82	Handbooks/Manuals
VF160-302	359.5409(4-9)	Drill books/Etc., By place
VF160-162	359.540973	United States
VF163-165	359.540971	Canada
VF166-168	359.540972	Mexico
VF169-170	359.5409728	Central America
VF172-173	359.5409729	West Indies
VF175-211	359.54098	South America
VF176-178	359.540982	Argentina
VF185-187	359.540983	Chile
VF188-190	359.5409861	Colombia
VF215-269	359.54094	Europe
VF228-230	359.540944	France
VF231-233	359.540943	Germany
VF234-236	359.540941	Great Britain
VF243-245	359.540945	Italy
VF252-254	359.540947	European Russia
VF255-257	359.540946	Spain
VF270-280	359.54095	Asia
VF277-279	359.540952	Japan
VF285-292	359.54096	Africa
VF295-298	359.54099(3-4)	Australia/New Zealand
VF300-302	359.54099(5-6)	Oceania
VF320-325	359.98	Naval artillery equipment
VF346-510	359.(8/98)	Systems/Facilities/Material
VF410	359.82/623.(4424)	Machine guns
VF520-530	359.98	Fire control/Instruments
VG	359.3	Minor services of navies
VG20-25	359.347	Chaplains
VG23	359.3470973	United States
VG25	359.34709(4-9)	In other countries
VG30-35	781.599/784.84	Music/Bands
VG33	781.599/784.84(0973)	United States
VG35	781.599/784.84 + 09(4-9)	In other countries
VG50-55	359.97	Coast Guard (Military duty)
VG53	359.970973	United States
VG55	359.9709(4-9)	In other countries
VG60-65	359.693	Postal service
VG63	359.6930973	United States
VG65	359.69309(4-9)	In other countries
VG70-85	359.983/623.856	Communications
VG70-75	623.8562	Telegraph
VG73	623.85620973	United States
VG75	623.856209(4-9)	In other countries
VG76-78	623.8564	Wireless telegraph/Radio/ Etc.
VG77	623.85640973	United States
VG78	623.856409(4-9)	In other countries
VG80-85	623.8563	Telephone
VG83	623.85630973	United States
VG85	623.856309(4-9)	In other countries
VG86-88	359.984	Underwater demolition
VG87	359.9840973	United States
VG88	359.98409(4-9)	In other countries
VG90-95	359.94	Naval aviation
VG93-94.7	359.940973	United States
VG95	359.9409(4-9)	In other countries
VG100-475	359.345	Medical service
VG100	359.3450(5/6)	Serials/Societies

LC	Dewey	Descriptor
VG103	359.34506	Congresses
VG121-224	359.34509(4-9)	Medical service, By place
VG123-125	359.3450973	United States
VG126-127	359.3450971	Canada
VG128-129	359.3450972	Mexico
VG130-131	359.34509728	Central America
VG132-133	350.34509729	West Indies
VG134-154	359.345098	South America
VG155-196	359.345094	Europe
VG157-164	359.3450941	Great Britain
VG171-172	359.3450944	France
VG173-174.5	359.3450943	Germany
VG179-180	359.3450945	Italy
VG185-186	350.3450947	European Russia
VG186.5	359.3450948	Scandinavia
VG187-188	359.3450946	Spain
VG199-213	359.345095	Asia
VG205-206	359.3450952	Japan
VG215-219	359.345096	Africa
VG221-222.5	359.345099(3-4)	Australia/New Zealand
VG223-224	359.345099(5-6)	Oceania
VG226-228	359.345092	Biography
VG230-235	359.34507	Education
VG240-245	359.345072	Research
VG280-285	359.345	Dental service
VG290-295	359.88	Medical supplies
VG410-450	359.72	Naval hospitals/Etc.
VG500-505	359.342	Public relations/Information
VG503	359.3420973	United States
VG505	359.34209(4-9)	In other countries
VG590-595	359.982/623.047	Civil/Construction engineering
VG593	359.982/623.047(0973)	United States
VG595	359.982/623.047 + 09(4-9)	In other countries
VG600-2000	359.34	Misc. noncombat services
VG2020-2029	359.346	Recreation services
VG2025-2026	359.3460973	United States
VG2029	359.34609(4-9)	In other countries
VK	387.5/623.89	Merchant Marine/ Navigation
VK1-4	387.5/623.89 + 0(5/6)	Serials/Societies, By language
VK5	387.5/623.89(06)	Congresses
VK15-124	387.509	Merchant Marine history
VK16	387.50901	Ancient
VK17	387.50902	Medieval
VK18-20	387.5090(23-4)	Modern
VK20	387.5	20th century
VK21-124	387.509(4-9)	Merchant Marine, By place
VK23-25	387.50973	United States
VK26-27	387.50971	Canada
VK28-29	387.50972	Mexico
VK30-31	387.509728	Central America
VK32-33	387.509729	West Indies
VK34-54	387.5098	South America
VK36-37	387.50982	Argentina
VK43-44	387.50983	Chile
VK54	387.50987	Venezuela
VK55-96	387.5094	Europe
VK57-64	387.50941	Great Britain
VK71-72	387.50944	France
VK73-74	387.50943	Germany
VK75-76	387.509495	Greece
VK77-78	387.509492	Netherlands
VK79-80	387.50945	Italy
VK83-84	387.509469	Portugal
VK85-86	387.50947	European Russia
VK86.5	387.50948	Scandinavia
VK87-88	387.50946	Spain
VK99-113	387.5095	Asia
VK105-106	387.50952	Japan
VK115-119	387.5096	Africa
VK121-122.5	387.5099(3-4)	Australia/New Zealand
VK123-124	387.5099(5-6)	Oceania
VK139-140	387.5092	Biography
VK160	387.5023	As a profession
VK200	623.888	Safety
VK205-215	623.88	Ship Command/Masters' manual
VK321-369.8	387.1	Harbors/Ports
VK369-.8	387.15	Marinas/Etc.
VK371-378	623.8884	Collisions
VK381-397	623.8561	Signaling
VK401-537	387.507/623.88	Education/Training
VK541-547	623.88	Seamanship
VK543	623.88	Helmsmanship
VK549-572	623.89	Science of navigation
VK549-555	623.8909	History
VK559.5	623.89076	Examinations/Questions
VK560-561	623.893	Electronic aids in navigation
VK563	623.8920212	Nautical tables/Etc.
VK570-571	387.52	Routes
VK572	623.8923	Dead reckoning
VK573-587	623.89(2-3)	Nautical instruments
VK588-597	526.99	Hydrographic surveying
VK600-794	623.8949	Tide/Current tables
VK607-794	623.89490916(2-7)	By place
VK607-609	623.8949091632	Arctic Ocean
VK610-680	623.894909163	Atlantic Ocean
VK619-621	623.89490916334	Baltic Sea
VK639-644	623.89490916336	English Channel
VK653-674	623.8949091638	Mediterranean Sea
VK685-701	623.894909165	Indian Ocean
VK715-756	623.894909164	Pacific Ocean
VK717	623.8949091644	North Pacific Ocean
VK725	623.8949091648	South Pacific
VK741-756	623.8949091642	East Pacific
VK759-792	623.894909163(4/6)	West Atlantic
VK798-997	623.8922	Sailing direction/Pilot guides
VK798	623.892205	Serials
VK800-803	623.892209	History
VK804-997	623.892216(3-7)	By place
VK810-880	623.89223	Atlantic Ocean
VK815-818	623.892236	North Sea
VK819-821.8	623.8922334	Baltic Sea
VK839-844	623.8922336	English Channel
VK853-874	623.892238	Mediterranean Sea
VK885-901	623.89225	Indian Ocean
VK915-956	623.89224	Pacific Ocean
VK917	623.892244	North Pacific Ocean
VK925	623.892248	South Pacific
VK941-956	623.89221642	East Pacific Ocean
VK959-992	623.8922163(4/6)	West Atlantic Ocean
VK1000-1249	623.8942	Lighthouses
VK1012	623.8944	Buoys/Markers
VK1015	623.894209	History
VK1021-1124	623.894209(4-9)	By place
VK1023-1025	623.89420973	United States
VK1026-1027	623.89420971	Canada
VK1028-1029	623.89420972	Mexico
VK1030-1031	623.894209728	Central America
VK1032-1033	623.894209729	West Indies

LC	Dewey	Descriptor	LC	Dewey	Descriptor
VK1034-1054	623.8942098	South America	VM34-54	623.81098	South America
VK1055-1096	623.8942094	Europe	VM36-37	623.810982	Argentina
VK1099-1113	623.8942095	Asia	VM43-44	623.810983	Chile
VK1115-1119	623.8942096	Africa	VM55-96	623.81094	Europe
VK1121-1122.5	623.8942099(3-4)	Australia/New Zealand	VM57-64	623.810941	Great Britain
VK1123-1124	623.8942099(5-6)	Oceania	VM71-72	623.810944	France
VK1150-1246	623.894(4/5)	Beacon/Buoy/Light lists	VM73-74.5	623.810943	Germany
VK1151-1185	623.894(4/5)094	Europe	VM75-76	623.8109495	Greece
VK1190-1199	623.894(4/5)096	Africa	VM79-80	623.810945	Italy
VK1203-1209	623.894(4/5)095	Asia	VM83-84	623.8109469	Portugal
VK1211-1212	623.894(4/5)099(3-4)	Australia/New Zealand	VM85-86	623.810947	European Russia
VK1221-1223	623.894(4/5)099(5-6)	Oceania	VM86.5	623.810948	Scandinavia
VK1225-1236	623.894(4/5)098	South America	VM87-88	623.810946	Spain
VK1237-1238	623.894(4/5)09728	Central America	VM99-113	623.81095	Asia
VK1239-1240	623.894(4/5)09729	West Indies	VM101-102	623.810951	China
VK1243-1244	623.894(4/5)0973	United States	VM105-106	623.810952	Japan
VK1245	623.894(4/5)0971	Canada	VM115-119	623.81096	Africa
VK1246	623.894(4/5)0972	Mexico	VM121-122.5	623.81099(3-4)	Australia/New Zealand
VK1250-1299-.6	623.888(5-6)	Shipwrecks/Fires	VM123-124	623.81099(5-6)	Oceania
VK1258	623.8886	Fire fighting/Prevention	VM139-140	623.81092	Biography
VK1270-1294	623.888(5-6) + 09(4-9)	Shipwrecks/Fires, By place	VM142-144	623.8184	Wooden construction
VK1270-1273	623.888(5-6)0973	United States	VM146-147	623.8182	Metal construction
VK1274-1276	623.888(5-6)0971	Canada	VM148	623.81844	Concrete construction
VK1277-1279	623.88(5-6) + 09(72-8)	Central/South America/ W. Indies	VM153-155	623.810287	Tonnage/Measurement
			VM156-163	623.8101	Theory/Principles
VK1280-1282	623.888(5-6)094	Europe	VM165-276	623.8107	Education
VK1283-1285	623.888(5-6)096	Africa	VM291	623.810299	Estimates
VK1286-1288	623.888(5-6)095	Asia	VM295-296	623.810(687/212)	Contracts/Specifications
VK1289-1291.3	623.888(5-6) + 099(3-4)	New Zealand/Australia	VM297	623.812	Designs
VK1292-1294	623.888(5-6) + 099(5-6)	Oceania	VM298	623.8101	Models
VK1300-1481	623.8887	Saving life/Property	VM298.5-301	338.4762382	Shipbuilding industry
VK1315	623.888709	History	VM311-466	623.82(1-9)	By type of vessel
VK1321-1424	623.888709(4-9)	By place	VM315	623.8204	Motor ships
VK1430	623.8887092	Biography	VM317	623.8728	Atomic/Nuclear ships
VK1460-1481	623.8887	Apparatus/Etc.	VM320-361	623.82(02/3)	Small craft
VK1491	387.55	Salvage	VM331-333	623.82(023/314)	Yachts
VK1500-1661	623.8922	Pilots/Piloting	VM340-349	623.8231	Motor boats/Launches
VK1515	623.892209	History	VM351-361	623.829	Small boats/Row boats
VK1521-1624	623.892(2-9) + (4-9)	By place	VM362	623.8204	Hydrofoils
VK1523-1525	623.892(2-9)73	United States	VM365-367	623.8257	Submarines
VK1526-1527	623.892(2-9)71	Canada	VM378-466	623.82(3-6)	By use
VK1528-1529	623.892(2-9)72	Mexico	VM381-385	623.8243	Passenger ships
VK1530-1531	623.892(2-9)728	Central America	VM391-395	623.8245	Cargo/Freight ships
VK1532-1533	623.892(2-9)729	West Indies	VM421	623.8234	Ferryboats
VK1534-1554	623.892(2-9)8	South America	VM461-.5	623.82436	River steamers
VK1555-1596	623.892(2-9)4	Europe	VM467	623.844	Ship joinery
VK1599-1613	623.892(2-9)5	Asia	VM470	623.86	Equipment/Fittings
VK1615-1619	623.892(2-9)6	Africa	VM471-479	623.85(03/2)	Electricity on ships
VK1621-1624	623.892(2-9) + 9(3-6)	Australia/New Zealand/ Oceania	VM480-.5	623.8504	Electronic apparatus
			VM481-482	623.85(3/4)	Heating/Sanitation/Etc.
VM	623.81	Naval architecture/ Engineering	VM491-493	623.852	Lighting
			VM503-505	623.8542	Water supply
VM1-4	623.810(5/6)	Serials/Societies	VM521-561	623.887	Propulsion
VM5	623.8106	Congresses	VM565	623.88	Steerage of ships
VM6	623.81074	Exhibitions/Museums	VM600-989	623.8	Marine engineering
VM12	623.81025	Directories	VM615-619	623.809	History
VM15-124	623.8109	History	VM621-724	623.809(4-9)	By place
VM16	623.810901	Ancient	VM623-625	623.80973	United States
VM17	623.810902	Medieval	VM626-627	623.80971	Canada
VM19	623.8109034	19th century	VM628-629	623.80972	Mexico
VM20	623.810904	20th century	VM630-631	623.809728	Central America
VM21-124	623.8109(4-9)	By place	VM632-633	623.809729	West Indies
VM23-25	623.810973	United States	VM634-654	623.8098	South America
VM26-27	623.810971	Canada	VM655-696	623.8094	Europe
VM28-29	623.810972	Mexico	VM657-664	623.80941	Great Britain
VM30-31	623.8109728	Central America	VM671-672	623.80944	France
VM32-33	623.8109729	West Indies	VM673-674.5	623.80943	Germany

LC	Dewey	Descriptor
VM675-676	623.809495	Greece
VM679-680	623.80945	Italy
VM683-684	623.809469	Portugal
VM685-686	623.80947	European Russia
VM686.5	623.80948	Scandinavia
VM687-688	623.80946	Spain
VM699-713	623.8095	Asia
VM705-706	623.80952	Japan
VM715-719	623.8096	Africa
VM721-722.5	623.8099(3-4)	Australia/New Zealand
VM723-724	623.8099(5-6)	Oceania
VM725-728	623.807	Education
VM731-779	623.87	Marine engines
VM741-750	623.8722	Boilers
VM753-759	623.873	Propellers/Gears/Etc.
VM770-771	623.8723	Gas/Oil/Diesel engines
VM773	623.8726	Electric propulsion
VM774-777	623.8728	Nuclear/Atomic engines
VM779	623.874	Fuels
VM781-861	623.86	Misc. appliances/Equipment
VM901-965	623.83	Shipyard equipment/Appliances
VM975-989	627.72	Diving
Z	011/020	Bibliography/Library Science
Z4-8	002.09	Books/Bookmaking, History
Z40-104.5	652	Writing
Z43-45	652.1/745.61	Calligraphy/Penmanship
Z49-51	652.3	Typewriters/Typewriting
Z53-102	653.(14)	Shorthand/Stenography
Z103-104.5	652.8	Cryptography
Z105.5-116	411.7	Paleography
Z116-265	686.2	Printing
Z119-.5	686.205	Serials
Z120-.5	686.206	Societies/Congresses
Z121	686.2074	Museums/Exhibitions
Z122-.5	686.207	Education
Z124-228	686.(1/209)	History of printing
Z133-225	686.209(4-9)	Printing history, By place
Z133-134	686.209436	Austria
Z135-136	686.209437	Czechoslovakia
Z137-138	686.209439	Hungary
Z144-145	686.20944	France
Z147-148	686.20943	Germany
Z151-.5	686.20941	Great Britain
Z152.6	686.209417	Ireland
Z153-154	686.209495	Greece
Z155-156	686.20945	Italy
Z159-160	686.209493	Belgium
Z161-162	686.209492	Netherlands
Z163-164	686.209438	Poland
Z165-166	686.20947	European Russia
Z167	686.2094897	Finland
Z168	686.209496	Baltic States
Z169-170	686.20948	Scandinavia
Z171-172	686.209469	Portugal
Z173-174	686.20946	Spain
Z175-176	686.209494	Switzerland
Z177-178	686.209561	Turkey
Z185-186	686.2095	Asia
Z195-196	686.2096	Africa
Z205-213	686.2097	America
Z206-207	686.20971	Canada
Z208-209	686.20973	United States
Z210-211	686.20972	Mexico
Z212-213	686.209(8/728-729)	S./Central America/West Indies
Z221-222	686.2099(3-6)	Australia/New Zealand/Oceania
Z231-232	686.2(092/06)	Printers/Printing companies
Z240-241.5	093	Incunabula
Z243-264.5	686.2023	Printing trade/Etc.
Z250	686.224	Kinds of type
Z265	686.4	Reproduction/Photography/Etc.
Z266-276	686.3	Bookbinding (General)
Z278-549	070.5/381.45002	Bookselling/Publishing
Z287-544	070.509(4-9)	Publishing, By place
Z291-444	070.5094	Europe
Z293-300	070.509436	Austria
Z301	070.509437	Czechoslovakia
Z302	070.509439	Hungary
Z303-310	070.50944	France
Z313-321	070.50943	Germany
Z323-330	070.50941	Great Britain
Z331	070.509417	Ireland
Z333	070.509495	Greece
Z338-345	070.50945	Italy
Z348-355	070.509493	Belgium
Z356-363	070.509492	Netherlands
Z365	070.509438	Poland
Z366-373	070.50947	European Russia
Z376-408	070.50948	Scandinavia
Z384-391	070.509489	Denmark
Z392-399	070.509481	Norway
Z400-407	070.509485	Sweden
Z408	070.5094897	Finland
Z410-417	070.50946	Spain
Z418-425	070.509469	Portugal
Z428-435	070.509494	Switzerland
Z439	070.5094977	Bulgaria
Z441	070.509498	Romania
Z443	070.509497	Yugoslavia
Z444	070.5094965	Albania
Z448-464	070.5095	Asia
Z449	070.5095694	Israel/Palestine
Z450	070.50955	Iran
Z451-458	070.50954	India
Z459	070.5095491	Pakistan
Z460	070.509598	Indonesia
Z461	070.509599	Philippines
Z462	070.50951	China
Z463	070.50952	Japan
Z465-470	070.5096	Africa
Z466	070.5096(1-2)	North Africa/Egypt
Z467	070.509676	East Africa
Z468	070.50966	West Africa
Z469	070.50968	South/Southern Africa
Z471-479	070.50973	United States
Z481-488	070.50971	Canada
Z491-498	070.50972	Mexico
Z501	070.509728	Central America
Z508-515	070.509729	West Indies
Z517-531	070.5098	South America
Z519	070.50982	Argentina
Z520	070.50984	Bolivia
Z521	070.50981	Brazil
Z522	070.50983	Chile
Z523	070.509861	Colombia
Z524	070.509866	Ecuador
Z525	070.50988	Guianas
Z528	070.509892	Paraguay

LC	Dewey	Descriptor	LC	Dewey	Descriptor
Z529	070.50985	Peru	Z831-832	025.00946	Spain
Z530	070.509895	Uruguay	Z833-834	025.009469	Portugal
Z531	070.50987	Venezuela	Z837-838	025.009494	Switzerland
Z533-543	070.5099(3-4)	Australia/New Zealand	Z838.5	025.0094965	Albania
Z544	070.5099(5-6)	Oceania	Z839	025.0094977	Bulgaria
Z551-656	351.824	Copyright (Nonlegal aspects)	Z840	025.009498	Romania
			Z841-.8	025.009497	Yugoslavia
Z657-659	323.445	Freedom of the press	Z843-844	025.00956	Near East
Z662-1000.5	027	Libraries	Z845-846	025.0095	Asia
Z665-718.8	020	Library Science	Z857-858	025.0096	Africa
Z674.7-.83	021.65	Library information networks	Z870-871	025.0099(3-6)	Australia/New Zealand/ Oceania
Z675	027.(1-8)	Types of libraries	Z881-980	025.31	Library catalogs
Z675.B8	027.69	Business/Industrial	Z987-997	026.1	Private libraries/Collecting
Z675.C5	027.67	Religious/Church	Z998-1000.5	017.(4/8)	Booksellers' catalogs/Prices
Z675.G7	027.5	Government libraries	Z1001-1121	011	General bibliography
Z675.H7	027.662	Hospital libraries	Z1001	011.001	Theory/Philosophy
Z675.P8	027.665	Prison libraries	Z1001.3	011.009	History
Z675.P85	027.2	Proprietary/Subscription	Z1003-.5	011.73	Choice of books
Z675.R4	027.3	Rental libraries	Z1006	016.(413/03)	Dictionaries/Encyclopedias
Z675.S3	027.8	School libraries	Z1007	016.34	Serials
Z678-.88	025.1	Library administration	Z1008	016.06	Societies/Congresses
Z678.9	025.3132	Automation	Z1011-1017	011.1	General bibliographies
Z681	025.12	Photography/Etc. (Reproduction)	Z1012-1017	011.09	General bibliographies, By date
Z687-716.1	025.(2-8)	The Collections-Processing/ Etc.	Z1019-1033	011.(3/4)	Special classes of books
			Z1035-.9	011.73	Best books
Z699-.5	025.04	Bibliographic databases	Z1036	016.0174	Booksellers' catalogs
Z700	025.7	Bookbinding	Z1039	013	For special people/Classes/ Etc.
Z720	025.0092	Biographies of librarians			
Z721-871	025.00(9/021)	History/Statistics	Z1041-1121	014	Anonyms/Pseudonyms
Z722-725	025.009	By date	Z1201-4980	015	National bibliography
Z731-871	025.009(1-9)	History/Statistics, By place	Z1201-1939	015.(7-8)	America (General)
Z731-733	025.00973	United States	Z1215-1363	015.73	United States
Z735-736	025.00971	Canada	Z1223.5-.6	015.7(4-9)	Municipal/State publications
Z739-740	025.00972	Mexico			
Z743-744	025.009728	Central America	Z1224.2-1231	016.81	American literature
Z753-754	025.009729	West Indies	Z1236-1249	016.973	History
Z759-760	025.0097299	Bermuda	Z1253-1354	016.97(4-9)	By state
Z765-766	025.0982	Argentina	Z1365-1401	015.71	Canada
Z767-768	025.00984	Bolivia	Z1411-1500	015.72(8)	Mexico/Central America
Z769-770	025.00981	Brazil	Z1501-1595	015.729	West Indies
Z771-772	025.00983	Chile	Z1601-1939	015.8	South America
Z773-774	025.009861	Colombia	Z2000-2959	015.4	Europe
Z775-776	025.009866	Ecuador	Z3001-3496	015.5	Asia
Z777-778	025.00988	Guianas	Z3013-3040	015.56	Near East/Arabia
Z779-780	025.009892	Paraguay	Z3041-3325	015.5	East Asia
Z781-782	025.00985	Peru	Z3221-3415	015.59	Southeast Asia
Z783-784	025.009895	Uruguay	Z3366-3370	015.55	Iran
Z785-786	025.00987	Venezuela	Z3401-3415	015.57	Asian Russia (Siberia)
Z791-792	025.00941	Great Britain	Z3461-3465	015.5662	Armenia
Z792.5	025.009417	Ireland	Z3466-3470	015.5692	Lebanon
Z793-794	025.009436	Austria	Z3476-3480	015.5694	Israel/Palestine
Z794.3	025.009439	Hungary	Z3481-3485	015.5691	Syria
Z795-796	025.009437	Czechoslovakia	Z3496	015.5645	Cyprus
Z797-798	025.00944	France	Z3501-3975	015.6	Africa
Z801-803	025.00943	Germany	Z4001-4980	015.9(3-6)	Australia/New Zealand/ Oceania
Z805-806	025.009495	Greece			
Z809-810	025.00945	Italy	Z5051-7999	015	Academic institutions
Z813-814	025.009493	Belgium	Z5060-5066	016.6291	Aerospace technology
Z815-816	025.009492	Netherlands	Z5069	016.11185	Aesthetics
Z817-818	025.009438	Poland	Z5071-5074	016.63	Agriculture
Z819-820	025.00947	European Russia	Z5095	016.05	Almanacs
Z823-824	025.009489	Denmark	Z5111-5119	016.301	Anthropology
Z825-826	025.009481	Norway	Z5131-5134	016.9301	Archaeology
Z827-828	025.009485	Sweden	Z5151-5154	016.52	Astronomy
Z829-830	025.0094897	Finland	Z5160-5164	016.3337924	Atomic energy

LC	Dewey	Descriptor	LC	Dewey	Descriptor
Z5167	016.670427	Automation	Z6011-6019	016.9104	Voyages/Travels
Z5170-5173	016.388342	Automobiles	Z6021-6027	016.(526/912)	Maps/Cartography
Z5180-5185	016.(5899/576)	Bacteriology/Microbiology	Z6031-6035	016.551	Geology
Z5256	016.595799	Bees	Z6041-6045	016.55	Geophysics
Z5275	016.7868848	Bells	Z6046	016.6661	Glass
Z5301-5319	012	Biography	Z6055	016.7392(2/3)	Gold/Silversmiths' work
Z5320-5323	016.574	Biology	Z6081	016.155282	Graphology
Z5331-5335	016.598	Birds	Z6121	016.79644	Gymnastics (P.Ed.)
Z5346-5349	016.305908161	The blind	Z6151-6155	016.(68/7455)	Handicraft
Z5351-5360	016.581	Botany	Z6201-6209	016.9	History
Z5440	016.5293	Calendars	Z6202	016.93	Ancient
Z5451-5452	016.62713	Canals	Z6203	016.9(4-9)	Medieval
Z5481	016.7954	Cards/Card playing	Z6204	016.9(4-9)	Modern
Z5491	016.59974428	Cats	Z6240	016.7982	Horses/Horsemanship
Z5521-5526	016.54	Chemistry	Z6250	016.64794	Hotels
Z5541	016.7941	Chess	Z6260	016.62082	Human engineering
Z5579-.5	016.909	Civilization	Z6270	016.641862	Ice cream
Z5601	016.6413373	Coffee	Z6297	016.67872	Synthetic Rubber
Z5640-5644	016.004	Computer science	Z6331-6335	016.66914(1/2)	Iron/Steel
Z5680	016.523	Cosmic physics	Z6366-6375	016.296	Jews
Z5691-5695	016.792026	Costume	Z6461-6485	016.3(27/41)	International law/Relations
Z5701	016.58317	Cotton	Z6465	016.(327/413)	Foreign relations
Z5703-.5	016.364	Criminology	Z6481-6485	016.34123	United Nations
Z5704	016.30590816	Physically handicapped	Z6511-6526	016.8	Literature
Z5705	016.03	Curiosities/Wonders	Z6511-6525	016.8	General literature
Z5706-5707	016.(3881762142/6362142)	Dairying	Z6651-6655	016.51	Mathematics
Z5710-5711	016.3942	Special days/Holidays/Etc.	Z6658-6676	016.61	Medicine
Z5721	016.305908161	Deaf-mutes	Z6662-6675	016.61(6-8)	By specialty
Z5725	016.3069	Death	Z6662-6663	016.61(1-2)	Anatomy/Physiology
Z5761	016.291216	Devil	Z6664	016.616	Internal medicine
Z5771-.4	011.7	Directories	Z6664.6	016.6171027	Sports medicine
Z5772	016.904	Disasters	Z6666-6667	016.617	Surgery
Z5775-5777	016.3309	Domestic economy	Z6668-.2	016.6176	Dentistry
Z5781-5785	016.792	Drama/Theater	Z6669	016.6177	Opthalmology
Z5811-5819	016.37	Education	Z6670	016.6165	Dermatology
Z5831-5839	016.(3337932/6213)	Electricity/Electronics	Z6671-.2	016.618(1-8)	Obstetrics/Gynecology
Z5841-5844	016.929(8/9)	Emblems	Z6671.5-.52	016.61892	Pediatrics
Z5848-5849	016.03	Encyclopedias	Z6673-.6	016.61(3/4)	Hygiene/Public health
Z5851-5855	016.62	Engineering	Z6674	016.636089	Veterinary medicine
Z5856-5860	016.5957	Entomology	Z6677-.2	016.3623	Mental retardation
Z5861-5863	016.3337	Environment	Z6678-6679	016.669	Metals
Z5865-5867	016.808803538	Erotic literature	Z6681-6685	016.5515	Meteorology
Z5873	016.17	Ethics	Z6704-6706	016.50282	Microscopy
Z5877	016.395	Etiquette	Z6721-6726	016.355	Military science
Z5883	016.9074	Exhibitions	Z6736-6740	016.6222	Mines/Mining
Z5885	016.6622	Explosives	Z6824	016.92997	Names
Z5896	016.3982(1-4)	Fables	Z6827	016.508	Nature
Z5906	016.(79686/3948)	Fencing/Dueling	Z6831-6836	016.359	Naval science
Z5916-5918	016.80883	Fiction	Z6837-6841	016.629045	Navigation
Z5931-5961	016.7	Fine arts	Z6866-6870	016.737	Numismatics
Z5941-5945	016.72	Architecture	Z6876-6880	016.133	Occult sciences
Z5946-5950	016.75	Painting	Z6900	016.61696	Parasitology
Z5951-5955	016.73	Sculpture	Z6905	016.36368	Parks
Z5970-5975	016.6392-3/799.1	Fish culture/Fishing	Z6915	016.55321	Peat
Z5980	016.92992	Flags	Z6935	016.7902	Performing arts
Z5981-5985	016.398	Folklore	Z6940-6964	016.07	Periodicals/Journalism
Z5986	016.3384764795	Food service	Z6972	016.55328	Petroleum
Z5990	016.0032	Forecasting	Z7001-7124	016.4(1)	Philology/Linguistics
Z5991	016.6349	Forestry	Z7125-7130	016.1	Philosophy
Z5993	016.3661	Freemasons	Z7134-7137	016.77	Photography
Z5994	016.3939	Funeral customs	Z7141-7145	016.53	Physics
Z5994.6	016.59(1-9)/016.6753	Fur/Animals	Z7155-7157	016.80881	Poetry
Z5995-.5	016.6454	Furniture	Z7161-7166	016.3(2)	Political/Social Sciences
Z5996-5997	016.635	Gardening	Z7179	016.6663	Pottery
Z5998	016.5538	Gems	Z7191	016.3989	Proverbs
Z6000	016.5261	Geodesy	Z7201-7205	016.15	Psychology
Z6001-6028	016.91	Geography/Travel/Maps	Z7215	016.6213848	Radar

LC	Dewey	Descriptor	LC	Dewey	Descriptor
Z7221-7225	016.3845	Radio	Z7757	016.2009(4-9)	By place
Z7231-7236	016.385	Railroads	Z7770-7772	016.20	Bible
Z7254	016.(3620425/61703)	Rehabilitation	Z7833-7836	016.29(2-9)	Religions (Non-Christian)
Z7291	016.3986	Riddles	Z7836	016.3982	Mythology
Z7295	016.3881	Roads	Z7837-7841	016.282	Roman Catholic Church
Z7335	016.55363	Salt	Z7842	016.2819	Russian/Eastern Orthodox
Z7401-7409	016.5	Science/Natural history	Z7843	016.(29641/3416)	Sabbath/Sacraments
Z7407	016.509(4-9)	Science, By place	Z7845	016.28(1-9)	Christian sects/Churches
Z7408	016.509(4-9)	Natural history, By place	Z7860-7864	016.2943	Buddhism
Z7421	016.92982	Seals (Device)	Z7876	016.529	Time/Timekeepers
Z7511-7516	016.79(6/3)	Sports/Amusements/ Recreation	Z7882	016.(39414/58379)	Tobacco/Smoking
			Z7890-7891	016.6159	Toxicology
Z7536	016.6168554	Stammering	Z7893	016.790133	Toys
Z7551-7555	016.31	Statistics	Z7925	016.3620425	Vocational rehabilitaton
Z7609-7610	016.641336	Sugar	Z7935	016.5537	Water supply
Z7615	016.36228	Suicide	Z7951	016.64122	Wine/Wine making
Z7631	016.79721	Swimming	Z7961-7965	016.3054	Women
Z7671-7675	016.003	System analysis/Etc.	Z7971-7975	016.(6363145/67731)	Wool
Z7711	016.(38455/621388)	Television	Z7991-7999	016.591	Zoology
Z7721	016.178	Temperance	Z7996	016.59	Taxonomy
Z7751-7865.5	016.2(912)	Theology/Religion	Z8001-8999	012	Personal bibliography

Dewey-LC Conversion Table

Dewey	LC	Descriptor	Dewey	LC	Descriptor
001	AZ	Scholarship/Learning/Errors	015.5662	Z3461-3465	Armenia
001.01	AZ101-(181)	Philosophy/Theory	015.5691	Z3481-3485	Syria
001.09	AZ501-908	By place	015.5692	Z3466-3470	Lebanon
001.09(72-8)	AZ517-588	Spanish America	015.5694	Z3476-3480	Israel/Palestine
001.090(1-4)	AZ(20)-(48)	By date	015.57	Z3401-3415	Asian Russia (Siberia)
001.090(1-4)	AZ200-361	History, By date	015.59	Z3221-3415	Southeast Asia
001.090(23-31)	AZ331	Renaissance	015.6	Z3501-3975	Africa
001.090(3-4)	AZ341-361	Modern	015.7(4-9)	Z1223.5-.6	Municipal/State publications
001.0901	AZ301-311	Ancient			
001.0902	AZ321	Medieval	015.71	Z1365-1401	Canada
001.094	AZ600-765	Europe	015.72(8)	Z1411-1500	Mexico/Central America
001.095	AZ770-795	Asia	015.729	Z1501-1595	West Indies
001.096	AZ800-821	Africa	015.73	Z1215-1363	United States
001.097	AZ501-516	North America	015.8	Z1601-1939	South America
001.0973	AZ503-513	United States	015.9(3-6)	Z4001-4980	Australia/New Zealand/ Oceania
001.099(3-6)	AZ850-908	Australia/New Zealand/ Oceania			
001.51	GR931-940	Signs and symbols	016	AI	Indexes
001.9	AZ999	Popular errors	016	AI3-19	Indexes, By language
001.942	TL789	UFOs	016.(413/03)	Z1006	Dictionaries/Encyclopedias
002.09	Z4-8	Books/Bookmaking, History	016.(5899/576)	Z5180-5185	Bacteriology/Microbiology
003.5	Q317-321	Bionics	016.003	Z7671-7675	System analysis/Etc.
003.5	Q300-385	Cybernetics	016.0032	Z5990	Forecasting
003.50(5/6)	Q300	Serials/Societies/Congresses	016.004	Z5640-5644	Computer science
003.503	Q304	Dictionaries/Encyclopedias	016.0174	Z1036	Booksellers' catalogs
003.507	Q316	Education	016.03	Z5705	Curiosities/Wonders
003.509	Q305	History	016.03	Z5848-5849	Encyclopedias
003.52	Q334-336	Perception	016.05	Z5095	Almanacs
003.54	Q350-385	Information theory	016.06	Z1008	Societies/Congresses
004	QA75-76.95	Calculating machines/ Computers	016.07	AI21	Newspaper indexes
004.0(5/6)	QA75.5	Serials/Societies/Congresses	016.07	Z6940-6964	Periodicals/Journalism
004.03	QA76.15	Dictionaries/Encyclopedias	016.1	Z7125-7130	Philosophy
004.09	QA76.17	History	016.11185	Z5069	Aesthetics
004.092	QA76.2	Biography	016.133	Z6876-6880	Occult sciences
006.3	Q334-336	Artificial intelligence	016.15	Z7201-7205	Psychology
011	Z	Bibliography	016.155282	Z6081	Graphology
011	Z1001-1121	General bibliography	016.17	Z5873	Ethics
011.(3/4)	Z1019-1033	Special classes of books	016.178	Z7721	Temperance
011.001	Z1001	Theory/Philosophy	016.2(912)	Z7751-7865.5	Theology/Religion
011.009	Z1001.3	History	016.20	Z7770-7772	Bible
011.09	Z1012-1017	General bibliography, By date	016.2009(4-9)	Z7757	By place
011.1	Z1011-1017	General bibliographies	016.28(1-9)	Z7845	Christian sects/Churches
011.7	AY2001	Compilation of directories	016.2819	Z7842	Russian/Eastern Orthodox
011.7	Z5771-.4	Directories	016.282	Z7837-7841	Roman Catholic Church
011.73	Z1003-.5	Choice of books	016.29(2-9)	Z7833-7836	Religions (Non-Christian)
011.73	Z1035-.9	Best books	016.291216	Z5761	Devil
012	Z8001-8999	Personal bibliography	016.2943	Z7860-7864	Buddhism
012	Z5301-5319	Biography	016.296	Z6366-6375	Jews
013	Z1039	For special people/ Classes/Etc.	016.29641	Z7843	Sabbath/Sacraments
014	Z1041-1121	Anonyms/Pseudonyms	016.3(2)	Z7161-7166	Political/Social Sciences
015	Z5051-7999	Academic institutions	016.301	Z5111-5119	Anthropology
015	Z1201-4980	National bibliography	016.3054	Z7961-7965	Women
015.(7-8)	Z1201-1939	America (General)	016.30590816	Z5704	Physically handicapped
015.4	Z2000-2959	Europe	016.305908161	Z5721	Deaf-mutes
015.5	Z3041-3325	East Asia	016.305908161	Z5346-5349	The blind
015.5	Z3001-3496	Asia	016.3069	Z5725	Death
015.55	Z3366-3370	Iran	016.31	Z7551-7555	Statistics
015.56	Z3013-3040	Near East/Arabia	016.327	Z6465	Foreign relations
015.5645	Z3496	Cyprus	016.327	Z6461-6485	International law/Relations
			016.3309	Z5775-5777	Domestic economy
			016.3337	Z5861-5863	Environment
			016.3337924	Z5160-5164	Atomic energy
			016.3337932	Z5831-5839	Electricity/Electronics
			016.3384764795	Z5986	Food service

Dewey	LC	Descriptor
016.34	Z1007	Serials
016.3409	K7000	Bibliographies
016.341	Z6461-6485	International law/Relations
016.34123	Z6481-6485	United Nations
016.3413	Z6465	Foreign relations
016.3416	Z7843	Sabbath/Sacraments
016.34942	KD51-59	Bibliography
016.34971	KE1-8	Bibliography
016.34973	KF1-8	Bibliography
016.355	Z6721-6726	Military science
016.359	Z6831-6836	Naval science
016.3620425	Z7254	Rehabilitation
016.3620425	Z7925	Vocational rehabilitaton
016.36228	Z7615	Suicide
016.3623	Z6677-.2	Mental retardation
016.36368	Z6905	Parks
016.364	Z5703-.5	Criminology
016.3661	Z5993	Freemasons
016.37	Z5811-5819	Education
016.3845	Z7221-7225	Radio
016.38455	Z7711	Television
016.385	Z7231-7236	Railroads
016.3881	Z7295	Roads
016.3881762142	Z5706-5707	Dairying
016.388342	Z5170-5173	Automobiles
016.3939	Z5994	Funeral customs
016.39414	Z7882	Tobacco/Smoking
016.3942	Z5710-5711	Special days/Holidays/Etc.
016.3948	Z5906	Fencing/Dueling
016.395	Z5877	Etiquette
016.398	Z5981-5985	Folklore
016.3982	Z7836	Mythology
016.3982(1-4)	Z5896	Fables
016.3986	Z7291	Riddles
016.3989	Z7191	Proverbs
016.4(1)	Z7001-7124	Philology/Linguistics
016.5	Z7401-7409	Science/Natural history
016.50282	Z6704-6706	Microscopy
016.508	Z6827	Nature
016.509(4-9)	Z7407	Science, By place
016.509(4-9)	Z7408	Natural history, By place
016.51	Z6651-6655	Mathematics
016.52	Z5151-5154	Astronomy
016.523	Z5680	Cosmic physics
016.526	Z6021-6027	Maps/Cartography
016.5261	Z6000	Geodesy
016.529	Z7876	Time/Timekeepers
016.5293	Z5440	Calendars
016.53	Z7141-7145	Physics
016.54	Z5521-5526	Chemistry
016.55	Z6041-6045	Geophysics
016.551	Z6031-6035	Geology
016.5515	Z6681-6685	Meteorology
016.55321	Z6915	Peat
016.55328	Z6972	Petroleum
016.55363	Z7335	Salt
016.5537	Z7935	Water supply
016.5538	Z5998	Gems
016.574	Z5320-5323	Biology
016.581	Z5351-5360	Botany
016.58317	Z5701	Cotton
016.58379	Z7882	Tobacco/Smoking
016.59	Z7996	Taxonomy
016.59(1-9)	Z5994.6	Fur/Animals
016.591	Z7991-7999	Zoology
016.5957	Z5856-5860	Entomology
016.595799	Z5256	Bees
016.598	Z5331-5335	Birds
016.59974428	Z5491	Cats
016.61	Z6658-6676	Medicine
016.61(1-2)	Z6662-6663	Anatomy/Physiology
016.61(3/4)	Z6673-.6	Hygiene/Public health
016.61(6-8)	Z6662-6675	By specialty
016.6159	Z7890-7891	Toxicology
016.616	Z6664	Internal medicine
016.6165	Z6670	Dermatology
016.6168554	Z7536	Stammering
016.61696	Z6900	Parasitology
016.617	Z6666-6667	Surgery
016.61703	Z7254	Rehabilitation
016.6171027	Z6664.6	Sports medicine
016.6176	Z6668-.2	Dentistry
016.6177	Z6669	Opthalmology
016.618(1-8)	Z6671-.2	Obstetrics/Gynecology
016.61892	Z6671.5-.52	Pediatrics
016.62	Z5851-5855	Engineering
016.62082	Z6260	Human engineering
016.6213	Z5831-5839	Electricity/Electronics
016.6213848	Z7215	Radar
016.621388	Z7711	Television
016.6222	Z6736-6740	Mines/Mining
016.62713	Z5451-5452	Canals
016.629045	Z6837-6841	Navigation
016.6291	Z5060-5066	Aerospace technology
016.63	Z5071-5074	Agriculture
016.6349	Z5991	Forestry
016.635	Z5996-5997	Gardening
016.636089	Z6674	Veterinary medicine
016.6362142	Z5706-5707	Dairying
016.6363145	Z7971-7975	Wool
016.639(2/3)	Z5970-5975	Fish culture/Fishing
016.64122	Z7951	Wine/Wine making
016.6641336	Z7609-7610	Sugar
016.6413373	Z5601	Coffee
016.641862	Z6270	Ice cream
016.6454	Z5995-.5	Furniture
016.64794	Z6250	Hotels
016.6622	Z5885	Explosives
016.6661	Z6046	Glass
016.6663	Z7179	Pottery
016.669	Z6678-6679	Metals
016.66914(1/2)	Z6331-6335	Iron/Steel
016.670427	Z5167	Automation
016.6753	Z5994.6	Fur/Animals
016.67731	Z7971-7975	Wool
016.67872	Z6297	Synthetic Rubber
016.68	Z6151-6155	Handicraft
016.7	Z5931-5961	Fine arts
016.72	Z5941-5945	Architecture
016.73	Z5951-5955	Sculpture
016.737	Z6866-6870	Numismatics
016.7392(2/3)	Z6055	Gold/Silversmiths' work
016.7455	Z6151-6155	Handicraft
016.75	Z5946-5950	Painting
016.77	Z7134-7137	Photography
016.7868848	Z5275	Bells
016.79(6/3)	Z7511-7516	Sports/Amusements/Recreation
016.790133	Z7893	Toys
016.7902	Z6935	Performing arts
016.792	Z5781-5785	Drama/Theater
016.792026	Z5691-5695	Costume
016.7941	Z5541	Chess
016.7954	Z5481	Cards/Card playing

Dewey	LC	Descriptor
016.79644	Z6121	Gymnastics (P.Ed.)
016.79686	Z5906	Fencing/Dueling
016.79721	Z7631	Swimming
016.7982	Z6240	Horses/Horsemanship
016.7991	Z5970-5975	Fish culture/Fishing
016.8	Z6511-6525	General literature
016.8	Z6511-6526	Literature
016.808803538	Z5865-5867	Erotic literature
016.80881	Z7155-7157	Poetry
016.80883	Z5916-5918	Fiction
016.81	Z1224.2-1231	American literature
016.9	Z6201-6209	History
016.9(4-9)	Z6204	Modern
016.9(4-9)	Z6203	Medieval
016.904	Z5772	Disasters
016.9074	Z5883	Exhibitions
016.909	Z5579-.5	Civilization
016.91	Z6001-6028	Geography/Travel/Maps
016.9104	Z6011-6019	Voyages/Travels
016.912	Z6021-6027	Maps/Cartography
016.929(8/9)	Z5841-5844	Emblems
016.92982	Z7421	Seals (Device)
016.92992	Z5980	Flags
016.92997	Z6824	Names
016.93	Z6202	Ancient
016.9301	Z5131-5134	Archaeology
016.97(4-9)	Z1253-1354	By state
016.973	Z1236-1249	History
017.(4/8)	Z998-1000.5	Booksellers' catalogs/Prices
020	Z665-718.8	Library Science
020	Z	Library Science
021.65	Z674.7-.83	Library information networks
022	CD981-985	Buildings/Furnishings
025.(2-8)	Z687-716.1	The Collections-Processing/Etc.
025.00 (9/021)	Z721-871	History/Statistics
025.009	Z722-725	By date
025.009(1-9)	Z731-871	History/Statistics, By place
025.0092	Z720	Biographies of librarians
025.00941	Z791-792	Great Britain
025.009417	Z792.5	Ireland
025.00943	Z801-803	Germany
025.009436	Z793-794	Austria
025.009437	Z795-796	Czechoslovakia
025.009438	Z817-818	Poland
025.009439	Z794.3	Hungary
025.00944	Z797-798	France
025.00945	Z809-810	Italy
025.009946	Z831-832	Spain
025.009469	Z833-834	Portugal
025.00947	Z819-820	European Russia
025.009481	Z825-826	Norway
025.009485	Z827-828	Sweden
025.009489	Z823-824	Denmark
025.0094897	Z829-830	Finland
025.009492	Z815-816	Netherlands
025.009493	Z813-814	Belgium
025.009494	Z837-838	Switzerland
025.009495	Z805-806	Greece
025.0094965	Z838.5	Albania
025.009497	Z841-.8	Yugoslavia
025.0094977	Z839	Bulgaria
025.009498	Z840	Romania
025.0095	Z845-846	Asia
025.00956	Z843-844	Near East
025.0096	Z857-858	Africa
025.00971	Z735-736	Canada
025.00972	Z739-740	Mexico
025.009728	Z743-744	Central America
025.009729	Z753-754	West Indies
025.0097299	Z759-760	Bermuda
025.00973	Z731-733	United States
025.00981	Z769-770	Brazil
025.00982	Z765-766	Argentina
025.00983	Z771-772	Chile
025.00984	Z767-768	Bolivia
025.00985	Z781-782	Peru
025.009861	Z773-774	Colombia
025.009866	Z775-776	Ecuador
025.00987	Z785-786	Venezuela
025.00988	Z777-778	Guianas
025.009892	Z779-780	Paraguay
025.009895	Z783-784	Uruguay
025.0099(3-6)	Z870-871	Australia/New Zealand/Oceania
025.04	Z699-.5	Bibliographic databases
025.1	Z678-.88	Library administration
025.12	Z681	Photography/Etc. (Reproduction)
025.31	Z881-980	Library catalogs
025.3132	Z678.9	Automation
025.7	Z700	Bookbinding
026.007	CD501-511	Education
026.1	Z987-997	Private libraries/Collecting
026.526	GA192-197.3	Map libraries/Collections
027	Z662-1000.5	Libraries
027	CD921-4280	Archives
027	CD1-511	Diplomatics
027	AG500-551	Information centers/Bureaus
027.(1-8)	Z675	Types of libraries
027.0(5-9)	AG551	Other countries
027.0(1-9)	CD1000-4280	National archives, By place
027.0(3-9)	CD101-392	Documents, By place
027.0(71-8)	AG531	Other American countries
027.001	CD46	Philosophy/Theory
027.001	CD947-972	Philosophy/Theory
027.0025	CD941	Directories
027.0028	CD973-976	Methods/Techniques
027.003	CD40	Dictionaries/Encyclopedias
027.003	CD945	Dictionaries/Encyclopedias
027.005	CD921	Serials/Societies
027.005	CD1-15	Serials
027.006	CD20-29	Societies/Congresses
027.006	CD921	Serials/Societies
027.007	CD987-988	Education
027.009	CD47	History
027.009	CD995-4280	History
027.0090	CD50-69	General diplomatics, By date
027.0090(1-4)	CD996-.4	By date
027.04	AG540	Europe
027.04	CD1000-2000	Europe
027.04	CD101-215	Europe
027.041	CD1040-1199.5	Great Britain
027.043	CD1220-1378.195	Germany
027.0436	CD1120-1149.5	Austria
027.0437	CD1150-1169.5	Czechoslovakia
027.0438	CD1740-1759.5	Poland
027.0439	CD1170-1189.5	Hungary
027.044	CD1190-1219.5	France
027.045	CD1400-1658	Italy
027.046	CD1850-1879.5	Spain
027.0469	CD1880-1899.5	Portugal

Dewey	LC	Descriptor
027.047	CD1710-1739.5	Russia
027.0481	CD1810-1829.5	Norway
027.0485	CD1830-1849.5	Sweden
027.0489	CD1770-1789.5	Denmark
027.04912	CD1790-1809.5	Iceland
027.0492	CD1690-1709.5	Netherlands
027.0493	CD1670-1689.5	Belgium
027.0494	CD1900-1929.5	Switzerland
027.0496	CD1930-1989.5	The Balkans
027.05	CD221-254	Asia
027.05	CD2001-2291	Asia
027.051	CD2030-2059.5	China
027.052	CD2160-2189.5	Japan
027.054	CD2080-2099.5	India
027.05694	CD2010-2919.5	Israel
027.06	CD255-269	Africa
027.06	CD2300-2491	Africa
027.07(4-9)	CD3070-3609	By state
027.071	CD331-332	Canada
027.071	CD3620-3649.6	Canada
027.072	CD333-334	Mexico
027.072	CD3650-3679.5	Mexico
027.0728	CD3690-3859.5	Central America
027.0728	CD335-350	Central America
027.0729	CD351-362	Caribbean area
027.0729	CD3860-3985	Caribbean area
027.073	CD3020-3615	United States
027.073	CD309-311	United States
027.073	AG521-527	United States
027.08	CD4000-4279.5	South America
027.08	CD365-392	South America
027.09(3-4)	CD271-290	Australia/New Zealand
027.09(3-4)	CD2500-2789.5	Australia/New Zealand
027.09(5-6)	CD291	Oceania
027.09(5-6)	CD2795	Oceania
027.2	Z675.P85	Proprietary/Subscription
027.3	Z675.R4	Rental libraries
027.5	Z675.G7	Government libraries
027.662	Z675.H7	Hospital libraries
027.665	Z675.P8	Prison libraries
027.67	Z675.C5	Religious/Church
027.69	Z675.B8	Business/Industrial
027.8	Z675.S3	School libraries
027/327.2	CD	Diplomatics/Archives/Seals
028.7	AG	Dictionaries/General reference
028.7	AG103-196	Reference, General
030	AE	Encyclopedias
030	AY	Yearbooks/Almanacs/Directories
030	AY30-1730	Almanacs
030	AG240-243	Wonders/Curiosities
030-039	AE5-88	Modern, By language
030-039	AE2-4	Early
030.9	AY30-39	History
030.9(4-9)	AY51-1730	By place
030.97	AY51-425	North America
030.971	AY410-425	Canada
030.9728	AY430-499	Central America
030.973	AY51-381	United States
030.993	AY1651-1652	New Zealand
030.994	AY1600-1636	Australia
031	AY410-425	Canada
031	AY51-381	United States
031.02	AG305-313	Notes/Queries
031/032	AE5-10	American/English
032	AY1600-1636	Australia

Dewey	LC	Descriptor
032	AY1651-1652	New Zealand
032	AY750-789	Great Britain
032.02	AG305-313	Notes/Queries
033.1	AY850-860	Germany
034.1	AY830-839	France
035.1	AY890-899	Italy
036	AE7-10	American, Other than English
036	AY430-499	Central America
036	AY600-729	South America
036	AY510-581	West Indies
036.1	AE61-65	Spanish
036.1	AY1000-1009	Spain
036.9	AY1010-1019	Portugal
0369.509728	AM314-322	Central America
038	AY950-989	Scandinavia
039.99	AY1671-1730	Oceania
050	AY	Yearbooks/Almanacs/Directories
050	AP	General periodicals
050	AP1	Periodicals, Polyglot
050	PN4832-4836	Magazines/Other periodicals
050	AI1	Periodical indexes
050-059	PN4699-4705	Serials
050.240396073	AP(270)-(271)	Afro-American
050.24042	AP(250)-(265)	Women's
050.2405(4-5)	AP200-230	Juvenile periodicals
051	AP2-9	English
051-059	AP2-95	By language
052	AP2-9	English
053.1	AP30-36.7	German
053.931	AP14-17	Dutch/Flemish
053.936	AP18	Afrikaans
054.1	AP20-28	French
055.1	AP37-39	Italian
055.91	AP86	Romanian
056.1	AP60-64	Spanish
056.9	AP65-68	Portuguese
057	AP50-58	Slavic
058	AP40-49	Scandinavian
058.94541	AP80	Finnish
059.89	AP85	Modern Greek
059.916	AP73-77	Celtic
059.924	AP91-93	Jewish
059.94511	AP82-83	Hungarian
060	AS2.5-4	Congresses
060	AS	Learned societies
060	HD2421-2429	Trade/Industrial associations
060.25	AS8	Directories
060.5	AS1-2	Serials
060.6	AS6	Organization
060.9	AS5	History
061-068	AS9-911	By place
061.(3-9)	AS21-36	United States
061.1	AS40-42	Canada
062	AS111-122	Great Britain
062-068	AS91-348	Europe
063	AS171-182	Germany
064	AS151-162	France
065	AS211-222	Italy
066.(9)	AS300-304	Spain/Portugal
067	AS251-262	European Russia
068.48	AS271-284	Scandinavia
068.495	AS191-202	Greece
068.5	AS401-599	Asia

Dewey	LC	Descriptor
068.51	AS441-452	China
068.52	AS541-552	Japan
068.54	AS461-472	India
068.6	AS600-699	Africa
068.728	AS60-70	Central America
068.729	AS71-75	West Indies
068.8	AS77-90	South America
068.9(3-6)	AS701-785	Australia/New Zealand/Oceania
069	AM	Museums/Collecting
069.(01)	AM111-157	Museology/Methods
069.05	AM1	Serials/Societies
069.083	AM8	Children's museums
069.09	AM10-101	History, By place
069.09(72-8)	AM23-35	Latin/Spanish America
069.094	AM40-70	Europe
069.0941	AM41-43	Great Britain
069.0943	AM49-51	Germany
069.0944	AM46-48	France
069.0945	AM54-55	Italy
069.0946(9)	AM65-66	Spain/Portugal
069.0948	AM61.5-64	Scandinavia
069.09495	AM52-53	Greece
069.09496	AM69	Balkan states
069.095	AM71-79	Asia
069.0951	AM72	China
069.0952	AM77-78	Japan
069.096	AM80-91	Africa
069.0971	AM21-22	Canada
069.0973	AM11-13	United States
069.0974	AM60	European Russia
069.099(3-6)	AM93-100	Australia/New Zealand/Oceania
069.5	AM200-401	Collectors/collecting
069.50(5/6)	AM200-207	Serials/Societies
069.509	AM301-396	Collecting, By place
069.509	AM221	History of collecting
069.5092	AM223	Biography
069.5094	AM342-371	Europe
069.50941	AM343-347	Great Britain
069.50943	AM350	Germany
069.50944	AM349	France
069.50946(9)	AM362-363	Spain/Portugal
069.50947	AM356	European Russia
069.5095	AM372-385	Asia
069.5096	AM387-389	Africa
069.50971	AM313	Canada
069.50972 (8/9)	AM314-329	Mexico/Central Amer./W.Indies
069.50973	AM303-311	United States
069.5098	AM330-341	South America
069.5099(3-6)	AM390-396	Australia/New Zealand/Oceania
069.53	N9100-9165	Art and war (Loss/Damage/Etc.)
069.54	N8750-9084	Protection/Cultivation of art
070.4	PN4722-4726	Collections
070.4	PN4699-5650	Journalism/Period press
070.4028	PN4775-4784	Practical Journalism/Techniques
070.403	PN4728	Dictionaries
070.406	PN4717	Congresses
070.406	PN4712-4715	Societies
070.407	PN4785-4823	Education
070.444	PN6700-6790	Comic books/Comic strips
070.449796	TR821	Sports journalism
070.49	TR820	Journalism

Dewey	LC	Descriptor
070.5	Z278-549	Bookselling/Publishing
070.509 (4-9)	Z287-544	Publishing, By place
070.5094	Z291-444	Europe
070.50941	Z323-330	Great Britain
070.509417	Z331	Ireland
070.50943	Z313-321	Germany
070.509436	Z293-300	Austria
070.509437	Z301	Czechoslovakia
070.509438	Z365	Poland
070.509439	Z302	Hungary
070.50944	Z303-310	France
070.50945	Z338-345	Italy
070.50946	Z410-417	Spain
070.509469	Z418-425	Portugal
070.50947	Z366-373	European Russia
070.50948	Z376-408	Scandinavia
070.509481	Z392-399	Norway
070.509485	Z400-407	Sweden
070.509489	Z384-391	Denmark
070.5094897	Z408	Finland
070.509492	Z356-363	Netherlands
070.509493	Z348-355	Belgium
070.509494	Z428-435	Switzerland
070.509495	Z333	Greece
070.5094965	Z444	Albania
070.509497	Z443	Yugoslavia
070.5094977	Z439	Bulgaria
070.509498	Z441	Romania
070.5095	Z448-464	Asia
070.50951	Z462	China
070.50952	Z463	Japan
070.50954	Z451-458	India
070.5095491	Z459	Pakistan
070.50955	Z450	Iran
070.5095694	Z449	Israel/Palestine
070.509598	Z460	Indonesia
070.509599	Z461	Philippines
070.5096	Z465-470	Africa
070.5096 (1-2)	Z466	North Africa/Egypt
070.50966	Z468	West Africa
070.509676	Z467	East Africa
070.50968	Z469	South/Southern Africa
070.50971	Z481-488	Canada
070.50972	Z491-498	Mexico
070.509728	Z501	Central America
070.50729	Z508-515	West Indies
070.50973	Z471-479	United States
070.509730687	KF3084	Publishing contracts
070.5098	Z517-531	South America
070.50981	Z521	Brazil
070.50982	Z519	Argentina
070.50983	Z522	Chile
070.50984	Z520	Bolivia
070.50985	Z529	Peru
070.509861	Z523	Colombia
070.509866	Z524	Ecuador
070.50987	Z531	Venezuela
070.50988	Z525	Guianas
070.509892	Z528	Paraguay
070.509895	Z530	Uruguay
070.5099 (3-4)	Z533-543	Australia/New Zealand
070.5099 (5-6)	Z544	Oceania
071-079	PN4840-5648	Journalism, By place
071.(3-9)	PN4841-4900	United States
071.1	PN4901-4920	Canada
072	PN5111-5160	Great Britain
073	PN5201-5220	Germany

Dewey	LC	Descriptor
073-078	PN5110-5355	Europe
074	PN5171-5790	France
077	PN5271-5280	European Russia
078	PN5280.5-5310	Scandinavia
079	PN5000-5106	South America
079	PN4930.5-4959	Caribbean/West Indies
079(56/174927)	PN5359	Near East/Arab countries
079.5	PN5360-5449	Asia
079.6	PN5450-5499	Africa
079.9 (4/3)	PN5511-5590	Australia/New Zealand
079.9 (5-6)	PN5620-5639	Oceania
080	AC	General collections
080	AC9	General collections
081/082	AC1-8	American/English collections
083.1	AC30-35	German collections
083.7	AC103-104	Yiddish
083.931	AC16-19	Dutch collections
084.1	AC20	French collections
085.1	AC40-45	Italian collections
086.(1/69)	AC70-75	Spanish/Portuguese
087	AC60-65	Slavic
088	AC50-55	Scandinavian
089.(7-9)	AC95	Other European
089.59	AC156-160	Indo-Chinese
089.911	AC111-125	Indo-Aryan
089.915	AC126-127	Persian
089.91992	AC132-133	Armenian
089.92	AC101-102	Semitic
089.927	AC105-106	Arabic
089.9435	AC140-141	Turkish
089.945	AC80-85	Finno-Ugrian
089.951	AC149-150	Chinese
089.956	AC145-146	Japanese
089.957	AC147-148	Korean
089.96	AC177-189	African
089.97	AC195	American Indian
089.992	AC166-167	Malay
089.9922	AC168-169	Indonesian
093	Z240-241.5	Incunabula
100	BD10-28	Philosophy, Introductions
100	B	Philosophy
100-999	LT	Textbooks
101	B53-67	Methodology
101.4	B49-50	Terminology
102.5	B35	Directories
103	B40-48	Dictionaries
103	B51	Encyclopedias
105	B1-8	Serials
105	B31	Yearbooks
106	B20	Congresses
106	B11-18	Societies
107	B52-59.5	Education
109.22	B104	Collective biography
110	BD95-131	Metaphysics
110-121	BD	Speculative philosophy
110-121.0202	BD30-38	Outlines/Etc.
110.202	BD131	Outlines/Etc.
111	BD300-450	Ontology
111.1	BD331	Being/Substance
111.5	BD398	Nothingness
111.6	BD411	Finite/Infinite
111.8	BD352	Attributes of being
111.82	BD396	Whole/Parts
111.85	BH	Aesthetics
111.8501	BH39-41	Philosophy
111.8503	BH56	Dictionaries/Encyclopedias
111.8505	BH1-8	Serials
111.8506	BH11-19	Societies/Congresses
111.8507	BH61-62	Education
111.8509	BH81-208	History
111.8509 (4-9)	BH221	By place
113	BD493-701	Cosmology
113.09	BD494-496	History
114	BD621-626	Space/Space and matter
114-117	BD620-655	Space/Time/Matter/Motion
115	BD632-638	Time/Space and time
116	BD652	Matter and motion/Force
117	BD652	Matter and motion/Force
117	BD646-648	Structure of matter and form
121	BD143-237	Epistemology
121.2	BD201	Limits of knowledge
121.3	BD181	Origin/Sources of knowledge
121.4	BD220	Objectivity
121.4	BD222	Subjectivity
121.6	BD215	Belief/Faith
121.6	BD183	Inquiry
121.65	BD182	Criterion
121.7	BD215	Belief/Faith
121.8	BD232	Value/Worth
122	BD530-595	Causation/Teleology
124	BD530-595	Causation/Teleology
128	BD450	Philosophical anthropology
133	BF1001-1389	Parapsychology
133	BF1404-1999	Occult sciences
133.025	BF1409	Directories
133.025	BF1024.4	Directories
133.03	BF1407	Dictionaries/Encyclopedias
133.03	BF1025	Dictionaries/Encyclopedias
133.05	BF1001-1008	Serials
133.06	BF1404	Congresses
133.06	BF1009-1021	Societies/Congresses
133.07	BF1040.5	Education
133.09	BF1028-.5	History
133.09	BF1421-1429	History
133.09(4-9)	BF1434	By place
133.092	BF1026-1027	Biography
133.092	BF1408-.2	Biography
133.1	BF1444-1486	Ghosts/Apparitions
133.3	BF1845-1999	Fortune-telling
133.3	BF1783-1815	Seers/Prophets
133.324 8	BF1745-1779	Oracles/Divinations
133.42	BF1501-1562	Demonology
133.422	BF1546-1550	Satanism
133.43	BF1562.5-1623	Witchcraft/Magic
133.5	BF1651-1729	Astrology
133.6	BF908-990	Palmistry
133.8	BF1111-1118	Hypnotism
133.82	BF1161-1175	Telepathy
133.9	BF1228-1389	Spiritualism
135.3	BF1074-1099	Dreaming
137	BF889-905	Graphology
138	BF839.8-861	Physiognomy
139	BF866-885	Phrenology
150	BF	Psychology
150.1	BF38-.8	Philosophy
150.14	BF32	Terminology
150.1943	BF199	Behaviorism
150.195	BF173-175.5	Psychoanalysis
150.1982	BF203	Gestalt
150.25	BF30	Directories
150.287	BF176-.5	Testing/Tests
150.3	BF31	Dictionaries/Encyclopedias

Dewey	LC	Descriptor
150.5	BF1-8	Serials
150.6	BF11-20	Societies/Congresses
150.7	BF77-80.7	Education
150.724	BF180-198.7	Experimental psychology
150.724	BF76.5	Research
150.9	BF81-105	History
150.9(4-9)	BF108	By place
150.92	BF109	Biography
152.1	BF231-299	Sensation
152.33	BF335-337	Habits
152.4	BF511-593	Emotion/Feeling
153.15	BF318-319.5	Learning
153.2	BF365-395	Association/Ideas
153.3	BF408-426	Imagination/Creativity
153.4	BF319.5-499	Cognition/Consciousness
153.42	BF441-449	Thought/Thinking
153.73	BF321-323	Apperception/Attention
153.8	BF501-504.3	Motivation
153.8	BF608-635	Will/Choice
153.9	BF431-433	Intelligence
154.2	BF315	Subconsciousness
154.4	BF207-210	Drugs/Electronic effects
154.64	BF1068-1073	Somnambulism/Sleep
155	BF712-724.85	Developmental psychology
155	BF697-.5	Differential psychology
155.2	BF818-839	Character
155.2	BF698	Personality
155.26	BF795-811	Temperament
155.28	BF698.4-.9	Personality assessment/Tests
155.3	BF692-.5	Sexual behavior (Psychology)
155.4	LB1101-1139	Child study
155.4	BF719-723	Infant/Child psychology
155.5	BF724-.85	Adolesence/Young adult
155.7	BF699-711	Genetic psychology
155.8	GN502-517	Psychological anthropology
155.89(4-9)	BF108	By place
155.9	BF353-.5	Environmental psychology
156	BF660-685	Comparative psychology
158	BF636-637	Applied psychology
158.7	HF5548.7-.85	Industrial psychology
160	BC	Logic
160-169	BC38-39	Modern
160-169.9	BC11-39	History
160-169.9(01/3)	BC25-32	Ancient
160-169.9(4-9)	BC39.5	Logic, By place
160-169.902	BC34-35	Medieval
160.(5/6)	BC4-5	Societies/Congresses
160.1	BC50-57	Methodology
160.202	BC101-117	Outlines/Etc.
160.3	BC9	Dictionaries/Encyclopedias
160.5	BC1	Serials
160.7	BC59	Education
161	BC80-99	Induction
162	BC60-78	Deduction
165	BC175	Fallacies
166	BC185	Syllogisms/Dilemma
167	BC183	Hypotheses
168	BC177	Reasoning/Argument
170	BJ991-1185	Textbooks, By language
170	BJ	Ethics
170.1	BJ37-60	Philosophy/Methodology
170.202	BJ1075-1077	Outlines/Etc.
170.3	BJ63	Dictionaries/Encyclopedias
170.5	BJ1-8	Serials
170.6	BJ19	Congresses

Dewey	LC	Descriptor
170.6	BJ10	Societies
170.7	BJ66-68	Education
170.9	BJ116-118	China/Japan
170.9	BJ71-982	History of ethics
170.9	BJ101-214	Ancient
170.9(4-9)	BJ351-982	History
170.90(23-31)	BJ271-285	Renaissance
170.90(3-4)	BJ301-982	Modern
170.902	BJ231-255	Medieval
170.932	BJ131-133	Egypt
170.935	BJ136-143	Assyria-Babylonia/Persia
170.937	BJ160-224	Greece/Rome
170.938	BJ160-224	Greece/Rome
170.941	BJ601-654	Great Britain
170.943	BJ751-759	Germany
170.9436	BJ591-594	Austria
170.9438	BJ847-850	Poland
170.9439	BJ805-808	Hungary
170.944	BJ701-704	France
170.945	BJ811-814	Italy
170.946	BJ911-914	Spain
170.9469	BJ921-924	Portugal
170.947	BJ851-854	European Russia
170.948	BJ861-864	Scandinavia
170.9481	BJ881-884	Norway
170.9485	BJ891-894	Sweden
170.9489	BJ871-874	Denmark
170.9492	BJ831-834	Netherlands
170.9493	BJ841-844	Belgium
170.9494	BJ941-944	Switzerland
170.9495	BJ801-804	Greece
170.94977	BJ595-598	Bulgaria
170.95	BJ961-964	Asia
170.951	BJ965-968	China
170.9519	BJ973-976	Korea
170.952	BJ971	Japan
170.954	BJ121-123	India
170.955	BJ136-143	Assyria-Babylonia/Persia
170.96	BJ980-982	Africa
170.971	BJ401-404	Canada
170.972	BJ421-424	Mexico
170.9728	BJ431-434	Central America
170.9729	BJ441-444	West Indies
170.973	BJ351-354	United States
170.98	BJ441-564	South America
174	BJ1725	Professional ethics
174.2	R723-726	Medical philosophy/Ethics
174.4	HF5387	Business ethics
176	HQ31-64	Sex instruction/Ethics
177.5	HT1561	Ethics of race questions
179. (8/9)	BJ1518-1535	Virtue/Vices/Character
180	B108-118	Ancient philosophy
181	B5017-5289	Philosophy, Asia
181	B121-162.7	Ancient oriental philosophy
181.043	B162	Buddhist, Ancient
181.044	B162.5	Jainist, Ancient
181.06	B154-159	Jewish, Ancient
181.09561	B162.6	Shinto, Ancient
181.09561	B135-138	Japanese, Ancient
181.1	B5135-5289	Philosophy, South/Eastern Asia
181.11(2-5)	B125-128	Chinese, Ancient
181.114	B162.7	Taoist, Ancient
181.119	B139.1-.4	Korean, Ancient
181.12	B135-138	Japanese, Ancient
181.2	B140-143	Egyptian, Ancient
181.3	B755-759	Jewish philosophers

Dewey	LC	Descriptor	Dewey	LC	Descriptor
181.3	B5055-5059	Israel/Palestine	200	BR	Christianity
181.4	B5130-5134	Philosophy, India	200.1	BL51-54	Philosophy of religion
181.4	B130-133	India, Ancient	200.25	BL35	Directories
181.5	B5070-5074	Philosophy, Iran	200.3	BL31	Dictionaries/Encyclopedias
181.5	B150-153	Iranian, Ancient	200.5	BL1-10	Serials
181.6	B145-148	Assyrian-Babylonian, Ancient	200.6	BL11-21	Societies/Congresses
			200.7	BL41-42	Education
181.6	B5040-5044	Philosophy, Iraq	200.8996073	E185.7	Religion
181.8	B5045-5054	Philosophy, Lebanon/Syria	200.92	BL71.5-72	Biography
181.9	B5060-5069	Philosophy, Jordan/Arabia	201	BR100-114	Philosophy
181.9	B149.2-.23	Armenian, Ancient	203	BR95-99	Encyclopedias/Dictionaries
182	B188-258	Greek, Ancient (First period)	205	BR1-9	Serials
			206	BR21-29	Societies
182-185	B165-491	Ancient Greek	206	BR41-43	Congresses
182-188	B165-708	Ancient occident philosophy	207	BV1607-1612	In public/Private schools
			207	BX8714	Education
182.7-183	B265-320	Greek, Ancient (Second period)	207	BX8111-8114	Education
			207	BX8561-8564	Education
183	B310-318	Greek, Ancient (Socratic)	207	BX9761-9764	Education
183.4	B504-623	Greco-Roman	207	BX8219-8227	Education
184	B350-398	Greek, Ancient (Plato)	207	BX9412-9413	Education
184-186	B335-491	Greek, Ancient (Third period)	207	BX9917-9923	Education
			207	BX9817-9823	Education
185	B400-491	Greek, Ancient (Aristotle)	207	BX5869-5876	Education
186-187	B504-623	Greco-Roman	207	BX6061-6064	Education
186.4	B630-708	Alexandrian/Early Christian	207	BX5041-5050	Education
189	B720-765	Medieval philosophy	207	BX7119-7127	Education
189.4	B734	Scholasticism	207	BX6113	Education
189.5	B728	Mystic philosophy	207	BX6219-6227	Education
190	B770-780	Renaissance	207	BX895-939	Education
190	B790-5739	Modern philosophy	207	BX7619-7627	Education
190	B630-708	Alexandrian/Early Christian	207	BX8917-8925	Education
191	B850-945	Philosophy, United States	207	BX8610	Education
191	B981-995	Philosophy, Canada	207	BX8012-8016	Education
192	B1111-1682	Philosophy, Great Britain	209	BR138-1500	History
193	B2521-3396	Philosophy, Germany/ Austria	209.(4-9)	BR500-1500	Christianity, By place
			209.0(1-2)	BR160.3-275	Early/Medieval
194	B1801-2430	Philosophy, France	209.0(1-4)	BR160-481	By period
195	B3551-3656	Philosophy, Italy	209.0(23-31)	BR280	Renaissance/Reformation
196.1	B4561-4568	Philosophy, Spain	209.0(3-4)	BR290-481	Modern
197	B4201-4279	Russia	209.2	BR1690-1725	Biography
198	B4301-4315	Scandinavia	209.41	BR740-799	Great Britain
198.1	B4411-4445	Norway	209.43	BR850-859	Germany
198.5	B4455-4495	Philosophy, Sweden	209.44	BR840-849	France
198.8	B4711-4715	Philosophy, Finland	209.46	BR1020-1029	Spain
198.9	B4591-4598	Philosophy, Portugal	209.47	BR930-939	European Russia
198.9	B4325-4395	Philosophy, Denmark	209.48	BR940-1019	Scandinavia
199.437	B4801-4805	Philosophy, Czechoslovakia	209.5	BR1060-1357	Asia
199.438	B4687-4691	Philosophy, Poland	209.51	BR1280-1297	China
199.439	B4811-4815	Philosophy, Hungary	209.519	BR1320-1337	Korea
199.4912	B4402-4406	Philosophy, Iceland	209.52	BR1300-1317	Japan
199.492	B4041-4095	Philosophy, Netherlands	209.54	BR1150-1156	India
199.492	B3801-4030	Philosophy, Low countries	209.59	BR1178-1261	Southeast Asia
199.493	B4151-4175	Philosophy, Belgium	209.6	BR1359-1470	Africa
199.494	B4625-4651	Philosophy, Switzerland	209.61	BR1369-1415	North Africa
199.495	B3500-3515	Philosophy, Greece	209.66	BR1460-1470	West Africa
199.4965	B4851-4855	Philosophy, Albania	209.67	BR1430	Central Africa
199.497	B4841-4845	Philosophy, Yugoslavia	209.676	BR1440-1445	East Africa
199.4977	B4831-4835	Philosophy, Bulgaria	209.68	BR1446-1458	Southern Africa
199.498	B4821-4825	Romania	209.72	BR610-615	Mexico
199.561	B4871-4875	Philosophy, Turkey	209.728	BR620-625	Central America
199.6	B5300-5679	Philosophy, Africa	209.729	BR640-655	Caribbean
199.72	B1001-1084	Philosophy, Latin America	209.73	BR513-563	United States
199.8	B1001-1084	Philosophy, Latin America	209.8	BR660-730	South America
199.9(3-6)	B5685-5739	Australia/New Zealand/ Oceania	209.9(3-6)	BR1480-1495	Australia/New Zealand/ Oceania
200	BL	Religion	209.98	BR1500	Polar regions

Dewey	LC	Descriptor	Dewey	LC	Descriptor
210	BL175-290	Natural theology	230-239	BT65-84	Doctrinal/Dogmatic/Systematic
211.4	BL2700-2790	Rationalism	230-280	PJ601-621	Christian Oriental
220	BS	Bible	230.(1-9)	BT1313-1480	History of doctrines/Movements
220	BS546-559	Bible stories			
220.(4-5)	BS1-355	Versions	230.(1-9)	BT1319-1480	By periods
220.(6-7)	BS410-680	Works about the Bible	230.01	BT40-55	Philosophical theology
220.07	BS585-613	Education	230.09	BT20-30	History
220.15	BS647-649	Prophecy	230.2	BX1746-1755	Theology/Doctrine
220.3	BS420-429	Concordances	230.342	BX5137-5140	Dogma
220.4	BS11-115	Early	230.373	BX5929-5930	Doctrines
220.5	BS125-355	Modern	230.42	BX9420-9422	Doctrine
220.52	BS405-408	Abridged	230.58	BX7250-7252	Special doctrines
220.520(1-9)6	BS390-399	Selections/Quotes	230.61	BX6330-6331	Doctrine
220.531092	PT1505	The Bible	231	BT98-180	God
220.6	BS500-534	Criticism/Interpretation	231.(1-3)	BT109-115	Trinity
220.7	BS482-498	Commentaries	231.3	BT117-123	Holy spirit
220.95	BS635-636	And history	231.4	BT130-157	Divine attributes
221	BS701-1830	Old Testament	231.72	BT94	Kingdom of God
221.(4-5)	BS701-1013	Texts and versions	231.73	BX2164-2167	Devotions to St. Joseph
221.07	BS1193-1195	Education	231.73	BX2160-2161	Devotions to Virgin Mary
221.09	BS1130-1136	History	231.73	BX2159	Devotions to Jesus
221.092	BS580	People in the Old Testament	231.765	BT695-748	Creation
221.4	BS705-815	Early	231.8	BT160-180	Theodicy
221.47	BS767-815	Latin	232	BT198-590	Christology
221.48	BS737-765	Ancient Greek	232.1	BT230-245	Messiahship
221.5	BS825-1013	Modern	232.8	BT250-270	Offices of Jesus Christ
221.520(1-9)3	BS1121-1128	Concordances	232.9	BT296-500	Life of Christ
221.520(1-9)6	BS1091-1099	Selections/Quotes	232.9(56-97)	BT400-420	Transfiguration to ascension
221.6	BS1160-1191	Criticism/Interpretation	232.901	BT306	Words of Jesus
221.65	BS1104	Harmonies	232.903	BT304	Character/Personality (Jesus)
221.7	BS1143-1158	Commentaries			
221.92	BS569-580	People of the Bible	232.91	BT610-640	Theology
222-224	BS1200-1830	Special parts	232.91	BT595-680	Mary
222.1	BS1221-1285	Pentateuch	232.91	BX2160-2161	Devotions to Virgin Mary
223	BS1401-1490	Political books	232.917	BT650-654	Miracles/Shrines
223	BS1455-1490	Wisdom literature	232.932	BX2164-2167	Devotions to St. Joseph
223.2	BS1419-1450	Psalms	232.95	BT340-500	Public life of Jesus
224	BS1501-1675	Prophetic books	232.95	BT306	Words of Jesus
225-228	BS1901-2970	New Testament	232.954	BS2415-2417	Teachings of Jesus
225.(4-5)	BS1901-2213	Texts and versions	232.954	BT373-378	Parables
225.(6-7)	BS2280-2545	Works about New Testament	232.954	BT380-382	Sermon on the Mount
225.07	BS2525-2544	Education	232.955	BT580	Miracles/Shrines
225.09	BS2315-2318	History	232.96	BT430-470	Passion
225.092	BS2430-2520	People of the Bible	232.96	BX2159	Devotions to Jesus
225.4	BS1937-2020	Early	232.966	BT587	Relics
225.5	BS2025-2213	Modern	233	BT700-745	Man
225.520(1-9)3	BS2301-2312	Concordances	234	BT750-810	Salvation
225.520(1-9)6	BS2260-2269	Selections/Quotes	234.13	BX6950	Healing
225.6	BS2350-2393	Criticism/Interpretation	234.9	BT809-810	Freedom/Predestination
225.7	BS2333-2348	Commentaries	235	BT960-985	Invisible world
225.92	BS569-580	People of the Bible	235.2	BX380	Saints
226-228	BS2547-2970	Special parts	235.2	BT683-694	Misc. saints
226.(2-5)	BS2549-2619	Gospels	235.3	BT968	Angels
226.6	BS2620-2629	Acts	235.4	BT975-981	Demons
226.8	BT373-378	Parables	236	BT819-891	Eschatology
226.9	BT380-382	Sermon on the Mount	236.2	BT899-940	Future life/Future state
226.9505	BS546-559	Bible stories	236.22	BT919-925	Immortality
227	BS2630-2638	Epistles	236.24	BT844-849	Heaven
227	BS2640-2815	Pauline Epistles	236.25	BT834-842	Hades
228	BS2820-2827	Apocalypse	236.9	BT875-891	End of world
229	BS2831-2970	Apocrypha	238	BT990-1010	Creeds/Etc.
229	BS1691-1830	Apocrypha	238	BT1029-1040	Catechisms
230	BS2397-2405	Theology of	238.2	BX1958-1968	Creeds/Catechisms
230	BT	Christian doctrinal theology	238.33	BX6074	Creeds
230	BS1192	Theology of	238.373	BX5939	Creeds
230-236	BT19-33	Doctrine and dogma	238.42	BX9428-9429	Creeds/Catechisms

185

Dewey	LC	Descriptor
238.46	BX8578	Creeds/Catechisms
238.5	BX9183-9184	Creeds/Catechisms
238.58	BX7235-7236	Creeds
238.61	BX6335-6336	Creeds/Catechisms
238.7	BX8335	Creeds/Catechisms
238.93	BX8649	Creeds/Catechisms
238.94	BX8733	Creeds/Catechism
238.97	BX8124	Creeds/Catechisms
239	BT1095-1253	Apologetics
239.009	BT1109-1115	History
241	BJ1238-1278.5	Christian ethics
241	BV4625-4780	Moral theology
241.2	BT95-97	Divine law
241.3	BV4625-4627	Sins/Vices
241.4	BV4630-4647	Virtues
241.5(2-4)	BV4650-4715	Biblical precepts
241.57	BV4720-4780	Church precepts
242	BV4800-4897	Meditation/Devotion
242	BX2178-2198	Meditations
242.802	BX2050-2155	Prayer books
246.55	BV150-168	Symbols
247	NA5050-5095	Ecclesiastical furnishings
247	BV775-777	Property
247.1	BV195-196	Altars
248	BV	Christian practical theology
248	BV4485-5099	Christian life
248.(4-5)	BV4520-4526	Religious duties
248.03	BV2.5	Dictionaries
248.05	BV1	Serials
248.22	BV5070-5095	Mysticism
248.24	BV4912-4950	Religious conversion
248.3	BV5-469	Worship
248.3	BV5-530	Worship
248.309	BV5	History
248.309	BV5-8	History
248.32	BV205-287	Prayer
248.463	BX2323	Pilgrimages
248.47	BV5099	Quietism
248.47	BV5015-5068	Asceticism
248.482	BX2380-2386	Religious life
248.482	BX2349-2377	Christian life
248.482	BX2347-2348	Practical religion
248.8(2-9)	BV4527-4599	For special persons
249	BV200	Family worship
249	BV4520-4526	Religious duties
251	BV4200-4317	Preaching/Homiletics
252	BV4239-4317	Sermons
252.02	BX1756	Sermons/Etc.
252.03	BX5008.11	Sermons
252.041	BX8066	Sermons
252.042	BX9426	Sermons
252.046	BX8577	Sermons
252.05	BX9178	Sermons
252.058	BX7233	Sermons
252.061	BX6332-6333	Sermons
252.067	BX6123	Sermons
252.091	BX9842-9843	Sermons
252.09134	BX9942-9943	Sermons
252.093	BX8639	Sermons
252.094	BX8724	Sermons
252.096	BX7733	Sermons
252.097	BX8127	Sermons
252.098	BX9777	Sermons
252.099	BX9876	Sermons
252.7	BX8333	Sermons
253	BV4000-4470	Pastoral theology
253.07	BV4019-4180	Education
253.2	BV4390-4399	Personal life
253.52	BV4012	Psychology
254.3	BV652.95-657	Mass media
254.7/262.933	BV775-777	Property
254.8	BV770-774	Church finance
255.(1-7)	BX2890-4192	Individual orders/Men
255.(1-7)	BX2433-2434	Superiors/Administration
255.(1-7)009	BX2460-2749	History
255.(1-7)009	BX2501-2749	By place
255.(1-7)0090(1-4)	BX2465-2475	By period
255.(1-7)0094	BX2631-2676	Europe
255.(1-7)0095	BX2677-2731	Asia
255.(1-7)0096	BX2732-2740	Africa
255.(1-7)00971	BX2527-2529	Canada
255.(1-7)00972	BX2530-2532	Mexico
255.(1-7)009728	BX2533-2547	Central America
255.(1-7)009729	BX2548-2560	Caribbean
255.(1-7)00973	BX2505-2525	United States
255.(1-7)0098	BX2561-2589	South America
255.(1-7)0099(3-6)	BX2747-2749	Australia/New Zealand/ Oceania
255.(1-7)06	BX2435-2438	Life/Rules
255.(1-7/9)	BX2400-4556	Monasticism/Orders
255.(8/98)	BX385-388	Monasticism
255.(8/98)	BX580-583	Monasticism
255.(8/98)	BX5970-5974	Religious orders
255.8	BX5971-5972	Men
255.9	BX4200-4250	General orders for women
255.9(1-7)	BX4262-4556	Individual orders for women
255.98	BX5973-5974	Women
259.8	BV1620-1652	Social life/Recreation
260	BV598-603	The church
260	BV590-1652	Ecclesiastical theology
261	BR115	And other subjects
261.2	BR127-128	And other religions
261.7	BV629-633	Church and state
261.7	BX1790-1795	And the state
261.72	BR1610-1617	Tolerance/Liberalism
261.8	HT910-921	Religion and slavery
261.83	HN30-39	Church and social problems
261.8309(4-9)	HN39	Religion/Etc., By place
261.832	HV530	The church and charity
262	BV646-651	Church polity
262	BV700-741	Parish/Congregation/ Authority
262.0068	BV652-.9	Church management
262.01947	BX515-558	Organization
262.02	BX1800-1920	Organization
262.033	BX6076	Organization
262.03411	BX5340-5355	Organization
262.03417	BX5540-5555	Organization
262.0342	BX5150-5182	Organization
262.0373	BX5950-5968	Organization
262.041	BX8071	Organization
262.042	BX9425	Organization
262.046	BX8576	Organization
262.05	BX9190-9195	Organization
262.058	BX7240-7246	Organization
262.061	BX6340-6346	Organization
262.07	BX8339-8346	Organization
262.091	BX9850	Organization
262.093	BX8657-8659	Organization
262.094	BX8737	Organization
262.095	BX6958	Organization
262.096	BX7740-7746	Organization
262.097	BX8126	Organization

Dewey	LC	Descriptor	Dewey	LC	Descriptor
262.098	BX9776	Organization	264.09134	BX9954	Sacraments
262.1	BX1905-1920	Priests/Bishops/Etc.	264.093	BX8655	Sacraments
262.13	BX1805-1815	Pope	264.093	BX8651	Liturgy/Ritual
262.13	BX950-961	Papacy	264.094	BX8735	Liturgy/Ritual
262.136	BX1818-1899	Curia Romana	264.094	BX8736	Sacraments
262.14	BV659-690	Clergy/Ministry	264.095	BX6960	Service/Liturgy
262.52	BX820-837	Councils	264.096	BX7737	Liturgy/Ritual
262.72	BX1-9	Church unity	264.097	BX8125	Liturgy/Ritual
263.042(3-9)	BX2320-2321	Shrines	264.2	BV290-530	Music/Hymns
263.4	BV107-133	Lord's day	264.2	BV343-520	Hymn books
263.9	BV30-135	Church year	264.36	BV823-828	Holy Communion
263.9	BV80-105	Fast days	265	BV800-838	Sacraments/Ordinances
263.9(1-7)	BV43-64	Feast days	265.1	BV800-813	Baptism
263.98	BV65-70	Saints' days	265.5	BV835-838	Marriage
264	BV198-199	Books/Liturgies	266	BV2000-3705	Missions
264	BV15-29	Public worship	266.(4-9)	BV2350-2595	Protestant
264	BV169-199	Liturgy/Rituals	266.(4-9)	BV2495-2525.2	By denomination
264	BV5-530	Worship	266.(4-9)09	BV2400-2595	History
264.019	BX377-378	Sacraments	266.02	BV2000-2121	General/Foreign
264.019	BX350-376	Liturgy and ritual	266.023	BV2750-3695	In specific countries
264.01947	BX560-573	Worship	266.02309(72-8)	BV2829-2853	Latin America
264.02	BX1970-2175	Liturgy and ritual	266.023091822	BV3147	Mediterranean region
264.02(1-9)	BX1999-2045	Special liturgical books	266.023094	BV2855-3145	Europe
264.02(1-9)	BX1980-1990	Books/Texts	266.0230941	BV2860-2875	Great Britain
264.02009(4-9)	BX1977	By place	266.0230943	BV2950-2957	Germany
264.020090(1-4)	BX1973-1975	By period	266.0230944	BV2940-2945	France
264.02036	BX2215-2239	Eucharist	266.0230945	BV2970-2975	Italy
264.0208	BX2200-2292	Sacraments	266.0230946	BV3120-3127	Spain
264.02084	BX2240	Ordination (Holy Order)	266.023095	BV3400-3457	East Asia
264.02085	BX2250-2254	Marriage	266.023095	BV3149-3487	Asia
264.02086	BX2260-2267	Penance	266.0230951	BV3410-3427	China
264.020864	BX2270	Absolution	266.0230952	BV3440-3457	Japan
264.020866	BX2279-2283	Indulgences	266.0230954	BV3260-3290	India
264.02091	BX2295-2310	Sacramentals	266.0230954	BV3250-3290	South Asia
264.023	BX2037	Sacramentaries	266.0230956	BV3160-3217	Near East
264.023	BX2169	Eucharistic devotions	266.0230957	BV3470-3487	North Asia
264.023	BX2015	Missals	266.0230958	BV3220-3240	Central Asia
264.024	BX2000	Breviaries	266.0230959	BV3298-3390	Southeast Asia
264.025	BX2030-2031	Pontificals	266.023096	BV3500-3630	Africa
264.025	BX2035	Rituals	266.023096(1-9)	BV3560-3625	Africa, By country
264.0272	BX2010	Holy week	266.0230971	BV2810-2820	Canada
264.03	BX5145	Prayer books	266.0230973	BV2762-2808	United States
264.033	BX6075	Liturgy and ritual	266.023099(3-4)	BV3650-3667	Australia/New Zealand
264.03411	BX5335-5337	Liturgy and ritual	266.023099(3-6)	BV3640-3680	Oceania
264.03417	BX5535-5537	Liturgy and ritual	266.023099(5-6)	BV3670-3680	Oceania
264.0342	BX5140.5-5147	Liturgy and ritual	266.0230998	BV3690-3695	Polar regions
264.035	BX5148-5149	Sacraments	266.2	BV2130-2300	Roman Catholic
264.03573	BX5949	Sacraments	266.373	BX5969	Missions
264.0373	BX5943-5945	Book of common prayer	266.93	BX8661	Missions
264.0373	BX5940	Liturgy and ritual	267	BV900-1450	Societies/Associations
264.038	BX5146	Psalter	267.3	BV1000-1220	YMCA
264.03873	BX5947-5948	Other rituals	267.5	BV1300-1393	YWCA
264.03873	BX5946	Psalter	267.613	BV1420-1430	YPSCE
264.041	BX8067	Liturgy/Ritual	268	BV1500-1579	Sunday schools
264.041	BX8072-8073	Sacraments	268	BV1460-1615	Religious education/ Schools
264.042	BX9427	Liturgy/Ritual			
264.046	BX8574-8575	Liturgy/Ritual/Devotions	268	LC361-629	Christian education
264.05	BX9188-9189	Sacraments	268	LA95-98	Christian education
264.05	BX9185-9187	Liturgy/Ritual	268.090(1-2)	LB125	Early Christian/Medieval
264.058	BX7237	Service/Liturgy	268.6	BV1534-1536	Teaching methods
264.058	BX7238-7239	Sacraments	268.82	BX895-939	Education
264.061	BX6337-6339	Liturgy/Ritual	268.828(3-9)	LC531-629	Protestant
264.067	BX6124.3-.6	Ordinances/Sacraments	268.8282	LC461-510	Roman Catholic
264.07	BX8336-8337	Worship/Liturgy/Ritual	268.83	BX6061-6064	Education
264.07	BX8338	Sacraments	268.8342	BX5041-5050	Education
264.091	BX9854	Sacraments	268.841	BX8012-8016	Education
264.09134	BX9953	Services	268.842	BX9412-9413	Education

Dewey	LC	Descriptor
268.846	BX8561-8564	Education
268.85	BX8917-8925	Education
268.858	BX7119-7127	Education
268.861	BX6219-6227	Education
268.8673	BX6113	Education
268.87	BX8219-8227	Education
268.891	BX9817-9823	Education
268.89134	BX9917-9923	Education
268.893	BX8610	Education
268.894	BX8714	Education
268.895	BX6917	Education
268.896	BX7619-7627	Education
268.897	BX8111-8114	Education
268.898	BX9761-9764	Education
269.2	BV3750-3799	Evangelism/Revivals
269.24	BX6475-6476	Meetings/Camps
270	BR117-126	Christian literature
270-273	BT1313-1480	History of doctrines/ Movements
270-273	BT1319-1480	By periods
270.(1-3)	BX1070-1176	590-1049
270.(1-4)	BR160.3-275	Early/Medieval
270.(1-5)	BX965-1397	By date
270.(1-82)	BR160-481	By date
270.(4-5)	BX1210-1263	1122-1305
270.(5-7)	BR280	Renaissance/Reformation
270.092	BX380	Saints
270.4	BX1178-1200	1049-1122
270.5	BX1304-1329	1447-1572
270.5	BX1270-1302	1305-1447
270.8	BR290-481	Modern
272	BR1600-1609	Persecutions/Martyrs
272.2	BX1700-1745	Inquisition
274-279	BR500-1500	Christianity, By place
274.1	BR740-799	Great Britain
274.3	BR850-859	Germany
274.4	BR840-849	France
274.6	BR1020-1029	Spain
274.7	BR930-939	European Russia
274.8	BR970-1019	Scandinavia
275	BR1060-1357	Asia
275.1	BR1280-1297	China
275.19	BR1320-1337	Korea
275.2	BR1300-1317	Japan
275.4	BR1150-1156	India
275.9	BR1178-1261	Southeast Asia
276	BR1359-1470	Africa
276.1	BR1369-1415	North Africa
276.6	BR1460-1470	West Africa
276.7	BR1430	Central Africa
276.76	BR1440-1445	East Africa
276.8	BR1446-1458	Southern Africa
277.2	BR610-615	Mexico
277.28	BR620-625	Central America
277.29	BR640-655	Caribbean
277.3	BR513-563	United States
278	BR660-730	South America
279.(3-6)	BR1480-1495	Australia/New Zealand/ Oceania
279.8	BR1500	Polar regions
280-289	BX	Christian church denominations
280.4	BX4872-4924	Pre-Reformation
280.4	BX4819-4821	Anti-Protestant
280.4	BX4818	And other Christians
280.4	BX4800-9999	Protestantism
280.40(5/6)	BX4800-4801	Serials/Societies
280.409	BX4804-4807	Protestantism, History
280.409(4-9)	BX4833-4861	Protestantism, By place
280.4092	BX4825-4827	Biography
280.4094	BX4837-4854	Europe
280.40941	BX4838-4840	Great Britain
280.40943	BX4844	Germany
280.40944	BX4843	France
280.40945	BX4851	Spain
280.40945	BX4847	Italy
280.40947	BX4849	European Russia
280.4095	BX4857	Asia
280.40972	BX4833	Mexico
280.409728	BX4833.5-4834	Central America
280.409729	BX4835	West Indies
280.4098	BX4836	South America
280.4099(3-6)	BX4861	Australia/New Zealand/ Oceania
281	BX100-754	Eastern/Oriental
281.9	BX200-754	Orthodox eastern
281.9(4-9)	BX650-754	Other areas
281.9(4-9)	BX400-754	Divisions
281.909	BX290-310	Eastern/Orthodox history
281.9092	BX390-359	Biography
281.943(6/9)	BX630-639	Austria/Hungary
281.947	BX460-605	Russian Orthodox
281.94709	BX485-492	History
281.94709(4-9)	BX494-500	By place
281.947092	BX575-577	Saints
281.947092	BX595-597	Biography
281.9495	BX610-619	Greek
282	BX1781-1789	And other churches
282	BX2325-2333	Saints
282	BX800-4795	Roman Catholic
282.(4-9)	BX1401-1695	By place
282.(4-9)	BX4600-4644	Churches by place
282.0(5/6)	BX800-816	Serials/Societies
282.03	BX841-847	Dictionaries
282.09	BX940-1745	History
282.090(1-4)	BX965-1397	By date
282.090(24-3)	BX1305-1329	1447-1572
282.090(34-4)	BX1365-1390	1789-
282.0902(3-4)	BX1270-1302	1305-1447
282.09021	BX1178-1200	1049-1122
282.09021	BX965-1176	590-1049
282.09022	BX1210-1263	1122-1305
282.0903(1-3)	BX1330-1361	1572-1789
282.092	BX4700-4705	Saint/Martyrs, Biographies
282.092	BX4650-4705	Biography
282.0922	BX4654-4660	Saints/Martyrs, Collected bios.
282.4	BX4627-4638	Europe
282.4	BX1490-1612	Europe
282.41	BX4631	Great Britain
282.41	BX1491-1514	Great Britain
282.43	BX4630	Germany
282.43	BX1534-1539	Germany
282.44	BX4629	France
282.44	BX1528-1533	France
282.45	BX1543-1548	Italy
282.45	BX4634	Italy
282.46	BX1583-1588	Spain
282.46	BX4636	Spain
282.469	BX4635	Portugal
282.47	BX1558-1560	European Russia
282.5	BX1615-1673	Asia
282.5	BX4640	Asia
282.5	BX1662-1670	East Asia

Dewey	LC	Descriptor
282.54	BX1643-1661	South Asia
282.56	BX1617-1636	Middle East
282.58	BX1637-1642	Central Asia
282.6	BX4642	Africa
282.6	BX1675-1682	Africa
282.71	BX4605	Canada
282.71	BX1419-1424	Canada
282.72	BX4610	Mexico
282.72	BX1427-1431	Mexico
282.728	BX1432-1447	Central America
282.728	BX4615	Central America
282.729	BX1448-1459	West Indies
282.729	BX4618	West Indies
282.73	BX4600-4603	United States
282.73	BX1404-1418	United States
282.8	BX1460-1489	South America
282.8	BX4620-4625	South America
282.9(3-6)	BX4644	Australia/New Zealand/ Oceania
282.9(3-6)	BX1685-1695	Australia/New Zealand/ Oceania
283	BX5001-6093	Anglican communion
283-289	BX4800-9999	Protestantism
283-289.09	BX4804-4807	Protestantism, History
283.(4-9)	BX5103-5110	By place
283.0(4-9)	BX5996-6030	By place (Abroad)
283.0(5/6)	BX5001-5002	Serials/Societies
283.090(1-5)	BX5005	Anglican history
283.3	BX6081-6083	Churches
283.3	BX6051-6093	Reformed Episcopal
283.30(5/6)	BX6051-6055	Serials/Societies
283.3092	BX6091-6093	Biography
283.309(34-4)	BX6065-6069	Episcopal Reformed, History
283.411	BX5210-5395	Episcopal Church in Scotland
283.411	BX5369-5370	Churches
283.411092	BX5390-5395	Biography
283.417	BX5410-5595	Church in Ireland
283.417	BX5569-5570	Churches
283.41709	BX5500-5510	Church in Ireland, History
283.417092	BX5590-5595	Biography
283.42	BX5127-5129	And other churches
283.42	BX5194-5195	Churches
283.42	BX5115-5126	Movements
283.42	BX5011-5740	Church of England
283.420(5/6)	BX5011-5023	Serials/Societies
283.42025	BX5031	Directories
283.4209	BX5051-5101	Church of England, History
283.4209(1-5)	BX5067-5101	By period
283.4209(4-9)	BX5600-5740	Church of England abroad
283.42092	BX5197-5199	Biography
283.420971	BX5617	Churches
283.420971	BX5610-5613	In Canada, History
283.420971	BX5601-5620	Anglican Church of Canada
283.4209710(5/6)	BX5601-5604	Serials/Societies
283.420971092	BX5619-5620	Biography
283.429	BX5596-5598	Anglican Church in Wales
283.5	BX5661-5680	Asia
283.6	BX5681-5700	Africa
283.7(3-9)09	BX5879-5919	Episcopal Church, History
283.7(3-9)09(34-4)	BX5881-5882	By period
283.7(4-9)	BX5885-5919	Episcopal Church, By place
283.73	BX5800-6093	Episcopal church
283.73	BX5926-5928	And other churches
283.73	BX5980-5983	Churches
283.73092	BX5990	Biography

Dewey	LC	Descriptor
283.837(5-9)	BX5869-5876	Education
283.9(3-4)	BX5701-5720	Australia/New Zealand
283.9(5-6)	BX5721-5740	Oceania
284.1	BX8075-8077	Individual churches
284.1	BX8063.7	Relations with others
284.1	BX8001-8080	Lutheran
284.1(4-9)	BX8020-8063	By place
284.10(5/6)	BX8001-8011	Serials/Etc.
284.109	BX8018-8063	Lutheran Church, History
284.1092	BX8079-8080	Biography
284.14	BX8025-8040	Other European areas
284.143	BX8020-8023	Germany
284.173	BX8041-8061	United States
284.2	BX9401-9640	Reformed/Calvinist
284.2(4-9)	BX9430-9640	Reformed/Calvinist, By place
284.205	BX9401	Serials
284.206	BX9403	Societies/Congresses
284.209	BX9415	Reformed/Calvinist history
284.2092	BX9417-9419	Biography
284.24	BX9430-9480	Europe
284.244	BX9450-9459	France
284.2492	BX9470-9479	Netherlands
284.2494	BX9430-9439	Switzerland
284.25	BX9615	Asia
284.26	BX9618-9640	Africa
284.271	BX9596	Canada
284.273	BX9495-9593	United States
284.3	BX4900-4906	Lollards/Wycliffites
284.3	BX4929-4946	Anabaptists
284.3	BX4913-4924	Hussites
284.4	BX4872-4893	Waldenses/Albiegenses
284.6	BX8581-8583	Branches/Churches
284.6	BX8551-8593	Moravian/United Brethren
284.6	BX8530	Moravian
284.6(4-9)	BX8566-8569	By place
284.60(5/6)	BX8551-8555	Serials/Societies
284.609	BX8565-8569	Moravian Church, History
284.6092	BX8591-8593	Biography
284.9	BX6195-6198	Arminians
285	BX9211-9215	Individual churches
285	BX8901-9225	Presbyterian
285.(1/2)(4-9)	BX8933-9169	By place
285.(1/2)(72-8)	BX9011-9043	Latin America
285.(1/2)4	BX9050-9140	Europe
285.(1/2)5	BX9150-9151	Asia
285.(1/2)6	BX9160-9162	Africa
285.(1/2)71	BX9001-9003	Canada
285.(1/2)9(3-6)	BX9168-9169	Australia/New Zealand/ Oceania
285.0(5/6)	BX8901-8907	Serials/Societies
285.09	BX8930-9169	Presbyterian, History
285.092	BX9220-9225	Biography
285.1	BX8935-8999	United States
285.136	BX8990-8998	Reformed Presbyterian
285.2	BX9052-9105	Great Britain
285.731	BX6801-6843	Christian Reformed
285.734	BX7451-7571	Evangelical and Reformed
285.8	BX7101-7260	Congregationalism
285.8	BX7255-7257	Individual churches
285.8(4-9)	BX7133-7228	Congregationalism, By place
285.80(5/6)	BX7101-7105	Serials/Societies
285.806	BX7106-7109	Congresses
285.809	BX7131-7228	Congregationalism, History
285.8092	BX7259-7260	Biography
285.834	BX9884-9886	United Church of Christ

Dewey	LC	Descriptor
285.84	BX7175-7210	Europe
285.85	BX7215-7216	Asia
285.86	BX7220-7222	Africa
285.87(3-9)	BX7135-7149	United States
285.871	BX7151-7173	Canada
285.89(3-6)	BX7225-7228	Australia/New Zealand/Oceania
285.9	BX9301-9365	Puritanism
285.9(4-9)	BX9331-9359	Puritanism, By place
285.90(5/6)	BX9301-9303	Serials/Societies
286.(1-5)	BX6480-6490	Individual churches
286.(1-5)	BX6349-6462	Branches
286.(1-5)	BX6201-6495	Baptist
286.1(4-9)	BX6233-6328	Baptists, By place
286.1(72/8)	BX6254-6273	Latin America
286.10(3/25)	BX6211-6213	Dictionaries/Directories
286.10(5/6)	BX6201-6206	Serials/Societies
286.109	BX6231-6328	History
286.1092	BX6493-6495	Biography
286.14	BX6275-6310	Europe
286.15	BX6315-6316	Asia
286.16	BX6320-6322	Africa
286.17(3-9)	BX6235-6249	United States
286.171	BX6251-6253	Canada
286.19(3-4)	BX6325-6326	Australia/New Zealand
286.19(5-6)	BX6327-6328	Oceania
286.5	BX7800-7843	German Baptist
286.6	BX7301-7343	Disciples of Christ
286.63	BX6751-6799	Christian church
286.7	BX6185	Individual churches
286.7	BX6101-6194	Adventists
286.70(5/6)	BX6101-6105	Serials/Societies
286.709	BX6115-6117	Adventists, History
286.7092	BX6191-6193	Biography
286.73	BX7020-7097	Church of God
286.73	BX6131-6184	Branches
286.73	BX6101-6193	Millerites
286.732	BX6151-6154	Seventh-Day Adventists
287	BX8380-8331	And other churches
287	BX8201-8495	Methodism
287	BX8481-8483	Individual churches
287.(1-8)	BX8350-8473	Branches
287.0(5/6)	BX8201-8207	Serials/Societies
287.09	BX8231-8328	History
287.092	BX8491-8495	Biography
287.1	BX8350-8359	Wesleyan
287.4	BX8370-8379	Primitive Methodist
287.6	BX8380-8389	United Methodist
287.63(2-3)	BX8390-8399	Methodist Episcopal
287.8	BX8435-8473	Black Methodist
287.8(4-9)	BX8233-8328	Methodism, By place
287.8(72-8)	BX8254-8273	Latin America
287.84	BX8275-8310	Europe
287.841	BX8276-8293	Great Britain
287.85	BX8315-8316	Asia
287.86	BX8320-8322	Africa
287.871	BX8251-8253	Canada
287.873	BX8235-8249	United States
287.89(3-6)	BX8325-8328	Australia/New Zealand/Oceania
287.92	BX9881-9883	United Church of Canada
287.96	BX9701-9743	Salvation Army
289.1	BX9801-9869	Unitarianism
289.1	BX9861-9863	Individual churches
289.1(4-9)	BX9833-9835	Unitarianism, By place
289.105	BX9801	Serials
289.106	BX9803-9807	Societies/Congresses
289.109	BX9831-9835	History
289.1092	BX9867-9869	Biography
289.134	BX9961-9962	Individual churches
289.134	BX9901-9969	Universalism
289.13405	BX9901	Serials
289.13406	BX9903-9907	Societies/Congresses
289.13409	BX9931-9935	Universalism, History
289.134092	BX9967-9969	Biography
289.173	BX9833	United States
289.3	BX8670-8687	Individual branches/Temples
289.3	BX8601-8695	Mormons
289.30(5/6)	BX8601-8605	Serials/Societies
289.309	BX8611-8617	History
289.32	BX8622-8631	Sacred books
289.4	BX8741-8743	Individual churches
289.4	BX8701-8749	New Jerusalem Church
289.405	BX8701	Serials
289.406	BX8703-8705	Societies/Congresses
289.409	BX8715-8719	History
289.4092	BX8747-8749	Biography
289.5	BX6901-6997	Christian Science
289.5	BX6980-6985	Individual churches
289.5	BX6950	Healing
289.50(5/6)	BX6901-6903	Serials/Societies
289.506	BX6905-6907	Congresses
289.509	BX6931-6935	Christian Science, History
289.5092	BX6990-6996	Biography
289.6	BX7601-7795	Society of Friends (Quakers)
289.6(4-9)	BX7633-7728	By place
289.6(72-8)	BX7655-7673	Latin America
289.605	BX7601-7606	Serials/Societies
289.606	BX7606.5-7608	Congresses
289.609	BX7630-7732	Friends, History
289.6092	BX7790-7795	Biography
289.63	BX7751-7783	Individual branches/Meetings
289.64	BX7675-7710	Europe
289.641	BX7676-7693	Great Britain
289.65	BX7715-7716	Asia
289.66	BX7720-7723	Africa
289.67(3-9)	BX7635-7649	United States
289.671	BX7650-7653	Canada
289.69(3-6)	BX7725-7728	Australia/New Zealand/Oceania
289.7	BX8101-8143	Mennonites
289.7	BX8131-8132	Individual churches
289.7(4-9)	BX8116-8119	Mennonites, By place
289.70(5/6)	BX8101-8105	Serials/Societies
289.703	BX8106	Dictionaries/Encyclopedias
289.709	BX8115-8119	History
289.7092	BX8141-8143	Biography
289.73	BX8129	Branches
289.771	BX8118.5-.7	Canada
289.773	BX8116-8118	United States
289.8	BX9751-9793	Shakers
289.8(4-9)	BX9766-9769	History, By place
289.80(5/6)	BX9751-9755	Serials/Societies
289.809	BX9765-9769	Shakers, History
289.8092	BX9791-9793	Biography
289.873	BX9766-9768	United States
289.9	BX9875-9877	United Brethren in Christ
289.9	BX7433-7435	Dukhobors
289.905	BX9875	Serials/Societies
289.9092	BX9877	Biography
289.92	BX8525-8528	Jehovah's Witnesses

Dewey	LC	Descriptor
289.94	BX8762-8780	Pentecostal churches
289.95	BX9887	United Evangelical Church
290-299	BL74-98	Religions of the world
291.(3/43)	BL550-619	Worship
291.09	BL660-2670	History
291.093	BL2320-2370	Mediterranean region
291.094	BL900-980	Other European religions
291.094	BL690-980	Europe
291.0956	BL660-687	Middle East
291.13	BL300-325	Myth
291.14	BL350-385	Classification of religions
291.172	BL410	Inter-relations of religions
291.175	BL239-265	Religion and science
291.1772	BL640	Religious liberty
291.1783	HN40	Non-Christian & social problems
291.17834567	HT910-921	Religion and slavery
291.2	BL425-490	Religious doctrines
291.23	BL500-547	Eschatology
291.4	BL624-627	Religious life
291.42	BL639	Religious conversion
291.5	BJ1188-1295	Religious ethics
291.61	BL635	Priests
291.63	BL633	Prophets
291.65	BL630-632	Religious organization
291.65	HS1525-1560	Religious societies
291.7	BL637	Missionaries
291.82	BL70-71	Sacred books
292	BL700-820	Classical religions/Myths
292-299	BL390	World religions
292.07	BL800-820	Roman
292.08	BL780-795	Greek
293	BL830-875	Germanic/Norse
293.41109	BX5300-5310	Church in Scotland, History
294	BL1000-2370	Asian/Oriental
294.3	BQ800-829	Persecutions
294.3	BQ	Buddhism
294.3(4-5)	BQ5485-5530	Precepts
294.3(657/435)	BQ6300-6388	Monasteries/Shrines
294.305	BQ1-10	Serials
294.306	BQ12-93	Societies/Clubs
294.306	BQ96-99	Financial institutions
294.307	BQ141-209	Religious education
294.307	BQ210-219	Research
294.309	BQ251-799	History
294.309(4-9)	BQ320-799	By place
294.309(7-8)	BQ720-760	America
294.3090(1-4)	BQ286-317	By period
294.3092	BQ840-999	Biography
294.3094	BQ700-709	Europe
294.3095	BQ610-699	Far East
294.30951	BQ620-649	China
294.309519	BQ650-669	Korea
294.30952	BQ670-699	Japan
294.30954	BQ330-349	India
294.3095493	BQ350-379	Sri Lanka
294.3095496	BQ380-396	Nepal
294.30958	BQ570-609	Central Asia
294.30959(4-7)	BQ440-509	Indochina
294.309591	BQ416-439	Burma
294.309593	BQ550-568	Thailand
294.309595	BQ540-549	Malaysia
294.309598	BQ510-539	Indonesia
294.3096	BQ710-719	Africa
294.30971	BQ740-749	Canada
294.30973	BQ730-739	United States
294.3099(3-6)	BQ770-799	Pacific area
294.33172	BQ4600-4610	Buddhism and other religions
294.3377	JC47-50	Oriental state
294.337832	BQ5851-5899	Welfare work
294.34	BQ5720-5845	Folklore
294.34	BQ4260-4263	Seal of 3 laws
294.34	BQ4061-4570	Doctrinal/Systematic
294.34	BQ4180-4565	Special doctrines
294.34	BQ4195-4250	Dharma
294.34(3-4)	BQ4911-5720	Practice/Worship
294.3409	BQ4080-4125	History
294.34211	BQ4620-4890	Pantheism
294.3423	BQ4475-4525	Eschatology
294.3435	BQ5130-5137	Temple
294.3436	BQ5700-5720	Festivals
294.3437	BQ5100-5125	Symbols
294.3437	BQ5070-5075	Altar/Etc.
294.3438	BQ5035-5065	Hymns/Chants
294.3438	BQ4965-5030	Ceremonies
294.344	BQ5360-5680	Religious life
294.3443	BQ5535-5594	Meditation/Prayer
294.34446	BQ6400-6495	Pilgrims
294.34447	BQ6200-6240	Asceticism
294.345	BQ4401-4430	Virtues/Vices
294.35	BJ1289	Buddhist ethics
294.361	BQ5140-5355	Ministry/Priesthood
294.363	BQ860-939	Buddha
294.3657	BQ6001-6160	Monasticism
294.37	BQ5901-5975	Missionary work
294.37	LC921-929.7	Buddhist education
294.382	BQ1100-3340	Tripitaka (Canon literature)
294.382(2-4)	BQ1170-3340	By version
294.39	BQ7001-9800	Modifications/Schools
294.391	BQ7100-7285	Theravada Buddhism
294.392	BQ8000-9800	Special sects
294.392	BQ7300-7522	Mahayana Buddhism
294.3923	BQ7530-7950	Lamaism
294.3926	BQ8500-8769	Pure Land
294.3927	BQ9250-9519	Zem
294.4	BL1300-1380	Jainism
294.409	BL1324-1327	By place
294.42	BL1356-1375	Doctrine
294.44	BL1376-1380	Practice/Worship
294.482	BL1310-1314.2	Sacred books
294.5	BL1100-1295	Hinduism
294.5	BJ121-123	India
294.52	BL1213.32-1215.7	Doctrines/Theology
294.5211	BL1216-1225	Pantheon/Deities
294.536	BL1239.72-.82	Festivals
294.54	BL1225.2-1243.58	Practice/Worship
294.5446	BL1239.32	Pilgrims
294.55	BL1271.2-1295	Sects/Cults
294.5657	BL1243.72-.78	Monasteries
294.5657	BL1238	Monasticism
294.57	BL1243.32-.36	Missionaries
294.592	BL1141.2-1142.6	Tantric texts
294.5921	BL1112.2-1137.5	Vedic texts
294.595	BL1141.2-1142.6	Tantric texts
295	BL1500-1590	Zoroastrianism
295.82	BL1510-1525	Sacred books
296	BM	Judaism
296.(12-8)	BM495-532	Rabbinical literature
296.0(5/6)	BM1	Serials/Societies
296.025	BM55-65	Directories
296.03	BM50	Dictionaries/Encyclopedias
296.05	BM11	Yearbooks
296.06	BM21-30	Societies/Congresses

Dewey	LC	Descriptor
296.076	BM51	Questions/Answers
296.09	BM150-449	History
296.09(4-9)	BM201-449	By place
296.090(34-4)	BM195	19th-20th centuries
296.0903(1-3)	BM193	16th-18th centuries
296.092	BM750-755	Biography
296.094	BM290-376	Europe
296.0941	BM292-305	Great Britain
296.0943	BM316-318	Germany
296.09436	BM307-309	Austria
296.09438	BM337-339	Poland
296.0944	BM313-315	France
296.0945	BM322-324	Italy
296.0946	BM354-356	Spain
296.09469	BM328-330	Portugal
296.0947	BM331-333	European Russia
296.0948	BM340-353	Scandinavia
296.09481	BM348-350	Norway
296.09485	BM351-353	Sweden
296.09489	BM342-344	Denmark
296.094897	BM334-336	Finland
296.09492	BM325-327	Netherlands
296.09493	BM310-312	Belgium
296.09494	BM357-359	Switzerland
296.09495	BM319-321	Greece
296.09497	BM373-375	Yugoslavia
296.094977	BM364-366	Bulgaria
296.09498	BM370-372	Romania
296.095	BM377-431	Asia
296.0951	BM423-425	China
296.0952	BM426-428	Japan
296.0953	BM393-395	Arabia
296.0954	BM406-410	India
296.0955	BM396-398	Iran
296.09567	BM386.4-.6	Iraq/Mesopotamia
296.09569(1/4)	BM387-389	Syria/Palestine
296.095694	BM390-392	Israel
296.09581	BM400	Afghanistan
296.096	BM432-440	Africa
296.0962	BM434-436	Egypt
296.0968	BM437	South Africa
296.0971	BM227-229	Canada
296.0972	BM230-232	Mexico
296.09728	BM233-247	Central America
296.09729	BM248-260	West Indies
296.0973	BM205-225	United States
296.098	BM261-289	South America
296.099(3-4)	BM443-445	Australia/New Zealand
296.099(5-6)	BM447-449	Oceania
296.1	BM480-488	Pre-Talmudic literature
296.12	BM497-509	Talmudic literature
296.14	BM510-518	Midrash
296.16	BM525-526	Cubala
296.18	BM520-523	Halacha
296.3	B755-759	Jewish philosophers
296.3	BM600-652	Dogmatic Judaism
296.33	BM615-625	Messiah
296.385	BJ1279-1287	Jewish ethics
296.42	BM730-747	Preaching
296.43	BM690-720	Festivals
296.65	BM653-655	Congregations/Temples
296.68	LC701-775	Jewish education
296.68	BM70-135	Education
296.7	BM650-747	Practice of Judaism
296.72	BM656-685	Worship
296.81	BM900-990	Samaritans
296.81	BM165-178	Ancient
296.82	BM180-185	Medieval
296.83	BM190-199	Modern
296.8332	BM198	Hasidism
296.8342	BM197.5	Conservative
297	BP	Islam
297.(3-4)	BP174-190	Practice/Worship
297.(8/9)	BP600-610	Other beliefs/Movements
297.03	BP40	Dictionaries/Encyclopedias
297.05	BP1-9	Serials
297.06	BP10-15	Societies/Congresses
297.07	BP42-48	Education
297.09	BP50-68	History
297.092	BP70-80	Biography
297.12	BP100-137	Sacred books
297.122	BP100-134	Koran
297.124	BP135-136	Hadith literature
297.1977	JC47-50	Oriental state
297.2	BP166	Theology
297.3(6/8)	BP186	Feasts/Festivals
297.35	BP187	Shrines
297.38	BP184	Ceremonies/Rites
297.4	BP188-190	Religious life
297.5	BJ1292	Islamic ethics
297.7	LC901-915	Islamic education
297.8	BP195-253	Other sects
297.82	BP192-194	Shiites
297.93	BP300-395	Bahaism
299.141(1-44)	BL2000-2032	India
299.1412	BL2035	Pakistan
299.16	BL900-980	Other European religions
299.2	BL1600-1710	Semitic religions
299.3	BJ131-133	Egypt
299.5	BL1000-2370	Asian/Oriental
299.5	BL1750-2375	Asian religions, By place
299.51	BL1800-1975	China
299.512	PL2458-2515.5	Confucian Canon
299.6	BL2400-2490	Africa
299.61	BL2462	North Africa
299.62	BL2420-2460	Egyptian
299.676	BL2464	East Africa
299.68	BL2463	Southern Africa
299.696	BL2465	West Africa
299.7	BL2520-2560	North America
299.8	BL2580-2592	South America
299.915	BL2270-2280	Iran
299.92	BL740-760	Etruscan
299.92	BL2670	Arctic
299.92	BL2600-2630	Oceania
299.934	BP500-585	Theosophy
299.935	BP595-597	Anthroposophy
299.95	BL2300	Siberia
299.95(8-95)	BL2050-2150	Southeast Asia
299.956	BL2200-2228	Japan
299.957	BL2230-2240	Korea
299.919	BL2290	Phrygia
300	H	Social sciences
300.1	H61	Theory/Method
300.25	H50	Directories
300.5	H1-9	Serials
300.6	H10-29	Societies/Congresses
300.7	H62	Education
300.711	H65-87	Schools
300.74	H63-64	Museums/Exhibits
300.9	H51-53	History
300.92	H57-59	Biography
301	HM	Sociology
301	GN	Anthropology

Dewey	LC	Descriptor	Dewey	LC	Descriptor
301.01	HM24-37	Theory/Etc.	304.2094897	GF604	Finland
301.01	GN33-34.3	Philosophy	304.209492	GF593-594	Netherlands
301.014	GN12	Terminology	304.209493	GF596-597	Belgium
301.03	HM17	Dictionaries/Encyclopedias	304.209494	GF631-632	Switzerland
301.03	GN11	Dictionaries/Encyclopedias	304.2094947	GF545	Alps
301.05	HM1-7	Serials	304.209495	GF581-582	Greece
301.05	GN1	Serials	304.209496	GF641-642	Balkan states
301.06	HM9-13	Societies/Congresses	304.2095	GF651-696	Asia
301.06	GN2-3	Societies/Congresses	304.20951	GF656-657	China
301.07	GN42-46	Education	304.209519	GF659	Korea
301.07(2)	HM45-48	Education/Research	304.2095214	GF666-667	Japan
301.074	HM41-43	Museums	304.209538	GF681-682	Saudi Arabia
301.074	GN35-41	Museums/Exhibitions	304.20954	GF661-662	India
301.09	HM19-22	History	304.2095491	GF664	Pakistan
301.09	GN17	History	304.20955	GF671-672	Iran
301.09(4-9)	HM22	By place	304.20956	GF670	Near East (General)
301.092	GN20-21	Biography	304.209561	GF678-679	Turkey
302	HM132	Interpersonal relations	304.209567	GF675	Iraq
302	HM251-291	Social psychology	304.2095691	GF687-688	Syria
302.2	HM258	Communication	304.2095694	GF685-686	Israel/Palestine
302.2244	LC149-160	Literacy/Illiteracy	304.20957	GF676-677	Asian Russia
302.33	HM281-283	Crowds/Violence	304.209581	GF674	Afghanistan
302.35	HD58.7-.95	Organizational behavior	304.209595	GF669	Malaysia
302.54	HM136-146	Individualism	304.2096	GF701-758	Africa
303-306	HM201-221	Social forces/Laws	304.20961	GF702-706	North Africa
303.372	HM216	Moral	304.20962	GF711-712	Egypt
303.375	HM263	Public relations/Propaganda	304.20966	GF740-758	West/South Africa
303.38	HM261	Public opinion	304.20967	GF730	Central Africa
303.483	Q175.4-.55	Impact on society	304.209676	GF720-729	East Africa
303.6	HM281-283	Crowds/Violence	304.20971	GF511-512	Canada
304.(6/8)	HB1951-2577	Population geography/ Migration	304.20972	GF516-517	Mexico
304.2	HM206-208	Environment	304.209728	GF521-522	Central America
304.2	GF	Human ecology	304.209729	GF526-527	West Indies
304.2(3-5)	GF51-71	Environmental influence	304.20973	GF503-504	United States
304.20(5/6)	GF1	Serials/Societies	304.2098	GF531-532	South America
304.2014	GF4.5	Terminology	304.2099(5-6)	GF851-852	Oceania
304.2025	GF5	Directories	304.20993	GF805-806	New Zealand
304.203	GF4	Dictionaries/Encyclopedias	304.20994	GF801-802	Australia
304.206	GF3	Congresses	304.20998	GF891	Arctic regions
304.209	GF13	History	304.28	GF75	Man in environment
304.209(4-9)	GF500-895	Human ecology, By place	304.5	GN280.7	Man as an animal
304.209(7/8)	GF500-532	America	304.6	HA38-39	Registration of vital events
304.20913	GF895	Tropics	304.6	HB848-3697	Demography/Vital events
304.209174927	GF698	Arab countries	304.6	HB1741-1947	Sex
304.2091822	GF541	Mediterranean region	304.6	HQ763-767.7	Family planning/Birth control
304.2092	GF15-16	Biography	304.60(5/6)	HB848-849	Serials/Societies/Congresses
304.2094	GF540-645	Europe	304.607	HB850	Education
304.20941	GF551-562	Great Britain	304.6071724	HB884	Developing countries
304.209411	GF555-556	Scotland	304.609	HB851-853	History
304.209415	GF563	Ireland	304.609	HB1961-2151	Population geography, By place
304.209416	GF561.562	Northern Ireland	304.609	HB3501-3697	Demography, By place
304.20942	GF552	England	304.609(4-9)	HB1751-1947	By place
304.20943	GF576-579	Germany	304.6091724	HB2160	Developing countries
304.209436	GF565-567	Austria	304.6092	HB855-865	Biography
304.209437	GF568	Czechoslovakia	304.609411	HB1837-1838	Scotland
304.209439	GF569	Hungary	304.609411	HB2047-2048	Scotland
304.20944	GF571-572	France	304.609411	HB3587-3588	Scotland
304.20945	GF586-587	Italy	304.609416	HB1838.5	Northern Ireland
304.20946	GF621-622	Spain	304.609416	HB2048.5	Northern Ireland
304.209469	GF623-624	Portugal	304.609416	HB3588.5	Northern Ireland
304.20947	GF601-602	European Russia	304.609417	HB2049-2050	Irish Republic
304.209474	GF547	Baltic region	304.609417	HB1839-1840	Irish Republic
304.20948	GF611	Scandinavia	304.609417	HB3589-3590	Irish Republic
304.209481	GF612-613	Norway	304.60942(9)	HB1835-1836	England/Wales
304.209485	GF614-615	Sweden	304.60942(9)	HB2045-2046	England/Wales
304.209489	GF616-617	Denmark			

Dewey	LC	Descriptor	Dewey	LC	Descriptor
304.60942(9)	HB3585-3586	England/Wales	304.609494	HB2083-2084	Switzerland
304.60943	HB2045-2056.5	Germany	304.609494	HB1873-1874	Switzerland
304.60943	HB1845-1846.5	Germany	304.609494	HB3623-3624	Switzerland
304.60943	HB3595-3596.5	Germany	304.609495	HB2092.5	Greece
304.609436	HB1841-1842	Austria	304.609495	HB1882.5	Greece
304.609436	HB2051-2052	Austria	304.609495	HB3632.5	Greece
304.609436	HB3591-3592	Austria	304.6094965	HB1876.5	Albania
304.60943648	HB1842.9	Liechtenstein	304.6094965	HB2086.5	Albania
304.60943648	HB2052.9	Liechtenstein	304.6094965	HB3626.5	Albania
304.60943648	HB3592.9	Liechtenstein	304.609497	HB2088.5	Yugoslavia
304.609437	HB2052.3	Czechoslovakia	304.609497	HB1878.5	Yugoslavia
304.609437	HB1842.3	Czechoslovakia	304.609497	HB3628.5	Yugoslavia
304.609437	HB3592.3	Czechoslovakia	304.6094977	HB1877-1878	Bulgaria
304.609438	HB1858.7	Poland	304.6094977	HB2087-2088	Bulgaria
304.609438	HB2068.7	Poland	304.6094977	HB3627-3628	Bulgaria
304.609438	HB3608.7	Poland	304.609498	HB1881-1882	Romania
304.609439	HB2052.5	Hungary	304.609498	HB2091-2092	Romania
304.609439	HB1842.5	Hungary	304.609498	HB3631-3632	Romania
304.609439	HB3592.5	Hungary	304.60951	HB1904	China
304.60944	HB2053-2054	France	304.60951	HB2114	China
304.60944	HB1843-1844	France	304.60951	HB3654	China
304.60944	HB3593-3594	France	304.60951249	HB2116	Taiwan
304.60944949	HB1844.5	Monaco	304.60951249	HB1906	Taiwan
304.60944949	HB2054.5	Monaco	304.60951249	HB3656	Taiwan
304.60944949	HB3594.5	Monaco	304.6095125	HB1907	Hong Kong
304.60945	HB1849-1850	Italy	304.6095125	HB2117	Hong Kong
304.60945	HB2059-2060	Italy	304.6095125	HB3657	Hong Kong
304.60945	HB3599-3600	Italy	304.6095126	HB2115	Macao
304.60946	HB2079-2080	Spain	304.6095126	HB1905	Macao
304.60946	HB1869-1870	Spain	304.6095126	HB3655	Macao
304.60946	HB3619-3620	Spain	304.609517	HB1902.8	Mongolia
304.609469	HB2081-2082	Portugal	304.609517	HB2112.8	Mongolia
304.609469	HB1871-1872	Portugal	304.609517	HB3652.8	Mongolia
304.609469	HB3621-3622	Portugal	304.609519	HB2112.5-.6	Korea/North Korea
304.6094698	HB2128.5	Madeira Islands	304.609519	HB1902.5-.6	Korea/North Korea
304.6094698	HB1918.5	Madeira Islands	304.609519	HB3652.5-.6	Korea/North Korea
304.6094698	HB3668.5	Madeira Islands	304.60952	HB1901-1902	Japan
304.6094699	HB1917.5	Azores	304.60952	HB2111-2112	Japan
304.6094699	HB2127.5	Azores	304.60952	HB3651-3652	Japan
304.6094699	HB3667.5	Azores	304.6095332	HB2094.9-2095	Yemen
304.60947	HB2067-2068	European Russia	304.6095332	HB1884.9-1885	Yemen
304.60947	HB1857-1858	European Russia	304.6095332	HB3634.9-3635	Yemen
304.60947	HB3607-3608	European Russia	304.6095353	HB2095.3	Oman
304.609481	HB2075-2076	Norway	304.6095353	HB1885.3	Oman
304.609481	HB1865-1866	Norway	304.6095353	HB3635.3	Oman
304.609481	HB3615-3616	Norway	304.6095357	HB1885.5	United Arab Emirates
304.609485	HB2077-2078	Sweden	304.6095357	HB2095.5	United Arab Emirates
304.609485	HB1867-1868	Sweden	304.6095357	HB3635.5	United Arab Emirates
304.609485	HB3617-3618	Sweden	304.6095363	HB2095.7	Qatar
304.609489	HB1861-1862	Denmark	304.6095363	HB1885.7	Qatar
304.609489	HB2071-2072	Denmark	304.6095363	HB3635.7	Qatar
304.609489	HB3611-3612	Denmark	304.6095365	HB2095.9	Bahrain
304.6094897	HB1858.3	Finland	304.6095365	HB1885.9	Bahrain
304.6094897	HB2068.3	Finland	304.6095365	HB3635.9	Bahrain
304.6094897	HB3608.3	Finland	304.6095367	HB2096	Kuwait
304.6094912	HB1863-1864	Iceland	304.6095367	HB1886	Kuwait
304.6094912	HB2073-2074	Iceland	304.6095367	HB3636	Kuwait
304.6094912	HB3613-3614	Iceland	304.609538	HB1884.7	Saudi Arabia
304.609492	HB1855-1856	Netherlands	304.609538	HB2094.7	Saudi Arabia
304.609492	HB2065-2066	Netherlands	304.609538	HB3634.7	Saudi Arabia
304.609492	HB3605-3606	Netherlands	304.60954	HB1889-1890	India
304.609493	HB2063-2064	Belgium	304.60954	HB2099-2100	India
304.609493	HB1853-1854	Belgium	304.60954	HB3639-3640	India
304.609493	HB3603-3604	Belgium	304.6095491	HB1890.5	Pakistan
304.6094935	HB1856.5	Luxembourg	304.6095491	HB2100.5	Pakistan
304.6094935	HB2066.5	Luxembourg	304.6095491	HB3640.5	Pakistan
304.6094935	HB3606.5	Luxembourg	304.6095492	HB1890.6	Bangladesh

Dewey	LC	Descriptor	Dewey	LC	Descriptor
304.6095492	HB2100.6	Bangladesh	304.609612	HB2121.6	Libya
304.6095492	HB3640.6	Bangladesh	304.609612	HB1911.6	Libya
304.6095493	HB1886.8	Sri Lanka	304.609612	HB3661.6	Libya
304.6095493	HB2096.8	Sri Lanka	304.60962	HB2121.7	Egypt
304.6095493	HB3636.8	Sri Lanka	304.60962	HB1911.7	Egypt
304.6095495	HB1921.5	Maldive Islands	304.60962	HB3661.7	Egypt
304.6095495	HB2131.5	Maldive Islands	304.609624	HB2121.8	Sudan
304.6095495	HB3671.5	Maldive Islands	304.609624	HB1911.8	Sudan
304.6095496	HB1886.9	Nepal	304.609624	HB3661.8	Sudan
304.6095496	HB2096.9	Nepal	304.60963	HB2122	Ethiopia
304.6095496	HB3636.9	Nepal	304.60963	HB1912	Ethiopia
304.6095498	HB1890.3	Bhutan	304.60963	HB3662	Ethiopia
304.6095498	HB2100.3	Bhutan	304.60964	HB1911.3	Morocco
304.6095498	HB3640.3	Bhutan	304.60964	HB2121.3	Morocco
304.60955	HB1886.4	Iran	304.60964	HB3661.3	Morocco
304.60955	HB2096.4	Iran	304.609642	HB2541.3	Morocco
304.60955	HB3636.4	Iran	304.609648	HB2127.4	Spanish Sahara
304.609561	HB2093.4	Turkey	304.609648	HB1917.4	Spanish Sahara
304.609561	HB3633.4	Turkey	304.609648	HB3667.4	Spanish Sahara
304.6095645	HB2093.5	Cyprus	304.609649	HB2129	Canary Islands
304.6095645	HB1883.5	Cyprus	304.609649	HB1919	Canary Islands
304.6095645	HB3633.5	Cyprus	304.609649	HB3669	Canary Islands
304.609567	HB2096.3	Iraq	304.60965	HB2121.4	Algeria
304.609567	HB1886.3	Iraq	304.60965	HB1911.4	Algeria
304.609567	HB3636.3	Iraq	304.60965	HB3661.4	Algeria
304.6095691	HB2093.7	Syria	304.609661	HB1916.6	Mauritania
304.6095691	HB1883.7	Syria	304.609661	HB2126.6	Mauritania
304.6095691	HB3633.7	Syria	304.609661	HB3666.6	Mauritania
304.6095692	HB2093.9	Lebanon	304.6096623	HB1916.3	Mali
304.6095692	HB1883.9	Lebanon	304.6096623	HB2126.3	Mali
304.6095692	HB3633.9	Lebanon	304.6096623	HB3666.3	Mali
304.6095694	HB2094	Israel/Palestine	304.6096625	HB1916.4	Burkina Faso
304.6095694	HB1884	Israel/Palestine	304.6096625	HB2126.4	Burkina Faso
304.6095694	HB3634	Israel/Palestine	304.6096625	HB3666.4	Burkina Faso
304.6095695	HB1884.3	Jordan	304.6096626	HB1915.9	Niger
304.6095695	HB2094.3	Jordan	304.6096626	HB2125.9	Niger
304.6095695	HB3634.3	Jordan	304.6096626	HB3665.9	Niger
304.609581	HB1886.6	Afghanistan	304.609663	HB1916.5	Senegal
304.609581	HB2096.6	Afghanistan	304.609663	HB2126.5	Senegal
304.609581	HB3636.6	Afghanistan	304.609663	HB3666.5	Senegal
304.609591	HB1886.7	Burma	304.609664	HB2126.9	Sierra Leone
304.609591	HB2096.7	Burma	304.609664	HB1916.9	Sierra Leone
304.609591	HB3636.7	Burma	304.609664	HB3666.9	Sierra Leone
304.609593	HB2104.55	Thailand	304.6096651	HB2127	Gambia
304.609593	HB1894.55	Thailand	304.6096651	HB1917	Gambia
304.609593	HB3644.55	Thailand	304.6096651	HB3667	Gambia
304.609594	HB1894.4	Laos	304.6096652	HB1916.2	Guinea-Bissau
304.609594	HB2104.4	Laos	304.6096652	HB2126.2	Guinea-Bissau
304.609594	HB3644.4	Laos	304.6096652	HB3666.2	Guinea-Bissau
304.609595	HB1894.6	Malaysia	304.6096657	HB1917.3	Guinea-Bissau
304.609595	HB2104.6	Malaysia	304.6096657	HB2127.3	Guinea-Bissau
304.609595	HB3644.6	Malaysia	304.6096657	HB3667.3	Guinea-Bissau
304.609596	HB2104.3	Cambodia	304.6096658	HB1919.5	Cape Verde Islands
304.609596	HB1894.3	Cambodia	304.6096658	HB2129.5	Cape Verde Islands
304.609596	HB3644.3	Cambodia	304.6096658	HB3669.5	Cape Verde Islands
304.609597	HB2104.5	Vietnam	304.6096662	HB2127.2	Liberia
304.609597	HB1894.5	Vietnam	304.6096662	HB1917.2	Liberia
304.609597	HB3644.5	Vietnam	304.6096662	HB3667.2	Liberia
304.609598	HB2107-2108	Indonesia	304.6096668	HB1916	Ivory Coast
304.609598	HB1897-1898	Indonesia	304.6096668	HB2126	Ivory Coast
304.609598	HB3647-3648	Indonesia	304.6096668	HB3666	Ivory Coast
304.609599	HB2109-2110	Philippine Islands	304.609667	HB1916.8	Ghana
304.609599	HB1899-1900	Philippine Islands	304.609667	HB2126.8	Ghana
304.609599	HB3649-3650	Philippine Islands	304.609667	HB3666.8	Ghana
304.609611	HB2121.5	Tunisia	304.6096681	HB1915.8	Togo
304.609611	HB1911.5	Tunisia	304.6096681	HB2125.8	Togo
304.609611	HB3661.5	Tunisia	304.6096681	HB3665.8	Togo

Dewey	LC	Descriptor
304.6096683	HB2125.7	Benin (Dahomey)
304.6096683	HB1915.7	Benin (Dahomey)
304.6096683	HB3665.7	Benin (Dahomey)
304.609669	HB2126.7	Nigeria
304.609669	HB1916.7	Nigeria
304.609669	HB3666.7	Nigeria
304.6096711	HB2125.4	Cameroon
304.6096711	HB1915.4	Cameroon
304.6096711	HB3665.4	Cameroon
304.6096715	HB2124.7	Sao Tome/Principe
304.6096715	HB1914.7	Sao Tome/Principe
304.6096715	HB3664.7	Sao Tome/Principe
304.6096718	HB1914.6	Equatorial Guinea
304.6096718	HB2124.6	Equatorial Guinea
304.6096718	HB3664.6	Equatorial Guinea
304.609672	HB2124.8	French Equatorial Africa
304.609672	HB1914.8	French Equatorial Africa
304.609672	HB3664.8	French Equatorial Africa
304.6096721	HB2124.9	Gabon
304.6096721	HB1914.9	Gabon
304.6096721	HB3664.9	Gabon
304.6096724	HB2125	Congo
304.6096724	HB1915	Congo
304.6096724	HB3665	Congo
304.609673	HB1914.4	Angola
304.609673	HB2124.4	Angola
304.609673	HB3664.4	Angola
304.6096741	HB2125.2	Central African Republic
304.6096741	HB1915.2	Central African Republic
304.6096741	HB3665.2	Central African Republic
304.6096743	HB1915.3	Chad
304.6096743	HB2125.3	Chad
304.6096743	HB3665.3	Chad
304.6096751	HB2124.5	Zaire
304.6096751	HB1914.5	Zaire
304.6096751	HB3664.5	Zaire
304.60967571	HB2122.7	Rwanda
304.60967571	HB1912.7	Rwanda
304.60967571	HB3662.7	Rwanda
304.60967572	HB1912.8	Burundi
304.60967572	HB2122.8	Burundi
304.60967572	HB3662.8	Burundi
304.6096761	HB2122.6	Uganda
304.6096761	HB1912.6	Uganda
304.6096761	HB3662.6	Uganda
304.6096762	HB1912.5	Kenya
304.6096762	HB2122.5	Kenya
304.6096762	HB3662.5	Kenya
304.6096771	HB2122.3	Djibouti
304.6096771	HB1912.3	Djibouti
304.6096771	HB3662.3	Djibouti
304.6096773	HB2122.2	Somalia
304.6096773	HB1912.2	Somalia
304.6096773	HB3662.2	Somalia
304.609678	HB2122.9	Tanzania
304.609678	HB1912.9	Tanzania
304.609678	HB3662.9	Tanzania
304.609679	HB1913	Mozambique
304.609679	HB2123	Mozambique
304.609679	HB3663	Mozambique
304.60968	HB1913.4	South Africa
304.60968	HB2123.4	South Africa
304.60968	HB3663.4	South Africa
304.6096881	HB2124.2	Namibia
304.6096881	HB1914.2	Namibia
304.6096881	HB3664.2	Namibia
304.6096883	HB1913.9	Botswana
304.6096883	HB2123.9	Botswana
304.6096883	HB3663.9	Botswana
304.6096885	HB2123.7	Lesotho
304.6096885	HB1913.7	Lesotho
304.6096885	HB3663.7	Lesotho
304.6096887	HB2123.8	Swaziland
304.6096887	HB1913.8	Swaziland
304.6096887	HB3663.8	Swaziland
304.609689	HB2123.5	Zimbabwe/Zambia/Malawi
304.609689	HB1913.5	Zimbabwe/Zambia/ Malawi
304.609689	HB3663.5	Zimbabwe/Zambia/Malawi
304.6096894	HB1913.6	Zambia
304.6096894	HB2123.6	Zambia
304.6096894	HB3663.6	Zambia
304.6096897	HB1914	Malawi
304.6096897	HB2124	Malawi
304.6096897	HB3664	Malawi
304.609691	HB1913.2	Madagascar
304.609691	HB2123.2	Madagascar
304.609691	HB3663.2	Madagascar
304.609694	HB1922.5	Comoro Islands
304.609694	HB2132.5	Comoro Islands
304.609694	HB3672.5	Comoro Islands
304.609696	HB2132	Seychelles
304.609696	HB1922	Seychelles
304.609696	HB3672	Seychelles
304.6096981	HB1923.5	Reunion
304.6096981	HB2133.5	Reunion
304.6096981	HB3673.5	Reunion
304.6096982	HB1923	Mauritius
304.6096982	HB2133	Mauritius
304.6096982	HB3673	Mauritius
304.609699	HB2134	Kerguelen Islands
304.609699	HB1924	Kerguelen Islands
304.609699	HB3674	Kerguelen Islands
304.6097(4-9)	HB1987	By city
304.6097(4-9)	HB1777	By city
304.6097(4-9)	HB1985	By state
304.6097(4-9)	HB1775	By state
304.6097(4-9)	HB3525	By state
304.6097(4-9)	HB3527	By city
304.60971	HB1779-1780	Canada
304.60971	HB1989-1990	Canada
304.60971	HB3529-3530	Canada
304.60972	HB1991-1992	Mexico
304.60972	HB1781-1782	Mexico
304.60972	HB3531-3532	Mexico
304.6097281	HB1999	Guatemala
304.6097281	HB1789	Guatemala
304.6097281	HB3539	Guatemala
304.6097282	HB1995-1996	Belize
304.6097282	HB1785-1786	Belize
304.6097282	HB3535-3536	Belize
304.6097283	HB1790	Honduras
304.6097283	HB2000	Honduras
304.6097283	HB3540	Honduras
304.6097284	HB1794	El Salvador
304.6097284	HB2004	El Salvador
304.6097284	HB3544	El Salvador
304.6097285	HB1791	Nicaragua
304.6097285	HB2001	Nicaragua
304.6097285	HB3541	Nicaragua
304.6097286	HB1787-1888	Costa Rica
304.6097286	HB1997-1998	Costa Rica
304.6097286	HB3537-3538	Costa Rica
304.6097287	HB1792-1793	Panama

Dewey	LC	Descriptor
304.6097287	HB2002-2003	Panama
304.6097287	HB3542-3543	Panama
304.60972875	HB1793.5	Panama Canal Zone
304.60972875	HB2003.5	Panama Canal Zone
304.60972875	HB3543.5	Panama Canal Zone
304.6097291	HB2009-2010	Cuba
304.6097291	HB1799-1800	Cuba
304.6097291	HB3549-3550	Cuba
304.6097292	HB1803-1804	Jamaica
304.6097292	HB2013-2014	Jamaica
304.6097292	HB3553-3554	Jamaica
304.6097293	HB2012	Dominican Republic
304.6097293	HB1802	Dominican Republic
304.6097293	HB3552	Dominican Republic
304.6097294	HB2011	Haiti
304.6097294	HB1801	Haiti
304.6097294	HB3551	Haiti
304.6097295	HB2015-2016	Puerto Rico
304.6097295	HB1805-1806	Puerto Rico
304.6097295	HB3555-3556	Puerto Rico
304.6097296	HB2007-2008	Bahamas
304.6097296	HB1797-1798	Bahamas
304.6097296	HB3547-3548	Bahamas
304.609729722	HB2016.3	Virgin Islands of the U.S.
304.609729722	HB1806.3	Virgin Islands of the U.S.
304.609729722	HB3556.3	Virgin Islands of the U.S.
304.60972973	HB2016.72	Anguilla
304.60972973	HB2016.78	Saint Kitts-Nevis
304.60972973	HB1806.72	Anguilla
304.60972973	HB1806.78	Saint Kitts-Nevis
304.60972973	HB3556.78	Saint Kitts-Nevis
304.60972973	HB3556.72	Anguilla
304.60972974	HB1806.74	Antigua/Barbuda
304.60972974	HB2016.74	Antigua/Barbuda
304.60972974	HB3556.74	Antigua/Barbuda
304.60972975	HB1806.76	Montserrat
304.60972975	HB2016.76	Montserrat
304.60972975	HB3556.76	Montserrat
304.60972976	HB2017.7	Guadeloupe
304.60972976	HB1807.7	Guadeloupe
304.60972976	HB3557.7	Guadeloupe
304.60972977	HB1807.39	Saint Martin
304.60972977	HB2017.385	Saba
304.60972977	HB2017.385	Saint Eustatius
304.60972977	HB2017.39	Saint Martin
304.60972977	HB1807.385	Saint Eustatius
304.60972977	HB1807.38	Saba
304.60972977	HB3557.38	Saba
304.60972977	HB3557.385	Saint Eustatius
304.60972977	HB3557.39	Saint Martin
304.60972981	HB2016.57	Barbados
304.60972981	HB1806.57	Barbados
304.60972981	HB3556.57	Barbados
304.60972982	HB1807.9	Martinique
304.60972982	HB2017.9	Martinique
304.60972982	HB3557.9	Martinique
304.60972983	HB2017	Trinidad/Tobago
304.60972983	HB1807	Trinidad/Tobago
304.60972983	HB3557	Trinidad/Tobago
304.609729841	HB2016.93	Dominica
304.609729841	HB1806.93	Dominica
304.609729841	HB3556.93	Dominica
304.609729843	HB1806.97	Saint Lucia
304.609729843	HB2016.97	Saint Lucia
304.609729843	HB3556.97	Saint Lucia
304.609729844	HB1806.99	Saint Vincent/ Grenadines
304.609729844	HB2016.99	Saint Vincent/ Grenadines
304.609729844	HB3556.99	Saint Vincent/Grenadines
304.609729845	HB1806.95	Grenada
304.609729845	HB2016.95	Grenada
304.609729845	HB3556.95	Grenada
304.60972986	HB2017.37	Curacao
304.60972986	HB1807.35	Aruba
304.60972986	HB1807.36	Bonaire
304.60972986	HB2017.36	Bonaire
304.60972986	HB1807.37	Curacao
304.60972986	HB2017.35	Aruba
304.60972986	HB3557.35	Aruba
304.60972986	HB3557.36	Bonaire
304.60972986	HB3557.37	Curacao
304.6097299	HB2128	Bermuda
304.6097299	HB1918	Bermuda
304.6097299	HB3668	Bermuda
304.60973	HB1755-1756	United States
304.60973	HB1965-1966	United States
304.60973	HB3505-3506	United States
304.60981	HB2023-2024	Brazil
304.60981	HB1813-1814	Brazil
304.60981	HB3563-3564	Brazil
304.60982	HB1809-1810	Argentina
304.60982	HB2019-2020	Argentina
304.60982	HB3559-3560	Argentina
304.60983	HB1815-1816	Chile
304.60983	HB2025-2026	Chile
304.60983	HB3565-3566	Chile
304.60984	HB2021-2022	Bolivia
304.60984	HB1811-1812	Bolivia
304.60984	HB3561-3562	Bolivia
304.60985	HB2035-2036	Peru
304.60985	HB1825-1826	Peru
304.60985	HB3575-3576	Peru
304.609861	HB2027-2028	Colombia
304.609861	HB1817-1818	Colombia
304.609861	HB3567-3568	Colombia
304.609866	HB2029-2030	Ecuador
304.609866	HB1819-1820	Ecuador
304.609866	HB3569-3570	Ecuador
304.60987	HB2039-2040	Venezuela
304.60987	HB1829-1830	Venezuela
304.60987	HB3579-3580	Venezuela
304.609881	HB1822.3	Guyana
304.609881	HB2032.3	Guyana
304.609881	HB3572.3	Guyana
304.609882	HB1822.7	French Guiana
304.609882	HB2032.7	French Guiana
304.609882	HB3572.7	French Guiana
304.609883	HB2032.5	Suriname
304.609883	HB1822.5	Suriname
304.609883	HB3572.5	Suriname
304.609892	HB2033-2034	Paraguay
304.609892	HB1823-1824	Paraguay
304.609892	HB3573-3574	Paraguay
304.609895	HB2037-2038	Uruguay
304.609895	HB1827-1828	Uruguay
304.609895	HB3577-3578	Uruguay
304.60993	HB2152.5	New Zealand
304.60993	HB1942.5	New Zealand
304.60993	HB3692.5	New Zealand
304.60994	HB1925-1926	Australia
304.60994	HB2135-2136	Australia
304.60994	HB3675-3676	Australia
304.609953	HB1942.8	Papua New Guinea

Dewey	LC	Descriptor	Dewey	LC	Descriptor
304.609953	HB2152.8	Papua New Guinea	304.6209469	HB1661-1662	Portugal
304.609953	HB3692.8	Papua New Guinea	304.62094698	HB1708.5	Madeira Islands
304.6099593	HB2153	Solomon Islands	304.62094699	HB1707.5	Azores
304.6099593	HB1943	Solomon Islands	304.620947	HB1647-1648	European Russia
304.6099593	HB3693	Solomon Islands	304.6209481	HB1655-1656	Norway
304.6099595	HB2153.4	Vanuatu	304.6209485	HB1657-1658	Sweden
304.6099595	HB1943.4	Vanuatu	304.6209489	HB1651-1652	Denmark
304.6099595	HB3693.4	Vanuatu	304.62094897	HB1648.3	Finland
304.6099597	HB2153.3	New Caledonia	304.62094912	HB1653-1654	Iceland
304.6099597	HB1943.3	New Caledonia	304.6209492	HB1645-1646	Netherlands
304.6099597	HB3693.3	New Caledonia	304.6209493	HB1643-1644	Belgium
304.6099611	HB2153.5	Fiji Islands	304.62094935	HB1646.5	Luxembourg
304.6099611	HB1943.5	Fiji Islands	304.6209494	HB1663-1664	Switzerland
304.6099611	HB3693.5	Fiji Islands	304.6209495	HB1672.5	Greece
304.6099612	HB2153.6	Tonga	304.62094965	HB1666.5	Albania
304.6099612	HB1943.6	Tonga	304.6209497	HB1668.5	Yugoslavia
304.6099612	HB3693.6	Tonga	304.62094977	HB1667-1668	Bulgaria
304.6099613	HB2153.7	American Samoa	304.6209498	HB1671-1672	Romania
304.6099613	HB1943.7	American Samoa	304.620951	HB1694	China
304.6099613	HB3693.7	American Samoa	304.620951249	HB1696	Taiwan
304.6099614	HB1943.8	Western Samoa	304.62095125	HB1697	Hong Kong
304.6099614	HB2153.8	Western Samoa	304.62095126	HB1695	Macao
304.6099614	HB3693.8	Western Samoa	304.6209517	HB1692.8	Mongolia
304.609962	HB1943.9	French Polynesia	304.6209519	HB1692.5-.6	Korea/North Korea
304.609962	HB2153.9	French Polynesia	304.620952	HB1691-1692	Japan
304.609962	HB3693.9	French Polynesia	304.62095332	HB1674.9-1675	Yemen
304.6099623	HB2153.65	Cook Islands	304.62095353	HB1675.3	Oman
304.6099623	HB1943.65	Cook Islands	304.62095357	HB1675.5	United Arab Emirates
304.6099623	HB3693.65	Cook Islands	304.62095363	HB1675.7	Qatar
304.609967	HB2152.7	Guam	304.62095365	HB1675.9	Bahrain
304.609967	HB1942.7	Guam	304.62095367	HB1676	Kuwait
304.609967	HB3692.7	Guam	304.6209538	HB1674.7	Saudi Arabia
304.6099681	HB2152.9	Kiribati (Gilbert Islands)	304.620954	HB1679-1680	India
304.6099681	HB1942.9	Kiribati (Gilbert Islands)	304.62095491	HB1680.5	Pakistan
304.6099681	HB3692.9	Kiribati (Gilbert Islands)	304.62095492	HB1680.6	Bangladesh
304.609971	HB1921	Falkland Islands	304.62095493	HB1676.8	Sri Lanka
304.609971	HB2131	Falkland Islands	304.62095495	HB1711.5	Maldive Islands
304.609971	HB3671	Falkland Islands	304.62095496	HB1676.9	Nepal
304.609973	HB2130	St. Helena	304.62095498	HB1680.3	Bhutan
304.609973	HB1920	St. Helena	304.620955	HB1676.4	Iran
304.609973	HB1920.5	Tristan da Cunha	304.6209561	HB1673.4	Turkey
304.609973	HB2130.5	Tristan da Cunha	304.62095645	HB1673.5	Cyprus
304.609973	HB3670.5	Tristan da Cunha	304.6209567	HB1676.3	Iraq
304.609973	HB3670	St. Helena	304.62095691	HB1673.7	Syria
304.60998(1-8)	HB2155	Polar regions	304.62095692	HB1673.9	Lebanon
304.60998(1-8)	HB1945	Polar regions	304.62095694	HB1674	Israel/Palestine
304.60998(1-8)	HB3695	Polar regions	304.62095695	HB1674.3	Jordan
304.609982	HB1946	Greenland	304.6209581	HB1676.6	Afghanistan
304.609982	HB2156	Greenland	304.6209591	HB1676.7	Burma
304.609982	HB3696	Greenland	304.6209593	HB1684.55	Thailand
304.61	HB1953	Population density	304.6209594	HB1684.4	Laos
304.62	HB1531-1737	Age distribution	304.6209595	HB1684.6	Malaysia
304.6209	HB1541-1737	By place	304.6209596	HB1684.3	Cambodia
304.6209411	HB1627-1628	Scotland	304.6209597	HB1684.5	Vietnam
304.6209416	HB1628.5	Northern Ireland	304.6209598	HB1687-1688	Indonesia
304.6209417	HB1629-1630	Irish Republic	304.6209599	HB1689-1690	Philippine Islands
304.620942(9)	HB1625-1626	England/Wales	304.6209611	HB1701.5	Tunisia
304.620943	HB1635-1636.5	Germany	304.6209612	HB1701.6	Libya
304.6209436	HB1631-1632	Austria	304.620962	HB1701.7	Egypt
304.62094364B	HB1632.9	Liechtenstein	304.6209624	HB1701.8	Sudan
304.6209437	HB1632.3	Czechoslovakia	304.620963	HB1702	Ethiopia
304.6209438	HB1648.7	Poland	304.620964	HB1701.3	Morocco
304.6209439	HB1632.5	Hungary	304.6209648	HB1707.4	Spanish Sahara
304.620944	HB1633-1634	France	304.6209649	HB1709	Canary Islands
304.620944949	HB1634.5	Monaco	304.620965	HB1701.4	Algeria
304.620945	HB1639-1640	Italy	304.6209661	HB1706.6	Mauritania
304.620946	HB1659-1660	Spain	304.62096623	HB1706.3	Mali

Dewey	LC	Descriptor
304.62096625	HB1706.4	Burkina Faso
304.62096626	HB1705.9	Niger
304.6209663	HB1706.5	Senegal
304.6209664	HB1706.9	Sierra Leone
304.62096651	HB1707	Gambia
304.62096652	HB1706.2	Guinea-Bissau
304.62096657	HB1707.3	Guinea-Bissau
304.62096658	HB1709.5	Cape Verde Islands
304.62096662	HB1707.2	Liberia
304.62096668	HB1706	Ivory Coast
304.6209667	HB1706.8	Ghana
304.62096681	HB1705.8	Togo
304.62096683	HB1705.7	Benin (Dahomey)
304.6209669	HB1706.7	Nigeria
304.62096711	HB1705.4	Cameroon
304.62096715	HB1704.7	Sao Tome/Principe
304.62096718	HB1704.6	Equatorial Guinea
304.6209672	HB1704.8	French Equatorial Africa
304.62096721	HB1704.9	Gabon
304.62096724	HB1705	Congo
304.6209673	HB1704.4	Angola
304.62096741	HB1705.2	Central African Republic
304.62096743	HB1705.3	Chad
304.62096751	HB1704.5	Zaire
304.620967571	HB1702.7	Rwanda
304.620967572	HB1702.8	Burundi
304.62096761	HB1702.6	Uganda
304.62096762	HB1702.5	Kenya
304.62096771	HB1702.3	Djibouti
304.62096773	HB1702.2	Somalia
304.6209678	HB1702.9	Tanzania
304.6209679	HB1703	Mozambique
304.620968	HB1703.4	South Africa
304.62096881	HB1704.2	Namibia
304.62096883	HB1703.9	Botswana
304.62096885	HB1703.7	Lesotho
304.62096887	HB1703.8	Swaziland
304.6209689	HB1703.5	Zimbabwe/Zambia/Malawi
304.62096894	HB1703.6	Zambia
304.62096897	HB1704	Malawi
304.6209691	HB1703.2	Madagascar
304.6209694	HB1712.5	Comoro Islands
304.6209696	HB1712	Seychelles
304.62096981	HB1713.5	Reunion
304.62096982	HB1713	Mauritius
304.6209699	HB1714	Kerguelen Islands
304.62097(4-9)	HB1567	By city
304.62097(4-9)	HB1565	By state
304.620971	HB1569-1570	Canada
304.620972	HB1571-1572	Mexico
304.62097281	HB1579	Guatemala
304.62097282	HB1575-1576	Belize
304.62097283	HB1580	Honduras
304.62097284	HB1584	El Salvador
304.62097285	HB1581	Nicaragua
304.62097286	HB1577-1578	Costa Rica
304.62097287	HB1582-1583	Panama
304.620972875	HB1583.5	Panama Canal Zone
304.62097291	HB1589-1590	Cuba
304.62097292	HB1593-1594	Jamaica
304.62097293	HB1592	Dominican Republic
304.62097294	HB1591	Haiti
304.62097294	HB1596.74	Antigua/Barbuda
304.62097295	HB1595-1596	Puerto Rico
304.62097296	HB1587-1588	Bahamas
304.6209729722	HB1596.3	Virgin Islands of the U.S.
304.620972973	HB1596.78	Saint Kitts-Nevis
304.620972973	HB1596.72	Anguilla
304.620972976	HB1597.7	Guadeloupe
304.620972977	HB1597.39	Saint Martin
304.620972977	HB1597.385	Saint Eustatius
304.620972977	HB1597.38	Saba
304.620972981	HB1596.57	Barbados
304.620972982	HB1597.9	Martinique
304.620972983	HB1597	Trinidad/Tobago
304.6209729841	HB1596.93	Dominica
304.6209729843	HB1596.97	Saint Lucia
304.6209729844	HB1596.99	Saint Vincent/Grenadines
304.6209729845	HB1596.95	Grenada
304.620972986	HB1597.35	Aruba
304.620972986	HB1597.36	Bonaire
304.620972986	HB1597.37	Curacao
304.62097299	HB1708	Bermuda
304.620973	HB1545-1546	United States
304.620975	HB1596.76	Montserrat
304.620981	HB1603-1604	Brazil
304.620982	HB1599-1600	Argentina
304.620983	HB1605-1606	Chile
304.620984	HB1601-1602	Bolivia
304.620985	HB1615-1616	Peru
304.6209861	HB1607-1608	Colombia
304.6209866	HB1609-1610	Ecuador
304.620987	HB1619-1620	Venezuela
304.6209881	HB1612.3	Guyana
304.6209882	HB1612.7	French Guiana
304.6209883	HB1612.5	Suriname
304.6209892	HB1613-1614	Paraguay
304.6209895	HB1617-1618	Uruguay
304.620993	HB1732.5	New Zealand
304.620994	HB1715-1716	Australia
304.6209953	HB1732.8	Papua New Guinea
304.62099593	HB1733	Solomon Islands
304.62099595	HB1733.4	Vanuatu
304.62099597	HB1733.3	New Caledonia
304.62099611	HB1733.5	Fiji Islands
304.62099612	HB1733.6	Tonga
304.62099613	HB1733.7	American Samoa
304.62099614	HB1733.8	Western Samoa
304.6209962	HB1733.9	French Polynesia
304.62099623	HB1733.65	Cook Islands
304.6209967	HB1732.7	Guam
304.62099681	HB1732.9	Kiribati (Gilbert Islands)
304.6209971	HB1711	Falkland Islands
304.6209973	HB1710.5	Tristan da Cunha
304.6209973	HB1710	St. Helena
304.620998(1-8)	HB1735	Polar regions
304.6209982	HB1736	Greenland
304.63	HB901-1108	Births/Fertility
304.63	HQ760-767.7	Family size
304.6309	HB911-1107	By place
304.6309(4-9)	HQ762	Family size, By place
304.63091724	HB1108	Developing countries
304.6309411	HB997-998	Scotland
304.6309416	HB998.5	Northern Ireland
304.6309417	HB999-1000	Irish Republic
304.630942(9)	HB995-996	England/Wales
304.630943	HB1004-1006.5	Germany
304.6309436	HB1001-1002	Austria
304.630943648	HB1002.9	Liechtenstein
304.6309437	HB1002.3	Czechoslovakia
304.6309438	HB1018.7	Poland
304.6309439	HB1002.5	Hungary

199

Dewey	LC	Descriptor	Dewey	LC	Descriptor
304.630944	HB1003-1004	France	304.630965	HB1071.4	Algeria
304.630944949	HB1004.5	Monaco	304.6309661	HB1076.6	Mauritania
304.630945	HB1009-1010	Italy	304.63096623	HB1076.3	Mali
304.630946	HB1029-1030	Spain	304.63096625	HB1076.4	Burkina Faso
304.6309469	HB1031-1032	Portugal	304.63096626	HB1075.9	Niger
304.63094698	HB1078.5	Madeira Islands	304.6309663	HB1076.5	Senegal
304.63094699	HB1077.5	Azores	304.6309664	HB1076.9	Sierra Leone
304.630947	HB1017-1018	European Russia	304.63096651	HB1077	Gambia
304.6309481	HB1025-1026	Norway	304.63096652	HB1076.2	Guinea-Bissau
304.6309485	HB1027-1028	Sweden	304.63096657	HB1077.3	Guinea-Bissau
304.6309489	HB1021-1022	Denmark	304.63096658	HB1079.5	Cape Verde Islands
304.63094897	HB1018.3	Finland	304.63096662	HB1077.2	Liberia
304.63094912	HB1023-1024	Iceland	304.63096668	HB1076	Ivory Coast
304.6309492	HB1015-1016	Netherlands	304.6309667	HB1076.8	Ghana
304.6309493	HB1013-1014	Belgium	304.63096681	HB1075.8	Togo
304.63094935	HB1016.5	Luxembourg	304.63096683	HB1075.7	Benin (Dahomey)
304.6309494	HB1033-1034	Switzerland	304.6309669	HB1076.7	Nigeria
304.63094965	HB1036.5	Albania	304.63096711	HB1075.4	Cameroon
304.6309497	HB1038.5	Yugoslavia	304.63096715	HB1074.7	Sao Tome/Principe
304.63094977	HB1037-1038	Bulgaria	304.63096718	HB1074.6	Equatorial Guinea
304.6309498	HB1041-1042	Romania	304.6309672	HB1074.8	French Equatorial Africa
304.630951	HB1064	China	304.63096721	HB1074.9	Gabon
304.630951249	HB1066	Taiwan	304.63096724	HB1075	Congo
304.63095125	HB1067	Hong Kong	304.6309673	HB1074.4	Angola
304.63095126	HB1065	Macao	304.63096741	HB1075.2	Central African Republic
304.6309517	HB1062.8	Mongolia	304.63096743	HB1075.3	Chad
304.6309519	HB1062.5-.6	Korea/North Korea	304.63096751	HB1074.5	Zaire
304.630952	HB1061-1062	Japan	304.6309657571	HB1072.7	Rwanda
304.63095332	HB1044.9-1045	Yemen	304.6309657572	HB1072.8	Burundi
304.63095353	HB1045.3	Oman	304.63096761	HB1072.6	Uganda
304.63095357	HB1045.5	United Arab Emirates	304.63096762	HB1072.5	Kenya
304.63095363	HB1045.7	Qatar	304.63096771	HB1072.3	Djibouti
304.63095365	HB1045.9	Bahrain	304.63096773	HB1072.2	Somalia
304.63095367	HB1046	Kuwait	304.6309678	HB1072.9	Tanzania
304.6309538	HB1044.7	Saudi Arabia	304.6309679	HB1073	Mozambique
304.630954	HB1049-1050	India	304.630968	HB1073.4	South Africa
304.63095491	HB1050.5	Pakistan	304.63096881	HB1074.2	Namibia
304.63095492	HB1050.6	Bangladesh	304.63096883	HB1073.9	Botswana
304.63095493	HB1046.8	Sri Lanka	304.63096885	HB1073.7	Lesotho
304.63095495	HB1081.5	Maldive Islands	304.63096887	HB1073.8	Swaziland
304.63095496	HB1046.9	Nepal	304.6309689	HB1073.5	Zimbabwe/Zambia/ Malawi
304.63095498	HB1050.3	Bhutan			
304.630955	HB1046.4	Iran	304.63096894	HB1073.6	Zambia
304.6309561	HB1043.4	Turkey	304.63096897	HB1074	Malawi
304.63095645	HB1043.5	Cyprus	304.6309691	HB1073.2	Madagascar
304.6309567	HB1046.3	Iraq	304.6309694	HB1082.5	Comoro Islands
304.63095691	HB1043.7	Syria	304.6309696	HB1082	Seychelles
304.63095692	HB1043.9	Lebanon	304.63096981	HB1083.5	Reunion
304.63095694	HB1044	Israel/Palestine	304.63096982	HB1803	Mauritius
304.63095695	HB1044.3	Jordan	304.6309699	HB1084	Kerguelen Islands
304.6309581	HB1046.6	Afghanistan	304.63097(4-9)	HB937	By city
304.6309591	HB1046.7	Burma	304.63097(4-9)	HB935	By state
304.6309593	HB1054.55	Thailand	304.630971	HB939-940	Canada
304.6309594	HB1054.4	Laos	304.630972	HB941-942	Mexico
304.6309595	HB1054.6	Malaysia	304.63097281	HB949	Guatemala
304.6309596	HB1054.3	Cambodia	304.63097282	HB945-946	Belize
304.6309597	HB1054.5	Vietnam	304.63097283	HB950	Honduras
304.6309598	HB1057-1058	Indonesia	304.63097284	HB954	El Salvador
304.6309599	HB1059-1060	Philippine Islands	304.63097285	HB951	Nicaragua
304.6309611	HB1071.5	Tunisia	304.63097286	HB947-948	Costa Rica
304.6309612	HB1071.6	Libya	304.63097287	HB952-953	Panama
304.630962	HB1071.7	Egypt	304.630972875	HB953.5	Panama Canal Zone
304.6309624	HB1071.8	Sudan	304.63097291	HB959-960	Cuba
304.630963	HB1072	Ethiopia	304.63097292	HB963-964	Jamaica
304.630964	HB1071.3	Morocco	304.63097293	HB962	Dominican Republic
304.6309648	HB1077.4	Spanish Sahara	304.63097294	HB961	Haiti
304.6309649	HB1079	Canary Islands	304.63097295	HB965-966	Puerto Rico

Dewey	LC	Descriptor
304.63097296	HB957-958	Bahamas
304.6309729722	HB966.3	Virgin Islands of the U.S.
304.630972973	HB966.78	Saint Kitts-Nevis
304.630972973	HB966.72	Anguilla
304.630972974	HB966.74	Antigua/Barbuda
304.630972975	HB966.76	Montserrat
304.630972976	HB967.7	Guadeloupe
304.630972977	HB967.39	Saint Martin
304.630972977	HB967.385	Saint Eustatius
304.630972977	HB967.38	Saba
304.630972981	HB966.57	Barbados
304.630972982	HB967.9	Martinique
304.630972983	HB967	Trinidad/Tobago
304.6309729841	HB966.93	Dominica
304.6309729843	HB966.97	Saint Lucia
304.6309729844	HB966.99	Saint Vincent/ Grenadines
304.6309729845	HB966.95	Grenada
304.630972986	HB967.35	Aruba
304.630972986	HB967.36	Bonaire
304.630972986	HB967.37	Curacao
304.63097299	HB1078	Bermuda
304.630973	HB915-916	United States
304.630981	HB973-974	Brazil
304.630982	HB969-970	Argentina
304.630983	HB975-976	Chile
304.630984	HB971-972	Bolivia
304.630985	HB985-986	Peru
304.6309861	HB977-978	Colombia
304.6309866	HB979-980	Ecuador
304.630987	HB989-990	Venezuela
304.6309881	HB982.3	Guyana
304.6309882	HB982.7	French Guiana
304.6309883	HB982.5	Suriname
304.6309892	HB983-984	Paraguay
304.6309895	HB987-988	Uruguay
304.630993	HB1102.5	New Zealand
304.630994	HB1085-1086	Australia
304.6309953	HB1102.8	Papua New Guinea
304.63099593	HB1103	Solomon Islands
304.63099595	HB1103.4	Vanuatu
304.63099597	HB1103.3	New Caledonia
304.63099611	HB1103.5	Fiji Islands
304.63099612	HB1103.6	Tonga
304.63099613	HB1103.7	American Samoa
304.63099614	HB1103.8	Western Samoa
304.6309962	HB1103.9	French Polynesia
304.63099623	HB1103.65	Cook Islands
304.6309967	HB1102.7	Guam
304.63099681	HB1102.9	Kiribati (Gilbert Islands)
304.6309971	HB1081	Falkland Islands
304.6309973	HB1080.5	Tristan da Cunha
304.6309973	HB1080	St. Helena
304.630998(1-8)	HB1105	Polar regions
304.6309982	HB1106	Greenland
304.64	HB1322	Life tables
304.64	HB1321-1528	Deaths
304.6409(3-9)	HB1331-1528	By place
304.64091724	HB1528	Developing countries
304.6409411	HB1417-1418	Scotland
304.6409416	HB1418.5	Northern Ireland
304.6409417	HB1419-1420	Irish Republic
304.640942(9)	HB1415-1416	England/Wales
304.640943	HB1425-1426.5	Germany
304.6409436	HB1421-1422	Austria
304.640943648	HB1422.9	Liechtenstein
304.6409437	HB1422.3	Czechoslovakia
304.6409438	HB1438.7	Poland
304.6409439	HB1422.5	Hungary
304.640944	HB1423-1424	France
304.640944949	HB1424.5	Monaco
304.640945	HB1429-1430	Italy
304.640946	HB1449-1450	Spain
304.6409469	HB1451-1452	Portugal
304.64094698	HB1498.5	Madeira Islands
304.64094699	HB1497.5	Azores
304.640947	HB1437-1438	European Russia
304.6409481	HB1445-1446	Norway
304.6409485	HB1447-1448	Sweden
304.6409489	HB1441-1442	Denmark
304.64094897	HB1438.3	Finland
304.64094912	HB1443-1444	Iceland
304.6409492	HB1435-1436	Netherlands
304.6409493	HB1433-1434	Belgium
304.64094935	HB1436.5	Luxembourg
304.6409494	HB1453-1454	Switzerland
304.6409495	HB1462.5	Greece
304.64094965	HB1456.5	Albania
304.6409497	HB1458.5	Yugoslavia
304.64094977	HB1457-1458	Bulgaria
304.6409498	HB1461-1462	Romania
304.640951	HB1484	China
304.640951249	HB1486	Taiwan
304.64095125	HB1487	Hong Kong
304.64095126	HB1485	Macao
304.6409517	HB1482.8	Mongolia
304.6409519	HB1482.5-.6	Korea/North Korea
304.640952	HB1481-1482	Japan
304.64095332	HB1464.9-1465	Yemen
304.64095353	HB1465.3	Oman
304.64095357	HB1465.5	United Arab Emirates
304.64095363	HB1465.7	Qatar
304.64095365	HB1465.9	Bahrain
304.64095367	HB1466	Kuwait
304.6409538	HB1464.7	Saudi Arabia
304.640954	HB1469-1470	India
304.64095491	HB1470.5	Pakistan
304.64095492	HB1470.6	Bangladesh
304.64095493	HB1466.8	Sri Lanka
304.64095495	HB1501.5	Maldive Islands
304.64095496	HB1466.9	Nepal
304.64095498	HB1470.3	Bhutan
304.640955	HB1466.4	Iran
304.6409561	HB1463.4	Turkey
304.64095645	HB1463.5	Cyprus
304.6409567	HB1466.3	Iraq
304.64095691	HB1463.7	Syria
304.64095692	HB1463.9	Lebanon
304.64095694	HB1464	Israel/Palestine
304.64095695	HB1464.3	Jordan
304.6409581	HB1466.6	Afghanistan
304.6409591	HB1466.7	Burma
304.6409593	HB1474.55	Thailand
304.6409594	HB1474.4	Laos
304.6409595	HB1474.6	Malaysia
304.6409596	HB1474.3	Cambodia
304.6409597	HB1474.5	Vietnam
304.6409598	HB1477-1478	Indonesia
304.6409599	HB1479-1480	Philippine Islands
304.6409611	HB1491.5	Tunisia
304.6409612	HB1491.6	Libya
304.640962	HB1491.7	Egypt
304.6409624	HB1491.8	Sudan
304.640963	HB1492	Ethiopia

Dewey	LC	Descriptor
304.640964	HB1491.3	Morocco
304.6409648	HB1497.4	Spanish Sahara
304.6409649	HB1499	Canary Islands
304.640965	HB1491.4	Algeria
304.6409661	HB1496.6	Mauritania
304.64096623	HB1496.3	Mali
304.64096625	HB1496.4	Burkina Faso
304.64096626	HB1495.9	Niger
304.6409663	HB1496.5	Senegal
304.64096664	HB1496.9	Sierra Leone
304.64096651	HB1497	Gambia
304.64096652	HB1496.2	Guinea-Bissau
304.64096657	HB1497.3	Guinea-Bissau
304.64096658	HB1499.5	Cape Verde Islands
304.64096662	HB1497.2	Liberia
304.6409668	HB1496	Ivory Coast
304.64096667	HB1496.8	Ghana
304.64096681	HB1495.8	Togo
304.64096683	HB1495.7	Benin (Dahomey)
304.6409669	HB1496.7	Nigeria
304.64096711	HB1495.4	Cameroon
304.64096715	HB1494.7	Sao Tome/Principe
304.64096718	HB1494.6	Equatorial Guinea
304.6409672	HB1494.8	French Equatorial Africa
304.64096721	HB1494.9	Gabon
304.64096724	HB1495	Congo
304.6409673	HB1494.4	Angola
304.64096741	HB1495.2	Central African Republic
304.64096743	HB1495.3	Chad
304.64096751	HB1494.5	Zaire
304.640967571	HB1492.7	Rwanda
304.640967572	HB1492.8	Burundi
304.64096761	HB1492.6	Uganda
304.64096762	HB1492.5	Kenya
304.64096771	HB1492.3	Djibouti
304.64096773	HB1492.2	Somalia
304.6409678	HB1492.9	Tanzania
304.6409679	HB1493	Mozambique
304.640968	HB1493.4	South Africa
304.64096881	HB1494.2	Namibia
304.64096883	HB1493.9	Botswana
304.64096885	HB1493.7	Lesotho
304.64096887	HB1493.8	Swaziland
304.6409689	HB1493.5	Zimbabwe/Zambia/ Malawi
304.64096894	HB1493.6	Zambia
304.64096897	HB1494	Malawi
304.6409691	HB1493.2	Madagascar
304.6409694	HB1502.5	Comoro Islands
304.6409696	HB1502	Seychelles
304.64096981	HB1503.5	Reunion
304.64096982	HB1503	Mauritius
304.6409699	HB1504	Kerguelen Islands
304.64097(4-9)	HB1355	By state
304.64097(4-9)	HB1357	By city
304.640971	HB1359-1360	Canada
304.640972	HB1361-1362	Mexico
304.64097281	HB1369	Guatemala
304.64097282	HB1365-1366	Belize
304.64097283	HB1370	Honduras
304.64097284	HB1374	El Salvador
304.64097285	HB1371	Nicaragua
304.64097286	HB1367-1368	Costa Rica
304.64097287	HB1372-1373	Panama
304.640972875	HB1373.5	Panama Canal Zone
304.64097291	HB1379-1380	Cuba
304.64097292	HB1383-1384	Jamaica
304.64097293	HB1382	Dominican Republic
304.64097294	HB1381	Haiti
304.64097295	HB1385-1386	Puerto Rico
304.64097296	HB1377-1378	Bahamas
304.6409729722	HB1386.3	Virgin Islands of the U.S.
304.640972973	HB1386.78	Saint Kitts-Nevis
304.640972973	HB1386.72	Anguilla
304.640972974	HB1386.74	Antigua/Barbuda
304.640972975	HB1386.76	Montserrat
304.640972976	HB1387.7	Guadeloupe
304.640972977	HB1387.38	Saba
304.640972977	HB1387.39	Saint Martin
304.640972977	HB1387.385	Saint Eustatius
304.640972981	HB1386.57	Barbados
304.640972982	HB1387.9	Martinique
304.640972983	HB1387	Trinidad/Tobago
304.6409729841	HB1386.93	Dominica
304.6409729843	HB1386.97	Saint Lucia
304.6409729844	HB1386.99	Saint Vincent/ Grenadines
304.6409729845	HB1386.95	Grenada
304.640972986	HB1387.35	Aruba
304.640972986	HB1387.36	Bonaire
304.640972986	HB1387.37	Curacao
304.64097299	HB1498	Bermuda
304.640973	HB1335	United States
304.640981	HB1393-1394	Brazil
304.640982	HB1389-1390	Argentina
304.640983	HB1395-1396	Chile
304.640984	HB1391-1392	Bolivia
304.640985	HB1405-1406	Peru
304.6409861	HB1397-1398	Colombia
304.6409866	HB1399-1400	Ecuador
304.640987	HB1409-1410	Venezuela
304.6409881	HB1402.3	Guyana
304.6409882	HB1402.7	French Guiana
304.6409883	HB1402.5	Suriname
304.6409892	HB1403-1404	Paraguay
304.6409895	HB1407-1408	Uruguay
304.640993	HB1522.5	New Zealand
304.640994	HB1505-1506	Australia
304.64409953	HB1522.8	Papua New Guinea
304.64099593	HB1523	Solomon Islands
304.64099595	HB1523.4	Vanuatu
304.64099597	HB1523.3	New Caledonia
304.64099611	HB1523.5	Fiji Islands
304.64099612	HB1523.6	Tonga
304.64099613	HB1523.7	American Samoa
304.64099614	HB1523.8	Western Samoa
304.6409962	HB1523.9	French Polynesia
304.64099623	HB1523.65	Cook Islands
304.6409967	HB1522.7	Guam
304.64099681	HB1522.9	Kiribati (Gilbert Islands)
304.6409971	HB1501	Falkland Islands
304.6409973	HB1500.5	Tristan da Cunha
304.6409973	HB1500	St. Helena
304.640998(1-8)	HB1525	Polar regions
304.6409982	HB1526	Greenland
304.6609495	HB1042.5	Greece
304.69561	HB1883.4	Turkey
304.809	HB1952	Internal migration
304.80902	D135-149	Migrations
305	HM131-134	Social groups
305	GN478-491.7	Social organization
305	GN495.4-498	Societal groups
305-307	HT	Communities/Classes/Races
305.05	HT51	Serials

Dewey	LC	Descriptor
305.06	HT53-55	Societies/Congresses
305.23	HQ781-784	Child life/Activities
305.23	HQ767.8-792.2	Children/Child development
305.230(5/6)	HQ767.8	Serials/Societies
305.2303	HQ767.84	Dictionaries/Encyclopedias
305.2306	HQ767.82	Congresses
305.2307	HQ767.85	Education
305.2309	HQ767.87	History
305.2309(4-9)	HQ792-.2	Conditions, By place
305.235	HQ799.5-.9	Young adults
305.235	HQ793-799.2	Youth/Adolescence
305.23509(4-9)	HQ799	Other countries
305.2350973	HQ796-798	United States
305.24	HQ799.95-.97	Adulthood
305.244	HQ1059.4-.5	Middle age
305.26	HQ1060-1064	Aged
305.3	HQ77.7-.9	Transsexualism
305.3	HQ1075-.5	Sex roles
305.31	HQ1088-1090.7	Men
305.4	HQ1101-2039	Women/Feminism
305.4	HQ1240-1399	Misc. aspects of women/Society
305.4(06/8)	HQ1871-2030.7	Women's clubs/Societies
305.407	HQ1180-1181	Education/Women's studies
305.409	HQ1121-1154	History
305.409(4-9)	HQ1402-1870.5	Women, By place
305.409(4-9)	HQ1451-1870.9	Other countries
305.40973	HQ1402-1439	United States
305.5	HT675-690	Classes from occupations
305.5	HT655-657	Commons
305.5	HT601-1445	Classes
305.5(5-6)09(4-9)	HT690	By place
305.505	HT601	Serials
305.506	HT603	Societies
305.509	HT607	History
305.5122	HT713-725	Caste system
305.522	HT641-657	Classes, By birth
305.522(2-3)	HT647-653	Royalty/Nobility
305.55	HT680-690	Middle class
305.555	HD1501-1540	Social classes (Agricultural)
305.567	HT851-1445	Slavery
305.56705	HT851	Serials
305.56706	HT853-855	Societies/Congresses
305.56709	HT861-867	History
305.56709(4-9)	HT1048-1445	Slavery, By place
305.567094	HT1155-1240	Europe
305.5670941	HT1161-1165	Great Britain
305.5670943	HT1181-1185	Germany
305.5670944	HT1176-1180	France
305.5670945	HT1191-1195	Italy
305.5670946	HT1216-1220	Spain
305.5670947	HT1206-1210	European Russia
305.56709492	HT1196-1205	Low Countries
305.56709494	HT1227-1228	Switzerland
305.56709495	HT1234	Greece
305.567095	HT1240.5-1315	Far East
305.5670951	HT1241-1245	China
305.5670952	HT1276-1280	Japan
305.56709599	HT1271-1275	Philippine Islands
305.567096	HT1321-1427	Africa
305.5670971	HT1051-1052	Canada
305.5670972	HT1053-1054	Mexico
305.56709728	HT1055-1056	Central America
305.56709729	HT1071-1119	West Indies
305.567098	HT1121-1152	South America

Dewey	LC	Descriptor
305.567099(3-6)	HT1431-1445	Australia/New Zealand/Oceania
305.8	HT1501-1595	Races
305.8	GN502-517	Psychological anthropology
305.8	GN537-673	Ethnic groups/Races
305.8	GN301-673	Ethnology/Social anthropology
305.8	GN378-395	Collected ethnographies
305.8(03-99)	HT1575-1595	By race
305.8(036/93)	HT1581-1589	Black/Hamitic
305.8005	HT1501	Serials
305.8006	HT1503-1505	Societies/Congresses
305.8007	HT1506	Education
305.8009	HT1507	History
305.8009	GN550-673	Ethnic groups/Races, By place
305.8009(728/8)	GN562-564	Central/South America
305.80094	GN575-585	Europe
305.80095	GN625-635	Asia
305.80096	GN643-661	Africa
305.80097	GN550-560	North America
305.80099(3-6)	GN662-671	Australia/New Zealand/Oceania
305.800998	GN673	Arctic
305.8034	HT1577	Aryan/Indo-European
305.8034	HT1575	Caucasian
305.896073	E185.61-.625	Black-White relations
305.896073	E185.86	Social/Moral conditions
305.90652	HQ800-.4	Single people
306	HM101-121	Civilization/Culture
306	GN357-367	Culture/Cultural processes
306	GN301-673	Ethnology/Social anthropology
306.089	JV305-317	Natives
306.2	GN492-495	Political anthropology
306.27	UH750-769	Social work/Welfare
306.3	HM211	Economic
306.3	GN448-450.7	Economic anthropology
306.36	HD6951-6957	Industrial sociology
306.365	HT751-815	Serfdom
306.36509(4-9)	HT781-815	Serfdom, By place
306.36509(4-9)	HT815	Other countries
306.365090(1-4)	HT775	By date
306.3650941	HT781	Great Britain
306.3650943	HT791-801	Germany
306.3650943(6/9)	HT803	Austria/Hungary
306.3650944	HT785	France
306.3650947	HT807-809	Russia
306.42	HM213	Intellectual
306.42	GN451-477.7	Intellectual life
306.46	HM221	Technological
306.46	GN406-442	Technology/Material culture
306.461	GN296	Medical anthropology
306.6	HM219	Religious
306.7	HQ461-470	Erotic literature
306.7	HQ12-449	Sexual life
306.7	HQ19-30.7	Sexuality/Sexual behavior
306.7081	HQ28	Men
306.7082	HQ29	Women
306.70835	HQ27-.5	Adolescents/Young adults
306.708351	HQ27.3	Boys
306.708352	HQ27.5	Girls
306.70846	HQ30	Aged
306.7087	HQ30.5	Handicapped
306.70877	HQ30.7	The sick
306.709	HQ12-18	Sexual life, History

Dewey	LC	Descriptor
306.709(3-9)	HQ18	By place
306.7090(1-4)	HQ13-16	By date
306.7092	HQ18.3-.32	Biography
306.734	HQ801-802.5	Courtship/Dating/Etc.
306.735	HQ961-967	Free love
306.74	HQ101-440.7	Prostitution
306.7409	HQ111-117	History
306.7409(4-9)	HQ141-270.7	Prostitution, By place
306.74094	HQ184-231.84	Europe
306.740941	HQ185-187.5	Great Britain
306.740943	HQ197-200.5	Germany
306.740944	HQ193-196	France
306.740945	HQ202-205	Italy
306.740946	HQ225-228	Spain
306.740947	HQ214-217	European Russia
306.7409492	HQ206-213.5	Low Countries
306.7409494	HQ230	Switzerland
306.7409495	HQ231.83	Greece
306.74095	HQ232.7-253	Far East
306.740951	HQ250	China
306.740952	HQ247	Japan
306.740954	HQ237-240	India
306.740955	HQ232.56	Iran
306.740956	HQ231.93-232.56	Middle East
306.7409567	HQ232.55	Iraq
306.74095694	HQ232.2	Israel
306.7409599	HQ245	Philippine Islands
306.74096	HQ257-269.3	Africa
306.740971	HQ147-150	Canada
306.740972	HQ151	Mexico
306.7409728	HQ153-159	Central America
306.7409729	HQ160-165.9	West Indies
306.740973	HQ143-146	United States
306.74098	HQ166-183	South America
306.74099(3-6)	HQ270-.43	Australia/New Zealand/Oceania
306.765	HQ74	Bisexuality
306.766	HQ75-76.8	Homosexuality/Lesbianism
306.77	HQ77	Transvestism
306.77(5-6)	HQ79	Sadism/Masochism/Fetishism
306.772	HQ447	Masturbation
306.8	HQ	Marriage/The family/Woman
306.8	HQ503-2039	The family/Marriage/Home
306.803	HQ9	Dictionaries/Encyclopedias
306.805	HQ1	Serials
306.806	HQ3/7	Societies/Congresses
306.807	HQ10-.5	Education
306.8089(03-99)	HQ525	By race/Nationality/Etc.
306.809	HQ515-518	Modern
306.809	HQ503-727	The family/Etc., History
306.809	HQ505-518	By date
306.809(4-9)	HQ531-727	The family/Marriage, By place
306.80901	HQ505-512	Ancient
306.80902	HQ513	Medieval
306.8094	HQ611-662.7	Europe
306.80941	HQ613-618.5	Great Britain
306.80943	HQ625-626.5	Germany
306.80944	HQ623-624	France
306.80945	HQ629-630	Italy
306.80946	HQ649-650	Spain
306.80947	HQ637-638	European Russia
306.809492	HQ631-636.5	Low Countries
306.809494	HQ653-654	Switzerland

Dewey	LC	Descriptor
306.809495	HQ662.5	Greece
306.8095	HQ666.7-687	Far East
306.80951	HQ684	China
306.80952	HQ681-682	Japan
306.80954	HQ669-670	India
306.80955	HQ666.4	Iran
306.80956	HQ663.3-666.4	Middle East
306.809567	HQ666.3	Iraq
306.8095694	HQ664	Israel/Palestine
306.809599	HQ679-680	Philippine Islands
306.8096	HQ691-697.4	Africa
306.80971	HQ559-560	Canada
306.80972	HQ561-562	Mexico
306.809728	HQ563-574	Central America
306.809729	HQ575-587.9	West Indies
306.80973	HQ535-557	United States
306.8098	HQ588-610	South America
306.8099(3-6)	HQ705-723.9	Australia/New Zealand/Oceania
306.81	HB1111-1317	Marriage
306.8109	HB1121-1317	Marriage, By place
306.8109411	HB1207-1208	Scotland
306.8109416	HB1208.5	Northern Ireland
306.8109417	HB1209-1210	Irish Republic
306.810942(9)	HB1205-1206	England/Wales
306.810943	HB1215-1216.5	Germany
306.8109436	HB1211-1212	Austria
306.810943648	HB1212.9	Liechtenstein
306.8109437	HB1212.3	Czechoslovakia
306.8109438	HB1228.7	Poland
306.8109439	HB1212.5	Hungary
306.810944	HB1213-1214	France
306.810944949	HB1214.5	Monaco
306.810945	HB1219-1220	Italy
306.810946	HB1239-1240	Spain
306.8109469	HB1241-1242	Portugal
306.81094698	HB1288.5	Madeira Islands
306.81094699	HB1287.5	Azores
306.810947	HB1227-1228	European Russia
306.8109481	HB1235-1236	Norway
306.8109485	HB1237-1238	Sweden
306.8109489	HB1231-1232	Denmark
306.81094897	HB1228.3	Finland
306.81094912	HB1233-1234	Iceland
306.8109492	HB1225-1226	Netherlands
306.8109493	HB1223-1224	Belgium
306.81094935	HB1226.5	Luxembourg
306.8109494	HB1243-1244	Switzerland
306.8109495	HB1252.5	Greece
306.81094965	HB1246.5	Albania
306.8109497	HB1248.5	Yugoslavia
306.81094977	HB1247-1248	Bulgaria
306.8109498	HB1251-1252	Romania
306.810951	HB1274	China
306.810951249	HB1276	Taiwan
306.81095125	HB1277	Hong Kong
306.81095126	HB1275	Macao
306.8109517	HB1272.8	Mongolia
306.8109519	HB1272.5-.6	Korea/North Korea
306.810952	HB1271-1272	Japan
306.81095332	HB1254.9-1255	Yemen
306.81095353	HB1255.3	Oman
306.81095357	HB1255.5	United Arab Emirates
306.81095363	HB1255.7	Qatar
306.81095365	HB1255.9	Bahrain
306.81095367	HB1256	Kuwait
306.8109538	HB1254.7	Saudi Arabia

Dewey	LC	Descriptor
306.810954	HB1259-1260	India
306.81095491	HB1260.5	Pakistan
306.81095492	HB1260.6	Bangladesh
306.81095493	HB1256.8	Sri Lanka
306.81095495	HB1291.5	Maldive Islands
306.81095496	HB1256.9	Nepal
306.81095498	HB1260.3	Bhutan
306.810955	HB1256.4	Iran
306.8109561	HB1253.4	Turkey
306.81095645	HB1253.5	Cyprus
306.8109567	HB1256.3	Iraq
306.81095691	HB1253.7	Syria
306.81095692	HB1253.9	Lebanon
306.81095694	HB1254	Israel/Palestine
306.81095695	HB1254.3	Jordan
306.8109581	HB1256.6	Afghanistan
306.8109591	HB1256.7	Burma
306.8109593	HB1264.55	Thailand
306.8109594	HB1264.4	Laos
306.8109595	HB1264.6	Malaysia
306.8109596	HB1264.3	Cambodia
306.8109597	HB1264.5	Vietnam
306.8109598	HB1267-1268	Indonesia
306.8109599	HB1269-1270	Philippine Islands
306.8109611	HB1281.5	Tunisia
306.8109612	HB1281.6	Libya
306.810962	HB1281.7	Egypt
306.8109624	HB1281.8	Sudan
306.810963	HB1282	Ethiopia
306.810964	HB1281.3	Morocco
306.8109648	HB1287.4	Spanish Sahara
306.8109649	HB1289	Canary Islands
306.810965	HB1281.4	Algeria
306.8109661	HB1286.6	Mauritania
306.81096623	HB1286.3	Mali
306.81096625	HB1286.4	Burkina Faso
306.81096626	HB1285.9	Niger
306.8109663	HB1286.5	Senegal
306.8109664	HB1286.9	Sierra Leone
306.81096651	HB1287	Gambia
306.81096652	HB1286.2	Guinea-Bissau
306.81096657	HB1287.3	Guinea-Bissau
306.81096658	HB1289.5	Cape Verde Islands
306.81096662	HB1287.2	Liberia
306.81096668	HB1286	Ivory Coast
306.8109667	HB1286.8	Ghana
306.81096681	HB1285.8	Togo
306.81096683	HB1285.7	Benin (Dahomey)
306.8109669	HB1286.7	Nigeria
306.81096711	HB1285.4	Cameroon
306.81096715	HB1284.7	Sao Tome/Principe
306.81096718	HB1284.6	Equatorial Guinea
306.8109672	HB1284.8	French Equatorial Africa
306.81096721	HB1284.9	Gabon
306.81096724	HB1285	Congo
306.8109673	HB1284.4	Angola
306.81096741	HB1285.2	Central African Republic
306.81096743	HB1285.3	Chad
306.81096751	HB1284.5	Zaire
306.810967571	HB1282.7	Rwanda
306.810967572	HB1282.8	Burundi
306.81096761	HB1282.6	Uganda
306.81096762	HB1282.5	Kenya
306.81096771	HB1282.3	Djibouti
306.81096773	HB1282.2	Somalia
306.8109678	HB1282.9	Tanzania
306.8109679	HB1283	Mozambique
306.810968	HB1283.4	South Africa
306.81096881	HB1284.2	Namibia
306.81096883	HB1283.9	Botswana
306.81096885	HB1283.7	Lesotho
306.81096887	HB1283.8	Swaziland
306.8109689	HB1283.5	Zimbabwe/Zambia/ Malawi
306.81096894	HB1283.6	Zambia
306.81096897	HB1284	Malawi
306.8109691	HB1283.2	Madagascar
306.8109694	HB1292.5	Comoro Islands
306.8109696	HB1292	Seychelles
306.81096981	HB1293.5	Reunion
306.81096982	HB1293	Mauritius
306.8109699	HB1294	Kerguelen Islands
306.81097(4-9)	HB1147	By city
306.81097(4-9)	HB1145	By state
306.810971	HB1149-1150	Canada
306.810972	HB1151-1152	Mexico
306.81097281	HB1159	Guatemala
306.81097282	HB1155-1156	Belize
306.81097283	HB1160	Honduras
306.81097284	HB1164	El Salvador
306.81097285	HB1161	Nicaragua
306.81097286	HB1157-1158	Costa Rica
306.81097287	HB1162-1163	Panama
306.810972875	HB1163.5	Panama Canal Zone
306.81097291	HB1169-1170	Cuba
306.81097292	HB1173-1174	Jamaica
306.81097293	HB1172	Dominican Republic
306.81097294	HB1171	Haiti
306.81097295	HB1175-1176	Puerto Rico
306.81097296	HB1167-1168	Bahamas
306.8109729722	HB1176.3	Virgin Islands of the U.S.
306.810972973	HB1176.72	Anguilla
306.810972973	HB1176.78	Saint Kitts-Nevis
306.810972974	HB1176.74	Antigua/Barbuda
306.810972975	HB1176.76	Montserrat
306.810972976	HB1177.7	Guadeloupe
306.810972977	HB1177.39	Saint Martin
306.810972977	HB1177.385	Saint Eustatius
306.810972977	HB1177.38	Saba
306.810972981	HB1176.57	Barbados
306.810972982	HB1177.9	Martinique
306.810972983	HB1177	Trinidad/Tobago
306.8109729841	HB1176.93	Dominica
306.8109729843	HB1176.97	Saint Lucia
306.8109729844	HB1176.99	Saint Vincent/ Grenadines
306.8109729845	HB1176.95	Grenada
306.810972986	HB1177.35	Aruba
306.810972986	HB1177.37	Curacao
306.810972986	HB1177.36	Bonaire
306.81097299	HB1288	Bermuda
306.810973	HB1125-1126	United States
306.810981	HB1183-1184	Brazil
306.810982	HB1179-1180	Argentina
306.810983	HB1185-1186	Chile
306.810984	HB1181-1182	Bolivia
306.810985	HB1195-1196	Peru
306.8109861	HB1187-1188	Colombia
306.8109866	HB1189-1190	Ecuador
306.810987	HB1199-1200	Venezuela
306.8109881	HB1192.3	Guyana
306.8109882	HB1192.7	French Guiana
306.8109883	HB1192.5	Suriname
306.8109892	HB1193-1194	Paraguay

Dewey	LC	Descriptor	Dewey	LC	Descriptor
306.8109895	HB1197-1198	Uruguay	307.212094912	HB2493-2494	Iceland
306.810993	HB1312.5	New Zealand	307.21209492	HB2485-2486	Netherlands
306.810994	HB1295-1296	Australia	307.21209493	HB2483-2484	Belgium
306.8109953	HB1312.8	Papua New Guinea	307.212094935	HB2486.5	Luxembourg
306.81099593	HB1313	Solomon Islands	307.21209494	HB2503-2504	Switzerland
306.81099595	HB1313.4	Vanuatu	307.21209495	HB2512.5	Greece
306.81099597	HB1313.3	New Caledonia	307.212094965	HB2506.5	Albania
306.81099611	HB1313.5	Fiji Islands	307.21209497	HB2508.5	Yugoslavia
306.81099612	HB1313.6	Tonga	307.212094977	HB2507-2508	Bulgaria
306.81099613	HB1313.7	American Samoa	307.21209498	HB2511-2512	Romania
306.81099614	HB1313.8	Western Samoa	307.2120951	HB2534	China
306.8109962	HB1313.9	French Polynesia	307.2120951249	HB2536	Taiwan
306.81099623	HB1313.65	Cook Islands	307.212095125	HB2537	Hong Kong
306.8109967	HB1312.7	Guam	307.212095126	HB2535	Macao
306.81099681	HB1312.9	Kiribati (Gilbert Islands)	307.21209517	HB2532.8	Mongolia
306.8109971	HB1291	Falkland Islands	307.21209519	HB2532.5-.6	Korea/North Korea
306.8109973	HB1290	St. Helena	307.2120952	HB2531-2532	Japan
306.8109973	HB1290.5	Tristan da Cunha	307.212095332	HB2514.9-2515	Yemen
306.810998(1-8)	HB1315	Polar regions	307.212095353	HB2515.3	Oman
306.8109982	HB1316	Greenland	307.212095357	HB2515.5	United Arab Emirates
306.84	HQ1018-1043	Misc. marriage situations	307.212095363	HB2515.7	Qatar
306.8423	HQ981-997	Polygamy/Polyandry	307.212095365	HB2515.9	Bahrain
306.856	HQ998-999	Unmarried mothers	307.212095367	HB2516	Kuwait
306.874	HQ755.7-759.92	Parents	307.21209538	HB2514.7	Saudi Arabia
306.8742	HQ756.-.5	Husbands/Fathers	307.2120954	HB2519-2520	India
306.8743	HQ759-.6	Wives	307.212095491	HB2520.5	Pakistan
306.88	HQ805-806	Desertion/Adultery	307.212095492	HB2520.6	Bangladesh
306.89	HQ811-960.7	Divorce	307.212095493	HB2516.8	Sri Lanka
306.8909(4-9)	HQ831-960.7	Divorce, By place	307.212095495	HB2551.5	Maldive Islands
306.8909(4-9)	HQ837-960.9	Other countries	307.212095496	HB2516.9	Nepal
306.890973	HQ833-836	United States	307.212095498	HB2520.3	Bhutan
306.9	HQ1073-.5	Death/Dying	307.2120955	HB2516.4	Iran
307	GF101-127	Settlements	307.21209561	HB2513.4	Turkey
307.12	HT390-395	Regional planning	307.212095645	HB2513.5	Cyprus
307.1207	HT165.5-.53	Education	307.21209567	HB2516.3	Iraq
307.1209(4-9)	HT395	Other countries	307.212095691	HB2513.7	Syria
307.120973	HT392-394	United States	307.212095692	HB2513.9	Lebanon
307.1216	HT165.5-169.9	City planning	307.212095694	HB2514	Israel/Palestine
307.1216	TD160-167	Planning/Laying out cities	307.212095695	HB2514.3	Jordan
307.121609(4-9)	HT167-169.5	By place	307.21209581	HB2516.6	Afghanistan
307.121609(4-9)	HT169-.5	Other countries	307.21209591	HB2516.7	Burma
307.12160973	HT167-168	United States	307.21209593	HB2524.55	Thailand
307.2	HB1955-1956	Urban/Rural migration	307.21209594	HB2524.4	Laos
307.212	HB2371-2577	Rural population	307.21209595	HB2524.6	Malaysia
307.21209(4-9)	HB2381-2577	By place	307.21209596	HB2524.3	Cambodia
307.21209411	HB2467-2468	Scotland	307.21209597	HB2524.5	Vietnam
307.21209416	HB2468.5	Northern Ireland	307.21209598	HB2527-2528	Indonesia
307.21209417	HB2469-2470	Irish Republic	307.21209599	HB2529-2530	Philippine Islands
307.2120942(9)	HB2465-2466	England/Wales	307.21209611	HB2541.5	Tunisia
307.2120943	HB2475-2476.5	Germany	307.21209612	HB2541.6	Libya
307.21209436	HB2471-2472	Austria	307.2120962	HB2541.7	Egypt
307.2120943648	HB2472.9	Liechtenstein	307.21209624	HB2541.8	Sudan
307.21209437	HB2472.3	Czechoslovakia	307.2120963	HB2542	Ethiopia
307.21209438	HB2488.7	Poland	307.21209648	HB2547.4	Spanish Sahara
307.21209439	HB2472.5	Hungary	307.21209649	HB2549	Canary Islands
307.2120944	HB2473-2474	France	307.2120965	HB2541.4	Algeria
307.2120944949	HB2474.5	Monaco	307.21209661	HB2546.6	Mauritania
307.2120945	HB2479-2480	Italy	307.212096623	HB2546.3	Mali
307.2120946	HB2499-2500	Spain	307.212096625	HB2546.4	Burkina Faso
307.21209469	HB2501-2502	Portugal	307.212096626	HB2545.9	Niger
307.212094698	HB2548.5	Madeira Islands	307.21209663	HB2546.5	Senegal
307.212094699	HB2547.5	Azores	307.21209664	HB2546.9	Sierra Leone
307.2120947	HB2487-2488	European Russia	307.212096651	HB2547	Gambia
307.21209481	HB2495-2496	Norway	307.212096652	HB2546.2	Guinea-Bissau
307.21209485	HB2497-2498	Sweden	307.212096657	HB2547.3	Guinea-Bissau
307.21209489	HB2491-2492	Denmark	307.212096658	HBw549.5	Cape Verde Islands
307.212094897	HB2488.3	Finland	307.212096662	HB2547.2	Liberia

Dewey	LC	Descriptor	Dewey	LC	Descriptor
307.212096668	HB2546	Ivory Coast	307.2120972983	HB2437	Trinidad/Tobago
307.21209667	HB2546.8	Ghana	307.21209729841	HB2436.93	Dominica
307.212096681	HB2545.8	Togo	307.21209729843	HB2436.97	Saint Lucia
307.212096683	HB2545.7	Benin (Dahomey)	307.21209729844	HB2436.99	Saint Vincent/
307.21209669	HB2546.7	Nigeria			Grenadines
307.212096711	HB2545.4	Cameroon	307.21209729845	HB2436.95	Grenada
307.212096715	HB2544.7	Sao Tome/Principe	307.2120972986	HB2437.37	Curacao
307.212096718	HB2544.6	Equatorial Guinea	307.2120972986	HB2437.36	Bonaire
307.21209672	HB2544.8	French Equatorial Africa	307.2120972986	HB2437.35	Aruba
307.212096721	HB2544.9	Gabon	307.212097299	HB2548	Bermuda
307.212096724	HB2545	Congo	307.2120973	HB2385-2386	United States
307.21209673	HB2544.4	Angola	307.2120981	HB2443-2444	Brazil
307.212096741	HB2545.2	Central African Republic	307.2120982	HB2439-2440	Argentina
307.212096743	HB2545.3	Chad	307.2120983	HB2445-2446	Chile
307.212096751	HB2544.5	Zaire	307.2120984	HB2441-2442	Bolivia
307.2120967571	HB2542.7	Rwanda	307.2120985	HB2455-2456	Peru
307.2120967572	HB2542.8	Burundi	307.21209861	HB2447-2448	Colombia
307.212096761	HB2542.6	Uganda	307.21209866	HB2449-2450	Ecuador
307.212096762	HB2542.5	Kenya	307.2120987	HB2459-2460	Venezuela
307.212096771	HB2542.3	Djibouti	307.21209881	HB2452.3	Guyana
307.212096773	HB2542.2	Somalia	307.21209882	HB2452.7	French Guiana
307.21209678	HB2542.9	Tanzania	307.21209883	HB2452.5	Suriname
307.21209679	HB2543	Mozambique	307.21209892	HB2453-2454	Paraguay
307.2120968	HB2543.4	South Africa	307.21209895	HB2457-2458	Uruguay
307.212096881	HB2544.2	Namibia	307.2120993	HB2572.5	New Zealand
307.212096883	HB2543.9	Botswana	307.2120994	HB2555-2556	Australia
307.212096885	HB2543.7	Lesotho	307.21209953	HB2572.8	Papua New Guinea
307.212096887	HB2543.8	Swaziland	307.212099593	HB2573	Solomon Islands
307.21209689	HB2543.5	Zimbabwe/Zambia/	307.212099595	HB2573.4	Vanuatu
		Malawi	307.212099597	HB2573.3	New Caledonia
307.212096894	HB2543.6	Zambia	307.212099611	HB2573.5	Fiji Islands
307.212096897	HB2544	Malawi	307.212099612	HB2573.6	Tonga
307.21209691	HB2543.2	Madagascar	307.212099613	HB2573.7	American Samoa
307.21209694	HB2552.5	Comoro Islands	307.212099614	HB2573.8	Western Samoa
307.21209696	HB2552	Seychelles	307.21209962	HB2573.9	French Polynesia
307.212096981	HB2553.5	Reunion	307.212099623	HB2573.65	Cook Islands
307.212096982	HB2553	Mauritius	307.21209967	HB2572.7	Guam
307.21209699	HB2554	Kerguelen Islands	307.212099681	HB2572.9	Kiribati (Gilbert Islands)
307.212097(4-9)	HB2407	By city	307.21209971	HB2551	Falkland Islands
307.212097(4-9)	HB2405	By state	307.21209973	HB2550	St. Helena
307.2120971	HB2409-2410	Canada	307.21209973	HB2550.5	Tristan da Cunha
307.2120972	HB2411-2412	Mexico	307.2120998(1-8)	HB2575	Polar regions
307.212097281	HB2419	Guatemala	307.21209982	HB2576	Greenland
307.212097282	HB2415-2416	Belize	307.216	HB2161-2367	Urban population
307.212097283	HB2420	Honduras	307.21609	HB2171-2367	By place
307.212097284	HB2424	El Salvador	307.21609411	HB2257-2258	Scotland
307.212097285	HB2421	Nicaragua	307.21609416	HB2258.5	Northern Ireland
307.212097286	HB2417-2418	Costa Rica	307.21609417	HB2259-2260	Irish Republic
307.212097287	HB2422-2423	Panama	307.2160942(9)	HB2255-2256	England/Wales
307.2120972875	HB2423.5	Panama Canal Zone	307.2160943	HB2265-2266.5	Germany
307.212097291	HB2429-2430	Cuba	307.21609436	HB2261-2262	Austria
307.212097292	HB2433-2434	Jamaica	307.2160943648	HB2262.9	Liechtenstein
307.212097293	HB2432	Dominican Republic	307.21609437	HB2262.3	Czechoslovakia
307.212097294	HB2431	Haiti	307.21609438	HB2278.7	Poland
307.212097295	HB2435-2436	Puerto Rico	307.21609439	HB2262.5	Hungary
307.212097296	HB2427-2428	Bahamas	307.2160944	HB2263-2264	France
307.21209729722	HB2436.3	Virgin Islands of the U.S.	307.2160944949	HB2264.5	Monaco
307.2120972973	HB2436.78	Saint Kitts-Nevis	307.2160945	HB2269-2270	Italy
307.2120972973	HB2436.72	Anguilla	307.2160946	HB2289-2290	Spain
307.2120972974	HB2436.74	Antigua/Barbuda	307.21609469	HB2291-2292	Portugal
307.2120972975	HB2436.76	Montserrat	307.216094698	HB2338.5	Madeira Islands
307.2120972976	HB2437.7	Guadeloupe	307.216094699	HB2337.5	Azores
307.2120972977	HB2437.38	Saba	307.2160947	HB2277-2278	European Russia
307.2120972977	HB2437.385	Saint Eustatius	307.21609481	HB2285-2286	Norway
307.2120972977	HB2437.39	Saint Martin	307.21609485	HB2287-2288	Sweden
307.2120972981	HB2436.57	Barbados	307.21609489	HB2281-2282	Denmark
307.2120972982	HB2437.9	Martinique	307.216094897	HB2278.3	Finland

Dewey	LC	Descriptor
307.216094912	HB2283-2284	Iceland
307.21609492	HB2275-2276	Netherlands
307.21609493	HB2273-2274	Belgium
307.216094935	HB2276.5	Luxembourg
307.21609494	HB2293-2294	Switzerland
307.21609495	HB2302.5	Greece
307.216094965	HB2296.5	Albania
307.21609497	HB2298.5	Yugoslavia
307.216094977	HB2297-2298	Bulgaria
307.21609498	HB2301-2302	Romania
307.2160951	HB2324	China
307.2160951249	HB2326	Taiwan
307.216095125	HB2327	Hong Kong
307.216095126	HB2325	Macao
307.21609517	HB2322.8	Mongolia
307.21609519	HB2322.5-.6	Korea/North Korea
307.2160952	HB2321-2322	Japan
307.216095332	HB2304.9-2305	Yemen
307.216095353	HB2305.3	Oman
307.216095357	HB2305.5	United Arab Emirates
307.216095363	HB2305.7	Qatar
307.216095365	HB2305.9	Bahrain
307.216095367	HB2306	Kuwait
307.21609538	HB2304.7	Saudi Arabia
307.2160954	HB2309-2310	India
307.216095491	HB2310.5	Pakistan
307.216095492	HB2310.6	Bangladesh
307.216095493	HB2306.8	Sri Lanka
307.216095495	HB2341.5	Maldive Islands
307.216095496	HB2306.9	Nepal
307.216095498	HB2310.3	Bhutan
307.2160955	HB2306.4	Iran
307.21609561	HB2303.4	Turkey
307.216095645	HB2303.5	Cyprus
307.21609567	HB2306.3	Iraq
307.216095691	HB2303.7	Syria
307.216095692	HB2303.9	Lebanon
307.216095694	HB2304	Israel/Palestine
307.216095695	HB2304.3	Jordan
307.21609581	HB2306.6	Afghanistan
307.21609591	HB2306.7	Burma
307.21609593	HB2314.55	Thailand
307.21609594	HB2314.4	Laos
307.21609595	HB2314.6	Malaysia
307.21609596	HB2314.3	Cambodia
307.21609597	HB2314.5	Vietnam
307.21609598	HB2317-2318	Indonesia
307.21609599	HB2319-2320	Philippine Islands
307.21609611	HB2331.5	Tunisia
307.21609612	HB2331.6	Libya
307.2160962	HB2331.7	Egypt
307.21609624	HB2331.8	Sudan
307.2160963	HB2332	Ethiopia
307.2160964	HB2331.3	Morocco
307.21609648	HB2337.4	Spanish Sahara
307.21609649	HB2339	Canary Islands
307.2160965	HB2331.4	Algeria
307.21609661	HB2336.6	Mauritania
307.216096623	HB2336.3	Mali
307.216096625	HB2336.4	Burkina Faso
307.216096626	HB2335.9	Niger
307.21609663	HB2336.5	Senegal
307.21609664	HB2336.9	Sierra Leone
307.216096651	HB2337	Gambia
307.216096652	HB2336.2	Guinea-Bissau
307.216096657	HB2337.3	Guinea-Bissau
307.216096658	HB2339.5	Cape Verde Islands
307.216096662	HB2337.2	Liberia
307.216096668	HB2336	Ivory Coast
307.21609667	HB2336.8	Ghana
307.216096681	HB2335.8	Togo
307.216096683	HB2335.7	Benin (Dahomey)
307.21609669	HB2336.7	Nigeria
307.216096711	HB2335.4	Cameroon
307.216096715	HB2334.7	Sao Tome/Principe
307.216096718	HB2334.6	Equatorial Guinea
307.21609672	HB2334.8	French Equatorial Africa
307.216096721	HB2334.9	Gabon
307.216096724	HB2335	Congo
307.21609673	HB2334.4	Angola
307.216096741	HB2335.2	Central African Republic
307.216096743	HB2335.3	Chad
307.216096751	HB2334.5	Zaire
307.2160967571	HB2332.7	Rwanda
307.2160967572	HB2332.8	Burundi
307.216096761	HB2332.6	Uganda
307.216096762	HB2332.5	Kenya
307.216096771	HB2332.3	Djibouti
307.216096773	HB2332.2	Somalia
307.21609678	HB2332.9	Tanzania
307.21609679	HB2333	Mozambique
307.2160968	HB2333.4	South Africa
307.216096881	HB2334.2	Namibia
307.216096883	HB2333.9	Botswana
307.216096885	HB2333.7	Lesotho
307.216096887	HB2333.8	Swaziland
307.21609689	HB2333.5	Zimbabwe/Zambia/Malawi
307.216096894	HB2333.6	Zambia
307.216096897	HB2334	Malawi
307.21609691	HB2333.2	Madagascar
307.21609694	HB2342.5	Comoro Islands
307.21609696	HB2342	Seychelles
307.216096981	HB2343.5	Reunion
307.216096982	HB2343	Mauritius
307.21609699	HB2344	Kerguelen Islands
307.216097(4-9)	HB2195	By state
307.216097(4-9)	HB2197	By city
307.2160971	HB2199-2200	Canada
307.2160972	HB2201-2202	Mexico
307.216097281	HB2209	Guatemala
307.216097282	HB2205-2206	Belize
307.216097283	HB2210	Honduras
307.216097284	HB2214	El Salvador
307.216097285	HB2211	Nicaragua
307.216097286	HB2207-2208	Costa Rica
307.216097287	HB2212-2213	Panama
307.216097287	HB2213.5	Panama Canal Zone
307.216097291	HB2219-2220	Cuba
307.216097292	HB2223-2224	Jamaica
307.216097293	HB2222	Dominican Republic
307.216097294	HB2221	Haiti
307.216097295	HB2225-2226	Puerto Rico
307.216097296	HB2217-2218	Bahamas
307.21609729722	HB2226.3	Virgin Islands of the U.S.
307.2160972973	HB2226.78	Saint Kitts-Nevis
307.2160972973	HB2226.72	Anguilla
307.2160972974	HB2226.74	Antigua/Barbuda
307.2160972975	HB2226.76	Montserrat
307.2160972976	HB2227.7	Guadeloupe
307.2160972977	HB2227.385	Saint Eustatius
307.2160972977	HB2227.38	Saba
307.2160972977	HB2227.39	Saint Martin
307.2160972981	HB2226.57	Barbados

Dewey	LC	Descriptor
307.2160972982	HB2227.9	Martinique
307.2160972983	HB2227	Trinidad/Tobago
307.21609729841	HB2226.93	Dominica
307.21609729843	HB2226.97	Saint Lucia
307.21609729844	HB2226.99	Saint Vincent/ Grenadines
307.21609729845	HB2226.95	Grenada
307.2160972986	HB2227.35	Aruba
307.2160972986	HB2227.36	Bonaire
307.2160972986	HB2227.37	Curacao
307.216097299	HB2338	Bermuda
307.2160973	HB2175-2176	United States
307.2160981	HB2233-2234	Brazil
307.2160982	HB2229-2230	Argentina
307.2160983	HB2235-2236	Chile
307.2160984	HB2231-2232	Bolivia
307.2160985	HB2245-2246	Peru
307.21609861	HB2237-2238	Colombia
307.21609866	HB2239-2240	Ecuador
307.2160987	HB2249-2250	Venezuela
307.21609881	HB2242.3	Guyana
307.21609882	HB2242.7	French Guiana
307.21609883	HB2242.5	Suriname
307.21609892	HB2243-2244	Paraguay
307.21609895	HB2247-2248	Uruguay
307.2160993	HB2362.5	New Zealand
307.2160994	HB2345-2346	Australia
307.21609953	HB2362.8	Papua New Guinea
307.216099593	HB2363	Solomon Islands
307.216099595	HB2363.4	Vanuatu
307.216099597	HB2363.3	New Caledonia
307.216099611	HB2363.5	Fiji Islands
307.216099612	HB2363.6	Tonga
307.216099613	HB2363.7	American Samoa
307.216099614	HB2363.8	Western Samoa
307.21609962	HB2363.9	French Polynesia
307.216099623	HB2363.65	Cook Islands
307.21609967	HB2362.7	Guam
307.216099681	HB2362.9	Kiribati (Gilbert Islands)
307.21609971	HB2341	Falkland Islands
307.21609973	HB2340.5	Tristan da Cunha
307.21609973	HB2340	St. Helena
307.2160998(1-8)	HB2365	Polar regions
307.21609982	HB2366	Greenland
307.26	HT381	Movement to country
307.3416	HT170-178	Urban renewal
307.341609(4-9)	HT178	Other countries
307.34160973	HT175-177	United States
307.72	HT401-485	Rural groups/Sociology
307.72	GF127	Rural settlements/ Geography
307.7205	HT401-403	Serials
307.7206	HT405-407	Societies/Congresses
307.7207	HT411	Education
307.7209	HT415	History
307.74	HT351	Suburban cities/Towns
307.76	HT201-221	City population (Life, etc.)
307.76	HT119	Modern cities
307.76	HT101-395	Urban sociology/ Groups/City
307.76	GF125	Cities/Urban geography
307.7603	HT108.5	Dictionaries/ Encyclopedias
307.7605	HT101-103	Serials
307.7606	HT105-107	Societies/Congresses
307.7607	HT109	Education/Museums
307.76072	HT110	Research

Dewey	LC	Descriptor
307.7609	HT111-149.5	History
307.7609(4-9)	HT121-149.5	Cities, By place
307.760902	HT115	Medieval cities
307.76091724	HT149.5	Developing countries
307.7609174927	HT147.5	Arab countries
307.76093	HT114	Ancient cities
307.76094	HT131-145	Europe
307.760941	HT133	Great Britain
307.760943	HT137	Germany
307.760944	HT135	France
307.76095	HT147	Asia
307.76096	HT148	Africa
307.760971	HT127	Canada
307.760972	HT127.7	Mexico
307.760972(8/9)	HT128-.5	Central America/West Indies
307.760973	HT123-.5	United States
307.76098	HT129	South America
307.76099(3-6)	HT149	Australia/New Zealand/Oceania
307.764	HT330-334	Metropolitan areas
307.768	HT169.55-.57	New towns
307.774	HQ970-972	Communal living
31(7.4-7.9)	HA251-730	By state
310	HA154-4737	Statistical data
310	HA154-155	Statistics (General)
310	HA	Statistics
310.(5/6)	HA1-15	Serials/Societies
310.1	HA29-31.9	Theory/Method
310.3	HA17	Dictionaries/ Encyclopedias
310.6	HA36-37	Organizations/Bureau
310.7	HA35	Education
310.9	HA19	History
310.92	HA22-23	Biography
314	HA1107	Europe
314-319	HA175-4737	By place
314.1	HA1121-1140	Great Britain/England
314.11	HA1151-1160	Scotland
314.15	HA1170.1-.5	Ireland
314.16	HA1141-1150	Northern Ireland
314.29	HA1161-1170	Wales
314.3	HA1231-1349	Germany
314.36	HA1171-1190	Austria
314.3648	HA1210.5	Liechtenstein
314.37	HA1191-1200	Czechoslovakia
314.38	HA1451-1460	Poland
314.39	HA1201-1210	Hungary
314.4	HA1211-1230	France
314.5	HA1361-1379	Italy
314.6	HA1541-1560	Spain
314.69	HA1571-1580	Portugal
314.698	HA2285	Madeira Islands
314.699	HA2280	Azores
314.7	HA1431-1450	European Russia
314.81	HA1501-1520	Norway
314.85	HA1521-1540	Sweden
314.89	HA1471-1490	Denmark
314.897	HA1450.5	Finland
314.912	HA1491-1500	Iceland
314.92	HA1381-1390	Netherlands
314.93	HA1391-1410	Belgium
314.935	HA1411-1420	Luxembourg
314.94	HA1591-1610	Switzerland
314.95	HA1351-1359	Greece
314.965	HA1620.5	Albania
314.971	HA1631-1635	Yugoslavia

Dewey	LC	Descriptor
314.977	HA1621-1630	Bulgaria
314.98	HA1641-1650	Romania
315	HA4551-4555	Asia
315.1	HA4631-4640	China
315.1249	HA4646-4650	Taiwan
315.125	HA4651-4655	Hong Kong
315.17	HA4630.8	Mongolia
315.19	HA4630.5-.6	Korea/North Korea
315.2	HA4621-4630	Japan
315.26	HA4641-4645	Macao
315.332	HA4564	Yemen
315.353	HA4565	Oman
315.357	HA4566	United Arab Emirates
315.363	HA4567	Qatar
315.365	HA4568	Bahrain
315.367	HA4569	Kuwait
315.38	HA4563	Saudi Arabia
315.4	HA4581-4590	India
315.491	HA4590.5	Pakistan
315.492	HA4590.6	Bangladesh
315.493	HA4570.8	Sri Lanka
315.495	HA2300	Maldive Islands
315.496	HA4570.9	Nepal
315.498	HA4590.3	Bautan
315.5	HA4570.2	Iran
315.61	HA4556.5	Turkey
315.645	HA4557	Cyprus
315.67	HA4570	Iraq
315.691	HA4558	Syria
315.692	HA4559	Lebanon
315.694	HA4560	Israel
315.695	HA4561	Jordan
315.81	HA4570.6	Afghanistan
315.91	HA4570.7	Burma
315.93	HA4600.55	Thailand
315.94	HA4600.4	Laos
315.95	HA4600.6	Malaysia
315.96	HA4600.3	Cambodia
315.97	HA4600.5	Vietnam
315.98	HA4601-4610	Indonesia
315.99	HA4611-4620	Philippine Islands
316.11	HA4684	Tunisia
316.12	HA4685	Libya
316.2	HA4686	Egypt
316.24	HA4687	Sudan
316.3	HA4689	Ethiopia
316.4	HA4682	Morocco
316.48	HA4737	Spanish Sahara
316.49	HA2287	Canary Islands
316.5	HA4683	Algeria
316.61	HA4730	Mauritania
316.623	HA4727	Mali
316.625	HA4728	Burkina Faso
316.626	HA4724	Niger
316.63	HA4729	Senegal
316.64	HA4733	Sierra Leone
316.651	HA4734	Gambia
316.652	HA4726	Guinea-Bissau
316.657	HA4736	Guinea-Bissau
316.658	HA2289	Cape Verde Islands
316.662	HA4735	Liberia
316.668	HA4725	Ivory Coast
316.67	HA4732	Ghana
316.681	HA4723	Togo
316.683	HA4722	Benin (Dahomey)
316.69	HA4731	Nigeria
316.711	HA4719	Cameroon
316.715	HA4713	Sao Tome/Principe
316.718	HA4712	Equatorial Guinea
316.72	HA4714	French Equatorial Africa
316.721	HA4715	Gabon
316.724	HA4716	Congo
316.73	HA4710	Angola
316.741	HA4717	Central African Republic
316.743	HA4718	Chad
316.751	HA4711	Zaire
316.7571	HA4695	Rwanda
316.7572	HA4696	Burundi
316.761	HA4694	Uganda
316.762	HA4693	Kenya
316.771	HA4691	Djibouti
316.773	HA4690	Somalia
316.78	HA4697	Tanzania
316.79	HA4698	Mozambique
316.8	HA4701	South Africa
316.881	HA4708	Namibia
316.883	HA4706	Botswana
316.885	HA4704	Lesotho
316.887	HA4705	Swaziland
316.89	HA4702	Zimbabwe/Zambia/ Malawi
316.894	HA4703	Zambia
316.897	HA4707	Malawi
316.91	HA4699	Madagascar
316.94	HA2303	Comoro Islands
316.96	HA2301	Seychelles
316.981	HA2307	Reunion
316.982	HA2305	Mauritius
316.99	HA2309	Kerguelen Islands
317.1	HA741-750	Canada
317.2	HA761-770	Mexico
317.281	HA811-820	Guatemala
317.282	HA791-800	Belize
317.283	HA821-830	Honduras
317.284	HA841-850	El Salvador
317.285	HA831-840	Nicaragua
317.286	HA801-810	Costa Rica
317.287	HA851-854	Panama
317.2875	HA855	Panama Canal Zone
317.2886	HA917	Netherlands Antilles
317.2981	HA865	Barbados
317.291	HA871-880	Cuba
317.292	HA891-900	Jamaica
317.293	HA886-890	Dominican Republic
317.294	HA881-885	Haiti
317.295	HA901-910	Puerto Rico
317.296	HA861	Bahamas
317.297	HA866	Leeward Islands
317.29722	HA911-915	Virgin Islands of the U.S.
317.2976	HA918.7	Guadeloupe
317.2982	HA918.9	Martinique
317.2983	HA867	Trinidad/Tobago
317.2984	HA868	Windward Islands
317.299	HA921-930	Bermuda
317.3	HA201-730	United States
318.1	HA971-990	Brazil
318.2	HA941-960	Argentina
318.3	HA991-1010	Chile
318.4	HA961-970	Bolivia
318.5	HA1051-1070	Peru
318.61	HA1011-1020	Colombia
318.66	HA1021-1030	Ecuador
318.7	HA1091-1100	Venezuela
318.81	HA1033	Guyana

Dewey	LC	Descriptor
318.82	HA1037	French Guiana
318.83	HA1035	Suriname
318.92	HA1041-1050	Paraguay
318.95	HA1071-1090	Uruguay
319.3	HA3171-3190	New Zealand
319.4	HA3001-3010	Australia
319.53	HA4013	Papua New Guinea
319.593	HA4014	Solomon Islands
319.595	HA4015.5	Vanuatu
319.597	HA4015	New Caledonia
319.611	HA4016	Fiji Islands
319.612	HA4017	Tonga
319.613	HA4018.5	American Samoa
319.614	HA4018.7	Western Samoa
319.623	HA4017.5	Cook Islands
319.67	HA4012	Guam
319.681	HA4016.7	Kiribati/Tuvalu (Gilbert and Ellice Islands)
319.711	HA2295	Falkland Islands
319.73	HA2291	St. Helena
319.82	HA740	Greenland
319.89	HA4020-.5	Polar regions
320	JA	Political science
320	JA83	Modern
320.011	JA71-80	Theory
320.011	JC	Political theory
320.03	JA61-64	Dictionaries/Encyclopedias
320.05	JA50-59	Yearbooks
320.05	JA1-26	Serials
320.06	JA27-34	Societies
320.06	JA35-.5	Congresses
320.07	JA86-89	Education
320.09	JA81-84	History
320.09(3-9)	JA84	By place
320.090(1-2)	JA82	Ancient/Medieval
320.092	JA92-98	Biography of writers
320.1	K3169	The state
320.1	JC325-341	Nature/Concept of the state
320.1	JC11-323	The state
320.1-323	JC501-628	Purpose/Relations of the state
320.54	JC311-323	Nationalism
320.8	JF751-786	Federal-State relations
320.932	JC66	Egypt
320.933	JC67	Hebrews
320.935	JC61	Assyro-Babylonian
320.9376	JC81-90	Rome
320.938	JC71-79	Greece
320.9495	JC91-95	Byzantine
321	K3285	Forms of government
321	JC348-497	Forms of the state
321	JC134-273	Treatises, By date
321	JC131-273	Treatises on the modern state
321.(4/8)	JC421-458	Democracy
321.023	JF751-786	Federal-State relations
321.03	JC359	Empire
321.04	JC361-363	The world state
321.06	JC352	City/State
321.07	HX806-810.5	Utopias/Ideal states
321.09	JC490-497	Change of form
321.1	JC31-46	Village
321.1	JC26-29	Tribal
321.1	JC20-46	The primitive state
321.1(2/4)	JC51-95	Ancient state
321.14	JC101-126	Medieval state
321.3	JC109-113	Feudal
321.5	JC411-417	Aristocracy
321.5	JC419	Oligarchy
321.6	JC374-393	Monarchy
321.8042	JF285	Election/Succession
321.92	JC474	Communistic state
321.94	JC481	Totalitarianism/Fascism
321.94	JC478	Corporate state
322.1	K3280-3282	Church and state
322.1	JC510-514	Church and state
322.2	HD8031	Labor in politics
323-324	JF800-1191	Political rights/Guaranties
323.(01)	JC571-609	Individual/Natural rights
323.0941	JN901-1097	Civil/Political rights
323.0973	JK1711-2246	Politics/Civil rights
323.34	HQ1236-.5	Women and the state/Rights
323.445	PN4735-4748	Relation to the state
323.445	Z657-659	Freedom of the press
323.6	JF800-823	Citizenship
323.60973	JK1751-1788	Citizenship
323.6230973	JK1800-1836	Naturalization
324.2	JF2011-2112	Political parties
324.241	JN1111-1129	Political parties
324.273	JK2251-2391	Political parties
324.273(2-8)	JK2301-2391	PArticular parties
324.60973	JK1846-1936	Suffrage
324.60973	JK1951-2225	Electoral/Ballot systems
324.62	JF825-943	Suffrage
324.63	JF1001-1043	Electoral systems/Voting
324.63	JF1051-1077	Representation
324.65	JF1091-1177	The ballot
324.66	JF1081-1085	Corruption/Electoral fraud
324.973	JS393-399	Suffrage/Elections
325	JV	Colonization/Migration
325.(1-2)	JV6001-9500	Immigration/Emigration
325.(1-2)05	JV6001-6006	Serials
325.(1-2)09	JV6021-6033	History
325.(4-9)	JV201-246	By area
325.(4-9)	JV6135-6149	To specific areas
325.(4-9)	JV6141-6149	Europe/Asia/Africa/Oceania
325.(41/241)	JV7600-7729	Great Britain
325.(411/2411)	JV7700-7709	Scotland
325.(415/2415)	JV7710-7719	Ireland
325.(43/243)	JV8000-8099	Germany
325.(436/2436)	JV7800-7899	Austria/Hungary
325.(438/2438)	JV8195	Poland
325.(44/244)	JV7900-7999	France
325.(45/245)	JV8130-8139	Italy
325.(46/246)	JV8250-8259	Spain
325.(469/2469)	JV8260-8269	Portugal
325.(47/247)	JV8180-8189	European Russia
325.(481/2481)	JV8210-8219	Norway
325.(485/2485)	JV8220-8229	Sweden
325.(489/2489)	JV8200-8209	Denmark
325.(4897/24897)	JV8193	Finland
325.(492/2492)	JV8150-8159	Netherlands
325.(493/2493)	JV8160-8169	Belgium
325.(4935/24935)	JV8175	Luxembourg
325.(494/2494)	JV8280-8289	Switzerland
325.(495/2495)	JV8110-8119	Greece
325.(496/2496)	JV8300-8339	Balkan states
325.(5/25)	JV8490-8749	Asia
325.(51/251)	JV8700-8709	China
325.(51249/251249)	JV8710-8719	Taiwan
325.(52/252)	JV8720-8729	Japan
325.(53/253)	JV8760	Arab countries
325.(54/254)	JV8500-8509	India

Dewey	LC	Descriptor
325.(56/256)	JV8739-8749	Near East
325.(6/26)	JV8790-9025	Africa
325.(72/271)	JV7200-7299	Canada
325.(72/272)	JV7400-7409	Mexico
325.(7281/27281)	JV7416	Guatemala
325.(7282/27282)	JV7347	British Honduras
325.(7283/27283)	JV7419	Honduras
325.(7284/27284)	JV7423	El Salvador
325.(7285/27285)	JV7426	Nicaragua
325.(7286/27286)	JV7413	Costa Rica
325.(7287/27287)	JV7429	Panama
325.(72875/272875)	JV7432	Panama Canal Zone
325.(729/2729)	JV7353-7359	Danish/Dutch/French Caribbean
325.(729/2729)	JV7320-7339	British West Indies
325.(7291/27291)	JV7370-7379	Cuba
325.(7293/27293)	JV7395	Dominican Republic
325.(7294/27294)	JV7393	Haiti
325.(7295/27295)	JV7380-7389	Puerto Rico
325.(729722/2729722)	JV7397	U.S. Virgin Islands
325.(73/273)	JV6403-7127	U.S. (Immigration/ Emigration)
325.(8/728)	JV6139	South/Central America
325.(81/281)	JV7460-7469	Brazil
325.(82/282)	JV7440-7449	Argentina
325.(83/283)	JV7470-7479	Chile
325.(84/284)	JV7450-7459	Bolivia
325.(85/285)	JV7510-7519	Peru
325.(861/2861)	JV7480-7489	Colombia
325.(866/2866)	JV7490-7499	Ecuador
325.(87/287)	JV7530-7539	Venezuela
325.(881/2881)	JV7346	British Guiana
325.(892/2892)	JV7500-7509	Paraguay
325.(895/2895)	JV7520-7529	Uruguay
325.(93/293)	JV9260-9269	New Zealand
325.(94/294)	JV9100-9259	Australia
325.1	JV6201-6348	Immigration
325.2	JV6061-6149	Emigration
325.2090(1-4)	JV6061-6081	History, By date
325.20901	JV6065-6066	Ancient
325.20902	JV6068-6069	Medieval
325.209032	JV6071-6072	17th century
325.20904	JV6080-6081	20th century
325.273	JV6431-6445	Emigration
325.3	JV351-381	Types of colonies
325.3	JV1-5399	Colonies and colonization
325.3(3-9)	JV500-5399	Colonizing nations
325.3(3-9)	JV261-291	Colonists by nationality/Race
325.301	JV51	Philosophy/Theory
325.305	JV1-9	Serials
325.306	JV10-21	Societies/Congresses
325.307	JV55-59	Education
325.309033	JV6074-6075	18th century
325.309034	JV6077-6078	19th century
325.31	JV412-485	Administration/ Organization
325.341	JV1000-1099	Great Britain
325.343	JV2000-2099	Germany
325.344	JV1800-1899	France
325.345	JV2200-2299	Italy
325.346(9)	JV4000-4299	Spain/Portugal
325.347	JV3000-3099	Russia
325.348(9)	JV3300-3399	Scandinavia/Denmark
325.349(2-3)	JV2500-2899	Netherlands/Belgium
325.352	JV5200-5299	Japan
325.373	JV500-599	United States
325.394	JV5300-5399	Australia
325.7	JV6137	To North America
325.7(4-9)	JV6905-7127	By state
325.73	JV6450-6479	Immigration
325.7306	JV6403-6405	Societies/Congresses
325.73089	JV6610-6895	By race/Nationality
325.9(5-6)/325.29(5-6)	JV9290-9500	Oceania
326	HT941-950	Law and slavery
326	HT1025-1037	Abolition of slavery
327	JX1305-1598	Foreign relations
327	JX1315-1395	Modern
327	JX1391-1395	20th century
327.(3-9)	JX1404-1598	By place
327.(4-9)	JX1705-1894	Diplomacy, By place
327.09	JX1305-1395	History
327.090(1-4)	JX1305-1395	By date
327.2	CD1-511	Diplomatics
327.2	JX1625-1896	Diplomacy/Diplomatic service
327.201	CD46	Philosophy/Theory
327.203	CD40	Dictionaries/ Encyclopedias
327.205	CD1-15	Serials
327.206	CD20-29	Societies/Congresses
327.209	CD47	History
327.209	JX1635-1662	History, By date
327.2090(1-5)	CD50-69	General diplomatics, By date
327.411	JX1787-1788	Scotland
327.411	JX1545	Scotland
327.415	JX1789-1790	Ireland
327.415	JX1546	Ireland
327.42	JX1783-1784	England
327.42	JX1543	England
327.43	JX1549	Germany
327.43	JX1795-1796	Germany
327.436	JX1791-1792	Austria
327.436	JX1547	Austria
327.437	JX1547.3	Czechoslovakia
327.437	JX1792.5	Czechoslovakia
327.438	JX1808.7	Poland
327.438	JX1555.7	Poland
327.439	JX1798.5	Hungary
327.439	JX1550.5	Hungary
327.44	JX1548	France
327.44	JX1793-1794	France
327.45	JX1799-1800	Italy
327.45	JX1551	Italy
327.46	JX1819-1820	Spain
327.469	JX1562	Portugal
327.469	JX1821-1822	Portugal
327.47	JX1555	European Russia
327.47	JX1807-1808	European Russia
327.481	JX1559	Norway
327.481	JX1815-1816	Norway
327.485	JX1817-1818	Sweden
327.485	JX1560	Sweden
327.489	JX1811-1812	Denmark
327.489	JX1557	Denmark
327.4897	JX1808.3	Finland
327.4897	JX1555.3	Finland
327.4912	JX1813-1814	Iceland
327.4912	JX1558	Iceland
327.492	JX1805-1806	Netherlands
327.492	JX1554	Netherlands/Holland
327.493	JX1803-1804	Belgium
327.493	JX1553	Belgium

Dewey	LC	Descriptor
327.4935	JX1554.5	Luxembourg
327.4935	JX1806.5	Luxembourg
327.494	JX1823-1824	Switzerland
327.494	JX1563	Switzerland
327.495	JX1550	Greece
327.495	JX1797-1798	Greece
327.4965	JX1826.5	Albania
327.497	JX1828.5	Yugoslavia
327.497	JX1564.5	Yugoslavia
327.4977	JX1827-1828	Bulgaria
327.4977	JX1564	Bulgaria
327.498	JX1831-1832	Romania
327.498	JX1566	Romania
327.51	JX1570	China
327.51	JX1837-1838	China
327.51249	JX1838.5	Taiwan
327.51249	JX1579.7	Taiwan
327.519	JX1577.5	Korea
327.52	JX1851-1852	Japan
327.52	JX1577	Japan
327.54	JX1839-1840	India
327.54	JX1571	India
327.55	JX1853-1854	Iran
327.55	JX1578	Iran
327.561	JX1568	Turkey
327.561	JX1825-1826	Turkey
327.59(3-7)	JX1841-1844	Indochina
327.59(3-6)	JX1572-1573	Indochina
327.593	JX1579.5	Thailand
327.598	JX1574	Indonesia
327.598	JX1845-1848	Indonesia
327.599	JX1576	Philippines
327.599	JX1849-1850	Philippines
327.62	JX1583	Egypt
327.62	JX1863-1864	Egypt
327.71	JX1515	Canada
327.71	JX1729-1730	Canada
327.72	JX1731-1732	Mexico
327.72	JX1516	Mexico
327.7281	JX1739	Guatemala
327.7281	JX1519	Guatemala
327.7282	JX1517.5	Belize
327.7283	JX1520	Honduras
327.7284	JX1744	El Salvador
327.7284	JX1523	El Salvador
327.7285	JX1741	Nicaragua
327.7285	JX1521	Nicaragua
327.7286	JX1737-1738	Costa Rica
327.7286	JX1518	Costa Rica
327.7287	JX1742-1743	Panama
327.7287	JX1522	Panama
327.72875	JX1522.5	Panama Canal Zone
327.72875	JX1743.5	Panama Canal Zone
327.7282	JX1735-1736	Belize/British Honduras
327.7291	JX1749-1750	Cuba
327.7291	JX1525	Cuba
327.7292	JX1753	Jamaica
327.7292	JX1527	Jamaica
327.7293	JX1752	Dominican Republic
327.7293	JX1526.5	Dominican Republic
327.7294	JX1751	Haiti
327.7294	JX1526	Haiti
327.7295	JX1528	Puerto Rico
327.7295	JX1755-1756	Puerto Rico
327.7296	JX1524.5	Bahamas
327.729722	JX1528.5	U.S. Virgin Islands
327.729722	JX1756.5	U.S. Virgin Islands

Dewey	LC	Descriptor
327.73	JX1405-1428	United States
327.73	JX1705-1725	United States
327.81	JX1533	Brazil
327.81	JX1763-1764	Brazil
327.82	JX1531	Argentina
327.82	JX1759-1760	Argentina
327.83	JX1534	Chile
327.84	JX1761-1762	Bolivia
327.84	JX1532	Bolivia
327.85	JX1775-1776	Peru
327.85	JX1539	Peru
327.861	JX1535	Colombia
327.861	JX1767-1768	Colombia
327.866	JX1536	Ecuador
327.866	JX1769-1770	Ecuador
327.87	JX1779-1780	Venezuela
327.87	JX1541	Venezuela
327.881	JX1537.1	Guyana
327.881	JX1772	Guyana
327.882	JX1537.5	French Guiana
327.882	JX1772.7	French Guiana
327.883	JX1772.5	Suriname
327.883	JX1537.3	Suriname
327.892	JX1773-1774	Paraguay
327.892	JX1538	Paraguay
327.895	JX1540	Uruguay
327.895	JX1777-1778	Uruguay
327.9(3-4)	JX1875-1876	New Zealand/Australia
327.9(3-4)	JX1589-1597	Australia/New Zealand
327.9(5-6)	JX1891-1894	Oceania
327.9(5-6)	JX1598	Oceania
328	JF201-723	Organs/Functions of government
328	J	Official documents/Gazettes
328	JF401-637	Legislation/Lawmaking
328.(4-9)	J100-981	Documents of other countries
328.(4-9)04	J10-981	Official documents
328.09	JF411-416	History
328.2	JF488-495	Initiative/Referendum
328.2	JF488-497	Direct legislation
328.2(4-9)	JF493-495	Direct legislation, By place
328.3	JF501-540.5	Legislative bodies
328.31	JF541-567	Upper house
328.32	JF601-637	Lower house
328.34	JF441-483	Legislative powers
328.37	JF424-427	Lawmaking
328.4	J301-462	Europe
328.41	J301-309	Great Britain
328.41	JN500-695	Parliament
328.411	KDC70-90	Legislation
328.416	KDE42-50	Legislation
328.417	KDK38-51	Legislation
328.42	KD125-180	Legislation
328.43	J351-383	Germany
328.436	J310-340	Austria/Hungary
328.44	J341-345	France
328.45	J388-389	Italy
328.46(9)	J409-411	Spain/Portugal
328.47	J397-400	European Russia
328.48	J402-406	Scandinavia
328.492	J391-395	Low Countries/Netherlands
328.494	J415-442	Switzerland
328.495	J385	Greece
328.496	J450-459	Balkans
328.4965	J450	Albania
328.497	J459	Yugoslavia

Dewey	LC	Descriptor
328.4977	J451-452	Bulgaria
328.5	J671-681	Far East
328.5	J500-693	Asia
328.51	J671	China
328.51249	J672	Taiwan
328.5125	J613	Hong Kong
328.519	J677-.5	Korea
328.52	J674	Japan
328.5332	J693.Y4	Yemen
328.5357	J693.U54	United Arab Emirates
328.5363	J693.Q37	Qatar
328.538	J693.S3	Saudi Arabia
328.54	J500-593	India
328.5491	J577	Pakistan
328.5492	J579	Bangladesh
328.5493	J611	Sri Lanka
328.5496	J625	Nepal
328.55	J688-689	Iran
328.561	J691	Turkey
328.5645	J612	Cyprus
328.567	J693.I6	Iraq
328.5691	J693.S8	Syria
328.5692	J693.L5	Lebanon
328.5694	J693.P2	Palestine/Israel
328.57	J655	Asian Russia
328.581	J685	Afghanistan
328.593	J681	Thailand
328.594	J643	Laos
328.5951	J615-618	Malaysia
328.596	J642	Cambodia
328.5965	J693.J6	Jordan
328.597	J644	Vietnam
328.598	J631	Indonesia
328.599	J661-663	Philippines
328.6	J700-881	Africa
328.611	J765	Tunisia
328.612	J826	Libya
328.62	J866	Egypt
328.624	J868	Sudan
328.63	J861	Ethiopia
328.64	J881	Morocco
328.642	J857	Tangier
328.65	J763	Algeria
328.661	J775	Mauritania
328.6623	J774	Mali
328.6625	J780	Burkina Faso
328.6626	J777	Niger
328.663	J779	Senegal
328.664	J747	Sierra Leone
328.6652	J771	Guinea-Bissau
328.6652	J850	Equitorial Guinea
328.6658	J844	Cape Verde Islands
328.6662	J875	Liberia
328.6668	J773	Ivory Coast
328.667	J741.G3	Ghana/Gold Coast
328.6681	J809	Togo
328.6683	J768	Benin (Dahomey)
328.669	J745-.7	Nigeria
328.6711	J805	Cameroon
328.6715	J851	Sao Tome/Principe
328.6721	J787	Gabon
328.6724	J786	Congo
328.673	J841	Angola
328.6741	J784	Central African Republic
328.6743	J785	Chad
328.6751	J831	Zaire
328.6757	J814-816	Ruanda-Urundi

Dewey	LC	Descriptor
328.6761	J732	Uganda
328.6762	J731	Kenya
328.6773	J825	Somalia
328.678	J801	Tanzania
328.6781	J733	Zanzibar
328.679	J849	Mozambique
328.68	J705-719	South Africa
328.6881	J812	Namibia
328.6883	J723	Botswana
328.6885	J722	Lesotho
328.6887	J720	Swaziland
328.6891	J725	Zimbabwe/Zambia/ Malawi
328.69	J758-759	Indian Ocean Islands
328.7(4-7)07	JK2484-2508	The legislature
328.7(4-9)	JK2430-2441	Legislation
328.7(4-9)04	J86-87	State documents
328.71	J100-125	Canada
328.71	JL131-179	The legislative
328.71	KE78-125	Legislation
328.72	J170-172	Mexico
328.728	J175-185	Central America
328.729	J166-168	Other Caribbean Islands
328.7291	J162-163	Cuba
328.7295	J164-165	Puerto Rico
328.73	J10	Continental Congress
328.73	JK1001-1447	Congress/Legislative branch
328.7301	J11-15	Congress (Annuals/ Record/Etc.)
328.7304	J10-87	United States, Official docs.
328.73071	JK1151-1276	Senate
328.73072	JK1304-1447	House of Representatives
328.73074	JK1166-1197	Constitutional powers
328.73074	JK1326-1391	Constitutional powers
328.7309	J21-34	Congress 1-14th
328.7309	J35-75	15th and later
328.7309	JK1021-1059	History
328.7507	JK9695-9704	Legislative
328.75071	JK9705-9710	Senate
328.75072	JK9711-9716	House of Representatives
328.8	J200-259	South America
328.9(5-6)	J951-981	Oceania
328.93	J941	New Zealand
328.94	J903-936	Australia
328.97	J753-755	Atlantic Ocean Islands
330	HB	Economics/Economic theory
330	HB71-74	Economics (General)
330.0(5/6)	HB1-9	Serials/Societies
330.0(5/6)	HC10-14	Serials/Societies
330.007	HJ203-209	Education
330.01	HB131-145	Methodology
330.025	HB63	Directories
330.03	HB61	Dictionaries/ Encyclopedias
330.03	HC15	Dictionaries/ Encyclopedias
330.06	HB21	Congresses
330.07	HC28	Education
330.09	HB75-130	History
330.1	HC26	Theory/Method
330.122	HB501	Capital/Capitalism
330.156	HB846-.8	Welfare theory
330.1543	HB135-145	Mathematical economics
330.16	HB251	Wealth
330.17	HB701-715	Property

Dewey	LC	Descriptor
330.9	HD	Economic history/Conditions
330.9	HC	Economic history/Conditions
330.9	HC54-60	20th century
330.9(1-9)	HC94-1085	By place
330.900112	HB3730	Economic forecasting
330.902	HC41-42	Middle Ages
330.903	HC51-53	16th-19th centuries
330.909	HC31-60	History
330.9092	HC29	Biography
330.917241	HC245-246	Commonwealth
330.93	HC31-39	Ancient
330.94	HC240-407	Europe
330.941	HC251-257	Great Britain
330.9417	HC258	Ireland
330.943	HC280-290	Germany
330.9436	HC261-270	Austria
330.9437	HC270.2-.295	Czechoslovakia
330.9438	HC340.3	Poland
330.944	HC271-280	France
330.945	HC301-310	Italy
330.946	HC381-390	Spain
330.9469	HC391-394	Portugal
330.947	HC331-340	European Russia
330.948	HC341-380	Scandinavia
330.9481	HC361-370	Norway
330.9485	HC371-380	Sweden
330.9489	HC351-360	Denmark
330.9492	HC321-329	Netherlands
330.9493	HC311-320	Belgium
330.94935	HC330	Luxembourg
330.9494	HC395-400	Switzerland
330.9495	HC291-300	Greece
330.9496	HC401-407	Balkans
330.94965	HC402	Albania
330.9497	HC407	Yugoslavia
330.94977	HC403	Bulgaria
330.9498	HC405	Romania
330.95	HC411-495	Asia
330.951	HC426-430	China
330.951249	HC430.5	Taiwan
330.9519	HC466-470	Korea
330.952	HC461-465	Japan
330.95332	HC415.34	Yemen
330.95353	HC415.35	Oman
330.95357	HC415.36	United Arab Emirates
330.95363	HC415.37	Qatar
330.95365	HC415.38	Bahrain
330.95367	HC415.39	Kuwait
330.9538	HC415.33	Saudi Arabia
330.954	HC431-440	India
330.95491	HC440.5	Pakistan
330.95492	HC440.8	Bangladesh
330.95493	HC424	Sri Lanka
330.95496	HC425	Nepal
330.955	HC471-480	Iran
330.9561	HC491-495	Turkey
330.9567	HC415.4	Iraq
330.95691	HC415.23	Syria
330.95692	HC415.24	Lebanon
330.95694	HC415.25	Israel/Palestine
330.95695	HC415.26	Jordan
330.9581	HC416-420	Afghanistan
330.9591	HC422	Burma
330.9593	HC445	Thailand
330.9594	HC443	Laos
330.9596	HC442	Cambodia
330.9597	HC444	Vietnam
330.9598	HC446-450	Indonesia
330.9599	HC451-460	Philippine Islands
330.96	HC800-1085	Africa
330.9611	HC820	Tunisia
330.9612	HC825	Libya
330.962	HC830	Egypt
330.9624	HC835	Sudan
330.963	HC845	Ethiopia
330.964	HC810	Morocco
330.965	HC815	Algeria
330.96626	HC1020	Niger
330.96652	HC1030	Guinea-Bissau
330.96668	HC1025	Ivory Coast
330.9669	HC1055	Nigeria
330.96711	HC995	Cameroon
330.96721	HC975	Gabon
330.96724	HC980	Congo
330.9673	HC950	Angola
330.96743	HC990	Chad
330.96751	HC955	Zaire
330.967571	HC875	Rwanda
330.967572	HC880	Burundi
330.96761	HC870	Uganda
330.96762	HC865	Kenya
330.96773	HC850	Somalia
330.9678	HC885	Tanzania
330.9679	HC890	Mozambique
330.968	HC905	South Africa
330.96887	HC925	Swaziland
330.9689	HC910	Zimbabwe (Southern Rhodesia)
330.96894	HC915	Zambia
330.9691	HC895	Madagascar
330.97(4-9)	HC107-110	By state
330.971	HC111-120	Canada
330.972	HC131-140	Mexico
330.9728	HC141-148	Central America
330.9729	HC151-158	West Indies
330.973	HC106.2-.8	United States
330.98	HC161-239	South America
330.981	HC186-189	Brazil
330.982	HC171-180	Argentina
330.983	HC191-195	Chile
330.984	HC181-185	Bolivia
330.985	HC226-230	Peru
330.9861	HC196-200	Colombia
330.9866	HC201-204	Ecuador
330.987	HC236-239	Venezuela
330.988	HC205-220	Guyanas
330.988(1-8)	HC721-740	Arctic regions
330.9892	HC221-225	Paraguay
330.9895	HC231-235	Uruguay
330.99(5-6)	HC681-688	Pacific Ocean Islands
330.993	HC661-670	New Zealand
330.994	HC601-610	Australia
330.997	HC592-595	Atlantic Ocean Islands
330.9982	HC110.5	Greenland
331	HD6958.5-6976	Industrial relations
331	HD4801-8943	Labor
331.(3-6)	HD6050-6305	Classes of labor
331.0112	HD5650-5660	Employees in management
331.09(4-9)	HD8045-8943	Labor, By place
331.094	HD8371-8650.5	Europe
331.0941	HD8381-8400	Great Britain
331.0943	HD8441-8460.5	Germany

Dewey	LC	Descriptor
331.0944	HD8421-8440	France
331.0945	HD8471-8490	Italy
331.0946	HD8581-8590	Spain
331.0947	HD8521-8530	European Russia
331.09492	HD8491-8520.5	Low Countries
331.09494	HD8601-8610	Switzerland
331.09495	HD8650.5	Greece
331.095	HD8670.7-8755	Far East
331.0951	HD8731-8740	China
331.0952	HD8721-8730	Japan
331.0954	HD8681-8690	India
331.0955	HD8670.2	Iran
331.0956	HD8651-8669	Middle East
331.09567	HD8670	Iraq
331.095694	HD8660	Israel/Palestine
331.09599	HD8711-8720	Philippine Islands
331.096	HD8771-8837	Africa
331.0971	HD8101-8110	Canada
331.0972	HD8111-8120	Mexico
331.09728	HD8126-8190	Central America
331.09729	HD8191-8250	West Indies
331.0973	HD8051-8085	United States
331.098	HD8251-8370	South America
331.099(3-6)	HD8841-8939.5	Australia/New Zealand/Oceania
331.1021	HD5711-5712	Statistics
331.107	HD5702	Education
331.117	HD4861-4895	Labor systems
331.11732	HD7795-8027	State labor
331.12	HD5701-6000.7	Labor market
331.12042	HD5713-.6	Manpower policy
331.1209(4-9)	HD5721-5851	Labor market, By place
331.12094	HD5764-5811.83	Europe
331.120941	HD5765-5767.5	Great Britain
331.120943	HD5777-5780.5	Germany
331.120944	HD5773-5776	France
331.120945	HD5782-5785	Italy
331.120946	HD5805-5808	Spain
331.120947	HD5794-5797	European Russia
331.1209492	HD5785.5-5793.5	Low Countries
331.1209494	HD5810	Switzerland
331.1209495	HD5811.83	Greece
331.12095	HD5812.7-5833	Far East
331.120951	HD5830	China
331.120952	HD5827	Japan
331.120954	HD5817-5820	India
331.120955	HD5812.56	Iran
331.120956	HD5811.93-5812.53	Middle East
331.1209567	HD5812.55	Iraq
331.12095694	HD5812.2	Israel/Palestine
331.1209599	HD5825	Philippine Islands
331.12096	HD5837-5849.3	Africa
331.120971	HD5727-5730	Canada
331.120972	HD5731	Mexico
331.1209728	HD5733.5-5739	Central America
331.1209729	HD5740.5-5745.9	West Indies
331.120973	HD5723-5726	United States
331.12098	HD5747-5763	South America
331.12099(3-6)	HD5850-.68	Australia/New Zealand/Oceania
331.127	HD5716-5717	Labor mobility
331.128	HD5860-6000.7	Labor/Employment agencies
331.12809(4-9)	HD5871-6000.7	Employment agencies, By place
331.137	HD5707.5-5710.2	Unemployment
331.21	HD6977-7080	Wages/Cost of living
331.21	HD4925	Family allowance
331.21	HD4906-5100.7	Wages
331.2101	HD4909-4912	Theory
331.21021	HD4915-4916	Statistics
331.216	HD4926-4928	Remuneration
331.2164	HD2970-3110	Profit sharing
331.2166	HD4964-4965	Professional salary/Fee
331.216409(4-9)	HD2981-3110.9	Profit sharing, By place
331.23	HD4917-4924	Minimum wage
331.2309(4-9)	HD4918-4924	Minimum wage, By place
331.252	HD7105-7110	Old age pensions
331.257	HD5106-5267	Hours
331.2572	HD5109	Flexible
331.2572	HD5110	Part time/Job sharing
331.2576	HD5260-5267	Vacations
331.25762	HD5115.5-.6	Sick leave
331.25763	HD5255-5257	Leave of absence
331.2592	HD5715-.5	Occupational training
331.2813	HD4938-4946	State labor wages
331.281331714	HD4965.2	Businessmen's executive salary
331.29(4-9)	HD4971-5100.7	Wages, By place
331.291724	HD4967	Wages, Developing countries
331.294	HD5014-5061.83	Europe
331.2941	HD5015-5017.5	Great Britain
331.2943	HD5027-5030.5	Germany
331.2944	HD5023-5026	France
331.2945	HD5032-5035	Italy
331.2946	HD5055-5058	Spain
331.29469	HD5059	Portugal
331.2947	HD5044-5047	European Russia
331.29492	HD5035.5-5043.5	Low Countries
331.29495	HD5061.83	Greece
331.295	HD5062.7-5083	Far East
331.2951	HD5080	China
331.2952	HD5077	Japan
331.2954	HD5067-5070	India
331.2955	HD5062.56	Iran
331.2956	HD5061.93-5062.53	Middle East
331.29567	HD5062.55	Iraq
331.295694	HD5062.2	Israel/Palestine
331.29599	HD5075	Philippine Islands
331.296	HD5088.3-5099.3	Africa
331.2971	HD4977-4980	Canada
331.2972	HD4981	Mexico
331.29728	HD4983.5-4989	Central America
331.29729	HD4990-4995.9	West Indies
331.2973	HD4973-4976	United States
331.298	HD4996-5013	South America
331.299(3-6)	HD5100-.68	Australia/New Zealand/Oceania
331.3(1-47)	HD6229-6276	Child/Youth labor
331.34	HD6276.5-6278	College students
331.39(4-8)	HD6279-6283	Middle East
331.4	HD6050-6220.7	Women
331.409(4-9)	HD6091-6220.7	Women's labor, By place
331.59	HD7255-7256	Disabled rehabilitation
331.6	HD6304-6305	Minorities
331.6396073	E185.8	Occupations
331.7	HB2581-2787	Professions/Occupations
331.7	HD9000-9999	Special industries and trades
331.7(1-9)	HD8039	Labor, By industry or trade
331.7009(4-9)	HB2591-2787	Professions, By place
331.7009411	HB2677-2678	Scotland
331.7009416	HB2678.5	Northern Ireland
331.7009417	HB2679-2680	Irish Republic

Dewey	LC	Descriptor	Dewey	LC	Descriptor
331.700942(9)	HB2675-2676	England/Wales	331.7009611	HB2751.5	Tunisia
331.700943	HB2685-2686.5	Germany	331.7009612	HB2751.6	Libya
331.7009436	HB2681-2682	Austria	331.700962	HB2751.7	Egypt
331.700943648	HB2682.9	Liechtenstein	331.7009624	HB2751.8	Sudan
331.7009437	HB2682.3	Czechoslovakia	331.700963	HB2752	Ethiopia
331.7009438	HB2698.7	Poland	331.700964	HB2751.3	Morocco
331.7009439	HB2682.5	Hungary	331.7009648	HB2757.4	Spanish Sahara
331.700944	HB2683-2684	France	331.7009649	HB2759	Canary Islands
331.700944949	HB2684.5	Monaco	331.700965	HB2751.4	Algeria
331.700945	HB2689-2690	Italy	331.7009661	HB2756.6	Mauritania
331.700946	HB2709-2710	Spain	331.70096623	HB2756.3	Mali
331.7009469	HB2711-2712	Portugal	331.70096625	HB2756.4	Burkina Faso
331.70094698	HB2758.5	Madeira Islands	331.70096626	HB2755.9	Niger
331.70094699	HB2757.5	Azores	331.7009663	HB2756.5	Senegal
331.700947	HB2697-2698	European Russia	331.7009664	HB2756.9	Sierra Leone
331.7009481	HB2705-2706	Norway	331.70096651	HB2757	Gambia
331.7009485	HB2707-2708	Sweden	331.70096652	HB2756.2	Guinea-Bissau
331.7009489	HB2701-2702	Denmark	331.70096657	HB2757.3	Guinea-Bissau
331.70094897	HB2698.3	Finland	331.70096658	HB2759.5	Cape Verde Islands
331.70094912	HB2703-2704	Iceland	331.70096662	HB2757.2	Liberia
331.7009492	HB2695-2696	Netherlands	331.70096668	HB2756	Ivory Coast
331.7009493	HB2693-2694	Belgium	331.7009667	HB2756.8	Ghana
331.70094935	HB2696.5	Luxembourg	331.70096681	HB2755.8	Togo
331.7009494	HB2713-2714	Switzerland	331.70096683	HB2755.7	Benin (Dahomey)
331.7009495	HB2722.5	Greece	331.7009669	HB2756.7	Nigeria
331.70094965	HB2716.5	Albania	331.70096711	HB2755.4	Cameroon
331.7009497	HB2718.5	Yugoslavia	331.70096715	HB2754.7	Sao Tome/Principe
331.70094977	HB2717-2718	Bulgaria	331.70096718	HB2754.6	Equatorial Guinea
331.7009498	HB2721-2722	Romania	331.7009672	HB2754.8	French Equatorial Africa
331.700951	HB2744	China	331.70096721	HB2754.9	Gabon
331.700951249	HB2746	Taiwan	331.70096724	HB2755	Congo
331.70095125	HB2747	Hong Kong	331.7009673	HB2754.4	Angola
331.70095126	HB2745	Macao	331.70096741	HB2755.2	Central African Republic
331.7009517	HB2742.8	Mongolia	331.70096743	HB2755.3	Chad
331.7009519	HB2742.5-.6	Korea/North Korea	331.70096751	HB2754.5	Zaire
331.700952	HB2741-2742	Japan	331.700967571	HB2752.7	Rwanda
331.70095332	HB2724.9-2725	Yemen	331.700967572	HB2752.8	Burundi
331.70095353	HB2725.3	Oman	331.70096761	HB2752.6	Uganda
331.70095357	HB2725.5	United Arab Emirates	331.70096762	HB2752.5	Kenya
331.70095363	HB2725.7	Qatar	331.70096771	HB2752.3	Djibouti
331.70095365	HB2725.9	Bahrain	331.70096773	HB2752.2	Somalia
331.70095367	HB2726	Kuwait	331.7009678	HB2752.9	Tanzania
331.7009538	HB2724.7	Saudi Arabia	331.7009679	HB2753	Mozambique
331.700954	HB2729-2730	India	331.700968	HB2753.4	South Africa
331.70095491	HB2730.5	Pakistan	331.70096881	HB2754.2	Namibia
331.70095492	HB2730.6	Bangladesh	331.70096883	HB2753.9	Botswana
331.70095493	HB2726.8	Sri Lanka	331.70096885	HB2753.7	Lesotho
331.70095495	HB2761.5	Maldive Islands	331.70096887	HB2753.8	Swaziland
331.70095496	HB2726.9	Nepal	331.7009689	HB2753.5	Zimbabwe/Zambia/ Malawi
331.70095498	HB2730.3	Bhutan			
331.700955	HB2726.4	Iran	331.70096894	HB2753.6	Zambia
331.7009561	HB2723.4	Turkey	331.70096897	HB2754	Malawi
331.70095645	HB2723.5	Cyprus	331.7009691	HB2753.2	Madagascar
331.7009567	HB2726.3	Iraq	331.7009694	HB2762.5	Comoro Islands
331.70095691	HB2723.7	Syria	331.7009696	HB2762	Seychelles
331.70095692	HB2723.9	Lebanon	331.70096981	HB2763.5	Reunion
331.70095694	HB2724	Israel/Palestine	331.70096982	HB2763	Mauritius
331.70095695	HB2724.3	Jordan	331.7009699	HB2764	Kerguelen Islands
331.7009581	HB2726.6	Afghanistan	331.70097(4-9)	HB2617	By city
331.7009591	HB2726.7	Burma	331.70097(4-9)	HB2615	By state
331.7009593	HB2734.55	Thailand	331.700971	HB2619-2620	Canada
331.7009594	HB2734.4	Laos	331.700972	HB2621-2622	Mexico
331.7009595	HB2734.6	Malaysia	331.70097281	HB2629	Guatemala
331.7009596	HB2734.3	Cambodia	331.70097282	HB2625-2626	Belize
331.7009597	HB2734.5	Vietnam	331.70097283	HB2630	Honduras
331.7009598	HB2737-2738	Indonesia	331.70097284	HB2634	El Salvador
331.7009599	HB2739-2740	Philippine Islands	331.70097285	HB2631	Nicaragua

Dewey	LC	Descriptor
331.70097286	HB2627-2628	Costa Rica
331.70097287	HB2632-2633	Panama
331.700972875	HB2633.5	Panama Canal Zone
331.70097291	HB2639-2640	Cuba
331.70097292	HB2643-2644	Jamaica
331.70097293	HB2642	Dominican Republic
331.70097294	HB2641	Haiti
331.70097295	HB2645-2646	Puerto Rico
331.70097296	HB2637-2638	Bahamas
331.7009729722	HB2646.3	Virgin Islands of the U.S.
331.700972973	HB2646.78	Saint Kitts-Nevis
331.700972973	HB2646.72	Anguilla
331.700972974	HB2646.74	Antigua/Barbuda
331.700972975	HB2646.76	Montserrat
331.700972976	HB2647.7	Guadeloupe
331.700972977	HB2647.39	Saint Martin
331.700972977	HB2647.385	Saint Eustatius
331.700972977	HB2647.38	Saba
331.700972981	HB2646.57	Barbados
331.700972982	HB2647.9	Martinique
331.700972983	HB2647	Trinidad/Tobago
331.7009729841	HB2646.93	Dominica
331.7009729843	HB2646.97	Saint Lucia
331.7009729844	HB2646.99	Saint Vincent/ Grenadines
331.7009729845	HB2646.95	Grenada
331.700972986	HB2647.36	Bonaire
331.700972986	HB2647.35	Aruba
331.700972986	HB2647.37	Curacao
331.70097299	HB2758	Bermuda
331.700973	HB2595-2596	United States
331.700981	HB2653-2654	Brazil
331.700982	HB2649-2650	Argentina
331.700983	HB2655-2656	Chile
331.700984	HB2651-2652	Bolivia
331.700985	HB2665-2666	Peru
331.7009861	HB2657-2658	Colombia
331.7009866	HB2659-2660	Ecuador
331.700987	HB2669-2670	Venezuela
331.7009881	HB2662.3	Guyana
331.7009882	HB2662.7	French Guiana
331.7009883	HB2662.5	Suriname
331.7009892	HB2663-2664	Paraguay
331.7009895	HB2667-2668	Uruguay
331.700993	HB2782.5	New Zealand
331.700994	HB2765-2766	Australia
331.7009953	HB2782.8	Papua New Guinea
331.70099593	HB2783	Solomon Islands
331.70099595	HB2783.4	Vanuatu
331.70099597	HB2783.3	New Caledonia
331.70099611	HB2783.5	Fiji Islands
331.70099612	HB2783.6	Tonga
331.70099613	HB2783.7	American Samoa
331.70099614	HB2783.8	Western Samoa
331.7009962	HB2783.9	French Polynesia
331.70099623	HB2783.65	Cook Islands
331.7009967	HB2782.7	Guam
331.70099681	HB2782.9	Kiribati (Gilbert Islands)
331.7009971	HB2761	Falkland Islands
331.7009973	HB2760.5	Tristan da Cunha
331.7009973	HB2760	St. Helena
331.700998(1-8)	HB2785	Polar regions
331.7009982	HB2786	Greenland
331.702	HF5381-5386	Vocational guidance
331.712	HD8038	Professions (General)
331.71208996073	E185.82	Afro-American professionals
331.8	HD6350-6940.7	Trade/Labor union
331.80(5/6)	HD6350	Serials/Societies
331.809	HD6451-6481	History
331.809(4-9)	HD6500-6940.5	Labor unions, By place
331.8094	HD6656-6795.5	Europe
331.80941	HD6661-6670	Great Britain
331.80943	HD6691-6700.5	Germany
331.80944	HD6681-6690	France
331.80945	HD6706-6715	Italy
331.80946	HD6761-6765	Spain
331.80947	HD6731-6735	European Russia
331.809492	HD6716-6730.5	Low Countries
331.809494	HD6771-6775	Switzerland
331.809495	HD6795.5	Greece
331.8095	HD6805.7-6851	Far East
331.80951	HD6836-6840	China
331.80952	HD6831-6835	Japan
331.80954	HD6811-6815	India
331.80955	HD6805.2	Iran
331.80956	HD6796.5-6804	Middle East
331.809567	HD6805	Iraq
331.8095694	HD6798.5	Israel/Palestine
331.809599	HD6826-6830	Philippine Islands
331.8096	HD6861-6888.5	Africa
331.80971	HD6521-6530	Canada
331.80972	HD6531-6535	Mexico
331.809728	HD6540.5-6570	Central America
331.809729	HD6571-6595.95	West Indies
331.80973	HD6500-6519	United States
331.8098	HD6596-6655	South America
331.8099(3-6)	HD6891-6938.9	Australia/New Zealand/Oceania
331.88113613	HV46-.2	Social workers' trade unions
331.88113711	LB2335.86-.88	Trade unions
331.88113711	LB2844.52-.63	Trade unions
331.89	HD5306-5474	Labor disputes/Strikes/Etc.
331.8909(4-9)	HD5321-5450.7	By place
331.8914	HD5481-5630.7	Arbitration/Conciliation
331.891409(4-9)	HD5501-5630.7	Arbitration, By place
332	HG	Finance
332.(1-3)	HG1811-2351	Special classes of banks
332.(26-178)	HG4301-4480.9	Trust services
332.(450212/042)	HG3853-3877	Tables/Cambistry
332.0(5/6)	HG1-52	Serials/Societies
332.021	HG176-.5	Statistics
332.024	HG7920-7933	Thrift/Saving
332.024	HG179	Personal finance
332.025	HG64-96	Directories
332.03	HG151	Dictionaries/ Encyclopedias
332.041	HD39-40.7	Capital/Capital investments
332.042	HG3879-3898	Intern'l. finance/ Banking/Etc.
332.06	HG63	Congresses
332.07	HG152	Education
332.09	HG171	History
332.092	HG172	Biography
332.1	HG1501-3550	Banking
332.1	HG1656	Reserves/Liquidity
332.10285	HG1709	Elecronic data processing
332.109(4-9)	HG2401-3550	Banking, By place
332.10973	HG2401-2626	United States
332.10973	HG2461-2491	History
332.10973021	HG2493	Statistics
332.11	HG1811-1855	Central banks
332.12	HG2301-2351	Clearing houses
332.123	HG1978-2031	Private banks

Dewey	LC	Descriptor
332.15	HG3879-3898	Intern'l. finance/ Banking/Etc.
332.16	HG1722	Mergers
332.1753	HG1641-1643	Loans/Bank credits
332.1752	HG1660	Accounts and deposits
332.178	HG2251-2256	Safe deposit companies
332.21	HG1881-1966	Savings banks
332.260(5/6)	HG4301-4305	Serials/Societies
332.26025	HG4307	Directories
332.2609	HG4311	History
332.2609(4-9)	HG4341-4480.9	Trust services, By place
332.2609(4-9)	HG4357-4480.9	Other countries
332.260973	HG4341-4356	United States
332.28	HG1975-1976	Development banks
332.31	HG2041-2051	Agriculture credit
332.32	HG2121-23156	S & L Associations
332.34	HG2070-2106	Pawn brokering
332.4	HG201-1496	Money
332.404(2-3)	HG315	Small coins
332.4044	HG348-353.5	Paper money
332.41	HD49-.5	Overproduction/Inflation
332.42(2-4)	HG261-312	Precious metals/Bullion
332.42042	HG361-363	Legal tender
332.423	HG401-421	International bimetallism
332.45	HG381-395	International currency
332.45	HG3810-4000	Foreign exchange
332.450(5/6)	HG3810	Serials/Societies
332.4501	HG3821-3823	Theory/Method
332.4503	HG3810.5	Dictionaries/ Encyclopedias
332.4509	HG3811-3815	History
332.45609(4-9)	HG3901-4000	Foreign exchange, By place
332.45609(4-9)	HG3861-3877	Tables, By place
332.46	HG321-329	Mints/Assaying
332.49(4-9)	HG451-1496	Money, By place
332.49(4-9)	HG656-1496	Other countries
332.4973	HG451-645	United States
332.4973	HG501-540	History, U.S. money
332.6	HG4501-6051	Investments
332.609(4-9)	HG4905-5993	Investment, By place
332.609(4-9)	HG5151-5992.7	Other countries
332.6097(4-9)	HG5125-5131	Local, By place
332.60973	HG4905-5131	United States
332.62	HG4621	Stock brokerage
332.620973	HG4928.5-4930.5	Investment companies/ Dealers
332.632	HG4651-4751	Securities
332.6327	HG4530	Mutual funds
332.63220973	HG4961-4965	Industrial securities
332.632320973	HG4931-4955	Government securities
332.64	HG4551-4598	Stock exchanges
332.645	HG6001-6051	Speculation
332.6722	HG1723	Bank stocks
332.673	HG4538	Foreign investments
332.7	HG3691-3769	Credit
332.722	HG2040	Mortgage credit agencies
332.76	HG1685-1703	Drafts/Checks
332.77	HG1655	Acceptances
332.82	HB531-551	Interest
332.82	HG1621-1638	Rate of interest
332.83	HB551	Usury
332.84	HG1651-1654	Discounts
332.9	HG335-341	Counterfeiting
333.01	HD1241-1339	Policy/Theory of distribution
333.1	HD1290-1291	Municipal ownership
333.13	HD1259-1265	Eminent domain

Dewey	LC	Descriptor
333.1309(4-9)	HD1262-1265	By place
333.1309(4-9)	HD1265	Other places
333.130973	HD1262-1263	United States
333.14	HD1301-1313	Agrarian socialism
333.2	HD1286-1289	Communal ownership
333.3	HD1241-1339	Land tenure
333.3	HD1326-1329	Large holdings
333.31	HD1332-1333.5	Land/Agrarian reform
333.322	HD1336-1339	Peasant/Small holdings
333.33	HD1334-1335	Consolidation of land holdings
333.33	HD1361-1395	Real estate business
333.335563	HD1478	Sharecropping
333.54	HD1330-1331	Landlord/Peasant
333.7(36-83)	HD1635-1702	Special classes of lands
333.7153	HD1580	Melioration/Reclamation
333.7153	HD1711-1741	Irrigation/Reclamation
333.72	S900-954	Conservation (Natural resorces)
333.72	QH75-77	Nature conservation
333.73	HD101-1395	Land use
333.730(5/6)	HD101-107	Serials/Societies
333.7301	HD108	Theory
333.7303	HD107.7-.8	Dictionaries/ Encyclopedias
333.7307	HD110	Education
333.7309	HD113-156	History
333.7309(4-9)	HD166-1130.5	Land use, By place
333.73090(3-4)	HD151-156	Modern
333.730901	HD113-139	Ancient
333.730902	HD141-150	Medieval
333.7309411	HD611-620	Scotland
333.7309416	HD620.5	Northern Ireland
333.7309417	HD621-630	Irish Republic
333.730942(9)	HD601-610	England/Wales
333.730943	HD651-660.5	Germany
333.7309436	HD631-640	Austria
333.730943648	HD640.9	Liechtenstein
333.7309437	HD640.3	Czechoslovakia
333.7309438	HD726-729.5	Poland
333.7309439	HD640.5	Hungary
333.730944	HD641-650	France
333.730944949	HD650.5	Monaco
333.730945	HD671-680	Italy
333.730946	HD771-780	Spain
333.7309469	HD781-790	Portugal
333.73094698	HD1028.5	Madeira Islands
333.73094699	HD1028	Azores
333.730947	HD711-720	European Russia
333.7309481	HD751-760	Norway
333.7309485	HD761-770	Sweden
333.7309489	HD731-740	Denmark
333.73094897	HD721-725	Finland
333.73094912	HD741-750	Iceland
333.7309492	HD701-710	Netherlands
333.7309493	HD691-700	Belgium
333.73094935	HD710.5	Luxembourg
333.7309494	HD791-800	Switzerland
333.7309495	HD840.5	Greece
333.73094965	HD810.5	Albania
333.7309497	HD821-825	Yugoslavia
333.73094977	HD811-820	Bulgaria
333.7309498	HD831-840	Romania
333.730951	HD921-930	China
333.730951249	HD936-940	Taiwan
333.73095125	HD941-945	Hong Kong
333.73095126	HD931-935	Macao

Dewey	LC	Descriptor	Dewey	LC	Descriptor
333.7309517	HD920.8	Mongolia	333.73096743	HD1008	Chad
333.7309519	HD920.5-.6	Korea/North Korea	333.73096751	HD1001	Zaire
333.730952	HD911-920	Japan	333.730967571	HD985	Rwanda
333.73095332	HD854-.5	Yemen	333.730967572	HD986	Burundi
333.73095353	HD855	Oman	333.73096761	HD984	Uganda
333.73095357	HD856	United Arab Emirates	333.73096762	HD983	Kenya
333.73095363	HD857	Qatar	333.73096771	HD981	Djibouti
333.73095365	HD858	Bahrain	333.73096773	HD980	Somalia
333.73095367	HD859	Kuwait	333.7309678	HD987	Tanzania
333.7309538	HD853	Saudi Arabia	333.7309679	HD988	Mozambique
333.730954	HD871-880	India	333.730968	HD991	South Africa
333.73095491	HD880.5	Pakistan	333.73096881	HD998	Namibia
333.73095492	HD880.6	Bangladesh	333.73096883	HD996	Botswana
333.73095493	HD860.8	Sri Lanka	333.73096885	HD994	Lesotho
333.73095495	HD1029.7	Maldive Islands	333.73096887	HD995	Swaziland
333.73095496	HD860.9	Nepal	333.7309689	HD992	Zimbabwe/Zambia/
333.73095498	HD880.3	Bhutan			Malawi
333.730955	HD860.2	Iran	333.73096894	HD993	Zambia
333.7309561	HD846.5	Turkey	333.73096897	HD997	Malawi
333.73095645	HD847	Cyprus	333.7309691	HD989	Madagascar
333.7309567	HD860	Iraq	333.7309694	HD1030	Comoro Islands
333.73095691	HD848	Syria	333.7309696	HD1029.9	Seychelles
333.73095692	HD849	Lebanon	333.73096981	HD1030.5	Reunion
333.73095694	HD850	Israel/Palestine	333.73096982	HD1030.3	Mauritius
333.73095695	HD851	Jordan	333.7309699	HD1030.7	Kerguelen Islands
333.7309581	HD860.6	Afghanistan	333.730971	HD311-320	Canada
333.7309591	HD860.7	Burma	333.730972	HD321-330	Mexico
333.7309593	HD890.55	Thailand	333.73097281	HD351-360	Guatemala
333.7309594	HD890.4	Laos	333.73097282	HD336-340	Belize
333.7309595	HD890.6	Malaysia	333.73097283	HD361-370	Honduras
333.7309596	HD890.3	Cambodia	333.73097284	HD391-400	El Salvador
333.7309597	HD890.5	Vietnam	333.73097285	HD371-380	Nicaragua
333.7309598	HD891-900	Indonesia	333.73097286	HD341-350	Costa Rica
333.7309599	HD901-910	Philippine Islands	333.73097287	HD381-385	Panama
333.7309611	HD974	Tunisia	333.730972875	HD386-390	Panama Canal Zone
333.7309612	HD975	Libya	333.73097291	HD411-420	Cuba
333.730962	HD976	Egypt	333.73097292	HD431-440	Jamaica
333.7309624	HD977	Sudan	333.73097293	HD426-430	Dominican Republic
333.730963	HD979	Ethiopia	333.73097294	HD421-425	Haiti
333.730964	HD972	Morocco	333.73097295	HD441-450	Puerto Rico
333.7309648	HD1027	Spanish Sahara	333.73097296	HD406-410	Bahamas
333.7309649	HD1028.7	Canary Islands	333.73309729722	HD450.3	Virgin Islands of the U.S.
333.730965	HD973	Algeria	333.730972973	HD453.8	Saint Kitts-Nevis
333.7309661	HD1020	Mauritania	333.730972973	HD453.2	Anguilla
333.73096623	HD1017	Mali	333.730972974	HD453.4	Antigua/Barbuda
333.73096625	HD1018	Burkina Faso	333.730972975	HD453.6	Montserrat
333.73096626	HD1014	Niger	333.730972976	HD458	Guadeloupe
333.7309663	HD1019	Senegal	333.730972977	HD456.8	Saba
333.7309664	HD1023	Sierra Leone	333.730972977	HD456.9	Saint Martin
333.73096651	HD1024	Gambia	333.730972977	HD456.85	Saint Eustatius
333.73096652	HD1016	Guinea-Bissau	333.730972981	HD451.5	Barbados
333.73096657	HD1026	Guinea-Bissau	333.730972982	HD459	Martinique
333.73096658	HD1028.9	Cape Verde Islands	333.7309729841	HD454.3	Dominica
333.73096662	HD1025	Liberia	333.7309729843	HD454.7	Saint Lucia
333.73096668	HD1015	Ivory Coast	333.7309729844	HD454.9	Saint Vincent/
333.7309667	HD1022	Ghana			Grenadines
333.73096681	HD1013	Togo	333.7309729845	HD454.5	Grenada
333.73096683	HD1012	Benin (Dahomey)	333.730972986	HD456.7	Curacao
333.7309669	HD1021	Nigeria	333.730972986	HD456.5	Aruba
333.73096711	HD1009	Cameroon	333.730972986	HD456.6	Bonaire
333.73096715	HD1003	Sao Tome/Principe	333.73097299	HD1028.3	Bermuda
333.73096718	HD1002	Equatorial Guinea	333.730973	HD170-279	United States
333.7309672	HD1004	French Equatorial Africa	333.730981	HD491-500	Brazil
333.73096721	HD1005	Gabon	333.730982	HD471-480	Argentina
333.73096724	HD1006	Congo	333.730983	HD501-510	Chile
333.7309673	HD1000	Angola	333.730984	HD481-490	Bolivia
333.73096741	HD1007	Central African Republic	333.730985	HD551-560	Peru

Dewey	LC	Descriptor
333.7309861	HD511-520	Colombia
333.7309866	HD521-530	Ecuador
333.730987	HD571-580	Venezuela
333.7309881	HD540.3	Guyana
333.7309882	HD540.7	French Guiana
333.7309883	HD540.5	Suriname
333.7309892	HD541-550	Paraguay
333.7309895	HD561-570	Uruguay
333.730993	HD1120.5	New Zealand
333.730994	HD1031-1040	Australia
333.7309953	HD1122	Papua New Guinea
333.73099593	HD1123	Solomon Islands
333.73099595	HD1125	Vanuatu
333.73099597	HD1124	New Caledonia
333.73099611	HD1126	Fiji Islands
333.73099612	HD1127	Tonga
333.73099613	HD1128	American Samoa
333.73099614	HD1129	Western Samoa
333.7309962	HD1129.5	French Polynesia
333.73099623	HD1127.5	Cook Islands
333.7309967	HD1121.5	Guam
333.73099681	HD1122.3	Kiribati (Gilbert Islands)
333.7309971	HD1029.5	Falkland Islands
333.7309973	HD1029	St. Helena
333.7309973	HD1029.3	Tristan da Cunha
333.730998(1-8)	HD1130	Polar regions
333.7309982	HD1130.5	Greenland
333.75	SD411-428	Conservation/Protection
333.7717	HT169.6-.9	Zoning
333.79	HD9502	Energy industry
333.7923	HD9681	Solar energy industry
333.7924	HD9698-.5	Nuclear power industry
333.88	HD9682	Geothermal industry
333.913	HD1711-1741	Irrigation/Reclamation
333.9164	HC92	Economics of the ocean
333.9516	QL81.5-84.28	Wildlife conservation
333.953	QK86	Conservation
334.09	HD3441-3570.9	Cooperation, By place
334.2	HG2032-2039	Cooperative banks
334.2	HG1968-1969	Trade/Union banks
334.5	HD3271-3410.9	Cooperative distribution
334.6.	HD2951-3575	Industrial cooperation
334.6	HD3120-3260.9	Cooperative production
334.60(5/6)	HD2951-2953	Serials/Societies
334.601	HD2961	Theory/Method
334.603	HD2954	Dictionaries/ Encyclopedias
334.607	HD2955	Education
334.609	HD2956	History
334.609(4-9)	HD3131-3260.9	Production, By place
334.681380109(4-9)	HD3281-3410.9	Distribution, By place
334.683	HD1491-.5	Cooperative agriculture
334.7	HS1501-1510	Benevolent/Friendly societies
335	HD1492-.5	Collective farms
335.(4/83)	HX	Socialism/Communism/Anarchism
335.(43/12)	HX626-780.7	Communism/Utopian Socialism
335.0014	HX18	Terminology
335.003	HX17	Dictionaries/ Encyclopedias
335.005	HX1-9	Serials
335.006	HX11-13	Societies/Congresses
335.007	HX19-.2	Education
335.009	HX21-54	History
335.009	HX36-44	Modern
335.009(4-9)	HX101-517.5	Other countries
335.009(4-9)	HX80-517.5	Socialism/Etc., By place
335.00902	HX31	Medieval
335.0093	HX26	Ancient
335.0094	HX236-375.5	Europe
335.00941	HX241-250	Great Britain
335.00943	HX271-280.5	Germany
335.00944	HX261-270	France
335.00945	HX286-295	Italy
335.00946	HX341-345	Spain
335.00947	HX311-315	European Russia
335.009492	HX296-310.5	Low Countries
335.009495	HX375.5	Greece
335.0095	HX385.7-431	Asia
335.00951	HX416-420	China
335.00952	HX411-415	Japan
335.00954	HX391-395	India
335.0095491	HX395.5	Pakistan
335.0095493	HX385.8	Sri Lanka
335.00956	HX376.5-385.2	Middle East
335.009599	HX406-410	Philippines
335.0096	HX436-468.5	Africa
335.00971	HX101-110	Canada
335.00972	HX111-115	Mexico
335.009728	HX116-150	Central America
335.009729	HX151-175.95	West Indies
335.00973	HX81-92	United States
335.0098	HX176-235	South America
335.0099(3-6)	HX471-518.5	Australia/New Zealand/Oceania
335.43	HX77	Democratic Centralism
335.4309	HX626-632	History
335.4309(4-9)	HX651-780.7	Communism, By place
335.43094	HX694-741.84	Europe
335.430941	HX695-697.5	Great Britain
335.430943	HX707-710.5	Germany
335.430944	HX703-706	France
335.430945	HX712-715	Italy
335.430946	HX735-738	Spain
335.430947	HX724-727	European Russia
335.4309492	HX715.5-723.5	Low Countries
335.4309495	HX741.83	Greece
335.43095	HX742.7-763	Asia
335.430951	HX760	China
335.430952	HX757	Japan
335.430954	HX747-750	India
335.43095491	HX750.5	Pakistan
335.43095493	HX742.8	Sri Lanka
335.430956	HX741.9-742.56	Middle East
335.4309599	HX755	Philippines
335.43096	HX767-779.3	Africa
335.430971	HX657-660	Canada
335.430972	HX661	Mexico
335.4309728	HX663-669	Central America
335.4309729	HX670-675.9	West Indies
335.430973	HX653-656	United States
335.43098	HX676-693	South America
335.43099(3-6)	HX780-.68	Australia/New Zealand/Oceania
335.7	HX51-54	Christian Socialism
335.83	HX821-970.7	Anarchism
335.8309(4-9)	HX841-970.7	Anarchism, By place
335.9	HX635	Management of collectives
336	HJ	Public finance
336	HJ2005-2216	The budget
336.(02/2)	HJ2240-3192.7	Revenue/Taxation
336.(1-3)	HJ2005-2347	Income/Expenditure

Dewey	LC	Descriptor
336.(16/272)	HJ5301-5508	Fees/Licenses/Stamp tax
336.(39/206)	HJ7451-7977	Expenditure
336.00(5/6)	HJ101-119	Serials/Societies
336.001	HJ131-132	Theory
336.001	HJ2005-2043	Theory
336.003	HJ120-129	Dictionaries/ Encyclopedias
336.01(3-4)	HJ9000-9694.7	Local finance
336.01(3-4)(4-9)	HJ9141-9694.7	Local finance, By place
336.01(3-4)(4-9)	HJ9350-9694.7	Other countries
336.01(3-4)0(5/6)	HJ9011-9109	Serials/Societies
336.01(3-4)097(4-9)	HJ9170-9343	U.S. local, By place
336.01(3-4)7(4-9)	HJ9141-9343	United States
336.09(4-9)	HJ210-1620	History/Conditions
336.090(3-4)	HJ230-240	Medieval/Modern
336.093	HJ213-227	Ancient
336.1	HJ3801-3844	Income other than taxation
336.1609(4-9)	HJ5323-5519	Other countries
336.1609(4-9)	HJ5321-5508	Fees/Licenses/Etc., By place
336.160973	HJ5321-5374	United States
336.17	HG6105-6270.9	Lotteries
336.1709	HG6105	History
336.1709(4-9)	HG6126-6270.9	Lotteries, By place
336.2	HJ3851-4939	Direct taxes
336.2	HJ5001-5225	Indirect taxes
336.2	HJ5521-5957	Other forms of tax
336.2(2-78)	HJ4101-4939	Specific direct taxes
336.2001	HJ2300-2323	Theory
336.2009	HJ2250-2279	History
336.200(5/6)	HJ2240	Serials/Etc.
336.20015195	HJ2351.4	Tax revenue estimating
336.2009(4-9)	HJ3871-4056.7	Direct taxes, By place
336.2009(4-9)	HJ2445-3192.7	Other countries
336.2009(4-9)	HJ5075-5508	Other countries
336.2009(4-9)	HJ5018-5225	Indirect taxes, By place
336.2009(4-9)	HJ2360-3192.7	Revenue/Taxation, By place
336.20097(4-9)	HJ2385-2442	Local, By place
336.200973	HJ5018-5074	United States
336.200973	HJ2360-2442	United States
336.201(3-4)	HJ9115-9123	Revenue/Tax
336.206	HJ2336-2337	Exemption
336.207	HJ5703-5797	Raw materials/ Manufacturing
336.22	HD1294-1295	Taxation
336.2209(4-9)	HJ4120-4449	Land/Real estate tax, By place
336.243	HD2753	Taxation of
336.276	HJ5801-5923	Inheritance/Transfer
336.27837	LC184-188	Schools/College taxation
336.278388	HJ5951-5957	Transportation/Traffic
336.293	HJ2326-2327	Progressive/Taxation
336.294	HJ2341-2343	Double taxation
336.3	HJ8003-8899	Public credit/Debts/Loans
336.309	HJ8003-8011	History
336.34	HJ8034	Public credits/Creditors
336.3409(4-9)	HJ8101-8899	Public credit, By place
336.344	HJ8046-8049	Borrowing/Forms of loans
336.363	HJ8055	Reduction/Liquidation
336.363	HJ8052	Amortization/Sinking funds
336.368	HJ8061-8079	Insolvency
336.3909(4-9)	HJ7660-7977	Other countries
336.3909(4-9)	HJ7531-7977	Expenditure, By place
336.3909(4-9)	HJ9125-9127	Expenditure
336.390973	HJ7531-7654	United States
336.4	HJ1000-1616	Europe
336.41	HJ1001-1039.7	Great Britain
336.43	HJ1101-1150.5	Germany
336.44	HJ1071-1099	France
336.45	HJ1156-1188	Italy
336.46	HJ1241-1249	Spain
336.47	HJ1205-1211.5	European Russia
336.492	HJ1190-1204.5	Low Countries
336.494	HJ1255-1264	Switzerland
336.495	HJ1151-1155	Greece
336.5	HJ1320.7-1425	Far East
336.51	HJ1401-1410	China
336.54	HJ1331-1340	India
336.55	HJ1318	Iran
336.56	HJ1302-1316	Middle East
336.567	HJ1317	Iraq
336.5694	HJ1306	Israel/Palestine
336.599	HJ1381-1390	Philippine Islands
336.6	HJ1441-1507	Africa
336.7(4-9)	HJ276-789	Local United States, By place
336.71	HJ790-799	Canada
336.72	HJ800-809	Mexico
336.728	HJ810-844	Central America
336.729	HJ844.3-889.5	West Indies
336.73	HJ241-789	United States
336.8	HJ890-999	South America
336.9(3-6)	HJ1511-1609.5	Australia/New Zealand/Oceania
338	HB241	Production
338	HB522-715	Income/Factor shares
338	HD28-88	Production
338	HD2321-4730.9	Industry
338	T58.7	Production/Productivity
338.(04/5)	HB615-715	Entrepreneurship/Risk
338.(2/4)	HD9506-9624	Mineral/Metal industries
338.02	HF1040-1054	Commodities
338.06	HD56-57.5	Industrial productivity
338.064	T173.2-174.5	Technology transfer/ Innovation
338.09(4-9)	HD58	Location of industry
338.091734	HD2330	Rural industry
338.1	HD1491-.5	Cooperative agriculture
338.1	HD1401-2210	Agriculture
338.106	HD1483-1486	Agricultural associations
338.13	S560-572	Farm economics/ Management
338.16	HD1470.5-1476	Size of farms
338.17	HD9000-9490	Agriculture, By product
338.176	SF84-.45	Economic zoology
338.181	HD1428-1431	International cooperation
338.3727	SH201-400.8	Fisheries
338.3727025	SH203	Directories
338.372703	SH201	Dictionaries/ Encyclopedias
338.372709	SH211	History
338.372709(4-9)	SH219-321	By place
338.372709163	SH213-.77	Atlantic Ocean
338.372709164	SH214-215	Pacific Ocean
338.372709165	SH216-.55	Indian Ocean
338.37270941	SH253-293	Europe
338.37270941	SH255-260	Great Britain
338.372709415	SH261-262	Ireland
338.37270943	SH271-272	Germany
338.372709436	SH263-264	Austria
338.37270944	SH269-270	France
338.37270945	SH277-278	Italy
338.37270946	SH285-286	Spain
338.372709469	SH281-282	Portugal

Dewey	LC	Descriptor
338.37270947	SH283-284	European Russia
338.372709481	SH279-280	Norway
338.372709485	SH287-288	Sweden
338.372709489	SH267-268	Denmark
338.372709492	SH275-276	Netherlands
338.372709493	SH265-266	Belgium
338.372709494	SH289-290	Switzerland
338.372709495	SH273-274	Greece
338.3727095	SH295-307	Asia
338.37270951	SH297-298	China
338.372709519	SH302.5-.7	Korea
338.37270952	SH301-302	Japan
338.37270954	SH299-300	India
338.37270955	SH303-304	Iran
338.372709561	SH291-292	Turkey
338.37270957	SH305-306	Siberia
338.3727096	SH311-315	Africa
338.37270962	SH313-314	Egypt
338.37270971	SH223-229	Canada
338.37270972	SH231	Mexico
338.372709728	SH232	Central America
338.372709729	SH233	West Indies
338.37270973	SH221-222	United States
338.3727098	SH234-251	South America
338.37270981	SH236	Brazil
338.37270982	SH235	Argentina
338.37270983	SH237	Chile
338.37270985	SH247	Peru
338.372709861	SH239	Colombia
338.372709866	SH241	Ecuador
338.37270987	SH251	Venezuela
338.372709881	SH242	Guyana
338.372709882	SH244	French Guiana
338.372709883	SH243	Suriname
338.372709892	SH245	Paraguay
338.372709895	SH249	Uruguay
338.3727099(5-6)	SH319	Oceania
338.37270993	SH318.5	New Zealand
338.37270994	SH317-318	Australia
338.372709982	SH268.G83	Greenland
338.372709989	SH320	Arctic regions
338.47	HD9680-9714	Mechanical/Electrical industries
338.47(001-999)	HD9980-9999	Other industries/Trades
338.473621	RJ33.5-.8	Practice of/Economics of
338.47624	HD9715-9717.5	Construction industry
338.4766	HD9650-9675	Chemical/Drugs industry
338.4767	HD9720-9975	Manufacturing industry
338.4762132	HD9684	Lighting industry
338.4762136	HD9707-9708.5	Optical/Photographic industries
338.47621381	HD9696	Electronic industy
338.476218	HD9700-9705.5	Machinery industry
338.4762382	VM298.5-301	Shipbuilding industry
338.47629046	HD9709-9714	Vehicle industry
338.47697	HD9683	Heating industry
338.4791	G155-180	Tourist trade
338.51	HD47-.4	Costs/Cost control
338.516	HB601	Profit
338.52	HB221-236	Price
338.52	HJ1391-1400	Japan
338.521	HB201-205	Value/Utility
338.5212	HB842-843	Demand
338.54	HB3711-3840	Business/Economic cycles
338.54209(4-9)	HB3741-4840	Business cycles, By place
338.6048	HB238	Competition
338.6048	HD41	Competition

Dewey	LC	Descriptor
338.6048	HF1414	Competition
338.6048	HF1413.5-1414	Boycotts/Competition
338.634	HD2331-2336	House industry
338.634	HD2337-2339	Sweating system
338.642	HD2340.8-2346	Small-medium industry/Artisans
338.644	HD2350.8-2356	Large industry/Factory system
338.7	HD2709-2932	Corporation/Cartels/Trusts
338.70(5/6)	HD2709-2711	Serials/Societies
338.703	HD2713	Dictionaries/ Encyclopedias
338.7068	HD2741-2748	Organization/ Administration
338.709	HD2770-2930.7	Corporations/Etc., By place
338.7094	HD2846-2891.83	Europe
338.70941	HD2846-2847.5	Great Britain
338.70943	HD2857-2860.5	Germany
338.70944	HD2853-2856	France
338.70945	HD2862-2865	Italy
338.70946	HD2885-2888	Spain
338.709469	HD2889	Portugal
338.70947	HD2874-2877	European Russia
338.709492	HD2865.5-2873.5	Low Countries
338.709495	HD2891.83	Greece
338.7095	HD2892.7-2913	Far East
338.70951	HD2910	China
338.70952	HD2907	Japan
338.70954	HD2897-2900	India
338.70955	HD2892.56	Iran
338.70956	HD2891.93-2892.53	Middle East
338.709567	HD2892.55	Iraq
338.7095694	HD2892.2	Israel/Palestine
338.709599	HD2905	Philippine Islands
338.7096	HD2918.3-2929.3	Africa
338.70971	HD2807-2810	Canada
338.70972	HD2811	Mexico
338.709728	HD2813.5-2819	Central America
338.709729	HD2820.5-2825.9	West Indies
338.70973	HD2771-2798	United States
338.7098	HD2827-2843	South America
338.7099(3-6)	HD2930-.68	Australia/New Zealand/Oceania
338.76	HD62.2-.8	Special enterprises
338.763	HD1493	Government owned/ Operated farms
338.8	HD2757-2768	Monopolies/Trusts/Etc.
338.9	HD72-88	Economic growth/Development
338.9	HD3860-4420.7	Government ownership
338.9	HD2329	Industrialization
338.9(1-9)	HC94-1085	By place
338.909(4-9)	HD4001-4420.7	Government ownership, By place
338.917241	HC245-246	Commonwealth
338.922	HD3641-3646	Subsidies
338.926	T173.2-174.5	Technology transfer/ Innovation
338.94	HC240-407	Europe
338.941	HC251-257	Great Britain
338.9417	HC258	Ireland
338.943	HC280-290	Germany
338.9436	HC261-270	Austria
338.9437	HC270.2-.295	Czechoslovakia
338.9438	HC340.3	Poland
338.944	HC271-280	France
338.945	HC301-310	Italy

Dewey	LC	Descriptor
338.946	HC381-390	Spain
338.9469	HC391-394	Portugal
338.947	HC331-340	European Russia
338.948	HC341-380	Scandinavia
338.9481	HC361-370	Norway
338.9485	HC371-380	Sweden
338.9489	HC351-360	Denmark
338.9492	HC321-329	Netherlands
338.9493	HC311-320	Belgium
338.94935	HC330	Luxembourg
338.9494	HC395-400	Switzerland
338.9495	HC291-300	Greece
338.9496	HC401-407	Balkans
338.94965	HC402	Albania
338.947	HC407	Yugoslavia
338.94977	HC403	Bulgaria
338.9498	HC405	Romania
338.95	HC411-495	Asia
338.951	HC426-430	China
338.951249	HC430.5	Taiwan
338.9519	HC466-470	Korea
338.952	HC461-465	Japan
338.95332	HC415.34	Yemen
338.95353	HC415.35	Oman
338.95357	HC415.36	United Arab Emirates
338.95363	HC415.37	Qatar
338.95365	HC415.38	Bahrain
338.95367	HC415.39	Kuwait
338.9538	HC415.33	Saudi Arabia
338.954	HC431-440	India
338.95491	HC440.5	Pakistan
338.95492	HC440.8	Bangladesh
338.95493	HC424	Sri Lanka
338.95496	HC425	Nepal
338.955	HC471-480	Iran
338.9561	HC491-495	Turkey
338.9567	HC415.4	Iraq
338.95691	HC415.23	Syria
338.95692	HC415.24	Lebanon
338.95694	HC415.25	Israel/Palestine
338.95695	HC415.26	Jordan
338.9581	HC416-420	Afghanistan
338.9591	HC422	Burma
338.9593	HC445	Thailand
338.9594	HC443	Laos
338.9596	HC442	Cambodia
338.9597	HC444	Vietnam
338.9598	HC446-450	Indonesia
338.9599	HC451-460	Philippine Islands
338.96	HC800-1085	Africa
338.9611	HC820	Tunisia
338.9612	HC825	Libya
338.962	HC830	Egypt
338.9624	HC835	Sudan
338.963	HC845	Ethiopia
338.964	HC810	Morocco
338.965	HC815	Algeria
338.96626	HC1020	Niger
338.96652	HC1030	Guinea-Bissau
338.96668	HC1025	Ivory Coast
338.9669	HC1055	Nigeria
338.96711	HC995	Cameroon
338.96721	HC975	Gabon
338.96724	HC980	Congo
338.9673	HC950	Angola
338.96743	HC990	Chad
338.96751	HC955	Zaire

Dewey	LC	Descriptor
338.967571	HC875	Rwanda
338.967572	HC880	Burundi
338.96761	HC870	Uganda
338.96762	HC865	Kenya
338.96773	HC850	Somalia
338.9678	HC885	Tanzania
338.9679	HC890	Mozambique
338.968	HC905	South Africa
338.96887	HC925	Swaziland
338.9689	HC910	Zimbabwe (Southern Rhodesia)
338.96894	HC915	Zambia
338.9691	HC895	Madagascar
338.97(4-9)	HC107-110	By state
338.971	HC111-120	Canada
338.972	HC131-140	Mexico
338.9728	HC141-148	Central America
338.9729	HC151-158	West Indies
338.973	HC106.2-.8	United States
338.98	HC161-239	South America
338.981	HC186-189	Brazil
338.982	HC171-180	Argentina
338.983	HC191-195	Chile
338.984	HC181-185	Bolivia
338.985	HC226-230	Peru
338.9861	HC196-200	Colombia
338.9866	HC201-204	Ecuador
338.987	HC236-239	Venezuela
338.988	HC205-220	Guyanas
338.9892	HC221-225	Paraguay
338.9895	HC231-235	Uruguay
338.99(5-6)	HC681-688	Pacific Ocean Islands
338.993	HC661-670	New Zealand
338.994	HC601-610	Australia
338.997	HC592-595	Atlantic Ocean Islands
338.998(1-8)	HC721-740	Arctic regions
338.9982	HC110.5	Greenland
339.2	HB251	Wealth
339.21	HB401	Rent
339.3	HB522-715	Income/Factor shares
339.42	HD6977-7080	Wages/Cost of living
339.43	HG7920-7933	Thrift/Saving
339.47	HB801-843	Consumption
339.5	HB3732	Economic stabilization
340	K237-264	The concept of law
340-349	K	Law (General)
340.(09/5)	K140-165	History of law
340.01	KF379-382	Jurisprudence/Philosophy
340.02	K181-184.7	Miscellany
340.023	K115-129	The legal profession
340.023	KD460-510	Legal profession
340.023411	KDC225-247	The legal profession
340.023417	KDK120-134	The legal profession
340.02371	KE330-372	Legal profession
340.02373	KF297-334	Legal profession
340.025	K68-70	Directories
340.025	KD336-340	Directories
340.02573	KF190-195	Directories
340.03	K48	Encyclopedias
340.03	K50-54	Dictionaries
340.03	KD313	Dictionaries
340.03	KD310	Encyclopedias
340.03	KF156	Law dictionaries
340.03	KF154	Encyclopedias
340.03	KDK84	Dictionaries
340.05	K1-36	Serials
340.05	K64	Yearbooks

Dewey	LC	Descriptor
340.05	KD325	Yearbooks
340.05	KF178	Yearbooks
340.06	K110	Bar associations
340.06	K175	Congresses
340.06	KD347	Congresses
340.06	KF202	Congresses
340.06	KF294	Law societies
340.06	KDK93	Societies
340.06071	KE359-372	The bar/Associations
340.06071	KE325	Legal institutes/Societies
340.06411	KDC220	Societies
340.0642	KD456	Societies
340.0642	KD345	Periodicals (Law associations)
340.07	K100-103	Legal education
340.07	KD417-452	Education
340.07	KE273-322	Education
340.07	KF262-292	Legal education
340.072	K85-88	Legal research
340.092	K170	Biography
340.09411	KDC270-320	History
340.09417	KDK141-161	History
340.0942	KD530-632	History
340.09429	KD9430	History
340.0973	KF350-374	History
340.1	K7021	Philosophy/Theory
340.1	K237-487	Philosophy/Theory of law
340.1	K325-328	Historical jurisprudence
340.1	KD640	Philosophy
340.1	KE427	Philosophy
340.109	K321-474	Legal theory
340.11	K270-274	Acts and events
340.11	K280-286	Sources of law
340.112	K400-474	Natural law
340.112	K330-344	Positivism
340.115	K368-380	Sociology of law/Jurisprudence
340.2	K540-5582	Comparative/International law
340.41103	KDC150-152	Dictionaries/Encyclopedias
340.5(2-9)	K583-591	Legal systems compared
340.52	K190-195	Primitive law
340.59	BP140-165	Islamic law
340.6	K7033	Congresses
340.9	K7625-7627	Jurisdiction
340.9	K7000-7720	Conflict of laws
340.9	K7030	History
340.9	K7680	Foreign judgments
340.9	JX6001-6953	Private (Conflict of laws)
340.901	JX6051-6053	Theory
340.903	K7015	Dictionaries/Encyclopedias
340.903	JX6041-6048	Dictionaries
340.905	JX6001-6008	Serials
340.906	K7019	Societies
340.906	JX6009-6025	Societies/Congresses
340.907	JX6085	Education
340.909	JX6071	History
340.909	JX6111-6242	By place
340.912	K7120-7197	Persons
340.913	K7120-7148	Status/Capacity
340.913	K7145-7148	Juristic persons
340.915	K7155-7197	Family law
340.915	JX6411-6433	Family
340.916	K7157-7178	Marriage
340.917	K7181-7192	Parent and child
340.918	K7197	Guardian and ward
340.92	K7260-7335	Obligations
340.92	JX6351	Contracts/Obligations
340.92(2-5)	K7265-7305	Contracts
340.929	K7310	Restitution/Quasi contracts
340.93	K7315-7335	Torts
340.94	K7200-7222	Property
340.94	JX6561-6570	Property
340.948	K7570-7582	Industrial property
340.948	K7550-7582	Intellectual property
340.9482	K7555-7557	Copyright
340.95	JX6501-6510	Inheritance/Succession
340.952	K7230-7245	Succession upon death
340.96	K7485-7495	Associations/Corporations
340.97	K7340-7512	Commercial law
340.97	K7350-7444	Commercial contracts
340.97	JX6271-6339	Commercial law (International)
340.972	K7350	Sale
340.982	K7380-7390	Banking/Loans
340.983	K7125-7140	Natural persons
340.986	K7470	Insurance
340.992	K7410-7418	Investments
340.996	K7360-7370	Negotiable instruments
341	K540-5582	Comparative/International law
341	JX	International law
341.0(9/1)	JX2001-3695	History/Theory
341.026	JX63-191	Documents/Cases
341.0267	JX1261-1283	Codification
341.0268(1-9)	JX221-1195	Cases, By place
341.02684	JX621-899	Europe
341.02685	JX900-1015	Asia
341.02686	JX1031-1145	Africa
341.026871	JX351-360	Canada
341.026872	JX361-370	Mexico
341.0268728	JX371-450	Central America
341.0268729	JX451-496	West Indies
341.026873	JX231-245	United States
341.02688	JX501-620	South America
341.02689(3-6)	JX1161-1195	Australia/New Zealand/Oceania
341.05	JX1-18	Serials
341.06	JX24-54	Societies/Congresses
341.0903(1-3)	JX2061-2182	1500-1713
341.0902	JX2041-2060	Medieval
341.09033	JX2206-2435	18th century
341.09034	JX2441-3085	19th century
341.0904	JX3091-3695	20th century
341.093(8/7)	JX2001-2035	Ancient (Greece/Rome)
341.22	JX1975	League of Nations
341.23	JX1976-1977	United Nations
341.245	KDZ1100-1199	Organization of American States
341.26	JX5401-5486	International responsibility
341.28	K3375	Colonial law
341.37	JX4161-4171	Treaties
341.47	K4135	Space law
341.482	JX4203-4270	Nationality/Citizenship
341.488	JX4275-4399	Asylum/Extradition
341.5	JX4471-5397	International disputes
341.522	JX1901-1995	International arbitration
341.52206	JX1905.5-1908	Societies
341.52206	JX1910-1935	Congresses
341.52209(1-9)	JX1961	By place
341.522090(1-4)	JX1941-1954	By date
341.55209	JX1937-1962	History

Dewey	LC	Descriptor	Dewey	LC	Descriptor
341.690268	D803-804	Atrocities	342.437029	JN2210-2229	Czechoslovakia
341.7	K7051-7054	International unification	342.438029	JN6750-6769	Poland
341.7566	JX4408-4449	Maritime law	342.44029	JN2301-3007	France
341.77	JX6708-6953	Criminal law	342.45029	JN5201-5697	Italy
342	K3150	Public law	342.46029	JN8101-8399	Spain
342	K3154-3367	Constitutional law	342.469029	JN8423-8661	Portugal
342	JC401-408	Constitutional	342.47029	JN6500-6747	European Russia
342	KE4120	Public law	342.48029	JN7001-7066	Scandinavia (General)
342.(5-9)029	JQ	Asia/Africa/Oceania (Admin./Etc.)	342.481029	JN7401-7695	Norway
342.(7-8)029	JL	Americas (Admin./Constitution)	342.485029	JN7721-7997	Sweden
342.0(5-68)	K3290-3367	Organs of government	342.489029	JN7101-7367	Denmark
342.02	K4700-4705	Government emergencies	342.4897029	JN7390-7399	Finland
342.02	K3171-3179	Constitutional principles	342.4912029	JN7300-7389	Iceland
342.029	K3161	Constitutional history	342.492029	JN5701-5999	The Netherlands
342.03288	K970	Victims compensation	342.493029	JN6101-6371	Belgium
342.04	K3185-3188	Structure of government	342.494029	JN8701-9599	Switzerland
342.0412	K3201-3205	Foreign relations	342.495029	JN5001-5191	Greece
342.05	K3310-3329	The legislature	342.496029	JN9600-9689	Balkan states
342.06	K3420-3431	Administrative organization	342.5029	JQ20-1825	Asia
342.062	K3332-3363	Heads of state	342.51029	JQ1519	China
342.066	K3400-3431	Administrative law	342.51249029	JQ1539	Taiwan
342.066	K3403-3416	The administrative process	342.5125029	JQ670-679	Hong Kong
342.068	K3440-3460	Civil service	342.519029	JQ1729-.5	Korea
342.08	K3290-3304	The people	342.52029	JQ1699	Japan
342.08	K3224-3278	Individual and state	342.53029	JQ1825.A75	Arabia
342.085	HT941-950	Law and slavery	342.53029	JQ1850	Arab countries
342.4029	JN1-97	Europe, General	342.5332029	JQ1825.Y4-.Y5	Yemen
342.4029	JN	Europe (Admin./Constitution)	342.5353029	JQ1825.O42	Oman
342.41029	JN101-1179	Great Britain	342.5357029	JQ1825.U5	United Arab Emirates
342.41029	JN111-248	Constitutional history	342.5363029	JQ1825.Q37	Qatar
342.410290(1-4)	JN128-237	By date	342.5365029	JQ1825.B34	Bahrain
342.410290(23-4)	JN175-237	Modern (1485-)	342.5367029	JQ1825.K8	Kuwait
342.411	KDC750-785	Constitutional law	342.538029	JQ1825.S3	Saudi Arabia
342.411029	JN1187-1371	Scotland	342.54029	JQ200-620	India
342.416	KDE410-462	Constitutional law	342.5491029	JQ540-559	Pakistan
342.416029	JN1572	Northern Ireland	342.5492029	JQ630-639	Bangladesh
342.417	KDK1200-1350	Constitutional law	342.5493029	JQ650-659	Sri Lanka
342.417029	JN1400-1571.5	Ireland	342.5496029	JQ1825.N4	Nepal
342.42	KD3930-4645	Constitutional law	342.55029	JQ1789	Iran
342.42	KD3981-3990	Constitutional law, General	342.561029	JQ1809	Turkey
342.42	KD3995-4018	Constitutional principles	342.5645029	JQ1825.C93	Cyprus
342.42024	KD4015-4018	Sources of law	342.567029	JQ1825.I7	Iraq
342.42024	KD3931-3932	Sources	342.5691029	JQ1825.S8	Syria
342.42029	KD3931-3966	History	342.5692029	JQ1825.L4	Lebanon
342.420290(1-4)	KD3938-3966	By date	342.5694029	JQ1825.P3	Israel/Palestine
342.4204	KD4185-4645	Organs of government	342.5695029	JQ1825.J6	Jordan
342.420412	KD4030	Foreign relations	342.57029	JQ1089-1199	Asian Russia
342.42042	KD680-685	Conflict of laws	342.581029	JQ1769	Afghanistan
342.42044	KD4000-4010	Separation of powers	342.59(7)029	JQ800-899	Vietnam/Indochina
342.4205	KD4190-4381	Parliament	342.593029	JQ1749	Thailand
342.4206	KD4430-4531	The Crown/Central government	342.594029	JQ950-959	Laos
342.4206	KD4435-4456	The Crown	342.595029	JQ710-719	Malaysia
342.4206(2-4)	KD4462	Prime Minister/Cabinet	342.596029	JQ930-939	Cambodia
342.4206(4/8)	KD4467-4531	Departments/Civil service	342.598029	JQ760-779	Indonesia
342.4208	KD4050-4139	Individual and state	342.599029	JQ1269-1419	Philippines
342.42083	KD4130-4139	Aliens	342.6029	JQ1870-3981	Africa
342.42083	KD4050-4058	Citizenship	342.71	KE4900-4934	Local government
342.42085	KD4080-4119	Civil rights	342.71	KE4125-4775	Constitutional law
342.4209	KD4746-4840	Local government	342.71029	JL1-500	Canada
342.4212	KD8860-9142	London	342.71029	JL11-65	Constitutional history
342.429029	JN1150-1159	Wales	342.710290(1-4)	JL41-65	By date
342.43029	JN3201-4980	Germany	342.71032	KE4228	Amending process
342.436029	JN1601-2199	Austria/Hungary	342.7104	KE4270-4285	Structure of government
			342.710412	KE4310	Foreign relations
			342.710418	KE5006-5010	Power of police
			342.710418	KE4335	Public policy/Police
			342.71042	KE470-474	Conflict of laws

Dewey	LC	Descriptor
342.71044	KE4526-4775	Organs of government
342.7105	KE4529-4665	The legislature
342.7106	KE4705-4765	The Crown/Executive branch
342.71066	KE5015-5036	Administrative procedure
342.71068	KE4940-4995	Civil service
342.71085	KE4345-4486	Civil rights
342.72029	JL1200-1299	Mexico
342.7281029	JL1480-1499	Guatemala
342.7282029	JL670-679	Belize
342.7283029	JL1520-1539	Honduras
342.7284029	JL1560-1579	El Salvador
342.7285029	JL1600-1619	Nicaragua
342.7286029	JL1440-1459	Costa Rica
342.7287029	JL1630-1679	Panama
342.7291029	JL1000-1019	Cuba
342.7292029	JL630-639	Jamaica
342.72921029	JL629.5	Cayman Islands
342.729375029	JL1120-1139	Santo Domingo
342.7294029	JL1080-1099	Haiti
342.7295029	JL1040-1059	Puerto Rico
342.7296029	JL610-619	Bahamas
342.72961029	JL659.5	Turks/Caicos Islands
342.7297029	JL640-649	Leeward Islands
342.72976029	JL820-829	Guadeloupe
342.72981029	JL620-629	Barbados
342.72982029	JL830-839	Martinique
342.72983029	JL650-659	Trinidad
342.72984029	JL660-669	Windward Islands
342.729845029	JL629.6	Grenada
342.72986029	JL770-779	Curacao
342.7299029	JL590-599	Bermuda
342.73	KF425-450	Principles/Concepts
342.73	KF4501-5130	Constitutional law
342.73001	KF4546-4554	Theory/Interpretation
342.7302	JK14-19	Charters/Constitutions
342.7302	KF4530	State constitutions
342.73023	KF4525-4528	The Constitution (Texts)
342.73024	KF4501-4515	Sources
342.73024	KF4581-4583	Sources of law
342.73024	KF350	Sources
342.73029	JK11-371	Constitutional history
342.73029	JK	U.S. (Admin./Constitutional hist.)
342.73029	KF4541-4545	Constitutional history
342.73032	KF4558	Amendments
342.73032	KF4555	Amending process
342.73041(8)	KF4695	Public policy/Police
342.730412	KF4650-4694	Foreign relations
342.730413	KF4635	Territories
342.730418	KF5399	Power of police
342.73042	JK310-331	Federal-State relations
342.73042	KF410-418	Conflict of law
342.73042	KF4600-4629	Federal-State relations
342.73044	JK305-306	Separation of powers
342.73044	KF4565-4578	Separation of powers
342.73044	KF4881-5130	Organs of government
342.7305	JK1061-1081	Constitutional powers
342.7305	KF4930-5005	The legislature
342.7306	KF5050-5125	Executive branch
342.73066	KF5401-5425	Administration and procedures
342.73068	KF5336-5398	Civil service
342.7307	KF4881-4921	Election law
342.7308	KF4700-4856	Individual and state
342.7308	KF4791-4856	Control of individuals
342.73082	JV6421-6429	Laws/Regulations
342.73082	KF4794-.5	Passports
342.73083	KF4800-4848	Aliens
342.73083	KF4700-4720	Citizenship
342.73085	KF4741-4783	Civil rights
342.730852	KF4865-4869	Church and state
342.73087	KF4788	Political parties
342.730872	KF8201-8228	Indians
342.7309	KF5300-5332	Local government
342.75029	JK9803-9993	Constitutional history
342.81029	JL2400-2499	Brazil
342.82029	JL2000-2099	Argentina
342.83029	JL2600-2699	Chile
342.84029	JL2200-2299	Bolivia
342.85029	JL3400-3499	Peru
342.861029	JL2800-2899	Colombia
342.866029	JL3000-3099	Ecuador
342.87029	JL3800-3899	Venezuela
342.881029	JL680-689	Guyana
342.882029	JL810-819	French Guiana
342.883029	JL780-789	Suriname
342.892029	JL3200-3299	Paraguay
342.895029	JL3600-3699	Uruguay
342.9(3-6)029	JQ3995-6651	Australia/New Zealand/Oceania
342.9711029	JL690-699	Falkland Islands
342.982029	JN7370-7379	Greenland
343.(3-9)0942	TE321-426	Laws, By place
343.0(66-68)/096	HE587-589	Taxation/Registration
343.0(96/66-68)	HE384-389	Control/Taxation
343.01	K4720-4760	National defense
343.01	UB461-736	Law
343.014	K4740-4760	Military criminal law
343.014	UB790-815	Military discipline/ Punishment
343.0143	UB840-867	Judiciary/Courts
343.0143	UB890	Procedure/Appeals
343.015	K4725-4734	Armed forces
343.015	JF1800	Military government
343.01822	UG130-135	Laws
343.019	VB790-815	Judiciary/Courts/Etc.
343.019	VB840-910	Discipline/Crimes/ Punishment
343.019	VB350-785	Naval law
343.02	K3476-3558	Public property
343.02	K3558-3560	Government property
343.025	K3514-3525	Public land
343.0252	K3511-3512	Eminent domain
343.03	K4430-4675	Public finance
343.036	K4453-4640	National revenue
343.04	K4456-4590	Taxation
343.043	K4650-4675	State/Local finance
343.052	K4501-4558	Income/Profit tax
343.053	K4568	Inheritance/Estate
343.054	K4560-4566	Property tax
343.0553	K4572-4580	Excise tax
343.056	K4600-4640	Tariffs
343.07	K3820-3823	Economics
343.07	K3840-4375	Business regulation
343.075	K3870-3918	Primary production
343.0775	TN215-257	Mining laws/Legislation
343.0786213	TK215-255	Laws/Legislation
343.078690	TH219-255	Laws/Legislation
343.08	K3941-3974	Trade and commerce
343.08	K3842-3862	Trade regulations
343.082	HF5833	Regulation
343.09	K3978-3990	Public utilities
343.09(4-5)	TG215-255	Bridge legislation and laws

Dewey	LC	Descriptor
343.093	K7430-7444	Carriers
343.093	K4011-4339	Transportation/ Communication
343.0942	K4028-4045	Roads
343.0942	K3492	Roads
343.0942	TE315-426	Laws and legislation
343.095	HE1051-1081	Government control
343.095	K4061-4070	Railroads
343.095	TF520-522	Service rules and regulations
343.096	K7449-7460	Maritime law
343.096	K1150-1231	Maritime law
343.0965	K4157-4180	Ships
343.0967	K4198-4200	Harbors/Ports
343.0967	K4182-4194	Navigation/Pilotage
343.097	K4091-4124	Aviation
343.0979	K4135	Space law
343.098	K4080	Local transportation
343.099	K4240-4343	Communication
343.0992	K4245-4279	Postal service
343.0994	K4301-4343	Telecommunication
343.0998	K4285-4290	The press
343.401	UB590-684	Europe
343.41103	KDC807-825	Public finance
343.41607	KDE235-282	Business regulation
343.41703	KDK1430-1526	Public finance
343.41707	KDK550-769	Business regulation
343.42(1-9)	KD5710-5752	Local finance
343.420(4-68)	KD5351-5694	Sources of national income
343.4201	KD5110-5133	Government emergencies/ War
343.4201	KD6338	Other defense agencies
343.4201	KD6240-6248	Auxiliary services (War time)
343.4201	KD6000-6355	National defense
343.4201(6-9)	KD6086-6228	Branches of service
343.42011	KD6355	Veterans
343.42013	KD6030-6335	Armed forces
343.42014	KD6250	Military discipline
343.42015	KD6335	Civil law/Armed forces
343.42015	KD6270-6332	Military criminal law
343.4202	KD1034-1195	Public property
343.42023	KD1465	Government personal property
343.42025	KD1090-1107	Public land
343.420252	KD1185-1189	Eminent domain
343.420256	KD1195	Public works
343.4203	KD5280-5752	Public finance
343.420309	KD5280	History
343.42032	KD5284-5286	Currency/Coinage
343.42032	KD5288	Foreign exchange
343.42034	KD5295	Public auditing
343.42034	KD5292	Budget
343.42036	KD5320-5694	National income
343.4203609	KD5320-5341	History
343.42037	KD5300	National debt
343.4204	KD5351-5605	Taxation
343.42053	KD1497	Estate planning
343.42056	KD5641-5694	Tariffs
343.4207	KD2200-2990	Business regulation
343.4207(6-7)	KD2241-2370	Primary production industries
343.42072	KD2204	Unfair trade practices
343.42072	KD2218-2220	Monopolies
343.420723	KD2212	Restraint of trade
343.42075	KD2230-2231	Weights/Measures/ Containers
343.42076	KD2241-2295	Agriculture/Forestry
343.4207692	KD2310-2315	Fishery
343.420775	KD2331-2370	Mining/Quarrying
343.42078	KD2375-2398	Manufacturing industries
343.4207833847664	KD2405-2430	Food processing industry
343.42078624	KD2435	Construction industry
343.4208	KD2455-2530	Commerce/Trade
343.4208	KD2204-2231	Trade regulations
343.42082	KD2206	Advertising
343.42082	KD2208-2209	Labeling
343.42083	KD2215	Price regulation
343.4209	KD2535-2560	Public utilities
343.4209(3-9)	KD2571-2915	Transportation/ Communication
343.4209(4-5)	KD1802	Carriage, By land
343.42093	KD1800-1847	Carriers
343.420942	KD1040-1048	Roads
343.42096	KD1811-1834	Carriage, By sea
343.42097	KD1804	Carriage, By air
343.4301	UB620-624	Germany
343.4401	UB615-619	France
343.4501	UB640-644	Italy
343.4601	UB660-664	Spain
343.46901	UB650-654	Portugal
343.4701	UB655-659	European Russia
343.49501	UB630-634	Greece
343.501	UB685-710	Asia
343.5101	UB690-694	China
343.5201	UB700-704	Japan
343.5401	UB695-699	India
343.601	UB715-729	Africa
343.7101	KE5460-5484	Government emergency
343.7101	KE6800-7240	National defense
343.7101	UB505-509	Canada
343.7102	KE5105-5420	Public property
343.71025	KE5184-5217	Public land law
343.7103	KE5600-6328	Public finance
343.7107	KE1589-2742	Business regulation
343.7107(6-7)	KE1671-1830	Primary production
343.710721	KE1631-1655	Competition
343.71075	KE1620-1622	Weights/Measures/ Containers
343.71076	KE1671-1745	Agriculture/Forestry
343.71076392	KE1760-1765	Fishing industry
343.71077	KE1790-1830	Mining/Quarrying/ Petroleum
343.71078	KE1840-1858	Manufacturing industries
343.7107833847664	KE1867-1906	Food processing industries
343.71078624	KE1915	Construction industry
343.7108	KE1935-1999	Trade/Commerce
343.7108	KE1591-1660	Trade regulation
343.71082	KE1616-1618	Labeling
343.71082	KE1610-1614	Advertising
343.7109	KE2020-2061	Public utilities
343.7109(3-9)	KE2071-2649	Transportation/ Communication
343.71093	KE1099-1135	Carriers
343.7201	UB510-514	Mexico
343.72801	UB515-519	Central America
343.72901	UB520-524	West Indies
343.7301	KF5900-6075.5	Government emergencies
343.7301	KF7201-7755	National defense/Military
343.7301(6-82)	KF7305-7335	Army
343.7301(6-82)	KF7631-7642	Army
343.7301(6-9)	KF7305-7479	Branches of service
343.73011	KF7701-7755	War veterans
343.73013	KF7250-7680	Armed forces

Dewey	LC	Descriptor
343.73014	KF7595-7596	Law enforcement
343.73014	KF7590	Military discipline
343.730143	KF7601-7679	Military criminal law
343.730143	KF7625-7659	Courts martial
343.730143	KF7665	Appellate
343.730146	KF7675-7677	Punishment
343.730146	KF7679	Probation
343.730184	KF7405-7430	Air Force
343.730184	KF7657	Air Force
343.73019	KF7646-7652	Navy
343.73019	KF7345-7375	Navy
343.7301996	KF7654	Marine Corps
343.7301996	KF7385-7395	Marine Corps
343.7301997	KF7659	Coast Guard
343.7301997	KF7485-7488.7	Services during war/ Emergency
343.7301997	KF7445-7479	Coast Guard
343.7302	KF5750-5857	Government property
343.7302	KF5750-5755	Administration
343.7302	KF5500-5865	Public property
343.73023	KF5820-5857	Personal property
343.73025	KF5760-5810	Land/Real property
343.73025	KF5601-5646	Public land law
343.730252	KF5599	Eminent domain
343.730253	KF5675-5677	Land grants
343.730253	KF5670-5673	Homesteads
343.7303	KF6200-6795	Public finance
343.73032	KF6201-6219	Currency/Coinage
343.73032	KF1033	Foreign-exchange
343.73034	KF6231-6236	Public auditing
343.73034	KF6221-6225	Budget
343.73036	KF6251-6708	National revenue
343.7303609	KF6251-6256	History
343.73037	KF6241-6245	Public debts
343.7304	KF6300-6328	Tax administration
343.7304	KF6329-6330	Exemption
343.7304	KF6298	Tax expenditures
343.7304	KF6296-6297	Tax planning
343.7304	KF6271-6645	Taxation
343.73042	KF6310-6316	Tax collection
343.73042	KF6320-6328	Procedures
343.73043	KF6720-6795	State/Local finance
343.7305	KF6335-6636	Kinds of taxes
343.73052	KF6351-6499	Income tax
343.730524	KF6566-6594	Taxes on capital and income
343.730526	KF6598-6636	Indirect taxes
343.73053	KF746-750	Estate planning
343.73054	KF6525-6558	Property tax
343.73056	KF6651-6708	Tariffs
343.7307	KF1600-2940	Business regulations
343.7307	KF1659-.1	Small business
343.7307(6-7)	KF1681-1873	Primary production
343.7307(6-7)	KF1681-1750	Agriculture/Forestry
343.73072	KF1631-1657	Monopolies
343.73072	KF1601-1611	Unfair trade practices
343.730721	KF3195-3198	Unfair competition
343.730723	KF1624-1625	Restraint of trade
343.730725	KF1626-1629	Price fixing
343.73075	KF1665-1666	Weights/Measures/ Containers
343.7307692	KF1770-1773	Fishery
343.73077	KF1801-1873	Mining/Quarrying/ Petroleum
343.73078	KF1875-1893	Manufacturing industry
343.73078624	KF1950	Construction industry
343.7308	KF1085-1086	Commodity exchanges
343.7308	KF1970-2057	Trade/Commerce
343.7308	KF1601-1666	Trade regulations
343.73082	KF1619-1620	Labeling
343.73082	KF1614-1617	Advertising
343.73088	KF1663	State/Trade barriers
343.7309	KF2076-2140	Public utilities
343.7309(4-5)	KF1092	By land
343.73093	KF1091-1137	Carriers
343.730942	KF5521-5536	Roads
343.73096	KF1096-1114	By sea
343.73097	KF1093	By air
343.801	UB530-589	South America
343.8201	UB530-534	Argentina
343.8301	UB545-549	Chile
343.86101	UB550-554	Colombia
343.8701	UB585-589	Venezuela
343.9(3-4)01	UB730-734.5	Australia/New Zealand
343.9(5-6)01	UB735-736	Oceania
344	K7585-7595	Social legislation
344	K1700-1970	Social legislation
344.(4-9)0413	RK5-15	Registration, By place
344.01	K1701-1841	Labor law
344.01712	K4360-4375	Professions
344.02	K1861-1929	Social insurance
344.03	K1960-1970	Public welfare
344.032	HV70-72	Public welfare laws
344.04	K3566-3609	Public health/Medical law
344.0413	RK4-15	Examination/Registration
344.042	K3651-3654	Alcohol
344.0423	K3625-3649	Food/Drugs/Cosmetics
344.04461	HV5081-5095	Alcoholism and the state
344.04633	SB970-.4	Policy
344.047	K3661-3674	Public safety
344.049	K3615-3617	Veterinary laws
344.063635	K3550-3553	Housing
344.07	K3740-3762	Education
344.09	K3770-3793	Science/Arts/Research
344.097	N8700-9165	Art and the state
344.411	KDC635-674	Social legislation
344.41104	KDC680-695	Health/Medical legislation
344.416	KDE320-348	Social legislation
344.417	KDK800-895	Social legislation
344.41704	KDK910-932	Medical/Health legislation
344.42	KD3000-3315	Social legislation
344.4201	KD3001-3177	Labor law
344.4201712	KD2940-2990	The professions
344.420189	KD1638-1642	Labor contracts
344.4202	KD3191-3273	Social insurance
344.4203	KD3291-3315	Public welfare
344.4203288	KD2007	Victim compensation
344.4204(6)	KD3351-3375	Public health/Pollution
344.42041	KD3395-3413	Medicine
344.42042	KD3466-3480	Alcohol
344.420423	KD3450-3462	Food/Drugs/Cosmetics
344.42047	KD3510	Accidents
344.420472	KD3494-3507	Hazards
344.42049	KD3420-3422	Veterinary medicine
344.4205	KD3490-3516	Public safety
344.420533	KD3492	Weapons/Firearms
344.420535	KD6340	Civil defense
344.420537	KD3515-3516	Fire
344.420542	KD3527	Gambling
344.4207	KD3600-3689	Education
344.4208	KD3758	Scientific/Cultural exchanges
344.4209	KD4650	National emblem/Seals
344.4209	KD4656-4657	Honors/Dignities

Dewey	LC	Descriptor
344.4209(5/7)	KD3710-3758	Science/Arts
344.42092	KD3753-3755	Archives
344.42092	KD3746	Libraries
344.42093	KD3736	Museums/Galleries
344.42097	KD3720-3731	The arts
344.42099	KD3525	Sports
344.42099	KD3523	Amusements
344.42907	KD9460	Education (Law)
344.71	KE3098-3542	Social law
344.7101712	KE2700-2742	The professions
344.710189	KE928-936	Labor contracts
344.71032	KE1229	Restitution
344.7103288	KE1312	Victims' compensation
344.7104(632)	KE3375-3635	Public health/Pollution
344.71041	KE3646-3660	Medical legislation
344.710423	KE3696-3725	Food/Drugs/Cosmetics
344.7105	KE3756-3778	Public safety
344.7107	KE3805-3917	Education
344.7109(5/7)	KE3950-4000	Science/Arts
344.73	KF3300-3750	Social legislation
344.7301	KF3301-3580	Labor law
344.7301712	KF2901-2940	The professions
344.73017613875	KF1121-1132	Maritime labor law
344.7301891	KF898-905	Labor contracts
344.7302	KF3600-3686	Social insurance
344.7303	KF3720-3745	Public welfare/Assistance
344.7303288	KF9763	Victims of crimes
344.7303288	KF1328	Victims' compensation
344.7304	KF3775-3813	Public health/Sanitation
344.73041	KF3821-3829	Medical legislation
344.73042	KF3901-3925	Alcohol
344.730423	KF3861-3894	Food/Drugs/Cosmetics
344.73047	KF3970	Accident control
344.730472	KF3945-3965	Hazardous items/Processes
344.73048	KF3832	Eugenics/Sterilization
344.73049	KF3835-3838	Veterinary medicine
344.7305	KF4850-4856	Internal security
344.7305	KF3941-3977	Public safety
344.73053(7/33)	KF3975-3977	Fire/Explosives
344.730533	KF3941-3942	Weapons/Firearms
344.730534	KF3750	Disaster relief
344.730535	KF7685	Civil defense
344.730542	KF1241	Gambling/Wagering contracts
344.730542	KF3992	Lotteries
344.7306	KF5865	Public works
344.73063635	KF5721-5740	Public housing/Redevelopment
344.73065515	KF5594	Meteorology
344.7307	KF4101-4258	Education
344.7307	KF4192	Other personnel
344.73074	KF4225-4258	Higher education
344.73074	KF4195-4223	Through high school
344.73076	KF4125-4143	School finance/Etc.
344.73078	KF4175-4190	Teachers
344.7307833847664	KF1900-1944	Food processing industry
344.73079	KF4150-4166	Students
344.730796	KF4124	Church and education
344.7308	KF4330	Scientific/Cultural exchanges
344.7309	KF5150	National emblems/Seals
344.7309	KF5153-5154	Honors/Awards
344.7309	KF5155-5156	Commemorative medals
344.7309(5/7)	KF4270-4330	Science/Arts
344.73092	KF4325	Archives
344.73092	KF4315-4319	Libraries
344.73093	KF4305	Museums/Galleries
344.73094	KF4310-4312	Monuments/Historical sites
344.73097	KF4288-4302	The arts
344.73099	KF3989	Sports
344.73099	KF3987	Amusements
345	K5000-5570	Criminal law
345.001	K5018-5022	Philosophy/Theory
345.009	K5032-5033	History
345.01	K5036-5048	Criminal jurisdiction
345.01	K5423	Jurisdiction
345.01	K5495-5497	Appellate/Etc.
345.02	K5090-5098	Forms of offense
345.02	K5165-5316	Offenses
345.02	K5055-5056	Criminal offense
345.04	K5064-5083	Criminal liability
345.05	K5412-5418	Principles of procedure
345.05	K5401-5570	Criminal procedure
345.0501	K5404	Philosophy/Theory
345.0509	K5409-5410	History
345.056	K5452-5453	Rights of suspects
345.06	K5465-5490	Evidence
345.072	K5430-5447	Preliminary proceedings
345.072	K5425	Indictment
345.075	K5460-5492	Trial
345.075	K5492	Jury
345.077	K5101-5136	Punishment
345.077	K5510-5570	Execution of sentence
345.08	K5575-5582	Juvenile criminal law
345.4110(7/5)	KDC910-948	Criminal law/Procedure
345.41107	KDC184-188	Trial (Civil/Criminal)
345.416(075)	KDE540-562	Criminal law/Procedure
345.4170(7/5)	KDK1750-1831	Criminal trial/Procedure
345.42	KD7850-8090	Criminal law
345.4205	KD8220-8464	Criminal procedure
345.4207	KD370-376	Criminal trials
345.429	KD9490	Criminal law
345.42907	KD9423	Criminal trials
345.71	KE8801-9440	Criminal law
345.7107	KE225-229	Criminal trials
345.73	KF9201-9461	Criminal law
345.7302	KF9300	Kinds of offenses
345.730232	KF9390-9456	Against government/Public
345.730233	KF6334	Tax evasion
345.730236	KF9460-9461	Through the mail
345.73025	KF9304-9345	Against persons
345.73026	KF9350-9379	Against property
345.7305	KF9641-9760	Criminal procedure
345.73052	KF9635	Extradition
345.730522	KF9630	Searches
345.730527	KF9625	Arrest
345.73056	KF9632	Bail
345.7306	KF9660-9677	Evidence
345.7307	KF9655-9688	Trial
345.7307	KF220-224	Criminal trials
345.73072	KF9645-9650	Arraignment
345.73072	KF9640-9642	Indictment
345.73075	KF9680	Jury
345.73077	KF9695	Pardon
345.73077	KF9225-9227	Punishment
345.73077	KF9725-9756	Execution of sentence
345.73077(2)	KF9685-9688	Judgment/Sentence
345.7308	KF9771-9827	Juvenile criminal law
346	K600-619	Private law
346	K623-968	Civil law
346.0(65-78)	HD3611-4730.9	Industry and the state
346.0(65-78)	HD3612	Regulation
346.012	K625-709	Persons
346.015	K670-709	Domestic relations

Dewey	LC	Descriptor
346.016	HQ1001-1006	Marriage and the state
346.02	K830-968	Obligations
346.02	K1024-1132	Commercial contracts
346.02(2-5)	K840-917	Contracts
346.029	K920	Restitution/Quasi contracts
346.03	K923-968	Torts
346.04	K720-792	Property
346.044	K3478-3486	Natural resources
346.045	K3531-3544	Regional/City planning
346.04691	K3496-3501	Water resources
346.04691	K4150-4235	Water
346.048	K1500-1578	Industrial property
346.048	K1401-1578	Intellectual property
346.0482	K1411-1485	Copyright
346.052	K805-821	Succession upon death
346.059	K795-798	Trusts and trustees
346.06	K1301-1366	Business associations
346.065	K1010-1016	Merchants/Business enterprises
346.07	K1000-1388	Commercial law
346.072	K1026-1045	Sale of goods
346.074	K1100-1104	Secured transactions
346.078	K1370-1388	Bankruptcy
346.08	K1066-1088	Banking
346.082	HG1725-1778	Banks and the state
346.086	HG8111-8123	Insurance (State supervision)
346.086	K1241-1287	Insurance
346.0862	K1226-1231	Marine insurance
346.08632	HG8901-8914	State supervision (Life ins.)
346.092	K1112-1116	Investments
346.096	K1054-1065	Negotiable instruments
346.4110(2/96)	KDC482-545	Obligations/Negotiable instruments
346.411012	KDC350-378	Persons
346.41104	KDC390-452	Property
346.411052	KDC462-470	Succession upon death
346.416012	KDE90-98	Persons
346.41604	KDE110-137	Property
346.416052	KDE145-151	Succession upon death
346.416059	KDE140-142	Trust/Trustees
346.417012	KDK185-205	Persons
346.41702	KDK370-437	Contracts
346.41703	KDK450-469	Torts
346.41704	KDK215-345	Property
346.417052	KDK360-365	Succession upon death
346.417059	KDK350-354	Trust/Trustees
346.420(4363/052)	KD966-992	Sale/Inheritance
346.42004	KD674	Equity
346.42013	KD723-746	Persons (Status/Capacity)
346.42015	KD750-785	Family law
346.4202	KD1621-1920	Types of contracts
346.4202	KD1554-1920	Contracts
346.4202	KD1621-1630	Commercial
346.42023	KD1610-1613	Government contracts
346.42024	KD1634	Service contracts
346.42025	KD1679-1685	Bailments
346.42029	KD2020-2024	Agency/Power of attorney
346.42029	KD1924	Quasi contracts
346.4203	KD1941-2004	Torts
346.4204	KD810-1465	Property
346.42043	KD821-1195	Real property/Land law
346.420432	KD833-960	Land tenure
346.420432	KD841-960	Estates
346.420432	KD833-1020.6	Real estate management/ Etc.
346.420432	KD810-815	Possession
346.420434	KD834-839	Feudal systems
346.4204364	KD1010-1016	Mortgages/Liens
346.42044	KD1035	Natural resources
346.42045	KD1125-1162	Planning/Zoning
346.4204691	KD1070	Water resources
346.42047	KD1205-1465	Personal property
346.42048	KD1261-1450	Intellectual/Industrial
346.42048	KD1238-1450	Intangible
346.42048	KD1450	Business names
346.420482	KD1281-1325	Copyright
346.420484	KD1345	Design protection
346.420486	KD1361-1413.3	Patent law
346.420488	KD1431-1445	Trademarks
346.42052	KD1497	Estate planning
346.42052	KD1500-1534	Succession upon death
346.42059	KD1480-1495	Trust/Trustees
346.4206	KD2040-2127	Associations
346.4206	KD2228	Trade associations
346.42064	KD2046-2054	Unincorporated associations
346.42064	KD2061-2062	Nonprofit
346.42065	KD2071-2127	Businesses/Companies
346.42066	KD2057-2127	Corporations
346.420682	KD2049-2054	Partnership
346.42072	KD1650-1675	Sale of goods
346.42073	KD1740-1742	Financial loans
346.42074	KD1752	Guaranty/Secured transactions
346.42078	KD2139-2172	Bankruptcy
346.42082	KD1715-1737	Banking
346.42086	KD1851-1913	Insurance
346.420862	KD1845-1847	Marine insurance
346.42092	KD1755-1763	Securities/Investments
346.42096	KD1695-1699	Negotiable instruments
346.71004	KE457	Equity
346.71012	KE498-606	Persons
346.71015	KE531-606	Family law
346.7102	KE850-1225	Contracts
346.7102	KE1328-1332	Agency
346.71023	KE899-906	Government contracts
346.71024	KE924	Service contracts
346.71025	KE970-972	Bailments
346.7103	KE1232-1309	Torts
346.7104	KE618-781	Property
346.71043	KE625-754	Real property
346.71045	KE5258-5284	Regional/City planning
346.7104691	KE5145-5165	Water resources
346.71047	KE765-781	Personal property
346.71048	KE2771-2998	Intellectual property
346.71052	KE806-833	Succession upon death
346.71059	KE787-799	Trusts
346.7106	KE1345-1465	Associations
346.71064	KE1351-1361	Unicorporated associations
346.71066	KE1369-1465	Corporations
346.71072	KE943-966	Sale of goods
346.71073	KE1030-1034	Loans
346.71074	KE1042-1056	Secured transactions
346.71078	KE1485-1520	Bankruptcy
346.71082	KE991-1026	Banking
346.71086	KE1141-1220	Insurance
346.71092	KE1060-1089	Investments
346.71096	KE980-986	Negotiable instruments
346.73004	KF398-400	Equity
346.73012	KF465-553	Persons
346.73013	KF465-485	Status/Capacity
346.73015	KF501-553	Family law
346.7302	KF871-890	Commercial/Mercantile contracts

Dewey	LC	Descriptor	Dewey	LC	Descriptor
346.7302	KF801-1241	Contracts	347.41705	KDK1580-1713	Courts (Procedure)
346.7302	KF807-839	Contracts (Principles)	347.41705	KDK1660-1713	Civil procedure
346.73023	KF841-869	Government contracts	347.41707	KDK102-106	Trials
346.73024	KF894	Service contracts	347.42	KD6335	Civil law/Armed forces
346.73025	KF939-951	Bailments	347.42	KD720-721	Civil law
346.73029	KF1341-1348	Power of attorney/Brokers	347.42	KD7100-7312	Justice after 1873
346.73029	KF1244	Restitution	347.42	KD4645	Judiciary
346.7303	KF1246-1327	Torts	347.42	KD6850-7640	Courts (Procedure)
346.7304	KF560-720	Property	347.42	KD6870-6992	Justice before 1873
346.73043	KF566-698	Real property	347.420(1-5)	KD7111-7312	Court organization/
346.730432	KF560-562	Ownership			Procedures
346.73044	KF5505-5508	Natural resources	347.42013	KD327-332	Judicial statistics
346.73045	KF5691-5710	Planning/Zoning	347.42017	KD512	Legal aid
346.7304691	KF5551-5590	Water resources	347.4205	KD411	Reporting
346.73047	KF701-720	Personal property	347.42055	KD318	Form books
346.73048	KF2971-3192	Intellectual property	347.4207	KD370-379.5	Trials
346.73048(6/8)	KF3091-3192	Patent law/Trademarks	347.4207	KD378-379.5	Civil trials
346.730482	KF2986-3080	Copyright	347.4209	KD7645-7647	Arbitration
346.730484	KF3086	Design protection	347.4209	KD6850-6855	History
346.73052	KF753-780	Succession upon death	347.429	KD9480	Courts and procedure
346.73052	KF746-750	Estate planning	347.7(4-9)02	JS381-385	Judiciary (City courts)
346.73059	KF726-745	Trusts	347.71	JL181-185	The judiciary
346.7306	KF1355-1480	Associations	347.71	KE495	Civil law
346.73064	KF1361-1380	Unincorporated	347.7101	KE8212-8332	Court organization
346.73064	KF1388-1389	Nonprofit corporations	347.7101	KE8200-8605	Courts
346.73064	KF1661	Trade associations	347.71013	KE198-206	Judicial statistics
346.73066	KF1384-1480	Corporations	347.71017	KE376-378	Legal aid
346.73066	KF1396-1477	Business corporations	347.7105	KE8341-8605	Civil procedure
346.73067	KF1480	Government-owned	347.710504	KE335-355	Practice of law
346.730682	KF1365-1380	Partnership	347.7107	KE234-237	Civil trials
346.73072	KF911-935	Sale of goods	347.7107	KE225-237	Trials
346.73073	KF1035-1040	Loans	347.7109	KE8618	Arbitration
346.73074	KF1045	Guaranty	347.7109	KE8615	Negotiated settlement
346.73074	KF1046-1062	Chattel mortgages/Liens	347.73	JK1507-1598	The Judiciary
346.73078	KF1501-1548	Bankruptcy	347.73	KF7680	Civil status
346.73082	KF966-1032	Banking	347.73	KF5130	Judiciary
346.73086	KF1146-1238	Insurance	347.730(1-5)	KF8700-9075	Courts/Procedure
346.730862	KF1135-1137	Marine insurance	347.730(1-5)	KF8711-8807	Court organization/
346.73092	KF1066-1083	Securities/Investments			Procedures
346.73096	KF956-962	Negotiable instruments	347.73013	KF180-185	Judicial statistics
347	K3367	The judiciary	347.73055	KF170	Form books
347	K2100-2385	Court procedures	347.731(4-6)	KF8770-8807	Judicial officers/Employees
347	JF700-723	Judiciary	347.7313	KF8732-8733	Administration (Courts)
347.0(72/52)	K7640-7646	Pleading/Motions	347.7317	KF336-337	Legal aid
347.01(2-7)	K2110-2155	Court organization/	347.732	JK1551-1598	Federal courts
		Procedure	347.7322	KF8754-8755	District/Circuit courts
347.012	K7625-7627	Jurisdiction	347.7324	KF8750-8752	Appeals courts
347.012	JF711	Prerogatives/Jurisdiction	347.7326	KF8741-8745	Supreme court
347.017	K133	Legal aid	347.7328	KF8760	Claims courts
347.02	JS185-188	Judiciary (City courts)	347.733	JK2521-2525	The judiciary
347.05	K2201-2385	Civil procedure	347.733	KF8736	State courts
347.05	K7616-7686	Civil procedure	347.734	KF8737	Local courts
347.052	K7650-7655	Parties	347.734(82/52)	KF8866-8885	Pleading/Motions
347.052	JF723	Jury system	347.735	KF8810-9075	Civil procedures
347.07	K540-546	Trials	347.7351	KF8820-8821	District courts
347.07	K7660-7673	Trial	347.7351	KF8816-8902	Court rules
347.077	K7681-7686	Remedies	347.7351	KF8858-8861	Jurisdiction
347.09	K2400-2405	Arbitration	347.7352	KF8890-8896	Parties
347.09	K2390	Negotiated settlement	347.7353	KF228	Civil suits
347.09	K7690	Arbitration	347.7353	KF8863-8865	Action/Process
347.41	JN751-829	Judiciary	347.736	KF8931-8969	Evidence
347.41103	KDC110-113	Courts of Appeal	347.737	KF8910-9075	Trial
347.41105	KDC875-902.6	Civil procedure	347.7372	KF8900-8902	Pretrial
347.41105	KDC840-948	Courts (Procedure)	347.7375	KF8911-8925	Trial practice
347.41107	KDC184-188	Trials (Civil/Criminal)	347.73752	KF8971-8986	Jury
347.41605	KDE525-530	Civil procedure	347.7377	KF8990-9002	Judgment
347.41605	KDE510-530	Courts (Procedure)	347.7377	KF9010-9039	Remedies

Dewey	LC	Descriptor	Dewey	LC	Descriptor
347.738	KF9050-9058	Appellate	349.493	KJK	Law of Belgium
347.738	KF9690	Appeals	349.4935	KKK0-499	Law of Luxembourg
347.739	KF9085	Arbitration	349.494	KKW	Law of Switzerland
347.739	KF9084	Negotiated settlement	349.495	KKE	Law of Greece
348.022	K7010-7011	Statutes	349.4965	KJG	Law of Albania
348.41604	KDE55-60	Law reports	349.497	KKZ	Law of Yugoslavia
348.41704	KDK61-80	Law reports	349.4977	KJM	Law of Bulgaria
348.42022	KD125-150	Statutes	349.498	KKR	Law of Romania
348.4204	KD190-300	Law reports, Etc.	349.561	KKX	Law of Turkey
348.429022	KD9407	Statutes	349.5645	KJN	Law of Cyprus
348.42904	KD9410-9417	Law reports	349.7	KDZ	North America
348.7(4-9)	KF165	Uniform state laws	349.7	KDZ0-999	General
348.7104	KE132-176	Law reports	349.7(41-987)	KFX	Law of United States cities
348.73	KF16-49	Legislative documents	349.71	KE	Law (Canada)
348.73022	KF50-90	Statutes	349.71(1-9)	KEZ	Law, Canadian cities
348.7304	KF255	Law reporting	349.71072	KE250-259	Legal research
348.7304	KF101-153	Law reports	349.711	KEB	Law, British Columbia
348.7304	KF260	Cases	349.7123	KEA	Law, Alberta
348.731	KF4520	Legislative history	349.7124	KES	Law, Saskatchewan
348.7322	KF8815	Statutes	349.7127	KEM	Law, Manitoba
349.(72/8)	KG0-999	Latin America, General	349.713	KEO	Law, Ontario
349.(72/8)	KG	Latin America	349.714	KEQ	Law, Quebec
349.4(2-9)	KD4746-4840	Local government	349.7151	KEN0-599	Law, New Brunswick
349.4(6-9)	KDK1910-1950	Local laws	349.716	KEN7400-7999	Law, Nova Scotia
349.411	KDC	Law (Scotland)	349.718	KEN1200-1799	Law, Newfoundland
349.411(2-9)	KDC980-990	Local laws	349.7188	KDZ4000-4499	St. Pierre and Miquelon
349.416	KDE	Law (Northern Ireland)	349.7191	KEY	Law, Yukon Territory
349.416(1-98)	KDE570-580	Local laws	349.7192	5400-5999	Law, Northwest Territories
349.417	KDK	Law (Ireland)	349.7192	KFZ1800-2399	Law of Northwest Territory
349.42	KD	Law (England)	349.72	KGF0-5999	General
349.42	KD691-703	General principles/Concepts	349.72	KGF	Mexico
349.42	KD5020-5025	Commonwealth/Empire	349.72(1-7)	KGF6200-9399	States
349.42	KD8850-9312	England	349.72(9)	KG3000-3999	Mexico/Central America
349.42(1-8)	KD8850-9150	Counties/Shires/Cities/Etc.	349.7212	KGF8900-8999	Tamaulipas
349.42(1-9)	KD8850-9355	Local laws	349.7213	KGF8000-8099	Nuevo Leon
349.42072	KD392-400	Legal research	349.7214	KGF6800-6899	Coahuila
349.4234	KDG	Law (Channel Islands, Britain)	349.7215	KGF7000-7099	Durango
349.42341	KDG220-380	Channel Islands, Jersey	349.7216	KGF6700-6799	Chihuahua
349.42342	KDG421-440	Channel Islands, Guernsey	349.7217	KGF8700-8799	Sonora
349.42345	KDG532-540	Channel Islands, Sark	349.7223	KGF6300-6399	Baja California/Baja California Norte
349.4279	KDG26-170	Isle of Man	349.7224	KGF6400-6499	Baja California Sur
349.429	KD9400-9500	Law of Wales	349.7232	KGF8600-8699	Sinaloa
349.429	KD9320-9355	Wales (Local law)	349.7234	KGF7900-7999	Nayarit
349.429(1-9)	KD9320-9325	Counties/Shires/Cities/Etc.	349.7235	KGF7400-7499	Jalisco
349.42903	KD9420	Law dictionaries	349.7236	KGF6900-6999	Colima
349.43	KK	Law of Germany	349.7237	KGF7700-7799	Michoacan
349.436	KJJ	Law of Austria	349.7241	KGF7100-7199	Guanajuato
349.43648	KKJ	Law of Liechtenstein	349.7242	KGF6200-6299	Aguascalientes
349.437	KJP	Law of Czechoslovakia	349.7243	KGF9300-9399	Zacatecas
349.438	KKP	Law of Poland	349.7244	KGF8500-8599	San Luis Potosi
349.439	KKF	Law of Hungary	349.7245	KGF8300-8399	Queretaro
349.44	KJV	Law of France	349.7246	KGF7300-7399	Hidalgo
349.44949	KKL	Law of Monaco	349.7247	KGF9000-9099	Tlaxcala
349.45	KKH	Law of Italy	349.7248	KGF8200-8299	Puebla
349.4549	KKS	Law of San Marino	349.7249	KGF7800-7899	Morelos
349.45634	KKY	Law of Vatican City	349.7252	KGF7500-7599	Mexico (State)
349.4585	1000-1499	Law of Malta	349.7253	KGF7600-7699	Mexico City (Federal District)
349.46	KKT	Law of Spain			
349.4679	KJH	Law of Andorra	349.7262	KGF9100-9199	Veracruz
349.469	KKQ	Law of Portugal	349.7263	KGF8800-8899	Tabasco
349.481	KKN	Law of Norway	349.7264	KGF6500-6599	Campeche
349.485	KKV	Law of Sweden	349.7265	KGF9200-9299	Yucatan
349.489	KJR	Law of Denmark	349.7267	KGF8400-8499	Quintana Roo
349.4897	KJT	Law of Finland	349.7273	KGF7200-7299	Guerrero
349.4912	KKG	Law of Iceland	349.7274	KGF8100-8199	Oaxaca
349.492	KKM	Law of Netherlands	349.7275	KGF6600-6699	Chiapas

Dewey	LC	Descriptor	Dewey	LC	Descriptor
349.7281	KGD0-5999	General	349.7285(1-32)	KGG6200-9499	Departments/Territory
349.7281	KGD	Guatemala	349.728511	KGG6800-6899	Chinandega
349.7281(1-84)	KGD6100-9899	Departments	349.728512	KGG7800-7899	Leon
349.72811	KGD9920-9939	Guatemala City	349.728513	KGG9600-9619	Managua (City)
349.72811	KGD7000-7099	Guatemala (Dept.)	349.728513	KGG8200-8299	Managua
349.72812	KGD7900-7999	Peten	349.728514	KGG8400-8499	Masaya
349.728131	KGD7300-7399	Izabal	349.728515	KGG7400-7499	Granada
349.728132	KGD9800-9899	Zacapa	349.728516	KGG6600-6699	Carazo
349.728141	KGD6500-6599	Chiquimula	349.728517	KGG9200-9299	Rivas
349.728142	KGD7500-7599	Jalapa	349.728521	KGG8800-8899	Nueva Segovia
349.728143	KGD7700-7799	Jutiapa	349.728522	KGG7600-7699	Jinotega
349.728144	KGD9100-9199	Santa Rosa	349.728523	KGG8000-8099	Madriz
349.728151	KGD6100-6199	Alta Verapaz	349.728524	KGG7200-7299	Estelf
349.728152	KGD6200-6299	Baja Verapaz	349.728525	KGG8600-8699	Matagalpa
349.728153	KGD6700-6799	El Progreso	349.728526	KGG6200-6299	Boaco
349.728161	KGD6300-6399	Chimaltenango	349.728527	KGG7000-7099	Chontales
349.728162	KGD8700-8799	Sacatepequez	349.728531	KGG9000-9099	Rio San Juan
349.728163	KGD6900-6999	Escuintla	349.728532	KGG6400-6499	Cabo Gracias a Dios
349.728164	KGD9300-9399	Solola	349.728532	KGG9400-9499	Zelaya
349.728165	KGD9500-9599	Suchitepequez	349.7286	KGB	Costa Rica
349.728171	KGD7100-7199	Huehuetenango	349.7286	KGB0-5999	General
349.728172	KGD8300-8399	Quiche	349.7286(1-7)	KGB6200-7499	Provinces
349.728181	KGD9700-9799	Totonicapan	349.72861	KGB7000-7099	Limon
349.728182	KGD8100-8199	Quezaltenango	349.72862	KGB6400-6499	Cartago
349.728183	KGD8500-8599	Retalhuleu	349.72863	KGB7400-7499	San Jose
349.728184	KGD8900-8999	San Marcos	349.72863	KGB8000-8019	San Jose (City)
349.7283	KGE	Honduras	349.72864	KGB6800-6899	Heredia
349.7283	KGE0-5999	General	349.72865	KGB6200-6299	Alajuela
349.7283(11-85)	KGE6100-9599	Departments	349.72866	KGB6600-6699	Guanacaste
349.728311	KGE7100-7199	Cortes	349.72867	KGB7200-7299	Puntarenas
349.728313	KGE6500-6599	Colon	349.7287	KGH	Panama
349.728314	KGE9500-9599	Yoro	349.7287	KGH0-5999	General
349.728315	KGE8100-8199	Islas de la Bahia	349.7287(1-5)	KGH6100-7799	Provinces
349.728315	KGE6100-6199	Atlantida	349.728711	KGH6300-6399	Chiriqui
349.72832	KGE7700-7799	Gracias a Dios	349.728712	KGH6100-6199	Bocas del Toro
349.72833	KGE8900-8999	Olancho	349.728721	KGH6500-6599	Cocle
349.72834	KGE7300-7399	El Paraiso	349.728722	KGH7700-7799	Veraguas
349.728351	KGE6300-6399	Choluteca	349.728723	KGH7300-7399	Los Santos
349.728352	KGE9300-9399	Valle	349.728724	KGH7100-7199	Herrera
349.72836	KGE8300-8399	La Paz	349.728731	KGH7840-7859	Panama City
349.728371	KGE9960-9979	Tegucigalpa	349.728731	KGH7500-7599	Panama
349.728371	KGE7500-7599	Francisco Morazan	349.728732	KGH6700-6799	Colon
349.728372	KGE6700-6799	Comayagua	349.728732	KGH7820-7839	Colon (City)
349.728381	KGE7900-7999	Intibuca	349.72874	KGH6900-6999	Darien
349.728382	KGE8500-8599	Lempira	349.72875	KGH9000-9499	Panama Canal Zone
349.728383	KGE8700-8799	Octepeque	349.7291	KGN0-5999	General
349.728384	KGE6900-6999	Copan	349.7291	KGN	Cuba
349.728385	KGE9100-9199	Santa Barbara	349.7291(1-67)	KGN6200-8899	Provinces
349.7284	KGC	El Salvador	349.72911	KGN8200-8299	Pina del Rio
349.7284(11-34)	KGC6200-8899	Departments	349.729123	KGN7200-7299	Havana (City)
349.728411	KGC6200-6299	Ahuachapan	349.729124	KGN7400-7499	Havana (Province)
349.728412	KGC9640-9659	Santa Ana (City)	349.72913	KGN8000-8099	Matanzas
349.728413	KGC8600-8699	Sonsonate	349.72914	KGN7900-7999	Las Villas
349.728421	KGC6600-6699	Chalatenango	349.729142	KGN8800-8899	Villa Clara
349.728422	KGC7000-7099	La Libertad	349.729143	KGN6600-6699	Cienfuegos
349.728423	KGC8000-8099	San Salvador	349.729145	KGN8400-8499	Sancti Spiritus
349.728423	KGC9600-9619	San Salvador (City)	349.729153	KGN6400-6499	Ciego de Avila
349.728424	KGC6800-6899	Cuscatlan	349.729156	KGN6200-6299	Camaguey
349.728425	KGC7200-7299	La Paz	349.72916	KGN8100-8199	Oriente
349.728426	KGC6400-6499	Cabanas	349.729162	KGN7800-7899	Las Tunas
349.728427	KGC8200-8299	San Vicente	349.729163	KGN6800-6899	Granma
349.728431	KGC8800-8899	Usulutan	349.729164	KGN7600-7699	Holguin
349.728432	KGC7800-7899	San Miguel	349.729165	KGN8600-8699	Santiago de Cuba
349.728433	KGC7600-7699	Morazan	349.729167	KGN7000-7099	Guantanamo
349.728434	KGC7400-7499	La Union	349.7292	KGT0-499	Jamaica
349.7285	KGG	Nicaragua	349.72921	KGM0-499	Cayman Islands
349.7285	KGG0-5999	General	349.7293	KGQ0-5999	General

Dewey	LC	Descriptor	Dewey	LC	Descriptor
349.7293	KGQ	Dominican Republic	349.72986	KGK1000-1499	Aruba
349.7293(2-85)	KGQ6200-8899	Provinces/National District	349.7299	KDZ2000-2499	Bermuda
349.729323	KGQ7600-7699	Pedernales	349.73	KF	Law (United States)
349.729324	KGQ6400-6499	Barahona	349.73072	KF240-246	Legal research
349.729325	KGQ6900-6999	Independencia	349.741	KFM0-599	Law of Maine
349.729342	KGQ8200-8299	San Juan	349.742	KFN1200-1799	Law of New Hampshire
349.729343	KGQ7100-7199	La Estrelleta (San Rafael)	349.743	KFV0-599	Law of Vermont
349.729345	KGQ6500-6599	Dajabon	349.744	KFM2400-2999	Law of Massachusetts
349.729352	KGQ7500-7599	Montecristi	349.745	KFR0-599	Law of Rhode Island
349.729353	KGQ8600-8699	Santiago Rodriguez	349.746	KFC3600-4199	Law of Connecticut
349.729356	KGQ8500-8599	Santiago	349.747	KFN5000-6199	Law of New York
349.729357	KGQ8800-8899	Valverde	349.748	KFP0-599	Law of Pennsylvania
349.729358	KGQ7800-7899	Puerto Plata	349.749	KFN1800-2399	Law of New Jersey
349.729362	KGQ6800-6899	Espaillat	349.75	KFZ8600-9199	Confederate States of America
349.729363	KGQ7900-7999	Salcedo			
349.729364	KGQ7400-7499	Maria Trinadad Sanchez	349.751	KFD0-599	Law of Delaware
349.729365	KGQ8000-8099	Samana	349.752	KFM1200-1799	Law of Maryland
349.729367	KGQ6600-6699	Duarte	349.753	KFD1200-1799	Law of District of Columbia
349.729369	KGQ7300-7399	La Vega	349.754	KFW1200-1799	Law of West Virginia
349.729372	KGQ6200-6299	Azua	349.755	KFV2400-2999	Law of Virginia
349.729373	KGQ7700-7799	Peravia	349.756	KFN7400-7999	Law of North Carolina
349.729374	KGQ8100-8199	San Cristobal	349.757	KFS1800-2399	Law of South Carolina
349.729375	KGQ8700-8799	Santo Domingo (National Dist.)	349.758	KFG0-599	Law of Georgia
			349.759	KFF0-599	Law of Florida
349.729382	KGQ8300-8399	San Pedro de Macoris	349.761	KFA0-599	Law of Alabama
349.729383	KGQ7200-7299	La Romana	349.762	KFM6600-7199	Law of Mississippi
349.729384	KGQ6700-6799	El Seibo	349.763	KFL0-599	Law of Louisiana
349.729385	KGQ7000-7099	La Altagracia	349.764	KFT1200-1799	Law of Texas
349.7294	KGS	Haiti	349.766	KFO1200-1799	Law of Oklahoma
349.7294	KGS0-5999	General	349.767	KFA3600-4199	Law of Arkansas
349.7294(2-6)	KGS6200-7899	Departments	349.768	KFT0-599	Law of Tennessee
349.72942	KGS7200-7299	Nord-Ouest	349.769	KFK1200-1799	Law of Kentucky
349.72943	KGS6800-6899	Nord	349.771	KFO0-599	Law of Ohio
349.72944	KGS6200-6299	Artibonite	349.772	KFI3000-3599	Law of Indiana
349.72945	KGS8000-8019	Port-au-Prince	349.773	KFI1200-1799	Law of Illinois
349.72945	KGS7400-7499	Ouest	349.774	KFM4200-4799	Law of Michigan
349.72946	KGS7600-7699	Sud	349.775	KFW2400-2999	Law of Wisconsin
349.7295	KGV0-5999	General	349.776	KFM5400-5999	Law of Minnesota
349.7295	KGV	Puerto Rico	349.777	KFI4200-4799	Law of Iowa
349.72951	KGV8100-8119	San Juan	349.778	KFM7800-8399	Law of Missouri
349.72952	KGV8000-8019	Bayamon	349.781	KFK0-599	Law of Kansas
349.72956	KGV8060-8079	Mayaguez	349.782	KFN0-599	Law of Nebraska
349.72957	KGV8080-8099	Ponce	349.783	KFS3000-3599	Law of South Dakota
349.7296	KGL0-499	Bahamas	349.784	KFN8600-9199	Law of North Dakota
349.72961	KGY0-499	Turks/Caicos Islands	349.786	KFM9000-9599	Law of Montana
349.729722	KGZ0-499	Virgin Islands of the U.S.	349.787	KFW4200-4799	Law of Wyoming
349.729725	KGL4000-4499	British Virgin Islands	349.788	KFC1800-2399	Law of Colorado
349.72973	KGJ7000-7499	Anguilla	349.789	KFN3600-4199	Law of New Mexico
349.72973	KGW2000-2499	St. Kitts/Nevis/Anguilla	349.791	KFA2400-2999	Law of Arizona
349.72974	KGK0-499	Antigua and Barbuda	349.792	KFU0-599	Law of Utah
349.72975	KGT2000-2499	Montserrat	349.793	KFN600-1199	Law of Nevada
349.72976	KGR3000-3499	French West Indies	349.794	KFC0-1199	Law of California
349.72976	KGR5000-5499	Guadeloupe	349.795	KFO2400-2919	Law of Oregon
349.72977	KGW8000-8499	St. Martin	349.796	KFI0-599	Law of Idaho
349.72977	KGW0-499	Saba	349.797	KFW0-599	Law of Washington
349.72977	KGW7000-7499	St. Eustatius	349.798	KFA1200-1799	Law of Alaska
349.72981	KGL1000-1499	Barbados	349.8	KH	South America
349.72982	KGT1000-1499	Martinique	349.8	KH0-999	General
349.72983	KGX0-499	Trinidad/Tobago	349.81	KHD0-5999	General
349.729841	KGP2000-2499	Dominica	349.81	KHD	Brazil
349.729843	KGW3000-3499	St. Lucia	349.81(1-7)	KHD6200-8999	States/Federal District
349.729844	KGW5000-5499	St. Vincent and the Grenadines	349.8112	KHD6200-6299	Acre
			349.8113	KHD6500-6599	Amazonas
349.729845	KGR4000-4499	Grenada	349.8114	KHD8500-8599	Roraima
349.72986	KGR1000-1499	Netherlands Antilles	349.8115	KHD7600-7699	Para
349.72986	KGP0-499	Curacao	349.8116	KHD6400-6499	Amapa
349.72986	KGL2000-2499	Bonaire	349.8121	KHD7300-7399	Maranhao

349 - 349

Dewey	LC	Descriptor	Dewey	LC	Descriptor
349.8122	KHD8000-8099	Piaui	349.8337	KHF7400-7499	Linares
349.8131	KHD6800-6899	Ceara	349.8338	KHF7900-7999	Nuble
349.8132	KHD8200-8299	Rio Grande do Norte	349.8339	KHF7100-7199	Concepcion
349.8133	KHD7700-7799	Paraiba	349.8341	KHF6700-6799	Bio-Bio
349.8134	KHD7900-7999	Pernambuco	349.8342	KHF6400-6499	Arauco
349.8135	KHD6300-6399	Alagoas	349.8345	KHF7700-7799	Malleco
349.8136	KHD7000-7099	Fernando de Noronha	349.8346	KHF6800-6899	Cautin
349.8141	KHD8800-8899	Sergipe	349.8352	KHF8500-8599	Valdivia
349.8142	KHD6600-6699	Bahia	349.8353	KHF8100-8199	Osorno
349.8151	KHD7500-7599	Minas Gerais	349.8354	KHF7500-7599	Llanquihue
349.8152	KHD6900-6999	Espirito Santo	349.8356	KHF6900-6999	Chiloe
349.8153	KHD8100-8199	Rio de Janeiro	349.83622	KHF6600-6699	Aysen
349.8153	KHD9800-9819	Rio de Janeiro (City)	349.8364	KHF7600-7699	Magallanes
349.8153	KHD7200-7299	Guanabara	349.84	KHC0-5999	General
349.8161	KHD9840-9859	Sao Paulo (City)	349.84	KHC	Bolivia
349.8161	KHD8700-8799	Sao Paulo	349.84(1-43)	KHC6200-7899	Departments
349.8162	KHD7800-7899	Parana	349.8412	KHC8020-8039	La Paz (City)
349.8164	KHD8600-8699	Santa Catarina	349.8412	KHC6800-6899	La Paz
349.817	KHD8900-8999	Mato Grosso do Sul	349.8413	KHC7000-7099	Oruro
349.8172	KHD7400-7499	Mato Grosso	349.8414	KHC7400-7499	Potosi
349.8173	KHD7100-7199	Goias	349.8423	KHC8000-8019	Cochabamba (City)
349.8174	KHD6700-6799	Brasilia (Federal District)	349.8423	KHC6400-6499	Cochabamba
349.8175	KHD8400-8499	Rondonia (Guapore)	349.8424	KHC6200-6299	Chuquisaca
349.82	KHA0-5999	General	349.8425	KHC7800-7899	Tarija
349.82	KHA	Argentina	349.843	KHC7600-7699	Santa Cruz
349.8211	KHA6200-8799	Buenos Aires (Federal Dist.)	349.8442	KHC6600-6699	El Beni
349.8212	KHA6300-6399	Buenos Aires (Province)	349.8443	KHC7200-7299	Pando
349.8213	KHA7300-7399	La Pampa (Eva Peron)	349.85	KHQ	Peru
349.8221	KHA6900-6999	Entre Rios	349.8512	KHQ8500-8599	Tumbes
349.8222	KHA6800-6899	Corrientes	349.8513	KHQ8100-8199	Piura
349.8223	KHA7700-7799	Misiones	349.8514	KHQ7500-7599	Lambayeque
349.8224	KHA8400-8499	Santa Fe	349.8516	KHQ7400-7499	La Libertad
349.8234	KHA6500-6599	Chaco (President Peron)	349.8521	KHQ6300-6399	Ancash
349.8235	KHA7000-7099	Formosa	349.8522	KHQ7100-7199	Huanuco
349.8241	KHA7200-7299	Jujuy	349.8522	KHQ6500-6599	Arequipa
349.8242	KHA8000-8099	Salta	349.8523	KHQ8000-8099	Pasco
349.8243	KHA8700-8799	Tucuman	349.8524	KHQ7300-7399	Junin
349.8245	KHA6400-6499	Catamarca	349.8525	KHQ7600-7699	Lima
349.8246	KHA7400-7499	La Rioja	349.8525	KHQ9680-9699	Lima (City)
349.8252	KHA8500-8599	Santiago del Estero	349.8525	KHQ6700-6799	Cajamarca
349.8254	KHA6700-6799	Cordoba	349.8526	KHQ9620-9639	Callao (City)
349.8262	KHA8200-8299	San Luis	349.8526	KHQ6800-6899	Callao
349.8263	KHA8100-8199	San Juan	349.8527	KHQ7200-7299	Ica
349.8264	KHA7600-7699	Mendoza	349.8528	KHQ7000-7099	Huancavelica
349.8272	KHA7800-7899	Neuquen	349.85292	KHQ6600-6699	Ayacucho
349.8273	KHA7900-7999	Rio Negro	349.85294	KHQ6400-6499	Apurimac
349.8274	KHA6600-6699	Chubut	349.8532	KHQ9600-9619	Arequipa (City)
349.8275	KHA8300-8399	Santa Cruz	349.8534	KHQ7900-7999	Moquegua
349.8276	KHA8600-8699	Tierra del Fuego	349.8535	KHQ8400-8499	Tacna
349.83	KHF0-5999	General	349.8536	KHQ8200-8299	Puno
349.83	KHF	Chile	349.8537	KHQ9660-9679	Cuzco (City)
349.83(1-6)	KHF6200-8699	Provinces	349.8537	KHQ6900-6999	Cuzco
349.8312	KHF8400-8499	Tarapaca	349.8542	KHQ7800-7899	Madre de Dios
349.8313	KHF6300-6399	Antofagasta	349.8543	KHQ7700-7799	Loreto
349.8313	KHF9600-9619	Antofagasta (City)	349.8545	KHQ8300-8399	San Martin
349.8314	KHF6500-6599	Atacama	349.8546	KHQ6200-6299	Amazonas
349.8323	KHF7200-7299	Coquimbo	349.861	KHH0-5999	General
349.8324	KHF6200-6299	Aconcagua	349.861	KHH	Colombia
349.83255	KHF9700-9719	Valparaiso (City)	349.861(12-8)	KHH6200-9399	Departments
349.83255	KHF8600-8699	Valparaiso/Easter Island	349.86112	KHH7400-7499	Cordoba
349.8331	KHF8200-8299	Santiago	349.86113	KHH8900-8999	Sucre
349.83315	KHF9640-9659	Santiago (City)	349.86114	KHH6700-6799	Bolivar
349.8332	KHF8000-8099	O'Higgins	349.86115	KHH6500-6599	Atlantico
349.8333	KHF7000-7099	Colchagua	349.86116	KHH8000-8099	Magdelena
349.8334	KHF7300-7399	Curico	349.86117	KHH7900-7999	La Guajira
349.8335	KHF8300-8399	Talca	349.86123	KHH7600-7699	El Cesar
349.8335	KHF7800-7899	Maule	349.86124	KHH8300-8399	Norte de Santander

Dewey	LC	Descriptor
349.86125	KHH8800-8899	Santander
349.86126	KHH6300-6399	Antioquia
349.86127	KHH7300-7399	Choco
349.86132	KHH8600-8699	Risaralda
349.86134	KHH8500-8599	Quindio
349.86135	KHH6900-6999	Caldas
349.86136	KHH9000-9099	Tolima
349.86137	KHH6800-6899	Boyaca
349.86138	KHH6400-6499	Arauca
349.86139	KHH9300-9399	Vichada
349.86143	KHH7100-7199	Casanore
349.86146	KHH7500-7599	Cundinamarca
349.86148	KHH6600-6699	Bogota (Special District)
349.86152	KHH9100-9199	Valle de Cauca
349.86153	KHH7200-7299	Cauca
349.86154	KHH7800-7899	Huila
349.86156	KHH8100-8199	Meta
349.86162	KHH8200-8299	Narino
349.86163	KHH8400-8499	Putamayo
349.86164	KHH7000-7099	Caqueta
349.86165	KHH9200-9299	Vaupes
349.86167	KHH7700-7799	Guainia
349.8617	KHH6200-6299	Amazonas
349.8618	KHH8700-8799	San Andres y Providencia
349.866	KHK0-5999	General
349.866	KHK	Ecuador
349.866(11-5)	KHK6100-9899	Provinces
349.86611	KHK6700-6799	Carchi
349.86612	KHK8100-8199	Imbabura
349.86613	KHK9960-9979	Quito (City)
349.86613	KHK9500-9599	Pichincha
349.86614	KHK7100-7199	Cotopaxi
349.86615	KHK9700-9799	Tungurahua
349.86616	KHK6300-6399	Bolivar
349.86617	KHK6900-6999	Chimborazo
349.86623	KHK6500-6599	Canar
349.86624	KHK6100-6199	Azuay
349.86625	KHK8300-8399	Loja
349.86631	KHK7300-7399	El Oro
349.86632	KHK7900-7999	Guayas
349.86633	KHK8500-8599	Los Rios
349.86634	KHK8700-8799	Manabi
349.86635	KHK7500-7599	Esmeraldas
349.86641	KHK9100-9199	Napo
349.86642	KHK9300-9399	Pastaza
349.86643	KHK8900-8999	Morona-Santiago
349.86644	KHK9800-9899	Zamora-Chinchipe
349.8665	KHK7700-7799	Galapagos Islands (Colon)
349.87	KHW	Venezuela
349.87	KHW0-5999	General
349.8712	KHW8100-8199	Tachira
349.8713	KHW7500-7599	Merida
349.8714	KHW8200-8299	Trujillo
349.8723	KHW8400-8499	Zulia
349.8724	KHW7200-7299	Falcon
349.8725	KHW7400-7499	Lara
349.8726	KHW8300-8399	Yaracuy
349.8732	KHW6800-6899	Carabobo
349.8734	KHW6500-6599	Aragua
349.8735	KHW7600-7699	Miranda
349.8742	KHW6400-6499	Apure
349.8743	KHW6600-6699	Barinas
349.8745	KHW7900-7999	Portuguesa
349.8746	KHW7000-7099	Cojedes
349.8747	KHW7300-7399	Guarico
349.8752	KHW6300-6399	Anzoategui
349.8753	KHW8000-8099	Sucre

Dewey	LC	Descriptor
349.8754	KHW7800-7899	Nueva Esparta
349.8756	KHW7700-7799	Monagas
349.8762	KHW7100-7199	Delta Amacuro
349.8763	KHW9660-9679	Ciudad Bolivar
349.8763	KHW6700-6799	Bolivar
349.8764	KHW6200-6299	Amazonas
349.877	KHW6900-6999	Carascas (Federal District)
349.881	KHN	Guyana
349.881	KHN0-5999	General
349.882	KHM0-5999	General
349.882	KHM	Guyane/French Guiana
349.883	KHS0-5999	General
349.883	KHS	Suriname
349.8831	KHS7000-7099	Nickerie
349.8832	KHS6600-6699	Coronie
349.8833	KHS7600-7699	Saramacca
349.8834	KHS7200-7299	Para
349.8835	KHS7400-7499	Paramaribo
349.8836	KHS7800-7899	Suriname
349.8837	KHS6400-6499	Commewijne
349.8838	KHS6800-6899	Marowijne
349.8839	KHS6200-6299	Brokopondo
349.892	KHP	Paraguay
349.892	KHP0-5999	General
349.892(1-27)	KHP6100-9399	Departments
349.892121	KHP6500-6599	Asuncion (Federal District)
349.892122	KHP7300-7399	Central
349.892123	KHP8900-8999	Paraguari
349.892124	KHP8500-8599	Neembucu
349.892125	KHP8300-8399	Misiones
349.892126	KHP8100-8199	Itapua
349.892127	KHP7100-7199	Caazapa
349.892128	KHP7900-7999	Guaira
349.892132	KHP6100-6199	Alto Parana
349.892134	KHP6900-6999	Caaguazu
349.892135	KHP7700-7799	Cordillera
349.892136	KHP9300-9399	San Pedro
349.892137	KHP6300-6399	Amambay
349.892138	KHP7500-7599	Concepcion
349.89224	KHP6700-6799	Boqueron
349.895	KHU	Uruguay
349.895	KHU0-5999	General
349.8951(1-36)	KHU6200-8099	Departments
349.89511	KHU6500-6599	Colonia
349.89512	KHU7700-7799	San Jose
349.89513	KHU7100-7199	Montevideo
349.89513	KHU9620-9639	Montevideo
349.89514	KHU6300-6399	Canalones
349.89515	KHU7000-7099	Maldonado
349.89516	KHU7500-7599	Rocha
349.89521	KHU6900-6999	Lavelleja
349.89522	KHU8000-8099	Treinta y Tres
349.89523	KHU6400-6499	Cerro Largo
349.89524	KHU6600-6699	Durazno
349.89525	KHU6800-6899	Florida
349.89526	KHU6700-6799	Flores
349.89527	KHU7800-7899	Soriano
349.89528	KHU7300-7399	Rio Negro
349.89531	KHU7200-7299	Paysandu
349.89531	KHU9640-9659	Paysandu
349.89532	KHU7900-7999	Tacuarembo
349.89534	KHU7400-7499	Rivera
349.89535	KHU9660-9679	Salto
349.89535	KHU7600-7699	Salto
349.89536	KHU6200-6299	Artigas
349.969	KFH0-599	Law of Hawaii
349.9711	KHL0-5999	General

Dewey	LC	Descriptor
349.9711	KHL	Falkland Islands
349.982	KDZ3000-3499	Greenland
350	JF1900	Federal districts
350-352	JF	Political administration
350-352	JF251-314	Executive
350-352.000202	JF107-109	Compends./Outlines/Etc.
350.3450947	VG185-186	European Russia
350.34509729	VG132-133	West Indies
350.714	HA38-39	Registration of vital events
351	JF201-723	Organs/Functions of government
351.(02/72)	HJ9-99.6	Documents, By place
351.003(4/6)	JF290-297	Term/Leaving office
351.00313	JF255	President
351.00322	JF260-261	Legislative power (Veto/Etc.)
351.00322	JF256	Military/War powers
351.00322	JF274	Appointments
351.00322	JF269	Treaty making
351.00322	JF265	Judicial/Pardoning power
351.00328	JF305-309	Privileges
351.00354	JF289	Oath/Inauguration
351.1	JF1601-1671	Officials/Bodies/Etc.
351.722	HJ2005-2216	The budget
351.72201	HJ2005-2043	Theory
351.724	HJ3231-5957	Taxation, Administration of
351.724001	HJ3241-3245	Theory
351.724009(4-9)	HJ3370-3696	Other countries
351.724009(4-9)	HJ3251-3696	Tax administration, By place
351.7246	HJ6603-7390	Customs administration
351.72460(5/6)	HJ6603-6605	Serials/Societies
351.724603	HJ6606-6607	Dictionaries/ Encyclopedias
351.724609(4-9)	HJ6750-7174.7	Other countries
351.724609(4-9)	HJ6620-7390	Administration, By place
351.72460973	HJ6620-6740	United States
351.74	HV7935-8025	Administration/ Organization
351.822	HG321-329	Mints/Assaying
351.824	Z551-656	Copyright (Nonlegal aspects)
351.871044	TD360	Water rates
351.89	JX1625-1896	Diplomacy/Diplomatic service
351.8909	JX1635-1662	History, By date
352	JS	Local government
352	JS141-231	Municipal government
352.(599/2599)	JV8683-8685	Philippines
352.0(72-8)000(5/6)	JS15	Other American areas
352.000(5/6)	JS13-37	Municipal serial documents
352.0001	JS50	Theory
352.0003	JS48	Dictionaries
352.0005	JS39-41	Serials
352.0006	JS42	Societies/Congresses
352.0007	JS49	Education
352.0009	JS55-67	History
352.008	JS141-163	Executive (Mayor/Etc.)
352.008097(4-9)	JS356-365	Executive (Mayor)
352.04	JS3000-69549	Europe
352.04000(5/6)	JS16-31	Europe
352.041	JS3001-4280	Great Britain
352.043	JS5301-5598	Germany
352.0436	JS4501-4650	Austria
352.0437	JS4721-4756	Czechoslovakia
352.0439	JS4661-4696	Hungary
352.044	JS4801-5249	France

Dewey	LC	Descriptor
352.045	JS5701-5925	Italy
352.046	JS6301-6335	Spain
352.0469	JS6341-6375	Portugal
352.047	JS6051-6120	European Russia
352.0481	JS6201-6235	Norway
352.0485	JS6251-6285	Sweden
352.0489	JS6151-6189	Denmark
352.0492	JS5931-5998	Netherlands
352.0493	JS6001-6048	Belgium
352.0494	JS6401-6889	Switzerland
352.0496	JS6900-6949	Balkan states
352.05	JS6950-7499	Asia
352.05000(5/6)	JS33	Asia
352.051	JS7351-7365	China
352.052	JS7371-7385	Japan
352.053	JS7510	Arab countries
352.054	JS7001-7090	India
352.0599	JS7300-7335	Philippines
352.06	JS7525-7829	Africa
352.06000(5/6)	JS35	Africa
352.07(4-9)	JS408-425	Other than municipal
352.07(4-9)	JS301-1583	United States (Local gov't.)
352.07(4-9)	JS304	Congresses
352.07(4-9)	JS431-1583	Municipalities (United States)
352.07(4-9)000(5/6)	JS13	United States
352.07(4-9)0005	JS301	Serials
352.07(4-9)0006	JS302-303	Societies
352.07(4-9)0009	JS309-323	History
352.071	JS1701-1800	Canada
352.071000(5/6)	JS14	Canada
352.0718	JS1811-1819	Newfoundland
352.072	JS2101-2143	Mexico
352.0728	JS2145-2219	Central America
352.0729	JS1840-2059	West Indies
352.08	JS2300-2778	South America
352.09(3-6)000(5/6)	JS37	Australia/New Zealand/ Oceania
352.09(5-6)	JS8450-8455	Oceania
352.093	JS8331-8399	New Zealand
352.094	JS8001-8310	Australia
353	JK	U.S. (Admin./Constitutional hist.)
353	JK404-1686	Governments/ Administration
353-354	JF31-36	History, By place
353.(1-87)	JK851-901	The departments
353.(1-87)	JK631-901	Departments/Civil service
353.(1-87)	J83-85	Department reports/ Documents
353.0003	JK9	Dictionaries
353.0005	J1	United States
353.0005	J1-9	Official gazettes
353.0005	JK1	Serials
353.0006	J10-87	United States, Official docs.
353.0006	JK3	Societies
353.00074	JK4	Exhibitions
353.001	JK765-770	Personnel administration
353.00123	JK771-849	Salaries/Pensions
353.0013	JK730-761	Appointments/Etc.
353.006	JK631-901	Departments/Civil service
353.00713	JK1606-1686	Government property
353.00722	HJ2050-2053	United States
353.00724	HJ3251-3361.9	United States
353.0089	JX1705-1725	United States
353.03	JK501-901	Executive
353.0313	JK511-609	The President

Dewey	LC	Descriptor
353.0318	JK609.5	The Vice President
353.035	J80-82	Presidential messages/ Documents
353.03509	J82	By President
353.04	JK610-616	The cabinet
353.2	HG2535-2543	Treasury/Currency comptroller
353.6	UA23.2-.6	Dept. of Defense
353.6	UB23-25	United States
353.7	VB23-25	United States
353.75	JK9661-9993	Confederate States
353.7503	JK9718-9719	Executive
353.81	S21	Federal documents
353.82	HF71-81	Ministries/Bureaus
353.9	JK2403-9501	State governments
353.9(7-9)	JK2701-9501	By state
353.9(7-9)	JK2443-2525	Administration
353.9(7-9)	JK2410-2411	Admission to statehood
353.9(7-9)0006	J86-87	State documents
353.9(7-9)00724	HJ3260-3361.9	By state
353.97(4-9)0313	JK2447-2474	The executive
353/354.(3-9) + 0005	J	Official documents/Gazettes
353/354.(4-9) + 0006	J10-981	Official documents
354.(3-9)0005	J1-9	Official gazettes
354.(3-9)061	CD70-79	Chancelleries, By place
354.(3-9)061007	CD501-511	Education
354.(4-9)	J100-981	Documents of other countries
354.(4-9)00722	HJ2054-2215	Other countries
354.(4-9)0089	JX1705-1894	Diplomacy, By place
354.(5-9)	JQ	Asia/Africa/Oceania (Admin./Etc.)
354.(7-8)	JL	Americas (Admin./ Constitution)
354.4	J301-462	Europe
354.4	JN1-97	Europe, General
354.4	JN	Europe (Admin./ Constitution)
354.40005	J7	Europe
354.41	J301-309	Great Britain
354.41	JN301-329	Government/Administration
354.41	JN101-1179	Great Britain
354.41000(5/6)	JN101-102	Serials/Societies/Etc.
354.4103	JN331-453	The executive
354.411	JN1187-1371	Scotland
354.4110089	JX1787-1788	Scotland
354.4150089	JX1789-1790	Ireland
354.416	JN1572	Northern Ireland
354.417	JN1400-1571.5	Ireland
354.420089	JX1783-1784	England
354.429	JN1150-1159	Wales
354.43	J351-383	Germany
354.43	JN3201-4980	Germany
354.430089	JX1795-1796	Germany
354.436	J310-340	Austria/Hungary
354.436	JN1601-2199	Austria/Hungary
354.4360089	JX1791-1792	Austria
354.437	JN2210-2229	Czechoslovakia
354.4370089	JX1792.5	Czechoslovakia
354.438	JN6750-6769	Poland
354.4380089	JX1808.7	Poland
354.4390089	JX1798.5	Hungary
354.44	J341-345	France
354.44	JN2301-3007	France
354.440089	JX1793-1794	France
354.45	J388-389	Italy
354.45	JN5201-5697	Italy

Dewey	LC	Descriptor
354.450089	JX1799-1800	Italy
354.46	JN8101-8399	Spain
354.46(9)	J409-411	Spain/Portugal
354.460089	JX1819-1820	Spain
354.469	JN8423-8661	Portugal
354.4690089	JX1821-1822	Portugal
354.47	J397-400	European Russia
354.47	JN6500-6747	European Russia
354.470089	JX1807-1808	European Russia
354.48	J402-406	Scandinavia
354.48	JN7001-7066	Scandinavia (General)
354.481	JN7401-7695	Norway
354.4810089	JX1815-1816	Norway
354.485	JN7721-7997	Sweden
354.4850089	JX1817-1818	Sweden
354.489	JN7101-7367	Denmark
354.4890089	JX1811-1812	Denmark
354.4897	JN7390-7399	Finland
354.48970089	JX1808.3	Finland
354.4912	JN7300-7389	Iceland
354.49120089	JX1813-1814	Iceland
354.492	J391-395	Low Countries/Netherlands
354.492	JN5701-5999	The Netherlands
354.4920089	JX1805-1806	Netherlands
354.493	JN6101-6371	Belgium
354.4930089	JX1803-1804	Belgium
354.49350089	JX1806.5	Luxembourg
354.494	J415-442	Switzerland
354.494	JN8701-9599	Switzerland
354.4940089	JX1823-1824	Switzerland
354.495	J385	Greece
354.495	JN5001-5191	Greece
354.4950089	JX1797-1798	Greece
354.496	J450-459	Balkans
354.496	JN9600-9689	Balkan states
354.4965	J450	Albania
354.49650089	JX1826.5	Albania
354.497	J459	Yugoslavia
354.4970089	JX1828.5	Yugoslavia
354.4977	J451-452	Bulgaria
354.49770089	JX1827-1828	Bulgaria
354.4980089	JX1831-1832	Romania
354.5	J500-693	Asia
354.5	J671-681	Far East
354.5	JQ20-1825	Asia
354.51	J671	China
354.51	JQ1519	China
354.510089	JX1837-1838	China
354.51249	JQ1539	Taiwan
354.51249	J672	Taiwan
354.512490089	JX1838.5	Taiwan
354.5125	JQ670-679	Hong Kong
354.5125	J613	Hong Kong
354.519	J677-.5	Korea
354.519	JQ1729-.5	Korea
354.52	J674	Japan
354.52	JQ1699	Japan
354.520089	JX1851-1852	Japan
354.53	JQ1825.A75	Arabia
354.53	JQ1850	Arab countries
354.5332	JQ1825.Y4-.Y5	Yemen
354.5332	J693.Y4	Yemen
354.5353	JQ1825.O42	Oman
354.5357	JQ1825.U5	United Arab Emirates
354.5357	J693.U54	United Arab Emirates
354.5363	JQ1825.Q37	Qatar
354.5363	J693.Q37	Qatar

Dewey	LC	Descriptor
354.7292	JL630-639	Jamaica
354.72920089	JX1753	Jamaica
354.72921	JL629.5	Cayman Islands
354.72930089	JX1752	Dominican Republic
354.729375	JL1120-1139	Santo Domingo
354.7294	JL1080-1099	Haiti
354.72940089	JX1751	Haiti
354.7295	J164-165	Puerto Rico
354.7295	JL1040-1059	Puerto Rico
354.72950089	JX1755-1756	Puerto Rico
354.7296	JL610-619	Bahamas
354.72961	JL659.5	Turks/Caicos Islands
354.7297	JL640-649	Leeward Islands
354.7297220089	JX1756.5	U.S. Virgin Islands
354.72976	JL820-829	Guadeloupe
354.72981	JL620-629	Barbados
354.72982	JL830-839	Martinique
354.72983	JL650-659	Trinidad
354.72984	JL660-669	Windward Islands
354.729845	JL629.6	Grenada
354.72986	JL770-779	Curacao
354.7299	JL590-599	Bermuda
354.8	J200-259	South America
354.80005	J6	South America
354.81	JL2400-2499	Brazil
354.810089	JX1763-1764	Brazil
354.82	JL2000-2099	Argentina
354.820089	JX1759-1760	Argentina
354.83	JL2600-2699	Chile
354.84	JL2200-2299	Bolivia
354.840089	JX1761-1762	Bolivia
354.85	JL3400-3499	Peru
354.850089	JX1775-1776	Peru
354.861	JL2800-2899	Colombia
354.8610089	JX1767-1768	Colombia
354.866	JL3000-3099	Ecuador
354.8660089	JX1769-1770	Ecuador
354.87	JL3800-3899	Venezuela
354.870089	JX1779-1780	Venezuela
354.881	JL680-689	Guyana
354.8810089	JX1772	Guyana
354.882	JL810-819	French Guiana
354.8820089	JX1772.7	French Guiana
354.883	JL780-789	Suriname
354.8830089	JX1772.5	Suriname
354.892	JL3200-3299	Paraguay
354.8920089	JX1773-1774	Paraguay
354.895	JL3600-3699	Uruguay
354.8950089	JX1777-1778	Uruguay
354.9(3-4)	JX1875-1876	New Zealand/Australia
354.9(3-6)	JQ3995-6651	Australia/New Zealand/ Oceania
354.9(5-6)	J951-981	Oceania
354.9(5-6)0089	JX1891-1894	Oceania
354.93	J941	New Zealand
354.94	J903-936	Australia
354.97	J753-755	Atlantic Ocean Islands
354.9711	JL690-699	Falkland Islands
354.982	JN7370-7379	Greenland
355	U	Military science (General)
355.(3-6)	UH	Other services
355.00(5/6)	U1-4	Serials/Societies
355.00148	U26	Symbols/Abbreviations
355.0021	UA19	Statistics
355.0023	UB147	Military service as a profession
355.00289	U380-385	Safety

Dewey	LC	Descriptor
355.003	U24-25	Dictionaries/ Encyclopedias
355.005	U9-10	Yearbooks/Almanacs
355.006	U7	Congresses
355.007	U400-717	Military education/Training
355.007	U400-403	History
355.007	U401-403	By date
355.0070(4-9)	U407-714	By place
355.00704	U505-630	Europe
355.007041	U510-549.3	Great Britain
355.007043	U570-574.54	Germany
355.0070436	U550-554	Austria
355.00705	U635-660	Asia
355.007051	U640-644	China
355.007052	U650-654	Japan
355.007054	U645-649	India
355.007055	U655-659	Iran
355.00706	U670-695	Africa
355.00707(4-9)	U409	By state
355.007071	U440-444	Canada
355.007072	U445-449	Mexico
355.0070728	U450-454	Central America
355.0070729	U455-459	West Indies
355.007073	U408-439	United States
355.00708	U465-499	South America
355.00709(3-6)	U700-714	Australia/New Zealand/ Oceania
355.00710747	U410-430	West Point/Etc.
355.0072	U390-395	Military research
355.0074	U13	Museums/Exhibitions
355.008996073	E185.63	Afro-American soldiers
355.009	D25	Military history
355.009	U27-43	History of military science
355.0090(1-4)	U29-42	By date
355.0090(3-4)	D214	Modern military history
355.0092	U51-55	Biography
355.00942	DA49-69	Military
355.009436	DB42-44	Military history
355.00945	DG480-499	Military history
355.00946	DP76-78	Military history
355.009469	DP547	Military history
355.009492	DJ124	Military history
355.009492	DH113	Military history
355.009493	DH540-545	Military history
355.009494	DQ59	Military history
355.009495	DF543	Military history
355.009495	DF765-775	Military history
355.009497	DR1250-1251	Military history
355.0094977	DR70	Military history
355.009498	DR219	Military history
355.009561	DR448	Military history
355.02	U21-22.3	War (Philosophy/ Psychology)
355.0215	UA11.5	Limited war
355.0215	U240	Small wars
355.03	UA12.5	Disarmament inspection
355.031	UA12	Mutual security
355.032	UA16	Military missions
355.0335	UA11	Military policy
355.07	U390-395	Military research
355.1	U750-773	Life/Manners/Customs/Etc.
355.1	UB147	Military service as a profession
355.113	UB420-425	Furloughs
355.13	UB790-815	Military discipline/ Punishment
355.13323	UB820-825	Military police

Dewey	LC	Descriptor
355.1334	UB780-789	Crimes/Offenses
355.134	UB430-435	Rewards
355.15	UC590-595	Flags/Colors
355.17	U350-365	Salutes/Ceremonials
355.183	UD317	Stream crossing
355.22	UA17.5	Manpower
355.223	UB320-338	Enlistment/Recruiting/Etc.
355.2236	UB320-336	Medical exams
355.22363	UB340-345	Compulsory service
355.225	UB350-355	Universal service
355.26	UA18	Industrial mobilization
355.26	UA929.5-.95	Industrial war damage/ Defense
355.28	UC15	Requisitions
355.28	UA910-915	Mobilization
355.3	UA	Armies (Organization/Etc.)
355.3	U11	Army lists
355.309	UA21-876	Organization, By place
355.3094	UA646-829	Europe
355.30941	UA647-668	Great Britain
355.30943	UA710-719	Germany
355.309436	UA670-679	Austria
355.30944	UA700-709	France
355.3095	UA830-853	Asia
355.30951	UA835-839.3	China
355.30952	UA845-849	Japan
355.30954	UA840-844	India
355.3096	UA855-868	Africa
355.3097	UA22-605	North America
355.3097(4-9)	UA50-549	By state
355.30971	UA600-602	Canada
355.30972	UA603-605	Mexico
355.309728	UA606-608	Central America
355.309729	UA609-611	West Indies
355.30973	UA23-585	United States
355.309741	UA230-239	Maine
355.309742	UA330-339	New Hampshire
355.309743	UA490-499	Vermont
355.309744	UA250-259	Massachusetts
355.309745	UA430-439	Rhode Island
355.309746	UA110-119	Connecticut
355.309747	UA360-369	New York
355.309748	UA420-429	Pennsylvania
355.309749	UA340-349	New Jersey
355.309751	UA120-129	Delaware
355.309752	UA240-249	Maryland
355.309753	UA130-139	District of Columbia
355.309754	UA520-529	West Virginia
355.309755	UA500-509	Virginia
355.309756	UA370-379	North Carolina
355.309757	UA440-449	South Carolina
355.309758	UA150-159	Georgia
355.309759	UA140-149	Florida
355.309761	UA50-59	Alabama
355.309762	UA280-289	Mississippi
355.309763	UA220-229	Louisiana
355.309764	UA470-479	Texas
355.309766	UA400-409	Oklahoma
355.309767	UA80-89	Arkansas
355.309768	UA460-469	Tennessee
355.309769	UA210-219	Kentucky
355.309771	UA390-399	Ohio
355.309772	UA180-189	Indiana
355.309773	UA170-179	Illinois
355.309774	UA260-269	Michigan
355.309775	UA530-539	Wisconsin
355.309776	UA270-279	Minnesota
355.309777	UA190-199	Iowa
355.309778	UA290-299	Missouri
355.309781	UA200-209	Kansas
355.309782	UA310-319	Nebraska
355.309783	UA450-459	South Dakota
355.309784	UA380-389	North Dakota
355.309786	UA300-309	Montana
355.309787	UA540-549	Wyoming
355.309788	UA100-109	Colorado
355.309789	UA350-359	New Mexico
355.309791	UA70-79	Arizona
355.309792	UA480-489	Utah
355.309793	UA320-329	Nevada
355.309794	UA90-99	California
355.309795	UA410-419	Oregon
355.309796	UA160-169	Idaho
355.309797	UA510-519	Washington
355.309798	UA60-69	Alaska
355.3098	UA612-645	South America
355.3099(3-6)	UA870-876	Australia/New Zealand/ Oceania
355.309969	UA159.1-.9	Hawaii
355.31	UA15	Armies of the world
355.33	UB200-235	Commanders/Staffs/ Headquarters
355.332	UB407-409	Warrant officers
355.332	UB410-415	Officers
355.34(37)	UB273-277	Propaganda/Sabotage
355.34(5/7)	UH630	Health/Morals
355.342	UH700-705	Public relations
355.342	UH800-910	Recreation/Information service
355.3432	UB250-271	Intelligence
355.3433	UB246-249	Security
355.345	UH70	Orderlies
355.345	UH650-655	Veterinary service
355.345	UH600-629.5	Hygiene/Sanitation
355.345	UH490-495	Nursing
355.345	UH500-505	Ambulances
355.345	UH487	Diet/Cooking for sick/ Wounded
355.345	UH201-630	Medical/Sanitary service
355.3450(5/6)	UH201	Serials/Societies
355.345028	UH510-515	Equipment
355.34506	UH205	Congresses
355.345068	UH400-485	Organization and service
355.3450711	UH398-399	Army medical schools
355.345072	UH399.5-.7	Research/Labs
355.345074	UH206	Museums/Exhibitions
355.34509	UH215-324	History
355.345092	UH341-347	Biography
355.345094	UH255-295	Europe
355.3450941	UH257-264	Great Britain
355.3450943	UH273-274	Germany
355.3450944	UH271-272	France
355.3450945	UH279-280	Italy
355.3450946	UH287-288	Spain
355.34509469	UH283-284	Portugal
355.3450947	UH285-286	European Russia
355.3450948	UH286.5	Scandinavia
355.34509495	UH275-276	Greece
355.3095	UH299-313	Asia
355.3450951	UH301-302	China
355.3450952	UH305-306	Japan
355.3450954	UH303-304	India
355.345096	UH315-319	Africa
355.3450971	UH226-227	Canada

Dewey	LC	Descriptor
355.3450972	UH228-229	Mexico
355.34509728	UH230-231	Central America
355.34509729	UH232-233	West Indies
355.3450973	UH223-225	United States
355.345098	UH234-254	South America
355.3450982	UH236-237	Argentina
355.3450983	UH243-244	Chile
355.34509861	UH245-246	Colombia
355.3450987	UH254	Venezuela
355.345099(3-4)	UH321-322.5	Australia/New Zealand
355.345099(5-6)	UH323-324	Oceania
355.346	UH800-910	Recreation/Information service
355.347	UH20-25	Chaplains
355.3480973	UA45	Women's reserves
355.35	U170-185	Field service/Encampments
355.35	U370-375	Garrison service
355.35	U190-195	Guard duty/Outposts/Etc.
355.352	UA14	Colonial/Native troops
355.352	U265	Military expeditions
355.37	UA13	General organization (Militia)
355.370973	UA42-560	Reserves/National Guard/Etc.
355.4	UA920-925	Attack/Defense plans
355.4	U250-255	Maneuvers
355.4	U161-163	Strategy
355.4(2/4)	UG443-449	Siege warfare (Attack/Defense)
355.4(8)	U280-313	Maneuvers/War games/Etc.
355.411	U168	Logistics
355.413	U220	Reconnaissance
355.42	U164-167.5	Tactics
355.422	U200	Debarkation/Landing maneuvers
355.422	U262	Commando tactics
355.422	U210	Skirmishing
355.423	U205	Stream crossing
355.424	UH87-100	Animals in military science
355.46	U260	Combined operations
355.46	U261	Amphibious warfare
355.47	UA985-997	Military geography/Charts
355.48	U719-740	Observations on special wars
355.49	JF1800	Military government
355.5	U320-328	Training/Military sports
355.5	U110-145	Handbooks
355.5	U400-717	Military education/Training
355.509	U400-403	History
355.509(4-9)	U407-714	By place
355.5090(1-4)	U401-403	By date
355.5094	U505-630	Europe
355.50941	U510-549.3	Great Britain
355.50943	U570-574.54	Germany
355.509436	U550-554	Austria
355.5095	U635-660	Asia
355.50951	U640-644	China
355.50952	U650-654	Japan
355.50954	U645-649	India
355.50955	U655-659	Iran
355.5096	U670-695	Africa
355.5097(4-9)	U409	By state
355.50971	U440-444	Canada
355.50972	U445-449	Mexico
355.509728	U450-454	Central America
355.509729	U455-459	West Indies
355.50973	U408-439	United States
355.5098	U465-499	South America
355.5099(3-6)	U700-714	Australia/New Zealand/Oceania
355.54	U900	Drill manuals for nonmilitary
355.547	U169	Drill manuals (Arms)
355.6	UB160-165	Records/Accounts/Etc.
355.6	UB	Military administration
355.6	UB337-338	Personnel classification
355.60(5/6)	UB1	Serials/Societies
355.609	UB15	History (General)
355.609(4-9)	UB21-124	By place
355.6094	UB55-95	Europe
355.60941	UB57-64	Great Britain
355.60943	UB73-74	Germany
355.60944	UB71-72	France
355.60945	UB79-80	Italy
355.60946	UB87-88	Spain
355.609469	UB83-84	Portugal
355.60947	UB85-86	European Russia
355.60948	UB86.5	Scandinavia
355.609495	UB75-76	Greece
355.6095	UB99-113	Asia
355.60951	UB101-102	China
355.60952	UB105-106	Japan
355.60954	UB103-104	India
355.6096	UB115-119	Africa
355.60971	UB26-27	Canada
355.60972	UB28-29	Mexico
355.609728	UB30-31	Central America
355.609729	UB32-33	West Indies
355.60973	UB23-25	United States
355.6098	UB34-54	South America
355.60982	UB36-37	Argentina
355.60983	UB43-44	Chile
355.609861	UB45-46	Colombia
355.60987	UB54	Venezuela
355.6099(3-4)	UB121-122.5	Australia/New Zealand
355.6099(5-6)	UB123-124	Oceania
355.61	UB180-197	Civilian personnel depts.
355.622	UA17	Costs/Budgets/Etc.
355.63	UB240-245	Inspection
355.693	UH80-85	Postal service
355.699	UH570	Treatment of dead
355.7	UA930	Strategic lines/Bases
355.71	UC400-440	Quarters/Barracks
355.8	UC260-267	Supplies
355.8	UC	Maintenance/Transportation
355.8	UC15	Requisitions
355.8	UF845	Telescopes/Binoculars
355.809	UC20-258	Organization, By place
355.8094	UC158-233	Europe
355.80941	UC184-187	Great Britain
355.80943	UC180-183	Germany
355.8095	UC234-245	Asia
355.80952	UC241	Japan
355.8096	UC247-253	Africa
355.80971	UC90-93	Canada
355.80972	UC94-97	Mexico
355.809728	UC98-99	Central America
355.809729	UC104-105	West Indies
355.80973	UC20-88	United States
355.8098	UC106-154	South America
355.8099(3-6)	UC255-258	Australia/New Zealand/Oceania
355.81	UC700-780	Subsistence
355.81	UC460-585	Clothing/Equipment

Dewey	LC	Descriptor	Dewey	LC	Descriptor
355.81	UF910	Bulletproof clothing	357.09(4-9)	UE21-124	By place
355.82	UF520-780	Ordnance	357.094	UE55-95	Europe
355.8209(4-9)	UF565	Other countries	357.0941	UE57-64	Great Britain
355.820973	UF563	United States	357.0943	UE73-74	Germany
355.8224	UF620	Machine guns	357.0944	UE71-72	France
355.824	UD380-425	Small arms	357.0945	UE79-80	Italy
355.824	UF560-780	Ordnance material	357.0946	UE87-88	Spain
355.824	UF520-537	Small arms	357.09469	UE83-84	Portugal
355.82513	UF750-770	Projectiles	357.0947	UE85-86	European Russia
355.85	UA940-945	Military communications	357.0948	UE86.5	Scandinavia
355/943	DD354-370	Military/Naval/Political	357.09495	UE75-76	Greece
355/943	DD99-120	Military/Naval/Political	357.095	UE99-113	Asia
356.1	UD	Infantry	357.0951	UE101-102	China
356.1	UD150-155	Manuals	357.0952	UE105-106	Japan
356.1	UD430	Militia/Reserves	357.0954	UE103-104	India
356.1	UD450-455	Mounted infantry	357.096	UE115-119	Africa
356.1(1-67)	UD450-485	Troops (By type)	357.0971	UE26-27	Canada
356.10(5/6)	UD1	Serials/Societies	357.0972	UE28-29	Mexico
356.109	UD157-302	Tactics/Maneuvers, By place	357.09728	UE30-31	Central America
356.109	UD15	History	357.09729	UE32-33	West Indies
356.109(4-9)	UD21-124	By place	357.0973	UE23-25	United States
356.1094	UD55-95	Europe	357.098	UE34-54	South America
356.10941	UD57-64	Great Britain	357.0982	UE36-37	Argentina
356.10943	UD73-74.5	Germany	357.0983	UE43-44	Chile
356.10944	UD71-72	France	357.09861	UE45-46	Colombia
356.10945	UD79-80	Italy	357.0987	UE54	Venezuela
356.10946	UD87-88	Spain	357.099(3-4)	UE121-122.5	Australia/New Zealand
356.109469	UD83-84	Portugal	357.099(5-6)	UE123-124	Oceania
356.10947	UD85-86	European Russia	357.1	UC600-695	Horses/Mules
356.10948	UD86.5	Scandinavia	357.1	UE144-145	Horse cavalry
356.109495	UD75-76	Greece	357.184	UE157-158	Tactics, Horse cavalry
356.1095	UD99-113	Asia	357.188	UE460-475	Horses/Equitation
356.10951	UD101-102	China	357.4099(5-6)	UE300-302	Oceania
356.10952	UD105-106	Japan	357.509(4-9)	UE160-302	Tactic/Maneuvers, By place
356.10954	UD103-104	India	357.5094	UE215-269	Europe
356.1096	UD115-119	Africa	357.50941	UE234-236	Great Britain
356.10971	UD26-27	Canada	357.50943	UE231-233.53	Germany
356.10972	UD28-29	Mexico	357.50944	UE228-230	France
356.109728	UD30-31	Central America	357.50945	UE243-245	Italy
356.109729	UD32-33	West Indies	357.50946	UE255-257	Spain
356.10973	UD23-25	United States	357.50947	UE252-254	European Russia
356.1098	UD34-54	South America	357.509495	UE237-239	Greece
356.10982	UD36-37	Argentina	357.5095	UE270-280	Asia
356.10983	UD43-44	Chile	357.50951	UE271-273	China
356.109861	UD45-46	Colombia	357.50952	UE277-279	Japan
356.10987	UD54	Venezuela	357.50954	UE274-276	India
356.1099(3-4)	UD121-122.5	Australia/New Zealand	357.5096	UE285-292	Africa
356.1099(5-6)	UD123-124	Oceania	357.50969	UE249-251	Portugal
356.164	UD470-475	Ski troops	357.50971	UE163-165	Canada
356.164	UD460-465	Mountain troops	357.50972	UE166-168	Mexico
356.166	UD480-485	Airborne/Parachute troops	357.509728	UE169-170	Central America
356.183	UD440-445	Field service	357.509729	UE172-173	West Indies
356.184	UD340-345	Bayonet drill	357.50973	UE160-162	United States
356.184	UD330-335	Firing	357.5098	UE175-211	South America
356.184	UD320-325	Manual of arms	357.50982	UE176-178	Argentina
356.186	UD370-375	Equipment	357.50983	UE185-187	Chile
356.189	UD10	Organization (General)	357.509861	UE188-190	Colombia
357	UE	Cavalry/Armor	357.5099(3-4)	UE295-298	Australia/New Zealand
357	UE150-155	Manuals	357.584	UE159	Armored/Mechanized cavalry
357	UE500	Camel troops			
357.(1/5)85	UE400-435	Training/Instructions/Etc.	357.584	UE360	Cavalry reconnaissance
357.(1/5)88	UE440-445	Equipment	358-359	UG500-565	Technical/Special troops
357.0(5/6)	UE1	Serials/Societies	358.0972	UE28-29	Mexico
357.043	UE10	Cavalry Organization (General)	358.1(2-6)	UF400-495	Artillery/Batteries (By type)
			358.12	UF	Artillery
357.09	UE15	History	358.12	UF150-155	Manuals
			358.12	UF356	Reserves/Militia

Dewey	LC	Descriptor
358.120(5/6)	UF1	Serials/Societies
358.1203	UF9	Dictionaries/Encyclopedias
358.12074	UF6	Museums/Exhibitions
358.1209	UF15	History (General)
358.1209(4-9)	UF21-124	By place
358.12094	UF55-95	Europe
358.120941	UF57-64	Great Britain
358.120943	UF73-74	Germany
358.120944	UF71-72	France
358.120945	UF79-80	Italy
358.120946	UF87-88	Spain
358.1209469	UF83-84	Portugal
358.120947	UF85-86	European Russia
358.120948	UF86.5	Scandinavia
358.1209495	UF75-76	Greece
358.12095	UF99-113	Asia
358.120951	UF101-102	China
358.120952	UF105-106	Japan
358.120954	UF103-104	India
358.12096	UF115-119	Africa
358.120971	UF26-27	Canada
358.1209728	UF30-31	Central America
358.1209729	UF32-33	West Indies
358.120973	UF23-25	United States
358.12098	UF34-54	South America
358.120982	UF36-37	Argentina
358.120983	UF43-44	Chile
358.1209861	UF45-46	Colombia
358.120987	UF54	Venezuela
358.12099(3-4)	UF121-122.5	Australia/New Zealand
358.12099(5-6)	UF123-124	Oceania
358.123	UF10	Artillery organization (General)
358.124	UF320	Stream crossing
358.12409(4-9)	UF157-302	Tactics/Maneuvers, By place
358.124094	UF215-269	Europe
358.1240941	UF234-236	Great Britain
358.1240943	UF231-233.53	Germany
358.1240944	UF228-230	France
358.1240945	UF243-245	Italy
358.1240946	UF255-257	Spain
358.12409469	UF249-251	Portugal
358.1240947	UF252-254	European Russia
358.12409495	UF237-239	Greece
358.124095	UF270-280	Asia
358.1240951	UF271-273	China
358.1240952	UF277-279	Japan
358.1240954	UF274-276	India
358.124096	UF285-292	Africa
358.1240971	UF163-165	Canada
358.1240972	UF166-168	Mexico
358.12409728	UF169-170	Central America
358.12409729	UF172-173	West Indies
358.1240973	UF160-162	United States
358.124098	UF175-211	South America
358.1240982	UF176-178	Argentina
358.1240983	UF185-187	Chile
358.12409861	UF188-190	Colombia
358.1240987	UF209-211	Venezuela
358.124099(3-4)	UF295-298	Australia/New Zealand
358.124099(5-6)	UF300-302	Oceania
358.125	UF340-345	Target practice
358.128	UF360-365	Equipment/Harness/Etc.
358.120972	UF28-29	Mexico
358.13	UF625	Antiaircraft guns

Dewey	LC	Descriptor
358.18	UE	Cavalry/Armor
358.18	UE10	Cavalry organization (General)
358.18	UE150-155	Manuals
358.18	UE147	Armor
358.180(5/6)	UE1	Serials/Societies
358.1809	UE15	History
358.1809(3-4)	UE121-122.5	Australia/New Zealand
358.1809(4-9)	UE21-124	By place
358.1809(5-6)	UE123-124	Oceania
358.18094	UE55-95	Europe
358.180941	UE57-64	Great Britain
358.180943	UE73-74	Germany
358.180944	UE71-72	France
358.180945	UE79-80	Italy
358.180946	UE87-88	Spain
358.1809469	UE83-84	Portugal
358.180947	UE85-86	European Russia
358.180948	UE86.5	Scandinavia
358.1809495	UE75-76	Greece
358.18095	UE99-113	Asia
358.180952	UE105-106	Japan
358.180954	UE103-104	India
358.18096	UE115-119	Africa
358.180971	UE26-27	Canada
358.1809728	UE30-31	Central America
358.1809729	UE32-33	West Indies
358.180973	UE23-25	United States
358.18098	UE34-54	South America
358.180982	UE36-37	Argentina
358.180983	UE43-44	Chile
358.1809861	UE45-46	Colombia
358.180987	UE54	Venezuela
358.184	UE360	Cavalry reconnaissance
358.184	UE159	Armored/Mechanized cavalry
358.18409(4-9)	UE160-302	Tactics/Maneuvers, By place
358.184094	UE215-269	Europe
358.1840941	UE234-236	Great Britain
358.1840943	UE231-233.53	Germany
358.1840944	UE228-230	France
358.1840945	UE243-245	Italy
358.1840946	UE255-257	Spain
358.18409469	UE249-251	Portugal
358.1840947	UE252-254	European Russia
358.18409495	UE237-239	Greece
358.184095	UE270-280	Asia
358.1840951	UE271-273	China
358.1840952	UE277-279	Japan
358.1840954	UE274-276	India
358.184096	UE285-292	Africa
358.1840971	UE163-165	Canada
358.1840972	UE166-168	Mexico
358.18409728	UE169-170	Central America
358.18409729	UE172-173	West Indies
358.1840973	UE160-162	United States
358.184098	UE175-211	South America
358.1840982	UE176-178	Argentina
358.1840983	UE185-187	Chile
358.18409861	UE188-190	Colombia
358.184099(3-4)	UE295-298	Australia/New Zealand
358.184099(5-6)	UE300-302	Oceania
358.185	UE400-435	Training/Instructions/Etc.
358.188	UE440-445	Equipment
358.2	UG360-390	Field engineering
358.22	UG150-155	Manuals

Dewey	LC	Descriptor	Dewey	LC	Descriptor
358.22	UG	Military engineering	359.00709(3-6)	V690-695	Australia/New Zealand/ Oceania
358.220(5/6)	UG1	Serials/Societies	359.0072	V390-395	Research
358.2206	UG5	Congresses	359.0074	V13	Exhibitions/Museums
358.2207	UG157	Education	359.008996073	E185.63	Afro-American seaman
358.22074	UG6	Museums/Exhibitions	359.009	D27	Naval history
358.2209	UG15	History	359.009	V25-55	History
358.2209(4-9)	UG21-124	By place	359.009(4-9)	V55	By place
358.22092	UG127-128	Biography	359.0090(1-4)	V29-53	History, By date
358.224	UG320-325	Maneuvers	359.0090(3-4)	D215	Modern naval history,
358.224	UG160-302	Tactics/Regulations			General
358.24	UB280-285	Cryptography	359.00901	V29-41	Ancient
358.24	UG570-613.5	Communication	359.00901	D95	Naval history
358.25	UC	Maintenance/Transportation	359.00902	D128	Naval
358.25	UC270-360	Transportation	359.00902	V43-46	Medieval
358.25	UF390	Motor transportation	359.00903(2/3)	V47	17th-18th centuries
358.34	UG447-.6	Chemical warfare	359.009034	V51	19th century
358.4	UG670-675	Manuals	359.0092	V61-64	Biography
358.4	UG622-1425	Air forces/Air warfare	359.00942	DA70-89.1	Naval
358.400(5/6)	UG622-623	Serials/Societies/Congresses	359.009436	DB45	Naval history
358.4003	UG628	Dictionaries/	359.00945	DG480-499	Naval
		Encyclopedias	359.00946	DP80-81	Naval history
358.4007	UG637-639	Education/Training	359.009469	DP550-551	Naval history
358.40071173	UG638.5	U.S. Air Force Academy	359.009492	DH121	Naval history
358.40074	UG623-624	Museums/Exhibitions	359.009492	DJ130-138	Naval history
358.4009	UG633-635	By place	359.009493	DH551	Naval history
358.4009	UG625	History	359.009495	DF765-787	Naval
358.4009(4-9)	UG635	Other countries	359.009495	DF544	Naval history
358.40092	UG626-.2	Biography	359.009497	DR1252-1253	Naval history
358.400942	DA89.5	Air Force	359.009498	DR225	Naval history
358.400973	UG633-634.5	United States	359.009561	DR451	Naval history
358.413	UG770-1045	Organization	359.1	V720-743	Life/Manners/Customs/Etc.
358.414	UG700-705	Tactics	359.1(6-7)	V310	Ceremonies/Honors
358.4145	UG730-735	Air defenses	359.13	VB840-910	Discipline/Crimes/
358.415	UG637-639	Education/Training			Punishment
358.418	UG1100-1425	Equipment/Supplies	359.13323	VB920-955	Military police
358.45	UG760-765	Aerial reconnaissance	359.134	VB330-335	Rewards
358.5	UG615-620	Motor vehicles	359.15	V305	Flags, Other countries
359	DD354-370	Military/Naval/Political	359.15	V300-305	Flags (Not signaling)
359	DD99-120	Military/Naval/Political	359.15	V303-304	Flags, United States
359	V53	20th century	359.28	VA48	Mobilization
359	V	Naval science	359.3	VG	Minor services of navies
359	V110-145	Handbooks	359.3	VD	Naval seamen
359	VA	Navies/Naval situations	359.309	VD15	History
359	VD150-155	Manuals	359.309(4-9)	VA49-750	By place
359.(32/8)	V750-995	War vessels/Material	359.309(4-9)	VD21-124	By place
359.(32/8)090(1-4)	V755-767	By period	359.3094	VA450-619	Europe
359.00(5/6)	V1-5	Serials/Societies	359.3094	VD55-96	Europe
359.006	V7	Congresses	359.30941	VA452-467	Great Britain
359.007	V400-699	Naval education/Training	359.30941	VD57-64	Great Britain
359.007	V402-409	By date	359.30943	VA510-519.39	Germany
359.007	V401-409	History	359.30943	VD79-80	Italy
359.0070(4-9)	V411-695	By place	359.30943	VD73-74.5	Germany
359.00704	V500-623	Europe	359.30944	VD71-72	France
359.007041	V510-530	Great Britain	359.30945	VA540-549	Italy
359.007043	V570-574	Germany	359.30946	VA580-589	Spain
359.00705	V630-650	Asia	359.30946	VD87-88	Spain
359.007051	V630-634	China	359.309469	VD83-84	Portugal
359.007052	V640-644	Japan	359.309469	VA560-569	Portugal
359.007054	V635-639	India	359.30947	VD85-86	European Russia
359.007055	V645-649	Iran	359.30947	VA570-579	European Russia
359.00706	V660-680	Africa	359.30948	VD86.5	Scandinavia
359.007071	V440-444	Canada	359.309492	VA530-539	Netherlands
359.007072	V445-449	Mexico	359.309495	VD75-76	Greece
359.0070728	V450-453	Central America	359.309495	VA520-529	Greece
359.0070729	V455-458	West Indies	359.3095	VD99-113	Asia
359.007073	V411-438	United States	359.3095	VA620-667	Asia
359.00708	V465-496	South America			

Dewey	LC	Descriptor	Dewey	LC	Descriptor
359.30951	VA630-639	China	359.3460973	VG2025-2026	United States
359.30951	VD101-102	China	359.347	VG20-25	Chaplains
359.30952	VD105-106	Japan	359.34709(4-9)	VG25	In other countries
359.30952	VA650-659	Japan	359.3470973	VG23	United States
359.3096	VD115-119	Africa	359.373	VA45	Militia/Reserves
359.30971	VA400-402	Canada			(Organization)
359.30971	VD26-27	Canada	359.42	V160-178	Strategy/Tactics
359.30972	VA403-405	Mexico	359.5	V260-265	Physical Training
359.30972	VD28-29	Mexico	359.5	V400-699	Naval education/Training
359.309728	VD30-31	Central America	359.509	V401-409	History
359.309728	VA406-407	Central America	359.509(4-9)	VD160-302	Drill regulations, By place
359.309729	VD32-33	West Indies	359.509(4-9)	V411-695	By place
359.309729	VA409-410	West Indies	359.5090(1-4)	V402-409	By date
359.30973	VD23-25	United States	359.5094	VD215-269	Europe
359.30973	VA49-395	United States	359.5094	VD228-230	France
359.3098	VA415-445	South America	359.5094	V500-623	Europe
359.3098	VD34-54	South America	359.50941	V510-530	Great Britain
359.30982	VA416-418	Argentina	359.50941	VD234-236	Great Britain
359.30983	VA425-427	Chile	359.50943	V570-574	Germany
359.309861	VA428-430	Colombia	359.50943	VD231-233	Germany
359.3099(3-4)	VD121-122.5	Australia/New Zealand	359.50946	VD255-257	Spain
359.3099(5-6)	VD123-124	Oceania	359.509469	VD249-251	Portugal
359.3099(5-6)	VA730-750	Oceania	359.5095	V630-650	Asia
359.30993	VA720-729	New Zealand	359.5095	VD270-280	Asia
359.30994	VA710-719	Australia	359.50951	V630-634	China
359.31	VB160	Administration (Fleets/Etc.)	359.50952	V640-644	Japan
359.323	VD400-405	Small boat service	359.50952	VD277-279	Japan
359.3253	V820-.5	Cruisers	359.50954	V635-639	India
359.3254	V825-.5	Destroyers	359.50955	V645-649	Iran
359.3255	V874-875	Aircraft carriers	359.5096	VD285-292	Africa
359.3257	V857-859	Submarines	359.5096	V660-680	Africa
359.3258	V830-840	Torpedo boats	359.50971	VD163-165	Canada
359.332	VB307-309	Warrant officers	359.50971	V440-444	Canada
359.332	VB310-315	Officers	359.50972	VD166-168	Mexico
359.338	VB260-275	Enlisted men	359.50972	V445-449	Mexico
359.34	VG600-2000	Misc. noncombat services	359.509728	V450-453	Central America
359.342	VG500-505	Public relations/Information	359.509728	VD169-170	Central America
359.34209(4-9)	VG505	In other countries	359.509729	VD172-173	West Indies
359.3420973	VG503	United States	359.509729	V455-458	West Indies
359.3432	VB230-250	Intelligence	359.50973	VD160-162	United States
359.345	VG280-285	Dental service	359.50973	V411-438	United States
359.345	VG100-475	Medical service	359.5098	V465-496	South America
359.3450(5/6)	VG100	Serials/Societies	359.5098	VD175-211	South America
359.34506	VG103	Congresses	359.5099(3-4)	VD295-298	Australia/New Zealand
359.34507	VG230-235	Education	359.5099(3-6)	V690-695	Australia/New Zealand/
359.345072	VG240-245	Research			Oceania
359.34509(4-9)	VG121-224	Medical service, By place	359.5099(5-6)	VD300-302	Oceania
359.345092	VG226-228	Biography	359.5409(4-9)	VF160-302	Drill books/Etc., By place
359.345094	VG155-196	Europe	359.54094	VF215-269	Europe
359.3450941	VG157-164	Great Britain	359.540941	VF234-236	Great Britain
359.3450943	VG173-174.5	Germany	359.540943	VF231-233	Germany
359.3450944	VG171-172	France	359.540944	VF228-230	France
359.3450945	VG179-180	Italy	359.540945	VF243-245	Italy
359.3450946	VG187-188	Spain	359.540946	VF255-257	Spain
359.3450948	VG186.5	Scandinavia	359.540947	VF252-254	European Russia
359.345095	VG199-213	Asia	359.54095	VF270-280	Asia
359.3450952	VG205-206	Japan	359.540952	VF277-279	Japan
359.345096	VG215-219	Africa	359.54096	VF285-292	Africa
359.3450971	VG126-127	Canada	359.540971	VF163-165	Canada
359.3450972	VG128-129	Mexico	359.540972	VF166-168	Mexico
359.34509728	VG130-131	Central America	359.5409728	VF169-170	Central America
359.3450973	VG123-125	United States	359.5409729	VF172-173	West Indies
359.345098	VG134-154	South America	359.540973	VF160-162	United States
359.345099(3-4)	VG221-222.5	Australia/New Zealand	359.54098	VF175-211	South America
359.345099(5-6)	VG223-224	Oceania	359.540982	VF176-178	Argentina
359.346	VG2020-2029	Recreation services	359.540983	VF185-187	Chile
359.34609(4-9)	VG2029	In other countries	359.5409861	VF188-190	Colombia

Dewey	LC	Descriptor	Dewey	LC	Descriptor
359.54099(3-4)	VF295-298	Australia/New Zealand	359.8209	VF15	History
359.54099(5-6)	VF300-302	Oceania	359.8209(4-9)	VF21-124	By place
359.547	VD320-345	Manual of arms/Bayonet/ Etc.	359.82094	VF55-96	Europe
			359.820941	VF57-64	Great Britain
359.6	VB	Naval administration	359.820943	VF73-74.5	Germany
359.609	VB15	History	359.820944	VF71-72	France
359.609(4-9)	VB21-124	By place	359.820945	VF79-80	Italy
359.6094	VB55-96	Europe	359.820946	VF87-88	Spain
359.60941	VB57-64	Great Britain	359.8209469	VF83-84	Portugal
359.60943	VB73-74.5	Germany	359.820947	VF85-86	European Russia
359.60944	VB71-72	France	359.820948	VF86.5	Scandinavia
359.60945	VB79-80	Italy	359.82095	VF101-113	Asia
359.60946	VB87-88	Spain	359.820952	VF105-106	Japan
359.609469	VB83-84	Portugal	359.8209561	VF111-112	Turkey
359.60947	VB85-86	European Russia	359.82096	VF115-119	Africa
359.609495	VB75-76	Greece	359.820971	VF26-27	Canada
359.6095	VB99-113	Asia	359.820972	VF28-29	Mexico
359.60951	VB101-102	China	359.8209728	VF30-31	Central America
359.60952	VB105-106	Japan	359.8209729	VF32-33	West Indies
359.6096	VB115-119	Africa	359.820973	VF23-25	United States
359.60971	VB26-27	Canada	359.82098	VF34-54	South America
359.60972	VB28-29	Mexico	359.820982	VF36-37	Argentina
359.609728	VB30-31	Central America	359.820983	VF43-44	Chile
359.609729	VB32-33	West Indies	359.8209861	VF45-46	Colombia
359.60973	VB23-25	United States	359.82099(3-4)	VF121-122.5	Australia/New Zealand
359.6098	VB34-54	South America	359.82099(5-6)	VF123-124	Oceania
359.60982	VB36-37	Argentina	359.824	VD350-355	Equipment/Small arms
359.60983	VB43-44	Chile	359.824424	VF410	Machine guns
359.609861	VB45-46	Colombia	359.88	VG290-295	Medical supplies
359.6099(3-4)	VB121-122.5	Australia/New Zealand	359.93	V210-214	Submarine warfare
359.6099(5-6)	VB123-124	Oceania	359.94	VG90-95	Naval aviation
359.61	VB257-258.5	Personnel management	359.9409(4-9)	VG95	In other countries
359.61	VB170-187	Civil department	359.940973	VG93-94.7	United States
359.62(2)	VC500-505	Ship records/Accounting	359.96	VE	Marines
359.622	VA20-25	Costs/Expenditures	359.9614	VE400-405	Uniforms
359.63	VB220-225	Inspection	359.96309	VE15	History
359.693	VG60-65	Postal service	359.96309(4-9)	VE21-124	By place
359.69309(4-9)	VG65	In other countries	359.963094	VE55-96	Europe
359.6930973	VG63	United States	359.9630941	VE57-64	Great Britain
359.7	V220-240	Stations/Ports/Bases/Yards	359.9630943	VE73-74.5	Germany
359.7	VC412-425	Navy yards/Stations	359.9630944	VE71-72	France
359.72	VG410-450	Naval hospitals/Etc.	359.9630945	VE79-80	Italy
359.8	VF346-510	Systems/Facilities/Material	359.9630946	VE87-88	Spain
359.8	VC270-279	Equipment of vessels	359.9630947	VE85-86	European Russia
359.8	V398	Electronic data processing	359.9630948	VE86.5	Scandinavia
359.8	VC260-268	Supplies/Stores	359.963095	VE99-113	Asia
359.8	VC	Naval maintenance	359.9630952	VE105-106	Japan
359.809(4-9)	VC20-258	Organization, By place	359.963096	VE115-119	Africa
359.8094	VC160-229	Europe	359.9630971	VE26-27	Canada
359.80941	VC184-187	Great Britain	359.9630972	VE28-29	Mexico
359.80943	VC180-183.53	Germany	359.96309728	VE30-31	Central America
359.8095	VC230-245	Asia	359.96309729	VE32-33	West Indies
359.80952	VC241	Japan	359.9630973	VE23-25	United States
359.8096	VC247-253	Africa	359.963098	VE34-54	South America
359.80971	VC90-93	Canada	359.963099(3-4)	VE121-122.5	Australia/New Zealand
359.80972	VC94-97	Mexico	359.963099(5-6)	VE123-124	Oceania
359.809728	VC98-99	Central America	359.9641	V215	Marine camouflage
359.809729	VC104-105	West Indies	359.9646	U261	Amphibious warfare
359.80973	VC20-65	United States	359.965	VE150-155	Handbooks/Manuals
359.8098	VC110-150	South America	359.965	VE430-435	Training camps
359.8099(3-6)	VC255-258	Australia/New Zealand/ Oceania	359.96509(4-9)	VE160-302	Drill regulations, By place
			359.965094	VE215-269	Europe
359.81	VC280-410	Clothing/Subsistence	359.9650941	VE234-236	Great Britain
359.82	VF150-155	Handbooks/Manuals	359.9650943	VE231-233	Germany
359.82	VF	Naval ordnance	359.9650944	VE228-230	France
359.820(5/6)	VF1	Serials/Societies	359.9650945	VE243-245	Italy
359.82074	VF6	Exhibitions/Museums	359.9650947	VE252-254	European Russia

Dewey	LC	Descriptor	Dewey	LC	Descriptor
359.9650952	VE277-279	Japan	361.30973	HV85-99	United States
359.965096	VE270-280	Asia	361.37	HV40.4-.42	Non-professional workers
359.965096	VE285-292	Africa	361.6	HV51-57	Public relief/Aid
359.9650971	VE163-165	Canada	361.7	HV48	Private relief/Aid
359.9650972	VE166-168	Mexico	361.7(4-6)	HV589-593	Other relief associations
359.96509728	VE169-170	Central America	361.70681	HV41.2-.9	Fund raising
359.96509729	VE172-173	West Indies	361.709	HV16-25	History of philanthropy
359.9650973	VE160-162	United States	361.75	HV530	The church and charity
359.965098	VE175-211	South America	361.77	HV560-583	Red Cross/Crescent
359.965099(3-4)	VE295-298	Australia/New Zealand	361.77	UH520-551	Relief societies
359.965099(5-6)	VE300-302	Oceania	361.77	UH535-537	Red Cross
359.9654	VE330-340	Manual of arms/ Shooting/Etc.	361.7709	HV568	History
			361.7709(4-9)	HV575-580	By place
359.96622	VE480-490	Accounting/Pay/ Allowances	361.77092	HV569	Biography
			361.9	HN8-19	History
359.9671	VE420-425	Quarters/Barracks	361.9(3-4)	HN13-18	Modern
359.96824	VE350-390	Equipment/Small arms	361.9(4-9)	HN50-981	Social problems, By place
359.97	VG50-55	Coast Guard (Military duty)	361.90(31-33)	HN14	Medieval to 1800
359.9707073	V437	Coast Guard	361.901	HN9-10	Ancient
359.9709(4-9)	VG55	In other countries	361.902	HN11	Medieval
359.970973	VG53	United States	361.9034	HN15-.5	19th century
359.98	VF520-530	Fire control/Instruments	361.904	HN16-18	20th century
359.98	VF346-510	Systems/Facilities/Material	361.91717	HN958-962	Communist countries
359.98	VF346-510	Systems/Facilities/Material	361.91724	HN978-981	Developing countries
359.98	VF320-325	Naval artillery equipment	361.941	HN381-400	Great Britain
359.9817	V990-995	Fleet Ballistic Missile Systems	361.9417	HN400.3	Ireland/Irish Republic
			361.943	HN441-460.5	Germany
359.982	VG590-595	Civil/Construction engineering	361.9436	HN401-420	Austria
			361.943648	HN420.9	Liechtenstein
359.98209(4-9)	VG595	In other countries	361.9437	HN420.3	Czechoslovakia
359.9820973	VG593	United States	361.9438	HN536-539.5	Poland
359.983	VG70-85	Communications	361.9439	HN420.5	Hungary
359.984	VG86-88	Underwater demolition	361.944	HN421-440	France
359.98409(4-9)	VG88	In other countries	361.944949	HN440.5	Monaco
359.9840973	VG87	United States	361.945	HN471-490	Italy
359.985	VC530-580	Transportation/Shipping	361.946	HN581-590	Spain
361	HN	Social history/Problems	361.9469	HN591-600	Portugal
361.(3/7)	HV40-525	Social work/Charities	361.94698	HN838.5	Madeira Islands
361.00(5/6)	HN1	Serials/Societies	361.94699	HN838	Azores
361.001	HN28	Theory	361.947	HN521-530	European Russia
361.0021	HN25	Statistics	361.9481	HN561-570	Norway
361.006	HN3	Congresses	361.9485	HN571-580	Sweden
361.007	HN29	Education	361.9489	HN541-550	Denmark
361.05	HV59-61	Institutional/Indoor relief	361.94897	HN531-535	Finland
361.05	HV65	Noninstitutional/Outdoor aid	361.94912	HN551-560	Iceland
			361.9492	HN511-520	Netherlands
361.1	HV	Social pathology/ Criminology	361.9493	HN501-510	Belgium
			361.94935	HN520.5	Luxembourg
361.1021	HV29	Statistics	361.9494	HN601-610	Switzerland
361.1025	HV7	Directories	361.9495	HN650.5	Greece
361.10285	HV29.2-.5	Computer applications	361.94965	HN620.5	Albania
361.103	HV12	Dictionaries/ Encyclopedias	361.9497	HN631-635	Yugoslavia
			361.94977	HN621-630	Bulgaria
361.105	HV1-4	Serials	361.9498	HN641-650	Romania
361.106	HV6	Societies	361.951	HN731-740	China
361.106	HV8	Congresses	361.951249	HN746-750	Taiwan
361.107	HV11	Education	361.95125	HN751-755	Hong Kong
361.1074	HV10	Exhibitions/Museums	361.9517	HN730.8	Mongolia
361.1076	HV11.5	Examinations/ Questions/Etc.	361.9519	HN730.5-.6	Korea/North Korea
			361.952	HN721-730	Japan
361.1092	HV27-28	Biography	361.95332	HN664-.5	Yemen
361.3023	HV10.5	Social work as a profession	361.95353	HN665	Oman
361.309(4-9)	HV101-520.5	Other countries	361.95357	HN666	United Arab Emirates
361.309(4-9)	HV85-520.5	Social work, By place	361.95363	HN667	Qatar
361.3091734	HV67	Rural social work	361.95365	HN668	Bahrain
361.3092	HV40.3-.32	Biography	361.95367	HN669	Kuwait
361.3097(4-9)	HV98-99	By state/City	361.9538	HN663	Saudi Arabia

Dewey	LC	Descriptor	Dewey	LC	Descriptor
361.954	HN681-690	India	361.9678	HN797	Tanzania
361.95491	HN690.5	Pakistan	361.9679	HN798	Mozambique
361.95492	HN690.6	Bangladesh	361.968	HN801	South Africa
361.95493	HN670.8	Sri Lanka	361.96881	HN808	Namibia
361.95495	HN839.7	Maldive Islands	361.96883	HN806	Botswana
361.95496	HN670.9	Nepal	361.96885	HN804	Lesotho
361.95498	HN690.3	Bhutan	361.96887	HN805	Swaziland
361.955	HN670.2	Iran	361.9689	HN802	Zimbabwe (Southern Rhodesia)
361.9561	HN656.5	Turkey			
361.95645	HN657	Cyprus	361.96894	HN803	Zambia (Northern Rhodesia)
361.9567	HN670	Iraq			
361.95691	HN658	Syria	361.96897	HN807	Malawi (Nyasaland)
361.95692	HN659	Lebanon	361.9694	HN840	Comoro Islands
361.95694	HN660	Israel/Palestine	361.9696	HN839.9	Seychelles
361.95695	HN661	Jordan	361.96981	HN840.5	Reunion
361.9581	HN670.6	Afghanistan	361.96982	HN840.3	Mauritius
361.9591	HN670.7	Burma	361.9699	HN840.7	Kerguelen Islands
361.9593	HN700.55	Thailand	361.971	HN101-110	Canada
361.9594	HN700.4	Laos	361.972	HN111-120	Mexico
361.9595	HN700.6	Malaysia	361.9728	HN131-140	Costa Rica
361.95955	HN700.68	Brunei	361.97281	HN141-150	Guatemala
361.95957	HN700.67	Singapore	361.97282	HN126-130	Belize
361.9596	HN700.3	Cambodia	361.97283	HN151-160	Honduras
361.9597	HN700.5	Vietnam	361.97284	HN181-190	El Salvador
361.9598	HN701-710	Indonesia	361.97285	HN161-170	Nicaragua
361.9599	HN711-720	Philippine Islands	361.97287	HN171-175	Panama
361.9611	HN784	Tunisia	361.972875	HN176-180	Panama Canal Zone
361.9612	HN785	Libya	361.97291	HN201-210	Cuba
361.962	HN786	Egypt	361.97292	HN221-230	Jamaica
361.9624	HN787	Sudan	361.97293	HN216-220	Dominican Republic
361.963	HN789	Ethiopia	361.97294	HN211-215	Haiti
361.964	HN782	Morocco	361.97295	HN231-240	Puerto Rico
361.9648	HN837	Spanish Sahara	361.97296	HN196-200	Bahamas
361.9649	HN838.7	Canary Islands	361.97297	HN244	Leeward Islands
361.965	HN783	Algeria	361.9729722	HN241	Virgin Islands of the U.S.
361.9661	HN830	Mauritania	361.972976	HN249	Guadeloupe
361.96623	HN827	Mali	361.972982	HN250	Martinique
361.96625	HN828	Burkina Faso	361.972983	HN246	Trinidad and Tobago
361.96626	HN824	Niger	361.972984	HN245	Windward Islands
361.9663	HN829	Senegal	361.972986	HN247	Netherlands Antilles
361.9664	HN833	Sierra Leone	361.97299	HN838.3	Bermuda
361.96651	HN834	Gambia	361.973	HN51-90	United States
361.96652	HN826	Guinea	361.98	HN940	Arctic regions
361.96657	HN836	Guinea-Bissau	361.981	HN281-290	Brazil
361.96658	HN838.9	Cape Verde Islands	361.982	HN261-270	Argentina
361.96662	HN835	Liberia	361.982	HN942.5	Greenland
361.96668	HN825	Ivory Coast	361.983	HN291-300	Chile
361.9667	HN832	Ghana	361.984	HN271-280	Bolivia
361.96681	HN823	Togo	361.985	HN341-350	Peru
361.96683	HN822	Benin (Dahomey)	361.9861	HN301-310	Colombia
361.9669	HN831	Nigeria	361.9866	HN311-320	Ecuador
361.96711	HN819	Cameroon	361.987	HN361-370	Venezuela
361.96715	HN813	Sao Tome/Principe	361.9881	HN330.3	Guyana
361.96718	HN812	Equatorial Guinea	361.9882	HN330.7	French Guiana
361.9672	HN814	French Equatorial Africa	361.9883	HN330.5	Suriname
361.96721	HN815	Gabon	361.989	HN942.7	Antarctic regions
361.96724	HN816	Congo	361.9892	HN331-340	Paraguay
361.9673	HN810	Angola	361.9895	HN351-360	Uruguay
361.96741	HN817	Central African Republic	361.993	HN930.5	New Zealand
361.96743	HN818	Chad	361.994	HN841-850	Australia
361.96751	HN811	Zaire	361.9953	HN932	Papua New Guinea
361.967571	HN795	Rwanda	361.99593	HN933	Solomon Islands
361.967572	HN796	Burundi	361.99595	HN935	Vanuatu
361.96761	HN794	Uganda	361.99597	HN934	New Caledonia
361.96762	HN793	Kenya	361.99611	HN936	Fiji Islands
361.96771	HN791	Djibouti	361.99612	HN937	Tonga
361.96773	HN790	Somalia	361.99613	HN938	American Samoa

Dewey	LC	Descriptor
361.99614	HN939	Western Samoa
361.9962	HN939.5	French Polynesia
361.9967	HN931.5	Guam
361.99681	HN932.3	Kiribati (Gilbert Islands)
361.9971	HN839.5	Falkland Islands
361.9973	HN839.3	Tristan da Cunha
361.9973	HN839	St. Helena
362	HV697-4959	Protection/Assistance/Relief
362.(3-4)	HV888-907	Handicapped children
362.(3-4)	HV1551-3024	Handicapped adults
362.1(1-6)	HV687-694	Medical charities/ Advice/Aid
362.11	RJ27-28	Hospitals/Clinics/Etc.
362.11	RG12-16	Hospitals/Clinics/Etc.
362.11	RK3-.5	Hospitals/Clinics/Etc.
362.11	RL20-21	Hospitals/Clinics/Etc.
362.11	RZ302-304	Hospitals/Clinics/Etc.
362.1109(4-9)	RJ27.2-.5	Hospitals, By place
362.1109(4-9)	RK3.5	Hospitals, By place
362.11097(4-9)	RJ27.5	By areas
362.110973	RJ27.2-.3	United States
362.1608697	UB356-385	Veterans/Soldiers' homes
362.1968	HV1570-.5	Developmentally disabled
362.20425	HV689-690	Psychiatric social work
362.29	HV4997-5000	Substance abuse
362.29(3-8)09(4-9)	HV5840	Other countries
362.29(3-8)09(4-9)	HV5825-5840	Drug habits, By place
362.29(3-8)0973	HV5825-5833	United States
362.29(3-9)	HV5800-5840	Drug habits/Abuse
362.2909(4-9)	HV4999.2-5000	By place
362.292	HV5001-5720.5	Alcoholism/Intemperance
362.29205	HV5001-5002	Serials
362.29206	HV5006-5009	Societies/Congresses
362.29209	HV5020-5025	History
362.29209(4-9)	HV5301-5720.5	Other countries
362.29209(4-9)	HV5285-5720.5	Alcoholism, By place
362.292092	HV5030-5032	Biography
362.2920973	HV5285-5298	United States
362.2927	HV5203-5247	Women and temperance reform
362.2928	HV5275-5283	Care/Rehabilitation
362.293	HV5813	Morphine
362.293	HV5816	Opium
362.296	HV5725-5770	Tobacco habit
362.296(4-9)	HV5770	Other countries
362.29609(4-9)	HV5755-5770	By place
362.2960973	HV5755-5768	United States
362.298	HV5810	Cocaine/Crack
362.3	HV891-901	Mentally handicapped
362.38	HV3004-3009.5	Mentally handicapped
362.3809(4-9)	HV3008	Other countries
362.380973	HV3006	United States
362.4	HV903-907	Physically handicapped
362.41	HV1571-2349	Blind
362.41	HV1597-.2	Deaf-blind
362.4109(4-9)	HV1783-2220.5	Blind persons, By place
362.4109(4-9)	HV1801-2220.5	Other countries
362.41092	HV1584	Biography
362.410973	HV1783-1796	United States
362.42	HV2350-2990.5	Deaf
362.4209(4-9)	HV2510-2990.5	Deaf persons, By place
362.42092	HV2373	Biography
362.420973	HV2510-2561	United States
362.4283	HV2402	Interpreters
362.4283	HV2502-2503	Communication devices for
362.48	HV3011-3024	Physically handicapped
362.4809(4-9)	HV3024	Other countries

Dewey	LC	Descriptor
362.4809(4-9)	HV3023-3024	By place
362.480973	HV3023	United States
362.5	HV4023-4470.7	City poor/Slums
362.5	HV4480-4630	Mendicancy/ Vagabondism/ Tramps
362.509(4-9)	HV4041-4170.7	By place
362.5091724	HV4173	Developing countries
362.5094	HV4084-4131.84	Europe
362.50941	HV4085-4087.5	Great Britain
362.50943	HV4097-4100	Germany
362.50944	HV4093-4096.5	France
362.50945	HV4102-4105	Italy
362.50946	HV4125-4128	Spain
362.50947	HV4114-4117	European Russia
362.509492	HV4105.5-4113.5	Low Countries
362.5095	HV4132.6-4153	Asia
362.50951	HV4150	China
362.50952	HV4147	Japan
362.50954	HV4137-4140	India
362.50956	HV4131.9-4132.56	Near East
362.5096	HV4157-4169.3	Africa
362.50971	HV4047-4050	Canada
362.50972	HV4051	Mexico
362.509728	HV4053-4059	Central America
362.509729	HV4060-4065.9	West Indies
362.50973	HV4043-4046	United States
362.5098	HV4066-4083	South America
362.5099(4-6)	HV4170-.68	Australia/New Zealand/ Oceania
362.58	HV680-685	Legal aid
362.6	HV1450-1493	Aged
362.609(4-9)	HV1457-1493	Aged, By place
362.61	HV1454-.2	Life care communities
362.7	HV701-1420.5	Children
362.7(3/6)	HV873-887	Destitute/Neglected/ Abandoned
362.70(5/6)	HV701-707	Serials/Societies/Congresses
362.7083	HV1421-1441	Young men/Women
362.709(4-9)	HV745-804	Other countries
362.709(4-9)	HV741-803	By place
362.70973	HV741-743	United States
362.712	HV851-861	Day care centers
362.73	HV835-847	Foundlings
362.7309(4-9)	HV880-887	Destitute, By place
362.730973	HV880-885	United States
362.732	HV862-866	Residential care/Group homes
362.732	HV959-1420.5	Orphans/Orphanages
362.73209(4-9)	HV971-1420.5	Orphanages, By place
362.7320973	HV971-995	United States
362.734	HV874.8-875.7	Adoption
362.8	HQ301-440.7	Rescue work
362.809(4-9)	HQ311-440.7	Rescue work, By place
362.82	HV697-700.7	Families
362.8209(4-9)	HV699-700	By place
362.8294	HV700.7	Unmarried fathers
362.8294	HV700.5	Unmarried mothers
362.83	HV1442-1448	Women
362.84(03-99)	HV3176-3199	Classed by race/Ethnic group
362.8496073	HV3181-3185	Afro-Americans
362.858	HV3025-3174	Classed by occupations
362.86	VB280-285	Pensions/Disability benefits
362.87	HV640-645	Refugee problems
362.88	HV6250-.4	Victims of crime
363.107	HV675-677	Accident prevention
363.11	HD7260-7780.8	Industrial hygiene

Dewey	LC	Descriptor
363.11	HD7262-7265.5	Accidents/Dangers
363.11	T54-55	Industrial accidents/Safety
363.119622	HV638	Mine disasters
363.2(89)	HV7551-8280.7	Police/Detectives
363.2025	HV7900	Directories
363.203	HV7901	Dictionaries/ Encyclopedias
363.207	HV7923	Education
363.209	HV7903-7909	History
363.209(4-9)	HV8130-8280.7	Police, By place
363.2092	HV7911	Biography
363.2094	HV8194-8217.7	Europe
363.20941	HV8195-8197.5	Great Britain
363.20943	HV8207-8210	Germany
363.20944	HV8203-8206	France
363.20945	HV8212-8215	Italy
363.20946	HV8235-8238	Spain
363.209469	HV8239	Portugal
363.20947	HV8224-8227	European Russia
363.209492	HV8215.5-8223.5	Low Countries
363.209495	HV8241.83	Greece
363.2095	HV8241.85-8263	Asia
363.20951	HV8260	China
363.20952	HV8257	Japan
363.20954	HV8247-8250	India
363.20956	HV8241.9-8242.56	Middle East
363.209599	HV8255	Philippines
363.2096	HV8267-8279.3	Africa
363.20971	HV8157-8160	Canada
363.20972	HV8161	Mexico
363.209728	HV8163-8169	Central America
363.209729	HV8170-8175.9	West Indies
363.20973	HV8130-8148	United States
363.2098	HV8176-8193	South America
363.2099(3-6)	HV8280-.68	Australia/New Zealand/ Oceania
363.23	HV8031-8080	Police duty/ Investigation/ Etc.
363.289	HV8081-8099	Private detectives
363.289	HV8290	Guards/Watchmen/Etc.
363.32	U230	Riot duty
363.33	HV7435-7439	Gun control
363.348	HV553-639	Disaster relief
363.34809(4-9)	HV555	Disaster relief, By place
363.349	HV599-639	Types of disasters
363.34928	HV636	Storms/Hurricanes/ Typhoons
363.34928	HV625-626	Droughts
363.34938	HV609-610	Floods
363.34958	HV599-600	Earthquakes
363.34958	HV638.5	Volcanoes
363.3498	N9100-9165	Art and war (Loss/ Damage/Etc.)
363.34988	HV639	War
363.35	UA926-929	Civil defense
363.37	HV620	Fires
363.44	HQ101-440.7	Prostitution
363.44	HQ280-285	Traffic in women
363.49	HV1449	Homosexuals
363.5	HD7285-7391	Housing
363.509(4-9)	HD7291-7390	Housing, By place
363.5091724	HD7391	Developing countries
363.5094	HD7332-7357.5	Europe
363.50941	HD7333-7335.5	Great Britain
363.50943	HD7339-.5	Germany
363.50944	HD7338	France
363.50945	HD7341	Italy
363.50946	HD7351	Spain
363.50947	HD7345	European Russia
363.509492	HD7342-7344.5	Low Countries
363.509494	HD7353	Switzerland
363.509495	HD7357.5	Greece
363.5095	HD7359.7-7371	Far East
363.50951	HD7368	China
363.50952	HD7367	Japan
363.50954	HD7361	India
363.50955	HD7359.2	Iran
363.50956	HD7358.25-.95	Middle East
363.509567	HD7359	Iraq
363.5095694	HD7358.45	Israel/Palestine
363.509599	HD7366	Philippine Islands
363.5096	HD7372.3-7378.4	Africa
363.50971	HD7305	Canada
363.50972	HD7306	Mexico
363.509728	HD7307.5-7313	Central America
363.509729	HD7314.5-7319.9	West Indies
363.50973	HD7293-7304	United States
363.5098	HD7321-7331	South America
363.5099(3-6)	HD7379-7388.9	Australia/New Zealand/ Oceania
363.6	HD2763-2768	Public utilities
363.61	TD201-500	Water supply
363.68	SB481-485	Parks/Public reservations
363.680(5/6)	SB481	Serials/Societies/Congresses
363.6809(4-9)	SB484-485	Other countries
363.680973	SB482-483	United States
363.69	NA105-109	Monuments (Preserve/Restore)
363.7288	TS214	Scrap metals
363.73	TD172-192	Environmental pollution
363.7387	QC882	Pollutants (Dust/ Smoke/Etc.)
363.7394	GC1080-1581	Marine pollution
363.74	TD891-893.5	Noise
363.8	HV630-635	Famines
363.883	HV694	Soup kitchens
363.92	HQ750-755.5	Eugenics
363.96	HQ760-767.7	Family size
363.96	HQ763-767.7	Family planning/Birth control
363.9609	HQ762	Family size, By place
364	HV6001-7220.5	Criminology
364	HV	Social pathology/ Criminology
364	HV7231-9481	Criminal justice admin.
364.(1/3)09(4-9)	HV6801-7220.5	Other countries
364.(1/3)09(4-9)	HV6774-7220.5	Crimes/Criminals, By place
364.(1/3)0973	HV6774-6795	United States
364.02109(4-9)	HV7245-7400	By place (Statistics/Etc.)
364.021094	HV7342-7367.7	Europe
364.0210941	HV7343-7345.5	Great Britain
364.0210943	HV7349-.5	Germany
364.0210944	HV7348	France
364.0210945	HV7351	Italy
364.0210946	HV7361	Spain
364.0210947	HV7355	European Russia
364.0210951	HV7378	China
364.0210952	HV7377	Japan
364.0210954	HV7371	India
364.0210956	HV7368.2-7369.2	Middle East
364.021096	HV7382-7388.4	Africa
364.021097(4-9)	HV7250-7300	By state
364.0210971	HV7315	Canada
364.0210972	HV7316	Mexico

Dewey	LC	Descriptor	Dewey	LC	Descriptor
364.02109728	HV7317-7323	Central America	364.2	HV6045-6054	Criminal type
364.02109729	HV7324-7329.9	West Indies	364.22	HV6150-6190	Environmental causes
364.0210973	HV7245-7300	United States	364.24	HV6121-6125	Hereditary causes
364.021098	HV7330-7341	South America	364.24	HV6065-6079	Criminal anthropometry
364.021099(3-6)	HV7389-7398.9	Australia/New Zealand/ Oceania	364.256	HV6191-6197	Caused by race/Nationality
364.0210995	HV7368-7381	Asia	364.3	HV6080-6113	Criminal psychology
364.03	HV6017	Encyclopedias/Dictionaries	364.3496073	E185.65	Crime
364.03	HV7411	Dictionaries/ Encyclopedias	364.36	HV9051-9230.7	Juvenile offenders
			364.360(5/6)	HV9051-9058	Serials/Societies/Congresses
364.05	HV7231-7239	Serials	364.3607	HV9068	Education
364.05	HV6001-6006	Serials	364.3609(4-9)	HV9101-9230.7	Juvenile offenders, By place
364.06	HV6008-6010	Societies/Congresses	364.3609(4-9)	HV9107-9230.7	Other countries
364.06	HV7240-7243	Societies/Congresses	364.360973	HV9103-9106	United States
364.07	HV6024	Education	364.6	HV8301-9920.5	Penology
364.072	HV7419.5	Research	364.6(3-8)	HV8545-8654	Forms of punishment
364.072	HV6024.5	Research	364.601	HV9261-9430.7	Reforming of adult prisoners
364.074	HV6011	Exhibitions/Museums	364.6021	HV8482-8488	Statistics
364.09	HV6018-6023	History of criminology	364.602109(72-8)	HV8484	Other American countries
364.1	HV6251-6773.3	Crimes and offenses	364.6021094	HV8485	Europe
364.106	HV6437-6453	Outlaws/Gangs/Etc.	364.6021095	HV8486	Asia
364.13	HV6254-6321	Political crimes	364.6021096	HV8487	Africa
364.1309(4-9)	HV6321	Other countries	364.60210971	HV8483	Canada
364.130973	HV6303-6316	United States	364.60210973	HV8482	United States
364.133	HJ2348.5	Tax evasion	364.60210994	HV8488	Australia
364.133	HJ6619	Smuggling	364.609	HV8497-8654	History
364.133	HV6337-6351	Offenses against the revenue	364.609(3-6)	HV9871-9918.9	Australia/New Zealand/ Oceania
364.134	HV6455-6471	Lynching	364.609(4-9)	HV9441-9920.5	Penology, By place
364.134	HV6323-6335	Offenses against justice	364.609(4-9)	HV9501-9920.5	Other countries
364.142	HV6419-6433	Against public safety	364.60902	HV8529-8532	Medieval
364.143	HV6486-6491	Disorderly conduct	364.60903	HV8508-8526	Ancient
364.143	HV6474-6485	Riots/Mobs/Unlawful assemblies	364.6094	HV9636-9775.7	Europe
364.143	HV6435-6492	Against the public order	364.60941	HV9641-9650	Great Britain
364.15	HV6493-6626.5	Against persons	364.60943	HV9671-9680.5	Germany
364.152	HV6499-6535	Murder/Homicide	364.60944	HV9661-9670	France
364.15209(4-9)	HV6518-6535	Murder, By place	364.60945	HV9686-9695	Italy
364.15209(4-9)	HV6535	Other countries	364.60946	HV9741-9745	Spain
364.1520973	HV6518-6534	United States	364.60947	HV9711-9715	European Russia
364.1522	HV6543-6548	Suicide	364.609492	HV9696-9710.5	Low Countries
364.1523	HV6537-6541	Infanticide	364.609495	HV9775.5	Greece
364.153	HV6584-6589	Seduction	364.6095	HV9785.7-9831	Asia
364.1532	HV6558-6569	Rape	364.60951	HV9816-9820	China
364.1534	HQ121-125	Regulation/And the law	364.60952	HV9811-9815	Japan
364.1534	HQ280-285	Traffic in women	364.60954	HV9791-9795	India
364.1536	HQ71-72	Sexual deviations/Crimes	364.60956	HV9776.5-9785.2	Middle East
364.154	HV6595-6604	Kidnapping	364.609599	HV9806-9810	Philippines
364.154	HV6571-6574	Abduction	364.6096	HV9836-9868.5	Africa
364.1555	HV6618	Bodily assault	364.60971	HV9501-9510	Canada
364.1555(3-4)	HV6625-6626.5	Abuse of persons	364.60972	HV9511-9515	Mexico
364.156	HV6629-6633	Against reputation/Honor	364.609728	HV9516-9550	Central America
364.16	HV6635-6700	Against property	364.609729	HV9551-9575.95	West Indies
364.162	HV6675-6685	Embezzlement/Forgery/Etc.	364.60973	HV9456-9481	United States
364.162	HV6646-6665	Theft	364.6098	HV9576-9635	South America
364.163	HV6691-6700	Frauds/Quacks/Etc.	364.66	HV8551-8586	Capital punishment
364.164	HV6638-.5	Arson	364.67	HV8593-8599	Torture
364.164	HV6666-6669	Vandalism	364.67	HV8613-8621	Flogging/Flagellation
364.164	HV6640	Bombings	364.9(4-9)	HV9960	In other countries
364.165	HV6688	Extortion	364.973	HV9950-9956	U.S. criminal justice admin.
364.168	HV6763-6771	Financial crimes	365	HV8935-8962	Penal colonies/ Transportation
364.168	HV6773-.3	Computer crimes	365	HV8705-8749	Imprisonment
364.17	HV6705-6722	Against public morals	365.01	HV8751-8931	Prison methods/Practice
364.172	HV6708-6722	Gambling	365.4092	HV8657-8658	Biography of prisoners
364.1791	HV6549-6555	Poisoning	365.601	HV8675-8686	Theory of punishment
364.2	HV6115-6190	Causes of crime/Etiology	365.641	HV9025	Prison violence
364.2	HV6035-6197	Criminal anthropology	365.7	HV8971-9018	Prison reform

Dewey	LC	Descriptor
366-367	HS	Societies (Secret/ Benevolent)
366.(1-5)	HS181-191	Anti-secret society
366.(1-5)	HS148	20th century
366.(1-5)	HS101-330.7	Secret societies
366.(1-5)03	HS119	Dictionaries/ Encyclopedias
366.(1-5)05	HS113	Yearbooks/Almanacs
366.(1-5)05	HS101-106	Serials
366.(1-5)06	HS110	Congresses
366.(1-5)09	HS125-148	History
366.(1-5)09(4-9)	HS201-330.7	Secret societies, By place
366.(1-5)09(4-9)	HS207-330.7	Other places
366.(1-5)090(2-31)	HS137	Medieval to 1600
366.(1-5)09033	HS146	18th century
366.(1-5)09034	HS147	19th century
366.(1-5)093	HS131	Ancient
366.(1-5)0973	HS203-206	United States
366.0(5/6)	HS1	Serials/Societies
366.025	HS17	Directories
366.05	HS8	Yearbooks
366.05	HS12	Dictionaries/ Encyclopedias
366.06	HS5	Congresses
366.09	HS25	History
366.09(4-9)	HS61-89	Organization, By place
366.09(728-8)	HS65	Central/South America
366.094	HS71	Other European countries
366.0941	HS67	Great Britain
366.095	HS81	Asia
366.096	HS84	Africa
366.0971	HS63	Canada
366.0973	HS61	United States
366.099(3-4)	HS87	Australia/New Zealand
366.099(5-6)	HS89	Oceania
366.1	HS351-929	Freemasons
366.1(6-7)	HS701-833	Other Masonic bodies
366.1025	HS381-390	Directories
366.103	HS375	Dictionaries/ Encyclopedias
366.105	HS365	Yearbooks
366.105	HS351-359	Serials
366.107	HS392-394	Education/Research
366.1089036	HS875-895	Freemasonry and blacks
366.109	HS403-420	History
366.109(4-9)	HS390	Other countries
366.109(4-9)	HS503-680.7	Freemasons, By place
366.109(4-9)	HS557-680.7	Other countries
366.1092	HS399-400	Biography
366.10973	HS503-539	United States
366.10973	HS383-387	United States
366.12	HS455-459	Rituals
366.18	HS851-859	Women in Masonry
366.2	HS1201-1350	Knights of Pythias
366.2025	HS1207-1213	Directories
366.203	HS1205	Dictionaries/ Encyclopedias
366.205	HS1201	Serials
366.209	HS1251-1261	By place
366.209	HS1219	History
366.209(4-9)	HS1261	Other countries
366.20973	HS1251-1254	United States
366.3	HS951-1179	Odd Fellows
366.3025	HS963-975	Directories
366.305	HS951-953	Serials
366.3089036	HS1171-1179	Odd Fellows and blacks
366.309	HS987-991	History

Dewey	LC	Descriptor
366.309(4-9)	HS1041-1051	Odd Fellows, By place
366.309(4-9)	HS1051	Other countries
366.30973	HS1041-1045	United States
366.38	HS1161	Women in Odd Fellows
367	HQ1871-2030.7	Women's clubs/Societies
367	HS2501-3365	Clubs
367.01	HS2521	Theory
367.025	HS2507-2515	Directories
367.05	HS2501-2503	Serials
367.4	HS3250-3270	Children's clubs
367.9(4-9)	HS2721-3200	Clubs, By place
367.9(4-9)	HS2731-3200	Other countries
367.973	HS2721-2725	United States
368	HG8011-9999	Insurance
368.(09-8)	HG9970	Auto insurance
368.(1-8)	HG9969.5-9999	Other insurance
368.0065	HG8075-8107	Insurance business
368.01	HG8779-8793	Actuarial science
368.093	HG9972	Aviation insurance
368.11	HG9651-9899	Fire insurance
368.1100(5/6)	HG9651-9655	Serials/Societies
368.110021	HG9663	Statistics
368.1100212	HG9689	Tables
368.110025	HG9657	Directories
368.11003	HG9657.5	Encyclopedias/Dictionaries
368.110068	HG9671-9731	Business/Management
368.11009	HG9660	History
368.11009(4-9)	HG9751-9866	Fire insurance, By place
368.11009(4-9)	HG9781-9866	Other places
368.1100973	HG9751-9780	United States
368.11014	HG9711-9725	Inspectors/Claims
368.11019	HG9733-9735	State regulations
368.122	HG9979	Disaster insurance
368.2(2-3)	HE961-971	Marine insurance/Damage
368.32	HG8751-9271	Life insurance
368.32	HG9271	Child life insurance
368.32	HG8799-8830	By class insured/By risk
368.32009(4-9)	HG8941-9200.5	Life insurance, By place
368.32019	HG8901-8914	State supervision (Life ins.)
368.32065	HG8835-8899	Life insurance business
368.362	HG9251-9262	Industrial life insurance
368.363	HG9201-9245	Mutual life insurance
368.382	HG9371-9399	Health insurance
368.384	HG9301-9343	Accident insurance
368.4	HG8205-8220	Government insurance
368.42	HD7101-7104	Public health insurance
368.424	HG9291-9295	Maternity insurance
368.43	HD7105-7110	Old age pensions
368.43	HD7088-7250.7	Social security/Insurance
368.430(5/6)	HD7088-7090	Serials/Societies
368.4303	HD7090.5	Encyclopedias/Dictionaries
368.4309	HD7121-7250.7	Social security, By place
368.43094	HD7164-7211.83	Europe
368.430941	HD7165-7167.5	Great Britain
368.430943	HD7177-7180.5	Germany
368.430944	HD7173-7176	France
368.430945	HD7182-7185	Italy
368.430946	HD7205-7208	Spain
368.430947	HD7194-7197	European Russia
368.4309492	HD7185.5-7193.5	Low Countries
368.4309494	HD7210	Switzerland
368.4309495	HD7211.83	Greece
368.43095	HD7212.7-7233	Far East
368.430951	HD7230	China
368.430952	HD7227	Japan
368.430954	HD7217-7220	India
368.430955	HD7212.56	Iran

Dewey	LC	Descriptor
368.430956	HD7211.93-7212.53	Middle East
368.4309567	HD7212.55	Iraq
368.43095694	HD7212.2	Israel/Palestine
368.4309599	HD7225	Philippine Islands
368.43096	HD7237-7249.3	Africa
368.430971	HD7127-7130	Canada
368.430972	HD7131	Mexico
368.4309728	HD7133.5-7139	Central America
368.4309729	HD7140-7145.9	West Indies
368.430973	HD7123-7126	United States
368.43098	HD7147-7163	South America
368.43099(3-6)	HD7250-.68	Australia/New Zealand/ Oceania
368.44	HD7095-7096	Unemployment insurance
368.5	HG9990	Liability
368.564	HG8053.5-8054.4	Malpractice insurance
368.8	HG9956-9969	Casualty insurance
368.8(3-4)	HG9997	Fidelity/Surety insurance
368.81	HG8059	Business insurance
368.854	HG1662	Insurance of deposits
368.88	HG9999	Title insurance
368.9(4-9)	HG8550-8740.5	Other countries
368.9(4-9)	HG8501-8740.5	Insurance, By place
368.973	HG8501-8540	United States
369	HS1355-3369	Other societies
369	HS	Societies (Secret/ Benevolent)
369.1	HS2321-2330	United States
369.12	E186.3-.99	Patriotic societies
369.2	HS2301-2460.7	Political/Patriotic societies
369.2	U56-59	Clubs
369.2(3-9)	V66-69	Clubs, By place
369.3(03-9)	HS1601-2265	Race societies
369.4(3/6)	HS3265-3270	Scouts/Scouting (General)
369.4(3/6)09(4-9)	HS3270	Scouting, By place
369.4(6-7)	HS3341-3365	Girls' societies
369.403	HS3252	Dictionaries/ Encyclopedias
369.406	HS3250-.2	Congresses
369.409	HS3254	History
369.409(4-9)	HS3260	Children's clubs, By place
369.4092	HS3256-.2	Biography
369.42	HS3301-3325	Boys' societies
369.42	HV877-878	Boys (Clubs/Etc.)
369.43	HS3312-3315	Boy Scouts
369.46	HV879	Girls (Societies/Etc.)
370	L	Education (General)
370-379	LC	Education (Special aspects)
370-379.091724	LC2601-2611	In developing countries
370.1	LB51-885	Theories by Date or Person
370.1	LB	Education/Theory/Practice
370.1	LB5-45	General
370.109(23-31)	LB175-375	Renaissance/Humanists
370.1090(1-2)	LB125	Early Christian/Medieval
370.1093	LB51-95	Ancient
370.1093(1-2)	LB472-475	16th-17th centuries
370.10933	LB501-575	18th century
370.10934	LB621-695	19th century
370.1094	LB775-885	20th century
370.11	LC1035-.8	Basic education
370.112	LC1001-1021	Humanistic/Liberal education
370.113	LC1081-1085	Industrial education
370.113	LC1500-1506	Vocational education
370.113	LC1037-.8	Career education
370.114	LC251-318	Moral education
370.114	LC251-951	Moral/Religious education

Dewey	LC	Descriptor
370.11409(4-9)	LC311-318	Moral education, By place
370.115	LC1090-1091	Political education
370.15	LB1050.9-1091	Educational psychology
370.19	LC65-245	Social aspects
370.19	LC225-.5	School and home
370.1931	LC215-238.4	And the community
370.19312	LC230-235	Parent-teacher associations
370.1934	LC189-214.53	Educational sociology
370.1934(6-8)	LC68-70	Demographic aspects
370.19341	LC65-67.68	Economic aspects
370.19341	LC142-148.5	Attendance
370.19344	LC212-.863	Discrimination
370.19349	LC71-120.4	And the state
370.194	LC5161-5163	Fundamental education
370.196	LC1099	Intercultural education
370.5	L10-94	By language/Place
370.5	L101	Yearbooks
370.5	L7-97	Serials
370.6	L106-107	Congresses
370.71	LB1705-2286	Training of teachers
370.73	LB1805-2151	State teachers' colleges
370.7309174927	LB2129	Arab countries
370.73094	LB2059-2124	Europe
370.730941	LB2061-2068	Great Britain
370.73095	LB2125-2128	Asia
370.73096	LB2130-2133	Africa
370.730971	LB1991-1998	Canada
370.730972	LB2001-2003	Mexico
370.7309728	LB2005-2019	Central America
370.7309729	LB2020-2032	West Indies
370.730973	LB1805-1987	United States
370.73098	LB2035-2058	South America
370.73099(3-4)	LB2135-2149	Australia/New Zealand
370.73099(5-6)	LB2150-2151	Oceania
370.74	L797-899	Exhibitions/Museums
370.74	LC6691	Traveling exhibits
370.74(4-9)	L801-899	By place
370.744	L818-885	Europe
370.745	L887-889	Asia
370.746	L890-891	Africa
370.7471	L805-806	Canada
370.7472	L808-809	Mexico
370.74728	L811-812	Central America
370.74729	L814-815	West Indies
370.7473	L801-803	United States
370.748	L816-817	South America
370.749(3-6)	L893-898	Australia/New Zealand/ Oceania
370.9(4-9)	L111-791	By place
370.94	L341-551	Europe
370.941	L341-359	Great Britain
370.9415	L346-348	Ireland
370.943	L401-410	Germany
370.9436	L361-366	Austria
370.9437	L385-387	Czechoslovakia
370.9439	L381-383	Hungary
370.944	L391-396	France
370.945	L421-426	Italy
370.946	L511-516	Spain
370.9469	L521-526	Portugal
370.947	L451-466	European Russia
370.9481	L491-496	Norway
370.9485	L501-506	Sweden
370.9489	L471-476	Denmark
370.94912	L481	Iceland
370.9492	L441-446	Netherlands
370.9493	L431-436	Belgium

Dewey	LC	Descriptor	Dewey	LC	Descriptor
370.9494	L531-536	Switzerland	371-379.095491	LA1155-1159	Pakistan
370.9495	L411-416	Greece	371-379.095492	LA1165-1169	Bangladesh
370.9497	L549-550	Yugoslavia	371-379.095493	LA1145-1149	Sri Lanka
370.94977	L541-542	Bulgaria	371-379.0955	LA1350-1354	Iran
370.9498	L545-546	Romania	371-379.0956	LA1045	Near East
370.95	L561-642	Asia	371-379.095645	LA1480-1484	Cyprus
370.951	L571-573	China	371-379.09567	LA1465-1469	Iraq
370.9519	L613-614	Korea	371-379.095691	LA1455-1459	Syria
370.952	L611-612	Japan	371-379.095692	LA1460-1464	Lebanon
370.954	L577-578	India	371-379.095694	LA1440-1444	Israel/Palestine
370.95491	L578.5-.6	Pakistan	371-379.095695	LA1470-1474	Jordan
370.955	L615-616	Iran	371-379.0957	LA1370-1394	Asian Russia
370.9561	L539-540	Turkey	371-379.09593	LA1220-1224	Thailand
370.9567	L627-628	Iraq	371-379.09594	LA1205-1209	Laos
370.95694	L631-632	Israel/Palestine	371-379.09595	LA1235-1239	Malaysia
370.957	L617-620	Asian Russia	371-379.09596	LA1190-1194	Cambodia
370.959(4-7)	L585-586	Indochina	371-379.09597	LA1180-1189	Vietnam
370.9595	L583-584	Malay Peninsula	371-379.09598	LA1270-1274	Indonesia
370.9598	L597-598	Indonesia	371-379.09599	LA1290-1299	Philippines
370.9599	L601-602	Philippines	371-379.096	LA1500-2090	Africa
370.96	L651-742	Africa	371-379.09611	LA1815-1819	Tunisia
370.97(4-9)	L116-219	Local, By place	371-379.09612	LA2070-2074	Libya
370.971	L221-223	Canada	371-379.0962	LA1645-1649	Egypt
370.972	L227-229	Mexico	371-379.09624	LA1810-1814	Sudan
370.9728	L231-249	Central America	371-379.0964	LA1940-1944	Morocco
370.9729	L251-267	West Indies	371-379.0965	LA1670-1674	Algeria
370.973	L111-219	United States	371-379.09664	LA1640-1644	Sierra Leone
370.98	L291-335	South America	371-379.096651	LA1620-1624	Gambia
370.99(3-6)	L750-791	Australia/New Zealand/	371-379.096662	LA1920-1924	Liberia
		Oceania	371-379.096667	LA1625-1629	Ghana
371-379. + (09)	LA	History of education	371-379.09669	LA1630-1634	Nigeria
371-379.09	LA190-2284	By place	371-379.096711	LA1850-1854	Cameroon
371-379.090(23-24)	LA106-108	Renaissance	371-379.09672	LA1780-1784	French Equatorial Africa
371-379.09(3-4)	LA2100-2189	Australia/New Zealand	371-379.096751	LA1910-1914	Zaire
371-379.090(1-4)	LA31-133	By date	371-379.096761	LA1565-1569	Uganda
371-379.09174927	LA1490-1493	Arab countries	371-379.096762	LA1560-1564	Kenya
371-379.092	LA2301-2396	Biography	371-379.09678	LA1840-1844	Tanzania
371-379.093	LA31-81	Ancient	371-379.0968	LA2010-2014	South Africa
371-379.093(8/7)	LA71-81	Classic (Greek/Roman)	371-379.096883	LA1600-1604	Botswana
371-379.0934	LA34-66	Oriental	371-379.096885	LA1545-1549	Lesotho
371-379.094	LA620-1040	Europe	371-379.096894	LA1595-1599	Zambia
371-379.0941	LA630-669.5	Great Britain	371-379.096897	LA1550-1554	Malawi
371-379.0943	LA720-779	Germany	371-379.09691	LA1790-1794	Madagascar
371-379.09436	LA670-679	Austria	371-379.0971	LA410-419	Canada
371-379.09438	LA840-844	Poland	371-379.0972	LA420-430	Mexico
371-379.09439	LA680-687	Hungary	371-379.09728	LA435-474	Central America
371-379.0944	LA690-716	France	371-379.09729	LA475-505	West Indies
371-379.0945	LA790-799	Italy	371-379.0973	LA201-398	United States
371-379.0946	LA910-919	Spain	371-379.098	LA540-609	South America
371-379.09469	LA920-929	Portugal	371-379.0981	LA555-559	Brazil
371-379.0947	LA830-838	European Russia	371-379.0982	LA545-549	Argentina
371-379.09481	LA890-899	Norway	371-379.0983	LA560-564	Chile
371-379.09485	LA900-909	Sweden	371-379.0984	LA550-554	Bolivia
371-379.09489	LA870-879	Denmark	371-379.0985	LA595-599	Peru
371-379.094912	LA880-889	Iceland	371-379.09861	LA565-569	Colombia
371-379.09492	LA820-820	Netherlands	371-379.09866	LA570-574	Ecuador
371-379.09493	LA810-819	Belgium	371-379.0987	LA605-609	Venezuela
371-379.09494	LA930-939	Switzerland	371-379.09881	LA575-579	Guyana
371-379.09495	LA780-789	Greece	371-379.09882	LA580-584	French Guiana
371-379.09497	LA1000-1009	Yugoslavia	371-379.09883	LA585-589	Suriname
371-379.094977	LA950-959	Bulgaria	371-379.09892	LA590-594	Paraguay
371-379.09498	LA970-979	Romania	371-379.09895	LA600-604	Uruguay
371-379.095	LA1050-1484	Asia	371-379.099(5-6)	LA2200-2270	Oceania
371-379.0951	LA1130-1134	China	371-379.0998(1-8)	LA2277-2279	Polar regions
371-379.09519	LA1330-1339	Korea	371-379.09982	LA2280-2284	Greenland
371-379.0952	LA1310-1319	Japan	371.(102/3)	LB1025-1050.7	Teaching (Principles/
371-379.0954	LA1150-1154	India			Practice)

Dewey	LC	Descriptor	Dewey	LC	Descriptor
371.01	LC73-97	Popular education	373-378.439	LF1551-1697	Hungary
371.01	LC59	Public school education	373-378.44	LF1711-2397	France
371.02	LC47-58.7	Private school education	373-378.45	LF3251-3897	Italy
371.04	LC45-.8	Nonformal education	373-378.46	LF4610-4827	Spain
371.1	LB2832-2844.1	Teaching personnel	373-378.469	LF4831-4887	Portugal
371.10023	LB1775-1785	Teaching as a profession	373-378.47	LF4211-4437	European Russia
371.104	LC72-.4	Academic freedom	373-378.481	LF4493-4537	Norway
371.122	LB1705-2286	Training of teachers	373-378.485	LF4539-4607	Sweden
371.2	LB2801-3095	School administration	373-378.489	LF4451-4487	Denmark
371.201	LB2831.6-.99	Administrative personnel	373-378.4897	LF1705-1709	Finland
371.232	LC5701-5771	Vacation	373-378.4912	LF4489-4491	Iceland
371.24	LB3525-3575	Special days	373-378.492	LF4071-4197	Netherlands
371.27	LB3050-3060.87	Tests/Measurements	373-378.493	LF3911-4067	Belgium
371.3	LC1031-1034.5	Competency based education	373-378.4935	LF4069	Luxemburg
371.32	LB3045-3048	Textbooks	373-378.494	LF4901-5047	Switzerland
371.32	LT	Textbooks	373-378.495	LF3211-3247	Greece
371.335	LB1042.5-1044.8	Audio visual education	373-378.5	LG21-395	Asia
371.38	LC6681	Education and travel	373-378.51	LG51-53	China
371.3944	LC25-33	Self-education	373-378.51249	LG55-57	Taiwan
371.4	LB1027.5-.9	Guidance/Counseling	373-378.519	LG281-285	Korea
371.5	LB3011-3095	Management/Discipline	373-378.52	LG240-277	Japan
371.6	LB3201-3325	Architecture/Equipment	373-378.53	LG31	Arabia
371.7	LB3401-3495	School hygiene	373-378.54	LG60-170.2	India
371.8	LB3602-3640	School life	373-378.5491	LG60-170.2	Pakistan
371.897	LH	College/School publications	373-378.5492	LG60-170.2	Bangladesh
371.897	TR818	School photography	373-378.5493	LG60-170.2	Sri Lanka
371.9	LC3950-4803	Exceptional children	373-378.5496	LG60-170.2	Nepal
371.9	LC4704-4803	Learning disabilities	373-378.55	LG291	Iran
371.9(1-4)	LC4001-4803	Handicapped children	373-378.561	LG321	Asia Minor
371.91	LC4501-4543	Physically handicapped	373-378.567	LG338	Iraq
371.911	HV1618-1708	Education of the blind	373-378.5691	LG361	Syria
371.912	HV2417-2500	Education of the deaf	373-378.5692	LG351-357	Lebanon
371.92	LC4580-4700	Mentally handicapped	373-378.5694	LG341-345	Israel
371.94	LC4165-4184	Mentally ill	373-378.57	LG301-320	Asian Russia
371.95	LC3991-4000	Gifted children	373-378.581	LG21	Afghanistan
371.967	LC4051-4100	Socially handicapped	373-378.59(3-7)	LG171-172	Indochina
371.97	LC3701-3740	Immigrants/Minorities	373-378.591	LG60-170.2	Burma
371.9768	LC2667-2674	Latin Americans	373-378.595	LG173	Malaysia
371.976872	LC2680-2688	Mexican Americans	373-378.598	LG181-184	Indonesia
371.97687295	LC2690-2698	Puerto Ricans	373-378.599	LG200-227	Philippines
371.9791497	LC3503-3520	Gypsies	373-378.6	LG401-681	Africa
371.979455	LC3530-3540	Lapps	373-378.6(5/11)	LG521	Algeria/Tunisia
371.9795	LC3001-3501	Asians	373-378.612	LG681	Libya
371.9796	LC2701-2913	Blacks	373-378.62	LG511	Egypt
372	LB1555-1601	Elementary education	373-378.624	LG513-514	Sudan
372-378	LC1390	Education of boys	373-378.63	LG401	Ethiopia
372.216	LB1140-.5	Nursery schools	373-378.64	LG631	Morocco
372.218	LB1141-1499	Kindergarten	373-378.66	LG481-491	West Africa
372.241	LB1501-1547	Primary education	373-378.6623	LG561	Mali
372.4	LB1049.9-1050.7	Reading (General)	373-378.663	LG551	Senegal
372.52	NC610-635	In elementary schools	373-378.6662	LG621	Liberia
372.86	GV201-555	Physical education/Training	373-378.672(4)	LG531	French Equatorial Africa/Congo
373	LB1603-1695	Secondary education	373-378.6751	LG615	Zaire
373-378.(5-9)	LG	Institutions, By place	373-378.67571	LG545	Rwanda
373-378.(561/474)	LF5051-5477	Turkey/Baltic	373-378.6761	LG421-423	Uganda
373-378.(7-8)	LE	Institutions, the Americas	373-378.6762	LG418	Kenya
373-378.4	LF	Institutions, Europe	373-378.678	LG468	Tanzania
373-378.41	LF20-1257	Great Britain	373-378.68	LG405-411	South Africa
373-378.411	LF960-1137	Scotland	373-378.689(7)	LG441	Zimbabwe/Zambia/ Malawi
373-378.415	LF800-957	Ireland	373-378.6891	LG461	Zimbabwe
373-378.42	LF20-797	England	373-378.6894	LG469	Zambia
373-378.429	LF1140-1257	Wales	373-378.691	LG541	Madagascar
373-378.43	LF2402-3197	Germany	373-378.71	LE3-5	Canada
373-378.436	LF1311-1537	Austria	373-378.72	LE7-9	Mexico
373-378.437	LF1541-1549	Czechoslovakia	373-378.728	LE11-13	Central America
373-378.438	LF4203-4209	Poland			

Dewey	LC	Descriptor
373-378.729	LE15-17	West Indies
373-378.8	LE21-78	South America
373-378.81	LE31-33	Brazil
373-378.82	LE21-23	Argentina
373-378.83	LE36-38	Chile
373-378.84	LE27-29	Bolivia
373-378.85	LE66-68	Peru
373-378.861	LE41-43	Colombia
373-378.866	LE46-48	Ecuador
373-378.87	LE76-78	Venezuela
373-378.88	LE51-59	Guianas
373-378.892	LE61-63	Paraguay
373-378.895	LE71-73	Uruguay
373-378.9(5-6)	LG961	Pacific islands
373-378.93	LG741-745	New Zealand
373-378.94	LG715-720	Australia
373-378.953	LG185-187	Papua New Guinea (Territory)
373.025	L900-991	Directories
373.025(4-9)	L901-991	By place
373.025174927	L967	Arab countries
373.0254	L914.5-957	Europe
373.02541	L915-918	Great Britain
373.025415	L919-920	Ireland
373.02543	L929-930	Germany
373.025436	L921-922	Austria
373.02544	L927-928	France
373.02545	L935-936	Italy
373.02546	L949-950	Spain
373.025469	L951-952	Portugal
373.02547	L941-942	European Russia
373.025481	L945-946	Norway
373.025485	L947-948	Sweden
373.025489	L943-944	Denmark
373.025492	L939-940	Netherlands
373.025493	L937-938	Belgium
373.025494	L953-954	Switzerland
373.025495	L931-932	Greece
373.0255	L960-961	Asia
373.0256	L970-971	Africa
373.02571	L905-906	Canada
373.02572	L907-908	Mexico
373.025728	L909-910	Central America
373.025729	L911-912	West Indies
373.02573	L901-903	United States
373.0258	L913-914	South America
373.0259(5-6)	L991	Oceania
373.02593	L985-986	New Zealand
373.02594	L981-982	Australia
373.113	LC1041-1048	Vocational education (General)
373.222	LC58-.7	Preparatory schools
373.241	LC6501-6560.4	Lyceums/Lecture courses
373.246	TT161-169	Industrial arts training
373.97(4-9)	LD7501	Secondary schools
374	LC5201-6660.4	Education extension/Adult
374	LC1660-1666	Adult education
374.22	HV547	Self-help groups
374.22	LC6601-6660.4	Reading circles
374.26	LC6571-6581	Radio/Television courses
374.4	LC5900-6101	Correspondence schools
376	LC1401-2571	Education of women
376.0(5/6)	LC1401	Serials/Societies
376.06	LC1402	Congresses
376.65	LC1551-1651	Higher education
376.9(4-9)	LC1751-2571	By place
376.90(1-4)	LC1421-1486	By date

Dewey	LC	Descriptor
376.90(1-4)	LC1701-2571	History
377	LC321-951	Religion/Education
377	LC107-120.4	Secularization
378	LB2300-2430	Higher education
378.(4-9)	LD7020-7251	Women's colleges
378.0(4/5)	LB2326.4-2330	Institutions
378.0025	L900-991	Directories
378.0025(4-9)	L901-991	By place
378.0025174927	L967	Arab countries
378.00254	L914.5-957	Europe
378.002541	L915-918	Great Britain
378.0025415	L919-920	Ireland
378.002543	L929-930	Germany
378.0025436	L921-922	Austria
378.002544	L927-928	France
378.002545	L935-936	Italy
378.002546	L949-950	Spain
378.0025469	L951-952	Portugal
378.002547	L941-942	European Russia
378.0025481	L945-946	Norway
378.0025485	L947-948	Sweden
378.0025489	L943-944	Denmark
378.0025492	L939-940	Netherlands
378.0025493	L937-938	Belgium
378.0025494	L953-954	Switzerland
378.0025495	L931-932	Greece
378.00255	L960-961	Asia
378.00256	L970-971	Africa
378.002571	L905-906	Canada
378.002572	L907-908	Mexico
378.0025728	L909-910	Central America
378.0025729	L911-912	West Indies
378.002573	L901-903	United States
378.00258	L913-914	South America
378.00259(5-6)	L991	Oceania
378.002593	L985-986	New Zealand
378.002594	L981-982	Australia
378.009	LA173-186	Higher education
378.0090(1-4)	LA177-186	By date
378.013	LC1051-1072	Professional education
378.103	LC237-238.4	And colleges/Universities
378.105	LB2351-2359	Admission requirements
378.107	LB2341-.8	Supervision/Administration
378.12	LB2331.7-2335.7	Teaching personnel
378.1543097(4-9)	LD6501	Junior colleges
378.1544	LC5501-5560	Evening schools
378.1553	LB2371-2372	Academic degrees
378.1554	LC6201-6401	University extension
378.168	LB2366-2367.6	College examinations
378.197	LB3497-3499	Universities/ Colleges/ Hygiene
378.199	LB2361-2365	Curriculum
378.3	LB2337.3-2340.8	Student finance
378.7(4-9)	LD13-7251	Universities/Colleges
379.(2/3)	LC165-182	Higher education and state
379.157	LB1771-1773	Certification (Teachers)
379.23	LC129-139	Compulsory education
380.03	HF1001-1002	Dictionaries/ Encyclopedias
380.1	HF5410-5417.5	Marketing/Distribution
380.1	HF	Commerce
380.10(5/6)	HF1-53	Serials/Societies
380.1021	HF1016-1017	Statistics
380.1025	HF54	Directories
380.106	HF55	Associations/Congresses
380.107	HF1101-1186	Commercial education

Dewey	LC	Descriptor
380.1070(4-9)	HF1131-1186	Commercial education, By place
380.1070(5/6)	HF1101	Serials/Societies
380.1070(72-8)	HF1135	Spanish America
380.10704	HF1140-1165	Europe
380.10705	HF1171	Asia
380.10706	HF1176	Africa
380.10706	HF1102	Congresses
380.107073	HF1131-1134	United States
380.10709	HF1108	History
380.10709(3-4)	HF1181-1186	Australia/New Zealand
380.1074	HF61	Museums
380.109	HF351	History
380.109(4-9)	HF3000-4050	Commerce, By place
380.1090(3-4)	HF479-499	Modern
380.10901	HF357-389	Ancient
380.10902	HF391-475	Medieval
380.1094	HF3491-3750.5	Europe
380.10941	HF3501-3530.5	Great Britain
380.10943	HF3561-3570.5	Germany
380.10944	HF3551-3560	France
380.10945	HF3581-3590	Italy
380.10946	HF3681-3690	Spain
380.10947	HF3621-3630	European Russia
380.109492	HF3590-3620.5	Low Countries
380.109494	HF3701-3710	Switzerland
380.109495	HF3750.5	Greece
380.1095	HF3770.3-3855	Far East
380.10951	HF3831-3840	China
380.10952	HF3821-3830	Japan
380.10954	HF3781-3790	India
380.10955	HF3770.2	Iran
380.10956	HF3756-3769	Middle East
380.109567	HF3770	Iraq
380.1095694	HF3760	Israel/Palestine
380.109599	HF3811-3820	Philippine Islands
380.1096	HF3872-3937	Africa
380.10971	HF3221-3230	Canada
380.10972	HF3231-3240	Mexico
380.109728	HF3246-3310	Central America
380.109729	HF3311-3369	West Indies
380.10973	HF3021-3031	History
380.10973	HF3000-3163	United States
380.10973021	HF3001-3006	Statistics
380.10973025	HF3010-3012	Directories
380.1098	HF3371-3490	South America
380.1099(3-6)	HF3941-4039.5	Australia/New Zealand/ Oceania
380.14159	SB442.8-443.4	Marketing (Florists/Etc.)
380.144	HQ280-285	Traffic in women
380.144	HT975-999	Slave trade
380.1457	N8600-8675	Dealers/Etc.
381	HF1401-1647	Commercial policies
381.0973	HF3151-3163	Local commerce
381.1	HF5429.7-5430.6	Shopping centers
381.1	HF5428-5429.6	Retail trade
381.1(42)	HF5460-5469.5	Stores/Mail order
381.18	HF5469.7-5481	Markets/Fairs
381.19	HF5482-.3	Secondhand trade
381.2	HF5419-5422	Wholesale trade
381.45002	Z278-549	Bookselling/Publishing
382	HF1371-1379	International trade
382.0973	HF3041-3050	Foreign commerce
382.17	HF1014	Balance of trade
382.3	HF1401-1647	Commercial policies
382.309(4-9)	HF1451-1647	Commercial policies, By place

Dewey	LC	Descriptor
382.5	HF1419-1420	Imports
382.6	HF1414.5-1417	Exports/Controls/Etc.
382.7	HF1701-2701	Tariff policy
382.709(4-9)	HF1750-2580.7	Tariff policy, By place
382.709(4-9)	HF1761-2580.9	Other countries
382.70973	HF1750-1757	United States
383	HE6000-7496	Postal services/Stamps
383.0(5/6)	HE6000-6025	Serials/Societies
383.03	HE6031-6035	Encyclopedias/Dictionaries
383.07	HE6036	Education
383.23	HE6182-6228	Stamps/Postmarks
383.41	HE6246-6278	International
383.49	HE6041-6055	History
383.49(4-9)	HE6300-7496	Postal service, By place
383.49(4-9)	HE6651-7496	Other countries
383.492	HE6061	Biography
383.4973	HE6300-6500	United States
384	HE	Transportation/ Communications
384.(1-7)	HE7601-8700.9	Telecommunications
384.03	HE7621-7625	Encyclopedias/Dictionaries
384.05	HE7601	Serials
384.06	HE7603-7604	Societies/Congresses
384.068	HE7661	Administration
384.09(4-9)	HE7761-8630.7	Telecommunications, By place
384.091724	HE8635	Developing countries
384.094	HE8081-8340.5	Europe
384.0941	HE8091-8120.5	Great Britain
384.0943	HE8151-8160.5	Germany
384.0944	HE8141-8150	France
384.0945	HE8171-8180	Italy
384.0946	HE8271-8280	Spain
384.0947	HE8211-8220	European Russia
384.09492	HE8181-8210.5	Low Countries
384.09494	HE8291-8300	Switzerland
384.09495	HE8340.5	Greece
384.095	HE8360.7-8445	Far East
384.0951	HE8421-8430	China
384.0952	HE8411-8420	Japan
384.0954	HE8371-8380	India
384.0955	HE8360.2	Iran
384.0956	HE8346-8359	Middle East
384.09567	HE8360	Iraq
384.095694	HE8350	Israel/Palestine
384.09599	HE8401-8410	Philippine Islands
384.096	HE8461-8527	Africa
384.0971	HE7811-7820	Canada
384.0972	HE7821-7830	Mexico
384.09728	HE7831-7900	Central America
384.09729	HE7901-7959	West Indies
384.0973	HE7761-7798	United States
384.098	HE7961-8080	South America
384.099(3-6)	HE8531-8629.5	Australia/New Zealand/ Oceania
384.1	HE7709-7741	Ocean cables
384.1	HE9723-9737	Signaling
384.1	TK5601-5681	Submarine telegraph
384.13	HE7681-7695	Rates/Finances
384.14	HE7669-7679	Codes
384.15	TK5301-5385	Plants/Stations/The line
384.15	TK5451-5468	The line
384.15	TK5501-5585	Systems/Instruments
384.5	HE8660-8688	Wireless
384.51	HE9719-9721	Satellite telecommunications
384.53	HE9713-9715	Wireless telephone industry

Dewey	LC	Descriptor
384.54	HE8690-8699	Radio
384.55	HE8700-.9	Television
384.6	HE8701-9680.7	Telephone industry
384.609(4-9)	HE8801-9680.7	Telephone industry, By place
384.609(4-9)	HE8861-9680.7	Other countries
384.60973	HE8801-8846	United States
384.63	HE8777-8779	Rates
385	HE1001-5600	Railways
385.0(5/6)	HE1001-1007	Serials/Societies
385.0(5/6)	TF1-4	Serials/Societies
385.021	HE2271-2273	Statistics
385.025	TF12	Directories
385.03	HE1009	Encyclopedias/Dictionaries
385.03	TF9	Encyclopedias/Dictionaries
385.06	TF5	Congresses
385.065	TF510-512	Organization of staff/Etc.
385.068	HE1601-2591	Administration
385.068	TF501-504	Serials/Societies
385.068	TF960-970	Operation and management
385.068	TF515	Records/Etc.
385.068	TF501-668	Railroad management
385.07	TF171-183	Education
385.07	TF518	Education
385.074	TF6	Exhibitions/Museums
385.09	HE1021	History
385.09	TF15-20	History
385.09(4-9)	HE2701-3560	Railroads, By place
385.09(4-9)	TF21-126	By place
385.092	TF139-140	Biography
385.0941	HE3011-3020	Great Britain
385.0941	TF57-64.5	Great Britain
385.09411	TF61-62	Scotland
385.09416	HE3041-3050	Northern Ireland
385.09417	TF59-.3	Ireland
385.0943	HE3071-3080.5	Germany
385.0943	TF73-74.5	Germany
385.09436	HE3051-3059.2	Austria
385.09436	TF65-.2	Austria
385.09437	HE3059.3	Czechoslovakia
385.09437	TF65.3-.4	Czechoslovakia
385.09438	HE3060.5	Poland
385.09438	TF95.P7	Poland
385.09439	HE3059.5	Hungary
385.09439	TF65.5-66	Hungary
385.0944	HE3061-3070	France
385.0944	TF71-72.5	France
385.0945	HE3091-3100	Italy
385.0945	TF79-80	Italy
385.0946	HE3191-3200	Spain
385.0946	TF87-88	Spain
385.09469	HE3201-3210	Portugal
385.09469	TF83-84.5	Portugal
385.0947	HE3131-3140	European Russia
385.0947	TF85-86	European Russia
385.0948	TF88.5	Scandinavia
385.09481	HE3171-3180	Norway
385.09481	TF81-82	Norway
385.09485	HE3181-3190	Sweden
385.09485	TF89-90	Sweden
385.09489	HE3151-3160	Denmark
385.09489	TF69-70	Denmark
385.094897	TF95.F5	Finland
385.094912	HE3161-3170	Iceland
385.09492	HE3121-3130	Netherlands
385.09492	TF77-78	Netherlands
385.09493	HE3111-3120	Belgium
385.09493	TF67-68	Belgium
385.09494	HE3211-3220	Switzerland
385.09494	TF91-92	Switzerland
385.09495	TF75-76	Greece
385.09496	TF95.A2	Balkans
385.09497	HE3241-3245	Yugoslavia
385.09497	TF95.Y8	Yugoslavia
385.094977	HE3231-3240	Bulgaria
385.09498	HE3251-3260	Romania
385.0951	HE3281-3290	China
385.0951	TF101-102	China
385.09519	HE3360.5	Korea/North Korea
385.0952	HE3351-3360	Japan
385.0952	TF105-106	Japan
385.09538	HE3380.3	Saudi Arabia
385.0954	HE3291-3300	India
385.0954	TF103-104	India
385.095491	HE3300.5	Pakistan
385.095491	TF104.5-.6	Pakistan
385.095492	HE3300.6	Bangladesh
385.095493	HE3300.3	Sri Lanka
385.095493	TF104.7-.8	Sri Lanka
385.0955	TF107-108	Iran
385.09561	TF111-112	Turkey
385.09567	TF113.I7	Iraq
385.095694	TF113.I75	Israel/Palestine
385.0957	TF109-110	Asian Russia
385.09594	HE3320.4	Laos
385.09595	HE3321-3330	Malaysia
385.09597	HE3320.3	Vietnam
385.09598	HE3331-3340	Indonesia
385.09598	TF113.I55	Indonesia
385.09599	HE3341-3350	Philippine Islands
385.09599	TF133.P6	Philippines
385.096	TF115-119	Africa
385.096(1-9)	TF119	Africa, By country
385.09611	HE3413	Tunisia
385.09612	HE3414	Libya
385.0962	HE3401-3410	Egypt
385.0962	TF117-118	Egypt
385.09624	HE3415	Sudan
385.0963	HE3416	Ethiopia
385.0964	HE3411	Morocco
385.09648	HE3458.2	Spanish Sahara
385.0965	HE3412	Algeria
385.09661	HE3452	Mauritania
385.096623	HE3449	Mali
385.096625	HE3450	Burkina Faso
385.096626	HE3446	Niger
385.09663	HE3451	Senegal
385.09664	HE3455	Sierra Leone
385.096651	HE3456	Gambia
385.096652	HE3448	Guinea-Bissau
385.096657	HE3458	Guinea-Bissau
385.096662	HE3457	Liberia
385.096668	HE3447	Ivory Coast
385.09667	HE3454	Ghana
385.096681	HE3445	Togo
385.096683	HE3444	Benin (Dahomey)
385.09669	HE3453	Nigeria
385.096711	HE3442	Cameroon
385.096715	HE3436	Sao Tome/Principe
385.096718	HE3435	Equatorial Guinea
385.09672	HE3437	French Equatorial Africa
385.096721	HE3438	Gabon
385.096724	HE3439	Congo
385.09673	HE3433	Angola

Dewey	LC	Descriptor
385.096743	HE3441	Chad
385.096751	HE3434	Zaire
385.0967571	HE3421	Rwanda
385.0967572	HE3422	Burundi
385.096761	HE3420	Uganda
385.096762	HE3419	Kenya
385.096773	HE3417	Somalia
385.09678	HE3423	Tanzania
385.09679	HE3424	Mozambique
385.0968	HE3426	South Africa
385.096881	HE3432.3	Namibia
385.096883	HE3431	Botswana
385.096885	HE3429	Lesotho
385.096887	HE3430	Swaziland
385.096894	HE3428	Zambia
385.096897	HE3432	Malawi
385.09691	HE3425	Madagascar
385.0971	HE2801-2810	Canada
385.0971	TF26-27	Canada
385.0972	HE2811-2820	Mexico
385.0972	TF28-29	Mexico
385.09728	TF30-31	Central America
385.097281	HE2836-2840	Guatemala
385.097282	HE2825.5	Belize
385.097283	HE2841-2845	Honduras
385.097284	HE2851-2855	El Salvador
385.097285	HE2846-2850	Nicaragua
385.097286	HE2831-2835	Costa Rica
385.09729	TF32-33	West Indies
385.097296	HE2860-2865	Bahamas
385.0973	HE2704-2791	United States
385.0973	TF23-25	United States
385.098	HE2891-3000	South America
385.0981	HE2921-2930	Brazil
385.0981	TF41-42	Brazil
385.0982	HE2901-2910	Argentina
385.0982	TF36-37	Argentina
385.0983	HE2931-2940	Chile
385.0983	TF43-44	Chile
385.0984	HE2911-2920	Bolivia
385.0984	TF38-39	Bolivia
385.0985	HE2971-2980	Peru
385.0985	TF52	Peru
385.09861	HE2941-2950	Colombia
385.09861	TF45-46	Colombia
385.09866	HE2951-2960	Ecuador
385.09866	TF47	Ecuador
385.0987	HE2991-3000	Venezuela
385.0987	TF54	Venezuela
385.09881	HE2962	Guyana
385.09881	TF48	Guyana
385.09882	HE2964	French Guiana
385.09882	TF50	French Guiana
385.09883	HE2963	Suriname
385.09883	TF49	Suriname
385.09892	HE2966-2970	Paraguay
385.09892	TF51	Paraguay
385.09895	HE2981-2990	Uruguay
385.09895	TF53	Uruguay
385.099(5-6)	TF123-124	Oceania
385.0993	HE3550.5	New Zealand
385.0993	TF122.5-.6	New Zealand
385.0994	HE3461-3550	Australia
385.0994	TF121-122	Australia
385.0998	TF125-126	Polar areas
385.1	HE2231-2261	Finance
385.1	HE1831-2220	Rates

Dewey	LC	Descriptor
385.2	HE1821-2591	Traffic
385.22	HE2561-2591	Passengers
385.22	HE2556	Baggage
385.22	HE2330-2345	Car service/Delay transit
385.22	HE1951-2100	Passenger
385.22	TF668	Dining car service
385.2209(4-9)	HE2351-2547	Passengers, By place
385.24	HE2301-2547	Freight
385.31	TF240-268	Permanent way/ Roadway/Track
385.314	TF305-308	Yards and terminals
385.314	TF270-300	Structures and buildings
385.314	TF315	Docks
385.363	TF975	Electric locomotives
385.5	HE3601-4043	Light rails
385.5	TF701-851	Municipal railways
385.5	TF670-851	Local and light railways
385.5(2-4)	TF677-851	By type
385.50(5/6)	HE3601	Serials/Societies
385.509(4-9)	HE3651-4043	Light rails, By place
386	HE380.8-971	Water transportation
386.(3-5)	HE380.8-560	Waterways
386.0(5/6)	HE380.8	Serials/Societies
386.09(4-9)	HE392.8-520.9	By place
386.09(4-9)	HE403.5-520.9	Other countries
386.0971	HE397-400	Canada
386.0972	HE401	Mexico
386.0973	HE392.8-398	United States
386.2	HE565	Tests of vessels
386.2234	TF320	Ferries
386.42	HE528-545	Interoceanic canals
386.42	TC773-788	Isthmain canal projects
386.43	TC791	Suez Canal
386.44	TC774-781	Panama Canal
386.6	HE5751-5870	Ferries
386.8	HE550-560	Ports
387	HE380.8-971	Water transportation
387.1	VK321-369.8	Harbors/Ports
387.15	VK369-.8	Marinas/Etc.
387.16	HE951-953	Port guides/Charges
387.5	HE730-943	Merchant Marine
387.5	VK	Merchant Marine/ Navigation
387.5	VK20	20th century
387.5	HE561-971	Shipping/Merchant Marine
387.5	HE737-738	Manuals
387.5(06)	HE562	Congresses
387.50(5/6)	HE561	Serials/Societies
387.50(5/6)	HE730-736	Serials/Societies
387.50(5/6)	VK1-4	Serials/Societies
387.5023	VK160	As a profession
387.503	HE567-568	Encyclopedias/Dictionaries
387.506	HE564	Associations of owners
387.506	VK5	Congresses
387.507	HE570	Education
387.507	VK401-537	Education/Training
387.509	VK15-124	Merchant Marine history
387.509(4-9)	VK21-124	Merchant Marine, By place
387.509(4-9)	HE745-943	Merchant Marine, By place
387.509(4-9)	HE769-937	Other countries
387.5090(23-4)	VK18-20	Modern
387.50901	VK16	Ancient
387.50902	VK17	Medieval
387.5091724	HE943	Developing countries
387.5092	HE568.9	Biography
387.5092	VK139-140	Biography
387.5094	VK55-96	Europe

261

Dewey	LC	Descriptor
387.50941	VK57-64	Great Britain
387.50943	VK73-74	Germany
387.50944	VK71-72	France
387.50945	VK79-80	Italy
387.50946	VK87-88	Spain
387.509469	VK83-84	Portugal
387.50947	VK85-86	European Russia
387.50948	VK86.5	Scandinavia
387.509492	VK77-78	Netherlands
387.509495	VK75-76	Greece
387.5095	VK99-113	Asia
387.50952	VK105-106	Japan
387.5096	VK115-119	Africa
387.50971	VK26-27	Canada
387.50972	VK28-29	Mexico
387.509728	VK30-31	Central America
387.509729	VK32-33	West Indies
387.50973	VK23-25	United States
387.50973	HE745-767	United States
387.5098	VK34-54	South America
387.50982	VK36-37	Argentina
387.50983	VK43-44	Chile
387.50987	VK54	Venezuela
387.5099(3-4)	VK121-122.5	Australia/New Zealand
387.5099(5-6)	VK123-124	Oceania
387.51	HE740-743	Subsidies
387.52	HE323-328	Ocean/Trade routes
387.52	VK570-571	Routes
387.544	HE593-601	Traffic/Freight
387.55	VK1491	Salvage
387.7	HE9761-9900	Air transportation
387.70(5/6)	HE9761-9765	Serials/Societies
387.703	HE9768-9769	Encyclopedias/Dictionaries
387.7068	HE9780-9789	Administration
387.709	HE9774-9775	History
387.709(4-9)	HE9801-9900	Air transportation, By place
387.7094	HE9842-9867.5	Europe
387.70941	HE9843-9845.5	Great Britain
387.70943	HE9849-.5	Germany
387.70944	HE9848	France
387.70945	HE9851	Italy
387.70946	HE9861	Spain
387.70947	HE9855	European Russia
387.709492	HE9852-9854.5	Low Countries
387.709494	HE9863	Switzerland
387.709495	HE9867.5	Greece
387.7095	HE9869.7-9881	Far East
387.70951	HE9878	China
387.70952	HE9877	Japan
387.70954	HE9871	India
387.70955	HE9869.2	Iran
387.70956	HE9868.2-.95	Middle East
387.709567	HE9869	Iraq
387.7095694	HE9868.45	Israel/Palestine
387.709599	HE9876	Philippine Islands
387.7096	HE9882.3-9888.4	Africa
387.70971	HE9815	Canada
387.70972	HE9816	Mexico
387.709728	HE9817.5-9823	Central America
387.709729	HE9824.5-9829.9	West Indies
387.70973	HE9803-9814	United States
387.7098	HE9830-9841	South America
387.7099(3-6)	HE9889-9898.9	Australia/New Zealand/ Oceania
388	HE	Transportation/ Communications
388.0(5/6)	HE1-8	Serials/Societies

Dewey	LC	Descriptor
388.01	HE147.5-149	Theory/Method
388.021	HE191.4-.5	Statistics
388.03	HE141	Encyclopedias/Dictionaries
388.042	HE199.9	Passenger traffic
388.044	HE5880-5990	Express service
388.044	HE199-.5	Freight
388.044	HF5484-5495	Warehousing/Storage
388.0440(5/6)	HE5880	Serials/Societies
388.04409(4-9)	HE5905-5990	Other countries
388.04409(4-9)	HE5893-5990	Express service, By place
388.0440973	HE5893-5904	United States
388.049	HE5889	Rates
388.06	HE11	Congresses
388.07	HE191.9-192	Education
388.074	HE13-.2	Museums/Exhibitions
388.09	HE159-181	History
388.092	HE151.4-.5	Biography
388.1	HE331-380	Roads/Highways/Traffic
388.13	HE379-380	Vehicular tunnels
388.132	HE374-377	Bridges
388.3	HE5601-5720	Automotive transportation
388.309(4-9)	HE5623-5720	Auto transportation, By place
388.314	HE369-373	Traffic surveys
388.3228	HE5746-5749	Stage lines
388.4	HE305-311	Urban transportation
388.4	HE4201-5600	Rapid transit
388.4	TA1205	Urban transportation systems
388.4	HE3601-4043	Light rails
388.40(5/6)	HE3601	Serials/Societies
388.40(5/6)	HE4201-4202	Serials/Societies
388.4068	HE4301-4391	Administration
388.409(4-9)	HE4401-5600	Rapid transit, By place
388.409(4-9)	HE3651-4043	Light rails, By place
388.409(4-9)	HE4501-5600	Other countries
388.40973	HE4401-4491	United States
388.41312	TA1245-1250	Signaling/Equipment
388.47	TA1225	Terminals
390-395	GT	Manners and customs
390.(1-4)	GT5320-6720	Customs of special classes
390.00(5/6)	GT1	Serials/Societies
390.001	GT61	Philosophy
390.003	GT31	Dictionaries/ Encyclopedias
390.006	GT3	Congresses
390.009	GT41	History of manners and customs
390.0092	GT51-53	Biography
390.2	GT5320-5680	By birth/Rank/Etc.
390.22	GT5010-5090	Royalty/Nobility
390.4	GT5750-6390	By occupation
391	GT500-2370	Dress/Fashion
391.0(1-4)	GT1710-1950	By class
391.009(3-9)	GT601-1605	By place
391.009(72-8)	GT623-716	Latin America
391.0090(1-4)	GT530-596	By date
391.0090(3-4)	GT580-596	Modern
391.00901	GT530-560	Ancient
391.00902	GT575	Medieval
391.0094	GT720-1330	Europe
391.0095	GT1370-1570	Asia
391.0096	GT1580-1589	Africa
391.0097	GT603-620	North America
391.0099(3-6)	GT1590-1599	Australia/New Zealand/ Oceania
391.4	GT2050-2370	Materials/Accessories

Dewey	LC	Descriptor
392	GT2400-3390	Customs of private life
392.(4-6)	GT2600-2810	Love/Sex/Marriage
392.13	HQ768-778.7	Child rearing
392.14	GT2450-2487	Children/Adolescence
392.36	GT170-474	Houses/Dwellings
392.36009(4-9)	GT201-384	Dwellings, By place
392.360090(1-4)	GT175-195	By date
392.360090(23-31)	GT185	Renaissance
392.360090(34-4)	GT195	1801-
392.3600901	GT175	Ancient
392.3600902	GT180	Medieval
392.3600903(1-3)	GT190	16th-18th centuries
392.3600941	GT285-294	Great Britain
392.3600941(6-7)	GT294.5-.6	Ireland
392.3600943	GT298.9-299	Germany
392.36009436	GT295-296	Austria
392.36009439	GT296.5-.6	Hungary
392.3600944	GT297-298	France
392.3600945	GT303-304	Italy
392.3600946	GT323-324	Spain
392.36009469	GT325-326	Portugal
392.3600947	GT311-312	Russia
392.36009481	GT319-320	Norway
392.36009485	GT321-322	Sweden
392.36009489	GT315-316	Denmark
392.360094912	GT317-318	Iceland
392.36009492	GT307-308	Netherlands
392.36009494	GT327-328	Switzerland
392.36009495	GT301-302	Greece
392.36009496	GT331-341	Balkan states
392.360095	GT343-372	Asia
392.3600951	GT365-366	China
392.36009519	GT369-370	Korea
392.3600952	GT367-368	Japan
392.3600954	GT351-352	India
392.360095493	GT352.5-.6	Sri Lanka
392.3600955	GT347-348	Iran
392.36009561	GT345-346	Turkey
392.36009567	GT346.5-.6	Iraq
392.360095691	GT344-.2	Syria
392.3600958	GT349-350	Central Asia
392.36009593	GT355-356	Thailand
392.36009595	GT357-358	Malaysia
392.36009598	GT359-360	Indonesia
392.36009599	GT361-362	Philippine Islands
392.360096	GT373-377	Africa
392.3600962	GT375-376	Egypt
392.3600971	GT228-229	Canada
392.3600972	GT231-232	Mexico
392.360097281	GT239-240	Guatemala
392.360097282	GT235-236	Belize
392.360097283	GT241-242	Honduras
392.360097284	GT246-.5	El Salvador
392.360097285	GT243-244	Nicaragua
392.360097286	GT237-238	Costa Rica
392.360097287	GT245-.5	Panama
392.360097291	GT251-252	Cuba
392.360097292	GT255-256	Jamaica
392.360097294	GT253-254	Haiti
392.360097295	GT257-.5	Puerto Rico
392.360097296	GT249-250	Bahamas
392.3600973	GT205-227	United States
392.3600981	GT265-266	Brazil
392.3600982	GT261-262	Argentina
392.3600983	GT267-268	Chile
392.3600984	GT263-264	Bolivia
392.3600985	GT277-278	Peru
392.36009861	GT269-270	Colombia
392.36009866	GT271-272	Ecuador
392.3600987	GT281-282	Venezuela
392.3600988	GT273-274	Guianas
392.36009892	GT275-276	Paraguay
392.36009895	GT279-280	Uruguay
392.360099(5-6)	GT383-384	Oceania
392.3600993	GT381-382	New Zealand
392.3600994	GT379-380	Australia
392.5	HQ745-746	Weddings
392.5	GT2660-2810	Marriage
392.509(3-9)	GT2701-2796	By place
393.1	GT3150-3390	Burial
394	GT3400-5090	Customs of public social life
394.(7-8)	UB880	Court of honor/Dueling
394.1	GT2805-2955	Eating/Drinking
394.26	GT3925-4995	Festivals/Holidays
394.4	JF289	Oath/Inauguration
395	BJ1801-2195	Etiquette
395.0(5/6)	BJ1801	Serials/Societies
395.0207	BJ1843	Satire/Etc.
395.03	BJ1815	Dictionaries/ Encyclopedias
395.09	BJ1821	History
395.22	HQ745-746	Weddings
395.3	BJ2021-2078	Entertaining/Hospitality
395.4	BJ2081-2100	Correspondence/Stationery
395.5	BJ2139-2156	Specific situations
395.53	GT485	Churches
395.53	BJ2018-2019.5	Church etiquette
395.59	BJ2195	Telephone etiquette
395.59	BJ2120-2128	Conversation etiquette
398	GR	Folklore
398.042	GR931-940	Signs and symbols
398.09(3-9)	GR100-390	By place
398.09(72/8)	GR114-133	Latin America
398.094	GR135-263	Europe
398.095	GR265-345	Asia
398.096	GR350-360	Africa
398.097	GR101-113	North America
398.099(3-6)	GR365-385	Australia/New Zealand/ Oceania
398.2	GR72-79	Folk literature (General)
398.2	PN1341-1347	Folk poetry
398.2	PN683-687	Legends
398.2042	PR951-981	Folk literature
398.20421	PS451-478	Folk literature
398.20431	PT881-951	Folk literature
398.2043109	PT883-890	History
398.2043931	PT5351-5395	Folk literature
398.2043936	PT6540-6545	Folk literature
398.204394	PT4829-4830	Folk literature
398.204395	PT7088-7089	Folk literature
398.2043961	PT7288	Novels/Fairy tales
398.20439691	PT7420-7438	Folk literature
398.20439691	PT7430-7438	Collections (Folk literature)
398.2043969109	PT7420-7426	History of folk literature
398.204397	PT9525-9542	Collections (Folk literature)
398.20439709	PT9509-9520	History
398.2043981	PT7900-7930	Folk literature
398.2043982	PT8600-8635	Folk literature
398.20441	PQ781-841	Folk literature
398.20451	PQ4186-4199	Folk literature
398.20461	PQ6155-6167	Folk literature
398.20469	PQ9121-9128	Folk literature
398.2049155	PK6426	Folk literature

Dewey	LC	Descriptor
398.204924	PJ5048	Folk literature
398.204927	PJ7680	Folk literature
398.204927	PJ7580	Folk literature
398.204951	PL2445-2446	Folk literature
398.204956	PL748-749	Folk literature
398.204957	PL968.2-.4	Folk literature
398.209	PN905-1008	Folk literature
398.2090(1-4)	PN953-963	By date
398.20938	PA3285	Folk literature
398.209485	PT9509-9542	Folk literature
398.209493	PT6200-6230	Folk literature
398.3	GR650-690	Geographical
398.35(3-4)	GR430-487	Relating to private life
398.353	GR880	Folk medicine
398.355	GR865-874	Transportation/Travel/ Commerce
398.355	GR890-910	Occupations
398.362	GR620-635	Cosmic phenomena
398.4	GR500-615	Supernatural beings/ Demonology
398.41	GR81	Folk beliefs/ Superstitions/ Etc.
398.46	GR700-860	Animals/Plants/Minerals
398.6	PN6366-6377	Riddles/Charades
398.9	PN6400-6525	Proverbs
398.9	PN6299-6308	Maxims
398.9	PN6269-6278	Aphorisms/Apothegms
400	P101-410	Language/Comparative philology
400	P	Philology/Linguistic
401	P101-106	Philosophy, By date
401	P33-41	Theory
403	P29	Encyclopedias/Dictionaries
405	P1-10	Serials
406	P11-23	Societies/Congresses
407	P51-59	Education
409	P61-81	History of philology
409.(4-9)	P81	By place
409.0(1-4)	P63-77	By date
410	P121-149	Science of language
410	P	Philology/Linguistic
410.1	P33-41	Theory
410.15	P583-610	Phonology
410.2	P721-725	Etymology
410.3	P29	Encyclopedias/Dictionaries
410.3028	P761-769	Lexicography
410.5	P575-769	Comparative grammar
410.5	P631-663	Parts of speech
410.5	P611-627	Morphology
410.5	P671	Syntax
410.5	P1-10	Serials
410.6	P11-23	Societies/Congresses
410.7	P51-59	Education
410.9	P61-81	History of philology
410.90(1-4)	P63-77	By date
411-499.1	CN900-1355	By place
411.7	CN120-740	Ancient
411.7	CN	Epigraphy/Inscriptions
411.7	CN120-760	By period
411.7	Z105.5-116	Paleography
411.70(5/6)	CN1	Serials/Societies
411.701	CN40-42	Philosophy/Theory
411.703	CN70	Dictionaries/ Encyclopedias
411.706	CN15	Congresses
411.707	CN50	Education
411.7074	CN25-30	Museums/Collections

Dewey	LC	Descriptor
411.709	CN55	History
412	P321	Etymology
413	P331-365.5	Comparative lexicography
413/423-490.3	AG1-90	Dictionaries
413/423-490.3	AG	Dictionaries
414	P215-240	Phonetics/Phonology
415	P151-152	Theory
415	P291-298	Syntax
415	P151-259	Grammar
415	P241-259	Morphology
415	P270-298	Parts of speech
415	P201-299	Comparative grammar
417	P901-1099	Extinct Asiatic/European
417.2	PM9001-9021	Secret languages (Slang/ Argot)
420	PE	English
420	PE1-71	Philology
420	PE1001-1400	Language
420	PE1001-1693	Modern
420	PE801-896	Early modern
420-480	P501-769	Indo-European philology
420-480. + (3)	P518	Encyclopedias/Dictionaries
420-480. + (9)	P541-551	History
420-480. + (5)	P501	Serials
420-480. + (6)	P503-505	Societies/Congresses
420-490.0803538	HQ461-470	Literature, By language
420.1	PE35-37	Philosophy/Theory
420.3	PE31	Encyclopedias
420.5	PE1-9	Serials
420.5	PE1001-1010	Serials
420.6	PE11-13	Societies/Congresses
420.6	PE1011	Societies
420.7	PE65-69	Education
420.7	PE1065-1069	Education
420.9	PE51-60	History
420.9	PE1075-1087	History
420.92	PE63-64	Biography
421-461.1	CN900-1130	Europe
421.1	CN960-997	Great Britain
421.1	CN1340-1355	Australia/New Zealand/ Oceania
421.1-499.11	CN805-865	By language
421.1-499.11	CN755-760	Medieval/modern inscriptions
421.5	PE1133-1168	Phonology
422	PE1571-1599	Etymology
423	PE1620-1693	Dictionaries
423.028	PE887-895	Lexicography
423.028	PE1601-1693	Lexicography
425	PE821-873	Grammar
425	PE1199-1359	Parts of speech
425	PE1171-1197	Morphology
425	PE1097-1105	Grammar
427	PE1700-3601	Geographic variation/ Dialects
427.02	PE524-531	Language
427.02	PE451-693	Middle English
427.02	PE501-523	Philology
427.022	PE561-569	Etymology
427.023	PE575-585	Dictionaries
427.023028	PE574-585	Lexicography
427.025	PE529-531	Grammar
427.027	PE688	Geographic variation/ Dialects
427.09	PE3701-3729	Slang
428.6	PE1117-1130	Readers
429	PE124-231	Language

Dewey	LC	Descriptor
429	PE101-123	Philology
429	PE101-408	Anglo-Saxon
429.2	PE261-269	Etymology
429.3	PE275-285	Dictionaries
429.3028	PE274-285	Lexicography
429.5	PE129-231	Grammar
429.7	PE287-299	Geographic variation/ Dialects
430	PF	Teutonic languages
430	PF3001-5999	German
430	PF4514-4595	Language
430	PF3073-3095	Language
430	PD73-361	Language
430	PF4501-4596	Early Modern German
430	PD	Germanic languages/ Literature
430.01	PD35	Philosophy/Theory
430.03	PD31	Encyclopedias
430.05	PD1-9	Serials
430.06	PD11-21	Societies/Congresses
430.07	PD65-69	Education
430.09	PD51-60	History
430.092	PD63-64	Biography
430.1	PF3035-3037	Philosophy/Theory
430.3	PF3031	Encyclopedias
430.5	PF3001-3009	Serials
430.6	PF3011-3019	Societies
430.6	PF3021	Congresses
430.7	PF3065-3069	Education
430.9	PF3051-3060	History
430.92	PF3063-3064	Biography
431.1	CN910-915	Austria
431.1	CN950-957	Germany
431.5	PF3131-3168	Phonology
432	PF3571-3599	Etymology
432	PD571-599	Etymology
433	PD625-660	Dictionaries
433	PF3620-3693	Dictionaries
433.028	PD601-660	Lexicography
433.028	PF3601-3693	Lexicography
435	PF3171-3197	Morphology
435	PD99-321	Grammar
435	PF3199-3335	Parts of speech
435	PF3097-3400	Grammar
437	PD700-777	Geographic variation/ Dialects
437.(1-6)	PF5000-5951	Dialects/Provincialisms
437.01	PF3801-3823	Philology
437.01	PF3824-3977	Language
437.01	PF3801-3991	Old High German
437.015	PF3831-3931	Grammar
437.02	PF4043-4350	Middle High German
437.02	PF4043-4111	Language
437.023	PF4333-4345	Dictionaries
437.023028	PF4327-4345	Lexicography
437.025	PF4061-4171	Grammar
437.09	PF5971-5999	Slang
437.947	PJ5111-5192	Yiddish
437.9473	PJ5117	Dictionaries
437.9475	PJ5115-5116.5	Grammar
439.(1-4)	PD1001-1350	Old Germanic
439.(5-6)	PD1543-1855	Language
439.(5-6)	PD1501-1541	Philology
439.(5-6)	PD1501-5929	North Germanic/ Scandinavian
439.(5-6)03	PD1519	Encyclopedias
439.(5-6)05	PD1501-1504	Serials
439.(5-6)06	PD1505-1507	Societies
439.(5-6)07	PD1535-1539	Education
439.(5-6)09	PD1525-1531	History
439.(5-6)092	PD1533-1534	Biography
439.(5-6)2	PD1801-1819	Etymology
439.(5-6)3028	PD1823	Lexicography
439.(5-6)5	PD1559-1701	Grammar
439.(5-6)7	PD1850-1893	Geographic variations/ Dialects
439.1	PF3992-3996	Language
439.1	PF3992-4000	Old Saxon
439.2	PF1401-1558	Frisian
439.2	PF1401-1411	Philology
439.2	PF1415-1497	Language
439.31	PF1001-1184	Flemish
439.31	PF1001-1023	Philology
439.31	PF1024-1125	Language
439.31	PF73-693	Language
439.31	PF1-979	Dutch
439.310(5/6)	PF1001-1003	Serials/Societies
439.3101	PF35-37	Philosophy/Theory
439.3103	PF31	Encyclopedias
439.3105	PF1-9	Serials
439.3106	PF11-19	Societies
439.3106	PF21	Congresses
439.3107	PF1019	Education
439.3107	PF65-69	Education
439.3109	PF51-60	History
439.3109	PF1015	History
439.31092	PF63-64	Biography
439.3115	PF131-168	Phonology
439.312	PF1161-1167	Etymology
439.312	PF571-599	Etymology
439.313	PF620-693	Dictionaries
439.313	PF1175-1184	Dictionaries
439.313028	PF601-693	Lexicography
439.315	PF1033-1125	Grammar
439.315	PF171-197	Morphology
439.315	PF199-335	Parts of speech
439.315	PF97	Grammar
439.317	PF700-979	Geographic variation/ Dialects
439.31709	PF951-979	Slang
439.6	PD2201-2392	Old Norse/Icelandic
439.6	PD2201-2223	Philology
439.6	PD2224-2392	Language
439.602	PD2361-2369	Etymology
439.603028	PD2376-2385	Lexicography
439.605	PD2229-2331	Grammar
439.607	PD2387-2392	Geographic variation/ Dialects
439.67	PD2483-2489	Old Norse dialects
439.69	PD2401-2447	Modern Icelandic
439.690(5/6)	PD2401	Serials/Societies
439.6907	PD2407	Education
439.6909	PD2409	History
439.692	PD2431	Etymology
439.693	PD2437	Dictionaries
439.695	PD2411-2423	Grammar
439.697	PD2447	Slang
439.7	PD5001-5071	Philology
439.7	PD5073-5400	Language
439.7	PD5001-5929	Swedish
439.701	PD5035	Philosophy/Theory
439.707	PD5065	Education
439.709	PD5051	History
439.709	PD5075	History

Dewey	LC	Descriptor
439.7092	PD5063-5064	Biography
439.72	PD5571-5599	Etymology
439.73	PD5625-5693	Dictionaries
439.73028	PD5611-5693	Lexicography
439.75	PD5101-5400	Grammar
439.77	PD5700-5929	Geographic variation/ Dialects
439.81	PD3073-3400	Language
439.81	PD3001-3929	Danish
439.81	PD3001-3071	Philology
439.810(5/6)	PD3001-3019	Serials/Societies
439.8101	PD3035	Philosophy/Theory
439.8107	PD3065	Education
439.8109	PD3075	History
439.8109	PD3051	History
439.81092	PD3063-3064	Biography
439.812	PD3571-3599	Etymology
439.813	PD3625-3693	Dictionaries
439.813028	PD3601-3693	Lexicography
439.815	PD3101-3400	Grammar
439.817	PD3901-3929	Slang
439.817	PD3700-3929	Geographic variation/ Dialects
439.82	PD2571-2578	Middle Norwegian
439.82	PD2501-2999	Norwegian
439.83	PD2601-2999	Modern
439.830(5/6)	PD2601	Serials/Societies
439.8307	PD2611-2612	Education
439.832	PD2683-2684	Etymology
439.833	PD2688-2695	Dictionaries
439.833028	PD2687-2695	Lexicography
439.835	PD2619-2673	Grammar
439.837	PD2696-2699	Geographic variation/ Dialects
439.837	PD2699	Slang
439.9	PD1115-1211	Gothic
439.909	PD1115	History
439.93	PD1193	Dictionaries
439.95	PD1119-1167	Grammar
440	PC2001-2071	Philology
440	PC	Romance languages
440	PC43-400	Languages
440	PC2001-3761	French
440	PC2073-2400	Language
440.01	PC21-23	Philosophy/Theory
440.03	PC19	Encyclopedias
440.05	PC1-5	Serials
440.06	PC6-11	Societies/Congresses
440.07	PC35-39	Education
440.1	PC2035	Philosophy/Theory
440.5	PC2001-2009	Serials
440.6	PC2011-2019	Societies
440.7	PC2065	Education
440.9	PC2051-2060	History
440.92	PC2063-2064	Biography
441.1	CN945-948	France
441.5	PC2131-2151	Phonology
442	PC301-319	Etymology
442	PC2571-2591	Etymology
443.(028)	PC2620-2693	Dictionaries/Lexicography
443.028	PC320-335	Lexicography
445	PC60-201	Grammar
445	PC2101-2400	Grammar
445	PC2171-2175	Morphology
445	PC2201-2321	Parts of speech
447	PC2700	Geographic variations
447	PC3721-3761	Slang

Dewey	LC	Descriptor
447-449	PC2700-3761	Dialects/Provincialisms/Etc.
447.00(5/6)	PC2701	Serials/Societies/Congresses
447.01	PC2801-2898	Old French
447.01	PC2813-2896	Language
447.012	PC2883-2886	Etymology
447.013028	PC2887-2895	Lexicography
447.015	PC2821-2873	Grammar
447.2	PC2761	Etymology
447.3028	PC2766	Lexicography
447.5	PC2721-2746	Grammar
447.9	PM7831-7875	Creole
448.6	PC2113-2117	Readers
449	PC3201-3366	Provencal (Old)
449	PC3371-3378	Language
449	PC3214-3273	Language
449	PC3201-3213	Philology
449	PC3371-3420	Neo-Provencal
449.0(5/6)	PC3201	Serials/Societies
449.09	PC3207	History
449.09	PC3215	History
449.092	PC3209	Biography
449.2	PC3283-3286	Etymology
449.3028	PC3287-3295	Lexicography
449.5	PC3219-3273	Grammar
449.7	PC3299	Slang
449.7	PC3296	Geographic variations
449.9	PC3801-3975	Catalan
449.9	PC3801-3813	Philology
449.9	PC3814-3873	Language
449.90(5/6)	PC3801	Serials/Societies
449.909	PC3815	History
449.909	PC3807	History
449.9092	PC3809	Biography
449.92	PC3883-3886	Etymology
449.93028	PC3887-3895	Lexicography
449.95	PC3819-3873	Grammar
450	PC1001-1977	Italian
450	PC1073-1693	Language
450	PC1001-1071	Philology
450.(5/6)	PC1001-1011	Serials/Societies
450.1	PC1035	Philosophy/Theory
450.7	PC1065	Education
450.9	PC1075	History
450.9	PC1051-1060	History
450.92	PC1063-1064	Biography
451.1	CN1010-1015	Italy
451.1	CN470-499	Ancient dialects of Italy
452	PC1571-1580	Etymology
453	PC1620-1645	Dictionaries
453.028	PC1620-1693	Lexicography
455	PC1099-1400	Grammar
457	PC1951-1977	Slang
457	PC1700-1977	Geographic variation/ Dialects
457.003	PC1704	Encyclopedias
457.009	PC1713-1718	History
459	PC601-623	Philology
459	PC601-872	Romanian
459	PC624-799	Language
459.0(5/6)	PC601-603	Serials/Societies
459.07	PC619	Education
459.09	PC625	History
459.09	PC615	History
459.2	PC761-767	Etymology
459.3028	PC775-784	Lexicography
459.5	PC631-725	Grammar
459.7	PC787-799	Geographic linguistics

Dewey	LC	Descriptor
459.7	PC799	Slang
459.9	PC901-949	Language
459.9	PC901-986	Romansh
459.90(5/6)	PC901	Serials/Societies
459.907	PC907	Education
459.909	PC905-906	History
459.9092	PC906	Biography
459.92	PC931	Etymology
459.93	PC937	Dictionaries
459.95	PC911-923	Grammar
459.97	PC949	Slang
459.97	PC941-949	Geographic variation/Dialects
460	PC4073-4693	Language
460	PC4001-4071	Philology
460	PC4001-4977	Spanish
460.1	PC4035	Philosophy/Theory
460.5	PC4001-4009	Serials
460.6	PC4011-4019	Societies
460.7	PC4065	Education
460.9	PC4051-4060	History
460.9	PC4075	History
460.92	PC4063-4064	Biography
461.1	CN1090-1095	Spain
461.107	PK11-13	Education
462	PC4571-4580	Etymology
463	PC4620-4645	Dictionaries
463.028	PC4620-4693	Lexicography
465	PC4099-4400	Grammar
467	PC4700-4941	Geographic variation/Dialects
467	PC4951-4977	Slang
469	PC5001-5041	Philology
469	PC5043-5231	Language
469	PC5001-5491	Portuguese
469.005	PC5001	Serials
469.006	PC5003	Societies
469.007	PC5035-5039	Education
469.009	PC5025-5034	History
469.2	PC5301-5315	Etymology
469.3	PC5325-5348	Dictionaries
469.3028	PC5320-5348	Lexicography
469.5	PC5061-5231	Grammar
469.7	PC5350-5498	Geographic variation/Dialects
469.709	PC5498	Slang
470	PA111-199	Greek/Latin languages
470	PA2001-2915	Latin philology/Language
470.143	PA195	Semantics
470.5	PA2001-2009	Serials
470.6	PA2011-2019	Societies
470.7	PA2061-2067	Education
470.76	PA119	Examination questions
470.9	PA2041-2055	History
470.9(4-9)	PA2055	History, By place
470.90(1-4)	PA2043-2052	By date
470.90(23-31)	PA2047	Renaissance
470.90(3-4)	PA2049-2052	Modern
470.903(2-3)	PA2051	17th-18th centuries
470.90(34-4)	PA2052	19th-20th centuries
470.902	PA2045	Medieval
471.1	CN340-740	Classical languages
471.1	CN510-740	Latin
471.1	CN530-730	By place
471.5	PA2111-2131	Phonology
471.5	PA121	Phonology
472	PA2341-2350	Etymology
472	PA191	Etymology
473	PA2361-2389	Dictionaries
473.028	PA2351-2359	Lexicography
475	PA2161-2281	Parts of speech
475	PA2133-2158	Morphology
475	PA2285-2297	Syntax
475	PA2071-2309	Grammar
475	PA111	Comparative grammar
475	PA141-155	Morphology
475	PA161	Syntax
477	PA2600-2748	Vulgar Latin
477	PA2391-2550	Ancient dialects of Italy
478	PA2901-2915	Modern Latin (1350-)
478	PA2311-2320	Style/Rhetoric
478	PA2801-2899	Medieval Latin
479	PA2420-2550	Italic dialects
480	PA	Classical (Greek/Latin)
480	PA67	20th century
480	PA1-895	Classical philology
480	PA227-379	Language
480	PA227-1179	Greek philology/Language
480	PA111-199	Greek/Latin languages
480.01	PA35-37	Philosophy/Theory
480.03	PA31	Encyclopedias/Dictionaries
480.05	PA1-9	Serials
480.06	PA11-23	Societies/Congresses
480.07	PA74-79	Education
480.09	PA51-72	History
480.09(4-9)	PA70	History, By place
480.090(1-4)	PA53-67	By date
480.090(23-31)	PA57	Renaissance
480.090(3-4)	PA59-67	Modern
480.0903(1-2)	PA61	16th-17th centuries
480.0903(2-3)	PA63	17th-18th centuries
480.0902	PA55	Medieval
480.09034	PA65	19th century
480.092	PA83-85	Biography
480.143	PA195	Semantics
480.7	PA231-241	Education
480.76	PA119	Examination questions
480.802	PA39-49	Criticism (Hermeneutics)
481	PA411-419	Prosody/Metrics
481.1	CN430	Cyprus
481.1	CN340-740	Classical languages
481.1	CN440-441	Egypt
481.1	CN410-415	Asia Minor
481.1	CN380-455	Classical Greek, By place
481.1	CN420	Crete
481.1	CN400	Asia
481.1	CN350-455	Classical Greek
481.5	PA265-281	Phonology
481.5	PA121	Phonology
482	PA191	Etymology
482	PA421-430	Etymology
483	PA441-459	Dictionaries
483.028	PA431-459	Lexicography
485	PA367-379	Syntax
485	PA303-361	Parts of speech
485	PA283-287	Morphology
485	PA251-379	Grammar
485	PA111	Comparative grammar
485	PA141-155	Morphology
485	PA161	Syntax
487	PA500-591	Dialects
487.3	PA1001-1179	Medieval/Modern Greek
487.30(7/9)	PA1041-1049	Education/History
487.303	PA1031	Encyclopedias/Dictionaries

Dewey	LC	Descriptor	Dewey	LC	Descriptor
487.305	PA1001-1009	Serials	491.35	PK1206-1215	Grammar
487.306	PA1011-1023	Societies/Congresses	491.37	PK1001-1095	Pali
487.315	PA1061-1071	Phonology	491.37	PK1001-1081	Philology
487.32	PA1111	Etymology	491.372	PK1083-1086	Etymology
487.33	PA1123-1145	Dictionaries	491.373	PK1089-1095	Dictionaries
487.35	PA1081-1089	Parts of speech	491.373028	PK1087-1093	Lexicography
487.35	PA1091-1097	Syntax	491.375	PK1017-1073	Grammar
487.35	PA1051-1099	Grammar	491.4	CN1170-1175	India
487.35	PA1076	Morphology	491.4	PK1501-2899	Modern Indo-Aryan
487.37	PA1151-1155	Dialects	491.4(1-9)	PK1550-2899	Dialects/Languages
487.38	PA1101-1105	Style/Rhetoric	491.41	PK2781-2790	Sindhi
487.4	CN350-455	Classical Greek	491.419	PK2261-2270	Lahnda
487.4	CN750-753	Early Christian inscriptions	491.42	PK2631-2659	Panjabi
487.4	PA600-695	Hellenistic Greek	491.43	PK1537	Dictionaries
487.4	PA700-895	Biblical Greek	491.43	PK1931-1970	Hindi language
487.4	PA700-791	Septuagint (Rabbinic Greek)	491.439	PK1971-1979	Urdu language
487.4	PA800-895	New Testament/Early Christian	491.44	PK1651-1730.46	Bengali
			491.45	PK1511-1523	Grammar
487.4	CN405	Near East	491.45	PK2561-2579.5	Oriya
487.43	PA881	Dictionaries	491.451	PL3851-4001	Assamese
487.45	PA813-857	Grammar	491.451	PK1550-1569	Assamese
488	PA401-407	Style/Rhetoric/Composition	491.454	PK1801-1831	Bihari
489.3	PA1001-1179	Medieval/Modern Greek	491.46	PK2351-2418	Marathi
489.30(7/9)	PA1041-1049	Education/History	491.47	PK1841-1859	Gujarati
489.303	PA1031	Encyclopedias/Dictionaries	491.479	PK2701-2709	Rajasthani
489.305	PA1001-1009	Serials	491.4797	PK2461-2479	Marawari
489.306	PA1011-1023	Societies/Congresses	491.48	PK2801-2891	Sinhalese
489.311	CN1000-1005	Greece	491.49	PK2591-2610	Pahari
489.315	PA1061-1071	Phonology	491.499	PK7070	Khowar
489.32	PA1111	Etymology	491.499	PK7050-7065	Kafir group
489.33	PA1123-1145	Dictionaries	491.499	PK7040-7045	Kohistani
489.35	PA1051-1099	Grammar	491.499	PK7021-7037	Kashmiri
489.35	PA1091-1097	Syntax	491.499	PK7001-7075	Dardic (Pisacha)
489.35	PA1076	Morphology	491.5	PK6001-6091	Philology
489.35	PA1081-1089	Parts of speech	491.5	PJ6201-6209	Persian
489.37	PA1151-1155	Dialects	491.5	PK6001-6996	Iranian philology/Literature
489.38	PA1101-1105	Style/Rhetoric	491.51	PK6121-6129	Old Persian
490	PJ	Oriental philology/Literature	491.52	PK6101-6118	Avestan
			491.53	PK6135-6199.5	Middle Iranian (Pahlavi)
491.(2-4)	PK101-185	Indo-Aryan languages	491.53	PJ6209	Dictionaries
491.(7-9)	PG	Slavic/Balto-Slavic/ Albanian	491.55	PK6201-6399	Language
			491.55	PK6201-6599	New Persian
491.(85-89)	PG7900-7925	Minor Slavic dialects	491.593	PK6701-6820	Afghan
491.1	PK1471-1490	Middle Indo-Aryan	491.6	PB1001-1013	Philology
491.1	PK1-14	Philology	491.6	PB2001-3029	Brittanic
491.1	PK15-79	Languages	491.6	PB1950	Pict (Pre-Celtic)
491.1	PK	Indo-Iranian languages	491.6	PB	Celtic languages
491.1(3/03)	PK14	Dictionaries/ Encyclopedias	491.6	PB3001-3029	Gaulish
			491.6	PB1014-1095	Celtic language
491.10(5/6)	PK1	Serials/Societies	491.6(2/3)	PB1101-1113	Philology
491.13	PK75-77	Dictionaries	491.6(2/3)	PB1101-1195	Gaelic
491.15	PK21-41	Grammar	491.6(2-3)	PB1114-1195	Gaelic language
491.2	PK207-379	Vedic	491.6(2-3)0(5/6)	PB1101	Serials/Societies
491.2	PK223-379	Language	491.6(2-3)01	PB1105	Philosophy
491.2	PK423-976	Language	491.6(2-3)07	PB1111	Education
491.2	PK401-420	Philology	491.6(2-3)09	PB1115	History
491.2	PK401-976	Sanskrit	491.6(2-3)09	PB1107	History
491.22	PK901-919	Etymology	491.6(2-3)092	PB1109	Biography
491.22	PK361-369	Etymology	491.6(2-3)2	PB1183-1185	Etymology
491.23	PK925-969	Dictionaries	491.6(2-3)3028	PB1187-1189	Lexicography
491.23	PK375-379	Dictionaries	491.6(2-3)5	PB1119-1171	Grammar
491.23028	PK920-969	Lexicography	491.60(5/6)	PB1001	Serials/Societies
491.25	PK231-313	Grammar	491.601	PB1005	Philosophy
491.25	PK501-811	Grammar	491.603	PB328	Dictionaries
491.3	PK1201-1409	Prakrit languages	491.605	PB1-5	Serials
491.33	PK1223-1225	Dictionaries	491.606	PB6-11	Societies/Congresses
			491.607	PB1011	Education

Dewey	LC	Descriptor
491.609	PB1007	History
491.609	PB1015	History
491.609	PB67.9	History/Criticism
491.6092	PB1009	Biography
491.62	PB1201-1213	Philology
491.62	PB1214-1299	Language
491.62	PB1201-1449	Irish
491.62	PB1083-1085	Etymology
491.620(5/6)	PB1201	Serials/Societies
491.6201	PB1205	Philosophy
491.6207	PB1211	Education
491.6209	PB1215	History
491.6209	PB1207	History
491.622	PB1283-1284	Etymology
491.623028	PB1287-1295	Lexicography
491.625	PB1221-1273	Grammar
491.627	PB1299	Slang
491.63	PB1501-1599	Language
491.63	PB1501-1709	Scottish Gaelic
491.63	PB1514-1599	Language
491.63	PB1501-1213	Philology
491.630(5/6)	PB1501	Serials/Societies
491.6301	PB1505	Philosophy
491.63028	PB1087-1089	Lexicography
491.6307	PB1511	Education
491.6309	PB1507	History
491.6309	PB1515	History
491.632	PB1583-1584	Etymology
491.633028	PB1587-1595	Lexicography
491.635	PB1521-1573	Grammar
491.64	PB1801-1888	Manx
491.64	PB1801-1847	Language
491.640(5/6)	PB1801	Serials/Societies
491.6407	PB1807	Education
491.6409	PB1809	History
491.64092	PB1806	Biography
491.645	PB1811-1847	Grammar
491.65	PB1019-1071	Grammar
491.66	PB2114-2199	Language
491.66	PB2101-2113	Philology
491.66	PB2101-2499	Welsh/Cymric
491.660(5/6)	PB2101	Serials/Societies
491.6601	PB2105	Philosophy
491.6607	PB2111	Education
491.6609	PB2115	History
491.6609	PB2107	History
491.66092	PB2109	Biography
491.662	PB2183-2184	Etymology
491.663028	PB2187-2195	Lexicography
491.665	PB2121-2173	Grammar
491.67	PB2501-2549	Language
491.67	PB2501-2621	Cornish
491.670(5/6)	PB2501	Serials/Societies
491.6707	PB2507	Education
491.6709	PB2509	History
491.67092	PB2506	Biography
491.675	PB2511-2547	Grammar
491.68	PB2801-2849	Language
491.68	PB2801-2931	Breton
491.680(5/6)	PB2001	Serials/Societies
491.680(5/6)	PB2801	Serials/Societies
491.6807	PB2005	Education
491.6807	PB2807	Education
491.6809	PB2007	History
491.6809	PB2809	History
491.68092	PB2806	Biography
491.682	PB2021	Etymology
491.683028	PB2023	Lexicography
491.685	PB2811-2847	Grammar
491.685	PB2009-2015	Grammar
491.7	PG2073-2850	Language
491.7	PG2001-2072	Philology
491.7	PG2001-3698	Russian
491.701	PG2035-2037	Philosophy/Theory
491.7011	CN1060-1065	European Russia
491.703	PG2031	Encyclopedias
491.705	PG2001-2009	Serials
491.706	PG2011-2019	Societies
491.706	PG2021	Congresses
491.707	PG2065-2069	Education
491.7092	PG2063-2064	Biography
491.715	PG2131-2161	Phonology
491.72	PG2571-2591	Etymology
491.73	PG2625-2693	Dictionaries
491.73028	PG2601-2693	Lexicography
491.75	PG2199-2321	Parts of speech
491.75	PG2171-2197	Morphology
491.75	PG2097-2127	Grammar
491.77	PG2700-2850	Geographic variation/Dialects
491.7709	PG2850	Slang
491.79	PG3801-3813	Philology
491.79	PG3801-3998	Ukranian
491.79	PG3814-3899	Language
491.793	PG3888-3894.5	Dictionaries
491.793028	PG3887-3894.5	Lexicography
491.795	PG3819-3881	Grammar
491.8	PG8001-9198	Balto-Slavic languages
491.8	PG1-7948	Slavic
491.8	PG1-41	Philology
491.8	PG43-400	Language
491.80(5/6)	PG1-11	Serials/Societies
491.801	PG21-23	Philosophy/Theory
491.807	PG35-39	Education
491.809	PG25-31	History
491.8092	PG33-34	Biography
491.81	PG801-823	Philology
491.81	PG824-993	Language
491.81	PG801-1158	Bulgarian
491.813	PG975-984	Dictionaries
491.815	PG831-925	Grammar
491.81701	PG601-698	Language
491.81701	PG601-789	Church Slavic
491.817015	PG661-698	Grammar
491.82	PG1224-1399	Language
491.82	PG1201-1223	Philology
491.82	PG301-319	Etymology
491.82	PG1201-1798	Serbo-Croatian
491.823(028)	PG1374-1384	Dictionaries/Lexicography
491.825	PG1229-1313	Grammar
491.827	PG1399	Slang
491.83	PG19	Encyclopedias
491.83	PG331-335	Dictionaries
491.83028	PG320-335	Lexicography
491.84	PG1801-1813	Philology
491.84	PG1801-1998	Slovenian
491.84	PG1814-1899	Language
491.843	PG1888-1894.5	Dictionaries
491.843028	PG1887-1894.5	Lexicography
491.845	PG1819-1881	Grammar
491.85	PG6001-7498	Polish
491.85	PG6001-6790	Philology/Language
491.85	PG59-97	Grammar
491.853028	PG6625-6638	Lexicography

Dewey	LC	Descriptor
491.857	PG6700-6790	Geographic variation/ Dialects
491.86	PG4004-4771	Language
491.86	PG4001-4599	Bohemian (Czech)
491.863	PG4625-4693	Dictionaries
491.863028	PG4601-4693	Lexicography
491.867	PG4700-4771	Geographic variation/ Dialects
491.87	PG5201-5598	Slovak
491.87	PG5201-5223	Philology
491.87	PG5224-5293	Language
491.87	PG350-400	Geographic variation/ Dialects
491.8709	PG400	Slang
491.873	PG5375-5384	Dictionaries
491.875	PG5231-5325	Grammar
491.88	PG5631-5659	Language
491.88	PG5631-5698	Sorbish/Wendish
491.91	PG8201-8208	Old Prussian
491.913	PG8206	Dictionaries
491.92	PG8501-8693	Philology/Language
491.92	PG8501-8798	Lithuanian
491.93	PG8801-9198	Lettish
491.93	PG8801-8993	Philology/Language
491.991	PG9501-9513	Philology
491.991	PG9501-9678	Albanian
491.991	PG9514-9599	Language
491.992	PK8001-8835	Armenian
491.992	PK8001-8499	Language
492	PJ4101-4197	West/North Semitic languages
492	PJ3001-3097	Semitic philology
492	PJ701-761	Languages
492	PJ701-908	Mohammedan
492-493	PJ1-187	Languages
492-493.(01)	PJ37	Philosophy/Theory
492-493.(02)	PJ183	Etymology
492-493.(03/3)	PJ31	Encyclopedias/Dictionaries
492-493.(05)	PJ1-10	Serials
492-493.(06)	PJ20-21	Congresses
492-493.(07)	PJ65-69	Education
492-493.(09)	PJ51-60	History
492-493.(092)	PJ63-64	Biography
492-493.(3028)	PJ187	Lexicography
492-493.(5)	PJ120-171	Grammar
492.0(5/6)	PJ3001-.5	Serials/Societies/Congresses
492.01	PJ3005	Philosophy/Theory
492.03	PJ3004	Dictionaries/ Encyclopedias
492.07	PJ3011-3013	Education
492.1	PJ3101-4083	East Semitic languages
492.1	PJ3101-3953	Assyriology
492.1	PJ3231-3595	Language
492.10(5/6)	PJ3101-3121	Serials/Societies
492.11	PJ3081-3095	Texts/Inscriptions
492.111	PJ3701-3941	Texts/Inscriptions
492.111	PJ3191-3225	Cuneiform writing
492.12	PJ3450-3471	Etymology
492.13	PJ3523-3547	Dictionaries
492.13028	PJ3511-3547	Lexicography
492.15	PJ3231-3311	Grammar
492.17	PJ3550-3595	Linguistic geography/ Dialects
492.2	PJ3065	Etymology
492.2	PJ5201-5329	Aramaic
492.211	PJ5208-5209	Texts/Inscriptions
492.29	PJ5211-5219	Biblical (Chaldaic)
492.29	PJ4860	Samaritan
492.29	PJ5271-5279	Samaritan
492.29	PJ5211-5289	West Aramaic
492.3	PJ5414-5493	Language
492.3	PJ3071-3075	Lexicography
492.3	PJ5401-5909	Syriac
492.3	PJ5401-5411	Philology
492.3	PJ5301-5329	East Aramaic
492.32	PJ5483	Etymology
492.33	PJ5490-5493	Dictionaries
492.35	PJ5419-5471	Grammar
492.37	PJ5701-5709	East Syriac (Nestorian)
492.37	PJ5801-5809	Neo-Syriac
492.37	PJ5711-5719	West Syriac (Jacobite)
492.4	PJ4543-4937	Language
492.4	PJ4501-4541	Philology
492.4	PJ4501-5192	Hebrew
492.401	PJ4521	Philosophy/Theory
492.403	PJ4519	Encyclopedias
492.405	PJ4501-4504	Serials
492.406	PJ4505-4509	Societies/Congresses
492.409	PJ4525-4531	History
492.411	CN745	Early Jewish inscriptions
492.411	PJ5034.4-.9	Inscriptions
492.411	CN1193-1194	Israel
492.415	PJ4576-4583	Phonology/Phonetics
492.42	PJ4801-4819	Etymology
492.43	PJ4825-4847	Dictionaries
492.43028	PJ4820-4847	Lexicography
492.45	PJ4601-4677	Morphology
492.45	PJ4553-4731	Grammar
492.47	PJ4855-4937	Dialects/Provincialisms
492.47	PJ5061-5192	Mixed Jewish dialects
492.47	PJ4901-4937	Talmudic (Mishnaic) Hebrew
492.472	PJ4931-4933	Etymology
492.473	PJ4935-4937	Dictionaries
492.473028	PJ4934-4937	Lexicography
492.475	PJ4911-4925	Grammar
492.5	PJ3021-3041	Grammar
492.5	PJ735-745	Grammar
492.6	PJ4150	Ugaritic
492.6	PJ4149	Moabite
492.6	PJ4171-4197	Phoenician-Punic
492.7	PJ6001-6071	Philology
492.7	PJ6701-6901	Modern Arabic dialects (North)
492.7	PJ6073-6697	Language
492.7	PJ6001-8517	Arabic
492.7	PJ6101-6199.5	Arabic
492.7(3/03)	PJ6031	Dictionaries/ Encyclopedias
492.70(5/6)	PJ6001-6021	Serials/Societies/Congresses
492.701	PJ6035	Philosophy/Theory
492.707	PJ6065-6069	Education
492.707	PJ6707	Education
492.711	PJ7593-7600	Inscriptions/Papyri
492.72	PJ6172-6199	Etymology
492.73	PJ6620-6680	Dictionaries
492.73	PJ6737	Dictionaries
492.73028	PJ6601-6680	Lexicography
492.75	PJ6101-6599	Grammar
492.77	PJ6810	Lebanon
492.77	PJ6751-6760	Spain
492.77	PJ6771-6799	Egypt
492.77	PJ6805-6808	Palestine
492.77	PJ6690-6695	Ancient Arabic

Dewey	LC	Descriptor
492.77	PJ6821-6830	Mesopotamia/Iraq
492.77	PJ6841-6880	Arabic peninsula
492.77	PJ6811-6820	Syria
492.773	PJ6795	Dictionaries
492.775	PJ6777-6785	Grammar
492.8	PJ8991-9293	Ethiopian languages
492.9	PJ5901-5909	South Semitic languages
492.9	PJ6950-7144	South Arabic
493	PJ701-908	Mohammedan
493	PJ701-761	Languages
493	PJ601-621	Christian Oriental
493.1	PJ1801-1921	Demotic literature
493.1	PJ1001-1989	Egyptology
493.1	PJ1111-1439	Language
493.1	PJ1091-1097	Hieroglyphic
493.101	PJ1035	Philosophy/Theory
493.103	PJ1031	Encyclopedias/Dictionaries
493.105	PJ1001-1009	Serials
493.106	PJ1011-1021	Societies/Congresses
493.109	PJ1051-1069	History
493.111	PJ1501-1571	Texts (Inscriptions/Papyri)
493.12	PJ1350-1371	Etymology
493.13	PJ1423-1439	Dictionaries
493.13028	PJ1401-1439	Lexicography
493.15	PJ1121-1201	Grammar
493.2	PJ2001-2199	Coptic
493.20(5/6)	PJ2001	Serials/Societies
493.207	PJ2019	Education
493.22	PJ2161	Etymology
493.23(028)	PJ2181	Dictionaries/Lexicography
493.25	PJ2029-2113	Grammar
493.3	PJ2369-2399	Berber languages
493.3	PJ2353-2367	Libyan languages
493.3	PJ2340-2399	Libyco/Berber languages
493.303	PJ2349	Dictionaries
493.32	PJ2347	Etymology
493.35	PJ2345	Grammar
493.5	PJ735-745	Grammar
493.5	PJ2401-2594	Cushitic languages
493.509	PJ2425-2594	By dialect
493.52	PJ2409	Etymology
493.53	PJ2413	Dictionaries
493.55	PJ2405	Grammar
494	PL1-481	Ulra-Altaic
494-499	PL	East Asian/African/ Oceanian
494.1	PL450-481	Tungus-Manchu
494.1	PL471-479	Manchu
494.2	PL400-431	Mongolian languages
494.2	PL401-409	Mongol language
494.3	PL63	Kipchak
494.3	PL65.B2	Balkar
494.3	PL61-65	Kipchak (Northwestern) group
494.3	PL65.T3	Tatar
494.3	PL21-396	Turkic languages
494.3	PL65.C74	Crimean Tatar
494.3	PL41-45	Siberian (Northeastern) group
494.3	PL31	Old Turkic
494.35	PJ6231-6239	Turkish
494.35	PL101-275	Turkish (Osmanic/Ottoman)
494.36	PL91-396	Oghuz (Southwestern) group
494.36	PL331-334	Turkmen
494.36	PL51-56	Chagatai (Southeastern) group

Dewey	LC	Descriptor
494.361	PL311-314	Azerbaijani
494.5	PH	Finno-Ugrian/Basque
494.5	PH561-569	Votish (Chudish, S.)
494.5	PH1-11	Philology
494.5	PH14	Language
494.501	PH5	Philosophy/Theory
494.505	PH1	Serials
494.507	PH11	Education
494.5092	PH9	Biography
494.51	PH1201-3718	Ugrian languages
494.51	PH1251-1409	Ob-Ugrian
494.511	PH2001-3718	Hungarian
494.511	PH2001-2071	Philology
494.511	PH2073-2800	Language
494.5113	PH2625-2693	Dictionaries
494.5113028	PH2601-2693	Lexicography
494.5115	PH2097-2410	Grammar
494.511709	PH2800	Slang
494.53	PH4	Encyclopedias
494.53	PH1001-1109	Permian
494.54	PH581-589	Livonian
494.54	PH501-509	Karelian
494.54	PH541-549	Vepsish (Chudish, N.)
494.541	PH131-225	Grammar
494.541	PH124-293	Language
494.541	PH101-123	Philology
494.541	PH101-498	Finnish
494.5410(5/6)	PH101-103	Serials/Societies
494.545	PH601-629	Language
494.545	PH601-688	Estonian
494.55	PH701-735	Lappish
494.55	PH21-41	Grammar
494.55	PH701-729	Language
494.56	PH751-779	Language
494.56	PH751-785	Mordvinian
494.56	PH801-809	Cheremissian
494.6	PM1-95	Hyperborean languages
494.6	PM	Hyperborean
494.6	PL495	Ainu
494.8	PL4601-4794	Dravidian languages
494.811	PL4751-4758.9	Tamil
494.812	PL4711-4718.9	Malayalam (Malabar)
494.814	PL4641-4659	Kannada/Kanarese
494.827	PL4771-4780.9	Telugu
495	PL4051-4054	Karen languages
495	PL491-495	Far eastern languages
495	PL3521-4001	Sino-Tibetan
495.1	PL1001-1940	Language
495.1	PL1891-1900	Mandarin
495.1	PL1001-(3208)	Chinese language
495.1-9	CN1150-1230	Asia
495.103	PL1031	Encyclopedias
495.105	PL1001-1010	Serials
495.106	PL1011-1021	Societies/Congresses
495.107	PL1065-1069	Education
495.109	PL1075-1083	History of the language
495.11	CN1160-1161	China
495.115	PL1201-1219	Phonology
495.12	PL1281-1315	Etymology
495.13	PL1420-1498	Dictionaries
495.13028	PL1401-1498	Lexicography
495.15	PL1099-1241	Grammar
495.17	PL1501-1940	Dialects
495.17	PL1731-1740	Cantonese
495.17	PL1861-1870	Hsiang (Hunanese)
495.17	PL1931-1940	Wu
495.4	PL3551-4001	Tibeto-Burman

Dewey	LC	Descriptor
495.4	PL3561-3801	Tibeto-Himalayan
495.4	PL3601-3775	Tibetan
495.4	PL3601-3651	Language
495.49	PL3781-3801	Himalayan languages
495.6	PL501-699	Language
495.6	PL501-889	Japanese
495.609	PL525-.6	History
495.611	CN1180-1181	Japan
495.611	PL750-751	Inscriptions
495.63	PL674.5-677.6	Dictionaries
495.65	PL531.3-532.5	Grammar
495.7	PL901-998	Korean language
495.7	PL901-949	Language
495.711	PL969.2-.4	Inscriptions
495.73	PL935-.6	Dictionaries
495.8	PL3851-4001	Burmese
495.8	PL3921-3988	Burmese
495.8	PL3921-3969	Languages
495.91	PL4111-4251	Thai languages
495.91	PL4151-4199	Language
495.91	PL4151-4209	Thai/Siamese
495.922	PL4371-4379	Vietnamese/Annamese
495.93	PL4281-4587	Austroasiatic languages
495.932	PL4301-4351	Mon-Khmer languages
495.95	PL4501-4587	Munda (Kolarian) languages
496	CN1300-1320	Africa
496	PL8015-8021	Languages, By country
496	PL8000-8009	Languages
496	PL8000-8839	African languages
496.(1-5)	PL8035-8839	Languages, Alphabetically
496.(1-5)	PL8024-8027	Families of languages
496.0(5/6)	PL8000-8002	Serials/Societies/Congresses
496.07	PL8004	Education
496.39	PL8025	Bantu
496.391	PJ5321-5329	Mandaean
496.5	PL8027	Sudanian
496.5	PL8008	Grammar
497	PM5001-7356	Of South America & West Indies
497	PM101-2711	American aboriginal
497	PM5071-5099	Of West Indies
497	PM	Indian languages
497	PM231-355	Of Canada/Newfoundland/ Etc.
497	PM421-501	Of United States and Mexico
497	PM3501-4566	Languages, Alphabetical
497	PM3001-4566	Of Mexico and Central America
497	PM3100-3281	Of Mexico, By state
497	PM3301-3393	Of Central America, By country
497.(1-9)	PM549-2711	Languages, Alphabetical
497.1	PM61-64	Eskimo
497.1	PM31-34	Aleut
498	PM5001-7356	Of South America & West Indies
498	PM5100-5295	Of South America
498.(2-4)	PM5301-7356	Languages, Alphabetical
499	CN1340-1355	Australia/New Zealand/ Oceania
499	PM8999	Picture languages (Isotype)
499	PL5001-7511	Languages of Oceania
499.(2/12/15)	PL5001-7101	Austronesian/Papuan/ Australian
499.12	PL6601-6621	Papuan languages
499.15	PL7001-7101	Australian languages
499.2	PL4401-4471	Malay languages
499.2(8/21)	PL5051-5490	Malayan (Indonesian)
499.21	PL5501-6135	Philippine languages
499.221	PL5071-5089	Indonesian
499.222	PL5161-5179	Javanese
499.28	PL5101-5139	Malay
499.4	PL6401-6551	Polynesian languages
499.5	PL6191-6341	Micronesian/Melanesian
499.92	PH5023-5259	Language
499.92	PH5001-5022	Philology
499.92	PH5001-5490	Basque
499.95	PJ4010-4041	Language
499.95	PJ4001-4083	Sumerian
499.950(5/6)	PJ4001-4007	Serials/Societies
499.953	PJ4037	Dictionaries
499.955	PJ4011-4025	Grammar
499.96	PK9001-9201	Caucasian languages
499.96	PK9201	Other languages
499.96	PK9101-9169	Georgian
499.960(5/6)	PK9001	Serials/Societies
499.9607	PK9005	Education
499.963	PK9125	Dictionaries
499.963	PK9025	Dictionaries
499.965	PK9106-9115	Grammar
499.965	PK9007-9015	Grammar
499.99	PM8001-8995	Artificial languages
499.99	PM	Artifical
499.992	PM8201-8298	Esperanto
500	Q	Science, General
500.5	QB500.25-.268	Universe/Space sciences
501	Q174-175.3	Philosophy/Methodology
501.2	Q177	Classification of the sciences
501.4	Q179	Terminology
502.22	Q161.7	Pictorial works
502.3	Q147-149	As a profession
502.5	Q145	Directories
502.8	Q184-185.7	Instruments/Apparatus
502.82	QH201-278.5	Microscopy
502.82(2-5)	QH211-212	Microscopes
502.820(5/6)	QH201	Serials/Societies/Congresses
502.85	Q183.9	Computers/Data processing
503	Q121-123	Encyclopedias/Dictionaries
505	Q1-9	Serials
506	Q10-101	Societies/Congresses
507	Q181-183.4	Education
507.2	Q179.9-180.7	Research
507.4	Q105	Museums/Exhibitions
508	Q115-116	Scientific voyages/ Expeditions
508	QH	Natural history/Biology
508	QH1-278.5	Natural history
508.(4-9)	QH101-198	Topographical divisions
508.0(5/6)	QH1-7	Serials/Societies/Congresses
508.014	QH83	Terminology
508.0222	QH46	Pictorial works
508.025	QH35	Directories
508.03	QH13	Dictionaries/ Encyclopedias
508.07	QH51-58	Education
508.074	QH70	Museums/Exhibitions
508.09	QH15-21	History
508.092	QH26-31	Biography
508.3(1-3)	QH84-198	Geographical distribution
508.314	QH84.8-89	Land
508.316(2-9)	QH90-100	Water/Aquatic biology

Dewey	LC	Descriptor
508.4	QH135-178	Europe
508.5	QH179-193	Asia
508.6	QH194-195	Africa
508.71	QH106-.2	Canada
508.72	QH107	Mexico
508.728	QH108	Central America
508.729	QH109	West Indies
508.73	QH104-105	United States
508.8	QH111-130	South America
508.9(3-6)	QH197-198	Australia/New Zealand/ Oceania
509	Q124.6-127.2	History
509.(3-4)	Q125-.2	Modern
509.(4-9)	Q127-.2	By place
509.01	Q124.95	Ancient
509.02	Q124.97	Medieval
509.2	Q141-143	Biography
510	QA	Mathematics
510.(5/6)	QA1	Serials/Societies/Congresses
510.(5/6)	QA75.5	Serials/Societies/Congresses
510.1	QA8-10.4	Philosophy
510.212	QA47-59	Tables
510.25	QA30	Directories
510.28	QA75-76.95	Calculating machines/ Computers
510.3	QA76.15	Dictionaries/ Encyclopedias
510.3	QA5	Dictionaries/ Encyclopedias
510.7	QA11-20	Education
510.9	QA76.17	History
510.9	QA21-27	History
510.9(4-9)	QA27	By place
510.90(3-4)	QA24-26	Modern
510.902	QA23	Medieval
510.92	QA28-29	Biography
510.92	QA76.2	Biography
510.93	QA22	Ancient
511.3	QA267-268.5	Machine theory
511.3	QA9-10.3	Mathematical logic
511.6	QA164-167.2	Combinatorial analysis
512	QA150-272	Algebra
512.00(5/6)	QA150	Serials/Societies/Congresses
512.007	QA159	Education
512.0076	QA157	Exercises/Examinations
512.2	QA171	Theory of groups
512.5	QA184-205	Linear/Multilinear algebra
512.7	QA241-.7	Number theory
512.94	QA211-218	Equation theory
513	QA101-141.8	Elementary math/ Arithmetic
514	QA611-614.97	Topology
515	QA299.6-433	Analysis
515	QA303-316	Calculus
515	QA401-425	Analytical methods
515.35	QA370-379	Differential equations
515.7	QA319-329.9	Functional analysis
516	QA440-699	Geometry
516.05	QA474	Plane geometry
516.06	QA475	Solid geometry
516.2	QA451-469	Elementary geometry
516.24	QA531-538	Trigonometry
516.3	QA551-563	Analytic geometry
516.35	QA564-608	Algebraic geometry
516.36	QA615-639	Infinitesimal geometry
516.36	QA641-660	Differential geometry
516.6	QA501-521	Descriptive geometry

Dewey	LC	Descriptor
519	T57-59	Applied mathematics
519.2	QA273-274.76	Probabilities
519.3	QA269-272	Game theory
519.5	QA276-280	Mathematical statistics
520	QB	Astronomy
520	QB495-991	Descriptive astronomy
520.(5/6)	QB1	Serials/Societies/Congresses
520.(5/6)	QB495	Serials/Societies/Congresses
520.1	QB14.5	Philosophy
520.23	QB51.5	As a profession
520.3	QB14	Dictionaries/ Encyclopedias
520.3	QB497	Dictionaries/ Encyclopedias
520.7	QB61-62.7	Education
520.74	QB2	Museums/Exhibitions
520.9	QB498-.2	History
520.9	QB15-34	History
520.90(3-4)	QB28-33	Modern
520.901	QB16-22	Ancient
520.902	QB23	Medieval
520.92	QB35-36	Biography
521	QB421	Double star theory
521	QB349-421	Theory/Celestial mechanics
521.4	QB361-407	Perturbations
522.1	QB4-.9	Observations
522.1	QB81-84	Observatories
522.19(1-9)	QB82	Observatories, By place
522.2	QB84.5-115	Astronomical instruments
522.6	QB121	Photography/Etc.
522.68	QB470	Infrared astronomy
522.68	QB468-480	Non-optical methods
522.682	QB475-479.3	Radio astronomy
522.684	QB480	Radar astronomy
522.6862	QB471-.7	Gamma ray
522.6863	QB472-473	X-ray astronomy
522.7	QB140-237	Practical/Spherical astronomy
522.9	QB151-168	Correction/Reduction
523.01	QB460-466	Astrophysics (General)
523.02	QB450	Cosmochemistry
523.1(2)	QB980-991	Cosmology/Cosmogony
523.111	QB136	Space/Astronautics in
523.1125	QB790-792	Interstellar matter
523.2	QB500.5-785	Solar system
523.3	QB391-399	Lunar theory
523.3	QB580-595	Moon
523.4	QB600-701	Planets
523.4	QB361-389	Planetary theory
523.5	QB740-759	Meteors/Meteorites
523.6	QB717-732	Comets
523.7	QB520-544	Sun
523.8	QB799-903	Stars
523.9	QB401-407	Satellites
526	GA	Cartography
526	QB283	Mathematical theory of earth
526	QE36	Geological maps
526.0(5/6)	GA101	Serials/Societies
526.0(5/6)	GA1	Serials/Societies
526.01	GA102.3	Philosophy
526.014	GA102.2	Terminology
526.0221	GA125-155	Map drawing/Modeling/Etc.
526.023	GA197.5	As a profession
526.025	GA102.25	Directories

Dewey	LC	Descriptor	Dewey	LC	Descriptor
526.03	GA102	Dictionaries/ Encyclopedias	530.42	QC175.4-.45	Superfluid physics
			530.44	QC717.6-718.8	Plasma physics/Ionized gases
526.06	GA101.2	Congresses	530.7	QC100.5-.8	Measuring instruments
526.07	GA102.5-.7	Education	530.81	QC101-114	Measurement (Length/ Area/Etc.)
526.07	GA2.7-.9	Education			
526.074	GA190	Exhibitions/Museums	530.81	QC81-114	Weights/Measures
526.09	GA3	History	530.810(5/6)	QC81	Serials/Societies/Congresses
526.1	QB275-343	Geodesy	530.8103	QC82	Dictionaries/ Encyclopedias
526.10(5/6)	QB275	Serials/Societies/Congresses			
526.1028 5	QB297	Computers/Data processing	530.81074	QC81.5	Museums/Exhibitions
526.103	QB279	Dictionaries/ Encyclopedias	530.8109	QC83-86	History
			530.812	QC90.8-94	Metric system
526.109	QB280.5	History	531	QC176-.9	Solids/Solid-state physics
526.1092	QB297.9-298	Biography	531-533	QC120-168.85	Experimental mechanics
526.3	QB301-328	Geodetic surveying	531.0(5/6)	QC120	Serials/Societies/Congresses
526.6	QB201-205	Geodetic astronomy	531.01515	QA801-939	Analytical mechanics
526.6	QB224.5-237	Longitude/Latitude	531.015150(5/6)	QA801	Serials/Societies/Congresses
526.7	QB330-339	Gravity determinations	531.1	QC133-136	Dynamics
526.8	GA110-115	Projection	531.11	QA843-871	Dynamics
526.982	GA109	Aerial cartography	531.112	QA841-842	Kinematics
526.99	VK588-597	Hydrographic surveying	531.12	QA821-835	Statics
528	QB7-9	Ephermerides	531.38	QA901-930	Mechanics of deformable bodies
529	QB209-224	Time (Sundials/ Sunsets/Etc.)			
			531.38	QA931-939	Elasticity/Plasticity
529	CE	Chronology/Calendars	531.6	QC72-73.8	Force/Energy
529.(3/4)	CE51-77	Medieval/Modern	532	QC138-168.85	Fluids/Fluid mechanics
529.(32/44)	CE81-85	Church/Religious	532.2	QC145.5-148.4	Hydrostatics/Floating bodies
529.0(5/6)	CE1	Serials/Societies			
529.03	CE4	Dictionaries/ Encyclopedias	532.5	QC175.3-.36	Kinetic liquid theory
			532.5	QC150-159	Fluid/Hydrodynamics
529.06	CE1.5	Congresses	532.5	TC160-181	Hydrodynamics/Etc.
529.09	CE6-8	History	533.2	QC167.5-168.85	Gas dynamics/Motion of gases
529.3	CE21-46	Ancient			
529.32(2-9)	CE31-39	Asian	533.6	QC161-167	Gases/Pneumatics
529.32207	CE46	Roman	533.7	QC175-.16	Kinetic gas theory
529.32208	CE42	Greek	534	QC221-246	Acoustics/Sound
530	QC	Physics	534.0(5/6)	QC221	Serials/Societies/Congresses
530	QC170-197	Atomic physics	534.07	QC226-227	Education
530	QC172-173.4	Matter/Antimatter	534.072	QC228	Laboratories
530.0(5/6)	QC1	Serials/Societies/Congresses	534.2	QC233	Propagation of sound
530.01	QC5.56-6.4	Philosophy/Methodology	534.23	QC242-.4	Underwater acoustics
530.014	QC6.8	Terminology/Nomenclature	534.5	QC231	Vibrations/Wave motion
530.023	QC29	Physics as a profession	534.5	QC235-241	Vibrations
530.025	QC16.2	Directories	534.55	QC244	Ultrasonics
530.028	QC53	Instruments/Apparatus	535	QC350-467	Optics/Light
530.0285	QC52	Computers/Data processing	535.(15/2)	QC446.15-.3	Quantum/Nonlinear optics
530.03	QC5	Dictionaries/ Encyclopedias	535.0(5/6)	QC350	Serials/Societies/Congresses
			535.028	QC370.5-379	Optical instruments/ Apparatus
530.07	QC30-47	Education			
530.072	QC51	Laboratories	535.07(2)	QC363-366	Education/Research
530.074	QC60	Museums/Exhibitions	535.2	QC392-449	Physical optics
530.09	QC6.9-9	History	535.220287	QC391	Photometry/ Microphotometry
530.09(4-9)	QC9	By place			
530.092	QC15-16	Biography	535.323	QC425-.4	Reflection
530.11	QC173.5-.65	Relativity	535.324	QC425.9-426.8	Refraction
530.12	QC173.96-174.52	Quantum theory/Mechanics	535.35	QC476.4-480.2	Luminescence
530.1207	QC20.52-.54	Education	535.4	QC449	Holography
530.122	QC174.3-.35	Matrix mechanics	535.4	QC414.8-417	Diffraction
530.124	QC174.2-.26	Wave mechanics	535.4	QC410.9-411	Interference
530.13	QC174.7-175.36	Statistical physics	535.52	QC440-446	Polarization
530.133	QC174.4-.43	Quantum statistics	535.6	QC494-496.9	Color
530.138	QC175.2-.25	Transport theory	535.84	QC450-464	Spectroscopy
530.14	QC173.68-.75	Field theory	536	QC251-338.5	Heat
530.143	QC174.45-.52	Quantum field theory	536.0(5/6)	QC251	Serials/Societies/Congresses
530.15	QC19.2-20.85	Mathematical physics	536.2	QC319.8-338.5	Heat transfer
530.150(5/6)	QC19.2	Serials/Societies/Congresses	536.23	QC320.8-323	Conduction
530.4175	QC176.82-.9	Thin films			

Dewey	LC	Descriptor
536.25	QC326-330	Convection
536.3	QC331-338.5	Radiation/Absorption/Cooling
536.4	QC301-310	Change of state
536.50287	QC270-275	Thermometers
536.6	QC290-297	Calorimeters
536.7	QC310.15-319	Thermodynamics
537	QC501-718.8	Electricity
537	QC669-675.8	Electromagnetism
537-538	QC501-766	Electricity/Magnetism
537.028	QC543-544	Instruments/Apparatus
537.2	QC570-596.9	Electrostatics/Friction
537.24	QC584-585.8	Dielectrics
537.5	QC685-689.5	Quantum electronics
537.534	QC676-678.6	Radio waves
537.534	QC660.5-678.6	Electric oscillations/Waves
537.6	QC630-648	Electrodynamics
537.6	QC601-625	Electric current
537.62	QC610.3-612	Electric conductivity
537.622	QC610.9-611.8	Semiconductor physics
537.67	QC679-680.5	Quantum electrodynamics
538	QC750-755.65	Magnetism
538.4	QC756.7-757.9	Magnets
538.7	QC811-849	Geomagnetism
538.70(5/6)	QC811	Serials/Societies/Congresses
538.78	QC825-826	Magnetic surveys
538.79	QC830-845	Magnetic observations
539.2	QC474-496.9	Radiation physics
539.20(5/6)	QC474	Serials/Societies/Congresses
539.7	QC791.9-792.8	Atomic energy
539.7	QC170-197	Atomic physics
539.7(2)	QC770-798	Nuclear/PArticle physics
539.70(5/6)	QC170	Serials/Societies/Congresses
539.70(5/6)	QC770	Serials/Societies/Congresses
539.7028	QC785.5-787	Instruments/Apparatus
539.7072	QC788-789.2	Research
539.72	QC793-.5	Elementary pArticle physics
539.7222	QC484.2-.6	Bremsstrahlung
539.7222	QC480.8-482.3	X-rays
539.7223	QC484.8-485.9	Cosmic ray physics
539.75	QC793.9-794.8	Nuclear interactions
539.752	QC794.95-798	Radioactivity/Substances
539.762	QC789.7-790.8	Nuclear fission
539.764	QC790.95-791.8	Nuclear fusion
540	QD	Chemistry
540.(5/6)	QD1	Serials/Societies/Congresses
540.1	QD6	Philosophy
540.112	QD23.3-26.5	Alchemy
540.14	QD7	Terminology
540.23	QD39.5	As a profession
540.25	QD23	Directories
540.3	QD4-5	Encyclopedias/Dictionaries
540.7	QD40-49	Education
540.74	QD2	Museums/Exhibitions
540.9	QD11-18	History
540.9(4-9)	QD18	By place
540.92	QD21-22	Biography
541	QD450-731	Physical/Theoretical chemistry
541.0(5/6)	QD450	Serials/Societies/Congresses
541.242	QD463-464	Atomic/Nuclear weights
541.28	QD462-.9	Quantum chemistry
541.33	QD506-508	Surface chemistry
541.34	QD540-549	Theory of solution
541.35	QD701-731	Photochemistry
541.36	QD510-536	Thermochemistry

Dewey	LC	Descriptor
541.37	QD273	Electrochemistry
541.37	QD551-562	Electrochemistry/Electrolysis
541.38	QD601-608	Nuclear/Radiochemistry
541.382	QD625-655	Radiation chemistry
541.39	QD501-505.5	Conditions/Law of reactions
542.1	QD51-63	Laboratories
543	QD71-142	Analytical chemistry
543.00(5/6)	QD71	Serials/Societies/Congresses
543.08	QD142	Water analysis
544	QD81-96	Qualitative analysis
545	QD101-117	Quantitative analysis
546	QD466-469	Chemical elements
546	QD146-197	Inorganic chemistry
546.(2-6)	QD181-197	Other elements
546.0(5/6)	QD146	Serials/Societies/Congresses
546.3	QD171-172	Metals
546.3	QD130-139	Technical analysis (Metals)
546.7	QD161-169	Nonmetals
547	QD241-441	Organic chemistry
547.00(5/6)	QD241	Serials/Societies/Congresses
547.05	QD410-412	Organometallic compounds
547.3	QD271-272	Organic analysis
547.4	QD300-315	Alphatic compounds
547.59	QD399-406	Heterocyclic compounds
547.6	QD330-341	Aromatic compounds
547.611	QD390-395	Condensed benzene rings
547.7	QD380-388	Polymers
547.76	QD375-377	Antibiotics
547.78	QD320-327	Carbohydrates
548	QD901-999	Crystallography
548.(5/81)	QD921-932	Crystal growth/Structure
548.(81/7)	QD911-915	Geometrical/Mathematical
548.0(5/6)	QD901	Serials/Societies/Congresses
548.8	QD931-947	Crystals, Physical properties
549	QE351-399.2	Mineralogy
549.0(5/6)	QE351	Serials/Societies/Congresses
549.012	QE388	Classification
549.1	QE367-369	Determinative mineralogy
549.13	QE371	Mineralogical chemistry
550	QC801-809	Geophysics/Cosmic physics
550.(5/6)	QC801	Serials/Societies/Congresses
550.5092	QC858	Biography
551	QE	Geology
551.(1-4/8)	QE500-625	Dynamic/Structural geology
551.(5/6)	QC851-999	Meteorology/Climatology
551.0(5/6)	QE1	Serials/Societies/Congresses
551.01	QE6	Philosophy
551.014	QE7	Terminology
551.023	QE34	As a profession
551.025	QE23	Directories
551.028	QE49.5	Instruments/Apparatus
551.0285	QE48.8	Computers/Data processing
551.03	QE5	Dictionaries/Encyclopedias
551.07	QE40-48	Education
551.072	QE49	Laboratories
551.074	QE51	Museums/Exhibitions
551.09	QE11-13	History
551.092	QE21-22	Biography
551.10(5/6)	QE500	Serials/Societies/Congresses
551.21	QE521.5-527	Volcanoes
551.22	QE531-545	Earthquakes/Seismology
551.23	QE528	Geysers/Hot springs/Etc.
551.3	QE517-.5	Dynamic geology
551.302	QE570	Weathering
551.303	QE571-597	Sedimentation

Dewey	LC	Descriptor
551.307	QE598-600.3	Earth/Mass movements
551.46	GC1000-1023	Marine resources
551.46	GC	Oceanography
551.46(1-9)	GC401-881	By place
551.46(5-6)	GC771-871	Pacific Ocean
551.4601	GC150-181	Physical oceanography
551.4601	GC109-149	Chemical oceanography
551.4601	GC100-103	Seawater
551.4607	GC63	Oceanographic expeditions
551.4607	GC65-78	Underwater exploration
551.46083	GC377-399	Marine sediments
551.46084	GC83-87.6	Submarine topography
551.4609	GC96-97.8	Estuarine oceanography
551.4600(5/6)	GC1	Serials/Societies
551.46001	GC10.2-.4	Philosophy
551.460014	GC9.2	Terminology
551.4600202	GC20	Outlines/Etc.
551.460023	GC30.5	As a profession
551.460028	GC41	Instruments/Apparatus
551.46003	GC9	Dictionaries/ Encyclopedias
551.46006	GC2	Congresses
551.46007	GC31-.7	Education
551.460072	GC57-59	Research
551.460074	GC35-.2	Museums/Exhibitions
551.46009	GC29-.2	History
551.460092	GC30	Biography
551.461	GC481-711	Atlantic Ocean
551.467	GC721-761	Indian Ocean
551.468	GC401-455	Arctic Ocean
551.469	GC461-462	Antarctic Ocean
551.47	GC200-376	Dynamics of the ocean
551.47	GC228.5-.6	Ocean circulation
551.47	GC190-.5	Ocean-atmosphere interaction
551.47	GC297-299	Water masses and ocean mixing
551.4701	GC229-296.8	Currents
551.4702	GC205-226	Waves
551.4708	GC300-376	Tides
551.5	QC878.5-879.59	Aeronomy
551.50(5/6)	QC851	Serials/Societies/Congresses
551.5014	QC854.2	Terminology
551.5028	QC875.5-876.7	Instruments
551.509	QC855-857	History
551.511	QC879.6-.8	Atmospheric chemistry
551.5113	QC882	Pollutants (Dust/ Smoke/ Etc.)
551.514	QC881-.2	Atmospheric shells
551.518	QC930.5-959	Wind
551.52	QC880-.4	Dynamic meteorology
551.52(5/7)	QC901-913	Temperature/Radiation
551.54	QC885-896	Atmospheric pressure
551.55	QC940.6-959	Storms/Cyclones
551.554	QC968-.2	Thunderstorms
551.56	QC974.5-976	Meteorological optics
551.56	QC960.5-969	Electrical phenomena
551.5632	QC966-.7	Lightning
551.57	QC915-929	Aqueous vapor
551.571	QC915-917	Humidity/Hygrometry
551.576	QC920.7-921.6	Clouds
551.577	QC924.5-926.2	Rainfall
551.6	QC980-999	Climatology/Weather
551.60(5/6)	QC980	Serials/Societies/Congresses
551.63	QC994.95-999	Weather forecasting
551.632	QC877-.5	Broadcasts/Warnings
551.635	QC972.6-973.8	Radio meteorology
551.6353	QC973.45-.8	Radar meteorology
551.65(1-9)	QC982-994.9	Geographic divisions
551.6513	QC993.5	Tropics
551.65143	QC993.6	Mountains
551.65154	QC993.7	Arid/Desert areas
551.65162	QC993.83-.9	Ocean/Maritime meteorology
551.654	QC989	Europe
551.655	QC990	Asia
551.656	QC991	Africa
551.6571	QC985-.5	Canada
551.6572(8)	QC986	Mexico/Central America
551.65729	QC987	West Indies
551.6573	QC983-984	United States
551.658	QC988	South America
551.659(3-6)	QC992-993	Australia/New Zealand/ Oceania
551.66	QH543-.2	Bio/Microclimatology
551.66	QC883.7-.86	Micrometerology
551.68	QC926.6-928.74	Weather/Cloud modification
551.69	QC884-.2	Paleoclimatology
551.7	QE640-699	Stratigraphy
551.7	QE914-932	Stratigraphic divisions
551.700(5/6)	QE640	Serials/Societies/Congresses
551.72	QE654-674	Paleozoic
551.72	QE915-920	Paleozoic
551.73	QE914	Precabrian
551.76	QE921-924	Mesozoic
551.76	QE675-688	Mesozoic
551.78	QE691-699	Cenozoic
551.78	QE925-931.3	Cenozoic
551.8	QE601-613.5	Structural geology
551.9	QE514-516.5	Geochemistry
552	QE420-499	Petrology
552.00(5/6)	QE420	Serials/Societies/Congresses
552.09(1-9)	QE443-456.5	Geographical divisions
552.094	QE451	Europe
552.095	QE452	Asia
552.096	QE453	Africa
552.0971	QE445.5-446	Canada
552.0972	QE446.5-.6	Mexico
552.09728	QE447	Central America
552.09729	QE448	West Indies
552.0973	QE444-445	United States
552.098	QE449	South America
552.099(5-6)	QE455	Oceania
552.0993	QE454.5-.6	New Zealand
552.0994	QE453.5-454	Australia
552.09981	QE456	Arctic regions
552.09989	QE456.5	Antarctic regions
552.1	QE461-462	Igneous rocks/Volcanic ash
552.4	QE475	Metamorphic rocks
552.5	QE471-.15	Sedimentary rocks
553	QE390-.2	Ore minerals
553.8	QE392-394	Precious stones
554	QE260-287.8	Europe
554-559	QE65-350.52	Geographical divisions
555	QE289-319	Asia
556	QE320-339	Africa
557	QE71-217	North America
557.(4-9)	QE81-182	By state
557.1	QE185-199	Canada
557.2	QE201-203	Mexico
557.28	QE210-217	Central America
557.29	QE220-226	West Indies
557.3	QE72-182	United States

Dewey	LC	Descriptor
557.41	QE119-120	Maine
557.42	QE139-140	New Hampshire
557.43	QE171-172	Vermont
557.44	QE123-124	Massachusetts
557.45	QE159-160	Rhode Island
557.46	QE93-94	Connecticut
557.47	QE145-146	New York
557.48	QE157-158	Pennsylvania
557.49	QE141-142	New Jersey
557.51	QE95-96	Delaware
557.52	QE121-122	Maryland
557.53	QE97-98	District of Columbia
557.54	QE177-178	West Virginia
557.55	QE173-174	Virginia
557.56	QE147-148	North Carolina
557.57	QE161-162	South Carolina
557.58	QE101-102	Georgia
557.59	QE99-100	Florida
557.61	QE81-82	Alabama
557.62	QE129-130	Mississippi
557.63	QE117-118	Louisiana
557.64	QE167-168	Texas
557.66	QE153-154	Oklahoma
557.67	QE87-88	Arkansas
557.68	QE165-166	Tennessee
557.69	QE115-116	Kentucky
557.71	QE151-152	Ohio
557.72	QE109-110	Indiana
557.73	QE105-106	Illinois
557.74	QE125-126	Michigan
557.75	QE179-180	Wisconsin
557.76	QE127-128	Minnesota
557.77	QE111-112	Iowa
557.78	QE131-132	Missouri
557.81	QE113-114	Kansas
557.82	QE135-136	Nebraska
557.83	QE163-164	South Dakota
557.84	QE149-150	North Dakota
557.86	QE133-134	Montana
557.87	QE181-182	Wyoming
557.88	QE91-92	Colorado
557.89	QE143-144	New Mexico
557.91	QE85-86	Arizona
557.92	QE169-170	Utah
557.93	QE137-138	Nevada
557.94	QE89-90	California
557.95	QE155-156	Oregon
557.96	QE103-104	Idaho
557.97	QE175-176	Washington
557.98	QE83-84	Alaska
558	QE230-251	South America
559.(3-6)	QE340-349	Australia/New Zealand/ Oceania
559.8(1/2)	QE70	Arctic regions/Greenland
559.89	QE350	Antarctic
560	QL88-.5	Extinct animals/Fossils
560	QE760.8-899	Paleozoology
560	QE701-760	Paleontology
560.(5/6)	QE760.8	Serials/Societies/Congresses
560.(5/6)	QE701	Serials/Societies/Congresses
560.17	QE724-742	Stratigraphic divisions
560.172	QE725-730	Paleozoic
560.176	QE731-734	Mesozoic
560.178	QE736-741.3	Cenozoic
560.9(1-9)	QE743-760	Geographical divisions
560.94	QE753-755	Europe
560.95	QE756	Asia

Dewey	LC	Descriptor
560.96	QE757	Africa
560.971	QE748	Canada
560.972	QE749	Mexico
560.9728	QE751	Central America
560.9729(9)	QE750	West Indies/Bermuda
560.973	QE746-747	United States
560.98	QE752	South America
560.99(3-6)	QE758-759	Australia/New Zealand/ Oceania
560.9981	QE744	Arctic regions
560.9989	QE760	Antarctic regions
561	QE901-996.5	Paleobotany
561.(2-93)	QE955-983	Systematic divisions
561.(3-4)	QE980-983	Angiospermophyta/ Magnoliophyta
561.0(5/6)	QE901	Serials/Societies/Congresses
561.19(1-9)	QE934-950	Geographical divisions
561.194	QE943-945	Europe
561.195	QE946	Asia
561.196	QE947	Africa
561.1971	QE938	Canada
561.1972	QE939	Mexico
561.19728	QE941	Central America
561.19729	QE940	West Indies
561.1973	QE936-937	United States
561.198	QE942	South America
561.199(5-6)	QE949	Oceania
561.1993	QE948.2	New Zealand
561.1994	QE948	Australia
561.19981	QE934	Arctic regions
561.19989	QE950	Antarctic regions
561.5	QE975-978	Gymnosperms/Pinophyta
562	QE767	Plankton
562-565	QE770-832	Invertebrates
566-569	QE840.5-882	Chordata/Vertebrates
572	GN537-673	Ethnic groups/Races
572	GN269-279	Race (General)
572.9	GN550-673	Ethnic groups/Races, By place
572.9(728/8)	GN562-564	Central/South America
572.94	GN575-585	Europe
572.95	GN625-635	Asia
572.96	GN643-661	Africa
572.97	GN550-560	North America
572.99(3-6)	GN662-671	Australia/New Zealand/ Oceania
572.998	GN673	Arctic
573	GN49-296	Physical anthropology/ Somatology
573	GN	Anthropology
573	GN221-263	Physiological anthropology
573.01	GN33-34.3	Philosophy
573.014	GN12	Terminology
573.03	GN11	Dictionaries/ Encyclopedias
573.05	GN1	Serials
573.06	GN2-3	Societies/Congresses
573.07	GN42-46	Education
573.074	GN35-41	Museums/Exhibitions
573.09	GN17	History
573.092	GN20-21	Biography
573.2	GN281-289	Human evolution
573.2	GN280.7	Man as an animal
573.22	GN62.8-263	Human variation
573.3	GN700-875	Prehistoric archaeology
573.3	GN282-286.7	Fossil man
573.314	GN209	Teeth

Dewey	LC	Descriptor	Dewey	LC	Descriptor
573.6	GN66-69	Body dimensions	575.13	QH443-450.5	Recombination mechanisms
573.6(3-7)	GN211	Sex organs	575.132	QH421-425	Hybridization
573.671	GN70-161	Skeleton	575.2	QH401-411	Variation
573.673	GN171	Muscular system	575.292	QH460-468	Mutations
573.677	GN191-199	Skin	576	QR	Microbiology
573.68	GN181-190	Nervous system/Brain	576.0(5/6)	QR1	Serials/Societies/Congresses
574	QH	Natural history/Biology	576.012	QR12	Classification
574	QH301-705	Biology	576.014	QR11	Terminology
574.0(5/6)	QH301	Serials/Societies/Congresses	576.0222	QR54	Pictorial works
574.01	QH331	Philosophy	576.028	QR65-71	Technique/Equipment
574.023	QH314	As a profession	576.03	QR9	Dictionaries/
574.03	QH302.5	Dictionaries/			Encyclopedias
		Encyclopedias	576.07	QR61-63	Education
574.07	QH315-320	Education	576.072	QR64-.8	Laboratories
574.072	QH321-323.2	Laboratories/Stations	576.09	QR21-22	History
574.09	QH305-.2	History	576.092	QR30-31	Biography
574.1	QH501-531	Life (Growth/ Respiration/	576.15	QR100-129	Microbial ecology
		Etc.)	576.62	QR353-.5	Rickettsias
574.16	QH471-489	Reproduction	576.64	QR355-502	Virology
574.191	QH650-659	Physical/Chemical agent	576.640(5/6)	QR355	Serials/Societies/Congresses
		effects	576.6483	QR351	Micro-organism of plants
574.1915	QH652-.7	Radiation	576.6484	QR301-327	Micro-organism of animals
574.19153	QH651	Light	577	QH325	Origin/Beginning of life
574.1916	QH653	Temperature	578	QH201-278.5	Microscopy
574.192	QD415-441	Biological chemistry	578.(6-9)	QH231-278.5	Preparation of objects
574.29	QR180-189.5	Immunology	579	QH61-63	Collecting/Preservation
574.292	QR186.5-6	Antigens	579	QL61-67	Collecting/Preservation
574.293	QR186.7-.85	Antibodies	580.742	QK75-77	Herbariums
574.295	QR187-.3	Antigen/Antibody reactions	580.744	QK71-73	Botanical gardens
574.295	QR186	Immune response	581	QK	Botany
574.3	QH491	Development/	581.0(5/6)	QK1	Serials/Societies/Congresses
		Morphogenesis	581.012	QK91-97	Classification
574.31	QH499	Regeneration	581.014	QK10	Terminology
574.33	QL951-991	Embryology	581.0222	QK98-.3	Pictorial/Illustrations
574.330(5/6)	QL951	Serials/Societies/Congresses	581.025	QK35	Directories
574.332	QH491	Development/	581.03	QK9	Dictionaries
		Morphogenesis	581.03	QK7	Encyclopedias
574.5	QH540-549	Ecology	581.07	QK51-57	Education
574.5(3-7)	QH545-549	Influence of factors	581.074	QK79-.5	Museums
574.50(5/6)	QH540	Serials/Societies/Congresses	581.09	QK15-21	History
574.5222	QH543-.2	Bio/Microclimatology	581.092	QK26-31	Biography
574.821(2)	QH611-623	Physical/Chemical	581.1	QK710-899	Plant physiology
		properties	581.1334	QK861-899	Phytochemistry
574.87	QH573-705	Cytology	581.15	QK980-989	Evolution of plants
574.870(5/6)	QH573	Serials/Societies/Congresses	581.16	QK825-830	Reproduction
574.87072	QH585-.5	Research/Culture	581.2	SB621-795	Plant pathology
574.872	QH591-601.2	Cell structure	581.4	QK640-673	Plant anatomy
574.876	QH604-.3	Cell regulation/Control	581.5	QK900-989	Plant ecology
574.876	QH631-647	Physiological properties	581.50(5/6)	QK900-.2	Serials/Societies/Congresses
574.8762	QH605-.3	Cell division	581.632	QK98.5	Edible plants
574.8765	QH671	Pathology and death	581.64	QK98.7	Dye plants
574.9(2-9)	QH92-95.59	Marine biology, By place	581.69	SB617-618	Poisonous plants
574.92	QH90-100	Water/Aquatic biology	581.69	QK100	Poisonous plants
574.92	QH91-95.59	Marine biology	581.72	QK78-.5	Laboratories
574.921	QH92-93.9	Atlantic Ocean	581.9(09-99)	QK101-474.5	Geographical distribution
574.92142	QH95.8	Coral reefs	581.9(09-99)	QK930-938	Physiographic regions
574.92169	QH95.9	Brackish/Saline water	581.90913	QK474.5	Tropics
574.924	QH95.58	Antarctic Ocean	581.90914	QK936-938	Land
574.925	QH95-.55	Pacific Ocean	581.90916(2-9)	QK930-935	Water
574.927	QH94-.7	Indian Ocean	581.92	QK102-105	Aquatic
574.928	QH95.56-.57	Arctic seas	581.95	QK341-379	Asia
574.929	QH96-100	Freshwater biology/	581.953	QK353	Arabia
		Limnology	581.959	QK360-368	Southeast Asia
574.999	QH327	Space biology	581.96	QK381-424	Africa
575	QH359-425	Evolution	581.97	QK281-339	Europe
575.1	QH426-470	Genetics	581.97(4-9)	QK145-195	By state
575.10(5/6)	QH426	Serials/Societies/Congresses	581.971	QK201-203	Canada

Dewey	LC	Descriptor
581.972	QK211	Mexico
581.9728	QK215-222	Central America
581.9729	QK225-231	West Indies
581.973	QK115-195	United States
581.98	QK241-273	South America
581.99(3-6)	QK431-473	Australia/New Zealand/Oceania
581.9981	QK474-.3	Arctic regions
581.9989	QK474.4	Antarctic regions
582	QK474.8-495	Spermatophyta/Phanerogams
582.1(6-7)	QK474.8-480	Trees/Shrubs
582.13	QK495	Angiosperms
585	QE975-978	Gymnosperms/Pinophyta
585	QK494-.5	Gymnosperms
585.114	QE980-983	Angiospermophyta/Magnoliophyta
586	QK504-635	Cryptogams
587	QK520-532	Pteridophyta (Ferns)
588	QK532.4-563.7	Bryophyta/Bryology
589.(3-4)	QK564-580.5	Algae/Algology
589.1	QK580.7-597.5	Lichens
589.2	QK600-635	Fungi
589.9	QR352-.5	Mycoplasmas
590.744	QL73-77.5	Menageries/Zoological gardens
591	QL	Zoology
591.0(5/6)	QL1	Serials/Societies/Congresses
591.014	QL10	Terminology
591.0222	QL46-.5	Pictorial/Illustrations
591.025	QL35	Directories
591.03	QL7-9	Encyclopedias/Dictionaries
591.07	QL51-58	Education
591.072	QL69	Laboratories
591.074	QL71	Museums/Exhibitions
591.09	QL15-21	History
591.092	QL26-31	Biography
591.4	QL801-950.9	Anatomy
591.4	QL799	Morphology
591.4(4-6)	QL871-881	Urogenital system
591.40(5/6)	QL801	Serials/Societies/Congresses
591.41	QL835-841	Vascular system
591.42	QL845-855	Respiratory organs
591.43	QL856-867	Digestive organs
591.47	QL821-831	Muscular/Skeletal
591.48	QL945-949	Sense organs
591.48	QL921-938	Nervous system
591.49	QL950-.9	Regional anatomy
591.5(3/6)	QL758-.5	Predation/Aggression
591.51	QL750-795	Animal behavior
591.510(5/6)	QL750	Serials/Societies/Congresses
591.52	QL753-755.5	Seasonal habits
591.69	QL100	Poisonous animals
591.9(09-99)	QL101-345	Geographical distribution
591.9(3-9)	QL150-345	Topographical divisions
591.90914	QL111-118	Land
591.90916(2-9)	QL120-149	Water
591.909163	QL127-135	Atlantic
591.9091632	QL126	Arctic ocean
591.909164	QL138	Pacific ocean
591.909165	QL137	Indian ocean
591.909167	QL126.5	Antarctic ocean
591.909169	QL139	Brackish water
591.909169(2-8)	QL141-149	Fresh water
591.94	QL253-298	Europe
591.95	QL300-334	Asia
591.96	QL336-337	Africa
591.97(4-9)	QL159-215	By state
591.971	QL219-221	Canada
591.972	QL225	Mexico
591.9728	QL227	Central America
591.9729	QL229	West Indies
591.973	QL155-215	United States
591.98	QL235-251	South America
591.99(3-6)	QL338-345	Australia/New Zealand/Oceania
592	QL362-599.82	Invertebrates
593.1	QL366-369.2	Protozoa
593.4	QL371-374.2	Porifera (Sponges)
593.5	QL375-379	Coelenterata
593.8	QL380-.8	Ctenophora
593.9	QL381-385.2	Echinodermata
594.6	QL401-432	Mollusca
595.1	QL386-394	Worms
595.2	QL434-599.82	Arthropoda
595.4	QL451-459.2	Arachnida (Spiders/Scorpions)
595.6(1/2)	QL449.5-.65	Millipedes/Centipedes
595.7	QL461-599.82	Insects
597	QL614-639.6	Fishes
597-599	QL605-739.3	Vertebrates/Chordates
597-599.00(5/6)	QL605	Serials/Societies/Congresses
597.0074	QL78-79	Public aquariums
597.0074	SF456-458.83	Fishes/Aquariums
597.6	QL667-668	Amphibians
597.9	QL640-666	Reptiles
598	QL671-699	Birds
599	QL700-739.3	Mammals
600	T	Technology
601	T14	Philosophy/Theory
601.48	T8	Symbols/Abbreviations
603	T9-10	Dictionaries/Encyclopedias
604.2	T351-385	Mechanical drawing
605	T1-5	Serials/Societies
606	T1-5	Serials/Societies
606	T6	Congresses
607	T66-69	History
607	T61-173	Technical education
607.(4-9)	T71-170	By place
607.2	T175-178	Industrial research
607.34	T391-999	Technical exhibitions
607.3409	T400-999	By city/Date
607.4	T105-147	Europe
607.41	T107-114	Great Britain
607.43	T123-124	Germany
607.44	T121-122	France
607.5	T149-163	Asia
607.51	T151-152	China
607.52	T155-156	Japan
607.6	T165-166	Africa
607.71	T76-77	Canada/Newfoundland
607.72	T78-79	Mexico
607.728	T80-81	Central America
607.729	T82-83	West Indies
607.73	T73-75	United States
607.8	T84-104	South America
607.9(3-6)	T167-170	Australia/New Zealand/Oceania
608	T201-342	Patents
608.0(5/6)	T201-203	Serials/Societies/Congresses
608.7	T212-323.3	By place
608.7	T215-323.3	History
608.74	T255-295	Europe

Dewey	LC	Descriptor	Dewey	LC	Descriptor
608.741	T257-264.5	Great Britain	610.730693	RT62	Practical nursing
608.743	T273-274.5	Germany	610.730698	RT84	Nurses' aides
608.744	T271-272.5	France	610.730699	RT86.3	Nurse/Patient relationship
608.75	T299-313	Asia	610.7307	RT71-81	Education
608.752	T305-306	Japan	610.73070(1-9)	RT79-81	Education, By place
608.76	T315-319	Africa	610.73070(4-9)	RT81	Other areas
608.771	T226-227	Canada	610.730707(4-9)	RT80	By state
608.772	T228-229	Mexico	610.7307073	RT79-80	United States
608.7728	T230-231	Central America	610.73072	RT81.5	Research/Experimentation
608.7729	T232-233	West Indies	610.73076	RT55	Problems/Exercises/Exams
608.773	T223-225	United States	610.7309	RT31	Nursing history
608.78	T234-254	South America	610.7309(4-9)	RT4-17	Nursing, By place
608.79 (3-4)	T321-322.6	Australia/New Zealand	610.73092	RT34-37	Biography
608.79(5-6)	T323-324	Oceania	610.73094	RT10-12	Europe
608.798	T325-326	Polar areas	610.73095	RT13	Asia
609	T15-33	History	610.73096	RT14	Africa
609.(1-9)	T21-31	By place	610.73097	RT4-7	North America
610	R	Medicine (General)	610.73097(4-9)	RT5	By state
610.1	R723-726	Medical philosophy/Ethics	610.730971	RT6	Canada
610.14	R123	Terminology/Nomenclature	610.730972(8-9)	RT7	Other American areas
610.21	RA407-409.5	Statistics	610.730973	RT4-5	United States
610.222	R120	Pictorial works	610.73098	RT8	South America
610.23	R728-733	Practice of medicine	610.73099(5-6)	RT17	Oceania
610.25	R711-713.97	Directories	610.730993	RT16	New Zealand
610.28	R856-857	Biomedical engineering	610.730994	RT15	Australia
610.285	R858-859.7	Computers in medicine	610.732	RT104	Private-duty nursing
610.3	R125	Encyclopedias	610.733	RT102	Institutional nursing
610.3	R121	Dictionaries	610.734	RT97	Public health nursing
610.5	R5-99.7	Serials/Societies	610.734	RT108	Red Cross nursing
610.5	R101	Yearbooks	610.7343	RT98	Community health nursing
610.6	R106	Congresses	610.7362	RJ245	Pediatric nursing
610.69	R690-697	Medicine as a profession	610.73677	RD99-.35	Surgical nursing
610.695	RA390	Medical missions/ Assistance	610.73678	RG951	Obstetric nursing
610.695	R687	Medical expeditions	610.7368	RJ502.3	Psychiatric nursing
610.695	R722-.32	Medical missionaries	610.73691	RC674	Cardiovascular disease nursing
610.7	R108	Laboratories/Institutes/Etc.	610.73692	RC735.5	Nursing
610.7(2)	R735-854	Medical education/Research	610.73699	RT95	Communicable disease nursing
610.70(1-9)	R741-832.5	By place			
610.70(7-8)	R741-769	America	610.9	R131-684	History
610.704	R771-804	Europe	610.9(3-9)	R150-684	By place
610.705	R810-821	Asia	610.90(1-4)	R134.8-149	By date
610.706	R822-824	Africa	610.90(24-31)	R146-147	15th-16th centuries
610.707	R743-749	North America	610.90(3-4)	R145-149	Modern
610.708	R757-769	South America	610.90(34-4)	R149	19th-20th centuries
610.709(3-4)	R831-832.5	Australia/New Zealand	610.902	R141-144	Medieval
610.72	R850-854	Research/Experimentation	610.903(2-3)	R148	17th-18th centuries
610.73	RM125	Nurses' manuals	610.93	R135-138.5	Ancient
610.73	RF52.5	Nursing	610.94	R484-575	Europe
610.73	RT	Nursing	610.941	R486-498.4	Great Britain
610.73(2-6)	RT89-120	Specialties	610.9417	R498.6-.9	Ireland
610.73(2-6)07	RT90-.3	Teaching	610.943	R509-512.5	Germany
610.730(5-6)	RT1	Serials/Societies	610.9436	R499-502	Austria
610.7301	RT84.5	Philosophy of	610.9438	R535-538	Poland
610.73019	RT86	Psychology of	610.944	R504-507	France
610.730202	RT52	Outlines/Syllabi/Etc.	610.945	R517-520	Italy
610.73021	RT29	Statistics/Surveys	610.946	R555-558	Spain
610.730218	RT85.4	Standards for care/ Audit/Etc.	610.9469	R559-562	Portugal
610.73023	RT82	The profession	610.947	R531-534	European Russia
610.73023	RT86.7-.75	Practice of	610.9481	R547-550	Norway
610.73025	RT25	Directories	610.9485	R551-554	Sweden
610.73028	RT44	Instruments/Apparatus/Etc.	610.9489	R539-542	Denmark
610.730285	RT50.5	Computer applications	610.94912	R543-546	Iceland
610.7303	RT21	Dictionaries/ Encyclopedias	610.9492	R526-529	Netherlands
			610.9493	R521-524	Belgium
			610.9494	R563-566	Switzerland
610.7306	RT3	Congresses	610.9495	R513-516	Greece

Dewey	LC	Descriptor
610.95	R581-644	Asia
610.951	R601-604	China
610.9519	R627-630	Korea
610.952	R623-626	Japan
610.9538	R591-594	Saudi Arabia
610.954	R605-608	India
610.95491	R604.2-.5	Pakistan
610.95493	R608.2-.5	Sri Lanka
610.955	R631-634	Iran
610.9561	R640-643	Turkey
610.957	R635-638	Asian Russia
610.959(3-7)	R609-612	Indochina
610.9598	R614-617	Indonesia
610.9599	R618-621	Philippines
610.96	R651-654	Africa
610.971	R461-464	Canada
610.972	R465-468	Mexico
610.9728	R469-472	Central America
610.9729	R473-476	West Indies
610.97(4-9)	R155-363	By state
610.973	R151-363	United States
610.98	R480-483	South America
610.99(5-6)	R681-684	Oceania
610.993	R675-678	New Zealand
610.994	R671-674	Australia
611	QM	Human anatomy
611.(018)	RB24-33	Pathological anatomy/ Histology
611.00(5/6)	QM1	Serials/Societies/Congresses
611.0014	QM81	Terminology
611.00222	QM25	Pictorial works
611.0025	QM17	Directories
611.003	QM7	Dictionaries/ Encyclopedias
611.007	QM30-33.3	Education
611.0072	QM41-43	Laboratories
611.0074	QM51	Museums/Exhibitions
611.009	QM11	History
611.0092	QM16	Biography
611.013	QM601-695	Embryology
611.018	QM550-577.8	Histology
611.0180(5/6)	QM550	Serials/Societies/Congresses
611.1	QM178-197	Vascular system
611.2	QM251-265	Respiration/Voice organs
611.3	QM301-367	Digestive organs
611.4	QM368-371	Glands
611.6	QM401-421	Urinary/Reproductive organs
611.7(1-5)	QM100-170	Musculoskeletal system
611.71	QM105-117	Skeleton/Osteology
611.73	QM151-170	Muscles
611.77	QM481-495	Integument
611.8(1-3)	QM451-471	Nervous system
611.8(4-8)	QM501-511	Sense organs
611.9	QM535-549	Regions of the body
612	QP	Physiology
612	RJ252	Physiology
612	RJ125-145	Child/Adolescent physiology
612	RB113	Physiological pathology
612.(4/7921)	QP190-246	Secretions (Milk/Sweat)
612.(46/6)	QP247-285	Urinary/Reproductive organs
612.00(5/6)	QP1	Serials/Societies/Congresses
612.0014	QP13	Terminology
612.0028	QP54-55	Instruments/Technique
612.003	QP11	Dictionaries/ Encyclopedias
612.007	QP39-47	Education
612.0072	QP51-53	Laboratories
612.009	QP21	History
612.0092	QP25-26	Biography
612.01426	QP135	Body temperature/ Regulation
612.0144	QP82-.2	Physiological adaptation
612.014465	RA1101	Cold
612.015	QP901-981	Experimental pharmacology
612.015	QP501-801	Animal biochemistry
612.0151	QP601-619	Enzymes
612.01524	QP531-535	Inorganic substances
612.01528	QP670-671	Pigments
612.0157	QP550-801	Organic substances
612.01575	QP561-563	Amino acids
612.01575	QP551-619	Proteins/Amino acids
612.01577	QP751-752	Lipids
612.01578	QP701-702	Carbohydrates
612.01579	QP620-625	Nucleic acids
612.01580(5/6)	QP901	Serials/Societies/Congresses
612.11	QP91-99.5	Blood
612.13	QP101-110	Circulation system
612.17	QP111-114	Heart
612.2	QP121-124	Respiratory organs
612.3	QP141-185.3	Nutrition
612.3	RJ206-235	Child/Adolescent feeding
612.3(1-6)	QP145-159	Physiology of digestive tract
612.391	QP136-139	Hunger/Thirst/Etc.
612.399	QP771-772	Vitamins
612.4	QP186-188.5	Glands/Endocrinology
612.405	QP571-572	Hormones
612.42	QP115	Lymphatic system
612.46	QP248-250.8	Urinary organs
612.6	QP251-285	Reproduction/Physiology of sex
612.6(5-8)	QP84-87	Growth to death
612.7(4-6)	QP301-321	Musculoskeletal system
612.8	QP351-495	Neurophysiology/ Psychology
612.8(4-8)	QP431-495	Senses
612.80(5/6)	QP351	Serials/Societies/Congresses
612.81	QP361-430	Nervous system
612.82	QP376-430	Brain
612.84	QP474-495	Vision
612.85	QP460-471	Hearing/Equilibrium
613	RA773-788	Personal health and hygiene
613	RA421-790.85	Prevention/Public health
613	RL87-94	Care/Hygiene
613-617	RA	Public aspects of medicine
613.0(5/6)	RA421	Serials/Societies
613.023	RA440.9	The profession
613.03	RA423	Dictionaries/ Encyclopedias
613.04	RA564.5-.9	By age group/Class/Etc.
613.04	RB210-212	Age/Sex influence on disease
613.0432	RJ240	Child immunization (General)
613.0432	RJ101-111	Hygiene/Care of children
613.06	RA422	Congresses
613.07	RA440-.8	Education
613.072	RA428-.5	Public health laboratories
613.072	RA440.85	Research
613.074	RA437-438	Museums/Exhibitions

Dewey	LC	Descriptor
613.076	RA430	Examinations
613.089	RA561-563	By ethnic group/Etc.
613.08996073	E185.88	Health
613.09	RA441-.5	World health
613.09	RA424	History
613.09(3-9)	RA443-558	By place
613.09(7-8)	RA443-482	America
613.092	RA424.4-.5	Biography
613.094	RA483-523	Europe
613.095	RA525-541	Asia
613.096	RA545-552	Africa
613.097	RA443-456	North America
613.0971	RA449-450	Canada
613.0972	RA451-452	Mexico
613.09728	RA453-454	Central America
613.09729	RA455-456	West Indies
613.0973	RA445-448.5	United States
613.098	RA457-482	South America
613.098	RA450.5-482	Latin America
613.10(5/6)	RA791-.2	Serials/Societies/Congresses
613.109(3-9)	RA801-954	By place
613.109(7/8)	RA801-844	America
613.1094	RA845-887	Europe
613.1095	RA891-934	Asia
613.1096	RA943-949	Africa
613.1097	RA802-816	North America
613.10971	RA809-810	Canada
613.10972	RA811-812	Mexico
613.109728	RA813-814	Central America
613.109729	RA815-816	West Indies
613.10973	RA804-807	United States
613.1098	RA817-844	South America
613.1099(5-6)	RA953-954	Pacific Islands
613.10993	RA952.5	New Zealand
613.10994	RA951-952	Australia
613.11	RA791-954	Climatology/Meteorology
613.122	RA794	Health resorts/Spas/Etc.
613.19(3-4)	GV450	Sunbathing/Nudism
613.620(5/6)	HD7260-.5	Serials/Societies
613.6207	HD7260.6-.62	Education
613.6209(4-9)	HD7651-7780.7	Industrial hygiene, By place
613.7	GV435-436.5	Physical tests
613.9	HQ31-64	Sex instruction/Ethics
613.9	HQ56-57.6	Teaching
613.9072	HQ60	Sex research
613.9081	HQ36	Men
613.9082	HQ46	Women
613.9083	HQ53	Children
613.90835	HQ35	Adolescents
613.90846	HQ55	Aged
613.9087	HQ54-.3	Handicapped adults
613.909(4-9)	HQ57.5-.6	Teaching sex, By place
613.94	RC888	Male contraception
613.94	RG136-.6	Contraception
613.942	RG138	Sterilization of women
614	RA1-418.5	Medicine and the state
614.(4-5)	RA421-790.85	Prevention/Public health
614.(4-5)0(5/6)	RA421	Serials/Societies
614.(4-5)023	RA440.9	The profession
614.(4-5)03	RA423	Dictionaries/ Encyclopedias
614.(4-5)04	RA564.5-.9	By age group/Class/Etc.
614.(4-5)06	RA422	Congresses
614.(4-5)07	RA440-.8	Education
614.(4-5)072	RA428-.5	Public health laboratories
614.(4-5)072	RA440.85	Research
614.(4-5)074	RA437-438	Museums/Exhibitions
614.(4-5)076	RA430	Examinations
614.(4-5)089	RA561-563	By ethnic group/Etc.
614.(4-5)09	RA424	History
614.(4-5)09	RA441-.5	World health
614.(4-5)09(3-9)	RA443-558	By place
614.(4-5)09(7-8)	RA443-482	America
614.(4-5)092	RA424.4-.5	Biography
614.(4-5)094	RA483-523	Europe
614.(4-5)095	RA525-541	Asia
614.(4-5)096	RA545-552	Africa
614.(4-5)097	RA443-456	North America
614.(4-5)0971	RA449-450	Canada
614.(4-5)0972	RA451-452	Mexico
614.(4-5)09728	RA453-454	Central America
614.(4-5)09729	RA455-456	West Indies
614.(4-5)0973	RA445-448.5	United States
614.(4-5)098	RA450.5-482	Latin America
614.(4-5)098	RA457-482	South America
614.(44-59)	RA643-645	Disease and public health
614.06	RA5-8	Health organizations
614.060(7-8)	RA10-237	America
614.0604	RA239-299	Europe
614.0605	RA303-340	Asia
614.0606	RA345-352	Africa
614.0607	RA10.7	North America
614.0607(4-9)	RA13	By city
614.0607(4-9)	RA15-182	By state
614.06071	RA184-186	Canada
614.06072	RA187-188	Mexico
614.06072(8/9)	RA191-194	Central America/West Indies
614.06073	RA11-182	United States
614.0608	RA198-235	South America
614.0609	RA10-388	Organization documents/ Reports
614.0609(3-6)	RA371-388	Australia/New Zealand/ Oceania
614.091734	RA771-.7	Rural health and hygiene
614.1	RA1148	Forensic psychology
614.1	RA1151	Forensic psychiatry
614.1	RA1001-1171	Forensic medicine
614.1	RA1055-1056	Medicolegal exam/ Testimony
614.10(5/6)	RA1001	Serials/Societies
614.10202	RA1028	Outlines
614.1021	RA1018.5	Statistics
614.103	RA1017	Dictionaries/ Encyclopedias
614.106	RA1016	Congresses
614.107	RA1027	Education
614.1072	RA1032-1038	Laboratories
614.1074	RA1042-.2	Museums/Exhibitions
614.109	RA1021-1022	History
614.1092	RA1025	Biography
614.4	RA648.5-653	Epidemics
614.4(3-8)	RA639-642	Transmission of disease
614.409(4-9)	RA650-653.5	By place
614.409(7-8)	RA650.5-.55	America
614.4094	RA650.6	Europe
614.4095	RA650.7	Asia
614.4096	RA650.8	Africa
614.4099(3-6)	RA650.9	Australia/New Zealand/ Oceania
614.44	RA404	Reporting cases of sickness
614.46	RA655-758	Quarantine
614.4609(4-9)	RA664-758	By place
614.46094	RA700-737	Europe

Dewey	LC	Descriptor
614.46095	RA738-751	Asia
614.46096	RA753-755	Africa
614.46097	RA664-677	North America
614.460971	RA671	Canada
614.460972	RA673	Mexico
614.4609728	RA675	Central America
614.4609729	RA677	West Indies
614.460973	RA665-667	United States
614.46098	RA678-699	South America
614.46099(3-4)	RA756-.5	Australia/New Zealand
614.46099(5-6)	RA758	Pacific islands
614.47	RA638	Immunization & public health
614.48	RA761-766	Disinfection/Sterilization
614.6	RA619-636.7	Undertaking/Cemeteries/Etc.
615.(1/5)	RV401-411	Materia medica/Therapeutics
615.(1/5)	RX601-675	Materia medica/Therapeutics
615.(2-3)	RS160-167	Pharmacognosy/Substances
615.(5)	RM	Pharmacology/Therapeutics
615.(5)0(5/6)	RM1	Serials/Societies
615.(5)014	RM38	Terminology/Nomenclature
615.(5)0202	RM106	Outlines/Syllabi/Etc.
615.(5)025	RM39	Directories
615.(5)03	RM36	Dictionaries/Encyclopedias
615.(5)05	RM16	Yearbooks
615.(5)06	RM21	Congresses
615.(5)07	RM108	Education
615.(5)072	RM111	Experimental therapeutics
615.(5)076	RM105	Problems/Exercises/Exams
615.(5)09	RM41-47	History
615.(5)09(4-9)	RM47	By place
615.(5)090(3-4)	RM45	Modern
615.(5)0901	RM43	Ancient
615.(5)0902	RM44	Medieval
615.(5)092	RM61-62	Biography
615.(5/8)	RM182-190	Other therapeutic procedures
615.1	RS	Pharmacy/Materia medica
615.1	RS153-441	Materia medica
615.10(5/6)	RS1	Serials/Societies
615.10012	RS53	Classification of drugs
615.10014	RS55	Terminology/Nomenclature/Etc.
615.10202	RS98	Outlines/Syllabi/Etc.
615.1023	RS100-.4	Practice/Economics
615.1023	RS122.5-.9	The profession
615.1025	RS74-76	Directories
615.1028	RS355-356	Pharmaceutical supplies
615.10285	RS122.2	Computer applications
615.103	RS51	Dictionaries/Encyclopedias
615.105	RS21	Yearbooks
615.106	RS3	Congresses
615.107	RS101-121.9	Education
615.1070(4-9)	RS110-121	Education, By place
615.1072	RS122	Research/Experimentation
615.1074	RS123	Museums/Exhibitions
615.1076	RS97	Problems/Examinations/Etc.
615.1078	RS93	Laboratory manuals
615.109	RS61-68	History
615.109(4-9)	RS67	By place
615.1090(3-4)	RS65	Modern
615.10901	RS63	Ancient
615.10902	RS64	Medieval
615.1092	RS71-73	Biography
615.11	RS139-141.9	Pharmacopoeias
615.11	RV415-431	Pharmacy
615.13	RS125-131.9	Formularies/Prescriptions/Etc.
615.13	RS151.2-.9	Dispensatories
615.14	RM139	Prescription writing
615.14	RM138	Drug prescribing
615.19	RS192-199	Pharmaceutical processes
615.19	RS400-431	Pharmaceutical chemistry
615.19	RS441	Drugs/Microscopical exam.
615.1901	RS189-190	Assay methods/Standardization
615.328	RM259	Vitamin therapy
615.329	RM409	Antibacterial agents
615.329	RM265-267	Antibiotic therapy
615.36	RM283-298	Endocrinotherapy/Organotherapy
615.37	RM270-282	Serum therapy/Immunotherapy
615.37	RM370-371	On the immune system
615.372	QR189-.5	Vaccines
615.5	RM121-127	Therapeutics
615.50202	RM122	Outlines/Syllabi/Etc.
615.5076	RM126	Problems/Exercises/Exams
615.5078	RM123	Laboratory manuals
615.53	RV	Medicine/Botanic/Eclectic/Etc.
615.53	RV1-9	Botanic/Thomsonian medicine
615.53	RV11-431	Eclectic medicine
615.53	RZ	Other systems of medicine
615.53	RZ409.7-999	Miscellaneous treatments
615.530(5/6)	RV1	Serials/Societies
615.530(5/6)	RV11	Serials/Societies
615.530202	RV52	Outlines/Syllabi/Etc.
615.5305	RV15	Yearbooks
615.5306	RV21	Congresses
615.5307	RV100-181	Education
615.53070(4-9)	RV100-181	By place
615.53070(7-8)	RV151	Other American regions
615.530704	RV170-181	Europe
615.530704(2-9)	RV181	Other European regions
615.5307041	RV171	Great Britain
615.530707	RV100-151	America
615.5307073	RV100-101	United States
615.53076	RV51	Problems/Exercises/Exams
615.5309	RV61	History of eclectic medicine
615.53092	RV7-8	Biography
615.53092	RV71-76	Biography
615.532	RX	Homeopathy
615.5320(5/6)	RX1	Serials/Societies
615.53201	RX81-85	Theory/Principles
615.532025	RX46	Directories
615.53203	RX41	Dictionaries/Encyclopedias
615.53205	RX11	Yearbooks
615.53206	RX21	Congresses
615.53207	RX91-101	Education
615.532076	RX73.3	Problems/Exercises/Exams
615.53209	RX51	History
615.532092	RX61-66	Biography
615.533	RZ301-399	Osteopathy
615.5330(5/6)	RZ301	Serials/Societies
615.5330202	RZ343.2	Outlines/Syllabi/Etc.
615.533023	RZ336	The profession

Dewey	LC	Descriptor	Dewey	LC	Descriptor
615.533025	RZ333	Directories	615.831	RM835-844	Phototherapy
615.53305	RZ311	Yearbooks	615.83106	RM831.5	Congresses
615.53306	RZ313	Congresses	615.832	RM865-868.5	Thermotherapy
615.53307	RZ337-338	Education	615.8325	RV211	Fevers
615.533076	RZ343	Problems/Exercises/Exams	615.8325	RX211	Fevers
615.53309	RZ321-325	Osteopathy, History	615.8329	RM863	Cryotherapy
615.53309(4-9)	RZ325	By place	615.836	RM733	Respiration as a remedy
615.533092	RZ331-332	Biography	615.836	RM824-827	Aerotherapy
615.534	RZ210-275	Chiropractic	615.84	RM845-862.5	Radiotherapy
615.5340(5/6)	RZ201	Serials/Societies	615.845	RM869-890	Electrotherapy
615.5340202	RZ243.2	Outlines/Syllabi/Etc.	615.851	RZ400-408	Mental healing
615.5340222	RZ235	Pictorial works	615.851	RZ430	Mesmerism/Animal
615.534023	RZ236	The profession			magnetism/Etc.
615.534023	RZ232.2-.4	Practice/Economics of	615.8515	RM735-.7	Occupational therapy
615.534025	RZ233	Directories	615.85153	RM736.7	Recreational therapy
615.53405	RZ211	Yearbooks	615.853	RM801-822	Hydrotherapy
615.53406	RZ213	Congresses	615.854	RM214-258	Diet therapy
615.53407	RZ237-238	Education	615.88	RZ510	Phrenology
615.534076	RZ243	Problems/Exercises/Exams	615.88	RZ600	Radiesthesia
615.53409	RZ221-225	Chiropractic, History	615.882	GR880	Folk medicine
615.53409(4-9)	RZ225	By place	615.886	RS250-252	Commercial preparations
615.534092	RZ231-232	Biography	615.886	RM671-.5	Patent medicines
615.535	RZ433-445	Naturopathy	615.9	RA1190-1270	Toxicology/Poisons
615.542	RJ434	Therapeutics	615.9(1-54)	RA1230-1270	Poisons, By type
615.542	RJ52-53	Therapeutics	615.90021	RA1215.5-.52	Statistics
615.542	RJ424	Therapeutics	615.9007	RA1198-.3	Education
615.58	RM260-263	Chemotherapy	615.90072	RA1199	Research
615.6	RM147-180	Administration of drugs	615.9009	RA1195-1197	History
615.7	RM300-666	Drugs and their actions	615.902	RA1229	Industrial toxicology
615.7	RM301.55	Drug metabolism	615.907	RA1221-1223	Examination for poisons
615.7	RM301.5	Pharmacokinetics	615.91	RA1245-1247	Gaseous poisons
615.704	RM301.3	Drug response/Special	615.92	RA1230-1231	Inorganic poisons
		factors	615.94	RA1255	Animal poisons
615.7045	RM302-.3	Drug interactions	615.95	RA1235-1242	Organic poisons
615.7072	RM301.25	Research	615.952	RA1250	Vegetable poisons
615.71	RM345-349	On the cardiovascular	615.954	RA1258-1260	Food poisons
		system	616	RC581-951	Internal medicine
615.718	RM335	On blood cells/Etc.			specialities
615.718	RM340	On blood coagulation	616	RC	Internal medicine
615.72	RM388-.5	On respiratory system	616-618	RV211-391	Diseases/Treatment/Etc.
615.73	RM355-365	On the digestive system	616-618	RX211-581	Diseases/Treatment/Etc.
615.761	RM375-377	On the urinary organs	616-618.(062)	RZ260-265	Diseases/Injuries/Treatment
615.766	RM380-386	On reproductive organs	616-618.(062)	RZ347-397.5	Diseases/Treatment/Etc.
615.773	RM312	On the skeletal muscles	616.(042/55)	RL793	Congential disorders/
615.778	RM303-309	Drugs acting on the skin			Moles/Etc.
615.78	RM315-333	Neuropsychopharmacology	616.(1-9)	RB157	Acquired disease
615.8(31/4)	RM831-862.5	Phototherapy/	616.(15/42)	RX305-309	Blood/Lymphatics/Etc.
		Radiotherapy/Etc.			diseases
615.82	RM930-931	Rehabilitation therapy	616.(151-7/42)	RX309	Individual diseases
615.82	RM695-890	Physical medicine/Therapy	616.003	RC41	Dictionaries/
615.820(6/5)	RM695	Serials/Societies			Encyclopedias
615.82023	RM705	The profession	616.01	QR46-47	Medical/Etc. microbiology
615.82023	RM713	Practice/Economics of	616.01	QR	Microbiology
615.82025	RM697	Directories	616.0100(5/6)	QR1	Serials/Societies/Congresses
615.82028	RM698-.5	Instruments/Apparatus/Etc.	616.010012	QR12	Classification
615.8203	RM696.5	Dictionaries/	616.010014	QR11	Terminology
		Encyclopedias	616.0100222	QR54	Pictorial works
615.8206	RM696	Congresses	616.010028	QR65-71	Technique/Equipment
615.8207	RM706-707	Education	616.01003	QR9	Dictionaries/
615.82072	RM708	Research			Encyclopedias
615.82076	RM701.6	Problems/Exercises/Exams	616.01007	QR61-63	Education
615.8209	RM699-.3	Physical medicine, History	616.010072	QR64-.8	Laboratories
615.8209(4-9)	RM699.3	Physical medicine, By place	616.01009	QR21-22	History
615.82092	RM699.5-.7	Biography	616.010092	QR30-31	Biography
615.822	RM719-727	Mechanotherapy	616.014	QR75-97	Bacteria
615.83	RM862.7	Ultrasonic therapy	616.024	RC81-82	Popular medicine
615.830(5/6)	RM831	Serials/Societies	616.025	RC86-88.9	Medical emergencies

Dewey	LC	Descriptor	Dewey	LC	Descriptor
616.029	R726.5-.8	Terminal care/Dying	616.206	RC735	Special therapies
616.042	RB155	Heredity/Medical genetics	616.207	RC711	Pathology
616.047	RB153-154	Infection (And resistance)	616.2075	RC733-734	Examination/Diagnosis
616.047	RB127-150	Manifestations of diseases	616.212	RF361	Rhinitis
616.0472	RB127	Pain	616.212	RF341-437	Rhinology
616.0473	RB131	Inflammation	616.21206	RF348-349	Therapeutics
616.07	RB	Pathology	616.212075	RF345	Examination/Diagnosis
616.0700(5/6)	RB1	Serials/Societies	616.22	RF526	Diseases of the vocal cords
616.070014	RB115	Terminology	616.22	RF522	Larynx neurological disorders
616.0700202	RB120	Outlines			
616.070025	RB10	Directories	616.22	RF460-547	Laryngology
616.07006	RB3	Congresses	616.22075	RF476	Examination/Diagnosis
616.07007	RB123-124	Education	616.23	RC778	Diseases of the bronchi
616.070076	RB119	Examinations	616.23	RF529	Diseases of the trachea
616.07009	RB15-.2	History	616.24	RC756-776	Diseases of the lungs
616.070092	RB16-17	Biography	616.25	RC751	Pleurisy
616.071	RB151-214	Theories of disease/Etiology	616.27	RC754	Diseases of the mediastinum
616.075	RC71-78.7	Examination/Diagnosis			
616.075	RB37-55.2	Clinical/Laboratory pathology	616.3	RV271-276	Digestive system diseases
			616.3	RX331-336	Diseases of digestive system
616.0757(5)	R895-920	Radiology/Nuclear medicine	616.3 (3-4)	RC816-840	Stomach/Duodenum diseases
616.0759	RB57	Autopsies			
616.078	RA1063-.4	Death determination/Etc.	616.31	RC815-.6	Diseases of the mouth
616.08	RC49-52	Psychosomatic medicine	616.31	RC810	Visceroptosis/Splanchnoptosis
616.08	RL701-751	Psychosomatic/Nerve disorders			
			616.313	RC168.M8	Mumps
616.1	RC666-701	Cardiovascular diseases	616.314	RF491-496	Tonsillitis/Etc.
616.1(1-8)	RC692-700	Diseases	616.32	RC815.7	Diseases of the esophagus
616.100(5/6)	RC666	Serials/Societies	616.32	RF481-499	Pharynx/Tonsil diseases
616.1003	RC666.3	Dictionaries/Encyclopedias	616.3206	RF483	Therapeutics
			616.32075	RF482	Examination/Diagnosis
616.1006	RC666.2	Congresses	616.33	RX332	Diseases of the stomach
616.1009	RC666.5	History	616.33	RC799-869	Gastroenterology
616.10092	RC666.7-.72	Biography	616.3300(5/6)	RC799	Serials/Societies
616.107	RC669.9	Pathology	616.330028	RC805	Instruments/Etc.
616.1075	RC670-.5	Examination/Diagnosis	616.3307	RC802.9	Pathology
616.12	RC681-688	Diseases of the heart	616.33075	RC803-805	Examination/Diagnosis
616.12(2-9)	RC685	Individual diseases (Heart)	616.34	RC860-862	Diseases of the intestines
616.12043	RC687	Congenital anomalies	616.34(2-4)	RC862	Other diseases
616.1206	RC683.8-684	Therapeutics	616.3428	RC861	Constipation
616.1207	RC682.9	Pathology	616.35	RX341-346	Diseases of the rectum
616.12075	RC683-.5	Examination/Diagnosis	616.35	RC864-866	Proctology
616.13	RC691-701	Diseases of the blood vessels	616.36(2-5)	RC848-858	Individual diseases (Liver)
			616.3607	RC846.9	Pathology
616.13	RX311-316	Diseases of circulatory system	616.36075	RC847	Examination/Diagnosis
			616.362	RC845-858	Diseases of the liver/Etc.
616.13	RV251-256	Circulatory system diseases	616.362	RX333	Diseases of the liver
616.13043	RC701	Congenital anomalies	616.39	RC627.5-632	Metabolic diseases
616.1307	RC691.4	Pathology	616.39	RC620-627	Nutritional diseases
616.13075	RC691.5-.6	Examination/Diagnosis	616.399	RA1116	Starvation
616.15	RC633-647.5	Blood diseases	616.4	RC648-665	Endocrine gland diseases
616.2	RX321-326	Diseases of respiratory system	616.47	RB140-.5	Growth disorders
			616.5	RL130-169	Glands/Hair/Nail Diseases
616.2	RV261-266	Respiratory system diseases	616.5	RV381-391	Diseases of the skin
616.2	RC705-779	Respiratory system diseases	616.5	RL	Dermatology
616.2	RC737-.5	Apnea	616.5	RX561-581	Diseases of the skin
616.2	RC742	Empyema	616.500(5/6)	RL1	Serials/Societies
616.2(01-49)	RC779	Other respiratory diseases	616.50014	RL39	Nomenclature/Terminology
616.2(2-3)	RF510-540	Larynx/Trachea/Etc.	616.500202	RL74.3	Outlines/Syllabi/Etc.
616.2(2-3)008	RF511	By age group/Class/Etc.	616.500222	RL81	Pictorial works
616.2(2-3)03	RF540	Rehabilitation	616.50025	RL43	Directories
616.2(2-3)07	RF511.5	Pathology	616.50028	RL55	Instruments
616.2(2-3)075	RF512-514	Examination/Diagnosis	616.5003	RL41	Dictionaries/Encyclopedias
616.201	RC746	Croup			
616.203	RC150-.9	Influenza	616.5005	RL26	Yearbooks
616.204	RC204	Whooping cough	616.5006	RL31	Congresses

Dewey	LC	Descriptor
616.5007	RL77	Education
616.50072	RL48-49	Laboratories
616.50074	RL46.9-47	Museums/Exhibitions
616.50076	RL74.2	Problems/Examinations/Etc.
616.5008(3-6)	RL73	By age group/Class/Etc.
616.5009	RL46	History
616.50092	RL46.2-.3	Biography
616.5027	RL79	Research/Experimentation
616.506	RL110-120	Therapeutics
616.51	RL231-241	Dermatitis
616.52	RL201-331	Skin inflammations/ Infections
616.521	RL251	Eczema
616.523	RL221	Boils/Etc.
616.524	RL283	Impetigo
616.526	RL321	Psoriasis
616.544	RL471	Verrucae/Warts
616.544	RL451	Scleroderma
616.544	RL435	Keratosis/Ichthyosis
616.544	RL401-489	Hypertrophies
616.544	RL411	Corns/Callosities
616.545	RL675	Chronic ulcers/Bedsores
616.546	RL431	Hypertrichosis
616.55	RL790	Pigmentations/Albinism
616.57	RL760-785	Diseases due to parasites
616.6	RC870-923	Urology
616.6	RG484-485	Female urology
616.6	RV281-286	Genitourinary system diseases
616.6	RX351-356	Genitourinary system diseases
616.6(5/8)	RC875-899.5	Diseases/Disorders of genitals
616.600(5/6)	RC870	Serials/Societies
616.60076	RC873	Examinations/Problems
616.60092	RC870.9-.92	Biography
616.607	RC873.9	Pathology
616.6075	RC874	Examination/Diagnosis
616.61	RC902-918	Diseases of the kidneys
616.61	RC922	Diseases of the ureters
616.61100(5/6)	RC902.A1	Serials/Societies
616.61006	RC902.A2	Congresses
616.6107	RC903.9	Pathology
616.61075	RC904	Examination/Diagnosis
616.612	RC907	Nephritis/Etc.
616.62	RC892	Diseases of the urethra
616.62	RC919-921	Diseases of the bladder
616.62(2-4)	RC921	Individual bladder diseases
616.622	RC916	Urinary calculi
616.624	RC901.8	Urinary tract infections
616.63	RC905	Albuminuria/Etc.
616.63	RC900-923	Diseases of the urinary organs
616.630028	RC901.5-.7	Instruments/Etc.
616.63043	RC923	Congenital anomalies
616.6307	RC900.9	Pathology
616.63075	RC901	Examination/Diagnosis
616.633	RC912	Pyuria
616.635	RC915	Uremia
616.65	RC899	Diseases of the prostate
616.65043	RC881.5-883.5	Congenital anomalies
616.66	RC896	Diseases of the penis
616.66	RC894	Diseases of the prepuce
616.67	RC897	Diseases of the scrotum
616.68	RC898-.3	Diseases of the testes/Etc.
616.692	RC889	Impotence/Infertility
616.7	RC925-935	Musculoskeletal system disease
616.77	RC924-.5	Connective tissue diseases
616.8	RV241-246	Nervous system diseases
616.8	RC346-429	Neurology
616.8	RC321-571	Neurology/Psychiatry
616.8	RX281-301	Diseases of the nervous system
616.835	RC180-181	Poliomyelitis
616.852	RC530-552	Neuroses
616.858	RC554-569.5	Personality disorders
616.8583	HQ71-72	Sexual deviations/Crimes
616.85834	HQ75-76.8	Homosexuality/Lesbianism
616.85835	HQ79	Sadism/Masochism/ Fetishism
616.8588	RC569.7-571	Mental retardation
616.86	HV5823-.5	Drug testing
616.86107	HV5045	Psychology of alcoholism
616.89	RC435-571	Psychiatry
616.89	RC512-571	Psychopathology
616.89(2-8)	RC512-528	Psychoses
616.89022	RJ502.5-503	Child/Adolescent psychiatry
616.8914	RC475-489	Psychotherapy
616.89162	RC490-499	Hypnotism/Suggestion therapy
616.8917	RC500-510	Psychoanalysis
616.9	RV221-225	Diseases/Specific infections
616.9	RC110-216	Infectious/Parasitic diseases
616.9	RX221-226	Diseases/Specific infection
616.912	RC183-.9	Smallpox
616.914	RC125	Chicken pox
616.916	RC182.R8	Rubella/German measles
616.917	RC182.S2	Scarlet fever
616.92	RC115-116	Bacterial diseases
616.92(2/5)	RC114-.7	Rickettsial diseases/Viruses
616.9222	RC199-.9	Typhus
616.9232	RC171-179	Plague (Bubonic)
616.927	RC182.S12	Salmonella infections
616.9272	RC187-197	Typhoid fever
616.928	RC206-216	Yellow fever
616.93	RC118-.7	Spirochetal/Protozoan diseases
616.9313	RC138-.9	Diphtheria
616.9318	RC185	Tetanus
616.932	RC126-134	Cholera
616.935	RC140	Dysentery
616.9362	RC156-166	Malaria
616.951	RC200-203	Venereal diseases
616.953	RC148	Hydrophobia/Rabies
616.96	RC688	Parasites
616.96	RC119-.7	Parasitic diseases
616.97	RC581-606	Immunological diseases
616.9802	RC1030-1160	Travel/Transportation medicine
616.98022	RC1000-1015	Submarine medicine
616.98023	RC970-971	Military medicine
616.98024	RC981-986	Naval medicine
616.9803	RC963-969	Industrial medicine
616.9881	RC955-958	Arctic medicine
616.9883	RC960-962	Tropical medicine
616.989	RC91-103	Diseases by physical agents
616.991	RC182.R4	Rheumatic fever
616.992	RD651-678	Neoplasms/Tumors/ Oncology
616.992	RC254-282	Neoplasms/Tumors/ Oncology

Dewey	LC	Descriptor
616.995	RC306-320.5	Tuberculosis
616.998	RC154-.9	Leprosy
617	RV301-311	Surgery
617	RD	Surgery
617	RX366-376	Surgery adapted to homeopathy
617.(8/52-531)	RV341-347	Ear/Nose/Throat diseases
617.(8/523/531)	RX441-456	Diseases of ear/Nose/Throat
617.00(5/6)	RD1	Societies/Serials
617.0014	RD16	Nomenclature/Etc.
617.0025	RD10	Directories of surgeons
617.003	RD17	Dictionaries/ Encyclopedias
617.005	RD9	Yearbooks
617.006	RD9.2	Congresses
617.007	RD28	Education
617.0072	RD29-.5	Research/Experimentation
617.01	RD98-.4	Surgical complications
617.023	RD27.4-.44	Practice of surgery/ Economics
617.023	RD27.5	Profession of surgery
617.023(4-9)	RD27.42-.44	By place
617.023(4-9)	RD27.44	Other areas
617.0237(4-9)	RD27.43	By state
617.02373	RD27.42-.43	United States
617.026	RD92-97.8	Emergency surgery
617.044	RD156	War wounds
617.06	RD736	Special therapies
617.07	RD57	Surgical pathology
617.09	RD19-27.3	History
617.09(4-9)	RD27.3	By place
617.090(3-4)	RD27	Modern
617.0901	RD23	Ancient
617.0901	RD22	Primitive
617.0902	RD25	Medieval
617.092	RD27.34-.35	Biography
617.1027	RC1200-1245	Sports medicine
617.1062	RZ270-275	Wounds/Injuries
617.11	RA1085	Burns
617.122	RA1091	Electricity
617.14	RA1121	Wounds/Injuries/Accidents
617.15	RD101-103	Fractures (General)
617.18	RA1071-1081	Asphyxia
617.21	RD59	Surgical/Traumatic shock
617.3	RD701-811	Orthopedic surgery
617.3(7-9)	RD761-789	Deformities/Disorders
617.300(5/6)	RD701	Societies/Serials
617.300202	RD732.7	Outlines/Syllabi/Etc.
617.300222	RD733.2	Pictorial works
617.30028	RD755-757	Orthopedic instruments/Etc.
617.30028	RD757	Other apparatus
617.3003	RD723	Dictionaries/ Encyclopedias
617.3005	RD711	Yearbooks
617.3006	RD715	Congresses
617.30076	RD732.6	Problems/Exercises/ Examination
617.3008	RD732.3	By age group/Class/Etc.
617.303	RD792-811	Physical rehabilitation
617.30300(5/6)	RD792	Serials/Societies
617.3030025	RD794	Directories
617.303006	RD792.5	Congresses
617.303007	RD807-809	Education
617.30309	RD795-.5	History
617.303092	RD796	Biography
617.30754	RD734	Examination/Diagnoses
617.309	RD725-726	History

Dewey	LC	Descriptor
617.309(4-9)	RD726	By place
617.3092	RD727-728	Biography
617.37	RD762	Posture disorders
617.371	RD763	Head/Neck
617.374	RD766	Trunk
617.375	RD768-771	Spine/Back
617.376	RD772	Hip
617.39	RD775-789	Extremities
617.397	RD776-778.5	Upper extremities/Arm
617.398	RD779-789	Lower extremities/Leg
617.4	RD520-599.5	Surgery by system/Organ
617.47	RD680-688	Locomotor system (Surgery)
617.470592	RD756	Artificial limbs
617.470592	RD755.5	Implants
617.5(1/3)	RV291	Diseases of the head/Neck
617.51	RF	Otorhinolaryngology
617.51(1-86)	RF49	Diseases
617.5100(5/6)	RF1	Serials/Societies
617.510014	RF24	Nomenclature/Etc.
617.510025	RF28	Directories
617.51003	RF23	Dictionaries/ Encyclopedias
617.51005	RF11	Yearbooks
617.51006	RF16	Congresses
617.510072	RF29-30	Laboratories
617.510074	RF32-33	Museums/Etc.
617.51008	RF47	By age group/Class/Etc.
617.510092	RF37-38	Biography
617.51044	RF50	Wounds/Injuries
617.51059	RF51-52	Surgery
617.5106	RF53-54	Therapeutics
617.51061	RF55	Materia medica/ Pharmacology
617.5107	RF47.5	Pathology
617.510754	RF48-.5	Examination/Diagnosis
617.5109	RF25-26	History
617.5109(4-9)	RF26	Otorhinolaryngology, By place
617.523	RF350	Surgery
617.523	RX451	Diseases of the nose
617.531	RF484-.5	Surgery
617.531	RX456	Diseases of the throat
617.533	RF516-517	Surgery
617.54	RV293	Chest/Abdomen diseases
617.54	RX360	Diseases of the chest
617.55	RV297	Diseases of the pelvis
617.55	RG482-483	Diseases of the pelvis
617.6	RK	Dentistry
617.6(07/3)	RK301-493	Oral/Dental pathology/ Diseases
617.600(5/6)	RK1	Serials/Societies
617.60014	RK28	Nomenclature
617.60019	RK53	Psychological aspects
617.600202	RK57.5	Outlines/Syllabi/Etc.
617.60021	RK52-.4	Statistics
617.60025	RK37	Directories
617.600285	RK240	Computer applications
617.6003	RK27	Dictionaries/ Encyclopedias
617.6005	RK16	Yearbooks
617.6006	RK21	Congresses
617.6007	RK71-231	Education
617.60072	RK38-39	Laboratories
617.60072	RK80	Research/Experimentation
617.60074	RK68-69	Museums/Exhibitions
617.60076	RK57	Problems/Examinations/Etc.

Dewey	LC	Descriptor
617.6008(3-6)	RK306	By age group/Class/Etc.
617.6008(3-6)	RK55	By age group/Class/Etc.
617.60089	RK55.3	By race/Ethnic group/Etc.
617.6009	RK29-34	History of dentistry
617.6009(4-9)	RK34	Dentistry, By place
617.60090(3-4)	RK33	Modern
617.600901	RK31	Ancient
617.600902	RK32	Medieval
617.60092	RK41-43	Biography
617.6044	RK490-493	Wounds/Injuries
617.605	RK529-535	Oral surgery
617.605	RK501-519	Operative dentistry
617.605008(3-6)	RK529.5	By age group/Class/Etc.
617.60592	RK533	Transplants
617.606	RK318-320	Therapeutics
617.6070(1-9)	RK86-231	Education, By place
617.60704	RK114-184	Europe
617.60705	RK186-207	Asia
617.60706	RK214-221	Africa
617.60707	RK86-106	North America
617.607071	RK98	Canada
617.607072	RK100	Mexico
617.6070728	RK102-103	Central America
617.6070729	RK105-106	West Indies
617.607073	RK91-97	United States
617.60708	RK111-113	South America
617.60709(5-6)	RK231	Oceania
617.607093	RK227.5	New Zealand
617.607094	RK227	Australia
617.63	RX540	Diseases of the teeth
617.6307	RK307	Pathology
617.630754	RK308-310	Examination/Diagnosis
617.632	RK361-450	Periodontics
617.634	RK340-341	Diseases of enamel/Dentine
617.6342	RK351-356	Endodontics
617.64	RK520-528	Orthodontics
617.66	RK531	Exodontics
617.67	RK331	Caries
617.69	RK641-667	Prosthetic dentistry
617.7	RV321-331	Diseases of the eye
617.7	RX410-431	Diseases of the eye
617.7	RE	Opthalmology
617.7(2-8)	RE46-52	Diseases of the eye
617.7(5/12)	RE91-94	Vision disorders/Blindness
617.700(5/6)	RE1	Serials/Societies
617.70014	RE20	Nomenclature/Terminology/Etc.
617.700222	RE71	Pictorial works
617.70025	RE22	Directories
617.70028	RE73	Instruments/Apparatus/Etc.
617.7003	RE21	Dictionaries/Encyclopedias
617.7005	RE6	Yearbooks
617.7006	RE11	Congresses
617.70072	RE56-58	Research/Experimentation
617.7023	RE72-.5	Practice of
617.7043	RE906	Congenital abnormalities
617.7059	RE80-87	Surgery
617.70754	RE75-79	Examination/Diagnosis
617.709	RE26-30	Ophthalmology, History
617.709(4-9)	RE30	By place
617.7092	RE31-36	Biography
617.713	RE831-840	Wounds/Injuries
617.719	RE328	Diseases of the sclera
617.719	RE336-340	Diseases of the cornea
617.72	RE350-355	Diseases of the uvea
617.73	RE551-661	Diseases of the retina

Dewey	LC	Descriptor
617.73	RE725-780	Neuro-ophthalmology
617.74	RE714-715	Diseases of the eyeball
617.741	RE871	Glaucoma
617.742	RE401-461	Diseases of the lens
617.746	RE501	Diseases of the vitreous body
617.75(2)	RE940-981	Optometry/Opticians
617.755	RE925-939	Errors of refraction
617.759075	RE918-921	Color vision tests/Charts
617.764	RE201-216	Lacrimal gland/Duct diseases
617.771	RE121-155	Diseases of the eyelids
617.773	RE310-326	Diseases of the conjunctiva
617.78	RE711	Diseases of the orbit
617.79	RE986-988	Artificial eyes
617.8	RF320	Deaf-mutism
617.8	RF110-320	Otology/Diseases of ear
617.8	RX446	Diseases of the ear
617.8(1-2)	RF175-200	External ear/Auricle diseases
617.800202	RF58	Outlines/Syllabi/Etc.
617.800222	RF145	Pictorial works
617.800222	RF81	Pictorial works
617.80028	RF298-310	Instruments/Etc.
617.80028	RF87	Instruments/Etc.
617.8007	RF62	Education
617.80076	RF57	Problems/Exercises/Etc.
617.80076	RF131-132	Examinations/Problems
617.8008(1-8)	RF122.5	By age group/Class/Etc.
617.80089	RF122.7	By race/Ethnic group/Etc.
617.801	RF155	Complications/Sequelae
617.8023	RF85-.7	Practice/Economics
617.8027	RF63	Research/Experimentation
617.804(2-3)	RF292	Hereditary deafness/Congenital
617.8059	RF295	Surgery
617.8059	RF126-127	Surgery
617.806	RF124	Therapeutics
617.80754	RF123	Examination/Diagnosis
617.809	RF110-111	Otology, History
617.809(4-9)	RF111	Otology, By place
617.84	RF220-228	Middle ear diseases
617.85	RF210	Tympanic membrane diseases
617.86	RF230	Eustachian tubes
617.87	RF235	Mastoid process diseases
617.882	RF260-275	Internal ear diseases
617.89	RF286-320	Audiology
617.8900(5-6)	RF286	Serials/Societies
617.8006	RF286.5	Congresses
617.890076	RF291.3	Problems/Exercises/Etc.
617.89008	RF291.5	By age group/Class/Etc.
617.91	RD32-33.9	Operative surgery
617.9101	RD91-.5	Sterilization (Operative)
617.917	RD63-73	Operating rooms/Instruments
617.919	RD49-52	Pre/Post operative care
617.919	RD58	Processes after operations
617.95	RD130	Prosthesis/Artificial organs
617.95	RD118-120.5	Plastic surgery
617.95	RD120.7-129.5	Transplantation
617.96	RD78.3-87.3	Anesthesiology
617.99	RD151-498	Military/Naval surgery
617.9909(3-9)	RD200-498	By place
617.99094	RD268-441	Europe
617.99095	RD445-476	Asia
617.99096	RD481-489	Africa

Dewey	LC	Descriptor
617.990971	RD216	Canada
617.990972	RD221	Mexico
617.9909728	RD224-225	Central America
617.9909729	RD231-232	West Indies
617.990973	RD200-214	United States
617.99098	RD235-267	South America
617.99099(5-6)	RD498	Oceania
617.990993	RD493.5	New Zealand
617.990994	RD493	Australia
618	RG	Gynecology and obstetrics
618	RV361-365	Gynecology/Obstetrics
618	RX460-476	Gynecology/Obstetrics
618.(2-3)	RG551-591	Pregnancy
618.(2-8)	RG500-991	Obstetrics
618.00(5/6)	RX460	Gyn. serials/Societies
618.07	RG77	Pathology
618.09(4-9)	RG67	Gynecology, By place
618.1	RG316	Diseases of the endrometrium
618.1(1-7)	RG211-485	Female genital organs/ Diseases
618.1(1/2)	RG421-481	Diseases of the ovary/ Oviducts
618.100(5/6)	RG1	Serials/Societies
618.10014	RG47	Nomenclature/Etc.
618.10019	RG103.5	Psychological aspects
618.100222	RG79	Pictorial works
618.10025	RG32-33	Directories of gynecologists
618.1003	RG45	Dictionaries/ Encyclopedias
618.1005	RG26	Yearbooks
618.1006	RG31	Congresses
618.10072	RG17-18	Laboratories/Institutes/Etc.
618.10074	RG21-.2	Museums/Exhibitions
618.1009	RG51-67	History of gynecology
618.100901	RG53	Primitive
618.100901	RG57-59	Ancient
618.100902	RG61	Medieval
618.10092	RG71-76	Biography
618.100939	RG55	Oriental
618.106	RG306	Therapeutics
618.10754	RG304	Examination/Diagnosis
618.14	RG301-391	Diseases of the uterus
618.14	RG310-314	Diseases of the cervix uteri
618.142	RG218	Infectious diseases
618.142	RG312	Cervicitis
618.143	RG314	Erosion
618.145	RG104-.6	Operative gynecology
618.15	RG268-272	Diseases of the vagina
618.16	RG261-266	Diseases of the vulva
618.17	RG159-208	Functional/Systemic disorders
618.172	RX467	Menstruation
618.173	RX471	Leucorrhea
618.175	RC884	Climacteric
618.175	RX469	Menopause
618.19	RG491-499	Diseases of the breast
618.2	RG950	Midwives
618.2	RX476	Obstetrics
618.200202	RG533	Outlines/Etc.
618.200222	RG520	Pictorial works
618.20025	RG504-505	Directories
618.20028	RG545	Instruments/Apparatus/Etc.
618.200285	RG547	Computer applications
618.20072	RG502	Laboratories/Institutes/Inc.
618.20076	RG532	Exercises/Exams/Problems
618.2009	RG511-518	History

Dewey	LC	Descriptor
618.20090(34-4)	RG516	19th-20th centuries
618.200901	RG512-513	Primitive/Ancient
618.200902	RG514	Medieval
618.200903(1-3)	RG515	Modern through 1800
618.20092	RG509-510	Biography
618.2019	RG560	Psychology aspects
618.2021	RG530-.3	Statistics
618.2061	RG528	Pharmacology
618.207	RG527-.5	Examination/Diagnosis
618.22	RG563-564	Examination/Diagnosis
618.24	RG559	Nutritional aspects
618.24	RJ91	Prenatal influence/Culture
618.25	RG567	Multiple pregnancy
618.25	RG696	Multiple birth
618.3	RG571-580	Diseases/Conditions
618.31	RG586	Extrauterine pregnancy
618.32	RG600-631	Embryo/Fetus
618.32(6-8)	RG629	Specific diseases of fetus
618.320754	RG628-.3	Examination/Diagnosis
618.392	RG648	Spontaneous abortion
618.397	RG649	Premature labor
618.4	RG651-721	Labor
618.42	RG671-693	Presentations/Positions
618.45	RG661	Natural childbirth
618.5	RG701-721	Complicated labor
618.51	RG705-707	Anomalies/Mechanical obstacles
618.53	RG709	Fetal size/Etc.
618.54	RG711	Hemorrhage
618.56	RG715	Placenta complications
618.58	RG719	Umbilical cord complications
618.58	RJ316	Umbilical diseases
618.7	RG801-871	Puerperal state
618.71	RG861-866	Lactation diseases
618.75	RG831	Convulsions/Eclampsia
618.76	RG851	Psychoses/Mental disorders
618.8	RG725-791	Obstetric operations
618.82	RG741	Extraction/Version
618.83	RG781	Embryotomy/Craniotomy
618.86	RG761	Cesarean section
618.89	RG730	Asepsis/Antisepsis
618.92	RJ	Pediatrics
618.92	RV375-377	Diseases of children
618.92	RX501-531	Diseases of children
618.92(1-9)	RJ254-320	Diseases
618.92(1-9)	RJ370-520	Diseases of children
618.92(1-9)061	RJ560-570	Materia medica
618.92(15/42)	RJ411-416	Hematology/Lymph diseases
618.92(6)	RJ401-406	Infectious/Parasitic diseases
618.92000(5/6)	RJ1	Serials/Societies
618.9200025	RJ29	Directories
618.9200028	RJ34	Instruments/Etc.
618.920003	RJ26	Dictionaries/ Encyclopedias
618.920005	RJ16	Yearbooks
618.920006	RJ21	Congresses
618.9200072	RJ31-32	Laboratories/Institutes/Etc.
618.920009	RJ36-42	History of pediatrics
618.920009(4-9)	RJ42	By place
618.9200090(3-4)	RJ40	Modern
618.92000901	RJ38	Ancient
618.92000902	RJ39	Medieval
618.9200092	RJ43	Biography
618.92002	RJ47.3-.4	Genetic aspects

Dewey	LC	Descriptor
618.920025	RJ370	Critical diseases/ Emergencies
618.92007	RJ50-51	Examination
618.920075	RJ255.5-.6	Examination/Diagnosis
618.9201	RJ251-325	Newborn infants
618.92011	RJ250	Premature infants
618.92011	RJ281	Low birth weight
618.92023	RJ33.5-.8	Practice of/Economics of
618.92023(4-9)	RJ33.6-.8	Practice, By place
618.92023(4-9)	RJ33.8	Other areas
618.920237(4-9)	RJ33.7	By region or state
618.92202373	RJ33.6-.7	United States
618.920977	RJ296	Ophthalmia/Conjunctivitis
618.921	RJ421-426	Cardiovascular system/ Diseases
618.921075	RJ423-.5	Examination/Diagnosis
618.9212	RJ269	Heart diseases/ Abnormalities
618.9215	RJ269.5-271	Hematologic diseases
618.922	RJ274	Hyaline membrane disease/Etc.
618.922	RJ431-436	Respiratory system diseases
618.922	RJ312	Respiratory diseases
618.922	RJ256	Asphyxia
618.922075	RJ433-.5	Examination/Diagnosis
618.923	RJ267	Colic
618.9231	RJ460-463	Diseases of the mouth
618.9233	RJ446-456	Gastroenterology
618.923623	RJ272	Hepatitis
618.923625	RJ276	Jaundice/Icterus
618.9239	RJ286	Metabolic disorder
618.9242	RJ418-420	Endocrine system diseases
618.925	RJ511-516	Diseases of the skin
618.926	RJ466-478.5	Urology
618.9261	RJ278	Kidney diseases
618.928	RJ486-496	Nervous system diseases
618.928	RJ290	Nervous system diseases
618.92842	RJ301	Paralysis
618.9289	RJ499-507	Mental disorders
618.9289(5-8)	RJ506	Specific disorders
618.9289000(5/6)	RJ499.A1	Serials/Societies
618.92890007	RJ500	Education
618.928900072	RJ500.2	Research
618.92890009(4-9)	RJ502	Other regions or countries
618.9289000973	RJ501	United States
618.92890009(4-9)	RJ501-502	Mental disorders, By place
618.92890025	RJ504.4	Crisis intervention
618.92891(2-8)	RJ505	Specific therapies
618.928914	RJ504-505	Child psychotherapy
618.928917	RJ504.2	Analysis
618.928918	RJ504.7	Chemotherapy
618.929	RJ275	Infectious diseases
618.9297	RJ386-.5	Allergy
618.92979	RJ385-387	Immunologic diseases
618.97	RC952-954.6	Geriatrics
620	TA	Engineering, General/Civil
620.00(5/6)	TA1-5	Serials/Societies/Congresses
620.00(687/28)	TA201-210	Contracting/Equipment
620.00148	TA11	Symbols/Abbreviations
620.00151	TA329-348	Mathematics
620.00222	TA174-175	Engineering drawing/ Designs
620.00228	TA177	Models
620.0023	TA157-158	The profession
620.0025	TA12	Directories
620.0028	TA165	Instruments

Dewey	LC	Descriptor
620.003	TA9	Dictionaries/ Encyclopedias
620.0046	TT151	Mending/Repairing
620.00492	TA77-78	Netherlands
620.0068	TA190-194	Management
620.00681	TA177.4-185	Economics
620.0072	TA160	Research
620.0078	TA152	Laboratory manuals
620.009	TA15-19	History
620.009(4-9)	TA21-126	By place
620.0092	TA139-140	Biography
620.00941	TA57-64.5	Great Britain
620.00943	TA73-74.5	Germany
620.009436	TA65-.2	Austria
620.009437	TA65.3-.4	Czechoslovakia
620.009439	TA65.5-66	Hungary
620.00944	TA71-72.5	France
620.00945	TA79-80	Italy
620.00946	TA87-88	Spain
620.009469	TA83-84.5	Portugal
620.00947	TA85-86	European Russia
620.00948	TA88.5	Scandinavia
620.009481	TA81-82	Norway
620.009485	TA89-90	Sweden
620.009489	TA69-70	Denmark
620.0094897	TA95.F5	Finland
620.009493	TA67-68	Belgium
620.009494	TA91-92	Switzerland
620.009495	TA75-76	Greece
620.009496	TA95.A2	Balkans
620.009497	TA95.Y8	Yugoslavia
620.00951	TA101-102	China
620.00952	TA105-106	Japan
620.00954	TA103-104	India
620.0095491	TA104.5-.6	Pakistan
620.0095493	TA104.7-.8	Sri Lanka
620.00955	TA107-108	Iran
620.009561	TA111-112	Turkey
620.009567	TA113.I7	Iraq
620.0095694	TA113.I75	Israel/Palestine
620.00957	TA109-110	Asian Russia
620.009598	TA113.I55	Indonesia
620.009599	TA113.P6	Philippines
620.0096	TA115-119	Africa
620.0096(1-9)	TA119	Africa, By country
620.00962	TA117-118	Egypt
620.00971	TA26-27	Canada
620.00972	TA28-29	Mexico
620.009728	TA30-31	Central America
620.009729	TA32-33	West Indies
620.00973	TA23-25	United States
620.00981	TA41-42	Brazil
620.00982	TA36-37	Argentina
620.00983	TA43-44	Chile
620.00984	TA38-39	Bolivia
620.00985	TA52	Peru
620.009861	TA45-46	Colombia
620.009866	TA47	Ecuador
620.00987	TA54	Venezuela
620.009881	TA48	Guyana
620.009882	TA50	French Guiana
620.009883	TA49	Suriname
620.009892	TA51	Paraguay
620.009895	TA53	Uruguay
620.0099(5-6)	TA123-124	Oceania
620.00993	TA122.5-.6	New Zealand
620.00994	TA121-122	Australia

Dewey	LC	Descriptor
620.00998	TA125-126	Polar areas
620.1	TJ170-173	Mechanics
620.1(2-9)	TA418.95-492	By type of material
620.10(3-7)	TA349-360	Applied mechanics
620.11	TA401-492	Materials
620.110(5/6)	TA401-.3	Serials/Societies/Congresses
620.110287	TA410-418.34	Testing
620.1103	TA402	Dictionaries/Encyclopedias
620.1107	TA404-.3	Education/Research
620.1109	TA402.5	By place
620.2(1-5)	TA365-367	Acoustical engineering
620.4162	TC1501-1645	Ocean engineering
620.41620(5/6)	TC1501	Serials/Societies
620.416206	TC1505	Congresses
620.82	T59.7-.77	Human engineering
621	HD9680-9714	Mechanical/Electrical industry
621	TJ	Mechanical engineering
621.(86/98)	TJ1425-1475	Lifting/Pressing machinery
621.0(5/6)	TJ1-4	Serials/Societies
621.01	TJ14	Philosophy
621.025	TJ11-13	Directories
621.0289	TJ166	Safety
621.0294	TJ168	General catalogs
621.03	TJ9	Dictionaries/Encyclopedias
621.06	TJ5	Congresses
621.07	TJ158-159	Education
621.074	TJ6	Exhibitions/Museums
621.09	TJ15-20	History
621.09(4-9)	TJ21-126	By place
621.092	TJ139-140	Biography
621.0941	TJ57-64.5	Great Britain
621.0943	TJ73-74.5	Germany
621.09436	TJ65-.2	Austria
621.09437	TJ65.3-.4	Czechoslovakia
621.09439	TJ65.5-66	Hungary
621.0944	TJ71-72.5	France
621.0945	TJ79-80	Italy
621.0946	TJ87-88	Spain
621.09469	TJ83-84.5	Portugal
621.0947	TJ85-86	European Russia
621.0948	TJ88.5	Scandinavia
621.09481	TJ81-82	Norway
621.09485	TJ89-90	Sweden
621.09489	TJ69-70	Denmark
621.094897	TJ95.F5	Finland
621.09492	TJ77-78	Netherlands
621.09493	TJ67-68	Belgium
621.09494	TJ91-92	Switzerland
621.09495	TJ75-76	Greece
621.09496	TJ95.A2	Balkans
621.09497	TJ95.Y8	Yugoslavia
621.0951	TJ101-102	China
621.0952	TJ105-106	Japan
621.0954	TJ103-104	India
621.095491	TJ104.5-.6	Pakistan
621.095493	TJ104.7-.8	Sri Lanka
621.0955	TJ107-108	Iran
621.09561	TJ111-112	Turkey
621.09567	TJ113.I7	Iraq
621.095694	TJ113.I75	Israel/Palestine
621.0957	TJ109-110	Asian Russia
621.09598	TJ113.I55	Indonesia
621.09599	TJ113.P6	Philippines
621.096	TJ115-119	Africa
621.096(1-9)	TJ119	Africa, By country
621.0962	TJ117-118	Egypt
621.0971	TJ26-27	Canada
621.0972	TJ28-29	Mexico
621.09728	TJ30-31	Central America
621.09729	TJ32-33	West Indies
621.0973	TJ23-25	United States
621.0981	TJ41-42	Brazil
621.0982	TJ36-37	Argentina
621.0983	TJ43-44	Chile
621.0984	TJ38-39	Bolivia
621.0985	TJ52	Peru
621.09861	TJ45-46	Colombia
621.09866	TJ47	Ecuador
621.0987	TJ54	Venezuela
621.09881	TJ48	Guyana
621.09882	TJ50	French Guiana
621.09883	TJ49	Suriname
621.09892	TJ51	Paraguay
621.09895	TJ53	Uruguay
621.099(5-6)	TJ123-124	Oceania
621.0993	TJ122.5-.6	New Zealand
621.0994	TJ121-122	Australia
621.0998	TJ125-126	Polar areas
621.1	TJ461-567	Steam engines
621.1	TJ268-280.5	Steam engineering
621.1(5-6)	TJ515-551	Design/Construction
621.1(5-6)	TJ700-740	Other steam engines
621.1(5-6)	TJ485-507	Special types
621.1(5-9)	TJ310-318	Types of boilers
621.18	TJ290-295	Construction
621.183	TJ320-358	Furnaces
621.183	TJ281-393	Boilers
621.185	TJ415-444	Pipe and fittings
621.197	TJ320-393	Details/Accessories
621.2	TJ840-935	Hydraulic machinery
621.3	TK	Electrical/Nuclear engineering
621.3(2-9)	TK4001-4101	Applications of electric power
621.30(5/6)	TK1-4	Serials/Societies
621.30221	TK431-451	Drawings
621.3025	TK12	Directories
621.3028	TK452-454.4	Apparatus/Materials
621.303	TK9	Dictionaries/Encyclopedias
621.306	TK5	Congresses
621.307	TK165-213	Education
621.3074	TK6	Exhibitions/Museums
621.309	TK15-18	History
621.309(4-9)	TK21-126	By place
621.30941	TK57-64.5	Great Britain
621.30943	TK73-74.5	Germany
621.309436	TK65-.2	Austria
621.309437	TK65.3-.4	Czechoslovakia
621.309439	TK65.5-66	Hungary
621.30944	TK71-72.5	France
621.30945	TK79-80	Italy
621.30946	TK87-88	Spain
621.309469	TK83-84.5	Portugal
621.30947	TK85-86	European Russia
621.30948	TK88.5	Scandinavia
621.309481	TK81-82	Norway
621.309485	TK89-90	Sweden
621.309489	TK69-70	Denmark
621.3094897	TK95.F5	Finland
621.309492	TK77-78	Netherlands

Dewey	LC	Descriptor	Dewey	LC	Descriptor
621.309493	TK67-68	Belgium	621.32094	TK4147-4148	Europe
621.309494	TK91-92	Switzerland	621.32095	TK4149-4150	Asia
621.309495	TK75-76	Greece	621.32096	TK4151-4152	Africa
621.309496	TK95.A2	Balkans	621.320971	TK4138-4139	Canada
621.309497	TK95.Y8	Yugoslavia	621.320972	TK4140	Mexico
621.30951	TK101-102	China	621.3209728	TK4141-4142	Central America
621.30952	TK105-106	Japan	621.3209729	TK4143-4144	West Indies
621.30954	TK103-104	India	621.320973	TK4135-4137	United States
621.3095491	TK104.5-.6	Pakistan	621.32098	TK4145-4146	South America
621.3095493	TK104.7-.8	Sri Lanka	621.32099(3-4)	TK4153-4154.5	Australia/New Zealand
621.30955	TK107-108	Iran	621.32099(5-6)	TK4155-4156	Oceania
621.309561	TK111-112	Turkey	621.325	TK4311-4335	Arc
621.309567	TK113.I7	Iraq	621.326	TK4341-4367	Incandescent
621.3095694	TK113.I75	Israel/Palestine	621.33	TF863-912	Construction
621.30957	TK109-110	Asian Russia	621.33	TF858-859	Electrification
621.309598	TK113.I55	Indonesia	621.33	TF855-1126	Electric railways
621.309599	TK113.P6	Philippines	621.362	TK4500	Infrared technology
621.3096	TK115-119	Africa	621.3692	QC447.9-448.2	Fiber optics
621.3096(1-9)	TK119	Africa, By country	621.37	TK401-415	Testing
621.30962	TK117-118	Egypt	621.37	TK275-277	Standards/Measurements
621.30971	TK26-27	Canada	621.373	TK301-396	Meters
621.30972	TK28-29	Mexico	621.38(5-7)	TK6201-6285	Plants/Stations/The line
621.309728	TK30-31	Central America	621.38(5-7)	TK6001-6525	Telephone
621.309729	TK32-33	West Indies	621.381	TK7800-8360	Electronics
621.30973	TK23-25	United States	621.3810(5/6)	TK7800-7801	Serials/Societies/Congresses
621.30981	TK41-42	Brazil	621.3810287	TK7878-7879	Electronic measurements
621.30982	TK36-37	Argentina	621.3813	TK7876	Microwaves
621.30983	TK43-44	Chile	621.3815	TK7867-7868	Circuits
621.30984	TK38-39	Bolivia	621.3815	TK7870-7872	Amplifiers/Tubes/Diodes
621.30985	TK52	Peru	621.381542	TK8300-8360	Photoelectronic devices
621.309861	TK45-46	Colombia	621.382	TK5101-6525	Telecommunication
621.309866	TK47	Ecuador	621.3828	TK5981-5986	Electroacoustics
621.30987	TK54	Venezuela	621.383	TK5301-5385	Plants/Stations/The line
621.309881	TK48	Guyana	621.383	TK5501-5585	Systems/Instruments
621.309882	TK50	French Guiana	621.383	TK5451-5468	The line
621.309883	TK49	Suriname	621.383	TK5107-5865	Telegraph
621.309892	TK51	Paraguay	621.383	TK5401-5491	Distribution/Construction
621.309895	TK53	Uruguay	621.3830(5/6)	TK5107	Serials/Societies/Etc.
621.3099(5-6)	TK123-124	Oceania	621.384	TK6540-6571.5	Radio
621.30993	TK122.5-.6	New Zealand	621.3841(1/8)	TK6560-6595	Receivers/Senders
621.30994	TK121-122	Australia	621.384135	TK6585-6592	Antennas
621.30998	TK125-126	Polar areas	621.3842	TK5700-5865	Radiotelegraph
621.3121	TK2896-2970	Production of electricity	621.3848	TK6573-6600	Radar
621.3121	TJ164	Power plants	621.38480(5/6)	TK6573	Serials/Societies/Congresses
621.3121	TK1001-1841	Production of electric energy	621.3850(5/6)	TK6001-6005	Serials/Societies/Congresses
			621.387	TK6401-6500	Systems/Instruments
621.3121	TK1041-1081	Production methods	621.387	TK6301-6397	Distribution/Construction
621.3121	TK1191-1841	Powerplants	621.388	TK6630-6720	Television
621.3121	TJ395-444	Powerplants	621.38800(5/6)	TK6630	Serials/Societies/Congresses
621.313	TK2411-2491	Generators	621.3883	TK6650-6655	Tubes/Antennas
621.313	TK2511-2541	Motors	621.38928	TK7018-7725	Bells/Alarms/Etc.
621.3132	TK2611-2699	Direct current	621.39	TK7885-7895	Computer engineering
621.3132	TK2000-2891	Dynamoelectric machinery/Etc.	621.39	TK7888.3	Digital
			621.390288	TK7887	Maintenance/Repair
621.3133	TK2711-2799	Alternating current	621.391	TK7889	Special computers
621.315	TK2805	Condensers	621.3919	TK7888	Analog
621.317	TJ212-225	Control engineering	621.397	TK7895	Tapes/Memory
621.317	TK2811-2891	Meters/Switches	621.4	TJ255-265	Heat engines
621.319	TK3001-3511	Distribution of electric power	621.4(2-3)	TJ731-830	Misc. motors/Engines
			621.4028	TK4601-4661	Electric heating
621.3191	TK3101-3171	Systems	621.433	TJ770-780	Gas engines
621.3193	TK3201-3351	Wiring/Cables	621.4356	TL780-785.8	Rockets
621.32	TP700-746	Illuminating industries	621.43560228	TL844	Model rockets
621.32	TK4125-4399	Electric lighting	621.436	TJ795-799	Diesel engines
621.32	TH7700-7975	Illumination, lighting	621.453	TJ823-827	Windmills
621.32(5-7)	TK4303-4391	Lighting systems	621.48	TK9001-9401	Nuclear engineering
621.3209(4-9)	TK4134-4156	By place	621.480(5/6)	TK9001-9006	Serials/Societies/Congresses

Dewey	LC	Descriptor
621.483	QC786.4-.8	Nuclear reactors for research
621.483	TK9202-9230ÿ ÿ ÿ	Nuclear reactors
621.4835	TK9151.4-9152.2	Radiation procedures
621.55	TJ940	Vacuum technology
621.6	TJ950-1030	Fans/Blowers/Air pumps
621.69	TJ900-925	Pumps
621.811	TJ181-210	Mechanical movements
621.811	TJ177	Machinery vibration
621.815	TJ227-240	Machine design
621.822	TJ1061-1073	Bearings
621.83	TJ189-204	Special gears
621.852	TJ1100-1119	Belts
621.862	TJ1357-1383	Hoisting
621.867	TJ1385-1418	Conveying
621.8672	TJ930-933	Pipelines
621.88	TJ1320-1340	Fastenings
621.9	TJ1125-1345	Machine shops
621.90(2/8)	TJ1180-1313	Machine/Handtools/Etc.
621.902	TJ1185-1191	Machine tools
621.9068	TJ1135-1150	Management
621.908	TJ1195-1201	Handtools
621.91(4)	TJ1345	Milling/Crushing
621.93	TJ1233-1240	Cutting/Sawing tools
622	TN	Mining engineering/ Metallurgy
622.0(5/6)	TN1-4	Serials/Societies
622.025	TN12	Directories
622.03	TN9-10	Dictionaries/ Encyclopedias
622.06	TN5	Congresses
622.07	TN165-213	Education
622.074	TN6	Exhibitions/Museums
622.09	TN15-19	History
622.09(4-9)	TN21-126	Mine engineering, By place
622.092	TN139-140	Biography
622.0941	TN57-64.5	Great Britain
622.0943	TN73-74.5	Germany
622.09436	TN65-.2	Austria
622.09437	TN65.3-.4	Czechoslovakia
622.09439	TN65.5-66	Hungary
622.0944	TN71-72.5	France
622.0945	TN79-80	Italy
622.0946	TN87-88	Spain
622.09469	TN83-84.5	Portugal
622.0947	TN85-86	European Russia
622.0948	TN88.5	Scandinavia
622.09481	TN81-82	Norway
622.09485	TN89-90	Sweden
622.09489	TN69-70	Denmark
622.094897	TN95.F5	Finland
622.09492	TN77-78	Netherlands
622.09493	TN67-68	Belgium
622.09494	TN91-92	Switzerland
622.09495	TN75-76	Greece
622.09496	TN95.A2	Balkans
622.09497	TN95.Y8	Yugoslavia
622.0951	TN101-102	China
622.0952	TN105-106	Japan
622.0954	TN103-104	India
622.095491	TN104.5-.6	Pakistan
622.095493	TN104.7-.8	Sri Lanka
622.0955	TN107-108	Iran
622.09561	TN111-112	Turkey
622.09567	TN113.I7	Iraq
622.095694	TN113.I75	Israel/Palestine
622.0957	TN109-110	Asian Russia
622.09598	TN113.I55	Indonesia
622.09599	TN113.P6	Philippines
622.096	TN115-119	Africa
622.096(1-9)	TN119	Africa, By country
622.0962	TN117-118	Egypt
622.0971	TN26-27	Canada
622.0972	TN28-29	Mexico
622.09728	TN30-31	Central America
622.09729	TN32-33	West Indies
622.0973	TN23-25	United States
622.0981	TN41-42	Brazil
622.0982	TN36-37	Argentina
622.0983	TN43-44	Chile
622.0984	TN38-39	Bolivia
622.0985	TN52	Peru
622.09861	TN45-46	Colombia
622.09866	TN47	Ecuador
622.0987	TN54	Venezuela
622.09881	TN48	Guyana
622.09882	TN50	French Guiana
622.09883	TN49	Suriname
622.09892	TN51	Paraguay
622.09895	TN53	Uruguay
622.099(5-6)	TN123-124	Oceania
622.0993	TN122.5-.6	New Zealand
622.0994	TN121-122	Australia
622.0998	TN125-126	Polar areas
622.18	TN270-271	Prospecting
622.2	TN272-274	Mines
622.2	TN345	Machinery/Tools/Etc.
622.2(2-9)	TN275-292	Practical mining operations
622.3(5-9)	TN948	Other nonmetallic minerals
622.33	TN799.5-948	Nonmetallic minerals
622.33(8-9)	TN845-859	Other natural carbons
622.334	TN800-842	Coal
622.338	TN860-879	Petroleum
622.3385	TN880-883	Natural gas
622.339	TN885	Amber/Fossil gums
622.34	TN400-580	Ores and mining
622.341	TN400-409	Iron ore
622.35	TN950-997	Building/Ornamental stones
622.361	TN941-943	Clay
622.3626	TN939	Sand/Gravel
622.363	TN899-909	Sodium salts, Soda deposits
622.3633	TN917	Borax/Borates
622.3635	TN946	Gypsum
622.3636	TN919	Potassium salts/Potash
622.364	TN913	Phosphates
622.364	TN911	Nitrates
622.365	TN936	Abrasives
622.3668	TN890	Sulphur
622.3672	TN930	Asbestos
622.3674	TN933	Mica
622.368	TN945	Cement materials
622.373	TN923-929	Mineral waters
622.48	TN343	Electrical engineering
622.6	TN331-342	Transportation
622.8	TN295-319	Safety and ventilation
623.(1-3)	UG360-390	Field engineering
623.(1-7)	UG	Military engineering
623.(75/888)	V380-386	Safety
623.0(5/6)	UG1	Serials/Societies
623.043	UG485	Electronics
623.045	UG450	Mechanical engineering
623.047	UG350	Hydraulic engineering
623.047	VG590-595	Civil/Construction engineering

Dewey	LC	Descriptor
623.04709(4-9)	VG595	In other countries
623.0470973	VG593	United States
623.06	UG5	Congresses
623.07	UG157	Education
623.074	UG6	Museums/Exhibitions
623.09	UG15	History
623.09(4-9)	UG21-124	By place
623.092	UG127-128	Biography
623.1	UG400-442	Fortification
623.4	UF520-780	Ordnance
623.4	UF560-780	Ordnance material
623.40287	UF890	Ordnance tests
623.409(4-9)	UF565	Other countries
623.40973	UF563	United States
623.44	UD380-425	Small arms
623.44	UF520-537	Small arms
623.44	U880-897	Guns
623.44(1-7)	U825-897	By type
623.44(2-3)	UD330-335	Firing
623.44074	U804	Museums/Exhibitions
623.4409	U800-897	History of arms/Armor
623.4409(4-9)	U818-823.5	By place
623.44090(1-4)	U805-815	By date
623.441	U850-870	Swords/Daggers
623.441	U877-878	Bows
623.441	U872	Lances/Spears
623.4424	UF620	Machine guns
623.4424	VF410	Machine guns
623.45115	UG490	Mines
623.4513	UF750-770	Projectiles
623.45195	V990-995	Fleet Ballistic Missle Systems
623.452	UF860-880	Explosives/Pyrotechnics
623.46	UF857	Range tables
623.46	UF848-856	Artillery instruments
623.51	UF820-830	Ballistics
623.55	UF800-805	Gunnery
623.62	UG330	Roads
623.63	UG345	Railroads
623.64	V220-240	Stations/Ports/Bases/Yards
623.67	UG335	Bridges
623.68	UG340	Tunnels
623.71	UG470-474	Military surveying/Mapping
623.72	UG476	Photography
623.73	UA940-945	Military communications
623.73	UG570-613.5	Communication
623.73(2-4)	UG590-613.5	Telegraph/Telephone
623.73(2/42)	UA980	Telegraphic connections
623.731	UG570-582	Signaling
623.7348	UG612-.5	Radar
623.74	UG615-620	Motor vehicles
623.75	U380-385	Safety
623.76	UG480	Electricity
623.8	VM600-989	Marine engineering
623.807	VM725-728	Education
623.809	VM615-619	History
623.809(4-9)	VM621-724	By place
623.8094	VM655-696	Europe
623.80941	VM657-664	Great Britain
623.80943	VM673-674.5	Germany
623.80944	VM671-672	France
623.80945	VM679-680	Italy
623.80946	VM687-688	Spain
623.809469	VM683-684	Portugal
623.80947	VM685-686	European Russia
623.80948	VM686.5	Scandinavia
623.809495	VM675-676	Greece
623.8095	VM699-713	Asia
623.80952	VM705-706	Japan
623.8096	VM715-719	Africa
623.80971	VM626-627	Canada
623.80972	VM628-629	Mexico
623.809728	VM630-631	Central America
623.809729	VM632-633	West Indies
623.80973	VM623-625	United States
623.8098	VM634-654	South America
623.8099(3-4)	VM721-722.5	Australia/New Zealand
623.8099(5-6)	VM723-724	Oceania
623.81	VM	Naval architecture/ Engineering
623.810(5/6)	VM1-4	Serials/Societies
623.810(687/212)	VM295-296	Contracts/Specifications
623.8101	VM298	Models
623.8101	VM156-163	Theory/Principles
623.81025	VM12	Directories
623.810287	VM153-155	Tonnage/Measurement
623.810299	VM291	Estimates
623.8106	VM5	Congresses
623.8107	VM165-276	Education
623.81074	VM6	Exhibitions/Museums
623.8109(4-9)	VM21-124	By place
623.810901	VM16	Ancient
623.810902	VM17	Medieval
623.8109034	VM19	19th century
623.810904	VM20	20th century
623.81092	VM139-140	Biography
623.81094	VM55-96	Europe
623.810941	VM57-64	Great Britain
623.810943	VM73-74.5	Germany
623.810944	VM71-72	France
623.810945	VM79-80	Italy
623.810946	VM87-88	Spain
623.8109469	VM83-84	Portugal
623.810947	VM85-86	European Russia
623.810948	VM86.5	Scandinavia
623.8109495	VM75-76	Greece
623.81095	VM99-113	Asia
623.810951	VM101-102	China
623.810952	VM105-106	Japan
623.81096	VM115-119	Africa
623.810971	VM26-27	Canada
623.810972	VM28-29	Mexico
623.8109728	VM30-31	Central America
623.8109729	VM32-33	West Indies
623.810973	VM23-25	United States
623.81098	VM34-54	South America
623.810982	VM36-37	Argentina
623.810983	VM43-44	Chile
623.81099(3-4)	VM121-122.5	Australia/New Zealand
623.81099(5-6)	VM123-124	Oceania
623.8109	VM15-124	History
623.812	VM297	Designs
623.818	V795-805.5	Construction/Materials
623.8182	VM146-147	Metal construction
623.8184	VM142-144	Wooden construction
623.81844	VM148	Concrete construction
623.82(02/3)	VM320-361	Small craft
623.82(023/314)	VM331-333	Yachts
623.82(1-9)	VM311-466	By type of vessel
623.82(3-6)	VM378-466	By use
623.8204	VM362	Hydrofoils
623.8204	VM315	Motor ships
623.8231	VM340-349	Motor boats/Launches
623.8234	VM421	Ferryboats

Dewey	LC	Descriptor
623.8243	VM381-385	Passenger ships
623.82436	VM461-.5	River steamers
623.8245	VM391-395	Cargo/Freight ships
623.825	V750-995	War vessels/Material
623.825090(1-4)	V755-767	By period
623.8251	VF	Naval ordnance
623.8251	VF	Naval ordnance
623.8251	VF	Naval ordnance
623.8251(096)	VF115-119	Africa
623.82510(5/6)	VF1	Serials/Societies
623.8251074	VF6	Exhibitions/Museums
623.825109	VF15	History
623.825109(4-9)	VF21-124	By place
623.8251094	VF55-96	Europe
623.82510941	VF57-64	Great Britain
623.82510943	VF73-74.5	Germany
623.82510944	VF71-72	France
623.82510945	VF79-80	Italy
623.82510946	VF87-88	Spain
623.825109469	VF83-84	Portugal
623.82510947	VF85-86	European Russia
623.82510948	VF86.5	Scandinavia
623.8251095	VF101-113	Asia
623.82510952	VF105-106	Japan
623.825109561	VF111-112	Turkey
623.82510971	VF26-27	Canada
623.82510972	VF28-29	Mexico
623.825109728	VF30-31	Central America
623.825109729	VF32-33	West Indies
623.82510973	VF23-25	United States
623.8251098	VF34-54	South America
623.82510982	VF36-37	Argentina
623.82510983	VF43-44	Chile
623.825109861	VF45-46	Colombia
623.8251099(3-4)	VF121-122.5	Australia/New Zealand
623.8251099(5-6)	VF123-124	Oceania
623.8253	V820-.5	Cruisers
623.8254	V825-.5	Destroyers
623.8255	V874-875	Aircraft carriers
623.8257	V857-859	Submarines
623.8257	VM365-367	Submarines
623.8258	V830-840	Torpedo boats
623.829	VM351-361	Small boats/Row boats
623.83	VC412-425	Navy yards/Stations
623.83	VM901-965	Shipyard equipment/Appliances
623.844	VM467	Ship joinery
623.85(03/2)	VM471-479	Electricity on ships
623.85(3/4)	VM481-482	Heating/Sanitation/Etc.
623.8504	VM480-.5	Electronic apparatus
623.852	VM491-493	Lighting
623.8542	VM503-505	Water supply
623.856	VG70-85	Communications
623.8561	VK381-397	Signaling
623.8561	V280-285	Naval signaling
623.8562	VG70-75	Telegraph
623.856209(4-9)	VG75	In other countries
623.85620973	VG73	United States
623.8563	VG80-85	Telephone
623.856309(4-9)	VG85	In other countries
623.85630973	VG83	United States
623.8564	VG76-78	Wireless telegraph/Radio/Etc.
623.856409(4-9)	VG78	In other countries
623.85640973	VG77	United States
623.86	SH344-.8	Methods/Gear
623.86	VM470	Equipment/Fittings
623.86	VM781-861	Misc. appliances/Equipment
623.87	VM731-779	Marine engines
623.8722	VM741-750	Boilers
623.8723	VM770-771	Gas/Oil/Diesel engines
623.8726	VM773	Electric propulsion
623.8728	VM317	Atomic/Nuclear ships
623.8728	VM774-777	Nuclear/Atomic engines
623.873	VM753-759	Propellers/Gears/Etc.
623.874	VM779	Fuels
623.88	VM565	Steerage of ships
623.88	VK401-537	Education/Training
623.88	VK205-215	Ship Command/Masters' manual
623.88	VK543	Helmsmanship
623.88	VK541-547	Seamanship
623.88(5-6) + 09(72-8)	VK1277-1279	Central/South America/W. Indies
623.887	VM521-561	Propulsion
623.888	SH343.9	Safety
623.888	V810	Damage control
623.888	VK200	Safety
623.888 (5-6)	VK1250-1299-.6	Shipwrecks/Fires
623.888(5-6) + 09(4-9)	VK1270-1294	Shipwrecks/Fires, By place
623.888(5-6) + 099(3-4)	VK1289-1291.3	New Zealand/Australia
623.888(5-6) + 099(5-6)	VK1292-1294	Oceania
623.888(5-6)094	VK1280-1282	Europe
623.888(5-6)095	VK1286-1288	Asia
623.888(5-6)096	VK1283-1285	Africa
623.888(5-6)0971	VK1274-1276	Canada
623.888(5-6)0973	VK1270-1273	United States
623.8884	VK371-378	Collisions
623.8886	VK1258	Fire fighting/Prevention
623.8887	VK1300-1481	Saving life/Property
623.8887	VK1460-1481	Apparatus/Etc.
623.888709	VK1315	History
623.888709(4-9)	VK1321-1424	By place
623.8887092	VK1430	Biography
623.89	SH343.8	Navigation
623.89	VK	Merchant Marine/Navigation
623.89	VK549-572	Science of navigation
623.89(2-3)	VK573-587	Nautical instruments
623.890(5/6)	VK1-4	Serials/Societies, By language
623.8906	VK5	Congresses
623.89076	VK559.5	Examinations/Questions
623.8909	VK549-555	History
623.892(2-9) + (4-9)	VK1521-1624	By place
623.892(2-9) + 9(3-6)	VK1621-1624	Australia/New Zealand/Oceania
623.892(2-9)4	VK1555-1596	Europe
623.892(2-9)5	VK1599-1613	Asia
623.892(2-9)6	VK1615-1619	Africa
623.892(2-9)71	VK1526-1527	Canada
623.892(2-9)72	VK1528-1529	Mexico
623.892(2-9)728	VK1530-1531	Central America
623.892(2-9)729	VK1532-1533	West Indies
623.892(2-9)73	VK1523-1525	United States
623.892(2-9)8	VK1534-1554	South America
623.8920212	VK563	Nautical tables/Etc.
623.8922	VK798-997	Sailing direction/Pilot guides
623.8922	VK1500-1661	Pilots/Piloting
623.892205	VK798	Serials
623.892209	VK800-803	History
623.892209	VK1515	History
623.8922(3-7)	VK804-997	By place

Dewey	LC	Descriptor
623.89223	VK810-880	Atlantic Ocean
623.89223(4/6)	VK959-992	West Atlantic Ocean
623.8922334	VK819-821.8	Baltic Sea
623.8922336	VK839-844	English Channel
623.8922336	VK815-818	North Sea
623.892238	VK853-874	Mediterranean Sea
623.89224	VK915-956	Pacific Ocean
623.892242	VK941-956	East Pacific Ocean
623.892244	VK917	North Pacific Ocean
623.892248	VK925	South Pacific
623.89225	VK885-901	Indian Ocean
623.89229	HE617-720	Interior navigation
623.89229(4-9)	HE623-720	Interior navigation, Place
623.89229(4-9)	HE635-720	Other countries
623.8922973	HE623-633	United States
623.8923	VK572	Dead reckoning
623.893	VK560-561	Electronic aids in navigation
623.894(4/5)	VK1150-1246	Beacon/Buoy/Light lists
623.894(4/5)094	VK1151-1185	Europe
623.894(4/5)095	VK1203-1209	Asia
623.894(4/5)096	VK1190-1199	Africa
623.894(4/5)0971	VK1245	Canada
623.894(4/5)0972	VK1246	Mexico
623.894(4/5)09728	VK1237-1238	Central America
623.894(4/5)09729	VK1239-1240	West Indies
623.894(4/5)0973	VK1243-1244	United States
623.894(4/5)098	VK1225-1236	South America
623.894(4/5)099(3-4)	VK1211-1212	Australia/New Zealand
623.894(4/5)099(5-6)	VK1221-1223	Oceania
623.8942	VK1000-1249	Lighthouses
623.894209	VK1015	History
623.894209(4-9)	VK1021-1124	By place
623.8942094	VK1055-1096	Europe
623.8942095	VK1099-1113	Asia
623.8942096	VK1115-1119	Africa
623.89420971	VK1026-1027	Canada
623.89420972	VK1028-1029	Mexico
623.894209728	VK1030-1031	Central America
623.894209729	VK1032-1033	West Indies
623.89420973	VK1023-1025	United States
623.8942098	VK1034-1054	South America
623.8942099(3-4)	VK1121-1122.5	Australia/New Zealand
623.8942099(5-6)	VK1123-1124	Oceania
623.8944	VK1012	Buoys/Markers
623.8949	VK600-794	Tide/Current tables
623.89490916(2-7)	VK607-794	By place
623.894909163	VK610-680	Atlantic Ocean
623.894909163(4/6)	VK759-792	West Atlantic
623.89490091632	VK607-609	Arctic Ocean
623.89490916334	VK619-621	Baltic Sea
623.89490916336	VK639-644	English Channel
623.89490091638	VK653-674	Mediterranean Sea
623.894909164	VK715-756	Pacific Ocean
623.89490091642	VK741-756	East Pacific
623.89490091644	VK717	North Pacific Ocean
623.89490091648	VK725	South Pacific
623.894909165	VK685-701	Indian Ocean
623.942	UG487	Infrared rays
624	TA	Engineering, General/Civil
624.(2-3)	TG	Bridge engineering
624.0(5/6)	TA1-5	Serials/Societies/Congresses
624.0(687/28)	TA201-210	Contracting/Equipment
624.0148	TA11	Symbols/Abbreviations
624.0151	TA329-348	Mathematics
624.0222	TA174-175	Engineering drawing/ Designs
624.0228	TA177	Models
624.023	TA157-158	The profession
624.025	TA12	Directories
624.028	TA165	Instruments
624.03	TA9	Dictionaries/ Encyclopedias
624.068	TA190-194	Management
624.0681	TA177.4-185	Economics
624.072	TA160	Research
624.078	TA152	Laboratory manuals
624.09	TA15-19	History
624.09(4-9)	TA21-126	By place
624.092	TA139-140	Biography
624.0941	TA57-64.5	Great Britain
624.0943	TA73-74.5	Germany
624.09436	TA65-.2	Austria
624.09437	TA65.3-.4	Czechoslovakia
624.09439	TA65.5-66	Hungary
624.0944	TA71-72.5	France
624.0945	TA79-80	Italy
624.0946	TA87-88	Spain
624.09469	TA83-84.5	Portugal
624.0947	TA85-86	European Russia
624.0948	TA88.5	Scandinavia
624.09481	TA81-82	Norway
624.09485	TA89-90	Sweden
624.09489	TA69-70	Denmark
624.094897	TA95.F5	Finland
624.09492	TA77-78	Netherlands
624.09493	TA67-68	Belgium
624.09494	TA91-92	Switzerland
624.09495	TA75-76	Greece
624.09496	TA95.A2	Balkans
624.09497	TA95.Y8	Yugoslavia
624.0951	TA101-102	China
624.0952	TA105-106	Japan
624.0954	TA103-104	India
624.095491	TA104.5-.6	Pakistan
624.095493	TA104.7-.8	Sri Lanka
624.0955	TA107-108	Iran
624.09561	TA111-112	Turkey
624.09567	TA113.I7	Iraq
624.095694	TA113.I75	Israel/Palestine
624.0957	TA109-110	Asian Russia
624.09598	TA113.I55	Indonesia
624.09599	TA113.P6	Philippines
624.096	TA115-119	Africa
624.096(1-9)	TA119	Africa, By country
624.0962	TA117-118	Egypt
624.0971	TA26-27	Canada
624.0972	TA28-29	Mexico
624.09728	TA30-31	Central America
624.09729	TA32-33	West Indies
624.0973	TA23-25	United States
624.0981	TA41-42	Brazil
624.0982	TA36-37	Argentina
624.0983	TA43-44	Chile
624.0984	TA38-39	Bolivia
624.0985	TA52	Peru
624.09861	TA45-46	Colombia
624.09866	TA47	Ecuador
624.0987	TA54	Venezuela
624.09881	TA48	Guyana
624.09882	TA50	French Guiana
624.09883	TA49	Suriname
624.09892	TA51	Paraguay
624.09895	TA53	Uruguay

Dewey	LC	Descriptor
624.099(5-6)	TA123-124	Oceania
624.0993	TA122.5-.6	New Zealand
624.0994	TA121-122	Australia
624.0998	TA125-126	Polar areas
624.1	TA630-695	Structural engineering
624.1(01/7)	TA645-656.5	Structural theory/Analysis
624.10(5/6)	TA630	Serials/Societies/Congresses
624.107(2)	TA638-.5	Education/Research
624.11	TA418.95-492	By type of material
624.15	TA705-770	Geology/Earthworks
624.15(3-8)	TA775-787	Foundations
624.1517	TA501-625	Surveying
624.1517028	TA562-595	Instruments/Methods
624.151707	TA535-538	Education
624.152	TA715-770	Earthworks/Excavations
624.1771	TA663-695	Design/Construction
624.1771	TA658-.6	Structural design
624.18	TA401-492	Materials
624.180(5/6)	TA401-.3	Serials/Societies/Congresses
624.180287	TA410-418.34	Testing
624.1803	TA402	Dictionaries/ Encyclopedias
624.1807	TA404-.3	Education/Research
624.1809	TA402.5	By place
624.183	TH5311-5511	Masonry/Bricklaying
624.19	TA800-820	Tunneling/Tunnels
624.193	TF230-238	Tunneling
624.20(212/687)	TG310	Specifications/Contracts
624.20(5/6)	TG1-4	Serials/Societies
624.201	TG265-270	Theory of structures, Bridges
624.20228	TG307	Models
624.2025	TG12	Directories
624.20287	TG305	Testing
624.20289	TG470	Accidents
624.20299	TG313	Estimates/Quantities/Costs
624.203	TG9	Dictionaries/ Encyclopedias
624.206	TG5	Congresses
624.2074	TG6	Exhibitions/Museums
624.209	TG15-20	History
624.209(3-9)	TG21-126	By place
624.2092	TG139-140	Biography
624.20941	TG57-64.5	Great Britain
624.20943	TG73-74.5	Germany
624.209436	TG65-.2	Austria
624.209437	TG65.3-.4	Czechoslovakia
624.209439	TG65.5-66	Hungary
624.20944	TG71-72.5	France
624.20945	TG79-80	Italy
624.20946	TG87-88	Spain
624.209469	TG83-84.5	Portugal
624.20947	TG85-86	European Russia
624.20948	TG88.5	Scandinavia
624.209481	TG81-82	Norway
624.209485	TG89-90	Sweden
624.209489	TG69-70	Denmark
624.2094897	TG95.F5	Finland
624.209492	TG77-78	Netherlands
624.209493	TG67-68	Belgium
624.209494	TG91-92	Switzerland
624.209495	TG75-76	Greece
624.209496	TG95.A2	Balkans
624.209497	TG95.Y8	Yugoslavia
624.20951	TG101-102	China
624.20952	TG105-106	Japan
624.20954	TG103-104	India

Dewey	LC	Descriptor
624.2095491	TG104.5-.6	Pakistan
624.2095493	TG104.7-.8	Sri Lanka
624.20955	TG107-108	Iran
624.209561	TG111-112	Turkey
624.209567	TG113.I7	Iraq
624.2095694	TG113.I75	Israel/Palestine
624.20957	TG109-110	Asian Russia
624.209598	TG113.I55	Indonesia
624.209599	TG113.P6	Philippines
624.2096	TG115-119	Africa
624.2096(1-9)	TG119	Africa, By country
624.20962	TG117-118	Egypt
624.20971	TG26-27	Canada
624.20972	TG28-29	Mexico
624.209728	TG30-31	Central America
624.209729	TG32-33	West Indies
624.20973	TG23-25	United States
624.20981	TG41-42	Brazil
624.20982	TG36-37	Argentina
624.20983	TG43-44	Chile
624.20984	TG38-39	Bolivia
624.20985	TG52	Peru
624.209861	TG45-46	Colombia
624.209866	TG47	Ecuador
624.20987	TG54	Venezuela
624.209881	TG48	Guyana
624.209882	TG50	French Guiana
624.209883	TG49	Suriname
624.209892	TG51	Paraguay
624.209895	TG53	Uruguay
624.2099(5-6)	TG123-124	Oceania
624.20993	TG122.5-.6	New Zealand
624.20994	TG121-122	Australia
624.20998	TG125-126	Polar areas
624.25	TG301-304	Bridge design and drafting
624.28	TG315	Maintenance/Repair
624.28	TG325	Abutments/Retaining walls
624.28	TG326	Details (Bearings/Etc.)
624.283	TG325.6	Floors
624.284	TG320	Bridge foundations
624.32	TG365-370	Trustle bridges
624.37	TG350-360	Beam and girder bridges
624.38	TG375-380	Trussed bridges
624.6	TG327-340	Arched bridges
625.(4-6)	TF670-851	Local and light railways
625.(4-6)	TF677-851	By type
625.(4-6)	TF701-851	Municipal railways
625.(7-8)	TE	Highway engineering
625.(74/88)	TE229-.8	Country roads/Paths/ Driveways
625.1	TF200-320	Railway construction
625.1	TF863-912	Construction
625.1	TF	Railroad engineering
625.1(1-2)	TF208	Preliminary operations
625.100(5/6)	TF1-4	Serials/Societies
625.10025	TF12	Directories
625.100289	TF610	Safety measures
625.1003	TF9	Encyclopedias/Dictionaries
625.1006	TF5	Congresses
625.1007	TF171-183	Education
625.10074	TF6	Exhibitions/Museums
625.1009	TF15-20	History
625.1009(4-9)	TF1021-1126	By country and system
625.1009(4-9)	TF21-126	By place
625.10092	TF139-140	Biography
625.100941	TF1057-1064.5	Great Britain
625.100941	TF57-64.5	Great Britain

Dewey	LC	Descriptor
625.2	TF550-606	Trains
625.2	TF371-498	Rolling stock and cars
625.2	TF340-498	Railroad equipment
625.23	TF668	Dining car service
625.26	TF975	Electric locomotives
625.263	TJ603-695	Locomotives
625.263	TF855-1126	Electric railways
625.7	TE279	Streets
625.7(042/94)	TE228	Safety and traffic control
625.70(212/687)	TE180	Specifications and contracts
625.70(5/6)	TE1-4	Serials/Societies
625.7025	TE12	Directories
625.70287	TE450	Hauling and traction tests
625.70299	TE183	Estimates/Quantities/Costs
625.703	TE9	Dictionaries/Encyclopedias
625.706	TE5	Congresses
625.7068	TE185	Records/Timekeeping/Etc.
625.707	TE191	Education
625.7074	TE6	Museums/Exhibitions
625.709	TE15-19	History
625.709(4-9)	TE21-126	By place
625.7092	TE139-140	Biography
625.70941	TE57-64.5	Great Britain
625.70943	TE73-74.5	Germany
625.709436	TE65-.2	Austria
625.709437	TE65.3-.4	Czechoslovakia
625.709439	TE65.5-66	Hungary
625.70944	TE71-72.5	France
625.70945	TE79-80	Italy
625.70946	TE87-88	Spain
625.709469	TE83-84.5	Portugal
625.70947	TE85-86	European Russia
625.70948	TE88.5	Scandinavia
625.709481	TE81-82	Norway
625.709485	TE89-90	Sweden
625.709489	TE69-70	Denmark
625.7094897	TE95.F5	Finland
625.709492	TE77-78	Netherlands
625.709493	TE67-68	Belgium
625.709494	TE91-92	Switzerland
625.709495	TE75-76	Greece
625.709496	TE95.A2	Balkans
625.709497	TE95.Y8	Yugoslavia
625.70951	TE101-102	China
625.70952	TE105-106	Japan
625.70954	TE103-104	India
625.7095491	TE104.5-.6	Pakistan
625.7095493	TE104.7-.8	Sri Lanka
625.70955	TE107-108	Iran
625.709561	TE111-112	Turkey
625.709567	TE113.I7	Iraq
625.7095694	TE113.I175	Israel/Palestine
625.70957	TE109-110	Asian Russia
625.709598	TE113.I55	Indonesia
625.709599	TE113.P6	Philippines
625.7096	TE115-119	Africa
625.7096(1-9)	TE119	Africa, By country
625.70962	TE117-118	Egypt
625.70971	TE26-27	Canada
625.70972	TE28-29	Mexico
625.709728	TE30-31	Central America
625.709729	TE32-33	West Indies
625.70973	TE23-25	United States
625.70981	TE41-42	Brazil
625.70982	TE36-37	Argentina
625.70983	TE43-44	Chile
625.70984	TE38-39	Bolivia
625.70985	TE52	Peru
625.709861	TE45-46	Colombia
625.709866	TE47	Ecuador
625.70987	TE54	Venezuela
625.709881	TE48	Guyana
625.709882	TE50	French Guiana
625.709883	TE49	Suriname
625.709892	TE51	Paraguay
625.709895	TE53	Uruguay
625.7099(5-6)	TE123-124	Oceania
625.70993	TE122.5	New Zealand
625.70994	TE121-122	Australia
625.70998	TE125-126	Polar areas
625.723	TE206-209.5	Location engineering
625.725	TE175	Highway design
625.73	TE210-227	Construction details
625.74	TE230-245	Special kinds of unpaved roads
625.763	TD868-870	Snow/Ice on streets
625.77	TE177-178	Roadside development
625.792	TE247	Ice roads/Crossings/Bridges
625.8	TE250-278.6	Pavements and paved roads
625.8(1-6)	TE200-205	Materials
625.88	TE280-295	Sidewalks/Footpaths/Flagging
625.888	TE298	Curbs/Curbstones
625.889	TE304	Trails
625.889	TE303	Equestrian roads
625.889	TE301	Bicycle paths
627	TC	Hydraulic engineering
627.0(5/6)	TC1-5	Serials/Societies/Congresses
627.03	TC9	Encyclopedias
627.07	TC157-.5	Education
627.072	TC158	Laboratories
627.074	TC6	Exhibitions/Museums
627.09	TC15-20	History
627.09(3-9)	TC21-126	By place
627.092	TC139-140	Biography
627.0941	TC57-64.5	Great Britain
627.09411	TC61-62	Scotland
627.09417	TC59-.3	Ireland
627.0943	TC73-74.5	Germany
627.09436	TC65-.2	Austria
627.09437	TC65.3-.4	Czechoslovakia
627.09438	TC95.P7	Poland
627.09439	TC65.5-66	Hungary
627.0944	TC71-72.5	France
627.0945	TC79-80	Italy
627.094591	TC104.5-.6	Pakistan
627.094593	TC104.7-.8	Sri Lanka
627.0946	TC85-86	Spain
627.09469	TC83-84.5	Portugal
627.0947	TC109-110	Asian Russia
627.0948	TC88.5	Scandinavia
627.09481	TC81-82	Norway
627.09485	TC89-90	Sweden
627.09489	TC69-70	Denmark
627.094897	TC95.F5	Finland
627.09492	TC77-78	Netherlands
627.09493	TC67-68	Belgium
627.09494	TC91-92	Switzerland
627.09495	TC75-76	Greece
627.09496	TC95.A2	Balkans
627.09497	TC95.Y8	Yugoslavia
627.0951	TC101-102	China
627.0952	TC105-106	Japan

Dewey	LC	Descriptor
627.0954	TC103-104	India
627.0955	TC107-108	Iran
627.09561	TC111-112	Turkey
627.09567	TC113.I7	Iraq
627.095694	TC113.I75	Israel/Palestine
627.09598	TC113.I55	Indonesia
627.09599	TC113.P6	Philippines
627.096	TC115	Africa, General
627.096(1-9)	TC119	Africa, By country
627.0962	TC117-118	Egypt
627.0971	TC26-27	Canada
627.0972	TC28-29	Mexico
627.09728	TC30-31	Central America
627.09729	TC32-33	West Indies
627.0973	TC23-25	United States
627.0981	TC41-42	Brazil
627.0982	TC36-37	Argentina
627.0983	TC43-44	Chile
627.0984	TC38-39	Bolivia
627.0985	TC52	Peru
627.09861	TC45-46	Colombia
627.09866	TC47	Ecuador
627.0987	TC54	Venezuela
627.09881	TC48	Guyana
627.09882	TC50	French Guiana
627.09883	TC49	Suriname
627.09892	TC51	Paraguay
627.09895	TC53	Uruguay
627.099(5-6)	TC123-124	Oceania
627.0993	TC122.5	New Zealand
627.0994	TC121-122	Australia
627.0998	TC125-126	Polar regions
627.13	TC601-791	Canals/Waterways
627.1309(4-9)	TC615-726	History, By place
627.130941	TC657-664.5	Great Britain
627.130943	TC673-674.5	Germany
627.1309436	TC665-.2	Austria
627.1309437	TC665.3-.4	Czechoslovakia
627.1309439	TC665.5-666	Hungary
627.130944	TC671-672.5	France
627.130945	TC679-680	Italy
627.130946	TC687-688	Spain
627.1309469	TC683-684.5	Portugal
627.130947	TC685-686	European Russia
627.130948	TC688.5	Scandinavia
627.1309481	TC681-682	Norway
627.1309485	TC689-690	Sweden
627.1309489	TC669-670	Denmark
627.13094897	TC695.F5	Finland
627.1309492	TC677-678	Netherlands
627.1309493	TC667-668	Belgium
627.1309494	TC691-692	Switzerland
627.1309495	TC675-676	Greece
627.1309496	TC695.A2	Balkans
627.1309497	TC695.Y8	Yugoslavia
627.130951	TC701-702	China
627.130952	TC705-706	Japan
627.130954	TC703-704	India
627.13095491	TC704.5-.6	Pakistan
627.13095493	TC704.7-.8	Sri Lanka
627.130955	TC707-708	Iran
627.1309561	TC711-712	Turkey
627.1309567	TC713.I7	Iraq
627.13095694	TC713.I75	Israel/Palestine
627.130957	TC709-710	Asian Russia
627.1309598	TC713.I55	Indonesia
627.1309599	TC713.P6	Philippines
627.13096	TC715	Africa
627.13096(1-9)	TC719	Africa, By country
627.130962	TC717-718	Egypt
627.130971	TC626-627	Canada
627.130972	TC628-629	Mexico
627.1309728	TC630-631	Central America
627.1309729	TC632-633	West Indies
627.130973	TC623-625	United States
627.130981	TC641-642	Brazil
627.130982	TC636-637	Argentina
627.130983	TC643-644	Chile
627.130984	TC638-639	Bolivia
627.130985	TC652	Peru
627.1309861	TC645-646	Colombia
627.1309866	TC647	Ecuador
627.130987	TC654	Venezuela
627.1309881	TC648	Guyana
627.1309882	TC650	French Guiana
627.1309883	TC649	Suriname
627.1309892	TC651	Paraguay
627.1309895	TC653	Uruguay
627.13099(5-6)	TC723-724	Oceania
627.130993	TC722.5	New Zealand
627.130994	TC721-722	Australia
627.130998	TC725-726	Polar areas
627.137	TC773-788	Isthmian canal projects
627.137	TC774-781	Panama Canal
627.137	TC791	Suez Canal
627.2	TC203-365	Harbors/Coast protective works
627.4	TC530-537	Protective works/Flood control
627.5	TC801-937	Irrigation/Land reclamation
627.509(4-9)	TC815-926	By place
627.50941	TC857-864.5	Great Britain
627.50943	TC873-874.5	Germany
627.509436	TC865-.2	Austria
627.509437	TC865.3-.4	Czechoslovakia
627.509439	TC865.5-866	Hungary
627.50944	TC871-872.5	France
627.50945	TC879-880	Italy
627.50946	TC887-888	Spain
627.509469	TC883-884.5	Portugal
627.50947	TC885-886	European Russia
627.50948	TC888.5	Scandinavia
627.509481	TC881-882	Norway
627.509485	TC889-890	Sweden
627.509489	TC869-870	Denmark
627.5094897	TC895.F5	Finland
627.509492	TC877-878	Netherlands
627.509493	TC867-868	Belgium
627.509494	TC891-892	Switzerland
627.509495	TC875-876	Greece
627.509496	TC895.A2	Balkans
627.509497	TC895.Y8	Yugoslavia
627.50951	TC901-902	China
627.50952	TC905-906	Japan
627.50954	TC903-904	India
627.5095491	TC904.5-.6	Pakistan
627.5095493	TC904.7-.8	Sri Lanka
627.50955	TC907-908	Iran
627.509561	TC911-912	Turkey
627.509567	TC913.I7	Iraq
627.5095694	TC913.I75	Israel/Palestine
627.50957	TC909-910	Asian Russia
627.509598	TC913.I55	Indonesia
627.509599	TC913.P6	Philippines

Dewey	LC	Descriptor
627.5096	TC915	Africa
627.5096(1-9)	TC919	Africa, By country
627.50962	TC917-918	Egypt
627.50971	TC826-827	Canada
627.50972	TC828-829	Mexico
627.509728	TC830-831	Central America
627.509729	TC832-833	West Indies
627.50973	TC823-825	United States
627.50981	TC841-842	Brazil
627.50982	TC836-837	Argentina
627.50983	TC843-844	Chile
627.50984	TC838-839	Bolivia
627.50985	TC852	Peru
627.509861	TC845-846	Colombia
627.509866	TC847	Ecuador
627.50987	TC854	Venezuela
627.509881	TC848	Guyana
627.509882	TC850	French Guiana
627.509883	TC849	Suriname
627.509892	TC851	Paraguay
627.509895	TC853	Uruguay
627.5099(5-6)	TC923-924	Oceania
627.50993	TC922.5	New Zealand
627.50994	TC921-922	Australia
627.50998	TC925-926	Polar areas
627.54	TC970-978	Drainage
627.7	TC195-201	Submarine building
627.702	TC183-201	Dredging/Preliminaries
627.72	VM975-989	Diving
627.8	TC540-558	Dams
627.922	TC375-381	Lighthouses
628	TD	Environmental engineering
628	TD158-167	Municipal engineering
628	RA565-600	Environmental health
628.0(5/6)	TD1-5	Serials/Societies/Congresses
628.023	TD156	As a profession
628.025	TD12	Directories
628.03	TD9	Dictionaries/Encyclopedias
628.074	TD6	Exhibitions/Museums
628.09	TD15-20	History
628.09(4-9)	TD21-126	By place
628.090(1-4)	TD16-20	By date
628.092	TD139-140	Biography
628.0941	TD57-64.5	Great Britain
628.0943	TD73-74.5	Germany
628.09436	TD65-.2	Austria
628.09437	TD65.3-.4	Czechoslovakia
628.09439	TD65.5-66	Hungary
628.0944	TD71-72.5	France
628.0945	TD79-80	Italy
628.0946	TD87-88	Spain
628.09469	TD83-84.5	Portugal
628.0947	TD85-86	European Russia
628.0948	TD88.5	Scandinavia
628.09481	TD81-82	Norway
628.09485	TD89-90	Sweden
628.09489	TD69-70	Denmark
628.094897	TD95.F5	Finland
628.09492	TD77-78	Netherlands
628.09493	TD67-68	Belgium
628.09494	TD91-92	Switzerland
628.09495	TD75-76	Greece
628.09496	TD95.A2	Balkans
628.09497	TD95.Y8	Yugoslavia
628.0951	TD101-102	China
628.0952	TD105-106	Japan
628.0954	TD103-104	India
628.095491	TD104.5-.6	Pakistan
628.095493	TD104.7-.8	Sri Lanka
628.0955	TD107-108	Iran
628.09561	TD111-112	Turkey
628.09567	TD113.I7	Iraq
628.095694	TD113.I75	Israel/Palestine
628.0957	TD109-110	Asian Russia
628.09598	TD113.I55	Indonesia
628.09599	TD113.P6	Philippines
628.096	TD115-119	Africa
628.096(1-9)	TD119	Africa, By country
628.0962	TD117-118	Egypt
628.0971	TD26-27	Canada
628.0972	TD28-29	Mexico
628.09728	TD30-31	Central America
628.09729	TD32-33	West Indies
628.0973	TD23-25	United States
628.0981	TD41-42	Brazil
628.0982	TD36-37	Argentina
628.0983	TD43-44	Chile
628.0984	TD38-39	Bolivia
628.0985	TD52	Peru
628.09861	TD45-46	Colombia
628.09866	TD47	Ecuador
628.0987	TD54	Venezuela
628.09881	TD48	Guyana
628.09882	TD50	French Guiana
628.09883	TD49	Suriname
628.09892	TD51	Paraguay
628.09895	TD53	Uruguay
628.099(5-6)	TD123-124	Oceania
628.0993	TD122.5-.6	New Zealand
628.0994	TD121-122	Australia
628.0998	TD125-126	Polar areas
628.1	TC401-526	River/Water supply engineering
628.1	TD201-500	Water supply
628.10(5/6)	TC401	Serials/Societies/Congresses
628.109	TC415-526	History, By place
628.109	TD215-220	History
628.109(4-9)	TD221-326	Water supply, By place
628.1090(1-4)	TD216-220	By date
628.10941	TD257-264.5	Great Britain
628.10941	TC457-464.5	Great Britain
628.10943	TC473-474.5	Germany
628.10943	TD273-274.5	Germany
628.109436	TD265-.2	Austria
628.109436	TC465-.2	Austria
628.109437	TD265.3-.4	Czechoslovakia
628.109437	TC465.3-.4	Czechoslovakia
628.109438	TC495.P7	Poland
628.109439	TC465.5-466	Hungary
628.109439	TD265.5-266	Hungary
628.10944	TC471-472.5	France
628.10944	TD271-272.5	France
628.10945	TD279-280	Italy
628.10946	TD287-288	Spain
628.10946	TC487-488	Spain
628.109469	TC483-484.5	Portugal
628.109469	TD283-284.5	Portugal
628.10947	TD285-286	European Russia
628.10947	TC485-486	European Russia
628.10948	TC488.5	Scandinavia
628.10948	TD288.5	Scandinavia
628.109481	TD281-282	Norway
628.109485	TC489-490	Sweden

Dewey	LC	Descriptor
628.109485	TD289-290	Sweden
628.109489	TD269-270	Denmark
628.109489	TC469-470	Denmark
628.1094897	TD295.F5	Finland
628.1094897	TC495.F5	Finland
628.109492	TD277-278	Netherlands
628.109492	TC477-478	Netherlands
628.109493	TC467-468	Belgium
628.109493	TD267-268	Belgium
628.109494	TC491-492	Switzerland
628.109494	TD291-292	Switzerland
628.109495	TD275-276	Greece
628.109495	TC475-476	Greece
628.109496	TD295.A2	Balkans
628.109496	TC495.A2	Balkans
628.109497	TD295.Y8	Yugoslavia
628.109497	TC495.Y8	Yugoslavia
628.10951	TC501-502	China
628.10951	TD301-302	China
628.10952	TC505-506	Japan
628.10952	TD305-306	Japan
628.10954	TC503-504	India
628.10954	TD303-304	India
628.1095491	TC504.5-.6	Pakistan
628.1095491	TD304.5-.6	Pakistan
628.1095493	TC504.7-.8	Sri Lanka
628.1095493	TD304.7-.8	Sri Lanka
628.10955	TC507-508	Iran
628.10955	TD307-308	Iran
628.109561	TC511-512	Turkey
628.109561	TD311-312	Turkey
628.109567	TD313.I7	Iraq
628.109567	TC513.I7	Iraq
628.1095694	TD313.I75	Israel/Palestine
628.1095694	TC513.I75	Israel/Palestine
628.10957	TD309-310	Asian Russia
628.10957	TC509-510	Asian Russia
628.109598	TD313.I55	Indonesia
628.109598	TC513.I55	Indonesia
628.109599	TC513.P6	Philippines
628.109599	TD313.P6	Philippines
628.1096	TD315-319	Africa
628.1096	TC515	Africa, General
628.1096(1-9)	TD319	Africa, By country
628.1096(1-9)	TC519	Africa, By country
628.10962	TC517-518	Egypt
628.10962	TD317-318	Egypt
628.10971	TD226-227	Canada
628.10971	TC426-427	Canada
628.10972	TC428-429	Mexico
628.10972	TD228-229	Mexico
628.109728	TD230-231	Central America
628.109728	TC430-431	Central America
628.109729	TC432-433	West Indies
628.109729	TD232-233	West Indies
628.10973	TD223-225	United States
628.10973	TC423-425	United States
628.10981	TC441-442	Brazil
628.10981	TD241-242	Brazil
628.10982	TD236-237	Argentina
628.10982	TC436-437	Argentina
628.10983	TC443-444	Chile
628.10983	TD243-244	Chile
628.10984	TD238-239	Bolivia
628.10984	TC438-439	Bolivia
628.10985	TC452	Peru
628.10985	TD252	Peru
628.109861	TD245-246	Colombia
628.109861	TC445-446	Colombia
628.109866	TD247	Ecuador
628.109866	TC447	Ecuador
628.10987	TD254	Venezuela
628.10987	TC454	Venezuela
628.109881	TC448	Guyana
628.109881	TD248	Guyana
628.109882	TD250	French Guiana
628.109882	TC450	French Guiana
628.109883	TD249	Suriname
628.109883	TC449	Suriname
628.109892	TD251	Paraguay
628.109892	TC451	Paraguay
628.109895	TD253	Uruguay
628.109895	TC453	Uruguay
628.1099(5-6)	TD323-324	Oceania
628.1099(5-6)	TC523-524	Oceania
628.10993	TD322.5-.6	New Zealand
628.10993	TC522.5	New Zealand
628.10994	TD321-322	Australia
628.10994	TC521-522	Australia
628.10998	TC525-526	Polar areas
628.10998	TD325-326	Polar areas
628.11	TD390-418	Sources of water supply
628.13	TD388-.5	Water conservation
628.14	TD481-491	Water distribution
628.16	TD365-387	Water quality
628.162	TD429	Water reuse
628.162	TD430-477	Water purification/Etc.
628.167	TD478-480.7	Saline water conversion
628.168	TD420-427	Water pollution
628.2	TD675-725	Sewers
628.2	TD662-670	Sewerage systems
628.3	TD730-737	Sewage
628.3	TD511-780	Sewage collection/ Sewerage
628.30(5/6)	TD511	Serials/Societies/Congresses
628.309	TD515-520	History
628.3090(4-9)	TD521-626	Sewerage, By place
628.3090(1-4)	TD516-520	By date
628.30941	TD557-564.5	Great Britain
628.30943	TD573-574.5	Germany
628.309436	TD565-.2	Austria
628.309437	TD565.3-.4	Czechoslovakia
628.309439	TD565.5-566	Hungary
628.30944	TD571-572.5	France
628.30945	TD579-580	Italy
628.30946	TD587-588	Spain
628.309469	TD583-584.5	Portugal
628.30947	TD585-586	European Russia
628.30948	TD588.5	Scandinavia
628.309481	TD581-582	Norway
628.309485	TD589-590	Sweden
628.309489	TD569-570	Denmark
628.3094897	TD595.F5	Finland
628.309492	TD577-578	Netherlands
628.309493	TD567-568	Belgium
628.309494	TD591-592	Switzerland
628.309495	TD575-576	Greece
628.309496	TD595.A2	Balkans
628.309497	TD595.Y8	Yugoslavia
628.30951	TD601-602	China
628.30952	TD605-606	Japan
628.30954	TD603-604	India
628.3095491	TD604.5-.6	Pakistan
628.3095493	TD604.7-.8	Sri Lanka

Dewey	LC	Descriptor
628.30955	TD607-608	Iran
628.309561	TD611-612	Turkey
628.309567	TD613.I7	Iraq
628.3095694	TD613.I175	Israel/Palestine
628.30957	TD609-610	Asian Russia
628.309598	TD613.I55	Indonesia
628.309599	TD613.P6	Philippines
628.3096	TD615-619	Africa
628.3096(1-9)	TD619	Africa, By country
628.30962	TD617-618	Egypt
628.30971	TD526-527	Canada
628.30972	TD528-529	Mexico
628.309728	TD530-531	Central America
628.309729	TD532-533	West Indies
628.30973	TD523-525	United States
628.30981	TD541-542	Brazil
628.30982	TD536-537	Argentina
628.30983	TD543-544	Chile
628.30984	TD538-539	Bolivia
628.30985	TD552	Peru
628.309861	TD545-546	Colombia
628.309866	TD547	Ecuador
628.30987	TD554	Venezuela
628.309881	TD548	Guyana
628.309882	TD550	French Guiana
628.309883	TD549	Suriname
628.309892	TD551	Paraguay
628.309895	TD553	Uruguay
628.3099(5-6)	TD623-624	Oceania
628.30993	TD622.5-.6	New Zealand
628.30994	TD621-622	Australia
628.30998	TD625-626	Polar areas
628.36	TD741-780	Sewage disposal
628.44	TD785-812	Municipal refuse/Solid wastes
628.440(5/6)	TD785	Serials/Societies/Congresses
628.440299	TD793.7	Estimates/Costs
628.44072	TD793.3	Research
628.4409(3-9)	TD789	Other countries
628.440973	TD788-.4	United States
628.442	TD794	Collection
628.445	TD795-812	Special disposal methods
628.46	TD813-870	Street cleaning/Litter
628.46028	TD860	Tools/Appliances
628.4609(3-9)	TD815-849	By place
628.46094	TD835-836	Europe
628.46095	TD838-839	Asia
628.46096	TD841-843	Africa
628.460971	TD820-822	Canada
628.460972	TD824-825	Mexico
628.4609728	TD826-827	Central America
628.4609729	TD829-830	West Indies
628.460973	TD817-819	United States
628.46098	TD832-833	South America
628.46099(3-6)	TD845-849	Australia/New Zealand/ Oceania
628.5	TD878-893.5	Special types of pollution
628.5	TD172-192	Environmental pollution
628.5028	TD192	Pollution control equipment
628.507(2)	TD178-.8	Education/Research
628.509	TD179	History
628.509(4-9)	TD179.5-190.7	By place
628.5094	TD186-.5	Europe
628.5095	TD187-.5	Asia
628.5096	TD188-.5	Africa
628.50971	TD182-.4	Canada
628.50972	TD182.6-.7	Mexico

Dewey	LC	Descriptor
628.509728	TD183-.5	Central America
628.509729	TD184-.5	West Indies
628.50973	TD180-181	United States
628.5098	TD185-.5	South America
628.5099(3-6)	TD189-.5	Australia/New Zealand/ Oceania
628.50998	TD190-.7	Polar regions
628.51	TD895-899	Industrial/Factory sanitation
628.53	TD881-890	Air
628.55	TD878-879	Soil
628.7	TD920-929	Rural sanitary engineering
629.(2/1)	TL	Motor vehicles/Aeronautics
629.04	TA1001-1280	Transportation engineering
629.040(5/6)	TA1001-1005	Serials/Societies/Congresses
629.04023	TA1160	As a profession
629.0403	TA1009	Dictionaries/ Encyclopedias
629.0407	TA1163	Education
629.0409	TA1015	History
629.0409(3-9)	TA1021-1126	By place
629.040941	TA1057-1064.5	Great Britain
629.040943	TA1073-1074.5	Germany
629.0409436	TA1065-.2	Austria
629.0409437	TA1065.3-.4	Czechoslovakia
629.0409439	TA1065.5-1066	Hungary
629.040944	TA1071-1072.5	France
629.040945	TA1079-1080	Italy
629.040946	TA1087-1088	Spain
629.0409469	TA1083-1084.5	Portugal
629.040947	TA1085-1086	European Russia
629.040948	TA1088.5	Scandinavia
629.0409481	TA1081-1082	Norway
629.0409485	TA1089-1090	Sweden
629.0409489	TA1069-1070	Denmark
629.04094897	TA1095.F5	Finland
629.0409492	TA1077-1078	Netherlands
629.0409493	TA1067-1068	Belgium
629.0409494	TA1091-1092	Switzerland
629.0409495	TA1075-1076	Greece
629.0409496	TA1095.A2	Balkans
629.0409497	TA1095.Y8	Yugoslavia
629.040951	TA1101-1102	China
629.040952	TA1105-1106	Japan
629.040954	TA1103-1104	India
629.04095491	TA1104.5-.6	Pakistan
629.04095493	TA1104.7-.8	Sri Lanka
629.040955	TA1107-1108	Iran
629.0409561	TA1111-1112	Turkey
629.0409567	TA1113.I7	Iraq
629.04095694	TA1113.I175	Israel/Palestine
629.040957	TA1109-1110	Asian Russia
629.0409598	TA1113.I55	Indonesia
629.0409599	TA1113.P6	Philippines
629.04096	TA1115-1119	Africa
629.04096(1-9)	TA1119	Africa, By country
629.040962	TA1117-1118	Egypt
629.040971	TA1026-1027	Canada
629.040972	TA1028-1029	Mexico
629.0409728	TA1030-1031	Central America
629.0409729	TA1032-1033	West Indies
629.040973	TA1023-1025	United States
629.040981	TA1041-1042	Brazil
629.040982	TA1036-1037	Argentina
629.040983	TA1043-1044	Chile
629.040984	TA1038-1039	Bolivia
629.040985	TA1052	Peru
629.0409861	TA1045-1046	Colombia

Dewey	LC	Descriptor
629.0409866	TA1047	Ecuador
629.040987	TA1054	Venezuela
629.0409881	TA1048	Guyana
629.0409882	TA1050	French Guiana
629.0409883	TA1049	Suriname
629.0409892	TA1051	Paraguay
629.0409895	TA1053	Uruguay
629.04099(5-6)	TA1123-1124	Oceania
629.040993	TA1122.5-.6	New Zealand
629.040994	TA1121-1122	Australia
629.040998	TA1125-1126	Polar areas
629.048	TC601-791	Canals/Waterways
629.04809(4-9)	TC615-726	History, By place
629.0480941	TC657-664.5	Great Britain
629.0480943	TC673-674.5	Germany
629.04809436	TC665-.2	Austria
629.04809437	TC665.3-.4	Czechoslovakia
629.04809439	TC665.5-666	Hungary
629.0480944	TC671-672.5	France
629.0480945	TC679-680	Italy
629.0480946	TC687-688	Spain
629.04809469	TC683-684.5	Portugal
629.0480947	TC685-686	European Russia
629.0480948	TC688.5	Scandinavia
629.04809481	TC681-682	Norway
629.04809485	TC689-690	Sweden
629.04809489	TC669-670	Denmark
629.048094897	TC695.F5	Finland
629.04809492	TC677-678	Netherlands
629.04809493	TC667-668	Belgium
629.04809494	TC691-692	Switzerland
629.04809495	TC675-676	Greece
629.04809496	TC695.A2	Balkans
629.04809497	TC695.Y8	Yugoslavia
629.0480951	TC701-702	China
629.0480952	TC705-706	Japan
629.0480954	TC703-704	India
629.048095491	TC704.5-.6	Pakistan
629.048095493	TC704.7-.8	Sri Lanka
629.0480955	TC707-708	Iran
629.04809561	TC711-712	Turkey
629.04809567	TC713.I7	Iraq
629.048095694	TC713.I75	Israel/Palestine
629.0480957	TC709-710	Asian Russia
629.04809598	TC713.I55	Indonesia
629.04809599	TC713.P6	Philippines
629.048096	TC715	Africa
629.048096(1-9)	TC719	Africa, By country
629.0480962	TC717-718	Egypt
629.0480971	TC626-627	Canada
629.0480972	TC628-629	Mexico
629.04809728	TC630-631	Central America
629.04809729	TC632-633	West Indies
629.0480973	TC623-625	United States
629.0480981	TC641-642	Brazil
629.0480982	TC636-637	Argentina
629.0480983	TC643-644	Chile
629.0480984	TC638-639	Bolivia
629.0480985	TC652	Peru
629.04809861	TC645-646	Colombia
629.04809866	TC647	Ecuador
629.0480987	TC654	Venezuela
629.04809881	TC648	Guyana
629.04809882	TC650	French Guiana
629.04809883	TC649	Suriname
629.04809892	TC651	Paraguay
629.04809895	TC653	Uruguay

Dewey	LC	Descriptor
629.048099(5-6)	TC723-724	Oceania
629.0480993	TC722.5	New Zealand
629.0480994	TC721-722	Australia
629.0480998	TC725-726	Polar areas
629.13	TL500-777	Aeronautics
629.13(251/5)	TL586-589.7	Navigation and instruments
629.1300(5/6)	TL500-505	Serials/Societies/Congresses
629.13009	TL515-516	History
629.13009(4-9)	TL521-532	By place
629.13009(72-8)	TL524-525	Mexico/West Indies/Latin Amer.
629.130092	TL539-540	Biography
629.130094	TL526	Europe
629.130095	TL527	Asia
629.130096	TL528	Africa
629.1300971	TL523	Canada
629.1300973	TL521-522	United States
629.130099(3-6)	TL529-530	Australia/New Zealand/ Oceania
629.130684	TL553.5	Accidents
629.1323	TL570-574	Aerodynamics
629.1324	TL556-558	Meteorology
629.1325	TL710-713	Flying
629.133	TL600-688	Aircraft type
629.1332	TL605-668	Lighter than air
629.1333	TL670-688	Heavier than air
629.135	TL692-694	Communication
629.1351	TL695-696	Electronic aids to navigation
629.136	TL725-733	Airways/Airports/Fields
629.2	TL1-480	Motor vehicles
629.20(5/6)	TL1-5	Serials/Societies
629.2025	TL12	Directories
629.203	TL9	Dictionaries
629.206	TL6	Congresses
629.2074	TL7	Exhibitions/Museums
629.209	TL15	History
629.209(4-9)	TL21-126	By place
629.2092	TL139-140	Biography
629.20941	TL57-64.5	Great Britain
629.20943	TL73-74.5	Germany
629.209436	TL65-.2	Austria
629.209437	TL65.3-.4	Czechoslovakia
629.209439	TL65.5-66	Hungary
629.20944	TL71-72.5	France
629.20945	TL79-80	Italy
629.20946	TL87-88	Spain
629.209469	TL83-84.5	Portugal
629.20947	TL85-86	European Russia
629.20948	TL88.5	Scandinavia
629.209481	TL81-82	Norway
629.209485	TL89-90	Sweden
629.209489	TL69-70	Denmark
629.2094897	TL95.F5	Finland
629.209492	TL77-78	Netherlands
629.209493	TL67-68	Belgium
629.209494	TL91-92	Switzerland
629.209495	TL75-76	Greece
629.209496	TL95.A2	Balkans
629.209497	TL95.Y8	Yugoslavia
629.20951	TL101-102	China
629.20952	TL105-106	Japan
629.20954	TL103-104	India
629.2095491	TL104.5-.6	Pakistan
629.2095493	TL104.7-.8	Sri Lanka
629.20955	TL107-108	Iran
629.209561	TL111-112	Turkey

Dewey	LC	Descriptor
629.209567	TL113.I7	Iraq
629.2095694	TL113.I75	Israel/Palestine
629.20957	TL109-110	Asian Russia
629.209598	TL113.I55	Indonesia
629.209599	TL113.P6	Philippines
629.2096	TL115-119	Africa
629.2096(1-9)	TL119	Africa, By country
629.20962	TL117-118	Egypt
629.20971	TL26-27	Canada
629.20972	TL28-29	Mexico
629.209728	TL30-31	Central America
629.209729	TL32-33	West Indies
629.20973	TL23-25	United States
629.20981	TL41-42	Brazil
629.20982	TL36-37	Argentina
629.20983	TL43-44	Chile
629.20984	TL38-39	Bolivia
629.20985	TL52	Peru
629.209861	TL45-46	Colombia
629.209866	TL47	Ecuador
629.20987	TL54	Venezuela
629.209881	TL48	Guyana
629.209882	TL50	French Guiana
629.209883	TL49	Suriname
629.209892	TL51	Paraguay
629.209895	TL53	Uruguay
629.2099(5-6)	TL123-124	Oceania
629.20993	TL122.5-.6	New Zealand
629.20994	TL121-122	Australia
629.20998	TL125-126	Polar areas
629.227	TL400-460	Cycles
629.2275	TL439-448	Motorcycles
629.23	TL240-275	Design/Construction/Equipment
629.250(1-9)	TL200-229	Automobiles (By power type)
629.283	TL151.5-.7	Operation (Driving)
629.4	TL787-4050	Astronautics/Space travel
629.4(5/11)	TL1050-1060	Astrodynamics/Flight mechanics
629.40289	TL867	Safety
629.4068	TL869	Contracts
629.407	TL845-849	Education
629.409(4-9)	TL789.8	By place
629.4507	TL1085	Space flight training
629.453	TL1065-1080	Space navigation
629.453	TL3000-3280	Astrionics/Electronics
629.455	TL799	Flights (By planet)
629.458	TL1090-1095	Piloting
629.46	TL796-798	Artificial satellites
629.47	TL795	Spaceships
629.47	TL870-873	Systems engineering
629.47(1/3)	TL875-940	Vehicle design/Construction
629.472	TL950-953	Materials (Vehicle)
629.474	TL1100-1102	Electric equipment on vehicles
629.4742	TL1082	Instruments
629.477	TL1500-1575	Human engineering/Life support
629.4774	TL945	Sterilization (Vehicle)
629.478	TL4000-4050	Ground support
630	SB	Plant culture
630-638	S	Agriculture
630-638	S519	Juvenile literature
630-638. + 097(4-9)	S22.7-131	By state
630-638. + 099(5-6)	S398-400	Oceania

Dewey	LC	Descriptor
630-638.(09071)	S133-164	Canada
630-638.(094)	S215-269	Europe
630-638.(0941)	S217-224	Great Britain
630-638.(09416)	S220.5-.6	Northern Ireland
630-638.(0943)	S231-232.6	Germany
630-638.(09436)	S225-226	Austria
630-638.(09439)	S227-228	Hungary
630-638.(0944)	S229-230	France
630-638.(0945)	S235-236	Italy
630-638.(0946)	S253-254	Spain
630-638.(09469)	S255-256	Portugal
630-638.(0947)	S241-242	European Russia
630-638.(09481)	S249-250	Norway
630-638.(09485)	S251-252	Sweden
630-638.(09489)	S245-246	Denmark
630-638.(094912)	S247-248	Iceland
630-638.(09492)	S239-240	Netherlands
630-638.(09493)	S237-238	Belgium
630-638.(09494)	S257-258	Switzerland
630-638.(09495)	S233-234	Greece
630-638.(09497)	S267-268	Yugoslavia
630-638.(094977)	S261-262	Bulgaria
630-638.(09498)	S265-266	Romania
630-638.(095)	S313-314	Asian Russia
630-638.(095)	S270-322	Asia
630-638.(0951)	S277-278	China
630-638.(09519)	S305-306	Korea
630-638.(0952)	S303-304	Japan
630-638.(0954)	S279-280	India
630-638.(095493)	S281-282	Sri Lanka
630-638.(0955)	S307-308	Iran
630-638.(09561)	S315-316	Turkey
630-638.(09593)	S293-294	Thailand
630-638.(09595)	S295-296	Malay peninsula
630-638.(09596)	S287-288	Cambodia
630-638.(09597)	S285-286	Vietnam
630-638.(09598)	S297-298	Indonesia
630-638.(09599)	S301-302	Philippine Islands
630-638.(096)	S323-338	Africa
630-638.(09611)	S346-.6	Tunisia
630-638.(0962)	S341-342	Egypt
630-638.(0963)	S325-326	Ethiopia
630-638.(0964)	S367-368	Morocco
630-638.(0965)	S345-346	Algeria
630-638.(0966)	S347-348	West Africa
630-638.(096662)	S365-366	Liberia
630-638.(096711)	S359-360	Cameroon
630-638.(09673)	S373-374	Angola
630-638.(096751)	S339-340	Zaire
630-638.(09678)	S357-358	Tanzania
630-638.(09679)	S371-372	Mozambique
630-638.(0968)	S328-338	South/Southern Africa
630-638.(09691)	S349-350	Madagascar
630-638.(0972)	S165-166	Mexico
630-638.(09728)	S167-174	Central America
630-638.(09729)	S175-183	West Indies
630-638.(097299)	S184	Bermuda
630-638.(0973)	S21-131	United States
630-638.(098)	S185-212	South America
630-638.(0981)	S191-192	Brazil
630-638.(0982)	S187-188	Argentina
630-638.(0983)	S193-194	Chile
630-638.(0984)	S189-190	Bolivia
630-638.(0985)	S207-208	Peru
630-638.(09861)	S195-196	Colombia
630-638.(09866)	S197-198	Ecuador
630-638.(0987)	S211-212	Venezuela

Dewey	LC	Descriptor	Dewey	LC	Descriptor
630-638.(0988)	S199-204	The Guianas	631.5	SB185.8	Planting/Harvesting
630-638.(09892)	S205-206	Paraguay	631.5	S602.5-604.37	Methods of culture
630-638.(09895)	S209-210	Uruguay	631.5(2-36)	SB119-124	Propagation
630-638.(0993)	S397.7-.8	New Zealand	631.52	SB118.5-.75	Nurseries
630-638.(0994)	S381-397.5	Australia	631.521	SB113-118.45	Seeds
630-638.06073	S22	National societies/	631.54	SB125	Training/Pruning
		Congresses	631.55	HD1549	Gleaning
630-638.09(4-9)	S21-400	Documents/Etc., By place	631.55	SB129	Harvesting/Curing
630.(5/6)	SB1-13	Serials/Societies	631.58	SB111	Tropical farming
630.208	S671-760	Farm machinery/	631.583	SB414.6-417	Greenhouses
		Engineering	631.585	SB126.5	Hydroponics
630.25	SB44	Directories	631.586	SB110	Dry farming
630.2515	S600-.7	Agricultural meteorology	631.6	S604.8-621.5	Melioration/Reclamation
630.3	SB45	Encyclopedias/Dictionaries	631.8	S631-667	Fertilizers/Soil
630.5	S1-19	Serials			improvement
630.6	SB16	Congresses	632	SB599-989	Pests/Diseases
630.6	S20	Societies	632	SB957-969.8	Resistance to pesticides
630.68	S560-572	Farm economics/	632.0(5/6)	SB599	Serials/Societies
		management	632.025	SB600.5	Directories
630.7	S530-559	Education	632.03	SB600	Dictionaries
630.7(2)	SB51-56	Education/Research	632.06	SB599.2	Congresses
630.72	S539.5-542	Research/Experimentation	632.09(4-9)	SB605	By place
630.74	SB57-60	Exhibitions/Museums	632.19	SB744.5-746	Pollution
630.9	SB19-29	Documents, By place	632.5	SB610-615	Weeds/Parasitic plants/Etc.
630.9	SB71-87	History	632.6	SB992-998	Economic zoology
630.9	S419-481	History	632.60(5/6)	SB992	Serials/Societies/Congresses
630.9(4-9)	S441-481	By place	632.609	SB993.3-993.34	By place
630.9(4-9)	SB87	Other countries	632.609(4-9)	SB993.34	Other countries
630.901	S421-431	Ancient	632.60973	SB993.3-32	United States
630.901	SB73-77	Ancient	632.68	SB995-996	Birds
630.902	SB79	Medieval	632.69	SB993.5-994	Mammals (Deer/Rabbits/
630.903(1-2)	S435	16th-17th centuries			Rats)
630.903(3-4)	S437	18th-19th centuries	632.7	SB818-945	Economic entomology
630.92	SB61-63	Biography	632.7(1-9)	SB945	Specific insects
630.94(1-9)	S469	Other European countries	632.9	SB950-989	Pest control/Disease remedy
630.941	SB23	Great Britain	632.94	SB935-955	Methods of application
630.941	S453-460.6	Great Britain	632.95	SB950.9-970.41	Pesticides
630.943	SB27	Germany	632.95(1-4)	SB951.145-952	By type/Name
630.943	S465-466	Germany	632.95042	SB952.5	Safety measures
630.944	S463-464	France	632.96	SB974-989	Organic control/Protection
630.944	SB25	France	633	SB183-317	Field crops
630.95	S470-471	Asia	633-635	SB421-439.8	Classes of plants
630.96	S472-473	Africa	633.00(5/6)	SB183	Serials/Societies
630.97(4-9)	S443-451	By state	633.006	SB183.2	Congresses
630.971	S451.5	Canada	633.1	SB188-192	Grain/Cereal
630.972	S451.7	Mexico	633.2	SB193-207	Forage/Feed crops
630.9728	S476	Central America	633.2(1-5)	SB197-202	Grasses
630.9729	S477	West Indies	633.3	SB203-205	Legumes
630.973	S441-451	United States	633.5	SB241-261	Textile/Fiber plants
630.973	SB19-21	United States			(Hemp/Etc.)
630.973	SB83-85	United States	633.58	SB281-283	Basketwork/Matwork plants
630.98	S474-475	South America	633.6	SB215-239	Sugar plants (Beets/Cane)
630.99(5-6)	S479-.3	Oceania	633.7	SB267-279	Alkaloidal (Cocao/Tea/
630.993	S478.5	New Zealand			Tobacco)
630.994	S478	Australia	633.8(3-4)	SB305-307	Condiments/Spices
630.998(1-8)	S480	Arctic regions	633.81	SB301-303	Aromatic (Jasmine/
631	S583-587.5	Agricultural chemistry			Lavender)
631.2	S770-790.3	Structures/Buildings	633.85	SB298-299	Oil-bearing/Wax (Poppy/
631.208	SB46	Calendars/Rules			Palm)
631.3	S671-760	Farm machinery/	633.86	SB285-287	Dye plants
		Engineering	633.88	SB293-295	Medicinia plant culture
631.3	TJ1480-1496	Agricultural machinery	633.895	SB290-291	Gum/Resin plants
631.4	S590-599.9	Soils/Soil science	633.898	SB292	Insecticidal plants
631.45	S622-627	Soil conservation	634	SB354-402	Fruits/Orchards
631.45	S900-954	Conservation (Natural	634.9	SD	Forestry
		resorces)	634.9	SD411-428	Conservation/Protection
631.45	S604.5-605.64	Agricultural conservation	634.90(5/6)	SD1	Serials/Societies

Dewey	LC	Descriptor
634.9028	SD388	Equipment/Etc.
634.907	SD250-381	Education
634.9072	SD356	Research/Experimentation
634.909	SD11-115	Documents, By place
634.9090(1-4)	SD131-247.5	History of forest conditions
634.9094	SD45-83	Europe
634.90941	SD45-50	Great Britain
634.909415	SD51-52	Ireland
634.90943	SD61-62	Germany
634.909436	SD53-54	Austria
634.90944	SD59-60	France
634.90945	SD67-68	Italy
634.90946	SD75-76	Spain
634.90947	SD73-74	European Russia
634.909485	SD77-78	Sweden
634.909494	SD79-80	Switzerland
634.909495	SD63-64	Greece
634.9095	SD85-97	Asia
634.90951	SD85-86	China
634.90952	SD89-90	Japan
634.90954	SD87-88	India
634.909599	SD93-94	Philippine islands
634.9096	SD99-105	Africa
634.9097(4-9)	SD12	By state
634.90971	SD13-14	Canada
634.90972	SD15-16	Mexico
634.909728	SD17-18	Central America
634.909729	SD19	West Indies
634.90973	SD11-12	United States
634.9098	SD21-44	South America
634.90981	SD27-28	Brazil
634.90982	SD23-24	Argentina
634.90983	SD29-30	Chile
634.90984	SD25-26	Bolivia
634.90985	SD39-40	Peru
634.90985	SD41-42	Uruguay
634.909861	SD31-32	Colombia
634.909866	SD33-34	Ecuador
634.90987	SD43-44	Venezuela
634.90988	SD35-36	Guianas
634.909892	SD37-38	Paraguay
634.9099(5-6)	SD115	Oceania
634.90993	SD112-113	New Zealand
634.90994	SD110-111	Australia
634.92	SD561-668	Administration policy
634.95	SD391-409.5	Silviculture
634.97	SD383-385	Description (Trees/Forests)
634.97	SD395-397	By type
634.98	SD430-557	Exploitation/Utilization
634.99	SB170-171	Tree crops
635	SB175-177	Food crops (Legumes/Etc.)
635	SB317.5-319.77	Horticulture
635	SB320-353	Vegetables
635	SB450.9-467	Gardens/Gardening
635.(1-2)	SB209-211	Root/Tuber crops
635.(1-8)	SB608	By plant type
635.(6/7)91	SB781-793	Effect of elements on
635.0483	SB414.6-417	Greenhouses
635.9	SB403-450.87	Flowers/Ornamentals
635.9074	SB441-.75	Flower shows/Exhibitions
635.92	SB603.5	Garden pests/Diseases
635.932	SB434	Perennials
635.964(2/7)	SB433-.34	Lawns/Turf
635.967	SB469-476	Landscape gardening
635.9676	SB439	Wild plants
635.97(6/7)9(3-6)	SB761-795	Trees/Shrubs (Pest/ Diseases)

Dewey	LC	Descriptor
635.976	SB435-437	Shrubs/Ornamental trees
635.9824	QH68	Terrariums/Vivariums
635.986	SB418-419.5	Container/Indoor gardening
636	SF61	Textbooks
636	SF63-75.3	Handbooks
636	SF	Animal culture
636	SF75.5	Juvenile works
636.(3-8)	SF409	Small animal culture
636.(5-8)	SF399-401	Other domesticated animals
636.(7-9)	SF402-405	Fur-bearing animals
636.00(5/6)	SF1	Serials/Societies
636.0025	SF23-27	Directories
636.003	SF21	Dictionaries/ Encyclopedias
636.005	SF19	Yearbooks
636.006	SF5	Congresses
636.007(2)	SF81-83	Education/Research
636.0074	SF114-121	Exhibitions
636.009(4-9)	SF15	Documents, Other countries
636.0092	SF31-33	Biography
636.00973	SF11-13	Documents, United States
636.01	SF84.82-85.6	Stock ranges
636.08(4-5)	SF95-99	Feeds/Feeding/Nutrition
636.0812	SF101-103.5	Branding/Etc.
636.082	SF105-109	Breeding
636.0885	SF405.5-407	Laboratory animals
636.0886	SF170-180	Working animals
636.0887	SF411-459	Pets
636.0887	SF459	Other animals
636.089	SF600-1100	Veterinary medicine
636.0890(5/6)	SF600-604	Serials/Societies
636.089014	SF610	Terminology
636.089025	SF611	Directories
636.08903	SF609	Dictionaries/ Encyclopedias
636.08906	SF605	Congresses
636.08907	SF775-779	Education
636.089074	SF606	Exhibitions
636.08909	SF615-724	History
636.089092	SF612-613	Biography
636.0894	SF740	Veterinary public health
636.08951	SF915-919.5	Pharmacology
636.0895892	SF914.5	Acupuncture
636.0896	SF910	Other diseases/Conditions
636.0896	SH171-179	Diseases/Adverse factors
636.0896(1-9)	SF951-997.5	Diseases of classes of animals
636.0896025	SF914.3-.4	Emergencies
636.08969	SF781-809	Communicable diseases
636.089696	SF810	Parasitology, By pest
636.0897	SF911-914	Surgery
636.08973	SF910.5	Orthopedics
636.09	SF41-55	History
636.09(4-9)	SF55	Other countries
636.0941	SF53	Great Britain
636.0973	SF51	United States
636.1	SF277-359.7	Horses
636.1(1-7)	SF290-293	Breeds
636.18	SF361	Donkeys
636.18	SF362	Mules
636.2	SF191-275	Cattle
636.2(2-8)	SF198-199	Breeds
636.2142	SF221-250	Dairying
636.3	SF371-379	Sheep
636.39	SF380-388	Goats
636.4	SF391-397.4	Swine
636.5	SF461-473	Birds

Dewey	LC	Descriptor
636.5	SF481-507	Poultry
636.6	SF511-513	Other birds
636.63	SF508-510	Game birds
636.7	SF421-440.2	Dogs
636.8	SF441-450	Cats
636.9322	SF451-455	Rabbits/Hares
637	SF250.5-275	Dairy Processing/Products
638	SF518	Insect rearing
638.1	SF521-539	Bee culture
638.2	SF541-560	Sericulture
638.5	SF561-562	Other insects
639.(1-4)	SH167	By species or class
639.(2-7)	SH400-.8	Seafood gathering
639.(2/8)	SH	Aquaculture/Fisheries/ Angling
639.(2/8)00(5/6)	SH1	Serials/Societies/Congresses
639.(2/8)006	SH3	Congresses
639.(2/8)0092	SH20	Biography
639.(2/8)00973	SH11	Documents, United States
639.(37-7)	SH191	Other (Not fish or shellfish)
639.2	SH387	Porpoises/Dolphins
639.2	SH201-400.8	Fisheries
639.2	SH364	Sea otters
639.2025	SH203	Directories
639.203	SH201	Dictionaries/ Encyclopedias
639.2068	SH328-329	Management
639.20688	SH337	Packing, Transporting
639.207(2)	SH332-.2	Education/Research
639.2074	SH338-343	Exhibitions
639.209	SH211	History
639.209(4-9)	SH219-321	By place
639.209163	SH213-.77	Atlantic Ocean
639.209164	SH214-215	Pacific Ocean
639.209165	SH216-.55	Indian Ocean
639.2094	SH253-293	Europe
639.20941	SH255-260	Great Britain
639.209415	SH261-262	Ireland
639.20943	SH271-272	Germany
639.209436	SH263-264	Austria
639.20944	SH269-270	France
639.20945	SH277-278	Italy
639.20946	SH285-286	Spain
639.209469	SH281-282	Portugal
639.20947	SH283-284	European Russia
639.209481	SH279-280	Norway
639.209485	SH287-288	Sweden
639.209489	SH267-268	Denmark
639.209492	SH275-276	Netherlands
639.209493	SH265-266	Belgium
639.209494	SH289-290	Switzerland
639.209495	SH273-274	Greece
639.2095	SH295-307	Asia
639.20951	SH297-298	China
639.209519	SH302.5-.7	Korea
639.20952	SH301-302	Japan
639.20954	SH299-300	India
639.20955	SH303-304	Iran
639.209561	SH291-292	Turkey
639.20957	SH305-306	Siberia
639.2096	SH311-315	Africa
639.20971	SH223-229	Canada
639.20972	SH231	Mexico
639.209728	SH232	Central America
639.209729	SH233	West Indies
639.20973	SH221-222	United States
639.2098	SH234-251	South America
639.20981	SH236	Brazil
639.20982	SH235	Argentina
639.20983	SH237	Chile
639.20985	SH247	Peru
639.209861	SH239	Colombia
639.209866	SH241	Ecuador
639.20987	SH251	Venezuela
639.209881	SH242	Guyana
639.209882	SH244	French Guiana
639.209883	SH243	Suriname
639.209892	SH245	Paraguay
639.209895	SH249	Uruguay
639.2099(5-6)	SH319	Oceania
639.20993	SH318.5	New Zealand
639.20994	SH317-318	Australia
639.209982	SH268.G83	Greenland
639.209989	SH320	Arctic regions
639.27(2-5)	SH346-351	Fishery for individual species
639.28	SH381-385	Whaling
639.29	SH360-363	Seal fisheries
639.3(1-4)	SH151-179	Fish culture
639.3(4)	SF456-458.83	Fishes/Aquariums
639.3789	SH185	Frog culture
639.4	SH365-380.92	Shellfish fisheries/Culture
639.4	SH371-374.52	Mollusks
639.409(4-9)	SH365-367	By place
639.412	SH375-377	Pearl fisheries
639.48	SH378-379	Freshwater mollusks
639.5	SH380-.92	Crustaceans
639.7	SH389-391.5	Algae culture/Seaweed
639.734	SH396	Sponge fisheries
639.7545	SH187	Leech culture
639.8	SH138	Mariculture
639.8	SH20.5-191	Aquaculture
639.8025	SH20.5	Directories
639.809	SH21	History (General)
639.809(4-9)	SH34-133	By place
639.8094	SH67-101	Europe
639.8095	SH103-117	Asia
639.8096	SH121-125	Africa
639.80971	SH37	Canada
639.80972	SH39	Mexico
639.809728	SH41-.5	Central America
639.809729	SH42-.5	West Indies
639.80973	SH34-36	United States
639.8098	SH43-65	South America
639.8099(3-4)	SH131	Australia/New Zealand
639.8099(5-6)	SH133	Oceania
639.89	SH393	Seagrasses
639.9	SK351-579	Wildlife management
639.90(5/6)	SK351	Serials/Societies
639.906	SK352	Congresses
639.909(4-9)	SK361-579	By place
639.9092	SK354	Biography
639.9094	SK503-543	Europe
639.90941	SK505-511	Great Britain
639.9095	SK553-567	Asia
639.9096	SK571-575	Africa
639.90971	SK470-471	Canada
639.90972	SK473	Mexico
639.909728	SK475	Central America
639.909729	SK477	West Indies
639.90973	SK361-465	United States
639.9098	SK479-501	South America
639.9099(3-6)	SK577-578	Australia/New Zealand/ Oceania

Dewey	LC	Descriptor
639.90998	SK579	Arctic/Antarctic
639.94	SH334.9-336.5	Processing
639.95	SK357	Game preserves/Refuges/Etc.
639.977	SH327.7	Conservation
640	TX	Home economics
640	TT697-910	Home arts/Homecrafts
640.(5/6)	TX1-5	Serials/Societies/Congresses
640.(5/6)	TT697	Serials/Societies
640.1	TX13	Theory/Philosophy
640.3	TX11	Dictionaries/Encyclopedias
640.7	TX165-286	Education
640.74	TX6	Exhibitions/Museums
640.9	TX15-19	History
640.9(4-9)	TX21-126	By place
640.94	TX55-95	Europe
640.941	TX57-64.5	Great Britain
640.9417	TX59.3	Ireland
640.943	TX73-74.5	Germany
640.9436	TX65-.2	Austria
640.944	TX71-72.5	France
640.945	TX79-80	Italy
640.946	TX87-88	Spain
640.947	TX85-86	European Russia
640.9481	TX81-82	Norway
640.9485	TX89-90	Sweden
640.9492	TX77-78	Netherlands
640.9494	TX91-92	Switzerland
640.9495	TX75-76	Greece
640.95	TX99-113	Asia
640.951	TX101-102	China
640.952	TX105-106	Japan
640.954	TX103-104	India
640.955	TX107-108	Iran
640.9561	TX111-112	Turkey/Asia Minor
640.957	TX109-110	Asian Russia
640.96	TX115-119	Africa
640.962	TX117-118	Egypt
640.971	TX26-27	Canada
640.972	TX28-29	Mexico
640.9728	TX30-31	Central America
640.9729	TX32-33	West Indies
640.973	TX22-25	United States
640.98	TX34-54	South America
640.981	TX41-42	Brazil
640.982	TX36-37	Argentina
640.983	TX43-44	Chile
640.984	TX38-39	Bolivia
640.985	TX52	Peru
640.9861	TX45-46	Colombia
640.9866	TX47	Ecuador
640.987	TX54	Venezuela
640.988	TX48-50	Guianas
640.9892	TX51	Paraguay
640.9895	TX53	Uruguay
640.99(5-6)	TX123-124	Oceania
640.993	TX122.5-.6	New Zealand
640.994	TX121-122	Australia
641	TX341-641	Nutrition/Foods/Food supply
641.013	TX631-641	Gastronomy
641.07	TX364-365	Education
641.1	TX551-560	Dietary studies/Etc.
641.2	TX412-415	Beverages
641.300287	TX501-597	Examination/Analysis
641.3009	TX515	History

Dewey	LC	Descriptor
641.303	TX391-401	Vegetable foods
641.306	TX371-389	Animal foods
641.31	TX356	Marketing for food economy
641.4	TX599-612	Preservation/Storage
641.4(6-7)	TX607-612	Chemical treatment
641.5	TX645-840	Cookery
641.5	TX703-725	Cookbooks
641.507	TX661-669	Education
641.55	TX821-840	Fast food/Picnics/Etc.
641.57	TX820	Cooking for large numbers
641.59(3-9)	TX360	Diet of special countries
641.592(03-9)	TX361	Diet of special groups
641.6	TX409	Baking powders/Etc.
641.6(3-7)	TX801-814	Preparation by food type
641.62(2-5)	TX726	Cookery with alcohol
641.6382	TX406-407	Condiments/Spices
641.66	TX743-759	Animal foods
641.7	TX681-693	Cooking Processes
641.8(53-65)	TX761-799	Baking/Confectionery
641.814	TX819	Condiments/Sauces/Etc.
641.84	TX818	Sandwiches
641.87	TX815-817	Beverages
642	TX727-739	Menus/Etc.
642.(6-8)	TX851-885	Dining-room service/Tables/Etc.
642.3	TX821-840	Fast food/Picnics/Etc.
642.5	TX901-953	Hotels/Restaurants/Etc.
643	TX298-399	The house
643.2	TX1100-1105	Mobile home living
643.3	TX653-655	Kitchen
643.3	TX656-658	Equipment/Appliances/Etc.
644.3	TH7700-7975	Illumination, lighting
646.(2/6)	TT720-730	Mending
646.(2/6)	TT151	Mending/Repairing
646.1	TT845	Tools/Supplies
646.2	TT700-715	Sewing/Needlework
646.2	TT699-715	Textile arts/Crafts
646.2044	TJ1501-1519	Sewing machines
646.21	TT387-410	Soft home furnishings
646.3	TX340	Clothing
646.4	TT570-630	Men's fashions
646.4	TT490-695	Clothing manufacture
646.40(5/6)	TT490	Serials/Societies
646.40088092	TT647	Ecclesiastical vestments
646.40212	TT499	Tables/Calculations/Etc.
646.404	TT500-565	Women's fashions
646.406	TT635-645	Children's clothing
646.42	TT670-678	Underwear
646.5	TT650-665	Millinery
646.724(2)	TT950-979	Barbering/Hairdressing
648	TX955-985	Bldg. operation/Housekeeping
648.1	TT980-999ÿ	Laundry work
649.(5/68)	LC37-44.3	Home education
649.1	HQ768-778.7	Child rearing
650	HF5001-6182	Business
651	HF5546-5548.6	Office management
651.2	HF5520-5541	Equipment
651.3	HF5500.2-5506	Personnel
651.7	HF5717-5746	Business communications
651.79	HE9751-9755	Messenger service
651.79	HE7511-7549	Pneumatic services
652	Z40-104.5	Writing
652.1	Z43-45	Calligraphy/Penmanship
652.3	Z49-51	Typewriters/Typewriting
652.8	Z103-104.5	Cryptography

Dewey	LC	Descriptor
653.(14)	Z53-102	Shorthand/Stenography
657	HF5601-5689	Accounting/Bookkeeping
657.(2)	HG1706-1708	Accounting/Bookkeeping
657.48	HG177	Liquidity
657.61	HJ9701-9995	Public accounting
657.610(5/6)	HJ9701-9741	Serials/Societies
657.6101	HJ9745-9769	Methods
657.6109(4-9)	HJ9801-9940	Public accounting, By place
657.6109(4-9)	HJ9921-9940	Other countries
657.61097(4-9)	HJ9817-9920	Local, By place
657.610973	HJ9801-9920	United States
658	HD28-70	Industrial management
658.(3/5)	HD45-.2	Control of industry/ Technology
658.1147	HD5650-5660	Employees in Management
658.15	HG4001-4280.7	Financial management
658.150(5/6)	HG4001-4007	Serials/Societies
658.1501	HG4011-4012	Theory/Method
658.15021	HG4027-.15	Statistics
658.15025	HG4009	Directories
658.1503	HG4008	Dictionaries/ Encyclopedias
658.1507	HG4014-4016	Education
658.1509	HG4017	History
658.1509(4-9)	HG4050-4280.7	Financial management, By place
658.1509(4-9)	HG4090-4280.7	Other countries
658.15097(3-9)	HG4050-4070	United States
658.155	HD61	Risk/Risk management
658.3	HF5549-.5	Personnel management
658.3128	HD66	Work groups/Team work
658.3254	HD7255-7256	Disabled rehabilitation
658.402	HD50	Delegation of authority
658.407	HD4965.2	Businessmen's executive salary
658.408	HD60-.5	Social responsibilities
658.5	TS155-174	Production management
658.562	HD62	Simplification/ Standardization
658.567	TP995-996	Utilization of wastes
658.568	HD3656-3790.9	Inspections
658.56809(4-9)	HD3661-3790	Inspections, By place
658.723	HD2365-2385	Contracting
658.788	HF5761-5780	Shipping/Delivery of goods
658.8	HF5410-5417.5	Marketing/Distribution
659	HD59-.2	Public relations/Publicity
659.1	HF5801-6182	Advertising
659.10(5/6)	HF5801-5802	Serials/Societies
659.101	HF5837-6146	Methods
659.1025	HF5804-5808	Directories
659.103	HF5803	Dictionaries/ Encyclopedias
659.106	HF5802.5	Congresses
659.107	HF5814-5815	Education
659.109	HF5811-5813	History
659.1092	HF5810	Biography
659.1125	HF6178-6182	Agencies
659.132	HF5871-6141	Newspaper/Magazine
659.13209	HF6103	History
659.13209(4-9)	HF5901-6097	Newspaper/Magazine, By place
659.133	HF5861-5863	Direct mail
659.293613	HV42	Mass media/Public relations
660	TP155-156	Chemical engineering
660	TP	Chemical technology
660.0(5/6)	TP1	Serials/Societies
660.025	TP12	Directories

Dewey	LC	Descriptor
660.03	TP9	Dictionaries/ Encyclopedias
660.06	TP5	Congresses
660.07	TP165-183	Education
660.074	TP6	Exhibitions/Museums
660.076	TP187-197	Laboratories
660.09	TP15-20	History
660.09(4-9)	TP21-126	Chemical technology, By place
660.092	TP139-140	Biography
660.0941	TP57-64.5	Great Britain
660.0943	TP73-74.5	Germany
660.09436	TP65-.2	Austria
660.09437	TP65.3-.4	Czechoslovakia
660.09439	TP65.5-66	Hungary
660.0944	TP71-72.5	France
660.0945	TP79-80	Italy
660.0946	TP87-88	Spain
660.09469	TP83-84.5	Portugal
660.0947	TP85-86	European Russia
660.0948	TP88.5	Scandinavia
660.09481	TP81-82	Norway
660.09485	TP89-90	Sweden
660.09489	TP69-70	Denmark
660.094897	TP95.F5	Finland
660.09492	TP77-78	Netherlands
660.09493	TP67-68	Belgium
660.09494	TP91-92	Switzerland
660.09495	TP75-76	Greece
660.09496	TP95.A2	Balkans
660.09497	TP95.Y8	Yugoslavia
660.0951	TP101-102	China
660.0952	TP105-106	Japan
660.0954	TP103-104	India
660.095491	TP104.5-.6	Pakistan
660.095493	TP104.7-.8	Sri Lanka
660.0955	TP107-108	Iran
660.09561	TP111-112	Turkey
660.09567	TP113.I7	Iraq
660.095694	TP113.I75	Israel/Palestine
660.0957	TP109-110	Asian Russia
660.09598	TP113.I55	Indonesia
660.09599	TP113.P6	Philippines
660.096	TP115-119	Africa
660.096(1-9)	TP119	Africa, By country
660.0962	TP117-118	Egypt
660.0971	TP26-27	Canada
660.0972	TP28-29	Mexico
660.09728	TP30-31	Central America
660.09729	TP32-33	West Indies
660.0973	TP23-25	United States
660.0981	TP41-42	Brazil
660.0982	TP36-37	Argentina
660.0983	TP43-44	Chile
660.0984	TP38-39	Bolivia
660.0985	TP52	Peru
660.09861	TP45-46	Colombia
660.09866	TP47	Ecuador
660.0987	TP54	Venezuela
660.09881	TP48	Guyana
660.09882	TP50	French Guiana
660.09883	TP49	Suriname
660.09892	TP51	Paraguay
660.09895	TP53	Uruguay
660.099(5-6)	TP123-124	Oceania
660.0993	TP122.5-.6	New Zealand
660.0994	TP121-122	Australia

Dewey	LC	Descriptor
660.0998	TP125-126	Polar areas
660.28(2-3)	TP157-159	Apparatus and supplies
660.2842(6-7)	TP363	Heating, drying, cooling
660.28449	QR151	Fermentation (Yeasts/Etc.)
660.2961	TP365	By products of combustion
660.29686	TP480-482	Low-temperature engineering
660.62	QR53-.5	Industrial microbiology
661	TP200-245	Chemicals
661	TP249-261	Industrial chemistry
661.(1-7)	TP245	Inorganic chemicals
661.(4-6)	TP230-240	Salts
661.03	TP222-223	Alkalies
661.2	TP217	Acids
661.8	TP950-994	Organic chemical industries
661.8	TP247-248	Organic chemicals/ Preparations
662	TP265-267	Chemistry of fire
662.(1-2)	TP267.5-301	Explosives and pyrotechnics
662.5	TP310	Matches
662.6	TP315-360	Fuel
662.65	TP997	Wood distillation
662.66	TP361	Inflammable liquids and gases
663.13	TP500-659	Fermentation industries
664	TP368-465	Food processing/ Manufacture
664.(34/9)	TS1950-1981	Meats/Lard/Etc.
664.0285(2/3)	TP490-498	Refrigeration/Icemaking
664.68	QR151	Fermentation (Yeasts/Etc.)
664.7	TS2120-2159	Cereals/Grain milling
664.72	TS2156-2159	Cereal products
664.725	TS2159	Individual cereals (Corn/Rice)
664.755	TS2157	Macaroni/Spaghetti
664.76	TS2158	Feeds
664.902	TS1960-1967	Butchering/Meat curing
665.(2-4)	TP670-699	Oils/Fats/Waxes
665.(3-4)	TP680-684	Vegetable oils/Fats/Waxes
665.(5-8)	TP361	Inflammable liquids and gases
665.4	TP685-699	Mineral oils/Fats/Waxes
665.5	TP690-692.5	Petroleum
665.706	TP751-762	Gas industry
666.(1-7)	TP785-871	Glass/Clay industries/Etc.
666.8(6-9)	TP870-873	Artificial stones/Gems
666.9	TP875-889	Cement industries/Lime/ Etc.
667.(4-5)	TP946-949.95	Inks
667.(6-7)	TP934-944	Paints/Pigments/Varnishes
668.4	TP1101-1185	Plastics (Manufacture)
668.4(2-5)	TP1150-1175	Processes
668.4(2-9)	TP1177-1185	By type
668.40(5/6)	TP1101-1105	Serials/Societies/Congresses
668.4025	TP1112	Directories
668.403	TP1110	Dictionaries/ Encyclopedias
668.4074	TP1107	Exhibitions/Museums
668.409	TP1116-1118	History
669	TS551-650	Metals
669	TN690-693	Metallography
669	TN	Mining engineering/ Metallurgy
669	TN600-799	Metallurgy
669.(1-7)	TN695-799	Types of metallurgy
669.0(5/6)	TN600-605	Serials/Societies/Congresses

Dewey	LC	Descriptor
669.025	TN612	Directories
669.0283	TN688	Hydrometallurgy
669.0284	TN681-687	Electrometallurgy
669.07	TN675.3	Education
669.09	TN615-620	History
669.09(4-9)	TN621-655	By place
669.2	TS720-770	Precious metals
669.725	TN895-897	Alkalies
669.8	TN672	Heat treatment of metals
669.92	HG321-329	Mints/Assaying
670	T55.4-60.8	Industrial engineering
670	TS	Manufacturing
670.(5/6)	T55.4-.45	Serials/Societies
670.(5/6)	TS1-5	Serials/Societies/Congresses
670.148	T55.52	Symbols/Abbreviations
670.23	T56.3	As a profession
670.25	T55.54	Directories
670.3	TS9	Dictionaries/ Encyclopedias
670.3	T55.5	Dictionaries/ Encyclopedias
670.42	T58.7	Production/Productivity
670.42	T57-59	Applied mathematics
670.427	T59.5	Automation
670.9	TS15	History
670.9	T55.6	History
670.9(4-9)	TS21-126	Manufacturing, By place
670.92	TS139-140	Biography
670.941	TS57-64.5	Great Britain
670.943	TS73-74.5	Germany
670.9436	TS65-.2	Austria
670.9437	TS65.3-.4	Czechoslovakia
670.9439	TS65.5-66	Hungary
670.944	TS71-72.5	France
670.945	TS79-80	Italy
670.946	TS87-88	Spain
670.9469	TS83-84.5	Portugal
670.947	TS85-86	European Russia
670.948	TS88.5	Scandinavia
670.9481	TS81-82	Norway
670.9485	TS89-90	Sweden
670.9489	TS69-70	Denmark
670.94897	TS95.F5	Finland
670.9492	TS77-78	Netherlands
670.9493	TS67-68	Belgium
670.9494	TS91-92	Switzerland
670.9495	TS75-76	Greece
670.9496	TS95.A2	Balkans
670.9497	TS95.Y8	Yugoslavia
670.951	TS101-102	China
670.952	TS105-106	Japan
670.954	TS103-104	India
670.95491	TS104.5-.6	Pakistan
670.95493	TS104.7-.8	Sri Lanka
670.955	TS107-108	Iran
670.9561	TS111-112	Turkey
670.9567	TS113.I7	Iraq
670.95694	TS113.I75	Israel/Palestine
670.957	TS109-110	Asian Russia
670.9598	TS113.I55	Indonesia
670.9599	TS113.P6	Philippines
670.96	TS115-119	Africa
670.96(1-9)	TS119	Africa, By country
670.962	TS117-118	Egypt
670.971	TS26-27	Canada
670.972	TS28-29	Mexico
670.9728	TS30-31	Central America

Dewey	LC	Descriptor
670.9729	TS32-33	West Indies
670.973	TS23-25	United States
670.981	TS41-42	Brazil
670.982	TS36-37	Argentina
670.983	TS43-44	Chile
670.984	TS38-39	Bolivia
670.985	TS52	Peru
670.9861	TS45-46	Colombia
670.9866	TS47	Ecuador
670.987	TS54	Venezuela
670.9881	TS48	Guyana
670.9882	TS50	French Guiana
670.9883	TS49	Suriname
670.9892	TS51	Paraguay
670.9895	TS53	Uruguay
670.99(5-6)	TS123-124	Oceania
670.993	TS122.5-.6	New Zealand
670.994	TS121-122	Australia
670.998	TS125-126	Polar areas
671	TS653-718	Metal finishing (General)
671	TS200-770	Metal manufacturing
671.0(5/6)	TS200	Serials/Societies/Congresses
671.2	TS228.99-239	Casting
671.332	TS225-.2	Forging
671.35	TS215	Metalworking machinery
671.5	TS226-228.9	Joining of metals
672	TS300-360	Iron/Steel
673	TS370-377	Nonferrous metals (General)
674	TS800-915	Wood technology/Lumber
674.0(5/6)	TS800-801	Serials/Societies
674.386	TS920-937	Chemical processing of wood
674.8	TS840-915	Wood products/Furniture
674.8	TS850-851	Machinery/Mills
674.80(5/6)	TS840	Serials/Societies
674.82	TS890	Barrels
674.88	TS1262-1268	Pens/Pencils
675	TS940-1067	Leather industries/Tanning
675	TS970-980	Kinds of leather
675.0(5/6)	TS940	Serials/Societies
675.3	TS1060-1067	Furs
676	TS1080-1268	Paper manufacture/Trade
676	TS1090-1096	Manufacturing
676.0(5/6)	TS1080	Serials/Societies/Congresses
676.12	TS1171-1177	Woodpulp industry
676.28(2-9)	TS1124-1165	Paper types
676.2823	TS1228-1268	Stationery
677	TS1300-1865	Textile industries
677	TP890-933	Textile processing
677.(1-5)	TS1540-1549	Textile fibers
677.00(5/6)	TS1300-1301	Serials/Societies/Congresses
677.028	TS1488-1520	Other processes
677.02822	TS1480-1487	Spinning
677.028245	TT679-695	Knit goods/Machine knitting
677.02864	TS1760-1768	Dry goods/Fabrics
677.1	TS1700-1750	Flax/Hemp/Jute
677.21	TS1550-1590	Cotton manufacture
677.31	TS1600-1635	Woolen manufacture
677.39	TS1640-1688	Silk manufacture
678.2	TS1870-1935	Rubber industry
679.7	TS2220-2283	Tobacco
679.7	TS2255	Nicotine (Preparation/Use)
679.7(2/3)	TS2260	Cigars/Cigarettes
681	TS500-518	Instrument manufacture
681.11(3-4)	TS540-549	Watches/Clocks
681.6	TS1262-1268	Pens/Pencils
683	TS400-405	Hardware
683.3	TS519-530	Locksmithing
683.4	TS532-538.5	Firearms
684.08	TT152-153	Workshops
684.104	TS840-915	Wood products/Furniture
684.104	TS880-889	Furniture
685	TS940-1067	Leather industries/Tanning
685.(4/2)	TS2160-2193	Gloves/Hats
685.1	TS1030-1035	Harnesses/Saddles
685.24	TS1060-1067	Furs
685.31	TS989-1025	Boots/Shoemaking
686.(1/209)	Z124-228	History of printing
686.2	Z116-265	Printing
686.2(092/06)	Z231-232	Printers/Printing companies
686.2023	Z243-264.5	Printing trade/Etc.
686.205	Z119-.5	Serials
686.206	Z120-.5	Societies/Congresses
686.207	Z122-.5	Education
686.2074	Z121	Museums/Exhibitions
686.209(4-9)	Z133-225	Printing history, By place
686.209(8/728-729)	Z212-213	S./Central America/West Indies
686.20941	Z151-.5	Great Britain
686.209417	Z152.6	Ireland
686.20943	Z147-148	Germany
686.209436	Z133-134	Austria
686.209437	Z135-136	Czechoslovakia
686.209438	Z163-164	Poland
686.209439	Z137-138	Hungary
686.20944	Z144-145	France
686.20945	Z155-156	Italy
686.20946	Z173-174	Spain
686.209469	Z171-172	Portugal
686.20947	Z165-166	European Russia
686.20948	Z169-170	Scandinavia
686.2094897	Z167	Finland
686.209492	Z161-162	Netherlands
686.209493	Z159-160	Belgium
686.209494	Z175-176	Switzerland
686.209495	Z153-154	Greece
686.209496	Z168	Baltic States
686.2095	Z185-186	Asia
686.209561	Z177-178	Turkey
686.2096	Z195-196	Africa
686.2097	Z205-213	America
686.20971	Z206-207	Canada
686.20972	Z210-211	Mexico
686.20973	Z208-209	United States
686.2099(3-6)	Z221-222	Australia/New Zealand/Oceania
686.224	Z250	Kinds of type
686.22544	TR1010	Phototypeset
686.232	TR925-1045	Photomechanical processes
686.2325	TR940-950	Photolithography
686.2325	TR930-937	Collotype process
686.2327	TR975	Halftone
686.2327	TR980	Photogravure/Intaglio process
686.2327	TR970	Photoengraving/Relief
686.3	Z266-276	Bookbinding (General)
686.4	Z265	Reproduction, Photography/Etc.
686.42	TR920-923	Blue print reproductions
686.44	TR1025-1045	Electrophotography
687	TT498	Factories
687.0212	TT499	Tables/Calculations/Etc.

Dewey	LC	Descriptor
687.081	TT570-630	Men's fashions
687.082	TT500-565	Women's fashions
687.083	TT635-645	Children's clothing
687.2	TT670-678	Underwear
687.4	TS2160-2193	Gloves/Hats
687.4	TT650-665	Millinery
688.1	TT154-.5	Models/Modelmaking
688.42	TS2270	Pipes
688.6	TS2001-2035	Carriage/Wagon making
688.8	TS195-198.8	Packaging
690	TH845-895	Engineering
690	TH	Building construction
690-697	TH5011-5701	By phase of work
690.(5-6)	TH4021-4221	Public
690.(5-8)	TH4021-4970	Buildings by type or use
690.0(5/6)	TH1-4	Serials/Societies
690.028	TH900-915	Equipment
690.0299	TH434-437	Estimates/Costs
690.03	TH9	Dictionaries/Encyclopedias
690.06	TH5	Congresses
690.07	TH165-213	Education
690.074	TH6	Exhibitions/Museums
690.09	TH15-126	History
690.09(3-9)	TH21-126	By place
690.090(1-4)	TH15-19	By date
690.092	TH139-140	Biography
690.0941	TH57-64.5	Great Britain
690.0943	TH73-74.5	Germany
690.09436	TH65-.2	Austria
690.09437	TH65.3-.4	Czechoslovakia
690.09439	TH65.5-66	Hungary
690.0944	TH71-72.5	France
690.0945	TH79-80	Italy
690.0946	TH87-88	Spain
690.09469	TH83-84.5	Portugal
690.0947	TH85-86	European Russia
690.0948	TH88.5	Scandinavia
690.09481	TH81-82	Norway
690.09485	TH89-90	Sweden
690.09489	TH69-70	Denmark
690.094897	TH95.F5	Finland
690.09492	TH77-78	Netherlands
690.09493	TH67-68	Belgium
690.09494	TH91-92	Switzerland
690.09495	TH75-76	Greece
690.09496	TH95.A2	Balkans
690.09497	TH95.Y8	Yugoslavia
690.0951	TH101-102	China
690.0952	TH105-106	Japan
690.0954	TH103-104	India
690.095491	TH104.5-.6	Pakistan
690.095493	TH104.7-.8	Sri Lanka
690.0955	TH107-108	Iran
690.09561	TH111-112	Turkey
690.09567	TH113.I7	Iraq
690.095694	TH113.I75	Israel/Palestine
690.0957	TH109-110	Asian Russia
690.09598	TH113.I55	Indonesia
690.09599	TH113.P6	Philippines
690.096	TH115-119	Africa
690.096(1-9)	TH119	Africa, By country
690.0962	TH117-118	Egypt
690.0971	TH26-27	Canada
690.0972	TH28-29	Mexico
690.09728	TH30-31	Central America
690.09729	TH32-33	West Indies

Dewey	LC	Descriptor
690.0973	TH23-25	United States
690.0981	TH41-42	Brazil
690.0982	TH36-37	Argentina
690.0983	TH43-44	Chile
690.0984	TH38-39	Bolivia
690.0985	TH52	Peru
690.09861	TH45-46	Colombia
690.09866	TH47	Ecuador
690.0987	TH54	Venezuela
690.09881	TH48	Guyana
690.09882	TH50	French Guiana
690.09883	TH49	Suriname
690.09892	TH51	Paraguay
690.09895	TH53	Uruguay
690.099(5-6)	TH123-124	Oceania
690.0993	TH122.5-.6	New Zealand
690.0994	TH121-122	Australia
690.0998	TH125-126	Polar areas
690.1	TH2031-3000	Details in design/Construction
690.11	TH2101	Foundations/Supports/Etc.
690.11	TH5201	Foundations
690.12	TH2201-2251	Walls
690.15	TH2281-2288	Chimneys
690.15	TH2391-2495	Roofs
690.16	TH2521-2529	Flooring
690.17	TH2531	Ceilings
690.182	TH2261-2279	Windows/Doors/Etc.
690.2	TH375-383	Building sites
690.22	TH9025-9745	Protection of buildings
690.24	TH3301-3411	Maintenance/Repair
690.52	TH4311	Commercial/Office
690.53	TH4451-4499	Storage/Warehouses
690.54	TH4511-4591	Factories
690.58	TH4711	Recreation
690.6	TH4221	Churches
690.8	TH4805-4850	Houses
690.8(6/92)	TH4911-4935	Farm buildings
691.95	TH1715	Insulation
693	TH1061-1725	Systems of construction
693.(1-2)	TH5311-5511	Masonry/Bricklaying
693.(1/5)	TH1199-1501	Masonry/Concrete
693.7	TH1610-1675	Metals
693.82	TH9111-9599	From fire, Fire prevention
693.82	TH1061-1093	Fire-resistive/Fireproof
694	TH5601-5691	Carpentry/Joinery
694.2	TH2301-2311	Framing
696-697	TH6010-6013	Fittings/Etc. Mechanical equip.
696.1	TH6101-6887	Plumbing and pipefitting
696.1(3/8)	TH6571-6675	House drainage
696.10288	TH6681-6685	Maintenance of plumbing
696.12	TH6521-6569	Water supply
696.182	TH6485-6500	Bathrooms
696.184	TH6507-6512	Kitchens
696.2	TH6800-6887	Gas supply
697	TH6014-6085	Environmental engineering
697	TH7005-7699	Heating and ventilation
697.(1-2)	TH7418-7458	Local heating
697.(1-8)	TH7201-7643	Heating of buildings
697.02	TH7418-7458	Local heating
697.03	TH7461-7638	Central heating
697.04	TH7400-7413	Heating by special fuels
697.3	TH7601-7635	Warm air heating
697.92	TH7647-7699	Ventilation of buildings
697.93	TH7687-7688	Air conditioning and cooling

Dewey	LC	Descriptor	Dewey	LC	Descriptor
698	TH8001-8581	Decoration	708.1(3-9)	N570-880	United States
698.1	TT320-324	House painting	708.1(3-9)	N5215-5220	United States
700	NX	Arts (General)	708.2	N1020-1560	Great Britain
700.74	NX800-820	Special art centers	708.3	N2210-2406	Germany
700.79	NX700-750	Patronage of the arts	708.3(6/7)	N1610-1710	Austria-Hungary/
701	N61-72	Theory/Philosophy			Czechoslovakia
701.18	N7475-7483	Art criticism	708.38	N3150-3165	Poland
701.8	N7430-7433	Technique/Composition	708.4	N2010-2180	France
701.8	N7430-7433	Technique/Composition	708.5	N2510-3065	Italy
702-709	N	Visual arts	708.6	N3410-3497	Spain
702.3	NX163	As a profession	708.69	N3210-3236	Portugal
702.3	N8350-8356	Art as a profession	708.7	N3310-3375	Russia
702.5	NX100-120	Directories	708.81	N3110-3135	Norway
702.5	N50-55	Directories	708.85	N3510-3570	Sweden
702.8	N8510-8553	Studios/Materials	708.89	N1880-1935	Denmark
702.88	N8555-8580	Art conservation	708.92	N2450-2505	Netherlands
703	NX70	Encyclopedias	708.93	N1750-1850	Belgium
703	NX80	Dictionaries	708.94	N3610-3655	Switzerland
703	N31-33	Encyclopedias/Dictionaries	708.95	N5284-5285	Asia
704.94(2-9)	N7560-8266	By subject	708.95	N3700-3750	Asia
704.948	NK1648-1678	Religious art	708.95	N2410-2425	Greece
704.948	NX654-694	Religious arts	708.952	N3735	Japan
704.9482	NK1650-1657	Christian	708.954	N3720-3730	India
704.9482	NX655-663	Christian art	708.96	N5289-5290	Africa
704.9489	NK1670-1678	Non-Christian	708.96	N3800-3885	Africa
704.9489	NX670-692	Non-Christian art	708.99(3-4)	N5295-5298	Australia/New Zealand
704.948943	NK1676	Buddhist	708.99(5-6)	N5299	Oceania
704.94896	NK1672	Jewish	708.99(5-6)	N3990	Oceania
704.94897	NK1674	Islamic	708.993	N3976-3980	New Zealand
705	NX1-9	Serials	708.994	N3910-3975	Australia
705	N1-9	Serials	709	NX440-600	History of the arts
706	NX20-50	Societies/Congresses	709	N5300-7418	Visual art history
706	N10-17	Societies	709	N6501-7413	By place
706	N21-23	Congresses	709	N7475-7483	Art criticism
707	NX280-410	Education	709.(3-9)	NX501-596	By place
707	N81-390	Education	709.0(1-49)	NX448-458	By date
707	N90-284	Art education, History	709.0(24-31)	N6370-6375	Renaissance/16th century
707.1	N325-333	Art schools	709.0(3-4)	N6350-6494	Modern art
707.10(7-8)	N331	Other American countries	709.01	N5310-5313	Primitive/Prehistoric
707.104	N332-333	Europe	709.01	N5315-5899	Ancient
707.1073	N328-330	United States	709.02	N5940-6311	Medieval art
707.11	N345-365	Art study (Other schools)	709.032	N6410-6415	17th century
707.2	N380-390	Study of art history	709.033	N6420-6425	18th century
707.4	NX420-430	Exhibitions	709.034	N6450-6465	19th century
707.4	N4397-4877	International exhibitions	709.04	N6485-6494	20th century
707.4	N4390-5098	Exhibitions	709.2	NX90	Biography
707.4(1-9)	N5015-5098	Other exhibitions, By place	709.2	N40-43	Biographies
707.44	N5050-5080	Europe	709.3(7-8)	N5603-5899	Classical art
707.441	N5051-5056	Great Britain	709.32	N5350-5351	Egypt
707.444	N5063-5069	France	709.33	N5460	Judea/Syria
707.45	N5085	Asia	709.37	N5740-5790	Italy
707.46	N5090	Africa	709.38	N5630-5720	Greece
707.473	N5015-5020	United States	709.392	N5480-5560	Asia Minor
707.49(5-6)	N5098	Oceania	709.3949	N5470	Arabia
707.493	N5097	New Zealand	709.4	NX542-571	Europe
707.494	N5095	Australia	709.4	N6767-6988.5	Europe
707.6	N340	Examinations	709.41	NX543-547	Great Britain
708	N4020-4025	Private collections	709.41	N6767-6868.5	Great Britain
708	N5200-5299	Private collections	709.43	NX550-.6	Germany
708	N4010-4015	Public collections	709.43	N6866-6868.5	Germany
708	N400-4040	Art museums/Galleries	709.436	NX548	Austria
708.(1/972-98)	N5213-5230	The Americas	709.44	NX549	France
708.(11/972-8)	N908-910	Cities of other American areas	709.44	N6847-6848.5	France
708.(2-8)	N5240-5280	Europe	709.45	NX552	Italy
708.(2-9)	N1010-3690	Europe	709.45	N6917-6918.5	Italy
708.(3-8)	N3690	Other European countries	709.46	NX562	Spain
			709.469	NX563	Portugal

Dewey	LC	Descriptor
709.47	NX556	European Russia
709.47	N6988-.5	European Russia
709.48	NX557-561	Scandinavia
709.481	NX560	Norway
709.485	NX561	Sweden
709.489	NX558	Denmark
709.4912	NX559	Iceland
709.492	NX554	Netherlands
709.492	N6948-.5	Netherlands
709.493	NX555	Belgium
709.494	NX564	Switzerland
709.495	NX551	Greece
709.496	NX566-569	Balkan states
709.5	NX572-586	Asia
709.5(6-61)	NX573-.7	Near East/Asia Minor
709.51	NX583	China
709.519	NX584.6	Korea
709.52	NX584	Japan
709.54	NX576	India
709.5491	NX576.7	Pakistan
709.5493	NX576.6	Sri Lanka
709.55	NX574	Iran
709.561	NX565	Turkey
709.5694	NX573.7	Israel/Palestine
709.57	NX575.7	Asian Russia
709.581	NX575.6	Afghanistan
709.593	NX578.7	Thailand
709.594	NX578.6.L3	Laos
709.595	NX579	Malaysia
709.596	NX578.6.C3	Cambodia
709.597	NX578.6.V5	Vietnam
709.598	NX580	Indonesia
709.599	NX581	Philippines
709.6	NX587-589.8	Africa
709.61	NX587.6-588.6	North Africa
709.62	NX588	Egypt
709.63	NX588.7	Ethiopia
709.66	NX589-.6	West Africa
709.676	NX588.8-.9	East Africa
709.68	NX589.7-.8	Southern Africa
709.71	NX513	Canada
709.72	NX514	Mexico
709.728	NX515-522	Central America
709.7281	NX518	Guatemala
709.7283	NX519	Honduras
709.7284	NX522	El Salvador
709.7285	NX520	Nicaragua
709.7286	NX517	Costa Rica
709.7287	NX521	Panama
709.729	NX523-529	West Indies
709.7291	NX525	Cuba
709.7292	NX527	Jamaica
709.7294	NX526	Haiti
709.7295	NX528	Puerto Rico
709.7296	NX524	Bahamas
709.73	NX503-512	United States
709.73	N6510-6512.5	United States
709.8	NX530-541	South America
709.81	NX533	Brazil
709.82	NX531	Argentina
709.83	NX534	Chile
709.84	NX532	Bolivia
709.85	NX539	Peru
709.861	NX535	Colombia
709.866	NX536	Ecuador
709.87	NX541	Venezuela
709.88	NX537-.4	Guianas

Dewey	LC	Descriptor
709.892	NX538	Paraguay
709.895	NX540	Uruguay
709.9(5-6)	NX595-596	Oceania
709.93	NX593	New Zealand
709.94	NX590-591	Australia
711	NA9000-9425	City planning/Aesthetics
711.0(5/6)	NA9000	Serials/Societies
711.023	NA9013	As a profession
711.06	NA9010	Congresses
711.07	NA9012	Education
711.074	NA9015-9016	Exhibitions
711.09	NA9090-9095	History
711.09(4-9)	NA9101-9284	City planning, By place
711.092	NA9080-9085	Biography
711.4	HT165.5-169.9	City planning
711.407	HT165.5-.53	Education
711.409(4-9)	HT167-169.5	By place
711.409(4-9)	HT169-.5	Other countries
711.40973	HT167-168	United States
714	NA9400-9425	Fountains
720	NA	Architecture
720.1	NA2500	Theory/Aesthetics
720.202	NA2530	Outlines/Syllabi/Etc.
720.212	NA2590	Tables/Etc.
720.222	NA2700-2725	Architectural drawing
720.23	NA1995-1997	As a profession
720.25	NA50-60.5	Directories
720.3	NA31	Encyclopedias/Dictionaries/Etc.
720.5	NA1-9	Serials
720.6	NA10-21	Societies/Congresses
720.7	NA2000-2320	Education
720.71	NA2300-2320	Special schools
720.710(4-9)	NA2320	Other countries
720.710(4-9)	NA2101-2284	Education, By place
720.710(7-8)	NA2305	Other American
720.7104	NA2310	Europe
720.71073	NA2300-2304	United States
720.74	NA2400-2460	Museums/Exhibitions
720.76	NA120-130	Examination/Licensing
720.79	NA2335-2360	Competitions
720.9(4-9)	NA701-1613	By place
720.92	NA40	Biography
720.94	NA950-1455	Europe
720.941	NA961-997	Great Britain
720.94209033	NA630	Queen Anne
720.943	NA1068-1088	Germany
720.9436	NA1001-1011.5	Austria
720.9437	NA1023-1034	Czechoslovakia
720.9438	NA1191	Poland
720.9439	NA1012-1022.5	Hungary
720.944	NA1041-1053	France
720.945	NA1111-1123	Italy
720.946	NA1301-1313	Spain
720.9469	NA1321-1333	Portugal
720.947	NA1181-1188	European Russia
720.948	NA1201-1293	Scandinavia
720.9481	NA1261-1273	Norway
720.9485	NA1281-1293	Sweden
720.9489	NA1211-1223	Denmark
720.94897	NA1193	Finland
720.94912	NA1241-1253	Iceland
720.9492	NA1131-1153	Netherlands
720.9493	NA1161-1173	Belgium
720.9494	NA1341-1353	Switzerland
720.9495	NA1091-1103	Greece
720.9497	NA1441-1453	Yugoslavia

Dewey	LC	Descriptor
720.94977	NA1381-1393	Bulgaria
720.9498	NA1421-1433	Romania
720.95	NA1460-1569.6	Asia
720.951	NA1540-1549.6	China
720.9519	NA1560-1569.6	Korea
720.952	NA1550-1559.6	Japan
720.9538	NA1470-1472	Saudi Arabia
720.954	NA1501-1510	India
720.95491	NA1510.7-.8	Pakistan
720.95493	NA1510.6-.63	Sri Lanka
720.955	NA1480-1489	Iran
720.9561	NA1361-1373	Turkey
720.9567	NA1467-1469	Iraq
720.95691	NA1489.6-.8	Syria
720.95692	NA1476.6-.8	Lebanon
720.95694	NA1477-1479	Israel/Palestine
720.95695	NA1479.6-.8	Jordan
720.958	NA1492.6-1499	Asian Russia (Siberia)
720.9581	NA1492-.3	Afghanistan
720.9591	NA1512-.3	Burma
720.9593	NA1521-1523	Thailand
720.9594	NA1516-.3	Laos
720.9595	NA1525-.6	Malaysia
720.9596	NA1515-.3	Cambodia
720.9597	NA1514-.3	Vietnam
720.9598	NA1526-.6	Indonesia
720.9599	NA1527-1532	Philippines
720.96	NA1580-1599	Africa
720.9611	NA1591	Tunisia
720.9612	NA1589	Libya
720.962	NA1581-1585	Egypt
720.963	NA1586	Ethiopia
720.964	NA1590	Morocco
720.965	NA1588	Algeria
720.966	NA1598-1599	West Africa
720.9676	NA1597-.6	East Africa
720.968	NA1591.7-1596.6	Southern Africa
720.971	NA740-749	Canada
720.972	NA750-759	Mexico
720.9728	NA760-790	Central America
720.97281	NA776-778	Guatemala
720.97283	NA779-781	Honduras
720.97284	NA788-790	El Salvador
720.97285	NA782-784	Nicaragua
720.97286	NA773-775	Costa Rica
720.97287	NA785-787	Panama
720.9729	NA791-815	West Indies
720.97291	NA803-805	Cuba
720.97292	NA809-810	Jamaica
720.97294	NA806-808	Haiti
720.97295	NA812-814	Puerto Rico
720.97296	NA800-802	Bahamas
720.973	NA705-738	United States
720.98	NA820-939	South America
720.981	NA850-859	Brazil
720.982	NA830-839	Argentina
720.983	NA860-869	Chile
720.984	NA840-849	Bolivia
720.985	NA910-919	Peru
720.9861	NA870-879	Colombia
720.9866	NA880-889	Ecuador
720.987	NA930-939	Venezuela
720.9881	NA895	Guyana
720.9882	NA897	French Guiana
720.9883	NA896	Suriname
720.9892	NA900-909	Paraguay
720.9895	NA920-929	Uruguay

Dewey	LC	Descriptor
720.99(5-6)	NA1610-1613	Oceania
720.993	NA1606-1608	New Zealand
720.994	NA1600-1605	Australia
721	NA2750-2790	Design
721	NA2835-3070	Architectual details/Motives
721-728	NA4100-8480	Classes of buildings
721.042	NA4150-4160	Classed by form (Basilicas/Etc.)
721.044	NA4100-4145	By material (Wood/Stone/Etc.)
721.044	NA7150-7180	Types of materials
721.04497	NA8480	Prefabricated buildings
722	NA210-340	Ancient
722	NA205	Primitive
722-724	NA200-1613	History
722.62	NA300-301	Etruscan
722.7	NA310-340	Roman
722.7	NA295-340	Italy
722.80938	NA280-283	Athens (Parthenon/Etc.)
723	NA350-489	Medieval
723.4	NA390-391	Romanesque
723.4	NA423	Norman
723.5	NA440-489	Gothic
724	NA500-680	Modern
724.1(2-4)	NA510	Renaissance (16th century)
724.1(6-9)	NA590	Baroque/Rococo
724.19	NA627-640	18th century
724.19	NA640	Georgian
724.2	NA600	Neoclassicism
724.3	NA610	Gothic revival
724.5	NA645-670	19th century
724.6	NA680	20th century
725	NA4170-7010	Public buildings
725	NA9320-9425	Ornamental structures
725-728	NA4170-8480	Classed by use
725.1	NA4180-4193	International (Hague/Etc.)
725.1	NA4195-4510	National/State/Municipal
725.1(1-9)	NA4420-4427	Government offices/Bureaus
725.109(4-9)	NA4201-4384	By place
725.1094	NA4283-4341	Europe
725.10941	NA4285-4293	Great Britain
725.10943	NA4299-4300.6	Germany
725.109436	NA4295	Austria
725.10944	NA4297	France
725.10945	NA4303	Italy
725.10946	NA4323	Spain
725.109469	NA4325	Portugal
725.10947	NA4311	European Russia
725.10948	NA4313-4321	Scandinavia
725.109481	NA4319	Norway
725.109485	NA4321	Sweden
725.109489	NA4315	Denmark
725.1094912	NA4317	Iceland
725.109492	NA4307	Netherlands
725.109493	NA4309	Belgium
725.109494	NA4327	Switzerland
725.109495	NA4301	Greece
725.109496	NA4331-4338	Balkan states
725.1095	NA4343-4372	Asia
725.1095(6-61)	NA4345-4346.6	Near East/Asia Minor
725.10951	NA4365	China
725.109519	NA4368.6	Korea
725.10952	NA4367	Japan
725.10954	NA4351	India
725.1095491	NA4353	Pakistan
725.1095493	NA4352.6	Sri Lanka

Dewey	LC	Descriptor
725.10955	NA4347	Iran
725.109561	NA4329	Turkey
725.1095694	NA4346.6	Israel/Palestine
725.10957	NA4350	Asian Russia
725.109581	NA4349.6	Afghanistan
725.109593	NA4356.6	Thailand
725.109594	NA4356.L3	Laos
725.109595	NA4357	Malaysia
725.109596	NA4356.C3	Cambodia
725.109597	NA4356.V5	Vietnam
725.109598	NA4359	Indonesia
725.109599	NA4361	Philippines
725.1096	NA4373-4378.6	Africa
725.10961	NA4374-.8	North Africa
725.10962	NA4375	Egypt
725.10963	NA4376.7	Ethiopia
725.10966	NA4377-.6	West Africa
725.109676	NA4376.8-.9	East Africa
725.10968	NA4378-.6	Southern Africa
725.10971	NA4229	Canada
725.10972	NA4231	Mexico
725.109728	NA4233-4246	Central America
725.1097281	NA4239	Guatemala
725.1097283	NA4241	Honduras
725.1097284	NA4246	El Salvador
725.1097285	NA4243	Nicaragua
725.1097286	NA4237	Costa Rica
725.1097287	NA4245	Panama
725.109729	NA4247-4258	West Indies
725.1097291	NA4251	Cuba
725.1097292	NA4255	Jamaica
725.1097294	NA4253	Haiti
725.1097295	NA4257	Puerto Rico
725.1097296	NA4249	Bahamas
725.10973	NA4205-4228	United States
725.1098	NA4259-4281	South America
725.10981	NA4265	Brazil
725.10982	NA4261	Argentina
725.10983	NA4267	Chile
725.10984	NA4263	Bolivia
725.10985	NA4277	Peru
725.109861	NA4269	Colombia
725.109866	NA4271	Ecuador
725.10987	NA4281	Venezuela
725.10988	NA4273-.4	Guianas
725.109892	NA4275	Paraguay
725.109895	NA4279	Uruguay
725.1099(5-6)	NA4383-4384	Oceania
725.10993	NA4381	New Zealand
725.10994	NA4379-4380	Australia
725.11	NA4410-4417	Capitols
725.1109(4-9)	NA4415	Other countries
725.110973	NA4411-4413	United States
725.13	NA4430-4437	City/Town halls
725.16	NA4450-4457	Post offices
725.17	NA4440-4447	Official residences
725.18	NA4490-4497	Police stations
725.18	NA490-497	Military (Walls/Gates/Etc.)
725.2	NA6210-6280	Commercial buildings
725.3	NA6290-6327	Transportation (Airports/Etc.)
725.3(5/6)	NA6330-6360	Grain elevators/Warehouses/Etc.
725.4	NA6400-6589	Industrial buildings
725.8	NA6800-6810	Recreational buildings
725.822	NA6815-6840	Theaters/Opera houses
725.94	NA9325-9330	War memorials

Dewey	LC	Descriptor
725.94	NA9335-9355	Monuments
725.94	NA9360-9380	Memorial/Triumphal arches
725.9409(4-9)	NA109	Other countries
725.940973	NA106-108	Monuments, United States
726	NB1750-1793	Religious monuments/Shrines
726	NA4590-6199	Religious buildings
726.(1-3)	NA4610-4710	Non-Christian
726.(1/4)	NA4830-4910	Special (Chapels/Shrines/Etc.)
726.0(5/6)	NA4590	Serials/Societies
726.06	NA4595	Congresses
726.09	NA5201-6113	Religious buildings, By place
726.0937	NA5523-5534.5	Czechoslovakia
726.0939	NA5512-5522.5	Hungary
726.094	NA5450-5955	Europe
726.0941	NA5461-5497	Great Britain
726.0943	NA5568-5588	Germany
726.09436	NA5501-5511.5	Austria
726.09438	NA5691	Poland
726.0944	NA5541-5553	France
726.0945	NA5611-5623	Italy
726.0946	NA5801-5813	Spain
726.09469	NA5821-5833	Portugal
726.0947	NA5681-5688	European Russia
726.0948	NA5701-5793	Scandinavia
726.09481	NA5761-5773	Norway
726.09485	NA5781-5793	Sweden
726.09489	NA5711-5723	Denmark
726.094897	NA5693	Finland
726.094912	NA5741-5753	Iceland
726.09492	NA5641-5638	Netherlands
726.09493	NA5661-5673	Belgium
726.09494	NA5841-5853	Switzerland
726.09495	NA5591-5603	Greece
726.09497	NA5881-5893	Bulgaria
726.09497	NA5941-5953	Yugoslavia
726.09498	NA5921-5933	Romania
726.095	NA5960-6069.6	Asia
726.0951	NA6040-6049.6	China
726.09519	NA6060-6069.6	Korea
726.0952	NA6050-6059.6	Japan
726.09538	NA5970-5972	Saudi Arabia
726.0954	NA6001-6010	India
726.095491	NA6010.7-.8	Pakistan
726.095493	NA6010.6-.63	Sri Lanka
726.0955	NA5980-5989	Iran
726.09561	NA5861-5873	Turkey
726.09567	NA5967-5969	Iraq
726.095691	NA5989.6-.8	Syria
726.095692	NA5976.6-.8	Lebanon
726.095694	NA5977-5979	Israel/Palestine
726.095695	NA5979.6-.8	Jordan
726.0957	NA5992.6-5999	Asian Russia (Siberia)
726.09581	NA5992-.3	Afghanistan
726.09591	NA6012-.3	Burma
726.09593	NA6021-1523	Thailand
726.09594	NA6016-.3	Laos
726.09595	NA6025-.6	Malaysia
726.09596	NA6015-.3	Cambodia
726.09597	NA6014-.3	Vietnam
726.09598	NA6026-.6	Indonesia
726.09599	NA6027-6029	Philippines
726.096	NA6080-6099	Africa
726.09611	NA6091-.6	Tunisia
726.09612	NA6089	Libya

Dewey	LC	Descriptor
726.0962	NA6081-6085	Egypt
726.0963	NA6086	Ethiopia
726.0964	NA6090	Morocco
726.0965	NA6088	Algeria
726.0966	NA6098-6099	West Africa
726.09676	NA6097-.6	East Africa
726.0968	NA6092-6096.6	Southern Africa
726.0971	NA5240-5249	Canada
726.0972	NA5250-5259	Mexico
726.09728	NA5260-5290	Central America
726.097281	NA5276-5278	Guatemala
726.097283	NA5279-5281	Honduras
726.097284	NA5288-5290	El Salvador
726.097285	NA5282-5284	Nicaragua
726.097286	NA5273-5275	Costa Rica
726.097287	NA5285-5287	Panama
726.09729	NA5291-5315	West Indies
726.097291	NA5303-5305	Cuba
726.097292	NA5309-5311	Jamaica
726.097294	NA5306-5308	Haiti
726.097295	NA5312-5314	Puerto Rico
726.097296	NA5300-5302	Bahamas
726.0973	NA5205-5238	United States
726.098	NA5320-5439	South America
726.0981	NA5350-5359	Brazil
726.0982	NA5330-5339	Argentina
726.0983	NA5360-5369	Chile
726.0984	NA5340-5349	Bolivia
726.0985	NA5410-5419	Peru
726.09861	NA5370-5379	Colombia
726.09866	NA5380-5389	Ecuador
726.0987	NA5430-5439	Venezuela
726.09881	NA5395	Guyana
726.09882	NA5397	French Guiana
726.09883	NA5396	Suriname
726.09892	NA5400-5409	Paraguay
726.09895	NA5420-5429	Uruguay
726.099(5-6)	NA6110-6113	Oceania
726.0993	NA6106-6108	New Zealand
726.0994	NA6100-6105	Australia
726.5(1-28)	NA5000	Interior decoration
726.509	NA4790-5095	Christian architecture, History
726.5090(1-4)	NA4817-4825	Christian architecture, By date
726.58(1-9)	NA4828-4829	By denomination
726.8	NA6120-6199	Sepulchral monuments
726.809	NA6149-6199	Sepulchrals, By place
726.8090(3-4)	NA6148	Modern
726.80901	NA6132-6142	Ancient
726.80902	NA6143-6147	Medieval
726.8094	NA6162-6178	Europe
726.80941	NA6163	Great Britain
726.80943	NA6166	Germany
726.80944	NA6165	France
726.80945	NA6167	Italy
726.80946	NA6174	Spain
726.80947	NA6170	European Russia
726.8095	NA6179-6190	Asia
726.80951	NA6188	China
726.809519	NA6189.5	Korea
726.80952	NA6189	Japan
726.80954	NA6183	India
726.8095491	NA6183.2	Pakistan
726.8095493	NA6183.5	Sri Lanka
726.8096	NA6191-6194	Africa
726.80962	NA6192	Egypt

Dewey	LC	Descriptor
726.80971	NA6153-6154	Canada
726.80972	NA6155	Mexico
726.809728	NA6154-6157	Central America
726.809729	NA6158-6159	West Indies
726.80973	NA6150-6152	United States
726.8098	NA6160-6161	South America
726.8099(5-6)	NA6198-6199	Oceania
726.80993	NA6197	New Zealand
726.80994	NA6195-6196	Australia
727	NA6590-6605	Educational buildings
727.6	NA6700	Museums
728	NA7100-7880	Domestic architecture
728.(1-31/8)	NA7511-7515	City houses
728.(37/6/8)	NA7560-7566	Country homes
728.0(5/6)	NA7100	Serials/Societies
728.06	NA7102	Congresses
728.09	NA7105	History
728.09(4-9)	NA7201-7476	Houses/Etc., By place
728.094	NA7325-7412	Europe
728.0941	NA7328-7342	Great Britain
728.0943	NA7349-7351.6	Germany
728.09436	NA7343	Austria
728.0944	NA7346	France
728.0945	NA7355	Italy
728.0946	NA7385	Spain
728.09469	NA7388	Portugal
728.0947	NA7367	European Russia
728.0948	NA7370-7382	Scandinavia
728.09481	NA7379	Norway
728.09485	NA7382	Sweden
728.09489	NA7373	Denmark
728.094912	NA7376	Iceland
728.09492	NA7361	Netherlands
728.09493	NA7364	Belgium
728.09494	NA7391	Switzerland
728.09495	NA7352	Greece
728.09496	NA7397-7412	Balkan states
728.095	NA7415-7459	Asia
728.095(6-61)	NA7418-7422	Near East/Asia Minor
728.0951	NA7448	China
728.09519	NA7453.6	Korea
728.0952	NA7451	Japan
728.0954	NA7427	India
728.095491	NA7431	Pakistan
728.095493	NA7430	Sri Lanka
728.0955	NA7421	Iran
728.09561	NA7394	Turkey
728.095694	NA7420	Israel/Palestine
728.0957	NA7425	Asian Russia
728.09581	NA7424.6	Afghanistan
728.09593	NA7435	Thailand
728.09594	NA7434.L3	Laos
728.09595	NA7436	Malaysia
728.09596	NA7434.C3	Cambodia
728.09597	NA7434.V5	Vietnam
728.09598	NA7439	Indonesia
728.09599	NA7442	Philippines
728.096	NA7460-7468.6	Africa
728.0961	NA7461-7465.6	North Africa
728.0962	NA7463	Egypt
728.0963	NA7465.7	Ethiopia
728.0966	NA7467-.6	West Africa
728.09676	NA7466-.6	East Africa
728.0968	NA7478-.6	Southern Africa
728.0971	NA7241	Canada
728.0972	NA7244	Mexico
728.09728	NA7247-7267	Central America

Dewey	LC	Descriptor
728.097281	NA7256	Guatemala
728.097283	NA7259	Honduras
728.097284	NA7267	El Salvador
728.097285	NA7262	Nicaragua
728.097286	NA7253	Costa Rica
728.097287	NA7265	Panama
728.09729	NA7268-7286	West Indies
728.097291	NA7274	Cuba
728.097292	NA7280	Jamaica
728.097294	NA7277	Haiti
728.097295	NA7283	Puerto Rico
728.097296	NA7271	Bahamas
728.0973	NA7205-7239	United States
728.098	NA7289-7322	South America
728.0981	NA7298	Brazil
728.0982	NA7292	Argentina
728.0983	NA7301	Chile
728.0984	NA7295	Bolivia
728.0985	NA7316	Peru
728.09861	NA7304	Colombia
728.09866	NA7307	Ecuador
728.0987	NA7322	Venezuela
728.0988	NA7310-.4	Guianas
728.09892	NA7313	Paraguay
728.09895	NA7319	Uruguay
728.099(5-6)	NA7483-7484	Oceania
728.0993	NA7481	New Zealand
728.0994	NA7479-7480	Australia
728.314	NA7860	Apartment houses/Flats
728.373	NA7570-7572.5	Suburban homes/ Bungalows
728.4	HS1238	Buildings/Halls
728.4	HS1029	Buildings/Halls
728.4	HS469	Buildings/Halls
728.4	HS162	Buildings/Halls
728.4	NA8050-8125	Guild houses
728.4	NA7910-8125	Clubhouses
728.5	NA7800-7850	Hotels/Inns
728.6	NA8200-8260	Farm architecture
728.7	NA7574-7579	Summerhouses/Vacation houses
728.8	NA7580-7596	Villas
728.8	NA7600-7625	Manor houses
728.8(1-2)	NA7710-7786	Castles/Palaces
728.9	NA8300-8392	Minor buildings/ Gates/Fences
729	NA3310-4050	Architectural decoration
729.09(4-9)	NA3501-3596	Decoration, By place
729.090(1-4)	NA3330-3485	Decoration, By date
729.090(3-4)	NA3450-3485	Modern
729.0901	NA3330-3370	Ancient
729.0902	NA3390-3420	Medieval
729.7	NA3750-3860	Mosaic/Terrazzo work
729.7074	NA3755	Museums/Exhibitions
729.7090(3-4)	NA3810-3850	Modern
729.70901	NA3760-3780	Ancient
729.70902	NA3788-3792	Medieval
730	NB	Sculpture
730.(5/6)	NB1	Serials
730.294	NB33-35	Catalogs/Trade catalogs
730.3	NB50	Dictionaries/ Encyclopedias
730.6	NB38	Congresses
730.7	NB1120-1133	Education
730.74	NB16-30	Museums/Exhibitions
730.9	NB60-1113	History
730.9	NB201-1113	By country
730.94	NB450-955	Europe
730.941	NB461-497	Great Britain
730.943	NB568-588	Germany
730.9436	NB501-511.5	Austria
730.9437	NB523-534.5	Czechoslovakia
730.9438	NB691	Poland
730.9439	NB512-522.5	Hungary
730.944	NB541-553	France
730.945	NB611-623	Italy
730.946	NB801-813	Spain
730.9469	NB821-833	Portugal
730.947	NB681-699	European Russia
730.948	NB701-793	Scandinavia
730.9481	NB761-773	Norway
730.9485	NB781-793	Sweden
730.9489	NB711-723	Denmark
730.94897	NB693	Finland
730.94912	NB741-753	Iceland
730.9492	NB641-653	Netherlands
730.9493	NB661-673	Belgium
730.9494	NB841-853	Switzerland
730.9495	NB591-603	Greece
730.9497	NB941-953	Yugoslavia
730.94977	NB818-893	Bulgaria
730.9498	NB921-933	Romania
730.95	NB960-1069.6	Asia
730.951	NB1040-1049.6	China
730.9519	NB1060-1069.6	Korea
730.952	NB1050-1059.6	Japan
730.9538	NB970-972	Saudi Arabia
730.954	NB1001-1010	India
730.95491	NB1010.7-.73	Pakistan
730.95493	NB1010.6-.63	Sri Lanka
730.955	NB980-989	Iran
730.9561	NB861-873	Turkey
730.9567	NB967-969	Iraq
730.95691	NB989.6-.8	Syria
730.95692	NB976.6-.8	Lebanon
730.95694	NB977-979	Israel/Palestine
730.95695	NB979.6-.8	Jordan
730.957	NB992.6-999	Asian Russia (Siberia)
730.9581	NB992-.3	Afghanistan
730.9591	NB1012-.3	Burma
730.9593	NB1021-1023	Thailand
730.9594	NB1016-.3	Laos
730.9595	NB1025-.6	Malaysia
730.9596	NB1015-.3	Cambodia
730.9597	NB1014-.3	Vietnam
730.9598	NB1026-.6	Indonesia
730.9599	NB1027-1032	Philippines
730.96	NB1080-1099	Africa
730.9611	NB1091	Tunisia
730.9612	NB1089	Libya
730.962	NB1081-1085	Egypt
730.963	NB1086	Ethiopia
730.964	NB1090	Morocco
730.965	NB1088	Algeria
730.966	NB1098-1099	West Africa
730.9676	NB1097-.6	East Africa
730.968	NB1092-1096.6	Southern Africa
730.971	NB240-249	Canada
730.972	NB250-259	Mexico
730.9728	NB260-290	Central America
730.97281	NB276-278	Guatemala
730.97283	NB279-281	Honduras
730.97284	NB288-290	El Salvador
730.97285	NB282-284	Nicaragua

Dewey	LC	Descriptor
730.97286	NB273-275	Costa Rica
730.97287	NB285-287	Panama
730.9729	NB291-215	West Indies
730.97291	NB303-305	Cuba
730.97292	NB309-311	Jamaica
730.97294	NB306-308	Haiti
730.97295	NB312-314	Puerto Rico
730.97296	NB300-302	Bahamas
730.973	NB205-238	United States
730.98	NB320-439	South America
730.981	NB350-359	Brazil
730.982	NB330-339	Argentina
730.983	NB360-369	Chile
730.984	NB340-349	Bolivia
730.985	NB410-419	Peru
730.9861	NB370-379	Colombia
730.9866	NB380-389	Ecuador
730.987	NB430-439	Venezuela
730.9881	NB395	Guyana
730.9882	NB397	French Guiana
730.9883	NB396	Suriname
730.9892	NB400-409	Paraguay
730.9895	NB420-429	Uruguay
730.99(5-6)	NB1110-1113	Oceania
730.993	NB1106-1108	New Zealand
730.994	NB1100-1105	Australia
731.028	NB1160-1195	Designs/Techniques
731.2	NB1208-1270	Materials
731.2	NB135-159	Special materials used
731.4(1/56-57)	NB1220-1240	Metals
731.452	NB1215	Concrete
731.456	NB135-143	Bronze
731.462	NB1250-1255	Wood
731.463	NB1208-1210	Stone
731.47	NB145-159	Terra cottas
731.47	NB1265-1793	Terra cotta
731.48	NB1199	Restoration
731.54	NB1280-1291	Sculpture in relief
731.55	NB1272	Mobiles
731.76	NB1330-1684	Sculptured monuments
731.7609(4-9)	NB1501-1684	Monuments, By place
731.8(2-9)	NB1910-1950	Special subjects
731.81	NB1312	Equestrian statues
731.82	NB1293-1310	Portrait sculpture
731.832	NB1940	Animals
731.834	NB1950	Plants
731.87	NB1920	Mythology
731.88	NB1910	Religious subjects
732	NB69-169	Ancient
732	NB61.5-64	Primitive/Prehistoric
733.3	NB90-105	Greek
733.5	NB115-120	Roman
734	NB170-180	Medieval
734.224	NB172	Byzantine
734.25	NB180	Gothic
735	NB185-198	Modern
736.5	NB1800-1880	Sepulchral monuments
737	CJ	Numismatics
737.22	CJ5501-6661	Medals/Medallions
737.22	CJ5723-5780	Medieval/Modern
737.220(5/6)	CJ5501-5502	Serials/Societies/Congresses
737.2201	CJ5517-5521	Philosophy/Theory
737.2207	CJ5525	Education
737.2209(4-9)	CJ5795-6661	Medals, By place
737.2209(72-8)	CJ5830-6090	Latin America
737.22093	CJ5581-5690	Ancient
737.220937	CJ5641-5685	Roman

Dewey	LC	Descriptor
737.220938	CJ5625	Greek
737.22094	CJ6091-6380	Europe
737.22095	CJ6381-6485	Asia
737.22096	CJ6491-6559	Africa
737.220973	CJ5801-5812	United States
737.22099(3-6)	CJ6561-6661	Australia/New Zealand/ Oceania
737.3	CJ4801-5450	Tokens
737.3	CJ4861-4889	Tokens, By period
737.30(5/6)	CJ4801	Serials/Societies
737.303	CJ4813	Dictionaries/ Encyclopedias
737.3074	CJ4805-4808	Exhibitions/Museums
737.309(4-9)	CJ4901-5336	By place
737.309(72-8)	CJ4921-4985	Latin America
737.3094	CJ5046-5185	Europe
737.3095	CJ5186-5243	Asia
737.3096	CJ5246-5275	Africa
737.30973	CJ4901-4910	United States
737.3098	CJ4986-5045	South America
737.3099(3-6)	CJ5281-5336	Australia/New Zealand/ Oceania
737.4	CJ1-4625	Coins
737.4	CJ1301-1397	African/Oriental
737.401	CJ53	Philosophy/Theory
737.4028	CJ109-119	Materials
737.403	CJ31	Yearbooks
737.405	CJ1-9	Serials
737.406	CJ14-27	Societies/Congresses
737.407	CJ55	Education
737.4074	CJ39-45	Exhibitions/Museums
737.409	CJ59-62	History
737.49(4-9)	CJ1800-4625	Coins, By place
737.49(4-9)	CJ1735-1743	Renaissance
737.49(4-9)	CJ1509-4625	Medieval and modern
737.49(4-9)	CJ1747-1758	Modern coins
737.49(4-9)	CJ1601-1715	Medieval/Modern, By place
737.49(72-8)	CJ1889-2449	Latin America
737.493	CJ201-1397	Ancient
737.493	CJ801-1139	Roman
737.493	CJ301-763	Greek
737.493(1-5)	CJ573-647	Asia
737.493(1-5)	CJ1087-1099	Asia
737.493(1-9)	CJ1021-1139	By place
737.493(2-9)	CJ425-763	By place
737.493(6/98)	CJ1101-1139	Europe
737.4937	CJ1021-1070	Italy
737.4937	CJ517-542	Italy
737.4938	CJ427-499	Greece
737.49397	CJ725-763	Africa
737.49397	CJ1071-1085	Africa
737.494	CJ2450-3369	Europe
737.49495	CJ1201-1291	Byzantine
737.495	CJ3370-3889	Asia
737.496	CJ3900-4389	Africa
737.4971	CJ1860-1879	Canada
737.4973	CJ1820-1845	United States
737.499(3-6)	CJ4400-4625	Australia/New Zealand/ Oceania
737.6	CD	Diplomatics/Archives/Seals
737.6	CD5001-6471	Seals (Numismatics)
737.601	CD5029-5041	Philosophy/Theory
737.6025	CD5053	Directories
737.6028	CD5085-5175	Technique
737.603	CD5055	Dictionaries/ Encyclopedias
737.605	CD5011	Yearbooks

Dewey	LC	Descriptor
737.605	CD5001	Serials
737.606	CD5005-5009	Societies/Congresses
737.607	CD5045	Education
737.6074	CD5017-5022	Museums/Exhibitions
737.609	CD5049	History of seals
737.6090(23-31)	CD5561	Renaissance
737.6090(3-4)	CD5575-6471	Modern
737.60901	CD5201-5391	Ancient
737.60902	CD5501-5557	Medieval
737.6092	CD5051-5052	Biography
737.6094	CD5871-6151	Europe
737.60941	CD5881-5899.1	Great Britain
737.60943	CD5941-5960.2	Germany
737.60944	CD5921-5939	France
737.60945	CD5971-5989	Italy
737.6095	CD6161-6295	Asia
737.60951	CD6171-6180	China
737.60952	CD6241-6250	Japan
737.60954	CD6191-6200	India
737.6096	CD6301-6365	Africa
737.609728	CD5621-5700	Central America
737.609729	CD5701-5741	West Indies
737.60973	CD5601-5619	United States
737.6098	CD5751-5870	South America
737.6099(3-6)	CD6371-6471	Australia/New Zealand/ Oceania
738	NK3700-4695	Ceramic arts
738	NK3900-3930	Modern
738-749	NK3600-9955	Misc. arts
738.03	NK3770	Dictionaries/ Encyclopedias
738.074	NK3712-3745	Exhibitions/Museums
738.09	NK3780-4184	History
738.09(4-9)	NK4001-4184	Ceramic arts, By place
738.0902	NK3870-3880	Medieval
738.092	NK4200	Biography
738.093	NK3800-3855	Ancient
738.2	NK4370-4584	Porcelain
738.3	NK4360-4367	Stoneware
738.3	NK4260-4340	Earthenware/Terra cotta
739	TT205-214	Metalworking
739	NK6400-8459	Metalwork
739.14	TT267	Soldering/Brazing
739.14	TT215-240	Ironworking/Forging
739.15	TT382-.8	Metal finishing
739.27	TS740-761	Jewelry
741	NC95	20th century
741.(09/9) + 5(6-61)	NC318-320	Near East/Asia Minor
741.(09/9) + 9(5-6)	NC375-376	Oceania
741.(09/9)(3-9)	NC101-376	History of drawings, By place
741.(09/9)4	NC225-415	Europe
741.(09/9)41	NC228-242	Great Britain
741.(09/9)43	NC249-251.6	Germany
741.(09/9)44	NC246	France
741.(09/9)45	NC255	Italy
741.(09/9)46	NC285	Spain
741.(09/9)469	NC288	Portugal
741.(09/9)47	NC267	European Russia
741.(09/9)48	NC270-282	Scandinavia
741.(09/9)481	NC279	Norway
741.(09/9)485	NC282	Sweden
741.(09/9)489	NC273	Denmark
741.(09/9)4912	NC276	Iceland
741.(09/9)494	NC291	Switzerland
741.(09/9)495	NC252	Greece
741.(09/9)496	NC297-308	Balkan states

Dewey	LC	Descriptor
741.(09/9)5	NC315-359	Asia
741.(09/9)51	NC348	China
741.(09/9)519	NC353.6	Korea
741.(09/9)52	NC351	Japan
741.(09/9)54	NC327	India
741.(09/9)5491	NC331	Pakistan
741.(09/9)5493	NC330	Sri Lanka
741.(09/9)55	NC321	Iran
741.(09/9)561	NC294	Turkey
741.(09/9)5694	NC320	Israel/Palestine
741.(09/9)57	NC325	Asian Russia
741.(09/9)581	NC324.6	Afghanistan
741.(09/9)593	NC335	Thailand
741.(09/9)594	NC334.L3	Laos
741.(09/9)595	NC336	Malaysia
741.(09/9)596	NC334.C3	Cambodia
741.(09/9)597	NC334.V5	Vietnam
741.(09/9)598	NC339	Indonesia
741.(09/9)599	NC342	Philippines
741.(09/9)6	NC360-368.6	Africa
741.(09/9)61	NC361-.8	North Africa
741.(09/9)62	NC363	Egypt
741.(09/9)63	NC365.7	Ethiopia
741.(09/9)66	NC367.6	West Africa
741.(09/9)676	NC366.6	East Africa
741.(09/9)68	NC368-.6	Southern Africa
741.(09/9)71	NC141	Canada
741.(09/9)72	NC144	Mexico
741.(09/9)728	NC147-167	Central America
741.(09/9)7281	NC156	Guatemala
741.(09/9)7283	NC159	Honduras
741.(09/9)7284	NC167	El Salvador
741.(09/9)7285	NC162	Nicaragua
741.(09/9)7286	NC153	Costa Rica
741.(09/9)7287	NC165	Panama
741.(09/9)729	NC168-186	West Indies
741.(09/9)7291	NC174	Cuba
741.(09/9)7292	NC180	Jamaica
741.(09/9)7294	NC177	Haiti
741.(09/9)7295	NC183	Puerto Rico
741.(09/9)7296	NC171	Bahamas
741.(09/9)73	NC105-139	United States
741.(09/9)8	NC189-222	South America
741.(09/9)81	NC198	Brazil
741.(09/9)82	NC192	Argentina
741.(09/9)83	NC201	Chile
741.(09/9)84	NC195	Bolivia
741.(09/9)85	NC216	Peru
741.(09/9)861	NC204	Colombia
741.(09/9)866	NC207	Ecuador
741.(09/9)87	NC222	Venezuela
741.(09/9)88	NC210-.4	Guianas
741.(09/9)892	NC213	Paraguay
741.(09/9)895	NC219	Uruguay
741.(09/9)93	NC372	New Zealand
741.(09/9)94	NC369-370	Australia
741.(6)	NC	Drawing/Illustration
741.(6)0294	NC37-38	Catalogs of drawings
741.(6)05	NC1	Serials
741.(6)06	NC5	Congresses
741.(6)074	NC15-17	Exhibitions
741.(6)074	NC20-33	Museums/Collections of drawing
741.(6)092	NC45	Biography
741.0202	NC597	Outlines/Syllabi/Etc.
741.07	NC390-584	History of drawing study
741.07	NC390-670	Education

Dewey	LC	Descriptor
741.070(4-9)	NC401-584	Study, By country
741.076	NC599	Examinations/Questions
741.09	NC50-376	History of drawing
741.090(23-31)	NC85	Renaissance/16th century
741.090(3-4)	NC80-95	Modern
741.0901	NC54	Primitive
741.0901	NC55-65	Ancient
741.0902	NC70-75	Medieval
741.09033	NC87	18th century
741.09034	NC90	19th century
741.09132	NC86	17th century
741.2	NC730-757	Technique
741.2	NC850-915	Graphic art materials
741.217	NC1920-1940	Copying/Enlarging of drawings
741.218	NC930	Conservation/Restoration
741.22	NC850	Charcoal
741.23	NC855-875	Crayon
741.235	NC880-885	Pastels
741.24	NC890-895	Pencil drawings
741.25	NC900	Silverpoint
741.26	NC905	Pen and ink
741.5	PN6700-6790	Comic books/Comic strips
741.5	NC1300-1766	Pictorial humor/ Caricature/Etc.
741.5(09/9) + (4-9)	NC1400-1762	Caricatures, By place
741.5(09/9) + (728/8)	NC1450-1460	Central/South America
741.5(09/9) + 9(3-4)	NC1750-1761	Australia/New Zealand
741.5(09/9)4	NC1465-1670	Europe
741.5(09/9)41	NC1470-1479	Great Britain
741.5(09/9)43	NC1500-1509	Germany
741.5(09/9)44	NC1490-1499	France
741.5(09/9)45	NC1520-1529	Italy
741.5(09/9)46(9)	NC1630-1649	Spain/Portugal
741.5(09/9)47	NC1570-1579	European Russia
741.5(09/9)495	NC1510-1519	Greece
741.5(09/9)5	NC1680-1729	Asia
741.5(09/9)51	NC1690-1699	China
741.5(09/9)52	NC1700-1709	Japan
741.5(09/9)54	NC1710-1719	India
741.5(09/9)6	NC1730-1749	Africa
741.5(09/9)71	NC1440-1449	Canada
741.5(09/9)73	NC1420-1429	United States
741.5(09/9)78	NC1580-1629	Scandinavia
741.50(5/6)	NC1300	Serials/Societies
741.5074	NC1310-1312	Exhibitions
741.5074	NC1313-1318	Museums/Collections
741.509	NC1325-1762	History
741.58	NC1765-1766	Motion picture cartoons
741.6	NC950-995.8	Illustration
741.6	NC997-1003	Commercial/Advertising art
741.60(5/6)	NC997.A1	Serials/Societies
741.6023	NC1001	As a profession
741.6025	NC999	Directories
741.606	NC997.A2	Congresses
741.607	NC1000	Education
741.6074	NC997.A4	Exhibitions
741.609	NC998-.4	History
741.609(4-9)	NC975-995.8	Illustration, By place
741.6092	NC999.2	Biography
741.674	NC1800-1855	Posters
741.684	NC1860-1890	Greeting cards/Invitations/ Etc.
741.685	NE965-.3	Tradesmen's cards/Billheads
741.7	NC910	Silhouettes (Cutting/Etc.)
743	NC760-825	Special subjects
743.4	NC765-776	Human figure

Dewey	LC	Descriptor
743.6	NC780-783	Animal drawing
743.7	NC805-815	Trees/Plants/Flowers
743.836	NC790-800	Landscapes
745	NK1135-1149	Arts and crafts
745	TT855-910	Decorative crafts
745	NK	Decorative arts
745.01	NK1505	Theory
745.0294	NK1133	Catalogs
745.03	NK30	Dictionaries
745.03	NK28	Encyclopedias
745.05	NK1135	Serials
745.05	NK1-9	Serials
745.06	NK1136	Societies
745.06	NK11-21	Societies/Congresses
745.07	NK50-440	Education
745.070(1-9)	NK101-376	Education, By place
745.0710(5-9)	NK430	Special schools, Other places
745.0710(71-8)	NK410	Special schools, America
745.07104	NK420	Special schools, Europe
745.074	NK530-570	Private collections
745.074	NK1137	Exhibitions
745.074	NK450-490	Museums/Galleries
745.074(5-9)	NK560	Other countries
745.074(71-8)	NK540	Other American countries
745.074(71-8)	NK470	Other American countries
745.0744	NK550	Europe
745.0744	NK475-480	Europe
745.07473	NK460	Galleries, United States
745.07473	NK530-535	Collections, United States
745.09	NK1140-1142	History
745.09	NK600-1133	History
745.09(4-9)	NK801-1094	By place
745.090(3-4)	NK750-789	Modern
745.0901	NK610-685	Ancient
745.0902	NK700-740	Medieval
745.092	NC45	Biography
745.093	NK605	Primitive
745.4	NK1160-1590	Decoration/Ornament/ Design
745.4	NC	Design
745.40(5/6)	NK1160	Serials/Societies
745.401	NC703	Design theory
745.40294	NC37-38	Catalogs of drawings
745.403	NK1165	Dictionaries
745.405	NC1	Serials
745.407	NK1170	Education
745.4074	NC15-17	Exhibitions
745.4074	NC20-33	Museums/Collections of drawings
745.44	NK1175-1496	History
745.441	NK1177-1250	Ancient/Primitive
745.442	NK1260-1295	Medieval
745.443	NK1330	15th-16th centuries
745.443	NK1340-1365	17th-18th centuries
745.4441	NK1370-1382	19th century
745.4442	NK1390-1394	20th century
745.5	TT	Handicrafts/Arts and crafts
745.50(5/6)	TT1	Serials/Societies
745.5025	TT12	Directories
745.503	TT9	Dictionaries/ Encyclopedias
745.5074	TT6	Exhibitions/Museums
745.509(4-9)	TT15-126	Handicrafts, By place
745.50941	TT57-64.5	Great Britain
745.50943	TT73-74.5	Germany
745.509436	TT65-.2	Austria

Dewey	LC	Descriptor
745.509437	TT65.3-.4	Czechoslovakia
745.509439	TT65.5-66	Hungary
745.50944	TT71-72.5	France
745.50945	TT79-80	Italy
745.50946	TT87-88	Spain
745.509469	TT83-84.5	Portugal
745.50947	TT85-86	European Russia
745.50948	TT88.5	Scandinavia
745.509481	TT81-82	Norway
745.509485	TT89-90	Sweden
745.509489	TT69-70	Denmark
745.5094897	TT95.F5	Finland
745.509492	TT77-78	Netherlands
745.509493	TT67-68	Belgium
745.509494	TT91-92	Switzerland
745.509495	TT75-76	Greece
745.509496	TT95.A2	Balkans
745.509497	TT95.Y8	Yugoslavia
745.50951	TT101-102	China
745.50952	TT105-106	Japan
745.50954	TT103-104	India
745.5095491	TT104.5-.6	Pakistan
745.5095493	TT104.7-.8	Sri Lanka
745.50955	TT107-108	Iran
745.509561	TT111-112	Turkey
745.509567	TT113.I7	Iraq
745.5095694	TT113.I75	Israel/Palestine
745.50957	TT109-110	Asian Russia
745.509598	TT113.I55	Indonesia
745.509599	TT113.P6	Philippines
745.5096	TT115-119	Africa
745.5096(1-9)	TT119	Africa, By country
745.50962	TT117-118	Egypt
745.50971	TT26-27	Canada
745.50972	TT28-29	Mexico
745.509728	TT30-31	Central America
745.509729	TT32-33	West Indies
745.50973	TT23-25	United States
745.50981	TT41-42	Brazil
745.50982	TT36-37	Argentina
745.50983	TT43-44	Chile
745.50984	TT38-39	Bolivia
745.50985	TT52	Peru
745.509861	TT45-46	Colombia
745.509866	TT47	Ecuador
745.50987	TT54	Venezuela
745.509881	TT48	Guyana
745.509882	TT50	French Guiana
745.509883	TT49	Suriname
745.509892	TT51	Paraguay
745.509895	TT53	Uruguay
745.5099(5-6)	TT123-124	Oceania
745.50993	TT122.5-.6	New Zealand
745.50994	TT121-122	Australia
745.50998	TT125-126	Polar areas
745.51	TT180-203	Woodworking
745.51	TT325-345	Wood finishing
745.51	NK9600-9699	Woodworking
745.531	TT290	Leatherwork
745.531	NK6200-6210	Leatherwork
745.572	TT297	Plastic crafts
745.584	TT288	Bone/Horn crafts
745.592	TT174-176	Toys/Etc. for children
745.592	NK9509-.8	Toys (Handicrafted)
745.61	NK3600-3640	Alphabets/Calligraphy/ Initials
745.61	TT360	Lettering/Etc.

Dewey	LC	Descriptor
745.61	Z43-45	Calligraphy/Penmanship
745.61	ND1455-1457	Calligraphy as painting
745.619(8-9)	NK3632-3639	Non-Roman
745.61978	NK3603-3631	Roman
745.67	ND2890-3416	Illuminating (Manuscripts/ Etc.)
745.67	ND3410-3416	Modern illuminated books
745.67074	ND2893	Exhibitions
745.6709	ND2900-3294	History
745.6709(4-9)	ND3001-3294	By place
745.67090(1-4)	ND2910-2990	By date
745.67090(23-31)	ND2990	Renaissance
745.670901	ND2910	Ancient
745.670902	ND2920-2980	Medieval
745.67092	ND2890	Biographical dictionaries
745.7	TT370	Coloring of stone/Etc.
745.723	TT310-315	Paint mixing/Spraying
745.723	TT300-382.8	Painting/Varnishing/Etc.
745.73	TT270	Stencil cutting
745.75	TT380	Gilding/Bronzing
745.92	SB449-450.87	Flower arrangements
746	NK8800-9505	Textile arts
746.3	NK2975-3096	Tapestries
746.4(3-4)	TT740-829	Decorative needlework
746.42	TT848-849	Hand weaving
746.92	NK4700-4890	Costume/Accessories
746.920(5/6)	NK4700-.5	Serials/Societies
746.920294	NK4799	Catalogs
746.92074	NK4701-4703	Exhibitions/Museums
746.9209	NK4706-4710	Costume history
746.9209(4-9)	NK4713-4796	Other countries
746.9209(72-8)	NK4712.5	Spanish/Latin America
746.920973	NK4712	United States
747	NK1700-3505	Interior/House decoration
747.(3-7)	NK2117-2121	Special areas/Parts of house
747.(5/3)	NK3175-3296	Upholstery/Wall hangings
747.0(5/6)	NK1700	Serials/Societies
747.023	NK2116-.2	As a profession
747.025	NK1750	Directories
747.0294	NK2265	Catalogs
747.07	NK2116.4-.6	Education
747.074	NK2210-2220	Exhibitions/Museums
747.2	NK1710-2096	History/Styles, By place
747.2(1-9)	NK2000-2096	Interior decoration, By place
747.20(3-4)	NK1860-1986	Modern
747.201	NK1720-1780	Ancient
747.202	NK1800-1840	Medieval
747.203(4-5)	NK1870	15th-16th centuries
747.203(6-7)	NK1880-1940	17th-18th centuries
747.2048	NK1960-1972	19th century
747.2049	NK1980-1986	20th century
747.24	NK2042-2071	Europe
747.25	NK2072-2086	Asia
747.26	NK2087-2089.8	Africa
747.27	NK2001	North America
747.271	NK2013	Canada
747.272	NK2014	Mexico
747.2728	NK2015-2022	Central America
747.2729	NK2023-2029	West Indies
747.273	NK2003-2012	United States
747.28	NK2030-2041	South America
747.29(3-6)	NK2090-2096	Australia/New Zealand/ Oceania
747.3	NK2140-2180	Decorative painting
747.3	NK3375-3496	Wallpapers
747.5	NK2775-2896	Rugs/Carpets

Dewey	LC	Descriptor	Dewey	LC	Descriptor
747.505	NK2775	Serials	755	ND1430-1432	Religious
747.5074	NK2780-2786	Exhibitions/Museums	757	ND1300-1337	Portraits
747.509(4-9)	NK2808-2896	Rugs/Carpets, By place	757	ND1290-1293	Human figure
747.8(5-7)	NK2195	Other buildings	757	ND1309.6	20th century
747.86	NK2190	Church decoration	757.09	ND1303-1327	History
748	NK5100-5440	Glass (Stained/Leaded/Etc.)	757.090(24-31)	ND1308	15th-16th centuries
748.6	NE2690	Engraving on glass	757.090(3-4)	ND1309-.6	Modern
749	NK2200-2750	Furniture	757.0901	ND1305	Ancient
749.03	NK2205	Dictionaries	757.0902	ND1307	Medieval
749.05	NK2200	Serials	757.09031	ND1309.2	16th century
749.07	NK2267-2268	Education	757.09032	ND1309.3	17th century
749.2(1-9)	NK2401-2694	Furniture, By place	757.09033	ND1309.4	18th century
749.20(1-5)	NK2270-2694	Furniture, History	757.09034	ND1309.5	19th century
749.3	NK2910	Screens	757.092	ND1328-1329	Biography
750	ND	Painting	757.094	ND1313-1324	Europe
750	ND1560-1625	Surfaces (Canvas/	757.0941	ND1314-.6	Great Britain
		Glass/Metal)	757.0943	ND1317-.6	Germany
750.294	ND40-45	Catalogs of paintings/Etc.	757.0944	ND1316-.6	France
750.3	ND31	Dictionaries	757.0945	ND1318-.6	Italy
750.3	ND30	Encyclopedias	757.0946(9)	ND1322-.6	Spain/Portugal
750.7	ND1115-1120	Education	757.0947	ND1320-.6	European Russia
751	ND1500-1660	Materials/Methods	757.09492	ND1319-.6	Netherlands
751.2	ND1510-1535	Pigments/Varnishes	757.095	ND1325-1327	Asia
751.3	ND1538-1539	Brushes/Knives	757.095(1/2)	ND1326-.6	China/Japan
751.4	ND1470-1495	Techniques	757.0973	ND1311-.9	Portraits, United States
751.4	ND1480-1482	Styles (Abstract/	757.7	ND1330-1337	Portrait miniatures
		Impressionism)	758.1	ND1340-1367	Landscape painting
751.422	ND1700-2495	Watercolor painting	758.109	ND1343-1367	History
751.42205	ND1700	Serials	758.109(3-9)	ND1351-1367	Landscape painting, By
751.42206	ND1711-1721	Societies			place
751.42207	ND2110-2115	Education	758.109(71-8)	ND1352	Other American
751.422074	ND1725-1735	Museums/Collections/	758.1094	ND1353-1364	Europe
		Exhibition	758.10941	ND1354-.6	Great Britain
751.42209	ND1760-2094	History	758.10943	ND1357-.6	Germany
751.42209(4-9)	ND1801-2094	Watercolors, By place	758.10944	ND1356-.6	France
751.422094	ND1925-2012	Europe	758.10945	ND1358-.6	Italy
751.4220941	ND1928-1942	Great Britain	758.10946(9)	ND1362-.6	Spain/Portugal
751.4220943	ND1949-1951.6	Germany	758.1095	ND1366-.96	Asia
751.4220944	ND1947	France	758.10973	ND1351-.6	United States
751.4220945	ND1955	Italy	758.2	ND1370-1373	Marine painting
751.4220946(9)	ND1985-1988	Spain/Portugal	758.3	ND1380-1383	Animals/Birds
751.4220947	ND1964	European Russia	758.3	ND1385-1388	Sport/Hunting/Fishing
751.42209492	ND1961	Netherlands	758.4	ND1390-1393	Still life
751.422095	ND2015-2059	Asia	758.42	ND1400-1403	Flowers/Fruit
751.422095(1-2)	ND2048-2051	China/Japan	759	ND34-38	Biography
751.4220973	ND1805-1839	United States	759	ND49-1113	History
751.422098	ND1889-1922	South America	759.(1-9)	ND204-1113	Painting, By place
751.42242	ND2190-2192	Human figure	759.(3-8)	ND450-955	Europe
751.42242	ND2200-2202	Portraits	759.0(2-6)	ND1480-1482	Styles(Abstract/
751.422432	ND2280-2282	Animals/Birds			Impressionism)
751.422435	ND2300-2302	Flowers/Fruit	759.01	ND70-130	Ancient
751.422435	ND2290-2292	Still life	759.02	ND140-146	Medieval
751.422436	ND2240-2243	Landscapes	759.0212	ND135	Early Christian
751.422437	ND2270-2272	Marine			(Catacombs/Etc.)
751.42248	ND2360-2362	Religious	759.03	ND170-172	Renaissance (15-16th
751.6	ND1630-1660	Conservation of paintings			centuries)
751.7	ND1560-1625	Surfaces (Canvas/	759.046	ND180-182	17th century
		Glass/Metal)	759.047	ND186-188	18th century
751.73	ND2550-2888	Mural painting	759.05	ND190-192	19th century
751.7309(4-9)	ND2601-2876	Mural painting, By place	759.06	ND195-196	20th century
751.73090(1-4)	ND2555-2590	By date	759.06(3-6)	ND160-196	Modern
751.74	ND2882	Dioramas	759.11	ND240-249	Canada
751.74	ND2880	Panoramas	759.13	ND205-238	United States
751.75	ND2885-2888	Scene painting (As the	759.2	ND461-497	Great Britain
		stage)	759.3	ND568-588	Germany
752	ND1486-1495	Color	759.36	ND501-511.5	Austria
753	ND1420-1422	Mythological/Symbolical	759.37	ND523-534.5	Czechoslovakia

Dewey	LC	Descriptor
759.38	ND691	Poland
759.39	ND512-522.5	Hungary
759.4	ND541-553	France
759.5	ND611-623	Italy
759.6	ND801-813	Spain
759.69	ND821-833	Portugal
759.7	ND681-699	European Russia
759.8	ND701-793	Scandinavia
759.81	ND761-773	Norway
759.85	ND781-793	Sweden
759.89	ND711-723	Denmark
759.897	ND693	Finland
759.95	ND591-603	Greece
759.95	ND960-1069.6	Asia
759.951	ND1040-1049.6	China
759.9519	ND1060-1069.6	Korea
759.952	ND1050-1059.6	Japan
759.9538	ND970-972	Saudi Arabia
759.954	ND1001-1010	India
759.95491	ND1010.7-.73	Pakistan
759.95493	ND1010.6-.63	Sri Lanka
759.955	ND980-989	Iran
759.9561	ND861-873	Turkey
759.9567	ND967-969	Iraq
759.95691	ND989.6-.8	Syria
759.95692	ND976.6-.8	Lebanon
759.95694	ND977-979	Israel/Palestine
759.95695	ND979-.8	Jordan
759.957	ND992.6-999	Asian Russia (Siberia)
759.9581	ND992-.3	Afghanistan
759.9591	ND1012-.3	Burma
759.9593	ND1021-1023	Thailand
759.9594	ND1016-.3	Laos
759.9595	ND1025-.6	Malaysia
759.9596	ND1015-.3	Cambodia
759.9597	ND1014-.3	Vietnam
759.9598	ND1026-.6	Indonesia
759.9599	ND1027-1029	Philippines
759.96	ND1080-1099	Africa
759.9611	ND1091	Tunisia
759.9612	ND1089	Libya
759.962	ND1081-1085	Egypt
759.963	ND1086	Ethiopia
759.964	ND1090	Morocco
759.965	ND1088	Algeria
759.966	ND1098-1099	West Africa
759.9676	ND1097-.6	East Africa
759.968	ND1092-1096.6	Southern Africa
759.972	ND250-259	Mexico
759.9728	ND260-290	Central America
759.97281	ND276-278	Guatemala
759.97283	ND279-281	Honduras
759.97284	ND288-290	El Salvador
759.97285	ND282-284	Nicaragua
759.97286	ND273-275	Costa Rica
759.97287	ND285-287	Panama
759.9729	ND291-315	West Indies
759.97291	ND303-305	Cuba
759.97292	ND309-311	Jamaica
759.97294	ND306-308	Haiti
759.97295	ND312-314	Puerto Rico
759.97296	ND300-302	Bahamas
759.98	ND320-439	South America
759.981	ND350-359	Brazil
759.982	ND330-339	Argentina
759.983	ND360-369	Chile
759.984	ND340-349	Bolivia
759.985	ND410-419	Peru
759.9861	ND370-379	Colombia
759.9866	ND380-389	Ecuador
759.987	ND430-439	Venezuela
759.9881	ND395	Guyana
759.9882	ND397	French Guiana
759.9883	ND396	Suriname
759.9892	ND400-409	Paraguay
759.9895	ND420-429	Uruguay
759.99(5-6)	ND1110-1113	Oceania
759.993	ND1106-1108	New Zealand
759.994	ND1100-1105	Australia
760	NE	Print media
760-767	NE1-978	Printmaking/Engraving
760.(5/6)	NE1	Serials/Societies
760.23	NE61	As a profession
760.25	NE30	Directories
760.278	NE820	Engravers' marks
760.28	NE977-978	Equipment/Apparatus
760.294	NE63-75	Catalogs (Sales/Dealers)
760.3	NE20	Encyclopedias
760.5	NE10	Yearbooks
760.6	NE3	Congresses
760.7	NE970-973	Education
760.74	NE42-59	Museums/Exhibitions
760.75	NE60	Organization (Gallery/Museum)
761.2	NE1095-1097	20th century
761.2	NE1000-1352	Wood engraving/Woodcuts
761.20(5/6)	NE1000	Serials/Societies
761.2074	NE1010-1012	Exhibitions
761.209	NE1030-1196	History
761.209(4-9)	NE1101-1196	Wood engraving, By place
761.2090(24-32)	NE1050-1055	15th-17th centuries
761.2090(3-4)	NE1048-1097	Modern
761.20901	NE1035	Ancient
761.20902	NE1040-1047	Medieval
761.209033	NE1085-1088	18th century
761.209034	NE1090-1093	19th century
761.8	NE1400-1879	Metal engraving
761.80(5/6)	NE1400	Serials/Societies
761.8074	NE1410-1412	Exhibitions
763	NE2250-2529	Lithography
763.0(5/6)	NE2250	Serials/Societies
763.025	NE2283	Directories
763.028	NE2490-2495	Equipment/Apparatus
763.0294	NE2280	Dealers' catalogs
763.07	NE2480	Education
763.074	NE2260-2275	Museums/Exhibitions
763.09	NE2295-2396	History
763.09(4-9)	NE2301-2396	Lithography, By place
763.09034	NE2297	19th century
763.0904	NE2298	20th century
763.092	NE2410	Biography
764.2	NE2500-2529	Chromolithography
764.8	NE2236-2240	Serigraphy (Silk screen print)
764.809(4-9)	NE2238-.5	Other countries
764.80973	NE2237-.5	United States
765	NE1400-1879	Metal engraving
765.0(5/6)	NE1400	Serials/Societies
765.074	NE1410-1412	Exhibitions
765.09	NE1430-1749	History
765.090(3-4)	NE1639-1749	Modern
765.0902	NE1637.5	Medieval
765.09023	NE1638	14th century
765.09024	NE1655-1656	15th century

Dewey	LC	Descriptor
765.09031	NE1665-1666	16th century
765.09032	NE1670-1690	17th century
765.09033	NE1710-1719	18th century
765.09034	NE1720.5-1739	19th century
765.0904	NE1740-1749	20th century
765.093	NE1637	Ancient
766.3	NE2230	Aquatint
766.3	NE1940-2230	Etching/Aquatint
766.30(5/6)	NE1940	Serials/Societies
766.30294	NE1960	Dealers' catalogs
766.3074	NE1945-1955	Museums/Exhibitions
766.309	NE1980-1998	History
766.3090(24-32)	NE1984-1985	15th-17th century folios/Etc.
766.309033	NE1990-1992	18th century folios/Etc.
766.309034	NE1994-1995	19th century folios/Etc.
766.30904	NE1997-1998	20th century folios/Etc.
767.2	NE1940-2230	Etching
767.20(5/6)	NE1940	Serials/Societies
767.2074	NE1945-1955	Museums/Exhibitions
767.209	NE1980-1998	History
767.209(4-9)	NE2001-2096	Etching/Etc., By place
767.2090(24-32)	NE1984-1985	15th-17th century folios/Etc.
767.209033	NE1990-1992	18th century folios/Etc.
767.209034	NE1994-1995	19th century folios/Etc.
767.20904	NE1997-1998	20th century folios/Etc.
767.2092	NE2110	Biography
767.2094	NE1960	Dealers' catalogs
767.3	NE2220-2225	Dry point
769	NE430-492	Modern
769	NE2800-2890	Printing of engravings
769	NE1850-1879	Color prints
769	NE1330-1336	Linoleum block prints
769	NE1350-1352	Other materials used
769	NE1310-1325	Japanese/Ukiyoe prints
769.0(5/6)	NE2800	Serials/Societies
769.074	NE1314-1318	Museums/Exhibitions
769.09	NE2802	History
769.09	NE1321-1323	History
769.092	NE2803	Biography
769.18	NE380	Conservation/Restoration
769.4	NE2239-.7	Special subjects
769.4	NE2141-2149	Special subjects
769.4	NE953-962	Special subjects
769.42	NE2453	Human figures
769.42	NE2142	Human figures
769.42	NE2239	Human figures
769.420216	NE218-310	Catalogs of engraved portraits
769.432	NE2239.2	Animals/Birds
769.432	NE2145	Animals/Birds
769.435	NE2239.(3-4)	Still life
769.435	NE2146-2147	Flowers/Fruit/Still life
769.435	NE953	Flowers/Fruit
769.436	NE2143	Landscapes
769.436	NE2454	Landscapes/Etc.
769.437	NE2144	Marine/Naval
769.437	NE957-.3	Naval/Marine prints
769.437	NE2239.1	Marine/Landscapes
769.44	NE2148	Architectural subjects
769.48	NE2452	Religious subjects
769.48	NE2239.6	Religious subjects
769.48	NE958-.3	Religious
769.48	NE2141	Religious
769.4949355	NE955-.3	Military
769.5	NE2715	Stationery engraving

Dewey	LC	Descriptor
769.9	NE400-794	History of printmaking
769.9(4-9)	NE1334	Other countries
769.9(4-9)	NE501-794	By place
769.90(23-31)	NE440-468	14th-16th centuries
769.901	NE405-420	Ancient
769.9032	NE475-476	17th century
769.9033	NE1855	18th century color prints
769.9033	NE480-481	18th century
769.9034	NE1857	19th century color prints
769.9034	NE485-486	19th century
769.904	NE1858	20th century color prints
769.904	NE490-492	20th century
769.92	NE800	Biography
769.949796	NE960-.3	Sports
769.973	NE1332	United States
770	TR	Photography
770	TR149	Juvenile
770.(5/6)	TR1	Serials/Societies
770.1	TR200-220	Theory of general processes
770.212	TR151	Tables/Formulas
770.232	TR154	As a profession
770.25	TR12	Directories
770.3	TR9	Dictionaries/ Encyclopedias
770.6	TR5	Congresses
770.7	TR161	Education
770.74	TR6	Exhibitions/Museums
770.76	TR162	Examinations/Questions
770.9	TR15	History
770.9(4-9)	TR21-126	By place
770.92	TR139-140	Biography
770.94	TR55-95	Europe
770.941	TR57-64.5	Great Britain
770.9415	TR59.3	Ireland
770.943	TR73-74.5	Germany
770.9436	TR65-.2	Austria
770.944	TR71-72.5	France
770.945	TR79-80	Italy
770.946	TR87-88	Spain
770.947	TR85-86	European Russia
770.9481	TR81-82	Norway
770.9485	TR89-90	Sweden
770.9492	TR77-78	Netherlands
770.9494	TR91-92	Switzerland
770.9495	TR75-76	Greece
770.95	TR99-113	Asia
770.951	TR101-102	China
770.952	TR105-106	Japan
770.954	TR103-104	India
770.955	TR107-108	Iran
770.9561	TR111-112	Turkey/Asia Minor
770.957	TR109-110	Asian Russia
770.96	TR115-119	Africa
770.962	TR117-118	Egypt
770.971	TR26-27	Canada
770.972	TR28-29	Mexico
770.9728	TR30-31	Central America
770.9729	TR32-33	West Indies
770.973	TR22-25	United States
770.98	TR34-54	South America
770.981	TR41-42	Brazil
770.982	TR36-37	Argentina
770.983	TR43-44	Chile
770.984	TR38-39	Bolivia
770.985	TR52	Peru
770.9861	TR45-46	Colombia
770.9866	TR47	Ecuador

Dewey	LC	Descriptor
770.987	TR54	Venezuela
770.988	TR48-50	Guianas
770.9892	TR51	Paraguay
770.9895	TR53	Uruguay
770.99(5-6)	TR123-124	Oceania
770.993	TR122.5-.6	New Zealand
770.994	TR121-122	Australia
771	TR268	Pinhole photography
771	TR196-199	Materials/Supplies/Etc.
771.1	TR550-581	Studio/Laboratory
771.3	TR250-265	Cameras
771.352	TR270	Lenses
771.4	TR900-923	Industrial production
771.44	TR905	Enlargements
771.44	TR910	Reductions
771.47	TR225	Recovery of wastes
771.532(2-4)	TR280-285	Plates/Films/Paper
772-774	TR287-500	Processing technique
778	TR624-835	Applied photography
778	TR640-685	Artistic
778.2	TR504-508	Transparencies/Diapositives
778.5	TR845-899	Cinematography
778.6	TR515-545	Color photography
778.6	TR977	Color process
778.72	TR590-605	Lighting
778.93	TR721-729	Nature
778.93(6-7)	TR786-810	Mountains/Travel/Submarine
778.99 (5-6)	TR692-780	Scientific/Technological
780	ML48-54.8	Librettos
780	ML3930	Literature (Children's)
780	M	Music
780-788	ML	Literature on music
780.1	ML3800-3923	Philosophy/Physics (Music)
780.15	MT90-145	Analytical guides
780.216	ML132	Graded lists
780.216	ML136-158	Catalogs
780.25	ML12-21	Directories
780.262	ML93-97	Manuscripts/Autographs
780.262	ML135	Manuscripts
780.262090(1-32)	M1490	In manuscript before 1700
780.262090(1-34)	M1.A1-.A15	Manuscription before 1860
780.264	M2-2.3	Musical sources
780.268	M1625-1626	Recitations (Accompaniment)
780.3	ML100-102	Dictionaries/Encyclopedias
780.5	ML1-5	Serials
780.6	ML25-28	Societies
780.7	MT	Musical instruction and study
780.77	MT20-32	Special methods
780.78	ML40-44	Programs
780.79	ML35-38	Festivals/Congresses
780.9	ML3880-3923	Criticism
780.9	ML159-3797	History/Criticism
780.9	MT2-5	History/Criticism
780.9(4-9)	ML198-350.5	History/Criticism, By place
780.90(32-4)	ML193-197	1600-
780.901	ML162-169	Ancient
780.902	ML170-190	Medieval
780.92	ML385-429	Biography
780.92	M3-3.1	Individual composers
780.92(2)	ML90	Writings of musicians
780.92(2)	ML105-109	Biobibliography
780.94	ML240-325	Europe
780.95	ML330-345	Asia

Dewey	LC	Descriptor
780.96	ML350-.5	Africa
780.971	ML205.9	Canada
780.972	ML210-.9	Mexico
780.9728	ML220	Central America
780.9729	ML207	West Indies
780.973	ML200-.9	United States
780.98	ML230-239	South America
781	ML29-31	Music foundations
781	MT6-7	Music theory
781.17	ML3845-3877	Aesthetics
781.3	M1470	Chance compositions
781.3	MT40-67	Composition
781.3	M5000	Unidentified compositions
781.3	ML430-455	Composition
781.36	MT68	Improvisation/Accompaniment
781.5	M1900-1980	Special songs
781.54(4-6)	M176.5	Radio/Televison
781.542	M176	Motion pictures (Music)
781.554	M1450	Dance music
781.55409	ML3400-3465	Dance music
781.556	MT95-100	Opera
781.5609	ML3300-3354	Program music
781.599	M1627-1853	National music
781.599	VG30-35	Music/Bands
781.59909	ML3545-3775	National music
781.59909(4-9)	VG35	In other countries
781.5990973	VG33	United States
781.65	M1366	Jazz ensembles
781.7	M1999-2199	Sacred vocal music
782	MT820-949	Singing/Voice culture
782	MT820-949	Singing/Voice culture
782-783	M1497-5000	Vocal music
782-788	MT	Musical instruction and study
782-788.009	MT2-5	History/Criticism
782.(1/4)	M1497-1998	Secular vocal music
782.0077	MT898-949	Children's techniques
782.009	ML1400-3275	Vocal music
782.009(4-9)	ML1410-1451	History vocal music, By place
782.0090(1-4)	ML1402-1406	History vocal music, By date
782.1	MT95-100	Opera
782.1	M1500-1527.8	Dramatic music
782.1	ML1700-2881	Dramatic music
782.109(4-9)	ML1710-1751	Dramatic music, By place
782.1090(1-4)	ML1702-1706	Dramatic music, By date
782.1094	ML1720-1749	Europe
782.10971	ML1713	Canada
782.10972	ML1715	Mexico
782.109728	ML1716	Central America
782.109729	ML1714	West Indies
782.10973	ML1711	United States
782.1098	ML1717	South America
782.2(3/4)	MT110-115	Oratorios/Cantatas
782.2209	ML2900-3275	Sacred vocal music
782.2209(4-9)	ML2910-2951	By place
782.22090(1-4)	ML2902-2906	By date
782.23	M2000-2007	Oratorios
782.24	M2020-2036	Choruses/Cantatas/Etc.
782.25	M2190-2196	Sacred vocal music (Children's)
782.25	M2198-2199	Gospel/Revival
782.27	M2115-2146	Hymnals
782.3	M2147-2188	Liturgy and ritual
782.3	M2010-2017.7	Services

Dewey	LC	Descriptor
782.3(22)009	ML3000-3197	Religious/Denominational
782.3(4-9)	M2188	Other non-Christian
782.322(1-8)	M2184	Other Christian churches
782.322(4-8)009	ML3100-3188	Protestant
782.322(4-89)	M2161-2183	Protestant churches
782.3222	M2147-2155.6	Roman Catholic
782.3222009	ML3002-3051	Roman Catholic
782.33	M2156-2160.87	Orthodox churches
782.36	M2186-2187	Jewish
782.402405(4-5)	M1990-1998	Secular music (Children's)
782.409	ML1600-2881	Secular vocal music
782.409	ML1610-1751	History secular music, By place
782.4090(1-4)	ML1602-1606	History secular music, By date
782.4094	ML1620-1649	Europe
782.40971	ML1613	Canada
782.40972	ML1615	Mexico
782.409728	ML1616	Central America
782.409729	ML1614	West Indies
782.40973	ML1611	United States
782.4098	ML1617	South America
782.4209	ML2500-2551	Songs
782.48	M1610	Cantatas (Unaccompanied)
782.5	M1608	Choruses (Sol-fa notation)
782.5	M1530-1546.5	Choruses (Orchestra/Ensemble)
782.5	M1547-1600	Choruses (Solo unaccompanied)
782.5	M1609	Unison choruses
782.5	M2060-2101.5	Choruses (Accompaniment)
782.509	ML1500-1554	Choral music
783	M1611-1624.8	Songs for one voice
783.0077	MT825-850	Systems/Methods
783.0077	MT898-949	Children's techniques
783.0077	MT855-883	Special techniques
783.0077	MT855-883	Special techniques
783.1(2/3)	M2018-2019.5	Duets/Trios (Solo voices)
783.109	ML2600-2770	Part songs
783.12	M1528-1529.5	Duets/Trios
783.2	M2101-2114.8	For one voice
783.209	ML2800-2862	Solo songs
784	MT73	Bands
784	MT70-71	Orchestras
784.(6-9)	MT733-.6	Band instruction
784.(8-9)	M1200-1269	Band
784.0077	MT825-850	Systems/Methods
784.02405(4-5)	M1375-1420	Instrumental music (Children's)
784.09	ML1300-1354	Band music
784.19	M6-1490	Instrumental music
784.1909(4-9)	ML460-1354	Instruments, By place
784.1909033	M990	18th century instruments
784.19094	ML489-522	Europe
784.190941	ML501	Great Britain
784.190943	ML499-500	Germany
784.1909436	ML491	Austria
784.1909437	ML493	Czechoslovakia
784.1909439	ML494	Hungary
784.190944	ML497	France
784.190945	ML503	Italy
784.190946	ML518	Spain
784.1909469	ML519	Portugal
784.190947	ML507-511	European Russia
784.190948	ML513-516	Scandinavia
784.1909481	ML515	Norway
784.1909485	ML516	Sweden
784.1909489	ML514	Denmark
784.1909492	ML505	Netherlands
784.1909493	ML496	Belgium
784.1909494	ML520	Switzerland
784.19095	ML531	China
784.19095	ML525	Asia
784.1909519	ML537	Korea
784.190952	ML535	Japan
784.1909538	ML527	Saudia Arabia
784.190954	ML533	India
784.190955	ML539	Iran
784.19096	ML544	Africa
784.19097	ML475-486	America
784.190971	ML478	Canada
784.190972	ML482	Mexico
784.1909728	ML484	Central America
784.1909729	ML480	West Indies
784.190973	ML476	United States
784.19098	ML486	South America
784.19099(3-6)	ML547	Australia/New Zealand/Oceania
784.193	MT170-810	Instrumental techniques
784.2	M1000-1075	Orchestra
784.207	MT730	Orchestral instruction
784.207	MT125-130	Orchestral music
784.209	ML1200-1270	Orchestral music
784.4	M1350-1353	Reduced orchestra
784.48	M1356-.2	Dance orchestra
784.7	M1100-1160	String orchestra
784.8(3-4)	M1270	File/Drum/Field music
784.84	VG30-35	Music/Bands
784.84	UH40-45	Bands
784.8409(4-9)	VG35	In other countries
784.840973	VG33	United States
785	MT140-145	Chamber music
785	MT728	Chamber music
785	MT70-71	Orchestras
785	MT73	Bands
785.009	ML1100-1165	Chamber music
785.12	M180-298.5	Duets
785.13	M300-386	Trios
785.14	M400-486	Quartets
785.15	M500-586	Quintets
785.16	M600-686	Sextets
785.17	M700-786	Septets
785.18	M800-886	Octets
785.19	M900-986	Nonets chamber music
786-788	M177-990	Solo instruments
786-788	M6-175	Solo instruments
786-788.09	ML549-1092	Instruments
786.(2/3)09	ML650-747	Piano/Clavichord
786.2193	MT220-255	Piano
786.5	M6-39	Organs/Pianos
786.509	ML550-649	Organs
786.5193	MT180-198	Organ
786.55193	MT200-208	Harmonium (Reed organ)
786.59193	MT192-.8	Electronic keyboard instruments
786.609	ML1050-1055	Mechanical/Other instruments
786.7	M1473	Electronic music
786.8	M145-175	Percussion instruments
786.809	ML1030-1040	Percussion instruments
786.8193	MT655-722	Percussion/Other instruments
787	M40-59	String instruments
787.(7-9)193	MT539-654	Plectral instruments

Dewey	LC	Descriptor
787.09	ML750-927	String instruments
787.193	MT259-338	String instruments
787.2193	MT260-279	Violin
787.3193	MT280-298	Viola
787.4193	MT300-318	Violoncello
787.5193	MT320-334	Double bass
787.7	M115-142	Plectral instuments
787.709	ML1000-1018	Plectral instruments
787.75193	MT620-634	Zither
787.84	M1360	Mandolin/Plectral instruments
787.84193	MT600-612	Mandolin
787.87193	MT580-599	Guitar
787.88193	MT560-570	Banjo
787.9193	MT540-557	Harp
788	M60-110	Wind instruments
788.09	ML930-990	Wind instruments
788.193	MT339-538	Wind instruments
788.3193	MT340-359	Flute
788.52193	MT360-376	Oboe
788.58193	MT400-408	Bassoon
788.62193	MT380-388	Clarinet (A/Bb/C/Eb, Etc.)
788.86	M1362	Accordion band
788.9193	MT418	Brass insturments
790-799	GV	Recreation/Leisure
790.068	GV182-.5	Recreational facilities
790.068	HN41-46	Community/Social centers
790.0680(5/6)	HN41	Serials/Societies
790.06809(4-9)	HN43-46	Community centers, By place
790.0680973	HN43-45	United States
790.069	GV181.35-.55	Recreation leadership
790.1	GV735	Umpires
790.13	GV1201.5	Hobbies (General)
790.132	AM200-501	Collectors/Collecting
790.1320(5/6)	AM200-207	Serials/Societies
790.13209	AM301-396	Collecting, By place
790.13209	AM221	History of collecting
790.132092	AM223	Biography
790.132094	AM342-371	Europe
790.1320941	AM343-347	Great Britain
790.1320943	AM350	Germany
790.1320944	AM349	France
790.1320946(9)	AM362-363	Spain/Portugal
790.1320947	AM356	European Russia
790.132095	AM372-385	Asia
790.132096	AM387-389	Africa
790.1320971	AM313	Canada
790.13209728	AM314-322	Central America
790.13209729	AM323-329	West Indies
790.1320973	AM303-311	United States
790.132098	AM330	South America
790.132099(3-6)	AM390-396	Australia/New Zealand/Oceania
790.133	GV1218.5-1220.7	Toys
790.2	PN1560-1590	Performing arts/Show business
790.2	PN1585-1589	Performing arts centers
790.203	PN1579	Dictionaries
790.205	PN1560-1569	Serials
790.206	PN1570-1575	Societies/Congresses
790.207	PN1576-1578	Education
790.209	PN1581	History
790.2092	PN1583	Biography
791	GV1800-1860	Circuses/Spectacles
791.12	M1365	Minstrel music
791.62	PN3203-3299	Tableaux/Pageants/Happenings
792	PN2000-3307	The theater
792.022	PN3175-3191	Colleges/School theatricals
792.0222	PN3151-3171	Amateur theatricals
792.025	PN2085-2091	The stage/Accessories
792.028	PN2061-2071	Art of acting
792.09	PN2100-2193	History
792.090(1-4)	PN2131-2193	By date
792.090(23-31)	PN2171-2179	Renaissance
792.090(3-4)	PN2181-2193	Modern
792.0901	PN2131-2145	Ancient
792.0902	PN2152-2160	Medieval
792.0938	PA3201-3251	Theater/Stage
792.094	PN2570-2859	Europe
792.0941	PN2575-2609	Great Britain
792.0943	PN2640-2659.5	Germany
792.0943(6/9)	PN2610-2618	Austria (Hungary)
792.0944	PN2620-2639	France
792.0945	PN2670-2688	Italy
792.0946	PN2780-2788	Spain
792.09469	PN2790-2798	Portugal
792.0947	PN2720-2728	European Russia
792.0948	PN2730-2778	Scandinavia
792.09492	PN2690-2719	Low Countries
792.09494	PN2800-2808	Switzerland
792.09495	PN2660-2668	Modern Greece
792.09496	PN2818.5-2858	Balkans
792.095	PN2860-2960	Asia
792.0951	PN2870-2878	China
792.09519	PN2930-2939.8	Korea
792.0952	PN2920-2928	Japan
792.095694	PN2919-.8	Israel/Palestine
792.096	PN2969-3000	Africa
792.0962	PN2970-2978	Egypt
792.0971	PN2300-2308.5	Canada
792.0972	PN2310-2318	Mexico
792.09728	PN2320-2384	Central America
792.09729	PN2390-2440	West Indies
792.0973	PN2220-2298	United States
792.098	PN2445-2554	South America
792.099(3-4)	PN3010-3018	Australia/New Zealand
792.099(5-6)	PN3030	Oceania
793	GV1199-1570	Games and amusements
793	GV1221-1469	Indoor games
793.02405(4-5)	GV1203-1218	Children's games
793.2	GV1470-1511	Parties
793.24	PN3209-3299	Tableaux/Pageants/Happenings
793.24	PN6366-6377	Riddles/Charades
793.3	GV1580-1799	Dancing
793.4	M1985	Musical games
793.8	GV1541-1561	Parlor magic/Tricks
794	GV1312-1469	Board games
795	GV1301-1311	Gambling
795.4	GV1232-1299	Card games
796	GV561-1198.995	Sports
796.(07/32363/33263)	GV346-350	School/College athletics
796.028	GV743-749	Sporting goods/Supplies
796.068	GV401-433	Sports facilities
796.07	GV201-555	Physical education/Training
796.077	GV711	Coaching
796.3	GV861-1017	Ball games
796.42	GV1060.5-1098	Track and field
796.44	GV460-555	Gymnastics
796.5	GV191.2-200.6	Outdoor recreation
796.5	GV200.5	Wilderness survival

Dewey	LC	Descriptor
796.51	GV199-.6	Hiking
796.522	GV199.8-200.3	Mountaineering
796.54	GV191.68-198.9	Camping
796.6	GV1040-1060.2	Bicycling/Motorcycling
796.7	GV1020-1034	Automobile travel
796.72068	TE305	Racetracks (Construction)
796.8	GV1101-1150.6	Fighting sports
796.812	GV1195-1198.995	Wrestling
796.9	GV840.7-857	Winter sports
797.(1-3)	GV770.3-840	Water sports
797.(1-3)	GV200.6	Water recreation
797.5	GV750-770	Air sports
798	SF294.2-.35	Sports
798.2	SF308.5-310.5	Horsemanship
798.24	SF294.5-297	Shows
798.4	SF321-359.7	Racing
799.1	Z5970-5975	Fish culture/Fishing
799.1	SH	Aquaculture/Fisheries/ Angling
799.12	SH454	Casting
799.12	SH401-691	Angling
799.12	SH455.4-458	Angling methods
799.120(5/6)	SH401	Serials/Societies
799.12028	SH447-453	Equipment/Tackle
799.1203	SH411	Dictionaries/ Encyclopedias
799.1206	SH403	Fishing clubs
799.1209	SH421	History
799.1209(7-8)	SH461-601	America
799.12092	SH414-415	Biography
799.12094	SH603-643	Europe
799.12095	SH651-667	Asia
799.12096	SH671-675	Africa
799.12097	SH462	North America
799.120971	SH571-572	Canada
799.120972	SH573	Mexico
799.1209728	SH575-576	Central America
799.1209729	SH577-578	West Indies
799.120973	SH463-565	United States
799.12098	SH579-601	South America
799.12099(3-6)	SH677-679	Australia/New Zealand/ Oceania
799.120998	SH669	Arctic/Antarctic
799.17	SH681-691	Angling for special fish
799.1755	SH687-688	Trout
799.1755	SH684-686.7	Salmon
799.1758	SH681	Bass
799.2	SK	Hunting sports
799.2	SK336	Varmint hunting (General)
799.20(5/6)	SK1	Serials/Societies/Congresses
799.20216	SK275	Catalogs
799.2022	SK271	Illustrations (Hunting scenes)
799.2025	SK12	Directories
799.2028	SK335	Decoys
799.2028	SK273-275	Equipment
799.2028	SK36.3	Flying
799.2028	SK36.2	Dressing/Skinning
799.2028	SK36.7	Poaching
799.2028(2-5)	SK274-.8	Guns/Ballistics
799.20282	SK281-293	Special types of hunting
799.203	SK11	Dictionaries/ Encyclopedias
799.205	SK7	Yearbooks
799.206	SK3	Hunting clubs
799.2074	SK276	Museums/Collections
799.209	SK21	History
799.2092	SK15-17	Biography
799.213	SK37-39.5	Shooting
799.215	SK36	Bow hunting
799.23	SK293	Ferreting
799.24	SK311-335	Bird hunting
799.242	SK323-325	Land birds
799.24209(4-9)	SK324	By country
799.243	SK327-329	Bay birds
799.244	SK331-335	Waterfowl
799.248(5-9)	SK325	By kind of bird
799.25(4-9)/.27(1-9)	SK341	Other games
799.25974442	SK284-287	Fox hunting
799.26	SK295-305	Big game, By animal type
799.29	SK40-267	By country
799.294	SK183-223	Europe
799.2941	SK185-191	Great Britain
799.295	SK231-247	Asia
799.296	SK251-255	Africa
799.297	SK40-157	North America
799.297(4-9)	SK47-145	By state
799.2971	SK151-152	Canada
799.2972	SK153	Mexico
799.29728	SK155	Central America
799.29729	SK157	West Indies
799.2973	SK41-145	United States
799.2975	SK43	The South
799.2978	SK45	The West
799.298	SK159-181	South America
799.299(5-6)	SK267	Oceania
799.2993	SK262	New Zealand
799.2994	SK261	Australia
799.29989	SK265	Arctic/Antarctic
799.3	GV1151-1190	Shooting/Archery
800	PN	Literature (General)
801	PN45-57	Theory/Philosophy
803	PN41-43	Dictionaries/ Encyclopedias
805	PN1-19	Serials, By language
806	PN20-30	Societies/Congresses
807	PN59-72	Education
807.0(1-9)	PN70-71	By place
808	PN500-519	Collections
808	PN35-37	Collections
808	PN6010-6790	Collections-General literature
808	PN167-171	Plagiarism
808.(8-9)	PN1865-1988	Special types
808.02	PN149.8-163	As a profession
808.02	PN101-245	Authorship
808.042	PE1402-1497	Rhetoric
808.04207	PE1404-1405	Education
808.0431	PF3410-3497	Rhetoric
808.043931	PF410-497	Rhetoric
808.066(001-999)03961	PT7195-7211	Scientific/ Learned
808.066(001-999)03961	PT7312-7318	Scientific/ Learned
808.0662	BR117-126	Christian literature
808.1	PN1010-1525	Poetry
808.1001	PN1031-1049	Theory/Philosophy
808.1003	PN1021	Dictionaries
808.1005	PN1010	Serials
808.1006	PN1012-1014	Societies/Congresses
808.132	PN1301-1333	Epic poetry
808.14	PN1351-1389	Lyric poetry
808.2	PN1660-1693	Technique/Dramatic composition
808.2	PN1600-3307	Drama

Dewey	LC	Descriptor
808.200(6/74)	PN1611-1620	Societies/Congresses/Museums
808.2001	PN1631-1633	Philosophy
808.2005	PN1600-1610	Serials
808.3	PN3355-3383	Technique/Authorship
808.3	PN3311-3503	Prose (Fiction)
808.3(1-8)	PN3428-3448	Special kinds of fiction
808.300(5/6)	PN3311-3319	Serials/Societies
808.3001	PN3329-3352	Philosophy/Theory
808.5	PN4001-4355	Oratory/Elocution
808.5001	PN4061	Philosophy/Theory
808.50025	PN4007	Directories
808.5003	PN4016	Dictionaries
808.5005	PN4001-4005	Serials
808.5006	PN4009	Societies
808.5007	PN4071-4095	Education
808.53	PN4177-4191	Debating
808.54	PN4199-4355	Recitations
808.8026	PN1551	The dialogue
808.803538	HQ450-471	Erotica
808.803538	HQ471	Pornography
808.803538	PN6233-6238	Anacreontic (Erotic/Pleasures)
808.80357	ML3930	Literature (Childrens)
808.808(06)	PN172-239	Technique/Composition/Rhetoric
808.81	PN6099-6110	Poetry
808.819	PN1065-1085	Special subjects
808.82	PN6110.5-6120	Drama
808.82	PN1997-1997.85	Plays/Scenarios/Etc.
808.82	PN1621-1623	Collections
808.822	PN1990-1992.92	Broadcasting
808.8222	PN1991-.9	Radio broadcasts
808.8225	PN1992-.92	Television broadcasts
808.823	PN1993-1999	Motion pictures
808.8245	PN1530	The monologue
808.83	PN6120.15-.95	Fiction
808.83	PZ	Fiction/Juvenile Belles-letter
808.83	PN3321-3324	Collections
808.84	PN6141-6145	Essays
808.851	PN6340-6348	Toasts
808.851	PN6121-6129	Orations
808.86	PN6130-6140	Letters
808.87	PN6147-6231	Wit and humor
808.87	PN6157-6222	By place
808.87	PN6183-6222	Other European countries
808.87	PN6173-6178	Great Britain
808.87	PN6157-6163	United States
808.879(1-3)	PN6231	By topic
808.882	PN6080-6095	Quotations
808.882	PN6259-6268	Anecdotes/Table talk
808.882	PN6279-6288	Epigrams
809	PN441-1009.5	Literary history
809	PN80-99	Criticism
809	PN851-883	Comparative literature
809	PN1720-1861	History
809	PN1008.2-1009.5	Juvenile literature (General)
809	PN86-94	History
809.(888/83)	PN692-694	Prose/Fiction
809.0(1-5)	PN610-779	By date
809.0(1-5)	PN1741-1861	By date
809.0(23-31)	PN1785-1801	Renaissance
809.0(3-32)	PN715-749	Renaissance (1500-1700)
809.0(3-4)	PN695-779	Modern
809.0(3-4)	PN1811-1861	Modern
809.00(5/6)	PN80-.5	Serials/Societies
809.01	PN1741	Ancient
809.01	PN610-649	Ancient
809.02	PN1751-1771	Medieval
809.02	PN661-694	Medieval to 1500
809.1	PN1105-1279	History/Criticism
809.102	PN688-691	Poetry
809.2	PN451-497	Biography
809.5	PN4021-4055	History
809.50(1-4)	PN4031-4051	By date
809.83	PN3451-3503	History of fiction
809.830(1-4)	PN3466-3503	By date
809.830(23-31)	PN3481	Renaissance
809.830(3-4)	PN3491-3503	Modern (18th-20th centuries)
809.8301	PN3466	Ancient
809.836	PN841	Black literature (General)
809.9(1-2)	PN599-605	Movements of literature
809.912	PN601	Realism/Naturalism
809.913	PN599	Idealism
809.9145	PN801-820	Romance literatures
809.9145	PN603	Romanticism
809.93522	BS535-537	As literature
810-818. + (5-54)09	PS221-228	20th century
810	PS	American literature
810.1	PS31	Philosophy
810.3	PS21	Encyclopedias/Dictionaries
810.5	PS1-3	Serials
810.6	PS5-7	Societies/Congresses
810.7	PS41-49	Education
810.9	PS55-79	Criticism
810.9	PS85-111	History
811-818	PR9175-9199	America
811-818	PR9200	Mexico
811-818	PR9180-9199.3	Canada
811-818	PR9210-9275	West Indies
811-818	PR9280-9298	Central America
811-818	PR9620-9639.2	New Zealand
811-818	PR9645-9670	Oceania
811-818	PR9300-9333	South America
811-818	PR9340-9408	Africa
811-818	PR9600-9619.3	Australia
811-818	PR9420-9570	Asia
811-818. + (0809282)	PZ5-8.3	American/English
811-818. + (1-2)09	PS185-195	17th-18th centuries
811-818. + (1-54)08	PS700-3576	Individual authors, By date
811-818. + (1-54)08	PS530-536.2	By date
811-818. + (1-54)09	PS185-228	By date
811-818. + (3-4)09	PS201-217	19th century
811-818.(008)	PS538-549	North
811-818.(008)	PS537-574	By place
811-818.(008)	PS501-688	Collections
811-818.(008)	PS551-559	South
811-818.(008)	PS561-572	West/Central
811-818.(009)	PS241-286	By place
811-818.(009)	PS153-490	History
811-818.(009)	PS271-285	West/Central
811-818.(009)	PS261-267	South
811-818.(009)	PS241-255	North
811-818.(0803)	PS163-169	Special subjects
811-818.(09308)	PS508-509	Special authors/Topics
811-818.(1)	PS700-893	Colonial period
811-818.(3-4)	PS991-(3390)	19th century
811-818.(52)	PS3500-3549	1900-1960
811-818.(54)	PS3550-3576	1961-
811-818.(99287)	PS147-152	Women authors
811-828.(009)	PS85-96	English
811-899.(0809282)	PZ5-90	Juvenile Belles-letters

Dewey	LC	Descriptor
811-899.(0809282)	PZ	Fiction/Juvenile Belles-letter
811. + (1-54)09	PS312-325	By date
811. + (5-54)09	PS323.5-325	20th century
811.(1-54)08	PS601-615	By date
811.(3-4)09	PS316	19th century
811.0(2-8)08	PS593	By form
811.0(2-8)09	PS309	By form
811.0(5/6)	PS301	Serials/Societies
811.0(5/6)	PS580	Serials/Societies
811.07	PS306-.5	Education
811.08	PS583-584	Collections
811.08	PS580-619	Poetry
811.09	PS301-325	Poetry
811.09(8-9)08	PS589-591	Authors (Special types)
811.093	PS310	By topic
811.09308	PS595	By subject
811.109	PS312	Colonial
812.(1-54)08	PS631-634	By date
812.(1-54)09	PS341-352	By date
812.(3-4)008	PS607-611	19th century
812.(3-4)09	PS343-345	19th century
812.(5-54)008	PS613-615	20th century
812.(5-54)09	PS350-352	20th century
812.0(2-5)008	PS627	Special forms/Topics
812.0(2-5)009	PS336	Special forms
812.003	PS330	Encyclopedias/Dictionaries
812.007	PS335	Education
812.008	PS623-634.5	Drama
812.009	PS330-352	Drama
812.0803	PS627	Special forms/Topics
812.09(8-9)008	PS628	Special authors
812.093	PS338	Special topics
812.1008	PS601	Colonial period
812.109	PS341	Colonial period
813	PZ1-4	Fiction in English
813.(1-54)09	PS375-379	By date
813.0(1-87)009	PS374	Special forms/Topics
813.009	PS370-379	Fiction
813.0093	PS374	Special forms/Topics
814.008	PS680-688	Essays
814.009	PS420-428	Essays
815.01(1-54)08	PS666-668	By date
815.01008	PS660-668	Oratory
815.01009	PS400-408	Oratory
816	PS126-138	Biography/Memoirs/Letters
816.008	PS670-678	Letters
816.009	PS410-418	Letters
817.009	PS430-438	Wit and humor/Satire
818(009)	PS126-138	Memoirs/Letters/Etc.
818.(1-54)0808	PS651-659	By date
818.(1-54)0809	PS367-369	By date
818.03009	PS409	Diaries
818.08(093)008	PS648	Special forms/Topics
818.0800(5/6)	PS360	Serials/Societies
818.0800(5/6)	PS642	Serials/Societies
818.08008	PS642-659.5	Prose
818.08009	PS360-379	Prose
818.080093	PS366	Special topics
818.0809(8-9)008	PS647	Special authors
818.3008	PS669	Diaries
820	PR	English literature
820.(1-914)	PR161-479	By date
820.3	PR19	Dictionaries/Encyclopedias
820.5	PR1-3	Serials
820.6	PR5-7	Societies/Congresses
820.7	PR31-55	Education
820.8	PR13-14	Collections
820.802	PN6081-6084	English
820.9	PR57-78	Criticism
820.9	PR81-990	History
820.9	PR1-56	Literary history/Criticism
820.928709	PR111-116	Women authors
821	PR1170-1227	Poetry
821-828	PR8700-8807	Ireland
821-828	PR8500-8697	Scotland
821-828	PR8309-8489	England
821-828	PR8900-8997	Wales
821-828	PR8309-9680	Provincial/Local
821-828	PR9090-9170	Europe
821-828	PR9080-9680	English literature abroad
821-828. + (9914)009	PR471-479	20th century
821-828. + (0809282)	PZ5-8.3	American/English
821-828. + (1-2)009	PR251-369	Medieval/Middle (1066-1500)
821-828. + (1-914)08	PR1119-1150	By date
821-828. + (3-914)009	PR401-479	Modern
821-828. + (5-6)009	PR441-449	18th century
821-828. + (5-6)08	PR1134-1139	18th century
821-828. + (7-8)009	PR451-469	19th century
821-828. + (7-8)08	PR1143-1145	19th century
821-828. + (9-914)08	PR1148-1150	20th century
821-828.(1)	PR1803-2165	Early/Middle English
821-828.(1-914)	PR1490-6076	Literature, By author/Date
821-828.(108)	PR1120	Medieval
821-828.(3)	PR2199-3195	English Renaissance (1500-1640)
821-828.(3009)	PR421-429	Elizabethan era (1066-1500)
821-828.(308)	PR1121-1125	Renaissance
821-828.(4-6)	PR3291-3785	17th-18th centuries
821-828.(4009)	PR431-439	17th century
821-828.(408)	PR1127-1131	17th century
821-828.(7-8)	PR3991-5990	19th century
821-828.008	PR1098-1369	Collections
821-828.0803	PR1111	Special topics
821-828.89(1-9)	PR1110	Authors (Special classes)
821-828.912	PR6000-6049	1900-1960
821-828.914	PR6050-6076	1961-
821.(1-2)09	PR311-369	Poetry
821.(1-3)09	PR521-529	15th-16th centuries
821.(1-914)08	PR1203-1227	By date
821.(1-914)09	PR521-611	By date
821.(5-6)08	PR1215-1219	18th century
821.(5-6)09	PR551-575	18th century
821.(7-8)08	PR1221-1223	19th century
821.(7-8)09	PR581-595	19th century
821.(9-914)08	PR1224-1227	20th century
821.(9-914)09	PR601-611	20th century
821.0(2-8)09(1-9)	PR1181-1195	Special forms/Subjects
821.0(5/6)	PR1170	Serials/Societies
821.005	PR500	Serials
821.032(1-2)09	PR321-347	Epics/Metrical
821.04(1-2)09	PR351-369	Lyric
821.08	PR1171-1174	Collections
821.09	PR500-681	Poetry
821.09(1-9)	PR505-508	Special topics
821.308	PR1207	Elizabethan era
821.309	PR531-539	Elizabethan era
821.408	PR1209-1213	17th century
821.409	PR541-549	17th century
822.(1-914)08	PR1260-1273	By date

Dewey	LC	Descriptor
822.(1-914)09	PR641-739	Drama (History/Critcism), By date
822.(5-6)009	PR701-719	18th century
822.(5-6)08	PR1269	18th century
822.(7-8)009	PR721-734	19th century
822.(7-8)08	PR1271	19th century
822.(9-914)009	PR735-739	20th century
822.(9-914)08	PR1272	20th century
822.0(2-57)008	PR1248-1259	Special types
822.0(2-57)009	PR631-635	Special forms/Topics
822.00(5/6)	PR621	Serials/Societies
822.003	PR623	Dictionaries
822.008	PR1241-1273	Drama
822.009	PR621-739	Drama
822.108	PR1260-1261	Medieval
822.109	PR641-644	Medieval
822.2(2-3)009	PR646-649	16th century
822.208	PR1262	Pre-Shakespeare
822.3009	PR651-658	Elizabethan era
822.308	PR1263	Elizabethan era
822.4009	PR671-698	17th century
822.408	PR1265.3-1266	17th century
823	PZ1-4	Fiction in English
823.(1-914)09	PR833-888	By date
823.(5-6)09	PR851-858	18th century
823.(7-8)09	PR861-878	19th century
823.(9-914)09	PR881-888	20th century
823.009	PR821-888	Fiction/The novel
823.009(1-9)	PR830	By topic
823.209	PR833	16th century
823.309	PR836-839	Elizabethan era
823.409	PR841-844	17th century
824.008	PR1361-1369	Essays
824.009	PR921-927	Essays
825.01008	PR1321-1329	Oratory
825.01009	PR901-907	Oratory
826.008	PR1341-1349	Letters
826.009	PR911-917	Letters
827.009	PR931-937	Wit and humor
828.(1-914)08	PR767-808	By date
828.(1-914)0808	PR1293-1307	By date
828.(5-6)0808	PR1297	18th century
828.(7-8)0808	PR1301-1304	19th century
828.(9-914)0808	PR1307	20th century
828.03008	PR1330	Diaries
828.03009	PR908	Diaries
828.0800(5/6)	PR750	Serials/Societies
828.08008	PR1281-1309	Prose (General)
828.08009	PR750-888	Prose
828.08009(1-9)	PR756	Special topics
828.30808	PR1293	16th century
828.40808	PR1295	17th century
829	PR171-236	Anglo-Saxon to 1066
829	PR1490-1799	Anglo-Saxon literature
829.1	PR201-217	Poetry
829.8	PR221-236	Prose
830	PT	Germanic/Teutonic literature
830.(1-3)08	PT1371-1372	By date, to 1500
830.1	PT49	Philosophy
830.1	PT45	Theory
830.202	PT95-101	Compends.
830.202	PT103	Outlines
830.3	PT41	Encyclopedias/Dictionaries
830.5	PT1-9	Serials
830.6	PT31	Congresses
830.6	PT21-29	Societies

Dewey	LC	Descriptor
830.7	PT51-65	Education
830.802	PN6090-6093	German
830.9	PT1-80	History/Criticism
831-838	PT3971	Oceania
831-838	PT3830-3837.5	Czechoslovakia
831-838	PT3961	Asia
831-838	PT3810-3828	Austria
831-838	PT3900-3919	North America/United States
831-838	PT3810-3895	Europe
831-838	PT3701-3971	Provincial/Colonial
831-838	PT3840-3848	Hungary
831-838	PT1-4897	German literature
831-838	PT3951	Africa
831-838	PT3860	Switzerland
831-838	PT3850-3858	European Russia
831-838	PT3808-3971	Outside Germany
831-838	PT3701-3807	Germany
831-838 + (9-914)08	PT1141	20th century
831-838. + (1-914)08	PT1121-1141	By date
831-838. + (2-4)09	PT76	Medieval to 1600
831-838. + (3-4)09	PT241-261	Renaissance (1440-1648)
831-838. + (3-9)09	PT236-405	Modern
831-838. + (5-6)09	PT271-279	17th-18th centuries
831-838. + (7-8)09	PT341-395	19th century
831-838. + (9-14)09	PT80	20th century
831-838. + (9-914)09	PT401-405	20th century
831-838. + 9(8-9)	PT170	Other classes of authors
831-838.(009)	PT83-871	History of literature
831-838.(009)	PT71-80	Criticism
831-838.(009)	PS106	German
831-838.(0092)	PT155	Collected biography
831-838.(0093)	PT134-149	Special subjects/Countries
831-838.(08)	PT1100-1479	Collections
831-838.(0809282)	PZ31-38	German
831-838.(093)	PT1110	Special subjects
831-838.(098924)	PT169	Jewish authors
831-838.(099287)	PT167	Women as authors
831-838.(1-914)09	PT171-405	By date
831-838.(109)	PT183	Old High German
831-838.(2)	PT1501-1695	Middle High German (1050-1500)
831-838.(208)	PT1375-1479	Middle High German-Collections
831-838.(209)	PT187-201	Middle High German
831-838.(209)	PT175-230	Medieval
831-838.(4-5)	PT1701-1797	1500-1700
831-838.(408)	PT1121	16th century
831-838.(508)	PT1126	17th century
831-838.(509)	PT77	17th century
831-838.(6-7)	PT1799-2592	1700-1870
831-838.(608)	PT1131	18th century
831-838.(609)	PT285-321	18th century
831-838.(609)	PT78	18th century
831-838.(708)	PT1136	19th century
831-838.(709)	PT79	19th century
831-838.(8-914)	PT2600-2653	1870-1960
831-838.(9-914)	PT1501-2688	By author/Date
831-838.(914)	PT2660-2688	1961-
831.(1-914)08	PT1163-1175	By date
831.(3-5)08	PT1163-1165	15th-17th centuries
831.(4-9)09	PT521-553	Modern poetry
831.(7-8)08	PT1171-1173	19th century
831.(9-914)08	PT1174-1175	20th century
831.03208	PT1411-1418	Epic poetry
831.03208	PT1179-1181	Epic poetry
831.032209	PT203-214	Epic poetry

Dewey	LC	Descriptor
839.403	PT4802	Encyclopedias/Dictionaries
839.407	PT4803	Education
839.409	PT4815	Collective biography
839.409	PT4805-4814	History
839.41	PT4846	To 1600
839.4108	PT4834-4836	Poetry
839.4109	PT4817-4820	Poetry
839.42	PT4848	19th century
839.42	PT4847	17th-18th centuries
839.4208	PT4837-4838	Drama
839.4209	PT4821	Drama
839.43	PT4849	20th century
839.4309	PT4823	Fiction
839.4808008	PT4839-4845	Prose
839.5(1-8) + (0809282)	PZ51-60.3	Scandinavian
839.6	PT7285-7287	Mythical sagas
839.6	PT7326-7338	By author (Pre-1540)
839.6	PT7281	Sagas of Norwegian colonies
839.6	PT7276-7279	Sagas of kings
839.6	PT7271-7272	Icelandic church sagas
839.6	PT7282	Sagas of Denmark/Sweden
839.6	PT7150-7157	By language
839.6	PT7269	Sagas of Icelandic families
839.6	PT7263-7296	Individual sagas/Histories
839.6	PT7101-7338	Old Norse (Icelandic/ Norwegian)
839.607	PT7135-7139	Education
839.608	PT7220-7262	Collections
839.608	PT7261-7296	Sagas
839.6080382	PT7298-7309	Religious works
839.609	PT7181-7188	Sagas
839.609	PT7101-7129	History/Criticism
839.609	PT7145-7149	Criticism
839.609	PT7150-7211	History
839.6108	PT7230-7252	Poetry
839.6109	PT7170-7174	Poetry
839.63	PT7288	Novels/Fairy tales
839.6808008	PT7255-7262	Prose
839.6808009	PT7177-7211	Prose
839.69	PT7525-7550	In other countries
839.69	PT7520-7521	Provincial
839.69	PT7351-7550	Modern Icelandic literature
839.69	PT7526-7545	North America
839.69(1-4)	PT7500-7511	By author/Date
839.69(1-4)09	PT7395-7402	History, By date
839.69(1-8)09	PT7410-7418	By form
839.6907	PT7370-7373	Education
839.6908	PT7451-7495	Collections
839.6909	PT7351-7418	History/Criticism
839.69108	PT7465-7467	Poetry
839.69208	PT7470-7477	Drama
839.69308	PT7485-7487	Fiction
839.69808008	PT7480-7495	Prose
839.699	PT7581-7599	Faroese literature
839.699	PT7586-7588	By date
839.699(1-8)	PT7590-7592	By form
839.69908	PT7593-7596	Collections
839.69909	PT7584	Biography (Collected)
839.7	PT9950-9952	Provincial
839.7	PT9201-9999	Swedish literature
839.7	PT9955-9999	In other countries
839.7	PT9980-9995	North America
839.7((7-74)	PT9870-9875	20th century
839.7(1-74)	PT9650-9881	By author/Date
839.7(1-74)09	PT9320-9370	By date
839.7(2-5)	PT9674-9715	16th-18th centuries
839.7(2-5)09	PT9345-9361	16th-18th centuries
839.7(7-74)09	PT9368-9370	20th century
839.707	PT9240-9245	Education
839.708	PT9550-9639	Collections
839.709	PT9260-9499	History
839.709	PT9305-9315	Biography/Etc.
839.709	PT9250-9254	Criticism
839.709	PT9201-9499	History/Criticism
839.71	PT9650-9651	Medieval
839.7108	PT9580-9599	Poetry
839.7109	PT9320-9339	Medieval to 1540
839.7109	PT9375-9405	Poetry
839.7208	PT9605-9625	Drama
839.7209	PT9415-9449	Drama
839.7308	PT9627-9630	Fiction
839.7309	PT9480-9492	Fiction
839.76	PT9725-9850	19th century
839.7609	PT9365-9367	19th century
839.7808008	PT9626-9630	Prose
839.7808009	PT9460-9492	Prose
839.81	PT8231-8250	North America
839.81	PT7601-8260	Danish literature
839.81	PT8211-8229	West Indies/Virgin Islands
839.81	PT8210-8260	In other countries
839.81	PT8205-8207	Provincial
839.81	PT8174-8175	20th century
839.81(1-74)	PT8050-8175	By author/Date
839.81(1-74)09	PT7760	20th century
839.81(1-74)09	PT7721-7760	By date
839.81(2-5)	PT8060-8098	16th-18th centuries
839.81(2-5)09	PT7741-7747	16th-18th centuries
839.8107	PT7640-7644	Education
839.8108	PT7950-8046	Collections
839.8109	PT7700-7710	Biography/Etc.
839.8109	PT7660-7869	History
839.8109	PT7601-7869	History/Criticism
839.8109	PT7650-7654	Criticism
839.811	PT8050	Medieval
839.81108	PT7975-7994	Poetry
839.81109	PT7770-7795	Poetry
839.81109	PT7721-7738	Medieval to 1500
839.81208	PT7999-8020	Drama
839.81209	PT7800-7832	Drama
839.81308	PT8022-8024	Fiction
839.81309	PT7847-7862	Fiction
839.816	PT8100-8167	19th century
839.81609	PT7751-7756	19th century
839.81808008	PT8021-8046	Prose
839.81808009	PT7835-7862	Prose
839.82	PT8301-9155	Norwegian literature
839.82	PT9100-9155	Norwegian (Provincial/ Foreign)
839.82	PT9131-9150	North America
839.82(1-74)	PT8750-8961	By author/Date
839.82(1-74)09	PT8425-8450	By date
839.82(2-5)	PT8750-8775	16th-18th centuries
839.82(7-74)	PT8949-8950	20th century
839.8207	PT8340-8344	Education
839.8208	PT8650-8733	Collections
839.8209	PT8301-8574	History/Criticism
839.8209	PT8350-8354	Criticism
839.8209	PT8405-8415	Biography/Etc.
839.82108	PT8675-8695	Poetry
839.82109	PT8460-8490	Poetry
839.82208	PT8699-8718	Drama
839.82209	PT8500-8534	Drama
839.82309	PT8555-8567	Fiction

Dewey	LC	Descriptor
839.826	PT8800-8942	19th century
839.82808008	PT8719-8722	Prose
839.82808009	PT8540-8567	Prose
839.83	PT9064-9094	By author
839.83	PT9000-9094	Landsmaal/New Norwegian
839.8308	PT9025-9055	Collections
839.8309	PT9000-9019	History/Criticism
840	PQ1-3999	French literature
840	PQ	Romance language literature
840.202	PQ115-128	Compendiums
840.3	PQ41	Encyclopedias
840.5	PQ1-19	Serials
840.6	PQ21-31	Societies/Congresses
840.7	PQ51-65	Education
840.802	PN6086-6089	French
840.9	PQ1-841	History/Criticism
840.9	PQ75	History
840.9	PQ100-771	History of French literature
840.9	PQ146-150	Authors, Biographies
840.900(1-914)	PQ82-96	By date
841-848	PQ3950-3959	South America/Central America
841-848	PQ3940-3949	West Indies
841-848	PQ3980-3989	Africa
841-848	PQ3960-3979	Asia
841-848	PQ3867	Scandinavia
841-848	PQ3865	European Russia
841-848	PQ3863	Italy
841-848	PQ3809-3999	By place
841-848	PQ3990-3999	Oceania
841-848	PQ3900-3919	Canada
841-848	PQ3890	Other Europe
841-848	PQ3810-3858	Belgium
841-848	PQ3870-3888	Switzerland
841-848	PQ3861	Germany
841-848	PQ3860	Netherlands
841-848	PQ3862	Great Britain
841-848. + (3-914)09	PQ226-307	Modern
841-848. + (7-8)09	PQ281-299	19th century
841-848.(008)	PQ1101-1413	Collections
841-848.(009)	PS102	French
841-848.(0809282)	PZ21-28	French
841-848.(1)	PQ1411-1545	1350-1400
841-848.(1-914)	PQ1411-2651	By author/Date
841-848.(109)	PQ151-221	Medieval
841-848.(2)	PQ1551-1595	14th-15th centuries
841-848.(2-3)08	PQ1121-1125	15th-16th centuries
841-848.(3)	PQ1600-1709	16th century
841-848.(3-9)	PQ1600-2651	Modern
841-848.(309)	PQ230-239	Renaissance/16th century
841-848.(4)	PQ1710-1935	17th century
841-848.(408)	PQ1126-1130	17th century
841-848.(409)	PQ241-251	17th century
841-848.(5)	PQ1947-2147	18th century
841-848.(508)	PQ1131-1135	18th century
841-848.(509)	PQ261-276	18th century
841-848.(7-8)	PQ2149-2551	19th century
841-848.(9-914)	PQ2600-2651	20th century
841-848.(908)	PQ1141	20th century
841-848.(909)	PQ305-307	20th century
841-848.8	PQ1300-1595	Old French, Collections
841.(3-8)09	PQ411-443	Modern (16-19th centuries)
841.032109	PQ201-205	Epics
841.08	PQ1308-1339	Poetry
841.08	PQ1161-1193	Poetry
841.109	PQ207-211	Poetry

Dewey	LC	Descriptor
841.9	PQ400-491	History of Poetry
842.(3-9)09	PQ516-558	Modern
842.008	PQ1211-1241	Drama
842.008	PQ1341-1365	Drama
842.009	PQ500-558	Drama, History
842.05161008	PQ1371-1385	Moralities/Farces
842.109	PQ511-515	Medieval
843.008	PQ1261-1275	Fiction
843.009	PQ631-671	Fiction
843.009	PQ601-771	Prose (Fiction)
843.9009	PQ611-629	Modern French Prose/Fiction
845.01008	PQ1281-1283	Oratory
848.08008	PQ1391	Prose
848.08008	PQ1243-1297	Prose
848.0809	PQ601-771	Prose
848.089009	PQ611-629	Modern French prose
849	PQ3870-3888	Switzerland
849	PQ3863	Italy
849	PQ3990-3999	Oceania
849	PQ3890	Other Europe
849	PQ3980-3989	Africa
849	PC3301-3359	Literature
849	PQ3960-3979	Asia
849	PQ3809-3999	By place
849	PQ3862	Great Britain
849	PQ3865	European Russia
849	PQ3950-3959	South America/Central America
849	PQ3801-3999	Provincial/Colonial
849	PQ3867	Scandinavia
849	PQ3810-3858	Belgium
849	PQ3860	Netherlands
849	PQ3861	Germany
849	PC3381-3415	Literature
849	PQ3900-3919	Canadia
849	PQ3940-3949	West Indies
849.09	PC3301-3321	History
849.9	PC3901-3947	Literature
849.909	PC3901-3917	History of literature
850	PQ4001-5991	Italian literature
850.(5/6)	PQ4001	Serials/Societies
850.3	PQ4006	Encyclopedias
850.7	PQ4013-4023	Education
850.8	PQ4003-4005	Collections
850.9	PQ4057-4059	Biography
850.9	PQ4035-4047	History
850.9	PQ4025-4034	Criticism
850.9	PQ4001-4199	History and criticism
851-858	PQ5901-5991	Provincial/Local/Colonial
851-858. + (3-9)09	PQ4077-4087	Modern
851-858.(008)	PQ4201-4263	Collections
851-858.(0809282)	PZ41-48	Italian
851-858.(1)	PQ4265-4556	Authors and works to 1400
851-858.(109)	PQ4064-4073	Medieval
851-858.(2-5)	PQ4561-4664	Individual authors (1400-1700)
851-858.(209)	PQ4075	Renaissance
851-858.(5-8)	PQ4675-4734	Individual authors (1701-1900)
851-858.(9-914)	PQ4800-4851	By author (20th century)
851.08	PQ4207-4225	Poetry
851.09	PQ4091-4130	Poetry
852.008	PQ4227-4245	Drama
852.009	PQ4133-4160	Drama
858.08008	PQ4247-4263	Prose
858.08009	PQ4161-4185	Prose

Dewey	LC	Descriptor
859	PC800-872	Literature
859.09	PC800-812	History
859.9	PC951-986	Literature
859.909	PC951	History
859.9092	PC953	Biography
860	PQ6001-8921	Spanish literature
860.3	PQ6006	Encyclopedias
860.5	PQ6001	Serials
860.6	PQ6002	Societies/Congresses
860.7	PQ6013-6020	Education
860.9	PQ6051-6055	Biography
860.9	PQ6031-6167	History of literature
861-838	PQ7071-7079	United States and Canada
861-868	PQ7550-7529	Panama
861-868	PQ7519	By author
861-868	PQ7797	By author
861-868	PQ7801-7819	Bolivia
861-868	PQ7819	By author
861-868	PQ8097	By author
861-868	PQ7510-7519	Nicaragua
861-868	PQ8519	By author
861-868	PQ8510-8519	Uruguay
861-868	PQ7900-8099	Chile
861-868	PQ7530-7539	El Salvador
861-868	PQ7500-7509	Honduras
861-868	PQ7539	By author
861-868	PQ7489	By author
861-868	PQ8239	By author
861-868	PQ8600-8619	Africa
861-868	PQ7471-7539	Central America
861-868	PQ8200-8219	Ecuador
861-868	PQ8219	By author
861-868	PQ8700-8899	Philippine Islands
861-868	PQ7451	Other islands
861-868	PQ7480-7489	Costa Rica
861-868	PQ8650-8911	Asia
861-868	PQ7499	By author
861-868	PQ8259	By author
861-868	PQ8230-8239	Guiana
861-868	PQ7600-7799	Argentine Republic
861-868	PQ7529	By author
861-868	PQ8250-8259	Paraguay
861-868	PQ8549	By author
861-868	PQ8160-8179	Colombia
861-868	PQ7551-8549	South America
861-868	PQ7490-7499	Guatemala
861-868	PQ8921	Australia/Pacific islands
861-868	PQ7509	By author
861-868	PQ8496-8497	By author
861-868	PQ8300-8499	Peru
861-868	PQ8530-8549	Venezuela
861-868	PQ8179	By author
861-868	PQ7370-7389	Cuba
861-868	PQ7420-7439	Puerto Rico
861-868	PQ7361-7451	West Indies
861-868	PQ7400-7409	Dominican Republic
861-868	PQ7079	Individual authors
861-868	PQ7389	Individual authors
861-868	PQ7409	By author
861-868	PQ7100-7300	Mexico
861-868	PQ7071-8560	America
861-868	PQ7081-8560	Spanish America
861-868	PQ7439	By author
861-868	PQ7296-7297	By author
861-868	PQ7310-7349	In the United States
861-868	PQ7000-8921	Provincial/Local/Colonial
861-868	PQ7000-7011	Spain

Dewey	LC	Descriptor
861-868	PQ7020-8921	Outside of Spain
861-868	PQ7031-7061	Europe
861-868. + (1-2)09	PQ6057-6060	Early to 1500
861-868. + (3-6)09	PQ6063-6072	Modern
861-868.(008)	PQ6171-6264	Collections
861-868.(008)	PQ6003-6005	Collections
861-868.(009)	PQ6001-6167	History/Criticism
861-868.(009)	PQ6022-6030	Criticism
861-868.(0809282)	PZ71-78	Spanish
861-868.(1-3)	PQ6271-6498	By author, To 1700
861-868.(4-5)	PQ6500-6576	By author, 1700-1868
861-868.(5-6)	PQ6600-6647	By author, 1868-
861.08	PQ6175-6215	Poetry
861.09	PQ6076-6098	Poetry
862.008	PQ6217-6239	Drama
862.009	PQ6099-6029	Drama
868.08008	PQ6247-6264	Prose
868.08009	PQ6131-6153	Prose
869	PQ9500-9699	Brazil
869	PQ9431-9470	Europe
869	PQ9400-9411	Portugal
869	PQ9400-9991	Provincial/Local/Colonial
869	PQ9471-9699	America
869	PQ9471-9479	United States/Canada
869	PQ9901	Africa
869	PQ9421-9991	Other countries
869	PQ9001-9991	Portuguese literature
869	PQ9951	Asia
869	PQ9991	Australia/Oceania
869.(1-2)	PQ9191-9260	By author, To 1700
869.(1-3)	PQ9696-9697	By author, To 1800
869.(1-4)09	PQ9035-9055	By date
869.(1-8) + (0809282)	PZ81-88	Portuguese
869.(3-4)	PQ9261	By author, 1701-
869.05	PQ9000-9001	Serials
869.06	PQ9002-9003	Societies/Congresses
869.07	PQ9008-9009.5	Education
869.08	PQ9004-9006	Collections
869.08	PQ9131-9187	Collections
869.09	PQ9001-9128	History and criticism
869.09	PQ9010-9023	History
869.09	PQ9027-9033	Biography
869.108	PQ9149-9163	Poetry
869.109	PQ9061-9081	Poetry
869.2008	PQ9164-9170	Drama
869.2009	PQ9083-9095	Drama
869.808008	PQ9172-9187	Prose
869.808009	PQ9097-9119	Prose
870.(5/6)	PA8001-8002	Serials/Societies/Congresses
871	PA185-190	Prosody/Metrics
871	PA2329-2340	Prosody/Metrics
871	PA3019-3022	Poetry
871-878	PA6001-6971	Latin/Ancient Roman literature
871-878. + (1-4)8	PA6119	By date
871-878.(08)	PA6202-6971	By author
871-878.(09)	PA2311-2320	Style/Rhetoric
871-878.(09)	PA6141-6144	Criticism/Interpretation
871-878.(1-4)09	PA6035-6043	By date
871-878.(109)	PA6041-6043	Empire period
871-878.(109)	PA6035	Early (To 240 B.C.)
871-878.(3-4)	PA8001-8595	Medieval/Modern Latin
871-878.(8)	PA6101-6140	Collections
871-878.(9)	PA6001-6095	Literary history
871-878.(9)	PA181-184	Style
871-878.0(3-4)	PA8050-8096	By form
871-878.0(3-4)08	PA8200-8595	By author/Date

Dewey	LC	Descriptor
871-878.0(3-4)08	PA8112-8117	By date
871-878.0(3-4)08	PA8120-8149	By form
871-878.0(3-4)08	PA8101-8199	Collections
871-878.0(3-4)09	PA8035-8043	By date
871-878.0(3-4)09	PA8001-8045	History/Criticism
871-878.0308	PA8200-8445	Medieval to 1350
871-878.0408	PA8450-8595	Modern (1350-)
871.0(1-4)08	PA6123	By date
871.0(3-4)	PA8050-8065	Poetry
871.0(3-4)08	PA8120-8133	Poetry
871.0108	PA6121-6135	Poetry
871.0109	PA6047-6063	Poetry
871.09	PA6142	Poetry
872	PA3024-3034	Drama
872.0(3-4)	PA8073-8079	Drama
872.0(3-4)08	PA8135-8142	Drama
872.0109	PA6067-6075	Drama
872.08	PA6137	Drama
872.09	PA6143	Drama
873.08	PA6125	Epic
874.08	PA6127	Lyric
878.0(3-4)008	PA8081-8096	Prose
878.0(3-4)0080008	PA8145	Prose/Fiction
878.0080008	PA6138-6139	Prose
878.0080009	PA6144	Prose
878.010080009	PA6081-6095	Prose
880	PA	Classical (Greek/Latin)
881	PA3019-3022	Poetry
881	PA185-190	Prosody/Metrics
881-888. + (2-3)08	PA5070-5075	Collections
881-888. + (2-3)09	PA5000-5040	History/Criticism
881-888. + 0(1-3)09	PA3081-3086	By date
881-888.(01)	PA3051-4500	Ancient Greek (to 600 A.D.)
881-888.(01)	PA3818-4500	By author (to 700 A.D.)
881-888.(0108)	PA3427	Roman (31 B.C.-100 A.D.)
881-888.(0108)	PA3423-3424	Hellenistic (300-31 B.C.)
881-888.(0108)	PA3423-3427	By date
881-888.(0108)	PA3401-3516	Printed editions
881-888.(0108)	PA3301-3371	Papyri/Ostraka
881-888.(0108)	PA3301-3516	Collections
881-888.(0109)	PA3051-3191	Literary history
881-888.(0109)	PA3086	Roman
881-888.(0109)	PA3531	Roman (31 B.C.-600 A.D.)
881-888.(0109)	PA3527	Hellenistic (300-31 B.C.)
881-888.(0109)	PA3081-3084	Hellenistic (300-31 B.C.)
881-888.(0208)	PA5170-5198	Collections
881-888.(0208)	PA5170-5172	By date
881-888.(0208)	PA5178-5179	By place
881-888.(0209)	PA5101-5167	History/Criticism
881-888.(03)	PA5201-5298	Renaissance and modern
881-888.(0308)	PA5270-5272	By date
881-888.(0308)	PA5270-5298	Collections
881-888.(0308)	PA5301-5610	By author/Date
881-888.(09)	PA3001-3044	Classical literature (History)
881-888.(09)	PA3005-3006	Biography (Collected)
881-888.(09)	PA401-407	Style/Rhetoric/Composition
881-888.(2)	PA5101-5395	Medieval/Byzantine
881-888.(2-3)	PA5000-5665	Byzantine/Modern Greek
881-888.(208)	PA5301-5395	Byzantine to 1600
881-888.(308)	PA5609-5610	Modern (1600-)
881-888.(309)	PA5201-5267	History/Criticism
881-888.(9)	PA181-184	Style
881-888.(9)	PA3520-3564	Criticism/Interpretation
881-888.0(3-4)	PA1106	Prosody/Metrics
881-888.0308	PA5650-5665	In other countries
881.0108	PA3431-3459	Poetry
881.0109	PA3092-3125	Poetry
881.0109	PA3537-3543	Poetry
881.0208	PA5180-5189	Poetry
881.0209	PA5150-5155	Poetry
881.0308	PA5280-5289	Poetry
881.0309	PA5259-5255	Poetry
882	PA3024-3034	Drama
882.0108	PA3461-3466	Drama
882.0109	PA3131-3136	Drama
882.0109	PA3545-3551	Drama
882.0208	PA5190-5194	Drama
882.0209	PA5160-5163	Drama
882.0308	PA5290-5294	Drama
882.0309	PA5260-5263	Drama
883.0108	PA3437-3439	Epic
883.0109	PA3105-3107.5	Epic poetry
884.0108	PA3443-3447	Lyric poetry
884.0109	PA3110-3111	Lyric poetry
885.0108	PA3479-3482	Oratory
885.0109	PA3561-3564	Oratories
887.0109	PA3160	Satire
887.0109	PA3161-3191	Comedy
887.0109	PA3553	Comedy
887.0208	PA5197-5198	Humor/Satire
887.0209	PA5167	Humor/Satire
887.0308	PA5297-5298	Humor/Satire
887.0309	PA5265	Humor/Satire
888.008	PA3035-3044	Prose
888.008	PA3035-3044	Prose
888.01008	PA3255-3273	Prose
888.010080008	PA3473-3515	Prose
888.010080008	PA3403	Prose
888.010080009	PA3556-3558	Prose
888.020080008	PA5195-5196	Prose/Fiction
888.020080009	PA5165	Prose/Fiction
888.030080008	PA5295-5296	Prose/Fiction
889	PA5000-5665	Byzantine/Modern Greek
889.(1-3)	PA5201-5298	Renaissance and modern
889.(1-3)08	PA5270-5298	Collections
889.(1-3)08	PA5270-5272	By date
889.(1-3)08	PA5301-5610	By author/Date
889.(1-3)08	PA5609-5610	Modern (1600-)
889.(1-3)08	PA5650-5665	In other countries
889.(1-3)09	PA5201-5267	History/Criticism
889.08	PA5070-5075	Collections
889.09	PA5000-5040	History/Criticism
889.1	PA5101-5395	Medieval/Byzantine
889.1	PA1106	Prosody/Metrics
889.1(1-3)08	PA5280-5289	Poetry
889.1(1-3)09	PA5259-5255	Poetry
889.108	PA5170-5198	Collections
889.108	PA5170-5172	By date
889.108	PA5178-5179	By place
889.108	PA5301-5395	Byzantine to 1600
889.109	PA5101-5167	History/Criticism
889.1108	PA5180-5189	Poetry
889.1109	PA5150-5155	Poetry
889.2(1-3)08	PA5290-5294	Drama
889.2(1-3)09	PA5260-5263	Drama
889.2108	PA5190-5194	Drama
889.2109	PA5160-5163	Drama
889.7(1-3)08	PA5297-5298	Humor/Satire
889.7(1-3)09	PA5265	Humor/Satire
889.7108	PA5197-5198	Humor/Satire
889.7109	PA5167	Humor/Satire
889.8(1-3)0808	PA5295-5296	Prose/Fiction
889.810808	PA5195-5196	Prose/Fiction

Dewey	LC	Descriptor
889.810809	PA5165	Prose/Fiction
890	PJ	Oriental philology/Literature
891.1	PK80-85	Literature
891.1	PK2902-2979	Indo-Aryan literature
891.10802309	PK2941-2943	Narratives
891.109	PK2911-2915	By date
891.109	PK2902-2947	History/Criticism
891.1109	PK2916-2929	Poetry
891.1209	PK2931-2933	Drama
891.1709	PK2945-2947	Wit/Humor
891.2	PK3591-4485	Sanskrit
891.2	PK3791-3799	By author
891.3	PK4990-5046	Prakrit/Jaina literature
891.37	PK4501-4681	Pali literature
891.4	PK5401-5471	Modern Indo-Aryan literature
891.43	PK2030-2142	Hindustani literature
891.439	PK2151-2212	Urdu literature
891.5	PK6001-6996	Iranian philology/Literature
891.509	PK6097-6099	History of literature
891.55	PK6450.9-6561	By author
891.55	PK6400-6599	Literature
891.55(808/3)08	PK6443	Prose/Fiction
891.55(808/3)09	PK6423	Prose/Fiction
891.5508	PK6428-6450	Collections
891.5509	PK6400-6427.6	History/Criticism
891.55108	PK6433-6439	Poetry
891.55109	PK6416-6420	Poetry
891.55208	PK6440	Drama
891.55209	PK6421-6422	Drama
891.6	PB1096-1100	Literature
891.6	PR8490-8499	Celtic
891.6(2-3)	PB1196-1200	Literature
891.62	PB1306-1449	Literature
891.6209	PB1306-1337	History
891.63	PB1605-1709	Literature
891.6309	PB1605-1613	History
891.64	PB1851-1888	Literature
891.66	PB2206-2450	Literature
891.6609	PB2206-2237	History
891.67	PB2551-2621	Literature
891.6709	PB2551-2552	History
891.68	PB2856-2931	Literature
891.6809	PB2856-2858	History
891.7	PG2900-3698	Literature
891.7(1-8) + (0809282)	PZ61-68	Russian
891.79	PG3900-3987	Literature
891.8	PG500-583	Literature
891.809	PG501-512	History
891.81	PG701-705	Literature
891.81	PG1000-1158	Literature
891.8109	PG1000-1012	History
891.82	PG1400-1696	Literature
891.8209	PG1400-1412	History
891.84	PG1900-1962	Literature
891.8409	PG1900-1962	History
891.85	PG7001-7446	Literature
891.85(1-8) + (0809282)	PZ69-70	Polish
891.8509	PG7012-7129	History
891.86	PG5000-5146	Literature
891.87	PG5400-5546	Literature
891.88	PG5661-5698	Literature
891.92	PG8701-8798	Literature
891.93	PG9000-9198	Literature
891.991	PG9601-9678	Literature
891.992	PK8601-8661	Europe
891.992	PK8561-8699	By place
891.992	PK8501-8835	Literature
891.992	PK8547-8548	By author
891.992	PK8681-8689	United States/Canada
891.9920(9/8)	PK8501-8546	History and collections
892	PJ806-908	Literature
892-893	PJ306-489	Oriental literature (General)
892-893.(08)	PJ347-489	Collections
892-893.(09)	PJ306-345	History
892.(09)	PJ3097	Literature (History/Criticism)
892.(7-9)	PJ8500-8517	In America
892.(7-9)	PJ8130-8167	In India/Pakistan
892.(7-9)	PJ8030-8129	In the Near East
892.(7-9)	PJ8395-8490	In Europe
892.(7-9)	PJ8025-8190	In Asia
892.(7-9)	PJ8025-8517	By place
892.(7-9)	PJ8195-8390	In Africa
892.1	PJ3601-3941	Literature
892.109	PJ3601-3671	History
892.3	PJ5601-5695	Literature
892.308	PJ5611-5647	Collections
892.309	PJ5601-5607	History
892.4	PJ5001-5060	Literature
892.4	PJ5049	By place
892.4(1-6)	PJ5016-5021	By period
892.4(1-6)	PJ5050-5060	By date/Author
892.4(1-8)	PJ5022-5033.9	By form
892.40(5/6)	PJ5001-5004	Serials/Societies/Congresses
892.407	PJ5007	Education
892.408	PJ5035-5047.9	Collections
892.409	PJ5008-5034.2	History
892.7	PJ7501-8517	Arabic literature
892.7(1-6)	PJ7526-7538	By date
892.7(1-6)	PJ7695.8-7876	By date/Author
892.7(1-6)08	PJ7611-7625	By date
892.7(1-8) + 0809282	PZ8.72-.78	Arabic
892.708	PJ7601-7680	Collections
892.709	PJ7501-7600	History/Criticism
892.7108	PJ7631-7661	Poetry
892.7109	PJ7541-7561	Poetry
892.7208	PJ7665	Drama
892.7209	PJ7565	Drama
892.77	PJ8000-8517	Provincial/Colonial/Local
892.780808	PJ7671-7677	Prose
892.780809	PJ7571-7577	Prose
893	PJ806-908	Literature
893.1	PJ1481-1921	Literature
893.109	PJ1481-1488	History
893.2	PJ2190-2199	Literature
893.7	PT9960-9975	Finland
894.2	PL410-419	Mongol literature
894.3(5-6)	PL248	By author
894.3(5-6)	PL201-248	Literature
894.511	PH3001-3445	Literature
894.51109	PH3012-3132	History
894.541	PH300-405	Literature
894.54109	PH300-337	History
894.545	PH630-671	Literature
894.55	PH731-735	Literature
894.56	PH781-785	Literature
895.1	PL2250-(3208)	Literature
895.1	PL1001-(3208)	Chinese Literature
895.1(1-52)	PL2661-2929.5	By author/Date
895.1(1-8)	PL3033-(3208)	In other countries
895.1(1-8)	PL3030-(3208)	Provincial/Local
895.1(1-8) + (0809282)	PZ8.82-.88	Chinese

Dewey	LC	Descriptor
895.1(1-8)08	PL2450-2653	Collections
895.103	PL2257	Encylopedias
895.105	PL2250-2251	Serials
895.106	PL2252-2253	Societies/Congresses
895.107	PL2258-2260	Education
895.1074	PL2253.5	Exhibitions/Museums
895.109	PL2263-2443	History
895.109	PL2250-2443	History/Criticism
895.109	PL2261-2262.2	Criticism
895.109	PL2458-2515.5	Confucian Canon
895.1092	PL2260-.52	Biography
895.10922	PL2277	Biography (Collective)
895.11	PL2661-2662	Early to 221 B.C.
895.1108	PL2517-2565.8	Poetry
895.1109	PL2306-2355.8	Poetry
895.12	PL2663-2669	221 B.C.-618 A.D.
895.1208	PL2566-2603	Drama
895.1209	PL2356-2393	Drama
895.13	PL2670-2677	618-907 (T'ang Dynasty)
895.1308	PL2625-2653	Fiction
895.1309	PL2415-2443	Fiction
895.1408	PL2606-2623	Essays
895.1409	PL2395-2413	Essays
895.142	PL2679-2687	Sung Dynasty (960-1279)
895.144	PL2688-2694	Yuan Dynasty (1260-1368)
895.146	PL2694.5-2698	Ming Dynasty (1368-1644)
895.148	PL2699-2735	Ch'ing Dynasty (1644-1912)
895.151	PL2735.5-2832.3	1912-1949
895.152	PL2832.5-2929.5	1949-
895.4	PL3701-3775	Literature
895.6	PL700-889	Literature
895.6(1-5)	PL784-866	By author/Date
895.6(1-8)	PL885-889	Local/In other countries
895.6(1-8) + (0809282)	PZ49.2-.8	Japanese
895.6(1-8)08	PL752-783	Collections
895.6(1-9) + (0809282)	PL751.5	Juvenile literature
895.6(44-5)	PL821-866	Showa (1926-)
895.6(808/3)08	PL770-777	Prose/Fiction
895.6(808/3)09	PL740-747	Prose/Fiction
895.605	PL700-701	Serials
895.606	PL702-703	Societies/Congresses
895.607	PL709-711	Education
895.6074	PL703.5	Museums/Exhibitions
895.609	PL700-751.5	History/Criticism
895.609	PL714-715	Criticism
895.609	PL716-751.5	History
895.6108	PL757-763	Poetry
895.6109	PL727-733	Poetry
895.614	PL787-789	Heian period (794-1185)
895.62(2-4)	PL790-792	Kamakura-Monoyama (1185-1600)
895.6208	PL764-769	Drama
895.6209	PL734-739	Drama
895.632	PL793-795	Early Edo (1600-1788)
895.634	PL796-799	Late Edo (1789-1867)
895.642	PL800-820	Meiji-Taisho (1868-1926)
895.7	PL950-998	Literature
895.7	PL901-998	Korean literature
895.7(1-4)	PL986-993	By author/Date
895.7(1-8)	PL997-998	Local/In other countries
895.7(1-8)	PL969.5	Juvenile literature
895.7(1-8) + (0809282)	PZ50.52-.58	Korean
895.7(1-8)08	PL969.8-985	Collections
895.7(808/3)08	PL980-981	Prose/Fiction
895.7(808/3)09	PL965-967	Prose/Fiction
895.705	PL950.2-.4	Serials
895.706	PL950.6-.8	Societies/Congesses
895.707	PL952-.4	Education
895.709	PL955-969.5	History
895.709	PL950.2-969.5	History/Criticism
895.71	PL987	Koryo period (935-1392)
895.7108	PL974-976.23	Poetry
895.7109	PL959-961.23	Poetry
895.72	PL989-.96	1598-1894
895.72	PL988	1392-1598
895.7208	PL977-979	Drama
895.7209	PL962-964	Drama
895.728	PL990-.96	1894-1919
895.73	PL951.6	Dictionaries/ Encyclopedias
895.73	PL991-.96	1919-1945
895.74	PL992-993	1945-
895.8	PL3970-3988	Literature
895.91	PL4200-4209	Literature
896	PL8009.5-8014	Literature
896	PL8000-8839	African Literature
899.92	PH5280-5490	Literature
899.95	PJ4045-4075	Literature
899.96	PK9160-9169	Literature
899.96	PK9030-9040	Literature, By language
900	D	History (General)
900	C	Auxiliary sciences of history
901	CB19	Philosophy
901	D16.7-.9	Philosophy of history
901	D16-.8	Methodology
902.22	CB13	Pictorial works
903	CB9	Dictionaries/ Encyclopedias
903	D9	Dictionaries
903	C8	Dictionaries/ Encyclopedias
903	DE5	Dictionaries
904.5	GB5000-5030	Natural disasters
905	D2	Yearbooks
905	CB3-4	Serials/Societies/Congresses
905	C4	Yearbooks
905	D1	Serials
905	DE1-4	Serials
906	D3	Congresses
906	C2	Societies
906	C3	Congresses
906	DE15	Education
906	CB3-4	Serials/Societies/Congresses
906	DE1-4	Societies
906	D1	Societies
966.101	DT554.65-.67	Ancient to 1903
907	C20	Education
907	CB20	Education
907	D16.2-16.5	Education
907.2	CB15-18	Historiography
907.2	D13-15	Historiography
907.2	DE8-9	Historiography
909	DE7	Biography
909	CB	History of civilization
909	CB23-151	World history, General
909	D17-24	World histories
909	D31-34	Political/Diplomatic history
909	CB311	Ancient history
909.(1-2)	D175-195	Latin Kingdom of Jerusalem
909.(4-6)	D219-234	1453-1648
909.(7-8)	D299-309	1789-1800

Dewey	LC	Descriptor
909.0(7-8)	D101-110	Medieval-Modern (General)
909.0(7/8)	D105	Political/Diplomatic
909.0(7/8)03	D101	Dictionaries
909.0(7/8)092	D107-110	Biography
909.04	CB195-481	Civilization and race
909.04	DE73	Ethnography
909.0491497	DX	Gypsies
909.04924	DS133-151	Jews outside Palestine/Israel
909.07	D164	Fourth crusade
909.07	D166	Sixth crusade
909.07	D167	Seventh crusade
909.07	D151-173	Crusades
909.07	D168	Eighth crusade
909.07	D165	Fifth crusade
909.07	D200-203	11th-15th centuries
909.07	D161	First crusade
909.07	D162	Second crusade
909.07	D163	Third crusade
909.07	D111-203	Medieval
909.07	D171-172	13th/15th century crusades
909.07	D131-134	Political
909.07	CB351-355	Medieval history
909.070(5/6)	D111	Serials/Societies
909.07024055	D169	Juvenile works
909.0703	D113-114	Dictionaries
909.0703	D151-155	Dictionaries
909.07072	D156.58	Historiography
909.07072	D116	Historiography
909.07092	D115	Biography
909.07092	D156	Biography
909.08	D205	Modern (1453-)
909.08	D217	Political/Diplomatic history
909.0803	D205	Dictionaries
909.08072	D206	Historiography
909.091724	D880-888	Developing countries
909.09174927	DS36-39.2	Arab countries
909.09174927	DS36.77-.88	Social life
909.09174927	DS37-39.2	History
909.091749270(5/6)	DS36-.28	Serials/Societies/Congresses
909.0917492703	DS36.55	Gazetteers/Directories
909.0917492704	DS36.9	Ethnography
909.091811	D890-893	Eastern Hemisphere
909.09638	DE80-100	History
909.09638	DE	Mediterranean/Greco-Roman
909.096380(4-7)	DE96	1453-1800
909.0963801	DE94	Medieval to 1453
909.0963808(1-24)	DE98	1801-1945
909.0963808(24-3)	DE100	1945-
909.09824	DS331-349.9	Indian Ocean region
909.1	D121-123	By date
909.6	D242-283	1601-1715
909.638	DE46-71	Civilization
909.7	D284-297	1715-1789
909.7	D295	Political/Military history
909.8(1-21)	D351-400	1801-1920
909.82	CB357-430	Modern history
909.82	D410-472	20th century
909.82	D431-436	Military/Naval history
910(4-9)	CC908-950	By place
910(4-9)	CC600-605	Boundary stones
910(4-9)	CC300-350	Crosses
910(4-9)	CC310-350	Crosses, By place
910(4-9)	CC700-705	Stone heaps
910(4-9)	CC900-950	Hill figures/Tombs
910(4-9)	CC960	Lanterns of the dead
910	G	Geography/Maps
910.01	G70-.4	Philosophy
910.014	G100.5-108.5	Toponymy
910.202	G149.9-153	Instructions/Guidebooks
910.23	G65	As a profession
910.25	G64	Directories
910.3	G63	Dictionaries/Encyclopedias
910.4	G460-503	To several parts
910.4	G369-503	Special voyages/Travels
910.4	G149-180	Travel and voyages (General)
910.40(5/6)	G149-.5	Serials/Societies/Congresses
910.4083	G570	Juvenile voyages and travels
910.41	G445	Flights around the world
910.45	G540-550	Seafaring life/Ocean travel
910.45	G521-539	Shipwreck/Buried treasure
910.45	G419-420	Circumnavigations
910.5	G1	Serials
910.6	G56	Congresses
910.6	G2-55	Societies
910.7(02)	G72-76.5	Education/Research
910.71	G77	Schools
910.74	G77.8-78	Museums/Exhibitions
910.9	G80-99	History
910.9	G200-336	Discoveries/Explorations
910.9(3-9)	G220-336	By nationality
910.91	DS36.59-.65	Travel
910.92	G67-69	Biography
910.942	G240-246	English
910.943	G260-266	German
910.944	G250-256	French
910.945	G270-276	Italian
910.946	G287-289	Spanish
910.9469	G280-286	Portuguese
910.947	G290-296	Russian
910.948	G300-306	Scandinavian
910.9481	G778-810	Norwegian regions
910.9492	G230-236	Dutch
910.951	G320-326	Chinese
910.952	G330-336	Japanese
910.957	G820-839	Siberia
910.973	G220-226	American
910.998	G600-839	Arctic explorations
910.998	G575-599	Polar regions
910.9982	G725-765	Greenland
910.9989	G845-890	Antarctica
911	DE23-31	Geography
911	G141	Historical geography
911.3	G905-910	Tropics (General)
911.37	G1980-1981	Roman Empire
911.37	G6700-6701	Roman Empire
911.73	G3701	History
911.81(3-4)	G912-922	Northern/Southern hemispheres
912	G	Geography/Maps
912	G9900-9980	Unlocalized
912	G1001-1046	World atlases
912	G3190-9980	Maps
912	QB65	Atlases/Charts
912	GA300-325	World maps/Atlases
912	QE36	Geological maps
912.(3-9)	G1100-3102	Atlases, By specific place
912.(3-9)	GA341-1776	Maps, By region or country
912.(72-8)	G1540-1542	Latin America (General)
912.(99/19)	G3190-3192	Celestial maps
912.01	G70-.4	Philosophy

Dewey	LC	Descriptor	Dewey	LC	Descriptor
912.015	G64	Directories	912.45	GA891-895	Italy
912.023	G65	As a profession	912.45	G1983-1989	Italy
912.03	G63	Dictionaries/ Encyclopedias	912.45	G6705-6773	Italy
			912.46	G1965-1969	Spain
912.05	G1	Serials	912.46	G6560-6563	Spain
912.06	G56	Congresses	912.46	GA1005	Spain
912.06	G2-55	Societies	912.4689	G6670-6672	Gibraltar
912.07(02)	G72-76.5	Education/Research	912.469	GA1011-1015	Portugal
912.071	G77	Schools	912.469	G6680-6694	Portugal
912.074	G77.8-78	Museums/Exhibitions	912.469	G1975-1979	Portugal
912.09	G80-99	History	912.47	GA931-935	European Russia
912.09	GA201-246	History	912.47	G7000-7342	European Russia
912.092	G67-69	Biography	912.47	G2110-2193	European Russia
912.191	G1054-1055	Polar regions (Atlases)	912.48	GA951-995	Scandinavia
912.19162	G2800-3064	Oceans (General)	912.481	G2065-2069	Norway
912.191734	GF127	Rural settlements/ Geography	912.481	G6940-6944	Norway
			912.481	GA981-985	Norway
912.192	G3250-3251	Temperate zones	912.485	GA991-995	Sweden
912.193	G1053	Tropics (Atlases)	912.485	G2070-2074	Sweden
912.193	G3240-3241	Tropics	912.485	G6950-6954	Sweden
912.1962	G1059-1061	Maritime atlases (General)	912.489	GA961-965	Denmark
912.1962	G9095-9794	Oceans (General)	912.489	G6920-6923	Denmark
912.1963	G9100-9177	Atlantic Ocean	912.489	G2055-2059	Denmark
912.1963	G2805-2839	Atlantic Ocean/Islands	912.4897	G2075-2079	Finland
912.1963	GA368-381	Atlantic Ocean area	912.4897	G6960-6963	Finland
912.19632	G3050-3064	Arctic Ocean	912.49(2-3)	G1850-1874	Low Countries
912.1964	GA383-390	Pacific Ocean area	912.49(2-3)	G5990-6023	Low Countries
912.1964	G9230-9762	Pacific Ocean	912.4912	G2060-2064	Iceland
912.1964	G2860-3012	Pacific Ocean	912.4912	GA971-975	Iceland
912.19642	G3012	East Pacific islands	912.4912	G6930-6934	Iceland
912.1965	GA392-397	Indian Ocean	912.492	GA921-925	Netherlands
912.1965	G9180-9217	Indian Ocean area	912.493	GA911-915	Belgium
912.1965	G2850-2857	Indian Ocean islands	912.494	G6035-6043	Alps/Switzerland
912.1967	G3100-3102	Antarctica	912.494	G1895-1899	Switzerland
912.19732	GF125	Cities/Urban geography	912.494	GA1021-1025	Switzerland
912.198(3-4)	G1050-1052	Northern/Southern hemispheres	912.495	G2000-2004	Greece
			912.495	GA881-885	Greece
912.1981(3-4)	G3210-3222	Northern/Southern hemispheres	912.495	G6810-6813	Greece
			912.496	GA1031-1075	Balkan states
912.19811	G5670-9084	Eastern Hemisphere/ Eurasia/Etc.	912.4965	G6830-6834	Albania
			912.4965	G2005-2009	Albania
912.19811	G1780-2799	Eastern Hemisphere/Eurasia	912.497	G6840-6877	Yugoslavia
912.19812	G1100-1779	America/Western Hemisphere	912.497	G2010-2032	Yugoslavia
			912.4977	G6890-6894	Bulgaria
912.19812	G3290-5668	Western Hemisphere	912.4977	G2040-2044	Bulgaria
912.4	G1791-2082	Europe	912.498	G2035-2039	Romania
912.4	G5700-6966	Europe	912.498	G6880-6883	Romania
912.4	GA781-1077	Europe	912.5	GA1081-1340	Asia
912.4090(1-4)	G1791-1799	Europe, By date	912.5	G2200-2444	Asia
912.41	G5740-5814	Great Britain	912.5	G7400-8198.54	Asia
912.41	G1807-1834	Great Britain/Ireland	912.51	G2305-2326	China
912.41	GA791-825	Great Britain	912.51	GA1121-1125	China
912.43	GA871-880	Germany	912.51	G7810-7892	China
912.43	G6070-6428	Germany	912.51249	G7910-7914	Taiwan
912.43	G1907-1924	Germany	912.51249	G2340-2344	Taiwan
912.436	G1935-1939	Austria	912.5125	G7940-7944	Hong Kong
912.436	G6490-6494	Austria	912.5173	G7895-7899	Mongolia
912.436	GA831-834	Austria	912.519	G7900-7907	Korea
912.437	G6510-6513	Czechoslovakia	912.519	G2330-2334	Korea
912.437	G1945-1949	Czechoslovakia	912.519	GA1251-1255	Korea
912.438	G1950-1954	Poland	912.52	G7950-7963	Japan
912.438	G6520-6523	Poland	912.52	GA1241-1245	Japan
912.439	G1940-1944	Hungary	912.52	G2353-2357	Japan
912.439	G6500-6503	Hungary	912.53	G2245-2249	Arabian peninsula
912.44	G5830-5973	France	912.53	GA1101-1105	Arabia
912.44	G1837-1844	France	912.53	G7520-7604	Arabian peninsula
912.44	GA861-865	France	912.54	G7650-7654	India

Dewey	LC	Descriptor
912.54	G2280-2284	India
912.54	GA1131-1135	India
912.5491	G7640-7644	Pakistan
912.5491	G2270-2274	Pakistan
912.5491	GA1136-1140	Pakistan
912.5492	G7645-7649	Bangladesh
912.5492	G2275-2279	Bangladesh
912.5493	G2290-2294	Sri Lanka
912.5493	G7750-7754	Sri Lanka
912.5496	G2295-2299	Nepal
912.5496	G7760-7764	Nepal
912.55	G7620-7624	Iran
912.55	GA1261-1265	Iran
912.55	G2255-2259	Iran
912.56	G7420-7623	Near East
912.561	G2210-2214	Turkey
912.561	GA1301-1305	Turkey
912.5645	G2215-2219	Cyprus
912.567	G2250-2254	Iraq
912.567	G7610-7614	Iraq
912.5691	GA1331-1335	Syria
912.5691	G2220-2224	Syria
912.5692	G2225-2229	Lebanon
912.5694	G2235-2239	Israel/Palestine
912.5694	G7500-7504	Israel/Palestine
912.5694	GA1321-1325	Israel/Palestine
912.5695	G2240-2244	Jordan
912.57	GA1271-1295	Asian Russia
912.581	G7630-7634	Afghanistan
912.581	G2265-2269	Afghanistan
912.59(4-7)	GA1141-1195	Indochina
912.591	G2285-2289	Burma
912.591	G7720-7724	Burma
912.593	G8025-8029	Thailand
912.593	G2375-2379	Thailand
912.594	G8015-8017	Laos
912.594	G2374.5-.54	Laos
912.595	GA1201-1205	Malaysia
912.595	G8030-8034	Malaysia
912.5957	G8040-8044	Singapore
912.596	G8010-8014	Cambodia
912.597	G2370-2374	Vietnam
912.597	G8020-8022	Vietnam
912.598	GA1221-1225	Indonesia
912.598	G8070-8132	Indonesia
912.599	G8060-8064	Philippines
912.599	GA1231-1235	Philippines
912.6	GA1341-1673	Africa
912.6	G2445-2739	Africa
912.6	G8200-8904	Africa
912.61	GA1348-1414	North Africa
912.61	G2455-2499	North Africa
912.611	G8250-8254	Tunisia
912.612	G8260-8264	Libya
912.62	G8300-8304	Egypt
912.63	G8330-8334	Ethiopia
912.64	G8230-8234	Morocco
912.65	G8240-8244	Algeria
912.66	G2640-2739	West Africa
912.66	GA1550-1603	West Africa
912.6626	G8770-8774	Niger
912.663	G8810-8814	Senegal
912.6662	G8880-8884	Liberia
912.6668	G8780-8784	Ivory Coast
912.667	G8850-8854	Ghana
912.6681	G8760-8764	Togo
912.669	G8840-8844	Nigeria

Dewey	LC	Descriptor
912.67	G2590-2639	Central Africa
912.67	GA1500-1543	Central Africa
912.6711	G8730-8734	Cameroon
912.6718	G8660-8664	Equatorial Guinea
912.673	G8640-8644	Angola
912.6743	G8720-8724	Chad
912.6751	G8650-8654	Zaire
912.6757(1/2)	G8425-8439	Rwanda/Burundi
912.676	GA1428-1499	East Africa
912.6761	G8420-8424	Uganda
912.6762	G8410-8414	Kenya
912.6773	G8350-8364	Somalia
912.678	G8440-8444	Tanzania
912.679	G8450-8454	Mozambique
912.68	GA1604-1673	Southern Africa
912.68	G8500-8542	South Africa
912.68	G2560-2584	Southern Africa
912.689	G8550-8562	Zimbabwe (Southern Rhodesia)
912.691	G8460-8464	Madagascar
912.7	G3300-5184	North America
912.7	G1105-1694	North America
912.7(4-5)	G3709.3-.32	Atlantic states
912.7(4-9)	GA409-460	By state and city
912.71	G1115-1193	Canada
912.71	GA471-475	Canada
912.71	G3400-3612	Canada
912.711	G3510-3514	British Columbia
912.712	G3470-3504	Prairie provinces
912.713	G3460-3464	Ontario
912.714	G3450-3454	Quebec
912.715	G3410-3412	Maritime provinces
912.718	G3600-3612	New Foundland/Labrador
912.7191	G3520-3524	Yukon
912.7192	G3530-3532	N.W. Territories
912.72	G4410-4763	Mexico
912.72	G1545-1549	Mexico
912.72	GA481-485	Mexico
912.728	G4800-4884	Central America
912.728	GA491-555	Central America
912.728	G1550-1594	Central America
912.7281	GA521-525	Guatemala
912.7283	GA531-535	Honduras
912.7284	GA551-555	El Salvador
912.7285	GA541-545	Nicaragua
912.7286	GA511-515	Costa Rica
912.7287	GA546-550	Panama
912.729	G4390-4392	Caribbean area
912.729	GA561-621	West Indies
912.729	G1600-1694	West Indies
912.729	G4900-5184	West Indies
912.729	G1535-1537	Caribbean area
912.7291	GA581-585	Cuba
912.7292	GA601-605	Jamaica
912.7294	GA591-595	Haiti
912.7295	GA611-615	Puerto Rico
912.7296	GA571-575	Bahamas
912.73	G1200-1534.24	United States
912.73	G3690-4383	United States
912.73	GA405-460	United States
912.74	G3715-3717	Northeast Atlantic states
912.74	G3720-3784	New England
912.74	G3790-3854	Mid-Atlantic states
912.75	G3870-3933	Southeast Atlantic states
912.76	G3935-3937	South Central states
912.76	G3990-4033	West South Central states
912.77	G4040-4042	Central states

Dewey	LC	Descriptor
912.77	G4070-4123	Old Northwest
912.78	G4220-4222	Rocky Mountain states
912.78	G4050-4052	The West
912.79	G4125-4203	Northwestern states
912.79	G4295-4364	Southwestern
912.795	G4240-4293	Pacific Northwest
912.798	G4370-4373	Alaska
912.8	G1700-1779	South America
912.8	GA641-775	South America
912.8	G5200-5668	South America
912.81	GA671-675	Brazil
912.82	G5350-5352	Argentina
912.82	GA651-655	Argentina
912.83	G5330-5334	Chili
912.83	GA681-685	Chile
912.84	GA661-665	Bolivia
912.85	GA751-755	Peru
912.85	G5310-5314	Peru
912.861	G5290-5294	Colombia
912.861	GA691-695	Colombia
912.866	GA701-705	Ecuador
912.866	G5300-5302	Ecuador
912.87	GA771-775	Venezuela
912.88	G5240-5274	Guianas
912.88	GA711-730	Guianas
912.892	GA741-745	Paraguay
912.895	GA761-765	Uruguay
912.9	G2740-2799	Australasia
912.9	G8950-9084	Australasia
912.9(5-6)	GA1771-1776	Oceania
912.93	G9080-9084	New Zealand
912.93	G2795-2799	New Zealand
912.93	GA1765-1769	New Zealand
912.94	GA1681-1685	Australia
912.94	G8960-9063	Australia
912.94	G2750-2793	Australia
912.95	G2870-2894	Melanesia
912.95	G8140-8192	New Guinea
912.96	G2970-2984	Polynesia
912.965	G2900-2934	Micronesia
912.969	G4380-4383	Hawaii/Sandwich Islands
912.982	G3380-3384	Greenland
912.982	G1110-1114	Greenland
912.989	G9800-9804	Antarctica
912.99	G1000.3-.5	Planets (Atlases)
912.991	G3195-3199	Moon
912.998	G3260-3272	Polar regions
913.(7-8)	DE23-31	Geography
913.304	DS153.2	Travel
913.304	DS103-107.4	Travel
913.5(04)	DS254.8-259.2	Geography/Travel
913.63(04)	DL6.7-11.5	Geography/Travel
913.6304	DL115-120	Travel
913.6304	DL415-419.2	Travel
913.6304	DL614.55-619.5	Travel
913.64(04)	DQ20-26	Geography/Travel
913.66(04)	DP520-526.5	Geography/Travel
913.6604	DP27-43.2	Geography/Travel
913.7	DG27-41	Geography
913.8(04)	DF27-41	Geography/Travel
913.81(04)	DR914-918	Geography/Travel
913.9204	DR421-429.4	Travel
913.94	DS44.9-49.7	Geography
913.94304	DS94	Travel
913.94404	DS80.2	Travel
913.94904	DS204.5-208	Travel
913.98(04)	DR57-61	Geography/Travel
913.98(04)	DR1218-1224	Geography/Travel
913.98(04)	DR11-16	Geography/Travel
913.9804	DR207-210	Travel
914	D901-980	Travel
914	DAW1010-1015	Travel
914.11	DA757-.7	Geography
914.1104	DA850-878	Travel
914.1504	DA969-988	Travel
914.204	DA600-632	Travel
914.29(04)	DA725-731.2	Geography/Travel
914.3	DAW1010-1015	Travel
914.3(04)	DD21.5-43	Travel
914.36(04)	DB20-27.5	Geography/Travel
914.364804	DB888	Travel
914.37(04)	DB2018-2022	Geography/Travel
914.38(04)	DK4045-4081	Geography/Travel
914.3804	DD314-320	Travel
914.3904	DB906.9-917	Travel
914.4(04)	DC20.5-29.3	Geography/Travel
914.5	DG421	Geography
914.504	DG421.5-430.2	Travel
914.6(04)	DP27-43.2	Geography/Travel
914.69(04)	DP520-526.5	Geography/Travel
914.7(04)	DJK11-18	Geography/Travel
914.7(04)	DK18.7-29	Geography/Travel
914.8(04)	DL6.7-11.5	Geography/Travel
914.81	G778-810	Norwegian regions
914.8104	DL415-419.2	Travel
914.8504	DL614.55-619.5	Travel
914.8904	DL115-120	Travel
914.89704	DL1015-.4	Travel
914.91204	DL309-315	Travel
914.92(04)	DJ30-40	Geography/Travel
914.9204	DH31-40	Travel
914.93(04)	DH430-435	Geography/Travel
914.94(04)	DQ20-26	Geography/Travel
914.95	DF518	Geography
914.9504	DF721-728	Travel
914.96(04)	DR11-16	Geography/Travel
914.965(04)	DR914-918	Geography/Travel
914.97(04)	DR1218-1224	Geography/Travel
914.977(04)	DR57-61	Geography/Travel
914.9804	DR207-210	Travel
915	DS5.9-10	Geography
915.304	DS204.5-208	Travel
915.5(04)	DS254.8-259.2	Geography/Travel
915.596	G2374	Cambodia
915.6	DS44.9-49.7	Geography
915.6104	DR421-429.4	Travel
915.69104	DS94	Travel
915.69204	DS80.2	Travel
915.69404	DS103-107.4	Travel
915.69504	DS153.2	Travel
915.7	G820-839	Siberia
917.04	E41	Travel
917.3	E179.5	Historical geography
917.304	E161.5-169	Travel
919.(3-6)04	DU19-23.5	Travel
919.4(04)	DU96.5-105.2	Geography/Travel
919.8	G575-599	Polar regions
919.8	G575-890	Arctic/Antarctic regions
919.82	G725-765	Greenland
919.89	G845-890	Antarctica
920	CT93-206	Collective, General
920	CT25-83	History of the literature
920	CT	Biography
920.0(4-9)	CT210-3150	National

Dewey	LC	Descriptor
920.009296073	E185.96-.97	Biography
920.04	CT759-1458	Europe
920.041	CT770-868	Great Britain
920.043	CT150-159	German
920.043	CT1050-1099	Germany
920.0437	CT190-199	Slavic
920.044	CT100-1018	France
920.044	CT140-149	French
920.045	CT160-169	Italian
920.046(9)	CT180-189	Spanish/Portuguese
920.048	CT170-179	Scandinavian
920.048	CT1240-1328	Scandinavia
920.0492	CT130-139	Dutch
920.0496	CT1399-1458	Balkan
920.05	CT1820-1848	Far East
920.05	CT1500-1919	Asia
920.056	CT1870-1919	Near East
920.06	CT1920-2750	Africa
920.071	CT280-310	Canada
920.072	CT550-558	Mexico
920.0728	CT570-638	Central America
920.0729	CT339-410	West Indies
920.073	CT210-275	United States
920.08	CT640-758	South America
920.09(3-6)	CT2800-3090	Australia/New Zealand/ Oceania
920.72	CT3200-3830	Women
920.7209(3-9)	CT3230-3830	Women, By place
921.0(73/41)	CT100-120	American/English
926.601	CR14-16	Philosophy/Theory
929.(2-5)	CS25-35	Lists
929.(82/92)	JC345-347	Flags/Seals/Etc.
929.1	CS	Genealogy
929.10(5/6)	CS1	Serials/Societies
929.1025	CS5	Directories
929.103	CS6	Dictionaries/ Encyclopedias
929.106	CS2	Congresses
929.10720(4-9)	CS42-2209	Genealogy, By place
929.10720(72-8)	CS100-110	Latin America
929.107204	CS400-1059	Europe
929.1072041	CS410-499	Great Britain
929.1072043	CS610-699	Germany
929.1072048	CS890-939	Scandinavia
929.10720492	CS780-839	Low Countries
929.107205	CS1080-1549	Asia
929.107206	CS1550-1779	Africa
929.1072071	CS80-90	Canada
929.1072073	CS42-71	United States
929.107209(3-6)	CS2000-2209	Australia/New Zealand/ Oceania
929.109	CS7	History
929.2	CS38-39	Family history
929.4	CS2300-3090	Personal/Family names
929.409(4-9)	CS2347-2357	By place
929.42	CS2385-2391	Surnames
929.4209(4-9)	CS3010-3090	By place
929.44	CS2367-2377	Forenames
929.4400(5/6)	DS80.A2	Serials/Societies
929.48	CR5745-5809	Scandinavia
929.6	CR	Heraldry
929.6	CR165-185	Law/Regulations
929.6	CR1179-3395	Family
929.60(5/6)	CR1	Serials/Societies
929.6025	CR11	Directories
929.603	CR13	Dictionaries/ Encyclopedias

Dewey	LC	Descriptor
929.606	CR2	Congresses
929.6076	CR9	Museums/Exhibitions
929.609	CR151-159	History
929.7	CR4501-6305	Knighthood
929.7	CR3599-4420	Titles/Nobility
929.7	CR4480-4485	Royalty
929.7(2-3/09)	CR4801-6305	By place
929.7095	CR6000-6150	Asia
929.7096	CR6160-6190	Africa
929.7097	CR6250-6261	North America
929.7098	CR6270-6305	South America
929.72	CR4801-4941	Great Britain
929.73	CR5100-5475	Germany
929.736	CR4951-5005	Austria
929.738	CR5713-5737	Poland
929.74	CR5025-5085	France
929.75	CR5500-5580	Italy
929.76	CR5819-5889	Spain
929.769	CR5900-5925	Portugal
929.77	CR5657-5703	Russia
929.795	CR5485-5489	Greece
929.82	CR1101-1131	Ecclesiastical/Sacred
929.82	CR51-79	Crests
929.82	CR91-93	Shields
929.92	CR191-1020	Public/Official heraldry
929.92	CR101-115	Flags
929.9209(3-9)	CR199-1020	By place
929.92094	CR489-739	Europe
929.920941	CR490-524	Great Britain
929.920943	CR550-559.2	Germany
929.920944	CR540-549	France
929.920946	CR670-679	Spain
929.920947	CR610-614	European Russia
929.92095	CR749-850	Asia
929.920951	CR760-769	China
929.920952	CR800-809	Japan
929.920954	CR570-579	Italy
929.92096	CR869-920	Africa
929.92097	CR199-229	North America
929.920971	CR210-219	Canada
929.920972	CR220-229	Mexico
929.9209728	CR230-294	Central America
929.9209729	CR304-350	West Indies
929.920973	CR200-209	United States
929.92098	CR369-479	South America
929.92099(3-6)	CR930-1020	Australia/New Zealand/ Oceania
93(4-9)	CB311	Ancient history
930	D51-95	Ancient history, General
930-998.004	CB203-281	By place
930-998.004	CB305-430	By date
930.0(5/6)	D51-53	Serials/Societies
930.0099	D55	Biography
930.03	D54	Dictionaries/ Encyclopedias
930.072	D56	Historiography
930.1	CC140	Forgeries
930.1	CC	Archaeology
930.1(1-6)	D65-90	Earliest
930.101	CC72-80.6	Philosophy/Theory
930.1023	CC107	As a profession
930.1025	CC120-125	Directories
930.1028	CC135-137	Preservation
930.103	CC70	Dictionaries/ Encyclopedias
930.105	CC1-15	Serials
930.106	CC20-51	Societies/Congresses

Dewey	LC	Descriptor	Dewey	LC	Descriptor
930.107	CC83-97	Education	936.3	DH	Low Countries/Belgium
930.1092	CC110-115	Biography	936.3	DB51-99.2	History, By date
931	DS741-748.76	China, Ancient to 420	936.3	DB51	Ancient
932	DT43-154	Egypt	936.3	DH141-162	Early/Medieval to 1384
932	DT43-154	Egypt	936.3	DD375-454	By date
932	DT63-.5	Pyramids	936.3	DJ51	Social life
932	DT74-107.87	History	936.3	DL443-535	History
932	DT83-93	Egypt, Ancient to 640	936.3	DL460-478	Early and Medieval to 1387
932.004	DT71	Ethnography	936.3	DL131-133	Social life
932.004	DT71	Ethnography	936.3	DL101-291	Denmark
933	DS153-154.9	Jordan	936.3	DL660-700.9	Early to 1523 (Union of Kalmar)
933	DS122-.8	Israel/Palestine, to 70			
933	DS101-151	Israel/Palestine	936.3	DL1-87	Scandinavia, General
933	DS154.2	Jordan, Ancient to 70	936.3	DL30-33	Social life
933	DS114-128.19	History	936.3	DB30	Social life
933	DS153.7-154.55	History	936.3	DL43-87	History
933.00(5/6)	DS153.A2-.A5	Serials/Societies	936.3	DL160-183.9	Early/Medieval to 1523
933.00(5/6)	DS101	Serials/Societies	936.3	DL401-596	Norway
933.0025	DS102.9	Directories	936.3	DL431-433	Social life
933.004	DS153.5-.55	Ethnography	936.3	DL601-991	Sweden
933.004	DS113-.8	Ethnography	936.3	DL61-65	To 1387 (Northmen/ Vikings)
933.03	DU420.22-.34	Dominion era (1908-)			
933.035	DU420.32-.34	1945-1969	936.3	DL61-87	By date
933.037	DU420.32-.34	1970-	936.3	DL613-635	Social life
934	DS421-486.8	India	936.3	DL643-879	History
934	DS451-.9	India, Ancient to 647	936.30(1-2)	DL160-263.3	By date
934	DS433-481	History	936.30(1-2)	DL460-535	By date
934.004	DS430-432	Ethnography	936.30(1-2)	DL660-879	By date
935	DS67-79.9	Iraq (Babylonia/ Mesopotamia)	936.300(5/6)	DL1	Serials/Societies
			936.300(5/6)	DL101	Serials/Societies
935	DS275-287.8	Iran, Ancient to 637	936.300(5/6)	DL601	Serials/Societies
935	DS270-318.85	History	936.300(5/6)	DL401-403	Serials/Societies
935	DS70.82-79.66	History	936.3003	DL605	Gazetteers/Dictionaries
935	DS71-75	Iraq, Ancient to 637	936.3003	DL105	Gazetteers/Dictionaries
935	DS251-326	Iran (Persia)	936.3003	DL443	Dictionaries
935.00(5/6)	DS251-.5	Serials/Societies/Congresses	936.3003	DL4	Gazetteers/Dictionaries
935.00(5/6)	DS67	Serials/Societies	936.3003	DL643	Dictionaries
935.003	DS67.8	Dictionaries/Gazetteers	936.3003	DL405	Gazetteers/Dictionaries
935.003	DS253	Gazetteers	936.3004	DL141-142	Ethnography
935.004	DS268-269	Ethnography	936.3004	DL639-641	Ethnography
935.004	DS70.8	Ethnography	936.3004	DL641	Ethnography
936	DG59	Areas outside Italy	936.3004	DL441-442	Ethnography
936.(1-2)	DA	History, Great Britain	936.3004	DL41-42	Ethnography
936.1	DA930-932	To 1172	936.3006	DL1.5	Congresses
936.1	DA775-826	By date	936.3007(2)	DL645	Education/Historiography
936.1	DA758-826	History	936.30072	DL445	Historiography
936.2	DA28-592	History	936.30099	DL644	Biography
936.2	DA129-592	By date	936.30099	DL444	Biography
936.2	DA129-162	Early-1065	936.4	DC60-64	Ancient
936.2	DA20-690	England	936.4	DC60-423	By date
936.3	DH141-207	By date	936.4	DC	France
936.3	DB881-898	Liechtenstein	936.4	DH571-692	By date
936.3	DH141-162	Early/Medieval to 1384	936.4	DH401-811	Belgium
936.3	DD341-454	History	936.4	DQ78-110	Early and Medieval to 1516
936.3	DJ151-292	By date	936.4	DH503-692	History
936.3	DJ151-152	Early and Medieval to 1555	936.4	DQ	Switzerland
936.3	DH141-207	By date	936.4	DC35-423	History
936.3	DH95-207	History	936.4	DH571-692	By date
936.3	DJ95-292	History	936.4	DQ36-39	Social life
936.3	DD121-124	Earliest to 481	936.4	D70	Celts
936.3	DB35-99.2	History	936.4	DH571-584	Early and Medieval to 1555
936.3	DD	Germany	936.4	DQ51-210	History
936.3	DB51-59	To Medieval	936.4	DC33	Social life
936.3	DD121-289	By date	936.4	DQ79-84	Celts and Romans (To 687)
936.3	DB891-894	History	936.40(1-2)	DQ78-210	By date
936.3	DH95-207	History	936.400(5/6)	DQ1	Serials/Societies
936.3	DD84-262	History	936.4003	DQ51	Dictionaries

Dewey	LC	Descriptor
936.4003	DQ14	Gazetteers/Dictionaries
936.4004	DQ48-49	Ethnography
936.4006	DQ2	Congresses
936.4007(2)	DQ52.8-.95	Historiography
936.40099	DQ52-.7	Biography
936.6	DP48-.9	Social life
936.6	DP91-96	Earliest to 711
936.6	DP532-.7	Social life
936.6	DP535-682.2	History
936.6	DP558-618	Early to 1143
936.6	DP1-402	Spain
936.6	DP501-802	Portugal
936.6	DP	Spain/Portugal
936.60(1-2)	DP91-272.4	History, By date
936.60(1-3)	DP558-682.2	By date
936.600(5/6)	DP1	Serials/Societies
936.600(5/6)	DP501	Serials/Societies/Congresses
936.60025	DP513	Directories
936.60025	DP11	Directories
936.6003	DP514	Gazetteers/Dictionaries
936.6003	DP535	Dictionaries
936.6003	DP12	Gazetteers/Dictionaries
936.6004	DP52-53	Ethnography
936.6004	DP533-534.5	Ehtnography
936.6006	DP2	Congresses
936.60072	DP63-.83	Historiography
936.60072	DP536.8-.96	Historiography
936.60099	DP536	Biography
936.60099	DP58	Biography
937	DE86-92	Ancient to 476
937	DG11-365	Roman Empire to 476
937	DG	Italy
937	DE	Mediterranean/Greco-Roman
937	DG201-365	History, Ancient Italy
937	DE46-71	Civilization
937	DE80-100	History
937-938	DE72	During life of Christ
937.(1-7)	DG70	Other towns
937.(1-7)	DG51-55	Areas inside Italy
937.(1-9)	DG51-59	Local history
937.(8-9)	DG59	Areas outside Italy
937.0(1-9)	DG221-365	By date
937.0(8-9)	DG311-365	Decline/Fall (284-476 AD)
937.00(5/6)	DE1-4	Serials/Societies
937.003	DE5	Dictionaries
937.003	DG16	Dictionaries
937.004	DG75-190	Ethnography
937.004	DE73	Ethnography
937.005	DG11	Serials
937.006	DG12.5	Congresses
937.006	DG12	Societies
937.007	DG206.5	Education
937.007	DE15	Education
937.0072	DE8-9	Historiography
937.0072	DG205-206	Historiography
937.0074	DG12.2-.3	Museums/Exhibitions
937.0099	DE7	Biography
937.0099	DG203-204	Biography
937.01	DG231-269	Kings/Republic (753-727 BC)
937.01	DG233-.9	Foundations/Kings (753-510 BC)
937.02	DG235-269	Republic (509-27 BC)
937.03	DG237-238	Conquest of Italy (343-290 BC)
937.04	DG241-253	Conquest of Med. (264-133 BC)
937.04	DG250-253	East/West Wars (200-133 BC)
937.04	DG242-249.4	Punic/Illyrain Wars (264-201)
937.05	DG261-267	Julius Caesar/Triumvirate
937.05	DG268-269	2nd Triumvirate (43-31 BC)
937.05	DG256-260	Marius/Sulla (111-78 BC)
937.05	DG253.5-269	Fall of Republic/New Empire
937.06	DG272	Civilization/Social life
937.06	DG269.5-365	Empire (27 BC-476 AD)
937.060099	DG274-.3	Biography
937.07	DG275-309.3	Constitutional Empire
937.5	DG221-225	Pre-Roman/Etruria/Etruscans
937.6	DG61-69	Rome (City) to 476
938	DE86-92	Ancient to 476
938	DF207-241	History
938	DE86-92	Ancient to 476
938	DE	Mediterranean/Greco-Roman
938	DE80-100	History
938	DE46-71	Civilization
938	DF10-289	Ancient Greece
938	DF	Greece
938	DE80-100	History
938.(1-9)	DF251-289	Local history/Description
938.0(1-9)	DF220-241	By date
938.00(5/6)	DE1-4	Serials/Societies
938.0025	DF16	Dictionaries
938.003	DE5	Dictionaries
938.004	DF135	Ethnography
938.005	DF10	Serials
938.006	DF11	Societies
938.007	DE15	Education
938.0072	DE8-9	Historiography
938.0074	DF11.2-.3	Museums/Exhibitions
938.0099	DE7	Biography
938.01	DF220-221	Mythical/Minoan/Mycenaean
938.02	DF222-224	Early/Tyrants (775-500 BC)
938.03	DF225-226	Persian wars (499-479 BC)
938.04	DF227-228	Athenian/Pericles (479-431 BC)
938.05	DF229-230	Peloponnesian War (431-404 BC)
938.07	DF233-.8	Macedonia/Philip (359-336 BC)
938.07	DF234-.9	Alexander the Great
938.07	DF231-232	Spartan/Theban (404-362 BC)
938.08	DF235-238.9	Hellenistic (323-146 BC)
938.09	DF239-241	Roman (146 BC-476 AD)
938.09	DE72	During life of Christ
938.1	DR954-960.5	Early
938.1	DR922	Social life
938.1	DR927-977.25	History
938.1	DR954-977.25	By date
938.1	DR901-998	Albania
938.100(5/6)	DR901	Serials/Societies
938.1003	DR907	Gazetteers/Dictionaries
938.1003	DR927	Dictionaries
938.1004	DR923-925	Ethnography
938.1006	DR903.5	Congresses
938.10099	DR928-934	Biography

Dewey	LC	Descriptor
939	DE72	During life of Christ
939.2	DR401-741	Turkey
939.2	DR432	Social life
939.2	DR481	Early to 1281/1453
939.2	DR436-603	History
939.2	DR481-603	By date
939.2	DS155-156	Asia Minor
939.200(5/6)	DR401	Serials/Societies
939.20025	DR413	Directories
939.2003	DR414	Gazetteers/Dictionaries
939.2003	DR436	Dictionaries
939.2004	DR434-435	Ethnography
939.2006	DR401.2	Congresses
939.2007(2)	DR438.8-.95	Education/Historiography
939.20099	DR438-.7	Biography
939.37	DS54-.95	Cyprus
939.37	DS54.6	Cyprus, Ancient to 640
939.37	DS54.6	To 1571
939.4	DS62.2-.25	Near East, Ancient to 640
939.4	DS61-66	Near East, History (General)
939.4	DS41-66	Near East
939.400(5/6)	DS41-.5	Serials/Societies/Congresses
939.4003	DS43	Gazetteers/Dictionaries
939.43	DS96-.2	Ancient to 640
939.43	DS94.9-98.3	History
939.43	DS92-99	Syria
939.4300(5/6)	DS92	Serials/Societies
939.430025	DS92.8	Directories
939.43003	DS92.6	Gazetteers
939.43004	DS94.7-.8	Ethnography
939.44	DS80.7-87.53	History
939.44	DS81-82	Lebanon, Ancient to 640
939.44	DS80-90	Lebanon
939.44003	DS80.A5	Gazetteers/Dictionaries
939.44004	DS80.5	Ethnography
939.49	DS221-244.63	History
939.49	DS201-248	Arabian peninsula/Saudi Arabia
939.49	DS38	Arab countries, Ancient to 622
939.49	DS231	Ancient to 622
939.4900(5/6)	DS201	Serials/Societies
939.49004	DS218-219	Ethnography
939.55	DS181-184	Ancient to 640
939.55	DS161-195.5	Armenia
939.6	DS327-329.4	Central Asia
939.6	DS358	Afghanistan, Ancient to 640
939.6	DS350-375	Afghanistan
939.7	DT160-177	North Africa
939.7	DT168-171	Ancient to 640
939.7	DT168-169.5	Carthaginian era
939.7	DT167-176	History
939.71	DT179.2-.9	Northwest Africa
939.71	DT283.7-295.55	History
939.71	DT301-330	Morocco
939.71	DT288	Algeria, Ancient to 647
939.71	DT301-330	Morocco
939.71	DT271-299	Algeria
939.71	DT271-299	Algeria
939.71	DT313.7-325.92	History
939.71	DT318	Morocco, Ancient to 647
939.71004	DT283-.6	Ethnography
939.71004	DT313-.6	Ethnography
939.71004	DT313-.6	Ethnography
939.71004	DT283-.6	Ethnography
939.73	DT241-269	Tunisia
939.73	DT253.4-264.49	History
939.73	DT258	Tunisia, Ancient to 647
939.73	DT241-269	Tunisia
939.73004	DT253-.2	Ethnography
939.73004	DT253-.2	Ethnography
939.74	DT211-239	Libya
939.74	DT228	Libya, Ancient to 644
939.74	DT223.2-236	History
939.74004	DT223-.2	Ethnography
939.74004	DT223-.2	Ethnography
939.8	DB921-957	History
939.8	DB927-957	By date
939.8	DB927.3	Ancient
939.8	DJK77	Pannonia
939.8	DB901-999	Hungary
939.8	DR65-93.34	History
939.8	DR215-267.5	History
939.8	DR1228	Social life
939.8	DR73.7-93.34	By date
939.8	DR	Balkan peninsula
939.8	DR63	Social life
939.8	DR51-98	Bulgaria
939.8	DR1232-1321	History
939.8	DR1202-2285	Yugoslavia
939.8	DR1259-1312	By date
939.8	DR1259-1265	Early and Medieval
939.8	DR238-239.22	Early Roman period
939.8	DR75-77.8	1st Bulgarian Empire (681-1018)
939.8	DR238-267.5	By date
939.8	DR201-296	Romania
939.8	DR74-81.6	Early and Medieval
939.8	DR212	Social life
939.8	DR22-23	Social life
939.8	DB920.5	Social life
939.800(5/6)	DR1202	Serials/Societies
939.800(5/6)	DR201	Serials/Societies
939.800(5/6)	DR1	Serials/Societies
939.800(5/6)	DR51	Serials/Societies
939.80025	DR1212	Directories
939.80025	DR53.7	Directories
939.8003	DR53	Gazetteers/Dictionaries
939.8003	DR5	Gazetteers/Dictionaries
939.8003	DR204	Gazetteers/Dictionaries
939.8003	DR65	Dictionaries
939.8003	DR1209	Gazetteers/Dictionaries
939.8003	DR215	Dictionaries
939.8004	DR213-214	Ethnography
939.8004	DR24-27	Ethnography
939.8004	DR64	Ethnography
939.8004	DR1229-1230	Ethnography
939.8006	DR1205	Congresses
939.8006	DR201.2	Congresses
939.8006	DR1.5	Congresses
939.8007(2)	DR216.7-.92	Education/Historiography
939.8007(2)	DR1239-1243	Education/Historiography
939.80072	DR66.7-.97	Education/Historiography
939.80074	DR51.3-.4	Museums/Exhibitions
939.80099	DR1233-1235	Biography
939.80099	DR216	Biography
939.80099	DR66	Biography
940	D900-1075	Europe, General
940	DAW1031-1051	History
940	DAW	Central Europe
940	DAW1001	Serials/Societies
940	DAW1024	Social life
940	DAW1004	Congresses

Dewey	LC	Descriptor
940	DAW1006	Gazetteers/Dictionaries
940-949	D965-975	By place
940-990	G369-370	Medieval voyages/Travels
940-990	G400-401	Travels, 1400-1520
940-990	G419-503	1521-
940.(1-21)	DAW1046	Early to 1500
940.(1-5)	DAW1046-1051	By date
940.(1-559)	D911-923	By date
940.(28-48)	DAW1048	1815-1918
940.(4/54)	E745	Military history
940.(45/545)	E746	Naval history
940.004	DAW1026-1028	Ethnography
940.1	CB351-355	Medieval history
940.2(1-7)	DAW1047	1500-1815
940.24	D251-270	30 Years' War
940.252	D274.5-.6	Anglo/French War
940.252	D275-276	War of Revolution (1667-1668)
940.252	D277-278	Dutch War
940.2525	D279-280	War of Grand Alliance
940.2532	D291-294	War of Austrian Succession
940.2534	D297	Seven Years' War
940.27	D304-309	French Revolution
940.3	D501-680	World War I
940.30222	D522-528	Pictures/Etc.
940.305	D501	Serials
940.306	D502	Societies
940.306	D504	Congresses
940.3074	D503	Museums/Exhibitions
940.3092	D507	Biography
940.311	D511-520	Causes
940.3144	D652-658	Reconstruction
940.32	D610-621	Diplomacy
940.4	D529-578	Military operations
940.41273	D570-578	United States
940.4143	D531-538	German
940.4144	D530-549	Western
940.4144	D540	Hungarian
940.4144	D544-545	Anglo/French combined
940.4144	D539	Austrian
940.4144	D548-549	French
940.4144	D546-547	English
940.4145	D569	Italian
940.4147	D551-559	Russian
940.4147	D550-569	Eastern
940.416	D566-568	Turkey/Near East
940.439	D641-651	Peace
940.44	D600-607	Aerial operations
940.45	D581-582	Anglo-German
940.45	D583-584	Franco-Austrian
940.45	D580-589	Naval operations
940.451	D590-595	Submarine
940.46	D663-680	Celebration/Monuments
940.467	D609	Registers of the dead
940.48(1-2)	D640	Personal narratives
940.5	DAW1049	1918-1945
940.5(1-2)	D720-728	Between World Wars
940.5(405/31)	D803-804	Atrocities
940.53	D731-838	World War II
940.5305	D731	Serials
940.5306	D734	Congresses
940.5306	D732	Societies
940.53074	D733	Museums/Exhibitions
940.53092	D736	Biography
940.5311	D741-742	Causes
940.5312	D812-821	Peace
940.53144	D824-829	Reconstruction
940.5316	D801	Alien enemies
940.532	D748-754	Diplomatic
940.5336	D802	Occupied areas
940.54	D755-769	Military operations
940.54002	D745	Satire/Caricature
940.541	D794	Cavalry
940.541	D793	Tank
940.54127(1/2)	D768	Canada/Mexico
940.541273	D769	United States
940.542	D756-769	By place
940.542(1-3)	D766	Balkan/Middle East/Africa
940.542(5-6)	D767	Far East/Pacific battles
940.5421	D765	Poland/Czechoslovakia/Etc.
940.5421	D756-763	Western
940.542141	D759-760	Great Britain
940.542143	D757	Germany
940.542144	D761-762	France
940.5421495	D766.3-.32	Greece
940.5421497	D766.6-.62	Yugoslavia
940.5421498	D766.4-.42	Romania
940.5423	D766.8-.97	Africa
940.5425	D767.2-.82	China/Japan/Philippines/Etc.
940.5425	D764-767	Eastern
940.5426	D767.9-.99	Pacific islands
940.544	D785-792	Aerial operations
940.545	D775	Anglo-Italian
940.545	D772.3	Russo-German
940.545	D770-779	Naval operations
940.545	D771-772	Anglo-German
940.5451	D778-784	Submarine operations
940.545952	D777	Japanese
940.545973	D773-774	American
940.546	D830-838	Celebrations
940.5467	D797	Registers of the dead
940.547	D805	Prisoners
940.547(5-6)	D806-807	Medical/Sanitation
940.5477	D809	Relief
940.548(1-2)	D811	Personal narrative
940.55	D839-845.2	Post war
940.55	D1050-1065	1945-
940.55	D1058-1065	Political/Diplomatic history
940.55(4-6)	D842.5-847	1945-1965
940.55(4-8)	DAW1050	1945-1989
940.55(6-9)	D848-850	1965-
940.550(5/6)	D839	Serials/Societies
940.55004	D1056	Ethnography
940.550099	D1070-1075	Biography
940.550099	D839.5-.7	Biography
940.5505	D1050	Serials
940.5506	D839.2	Congresses
940.5507	D1050.8-.82	Education
940.558-	DAW1051	1989-
941	DA	History, Great Britain
941.(6-9)	DA990-995	Local history
941.0(6-85)	DA10-18	Empire/Commonwealth
941.1	DA750-890	Scotland
941.1	DA758-826	History
941.1(1-4)	DA880-890	Local history
941.10(1-8)	DA775-826	By date
941.10(2-4)	DA783	1278-1488
941.10(4-5)	DA784-790	1488-1603
941.10(61-69)	DA800-807	1603-1707
941.10(69-73)	DA809-814	1707-1800
941.10(73-81)	DA815-818	19th century
941.100(5/6)	DA750	Serials/Societies

Dewey	LC	Descriptor
941.1005	DA753	Yearbooks
941.10074	DA751-.5	Museums/Exhibitions
941.101	DA778	844-1057
941.102	DA779-782	1057-1278
941.108(2-5)	DA821-826	20th century
941.5	DA900-995	Ireland
941.5	DA909-965	History
941.5(1-84)	DA930-965	By date
941.50(3-5)	DA933-937	1172-1603
941.500(5/6)	DA900	Serials/Societies
941.501	DA930-932	To 1172
941.506	DA938-946	17th century
941.507	DA947-949	18th century
941.5081	DA950-958	19th century
941.5082	DA959-965	20th century
942	DA20-690	England
942	DA40-47	Political/Diplomatic
942	DA110-115	Social life
942	DA28-592	History
942.(1-8)	DA670	Local history
942.(2-8)	DA690	Other cities/Towns
942.0(1-8)	DA129-592	By date
942.0(2-46)	DA170-260	1066-1485
942.0(5-8)	DA300-592	1485-
942.00(5-6)	DA20-22	Serials/Societies
942.004	DA120-125	Ethnography
942.0099	DA28	Biography
942.01	DA129-162	Early-1065
942.05	DA310-360	Tudors (1485-1603)
942.052	DA331-339	Henry VIII
942.055	DA350-360	Elizabeth I (1558-1603)
942.06	DA370-462	1603-1702
942.06(1-2)	DA400-429	Civil War/Commonwealth
942.06(1-2)	DA385-398	Stuarts (Early)
942.06(4-9)	DA430-462	Stuarts (Late)
942.071	DA499	George I (1714-1727)
942.072	DA500	George II (1727-1760)
942.073	DA505-522	George III (1760-1820)
942.074	DA537-538	George IV (1820-1830)
942.075	DA539-542	William IV (1830-1837)
942.08(2-5)	DA566-592	20th century
942.081	DA550-565	Victoria (1837-1901)
942.1	DA675-689	London
942.1	DA677-684	History
942.1(3-7)	DA685	Parishes
942.2526	D281-283	War of Spanish Succession
942.9	DA713.5-722.1	History
942.9	DA711.5	Social life
942.9	DA700-745	Wales
942.900(5/6)	DA700	Serials/Societies
942.9004	DA712	Ethnography
942.90099	DA710	Biography
943	DD301-454	Prussia
943	DD341-454	History
943	DD	Germany
943	DAW1024	Social life
943	DD84-262	History
943	DAW1031-1051	History
943	DAW	Central Europe
943.(004)	DD51-78	Social life/Ethnography
943.(004)	DD335-339	Social life/Ethnography
943.(1)1-5	DD801	By state/Province
943.(1-5)	DD701-901	Local history
943.(7-9)	DB	Austria/Hungary/Czechoslovakia
943.0(1-43)	DD375-387	To 1640
943.0(1-76)	DD375-454	By date
943.0(1-87)	DD121-289	By date
943.0(13-25)	DD126-155	Medieval Empire (481-1273)
943.0(13-29)	DD125-174.6	To 1519
943.0(3-7)	DD175-289	1519-
943.0(34-57)	DD389-454	1640-
943.0(43-6)	DD190-199	1648-1815
943.0(6-84)	DD201-289	19th century-
943.0(6-84)	DD415-446	19th century
943.0(7-82)	DD206-216	1815-1871
943.000(5/6)	DAW1001	Serials/Societies
943.0003	DAW1006	Gazetteers/Dictionaries
943.0006	DAW1004	Congresses
943.0025	DD15.5	Directories
943.003	DD14	Gazetteers/Dictionaries
943.003	DD341	Dictionaries
943.003	DD308	Gazetteers/Dictionaries
943.003	DD84	Dictionaries
943.004	DAW1026-1028	Ethnography
943.005	DD301	Serials
943.005	DD1	Serials
943.006	DD2	Societies
943.006	DD302	Societies
943.0072	DD86	Historiography
943.0072	DD345	Historiography
943.0074	DD1.5-.6	Museums/Exhibitions
943.0099	DD85-.8	Biography
943.0099	DD343-.8	Biography
943.012	DD121-124	Earliest to 481
943.013	DD128	Merovingians (481-752)
943.014	DD129-135	Carolingians (752-911)
943.02(6-7)	DD156-174	House of Habsburg/Luxemburg
943.02(6-9)	DD156-174.6	1273-1519
943.021	DD127-135	481-918
943.022	DD136-144	919-1125
943.022	DD136-140.7	House of Saxony (919-1024)
943.023	DD141-144	House of Franconia (1024-1125)
943.024	DD145-155	Hohenstaufen (1125-1273)
943.03	DD175-189	1519-1648 (Reformation/Counter)
943.031	DD181-183	Peasants' War (1524-1525)
943.031	DD184	Schmalkaldic League (1530-1547)
943.041	DD189	Thirty Years' War (1618-1648)
943.05	DD390-414.9	17th-18th centuries
943.05(3-4)	DD406-407.5	Silesian Wars (1740-1745)
943.055	DD409-412.8	Seven Years' War (1756-1763)
943.07(3-6)	DD423	Confederation (1816-1866)
943.076	DD436-440	Austro-Prussian War (1866)
943.08(3-4)	DD448-451	1871-1918 (New Empire)
943.08(3-4)	DD217-231	New Empire (1871-1918)
943.08(5-7)	DD233-289	Revolution/Republic
943.081	DD442	North German Confederation
943.082	DD446	Franco-German War (1870-1871)
943.084	DD228.8	World War I (1914-1918)
943.085	DD452-454	Between World Wars
943.086	DD253-256.5	Hitler
943.086	DD256	World War II
943.087	DD258-262	West Germany
943.087	DD257-.4	Allied occupation (1945-)

Dewey	LC	Descriptor
943.1087	DD280-289	East Germany
943.155	DD851-900	Berlin
943.5518	DD900.2	Bonn
943.6	DB1-879	Austria
943.6	DB	Austria/Hungary/Czechoslovakia
943.6	DB35-99.2	History
943.6	DB30	Social life
943.6(1-3)	DB101-879	Local history/Description
943.60(2-4)	DB51-99.2	History, By date
943.60(3-53)	DB80-99.2	19th-20th centuries
943.600(5/6)	DB1-5	Serials/Societies
943.6003	DB14	Gazetteers
943.6003	DB35	Dictionaries
943.6004	DB33-34	Ethnography
943.60072	DB36.8-.9	Historiography
943.60099	DB36-.7	Biography
943.602	DB51-59	To Medieval
943.6022	DB51	481-976
943.6024	DB56-57	1246-1273
943.6025	DB58-59	1273-1500
943.603	DB65.2-77	1521-1815
943.6043	DB83	Revolution (1848)
943.605	DB96-99.2	Republic (1918-)
943.6052	DB99-.1	WW II/Occupation (1938-1955)
943.6053	DB99.2	1955-
943.613	DB841-860	Vienna
943.648	DB891-894	History
943.648	DB881-898	Liechtenstein
943.64800(5/6)	DB881	Serials/Societies
943.7	DB2044-2232	History
943.7	DB2000-3150	Czechoslovakia
943.7(1-3)	DB2300-2650	Local history/Description
943.700(5/6)	DB2000	Serials/Societies
943.70025	DB2009	Directories
943.7003	DB2007	Gazetteers/Dictionaries
943.7004	DB2040-2043	Ethnography
943.7006	DB2003	Congresses
943.70074	DB2001-2002	Museums/Exhibitions
943.702(1-24)	DB2080-2133	Early to 1526
943.7021	DB2085-2088	To 904 (Great Moravian Empire)
943.7022	DB2088.7-2133	907-1526
943.7022(3-4)	DB2135-2181	Hapsburg rule (1526-1918)
943.70223	DB2088.7-2091	907-1306 (Premyslid Dynasty)
943.70224	DB2095-2111	1306-1526 (Luxembourg Dynasty)
943.7023	DB2145-2171	1526-1815
943.70232	DB2145-2151	1526-1620
943.70233	DB2155-2171	1620-1800
943.7024	DB2175-2182	1815-1915
943.703	DB2185-2211	1918-1945
943.7032	DB2195-2202	1918-1939 (Republic)
943.7033	DB2205-2211	1939-1945 (World War II)
943.704	DB2215-2232	1945-
943.7042	DB2215-2222	1945-1968 (Reform/Repression)
943.7043	DB2225-2232	1968-
943.712	DB2600-2649	Prague
943.72	DB2300-2421	Moravia
943.73	DB2700-3150	Slovakia
943.8	DK4123-4442	History
943.8	DK4010-4800	Poland
943.8	DK	Russia/Poland
943.8(1-6)	DK4600-4800	Local history/Description
943.80(4-5)0099	DK4419-4420	Biography
943.800(5/6)	DK4010	Serials/Societies
943.8003	DK4030	Gazetteers/Dictionaries
943.8004	DK4120-4122	Ethnography
943.8006	DK4018	Congresses
943.80072	DK4139	Historiography
943.80099	DK4130-4138	Biography
943.802	DK4186-4348	Early to 1795
943.802(2-3)	DK4189-4289	To 1572
943.802(4-5)	DK4290-4328	1572-1763
943.8022	DK4210	To 960
943.8022	DK4211-4249	960-1386
943.8023	DK4249.7-4289	1386-1575
943.8025	DK4328.9-4348	Partition (1763-1795)
943.803	DK4348.5-4395	1795-1918
943.8033	DK4366-4378	Revolution (1863-1864)
943.8033	DK4379.5-4395	1864-1918
943.804	DK4409.4	Coup D'Etat (1926)
943.804	DK4404-4409	Wars (1918-1921)
943.804(4-53)	DK4397-4420	1918-1945
943.805(4-)	DK4429-4442	1945- (People's Republic)
943.805092	DK4434-4435	Biography
943.8053	DK4410-4415	1939-1945
943.82	DK4650-4685	Gdansk (Danzig)
943.84	DK4610-4645	Warsaw (Warszawa)
943.86	DK4700-4735	Krakow (Cracow)
943.9	DB921-957	History
943.9	DB901-999	Hungary
943.9	DB927-957	By date
943.9	DB920.5	Social life
943.9(1-9)	DB974.9-999	Local history/Description
943.90(43-53)	DB947-957	20th century
943.900(5/6)	DB901	Serials/Societies
943.9003	DB904	Dictionaries/Gazetteers
943.9003	DB921	Dictionaries
943.9004	DB919	Ethnography
943.90099	DB922	Biography
943.902	DB929-.9	Arpad Dynasty (894-1301)
943.903	DB930-931.9	Elective kings (1301-1526)
943.904	DB932-933	1526-1918 (Turkish/Hapsburgs)
943.9041	DB932-.3	1526-1686 (Turkish)
943.9042	DB932.5-934	1686-1918 (Hapsburgs)
943.9043	DB933-945	1867-1918 (Austria-Hungary)
943.9043	DB940-945	1849-1900
943.9051	DB955	1918-1945
943.9052	DB956-957	1945-1956 (Revolution of 1956)
943.9053	DB956	1953-
943.912	DB981-999	Budapest
944	DC35-423	History
944	DC	France
944	DC33	Social life
944.(1-9)	DC600-801	Local history/Description
944.0(1-83)	DC60-423	By date
944.0025	DC15	Directories
944.003	DC35	Dictionaries
944.003	DC14	Dictionaries/Gazetteers
944.004	DC34-.5	Ethnography
944.005	DC1	Serials
944.006	DC2	Societies
944.007	DC36.9-.985	Education
944.0099	DC36-.8	Biography
944.013	DC64.7-69.85	Merovingian Dynasty (486-751)

Dewey	LC	Descriptor
944.014	DC70-73.9	Carolingian Dynasty (751-987)
944.02	DC82-120	987-1589 (Royal power)
944.021	DC82-94	House of Capet (987-1328)
944.022	DC87-.7	Philip I-Louis VII (1060-1180)
944.023	DC90-91.6	Philip II-Louis IX (1180-1270)
944.024	DC91.7-93.7	Philip III-Charles IV
944.025	DC95-109	House of Valois (1328-1589)
944.026	DC101-105.9	Charles VI, VII (1380-1461)
944.027	DC106-109	Louis XI-Louis XII (1461-1515)
944.028	DC110-120	House of Angouleme (1515-1589)
944.03	DC120.8-138	Bourbons (1589-1789)
944.03(4-5)	DC133-138	Louis XV, XVI (1715-1789)
944.031	DC122-.9	Henry IV (1589-1610)
944.032	DC123-.9	Louis XIII (1610-1643)
944.04	DC139-249	Revolution & Napoleon
944.041	DC161-185.9	Assemblies
944.042	DC175-190.8	First Republic (1792-1799)
944.043	DC175-185.9	Nat'l. convention (1792-1795)
944.044	DC183-185	Reign of Terror (1793-1794)
944.045	DC186-190.8	Directory (1795-1799)
944.046	DC191-193.8	Consulate (1799-1804)
944.05	DC197-218	First Empire (1804-1815)
944.06	DC256-260	Restoration (1815-1830)
944.061	DC256-257	Louis XVIII (1815-1830)
944.062	DC258-259.5	Charles X (1824-1830)
944.063	DC266	Louis Philippe (1830-1848)
944.07	DC270-280	Second Republic/Empire (1848-1870)
944.08	DC281-423	1870 to present
944.081	DC334-354.9	Third Republic (1870-1945)
944.0812	DC281-354	1870-1899 (Paris Commune)
944.0814	DC385	World War I (1914-1918)
944.0815	DC389-396	Between wars (1918-1939)
944.0816	DC397	World War II (1940-1946)
944.082	DC398-409	Fourth Republic (1947-1958)
944.083	DC411-423	Fifth Republic (1958-)
944.36	DC701-790	Paris
944.949	DC941-947	Monaco
945	DG	Italy
945	DG401-583	Medieval/Modern (476-)
945	DG461-583	History
945.(1-3)	DG600-684.72	Northern Italy
945.(5-6)	DG691-817.3	Central Italy
945.(7-8)	DG819-875	Southern Italy
945.0(1-4)	DG503-529	476-1268
945.0(1-5)	DG500-537	Medieval (476-1492)
945.0(1-9)	DG500-583	By date
945.0(3-4)	DG520-529	German emperors (962-1268)
945.0(4-5)	DG530-537.8	1268-1492
945.0(6-9)	DG538-583	1492-
945.0(84-91)	DG555-575	Monarchy (1871-1947)
945.0025	DG413	Directories
945.003	DG415	Gazetteers/Dictionaries
945.003	DG461	Dictionaries
945.004	DG455-457	Ethnography
945.005	DG401	Serials
945.006	DG402	Societies
945.007	DG465.8	Education
945.0072	DG465-.7	Historiography
945.0099	DG463-.8	Biography
945.01	DG510	Byzantine exarchate (553-568)
945.01	DG511-514.7	Lombard kingdom
945.01	DG506-509	Goth kingdom (489-553)
945.02	DG515-529	Frankish emperors (774-962)
945.05	DG532-537.8	Renaissance
945.07	DG539-545.8	16th-18th centuries
945.08(2-4)	DG551-564	19th century
945.082	DG548-549	Kingdom of Italy
945.082	DG546-549	Napoleonic (1792-1815)
945.083	DG552-554.5	Risorgimento (1848-1871)
945.084	DG553-.5	Austro-Sardinian War
945.091	DG571-572	Fascism (1919-1945)
945.092	DG576-579	Republic (1948-)
945.1	DG610-618.75	Piedmont
945.182	DG631-645	Genoa
945.2	DG651-664.5	Milan/Lombardy
945.31	DG670-684.72	Venice
945.5	DG731-759.3	Tuscany/Florence
945.632	DG803-818	Modern Rome
945.634	DG791-800	Papal states/Vatican
945.73	DG840-857.5	Naples
945.8(1-2)	DG861-875	Sicily
945.8(5)	DG831	Sicily/Malta
945.85	DG987-999	Malta/Maltese islands
946	DP1-402	Spain
946	DP48-.9	Social life
946.(1-88)	DP285-402	Local history/Description
946.(9)	DP	Spain/Portugal
946.0(1-8)	DP91-272.4	History, By period (711-1516)
946.0(2-3)	DP97.3-160.8	
946.0(4-8)	DP161-272.4	Modern Spain (1516-)
946.0(6-74)	DP201-232.6	19th century
946.0(74-8)	DP233-272.4	1886-
946.00(5/6)	DP1	Serials/Societies
946.0025	DP11	Directories
946.003	DP12	Gazetteers/Dictionaries
946.004	DP52-53	Ethnography
946.006	DP2	Congresses
946.0072	DP63-.83	Historiography
946.0099	DP58	Biography
946.01	DP91-96	Earliest to 711
946.03	DP161.5-166	Fernando V/Isabel I (1479-1516)
946.04	DP170-189	Habsburgs (1516-1700)
946.054	DP192-200.8	Bourbons (1700-1808)
946.06	DP204-208	Napoleonic period (1808-1814)
946.07(3-4)	DP222-232.6	1868-1886
946.072	DP212-220	Bourbon restoration (1814-1868)
946.081	DP250-269.9	Second Republic (1931-1939)
946.082	DP269.97-271	1939-1975 (Franco)
946.083	DP272-.4	1975-
946.41	DP350-374	Madrid
946.7	DB2017-2022	Social life
946.79	DC921-930	Andorra
946.9	DP501-802	Portugal
946.9	DP535-682.2	History

Dewey	LC	Descriptor
946.9	DP532-.7	Social life
946.9(1-9)	DP702-802	Local history/Description
946.90(1-2)	DP568-629	House of Burgundy (1095-1640)
946.90(1-4)	DP558-682.2	By date
946.90(2-4)	DP620-682.2	1580-
946.900(5/6)	DP501	Serials/Societies/Congresses
946.90025	DP513	Directories
946.9003	DP535	Dictionaries
946.9003	DP514	Gazetteers/Dictionaries
946.9004	DP533-534.5	Ehtnography
946.90072	DP536.8-.96	Historiography
946.90099	DP536	Biography
946.901	DP558-618	Early to 1143
946.902	DP622-629	1580-1640 (Spanish Dynasty)
946.903(2-4)	DP632-644.9	House of Braganza (1640-1816)
946.903(4-6)	DP645-669	1816-1908
946.9035	DP650-657	Revolution/Wars of 1820-1840
946.904	DP670-682.2	20th century
946.904	DP674-682.2	Revolution/Republic (1910-)
946.9425	DP752-776	Lisbon
947	DJK	Eastern Europe (General)
947	DJK24	Social life
947	DK510-651	Russia
947	DK32-.7	Social life
947	DK	Russia/Poland
947	DK1-949.5	Russia (Soviet Union)
947	DK36-290.3	History
947.(2-9)	DK501-949.5	Local history/Description
947.0(1-45)	DK70-112	To 1613
947.0(46-83)	DK112.8-264.8	House of Romanov (1613-1917)
947.00(5/6)	DK1	Serials/Societies
947.000(5/6)	DJK1	Serials/Societies
947.0003	DJK6	Gazetteers/Dictionaries
947.0004	DJK26-28	Ethnography
947.0006	DJK1.5	Congresses
947.0007	DJK35-36	Education
947.00072	DJK32-34	Historiography
947.00099	DJK31	Biography
947.003	DK14	Gazetteers/Dictionaries
947.004	DK33-35	Ethnography
947.006	DK2.5	Congresses
947.05	DL733-743	Northern War (1700-1721)
947.08(4-54)	DK266-290.3	Soviet regime (1917-)
947.08400(5-)	DK266.A2	Serials/Etc.
947.0840072	DK266.A33	Historiography
947.0841	DK265-.95	Revolution (1917-1921)
947.0842	DK267-273	Stalin (1925-1953)
947.0842	DK273	World War II (1939-1945)
947.085(2-3)	DK274-282	1953-1982
947.0854	DK285-290	1982-
947.312	DK588-609	Moscow
947.4	DK502.3-.7	Baltic States
947.41	DK503-.95	Estonia
947.43	DK504-.95	Latvia
947.45	DK541-579	Leningrad
947.5	DK505-.95	Lithuania
947.65	DK507-.95	Belorussia
947.652	DK507.92-.939	Minsk
947.7	DJK61-66	Black Sea region
947.71	DK508-.95	Ukraine
947.714	DK508.92-.939	Kiev

Dewey	LC	Descriptor
947.718	DJK71-76	Carpathian Mountain region
947.75	DK509.1-.95	Moldavia/Bessarabia
947.91	DK690-699.5	Azerbaijan
947.92	DK680-689.5	Armenia
947.95	DK670-679.5	Georgia
948	DL1-87	Scandinavia, General
948	DL43-87	History
948	DL30-33	Social life
948.(2-8)	DL576-596	Local history/Description
948.(6-8)	DL971-991	Local history/Description
948.0(1-2)	DL61-65	To 1387 (Northmen/Vikings)
948.0(1-8)	DL61-87	By date
948.0(3-7)	DL75-81	1387-1900
948.00(5/6)	DL1	Series/Societies
948.003	DL4	Gazetteers/Dictionaries
948.004	DL41-42	Ethnography
948.006	DL1.5	Congresses
948.08	DL83-87	1901-
948.1	DL443-535	History
948.1	DL401-596	Norway
948.1	DL4?1-433	Social life
948.1	G778-810	Norwegian regions
948.10(1-4)	DL460-535	By date
948.100(5/6)	DL401-403	Serials/Societies
948.1003	DL405	Gazetteers/Dictionaries
948.1003	DL443	Dictionaries
948.1004	DL441-442	Ethnography
948.10072	DL445	Historiography
948.10099	DL444	Biography
948.101	DL460-478	Early and Medieval to 1387
948.102	DL480-502	1387-1814 (Union of Kalmar)
948.103	DL500-502	Union with Sweden (1814)
948.103	DL503-526	19th century
948.104	DL527-535	20th century (World War II)
948.1041	DL525	Dissolution of Union (1905)
948.23	DL581	Oslo (Christiania)
948.5	DL601-991	Sweden
948.5	DL613-635	Social life
948.5	DL643-879	History
948.50(1-5)	DL660-879	By date
948.50(2-5)	DL701-879	Modern (1523-)
948.500(5/6)	DL601	Serials/Societies
948.5003	DL643	Dictionaries
948.5003	DL605	Gazetteers/Dictionaries
948.5004	DL639-641	Ethnography
948.5007(2)	DL645	Education/Historiography
948.501	DL660-700.9	Early to 1523 (Union of Kalmar)
948.502	DL701-719.9	1523-1654 (Vasa Dynasty)
948.503	DL721-743	Zweibrucken Dynasty (1654-1718)
948.503	DL747-805	1718-1818
948.503	DL805	Union with Norway (1814)
948.504	DL807-859	1814-1907
948.505	DL860-879	20th century
948.73	DL976	Stockholm
948.9	DL101-291	Denmark
948.9	DL131-133	Social life
948.9(1-5)	DL269-291	Local history/Description
948.90(1-2)	DL160-183.9	Early/Medieval to 1523
948.90(1-2)	DL174-183.9	1241-1523 (Union of Kalmar)
948.90(1-5)	DL160-263.3	By date
948.90(3-5)	DL184-263.3	Modern 1523-
948.900(5/6)	DL101	Serials/Societies

Dewey	LC	Descriptor
948.9003	DL105	Gazetteers/Dictionaries
948.9004	DL141-142	Ethnography
948.90099	DL644	Biography
948.901	DL162-173.8	750-1241 (Norwegian rule)
948.903	DL193-199.8	1670-1808
948.903	DL185-192.8	1523-1670 (War with Sweden)
948.903	DL196.6	Northern War (1799-1721)
948.904	DL201-249	1808-1906
948.904	DL217-239.6	Schleswig-Holstein Wars
948.905	DL250-263.3	20th century
948.913	DL276	Copenhagen
948.97	DL1002-1180	Finland
948.97	DL1024-1141.6	History
948.97	DL1017	Social life
948.97(1-7)	DL1170-1180	Local history/Description
948.970(1-34)	DL1050-1141.6	By date
948.970(1-34)	DL1055-1141.6	Modern (1523-)
948.9700(5/6)	DL1002	Serials/Societies
948.97003	DL1007	Gazetteers/Dictionaries
948.97004	DL1018-1020	Ethnography
948.97006	DL1004	Congresses
948.97007(2)	DL1025-1027	Education/Historiography
948.970099	DL1024	Biography
948.9701	DL1058-1063	1523-1809
948.9701	DL1050-1052.9	Early to 1523
948.9702	DL1065-.805	1809-1917 (Russian period)
948.9703	DL1066-1141.6	20th century
948.971	DL1175-.95	Helsinki (Helsingfors)
949.12	DL351-380	History
949.12	DL301-398	Iceland
949.120(1-2)	DL351-356	Early to 1540
949.120(3-4)	DL365-373	1801-1918
949.120(4-5)	DL375	1918-
949.1200(5/6)	DL301	Serials/Societies
949.12003	DL304	Gazetteers
949.12004	DL331-334	Ethnography
949.1203	DL357-360	1540-1800
949.2	DJ	Netherlands (Holland)
949.2	DH71	Social life
949.2	DH95-207	History
949.2	DH	Low Countries (General)/Belgium
949.2	DH95-207	History
949.2	DJ95-292	History
949.2	DJ51	Social life
949.2(1-4)	DJ401-411	Local history/Description
949.20(1-2)	DH171-184	House of Burgundy (1384-1555)
949.20(1-2)	DJ151-152	Early and medieval to 1555
949.20(1-7)	DJ151-292	By date
949.20(2-7)	DH141-207	By date
949.20(2-7)	DH141-207	By date
949.20(3-4)	DJ154-210	1555-1795 (United Provinces)
949.20(5-6)	DJ241-263	1815-1890
949.20(5-7)	DJ215-292	19th-20th centuries
949.20(5-7)0099	DJ219	Biographies
949.20(6-71)	DJ281-283	Willhelmina (1890-1948)
949.200(5/6)	DJ1	Serials/Societies
949.200(5/6)	DH1	Serials/Societies
949.2003	DH101	Dictionaries
949.2003	DJ101	Dictionaries
949.2003	DH14	Gazetteers/Dictionaries
949.2003	DJ14	Gazetteers/Dictionaries
949.2004	DJ91-92	Ethnography
949.2004	DH91	Ethnography
949.20099	DJ103-106	Biography
949.20099	DH103	Biography
949.201	DH141-162	Early/Medieval to 1384
949.203	DH185-207	Wars/Independence (1555-1648)
949.204	DJ193	Anglo-Dutch War (1672-1674)
949.204	DJ196-199.2	Stadtholders (1702-1747)
949.204	DJ180-182	Anglo-Dutch (1652-1667)
949.204	DJ190-191	War with France (1672-1678)
949.204	DJ205-206	Anglo-Dutch War (1780-1784)
949.205	DJ226	Kingdom of Holland (1806-1810)
949.205	DJ228	Union with France (1810-1813)
949.205	DJ236	Netherlands kingdom (1813-1830)
949.205	DJ211	Batavian Republic (1795-1806)
949.2071	DJ287	World War II (1939-1948)
949.2071	DJ286	Between wars (1918-1939)
949.2071	DJ285	World War I (1914-1918)
949.2072	DJ288-289	Juliana (1948-1980)
949.2073	DJ290-292	Beatrix (1980-)
949.2352	DJ411.A5-59	Amsterdam
949.3	DH401-811	Belgium
949.3	DH503-692	History
949.3	DH471	Social life
949.3	DH401-811	Belgium
949.3(1-48)	DH801-811	Local history/Description
949.30(1-2)	DH571-584	Early and Medieval to 1555
949.30(1-4)	DH571-692	By date
949.30(2-3)	DH620-676	1794-1909 (French era)
949.300(5/6)	DH401	Serials/Societies
949.3003	DH511	Dictionaries
949.3003	DH414	Dictionaries/Gazetteers
949.3004	DH491-492	Ethnography
949.30099	DH513-516	Biography
949.302	DH585-619	1555-1794 (Austrian era)
949.304	DH677-692	20th century
949.332	DH802-809.95	Brussels
949.35	DH901-925	Luxembourg
949.4	DQ	Switzerland
949.4	DQ36-39	Social life
949.4	DQ51-210	History
949.4(3-79)	DQ301-851	Local history/Description
949.40(1-3)	DQ78-110	Early and Medieval to 1516
949.40(1-7)	DQ78-210	By date
949.40(2-3)	DQ88-110	1291-1516 (Independence)
949.40(3-4)	DQ111-123	1516-1798
949.40(5-6)	DQ124-191	19th century
949.400(5/6)	DQ1	Serials/Societies
949.4003	DQ14	Gazetteers/Dictionaries
949.4003	DQ51	Dictionaries
949.4004	DQ48-49	Ethnography
949.4006	DQ2	Congresses
949.4007(2)	DQ52.8-.95	Historiography
949.40099	DQ52-.7	Biography
949.401	DQ85-87	Carlovingian/German (687-1291)
949.405	DQ131-151	Helvetic Republic (1798-1803)
949.406	DQ154-191	Sonderbund (1815-1900)
949.407	DQ201-210	20th century
949.47	DQ820-829	Alps

Dewey	LC	Descriptor
949.5	DF548	Empire/Papacy (Political)
949.5	DF750-854.32	History
949.5	DF	Greece
949.5(1-7)	DF901	Provinces/Islands
949.5(1-7)	DF895-951	Local history
949.50(1-2)	DF553-599.5	Eastern Empire (323/476-1057)
949.50(1-4)	DF550-649	History
949.50(1-4)	DF501-649	Byzantine Empire (323-1453)
949.50(1-4)00(5/6)	DF501	Serials/Societies
949.50(1-4)004	DF542-.4	Ethnography
949.50(1-4)006	DF501.5	Congresses
949.50(1-4)007	DF505.8-.82	Education
949.50(1-4)0072	DF505-.7	Historiography
949.50(1-4)0099	DF506-.5	Biography
949.50(3-4)	DF599.8-649	1057-1453
949.50(5-7)	DF801-854.32	By date
949.50(5-7)	DF701-854.32	Modern Greece
949.50(5-7)00(5/6)	DF701	Serials/Societies/etc.
949.50(5-7)004	DF741-748	Ethnography
949.50(6-7)	DF833-854.32	20th century
949.501	DF557	Constantine the Great (323-337)
949.504	DF630-649	Palaeologi (1261-1453)
949.504	DF645-649	Fall of Constantinople (1453)
949.504	DF610-629	Latin Empire (1204-1261)
949.505	DF801-.9	Turkish rule (1453-1821)
949.506	DF816-818	Kapodistrias (1827-1831)
949.506	DF804-815	War of Independence (1821-1829)
949.506	DF803-832	1821-1913
949.5073	DF848	Republic (1924-1935)
949.512	DF915-936	Athens
949.6	DR63	Social life
949.6	DR22-23	Social life
949.6	DR	Balkan peninsula
949.6	DJK76.2-.8	Danube River valley
949.6	DR32-48.5	History
949.600(5/6)	DR1	Serials/Societies
949.6003	DR5	Gazetteers/Dictionaries
949.6003	DR32	Dictionaries
949.6004	DR24-27	Ethnography
949.6006	DR1.5	Congresses
949.60092	DR33	Biography
949.61	DR50-.84	Thrace
949.610(2-3)	DR45-48	1900 to present
949.6101(1-4)	DR39	Ancient to Medieval to 1500
949.61015	DR41-43	1500-1900 (Ottoman Empire)
949.618	DR716-739	Istanbul (Constantinople)
949.65	DR901-998	Albania
949.65	DR927-977.25	History
949.65	DR922	Social life
949.650(1-3)	DR954-977.25	By date
949.650(2-3)	DR970-977.25	1912-
949.6500(5/6)	DR901	Serials/Societies
949.65003	DR927	Dictionaries
949.65003	DR907	Gazetteers/Dictionaries
949.65004	DR923-925	Ethnography
949.65006	DR903.5	Congresses
949.650099	DR928-934	Biography
949.6501	DR961-969	1912 (Turkish rule)
949.7	DR1228	Social life
949.7	DR1202-2285	Yugoslavia
949.7	DR1232-1321	History
949.7(1-6)	DR1350-2285	Local history/Description
949.70(1-2)	DR1259-1312	By date
949.700(5/6)	DR1202	Serials/Societies
949.70025	DR1212	Directories
949.7003	DR1209	Gazetteers/Dictionaries
949.7004	DR1229-1230	Ethnography
949.7006	DR1205	Congresses
949.7007(2)	DR1239-1243	Education/Historiography
949.70099	DR1233-1235	Biography
949.701	DR1266-1280	1500 to 1918
949.701	DR1259-1265	Early and Medieval
949.702	DR1281-1312	1918-
949.71	DR1932-2125	Serbia
949.72	DR1502-1645	Croatia
949.73	DR1352-1485	Slovenia
949.742	DR1652-1785	Bosnia and Hercegovina
949.745	DR1802-1928	Montenegro
949.76	DR2152-2285	Macedonia
949.77	DR65-93.34	History
949.77	DR51-98	Bulgaria
949.77(2-8)	DR95-98	Local history/Description
949.770(1-3)	DR73.7-93.34	By date
949.7700(5/6)	DR51	Serials/Societies
949.770025	DR53.7	Directories
949.77003	DR65	Dictionaries
949.77003	DR53	Gazetteers/Dictionaries
949.77004	DR64	Ethnography
949.770072	DR66.7-.97	Historiography
949.770074	DR51.3-.4	Museums/Exhibitions
949.770099	DR66	Biography
949.7701	DR74-81.6	Early and Medieval
949.77013	DR75-77.8	1st Bulgarian Empire (681-1018)
949.77014	DR79-80.8	1018-1396 (2nd Empire)
949.77015	DR82-.5	Turk rule/Uprising (1396-1878)
949.7702	DR84.9-89.8	1878-1946
949.7703	DR89.9-93.34	1946-
949.773	DR97	Sofia
949.8	DR212	Social life
949.8	DR201-296	Romania
949.80(1-3)	DR238-267.5	By date
949.80(1-3)	DR215-267.5	History
949.80(2-4)	DR279-296	Local history/Description
949.800(5/6)	DR201	Serials/Societies
949.8003	DR215	Dictionaries
949.8003	DR204	Gazetteers/Dictionaries
949.8004	DR213-214	Ethnography
949.8006	DR201.2	Congresses
949.8007(2)	DR216.7-.92	Education/Historiography
949.80099	DR216	Biography
949.801 5	DR241-.5	Phanariote Regime (1601-1822)
949.8016	DR242-250	1822-1866
949.802	DR250-266	1881-1944
949.803	DR267-.5	1944-
949.82	DR286	Bucharest
949.84	DR279-280.74	Transylvania
949.98	DF901.C78-.C89	Crete
950	DS	Asia
950	DS31-35.2	Asia (General)
950.0(5/6)	DS1-3	Serials/Societies
950.03	DS4	Gazetteers/Dictionaries
950.04	DS13-28	Ethnography
950.1	DS33.5	Ancient to 1162

Dewey	LC	Descriptor	Dewey	LC	Descriptor
950.2	DS33.5	Mongol/Tatar eras (1162-1480)	953.004	DS218-219	Ethnography
			953.02	DS38.1-.7	622-1517
950.3	DS33.7	European entry (1480-1905)	953.02	DS232-238.7	622-1517
950.4	DS34	1905-	953.03	DS38.8	Ottoman Empire (1517-1740)
950.41	DS34	1905-1945			
950.424	DS34	1945-1949	953.03	DS239-241	Ottoman Empire (1517-1740)
950.425	DS34	1950-1959			
950.426	DS34	1960-1969	953.04	DS38.9	1740-1926
950.427	DS34	1970-1979	953.05	DS39	1926-
950.428	DS34	1980-	953.052	DS39	1926-1964
951	DS701-799.9	China	953.053	DS39	1964-
951.(1-6)	DS781-796	Local history/Description	954	DS433-481	History
951.015	DS748.45-.76	420-581	954	DS421-486.8	India
951.016	DS749.2-.29	Sui Dynasty (581-618)	954.(1-8)	DS483-486.8	Local history/Description
951.017	DS749.3-.47	T'ang Dynasty (618-907)	954.004	DS430-432	Ethnography
951.018	DS749.5-.76	907-960	954.02	DS451-473.5	647-1785
951.02	DS750.52-753.7	960-1644	954.021	DS451	647-997
951.024	DS751-.6	Sung Dynasty (960-1279)	954.022	DS452-458.7	Moslem conquests (997-1206)
951.025	DS752-.6	Yuan Dynasty (1271-1368)			
951.026	DS753-.7	Ming Dynasty (1368-1644)	954.0223	DS458-.3	Ghazni Dynasty (997-1196)
951.03	DS753.82-773.6	Ch'ing Dynasty (1644-1912)	954.0225	DS458.5-.7	Ghor Dynasty (1196-1206)
			954.023	DS459-.52	1206-1414
951.032	DS753.82-754.84	1644-1795	954.0232	DS459-.15	Delhi slave kings (1206-1290)
951.033	DS755-757.7	1796-1850 (Opium War)			
951.034	DS758.7-759.4	Taiping Rebellion (1850-1864)	954.0234	DS459.2-.3	Khilji Dynasty (1290-1320)
			954.0236	DS459.4-.52	Tughlak Dynasty (1320-1414)
951.035	DS763.5-773.23	1864-1911 (Boxer Rebellion)			
			954.024	DS459.6-.95	1414-1526
951.036	DS773.32-.6	Revolution (1911-1912)	954.0242	DS459.6	Sayyid Dynasty (1414-1451)
951.04	DS773.83-777.544	Republic (1912-1949)			
951.041	DS773.83-777.46	1912-1927	954.0245	DS459.7-.95	Lodi Dynasty (1451-1526)
951.042	DS777.47-.544	Nationalist era (1927-1949)	954.025	DS461-.9	Mogul Empire (1526-1707)
951.05	DS777.545-779.29	People's Republic (1949-)	954.0252	DS461.1	Babur Reign (1526-1530)
951.249	DS798.92-799.9	Taiwan/Formosa	954.0253	DS461.2	Humayun (1530-1556)
951.24902	DS799.64-.66	Ancient to 1683	954.0256	DS461.5	Jahangir Reign (1605-1627)
951.24903	DS799.64-.66	Chinese era (1683-1895)	954.0257	DS461.6	Shahjahan Reign (1628-1658)
951.24904	DS799.69-.72	Japanese era (1895-1945)			
951.24905	DS799.77-.833	Nationalist China (1945-)	954.0258	DS461.7	Aurangzib Reign (1658-1707)
951.5	DS785-786	Tibet			
951.73	DS798	Outer Mongolia	954.029	DS461.8	European entry (1707-1785)
951.8	DS781-784.2	Manchuria	954.0292	DS461.8	1707-1744
951.9	DS901-937	Korea	954.0294	DS461.8	Anglo-French War (1744-1757)
951.901	DS911-912.43	Ancient to 1392			
951.902	DS913-915.5	Yi Dynasty (1392-1910)	954.0296	DS463-472.9	1757-1772
951.903	DS916.525-.58	Japanese era (1910-1945)	954.0298	DS473-.5	Governor Hastings (1772-1785)
951.904	DS916.6-922.42	1945-			
951.9041	DS916.6-.92	1945-1950	954.03	DS474-480.83	British period (1785-1947)
951.9042	DS918-921.8	Korean War (1950-1953)	954.031	DS474-478.3	East India Co. (1785-1858)
951.9043	DS922-.42	1953-	954.035	DS479-480.83	Crown rule (1858-1947)
952	DS801-897	Japan	954.042	DS480.84-.85	Jawaharlal Nehru (1947-1964)
952.01	DS851-856.72	Ancient to 1185			
952.02	DS856.75-881.84	Feudal era (1185-1868)	954.043	DS480.852	Lal Bahadur Shastri (1964-1966)
952.021	DS856.75-861	Kamakura era (1185-1334)			
952.022	DS863-865.5	Namboku era (1334-1392)	954.045	DS480.852	Indira Gandhi (1966-1977)
952.023	DS868-869.6	Muromachi era (1392-1573)	954.05	DS480.853	1971-
952.024	DS869.5-.6	Momoyama era (1573-1603)	954.799	DS498-.8	Goa
			954.91	DS376-392.2	Pakistan
952.025	DS870-881.84	Takugawa era (1603-1868)	954.9104	DS384-387	West/East Union (1947-1971)
952.03	DS881.85-888.5	1868-1945			
952.031	DS881.98-884	Meiji era (1868-1912)	954.9105	DS388	1971-
952.032	DS885.8-888	Taisho era (1912-1926)	954.92	DS393-396.9	Bangladesh
952.033	DS888.15-890	Showa era (1926-1945)	954.9204	DS395	East/West Union (1947-1971)
952.04	DS888.84-890.3	1945-			
953	DS221-244.63	History	954.9205	DS395.5-.7	1971-
953	DS201-248	Arabian peninsula/Saudi Arabia	954.93	DS488-490	Sri Lanka
			954.9301	DS489.6-.73	Ancient to 1795
953.00(5/6)	DS201	Serials/Societies	954.9302	DS489.7-.73	British era (1795-1948)

Dewey	LC	Descriptor
954.9303	DS489.8-.86	1948-
954.96	DS493-495.8	Nepal
955	DS270-318.85	History
955	DS251-326	Iran (Persia)
955.00(5/6)	DS251-.5	Serials/Societies/Congresses
955.003	DS253	Gazetteers
955.004	DS268-269	Ethnography
955.02	DS288-290	637-1499 (Foreign rule)
955.03	DS292-297	Persian dynasties (1499-1794)
955.04	DS298-311	1794-1906
955.05	DS313-318.85	1906-
955.051	DS313-316	1906-1925
955.054	DS318.72-.85	1979-
956	DS61-66	Near East, History (General)
956	DS41-66	Near East
956.(1-8)	DS155-156	Asia Minor
956.(2-6)	DR701-741	Local history/Description
956.00(5/6)	DS41-.5	Serials/Societies/Congresses
956.003	DS43	Gazetteers/Dictionaries
956.01	DS62.4	To 1900
956.015	DS62.4	1300-1900 (Ottoman Empire)
956.02	DS62.4	1900-1918
956.0254	DS461.3-.4	Akbar Reign (1556-1605)
956.03	DS62.4	1918-1945
956.04	DS62.4	1945-1980
956.04	DS242-244.5	1740-1926 (Freedom from Turks)
956.042	DS62.4	Arab/Israel War (1948-1949)
956.044	DS62.4	Arab/Israel War (1956)
956.046	DS62.4	Arab/Israel War (1967)
956.048	DS62.4	Arab/Israel War (1973)
956.05	DS62.4	1980-
956.05	DS244.512-.63	1926-
956.052	DS316.2-317	Reza Shah Pahlavi (1925-1941)
956.052	DS244.512-.56	1926-1964
956.053	DS244.6-.63	1964-
956.1	DR436-603	History
956.1	DR401-741	Turkey
956.1	DR432	Social life
956.10(1-3)	DR481-603	By date
956.100(5/6)	DR401	Serials/Societies
956.10025	DR413	Directories
956.1003	DR436	Dictionaries
956.1003	DR414	Gazetteers/Dictionaries
956.1004	DR434-435	Ethnography
956.1006	DR401.2	Congresses
956.1007(2)	DR438.8-.95	Education/Historiography
956.10099	DR438-.7	Biography
956.101(3-4)	DR481	Early to 1281/1453
956.1015	DR515-516	1570-1571 (Cyprian War)
956.1015	DR511-529	1566-1640
956.1015	DR531-555.7	1640-1789
956.102-	DR576-603	20th century republic
956.45	DS54-.95	Cyprus
956.4501	DS54.6	To 1571
956.4502	DS54.7	1571-1878
956.4503	DS54.8-.83	British era (1878-1960)
956.4504	DS54.9	1960-
956.60(2-39)	DS195-.5	1901-
956.601(3-5)	DS186-188	428-1522
956.6015	DS191-193	1522-1800 (Ottoman Empire)
956.6015	DS194-.5	1801-1900
956.62	DS161-195.5	Armenia
956.620072	DS174-.9	Historiography
956.7	DS67-79.9	Iraq (Babylonia/Mesopotamia)
956.7	DS70.82-79.66	History
956.700(5/6)	DS67	Serials/Societies
956.7003	DS67.8	Dictionaries/Gazetteers
956.7004	DS70.8	Ethnography
956.702	DS76-.4	637-1553
956.703	DS77	Ottoman Empire (1553-1920)
956.704	DS79	1920-
956.7041	DS79.5	Mandate period (1920-1932)
956.7042	DS79.52-.53	Monarchy (1932-1958)
956.7043	DS79.65	Republic (1958-)
956.91	DS92-99	Syria
956.91	DS94.9-98.3	History
956.91(2-44)	DS99	Local history/Description
956.9100(5/6)	DS92	Serials/Societies
956.910025	DS92.8	Directories
956.91003	DS92.6	Gazetteers
956.91004	DS94.7-.8	Ethnography
956.9102	DS97-.4	640-1516
956.9103	DS97.5-.6	Ottoman Empire (1516-1920)
956.9104	DS98-.3	1920-
956.91041	DS98	Mandate period (1920-1945)
956.91042	DS98	Republic (1945-)
956.92	DS80-90	Lebanon
956.92	DS80.7-87.53	History
956.9200(5/6)	DS80.A2	Serials/Societies
956.92003	DS80.A5	Gazetteers/Dictionaries
956.92004	DS80.5	Ethnography
956.9203	DS83-85	640-1926
956.92032	DS83	640-1517
956.92034	DS84-85	Ottoman Empire (1517-1920)
956.92035	DS86	Mandate period (1920-1941)
956.9204	DS86	1926-
956.92042	DS86	1926-1941
956.92043	DS87-.53	1941-
956.92044	DS87.53	1975- (Civil War)
956.94	DS114-128.19	History
956.94	DS101-151	Israel/Palestine
956.9400(5/6)	DS101	Serials/Societies
956.940025	DS102.9	Directories
956.94004	DS113-.8	Ethnography
956.9402	DS122.9-123.5	Mishnaic/Talmudic eras (70-640)
956.9403	DS124-125.5	640-1917 (Ottoman Empire)
956.9404	DS126-.4	British era (1917-1948)
956.9405	DS126.5-128	1948-
956.94052	DS126.5-127	1948-1967
956.94053	DS127-128	1967-1974
956.94054	DS127-128	1974-
956.9442	DS109-.94	Jerusalem
956.95	DS153.7-154.55	History
956.95	DS153-154.9	Jordan
956.95(1-8)	DS154.9	Local history
956.9500(5/6)	DS153.A2-.A5	Serials/Societies
956.95004	DS153.5-.55	Ethnography
956.9502	DS154.3	70-640
956.9503	DS154.4	640-1923 (Ottoman Empire)

Dewey	LC	Descriptor
956.9504	DS154.5-.55	1923-
956.95042	DS154.5	Mandate period (1923-1946)
956.95043	DS154.5	Hashemite kingdom (1946-)
956.95044	DS154.55	1967-
957	DK501-949.5	Local history/Description
957	DK751-781	Siberia
957	G820-839	Siberia
958	DS327-329.4	Central Asia
958.1	DS350-375	Afghanistan
958.101	DS358	640-1221
958.102	DS358	1221-1709
958.103	DS358-368	1709-1919
958.104	DS369-371.2	1919-
958.1043	DS369.4-371	Muhammad Zahir Shah (1933-1973)
958.1044	DS371.2	Republic (1973-1978)
958.4	DK845-860	Asian Russia/West Turkestan
958.43	DK911-919.5	Kirghiz/Kirghizia
958.45	DK901-909.5	Kazakh/Kazakhstan
958.5	DK931-939.5	Turkmen/Turkmenia
958.6	DK921-929.5	Tajik/Tadzhikistan
958.7	DK941-949.5	Uzbek/Uzbekistan
959	DS520-589	Southeast Asia
959.1	DS527-530.9	Burma
959.102	DS529.2-.3	Ancient to 1826
959.103	DS529.7	British conquest (1826-1885)
959.104	DS530-.32	British era (1886-1948)
959.105	DS530.4-.53	1948-
959.3	DS561-589	Thailand
959.302	DS576-577	Ancient to 1782
959.3021	DS576-577	Ancient to 1219
959.303	DS577-582	1782-1910 (Rama I-V)
959.304	DS583-586	1910- (Rama VI-)
959.4	DS555-.98	Laos
959.403	DS556.6-.73	Ancient to 1949
959.404	DS559.7-.86	1949-
959.5	DS591-599	Malaysia
959.5(1-7)	DS597.22-599	Local history/Description
959.503	DS596.5-.63	Ancient to 1946
959.504	DS597-.215	1946-1963
959.505	DS597.2-.215	1963- (Federation period)
959.55	DS650-.99	Brunei
959.6	DS554-.98	Cambodia
959.603	DS554.6-.73	Ancient to 1949
959.604	DS554.7-.842	1949-
959.7	DS556-559.93	Vietnam
959.703	DS556.6-.83	Ancient to 1949
959.704	DS556.8-559.916	1949-
959.7041	DS556-.83	Indochinese War (1946-1954)
959.7042	DS556-.93	1954-1961
959.7043	DS557-559.8	Vietnamese War (1961-1975)
959.70434	E745	Military history
959.704345	E746	Naval history
959.7044	DS559.912-.916	1975-
959.8	DS600-649	Indonesia
959.81	DS646.1-.15	Sumatra
959.82	DS646.17-.29	Java
959.83	DS646.3-.34	Borneo
959.84	DS646.4-.49	Celebes/Sulawesi
959.85	DS646.6-.69	Moluccas/Maluku
959.86	DS646.5-.59	Timor

Dewey	LC	Descriptor
959.9	DS667-686.6	History
959.9	DS651-689	Philippines
959.9004	DS665-666	Ethnography
959.901	DS673.8	Ancient to 1564
959.902	DS674-678	Spanish era (1564-1898)
959.903	DS679-686.4	United States era (1898-1946)
959.904	DS686.5-.6	Republic (1946-)
960	DT	Africa
960	DT17-39	General history
960.04	DT15-16	Ethnography
960.1	DT24	Ancient to 640
960.2	DT25	640-1885
960.21	DT25	640-1450
960.22	DT25-57	1450-1799
960.23	DT28	1800-1885
960.3	DT29-30.5	1885-
960.31	DT29	1885-1945
960.32	DT30-.5	1945-
961	DT167-176	History
961	DT160-177	North Africa
961	DT211-346	Libya/Tunisia
961	DT160-177	North Africa
961	DT167-176	History
961.02	DT172-176	Arab/Ottoman rule (640-1830)
961.022	DT173	Arab era (640-1520)
961.023	DT174	Ottoman Empire (1520-1830)
961.03	DT176	European entry (1830-1950)
961.04	DT176	1950-
961.045	DT176	1950-1959
961.046	DT176	1960-1969
961.047	DT176	1970-1979
961.048	DT176	1980-1989
961.049	DT176	1990-
961.1	DT253.4-264.49	History
961.1	DT253.4-264.49	History
961.1	DT241-269	Tunisia
961.1004	DT253-.2	Ethnography
961.102	DT259	Arab era (647-1516)
961.103	DT261-263.76	Ottoman Empire (1516-1881)
961.104	DT263.9-264.3	1881-1956
961.105	DT264.35-.49	1956-
961.1051	DT264.35-.364	Habib Bourguiba (1956-1987)
961.1052	DT264.35-.49	1987-
961.2	DT223.2-236	History
961.2	DT211-239	Libya
961.2004	DT223-.2	Ethnography
961.202	DT229-231	Arab/Ottoman eras (644-1911)
961.203	DT235	Italian era (1911-1952)
961.204	DT235.5-236	1952-
961.2041	DT235.5	Idris I (1952-1969)
961.2042	DT236	Muammar Qaddafi (1969-)
962	DT43-154	Egypt
962.(5-9)	DT159.6-.9	Local history/Description
962.0(2-55)	DT74-107.87	History
962.0(2-55)	DT74-107.87	History
962.004	DT71	Ethnography
962.02	DT95-96.7	Arab era (640-1517)
962.03	DT97-106	Ottoman Empire (1517-1882)
962.04	DT107-.8	British era (1882-1922)

Dewey	LC	Descriptor	Dewey	LC	Descriptor
962.05	DT107.8-.87	1922-	966.23004	DT551.42-.45	Ethnography
962.051	DT107.8	Faud I (1922-1936)	966.2301	DT551.65	Ancient to 1902
962.052	DT107.82	Faruk/Regency (1936-1952)	966.2303	DT551.7-.72	French Sudan (1902-1960)
962.053	DT107.83	Naguib/Nasser (1953-1970)	966.2305	DT551.8-.82	1960-
962.054	DT107.85	Anwar Sadat (1970-1981)	966.25	DT555-.9	Burkina Faso (Upper Volta)
962.055	DT107.87	1981-	966.25	DT555.52-.83	History
962.4	DT154.1-159.9	Sudan	966.25004	DT555.42-.45	Ethnography
962.4	DT155.3-157.67	History	966.2501	DT555.65-.67	Ancient to 1897
962.4004	DT155-.2	Ethnography	966.2503	DT555.75-.77	French era (1897-1960)
962.401	DT156	Ancient to 500	966.2505	DT555.8-.83	1960-
962.402	DT156-.3	500-1820	966.26	DT547-.9	Niger
962.4022	DT156-.3	Christian kingdoms (500-1504)	966.26	DT547.5-.83	History
962.4023	DT156.3	Funj Sultanate (1504-1820)	966.26004	DT547.42-.45	Ethnography
962.403	DT156.4-.7	Anglo/Egyptian era (1820-1956)	966.2601	DT547.65	Ancient to 1900
			966.2603	DT547.75	French era (1900-1960)
962.404	DT157-.67	1956-	966.2605	DT547.8-.83	1960-
963	DT371-398	Ethiopia	966.3	DT549.47-.83	History
963	DT380.5-387.954	History	966.3	DT549-.9	Senegal
963.004	DT380-.4	Ethnography	966.3004	DT549.42-.45	Ethnography
963.01	DT383	Ancient to 640	966.301	DT549.7-.73	Ancient to 1895
963.02	DT383	640-1543	966.303	DT549.75-.77	French era (1895-1960)
963.03	DT384-386	1543-1855 (John IV)	966.305	DT549.8-.83	1960-
963.04	DT386.3-387.3	1855-1913 (Theodore II)	966.4	DT516.5-.82	History
963.05	DT387.5-.92	1913-1941 (WW I - WW II)	966.4	DT516-.9	Sierra Leone
963.05(4-5)	DT387.7-.92	Haile Selassie (1917-1974)	966.4004	DT516.42-.45	Ethnography
963.06	DT387.9-.92	1941-1974 (WW II and after)	966.401	DT516.65	Ancient to 1787
963.07	DT387.95-.954	1974-	966.402	DT516.7-.72	British era (1787-1896)
963.5	DT391-398	Eritrea	966.403	DT516.7-.72	1896-1961 (Protectorate)
964	DT179.2-.9	Northwest Africa	966.404	DT516.8-.82	1961-
964	DT211-346	Morocco	966.5	DT591-615.9	Portuguese West Africa
964	DT301-330	Morocco	966.5012	DT509.65-.7	British era (1807-1965)
964.0(2-5)	DT313.7-325.92	History	966.51	DT509.5-.83	History
964.0(2-5)	DT313.7-325.92	History	966.51	DT509-.9	Gambia
964.004	DT313-.6	Ethnography	966.51004	DT509.42-.45	Ethnography
964.02	DT319-323.5	Arab/Berber eras (647-1830)	966.5101	DT509.65	Ancient to 1806
964.03	DT324-.92	1830-1899	966.5103	DT509.8-.83	1965-
964.04	DT324-.92	1900-1956	966.52	DT477	Guinea
964.05	DT325-.92	1956-	966.52	DT543-.9	Guinea
964.9	DT669-671	West Coast islands	966.52	DT543.5-.827	History
965	DT283.7-295.55	History	966.52004	DT543.42-.45	Ethnography
965	DT271-299	Algeria	966.5201	DT543.65	Ancient to 1882
965	DT283.7-295.55	History	966.5203	DT543.75-.77	French era (1882-1958)
965.(1-7)	DT298-299	Local history/Description	966.5205	DT543.8-.827	1958-
965.004	DT283-.6	Ethnography	966.57	DT613-.9	Guinea-Bissau
965.02	DT289-292	Arab/Berber/Ottoman (647-1830)	966.57	DT479	Guinea-Bissau
			966.57	DT613.5-.83	History
965.03	DT294-295.3	French era (1830-1962)	966.57004	DT613.42-.45	Ethnography
965.04	DT294.5-295.3	1900-1962	966.5701	DT613.65	Ancient to 1879
965.05	DT295.5-.55	1962-	966.5702	DT613.75-.78	Portuguese era (1879-1974)
966	DT331-346	Sahara	966.5703	DT613.8-.83	1974-
966	DT491-516.9	British West Africa	966.58	DT669-671	West Coast islands
966	DT470-671	West Africa	966.58	DT671.C25-.C28	History
966	DT548	West Sahara	966.58	DT671.C2-.C29	Cape Verde
966	DT521-555.9	French West Africa (Sahara)	966.580(1-2)	DT671.C265	Early to 1975
			966.58004	DT671.C242-.C245	Ethnography
966.1	DT554-.9	Mauritania	966.5803	DT671.C28	1975-
966.1	DT554.52-.83	History	966.62	DT621-637	Liberia
966.1004	DT554.42-.45	Ethnography	966.62	DT630.8-636.53	History
966.1016	DT554.65-.67	300-1200 (Ghana Empire)	966.62004	DT630-.5	Ethnography
966.1017	DT554.65-.67	1200-1500 (Mali Empire)	966.6201	DT633-.3	Ancient to 1847
966.103	DT554.75-.77	French era (1903-1960)	966.6202	DT634-.3	1847-1945
966.105	DT554.8-.83	1960-	966.6203	DT635-636.53	1945-
966.23	DT551-.9	Mali (French Sudan)	966.68	DT545-.9	Ivory Coast
966.23	DT551.5-.82	History	966.68	DT545.52-.82	History
			966.68004	DT545.42-.45	Ethnography
			966.6801	DT545.7-.73	Ancient to 1904
			966.6805	DT545.8-.83	1960-

Dewey	LC	Descriptor
966.6903	DT545.75-.77	French era (1904-1960)
966.7	DT509.97-512.9	Ghana
966.7	DT510.5-512.34	History
966.7004	DT510.42-.43	Ethnography
966.701	DT511-.3	Ancient to 1874
966.705	DT512-.34	1957-
966.81	DT582-.9	Togo
966.81	DT582.5-.82	History
966.81004	DT582.42-.45	Ethnography
966.8101	DT582.65	Ancient to 1894
966.8102	DT582.7	German era (1894-1914)
966.8103	DT582.75	Anglo-French era (1914-1960)
966.8104	DT582.8-.82	1960-
966.83	DT541.5-.845	History
966.83	DT541-.9	Benin
966.83004	DT541.42-.45	Ethnography
966.8301	DT541.65-.67	Ancient to 1904
966.83018	DT541.65-.67	Dahomey kingdom (1600-1904)
966.8303	DT541.75	French era (1904-1960)
966.8305	DT541.8-.845	1960-
966.9	DT515.53-.84	History
966.9	DT515-.9	Nigeria
966.9004	DT515.42-.45	Ethnography
966.901	DT515.65-.73	Ancient to 1886
966.903	DT515.7-.77	British era (1886-1960)
966.905	DT515.8-.84	1960-
967	DT348-363.3	Central Sub-Sahara
967	DT2831-2864	British Central Africa
967	DT521-555.9	French West Africa (Sahara)
967.11	DT561-581	Cameroon
967.11	DT572-578.4	History
967.11004	DT570-571	Ethnography
967.1101	DT574-575	Ancient to 1884
967.1102	DT574-575	1884-1916 (German era)
967.1103	DT574-575	Anglo/French era (1916-1959)
967.1104	DT575.5-578.4	1960-
967.15	DT591-615.9	Portuguese West Africa
967.15	DT615-.9	Sao Tome & Principe
967.15	DT615.5-.8	History
967.15004	DT615.42-.45	Ethnography
967.1501	DT615.65-.7	Ancient to 1975
967.1502	DT615.8	Republic 1975-
967.18	DT620-.9	Equatorial (Spanish) Guinea
967.18	DT620.46-.83	History
967.18004	DT620.42-.45	Ethnography
967.1801	DT620.65-.67	Ancient to 1469
967.1802	DT620.65-.73	European eras (1469-1968)
967.2	DT639	Congo River area
967.21	DT546.1-.19	Gabon
967.21	DT546.15-.183	History
967.21004	DT546.142-.145	Ethnography
967.2101	DT546.165	Ancient to 1839
967.2102	DT546.165-.175	French era (1839-1960)
967.2104	DT546.18-.183	1960-
967.24	DT546.25-.283	History
967.24	DT546.2-.29	Republic of the Congo
967.24004	DT546.242-.245	Ethnography
967.2401	DT546.265-.267	Ancient to 1885
967.2403	DT546.265-.275	Middle Congo era (1885-1960)
967.2405	DT546.28-.283	1960-
967.3	DT1251-1465	Angola
967.3	DT1341-1436	History
967.3004	DT1304-1308	Ethnography
967.301	DT1357-1369	Ancient to 1648
967.302	DT1373-1382	1648-1899
967.303	DT1385-1417	1900-1975
967.304	DT1420-1436	1975-
967.41	DT546.3-.39	Central African Republic
967.41	DT546.348-.384	History
967.41004	DT546.342-.345	Ethnography
967.4101	DT546.365	Ancient to 1890
967.4103	DT546.365-.37	Ubangi-Shari era (1890-1960)
967.4105	DT546.375-.384	1960-
967.43	DT546.4-.49	Chad
967.43	DT546.457-.483	History
967.43004	DT546.422-.445	Ethnography
967.4301	DT546.47-.473	Ancient to 1850
967.4302	DT546.47-.477	French era (1850-1960)
967.4304	DT546.48-.483	1960-
967.51	DT641-665	Zaire
967.51	DT650.2-683	History
967.51(1-8)	DT665	Local history/Description
967.51004	DT649.5-650	Ethnography
967.5101	DT654-.3	Ancient to 1885
967.5102	DT655-657.2	Belgian era (1885-1960)
967.5103	DT658-.25	1960-
967.571	DT450.26-.437	History
967.571	DT450-.49	Rwanda
967.571004	DT450.24-.25	Ethnography
967.57104	DT450.435-.437	1962-
967.572	DT450.5-.95	Burundi
967.572	DT450.66-.855	History
967.572004	DT450.64-.65	Ethnography
967.57204	DT450.85-.855	1962-
967.6	DT365-469	East Africa
967.6	DT421-432.5	British East Africa
967.60(1-4)	DT365.5-.8	History
967.601	DT365.65	Ancient to 1894
967.603	DT365.7-.75	1894-1961
967.604	DT365.8	1961-
967.61	DT433.252-.287	History
967.61	DT433.2-.29	Uganda
967.61004	DT433.242-.245	Ethnography
967.6101	DT433.265-.267	Ancient to 1894
967.6103	DT433.27-.273	British era (1894-1962)
967.6104	DT433.275-.287	1962-
967.71	DT411-.9	Djibouti
967.71	DT411.5-.83	History
967.71004	DT411.42-.45	Ethnography
967.7101	DT411.65	Ancient to 1881
967.7103	DT411.75-.77	French era (1881-1977)
967.7104	DT411.8-.83	1977-
967.73	DT401-409	Somalia
967.73	DT402.5-407.3	History
967.73004	DT402.3-.45	Ethnography
967.7301	DT403.5-.7	Ancient to 1884
967.7303	DT404-406.3	British/Italian era (1884-1960)
967.7305	DT407-.3	1960-
967.8	DT436-449	Tanzania
967.8	DT443.5-448.25	History
967.8004	DT443-.2	Ethnography
967.9	DT3291-3415	Mozambique
967.9	DT3330-3398	History
967.9004	DT3324-3328	Ethnography
967.901	DT3345-3359	Ancient to 1648
967.902	DT3361-3383	1648-1900 (Portuguese era)
967.903	DT3383-3387	1900-1975

Dewey	LC	Descriptor
967.905	DT3389-3398	1975-
968	DT1062-1177	History
968	DT1701-2405	South Africa
968	DT1001-1190	Southern Africa
968	DT2035-2054	History
968	DT1772-1969	History
968.(2-9)	DT1190	Local history
968.004	DT1054-1058	Ethnography
968.004	DT1754-1770	Ethnography
968.02	DT1807-1810	Ancient to 1488
968.02	DT1107-1123	Ancient to 1488
968.03	DT1107-1123	European entry (1488-1814)
968.03	DT1807-1845	European entry (1488-1814)
968.04	DT1837-1922	1814-1910
968.04	DT1107-1144	1814-1910
968.041	DT1837-1845	1814-1835 (Mfecane/ Difaqane)
968.041	DT1107-1123	1814-1835 (Mfecane/ Difaqane)
968.042	DT1853	Great trek (1834-1838)
968.042	DT1107-1123	Great trek (1835-1838)
968.044	DT1853-1861	1838-1854
968.044	DT1107-1123	1838-1854
968.045	DT1861-1889	1854-1899
968.045	DT1107-1123	1854-1899
968.048	DT1125-1144	2nd Anglo-Boer War (1899-1902)
968.048	DT1890-1920	2nd Anglo-Boer War (1899-1902)
968.049	DT1921-1922	1902-1910
968.049	DT1125-1144	1902-1910
968.05	DT1924-1941	Union (1910-1961)
968.05	DT1144-1147	Union (1910-1961)
968.06	DT1945-1969	Republic (1961-)
968.06	DT1147-1177	Republic (1961-)
968.2	DT2325-2378	History
968.2	DT2291-2378	Transvaal
968.20(5-6)	DT2375-2378	Union/Republic (1910-)
968.2004	DT2322	Ethnography
968.203	DT2332-2344	Ancient to 1835
968.204	DT2332-2371	1835-1910
968.2042	DT2342	Great trek (1835-1852)
968.2045	DT2344-2359	South Africa (1852-1877)
968.2046	DT2354-2359	British era (1877-1881)
968.2048	DT2361-2368	2nd Anglo-Boer War (1899-1902)
968.2049	DT2371	Transvaal Colony (1902-1910)
968.4	DT2225-2278	History
968.4	DT2181-2278	Natal
968.40(5-6)	DT2270-2278	Union/Republic (1910-)
968.4004	DT2222	Ethnography
968.403	DT2232-2238	Ancient to 1824
968.404	DT2232-2267	1824-1910 (Zululand)
968.4041	DT2240	British entry (1824-1835)
968.4042	DT2242	Great trek (1835-1843)
968.4045	DT2250-2263	British colony (1843-1899)
968.4048	DT2265	2nd Anglo-Boer War (1899-1902)
968.4049	DT2267	1902-1910
968.5	DT2105-2145	History
968.5	DT2075-2145	Orange Free State
968.50(5-6)	DT2142-2145	Union/Republic (1910-)
968.5004	DT2102	Ethnography
968.503	DT2112-2118	Ancient to 1828
968.504	DT2118-2139	1828-1910
968.5042	DT2120	1835-1854 (Great trek)
968.5045	DT2124-2137	Orange Free State (1854-1899)
968.5048	DT2137-2139	2nd Anglo-Boer War (1899-1902)
968.5049	DT2139	Orange River Colony(1902-1910)
968.7	DT1991-2054	Cape of Good Hope (Province)
968.70(5-6)	DT2051-2054	Union/Republic (1910-)
968.7004	DT2032	Ethnography
968.703	DT2042-2044	European entry (1488-1814)
968.704	DT2042-2049	1806-1920
968.7042	DT2042-2044	British control (1806-1854)
968.7045	DT2042-2044	Self-government (1854-1899)
968.7048	DT2046-2049	2nd Anglo-Boer War (1899-1902)
968.81	DT1564-1648	History
968.81	DT1501-1685	Namibia
968.81004	DT1554-1558	Ethnography
968.8101	DT1587-1601	Ancient to 1884
968.8102	DT1603-1622	German era (1884-1915)
968.8103	DT1625-1648	South African era (1915-)
968.83	DT2421-2525	Botswana
968.83	DT2464-2502	History
968.83004	DT2454-2458	Ethnography
968.8301	DT2483-2488	Ancient to 1885
968.8302	DT2490-2493	Bechuanaland (1885-1966)
968.8303	DT2496-2502	1966-
968.85	DT2541-2686	Lesotho (Basutoland)
968.85	DT2604-2660	History
968.85004	DT2592-2596	Ethnography
968.8501	DT2630-2636	Ancient to 1868
968.8502	DT2638-2648	Basutoland (1868-1966)
968.8503	DT2652-2660	1966-
968.87	DT2701-2825	Swaziland
968.87	DT2754-2806	History
968.87004	DT2744-2746	Ethnography
968.8701	DT2777-2786	Ancient to 1840
968.8702	DT2777-2795	British era (1840-1968)
968.8703	DT2797-2806	1968-
968.91	DT2914-3000	History
968.91	DT2871-3025	Zimbabwe
968.91004	DT2910-2913	Ethnography
968.9101	DT2937-2957	Ancient to 1889
968.9102	DT2959-2975	British era (1889-1953)
968.9103	DT2976-2979	Confederation (1953-1963)
968.9104	DT2981-2994	Rhodesia (1964-1980)
968.9105	DT2996-3000	Republic (1980-)
968.94	DT3064-3119	History
968.94	DT3031-3145	Zambia
968.94004	DT3054-3058	Ethnography
968.9401	DT3079-3089	Ancient to 1890
968.9402	DT3091-3106	British era (1890-1953)
968.9403	DT3108-3111	Federation (1953-1963)
968.9404	DT3113-3119	Republic (1946-)
968.97	DT3194-3237	History
968.97	DT3161-3257	Malawi
968.97004	DT3189-3192	Ethnography
968.9701	DT3211-3214	Ancient to 1891
968.9702	DT3216-3225	Nyasaland (1891-1953)
968.9703	DT3227-3230	Federation (1953-1963)
968.9704	DT3232-3237	1964-
969	DT468-469	Islands (East African coast)
969.1	DT469.M21-.M38	Madagascar
969.101	DT469.M31-.M335	Ancient to 1895
969.103	DT469.M34-.M342	French era (1895-1960)

Dewey	LC	Descriptor	Dewey	LC	Descriptor
969.105	DT469.M343-.M345	1960-	971.95	F1101-1105.5	Franklin
969.4	DT469.M497	Mayotte	972.(8/9)01	E65	Latin America (General)
969.6	DT469.S4-.S49	Seychelles	972.0(1-8)	F1201-1392	Mexico
969.8	DT469.M39	Mascarene Islands	972.01	E141	Earliest to 1606
969.81	DT469.R3-.R5	Reunion	972.02	E143	Latin America (1607-1810)
969.8102	DT469.R44-.R453	Ancient to 1946	972.8	F1421-1577	Central America
969.8104	DT469.R455-.R458	As a French dept. (1946-)	972.8	F975	Central America
969.82	DT469.M4-.M495	Mauritius	972.81	F1461-1477	Guatemala
969.8201	DT469.M465-.M467	Ancient to 1810	972.83	F1501-1517	Honduras
969.8202	DT469.M47-.M473	British rule (1810-1968)	972.83	F1441-1457	British Honduras
969.8203	DT469.M48-.M483	1968-	972.84	F1481-1497	El Salvador
970	E16-18.85	History	972.85	F1521-1537	Nicaragua
970	E18.7	Juvenile works	972.86	F1541-1557	Costa Rica
970	E31-45	North America	972.87	F1561-1577	Panama
970	E	America	972.9	F1601-2175	West Indies
970	E38.5	Juvenile works	972.9	F1741-1991	Greater Antilles
970	E40	Civilization/Social life	972.9	F2161-2175	Caribbean Sea/Spanish Main
970	E141-143	Description			
970	E45	History	972.9	F2001-2151	Lesser Antilles
970.00(5/6)	E31	Serials/Societies	972.91	F1751-1849	Cuba
970.00(5/6)	E11	Serials/Societies	972.92	F1861-1896	Jamaica
970.003	E14	Dictionaries/Gazetteers	972.93	F1931-1940	Dominican Republic
970.003	E35	Dictionaries/Gazetteers	972.94	F1912-1930	Haiti (Republic)
970.004	E29	Populations	972.94	F1900-1940	Haiti
970.00497	E77-99	Indians (North America)	972.95	F1951-1983	Puerto Rico
970.007	E16.5	Education	972.96	F1650-1660	Bahamas
970.0072	E16	Historiography	972.97	F2006	Leeward Islands
970.0099	E17	Biography	972.972	F2136	Virgin Islands
970.00992	E36	Biography (Collective)	972.976	F2151	French West Indies
970.01(5-9)	E101-135	Discovery/Early explorations	972.984	F2011	Windward Islands
			972.986	F2141	Netherlands West Indies
970.01(6-9)	E121-135	Post-Columbian	972.99	F1630-1640	Bermuda
970.011	E103-110	Pre-Columbian period	973	E171-183.9	History
970.011	E51-74	Pre-Columbian America/ Indians	973	E151-839	United States
			973.(1-732)0496	E185.18	Free Negroes/South before 1863
970.01100(5/6)	E51	Serials/Societies			
970.0110074	E56	Museums/Exhibitions	973.(1-9)0496	E185.18-.3	History, By date
970.013	E105	Norse/Vinland	973.(318-68)	E301-453	Revolution-Civil War (1775-1861)
970.015	E111-120	Columbus			
970.016	E123-125	Spanish/Portuguese	973.(318-68)	E303-440.5	By date
970.017	E127-129	English	973.(4-6)099	E302.5-.6	Biographies
970.018	E131-133	French	973.(46-58)	E337.8-400	Early 19th century (1801-1845)
971	F1001-1035	Canada			
971-989	F	The Americas	973.(46-89)	E337.5-400	19th century
971.1	F1090	Rocky Mountains of Canada	973.(46-89)099	E339-340	Biography
			973.(521/621)	E302.1	Political history
971.1	F1086-1089.7	British Columbia	973.(7-82)0496	E185.2	1863-1877
971.23	F1075-1080	Alberta	973.(83-927)0496	E185.3	1877-
971.24	F1070-1074.7	Saskatchewan	973.0(5/6)	E151	Serials/Societies
971.27	F1061-1065	Manitoba	973.0072	E175-.4	Historiography
971.273	F1067	Assiniboine Region	973.025	E154.5-.7	Directories
971.3	F1056-1059.7	Ontario	973.03	E154	Gazetteers
971.4	F1050	St. Lawrence Gulf and valley	973.03	E174	Dictionaries/ Encyclopedias
			973.04	E184-185.97	Population elements
971.4	F1051-1055	Quebec	973.0496	E185-.93	Afro-Americans
971.5	F1035.8	Maritime provinces	973.05	E171	Serials
971.51	F1041-1045	New Brunswick	973.06	E172	Societies
971.6	F1036-1040	Nova Scotia	973.099	E176-.8	Biography
971.7	F1046-1049.7	Prince Edward Island	973.2	E186-199	Colonial history
971.8	F1121-1139	Newfoundland	973.2(1-4)	E191	1607-1689
971.82	F1136-1139	Labrador	973.2(1-7)	E191-199	By date
971.82	F1140	Labrador peninsula	973.2(5-7)	E195-199	1689-1775
971.88	F1170	Saint Pierre/Miquelon	973.20(5/6)	E186-.99	Serials/Societies
971.91	F1091-1095.5	Yukon	973.2099	E187.5	Biographies
971.92	F1060-.92	Canadian Northwest	973.25	E196	King William's War (1689-1697)
971.93	F1096-1100.5	Mackenzie			
971.94	F1106-1110.5	Keewatin			

Dewey	LC	Descriptor
973.25	E197	Queen Anne's War (1702-1713)
973.26	E198	King George's War (1744-1748)
973.26	E199	French & Indian War (1755-1763)
973.3	E201-298	The Revolution (1775-1783)
973.30082	E276	Women & the war
973.3022	E295-298	Illustrative material
973.305	E201	Serials
973.306	E202-.99	Societies
973.3099	E206-207	Biography
973.31	E210-216	Political history
973.312	J10	Continental Congress
973.313	E221	Declaration of Independence
973.317	E249	Treaty of Paris (1783)
973.318	E303-309	1775-1789 (The Confederation)
973.33(1-9)	E231-239	Campaigns, By year
973.33(1-9)	E241	Individual battles
973.34	E251-268	Armies/Troops
973.34(4-5)	E255-265	American army
973.34(4-5)	E263	By state
973.341	E267-268	British army
973.346	E265	Auxiliaries
973.35	E271	Naval history
973.36	E285-286	Celebrations/Exhibits
973.37(1-2)	E281	Prisoners/Prisons
973.375	E283	Medical services
973.38	E275	Personal accounts
973.38(1-6)	E278	Loyalists/Traitors
973.38(5-6)	E279-280	Secret service/Spies
973.4	E310-337	1789-1809 (Constitutional era)
973.4(1-3)	E311-320	Washington (1789-1797)
973.4(4-8)	E321-330	John Adams (1797-1801)
973.44	E323	French dispute (1796-1800)
973.46	E331-337	Jefferson (1801-1809)
973.46	E333	Louisiana Purchase (1803)
973.47	E335	War with Tripoli (1801-1805)
973.51	E341-370	Madison (1809-1817)
973.52	E351-364.9	War of 1812
973.53	E365	War with Algeria (1815)
973.54	E373	Missouri Compromise (1820)
973.54	E374	Annexation of Florida (1819)
973.54	E371-375	Monroe (1817-1825)
973.55	E376-380	John Quincy Adams (1825-1829)
973.56	E381-385	Jackson (1829-1837)
973.561	E384.3	Nullification
973.57	E386-390	Van Buren (1837-1841)
973.58	E396-400	Tyler (1841-1845)
973.58	E391-392	William H. Harrison (1841)
973.6	E415.6-440.5	1845-1861
973.6(3-4)	E423	Slavery question (1849-1853)
973.6099	E415.8-.9	Biography
973.61	E416-420	Polk (1845-1849)
973.62	E408	Mexican Cession of 1848
973.62	E401-415.2	War with Mexico (1845-1848)
973.63	E421-423	Taylor (1849-1850)
973.64	E426-430	Fillmore (1850-1853)
973.66	E433	Slavery question (1853-1857)
973.66	E431-435	Pierce (1853-1857)
973.68	E438	Slavery question (1857-1861)
973.68	E436-440.5	Buchanan (1857-1861)
973.7	E456-655	Civil War (1861-1865)
973.7	E456-459	Lincoln (1861-1865)
973.7	E461-655	Civil War (1861-1865)
973.713	E482-489	Confederate States
973.713	JK9778-9799	Secession of states
973.714	E185.5-.89	Emancipation
973.7140(5/6)	E185.5	Serials/Societies
973.742	UA580-585	Confederacy
973.757	V438	Confederate States
973.757	VA393-395	Confederate States Navy
973.8	E660-738	1865-1900
973.8(1-2)	E668	Reconstruction (1865-1877)
973.8099	E663-664	Biography
973.81	E666-670	Johnson (1865-1869)
973.81	E669	Alaska Purchase (1867)
973.82	E671-680	Grant (1869-1877)
973.83	E681-685	Hayes (1877-1881)
973.84	E691-695	Arthur (1881-1885)
973.84	E686-687.9	Garfield (1881)
973.85	E696-700	Cleveland (1885-1889)
973.86	E701-705	Benjamin Harrison (1889-1893)
973.87	E706-710	Cleveland (1893-1897)
973.88	E749	McKinley (1901)
973.88	E711-751	McKinley (1897-1901)
973.89	E714-735	Spanish-American War (1898)
973.892	E661.7	Diplomacy
973.9	E743-.5	Political history
973.9	E740-839	20th century
973.90(5/6)	E740	Serials/Societies
973.9099	E747-748	Biography
973.91(3-6)	E784	1919-1933
973.911	E756-760	T. Roosevelt (1901-1909)
973.912	E761-765	Taft (1909-1913)
973.913	E780	World War I (Internal)
973.913	E768	Virgin Islands Purchase (1917)
973.913	E766-783	Wilson (1913-1921)
973.914	E785-786	Harding (1921-1923)
973.915	E791-796	Coolidge (1923-1929)
973.916	E801-805	Hoover (1929-1933)
973.917	E806-812	F.D. Roosevelt (1933-1945)
973.918	E813-816	Truman (1945-1953)
973.921	E835-839	Eisenhower (1953-1961)
974	F106	Middle Atlantic States
974	F1-15	New England
974-979	E159	Monuments
974-979. + (0496)	E185.9-.93	By region/State
974-979.03	E230.5	By region
974.1	F16-30	Maine
974.2	F31-45	New Hampshire
974.3	F46-60	Vermont
974.4	F61-75	Massachusetts
974.5	F76-90	Rhode Island
974.6	F91-105	Connecticut
974.7	F116-130	New York
974.8	F146-160	Pennsylvania
974.9	F131-145	New Jersey
975	F206-220	South Atlantic States

Dewey	LC	Descriptor
975.1	F161-175	Delaware
975.2	F176-190	Maryland
975.3	F191-205	District of Columbia
975.4	F236-250	West Virginia
975.5	F221-235	Virginia
975.6	F251-265	North Carolina
975.7	F266-280	South Carolina
975.8	F281-295	Georgia
975.9	F306-320	Florida
975.9-976.4	F296-301	Gulf states
976.1	F321-335	Alabama
976.2	F336-350	Mississippi
976.3	F366-380	Louisiana
976.4	F381-395	Texas
976.6	F691-705	Oklahoma
976.7	F406-420	Arkansas
976.8	F431-445	Tennessee
976.9	F446-460	Kentucky
977	F476-485	Old Northwest/N.W. Territory
977	F516-520	Ohio River and valley
977	F561-575	Michigan
977	F597	Upper Mississippi valley
977	F396	Lower Mississippi valley
977	F351-355	Mississippi River and valley
977.1	F486-500	Ohio
977.2	F521-535	Indiana
977.3	F536-550	Illinois
977.5	F576-590	Wisconsin
977.6	F601-615	Minnesota
977.7	F616-630	Iowa
977.8	F461-475	Missouri
977/978	F591-596	West/Trans-Mississippi region
978	F598	Missouri River valley
978.(752)	F721-722	Rocky Mountains/Yellowstone Park
978.1	F676-690	Kansas
978.2	F661-675	Nebraska
978.3	F646-660	South Dakota
978.4	F631-645	North Dakota
978.6	F726-740	Montana
978.7	F756-770	Wyoming
978.8	F771-785	Colorado
978.9	F791-805	New Mexico
979	F851	Pacific states
979.(13)	F786-788	New Southwest/Colorado River
979.1	F806-820	Arizona
979.2	F821-835	Utah
979.3	F836-850	Nevada
979.33	E230-241	Military operations
979.4	F856-870	California
979.5	F871-885	Oregon
979.6	F741-755	Idaho
979.7	F886-900	Washington
979.7	F852-853	Columbia River and valley
979.8	F904-915	Alaska
980	F1401-1419	Latin/Spanish America (General)
980	E16-18.85	History
980	F2201-2239	South America
980	E18.7	Juvenile works
980	E	America
980.00(5/6)	E11	Serials/Societies
980.003	E14	Dictionaries/Gazetteers
980.004	E29	Populations
980.007	E16.5	Education
980.0072	E16	Historiography
980.0099	E17	Biography
980.01	E65	Latin America (General)
980.013	E101-135	Discovery/Early explorations
981	F2501-2659	Brazil
982	F2801-3021	Argentina
983	F3051-3285	Chile
984	F3301-3559	Bolivia
985	F3401-3619	Peru
986.1	F2251-2299	Colombia
986.6	F3701-3799	Ecuador
987	F2016	Venezuela coast islands
987	F2301-2349	Venezuela
988	F2351	Guiana
988.1	F2361-2391	British Guiana
988.2	F2441-2471	French Guiana
988.3	F2401-2431	Suriname
989.2	F2661-2699	Paraguay
989.5	F2701-2799	Uruguay
993	DU419-422	History
993	DU400-430	New Zealand
993-996	DU28.11-66	History
993-996	DU	Oceania/Australia/New Zealand
993-996.00(5/6)	DU1	Serials/Societies
993-996.003	DU10	Gazetteers/Dictionaries
993.004	DU422.5-424.5	Ethnography
993.01	DU420.12-.14	Ancient to 1840
993.02	DU420.16-.24	Colonial era (1840-1908)
993.02(2-3)	DU420.16-.24	Self-government (1853-1908)
993.021	DU420.16-.18	Crown colony (1840-1853)
993.031	DU420.22-.24	1908-1918
993.032	DU420.26-.28	1918-1945
994	DU98-117.2	History
994	DU80-398	Australia
994.004	DU120-125	Ethnography
994.01	DU98.1	Ancient to 1788
994.02	DU114-115.2	British settlement (1788-1851)
994.03	DU114-115.2	Self-government (1851-1901)
994.04	DU116-117.2	Commonwealth (1901-)
994.04(1-2)	DU116-.2	1900-1945
994.05	DU116.9-117.2	1945-1966
994.06	DU116.9-117.2	1966-
994.1	DU350-380	Western Australia
994.2	DU390	Central Australia
994.23	DU300-330	South Australia
994.29	DU392-398	Northern territory
994.3	DU250-280	Queensland
994.4	DU150-180	New South Wales
994.5	DU200-230	Victoria
994.6	DU182-198	Tasmania
994.7	DU145	Canberra
995	DU490	Melanesia (General)
995	DU739-747	New Guinea
995-996	DU520-950	Island groups
995.3	DU740	Papua New Guinea
995.8	DU550-553	Bismarck Archipelago
995.93	DU850	Solomon Islands
995.95	DU760	Vanuatu (New Hebrides)
995.97	DU720	New Caledonia
996	DU510	Polynesia (General)

Dewey	LC	Descriptor	Dewey	LC	Descriptor
996.1(3-4)	DU810-819	Western/American Samoa	996.9	DU620-629	Hawaiian Islands
996.11	DU600	Fiji Islands	996.9	DU625-627.83	History
996.12	DU880	Tonga (Friendly Islands)	996.9003	DU622	Gazetteers
996.15	DU910	Tokelau (Union Islands)	996.9004	DU624.6-.7	Ethnography
996.16	DU920	Wallis and Futuna Islands	996.90099	DU624.9-.96	Biography
996.18	DU800	Pitcairn Island	996.902	DU627-.2	Early to 1898
996.21	DU870	Society Islands (Tahiti)	996.903	DU627.5-.7	1900-1959 (Territory)
996.31	DU700-701	Marquesas Islands	996.904	DU627.8-.83	State (1959-)
996.4	DU650	Line Islands	997.1	F3031	Falkland Islands
996.5	DU500	Micronesia (General)	997.3	DT671.T8	Tristan da Cunha
996.6	DU560-568	Caroline Islands	997.3	DT671.S2	St. Helena
996.6	DU780	Pelew (Palau) Islands	998	G575-890	Arctic/Antarctic regions
996.7	DU640-648	Mariana Islands	998	G575-599	Polar regions
996.81	DU615	Kiribati (Gilbert Islands)	998.2	G725-765	Greenland
996.81	DU790	Phoenix Islands	998.9	G845-890	Antarctica
996.83	DU710	Marshall Islands	999	QB54	Extraterrestrial life